S0-BZF-133

South America
on a shoestring

South America on a Shoestring

Published by
Lonely Planet Publications
PO Box 88, South Yarra, Victoria 3141, Australia
Lonely Planet Publications
PO Box 2001A, Berkeley, CA 94702, USA

Cover design by
Graham Imeson

Illustrations by
Dennis Sheehan

First published
January 1980

This edition
October 1986

National Library of Australia
Cataloguing in Publication Data

Crowther, Geoff, 1944–
South America on a Shoestring

3rd ed.
Includes index
ISBN 0 908086 75 X.

1. South America – Description and travel – 1981 – Guide-books. 2. Latin America – Description and travel
– 1981 – Guidebooks. I. Title

918'.0438

©Geoff Crowther

All rights reserved. No part of this publication may be reproduced, stored in a retrieval system or transmitted in
any form by any means, electronic, mechanical, photcopying, recording or otherwise, except brief extracts for
the purpose of review, without the written permission of the publisher and the copyright owner.
Printed in Singapore by Singapore National Printers Ltd.

Geoff Crowther

Born on the Ides of March in Yorkshire, England. Geoff took to his heels early on in the search for the miraculous. The lure of the unknown took him to Kabul, Kathmandu and Lamu in the days before the overland tour bus companies began digging up the dirt along the tracks of Africa. His experiences there led him to join the now legendary but sadly defunct alternative information centre BIT in London in the early '70s. Here he put together their guides, *Overland to India and Australia* and *Overland through Africa*.

Three years and several dingy basement flats later he developed the classic symptoms of a 'burned-out BIT worker' and fled north for a period of healthy living on the bleak, wind-swept mountainsides of rural Cumbria. In 1977 he wrote his first guide for Lonely Planet – *Africa on the Cheap* – followed by *South America on a Shoestring* and *Korea & Taiwan – a travel survival kit*. He has also co-authored *India – a travel survival kit* and *Malaysia,*

Singapore & Brunei – a travel survival kit. When not crashing through the bush in search of gorillas in the Ruwenzoris, tramping over Inca trails in the high Andes or pitting his wits against Indian bureaucracy he lives in a banana shed with 치롱보 in the rain forests of New South Wales and spends his time pursuing noxious weeds, trying to get a house built and brewing mango wine.

Acknowledgements

A lot of people contributed towards this edition and I'm extremely grateful to everyone who took the time and trouble to write in with comments, update material, facts about areas not previously covered, street maps and timetables. It's been very encouraging to read it all and a pleasure to incorporate it into this new edition. Those of you who felt that some of the countries were thinly covered in the last edition, Brazil, Uruguay and Chile in particular, will be pleased to find that those chapters have been completely re-written and considerably expanded. A list of travellers who have written to us is included at the back of this book. Many thanks.

There are several other people who I would like to specially thank for making our long 1985 trip to South America such a pleasure. Thanks to Maureen and Tony Wheeler for welcoming us to their *pied a terre* in Berkeley, California, while they themselves returned from South America; and on the return trip, to Camille Coyne, Sam Lipson, Greg Rogers, Elizabeth Kim and Tom of Lonely Planet (USA), for being such good friends and for their matchless hospitality and help in many different ways.

In Australia I must thank the Lonely Planet team especially Andy Neilson and Marianne Poole for forwarding on feedback letters to my many different mailing addresses and Graham Imeson and Fiona Boyes for their hard work in helping to put all the new maps together.

In South America I'd like to thank Uli Kling (W Germany) for a lot of laughs and friendship in San Pedro de Atacama, Chile; Gianfranco di Palma (Italy) for his humour, companionship and sensitive point of view through the Chilean Lake

District; Raul Arroya (Chile) for falling over backwards to make his home a home-from-home for us and many other travellers in Puerto Montt (thankyou Raul, may you prosper!); Penny Stuckey (UK) and Bruce Anderson (Australia) for their companionship and humour in Montevideo, Uruguay, while they waited for money to come through which had been sent to Paraguay (Paraguay? Uruguay? What's the difference to an Australian bank clerk!?) and for helping Hyung Pun get her visas after I had left for Brazil; Au Yun Kwang (Korea) for a cordon blue authentic Korean feast aboard his ship the *Easter Bay* in Montevideo harbour (until we were turfed off by customs officials because they thought Hyung Pun was whoring) and for giving her some Korean novels (ever tried to find Korean language books in Montevideo?); Robin Fall, Heather Betts and the rest of the *Project Raleigh* crowd (UK) for their commitment to Bolivian wildlife and late-night discos!; Claude Berniquez (Canada) for his incredible enthusiasm, generosity, companionship and the simple pleasure of travelling with someone who lives to travel; James Hickman and his buddies from Oxford University UK, who, in the course of a train journey from Puno to Cuzco, finally realised that there was some vague resemblance between the man they were talking to and the Rasputin-like photograph on the first page of several books which they'd used to take them round the world (thanks for your many letters!), and finally Margarita (Peru) and William Kaiser (USA) for one of the mellowest places I've ever stayed in (the *Hostal Qoñi Unu* in Aguas Calientes down the line from Machu Picchu). Good luck to you both.

This book was written in Kilnhurst Cottage, Todmorden, UK, just as the snow was beginning to clothe the hill farms and moors in a crisp, white winter coat. Thankyou Dr & Mrs Heather Grieve for your hospitality, smiling faces and the loan whenever requested of your slide projector, typewriter and telephone. It's all very much appreciated. The book was typed on a *Kaypro 2* micro-computer loaned to me by Lonely Planet and run on 240 volts AC. Half way through the book, the local power station burned down and, when the power was cut off, I lost several files. This is life on the grid. I think I prefer my solar-powered system in Australia. At least you get several days advance warning of a power cut.

From the Publisher
Back at Lonely Planet Richmond, where everything comes together, rabbit stamps and champagne will be awarded to: Hugh Finlay for organising reader's information and first editing; Lindy Cameron for final editing, proof reading and overseeing; Ann Logan for the professional typesetting; Dennis Sheehan (Esq) for the illustrations and paste-up; Sue Mitra and Richard Everist for helping with the fiddly bits; Todd Pierce and Fiona Boyes for sticking down the fiddly bits; and Andy Neilson for everything else.

A Request
All travel guides rely on new information to stay up-to-date. Things change – prices go up, good places go bad, new places open up – nothing stays the same. So if you find things better, worse, cheaper, more expensive, or simply different, please write and tell us and help make the next edition even better. The nitty-gritty info we get from travellers about the current situation in this part of the world is invaluable so any details you have on hotels, restaurants, *peñas, casas de cambio*, Inca ruins, transport schedules, prices, journey times and street maps will be put to good use. As usual, the most useful letters will be rewarded with a free copy of the next edition, or another LP guide if you prefer.

Contents

Introduction

Generalising about an area which extends thousands of miles from the USA-Mexican border almost to Antarctica; which includes 21 countries with diverse and impressive Indian cultures, Spanish, Portuguese, Dutch, British and French colonial legacies; and is home to societies which are a cultural mosaic of Indians, Europeans, Africans, Caribbeans, and Asians – is a risky business! This diversity does, however, make one statement a safe bet: Central and South America is a winner for budget travellers whatever their interests.

Your interest is mountains? The towering Andes are a trekker's and climber's paradise. Beaches? Depending on your budget and your energy, choose from untouched tropical islands to Rio's famed Copacabana. Cities? Depending on your nerves there are roaring cosmopolitan mega-cities or quiet colonial backwaters, frozen in time. History? There's mysterious Machu Picchu or massive Spanish forts built to repel buccaneers like Francis Drake. Jungles? Rivers? Wildlife?

The next piece of good news is that none of these sights, potential adventures and experiences need cost you an arm and a leg. Many of these countries are afflicted with horrific inflation (in Bolivia in mid-1985 it reached 3000%) so if you travel with a so-called 'hard' currency many things will seem cheap to you, even if they don't for the unfortunate locals. In most Latin American countries it's possible to find a roof over your head for around US$1 to $4 per night. Bus rides are cheap, and so, often, are airfares.

Despite all these advantages, however, it seems Latin America still has something of a PR problem. The unfortunate images some people have are of jackbooted communists and/or fascists, frequent coups, and institutional crime and corruption. Like many misconceptions this is partly true, but, and it's a big but, this is only a part of the picture. If you use a moderate degree of good sense and caution you're unlikely to have any problems.

It's obviously a good idea to avoid the Honduras-Nicaragua border regions but within Nicaragua itself there are still many opportunities for interesting and secure travel. Parts of Rio de Janeiro have well-founded reputations for theft – but so has the Paris Metro, not to mention various 'suburbs' in North American cities. In general, political developments within Latin America are no more likely to affect tourists than they are in most other parts of the world.

Central and South America offers extraordinary cultural and geographic variety. The differences between Peruvians in the ancient Inca capital of Cuzco and the sybaritic Brazilians on the beaches of Rio are as great as those between a Greek farmer and a San Franciscan. Latin America is a great place to travel. Find out for yourself. And get there before the hordes.

Facts for the Visitor

PAPERWORK

The essential documents are a passport and an International Health Certificate. If you already have a passport, make sure it's valid for a reasonably long period of time and has plenty of blank pages on which stamp-happy immigration officials can do their bit. Whoever supplies you with your vaccinations will provide you with the Health Certificate. If you're taking your own transport or contemplating doing any driving then you should also take an International Driving Licence. Any national motoring organisation will fix you up with this provided you have a driving licence for your own country. The cost of these licences is generally about US$5.

An International Student Identity Card (ISIC) is also very useful in some places for getting reductions on entry charges to archaeological sites and museums. At times it will also entitle you to reductions on the cost of airline tickets though basically – unlike Africa, the Middle East and Asia – it's of limited use in Latin America. If you're not strictly entitled to one it's often possible to get hold of an ISIC by (temporarily) enrolling in a full-time course at one institution or another. It's also sometimes possible to get hold of one if you book a flight with one of the 'bucket shop' ticket agencies that have proliferated in certain cities in Europe and North America. Another possibility is to buy a fake card (average price around US$10). There always seems to be someone selling them wherever travellers collect in numbers but examine them carefully before buying as they vary a great deal in quality.

Another useful document is a Youth Hostels Association membership card, particularly if you are heading down to Chile, Argentina and Uruguay where accommodation charges in any place other than a Youth Hostel tend to be high.

VISAS

Visas are a stamp in your passport permitting you to enter a country and stay there for a specified period of time. They are obtained from the embassy or consulate of the appropriate country either before you set out or along the way. It's best to get them along the way, especially if your travel plans are not fixed, but keep your ear to the ground about the best places to get them. Two different consulates of the same country may have different requirements before they will issue a visa: the fee might be different; one might want to see how much money you have whereas another won't ask; one might issue them on the spot whereas another might tell you to come back in two days time.

Whatever you do, don't turn up at a border without a visa if you know that you'll need one unless you're absolutely sure you can get one at the border. If you do this you'll find yourself tramping back to the nearest consulate for a visa before you're allowed across. Very few, if any, visas are required by nationals of most European countries and Japan but people from the USA, Australia and New Zealand require quite a few. If you're one of these nationalities, take a cache of passport-size photographs with you when you set off – 24 should see you through.

British passport holders still have problems getting visas for Argentina. It's generally true to say that the further away from Argentina you are, the harder it is to get a visa. At the consulate in San Francisco, for example, they won't even accept an application. In Santiago, Chile, they'll tell you it takes about 1½ months. In Puerto Montt, Chile, you might get one in as little as 15 days. In

Montevideo, Uruguay, it takes 15 days to get a transit visa but longer for a tourist visa.

Getting visas is usually no problem though you may be asked, either verbally or on the application form, how much money you are carrying. If you don't have what officialdom considers as 'sufficient funds' for your proposed length of stay either when applying for a visa or on arrival, then the amount of time they give you may be reduced. This generally doesn't create any difficulties since you can always renew your visa at an immigration office inside the country by showing, if necessary, your own and someone else's travellers' cheques artfully combined. I've never seen signatures being scrutinised.

The biggest problem you're likely to encounter regarding visas and entry to countries is the onward ticket requirement. Some countries, it seems, are so suspicious about your motives for wanting to go there that they demand you have a ticket out of the country before they will let you in. They may demand to see this ticket either when you apply for a visa or on entry. The countries which presently demand this are Panama, Colombia, Venezuela and the three Guianas. This doesn't create any problems if you're going to leave from the same place you arrived but if you want to enter at one point and leave at another then it can sometimes be a headache.

There are two ways round it. The most flexible is to buy an MCO (Miscellaneous Charges Order) for, say, US$100. An MCO is rather like having a deposit account with an airline and it looks like an airline ticket but it isn't for any specific flight. It can be refunded in full or exchanged for a specific flight ticket either with the airline you bought it from or with any other airline which is a member of IATA. Most consular and immigration officials accept an MCO as an onward ticket. The second way to get round an onward ticket is to buy the

cheapest available ticket out of a country and then refund it later on. If you decide to do this then make sure it is the cheapest and that you can get a refund without waiting months for it – and don't forget to ask specifically where you can get a refund (some airlines will only refund tickets at the office where you bought them and sometimes only at their head office). Note that if you're flying from either Costa Rica or Panama to either Colombia or Venezuela, travel agents and airlines will only sell you a one-way ticket if you already have an onward ticket. If you don't want to buy a return ticket you must work out what you're going to do about an onward ticket first.

MONEY

Bring as much of this wonderful stuff as possible. US dollars are probably the best currency to take with you. Others like the pound sterling, yen and deutschmark are certainly acceptable in banks and *casas de cambio* (change houses) but in terms of every day versatility the US dollar is best. Everyone knows the exchange rate of the US dollar but few people know the exchange rates for the others without having to check with the banks. Avoid taking Australian or Canadian dollars. Exchange rates for these are poor. Take the bulk of your money as travellers' cheques but avoid buying them from small banks which may have only a few overseas branches as you might find them impossible to change in many places. American Express, Thomas Cook or First National City Bank cheques are among the most well known and in most cases they offer instant replacement in case of loss or theft. Keep a record of the cheque numbers and the original bill of sale for the cheques in a safe place in case of theft. Replacement is a whole lot quicker if you can produce these.

Even so, replacement in case of loss or theft can take time if you look like you've just crawled off the Inca Trail (freaky),

because so many travellers have been selling their cheques on the street market (black market) or simply pretending to lose them and then demanding a replacement set. This is particularly the case with American Express. Indeed, quite a few banks and casas de cambio, particularly in Peru, are either refusing to change American Express travellers' cheques or demanding a photostat of the first few pages of your passport when they do. There are similar problems with Thomas Cook cheques in Venezuela.

Whatever sort you decide on don't take too many large denominations – have plenty of US$20 and US$50s – otherwise you may well find yourself with large amounts of excess currency when you want to leave a country and find that you can only reconvert it at a poor rate of exchange.

Apart from cheques, you should take some cash with you – say, up to US$200 – because it's not always possible to change travellers' cheques in small places or when the banks are closed. It's also more convenient to change a few dollar bills just before you leave a country rather than a hefty US$20 or US$50 travellers' cheque. There are some countries (eg Chile and Uruguay) where you can exchange US dollar travellers cheques for US dollars cash at banks and casas de cambio. This means you can top up on cash from time to time without having to carry it all with you from the day you set off. It's obviously much safer to do this.

Cash, of course, comes into its own when there is a street market for currency, where the exchange rate for the US dollar can be much higher than that offered by either the banks or the casas de cambio. There is now a street rate for US dollars in all Latin American countries except Ecuador and Uruguay. The reason for this is the inability of many of these countries to finance their overseas debt repayments (massive in the case of Argentina, Brazil and Mexico) and this in turn has been brought about by the very high value of the US dollar (which pushes up rates of interest charged on the loans) and by the world-wide recession. Inflation has gone through the roof in some countries – in Bolivia, in mid-1985, it reached 3000%! Argentina, Peru and Brazil weren't too far behind Bolivia though their inflation rates were only in three figures and Argentina has apparently now come to grips with the problem. Nicaragua is also in dire straits but that is mainly as a result of US political and military pressure.

In some countries you can obtain the current street rate by simply going to a casa de cambio or travel agent rather than a bank. This is the case in Brazil and Paraguay and, to some extent, Peru. In other countries you will have to change on the street, at a hotel or in shops which sell imported goods (shops selling electrical and electronic goods and pharmacies are two of the most obvious). If you have to literally change on the street you need to observe a few precautions. Be discreet for a start – it's generally illegal to change on the street though you wouldn't know it in some places. Have the exact amount you want to change handy – avoid pulling out large wads of notes. Be very wary of sleight-of-hand tricks – insist on personally counting out the notes you are handed one by one. Don't let anyone else do this for you and don't hand over your dollar bills until you're satisfied you have the exact amount agreed to. Some operators are so sharp they'd have the shoes off your feet while you were tying up the laces.

One common trick is to hand you the agreed amount minus a few pesos or whatever to make sure that when you've counted it out you will complain that it's short. They take it back, count it out again, discover the 'mistake', top it up and hand it back to you, spiriting away all but one of the largest bills in the process. As you've just counted it the temptation is to be satisfied with what you're handed back. Don't be. Count it again. And don't

allow yourself to be distracted by supposed alarms like 'police' or 'danger'.

This advice is all very well except that in some countries (eg Brazil, Bolivia and Peru) it may be impossible to count it all out because of the sheer number of bills. In mid-1985, travellers in Bolivia were carrying plastic garbage bin liners around with them because only these were large enough to accommodate the number of bills you were handed after changing US$20 on the street.

Because inflation in this region is on such an unbelievable scale, unrivalled anywhere else in the world, it would be much easier to write a complete book on Tanzania, Uganda or Bangladesh than to quote realistic prices for most South and Central American countries. It is impossible to keep up with prices in economies like these. Even if you quote things in US dollars, as soon as there is a devaluation or food and fuel prices are doubled, tripled, quadrupled or whatever (Bolivia increased the price of fuel by 1000% in late-1985!), then things go haywire. What it means to travellers is that, at the beginning of a price hike, essentials are relatively expensive but as the value of local currency drops over the following months, life gets much cheaper for those with hard currency to spend. The difference can be as much as half. While these factors make it a nightmare to quote prices, one thing stays the same: if a hotel or restaurant was cheap before prices were increased, it's still going to be cheap afterwards relative to the prices of other hotels and restaurants.

If you run out of money while you're away and need more, ask your bank back home to send a draft to you (assuming you have money in your account there). Make sure you specify the city and the bank branch. Transferred by cable, money should reach you in a few days, but you can run into complications even with supposedly reliable banks. If you do it by mail it will take at least two weeks and often longer. Some banks will hang on to transferred funds and keep telling you they haven't received it yet because there's money to be made on the interest accruing from hard currency deposits. Whether it's the bank that makes it or one of the bank's officials is a debatable topic.

Some countries will only give you your money in the local currency; others will let you have it in US dollars. Find out what the score is before you request a transfer or you could lose a fair amount of money if there's an appreciable difference between the official and unofficial exchange rates. Some of the Central American republics, (Venezuela, Ecuador, Chile and Uruguay) will let you have it in dollars. Other countries like Brazil will only let you have some of it in dollars and will give you the rest of it in the local currency.

If you've taken your entire worldly assets with you and haven't another penny anywhere in the world you can put your hands on then you'll either have to find a job, if possible, or go to your nearest embassy and be repatriated. If repatriation is the order of the day, bear in mind that many embassies take your passport off you and don't give it back until you repay the debt – and they'll fly you back in full-fare tourist class. French embassies won't do this and US embassies are getting more and more reluctant.

A credit card can be very useful if you have one, particularly the sort that allows you to withdraw a certain amount of money every now and then, that you can use for buying travellers' cheques (American Express and Visa will allow you to do this). You'd be surprised how many apparently impecunious travellers have a credit card lurking somewhere on their person. It's also very useful where you are required to show 'sufficient funds' for visa or entry purposes.

Everyone has a preferred way to carry money. Some do it in a money belt; others in 'hidden' pockets sewn onto the inside of trousers; and others in a pouch hung around their neck. There isn't any foolproof way though some are better than others. If you put it in a pouch around your neck, incorporate a length of guitar string into the strap so that it can't be cut without you being alerted. All the same, there's no substitute for keeping your wits about you.

As far as bargaining goes, probably the only things you'll have to haggle over are long-term accommodation and purchases from markets, particularly hand-crafted goods. Remember that as a tourist you represent money to local people and in some places it may be virtually impossible to get a trader to lower his or her prices. This applies where there are a lot of tourists passing through. The traders know that even if you won't pay the price asked, then sooner or later somebody else will. Patience, humour and the ability to speak the local language can certainly help but you shouldn't expect too much.

BAGGAGE

Travel light. An overweight pack will quickly become a nightmare particularly if it's hot. Don't join that diminishing minority of travellers who stagger around in a pool of sweat, dwarfed by an enormous pack containing everything they could possibly think of including the kitchen sink.

Despite lingering prejudice among border officials, a backpack is preferable to an overnight bag as the latter screws up your balance. Get hold of one which will take some rough handling – overland travel destroys packs rapidly. Make sure the straps and buckles are sewn on securely and strengthen them if necessary before you leave. Whether you take a pack with or without a frame is up to you, but I find a pack with an internal frame much more convenient. *Berghaus* makes some of the best internal-framed packs. The best stockist in the UK is probably the YHA Adventure Centre, 14 Southampton St, London, WC2 (tel 01 836 8541). Take a strong plastic bag with you that will completely enclose your pack and use it on dusty journeys whether your pack is in the luggage compartment or strapped on the roof. If you don't you'll be shaking dust off your belongings for the next week.

A sleeping bag is more or less essential. At 3000 metres and higher it gets very cold at night and not all budget hotels provide sufficient blankets. You'll be glad of it too on long train, bus or truck journeys as a supplement to wooden benches and sacks of potatoes. A sheet sleeping bag is also useful when it's too hot to use a normal one. It's cool and keeps the mosquitoes off.

Although you'll need to cope with both hot and cold climates you can keep the weight of your pack down by initially taking only clothes for hot and temperate climates and buying things like a sweater and poncho when you need them in places like Ecuador, Peru and Bolivia. You'll find these relatively cheap compared with the prices you'd have to pay back home and the quality is usually very good.

Some people take a small tent and portable stove and though they're useful they do represent extra weight. They'll certainly give you a little more independence in out-of-the-way places. On the other hand, if you're not thinking of doing too much camping, equipment can be hired in many places where mountain trekking is popular, such as the Inca Trail in Peru.

Don't forget the small essentials: a combination pocket knife or Swiss Army knife; needle and cotton and small pair of scissors; a padlock; oral contraceptives (if used); a supply of anti-malarial pills; one or two good long novels. Most toilet articles (toilet paper, toothbrushes, paste, shaving cream, shampoo, tampons, etc) are easily found in all the large cities and even in small towns. Washing powder is available at virtually any *tienda* (small general store) in small packs which are just sufficient to do a pile of washing.

HEALTH

Useful books to browse through are *The Traveller's Health Guide* by Dr A C Turner, published by Roger Lascelles in the UK; and *The Preservation of Personal Health in Warm Climates* published by the Ross Institute of Tropical Hygiene, London, UK. Both books tell you all you'd ever need to know.

Vaccinations Officially, before you're allowed to enter most countries in Latin America you're required to have a valid International Health Certificate as proof that you're not the carrier of any of the old favourites which used to decimate populations in the days of yore. The essential vaccinations are cholera and yellow fever. In addition to these compulsory ones, you're strongly advised to be vaccinated against typhoid, paratyphoid, tetanus, polio and tuberculosis. Some people also take in a jab for hepatitis. At no border or airport anywhere in Latin America was I asked for this certificate but you'd be ill-advised to neglect vaccination on account of this.

If you've been living all your life in a western country you're probably already protected against polio and tuberculosis since it's likely you were vaccinated at school. Typhoid, paratyphoid and tetanus are often given in the one jab as a 'cocktail' called TABT but this practice is being discontinued and they're reverting to single jabs for each. You need to plan at least a month ahead, because not only can't they all be given at the same time but typhoid and tetanus both require booster shots two to four weeks after the first injections. The effect of the vaccines vary with different people and with the skill of the doctor or nurse. Typhoid and cholera often leave you with a stiff arm if you've not had them before. The others have little or no side-effect.

The International Vaccination Certificate covers cholera, yellow fever and typhoid. Their validity is as follows: cholera, six months; yellow fever, 10 years; typhoid/paratyphoid, one year. Tetanus, polio, tuberculosis and hepatitis are not included since they are not compulsory. Their effectiveness is as follows: tetanus, variable, usually about two years; polio and tuberculosis, for life; hepatitis, up to six months but its effectiveness varies – some medics say it's not worth it at all.

Your local doctor will arrange a course of injections for you if you live outside a city. Some large cities have vaccination centres which you can find by checking the telephone book.

If you're in London you can get vaccinations from one of the following places:

Hospital for Tropical Diseases, 4 St Pancras Way, London NW1 (tel 01-387 4411). Injections here are free but they're often booked up a month ahead.

West London Designated Vaccination Centre, 53 Great Cumberland Place, London W1 (tel 01-262 6456). No appointment is necessary – just turn up. The fees vary depending on the vaccine.

British Airways Immunisation Centre, Victoria Terminal, Buckingham Palace Rd, London SW1 (tel 01-834 2323). Try to book a few days in advance here otherwise you might have to wait around for a few hours before they can fit you in.

British Airways Medical Centre, Speedbird House, Heathrow Airport, Hounslow, Middlesex (tel 01-759 5511).

In Belgium try one of the following:

Ministere de la Sante Publique et de la Famille, Cite Administrative de l'État, Quartier de l'Esplanade, 1000 Brussel.

Centre Medical du Ministere des Affaires Etrangeres, 9 Rue Brederode, 1000 Brussel.

In France there is:

Direction Departmentale d'Action Santaire et Sociale, 57 Boulevard de Sevastapol, 75001 Paris (tel 508 9690).

Institut Pasteur, 25 Rue du Docteur Roux, 75015 Paris (tel 566 5800).

L'Institut d'Hygiene, 2 Quai du Cheval Blanc, 1200 Geneva (tel 022-43 8075).

In Holland try:

Any **GGD** office or the **Academical Medical Centre**, Amsterdam.

It's unlikely you'll be asked, but if you turn up at borders/airports with expired certificates they may insist on you having the relevant jab before being allowed to enter.

General Health Get your teeth checked and treated if necessary before you set out. Dentists are few and far between and treatment is expensive.

The two main things which are likely to affect your general health while abroad are diet and climate. Cheap food bought in cafés and street stands tends to be overcooked, very starchy (mainly corn or maize) and lacking in protein, vitamins and calcium. Over a period of time the latter two, when combined with a lack of exercise for the gums, can seriously affect the health of your teeth. Make sure you supplement the cooked food you buy with milk or yoghurt (where available and pasteurised) and fresh fruit. Exercise your gums by chewing liquorice root or a twig. Read up a little on dietary requirements before you set off. Avoid untreated milk and milk products – in many countries herds are not screened for brucellosis or tuberculosis. Fortunately, it's often possible to buy refrigerated cartons of pasteurised milk.

In hot climates you sweat a great deal and so lose a lot of water and salt. Make sure your drink sufficient liquid and have enough salt in your food to make good the losses (a teaspoon of salt a day is sufficient). If you don't make up the loss you run the risk of suffering from heat exhaustion and cramps. Heat can make you impatient and irritable especially if you're a speedy person. Try to take things at a slower pace.

Hot dry air will make your hair brittle and may cause it to thin out. Oil it frequently with refined coconut oil. Keep your skin clean. Even the most basic *hospedajes* have showers. Good sunglasses are a virtual necessity. If you arrive without a pair or lose/break the pair you have, you can buy them all over the continent. US$6 should buy you an excellent pair from a street seller.

Take great care of cuts, grazes or skin infections otherwise they tend to persist and get worse. If they're wet, bandage them up. Open sores attract flies and there are plenty of those. Change bandages daily and use antiseptic cream if necessary. A troublesome, though temporary, skin condition that many people from temperate climates come across initially is prickly heat. Many tiny, itchy blisters form on one or more parts of your body – usually where your skin is thickest, like on your hands. They are sweat droplets which are trapped under the skin because your pores aren't large enough or haven't opened sufficiently to cope with the greater volume of sweat. Anything which promotes sweating – exercise, a lot of tea, coffee, alcohol – makes it worse. Keep your skin aired and dry. Reduce clothing to a loose fitting minimum and keep out of direct sunlight. The use of calamine lotion or zinc oxide based talcum powder helps to soothe the skin. Apart from that there isn't much else you can do about it. It's just an acclimatisation problem that usually doesn't persist. Other than on a beach, avoid walking around on bare feet as you could pick up hookworm which is widespread in some areas. If swimming on a rocky beach keep an eye out for sea-urchins.

Remember that adjustment to the outlook, habits, social customs, etc of different people can be a strain on your own outlook, prejudices and temperament. Many travellers suffer from some degree of culture shock – something you can get on returning too if you've been away a long time. Culture shock can be at its most severe if you fly direct from your own country to one you have never visited before. Heat tends to exaggerate petty irritations that would pass unnoticed in a more temperate climate. Exhausting all-night-all-day bus journeys over bad roads don't help if you're feeling this way. Make sure you get enough sleep.

Drinking Water Most cities have a decent, chlorinated water supply and you can drink from the tap but outside these areas avoid unboiled water or ice, especially during the rainy season. Rivers can be contaminated by communities living further up the valleys so if you're walking in the mountains get your supply from the springs or small streams. Unboiled water is a major source of diarrhoea and hepatitis. The other major sources are salads that have been washed in contaminated water and eating unpeeled fruit that's been handled by someone who has one of these infections. Where possible stick to tea, *maté*, coffee, mineral water and other soft drinks (carbonated – in Spanish *con gas*) or beer. Peel fruit before eating it. Your susceptibility to getting infections will depend to a large extent on the conditions you've been used to at home and the sort of food you eat.

If you have to use water and you're not sure about its purity use water purifying tablets such as *Halazone*, *Sterotabs* or *Potable Aqua*. These are effective against most micro-organisms but not against amoebic dysentery. To kill these you need an iodine-based steriliser. The only trouble with the latter is that they make the water taste foul. The best way to purify water is, of course, to boil it for a little while.

Medical supplies, including most drugs, are available without prescription at pharmacies all over the continent so there's not much point in bringing everything you might conceivably need with you but note that the prices can vary considerably. In Peru, Bolivia and Brazil they tend to be quite cheap but in Argentina four tabs of an antibiotic can cost US$20 and you need enough for a seven to 10 day course!! Don't rely on the pharmacists having much medical knowledge – they'll naturally recommend the most expensive drugs. South America, in common with other third world countries, is used as a dumping ground by pharmaceutical companies for drugs which have been banned in the industrialised world. Bear this in mind when buying drugs from a pharmacy.

Mountain Sickness (Soroche) Some people suffer from this on the altiplano of Ecuador, Peru and Bolivia (average height 3000 to 4000 metres). Rapid ascent from sea level, over-exertion and lack of physical fitness can bring on the symptoms which include headache, dizziness, loss of appetite, nausea and vomiting. Breathlessness and heart pounding are quite normal at these altitudes due to the lack of oxygen and are not part of mountain sickness. Most people acclimatise within a week but the process can go on for up to six months and during this period it's normal to feel relatively breathless on exertion. If you do get mountain sickness the best treatment is quite simple: get down to a lower altitude. A pain-killer for headache and an anti-emetic for vomiting will also help. Oxygen will give relief and you can sometimes find it in the more expensive hotels but you're unlikely to find it in cheaper accommodation.

An excellent remedy for both soroche and the normal breathlessness and heart pounding is 'maté de coca' – tea made from coca leaves – which you can get in most cafés in Peru and Bolivia (but not in Ecuador, as this country has outlawed its cultivation). You can also buy the leaves legally in most *tiendas* (small general stores) throughout Peru and Bolivia for US$4 to $5 per kilo or from herbal stalls which you can find in every market.

The practice of chewing coca leaves goes back centuries and is still common among the Indians of the Andean altiplano. By dulling the pangs of hunger, cold, thirst and fatigue, coca will give you that extra stamina to take the altitude in your stride and enable you to do some serious walking in the mountains. Remember that you must chew the leaves with a little ash (or bicarbonate of soda). The mild alkali will allow the cocaine to be leached out of the leaves. Without the ash there will be very little effect and you'll be wasting your time.

Diarrhoea and Dysentery (Montezuma's Revenge, the Inca Two-Step and other endearing terms). Sooner or later, unless you're quite exceptional, you'll get a bout of diarrhoea so accept it as inevitable and know how to deal with it. Diarrhoea doesn't always mean you've caught something – it can be merely the result of a change of food. If you've spent most of your life living out of plastic-wrapped packages and tins from the supermarket it's going to take time for you to adjust. Most gut infections (and hepatitis) are spread by one or other of the following: infected urine or faeces contaminating water supplies; people with dirty hands preparing food; droplet infection from sneezing, coughing or spitting; and flies. Sanitary fittings and systems in Latin America are not built to take quantities of paper so instead of being flushed away it's thrown into the corner by the pan. When you've seen a few of these toilets, particularly ones which aren't cleaned out regularly, you'll realise why flies are such a health hazard. In many places there aren't any toilets so people use a convenient corner. To maintain balance though, I should point out that only once in nearly a year did I get diarrhoea although my travelling companions did get it a little more often. We were pretty fastidious but we ate in the cheapest cafés all along the line.

Avoid rushing off to the chemist and filling yourself with anti-biotics at the first sign of a loose gut. It's a harsh way to treat your body and, if misused, the bugs will build up a tolerance to the drugs. Try to starve the bugs out first. Eat nothing and rest. Avoid travelling and drink plenty of liquid (tea or *maté* without sugar or milk). Many cafés in Latin America serve camomile tea (called *té de manzanilla*) which is excellent for this; or drink *agua minerale*. About 24 to 48 hours should do the trick. If you really can't hack starving, keep to a small diet of yoghurt, lemons, boiled vegetables and tea with no sugar or milk.

If starving doesn't work or if you really have to move on and can't rest, there is a whole range of drugs available. *Lomotil* is probably one of the best though it's come under fire recently in medical literature. The dosage is two tabs three times daily for two days. If you can't find that then try *Pesulin* or *Pesulin-O* (the latter is the same except with the addition of tincture of opium). The dosage is two teaspoons four times daily for five days.

If you have no luck with either of these then move onto anti-biotics or see a doctor. There are many different varieties of anti-biotics and you almost need to be a biochemist to know what the differences between them are. They include *Tetracyclin*, *Chlorostrep*, *Typhstrep*, *Sulphatriad*, *Streptomagma* and *Thiazole* to name just a few. If possible, have a word with the pharmacist about the best one to take. Avoid *Enterovioform* which used to be sold widely in Europe but which is next to useless for treating gut ailments and is suspected of causing optic nerve damage. With anti-biotics, keep to the correct dosage. Over-use will do you more harm than good.

After a severe bout of diarrhoea or dysentery you will be dehydrated. This often causes painful cramps. Relieve these by drinking fruit juices or tea in which a small spoonful of salt has been dissolved. Maintaining a correct salt balance in your blood stream is important.

If you're unfortunate enough to contract dysentery there are two types: bacillic, the most common, acute and rarely persistent; and amoebic, persistent and more difficult to treat. Both are characterised by very liquid shit containing blood and/or excessive amounts of mucus. It's painful and strained (ah, travellers' tales!). With bacillic dysentery an attack comes suddenly and is accompanied by fever, nausea and painful muscular spasms. It responds well to antibiotics or other specific drugs.

Amoebic dysentery builds up more slowly but is more dangerous so get it treated as soon as possible. The best thing is to see a doctor. If that's not possible *Flagyl* is the most commonly prescribed drug. The dosage is six tabs per day for five to seven days. *Flagyl* is both an antibiotic and an anti-parasitic drug. It is also used for the treatment of giardiasis and trichomoniasis but should not be taken by pregnant women.

Hepatitis This is a liver disease caused by a virus. There are basically two types – infectious hepatitis (known as Type A) and serum hepatitis (known as Type B). The one you're most likely to pick up is Type A. It's a very contagious disease and you pick it up by drinking water, eating food or using cutlery or crockery that's been contaminated by an infected person. Foods to avoid are salads (unless you know they have been washed thoroughly in purified or chlorinated water) and unpeeled fruits that may have been handled by someone with dirty hands. It's also possible to pick it up by sharing a towel or toothbrush with an infected person.

Symptoms appear 15 to 50 days after infection (generally around 25 days) and consist of fever, loss of appetite, nausea, depression, complete lack of energy and pains around the base of your rib cage. Your skin will turn progressively yellow and the whites of your eyes yellow to orange. The easiest way to keep a check on the situation is to watch the colour of your eyes and urine. If you have the disease, the colour of your urine will be deep orange no matter how much liquid you have drunk – if you haven't drunk too much liquid or have been sweating a lot then don't jump to conclusions. Check it out by drinking a whole lot of liquid all at once (and not beer!). If it's still orange then you've got problems. The only thing you can do about it is rest, but if it gets really bad then cash in that medical insurance you bought when you set off and fly back home. Seeking medical attention is probably a waste of time and money. They can do tests which will tell you how bad it is but that's about it. Most travellers don't need telling. They can feel it! Think seriously about that gamma globulin vaccination before you leave home.

Area of Malaria Risk
in South America

Area of
Yellow Fever Risk
in South America

Malaria This is prevalent throughout most of Latin America, except on the Andean altiplano and parts of Mexico, Costa Rica, Venezuela, Chile, Brazil, Argentina and Uruguay (see map). It's spread by mosquitoes which transmit the parasite which causes the disease. You only have to be bitten by one mosquito carrying the parasite to contract the disease. Avoid it by taking a malarial prophylactic which kills the parasites if they get into your bloodstream. There is no vaccination for malaria. You need to start taking anti-malarial tablets about two weeks before you enter a malarial area and continue for about two weeks after leaving the area. Virtually any chemist will get you a supply without prescription in Latin America.

Yellow Fever Endemic in Panama, Venezuela, Colombia, Ecuador, Peru, Bolivia, the Guianas and Brazil (see map). Again this is spread by mosquitoes which transmit the disease when they bite you. Make sure your yellow fever vaccination is up to date – it's valid for 10 years.

It's easy enough to protect yourself from malaria and yellow fever but mosquitoes themselves are another kettle of fish. There are several ways of keeping the little bastards at bay. One is to use an insect repellent which you apply to your skin every few hours or whenever necessary. Try to choose one which contains DET (diethyl toluamide) or DMP (dimethyl phthalate).

One quite effective repellent which you'll find all over Latin America is *Autan*. Another you might come across is called *Off*. You might have difficulty locating them in rural areas so stock up in cities. There is no need to take vast supplies with you when you set off. Another effective deterrent, particularly when you're asleep, is to position your bed under a fan, where there is one. Mosquitoes don't like moving air currents and tend to stay on the walls.

If there are no large gaps in the room where you intend to sleep, an extermination campaign with a book or rolled-up newspaper will reduce the chances of you being bitten. Don't forget under the bed or inside cupboards! Of course there's always at least one sly bastard that will escape detection. If there's no fan, you will hear its evil little whine shortly after the light goes out! Mosquito bites can be troublesome until your skin adjusts. It's probably useless to say but don't scratch them. You'll make them worse and if you open them up they stand the chance of being infected by something else.

Bugs and other things Small scorpions tend to drop out of tiled roofs around the onset of the rainy season. Keep an eye out for them and shake out your boots before putting them on in the morning. If you get head lice, wash your hair with shampoo containing benzene hexachloride (eg *Lorexane*). Body lice are best dealt with by shaving off affected hair and throwing away whatever article of clothing was nearest your skin, or washing it in the same type of shampoo you would use for your hair. Treat scabies with a lotion of benzoyl benzoate obtained from any chemist (go easy on the stuff around your genitals and asshole – it really stings there but nowhere else). Meat-eaters remember that the flesh of pigs and cattle may contain the encysted eggs of tapeworms. Make sure it's very well cooked.

There is a very minor possibility of contracting Chagas' Disease (a variety of trypanosomiasis) in the lowland areas of the countries surrounding the Amazon basin if you sleep on the dirt floors of adobe or thatched huts. It's spread by the assassin bug (*vinchuca* in Spanish and *barbeiro* in Portuguese) which lives in cracks in mud walls and in thatch. Sleep under a mosquito net in places like this.

If you're into herbal medicines you could supplement your Potter's and Culpepper's by keeping an eye out for booklets on Indian remedies such as:

Antiguo Formulario 'Azteca' de Yerbas Medicinales found in Mexico and Guatemala. Similar booklets can be found on Inca remedies in Peru – the best place to look is on Av Abancay in Lima.

Health Insurance Get some! You may never need it but if you do it's worth a million. Medical treatment is expensive. There are a lot of travel insurance policies available and any travel agent will be able to recommend one. Get enough to cover any possible injury/illness and preferably one with a 'fly-you-home' clause in case you've got to get home for treatment. Make sure it will cover you for any money you would lose on a booked flight ticket. Most policies cover the cost of flying your travelling companion back with you if necessary.

MAIL

Have letters sent to you c/o *Lista de Correos* followed by the name of the city and country you want to pick them up in. Mail addressed in this way will always be sent to the main post office in the city that it's addressed to. Instead of using the post offices you can use American Express if you have their cheques as they operate a mail service for customers. Some embassies will also hold mail for their citizens. Among them are Australia, Canada, West Germany, Israel, Switzerland and the USA. British embassies will no longer hold mail. Any letters addressed for collection to a British embassy will be sent to the main post office.

To collect mail from a post office (or from Amex or an embassy) you need to produce your passport as proof of your identity. Most post offices hold mail for one to two months (in Mexico only 10 days according to recent reports) after which, if they're not collected, they get sent back to the country of origin. The service is free in most places, but in some countries you may have to pay a few cents for each letter.

In large places where there is a lot of

traffic, letters are generally sorted into alphabetical order. In small places they're often lumped together in one box. Sometimes you're allowed to sort through them yourself. In other places an employee will do the sorting in front of you.

If you're not getting expected letters ask them to check under every conceivable combination of your initials not forgetting they might also be under 'M' (for Mr, Ms, etc) or 'S' (for Señor, Señora). In Managua I once collected three letters: the first I found under 'C'; the second under 'G' and the third under 'S'.

This sort of confusion isn't as widespread as many people believe though most travellers will have a story to tell about mail. The confusion arises over the different systems of naming. In a Latin country, if you were called Juan García Moreno, for example, 'Juan' would be your Christian or given name, Garcia your father's name, and Moreno your mother's name. A post office employee would file such a letter under 'G'. In a non-Latin country, of course, it would be filed under 'M'. To avoid this confusion address a letter in block capitals, leave out all titles (Mr, Mrs, Señor, etc) and underline your surname.

Sending parcels back home can be a pain in the neck in many countries as you have to have the contents inspected and passed by a customs officer before they can be accepted by a postal clerk. So don't wander down to the post office with a neatly sealed parcel otherwise you're going to feel very frustrated. Also, in Peru and Bolivia the parcel must finally be stitched up in linen before it can be accepted by a postal clerk.

All the requisites for wrapping and stitching up parcels can generally be found either on the pavement outside a post office or inside it. Anyone who's been to India will remember the joys of this little operation very well! In some countries the place where you post parcels abroad is different from the main post office.

LANGUAGE

Spanish is the language of the vast majority of people in all of Latin America except in Brazil where it is Portuguese. To set off without, at the very least, a working knowledge of those languages is very short-sighted. You'll meet people all over the continent who will want to speak with you, exchange views, ask you what's happening where you come from, tell you what's happening where they live, or just have a light social evening laughing and joking about nothing in particular over a bottle of wine or a few beers. If you can't speak their language these exchanges will be limited to a few cliches and you'll start to feel trapped inside a cultural and linguistic bubble.

All this is quite apart from the obvious practical value of speaking the language in order to find your way around, a place to stay, order things in restaurants, buy a bus ticket, bargain for items in markets and get yourself out of potential hassles.

A few months before you go attend an evening course in Spanish or Portuguese. If you can't do that then buy a phrase book and grammar book and learn from that, or borrow a record/cassette course from your local library – buying them individually can be expensive; *Linguaphone* courses, for example, cost around US$140.

Try to find someone who comes from Latin America and ask them if you can come and practice your Spanish/Portuguese with them once or twice a week. And when you finally get to Latin America don't worry about making grammatical mistakes or using the wrong word. If people see you're trying, they'll help you out and you can both laugh about your occasionally unfortunate choice of words.

Spanish-speaking people are not at all snobbish about their language. They don't regard people who speak Spanish poorly with disdain. They're more than delighted that a foreigner has taken the time and trouble to try and learn something about their language. Communication is what they look for, not perfect pronunciation and grammar.

It's a good idea to set yourself a target of learning a few new words each day since, when you know off by heart all the standard phrases for finding your way about, there's a temptation to be satisfied with that and get stuck in a rut. It's a common trap.

Accents and pronunciation can vary considerably from one country to the next. In some places such as Mexico and Peru it's quite clear. In others, such as Nicaragua, it's spoken fairly lazily with the 'g' being dropped so that Managua, the capital, becomes 'Manawa' and Nicaragua becomes 'Nicarawa'. The speed with which people talk also varies; Puerto Rican is virtually impossible to understand unless you come from there. Chileans, too, speak it at speed and somewhat lazily so that many phrases resemble Portuguese.

Words used for the same item sometimes differ. In Mexico and much of Central America the word for 'matches' is *cerillos*, but in South America it's the mediaeval Spanish word *fosforos*. The word for 'toilet' is generally *servicio* or *baño* but can also be *urinario*, *sanitario*, *retrete*, *excusado*, *hombres* or *señoras*. Remember that there are significant differences between the Spanish spoken in Spain and that spoken in South America. 'Z' and 'c' before 'e' are pronounced 'th' in Spain but are all 's' or 'c' in Spanish America. What is pretty standard throughout Spanish-speaking America is that personal pronouns (I, you, he, she, we, they) are rarely used, being implied in the verb, and that 'll' is pronounced as a 'y' rather than the more correct 'ly'. It takes a little more time to get used to this vernacular.

You may hear it said that Portuguese is very similar to Spanish and so if you know the latter it's possible to get by in Brazil by using that language. Our own experience of this was that although it's more than likely a Portuguese speaker will understand someone speaking Spanish, you can't understand the response! Although there are similarities, they are different languages with different words, phrases and pronunciation so you can't really get around Brazil with Spanish, though if you already know Spanish well then it will give you a head start in Portuguese.

Apart from Spanish and Portuguese, there are large areas where various Indian languages are spoken and others where Creole English is predominant. The main Indian languages are Yaqui (Northern Mexico), Nahuatl (Central Mexico), Maya (Yucatan Peninsula, Mexico and Guatemala), Chibcha (Colombia), Quechua (Ecuador and Peru) and Aymara (Southern Peru and Bolivia).

Because many Indians never see the inside of a secondary school or even a primary school and remain largely isolated from the mainstream of life in many countries – particularly in Guatemala, Peru and Bolivia – they speak only their own language and cannot speak Spanish. When you realise that they comprise up to 50% of the population in some countries, it's as well to consider learning a little of one or two of their languages if you're thinking of spending any amount of time there. This might be difficult outside Latin America itself as phrase books/grammar books/courses will be very thin on the ground. Only in the last couple of years, despite a 50% Indian population, has Quechua been made an official language alongside Spanish in Peru.

One neat little phrase book you'll come across in the Yucatan and Guatemala is *300 Phrases in Common Use in Mayan, English and Spanish* which costs just a few cents. It's available in bookstores and hotels. If you can't find one it's published by Abelardo Fuente Vega, Calle 59 No 454, Mérida, Mexico. Creole English is spoken by black people living on the Caribbean coasts of Belize, Honduras, Nicaragua, Costa Rica, Panama, Guyana and the Colombian islands of San Andrés and Providencia, though many are bilingual and also speak Spanish.

ACCOMMODATION

In most Latin American countries it's usually possible to find a roof over your head for around US$1 to $4 per night. Obviously a great deal depends on what you're prepared to be satisfied with in terms of comfort, facilities, services and cleanliness; how much running around you're prepared to do particularly after a long journey; and whether you're in a city or a small town. In general, however, it's true to say that budget accommodation in South America is good value for money.

The cheapest places are the *hospedajes*, *casas de huespedes*, *hosterias*, *youth hostels* or *dormitorios* (the names change depending on the country you are in). They're usually fairly basic, providing only a bed and a table and chair in an otherwise bare room. Usually a clean sheet or two and a blanket are provided and in hot climates there will be a fan. You won't, however, get heating for this price in cold climates. Showers and toilets are communal but even very cheap places may well have hot water.

Standards of cleanliness vary widely. I've stayed in some spotless *hospedajes* with sheets and blankets provided for no more than US$2. There's little point in trying to quote average costs for various countries since inflation, devaluations and other factors render such figures obsolete as soon as they are printed.

Hotels and *pensiones* are generally a little more expensive than *hospedajes* though the distinction is often academic. Most pensiones tend to have slightly better facilities and the services are of a higher standard. For a dollar more than you would pay in an *hospedaje* you will probably have your own private shower and toilet in a *pension* or hotel. Quite a few hotels and *pensiones* have their own restaurant.

In some countries (especially in the southern parts of Chile and Argentina) the best and cheapest places to stay are with local families. These are usually excellent value, have hot water and you share the lounge with the family.

You will find that in many of the cheapest places accommodation has been maximised by the construction of hardboard partitions across what was once just one room. These partitions often do not reach the ceiling so although you can't see the other occupants you can certainly hear them – and vice versa. If the place doubles as a brothel then you will be in for several hours of sighs, cries and giggles, the doors banging, the toilets flushing and the customers arguing about the price. If you're well rested, this probably won't bother you too much but if you've just completed an exhausting journey on a bus or train then you might find it a bit trying. Complaining inevitably falls on deaf ears. Latin Americans like their noise. Indeed they appear to be immune to it whatever the volume. And talking of volume – if you don't like TVs turned up to full blast then make sure you get a room well away from the foyer or the TV lounge where there is one. It only goes off when the programmes finish. It isn't just in hotels, however, where noise will shatter your ear drums night and day. Wait till you've been on a long bus journey where the driver has only one cassette tape.

In Brazil the price of most hotels includes breakfast. The quality and quantity of this obviously depends on the type of hotel you stay in and sometimes on its location. In the very cheapest hotels it's often just a cup of coffee and maybe a piece of bread (with butter or jam/marmalade) or a couple of biscuits. If you pay more your breakfast may well be a whole buffet consisting of cooked sliced meats, fruit juice, fruit slices, bread, butter and jelly, biscuits and a pot of coffee. It's worth thinking about paying a little extra for a place which offers a good breakfast because you'll rarely be able to pick this up for the same price in a restaurant.

FOOD

As long as you stick to food stalls and small cafés where local people go, you can generally eat a reasonable meal for US$1 or a little more. Most cafés in Spanish America put on a cheap set-meal both at lunch time (known as *comida corrida* or *almuerzo*) and at dinner time (known as *comida* or *cena*). Breakfast (*desayuno*) is rarely a set-meal and you generally order whatever you feel like eating, though in many countries special stuffed pasties (known variously as *empanadas* or *salteñas*) are available at this time of day. They are similar to Cornish pasties except that they're stuffed with vegetables, vegetables and chicken, or vegetables and beef. They're often delicious and two or three of them with a coffee should set you up for the morning.

Lunch is the largest meal of the day. The only trouble with comida corrida/almuerzo and cena is that they tend to be almost exactly the same wherever you are in Latin America so you can get bored with them. They consist of a soup (usually of potato or maize with a bit of meat thrown in), a main course of rice with chicken or a slice of grilled beef/goat/llama and a sweet. In Central America they tend to be very starchy, maize being the staple diet of the vast majority of the people.

Before you get to the point where you never want to see another tortilla, try the variations on this theme such as *tostadas* (deep-fried tortillas served with a vegetable or meat-based chutney) and *enchiladas* (steamed and stuffed tortillas). There's very little variety in vegetables until you start paying considerably more for your food.

In Brazil, *lanches* will be the main meal of a budget traveller's day. It's the midday meal served in a million restaurants and almost identical wherever

you buy it. It consists of soup and a main course of rice, boiled black beans (the famous *feijão*), grilled or barbequed beef/lamb/chicken and manioc flour. There is occasionally a vegetable dish and a sweet. It can be very dry unless you're given sufficient black beans to juice up the mountain of rice which is provided. There is no such cheap set meal in the evening and meals at that time of day are more expensive.

On Saturday at lunchtimes most restaurants offer the traditional *feijoada completa*, a huge banquet of a meal which basically consists of the same ingredients as a *lanch* but with much more variety of meats and with vegetables. Eat one of these and you won't be eating again until well into the following day.

You don't have to eat the standard meal of the day, of course, and over the last few years things have been changing rapidly as far as choice of food goes. This is particularly true of places which are popular with travellers. Even in small places such as Antigua and Panajachel (Guatemala), Baños (Ecuador), Cuzco and Puno (Peru) you could almost be on Telegraph Avenue in Berkeley, California.

There are thousands of regional specialities which you can try for just a dollar or two more. As well as South America's answer to Colonel Sanders – *pollo a la brasa* – which can be found almost anywhere though it varies considerably in quality and greasiness, there's always good seafood available in coastal towns. The larger cities, of course, have the whole gamut of restaurants offering everything from Korean *kimchi* to Lebanese *shish kebab*, though these restuarants are noticably more expensive.

Even if you're a vegetarian you'll have little problem finding food in the main population centres. Vegetarianism is a growing movement in South America and it isn't confined to Hari Krishna devotees though this movement does have some excellent cheap restaurants which are very popular with both travellers and local people. If you can't find one, just tell the waiter at an ordinary restaurant that you don't want meat and will they put something with vegetables together for you. Most will come up with an acceptable spread.

Every town has a market where a wide variety of fruit and vegetables can be bought. They're usually cheap and plentiful – bananas, coconuts, melons, guavas, papino, sipote, mangoes, oranges, mandarins, grapefruit, avocados, peaches, pomegranates, prickly pears, apples, etc, depending on season and location.

Most fizzy drinks – *gaseosas* and *refrescos* – seem to contain nauseating amounts of sugar and after a while you may prefer to stick to *agua minerale* (carbonated mineral water). Two varieties which contain less sugar and more actual fruit juice are *Squirt* and *Boing* – found in Mexico, Guatemala and sometimes Nicaragua. Coca-Cola and Pepsi are, of course, ubiquitous, except in Peru where they have their own home-grown variety called *Inca Cola*. A suitable word to describe the taste of this stuff eludes me – boiled lollipops is a fair approximation.

Bottled lager-type beers are sold in most cafés. There are many different varieties in each country so you'll have to check them out to see which you prefer. Beer usually costs twice the price of a soft drink (between 70 cents and US$1, sometimes more). These days there are quite a few bars which offer draught beer (known as *chopp* – pronounced 'shop') which is cheaper than the bottled beer and often just as good. Spirits include tequila and mescal (Mexico), rum (Central America, Venezuela, Colombia, Ecuador and Peru), pisco and aguardiente (Peru and Bolivia). A bottle of something which won't rot your guts shouldn't cost more than US$2 to $3.

Wine is produced in Mexico, Chile, Peru, Bolivia, Argentina and Brazil. Some of the Chilean and Brazilian wines are as good as you'll find anywhere in the world and even the Bolivian wines produced in the Tarija region are excellent. Chilean wines are definitely the cheapest (though only in Chile – elsewhere they cost two to three times what they cost in their country of origin).

Asunción and Puerto Stroessner in Paraguay are duty-free cities where you can buy all the types of spirits you would expect to find in an airport duty-free shop. It's amazing that you can buy a litre bottle of Johnny Walker Red Label there for about US$4. How can profit possibly be made on that when it has to come all the way from Scotland?!

SOMEONE TO TRAVEL WITH

It's a fact of travelling life that overlanding is rarely a solo activity and this is particularly true of the 'Gringo Trail' – an endearing term for the route which most travellers take through Central America and down the Andes to Tierra del Fuego.

Even if you start out by yourself, you'll inevitably meet other people along the road heading in the same or a similar direction with whom you can team up for a while if the mood takes you or you like each other's company. The most likely places are hotels where many travellers congregate, beaches, buses, trains, archaeological sites, cafés and fiestas – in other words, just about everywhere along the main route.

Travellers are thin on the ground in Argentina, parts of Brazil, the Guianas and Venezuela. In Brazil, it's not just because it's so big, but because there are so many ways to travel though it.

If you'd prefer to set off with someone, student travel notice boards are particularly good things to keep an eye on. The same goes for Youth Hostel office notice boards in large cities. If you're in London, try looking in the weekly publications, *Time Out, London Alternative Magazine (LAM)*, and *The News & Travel Magazine* (formerly the *Australasian Express*). The latter two are free. In New York, try either the New York Student Centre, Hotel Empire, Broadway and 63rd Street (tel 212 695 0291), or get hold of something like the *Village Voice*.

A WARNING

Theft is a big problem in some countries especially Colombia and Peru and some cities of Brazil. On buses and trains you must keep an eye on your baggage at all times. This is especially important at night. Don't fall asleep in a railway compartment unless a friend is watching you and your gear. You'll wake up with everything gone. When a bus stops, if you can't see what's happening to your gear then get off and have a look. Don't take things for granted.

On the street, in markets and other crowded places use only the front pockets of your trousers and don't carry a shoulder bag unless it's in front of you. The number of travellers I've seen with slashed bags doesn't bear recalling.

At bus stations be especially wary of team-work thievery and don't fall for a ruse which is going to distract you from looking after your belongings. It only takes a few seconds of inattention for a thief to be halfway down the street with your bags. Remember that it's a lucky traveller who gets through Latin America without having anything stolen.

It's now common in Lima and Cuzco (Peru) for a gang of thieves to come up behind a traveller and squirt something onto the back of your shoulder which makes a real mess (hair shampoo is common). One of them points it out to you and while you busy yourself thinking what the hell it is and trying to get it off the other members of the team slash your bag or simply relieve you of whatever it is

that you're carrying and run off down the street. Yes, it's happened to me too. But the thief didn't get what he wanted because Hyung Pun tripped him up and he fell flat on his face. If this happens to you forget about the crap on your shoulder and get moving. There are always two or three of them.

We've also heard of a spate of robberies (some of them armed) on the Inca Trail from Km 88 to Machu Picchu. It's advisable not to go alone but even that isn't protection at times. Groups have also been robbed.

The authorities in Peru have increased policing considerably in tourist areas over the last couple of years especially on the trains so it's not quite as bad as it used to be in some areas. All the same, there's no substitute for vigilance.

In Brazil it's mainly on the beaches of Rio that you'll encounter trouble. There, gangs of youth and even children roam the beaches watching for anyone who leaves anything unattended. As soon as that happens, it's gone.

With this in mind, it's a very good idea to get some baggage insurance before you set off. Make sure that if there are any clauses in the policy limiting the amount that can be claimed on any article that the amount is sufficient to cover the replacement of such things as cameras and watches or a cassette player if you're carrying these things. If you have anything stolen you generally have to inform the insurance company by air-mail letter and go to the police within 24 hours to report the loss or theft. At the police station you complete a *denunciacion* (statement) and a copy of this is given to you. You must produce this when you make a claim from the insurance company. Usually the denunciacion has to be made on special paper known as *papel sellado* (stamped paper) which you buy beforehand for a few cents at any shop selling stationery.

In city police stations you might be able to find someone who can speak English and is willing to act as a translator, but in most cases this won't be the case so you'll either have to speak Spanish or provide your own translator. Have a list prepared of what has been stolen plus what the various items are worth. When you make a claim, especially for a valuable item, the insurance company generally demands that you produce a receipt to prove that you bought it in the first place.

In Peru the procedure for reporting a loss or theft is slightly more complicated if it includes your passport or travellers' cheques. In such cases you need *papel sellado* from a stationer's plus *forma copia certificado de guardia civil*, which is a special kind of paper available only from the Banco de la Nacion. Take both of these types of paper to the local PIP (investigative police). After your statement has been typed out on the two kinds of paper they both have to be rubber stamped and signed by the chief. Until you get your passport and visa card replaced, these two forms are your only form of ID and proof of loss. If your theft or loss occurs on a weekend, when it's impossible to buy the *forma copia*, report it to the PIP and carry on with the rest on Monday. Remember that the guardia is organised on a regional basis and a *denunciacion* must be made at the place where the loss occurred. If you were in transit and don't know precisely where the loss occurred it's best to say it happened on arrival to avoid any complications.

It can be expensive replacing a stolen/ lost passport. Apart from the cost of backtracking to the nearest embassy or consulate there will be telex charges to your home country to check on details of your previous passport plus the cost of a new passport.

BOOKS

Before you set off it's a good idea to read a few books about South America. This way you get a good idea of what places are worth visiting and an understanding of their culture. The following are suggested:

A History Of Latin America by George Pendle (Penguin). This is a pocket-sized account of the period from the Conquest to the present and is very readable though it contains hardly anything about pre-Conquest history.

Open Veins of Latin America: Five Centuries of the Pillage of a Continent by Eduardo Galeano (Monthly Review Press, NY and London, 1973). This is probably one of the best books written on Latin America. It covers the cultural, social and political struggles of the continent and is highly recommended.

The Ancient Sun Kingdoms of the Americas by Victor Wolfgang von Hagen (Paladin). One of the most readable accounts of the Aztec, Maya and Inca civilisations written to date. It's packed with details about the every day life, architecture, religions, agriculture, trade and political organisation of these cultures. There are also plenty of black and white photographs and maps. The author has written several books on the same theme.

The Maya by Michael D Coe (Penguin 1971). Contains a very detailed account of the civilisation of these people with some excellent black and white photographs but it's very dry and academic. A similar book is *The Aztecs of Mexico* by George C Valiant (Penguin).

A History of the Conquest of Mexico by W H Prescott. This is the standard work on the subject and well worth reading. The author has also written *History of the Conquest of Peru* though many people prefer John Hemming's *Conquest of the Incas* (Harcourt-Brace-Jovanovich, 1970). The latter gives some excellent insights into the Spanish Conquest.

The Conquest of New Spain by J M Cohen (Penguin, 1963). This is a translation of *Historia verdadera de la Conquista de la Nueva España* by Bernal Diaz del Castillo, one of the people who accompanied Cortés in his conquest of Mexico. It's the most readable translation of this book and cuts out a lot of repetition and extraneous detail as well as having several good maps (you may come across another translation by A P Maudslay which was done about 70 years ago but it's much less readable).

Lost City of the Inca: The Story of Machu Picchu and its Builders (New York, 1948) and *Across South America* (Houghton Mifflin, 1911) are two books written by Hiram Bingham, the discoverer of Machu Picchu. Probably the best place to find them is in a large library though I saw paperback editions of them for sale in Cuzco in 1985.

The Caste War of the Yucatán by Nelson Reed (Stanford University Press, 1964). This is an excellent account of the history of the Mayan uprisings against first Spanish and then Mexican central government rule.

Guatemala – Another Vietnam? by Thomas and Marjorie Melville (Pelican 1971). Written by two people who were once Roman Catholic missionaries in that country but who became identified with the cause of revolutionary land reform. They were eventually expelled from both Guatemala and the church and narrowly missed execution at the hands of the Guatemalan secret police in Mexico. It's well worth reading especially in the light of recent events there.

The Kingdom of the Sun by Luis Martin. The author is a Spaniard who teaches at a US university and who has lived and taught in Peru. The book lays bare, in an unsensational manner, the rapacious attitude the Spanish had towards the people and land of the new colonies.

Revolution and Counter Revolution in Chile by Michel Raptis (Allison and Busby, 1974). This is a brief and readable account of the development and overthrow of the Chilean revolution under Allende's presidency.

Narcotic Plants – Their Origins and Uses by William Emboden (Studio Vista, 1972). Written by an ethno-botanist, this book contains some very interesting descriptions and information about this class of South American plants – coca, yage, marijuana, datura, etc – with excellent colour photographs.

Cut Stones and Crossroads – A Journey in the Two Worlds of Peru by Ronald Wright (The Viking Press; Penguin 1984). Wright, an archaeologist, presents an entertaining, personal account of his journey through Peru and an insight into the country's dual personality – its proud Inca heritage and today's struggling emerging nation.

Other Guides

In a guide book of this size and scope we can't possibly cover every conceivable aspect of travel in Latin America so if you have a particular interest you'd like to pursue or need greater detail on the more remote places then you may want to supplement this with one or more of the following:

The South American Handbook edited by John Brooks (Trade and Travel Publications, Bath, UK). This is regarded by many as the standard work on the area since it contains the most amazing and comprehensive collection of information you will find anywhere ranging from the smallest villages to the largest cities. It is good and will double as a novel on those long train or bus journeys but it's also very pricey. As well as practical information it has excellent sections on history, geography, politics and the people of the various countries.

I do have a few criticisms of it, however. It's marketed on the basis that it is updated annually but this is clearly only partially true. Quite a bit gets added each year but very little gets deleted. What is more serious is the lack of street plans for all but the capital cities and even then most of them cover such a small area that they are of very limited use.

Finally, because it caters for every type of traveller from the jet-set to the impecunious, there's a lot of information which is of little or no use to budget travellers. Indeed, some sections, especially the hotel and restaurant sections of large cities, are so over-whelmingly exhaustive that it's impossible to make a reasoned choice.

A series of guide books which are well worth considering if you're thinking of doing any walking in the mountains or getting right off the beaten track are those written by George and Hilary Bradt. They include the following: *Backpacking in Mexico & Central America, Backpacking in Venezuela, Colombia & Ecuador, Backpacking in Peru & Bolivia, Backpacking in Chile & Argentina plus the Falkland Islands*, and *South America: River Trips*. These books contain excellent first-hand descriptions of numerous trails together with maps. Some are better than others.

Another excellent guide to walking in the mountains of Peru is *Trails of the Cordilleras Blanca & Huayhuash of Peru* by Jim Bartle. Like the Bradt's books, this one contains excellent descriptions of the various trails together with maps and a number of colour photographs which will certainly encourage you to go there.

If you're planning on taking your own vehicle then *Overland and Beyond* by Theresa and Jonathan Hewat is well worth having a look at. It is written by two people who took their own VW Kombi round the world for three and a half years. The book is packed with practical information.

Other guides which are worth looking at are *People's Guide to Mexico* by Carl Franz (John Muir Publications) which is an extremely witty and meaty 380-page guide containing everything you'd ever want to know about travelling and living in that country, and *Mexico – a travel survival kit* by Doug Richmond (Lonely Planet Publications) which is a much more specific guide to that country written by someone who has spent half his life there. It's packed with street plans and has several wraps of colour photographs. Similarly *Ecuador & The Galápagos Islands – a travel survival kit* by Rob Rachowiecki (Lonely Planet Publications, 1986) gives a good insight and a lot of detail into that country.

One last guide which has been recommended is *A Traveller's Guide to El Dorado & the Inca Empire* by Lynn Meisch (Headlands Press & Penguin). This is principally a guide for people who have more than a passing interest in Andean weaving techniques since this subject takes up about half of the book. It's very good on that but thin on other practical details.

Periodicals

South American Explorer published by South American Explorers Club, Av Portugal 146, Lima, Peru, is a quarterly with an annual subscription of US$10 plus US$5 for overseas mail. The magazine is free to members of the club who pay an annual subscription of US$25. The club provides services, support and information to travellers, scientific researchers, mountaineers and explorers as well as selling a wide range of books, guides and maps dealing with South America. The magazine is well worth subscribing to. The Club's addresses for mail are: 2239 E Colfax Av 205, Denver, Co 80206, USA; and Casilla 3714, Lima, Peru.

Adventurer's Club News published by the Adventurers Club of Los Angeles, 706 West Pico Boulevard, LA Ca 90017. This is published monthly and sent free to members. It contains articles of interest to travellers and is a good source of information on many parts of the world.

MAPS

The best maps of South America you're ever likely to lay hands on have been printed recently by an independent cartographer, Kevin Healey, of Melbourne, Australia. The southern half of the continent consists of two sheets on a scale of 1:5,000,000 (ie twice as big as Bartholomews which is on a scale of 1:10,000,000). Not only are they the best I've ever seen but there are numerous inserts, which don't clutter up the maps in any way, featuring important geographical features, archaeological sites and historical events. They're available from many booksellers.

If you can't get hold of these two maps then Bartholomews *America, South* is the next best bet, though you should be wary of some of the roads marked on this map, especially in Amazonia.

One of the best maps of Mexico and Central America that I've come across is published by Rand McNally, but if you want more detail of individual Central American republics then it's a good idea to visit the national tourist organisation of the country concerned and get larger scale maps. Excellent maps of Mexico are produced by the national tourist organisation of Mexico. They're free of charge. Texaco also produces a good map of Mexico which is also free.

Getting There

North Americans, of course, can simply hitch hike or take a bus or train and be in Mexico in a few hours. Travellers from the rest of the world (and North Americans who want to go directly to South America) will first have to think about flying. As with all travelling which involves flying, this requires some forethought and legwork if you are going to do it as cheaply as possible. There are a bewildering number of possibilities and airline ticket deals available and there's no one magic key which will instantly reveal all about this market.

There are a lot of factors to consider. Principal among them are: the country you live in; what travel agencies you have access to; whether you can buy your ticket in advance; how flexible you can be about your travelling arrangements; how old you are (it's to your advantage if you are 26-years-old or under); and whether you have a student card. While there are certain ways to go about getting the best deal you should nevertheless remember the old adage that no matter how little you paid for your ticket you will inevitably meet someone, somewhere who paid less.

The first thing to do is equip yourself with as much information as possible. One of the best sources about cheap fares and fare deals all over the world is the monthly magazine, *Business Traveller*, available from news stands in most developed countries or direct from 60/61 Fleet St, London EC4, UK, and from 13th Floor, 200 Lockhart Rd, Hong Kong. Others are the *Trailfinder* magazine, free from the Trailfinders Travel Centre, 48 Earls Court Rd, London W8 6EJ, UK; the London weekly entertainment guide, *Time Out*, available from news stands in London or from Tower House, Southampton St, London WC2E 7HD, UK; *LAM*, London's free weekly magazine

for entertainment, travel and jobs, available at underground stations or ring 01-743 6413 for details of the nearest pick-up point; and *The News & Travel Magazine (TNT)* (formerly the *Australasian Express*), also a free weekly magazine which you can pick up at underground stations or from 52 Earls Court Road, London W8 (tel 01-937 3985).

When you're hunting around for cheap tickets it helps to be fimiliar with ticketing jargon. The main terms you need to know about are:

APEX (and Super-APEX) This means Advance Purchase Excursion and must be bought 14 days to two months in advance. These tickets are usually only available on a return basis. There are minimum and maximum stay requirements, no stop-overs are allowed and there are cancellation charges.

Excursion Fares These are priced mid-way between APEX and full economy fare. There are no advance booking requirements but a minimum stay abroad is often obligatory. Their advantage over APEX is that you can change your bookings and/or stop-overs without surcharge.

Point-to-Point This is a discount ticket which can be bought on some routes in return for the passenger waiving his or her rights to stop-over.

ITX This means Independent Inclusive Tour Excursion and is often available on tickets to popular holiday destinations. It's officially only available as a holiday package deal which includes hotel accommodation but many agents will sell you one of these for the flight only and issue you with phoney hotel vouchers in case you're challenged at the airport (very rare).

Economy Class Symbolised by 'Y' on the airline ticket, this is the full economy fare. Tickets are valid for 12 months.

Budget Fare These can be booked at least three weeks in advance but the actual travel date is not confirmed until seven days prior to travel. There are cancellation charges.

MCO This means Miscellaneous Charges Order. It is a voucher which looks like an airline ticket but without any destination or date on it and is exchangeable with any IATA airline for specific flights. It's principal use for travellers is as an alternative to an onward ticket. It's obviously much more flexible than a ticket for a specific flight in those countries which demand an onward ticket, such as Panama, Colombia, Venezuela, Guyana and Trinidad.

IATA International Air Transport Association which, to all intents and purposes, is a price-fixing cartel to which most airlines belong. It's success at suppressing so-called illegal discounting of tickets has been severely curtailed in the last few years because of falling business, independent budget airlines like Laker (now defunct), Virgin and People's Express, and the unwillingness of the many Asian airlines to toe the line. Most American airlines have also terminated their membership.

Stand-By This can be one of the cheapest ways of flying though APEX may well be even cheaper. You simply turn up at the airport or, in some cases, at an airline's city centre terminal without a ticket and if there are spare seats available on the flight you want, then you get them at a considerable discount. It's become such a common thing since the early 1970s that most airline counters now have a special stand-by section. To give yourself the best chance of getting on a flight on the day of your choice, get there as early as possible and have your name placed on the waiting lists. It's first come, first served.

There is a whole grab-bag full of other terms which airlines invent from time to time to ginger up business but they're basically all variations of the above with discounts being offered in return for accepting various conditions.

All these discounted tickets are

those which the airlines officially sanction. There are, however, unofficially discounted tickets available through certain travel agents – known in the trade as 'bucket shops'. Despite all the airlines' self-righteous protestations to the contrary, the tickets which these bucket shops sell are released by the airlines through selected travel agents for sale at a considerable discount. These are tickets which the airlines know or predict they won't be able to sell through their normal channels. The rationale behind it all is that it's better for the airlines to fill as many seats as posssible rather than see their planes leave half empty even if some of the passengers are travelling on tickets which have cost them less (far less in some cases) than what the airlines were officially prepared to offer.

Generally bucket shops sell tickets at prices lower than what an APEX ticket would cost but without the advance purchase or cancellation penalty requirements (though some agents do have their own penalties for cancellation). Most of the bucket shops are well-established and scrupulous but there are one or two which are not, so use a little caution when buying a ticket. It's not unknown for fly-by-night operators to set up office, take money (on deposit or in full), and then disappear before they've given you a ticket. Most bucket shops insist on a deposit for a ticket but you should never hand over the full amount until you have the ticket in your hands. Tickets bought from a bucket shop are indistinguishable from those bought from an airline despite the nonsense which some people and some airlines will tell you. The only thing you need to watch is that if you're travelling on a ticket which has been discounted because you are a student then make sure you have a student card with you or you may be required to pay the difference on arrival at the airport.

In Europe, two of the best places for buying cheap tickets are London and Amsterdam. In both places there are more bucket shops than you can point a stick at and their services and prices are well advertised. In Asia the cheapest places are Hong Kong and Penang (Malaysia) with Singapore and Bangkok (Thailand) trailing behind those.

Australians and New Zealanders are unlucky because officially there are no bucket shops since discounting tickets is illegal and few agents are willing to do it. Their governments have adopted a protectionist policy for their own respective airlines. Of course, it does happen but it's not easy to find. The Australian government even attempted to prosecute Singapore Airlines some time ago for selling discounted tickets through certain agents. The case was dropped when the Singapore government started to make noises about withdrawing landing rights for Qantas in Singapore.

In the USA, deregulation has made it much easier for travellers to find cheap tickets so all you need do is spend a day or two comparing prices at different travel agents. I've always found Student Council Travel Services in the States pretty clued-up about the cheapest tickets and routes so make sure you include them in your rounds of the agents. They have offices at: 205 East 42nd St (tel 212-661 1450) and 356 West 34th St, (tel 212-239 4257), both in New York; 1093 Broxton Avenue, Los Angeles (tel 213 208 3551); 5500 Atherton, Long Beach (tel 213-598 3338); UCSD Student Center, B-023, La Jolla (tel 619-452 0630) and 4429 Cass St (tel 619-270 6401) both in San Diego; 312 Sutter St, San Francisco (tel 415-421 3473); 2511 Channing Way, Berkeley (tel 415 848 8604); 729 Boylston St, Suite 201, Boston (tel 617-266 1926); and 1314 Northeast 43rd St, Seattle (tel 206-632 2448).

Having located the best place to buy your ticket, the next thing to do is decide whether you're going to fix up all your tickets from your home base or simply buy a one-way ticket to some destination in the Americas and take it from there. A return ticket is always cheaper than two single tickets unless the only flying you plan to do is between Europe and America and vice versa on stand-by. Also, with few exceptions, it's always cheaper to add on places to a long-haul ticket rather than buy a straight A to B ticket and start all over again at the other end.

Buying airline tickets in some American countries is a decidedly uneconomic proposition because of government sales taxes on airline tickets which range from 3% to 21%! Details of these taxes can be found under the Money sections in the various country chapters. There is perhaps one exception to this and that is in Costa Rica where cheap tickets are available from *OTEJ*, a student organisation.

The only other things you have to decide are where to fly to in America and what to do about onward ticket requirements. If you are coming from Europe or Australasia and want to work your way overland down through Central America then the cheapest options are generally to fly to a city in the southern states of the USA such as San Francisco, Los Angeles or Houston. From Europe, however, also look into the cost of flights direct to Mexico as there may be very little difference. If you don't want to go through Central America then the cheapest places to fly to are various cities in Colombia and Venezuela.

If you do decide to fly direct to Colombia or Venezuela remember that both countries demand onward tickets before they will allow you in. This being the case, travel agents won't sell you a single ticket to those countries unless you already have an onward ticket (or MCO). If you don't have this then you'll have to buy a return ticket.

In the examples given of the costs of getting from Australasia, Asia and Europe to the Americas, you should bear in mind that different agents offer different deals; the cost of a ticket often depends on whether you fly peak, shoulder or low season; and that air fares are always on the increase so treat them only as a guideline.

From Australasia

From Australia the cheapest way to get to the Americas is to fly to Los Angeles or San Fransisco from Sydney or Melbourne. The full one-way economy fare is A$1526 but the return APEX fare is A$1392 (off-peak), A$1749 (shoulder) and A$1938 (peak).

If you want to fly direct to South America then just about your only option is to fly Sydney/Melbourne/Brisbane to Santiago (Chile) via Tahiti and Easter Island by a combination of *UTA/Qantas* and *LAN-Chile*. *Qantas* fly once weekly Melbourne-Sydney-Tahiti on Fridays. *UTA* fly once weekly Sydney-Tahiti also on Fridays. Both these flights connect with the once weekly *LAN-Chile* flight to Santiago on Saturdays calling at Easter Island. You can stop off at the island if you like but you will be there for a week before you can get the next flight on to Santiago.

Starting from New Zealand there are flights from Auckland to Tahiti on Wednesdays and Fridays (*Air New Zealand*) and Thursdays (*UTA*). Like the flights from Australia, the Friday flight from Auckland connects with the *LAN-Chile* flight to Santiago on the Saturday.

The fares are as follows: Sydney-Santiago – A$1060 (APEX one way); A$1720 (Economy return excursion fare except Xmas/New Year); A$1950 (Economy return excursion fare Xmas/New Year); A$1400 (Normal economy fare one-way). Melbourne/Brisbane-Santiago – A$1110 (APEX one-way); A$1780 (Economy return excursion fare except Xmas/New Year); A$2010 (Economy return excursion fare Xmas/New Year); A$1460 (Normal economy fare one-way). Auckland-Santiago – NZ$2323 (Economy return excursion fare

April/May); NZ$2516 (Economy return excursion fare rest of year); NZ$1850 (Normal economy fare one-way).

For more information on these flights contact the *LAN-Chile* offices at 10th Floor, American Express Tower, 388 George St, Sydney 2000 (tel 02-231 1355); or the *UTA* offices at 33 Bligh St, Sydney 2000 (tel 02-233 3277); 459 Collins St, Melbourne (tel 61 2041), and 331 Queen St, Brisbane (tel 221 5655).

The other thing you should enquire about if you are starting from Australia or New Zealand and intend to go on from South America to Europe and then back home are Round the World tickets. There are some excellent deals available on this sort of ticket and you may be able to pick up one of these for less than the cost of a return excursion fare to South America! With Round the World tickets you must keep going in one direction – you cannot back-track – but you are allowed a certain number of stop-overs. The number of stops often depends on the price of the ticket, but is usually at least five. Tickets are valid for a year and you can even extend their validity beyond a year in some cases by paying the difference between the price at which you bought the ticket and the current price of the same.

I can recommend these tickets having had experience with one. I bought it in Brisbane for A$1850 with the routing: Brisbane-Auckland-Honolulu-LA-San Francisco-London-Nairobi-Harare-Perth-Sydney. From San Francisco I went surface down to South America and from London to Harare I also went surface and even managed to sell the London-Nairobi-Harare sector in London (otherwise I would have had to throw it away).

An excellent travel agent in Sydney run by two very friendly and helpful travellers, Gerry Virtue and Chris Dewhirst, is at 28 Market St. These people really understand the airline pricing system and how to get the best out of it. Otherwise try one of the

Student Travel Australia (STA) offices which are also very good. They are at: 220 Faraday St, Carlton, Melbourne, Vic 3053 (tel 03-347 6911); Union Building, University of Tasmania, Hobart (tel 002-34 1850); 1A Lee St, Railway Square, Sydney 2000 (tel 02-212 1255); Level 4, The Arcade, Union House, Adelaide University, Adelaide (tel 08-223 6620); Hackett Hall, University of WA, Perth (tel 09-380 2302); Concessions Building, Australian National University, Canberra (tel 062-470 8005); Shop 2, Societe General House, 40 Creek St, Brisbane, 4000 (tel 07 221 9629). In Brisbane you should also check out the Brisbane Flight Centre, Shop 23, Post Office Square, 260-280 Queen St, Brisbane (tel 07-229 9211).

From Asia

From Hong Kong the cheapest flights are to Los Angeles and San Francisco. The full one-way economy fare is US$678 but there are return excursion fares for US$978 (high season) and US$890 (low). Advance purchase one-way fares with a stopover in Honolulu or Tahiti are US$489 (high) and US$445 (low).

From Japan the cheapest flights are again to Los Angeles and San Fransisco. The full one-way economy fare is US$799 (Y 211,700) but the return APEX fares are US$943 (Y250,000) (peak) and US$939 (Y 249,000) (off-peak).

From Singapore to Los Angeles or San Fransisco the full one-way economy fare is US$1100 but the return excursion fares are available for US$1540 (peak) and US$1397 (off-peak). One way advance purchase fares are US$770 (peak) and US$699 (off-peak). It's well worth hunting around the travel agents as you may well be able to find something cheaper. One of the best places to try is Airmaster Travel, Tan Kong Building, 87-C Bukit Timah Rd.

From Europe

If you simply want to fly from Europe to

the USA one-way then there's no point in going to a bucket shop for a ticket since you won't get one any cheaper than going stand-by. If, however, you want a return ticket then it's often possible to save money by going to the bucket shops since many of them offer return tickets for less than the price of two single stand-by fares. Almost all the airlines operating between major European cities and the USA offer stand-by fares. It's a good idea to ring around the airlines the night before departure to check seat availability and get to the terminal of the airline you choose as soon as it opens in the morning.

There's an excellent choice of flights from London and the cheapest at present is London-New York by *Virgin Atlantic* (an off-shoot of Virgin Records) which costs £129 one-way. For bookings and seat availability ring 01-200 0200. You should also check out *People's Express* which flies London-Newark (across the river from New York). Many bucket shops offer return tickets on this routing for less than the price of two *Virgin Atlantic* one-way tickets so check them out if that's what you want.

Current fares from London to various USA cities are as follows:

City	One-way	Return
New York	£129-175	£239-315
Houston/Dallas	£162-168	£324-336
LA/San Francisco	£168-239	£336-408
Miami	–	£340

If you want to go direct from Europe to Latin America then there are a whole range of possibilities and it's here that bucket shops come into their own. The cheapest places to fly to are generally Barranquilla, Bogotá and Cartagena (Colombia) and Caracas (Venezuela).

The current fares from London are:

To – City	One-way	Return
Mexico City	£220-315	£430-482
Bogotá	£190-212	£380-424
Caracas	£180	£360
Quito	£199-307	£398-456
Lima	£205-253	£410-460
Buenos Aires	£247-276	£494-551
Rio de Janeiro	£232-318	£464-555
Recife	–	£452

Similar fares are available from other European cities but there are one or two outstanding bargains. One company which is very popular both with travellers destined for Africa as well as South America is *Point Air-Mulhouse*, 4 Rue des Orphelins, 68200 Mulhouse, France (tel 89-42 44 61), and 54 Rue des Ecoles, 75006 Paris, France. This company is a travel club though anyone is entitled to join for a small fee. It offers no-frills flights to various Latin American destinations including Lima and La Paz. For further details of their schedules and fares write (in French) for their brochure. You need to book seats as far in advance as possible with this company as there's often a heavy demand for tickets.

Another alternative, which quite a few people from central Europe are taking, are the cheap *Aeroflot* or *Interflug* flights from East Berlin to Lima via Cuba.

GETTING THROUGH THE USA

Hitch Hiking The ease with which you can hitch hike in the United States varies quite a bit from one part to another. It's not very easy in New York and New Jersey states or in the Mid-West. Elsewhere it's pretty good. As in Europe, it's illegal to hitch on the interstate roads themselves – you must keep to the ramps and access roads. Display your national flag on the front of your rucksack – this definitely helps to secure lifts. With luck you should be able to make it from New York to the Mexican border in five or six days. If you're looking for a confirmed or share-expenses lift in New York try:

Ride Bulletin Board, 130 West 24th St (tel 212 989 0153).

People's Transit (tel 1 800 547 0933) – this place matches up drivers with riders to all parts of the USA.

New York Ride Center, 159 West 33rd St (tel 99-279 3870) – also known as the Grey Rabbit Ride Center. This place verges on the commercial and all the rides are share-expenses lifts.

A Free Car – 'Drive-Away Schemes

Delivering a car from one point to another in the USA is a well-known method of transport for people who have a driving licence but no car. The way it works is that the owner of the car who wants it delivered from A to B but is unable to do it himself/herself contacts a 'drive-away' agency which then arranges for someone else to do the driving. That's where you come in. There are 'drive-away' agencies in all the major towns and cities and they usually have plenty of cars which need moving.

What you have to do is ring round the various agencies until you find one which has a car that needs to be delivered in the direction you want to go. The busiest routes are from east to west (and vice versa) and north to south. On these routes it's possible to pick up something the same day you start ringing around. On other routes you may have to wait around for a day or two until something turns up or even compromise a little on the exact route you had in mind.

You need a driving licence from your own country and preferably an International Driving Permit too although the latter isn't strictly necessary. The agency will also ask you for a reference from someone who is a resident in the USA but if you don't know anyone then they're generally satisfied with taking details of your passport. You have to sign a contract which gives you a fixed number of days in which to deliver the car but it's sometimes possible to re-negotiate this with the owners if they're willing.

If the car breaks down en route you have to contact the owners or the agency and they'll extend the time of delivery. A US$50 deposit is taken from you by the agency and refunded in full on delivery. The first tankful of gas is usually provided free (owners often give you extra if they take a liking to you – we even got put up for the night as well!). After that it's up to you to do the driving and pay for the gas. If you share a car in this way with other travellers you can get through the States for next to nothing.

All the 'drive away' agencies advertise in the local papers under the heading 'Drive-Away'. They also have a listing in the phone books.

Bus Both *Greyhound* and *Trailways* run long-distance buses to just about everywhere imaginable in the States and also to Mexico City. They have their own large terminals in most places with cafés, bars and baggage deposit lockers. During the summer months they often have fare promotion deals for seven days, 15 days and 30 days which give unlimited travel during the allotted period. There's also *Green Tortoise Line* which are similar to the now defunct *Magic Bus* which used to operate in Europe.

Getting Around

BUS

Road transport, especially by bus, is very well developed throughout Latin America and even the smallest places are accessible. The state of the roads and the quality of the buses is, however, another story. The two combined would provide any novelist with enough material to fill a hundred books and you'll certainly never be short of things to write home to your friends about. Virtually all the major roads and many of the minor ones throughout Central America are paved and in good repair; buses are generally quick, comfortable and reliable and, at least in the major cities and towns, all buses arrive and depart from a central terminal.

All the various bus companies maintain ticket offices at these terminals and have information boards posted where you can see at a glance how many routes they cover, departure times, prices and whether the bus is a direct one or otherwise. Where this is not the case, the addresses of the various bus stations have been given under the appropriate town and their location marked on the town plans. Seats on buses are numbered and booked in advance but, except on the major routes between large cities, it's unlikely that a bus will be fully booked up to within an hour of departure.

Until the civil war in El Salvador took on its present dimensions and the Sandinista government threw out Somoza in Nicaragua, there used to be international buses, notably *TICA* and *Sirca*, all the way from Mexico City to Panama City via Guatemala City, San Salvador, Tegucigalpa, Managua and San José. *TICA* have now suspended their services and only run between San José and Panama City. *Sirca* have likewise suspended most of their services and now only run between Managua and San José. So, to get from one country to another these days you have to take local buses to the border and change to another. This sometimes involves walking some distance.

The only exceptions you're likely to come across regarding what's been said about Central American road and bus conditions are to be found in northern Guatemala, Nicaragua north of the lakes (largely off-limits to foreigners at present) and rural Costa Rica. In Guatemala the roads from the Belize border to Tikal, Tikal to Flores and Flores to Puerto Barrios are atrocious and the buses look like retired 18th century tanks. In Nicaragua and Costa Rica bad road conditions are generally due to the rainy season when roads and sometimes bridges get washed out. In the dry season they're generally okay after repair even when unsurfaced. There is still no road connection between Central America and South America through the Darien jungle on the border between Panama and Colombia. The Pan American Highway comes to an end about 80 km beyond Panama City and doesn't start again until you're well inside Colombia.

There are a number of possibilities of bridging this gap either by plane or a combination of boats and walking. Details are given in the Panama chapter.

Generalising about bus and road conditions in South America is much more difficult, if only because it's such a vast area with such a wide range of geographical and climatic conditions. Certainly some of the worst roads are to be found in the highlands of Peru (average height 3500 metres) where in places the only thing which distinguishes a road from a river bed is the absence of water.

Buses are stripped to their bare essentials, tyres usually haven't seen tread for years and they all seem to be held together by the double set of springs at the back, which makes the suspension rock-hard and ensures that each and every bump is transmitted directly to your backside. Seats are numbered – after a fashion – and bookable in advance but that's just the start. When all the seats are taken the corridor is then packed to capacity and beyond, and the roof is loaded with cargo to at least half the height of the bus and topped by the occasional goat.

You start to have serious doubts whether you'll ever get there and suffer from moments of sheer panic when you hit a pot-hole or a section of road with the wrong camber and the whole caboose lurches alarmingly over to one side. But somehow, 18 hours or so later, after enduring this fetid human sardine can, you're spat out onto the pavement feeling like a jellied mixture of death warmed up and super-tenderised steak. However, after a shower and a long rest punctuated by vivid recollections, you wake up and start laughing about it, remembering how beautiful the mountains and valleys were even through your bleary eyes. Then you're ready for the next leg of the journey – well, almost!

Similar stretches of road can be found in parts of Colombia and Bolivia and again in the Brazilian jungle where roads are characterised more by vast seas of red dust (or yawning oceans of thick mud after rain) rather than pot-holes or boulders. Overtaking from behind a dust-storm where visibility rarely exceeds a few metres, with trucks carrying umpteen tonnes of lumber coming the other way, can be a hazardous business. One fondly hopes and eventually comes to believe that the Brazilians have some mysterious sixth sense about these things. You'd better believe it, otherwise you might end up adding a touch of colour to the end of a mahogany log.

Elsewhere on the sub-continent the roads are generally excellent and this is particularly true of Chile, Argentina, Uruguay, Brazil and most of Venezuela. In all these countries and in Bolivia the bus terminals are centralised but in Colombia, Ecuador, Peru and Paraguay this is often not the case though things are

changing rapidly in Colombia and Paraguay.

Buses vary from the super-de-luxe Mercedes-Benz coaches found in Argentina, Brazil, Chile, Venezuela and parts of Bolivia to sardine tins like those which run in many parts of the Peruvian highlands. Obviously the sort of buses you find on any particular route depends a great deal on the state of the road. All the same, one company will sometimes run a mixture of new and geriatric buses on the same route and there's no way of knowing which you're going to get until it turns up. Don't make the mistake of assuming that because you see a company running new buses along a certain route that you'll necessarily get one too.

Chile, Argentina, Uruguay and Brazil offer sleeper buses on long hauls. These usually go at night and cost twice as much as the ordinary buses. They're not really worth it unless you have money to burn as the ordinary buses are very comfortable especially in comparison with buses in the Peruvian Andes.

TRAINS

The Central and South American railways cover some of the most spectacular routes in the world. Where they occur they're invariably cheaper than buses (even in first class) but they're also slower. Some that you shouldn't miss if you're going that way are:

Chihuahua-Los Mochis (Mexico) on the Pacific coast via the Barranca del Cobre – comparable to the USA's Grand Canyon.
Santa Marta-Bogotá (Colombia) – slow rise from sea level to the capital at 2640 metres.
Lima-Huancayo (Peru) – rapid rise from sea level to Andean altiplano at about 3200 metres, via the 4600 metre Croya pass. It is one of the highest railways in the world.
Puno/Juliaca-Arequipa (Peru) – similar to the last and including another 4600 metre pass.

La Paz-Arica (Bolivia-Chile) – 4000 metres down to sea level via the Lauca National Park.
La Paz-Calama (Bolivia-Chile) – 4000 metres down to sea level. Spectacular lunar-type landscapes and extinct volcanoes.

Many railways were not built to carry passengers but to service the needs of mining concerns and banana or coffee plantations and so are of limited or no use to travellers. There are quite a few such lines in the Central American republics and Chile.

In South America there are generally three types of trains. The first is the *ferrobus* which is a relatively fast, diesel-powered single or double car which caters for passengers going from A to B but not intermediate stations. They stop only occasionally and at main stations and meals are often available on board. You must book in advance (a day or so will be adequate). These are the most expensive trains and the preferred means of transport in Bolivia. They're excellent value.

The second type are the *tren rapide* which are more like ordinary trains and pulled by either a diesel or steam engine. They're relatively fast, have a limited number of stops and generally cost a little less than a *ferrobus*.

The third type are ordinary passenger trains, sometimes called *expreso* ('express' is a relative term in Spanish America particularly with respect to trains), which are slower, stop at most stations en route and cost less. There are generally two classes with 2nd class being very crowded. Lastly there are mixed passenger and freight trains which take everything and everyone, stop at every station and a lot of other places besides, take forever to get to their destination and are dirt cheap.

AIR

Because of the vast distances between

centres of population and the barriers imposed on overland communications by geography, South America was one of the first places to develop internal air services. There is an extensive pattern of internal flights especially in the Andean countries and prices are surprisingly low; they're often little more than the bus fare. After several 18 hour-plus bus journeys across the mountains over atrocious roads you may decide here and there, as many travellers do, that you can't face another and take a flight.

There are one or two points you should bear in mind relating especially to Peru and Bolivia, however. First, planes rarely depart on time and can be up to half a day late. Second, the concept of queueing for a boarding pass is virtually unknown. In practice, if your baggage is on the scales, you get served. Watch the locals: you'll soon suss out the 'system'. Third, *AeroPeru* and *Lloyd Aereo Boliviano* are notorious for cancelling planes at a moment's notice, so a backlog of passengers builds up, all of whom are intent on getting on the next flight. This is clearly impossible but that doesn't deter them so it's bedlam at the check-in counter. The most aggressive, most devious and those with least baggage are the ones who come out of this ordeal smiling, unless the airline lays on an additional plane. In Peru, the most notorious spot for this is Ayacucho which is perhaps fortunate as it's a pleasant place to stay for a few days but still disastrous if you're going to Lima to catch a connecting international flight.

In Peru you must re-confirm flights 48 hours before departure regardless of what anyone tells you to the contrary. Neglect to do this and you probably won't have a seat even though you have been told it is confirmed.

Internal flights in Chile, Argentina, Brazil and Venezuela tend to be considerably more expensive. You may hear stories about free flights on board military aircraft from time to time. Yes, some people still do make it but these flights are like hen's teeth.

Quite a few travellers buy Air Passes (the Brazil Air Pass being one of the most popular). For a fixed sum these passes give you unlimited air travel inside a country for 14 or 21 days but they must be bought outside the country in hard currency. The Brazil Air Pass costs US$250 for 14 days and US$330 for 21 days. They're good value in terms of mileage or if your time is limited but they do have two distinct disadvantages. The first is that once you start using one then you're locked into a schedule and you can't spend an extra few days in a place which you take a liking to. The second is that airports are often a long way from the city centres so if you get there late at night or have to set off very early in the morning then you're at the mercy of the taxi drivers. Three or four days of this and you can tot up quite a bill in taxi fares. There are public buses to all the airports in Brazil but they generally only run from 7-8 am to 8-9 pm – if that.

HITCHING

It's possible to hitch all over Central and South America but in many countries if you're looking for free lifts you'll be there a *long* time. Countries where this doesn't apply are Argentina (except Patagonia), Chile (except south of Puerto Montt where there are very few roads), Uruguay and parts of Brazil. In the latter it's easy most of the time.

Elsewhere free lifts are the exception rather than the rule as hitching is a recognised form of public transport, especially among poor people and in the highlands where buses can be infrequent. There are more or less fixed fares over certain routes (just ask the other people what they're paying) and these are generally less than the bus fare would be but can be the same in some places. You get a better view from the top of a lorry and people tend to be more friendly but if you're hitching on the altiplano in the

Andean countries take some warm clothing with you. Once the sun goes down or is obscured by mountains it gets *very* cold.

There's no need to stand at the side of the road waiting for a lift unless this happens to be convenient for you. Virtually every town has its central lorry park often located close to or in the market. Ask around here for a lorry going in the direction you want to take and how much it will cost and be there about half an hour before the driver says he's going. If the driver has as many passengers as he wants then you'll leave more or less on time. If not it's probable that you'll get a guided tour of the town as the driver hunts for more passengers.

TAKING YOUR OWN VEHICLE

The only time I've ever taken my own wheels with me was one time when I drove a 1938 Wolseley to Afghanistan – and back – but I'd be reluctant to do it again because I found that it soaked up a considerable amount of time in maintenance and repairs and involved a lot of pre-trip preparation.

I didn't find it particularly cheap either – for a start, you can't hitch-hike if you have your own wheels. Nevertheless, quite a few people do go to the trouble of taking their own transport with them. One of the first people I ever met who'd driven a VW Kombi around the world was Jonathon Hewat. He wrote a book called, *Overland and Beyond*, (Roger Lascelles, 47 York Rd, Brentford, Middx TW8 0QP, UK; £2.50) which is well worth reading if you're contemplating such a trip. Jonathon had the following comments:

Costs. Astronomical however you look at it! The whole process is rife with problems and is the worst part of any overland trip. If you try to sell the van instead of shipping it and then buy another one on the other side, you will have equal hassles with carnet rules and regulations, and fitting out another vehicle as a home-on-wheels is likely to be difficult except in the USA or in Australia. You will find that there are hidden extras such as landing, port and unloading charges (we averaged around US$100 per shipping on top of freight costs).

Thieves abound in profusion on every dock. Stay with your vehicle the entire time, *day and night*. If you ignore this almost certainly something will be stolen. If you're shipping your van with all your belongings in it (a) remove everything 'removable' from the exterior – horns, hubcaps, wipers, wing mirrors, etc. If you don't someone else will; (b) seal the living area from the driving cab; (c) draw all curtains in the living area so that no-one can see in; (d) remove everything from the driver's cab – mirrors, fan, cassette player, ashtray, compass, contents of glove compartment; (e) double-lock living area doors, having padlocked all interior cupboards. All this may sound excessive. It isn't. During our entire journey we did not meet a single traveller who had not had something stolen – usually while shipping.

That's one point of view, but recently I had a letter from another friend, Dr Norbert Holtschmidt, who is presently on his way round the world in quite a large truck. He painted a completely different picture and suggested that the comments which were made in the previous edition were partly nonsense and partly obsolete. He writes:

First of all, to go from North to South America or vice versa you have other options than just those between Panama and Colombia. And cheaper ones too such as between Guayaquil and Baltimore (USA). *Transnave* charged us less than US$300 for our van (a VW would have been US$200). And then, even our shipping costs from Australia (US$1900) will pay for themselves within the nine to 10 months we shall spend on this half of the continent simply because of the saving on accommodation, food and transport (diesel fuel is usually cheap).

Driving the last four months, for example, we averaged US$500 per month for all our costs including not only food and transport for two but an 18-day trip to Galapagos and a five-day shipping of our van and ourselves from Manaus to Belém as well. Compare it with your costs considering inflation in the meantime. I guess even after adding US$200 as part of shipping costs we are competing very well.

As far as safety in ports is concerned, we've never had any problems. Not even in Callao when we arrived three days after the van. But then we blocked off the whole van and separated the driver's cab from the living section – it's easy if you think ahead and take a few precautions. And what about theft in Peru and Colombia? As a backpacker you have to find yourself a safe hotel or other place to leave your gear and you have to watch it very carefully when travelling by bus or train. For us it's much easier: at least while driving, theft is impossible. And for overnighting we do not need to stay in populated, touristed (spoilt) areas where they are already waiting for you. We usually stay in rural districts which are much safer. And in places notorious for robbery like Bogotá and Lima, there are always churches or foreign schools if you don't fancy the police stations.

And finally the independence to stay where you like. What about a night among the ruins of Sacsayhuaman, next to an ancient Indio cemetery, or beside the ruins of Wilka Wayna. Or, to choose another country: what did you really see of the beauties of the Gran Sabana in southern Venezuela? Could you ask the bus or the truck driver to stop at the marvellous Salto Jaspe to see the cascades flowing down the black and red stones? Or could you have a close look at Salto Kama or Salto del Danto on the same route?

And not to forget health. We always have sterile water instead of diarrhoea. You see, there are not only disadvantages.

I'd readily agree that he makes some very valid points but then I don't go travelling in order to feel secure nor would I swap the countless memories of scenes I got involved in by being able to take off into the bush or the mountains whenever I felt like it without having to arrange safe garaging for a vehicle and contents. And I probably wouldn't have met half the people that I did had I not used public transport and stayed in cheap hotels. Not only that, but if I felt I could see a lot more by spending only a little more than I would by taking public transport then I'd hire a car and hunt round the budget hotels for a few people to share it with. Hiring the occasional car isn't that expensive especially as you can pay in local currency.

In the end I suppose it comes down to a question of personal choice.

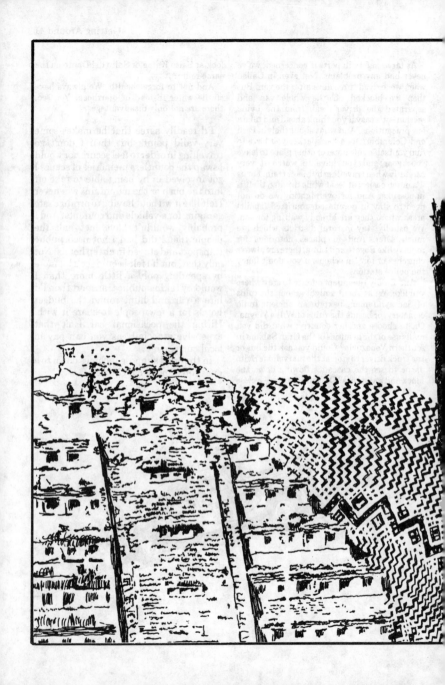

Mexico

DENNIS '82

Mexico

Mexico is one of Latin America's most interesting countries with so many different facets you could spend a lifetime here and still only get to know a small part of the whole. It's incredible how just crossing the Rio Grande from the USA takes you not only into another country but into a completely different world. They're as alike as chalk and cheese.

Unlike the United States, whose people are mostly of European or African descent, Mexico's population of some 70 million consists largely of *mestizos* – people of mixed Spanish and Indian blood. Conquest of the region by a European nation didn't result, in this case, in the attempted genocide or enslavement of the indigenous people. Not that the Indians were treated as equal partners in the new colony – they were not – but there was large scale intermarriage and interbreeding. In contrast to the United States where surviving Indian tribes are now an insignificant part of the nation, in Mexico there are still millions of more or less pure bloods who retain their own customs, cultural heritage and languages. Many tribes remain semi-autonomous on the fringes of the mainstream.

The contrasts don't end there. Of course it's possible to find extreme poverty close to conspicuous wealth in the United States too but in Mexico the gap can be enormous. Unemployment and under-employment in Mexico is estimated to be a staggering 50% and yet the country sits on top of vast oil reserves which, elsewhere in the world, have made countries rich beyond their wildest dreams. No wonder so many Mexicans attempt to cross the border illegally to find work in the United States. At least there's a chance there.

Nevertheless, as is often the case in poor countries, people are generally warm and easy-going and respond encouragingly to any visitor who makes an effort to speak their language and learn something of the customs.

44

Like Mesopotamia, the Nile and Indus Valleys, Mexico was one of the ancient cradles of civilisation with a recorded history stretching back as far as 3000 BC. That civilisation was able to develop unaffected by events in the rest of the world right up to the beginning of the 16th century, yet when contact was made the effect was devastating.

The indigenous peoples who made a lasting impact include the Olmec (800 BC to 600 AD) who inhabited the Vera Cruz, Tabasco, Oaxaca and highland Guatemalan areas. They are famous for their huge carved stone figures character-ised by flat noses, thick sensual lips and slit-like eyes. Their influence is visible on the very earliest relics at Monte Albán – a vast, artificially-flattened mountain-top ceremonial centre outside of Oaxaca which has played host to a succession of pre-Colombian civilisations which grew up on Mexican soil.

Further north in the valley of Anáhuac (where Mexico City stands today) another tribe, the Toltec, developed a civilisation (200 BC to 900 AD) which left one of the ancient world's most impressive mon-uments – the Pyramids of Teotihuacán. These are only part of what was once an immense ceremonial city covering some 27 square km. Other gems to be dis-covered there are the remains of temples to Tlaloc, the rain god, and Quetzalcoatl, the plumed serpent god. In common with their rivals at the time, the Toltec possessed ideographic writing, a type of paper book and a concept of time based on two calendars. The first of these was a divinatory calendar based on a 260-day count and another for everyday use based on a 360-day count. The two interlocked to coincide once every 52 years.

The first phase of Toltec expansion came to an end around 900 AD after which its centre moved south to places like Tula and parts of the Yucatán. Wholesale migrations, it seems, were not just a feature of ancient Asian civil-isations.

As a result of these migrations, the Toltec came into contact with the Mayan tribes who, by then, had also undertaken a migration from their original lands in the jungles and highlands of central America. The contact proved fertile for both groups as the ruins of the various Mayan cities in northern Yucatán indicate. It was during these various migrations that Tlaloc, known as Chac to the Mayans, became the foremost deity. His reclining image is found in almost all of the ruined cities of the Yucatán.

There were many other groups such as the Mixtec, Zapotec and Totonac who developed their own forms of civilisation at much the same time. It was all to become the heritage of the Aztec by the time this group made their appearance as an organised tribe around 1200 AD.

The Aztec came onto the pages of history as a small tribe who took over a number of islands on Lake Texcoco. There they grew crops on floating islands made out of woven reed baskets about three metres in diameter, filled with earth and anchored to the shallow lake bed. Roots penetrating through the bottom of the baskets eventually fixed each one of these in place. On these the Aztecs were able to grow all their food until conquest opened up more land for them on the shores of the lake. The remains of this method of cultivation can be seen today at Xochimilco, a southern suburb of Mexico City.

The structure of Aztec society was similar to that of other neighbouring tribes. It consisted predominantly of maize farmers who belonged to a kind of clan with a tribal council and an elected headman. From among the various clans, certain members of the councils were selected as advisors to the tribal chief (generally dubbed as the 'emperor' by westerners in the later history of the tribe). These advisors were responsible for electing the next leader on the death of the old one. New leaders could be chosen from among the brothers of the previous

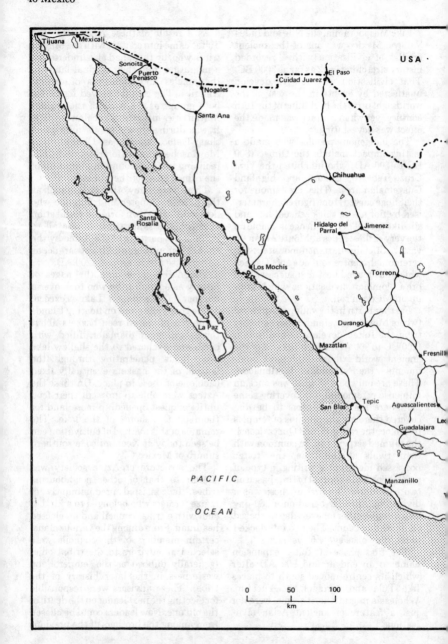

Mexico

leader or, if there were none, from among his nephews.

In common with neighbouring tribes, maize and its cultivation was the most important activity of Aztec life. The day began and ended with maize and for the common people, much of the day was taken up in the time-consuming process of preparing *tortillas*. Unlike the Incas in South America who cultivated potatoes as well as maize, and the Mayas who took advantage of a whole variety of fruit and other forest products, the Aztecs were entirely at the mercy of the maize harvest. Their agriculture was not as highly developed as that of the Incas and they knew little about fertilisers or irrigation.

Their religion was centred around maize and a successful harvest depended on gaining the favour of the rain god, Tlaloc. This in turn depended on a constant supply of sacrificial victims whose hearts would be gouged out of their bodies and offered to the god. The only way of assuring a constant supply of victims for this purpose was to wage war and in time, perpetual war became the Aztecs' assurance that life would continue. By the time Cortés arrived, the scale on which these sacrifices took place had become obsessive. This explains in part why many of the 400 or so tribes which the Aztec had conquered were more than willing to become allies of Cortés to bring down the 'empire'. They were not to know that they would very shortly be exchanging one form of bondage for another.

For its time, the Aztec capital, Tenochtitlán, was a remarkable example of advanced urban planning with fresh water and sanitation systems far better than anything Europe possessed until the 18th century. It covered an area of two square km, had a population of over 300,000 (larger than London or Paris at the time), and was connected to the mainland by four causeways. The latter served not just as access routes but also as dykes. Lake Texcoco has no natural

outlets so heavy rain could cause a rapid rise in the level of the lake. The causeways also served to minimise the effect of waves whipped up whenever there was high wind.

As in Venice, there were many interconnecting canals which honeycombed the city. At its centre, enclosed by high walls, were the magnificent temples of Huitzilopochtli, Tlaloc and Xipe, Moctezuma's palace, the ball court, the quarters of the military order known as the Eagle Knights, and a huge market. The temples were visible from far away and by all accounts, the Spaniards could hardly believe their eyes when the city was first sighted.

Sadly, hardly anything remains of this city as Cortés razed it and the stones were used to construct the Spanish city which rose on the same site. Very little remains of Lake Texcoco too, which has been drained several times in the last 400 years. There is, however, an excellent reconstruction of the city in the Museum of Anthropology in Mexico City.

Cortés small band of around 500 desperadoes and opportunists with their few horses couldn't have arrived on the coast at a more opportune moment. An Aztec legend had it that the god, Quetzalcoatl, had once been ruler of a kingdom in Mexico, lost it in battle, and then sailed away across the Gulf vowing to return one day on his birthday. According to the Aztec calendar, 1519 happened to be one such date and when Cortés arrived in Tenochtitlán along with his 4,000 or so Tlaxcala Indian allies he was welcomed as the returning god and showered with gifts. The awe in which the Spaniards – and especially their horses – were held lasted just long enough for them to manoeuvre into a position where they were able to make Moctezuma a prisoner within his own palace and to effectively take control.

The apparent ease with which all this was accomplished, however, was illusory. Not only had Cortés to rush back to the coast for a while to deal with a punitive expedition sent out by the Governor of Cuba to re-assert royal control, but on returning to Tenochtitlán, he found the Aztec in revolt. A skirmish was fought shortly after this in which Moctezuma was stoned to death by his own people and a new leader elected. Control was rapidly slipping from Cortés hands and a retreat was imperative. It was intended to be secret but a watchful Indian woman raised the alarm and in the ensuing battle thousands of Cortés' Indian allies and many hundreds of his own Spanish troops were killed and the treasure they had accumulated was lost in the lake. The retreat became known in Mexican history as the 'Noche Triste'.

Undaunted, Cortés returned the following year with reinforcements and after many battles with various Indian tribes and a naval blockade of Tenochtitlán lasting several months, the Aztec were finally defeated. Almost immediately, the Spanish began an intensive campaign to obliterate the Indian way of life, their religions and customs, and to lay a Spanish veneer over the whole country. The Catholic Church was their principal assistant. 'Saints' and 'miracles' were discovered in the most convenient situations in order to effect conversion of the millions. The Indian gods were simply re-named to fit acceptably into the Catholic pantheon of martyrs, angels and saints and, although it may have looked convincing, in practice it was very superficial. This is very obvious even today. No-where outside of Ecuador, Peru and Bolivia is Catholicism so obviously a mixture of pagan and Christian elements.

On a secular level, the cities of Tenochtitlán and the Mayan cities of the Yucatán were torn down to provide building stone for the new Spanish cities and churches which rose in their place. Indian tribal records were burnt, new plants and animals introduced and mines opened. Land was distributed in a lavish manner among the *conquistadores* and many of them ended up fabulously wealthy within just a few short years. A rigid economic order was imposed on the new colony whereby everything was designed in Spain, controlled by Spain and operated in a manner which would best benefit Spain regardless of the effect this might have in Mexico. It should be remembered that the Spanish were only just completing the re-conquest of Spain from the Moors at the time and were at the height of their confidence.

The colonial period was to last some 300 years during which time the colony was milked for all that it could produce. Trade with any nation other than Spain was rigidly controlled and non-Spanish immigration was prohibited. The trade restrictions were particularly irksome to locally-born Spanish and *mestizos* since it made many products prohibitively expensive and involved long delays in delivery.

Naturally, Spain couldn't keep things this way forever and a lively smuggling tradition grew up and flourished alongside the 'legitimate' trade. This involved goods which originated in China and the East Indies just as much as the industrial products of Britain, France and Holland. The regulation which generated the most resentment, however, was the one which decreed that only the *Peninsulares*, Spaniards born in Spain, were allowed to hold high office in the colonies.

In the end, the many indignities became intolerable for the *criollos* (the Spanish born in Mexico) and the standard of revolt was raised by a priest, Miguel Hidalgo, and a captain of the colonial army, Ignacio Allende. The rebels came very close to success but were captured by the royalist troops, executed, and their heads stuck on spikes outside the Alhondiga (the granary at Guanajuato). Nevertheless, Spain's days were numbered and 11 years later independence became a reality when Agusti'n Iturbide switched sides and the royalist troops were defeated.

The centuries of colonial exploitation with their attendant lack of economic and political development, however, were soon to take their toll. Stability in Mexico, as in Central and South America, was to be a long time in coming.

At independence, Mexico stretched from Panama to Oregon. The various Central American republics quickly went their own way after the collapse of Iturbide's short-lived 'empire' and with corruption and mismanagement the order of the day, what wealth Mexico had was soon squandered and the country forced to default on its foreign loans. Then, in 1836, Texas revolted and declared itself an independent republic.

The army which was sent north, under the command of Santa Ana, to re-assert Mexican control was defeated and shortly afterwards Texas was annexed by the United States. The annexation rankled and this, together with the impasse over unpaid debts, border provocations and other differences, led to war between Mexico and the United States in 1846. Santa Ana, who had been exiled in disgrace to Cuba following the loss of Texas, persuaded the US government to smuggle him into Mexico where he promised to persuade the authorities to call off the hostilities on terms favourable to the United States. Once there, however, he persuaded the Mexican government to make him commander-in-chief and also president. Military analysts at the time predicted a Mexican victory but ineptitude lost the day. Mexico City was occupied in 1847 and the Mexicans were forced to cede a huge slice of their northern territory to the US. This land subsequently became the states of California, Arizona, Utah, Nevada and parts of Colorado, New Mexico and Wyoming.

Santa Ana retained the presidency until thrown out in 1857, when a period of reform began under the presidency of Benito Juárez, a Zapote Indian from the town of Guelatao outside Oaxaca. His programme of popular education, freedom of the press and speech, civil marriage, the separation of the church and state, and the redistribution of church lands and property was hotly contested by the conservatives. Civil war broke out and lasted for three years, finally ending with victory for Juárez.

His troubles were not over however. The war had emptied the treasury and Juárez was forced to suspend payment of the national debt. The creditor nations – Britain, France and Spain – landed troops at Vera Cruz to enforce payment and, having done so, the British and Spanish withdrew. The French, however, had grander schemes in mind and pushed on to occupy Mexico City after which they installed Maximillian von Hapsburg of Austria as Emperor of Mexico. Juárez took to guerrilla warfare to oppose the French but it was not until the civil war in the United States had ended and Washington insisted that the French leave Mexico that Juárez could resume the presidency. Maximillian was abandoned by his sponsor the French emperor, Napoleon III, and was shot along with his generals at Querétaro.

Juárez died a natural death five years later and was succeeded by another liberal, Lerdo de Tejada. His presidency lasted only a short time and he was overthrown by Porfirio Díaz who, as dictator, was to rule Mexico for the next 34 years. Díaz initiated a programme of industrialisation which included the construction of railways and roads and the erection of oil wells. In doing this he handed out concessions to foreign capitalists (always with a substantial rake-off for himself and his supporters) in such abundance that by the time he was overthrown foreigners owned virtually everything which was worth the bother.

All this was done at the expense of the poor. Whole tribes were forced off the land they had farmed since Aztec times. The *campesinos* were prohibited from leaving their employers without permission.

Strikes and labour unions were banned, the press silenced and political opposition brutally suppressed by any means deemed necessary by the secret police.

The inevitable revolution broke out in 1911 and lasted until 1927 though there were outbreaks of violence right up until 1930. The revolution was spearheaded by Carranza, the Governor of Coahuila, Obregón from Sonora, Pancho Villa from Chihuahua and Emiliano Zapata from the south. Their objectives were the destruction of the *haciendas*, redistribution of the land and the alleviation of the wretched poverty into which most people had sunk. Though the revolution was successful it was not accomplished before years of anarchy, bloodshed and banditry had taken their toll. It's this period of Mexican history which has been immortalised in numerous Hollywood movies. Although times have changed, the image of Mexico as a land of bandits decked out in crossed bandoliers and huge hats riding sinewy horses has stuck, and is how many people who have never visited the country imagine it to be.

The revolution was eventually institutionalised in the *Partido Revolucionario Institutional* (PRI) following the election of Obregón as president and since then Mexico has enjoyed a stable government. The large estates have been divided up into *ejidos* (communal lands) and smallholdings, irrigation has been promoted, wages raised, education made available to all and oil wells, airports, electricity and other important industries nationalised.

It all sounds impressive and with Mexico now one of the world's largest exporters of oil it might be expected that the average peasant now enjoys a reasonable standard of living. In some ways this is true, but in other ways, the expectations of the revolution have fallen far short of being realised. Mexico has an ability to squander enormous amounts of money on ill-considered, ill-conceived, uncompleted or unnecessary projects and its national debt, which is touching US$1000 billion, is one of the largest in the world. It obviously will never be able to repay it.

The average peasant still has to make do with a very basic diet of *tortillas*, beans and rice; live in a thatched shack without windows, running water or sanitation; is still often illiterate and has to work long hours. There are no home comforts and it's a hard life.

There is also the enduring colonial legacy of corruption. Almost everyone in public office from government ministers down to traffic cops regards it as their right to make as much money as they see fit out of bribery, although here it goes under the euphemism of *mordida* ('little bite'). It's a national institution and goes all the way from the dollar a customs inspector may ask for what should be a free stamp in your passport, to the millions which government ministers and their friends may be paid for pulling strings or turning a blind eye to sharp practices.

On the other hand, the harshness of life and the corruption and exploitation have given its artists a brilliant understanding of satire. While you are in Mexico, make sure you see Diego Rivera's monumental paintings in the National Palace in Mexico City and Orozco's work in the Government Palace and the Hospicio Cabañas in Guadalajara. It's some of the most powerful stuff you're ever likely to come across.

VISAS

Visas are not required by anyone but everyone must have a Tourist Card. These are issued by embassies, consulates and most airline offices or you can get them at the border. They are free and, depending on your nationality, are valid for a stay of either 30 or 90 days (180 days for US citizens). The 30-day Tourist Cards are extendable up to a total of 90 days. US and Canadian citizens don't even require passports – just some proof of nationality.

Citizens of Chile, Lebanon and South Africa need special government permission before being allowed into the country.

Extensions of stay take at least two days to process but can take longer so if you have the option, get a 90-day Tourist Card at the outset. If you get your Tourist Card at the border you may well be asked for US$1 despite the fact that it is clearly stamped 'gratis'. You're not obliged to pay it but if you want 90 days instead of 30 then hand that dollar over.

Guatemalan visas The best place to get these are in Mexico City although there are consulates in Comitán and Chetumal closer to the border. They cost US$10.

MONEY
US$1 = M$390 up to M$505 (rising constantly)

The unit of currency is the Mexican peso (M$) = 100 centavos. There is no restriction on the import or export of local currency and there's a free market for the peso so there's no blackmarket. Change your money at banks or casas de cambio. Cash is much more useful than travellers' cheques, which you may have difficulty changing at many banks. Inflation is high and the exchange rate of the peso is constantly escalating against the dollar so you're advised to change only enough money to get you through a few days at a time. Don't bring Canadian dollars to Mexico – the exchange rates are poor and it's sometimes not even possible to change them.

It's very difficult to buy US dollars in Mexico as no-one wants to part with them. The only place which we have heard of that will, is the casa de cambio on Calle Rio Teber, behind the Sheraton Hotel (itself on Paseo de la Reforma) in Mexico City. To buy dollars there you must have US dollar travellers' cheques and even then you can only buy up to a maximum of US$300.

INFORMATION
Mexico is one of the world's most tourist-conscious nations and maintains information offices in many North American cities, most West European and Australasian capitals and in Japan. A request for information usually results in the delivery of a huge parcel of glossy leaflets, maps and other information. Most of it is quite useful in planning where you are going to go.

Apart from these external offices, most Mexican towns of any size or interest have their own tourist offices which are usually good and almost always have a map of the town though sometimes they're a little sketchy. The national HQ is at Calle Masaryk 172 between Hegel and Emerson, Colonia Polanco, at the back of Chapultepec Park, Mexico City, but it isn't really worth going there as there are two more convenient branch offices in the centre of the city.

Two helpful publications are *The Gazer – El Miron* and *This Week – Una Semana*. The first is a weekly magazine in Spanish and English which has information on hotels, bars, airlines, banks, maps, sightseeing suggestions and useful addresses and is free from hotels, bars, restaurants, travel agents and the like. The latter is similar and also free.

MAIL
Postage rates can be very high in Mexico so don't rush off to the post office with huge parcels under the impression that you'll be able to send them home for a song.

Letters sent to a *lista de correos* for collection are only kept for 10 days in most places so this is going to require some fine tuning among your friends back home.

WORK
At one time it was fairly easy to make some money by teaching English in Mexico but this isn't the case any more. Jobs are hard to find even for qualified

people. (It's officially illegal to work in Mexico without a work permit). If you are thinking of working then you'd be well advised to fix something up before you set off. Respectable institutions pay up to US$10 per hour but they will only take qualified and experienced staff.

Learning Spanish, on the other hand, is becoming increasingly popular not only in Mexico but in Guatemala.

MAPS

A good road map of Mexico is essential if you are going to be spending any amount of time in the country and especially if you are going to be doing most of your travelling by bus. There are hundreds of different bus companies between the major cities and the choice of routes can be bewildering without a map. A number of oil companies offer quite adequate free maps but the best are probably those put out by the Mexican Automobile Association, Chapultepec 276, Mexico City; and the Dirección General de Geográfia y Meterología, Avenida Observatorio 192, Mexico City 18, which is near the Observatorio metro station.

GETTING THERE

Since Mexico is one of the cheapest places to get to from North America and Europe, details of international flights to the country and overland transport from the USA are dealt with in the introductory Facts for the Visitor chapter.

The only international flight which will be mentioned here is the one to Cuba. For those who would like to make the detour to Cuba then Mexico is the cheapest place to fly from. There are flights from both Mexico City and Mérida, the latter being the cheaper. Check with *Cubana de Aviación*, Avenida Melchor Ocampo 469, Mexico City (near the Chapultepec end); and with *SETEJ*, Hamburgo 273, Zona Rosa, Mexico City, for the cheapest flights. SETEJ often organises charter flights and so can offer cheaper fares than you would normally get through the airlines themselves. This organisation will willingly send you details of their current programme through the mail. There is a Cuban embassy in Mexico City and a consulate in Mérida where you can get visas.

GETTING AROUND
Air

The two major carriers on the internal routes are *Aeromexico*, Paseo de la

Reforma 64, Mexico City; and *Mexicana*, on the corner of Avenida Juárez and Balderas, Mexico City. The former also covers the international routes. Between them these two companies have flights to most of the larger cities of Mexico.

Two smaller carriers are *Aerocaribe* which connects the Yucatán resorts of Cancún and Chetumal; and *Aeroviasa Oaxaqueñas* which has daily flights between Oaxaca and Puerto Escondido on the Pacific coast. The latter is worth considering if you don't fancy what can often be a 12-hour bus ride over rough and hair-raising roads and it's very cheap.

Bus

Mexico has an excellent system of paved roads even in rural areas. The bus network is equally good and is one of the best in Latin America. On long-distance routes there are generally both 1st and 2nd class buses. The former are fast, comfortable, stop only occasionally for a meal break and are more expensive. Choose them for long journeys. The 2nd class buses are generally older, often crowded and stop frequently to pick up and put down passengers. They cost around 10% less than the 1st class buses. Seats are numbered on the 1st class buses and on some of the 2nd class buses. Booking in advance is advisable although it's unlikely that buses will be fully booked within an hour or two of departure except around Christmas, New Year and Easter when there's heavy demand for seats.

Almost all large cities and many smaller ones have purpose-built central bus terminals where all the various bus companies have their offices so it's simplicity itself finding the bus you want. Destinations and ticket prices are usually prominently displayed so even if your command of Spanish isn't up to much you'll rarely have any problems. These terminals usually have good facilities such as toilets, bookshops, restaurants and left-luggage facilities. If you go to the

toilets there then have some small change ready as tipping the attendant is more or less obligatory. Where there are several bus companies on any particular run make sure you know which route they are going to take. Some may call at out-of-the-way places en route and increase the journey time. You might not mind this at all if you're in no hurry but otherwise it could be a source of frustration.

When you are buying tickets it helps to be familiar with a number of words which are often used in conjunction with the timetables:

asiento	seat
boleto	ticket
corto	short route (similar to *directo*)
cuota	via freeway/motorway (ie fastest route)
directo	direct
llegada	arrival
puntos intermedios	intermediate points
regreso	return
salida	departure
1a	1st class
2a	2nd class

A comprehensive list of bus schedules, journey times and fares is obviously outside the scope of a book of this nature and wouldn't be particularly useful or viable in any case since, although journey times remain much the same, schedules and fares change constantly. Fares, however, are very cheap and certainly aren't going to burn a hole in your pocket. 1st class buses cost about US$0.01 per km and 2nd class buses slightly less.

Train

Trains are generally cheaper than buses even if you travel in 1st class. The exception is where there are such things as *autovía* – special luxury carriages with their own diesel engine, found on certain tourist routes. In South America they would generally be called *ferrobus*. They are, however, much slower than buses. Rail fares are subsidised by the government so 2nd class is often very crowded, noisy and uncomfortable. It's better to pay the little bit extra and travel 1st class. On long hauls there are buffet cars and sleeping compartments. The latter are said to be air-conditioned but you should take this with a pinch of salt because often it doesn't work so during the day it can get as hot as hell in there. Indeed, you may well find that people with sleeping compartments ride between the carriages during the day because it's cooler (though often very dusty!).

If you're coming in from the USA you can pick up Mexican railways at the border towns of Mexicali/Calexico, Nogales, Cuidad Juárez/El Paso, Ojinga/Presidio, Piedras Negras/Eagle Pass, Nuevo Laredo/Laredo and Matamoros/Brownsville.

There is one rail journey in Mexico which you shouldn't miss if it's possible to fit it into your route, and that's the one between Chihuahua and Los Mochis via the Barranca del Cobre which is comparable with the Grand Canyon in the States. The journey is one of the most spectacular in the world and includes 30 bridges and 10 tunnels. There are three types of train available – the *autovía*, the more expensive *vistatren* (a carriage fitted with observation domes), and the ordinary train. The first two are for sightseers and go during the day. The latter is for people who simply want to get from A to B and goes at night. The exact departure times are often changed so you're well advised to go to the station personally the day before to check the current schedule and to buy a ticket. Don't buy tickets from travel agents in town or you could end up looking at a useless ticket and an empty track.

Going to the station at either town involves a little effort since this railway has its own stations (*Estación al Pacífico*) both of which are on the outskirts of the towns. The fare on the *autovía* is US$12.50 and the journey takes about 12 hours. If you can't afford this there are ordinary

2nd class trains on some days between the two places which go during the day but they often get to the most spectacular parts of the journey during the hours of darkness.

A few other trains you might find useful are:

Ciudad Juárez-Chihuahua The fare is US$1.10 (2nd class) and the journey takes about 4½ hours.

Tepic-Guadalajara The fares are US$0.75 (2nd class) and US$1.70 (1st class).

Guadalajara-Guanajuato The fare is US$1 (2nd class) and the journey takes about seven hours but you must change trains so it's more convenient to go by bus.

Mexico City-Oaxaca The fare is US$1.25 (2nd class) and takes 17 hours but can be very late.

Palenque-Mérida This train which originates in Mexico City is a convenient way of getting from Palenque to the Yucatán without having to backtrack to Villahermosa for a bus to Mérida but it's often way behind schedule. There is a train in either direction daily. The fares are US$1.80 (2nd class) and US$3.80 (1st class) and it takes about 12 hours. Be careful of robberies on this train. If you're alone, don't sleep; if you're in a group then keep someone on guard.

Ferries

The only ferries of interest to travellers are those from Baja California to the mainland and those from the north-east tip of the Yucatán to the islands of Isla Mujeres and Cozumel.

To/From Baja California There are ferries between Santa Rosalía and Guaymas (from Santa Rosalía on Tuesdays, Thursdays and Sundays in the evening and from Guaymas on the same days at about 12 noon, journey time six hours); between La Paz and Topolobampo (from La Paz on Mondays, Saturdays and Sundays in the evening and from Topolobampo on the same days in the mornings, journey time 11 hours, frequently cancelled because of insufficient passengers); between La Paz and Mazatlán (daily in either direction except on Mondays from La Paz and Sundays from Mazatlán, journey time 16 hours, the most popular ferry so make advance reservations as demand for tickets is high); and between Cabo San Lucas and Puerto Vallarta (from Cabo San Lucas on Wednesdays and Sundays in the late afternoon and from Puerto Vallarta on Saturdays also in the late afternoon).

Yucatán Ferries

Puerto Juárez-Isla Mujeres There are daily ferries at 8 and 11 am, 1, 3, 5 and 7 pm (at 7 and 10 am, 12 noon and 2, 4 and 6 pm from Isla Mujeres). The fare is a few cents.

Punta Sam-Isla Mujeres Ferries depart three or four times a day in either direction and take about 45 minutes. Punta Sam is about five km from Puerto Juárez and there are plenty of local buses between the two places.

Playa del Carmen-Cozumel There are ferries four or five times daily in either direction (the last at 4 pm). The journey takes about 1½ hours. There are buses from both Tulum and Puerto Juárez to Playa del Carmen.

Because of its size, geography and communication networks, Mexico lends itself to treatment by area. In the sections which follow, the country has been divided up into: the North-West; the North-East; Mexico City; the Centre; and the South.

The North-West

Baja California, Chihuahua, Guaymas, Los Mochis, Mazatlán, Guadalajara, Tepic & the Pacific beaches of San Blas & Santa Cruz.

BAJA CALIFORNIA

Most of the settlements of Baja California, along with the earliest settlements in the US state of the same name, were founded by Jesuits who created what was virtually an autonomous region during the colonial period until they were expelled by the Spanish Crown in 1768.

It's a wild, hot, dry and generally desolate peninsula which the 20th century has largely passed by. If you're on a tight budget it might be best to think twice about coming here as there are few cheap hotels and restaurants. Ferries to the mainland operate from Santa Rosalía, La Paz and Cabo San Lucas.

On the way down the peninsula you can visit the old Jesuit settlements. In **San Ignacio** there are only two places to stay and both are expensive but *Posada San Ignacio* (known as Oscar's Place) is the better of the two. In **Mulengé** the *Hotel Hacienda* costs US$13 a double. In **Loreto**, once the headquarters of the Jesuits and the de facto capital of California, all the hotels are outrageously priced. And in **Mission de San Javier** there are some excellent examples of Jesuit stone construction.

LA PAZ

The capital of Baja California del Sur, La Paz is the peninsula's largest town and was once a pearl fishing centre. The pearls have all gone and it's now a hotel construction boom town of little interest except that it's from there that ferries leave for Los Mochis and Mazatlán.

Places to Stay

Most of the budget hotels are around the zócala or within a few minutes walk of it. The oldest of the travellers' haunts is the

Hotel Yeneka, Madero between the zócalo and 16 de Septiembre. It used to be inexpensive but it was refurbished two or three years ago so it now costs US$7.40 a double. It's reasonable value for what you get. Cheaper is the *Hotel Posada San Miguel*, Belesario Dominguez near the junction with 16 de Septiembre and next to the old market. A double costs US$3.90.

Others which you can try are the *Pension California Casa de Huespedes*, Degollado between Madero and Revolucion de 1910; and the *Hotel Ulloa*, Serdán between Bravo and Ocampo (at night there's a sign saying 'Brandy Presidente Hotel').

Avoid the *Casa de Huespedes La Flores*, Revolucion de 1910 between the zócalo and 16 de Septiembre. It costs US$3 to $4 a double but it's noisy and full of cockroaches (it shares premises with a bath-house so it's not surprising there are plenty of roaches).

Places to Eat

The cheapest place to find a meal in La Paz is at the markets where there are quite a few inexpensive cafés. Try the ones at Degollado and Revolucion de 1910 (the best) and on Bravo between Prieto and Ramirez.

Near the plaza the best place to eat is the *Café Olimpia* opposite the Hotel La Purisima on 16 de Septiembre between Revolucion de 1910 and Serdán. The restaurant is popular with local people so it can be difficult to get a seat at times.

Other places you might like to try include the *Restaurant de la Rosa* next to the Ceilo Azul; and the *Antojitos El Mexicano* on 16 de Septiembre near Serdán, where *comida corrida* is excellent value.

CHIHUAHUA

Chihuahua is the capital of the state of the same name and the place which gave its name to the famous small dogs. It isn't a particularly interesting place in its own

right but it's a convenient overnight stop if you're heading north or south. Its main interest to travellers is that you can catch the train through the spectacular Barranca del Cobre to Los Mochis from there. The trip is highly recommended and very popular.

Information

There are two railway stations in Chihuahua. The first services the El Paso/Ciudad Juárez line and the other services the line to Los Mochis via the Barranca del Cobre. The latter is on the south side of town behind the jail and a long walk (about one hour) from the centre of town. Take a taxi or bus. Book the train to Los Mochis in advance, and from the station rather than from a travel agent.

While in Chihuahua, it's worth visiting the **Pancho Villa Museum**. To get there follow Calle 8, till its name changes to Ocampo and then stay on this street until you reach the triangular shaped Parque Lerdo. Turn left onto Paseo Bolívar, then right onto Calle 10 and the museum is on Calle 10 another five blocks up. If you don't fancy the walk, take a taxi (about US$2).

The bus terminal is five blocks from the cathedral.

Places to Stay

One of the cheapest places is the *Casa de Huespedes Libertad*, Libertad between Calle 10 and Ocampo, which is small and often full but cheap. Another is the *Hotel Maceya*, Calle 6 at the junction with Doblado. It's popular with truckies and agricultural workers and costs US$2.25 a double but it's over a bar – 'bring earplugs and sleeping pills'.

Another which is cheap is the *Hotel Reforma*, Victoria between Ocampo and Calle 12. It's a pleasant, clean house run by friendly staff and is good value for money.

If you want something mid-range then try the *Hotel Francis* which is clean and friendly and costs US$7 a double; or the *Hotel Turisto* on Avenida Juárez, which costs US$5 for a large, bright and comfortable double room.

Places to Eat

Two good places which are inexpensive are the *Cafeteria Rosavel*, Calle 10 at Articulo 123, which is popular with local people; and the *Loncheria*, Calle 10 between Progresso and Carillo, which is mainly a sandwich shop but does have other food too.

You can also find cheap food at the market which is two blocks from the bus terminal along Progresso. For a splurge try the *La Parilla*, Victoria between Ocampo and Calle 4.

Dino's Pizza, between the Hyatt and the zócala has been recommended.

GUADALAJARA

Guadalajara is one of Mexico's finest large cities and because of its year-round temperate climate it's very popular with North Americans who go there to visit and study in one of the many educational institutions.

Founded in 1530 and with a population now exceeding 2½ million, it has some very fine colonial buildings, graceful *portales*, numerous old shady plazas and is one of the best places to see Orozco's murals.

Information

The tourist office is at Juárez 638 in the premises of the Ex-convento del Carmen (same site as the Bellas Artes centre). It has free maps of the city and can recommend cheap places to stay. There is also an information desk in the Palacio del Gobierno which fronts on to the Plaza Mayor.

Things to See

Orozco's murals are an important attraction of Guadalajara. Examples can be seen at the University, Avenida Juárez at Tolsa; the Palacio del Gobierno, Plaza

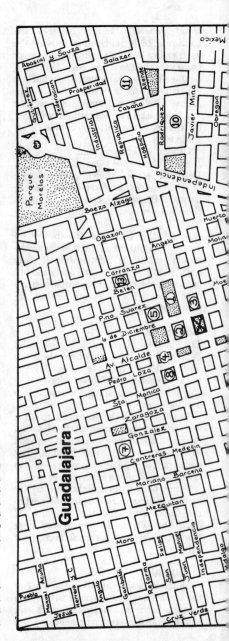

Mayor; the **Museo Taller José Clemente Orozco**; and at the huge Hospicio Cabañas near the central market, which is an enormous building with over 20 patios and is floodlit at night. It contains some of Orozco's finest work and still functions as an orphanage.

The **Teatro Degollado**, Degollado between Hidalgo and Morelos, has performances of folk music and dancing every Sunday at 10 am which are well worth the effort to go and see. No two performances are the same. The best seats are those in the boxes above the main floor. Tickets for these are also cheaper than those for the main floor. The theatre itself is one of Guadalajara's gems.

If you'd like to see a display of high quality handicrafts (some of which are for sale), go to the **Casa de Artesanías** at the north-western edge of the Parque Azul. The park itself is worth a visit if you want to get away from the noise and fumes for a while. It contains some incredible flowering trees but the zoo is depressing. Entry costs a few cents.

Museums which are worth visiting include the **Museo Regional de Guadalajara**, Liceo between Independencia and Hidalgo (mainly paintings of former colonial officials but a beautiful building which was once a seminary); and the **Archeological Museum of Western Mexico**, Plaza Juárez (open Monday to Saturday from 9 am to 1 pm and 4 to 6 pm, entry is free).

Make a point of spending an afternoon in the Plaza de las Mariachis (also known as the Plaza Tapatio) at the side of the Mercado Libertad where the *mariachis* practice in preparation for their evening rounds. This type of music originated in Guadalajara in the mid-19th century and originally catered for weddings and the like. These days they make a living playing mainly to customers in restaurants and bars, of which there are plenty around the plaza.

Don't forget to have a wander through the Mercado Libertad near the junction with Juárez and Calzada Independencia. It's an enormous building enclosing several patios on different levels and much larger than the main market in Mexico City. You can buy almost anything imaginable.

Places to Stay

Although there are plenty of hotels around the bus terminal and railway station it's not a particularly pleasant area to stay in. The hotels are just as expensive as others much closer to the Plaza Mayor so it's worth the 10 to 15 minute walk to the centre.

Two modestly priced hotels close to the centre are the *Hotel Hamilton*, Madero 381 between Ocampo and Galeana, which is clean and friendly and costs US$5.45 a double; and the *Hotel Imperio*, opposite the Mercado Libertad one block from the Plaza de los Mariachis.

Another in this area which has been recommended is the *Posada de la Plata*, Lopez Cotilla close to the Ex-convento del Carmen (tourist office). There are plenty of other cheaper hotels along the Calzada Independencia toward the bus terminal though they tend to be noisy as this is a main thoroughfare.

If you don't want to walk too far from the bus terminal then try the *Pension Jalisco*, Calle Balderas. It's clean, quiet, friendly and is very reasonably priced. The *Hotel Celta*, Calle Balderas almost directly in front of the Palacio Jalisco, is also quiet and clean and good value.

Another recommendation is the *Hotel San José*, 5 de Febrero opposite the bus terminal. There are plenty of others around the San José but few of them are what you would call inexpensive.

The *Hotel Suites Perla* on Gallardo not far from the Plaza Minerva, has been recommended with two-room suites for US$4, and if you stay for seven days, you are only charged for six.

Places to Eat

You can pick up excellent cheap meals at

any number of the cafés along Calle Los Angeles near the bus station; at the Mercado Libertad (good fish dinners upstairs); and at the *Carnes Asadas en su Jugo*, which is a large restaurant in the small market on Hidalgo between Sta Monica and Zaragoza.

Another place which is recommended is the snack bar in the *Instituto Cultural Mexico*, on the corner of Tolsa and Miguel Blanco. It's open to all and serves inexpensive food.

One of the best vegetarian restaurants in the city is the *Gran Comedor Vegetariano*, Lopez Cotilla between 8 de Julio and Martinez. It's easy to miss but worth finding because it does serve excellent inexpensive food.

For something slightly up-market try the *El Greco*, Lopez Cotilla at Penitenciaria. It's a popular place with local businessmen at lunch times. If you really want to splurge then head for *La Cava*, Priciliano Sanchez near Galeana. It has an atmosphere which is hard to beat as it's located in an historical monument and although it's expensive, the food is excellent. The entrance on Sanchez is through the *Cachee* boutique.

For somewhere to go in the evening try *La Peña*, on the corner of Lopez Cotilla and Emerson. It blasts off at 7 pm and goes on past midnight. Entry costs about US$0.50 and although food and drink is a little expensive it's still relatively modest.

AROUND GUADALAJARA

It's worth spending a couple of days or so at **Lake Chapala**, about 50 km south-east of Guadalajara, despite the fact that the town of Chapala and several of the nearby villages have been swamped by retired North Americans – about 30,000 of them!! The lake is said to be so polluted now that swimming is not recommended.

One of the cheapest places to stay in Chapala is the *Huespedes las Palmitas* behind the plaza which costs about US$2 a double but it's poor value. Much better is the colonial style *Hotel Lido* on the main street which is clean and costs US$3.15 a double.

If Chapala isn't to your liking then try either **Ajijic**, a smaller, more Indian village, 15 minutes by bus from Chapala, or **Jocotepec**, an Indian fishing village beyond Ajijic. For a place to stay in Ajijic try the *La Playita*, Calle Hidalgo 12B, which offers very basic but cheap accommodation. In the evenings try the *Teheban* which is a popular bar among foreign artisans living in the area. The cheapest place to stay in Jocotepec is the new *casa de huespedes* at Calle Matamoros 83 (on the same street as the bus station). In the evenings try the *Ramón's Bar* which is popular with expatriates.

There are hot springs on the lake at **San Juan Cosalá** (small entry charge) which some travellers have recommended. Should you decide not to go to Chapala there are other thermal springs at **Baños de los Canachos** north of Guadalajara.

GUAYMAS

This fishing and boat-building port on the Gulf of California is of little interest in itself but you might have to spend a night there on your way down the west coast. It's also the terminal for ferries from Santa Rosalía in Baja California.

Places to Stay & Eat

There are very few budget hotels in Guaymas so the choice is severely limited. The best bet is probably the *Casa de Huespedes* on Serdan between Calles 25 and 26.

For a place to eat try the *La Flor de Michoacán*, Calle 19 across the road from the market, which does good, inexpensive tacos. There's also the small market on Calle 19 at Rodriguez where there are several inexpensive cafés. Avoid seafood restaurants in Guaymas as they're all pretty expensive, though if you want to splurge you could try the *Hotel Impala*, on the corner of Rodriguez and Calle 29. It's expensive but the food is good.

LOS MOCHIS

The main reason that travellers go to Los Mochis is to take the train to Chihuahua through the Barranca del Cobre (or to stay overnight having come in the opposite direction). You could also find yourself spending the night there after taking the ferry from La Paz, Baja California. Ferries from La Paz actually dock at **Topolobampo**, a half-hour bus ride from Los Mochis.

The railway station for Chihuahua is a long way from the centre of Los Mochis so you will need to take either a taxi or a local bus. From Los Mochis the bus goes from near the *Tres Estrellas* bus station on Obregón and costs a few cents. It's painted green.

If you arrive from Chihuahua late at night, it's possible to go on by bus to Mazatlán rather than stay in Los Mochis.

Places to Stay & Eat

As with Guaymas, there are very few cheap places to stay in Los Mochis. The best and cheapest is probably the *Casa de Huespedes* on Obregón near the market. If it is full then try the *Los Arcos Hotel*, Allende near the junction with Obregón, which is a moderately priced, good value hotel. It fills up quickly so you need to get moving as soon as you get off the train.

The cheapest place to eat is at one of the small restaurants in the market on Independencia between Degollado and Zapata. Otherwise try the *Rio Rosa*, Obregón opposite the *Tres Estrellas* bus terminal, which has excellent, reasonably priced food.

CREEL

A lot of travellers who take the Barranca del Cobre train get off at this small village at the upper end of the canyon, since beyond this point the line goes across relatively flat and uninteresting country. If you get off here, a cheap place to stay is the *Hotel Korachi*. It's a very small place near the station and is often full so it's worth making a call from Los Mochis to

book a room before you set off if possible. The toilets here can be a 'real blow on the nose' as one traveller put it.

Margarita's Casa de Huespedes is right on the plaza príncipal between the two churches. It costs US$2 per night and cheap meals are available. The owner also has a truck which a small group can hire.

There is camping at the lake, seven km from the station.

Cheap meals are available from the *Café El Manzano* next to the railway station. Creel can be very cold in winter (it's at 2300 metres), so take warm clothes.

MAZATLÁN

Mazatlán is the largest port on the Pacific coast and an important industrial centre, yet it also has surprisingly good beaches a few minutes walk from the centre and is a popular resort for some North Americans. There are daily ferries to La Paz (Baja California).

The city gives the impression of having been founded early in the colonial era but in fact it's fairly recent, dating from the time of Maximillian's ill-fated empire when it was used by Germans bringing machinery to Mexico. It's unlikely you would stay there for the beaches alone as there are much better ones further south.

Places to Stay

One of the cheapest places is the *Hotel Victoria*, Azuela at Estrada, which costs around US$1 a single. Also in the same price range is the *Casa Familiar Aurora*, Azuela between Estrada and Ocampo, though it's cheaper if you have a group.

Going up in price, the *Hotel Milan* is worth a try and costs just over US$2 a single. The *Hotel Vialta*, Azuela between Hidalgo and Estrada, is similar in standard but costs about US$2.50 a single.

If those two are full then try the *Hotel San Lorenzo*, 21 de Marzo between

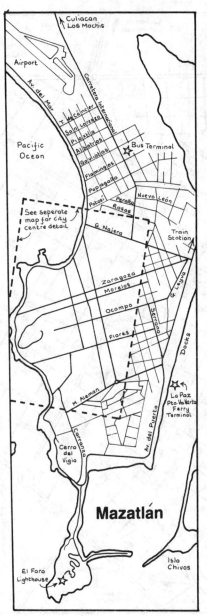

Mazatlán

Serdán and Azuela. You can generally find a room here because it's on a side street so it doesn't fill up that quickly.

Fairly close to the bus terminal is the *Hotel Esperanza*, Carretera Internacional, which costs US$6 a double but is very noisy and has weak pressure in the (hot) showers. To get there turn left along Río Tamazula coming out of the front of the bus station and carry on until you get to the traffic lights. It's on the left across the street from the traffic lights.

Another place which has been recommended as being fairly cheap is the *Hotel de Suprema*, on the corner of Azuela and Estrada, which is basic but costs only US$4.50 a double.

The *Hotel Santa Barbara* one block from the beach in the old part of town, has rooms with bath and fan for US$4. It's run by a very friendly family.

Places to Eat

Mazatlán is a place where you can eat seafood without burning a hole in your pocket. Try the cafés upstairs at the market where they offer good, inexpensive fish dishes. Another seafood restaurant which has been recommend is *Alberto's Restaurant*, Albatros and Av de Mar. It serves consistently good, inexpensive seafood (fish for less than US$2, shrimp cocktail for less than US$1).

The *Restaurant Dony*, 5 de Mayo at Escobedo, used to be an excellent place for a meal but recent reports suggest that the quality and service have gone way downhill. It's still moderately priced. Instead, try the *Restaurant Los Faroles*, Flores and Carnival, which has moderately priced Mexican food and generous portions.

For vaguely Chinese food (Mexican-Chinese) try the *Café Oriental*, Serdán between Estrada and Ocampo which specialises in chop sueys. Prices are moderate.

There are quite a few cafés and bars where people hang out (usually well-heeled tourists) but they are all ridiculously

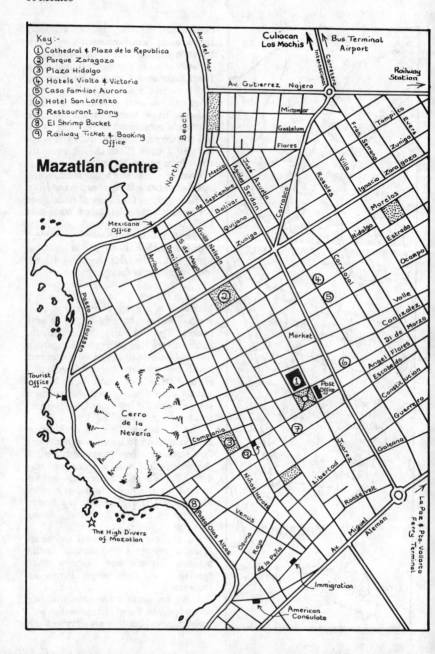

Key :-
① Cathedral & Plaza de la Republica
② Parque Zaragoza
③ Plaza Hidalgo
④ Hotels Vialta & Victoria
⑤ Casa Familiar Aurora
⑥ Hotel San Lorenzo
⑦ Restaurant Dony
⑧ El Shrimp Bucket
⑨ Railway Ticket & Booking Office

Mazatlán Centre

Culiacan Los Mochis

Bus Terminal Airport

Railway Station

Av. del Mar

Av. Gutierrez Najera

Carretera Internacional

North Beach

Mexicana Office

Mexico

Aquiles Serdan

José Arzello

Carrasco

Rosales

Fran Serrano

Villa

Tampico Evers

Zuniga

Ignacio Zaragoza

16 de Septiembre

Bolivar

Quijano

Zuniga

Guille Nelson

5 de Mayo

Arribo

Dominguez

Miramar

Gastelum

Flores

Morelos

Hidalgo

Estrada

Ocampo

Valle

Canizalez

21 de Marzo

Angel Flores

Escobedo

Constitucion

Guerrero

Galeana

Corrojal

Paseo Claussen

Tourist Office

Cerro de la Neveria

Complania

Market

Post Office

①

⑦

⑨

③

②

④

⑤

⑥

Juarez

Libertad

Roosevelt

Miguel Aleman

La Paz & Pto. Vallarta Ferry Terminal

The High Divers of Mazatlan

⑧

Paseo Olas Altas

Venus

Osuna

Rojo

de la Peña

Ninos Heroes

Immigration

American Consulate

expensive. Avoid the *Shrimp Bucket* for one. *Señor Frog* is similar.

SAN BLAS

For many years this town, about 33 km from Tepic, has been popular with young North Americans who go there to spend their college vacations sunbathing, swimming and surfing – though there's better surf further south around Santa Cruz. Unfortunately, because it has been the focus of many people's attention for years, prices have risen considerably though there are still some relatively inexpensive places to stay. Some travellers knock the place saying that it's played-out, but it has nevertheless managed to retain a certain degree of charm though not to the same extent as Santa Cruz.

The town has a long history, as the ruins in the centre and the old fort outside town suggest. The Spanish used it as a ship-building centre in the days when the trans-Pacific trade was being developed between the Philippines and Mexico.

There is a bank in San Blas which will change travellers' cheques.

Things to See

The old Spanish fortress is worth a visit although the vegetation is gradually taking over.

Jungle trips are available from San Blas by boat and although they cost US\$9 to \$18 per boat (six people to a boat) they are said to be worth it. The trips last about three hours and give you the opportunity to see many different water birds, reptiles and some incredible scenery. If you do go on one of them then take insect repellent with you as there are a lot of sand fleas which can make life unpleasant.

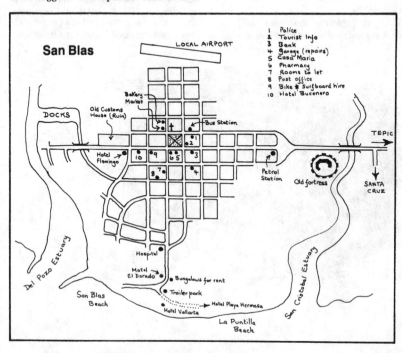

San Blas

1 Police
2 Tourist Info
3 Bank
4 Garage (repairs)
5 Casa Maria
6 Pharmacy
7 Rooms to let
8 Post office
9 Bike & Surfboard hire
10 Hotel Bucenero

LOCAL AIRPORT

DOCKS

Bakery
Market

Old Customs
House (Ruin)

Bus Station

TEPIC

Hotel
Flamingo

Petrol
Station

Old fortress

SANTA
CRUZ

Del Pozo Estuary

Hospital

Hotel
El Dorado

Bungalows for rent

Trailer park

San Blas
Beach

Hotel Vallarta

Hotel Playa Hermosa

San Cristobal Estuary

La Puntilla
Beach

Places to Stay

The most popular place among budget travellers is the *Casa Maria* on the main plaza. It's basic and costs US$4.35 a double without own shower and toilet and US$6.50 a double with own toilet facilities. It also has some rooms for US$2. If it's full then ask about slinging up a hammock at one of the beach restaurants and locking up your gear during the day. You can camp at *Motel Camping El Dorado* on the road to the beach but it costs US$2.75 or US$4.55 a double for a simple cabin. You can lock up gear during the day.

The two hotels on the main street, the *Hotel Flamingo* and *Hotel Bucanero* now cost US$6 and US$7 a double respectively making them relatively expensive. They're both fairly pleasant if you can afford the charges and the rooms face on to shady courtyards.

Getting There

Buses to Tepic run four times daily, the first around 6.30 am and the last around 4 pm. You can also get direct buses to Guadalajara twice daily, the first in the early morning and the second in the late afternoon – departure times vary so make enquiries. Local buses run down the coast to Santa Cruz usually three times daily. Again, departure times vary so make enquiries.

SANTA CRUZ

Further down the coast from San Blas, Santa Cruz is a much smaller and more mellow village with better prospects for finding cheaper accommodation. It has a pebble beach and so is unlikely to be 'developed' in the same way as San Blas and there are no hotels, as such, in town. The nearest sandy beach is at Miramar about one km north. It's a very pleasant cove and there are restaurants which serve excellent seafood. On the other hand, quite a few travellers have written to recommend the beach at Los Cocos about four km north of Santa Cruz which they say is beautiful and very quiet and

that you'll often be the only gringo there.

The post office is at *Lupita's* general store. They'll keep *lista de correos* letters indefinitely. This store also has all the foodstuffs you're likely to want if you're putting your own food together.

Watch out for the vicious blackflies which at certain times of the day descend on the beaches at Santa Cruz.

Places to Stay
The thing to do in Santa Cruz is to ask around for a *palapa*, a sort of large hut constructed of bamboo containing one or more string beds and basic cooking facilities – usually a mud fireplace/oven. Some have electricity connected, others don't. Washing facilities generally consist of just the use of a tap or a bucket of cold water. The rent for these places is usually the same regardless of the number of people who stay in one. If you have valuables then it's best to give them to the person renting the place for safe-keeping while you are out as there is no way of securing them otherwise. Two women to ask for are Rosalita, at the Bakery, and Irma Linda; both are very friendly.

If neither has a room ask at the *Lupita* general store or at *Raoul's* café next door where many travellers gather in the evenings to eat, drink and talk. Almost anyone you meet there will be able to give you a lead on a place to rent.

If you can't find anything then check at the *Restaurant Belmont* on the plaza and ask for Jorge. He has a number of concrete boxes down on the beach which he rents out for US$4.35 a night and he also runs a little thatched bar/restaurant there which has the cheapest beer in the village. You can also camp down there for US$1 and lock up your gear with him during the day. The Belmont may also have a few rooms but they're not cheap.

If you decide to stay at Los Cocos further up the coast there is a hotel for about US$1.50 per person and a good restaurant.

Places to Eat
In the village itself the best place to eat is the *Belmont* which offers meals but they're expensive.

If you want seafood then go to one of the restaurants on the beach at Miramar about one km north. None of them are particularly cheap but they do offer very good food.

Getting There
It's easy enough to get into Santa Cruz from Tepic by local bus – there are several every day – but strangely, going in the opposite direction, it can be difficult to get a bus out. They do exist but if, after several hours of waiting in vain, you get that stranded feeling then take a bus to San Blas. Buses to Guadalajara and Tepic operate on a more predictable schedule. Local buses from Santa Cruz to San Blas run three or four times daily, the first in the early morning and the last in the late afternoon.

The North-East

Guanajuato, Monterrey, Queretaro, San Luis Potosí & San Miguel de Allende.

GUANAJUATO
Guanajuato is one of the most enchanting places in Mexico and a hot favourite with all visitors to the country. Built in a steep-sided canyon amid wild and beautiful mountains, it has been an important silver mining centre since the metal was first discovered back in 1548. The wealth which the mines generated has left its mark on the many public buildings, churches, private mansions and numerous exquisite little shady plazas which today make it Mexico's finest colonial gem.

Its narrow twisting streets follow the steep contours of the canyon and often end in steps cut into the rock. Some of them are so narrow, particularly the famous Street of the Kiss, that opposite balconies almost touch one another. Walking through the streets is a delightful experience – you'd be hard pressed to find its equal anywhere else in the world.

The town even has an underground road – the *calle subterráneo* – which runs almost the whole length of what is virtually Guanajuato's only main street. Constructed after a particularly bad flash flood in 1905, it's now used to divert through-traffic and minimise congestion in the town's centre. Several hundred metres above it, a ring road encircling the town has been constructed. From there you can enjoy panoramic views of all of Guanajuato.

It was in Guanajuato that Hidalgo and others raised the standard of revolt against the Spanish and where the Royalist garrison, holed up inside the Alhondiga, were slaughtered to a man by the patriots. When the Spanish re-took the city, the heads of Hidalgo, Allende, Aldama and Jimenez were stuck on spikes at the four corners of the building in revenge for the slaughter. Guanajuato was also Diego Rivera's home town though his brilliance wasn't recognised there until after his death, as is often the case with great artists.

Things to See

The city is so steeped in history that almost everywhere you go you'll find something of interest. One of the most important monuments is the **Alhóndiga de Granadita**, a massive building constructed originally as a granary but later turned into a fortress during the struggle for independence. It has now been converted into a museum displaying folk art, paintings and other memorabilia relating to the history of the city. There's a small entry charge.

The gory collection of mummies in the museum at the **Panteón** near the railway station is another popular attraction. For years corpses have been placed in niches in the cemetery where they shrivel slowly

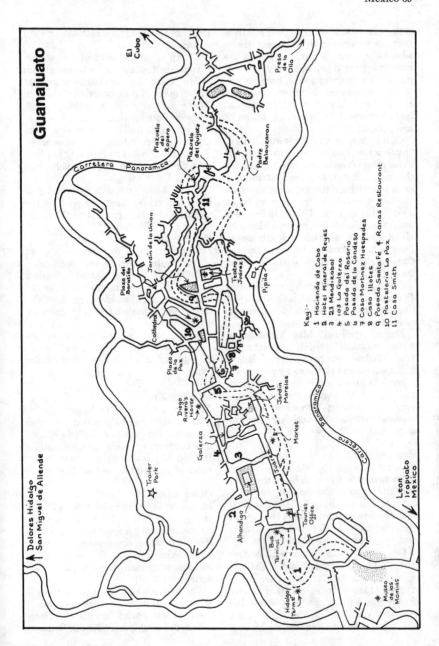

Guanajuato

Key:-
1 Hacienda de Cobo
2 Hotel Mineral de Reyes
3 23 Mendizabal
4 103 La Galerza
5 Posada del Rosario
6 Posada de la Condesa
7 Casa Martinez Huespedes
8 Casa Illotes
9 Posada Santa Fé † Ranas Restaurant
10 Pasteleria La Paz
11 Casa Smith

rather than rot. As long as their relatives continue to come up with the rent, that's where they stay. If not, the bodies are removed after a number of years and placed in a common grave. Some of the more unusual ones, however, have been rescued and placed in the museum, including one of a miner still in his boots and overall!

Of the churches that are worth visiting, La Valenciana, five km out of town near the silver mine of the same name, is probably the best. It's the most outstanding example of Churrigueresque architecture in Mexico and the interior is every bit as good as the exterior. There are frequent buses from the centre of town which take about 10 minutes. Others worth seeing include San Francisco (17th century), La Compañia (18th century Jesuit) and San Diego (17th century).

Diego Rivera's former house at Positos 47 is now a museum and has a display of the sketches for his famous murals as well as a number of his paintings.

During April and May, Guanajuato hosts the annual International Cervantes Festival when there are plays and dances in the streets and plazas along with many other activities. If you're here at that time don't miss it although accommodation is very tight. During November there's a cultural festival with activities such as mime and ballet shows.

Places to Stay

Because Guanajuato is a major tourist attraction, prices tend to be on the steep side and many of the cheaper places are often full. If you have difficulty finding something in your price range then ask at the tourist office. The staff are friendly and can often suggest cheap places.

One very popular place with budget travellers is the *Posada Kloster*, Calle de Alonso 32 near the Plaza de la Paz. This is a very pleasant old place run by an elderly couple who keep it spotlessly clean. It's excellent value at US$3 a single. If it's full, try either the *Casa Smith*, Manuel

Doblado 1; or the *Posada del Rosario*, Av Juárez 31.

Cheap rooms in student houses are sometimes available at *La Galarza* (also called Calle de los Positos) and at *Mendizabal 23* (also called Granaditas). There are no signs at either so ask upstairs. Both are close to the Alhóndiga.

If you can't find a place at any of the above then you'll have to go up-market. The *Hotel Mineral de Reyes*, 5 de Mayo past the Alhóndiga, is reasonably good value at US$7 a single.

If you have your own camping gear there is a trailer (caravan) park on the outskirts of town – marked on the map.

Places to Eat

For a good choice of food, try one or other of the restaurants in the open-sided building next to the Mercado Hidalgo. They're all cheap and no two have the same menu. For breakfast try one of the small cafés in the bus terminal which are good value.

A good bar to go to is the one on the Jardín Unión opposite the Agora. There's no sign but it's in a painted red-brick building.

MONTERREY

Monterrey is the third largest city in Mexico and one of the country's major industrial centres. Although it was founded over 400 years ago there's precious little of the old city surviving and there's not much of interest for the traveller.

Places to Stay

Monterrey is an expensive town with few cheap places to stay. It's a transport hub for the area and a magnet for people from the surrounding countryside who come here looking for work. This is one of the reasons why many cheap places are permanently full.

The best place to find a cheap room is around the bus terminal, where some of the cheapest places include the *Hotel America*, Cuauhtémoc between Reforma

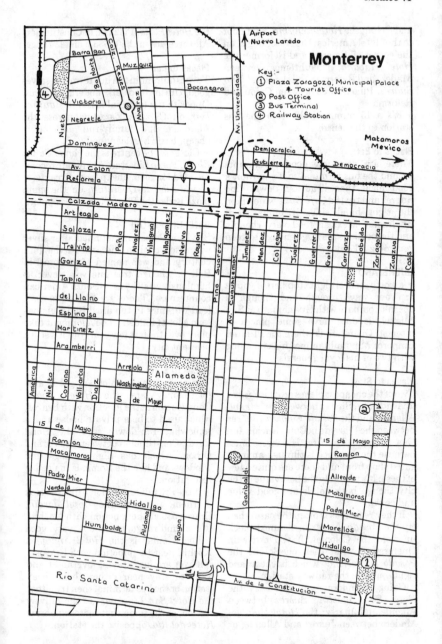

and Colón; the *Hotel Reforma*, next door to the Hotel America; the *Hotel Regis*, on the corner of Jimenez and Reforma; the *Hotel Habana*, Cuauhtémoc between Madero and Reforma; and the *Hotel Pino Suarez*, Pino Suarez between Colón and Reforma.

It's a 15 minute walk from the bus station to the centre.

Places to Eat
There are very few good restaurants around the bus terminal so if you want a good meal then head off down Pino Suarez and try the *Café Galis* which is on the right hand side. It offers good, wholesome Mexican food very cheaply and the portions are large enough to keep you going all day.

QUERÉTARO
It's worth an overnight stop here if you're on your way through and though it doesn't compare with Guanajuato or San Miguel, it does have some places of interest. Querétaro is where the ill-fated Emperor Maximillian met his end along with two of his loyal generals.

Places to Stay
Two of the cheapest places are the *Posada la Academia*, Suarez between Juárez and Allende; and the *Posada Colonial*, Juárez between the Plaza de la Constitución and Gen Arteaga. The first is easy to miss because the entrance is through an iron-gated shop front and there are quite a few of these. It's probably the best value in the city though both hotels are good value and cheap.

If they're full (as is often the case) then try the *Posada Juárez* in the next block up from the Colonial. If you arrive in Querétaro by rail then check out the *Posada la Nacional* which is cheap and right opposite the railway station.

Going up-market, you could try the *Hotel San Agustín*, Suarez between Allende and Juárez; the *Hotel Hidalgo*, Madero between Juárez and Allende; or

the *Hotel Plaza*, Plaza de la Constitución. All three are in the US$5 a single range.

Places to Eat
The restaurant in the bus terminal serves good, fresh food at moderate prices. Opposite the terminal is the *Restaurant Izar* on Calzada Zaragoza across the Alameda. It's family-run and offers cheap, basic Mexican food.

Closer to the centre is the *Fonda Santa Elena*, Paseo Libertad, a tiny café recommended for good, cheap food. Breakfasts at the *Flor de Querétaro* on the main plaza under the Plaza Hotel are popular.

SAN LUIS POTOSÍ
San Luis Potosí was founded after silver was discovered in the area in the 16th century and was named after Potosí in Bolivia, though this one was never as fabulously wealthy as its South American counterpart. There are also important lead workings in the area. San Luis has seen a lot of industrial development take place over the last few years but it's still a pleasant city.

Places to Stay
Two cheap places which are good value for money are the *Hotel Roma*, Constitución at the junction with Bravos, which used to be a private house and is somewhat run-down; and the *Hotel Royal*, Constitución between Bravos and Othón, which has high ceilings and windows and like the Roma, is in need of restoration.

If they're full or you don't like the look of them, then try the *Hotel Jardín*, Bravos 530 at the junction with Xochitl. It's a mid-range hotel but very good value. Similar is the *Hotel Anáhuac*, Xochitl near the junction with Bravos.

If you are just staying overnight and want to stay near either the railway station or the bus terminal then try either the *Hotel San Luis*, next to the railway station, or the somewhat more expensive *Hotel del Río*, opposite the station.

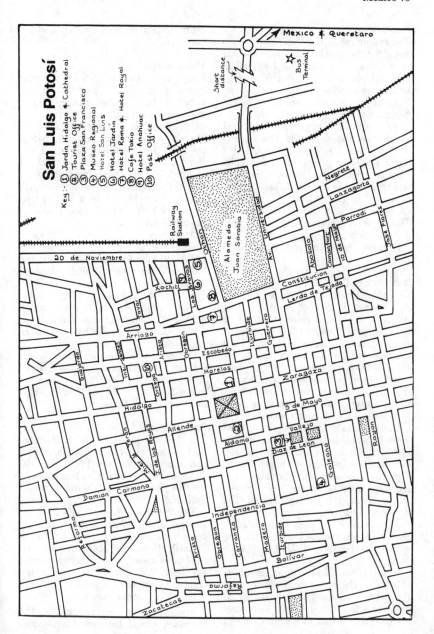

San Luis Potosí

Key:
1. Jardín Hidalgo + Cathedral
2. Tourist Office
3. Plaza San Francisco
4. Museo Regional
5. Hotel San Luis
6. Hotel Jardín
7. Hotel Roma + Hotel Royal
8. Cafe Tokio
9. Hotel Anahuac
10. Post Office

Places to Eat

The restaurant in the *Hotel San Luis* is one of the cheapest but the food is nothing special. For a wider choice and better food try the *Tortaria la Ideal*, Bravos near the junction with Xochitl and close to the Hotel Jardín. It's supposed to be open 24 hours a day and it's inexpensive.

The *Regis Restaurant* near the Hotel Jardín, on the corner of Bravos and Arreaga, has also been suggested. It's clean and the prices are reasonable. Another restaurant which has been recommended is the *Café Tokio*, Othón 415 near Constitución, which, despite its name, serves very good Mexican food. The service is quick and the place is very popular with local people. You can also get good American-style breakfasts there.

SAN MIGUEL DE ALLENDE

Like Guanajuato, Patzcuaro and Taxco, San Miguel is one of Mexico's most picturesque colonial gems. Much of its beauty stems from the fact that many rich people from Guanajuato once built their homes there. Despite the mountainous terrain the streets are nowhere near as steep as those in Guanajuato but they are snakelike and many are cobbled. It's a very popular destination with travellers and with good reason.

Unfortunately for those on a tight budget, San Miguel has a large community of retired North Americans so prices tend to be much higher than you might expect. The town is also very popular as a language learning centre, the *Instituto Allende* being the principal school. The *Academia Hispano*, opposite the Hotel San Sebastian has been recommended. Four-week courses cost US$240 but living with a local family costs US$9 to $12 per day.

In recognition of its beauty and irreplaceable value, the government has declared the town a national monument so all building alterations and new structures are carefully vetted to ensure they will conform with the traditional character of the town.

Places to Stay

Keeping in mind that there's hardly anything in San Miguel which can genuinely be described as cheap, there are some places which won't burn a hole in your pocket. Among them is the *Posada de las Monjas*, in the old part of town on Canal between Quebrada and Benificencia, which was formerly a convent. The older part is more attractive than the new so ask for a room there as it's also cheaper. There's an attached restaurant which serves good food at moderate prices.

Also very good value is the *Hotel Saulto*, Hernandez Marcias, which costs US$3.90/$5.30 for singles/doubles and has good cheap meals. There is a discount if you stay for a week or more. The *Hotel San Sebastian* has also been highly recommended. The staff are friendly, prices are moderate at about US$1.80 per person and some rooms have a kitchen and stove.

Other former cheapies such as the *Quinta Loreto*, Loreto; and the *Casa de Huespedes Felix*, Codo 30, are now quite expensive. Expect to pay US$7 a single and up if you go there.

Places to Eat

The cheapest places to eat are the cafés next to the *Flecha Amarilla* bus station and those around the Plaza Allende. There's also a good little place between the *Pan y Vino* sign and the dairy shop on Calle Reloj.

The *Posada la Fuente*, Calle Umaran, is popular with young people especially those who are in San Miguel to learn Spanish. Prices are above average and the food is mainly North American style. For breakfast, the restaurant at the *Qunita Loreto* is very popular and good value – North American-style.

Another good restaurant is the *Carrusel*, Canal between Macias and

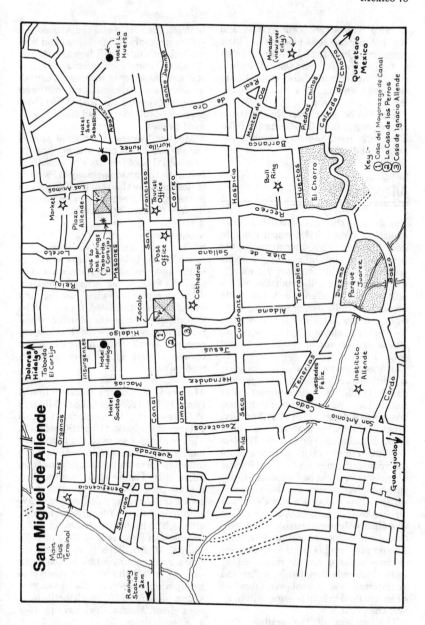

San Miguel de Allende

Key:-
① Casa del Mayorazgo de Canal
② La Casa de los Perros
③ Casa de Ignacio Allende

Hidalgo. This serves both Mexican and North-American style food but is a little expensive. One of the best places to sit around with a drink and watch the world go by is the *Terraza*, Calle Correo close to the plaza and next to the Parroquia, though it isn't cheap.

You can have lunch at the American Legion, across from the Huespedes Felix. They have good hamburgers, chile con carne and drinks.

Mexico City

Founded on the site of the old Aztec capital of Tenochtitlán, which was torn down to provide building stones for the new Spanish city, Mexico City is today possibly the world's largest city. Officially there are some 18 million inhabitants but official figures often don't take into account the millions more who live in the slums on the outskirts. It's a vibrant, thoroughly enjoyable place with an almost endless list of things to do and see.

It does have its drawbacks, however. It's fairly expensive, the smog is legendary and the traffic noise can be unbearable at certain times of the day. Not only that, but it was a dodgy place to build a city. Much of the Valley of Mexico was, until colonial times, taken up by Lake Texcoco. Very little remains of this lake today since the Spanish drained most of it but it takes a long time for a lake bed of this size to dry out completely and the land is still sinking. This makes it a very dangerous place to be when earthquakes strike. This was clearly demonstrated in the earthquake which hit the city in late 1985. Thousands of people lost their lives, most of them buried under the rubble. Many more thousands were left homeless and an international appeal was launched which resulted in help pouring in from all over the world.

The nucleus of the original city,

between the zócalo and the Alameda, is still remarkably well preserved and jam-packed with interest. Elsewhere demolition and reconstruction have been, and still are, the order of the day though it's unlikely that Mexico City will ever acquire a sky-line like that of São Paulo because of subsidence and the danger of earthquakes.

Many influences have been at work in the shaping of the city, and not just the Spanish. One of the city's most notable features – the broad, landscaped Paseo de la Reforma – was laid out by Maximillian in the mid-19th century during his brief reign as Emperor of Mexico.

Information

NB A terrific amount of damage was caused by the 1985 earthquake especially in the area around the Alameda and in the Zona Rosa. So far we haven't had any detailed reports of what remains and what has been destroyed. It may well be that many of the places we describe and recommend no longer exist. If this is the case, please write to us and we'll insert an update supplement as soon as things become clear.

The head office of the Mexican Tourist Board (tel 250 8555) is at Calle Masaryk 172 between Hegel and Emerson, Colonia Polanco at the back of Chapultepec Park. This is a long way from the centre and hardly worth the trek since the branch offices closer to the centre carry the same information. The one which most travellers use is in the CONASUPO building on the corner of Reforma and Juárez. They have good maps and are friendly and helpful, although no English is spoken.

American Express is at Hamburgo 75 (tel 533 20 20), Zona Rosa. If you use Amex as a mailing address then make sure you have their cheques or credit card handy when collecting. They have been known to charge US$3 for a letter if you're not a client. Thomas Cook have an office at Avenida Juárez 88.

Banking hours are from Monday to Friday from 9 am to 1 pm and (head offices only) Saturdays from 9 am to 12.30 pm.

SETEJ, Hamburgo 273 (tel 514 42 31/ 511 66 91), is the Mexican student organisation which can arrange cheap airline tickets and deal with ISIS insurance claims. They also have a hostel.

Embassies

Australia

Paseo de la Reforma 195 (5th floor) (tel 566 30 55)

Britain

Calle Rio Lerma 71 (tel 511 48 80). If you need a visa for Belize enquire about it here.

Canada

Rubén Darío 529 on the corner of Tres Picos (near Chapultepec) (tel 254 3288)

Cuba

Francisco Marquez 160, Colonia Condesa

West Germany

Byron 737, Colonia Rincón del Bosque (tel 545 66 55)

Guatemala

1025 Explanada, Lomas Chapultepec. Open from 9 am to 1.30 pm Monday to Friday. Visas cost US$10 and are generally issued while you wait.

Honduras

87 Reforma (2nd floor). Visas are issued while you wait. (Also the address of the Honduran airline TAN SAHASA)

Nicaragua

Calle Culiacán 58

USA

Reforma 305

Things to Do & See

Zócalo Although the zócalo in Mexico City is the oldest and one of the largest town squares in Latin America it's also one of the most drab. The trees which used to grow there were cut down in one of the revolutions and never replaced. It's now just a paved non-entity. Around it, however, are some of the city's most important public buildings.

Occupying virtually the whole of the north side is the **National Cathedral**. Construction began in 1573 and the

building was completed in 1667. It's certainly impressive as far as its size goes but otherwise it's a mish-mash of various styles and not particularly interesting. To its right is a smaller, separate church with an amazing Churrigueresque facade. This is the **Sagrario Metropolitano** which serves as the local parish church.

On the east side of the zócalo is the **National Palace** with a stunning collection of ballrooms, salons and audience halls built at different times over a 250 year period. Most of it is open to the public but the major attraction is Diego Rivera's powerful and unforgettable murals, work on which occupied him for almost a quarter of a century. Whatever else you do, don't miss these. The building also contains the **Museo Juárez** which is open Monday to Friday from 10 am to 7 pm. It has a collection of exhibits related to the life and times of Mexico's greatest reformer, Benito Juárez.

On the corner between the Cathedral and the National Palace is an Aztec site which is being excavated but it's only of minor interest and most of the finds have been transferred to the Museum of Anthropology in Chapultepec Park.

South of the zócalo, on the corner of Pino Surez and Salvador, is the **Museo de la Ciudad de Mexico** which has a fine collection of items ranging from pre-Aztec times to Pancho Villa, as well as a geological display of the Valley of Mexico. It should interest even those who normally don't take to museums. Entry is free.

Alameda In contrast to the zócalo, the Alameda is a pleasant, leafy park though it has had a gory history. It was once the place where victims of the Inquisition were burnt at the stake. On the east side of the Alameda stands the **Palacio de Bellas Artes** which not only puts on the best folklore ballets in the country but also houses one of the best art galleries in Mexico with works by Rivera, Orozco, Siquerios, Tamayo and O'Gorman. If you have an interest in art then it's well worth

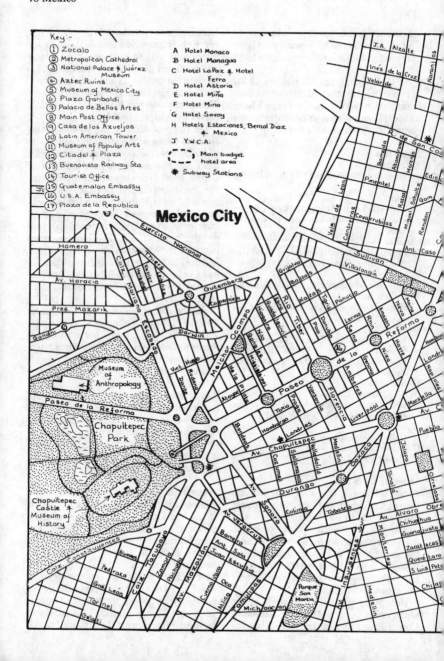

Key:-
1. Zócalo
2. Metropolitan Cathedral
3. National Palace & Juárez Museum
4. Aztec Ruins
5. Museum of Mexico City
6. Plaza Garibaldi
7. Palacio de Bellas Artes
8. Main Post Office
9. Casa de los Azueljos
10. Latin American Tower
11. Museum of Popular Arts
12. Citadel & Plaza
13. Buenavista Railway Sta.
14. Tourist Office
15. Guatemalan Embassy
16. U.S.A. Embassy
17. Plaza de la Republica

A. Hotel Monaco
B. Hotel Managua
C. Hotel La Paz & Hotel Ferro
D. Hotel Astoria
E. Hotel Miña
F. Hotel Mina
G. Hotel Savoy
H. Hotels Estaciones, Bernal Diaz & Mexico
J. Y.W.C.A.

- - - Main budget hotel area
✳ Subway Stations

Mexico City

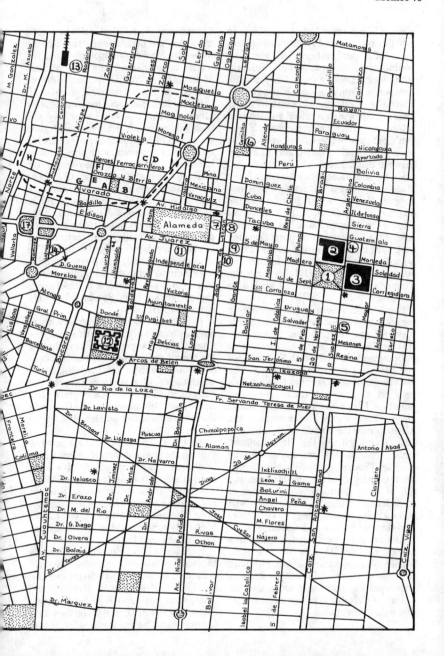

visiting and is open daily from 10 am to 5.30 pm and on Sundays from 10 am to 2 pm. Ballet performances are given on Wednesdays, Saturdays and Sundays with tickets ranging from US$5 to $10, cheaper on Sundays – book in advance. The museum also has a beautiful Tiffany glass curtain which is raised and lowered before and after performances. If you don't go to one of these then you can also see it for a small fee on Sunday mornings between 9 and 10 am.

On the south side of the Alameda is the **Museo de Artes e Industrias Populares**, Avenida Juárez, which has fascinating displays of popular arts and crafts from all over the country. It also has articles for sale. This museum was quite probably destroyed in the 1985 earthquake. There is another good artisan centre behind San Juan de Dios across Hidalgo from the Alameda where you can pick up Indian weaving.

South of the Palacio de Bellas Artes is the **Torre Latinoamericana** which remarkably survived the earthquake. There are spectacular views from the top of this building and it's well worth the small fee you have to pay to get to the top. The views are best after rain has fallen as this gets rid of some of the ever-present pollution. It's particularly spectacular at night. Three or four blocks north of the Alameda near the junction of San Juan de Letran and Peru is the **Plaza Garibaldi** which you should get along to one evening. Though best on Saturday nights, it's a very lively place any evening. It's full of bars, restaurants and scores of traditionally-dressed *mariachis* who make a living playing songs for customers who throng the bars and restaurants.

Another place worth a visit is the **Casa de los Azulejos** (House of Tiles) on Madero, one block from Letran. This is an example of *mudejar* decoration and was once a private mansion belonging to the Counts of Orizaba. It is now a restaurant of the Sanborn chain.

Chapultepec Park Most of the city's museums are here. Among them is the **Museo Nacional de Antropología** which is a strong contender for the title of Best Museum in the World. You need to devote at least one whole day to this place. In all there are 23 display halls but, unlike most museums, this one won't ever bore you with kilometre after kilometre of glass showcases filled with pottery. It really is a spectacular museum and the exhibits have been very imaginatively displayed. There is also plenty of information about the exhibits from maps and diagrams to photographs and historical precis. While naturally most people concentrate on the pre-Colombian sections, make sure you don't miss the excellent folk costume and life-style displays on the 1st floor. The museum is open daily Tuesday to Saturday from 9 am to 7 pm and on Sundays from 10 am to 6 pm. There is a small entry charge (cheapest on Sundays but very crowded then).

The **Museo Nacional de Historía** with its large collection of items dating from the Conquest to the present day, including the beautifully restored residence of Maximillian and his wife Carlotta, is well worth a visit. It's open from 9 am to 6 pm daily except Tuesdays. Entry costs a few cents. Near this museum is the **Galeria de Historía** which is also worth a visit. Entry is free.

Art buffs should also make a point of visiting the **Museo de Arte Moderno** which is also in Chapultepec Park. It's open from 11 am to 6 pm daily except Monday and entry costs a few cents. Student reductions on entry charges to museums in Mexico are only possible if you have a Mexican student card so you might as well forget about them.

In the south of the city is the **Anahuacalli Museum** containing Diego Riveras' collection of Mayan artefacts and the building itself is done in Mayan style. There's no bus service so take a taxi. There's also a museum in his house which has been kept the way it was when he was living there. Take a blue line metro to Estacion General Anaya.

Xochimilco This is essentially a separate town to the south-east of Mexico City and very popular with local people who flock there at weekends for picnics. It's there you can see the remains of the floating gardens which once covered large areas of Lake Texcoco during Aztec times. At Xochimilco there is a maze of canals which meander through flower, fruit and vegetable gardens. You can hire punts and a poler to explore the area though some travellers suggest it's hardly worth it and that you can see almost as much by taking a bus to the gardens and strolling around on foot. If you do hire a boat they cost about US$1 per person.

Mexico University Some travellers have suggested a visit there saying that it's well worth it. The University is one of the largest in the world with over 300,000 students. It's a town within a town and there are some beautiful murals to be seen.

Markets One of the best daily markets is the Lagunilla, on the corner of Allende and Rayon (metro to Allende), which is housed in two fairly large buildings and has a whole range of stuff for sale, especially practical items. On Sunday it's worth going to the huge open-air bazaar close by which has every conceivable thing for sale. It isn't particularly cheap but it's an antique collector's paradise and it is still possible to pick up things which might be worth a small fortune back home. Check it out.

Places to Stay

Inflation and redevelopment have made Mexico City an expensive city to stay in so be prepared to pay considerably more than you might have to in other Mexican cities. However, the worst blow to budget accommodation may have been dealt by the devastating earthquake which struck Mexico City in late 1985. Until the situation becomes clearer we will continue to describe cheaper hotels which were there before the earthquake. If any of them have disappeared by the time you get there please let us know and we'll insert a supplement as soon as possible.

There are still a number of cheapies in the back streets around the Plaza Garibaldi but it's a fairly rough area and many of the hotels are dark and depressing. Quite a few travellers use the *Hotel Moderno*, Calle de los Incas, which has clean sheets and plenty of hot water. It costs about US$3/$6 a single/double with own shower and toilet. A similar place and one which is very popular with seasoned travellers is *Hotel Monte Carlo*, Calle Uruguay 69, south of the Zócalo. It's very good value at US$3/$6 a single/double. You might also like to try the *Hotel Fleming*, Revillagigedo 35 south of the Alameda, which is about the same price.

Also suggested in this area is the *Hotel Capitol*, Uruguay 12, which is shabby but clean and reasonable value at US$3.25/$4.10 a single/double. Half the guests there are permanent. Another traveller wrote enthusiastically about the *Hotel Juárez*, Callejon de 5 de Mayo 17, which is a block and a half from the zócalo towards the Alameda. It's been newly renovated, provides bottled water, has all-marble toilets and costs under US$7 a night.

The area where most travellers stay, however, is in the triangle bounded by Reforma, Insurgentes Norte and Moctezuma. Many of the hotels there are often full so you may have to do some legwork before you find a room. One of the best streets to start on in this area is Calle Bernal Díaz, close to and more or less parallel to, Insurgentes Norte. Along this street there are the *Hotel Estaciones*, Bernal Díaz 17, which costs US$7 a double; the *Hotel Bernal Díaz* and the *Hotel Mexico*.

If you have no luck with these then head off down Alvorado towards the

Alameda and turn up Zaragoza where you can check out the *Hotel Savoy* and the *Hotel Miña* (on the corner of Miña and Salgado). On Miña itself there is also the *Hotel La Paz* and the *Hotel Ferro*, and close to them on Zarco just off Miña is the *Hotel Astoria*. This last bunch of hotels is now quite expensive.

Another place which has been recommended in this area is the *Hotel Manolete*, Lerdo, which costs US$2.50 a double without bath and US$3 a double with own shower and toilet. Similar is the *Hotel Moctezuma*, Zarco. The *Hotel Principal*, Bolivar 29, between the Alameda and the zócalo has clean, comfortable rooms for US$4.

The *Hotel Americas*, Lerdo and Moctezuma, charges US$3 a double with own shower and toilet; and the *Hotel Polly*, on the corner of Orozco and Zaragoza, costs US$3.50/$4.50 a single/double with own shower and toilet. The *Hotel Imperial*, Edison, has also been recommended as clean and quiet and costs US$4.50 a double with own bathroom.

For something a little up-market, try the *Hotel Lepanto*, Guerrero 90, which is clean, comfortable and air-conditioned and costs US$6 to $7 a single depending on the room, with own private shower and toilet. Don't take the prices of these hotels as gospel though, as every time the ravages of inflation make accommodation cheap for those with US dollars to spend, up goes the price.

Outside this area try the *Casa de los Amigos*, Ignacio Mariscal 132 two blocks from the Revolution Monument metro station, which is run by Quakers and costs US$2 per person in dormitory accommodation (sexes separated); the *SETEJ Youth Hostel*, Cozumel 57 near Chapultepec Park and close to the Sevilla metro station, which costs US$2.50 per night; and the *Casa de Gonzales*, Rio Sena 69, Colonia Cuauhtemoc, off Reforma and two blocks from the US embassy, which is very clean, has hot showers and meals available. The owner Señor Gonzales speaks excellent English and is very hospitable. Note that the Youth Hostel has a midnight curfew.

One traveller recommended the *Hotel Londres* at Plaza Buenavista 5, close to the blue line metro station Revolution, as being a good place with clean sheets every day, private bath and friendly staff. A double room costs US$4.50.

There's another Youth Hostel in the Olympic Village near the University but it will take you all day to find it and isn't worth the hassle.

Places to Eat

There are thousands of restaurants scattered around the downtown area of Mexico City but if you want a cheap meal then stay off the main drags. There is a good collection of both cheap and expensive restaurants in the Plaza Garibaldi area as well as along Rosales which joins Reforma at Juárez. Along the latter you could try the *Restaurant Leo* which does *quesedillas*, *enchillados* and *milanesas*; or the *Café Rosales* which offers Americanised Chinese food. Also on this street try the *Restaurant Nacional* which offers inexpensive, traditional Mexican food.

There's another bunch of typical Mexican restaurants on the top side of the Alameda near the Plaza Santa Anita on Hidalgo. Recommended is the *Restaurant Fonda Santa Anita*.

In the Chapultepec area or the Zona Rosa check out the restaurants at Insurgentes Plaza (off Reforma and down Genova). There's a whole range of restaurants there, from *Burger King* and *Kentucky Fried Chicken* upwards.

Getting There & Around

Long Distance Buses There are four bus terminals which serve the north, west, east and south of the country. Quite a few of the 1st class bus companies also maintain booking offices at their former terminals closer to the city centre.

The *Central Autobuses del Norte*, Avenida Cien Metros 4907, handles all buses going north of Mexico City including those to the US border. There are over 30 companies represented here. To get there (without a rucksack) take the metro to Potrero and it's two blocks from there.

The *Central Autobuses del Sur*, Tlalpan 2205, serves the Cuernavaca, Acapulco and Zihuantanejo routes. It's opposite the Taxqueña metro station.

The *Central Autobuses del Poniente* covers the routes west of Mexico City. It's opposite the Observatorio metro station.

The *Central Autobuses del Oriente*, Calzada Zaragoza, handles the buses to Oaxaca, Vera Cruz, Villahermosa, the Yucatán peninsula and Chiapas. It's opposite the San Lázaro metro station. The buses at this terminal are likely to be booked solidly two weeks before Christmas so if you want to travel at that time book as far in advance as possible.

ADO (tel 566 0055, 546 7448), one of the best of the 1st class bus companies, still has a booking office at Buenavista 9 off Hidalgo/Av Ribera de San Cosme.

Public Buses These should be avoided at rush hours as the overcrowding and congestion is horrific. At other times of day they can be useful and save you a lot of money. Some of the most useful are:

To/From Chapultepec Along Reforma to the zócalo. Nos 55, 76 and 100.

To Airport Nos 20 and 24 going east along Avenida Donceles (one block north of the zócalo). Change at Airport Square and take No 43 going north.

To Central Autobuses del Sur (Southern Bus Terminal) Nos 29, 29A and 31 going down Avenida Bolívar. Get off when the bus passes the Perifirico (ring road) and it's a five minute walk from there. The alternative is colectivo No 2 from the small streets south of the zócalo.

To Central Autobuses del Norte (Northern Bus Terminal) Buses marked 'Cien Metros' and 'Terminal del Norte' go directly there

or take No 7B or 70 from the corner of Bucareli and Avenida Juárez.

Taxis These are metered but there's no guarantee that the meters will be used so agree to the fare before you set off. Make sure you know not only the address of the place you want to go to but the district (*colonia*) too as there are many streets with the same names in different districts.

At both the airport and the two bus terminals there are prominent, government controlled ticket booths for the taxis. You have to buy your ticket here and the price is determined by a zoning system. This is all very well but you'll hardly ever get a taxi driver to take you anywhere for the prices you pay at these booths. Always expect to pay a surcharge (which will depend on your negotiating skills). Taxis from the airport are particularly bad about this so it's better to take the yellow VW minibuses run by *Setta* to the centre of the city. Tickets for these buses are sold in front of the airport terminal building.

Metro Like many vast Latin American cities, Mexico has an underground railway (metro). It's very quiet, fast and cheap (journeys cost just a few cents – same price regardless of the distance you travel) but it gets incredibly crowded at rush hours. At all times be very, very careful about pickpockets and bag slashers. They're very professional about it. You can only travel on the metro with rucksacks or heavy bags between 9 am and 4 pm. Officials or police will turn you back at the barriers if you are carrying anything of this nature at other times, so you won't be able to use the metro to get to the airport or bus terminals.

AROUND MEXICO CITY
Teotihuacán
Some of the most spectacular monuments in the world are at Teotihuacán and shouldn't be missed for anything. They include the Pyramids of the Sun and the Moon – the largest man-made structures

on the American continent. The Pyramid of the Sun covers almost the same area as the Great Pyramid of Cheops in Egypt. In addition to the pyramids there are the Palaces to Quetzalcoatl, Tlaloc and other gods as well as vast courts, halls and terraces.

The city which flourished here centuries before the Aztecs rose to prominence, covered an area of almost 23 square km! Most of the structures have been excavated and restored and there's also a small museum on the site which is worth visiting. The site is awash with *al fresco* soft drink sellers, trinket sellers and hustlers in general but they tend to pester the package tourists rather than individual travellers. There is a small entry fee to the site. There is a *son et lumiere* in English at the pyramids at 7.15 pm. It costs about US$1 and is said to be worth it.

To get to Teotihuacán take either a *Lineas Teotihuacán* bus (every 15 minutes or so) from the Central Autobuses del Norte (Northern Bus Terminal) or take the metro to Indios Verdes and then catch a 1st class bus from there to Teotihuacán. Buses leave every 30 minutes or so and cost about US$1. The journey takes about 1½ hours. Buses back to Mexico City are best caught in front of the site museum.

If you want to stay in Teotihuacán village for the night rather than go back to Mexico City then ask for *Posada y Restaurant Silverio* which is 200 metres from the plaza. It costs about US$3 a double and you can buy good food here, or there are other restaurants on the plaza.

Tula

This is the most important Toltec site in Mexico and includes ball courts, pyramids and the famous stone warriors, which are over six metres high. (Photographs of the warriors are often used in tourist literature). There is also a good museum and there's a small entry charge to the site.

The best way to get there is to take a bus from the Northern Bus Terminal. There

are buses every 15 minutes or so and the journey takes about two hours. There's also a train which leaves from Buenavista station at 8 am and returns at 8.35 pm but it is often late.

PUEBLA

Probably the only reason to stay in Puebla is to visit Cholula where there is a pyramid and other interesting churches. It's about 20 minutes by bus from the corner of 8 Poniente and 7 Norte.

Places to Stay

The *Latino*, next to the first class bus terminal is okay at US$4 with hot water. Closer to the main square is the *Ritz* which is more basic and doesn't have hot water.

For somewhere to eat, try the places on the street between *ADO* and the main square.

The Centre

Acapulco, Cuernavaca, Pátczuaro & Taxco

ACAPULCO

Acapulco is of course the most famous Mexican resort town. It has also provided the backdrop to numerous movies and TV programmes. It wasn't until after WW II however, that the boom took off. Back in colonial days it was an important port through which most of the trade from the Orient passed, but after independence it became a backwater and remained that way until a road was constructed to Mexico City in the late 1920s. Today it's not only a resort town but has also regained its stature as one of Mexico's most important ports.

The city stretches about 16 km along a series of bays and cliffs and climbs up into the hills behind.

Things to See

Naturally most people go to Acapulco

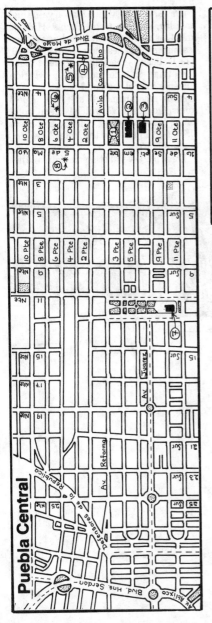

1 Plaza de Armas
2 Cathedral
3 Post Office, Tourist Office & Casa de la Cultura
4 Mercado El Parian & ADO Bus Terminal
5 Museo del Estado 'Casa del Alfeñique'
6 Museo de la Revolución 'Casa de los Serdán'
7 Museo de Historia Natural (Acuario Municipal)
8 Capilla de Rosario (Templo de Santo Domingo)

for the beaches and the surf but the high divers at La Quebrada are perhaps no less famous. It's worth going along one evening to see them. To get there you can either walk via Calle Quebrada from the Zócalo or take a bus and get off at El Mirador. Expect to throw in a contribution when the hat comes round.

There are a number of lagoons along the coast close to Acapulco which are chock full of wildlife and tropical flowers. Two of the best are **Laguna Coyuca**, north of Acapulco near the Playa Pie de la Cuesta; and the **Laguna Tres Palos**, south of the city near Puerto Marques. A trip to either can be very interesting but unfortunately they cost quite a lot these days. Expect to pay up to US$26 for a boat (shared between however many people you can round up).

The old star-shaped Spanish fort of San Diego is worth a look though you need to check on opening times because it's not normally open to the public. Situated close to the centre of the city, it was there that the last battle in the struggle for independence was fought.

Places to Stay

If you have the impression that Acapulco offers only super-luxury hotels then you'll be pleasantly surprised to hear that there are also plenty of cheap places to stay in the old part of the city around the zócalo.

Four of the most popular are the *Hotel del Patio*, on the corner of Guerrero and Progresso; the *Hotel Sanchez Romero*, Roberto Posada 9, down the hill towards the Cathedral from the Patio, with its own restaurant and balcony overlooking the street (easy to miss as the sign is only visible from the opposite side of the street); the *Hotel Isabel*, on the corner of

La Paz and Valle, which is good value and popular; and the *Hotel Pachis*, Hidalgo and Quebrada, which also has its own restaurant. All these hotels cost US$4.70. The Isabel was specially designed to take advantage of the natural convection currents to cool the building.

Also recommended are the *Hotel Rojas*, Quebrada 27, which is clean, good value, has a pleasant balcony and costs US$3.50 a single; and the *Hotel Angelita*, Quebrada 87.

There are several other cheapies in this

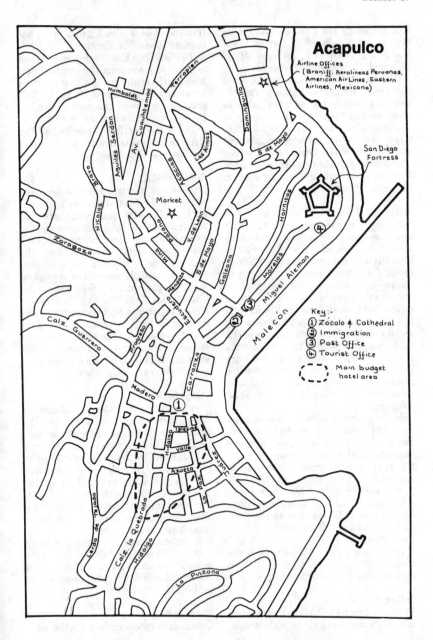

Acapulco

Airline Offices
(Braniff, Aerolineas Peruanas,
American Air Lines, Eastern
Airlines, Mexicana)

San Diego Fortress

Key:-
① Zocalo & Cathedral
② Immigration
③ Post Office
④ Tourist Office
--- Main budget
hotel area

area including the *Casa de Huespedes Concha*, Quebrada 25, a former townhouse but often full; and the *Hotel Mariscal*, Hidalgo and Quebrada.

Close to the Flecha Roja bus terminal there are a number of cheap places but they're generally not as good value as those around the zócalo. Exceptions to this general rule are the *La Casa del Río*, an old-fashioned place which is good but often full; and the *Casa de Huespedes María Elonia*, on the first floor of an office building – look out for the paint shop on the ground floor.

Places to Eat

For a very inexpensive meal you can't really beat the cafés in the market which is near the back entrance of the Flecha Roja bus terminal and over the pedestrian footbridge. Things open up very early in the morning. Close by is the restaurant opposite the Canada shoe shop and to the right of the bus exit from the Flecha Roja bus terminal. It operates 24 hours a day and is very popular with local people. The food often comes with the restaurant's home-made chili sauce which will burn your lips clean off if you're not used to this sort of thing so if you don't want it then remember to order food *sin salsa colorado*.

In the centre of town on Juárez a few metres from the Zócalo try the *Restaurant San Carlos*. It offers barbecued meat and seafood dishes and the prices are moderate. It's popular with gringos who stay in Acapulco a long time but is rarely patronised by other tourists. There is also a number of seafood restaurants along Azueta near Milla which advertise their daily specials on blackboards outside. Take your pick.

On Azueta near La Quebrada is the *Restaurant Marisco's Milla* with good service, good food and good prices.

Getting Around

The second class Flecha Roja bus terminal is about 20 minutes walk from the zócalo.

If you don't want to walk it then take a bus marked 'Zócalo' or 'Centro'.

The first class Estrella de Oro terminal is about four km from the centre. Local buses to the centre go right past the front entrance of the terminal. To get back to this terminal from the centre, catch a Cine-Rio bus at the stop above Sanborn's.

The Cine-Rio Basic bus across the street from the zócalo, will take you out to the beach at Conchessa.

CUERNAVACA

Cuernavaca has traditionally been the retreat of the Mexican rulers and their retinues. The Aztec emperors, Cortés and Maximillian all came here during the summer months. Since independence it's been government ministers and the wealthy who've kept up the tradition. With the completion of the *autopista* many people commute the 75 km daily into Mexico City. The city also has the largest expatriate North American community in Mexico outside of Chapala near Guadalajara. The price of accommodation and food generally reflect this state of affairs so think twice about going there if you're on a tight budget.

Things to See

Cortés' Palace is now the **Museo de Cuauhtémoc** though until 1967 it was the State Legislature. It's one of the best regional museums in Mexico and features displays ranging from palaeontology to contemporary Indian culture as well as a beautiful Diego Rivera mural, on the rear balcony, depicting the conquest of Mexico. The museum is on the plaza and there is a small entry charge. Spend a few hours there if you have the time.

If you're interested in crafts then pay a visit to FONART on Salazar close to the museum which has a good collection of household items, wood carvings, woven baskets and fabrics.

Places to Stay

Cuernavaca caters mainly for the well-heeled and isn't a place where the budget traveller should spend too much time. One of the few places which does qualify as a budget hotel is the *Casa de Huespedes Dora*, Calle Leyva between Las Casas and Abosolo, which has constant hot water (there's an attached bath house) but we've received bad reports about it recently. If you don't like the look of it then try the *Casa de Huespedes Marilu*, *Hotel America* or the *Posada San José*, all within 50 metres of each other along Aragon y León between Morelos and Matamoros. They're all similar in standard and fairly pleasant though the San José is the cheapest of them.

If all these are full then you can try the moderately priced *Hotel Penalba*, Matamoros between Degollado and Aragon y León.

Places to Eat

For a very cheap meal try the *Tacos Caballero* in the Flecha Roja bus terminal. Nearer to the centre on Rayón near Galeana are the *Restaurant Bar Acuario* and *El Tepa*. Both are moderately priced and popular with clerks and other government workers.

PÁTZCUARO

In contrast to Cuernavaca, Pátzcuaro is a much mellower town which hasn't been unduly affected by tourism. Not only does it have a similar climate to Cuernavaca but it's full of beautiful historical buildings, has two lively plazas and a lake-side location. These together with its narrow cobbled streets help to make it one of Mexico's most picturesque towns.

Things to See

Make sure you see the unfinished **Basílica** begun by Vasco de Quiroga in 1540. It contains an image of the Virgin Mary made from cornstalk pith and orchid juice which attracts pilgrims from all over the country on the eighth day of every month. Two other religious buildings

which are worth visiting are **La Compañía**, a restored Jesuit church at the top of Calle Portugal; and the monastery on Calle Lerín which has murals by Juan O'Gorman.

The **Museum of Popular and Regional Arts** in the Colegio de San Nicholas is one of the best of its kind in Mexico and also has the remains of a pre-Colombian town and pyramid in the precincts. There is a small entry fee. Close to this is the **Casa de Once Patios** on Larín between Ensen'anza and Cos, once a convent but now serving as workshops for weavers and laquerware workers. There are also shops there where you can purchase such items.

One of the most enjoyable things to do in Pátzcuaro is to take a trip to one or more of the inhabited islands on Lake Pátzcuaro. The most popular is Janitzio which has a huge, ugly monument to Morelos on it but is otherwise quite interesting. Boats leave from the Embarcadero about one km from the main plaza. The trip takes about 45 minutes and costs US$1. There are also less frequent boats to Tecuen, Yunuen and Pacanda which leave when there is sufficient demand (a minimum of 15 passengers is usually required).

Festival

The Fiesta of the Immaculate Conception on 8 December is a big event in this town and attracts pilgrims from all over the state. Accommodation is at a premium at that time so make sure you get there well before then or be prepared to commute from Morelia.

Places to Stay

One of the best places, though not the cheapest, is the moderately priced *Hotel Blanquita*, Volador 4 on the market square, which is clean, quiet and comfortable and has hot showers. It can be difficult to find on market days as it gets hidden behind the stalls. Slightly cheaper but very pleasant is the *Hotel El Artillero*, Quiroga between Zaragoza and Tena.

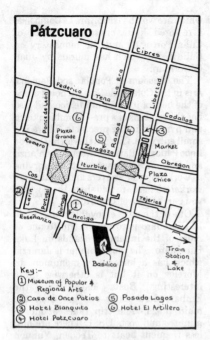

Pátzcuaro

Key:-
1. Museum of Popular & Regional Arts
2. Casa de Once Patios
3. Hotel Blanquita
4. Hotel Pátzcuaro
5. Posada Lagos
6. Hotel El Artillero

The hotel was once a mansion.

The *Hotel Pátzcuaro*, Calle Ramos less than one block from the Plaza Chica between Tena and Zaragoza, also used to be popular and has friendly staff but recent reports suggest that it's up for sale and that the owner is allowing it to fall into disrepair.

Another place, recommended in the past where quite a few travellers stay, is the *Posada Lagos*, Zaragoza 14 between the two plazas. Despite the sign in the lobby, there is no restaurant.

If all these places are full then there are a few hotels on the Plaza Chica opposite the Flecha Amarilla bus station which range from inexpensive to moderately priced. They are the *Hotel Posada de la Rosa, San Agustín* and the *Hotel Concordia*.

Places to Eat

It's hard to beat the restaurant in the same building as the *Hotel Blanquita* for a cheap fish meal though the price of white fish is rising steadily because of over-fishing in Lake Pátzcuaro. There are other cheap cafés in the immediate area.

Also reasonably good value is the restaurant in the *Gran Hotel*, Plaza Chica where the soups are particularly good. For a leisurely breakfast try the restaurant in the *Hotel Mesón Iturbide*, on the corner of Iturbide and the Plaza Principal. It's a pleasant, traditional restaurant and is inexpensive.

TAXCO

Like Guanajuato and San Miguel de Allende, Taxco has been declared a national monument and many people consider it to be the most picturesque. As with the others it was built on steep hillsides and its narrow, winding streets – many of them paved with patterned cobbles – are full of colonial houses, mansions, churches and other public buildings. It's a photographer's paradise and though today it has a population of some 60,000, it very nearly became a ghost town not so long ago. It's prosperity was based on silver mining but it wasn't until the early 18th century when a French prospector named José de la Borda discovered the richest veins that it really began to boom. Most of the town dates from that period.

The majority of the mines were exhausted by the beginning of the 20th century and as they closed one by one, the population began to dwindle and the town took on an air of neglect.

It was rescued largely through the efforts of William Spratling, an American who went there to write a book but ended up training the local youth as silversmiths. As a result, although there's only one silver mine which remains operational, the town has become famous for its silverware and jewellery. The wealth which this generates has led to the restoration of much of the town.

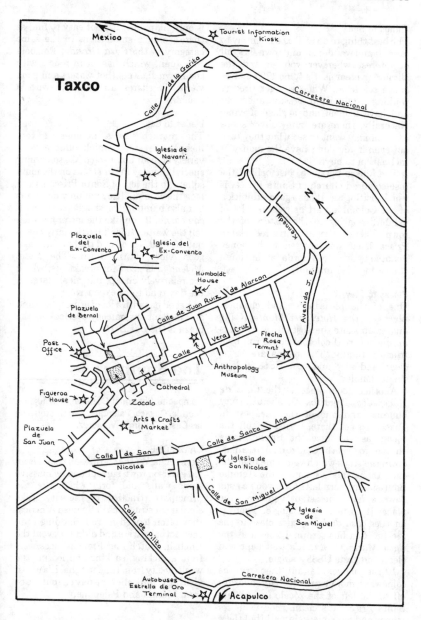

Things to See

The best thing to do in Taxco is simply to take off and wander around town. It's full of interest wherever you go and the climate is ideal as it's some 1700 metres above sea level. When you get tired of walking just duck into a restaurant or bar and have a meal and a glass of wine. Naturally, there are many silver shops and you may want to see what they turn out even if you don't have the money or inclination to buy.

The **Museo Spratling**, just behind the rose-coloured church of Santa Prisca, is worth visiting too. It has a good exhibition of pre-Colombian art as well as a lot of exhibits relating to the history of the town. There's a small entry fee. Santa Prisca itself was erected with money donated by José de la Borda (at the time a staggering M$7 million!).

Places to Stay

One of the pleasantest and cheapest places is the *Hotel del Monte*, Calle Juárez opposite the post office, which is an unconverted colonial house run by a friendly family. The rooms are large, clean and airy and cost US$3.50/$5 a single/double.

Another good place is the *Casa de Huespedes*, Pajaritos 23, a multi-story building and one of the cheapest in Taxco. To get there, turn right off the zócalo as you face the Santa Prisca church, go past the Centro de Artesanias, down the steps which you come to at the end, then walk as far as the Templo Bautista and turn left. After you've gone down a few more steps you'll see the place. It costs US$3 a single. There is another *casa de huespedes* close to the Flecha Roja bus terminal known as the *Casa Maria Crista*. It's well kept and clean and costs US$3 a single.

If the above are full then try the somewhat more expensive *Hotel Jardín* off to the left of the zócalo as you face Santa Prisca. It's clean, good value for money and has a pleasant patio but there

is only six rooms. It's not easy to find as there's only a small sign. In the same category is the *Casa Grande*, Plazuela San Juan, which has clean rooms with their own showers (hot water) and good views. It shares an entrance with a cinema.

Places to Eat

The market has a number of very inexpensive stalls which offer a wide variety of foods but if you'd like something special then try *Pizza Dama* on the main square to the left of Santa Prisca as you face the church. They not only do pizzas but also hamburgers, spaghetti and *chili con carne*. If you like the latter hot then tell the waiter. It isn't particularly cheap but the food is good and the balcony has a good view of the town. The *Hotel Meléndez* is good for breakfasts, which are relatively cheap, but meals later in the day tend to be expensive.

A good bar with a lot of atmosphere and an excellent low balcony overlooking the plaza is the *Bar Berta*.

The South

Campeche, Chetumal, Cozumel, Isla Mujeres, Mérida, Oaxaca, Palenque, San Cristóbal de las Casas, Tulum & Veracruz.

CAMPECHE

Campeche, on the Caribbean coast, is an old garrison town surrounded by massive stone walls and forts which are the principal attraction of the city. Like similar constructions in Spanish America, they often looked more forbidding than they actually were and didn't prevent the English, Dutch and French buccaneers from attacking, sacking and looting the wealthy city from time to time. It's worth visiting Campeche for a day en route to or from Mérida and Palenque.

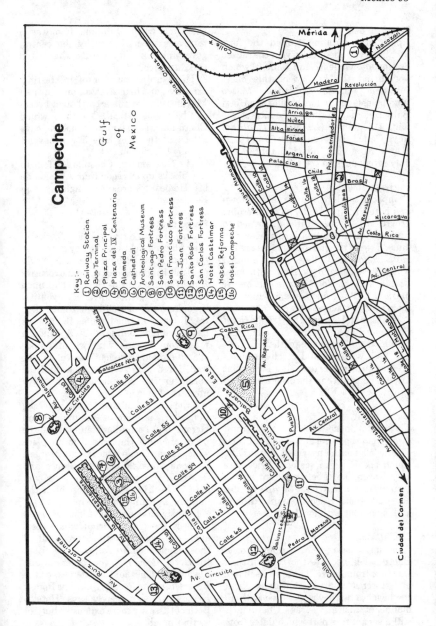

Campeche

Gulf of Mexico

Key:-
1. Railway Station
2. Bus Terminal
3. Plaza Principal
4. Plaza del IV Centenario
5. Alameda
6. Cathedral
7. Archeological Museum
8. Santiago Fortress
9. San Pedro Fortress
10. San Francisco Fortress
11. San Juan Fortress
12. Santa Rosa Fortress
13. San Carlos Fortress
14. Hotel Castelmar
15. Hotel Reforma
16. Hotel Campeche

Mérida

Nacozari

Ciudad del Carmen

Things to See

Apart from strolling around the fortifications you should also visit the **Museo de História**, Calle 57 and Calle 8, which documents the history of this once-turbulent port; and the **Museo Antropología** in the fort behind the Hotel Baluartes. The former residence of the King's Lieutenant (*La Casa de Tiente del Rey*), Calle 14 between Calles 59 and 61, is also worth a visit though the interior is only rarely open to the public.

Places to Stay

Campeche tends to be an expensive town and hotels fill up rapidly as the morning progresses. It's very difficult indeed to find anywhere to stay during May and June. Two of the cheapest places are the *Hotel Reforma*, Calle 8 near Calle 57, which is basic and popular with local people; and the *Hotel Campeche*, on the plaza at Calle 57 and Calle 8, which has rooms with attached shower.

If these hotels are full then try the *Hotel Castlemar*, on the corner of Calle 8 and 61, which has large rooms with thick walls and high windows and catches the sea breezes to some extent. It's somewhat more expensive than the others but good value.

Places to Eat

The market outside the city walls furthest away from the shore at the end of Calles 57 and 59 has many small restaurants which specialise in seafood. Prices are very reasonable. The restaurant on the ground floor of the *Hotel Campeche* also does excellent reasonably-priced food and is popular with local people.

CHETUMAL

The only reason most people go to Chetumal is because they are on their way to or from Belize. The town itself is of little interest and you can forget about the beaches as they're polluted with all manner of trash and sewage. Chetumal is still a sort of free port which dates from the time when Quintana Roo was a territory ruled directly by the central government but it's hardly what you'd call duty-free.

There are a number of interesting, extensive, and in most cases, unexcavated Mayan ruins in the area though access can be problematical. One thing which Chetumal is good for is hammocks – have a look at the ones here if you haven't already bought one.

The Guatemalan Consulate is four to five blocks up Obregón from Avenida de los Heroes towards the highway and Belize.

Places to Stay

There are not too many cheap places and they fill up quickly as the day goes on so find a room as soon as you get there. You'll probably have most luck at the inexpensive *Hotel Doris*, Av de los Heroes 41A, which has been a long-time travellers favourite. If you're a tall or well-built person then tread lightly in this hotel as the fittings have a habit of coming adrift. A giant of a man from Florida with whom I once shared a room there had the sink off the wall, his bed in several pieces and the bannister rail demolished within five minutes of arrival.

If the Doris is full then try the *Hotel Big Ben* which is more or less opposite on Heroes. It's of a similar standard and the prices are much the same. Another place which is very cheap is the *Posada Margot*, Av 5 de Mayo 26 between Blanco and Ochoa. If you want to get in there you need to check in as early as possible in the morning as it fills up quickly.

Slightly more expensive but very good value is the *Hotel Barudi* which costs US$5 a single with own bathroom. If all those mentioned are full then try either the *Hotel Alcoces*, on the corner of Calle Lazaro Cardenes and Av Heroes; or the *Hotel Quintano Roo*, on Quintana Roo off Heroes (the sign merely says 'Hotel'). Both of these are more expensive but not by that much.

AROUND CHETUMAL
Mayan Ruins

There are sites both to the west and north of Chetumal. The ones to the west are near Francisco Villa and Xpujil about half way between Chetumal and Francisco Escárcega. The first is **Kohunlich**, about seven km south of the main road just before the town of Francisco Villa, where there is an unusual pyramid decorated with masks which still bear some of their original colouring.

Seven km past Xpujil is **Becán**, the largest of the sites with huge, ruined temples and plazas and a ball court largely overgrown by jungle. Much of the site remains unexcavated. About two km beyond Becán and off down a dirt road

some 10 minutes is **Chicana** which has a very interesting Toltec/Maya temple with its main entrance built in the shape of the fanged jaws of the plumed serpent.

There is no direct public transport to any of these ruins so you either have to walk or arrange private transport from Xpujil. Hitching isn't really practical as there are so few cars. There is one daily bus in either direction between Chetumal and Francisco Villa/Xpujil.

North of Chetumal there are the three unexcavated sites of **Ichpaatun** (13 km), **Oxtancah** (14 km) and **Nohochmul** (20 km). Again, there is no direct public transport to the sites.

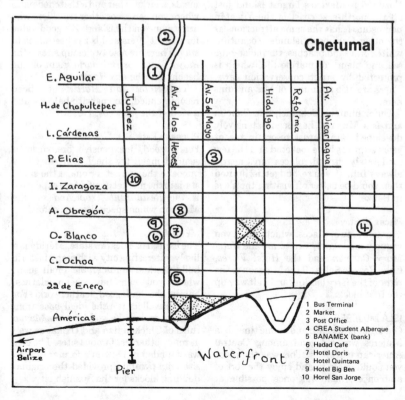

1 Bus Terminal
2 Market
3 Post Office
4 CREA Student Alberque
5 BANAMEX (bank)
6 Hadad Cafe
7 Hotel Doris
8 Hotel Quintana
9 Hotel Big Ben
10 Horel San Jorge

Laguna Bacalar (Laguna de Siete Colores)
About 20 km north of Chetumal is the 40
km-long lake of Bacalar with fantastic
clear blue water and white sand. There
are cheap *casas de huespedes* in the
village of Bacalar near the old Spanish
fort as well as a camping ground with
toilets and showers about 100 metres from
the lagoon. Prices are very reasonable.

To the north is the **Cenote Azul** which is
over 70 metres deep. Be sure to visit it if
you get the chance (it's just off the
Chetumal-Tulum road). There are regular
minibuses between Chetumal and Bacalar
which leave from just outside the bus
terminal.

COZUMEL
Cozumel is Mexico's largest island just
off the north-east coast of the Yucatán
peninsula. It has the same attractions as
the other Caribbean islands – beautiful
white coral sand beaches, turquoise-blue
sea and plenty of marine life, which is
protected by strict conservation laws.
There are also a number of Mayan ruins
here.

Unfortunately, Cozumel, like Cancún
and Isla Mujeres, has been extensively
developed as a tourist resort in recent
years so prices have rocketed and the few
moderately priced places are nearly
always full. If you're budget is limited
then you'd be better off visiting the Cays
in Belize.

Places to Stay
The only two places which are even
vaguely moderately priced are the *Hotel
Mary Carmen* and the *Hotel Flores*,
Calle Rosado Salas off the Malecón to the
right of the ferry landing and half way up
the first block.

ISLA MUJERES
Old legends die hard and at one time, Isla
Mujeres was a legend among Central
American travellers. This was the place
you could come to and enjoy the sort of
ambience which was once possible at

Cozumel, but for a song. That is no longer
true. It's now almost as expensive as
Cozumel and caters for North Americans
on package tours and the like. To add to
this, all the palm trees have been cut
down because they were diseased.

The best time to visit the island is
between April and November – the so-
called 'off season'. You can rent bicycles
(30 cents an hour) and mopeds (50 cents)
at several places in town.

Places to Stay
The only place which is remotely
affordable if you're on a tight budget is
the *Poc-na Hostel* where you can rent a
bunk or hammock for about US$2 per
night – more if you need sheets. It offers
meals, snacks, a bar and a thatched patio
where you can meet other travellers who
are staying on the island. It's good value
for what it offers and is the best place to
stay. There are also two camp sites – the
Playa Cocoteros Balneario, right on the
beach; and the *Las Hamacas*.

The *Hotel San Martin* has been
recommended. Rooms with balcony and
a view of the jetty cost US$5.

Places to Eat
For a good, inexpensive breakfast or
seafood meal, try the *Loncheria Chely*
opposite the market, or one of the small
stalls in the market itself. More expensive
is the *Restaurant Tropicana* on the
Malecón which specialises in seafood.

MÉRIDA
The capital of Yucatán state, Mérida is a
lively, interesting city with many historic
buildings and innumerable small shops
where you can buy cheap clothes,
hammocks and good leatherwork. For
most travellers it's the ideal base from
which to explore the world-famous Mayan
ruins of Chichén Itzá and Uxmal as well
as many other less famous sites. The city
was founded in 1542 on a former Mayan
site – its pyramid provided the original
building blocks for the Spanish city.

More recently, Mérida became a very prosperous city based on *henequén*, a fibre used to make rope and similar cordage. Those days are gone but the wealth which it brought enabled merchants to build themselves large mansions in the city and many of these are now open to the public.

Things to See

Of the buildings on the main plaza which are worth visiting, the **Casa de Montejo**, originally built in 1549 and rebuilt in 1850, is the best. It's open to the public in the afternoons daily except Sundays. There's a small admission charge. The **Cathedral** may also be worth a visit but it's fairly plain and not that interesting.

Away from the plaza, the most interesting street is the **Paseo de Montejo** (or Calle 56A) which is full of the imposing homes of Mérida's rich merchants built during the second half of the 19th century when henequén was the city's foremost export. One of the most pleasant ways of touring this street is to hire a *calesa*, a horse-drawn carriage. These are not as expensive as you might suppose, but make sure you fix the price before you set off.

It's worth spending some time at the **Museo de Arqueología**, on the corner of Calles 43 and 58. It's open Tuesday to Saturday from 8 am to 2 pm and on Sundays from 8 am to 8 pm.

Those with an interest in handicrafts should visit the **Casa de las Artesanías**, Calle 63 between Calles 64 and 66. There is an excellent selection of just about every craft produced in the Yucatán and prices are reasonable. The entrance is through the patio of an art school. Check out the hammocks there if you haven't already got one.

The murals in the Government Palace in the Plaza Hidalgo are reportedly worth seeing.

Hammocks Sr G Tuyub, Calle 28 between 15 and 13, Tixkokob, just out of Mérida,

makes hammocks of your choice and dyes them with natural colours. You can meet him on the main plaza and try to bargain.

Places to Stay

Despite its popularity with more well-heeled tourists, Mérida has a good selection of cheapies. Most charge around US$4.50 to $5 a double. One of the most popular at present and one of the cheapest is the *Casa de Huespedes*, Calle 62 No 507 between Calles 63 and 65. It's basic and some of the rooms are grubby and there are only cold showers but it's a 200-year-old hotel and only half a block from the main plaza. The exact price depends on what room you get but, at US$2/$4 a single/double, you'll be lucky to find anything cheaper than this.

If that one is full there is a choice of three others fairly close to the plaza which are used by many travellers. They are the *Hotel America*, Calle 67 between Calles 58 and 60; the *Hotel Oviedo*, Calle 62 between Calles 65 and 67; and the *Hotel La Paz*, Calle 62 between Calles 65 and 67. These are all very similar and offer much the same facilities for around US$4.50 to $5 a double. Single rooms are also available.

Another hotel which is also popular with travellers is the somewhat more expensive *Hotel Margarita*, Calle 66 No 506 between Calles 61 and 63. It's clean, friendly, has hot water and costs US$7 a double. Singles are also available. In the same block and of a similar standard and price is the *Hotel Latino*, Calle 66 No 505. It's very clean and has friendly staff.

Over near the bus terminal is another bunch of cheapies. One which has been enthusiastically recommended is the new *Hospedaje Casa Becil*, Calle 67 between Calles 66 and 68. It has large, very clean rooms, hot showers and even a TV lounge and costs US$4.50 a double. Similar is the *San Pablo Hotel*, on the corner of Calle 69 and 70; the *Hotel San Jorge* and the *Hotel San Fernando*, both of them on Calle 69 between 68 and 70. The quietest rooms in all these hotels are the ones at the back. Another in this area which has been recommended is the *Hospedaje Uxmal*, Calle 69, which is inexpensive. The *Hotel Cayre*, a few doors from the San Pablo, is considerably more expensive.

Places to Eat

The restaurant on the ground floor of the *Hotel America* offers good, inexpensive meals and there's a fairly wide choice of dishes available. Also well worth trying is the *Restaurant Astor*, Calle 60 between Calles 65 and 67, which offers barbecued chicken, salads, *tortillas* and drinks. Half a chicken plus the rest shouldn't cost you more than US$1.75.

In the past we recommended *La Mil Tortas*, Calle 62 between Calles 65 and 67, for their huge piping hot tortas, but it seems times have changed. One recent correspondent said that their tortas were now neither large nor piping hot and that the place had a plastic atmosphere to it and was moderately expensive. Perhaps they had a bad night and this wasn't typical. Check it out.

If you want to splurge in delightful surroundings then head for the Plaza Hidalgo (also known as the Plaza de Jesús) which is on Calle 60 between Calles 59 and 61. This has been turned into a pedestrian precinct and is full of sidewalk cafés. Food and drink will be brought to your table from either the *Hotel España* or the *Hotel Caribe* – depending on where you sit. It isn't cheap but it is an ideal place to while away the evening with eating, talking and drinking.

Getting There & Around

The bus terminal on Calle 69 between Calles 68 and 70 handles both first and second class buses. This is where you will find the buses to Chichén Itzá and Uxmal.

Bus No 79 goes to the airport and is marked *Aviación*. A taxi there will cost about US$5.

AROUND MÉRIDA
The Mayan Ruins

The Yucatán peninsula is studded with Mayan ruins and even if you're not an archaeology buff you'll find them fascinating. Many of them have had the jungle cleared from around them and have been restored as far as possible. The ruins are maintained by the government and there's a small entry charge to each site. The main sites are easily accessible by public buses but for the more remote sites you really need your own transport as many of them have not yet been excavated or even cleared.

Chichén Itzá These are some of the most extensive Mayan ruins in the Yucatán peninsula and they're truly magnificent. Scattered over about five sq km of cleared scrub-forest they include numerous temples, pyramids, ball courts and palaces adorned with beautiful sculptures. One of the pyramids has an internal chamber containing a red-painted jaguar. It can be visited between 11.30 am and 1 pm and again between 4 and 5 pm. Electric lights have been installed.

Near the main ruins is the Cenote Sagrado (Well of Sacrifice) which has been dredged on a number of occasions to yield a vast quantity of gold, copper, jade and pottery items as well as animal and human bones. Chichén Itzá is open daily from 6 am to 5 pm but if you want to avoid the guided tour groups then get there as early as possible. You need at least a whole day to explore these ruins.

Buses from Mérida to Chichén Itzá depart at 8.30 am and the journey takes 2½ hours. The fare is US$1.50. If you don't want to go back to Mérida there is a *cabaña* park near the site where you can sling a hammock for a reasonable fee and a camp site (motorcamp) about five km west of the site where you can rent a tent for the night. In the village of Piste, two km from the ruins, there is a campsite and the *Posada Novela* with double rooms for US$5.50.

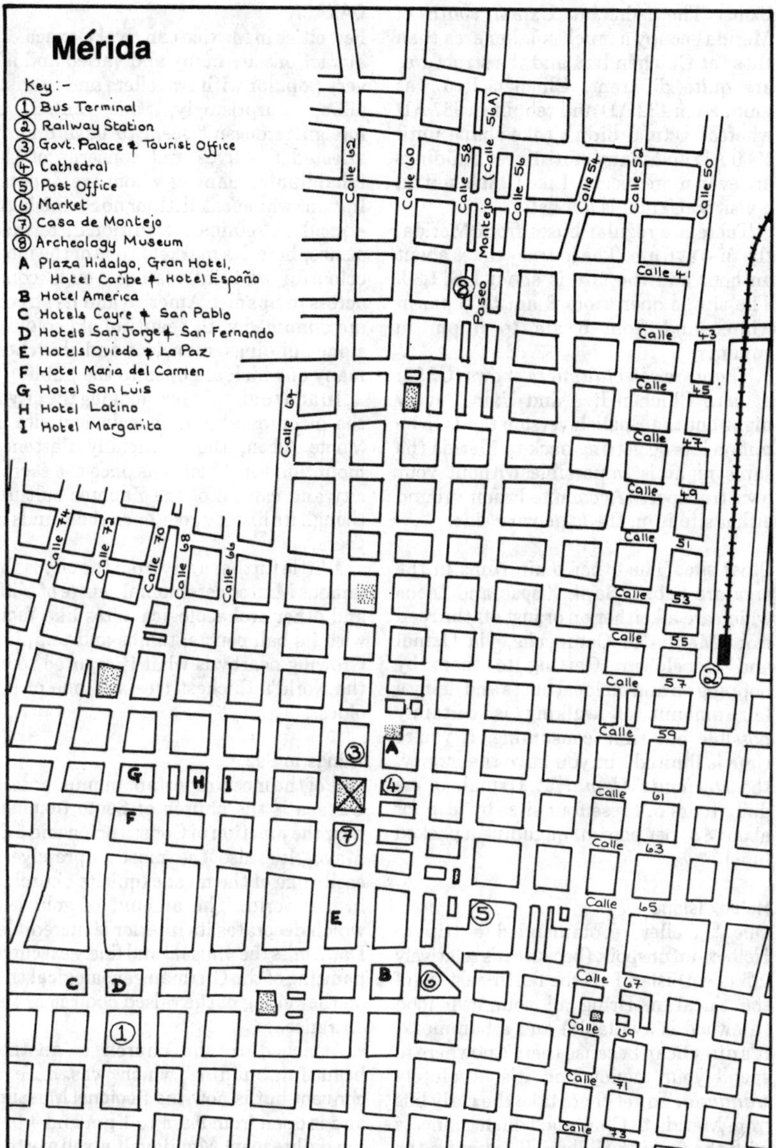

Mérida
Key:-
1 Bus Terminal
2 Railway Station
3 Govt. Palace & Tourist Office
4 Cathedral
5 Post Office
6 Market
7 Casa de Montejo
8 Archeology Museum
A Plaza Hidalgo, Gran Hotel, Hotel Caribe & Hotel España
B Hotel America
C Hotels Cayre & San Pablo
D Hotels San Jorge & San Fernando
E Hotels Oviedo & La Paz
F Hotel Maria del Carmen
G Hotel San Luis
H Hotel Latino
I Hotel Margarita
Calle 62
Calle 60
Calle 58
Paseo Montejo (Calle 56A)
Calle 56
Calle 54
Calle 52
Calle 50
Calle 41
Calle 43
Calle 45
Calle 47
Calle 49
Calle 51
Calle 53
Calle 55
Calle 57
Calle 59
Calle 61
Calle 63
Calle 65
Calle 67
Calle 69
Calle 71
Calle 73
Calle 64
Calle 74
Calle 72
Calle 70
Calle 68
Calle 66

Uxmal The ruins at Uxmal south of Mérida occupy a much smaller area than those at Chichén Itzá and the structures are quite different. Chichén Itzá was founded in 432 AD and rebuilt in 987 AD whereas Uxmal didn't take shape until 1000 AD and many of its finest buildings are even more recent. Like Chichén Itzá, a visit to Uxmal is a must.

There are regular buses from Mérida, the first at 6 am. The journey takes about an hour and the fare is about US$1.30. The site is open from 8 am to 5 pm in winter and from 6 am to 6 pm in summer.

There are *son et lumiere* shows (US$2) at both Chichén Itzá and Uxmal every night but the English version tends to be put on late so getting back to Mérida the same night is impossible without your own transport. Accommodation around either site is on the expensive side.

Other sites The other main ruins in the area are **Kabah, Sayil, Xlapac** and **Labná** which are all either on or just off the road from Mérida to Campeche, via Uxmal and Hopelchen. Getting to them by hopping on and off local buses and doing a fair amount of walking is certainly possible but time consuming. If you're time is limited but you have the money, the *Hacienda Uxmal* at Uxmal, offers daily tours of these four sites by jeep for about $20 per person, including a packed lunch.

Holbox Island

One traveller recommended a trip to Holbox, an unspoilt (because it's relatively unknown) island off the north-east tip of the Yucatán. Bring all your own food (firewood is available) and a hammock. It's dirt cheap because there's nowhere to spend your money and it's absolutely 'ranquilo. To get there take the early bus from Mérida to Chiquilá, which connects with the ferry to Holbox. If you miss the ferry, a private launch will cost from US$3 to $5.

OAXACA

Few cities in Mexico can rival Oaxaca. Its attractions are many and varied and it's very popular with travellers and tourists alike. Surprisingly, this influx of foreigners doesn't seem to have unduly affected the lives and concerns of the inhabitants, many of whom are Zapotec Indians who speak little or no Spanish. As a result it retains a traditional, relaxed atmosphere. Its market is one of the most colourful and interesting you'll come across in Spanish America and its streets are crammed with beautiful old colonial stone buildings, mansions and churches, many of which are open to the public.

To add to all this, overlooking the city is the incomparable archaeological site of **Monte Albán**, the artificially flattened mountain top which was once the sacred city and capital of the Zapotec culture, though its history goes back thousands of years.

A little further away from the city is the famous Mixtec ceremonial centre of **Mitla** and other archaeological sites like **Yagul** with its ball courts, tombs and temples. Growing nearby is what is reputed to be the world's thickest tree and one of it's oldest.

Things to See

One of the most important monuments in Oaxaca is the church of **Santo Domingo** near the junction of Constitución and 5 de Mayo. It's also the most impressive – easily one of the most exquisite churches in the world. The amount of gold leaf which decorates its interior is incredible. Don't miss the unusual and finely executed painting of the Guzmán genealogical tree on the ceiling of the raised choir near the entrance.

Attached to the church is another beautiful building which was once a convent but is now the **Regional Museum** and is open from 9 am to 1 pm and 4 to 7 pm daily except Monday. It's well worth a visit and has a collection of treasures excavated from Monte Albán and Mitla.

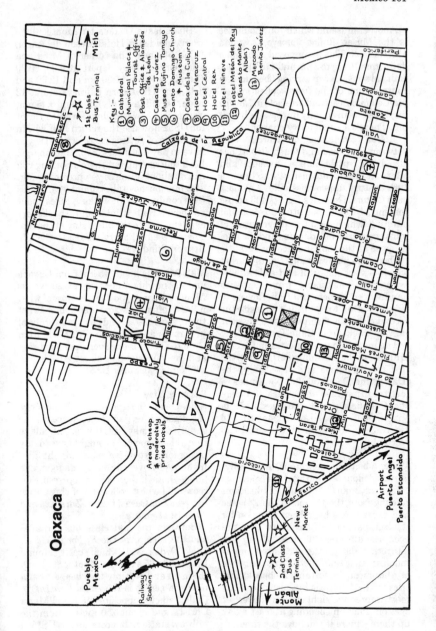

Oaxaca

Key:—
① Cathedral
② Municipal Palace ★
  Tourist Office
③ Post Office ★ Alameda
  de León
⊕ Casa de Juárez
④ Museo Rufino Tamayo
⑤ Santo Domingo Church
  ★ Museum
⑥ Casa de la Cultura
⑦ Hotel Veracruz
⑧ Hotel Central
⑨ Hotel Rex
⑩ Hotel Nineve
⑪ Hotel Mesón del Rey
  (Buses to Monte
  Albán)
⑫ Mercado Benito Juárez

1st Class
Bus Terminal

Área of cheap
★ moderately
★ priced hotels

Another museum which you should see is the **Museo Rufino Tamayo**, Avenida Morelos 503. This is supposed to be open daily from 10 am to 2 pm and 4 to 7 pm but isn't always. Keep trying because it contains one of the finest collections of pre-Colombian art and artefacts in Mexico displayed in an equally impressive building. There's a small entry charge.

Juárez' old house on García Vigil between Carranza and Quetzalcoatl has also been turned into a museum and offers an interesting insight into life in a 19th century upper class villa. The **Casa de la Cultura**, Gonzales Ortega 403 across the end of Colón, is a stunning colonial building which hosts a programme of music concerts, folk dancing and the like. Enquire at the tourist office for details.

Oaxaca is justly famous for its market which is very colourful and sells almost everything imaginable from herbs to hand-woven carpets and from flowers to jewellery. Don't miss it. It's opposite the second class bus terminal just across the railway tracks from Calle Trujano.

The most important fiestas in Oaxaca are those of the Los Lunes del Cerro on the first two Mondays after 16th July; the 'Day of the Dead' on 2nd November (a folk tradition that dates back to before the Conquest); and the Fiesta de la Virgen de la Soledad which starts on 16 December and continues until 23 December.

Monte Albán This enormous, artificially-flattened mountain top was the ceremonial centre of many different civilisations ranging from the Olmec to the Zapotec and excavations have been going on for the best part of half a century. The site occupies an area of some 40 sq km altogether though the excavated area is much smaller than this. It's not only one of the most important archaeological sites in the Americas but also one of the most impressive sights you will ever set eyes on. Plan on spending at least a day up there – more if you have the time.

Buses leave Oaxaca for Monte Albán from outside the Hotel Mesón del Angel, Mina 518 near the corner of Mina and Díaz Ordaz. They depart at 9.30, 10.30 (Sundays only), 11.30 am and 12.30 and 3.45 pm. The return journeys are at 12 noon, 1 (Sundays only), 2, 4 and 5.45 pm. You must, however, buy a return ticket for US$2 and use the return half within 2½ hours of getting there otherwise you have to pay a further US$0.50 surcharge. It's a tourist trap but there's nothing you can do about it unless you prefer to walk. The bus journey takes about 30 minutes (less coming down); walking takes about an hour. Soft drinks and snacks are available where the buses stop at the top. There's a small entry charge to the site (less on Sundays).

Mitla Mitla is about 45 km from Oaxaca and is nowhere near as extensive as Monte Albán so you can see most of what it has to offer in two or three hours. To get there, go to the second class bus terminal in Oaxaca and take a bus to Mitla from Gate 15. There is one every half hour or so and the journey takes about 1-1/2 hours. The fare is just over US$1.

Places to Stay

Since Oaxaca is so popular with travellers the demand for rooms often exceeds the supply so it may initially be difficult to find a cheap room. You might have to stay in a more expensive place for the first night or pay over the odds for a room in a budget hotel if there's a lot of pressure for rooms. The best collection of cheapies is between Las Casas, Ordaz, Zaragoza and 20 de Septiembre.

Between the 2nd class bus terminal and the zócalo try the *El Fortin Hotel*, Díaz Ordaz 312 which costs around US$4.50 to $5 a double. Another to try in this area and possibly the cheapest hotel near the centre is the *Hotel San Diego*, Calle Palacios opposite the Hotel Maria Christa and about 250 metres from the railway station. It costs about US$3 a double there without your own bathroom.

Two others to try are the *Hotel Tipico*, Calle 20 de Noviembre between Mina and Zaragoza, which is very good value and has hot water in the showers; and the *Hotel Central*, Calle 20 de Noviembre, which is clean, secure, has hot water and is good value at US$4 a single.

Further over towards the zócalo is the *Hotel Rex*, Calle de las Casas 308. This is a long-time favourite with travellers and costs US$2.50 to $3 a single without own bath and US$8.10 a double with own bath and hot water. The hotel has a friendly manager. Some travellers prefer the *Hotel Rivera* just opposite the central market which has huge clean rooms and hot showers. It generally works out cheaper than staying at the Rex and is certainly good value for money.

Also close to the zócalo on G Diaz Orclaz, the *Hotel San Fernando* has been recommended. Good clean, sunny rooms for US$4.

Outside these areas is the *Posada Margarita*, Calle Abasolo between Calles Alcala and 5 de Mayo. It's become very popular with travellers over the last two years or so. The price you pay depends on what room you take but it's inexpensive.

If all these places are full then you'll have to try one of the up-market hotels until you can move to one of the cheapies. Moderately priced hotels include the *Hotel Jimenez*, Mier y Terran between Trujano and Hidalgo; the *Hotel del Pacifico*, Trujano 420 at the junction with Mier y Terran; and the *Hotel Ninive*, Periferico and Las Casas.

If you have the money and want to splurge there's the *Hotel Monte Albán*, housed in a beautiful old mansion opposite the cathedral but it's very expensive. Bring your own credit card.

Places to Eat

As with the hotels, many of the cheapest restaurants are clustered around the second class bus terminal especially along Las Casas, Trujano and Hidalgo. In the centre of the market itself next to the second class bus terminal try the *Comedor Chonita* or the *Comedor Ocotlán*.

The *Hippocampo Restaurant*, off 20 de Noviembre on the left hand side one block before the Av Independencia, has been recommended by many travellers. You can get huge meals with salad and bread for less than US$1. It's very popular with travellers and locals alike. *Pizza Rick's* near the zócalo on the corner with Independencia is also good value. Large pizzas which will feed two to three people cost about US$3.50.

PALENQUE

Palenque is the site of some of the most spectacular and romantically set Mayan ruins in Central America. As at Tikal (Guatemala) and Copán (Honduras), they were built in thickly-forested hill country and the inspiration which the sculptors of this city drew from the wildlife is plain to see. Discovered intact in the Pyramid of the Inscriptions was a funerary crypt with a sarcophagus of the Sun God.

Going down into the crypt is every bit as exciting as climbing up inside the Cheops pyramid in Egypt. It has electric light these days so you don't need torches. Elsewhere on this site is some of the most beautiful sculptural work to be seen at any Mayan site. The city was abandoned around the 12th century AD and not re-discovered until the late 19th century. It's a magic place and travellers flock there by the thousands.

The ruins are about eight km from the village of Palenque. Local buses travel between the village and the site fairly frequently but not according to any set schedule (they leave when full). When it's raining, they're often cancelled. There's a small entry charge to the site.

Places to Stay

In the last few years the hotels in Palenque have been hiking their prices to the limits of what the market will tolerate so it works out very expensive to stay in the village itself. Many travellers have also been commenting about the indifferent or even surly nature of hotel managers.

The cheapest and friendliest places to stay are the two camp sites on the way to the ruins where you can either sling up a hammock in a *palapa* or rent/pitch a tent. The better of the two is the *Mayabell Camping* though the restaurant is expensive. The other is the *Tulcan Camping*. Both charge less than US$1 but beware of thieves. If you hear something which sounds like King Kong roaring away in the jungle at night, relax – it's the monkeys enjoying themselves.

In the village itself you could try the *Hotel Regional*, which is on the corner of

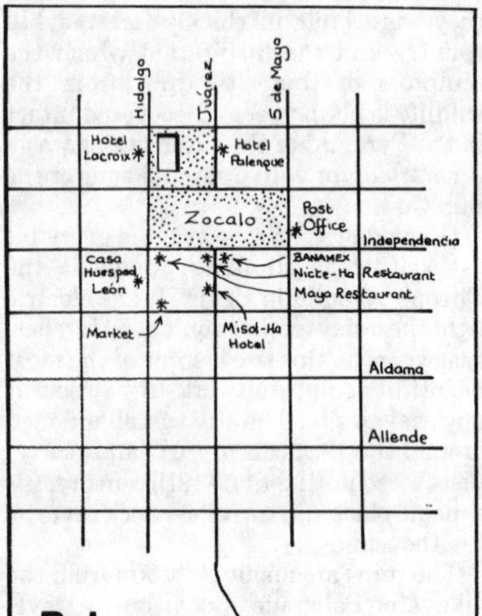

Palenque

Juárez and Allende and costs US$6 a double. Another place, the *Posada Alicia*, is a little way out of town but pleasant. To get there, turn right after the Huespedes León coming from the zócalo, go down to the church and turn left, then walk straight on for another 300 metres. The *Casa Huespedes León*, Hidalgo about half a block from the zócalo, is also worth trying.

The other hotels in Palenque are out of the range of the budget traveller.

Places to Eat

At most of the restaurants in Palenque, if you look like a gringo, you'll be charged gringo prices so always check prices before you eat. One place which has been recommended is the small restaurant below the Hotel Avenida. They serve good, inexpensive food.

The hotel between Mayabell Camping and the ruins has a reasonable breakfast.

Getting There

Many people come to Palenque from Villahermosa. If you do this then remember that there is only one bus in either direction daily at 7 am. *ADO* buses in Palenque leave from Hidalgo just past the Plaza Mayor (zócalo). Buses to San Cristóbal de las Casas leave from outside the Hotel Avenida.

There are buses to Mérida from Palenque and they are probably the best way of getting there, even though they arrive in the wee hours of the morning and you're not going to have much choice of places to stay. The train to Mérida is often several hours late (it starts from Mexico City), and gets very crowded and takes 15 hours, as against 6 to 8 hours by bus. The station in Palenque is quite a way from the village. Take a colectivo or start walking early.

AROUND PALENQUE

Agua Azul National Park

Fifty-five km from Palenque, en route to San Cristóbal de las Casas, is Agua Azul

National Park which is well worth visiting. There is a series of beautiful waterfalls stretching over nearly seven km with, as the name of the park implies, crystal-clear blue water. Swimming is permitted and there's a camp site where you can camp for less than US$1. There's also a small entry charge to the park. Food can be bought in the village from several small shops. Buses between Palenque and Agua Azul cost about US$0.75 and take about 1½ hours.

SAN CRISTÓBAL DE LAS CASAS

In a high mountain valley at over 2100 metres, San Cristóbal is very popular with travellers and there's a small resident community of westerners there. The area is populated by colourful Tzotzil and Tzeltal-speaking Indians who outnumber Spanish speakers by two to one. The various groups wear their own unique and characteristic tunics and their religion is still far more pagan than Christian.

The area was the scene of Indian insurrections throughout much of the 19th and early 20th centuries. The government has been making major efforts to integrate these people into the money economy but changing centuries-old customs and habits is proving to be a slow process. You're advised to tread warily in the outlying villages and don't take anything for granted, especially regarding photography.

San Cristóbal was founded in 1528 and named after its second bishop, Las Casas, who made a big nuisance of himself with the colonial authorities by petitioning the King of Spain to outlaw the excesses which the successors to the *conquistadores* were perpetrating on the Indians. It's a town full of churches and low-standing houses with small, barred windows and red-tiled roofs. It has an atmosphere which is quite unique in Mexico.

Information

You cannot get a Tourist Card or visa renewed in San Cristóbal. If you need to do this then it's probably easier to go into Guatemala for a few days and then return (unless you're one of those people who need a visa for Guatemala, in which case it will cost you US$10).

There is a laundromat on B Dominguez one block east and then one block north of the plaza.

Things to See

One of the main drawcards of San Cristóbal is the daily market which attracts Indians from all over the area. It's quite a sight to see them en masse dressed in their amazing variety of costumes. The best time to go is in the morning.

The **Museo Na Bolom**, Vicente Guerrero 33, is worth a visit. It has a fascinating collection of artefacts and photographs of the Lacandón Indians with a description of their history and way of life. It's set in a beautiful old house complete with gardens and is open from 4 to 5.30 pm daily except Monday. There is a small entry charge. It also has a guest house and library and a weaving cooperative works from there.

Places to Stay

There are plenty of cheap places in San Cristóbal. A popular spot is the *Posada Abuelito*, Tapachula near the junction with Tuxtla, which has dormitory-style accommodation but you need your own sleeping gear. It's a friendly place and one of the cheapest in town with hot water 24-hours a day.

Similar is the *Casa de Huespedes Margarita*, Guadelupe between Dominguez and Colón, once a private mansion. It has mixed dormitory accommodation with large comfortable beds, blankets and hot water and costs US$3 per person. Many travellers recommend it warmly and it has quite a reasonable restaurant.

Another which you can try in the same range is the *Casa de Huespedes Pola*, Insurgentes at Pino Suarez close to the

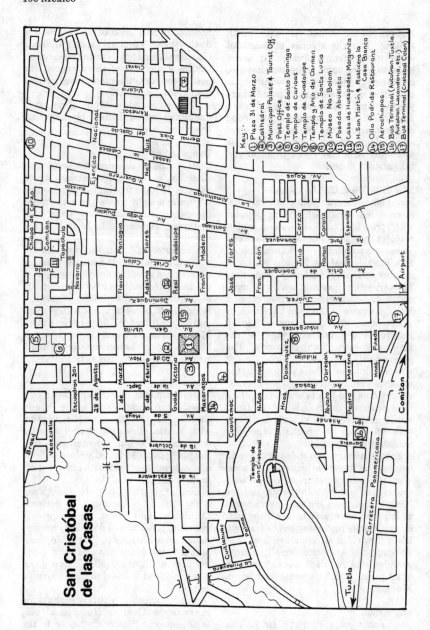

San Cristóbal de las Casas

Key:-
1. Plaza 31 de Marzo
2. Cathedral
3. Municipal Palace & Tourist Off.
4. Post Office
5. Templo de Santo Domingo
6. Templo de Caribas
7. Templo de Guadalupe
8. Templo y Arco del Carmen
9. Templo de Santa Lucia
10. Museo Na - Bolom
11. Posada Abuelita
12. Casa de Huespedes Margarita
13. H. San Martín & Rosticería la Casa Blanca
14. Olla Podrida Restaurant
15. Aerochiapas
16. Bus Terminal (Autotran, Tuxtla, Autotran Lacandonia, etc.)
17. Bus Terminal (Cristobal Colon)

bus stations. It's very basic but it does have hot water in the afternoons and costs US$2.50 a double.

Somewhat more expensive but perhaps one of the nicest places to stay in San Cristóbal is *La Carpintería* (no sign), Av Gral Utrilla and Calle Flavio A Paniagua. This has small pinewood cabins built around the carpenter's courtyard. The owner, Don Jaime, is a very friendly man. It's inexpensive and there are hot showers available (extra). One traveller recently reported however that there were no cabins and the smell was mildew and not pine.

In the same bracket is the *Posada El Cerrillo*, on the corner of Ejercito Nacional and Av B Dominguez. It's clean and friendly, has hot water all day and the prices are very moderate.

Other places you might like to check out are Sra Mercedes' rooms at Calle 1 de Marzo 59 which cost about US$1.50 each; and the *Hotel San Martín*, Guadelupe between Utrilla and B Dominguez one block from the plaza. The rooms on the top floor are the best. It's often full in the summer.

You can camp at the *El Ranchero* about one km from town. It costs about US$1 each, either in a *cabaña* or with your own tent.

Places to Eat

The *Normita*, Dr José Flores near Juárez, is one of the best cheap places. Try their *pozole* or *huevos Motulenos*. The restaurant has a very pleasant atmosphere and is open in the afternoons and evenings. *El Mural*, Diego Mazariegos between Matamoros and Allende, offers good, cheap, five-course meals. The owners are very friendly people.

The *Baños Mercedarios*, 1 de Marzo 55, is not only a bath-house and cheap pension where you can get a shower if your hotel doesn't have hot water, but a place where you can get a good, filling meal. Again, the owners are friendly.

Probably the most popular place in town is *Olla Podrida*, on the corner of Allende and Diego Mazariegos. It's a gringo hang-out with an arts and crafts shop and a useful noticeboard where you can find out about what's happening, houses for rent and lifts. They offer vegetarian dishes, yoghurt, whole-meal bread, *quiche lorraine* and *chili con carne* among other things. You can eat either inside or out on the patio. The owners are North Americans.

For breakfast, eggs and toast, or for a coffee during the day, try the *Central*, Madero between Insurgentes and Juárez. It's popular with visitors and locals alike. You can have a game of chess or dominoes and it's open from 8 am to 11 pm daily.

The restaurant with no name opposite Los Arcos on Diego Moyariegos, one block from the plaza, is a little expensive but recommended. The *Los Arcos* is cheaper but not as good.

There are a number of discos and other places where you can pick up some music in the evenings. *Discotheque Diego's*, on the corner of 1 de Marzo and 16 de Septiembre, is open Thursday to Sunday from 8.30 pm until 2 or 3 am. The entry fee entitles you to a free drink. There's also a disco every night at the *Hotel Rincón del Arco*, Ejercito Nacional near Vicente Guerrero. There is sometimes live music at both the *Posada Diego de Mazariegos* and the *Olla Podrida*.

Getting There

There are buses direct to Palenque from San Cristóbal but you must buy a ticket the day before or you'll get up at dawn only to find there are no seats left.

AROUND SAN CRISTÓBAL

Many of San Cristóbal's attractions lie outside the town in the surrounding villages. Each has a Sunday market. Remember to ask for permission from the municipal authorities in these towns and villages before entering any church or taking photographs. Some places make a charge for the latter.

Villages worth seeing are **San Juan Chamula** (10 km from San Cristóbal) – dolls, bags, purses and musical instruments; **Zinacantán** (11 km); **Tenejapa** – fine weaving and embroidery; **Huistán** (36 km) – weaving centre; **San Andrés Larrainzar** (27 km) – brocade and hat making; **San Pedro Chenalhó** (37 km); and **Amatenango del Valle** (37 km) – unglazed ceramics.

Buses connect most of these villages with San Cristóbal though you may have to walk part of the way to some of them. It's possible to hire horses and guides from *Na Bolom* and ride to some of the nearer villages.

If you're going to be spending any time at all in San Cristóbal then it's worth buying a copy of Mike Shawcross' book, *San Cristóbal de las Casas: City and Area Guide*, which is on sale in many places including the Olla Podrida restaurant.

TULUM

The Mayan ruins of Tulum half-way between Cancún and Chetumal have become very popular with travellers in recent years. Whatever time of year you go you'll find a sizeable gathering of them camping along the beach. So far it's a long way from being over-run but the government does have plans to develop it into a tourist resort complete with airport and all the ancillary services although nothing has been done about it yet. The ruins themselves are unusual in having once been a fortress instead of a ceremonial centre. There's a small entry fee. There are also some good ruins to see at Cobá, 42 km away, but they're difficult to get to.

The mosquitos in Tulum can be vicious, particularly in September. There are some good snorkelling possibilities along the coast 10 km north of Tulum at Xelhá.

Places to Stay

Unless you intend to camp on the beach then it's best to look for a place to rent on a monthly basis. There are quite a few of these. If you don't have a tent then head for Santa Fé, the main hang-out. The *Mirador* has *cabañas* with good kitchen facilities, but no toilets, which cost US$1.50 per person per night. You need your own hammock.

There is a similar *cabaña* site but with far less people south of Playa Carmen. The road there is unmarked except for a sign saying *Restaurant Lafitte*. When you get there, another one km further south along the beach will bring you to Xcholococo where the *cabañas* cost the same as those at *Mirador*.

VERACRUZ

This is Mexico's most important port city and the one which has taken the brunt of many invasions, principally by the French and the United States. Like other coastal cities of strategic importance, the Spanish provided Veracruz with a huge fortress to protect it. This is the Ulúa fortress and, like others similar to it, the Spanish regarded it as impregnable. It probably was but it didn't prevent invaders from taking the city, especially the North Americans who, under General Scott, demolished the city block by block in 1847 until the Mexican garrison surrendered. An assault on the fortress was therefore unnecessary. Ulúa is now open to the public and is Veracruz's principal attraction. It's well worth spending a day exploring the fort. There's a small entry charge. Take a torch with you if you want to explore the dungeons as the authorities are niggardly with their provision of electric lights. Other than the fortress, Veracruz has little of interest for the traveller.

The tourist office is on the zócalo and the staff are friendly and have good maps.

Places to Stay

Most of the cheap places are near the bus terminal which is quite a long way from

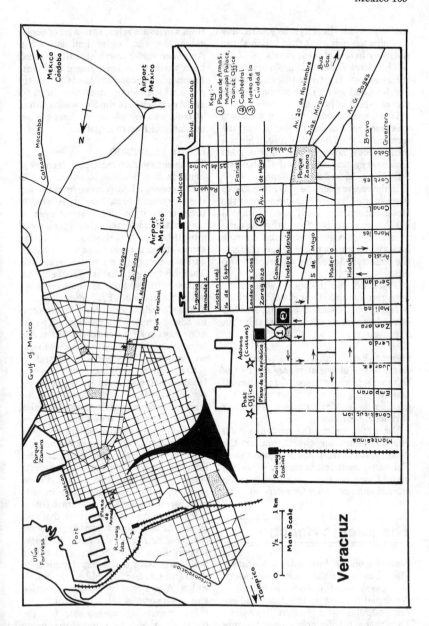

Veracruz

Key :-
① Plaza de Armas, Municipal Palace, Tourist Office
② Cathedral
③ Museo de la Ciudad

Main Scale
0   ½   1 km

the centre of the city. If you're only stopping to see the fort then you might as well stay in one of these hotels.

The *Hotel Tabasco* is probably one of the cheapest. It's three blocks from the bus terminal along Díaz Mirón towards the city centre past the Hotel Central. Prices are moderate. Further on down this same road about 12 blocks from the terminal is the *Hotel Avenida*. This is a multi-storey hotel so you have a good chance of getting a room if the Tabasco is full. Again, prices are moderate.

In the centre itself the only really cheap place is the *Casa de Huespedes* near the Hotel Rias which itself is on Zaragoza near Lerdo across from the Aduana Maritima. It's a simple and small rooming house which caters mainly to people from the country. Make sure your room has a fan.

Two others on the zócalo which have been recommended are the *Ortiz*, which is family-run, clean and cheap; and the *Hotel Imperial* which is a bit shabby but friendly.

Places to Eat

Some of the cheapest places are by the fish market, where there is a row of small cafés offering cheap seafood meals. Try the *Día de la Marina* which is popular with local families.

For a splurge, try the *Restaurant La Paella*, behind the church and on the plaza. It isn't cheap but it is good value. The other restaurants on the plaza are mainly for having a drink and hanging around and not really for eating at.

The Pacific Beaches

Puerto Escondido, Puerto Angel & Arista

These beaches on the Pacific coast south of Oaxaca are the last surviving un-developed beaches on this coast and are very popular with budget travellers. They're the sort of beaches where the only things to do are relax, read a lot of books, catch the sun, swim and surf. Any American surfer worth his salt will have been there or at least heard of Puerto Escondido. Escondido tends to be the place which North Americans head for and Angel is where the Europeans camp. There's usually plenty of cheap weed available in Puerto Angel.

PUERTO ESCONDIDO

The cheapest and most popular way of living in Escondido is to rent a *cabaña* and there are a lot to choose from both on the beach and back from it. A word of warning though: don't leave gear in unwatched or isolated *cabañas* or it could grow legs. The best way to avoid having things stolen is to rent a *cabaña* which is part of a compound where the owners live. That way you get what is effectively a 24-hour security system. Mosquito nets are advisable in Puerto Escondido.

The Cabañas Cortéz have been recommended by quite a few travellers. They're a fair way back from the beach but said to be much more pleasant than those right on the beach. They're set in a beautiful garden, have cooking and washing facilities and cost about US$1 per person per night. Also recommended is the *Neptun Cabañas* next to the beach which is also a camp site and has showers, cooking facilities and mosquito nets. The *cabañas* cost US$2 per person. On Calle Alfonso Perez Gasga going uphill away from the beach is *Cabañas Macuilxochitl*, which is a good place to relax and meet people. The cabañas have mosquito nets and there's an excellent restaurant there.

If you prefer a hotel room then there is a choice of cheap places, two of these being the *Casa de Huespedes Las Los Costas Precios Economicos*, quite a mouthful but inexpensive and a popular place to stay; and *La Posada*, right on the beach, which offers hostel type accommodation and has its own cheap restaurant.

For something up-market, try the *Hotel Roca Mar*, a three storey green building with an empty shop on the ground floor. Try to get a room on the top floor as these have both the views and the sea breezes.

For food, one of the most popular places is *La Palapa* on the hill above the Roca Mar. It's looking tatty these days but the seafood is still excellent. The prices are a bit on the high side but it's still good value. Another which is worth trying is the *Bucanero* on the main street (2nd storey) where you can get eggs any style for breakfast for under US$1. It's a good place to meet up with other travellers coming from or going to Guatemala, though as one traveller commented: 'the cliques which form here are hard to penetrate.' You can find typical Mexican food at the *Restaurant Crucer* opposite the bus station.

For reading matter, the *Paperback Shack* has a very good selection of English-language books.

PUERTO ANGEL

Puerto Angel is even more laid back than Escondido and is really only a small fishing village though it once served the coffee plantations in the hinterland. Most of the beaches near the village are just sandy coves but there's a long isolated beach about two km over the hills complete with shacks that you can rent, a few small cafés and much fine weed. It's very mellow and there are no hassles.

There are a couple of hotels in the village if you need somewhere to stay while you find a *cabaña*. They are the *Hotel Sonaya* overlooking Cemeterio beach; and *La Posada Cañon Devata* on Playa Panteón which is run by a Californian *gringa*.

ARISTA

Arista isn't anywhere near as well-trodden as the other two but is very pleasant and mellow. There aren't really any *cabañas* so what you have to do is sling up a hammock at one or other of the small restaurants along the beach. This should cost you less than 50 cents a night. You can also camp out on the beach. Good seafood is available at the cafés.

Getting There

You can get to Puerto Escondido either by flying from Oaxaca with *Aerovíasa Oaxaqueñas* (several flights per day, about US$25) or by taking the *Flecha Roja* or *Oaxaca Pacífico* buses over an incredible, hair-raising rough mountain road which zig-zags all over the place. Make sure you take a first class bus on this route – the second class buses are a nightmare. Buses take about 12 hours depending on the weather. You can also get to Escondido by *Flecha Roja* second class bus from Acapulco which takes six to seven hours but isn't recommended. If you arrive in Escondido by plane, there are VW minibuses between the airstrip and the town.

Local buses, colectivos and trucks run between Puerto Escondido, Puerto Angel and Arista.

Central America

Belize

Belize is a delightful anomaly in Latin America, being very much a mainland extension of Caribbean culture. This way of life is mirrored elsewhere in Central America only in small pockets of the eastern coasts of Honduras, Nicaragua and Costa Rica. The reasons for this are found in its history and, to some extent, its geography as much of the low-lying land was, until fairly recently, malarial mangrove swamp.

The first European settlers were a motley collection of English buccaneers, bankrupt planters and adventurers who came across from Jamaica with their black slaves in the 1640s to cut logwood, which was then a source of textile dyes. From time to time they would be driven out by the Spanish, but each time they returned. The threat of eviction by the Spaniards was finally removed in 1798 when a strong Spanish naval force was decisively beaten off, at St George's Cay, by the settlers.

Up until that time Britain had somewhat half-heartedly attempted to protect the interests of the settlers by treaties with Spain but despite the naval victory, made no attempt to annex the country. This failure to declare the area a colony led to claims by both Mexico and Guatemala following their independence from Spain in 1821, on the grounds that they were the successors to the Spanish Empire. The settlers however, had other ideas and maintained that the territory had become British by conquest following the naval engagement of 1798.

Years of dispute over sovereignty followed and although Mexico renounced its claims by treaty in 1893, Guatemala has consistently refused to do so and has on numerous occasions threatened a military takeover. Many attempts were made to find a diplomatic solution to the problem during the 1960s and '70s but all came to grief and frequently led to the recall of ambassadors.

Undoubtedly part of the reason for the

impasse is that the question of Belizean sovereignty is too convenient an issue for the military rulers of Guatemala to ditch since it serves to divert attention away from the country's internal problems. At the same time, Belizeans have little stomach for compromise with a military regime whose human rights record is appalling, and even less inclination to contemplate becoming even an autonomous region of a country in which they would effectively be second-class citizens. Ask almost anyone you meet.

A secret attempt by Britain and Guatemala to settle the dispute in the late 1970s, which would have involved redrawing the borders of Belize and a considerable loss of territory, led to all hell breaking loose in the colony when news of the plan leaked out to the press.

The threat of Guatemalan military action for many years delayed the granting of independence to the colony and demanded the presence of the British Army there. Internal self-government was granted in 1964 but it was not until August 1981 that the country felt confident enough to accept independence after mutual defence pacts had been agreed upon with a number of other Caribbean Commonwealth countries and the UN had voted to accept Belize as an independent nation. Independence celebrations were followed by the breaking of diplomatic relations between Guatemala and Britain yet again. For a while the border between Belize and Guatemala was closed but has subsequently re-opened.

Long before European settlers arrived there the mountains along the Guatemalan border were part of the lands occupied by the Old Maya civilisation (4th to 9th centuries AD). These people left a number of temples and ceremonial sites, the ruins of which are well worth visiting. They include Altun Ha, 50 km north-west of Belize City; Xunantunich near Benque Viejo; and Labantun in the far south of the country. The descendants of these

people still inhabit the area and make up around 17% of the population. The remainder of the population of around 150,000 consists mainly of Creoles – the descendants of black slaves who were brought across from Jamaica during the 17th and 18th centuries – plus a smaller group of indigenous Black Caribs who speak a language of their own and are found mostly in the towns and villages of the southern coastal area.

There are also minority groups of various European nationalities, principally German-speaking Mennonite farmers, North Americans, and others from the Middle East, China and neighbouring Latin American republics. English is the majority language with Spanish speakers making up some 15% of the population. On the other hand, many people are bilingual and quite a few are trilingual.

The land itself consists mainly of lush, richly forested low-lying ground, honeycombed with rivers and mangrove swamps but with mountains rising in the west and south to a height of 1000 metres. The most remarkable geographical feature of Belize, however, is the almost continuous chain of reefs and cays (small islands formed by the growth of coral) which lie between 15 and 60 km offshore. It's the longest coral reef in the world after the Great Barrier Reef of Australia. Most of the islands are very small and uninhabited but the larger ones support fishermen and skin divers and are very popular with travellers and campers. Many have beautiful beaches with crystal-clear water which is superb for swimming and snorkelling. Equipment is for hire on most of the larger cays. Don't miss this country – you'll love it!

VISAS

Required by all except nationals of Commonwealth countries, Belgians and nationals of the USA. Some travellers who require visas have been able to get them at the border but others have been turned back so it's best to make sure you get one in advance. It's also a lot cheaper

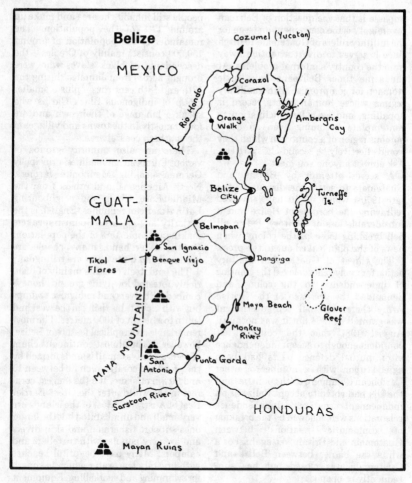

Belize

MEXICO

Cozumel (Yucatan)

Rio Hondo

Corazol

Orange Walk

Ambergris Cay

GUAT-MALA

Belize City

Turneffe Is.

Belmopan

San Ignacio
Benque Viejo

Tikal
Flores

Dangriga

MAYA MOUNTAINS

Maya Beach

Glover Reef

Monkey River

San Antonio

Punta Gorda

Sarstoon River

HONDURAS

▲ Mayan Ruins

that way – visas issued to the lucky few at the border have cost B$20! The length of stay you're given at the border varies but is usually three to four weeks. This can be extended at immigration in Belize City. You might be asked to show that you have 'sufficient funds' for your stay but the check is random.

Visas in Mexico City cost US$7. In Mérida they cost US$9 and can take two days to issue.

Following independence from Britain in August 1981, diplomatic relations between Guatemala and the UK were broken and the Belize/Guatemalan border closed for a time. The border between the two countries is now open (daily between 8 am and 6 pm) but there are no Guatemalan consulates in Belize. If you're heading for Guatemala after Belize then make sure you get your Guatemalan visa (where necessary) before entering Belize. The nearest consulate is in Mérida. There are others in Honduras.

The Honduran Consulate in Belize City is at 20 Park St. There are also Mexican and El Salvadorean consulates which can be found in the locations marked on the street plan of Belize City.

MONEY
US$1 = B$2

The unit of currency is the Belizean dollar (B$) = 100 cents. The currency is tied to the US dollar. Although it's becoming rarer, you may still hear prices expressed in pre-decimal English terms in some places – shilling (25 cents), or in US terms – nickel, dime and quarter. Belizean money is virtually unexchangeable outside the country except in Chetumal, Mexico.

There is a blackmarket of sorts but it's not easy to find. If you do come across it you may be offered up to US$1 = B$2.10.

The airport departure tax on international flights is B$8.

GETTING THERE & AROUND
Air
Quite a number of short international flights are available from Belize, mainly to neighbouring Central American republics and to Miami. Airlines serving the country include *Air Florida, Belize Airways, TAN, SAHSA, TACA* and *Aeromexico*. Most of the airlines have their offices on Queen St. The international airport is 15 km from the centre of town and buses and taxis are available.

For internal flights contact *Maya Airways*, 6 Fort St, Belize City, or travel agents elsewhere in the country.

Bus
There are the following internal bus services including services to Chetumal in Mexico:

Belize City-Benque Viejo Operated by *Novelo's Bus Service*, West Collect Canal. The fare is US$2, journey time 3½ hours. Monday – hourly from 12 noon to 4 pm; Tuesday and Thursday – 1, 2 and 3 pm; Friday – 1, 2, 3 and 4 pm; Saturday – 12 noon, 1, 2, 2.30, 3 and 4 pm; Sunday – 1 and 2 pm.

Belize City-Chetumal Operated by *Venus Bus Lines*, Magazine Rd. The fare is US$3.50, journey time 5½ hours. Daily at 6, 8.30, 11 am and 12.30 pm. Also by *Batty Bus Service*, 54 East Collect Canal. The fare is US$3.50. Daily at 6, 6.30, 9.30 am and 1 and 5 pm.

Belize City-Corozal Operated by *Venus Bus Lines*. The fare is US$3, journey time four hours. Daily at 6, 8.30, and 11 am and 3, 4 and 6 pm.

Belize City-Dangriga Operated by *Z-Lines Bus Service*, Magazine Rd. The fare is US$4, journey time four hours. Mondays to Saturdays at 1 and 4 pm and on Sundays at 1 and 3 pm.

Belize City-Mango Creek-Punta Gorda Operated by *Southern Transport*, James Bus Service, Pound Yard Bridge. The fare is US$5.75 to Mango Creek and US$7.50 to Punta Gorda, journey time about 10 hours. Monday at 8 am; Tuesday, Wednesday, Friday at 6 am; and Saturday at 9 am.

Belize City-Orange Walk Operated by *Urbina Bus Service*, Cinderella Plaza. The fare is US$2.50. Journey time 2½ hours. Daily at 11 am; Monday to Saturday at 1, 2 and 3 pm; and on Sunday at 7 pm.

Belize City-San Ignacio Operated by *Batty Bus Service*. The fare is US$1.40. Monday at 6.30, 9 and 10.30 am; Tuesday to Saturday at 9 and 10.30 am; and Sunday at 7.30, 8.30, 9.30 and 10.30 am.

If you're heading to Belize City from any of those places already mentioned, the departure times and terminal locations are:

Benque Viejo-Belize City *Novelo's Bus Service*, 119 George St. Monday at 4, 4.30, 5 and 5.30 am; Tuesday to Thursday at 4.30, 5, 5.30 and 6 am; Friday at 4.30, 5, 5.30, 6, 6.30 and 11 am; Saturday at 4, 4.30, 5 and 5.30 am; and on Sunday at 6 and 7 am.

Chetumal-Belize City *Batty Bus Service*, Bus Terminal, Chetumal. Monday to Saturday at 6.30 and 9.30 am, 1.30, 3 and 5 pm, and on Sunday at 9.30 am and 1, 1.30, 2 and 4 pm. Also *Venus Bus Service*, Bus Terminal, Chetumal. Daily at 8.30 am, 2 and 4 pm.

Corozal-Belize City *Venus Bus Service*, Gilharry Bus Terminal, Corozal. Monday to Saturday at 4 and 6 am and 3 pm and on Sunday at 7 and 10 am and 3 pm.

Dangriga-Belize City *Z-Lines Bus Service*, Bus Terminal, Dangriga. Monday to Saturday at 5.30 and 8.30 am and on Sunday at 8 and 10 am.

Punta Gorda-Belize City *Southern Transport*, James Bus Service, Bus Terminal, Punta Gorda. Tuesday, Thursday, Friday and Sunday at 6 am.

Orange Walk-Belize City *Urbina Bus Service*, Urbina's Gas Station, Orange Walk. Monday to Saturday at 5, 6.30 and 7 am.

San Ignacio-Belize City *Batty Bus Service*, front of the Police Station, San Ignacio. Monday at 12 noon, 1.30 and 3.30 pm; Tuesday to Saturday at 1.30 and 3.30 pm and on Sunday at 1, 2.30, 3 and 4 pm.

If you're heading for Guatemala you can pick up colectivos either in San Ignacio or Benque Viejo which will take you all the way to Melchor de Mencos, the first Guatemalan town, where they wait for you at the passport controls. The fare should be US$1.50. The bus service out of Melchor is irregular at the best of times though there are generally several buses per day to Santa Elena/Flores and usually two per day direct to Tikal. If you can't find a direct bus to Tikal you will have to change at the cross-roads about half way. Avoid getting stuck in Melchor by setting out as early as possible in the day from Belize. Hitching out of Melchor is hard work as there's hardly any traffic.

Boats
From Belize to the Cays or Guatemala, the following services operate:
Belize-Ambergris Cay (57 km) The regular scheduled boat is the *Sea Otter*, which departs from the Customs Wharf on Mondays, Tuesdays, Thursdays and Fridays at 3.30 pm. It leaves San Pedro, Ambergris Cay, on the same days at 7 am. The fare is US$5 and the journey takes from five to nine hours. If you don't fancy this there are flights for US$16.

Belize-Cay Caulker (45 km) The regular scheduled boat is the *Mermaid* which departs from the Customs Wharf on Mondays and Fridays at 3 pm and from Cay Caulker on Mondays and Fridays at 7 am, and on Sundays at 3 pm. The fare is US$4 in advance or US$5 on the boat and the journey takes about 2½ hours.

There are also several private boats which leave daily from the wharf in front of *Mom 's Restaurant* to Cay Caulker and less frequent ones to Ambergris Cay and other cays. Contact 'Chocolate' at Mom's Restaurant (or look on the notice board there); or the man from *Edith's Hotel*. Chocolate's boat costs US$7.50. The man from Edith's costs US$5. These boats usually leave from the wharf near Mom's around 11 am and from Cay Caulker at 7 am. The journey takes about an hour. There are also cheaper but slower mail boats (but not on Sundays) – enquire at the office on North Front St just past the fire station.

Boat connections between the cays themselves are very irregular and it's often easier to go via Belize.

Punta Gorda-Livingston-Puerto Barrios (Guatemala) Quite a few travellers use this route as a kind of back entrance to Honduras or to reach Guatemala City via the Rio Dulce and Lake Izabal without having to go through Flores. Three ferries cover the route – the *MV Punta Gorda, MV Punta Palma* and *MV Punta Cocoli*. One or other of the boats leaves Punta Gorda on Tuesdays, Thursdays and Saturdays at 4 pm. The fare is US$5 and tickets are available from Miramar Hotel, 95 Front St, Punta Gorda. In the opposite direction the schedule is not as predictable and although there are three boats per week, it's best to make enquiries in Puerto Barrios or Livingston.

There are occasional cargo boats which ply between Belize and Puerto Cortes in Honduras which will sometimes take a few passengers. Make enquiries at the docks about departure times. There is a Honduran Consulate in Belize City if you need a visa.

Belize City

Although no longer officially the capital, Belize City retains that position in all but name. If you ignore the Guianas, it's the smallest 'capital' city you'll come across anywhere in Central or South America and is very easy-going. You'll rarely meet anyone who comes away from this weather-board and corrugated-iron-roofed town with its air of benign neglect with anything other than good memories.

Places to Stay
If you're coming from Mexico or Guatemala then prepare yourself for a mild shock. At the beginning of 1985 hotel rates in Belize just about doubled. You're going to find it quite expensive after neighbouring countries. You can reduce the cost a bit by hunting round for a room in a private house but still expect to pay US$5 a single.

The cheapest place is the Chinese-run *Han's Guest House*, Queen St near the junction with Eve St, but be prepared for

skid-row conditions. That's how most travellers describe it though another redeemed it by saying it was 'safe and friendly – even the rat!' It costs US$3 a single, US$4 to $5 a double and US$6 a triple without fan. Fans are US$1 extra.

A better place is *Marin's Travelodge*, Craig St near the junction with Eve St, which is very secure and friendly and costs US$4 a single and US$6.30 to $8 a double. There is a baggage safe deposit. Similar in price is the *Hotel Belice*, Orange St, which costs US$6 a double with shared bath. Your belongings are safe here as there's a locked grill at the entrance.

Considerably more expensive is the *Hotel Belcove*, 9 Regent St West (not the same as Regent St). Rooms cost US$10/$16 a single/double with own bathroom. It has a good location with a verandah overlooking the river.

Others which have been recommended in the past are *Dim's Mira Rio Bar Restaurant & Hotel*, North Front St with a good verandah overlooking the river which is a nice place to sit and relax; *Hotel Dianne*, corner of George and Prince Sts; and the *Sunshine Hotel*, North Front St.

Avoid the *Luxury Hotel* as we've received quite a few reports of robberies there.

Places to Eat
Mom's Restaurant is still the most popular gringo hang-out with fish dinners for US$2.50; roast beef, potatoes, salad and bread for $3.50; beef, rice, beans and salad for $3; and very good though somewhat expensive breakfasts for US$2. The notice board is still the best in Belize if there's anything you want to know. Ask there for 'Chocolate', if you want a boat to Cay Caulker.

Other restaurants which are recommended include the *Hong Kong Restaurant*, Queen St, which serves excellent Chinese food (as you might expect) at reasonable prices, and the *Golden Dragon*,

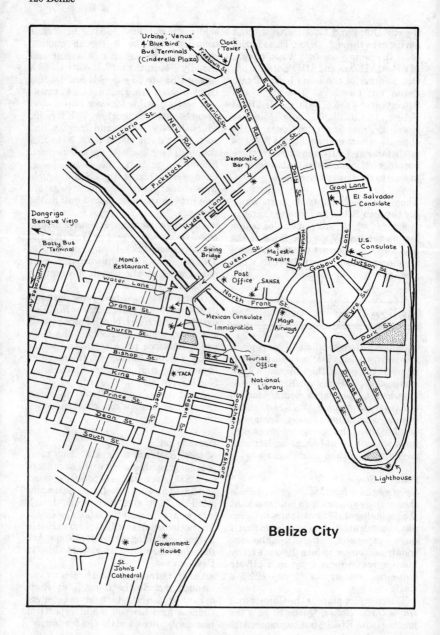

Belize City

off Queen St, which is similar. For home-baked pies and cakes go to *DIT's*, King St, which is the best in town for this kind of food.

If you want a splurge try either the *Fort George Chicken Salad* or the *Upstairs Café*, Queen St one block from the bridge, which has a pleasant balcony. The latter has expensive sea food (US$7 to $10) and T-bone steaks with potatoes and salad for around US$5.

There are plenty of good local corner bars where you can drink beer and talk to local people and play darts or billiards while listening to reggae pounding out on the jukebox. One good place is the *Democratic Bar*, 69 Hyde's Lane, which used to be on Queen St until it was burnt down in a fire which took half the street with it.

Beers costs US$1 per bottle everywhere and soft-drinks are about half the price. The two local brews are called *Belikin* and *Charger* but there are frequent shortages as the brewery seems incapable of keeping up with the local thirst. You might have to drink the more expensive English, Irish or American beers occasionally (up to US$3 per bottle!).

If you're looking for a night out or want to pick up some live music then the *102 Lounge Disco Bar* (formerly the Continental Hotel) on the west side of town, on Cemetery Rd past the bus station, is where many people go. It's popular with both locals and travellers as well as British Army personnel.

Getting Around

Airport The RAF operates a bus four times daily – in the mornings and at 12 noon, 6 pm and 11.45 pm which is available to everyone and costs US$0.50. Taxis charge US$10.

A Warning

Belize City used to be an exceptionally easy-going place but things appear to be changing. We've had quite a few reports of robberies, some of them in broad daylight right by the swing bridge outside *Mom's*. Be careful.

BENQUE VIEJO

Benque Viejo is the last town in Belize you pass through on the way to the Guatemalan border. It's also close to the Mayan ruins of Xunantunich. To get there head for the ferry across the river (free) at San José Succotz, about one km from town. From there the ruins are a two km walk along an obvious track. Entry to the ruins cost US$0.50.

If you'd like to stay overnight near the ruins the best place is the *Buena Vista Pyramid Cabins* at San José Succotz run by Betty Alden. The cabins, which have their own kitchens and are 10 minutes from the ferry and Novelo's bus line, are on a quiet farm in view of the ruins. Horses are available for hire to tour the ruins or to go exploring the jungle. If you prefer to stay in Benque Viejo itself then the *Hotel Roxi*, St Joseph St, is recommended.

DANGRIGA (formerly Stann Creek)

Budget hotels are at a premium. One of the best deals you'll find is at *Lucy's Hotel & Club* just over the river, where it's possible to get a small single room for US$5. The *Riverside Hotel* will set you back US$10 a double but it does have what is probably the best restaurant.

Near Dangriga is the small resort of Placencia which can be reached by truck from Mango Creek, followed by a short boat journey. The hotels there are expensive though and the only cheap accommodation you'll find is in private houses.

PUNTA GORDA

This town on the southern coast of Belize was highly recommended by one traveller who stayed there recently in a rented house. He described it as 'so different from Belize City and Dangriga – unpolluted sea, palm trees everywhere and friendly people'. He also said that if you're looking for somewhere to hang around for a while then this was a good place to find work. There are many North Americans around this area who are in the process of setting up farms and are desperate for workers prepared to stay for more than just a few days. The best time to make their acquaintance is on Saturday mornings at the market – they're not much in evidence at other times. This same traveller said that his friend had found a job there as a caretaker on an uninhabited island further up the coast!

Places to Stay

If you just need to stay overnight then the following hotels have been recommended: *Fosters Hotel*, 19 Main St has rooms for US$4.20 sharing; *Hotel Isabel*, Front St, costs US$4.20 sharing and US$2.10 per person in dormitory accommodation; and *Man Mans 5 Star Cookshop*, West St, is unlikely sounding but has eats and accommodation out back in huts for US$1.50 sharing.

SAN IGNACIO

Known as Cayo by locals, this town is a good base for walking trips into the mountains, especially around Pine Ridge.

Places to Stay

There's a delightful place to stay if you'd like to relax for a few days, see something of the wild-life and visit the ruins of Xunantunich. It's the *Jamal Ranch Cottages* (tel 092 2164 between 8 am and 4 pm) (P O Box 46), just over one km from the town. If you're walking then take the first left after the Esso station coming from Belize City.

The 150 acre ranch on the Macal River, part of which is cultivated and part natural, is run by Bart and Suzi Mickler, a North American couple. You stay in Mayan-style thatched cottages with mosquito nets and there's a lounge, bar and cooking facilities. The cottages cost US$5/$7.50 a single/double or you can camp with your own tent for US$2.50.

If you don't want to put your own food together then meals are available (all made with fresh vegetables straight from the gardens) at US$2 to $3 (breakfast or lunch) and US$3 to $5 (dinner). Suzi previously ran *Suzi's Panqueques* in Huehuetenango, Guatemala, around 1977. They frequently have film and live local music nights and offer guided tours to Xunantunich and Mountain Pine Ridge. Horses and canoes can also be hired. Many travellers have recommended this place.

In San Ignacio itself, try the family-run *Hi-Et Hotel* on West St right in the centre of town, which is spotless and has rooms for US$3.60 per person with shared bathroom. There is also *Elvira's* which is not officially a guest house but has rooms somewhat cheaper than the Hi-Et Hotel. To get to the latter turn left just before the Central Hotel, then take the third street on the right. If you get lost, just ask – everyone knows the place. They also have good cheap meals.

As well as these two there is the *Balmoral Hotel* which has reasonably priced rooms, and the *San Ignacio Hotel* which is pleasant but very expensive at US$10/$16 a single/double. The *Central Hotel*, 24 Burns Ave, is scruffy and noisy but some travellers have managed to get a bed there for as little as US$3, though the usual price is US$7 a single.

THE CAYS
Ambergris Cay

This is the most northerly cay and is regarded by many as the best though the sea around there sometimes gets clogged up with seaweed. It offers superb beaches, excellent opportunities for snorkelling and scuba diving, and glass-bottomed boats for hire to explore the coral formations. Unlike Cay Caulker, the beaches don't suffer from sand flies and mosquitoes and the lifestyle is very laid-back. For 'alternative lifestyle reef and fishing trips' contact Fido Badillo, next door to the Milos Hotel.

Places to Stay One of the cheapest places is *Ruby's* which is on the beach and costs US$3.25 a single (there's only one single) and US$6.50 a double. Quite a lot of travellers stay there.

Everything else is quite expensive. Try *Lily's Caribeña* which is US$7.50/$12.50 a single/double. Another you can try is *Milos Hotel* next door to the very expensive Paradise Hotel. It's right on the beach and charges US$20 to $22.50 a double per week with shared facilities and rooms with their own shower for US$3 per week extra. It's very clean and friendly (except for the washing facilities which are dirty). It has its own bar (with cheap beer and rum), a colour TV and pool tables. Groceries can be bought there too. There are other places with similar prices but none of them are right on the beach.

Cay Caulker

Cay Caulker is considerably more 'developed' than Ambergris Cay but easier to get to as it's connected to Belize City by several private boats which make the trip daily as well as a scheduled twice weekly launch. The beach, however, does suffer from nasty sand flies which you don't find on Ambergris Cay.

Snorkelling gear is available for hire from a number of places. There's also wind surfing gear available for US$4 per hour or US$15 per day, with lessons for US$5 excluding the cost of hiring gear. Scuba divers should contact the American couple who live behind the soccer field. They rent equipment for US$20 per dive (or US$5 per dive after the first). Boat hire costs US$30 for a group and they also offer a complete course of lessons (three days) leading to a certificate for US$75.

Places to Stay A popular place for short-term visitors is *Mrs Rivas* where you can get rooms for US$5. She also offers lobster meals for around US$3 per person. *Tony Vegas* is another long-time favourite where rooms cost US$5 a double or you

can camp for US$2.50 per night including tent hire. Tony organises snorkelling trips at US$3.50 per person for the boat and US$1.50 each for the equipment. You must have a group together but this is easy to arrange.

The *Martinez Hotel* has a variety of rooms from US$2.50/$6 a single/double, the latter with own shower and fan. It's very pleasant but many of the rooms are next to or over the bar which rages to a loud juke box until 2 am on Saturday nights. Lobster meals there cost US$3. Other places which have been recommended are *Tom's Hotel* which has rooms for US$6 a double and the *Vegas Far Inn* where you can camp for US$2 per person.

For long-stay visitors there are a number of small houses for rent which cost between US$50 and US$150 per month. Ask around.

Apart from the places to eat already mentioned there are quite a few others which offer seafood meals at roughly the same price. Just ask around. You normally have to make arrangements in the morning. *Sid's* and *Marlin's* have been recommended.

MAYAN RUINS

Very little excavation of the Mayan ruins has been carried out in Belize though there has been the occasional spectacular find. One of these was the head of a sun-god made of jade and weighing about three kg, unearthed in Altun Ha in 1969. Unfortunately, you won't be able to see this relic as it's kept in the vaults of the Royal Bank of Canada in Belize City! Part of Labantun in the far south was excavated in 1970 but since then nothing has happened and the area which was cleared is rapidly being overgrown. The ruins of Xunantunich near Benque Viejo are worth visiting if you have the time. The spectacular main temple there has a carved stone astronomical frieze.

INDIAN VILLAGES

Two colourful Kekchi villages which you might like to visit are **San Antonio** and **San Pedro Colombia** in the foothills of the Maya Mountains west of Dangriga. Both have many interesting religious festivals, the best of which is San Luis Rey on 5 August. Getting there can be a problem as there are no buses, but if you contact a Mr Wagner in Dangriga you might be able to get a lift without burning a hole in your pocket. The ruins of Labantun are close to San Pedro Colombia.

Costa Rica

One of the smallest of the Central American republics and the most prosperous, Costa Rica is unique in having a population which consists principally of *blancos* – people of unmixed Spanish and other European origin. Only in the provinces of Limón and, to a lesser extent, Puntarenas are there sizable minority groups of different ancestry. In both these areas there is a steadily diminishing number of black people of Jamaican origin (about 30%), whose forebears were brought in to work the banana plantations.

There are very few pure blooded Indians in Costa Rica because most of them were wiped out by the diseases introduced by the Spanish shortly after the Conquest.

Other features which set Costa Rica apart are the very high literacy rate and the absence of an army. The latter was abolished in 1948 (which is quite a feat for a Latin American country – or any other country for that matter!), though there is still a paramilitary National Guard. Costa Rica is one of the few real democracies in this part of the world.

From the Conquest until fairly recent times the country remained a poor and relatively isolated backwater populated by only a few Spanish settlers who farmed the lands of the Meseta Central. These early settlers were unable to parcel out the land into huge estates as was done in many other places in Central America because the Indian population, whose free (or cheap) labour would normally have been exploited on these feudal estates, was almost wiped out. As a result, Costa Rica never suffered from the problems of grossly unequal land distribution which have led to so much violence in the other republics.

Following independence from Spain and brief annexation to the Mexican

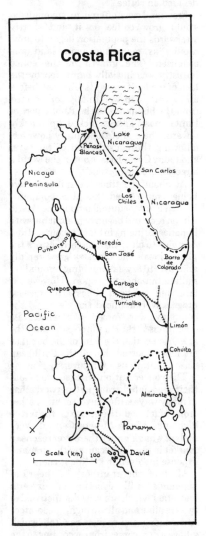

Empire of Iturbide, the government looked around for a suitable cash crop which would provide the country with a

reasonable income. They eventually decided on coffee.

Free land was offered to anyone who would grow coffee on it and shortly afterwards the population began to grow rapidly as more and more land was colonised. The growth of the coffee industry was initially hampered by the lack of roads. It was as late as 1846 before an ox-cart road was finally constructed from the highlands to the Pacific port of Puntarenas. Things picked up quickly towards the end of the century however, following the construction of railways, and today Costa Rica is one of the world's largest coffee exporters.

At about the time the railways were being constructed, the US company, United Fruit, acquired land in the Puerto Limón area and began to plant it out with bananas, bringing in black labourers from Jamaica to clear the jungle and work the plantations. The industry grew rapidly and by 1913 was providing around 11 million bunches for export. However, it later fell on hard times after disease progressively reduced the yield and the company was forced to transfer its operations to the Pacific coast. This is the area from which the bulk of the bananas are now exported though the Caribbean coast plantations are recovering slowly.

The concentration on cash crops and their associated transport networks has in many ways stifled investment in other crops which could be grown on the fertile highlands of the Meseta Central. Very little of what is grown there ever reaches a market in the city because of the time and expense involved in getting it there.

Most of the transport in the rural highlands still consists of ox-carts (carretas) which are very distinctive. No two are alike and all are highly decorated. Aficionados claim they can tell which village a cart comes from according to the pattern on it, in the same way that you can tell which village Guatemalan Indians come from according to the pattern of the weaving in their clothes.

In more recent years, many North Americans have settled in or retired to Costa Rica. Their influence has had a considerable effect on the country, especially on San José and the surrounding area.

Because of the very limited settlement which took place in Costa Rica until recent times, the country is a mecca for outdoor types, beach freaks and jungle lovers rather than those in search of ruins, Indian communities and colonial cities. It's an exceptionally beautiful country, very green with numerous volcanos, some of which are still active. It has plenty of ideal highland walking country, jungles packed with wildlife and some of the best beaches in the world.

Much of the country is still covered with forest. The best time to go walking is between December and May (the dry season) as at other times the roads frequently turn into thick mud. The Caribbean side of the mountains and its coast receive the most rain – on average 300 days a year – so take appropriate clothing with you.

VISAS

Required by all except nationals of most West European countries (except France and the Irish Republic), Canada, Israel and Japan. The cost of visas seems to vary widely. Various Australian travellers have reported fees of US$20, $10 and $5 (the latter in Honduras)! Tourist Cards, valid for 30 days and extendable up to a total of six months, cost US$2. There is an entry tax of US$0.20 and exit tax of US$1.

If you stay more than 30 days you must get an exit permit from immigration in San José for which there is a fee. In addition, all male visitors who stay more than 30 days are required to go to the Supreme Court to have their name checked in the *libro obligados* to make sure they haven't fathered a child! A certificate must be obtained confirming this.

You must have an onward ticket to enter the country but it's sufficient to have a bus ticket from the town nearest the border to the border, though at the Peñas Blancas border (Costa Rica/Nicaragua) they sometimes demand you have a ticket from San José to the border.

There are heavy searches at the border on entering (they're looking for drugs). Also, if arriving overland, blood tests are made for malarial control and a certificate and drugs issued.

The borders are open daily from 7 am to 12 noon, 1 to 5 pm and 6 to 10 pm.

MONEY
US$1 = 52.75 colónes (official)

The unit of currency is the colón = 100 centavos. It is presently floating against the US dollar. There is a free money market at the *casas de cambio* but few of them will take travellers' cheques. The average rate of exchange is 50 to 52 colónes. The Banco de Lyon will change travellers' cheques but charges 10 colónes commission.

You may be told in some banks that it is possible to cash US dollar travellers' cheques into cash dollars. Don't believe it. You're probably being set up as one traveller was recently. They conned him into handing them US$200 in cheques and then gave him colónes in return. Several hours and many angry words later they finally gave him US$50 cash and the rest in colónes.

What you certainly *can* do in Costa Rica is re-exchange up to US$50 worth of colónes back into dollars when you leave the country. The transaction will be stamped into your passport so that you can't do it twice.

The airport tax for international flights is now US$6 unless you have been in the country less than 48 hours, in which case it is US$1.30.

GETTING THERE
To/From South America
If you haven't already got a ticket from either Costa Rica or Panama to a South American country and you don't intend going through the Darien Gap, then

before you do anything else, get down to *OTEC* (Organización Turistica Estudiantil y Juvenil Costarricense), Avenida 3 between Calles 3 and 5, San José (tel 220866). This has been set up to cater for young travellers and has the best information in Costa Rica on cheap flights. Many travellers have recommended them and you can get some really good deals, especially if you have a student card and you're under 26 years old. One traveller recently picked up a San José-Quito (Ecuador) ticket for US$84 – the usual price is US$226. Even if you're going on to Panama first, it might well be worth getting a ticket there.

There are a number of other reasons why it is worth thinking about flying from Costa Rica rather than Panama. One is that before you can get into Panama you need an onward ticket. *TICA* bus tickets for Panama City-San José or David-San José or *Tracopa* David-San José tickets are acceptable for this but unless you intend to return to Panama on your way back from South America, you will be throwing away up to US$16. (The *Tracopa* David-San José ticket is the cheapest). The return halves of these bus tickets are in theory refundable but in practice, only at the office of issue and usually only after 30 days notice minus a cancellation fee. You may, of course, be able to find another traveller in South America who would be willing to buy the return half.

The other consideration about Panama is the cost of living, which is high compared to Costa Rica. The longer you spend hunting round for a cheap ticket and waiting for visas (where necessary), the more money you will spend.

Remember that if you choose to fly into Colombia then you are going to need an onward ticket from that country before you apply for a visa (where necessary). Indeed, no airline in either Costa Rica or Panama will sell you a one-way ticket to Colombia or Venezuela unless you already have an onward ticket from one or the other of those countries.

You can get a refund on the return half of a ticket in Colombia once through passport control though you may only be paid in pesos. The same applies for *COPA* which isn't a member of IATA. Take the return half to one of their offices in Cartagena (Calle Santos de Piedra 3466 near the Plaza Bolívar), Barranquilla, Cali or Medellín. Barranquilla is best since that's their head office and applications for refunds have to be referred to this office. The refund will be in pesos. Tickets from airlines which are not members of IATA (such as *COPA*) are not transferable to airlines which are members of that organisation.

To/From Nicaragua

TICA bus has suspended its services from Managua to San José and now only covers the San José-Panama City route. The only international bus between San José and Managua is by *Sirca* which leaves daily at 6 am and costs US$6.55 one-way. You can save a few dollars by doing the journey in stages but if you're coming from Managua, there are only two buses per day from Peñas Blancas to San José at 11.30 am and 3 pm (US$2.70) though there are others from Peñas Blancas to intermediate stops such as Liberia. Expect heavy searches at the border (they're mainly looking for drugs).

To/From Panama

TICA (office at Avenida 4, Calle 9) is the main international bus between Costa Rica and Panama. There is a daily bus in either direction between San José and Panama which costs US$16 and takes 19½ hours. You need to reserve a seat as far in advance as possible because there's heavy demand for tickets.

There are other buses which go from San José to the border and to David and Canoas. *Tracopa* (office on Avenida 16 near the Atlantic Railway Station, San José) have several departures daily to the border but only the 7.30-8 am bus goes to David (US$8.75, 13 hours) and the 11 am bus goes to Canoas (US$5.40). There's heavy demand for tickets so book as far in advance as possible. From the border to David there are frequent minibuses which cost US$1.25.

From David there are two express buses daily to Panama City which take about 5½ hours, and 10 daily ordinary buses, the first at 7 am and the last at 7 pm.

Remember that you must have an onward ticket to enter Panama. A return bus ticket is the cheapest way of satisfying this requirement.

GETTING AROUND
Bus
San José-Limón *Coupé Limón* and *Transportes del Atlantico* (terminal at Avenida 3 between Calles 17 and 19) and *Co-operlimón* (terminal at Avenida 3 between Calles 19 and 21) all have daily departures which take about four hours. For the best views sit on the right hand side of the bus coming out of San José.

San José-Cartago There are departures every five minutes or so to the former capital from the terminal on the corner of Avenida Central and 2 at Calle 13. The fare is about US$0.20.

San José-Puntarenas There are buses every 15 minutes or so from the terminal at Avenida 9 and Calle 12. The journey takes about 1½ hours.

San José-Quepos There are frequent buses from the terminal at the corner of Avenidas 1 and 3 at Calle 16. The journey takes about five hours.

Train
The two main railway lines in Costa Rica run from San José to the Caribbean port of Limón via Cartago, Turrialba and Siquirres; and from San José to the Pacific port of Puntarenas. Trains are slower than the buses and they tend to cost a little more but they make for interesting rides and superb views as they descend from the highlands to the coast.

There are two railway stations in San José: the Northern Railway Station (or Atlantic Station) on the east side of the Parque Nacional for trains to Limón; and the Ferrocarril Eléctrico al Pacífico in the southern part of the city along the Avenida 20, for trains to Puntarenas. A city bus to the latter will be marked 'Paso Ancho'.

From San José to Limón there is a daily train at 12 noon which costs US$1.85 and takes six hours. In the opposite direction it leaves at 6 am and takes up to nine hours. It's a beautiful journey with great views.

From San José to Puntarenas there are daily departures at 6.30 am, 10 am, 3 and 6 pm (with an additional train on Saturdays at 12.55 pm). From Puntarenas there are daily departures at 6 am, 8 am, 12 noon, 3 and 6 pm. The fare is US$1.50 and the journey takes about four hours.

Snacks and drinks are available either on the trains or at stops en route.

Puerto Limón

Puerto Limón is built on the site where Colombus landed on his fourth and last voyage of discovery. It has a predominantly black population and is one of Costa Rica's most important ports. It owes its present size to the Standard Fruit Company which had huge banana plantations along the coast in the late 19th and early 20th centuries.

Information
There is a bank in Limón where you can change travellers' cheques but it can take up to two hours – the cheques are scrutinised minutely. There is no longer any bank in Cahuita so if you are heading there make sure you have enough local currency before leaving Pto Limón.

Places to Stay
Pto Limón is a relatively expensive town

so don't expect too much in the way of bargains in budget accommodation.

Some of the cheapest places are the *Pension Dorita*, which costs US$1.65 per person but can be noisy because of the thin partition walls; the *Lincoln*, Avenida 5 between Calles 2 and 3; the *Wong*; the *Hawaii* and the *Libia*.

Better, but still nothing special although it is clean, is the *Pension El Sauce*, one block from the main square, which costs US$4.70 a double.

Places to Eat

Good places include the *Restaurant La Chucheca*, which has very cheap breakfasts and comidas; and the *Harbour Restaurant* where the meals of the day are recommended.

AROUND PUERTO LIMÓN
To the North

The main places of interest in this direction are Tortuguero Island, Barra del Colorado and Los Chiles. This is riverine jungle country stacked with wildlife and the area has been declared a National Park.

Tortuguero Island, the first place of interest going up the coast, is a green-turtle sanctuary where from April to August, between 8 pm and 4 am, you can watch turtles come up on the beach to lay their eggs. There are rooms to rent for about US$2 a double and a watch hut on the beach at the entrance to the National Park where you can sleep free. Meals at the nearby café cost about US$1 for rice, meat, beans and salad. It's a very pleasant place to stay for a while.

Further north is **Barra del Colorado** and **Los Chiles** which are reached by a fascinating boat trip along jungle-fringed rivers where you are more than likely to see alligators and other animals. If you get as far as Los Chiles on the Río Frio, the *Pension Onassis* (with an attached restaurant called – believe it or not! – *Jackie*) is recommended. It's about 150 metres from the boat dock.

Getting There To get to all these places from Limón you must first get a bus to Moín. They run every hour from 5.45 am to 5.45 pm daily and the journey takes about half an hour. From Moín to Tortuguero Island there is a government launch which departs at 9 am on Thursdays and Saturdays and costs US$0.55. In the opposite direction it departs at the same time on Fridays and Sundays. The journey takes between six and eight hours. There's also a tourist launch which costs US$3.10, and irregular cargo boats which you can sometimes get onto.

From Moín to Barra del Colorado there is a fast daily launch (except on Wednesdays), which costs US$2, or much slower (about a one day journey) freight boats which are more interesting but cost around US$5. One freight boat which takes passengers is the *Japdeva* – speak to the captain down at the dock.

If you go first to Tortuguero Island and get stuck for transport to Barra ask the National Park rangers if they can help out with boat transport – they often can. There is an airstrip at Barra and flights to Puerto Limón on Tuesdays and Fridays and to San José on Mondays and Saturdays cost US$20.

Getting to Los Chiles can be more tricky. The most interesting way is by boat through the jungles but finding such a boat can take time. There is a bus from San José but it takes at least eight hours and it's a very rough ride. The alternative is to fly. There are daily flights from San José, except on Sundays, for US$15.

To the South

The most popular place to the south is **Cahuita** beach, which has a National Park nearby. Both are popular with backpackers but avoid Cahuita on public holidays if possible as it can get very crowded. It is notable for having one beach of white sand and another of black sand and there's a wrecked Spanish galleon on a coral reef which you can get to without having to hire a boat.

Places to Stay & Eat Most travellers stay in cabins either on or close to the beach. There are quite a few of these but hardly any have signs so you need to ask around. The ones on the black sand beach tend to be cheaper (just over US$1 per person – enquire past the Café Daisy, a 15 minute walk from town) than on the white sand beach (US$3 per person). Cabins at US$3 would include shower and basic cooking facilities as a rule. *Jenny's* cabins are popular. Otherwise ask around at the *Bar Vaz*. Señor Letty also has cabins which are cheap and clean.

For somewhere to stay in Cahuita while you find a cabin, try the *Hotel Cahuita* which costs US$6.35 a double without bath and US$12.60 a double with own bath and including tax (10%). Other places to try are the *Victoria* and the *Belo Horizonte*.

You can get very good, cheap food from the *Sol y Mar* opposite the Hotel Cahuita for around US$1.60. *Miss Bertha's* at the end of the beach has also been recommended.

Be careful of thieves while you're on the beach.

Getting There Buses depart from Puerto Limón for Cahuita daily at 5 am, 10 am and 1 pm. The fare is US$1 and the journey takes about one hour along a surfaced road.

If you find Cahuita a bit too much like Bognor Regis then continue further down the coast to Puerto Vargas which is much quieter and you can camp free. There are buses from Cahuita which will take you most of the way.

PUNTARENAS

This is the main port on the Pacific coast and a popular beach resort for Josefiños (as residents of San José are known) but the beaches are dirty so most people head for **Puerto Quepos** or the even more tranquil **Playas Manuel Antonio**. If you are looking for something really out of the

way then head for Montezuma on the Nicoya Peninsula. There's a beautiful deserted beach with nearby waterfall, the village is very small – only about 100 people and they are very friendly. To get there, take the ferry from behind the market in Puntarenas and then a bus which goes to Cobano, another village about five km from Montezuma. Walk or take a taxi from there. There's a hotel in Montezuma which costs US$3 per person plus a number of small cabins for about US$1.45 per person.

Places to Stay

In Puntarenas try either the *Hotel Condor*, opposite the bus terminal which isn't too bad and costs US$1.65 per person; or the *Hotel Verano*, Calle 3 off Avenida 1, which costs US$2.10 a single with own bath and fan.

In Puerto Quepos, try either the *Hotel America* or the *Hotel Lima* on the road out towards Playas Manuel Antonio. Other cheapies are the *Hotel Viña del Mar* and the *Hotel Quepos*. For good seafood try the *Los Almendros*.

In Playas Manuel Antonio you can rent cabins from either *Sombra y Mar* or *Manuel Antonio Cabiñas* for about US$1 per person. The owners of the former are friendly and if you're short of funds, they'll let you sling up a hammock or camp free. Food on this beach tends to be expensive because most of it comes from Quepos.

AROUND PUNTARENAS
Monte Cerde Cloud Forest National Park

The best time to visit this exceptionally beautiful park, which is close to Puntarenas, is during March and April. The thing to do if you want to avoid staying in Puntarenas overnight is to take the 10 am train from San José which connects with the bus to Barranca at 2.15 pm. Get off at Santa Elena and stay at the *Flor y Mar Pension* (tel 611887) which is about four km from the town. It's run by a friendly North American who will pick you up (at a cost) from Santa Elena if you call. It costs US$2.30 including board (plenty of fresh cheese and milk available).

The entrance to the National Park is about one km back towards Santa Elena and the entry fee is US$2.50 – a bit steep but well worth it.

San José

The capital of Costa Rica with a population of around 800,000, San José is a very modern and Americanised city but pleasant and interesting nevertheless. It was founded fairly recently (1737) and didn't become the capital until 1823. Before that, the capital was at Cartago, a small city about 23 km from San José which has twice been destroyed by earthquake.

Information

The tourist office is at Plaza de la Cultura in the underground shopping mall at Avenida 2 between Calles 3 and 5. It's open on weekdays, the staff are helpful and they have free maps of San José and other places.

The casa de cambio opposite the tourist office is open on Saturday from 9 am to 3 pm and on Sunday from 9 am to 1 pm.

The National Parks office is inside the zoo at Parque Simon Bolívar, Avenida 11 and Calle 11. Call in for information on the National Parks. They have some very good material and a brochure for US$1.

For airline tickets, *OTEC* (Organización Turística Estudiantil y Juvenil Costarricense), Avenida 3 between Calles 3 and 5, is the best place to buy them, even if you don't have a student card. It's been recommended by many travellers. They also have the best information on San José and offer hostel type accommodation. English, French and Italian is spoken.

The Colombian Embassy is on the corner of Avenida 5 and Calle 5, Edificio La Vifia (2nd floor). The Nicaraguan Embassy is at Avenida Central between Calles 23 and 25 in the California district and visas are generally issued while you wait.

San José

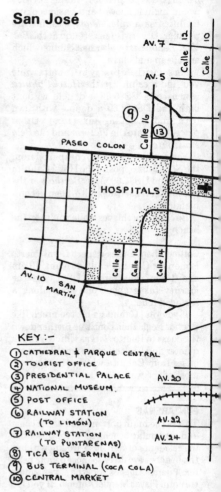

KEY :—
1. CATHEDRAL & PARQUE CENTRAL
2. TOURIST OFFICE
3. PRESIDENTIAL PALACE
4. NATIONAL MUSEUM
5. POST OFFICE
6. RAILWAY STATION (TO LIMÓN)
7. RAILWAY STATION (TO PUNTARENAS)
8. TICA BUS TERMINAL
9. BUS TERMINAL (COCA COLA)
10. CENTRAL MARKET

American Express have an office at Calle 1 between Av Central and Avenida 1.

For English language books try either *The Bookshop*, Avenida 1 between Calles 1 and 3; or *Lehmann*, Avenida Central.

Sirca bus office (for San José-Managua buses) is now at the corner of Avenida 2 and Calle 11.

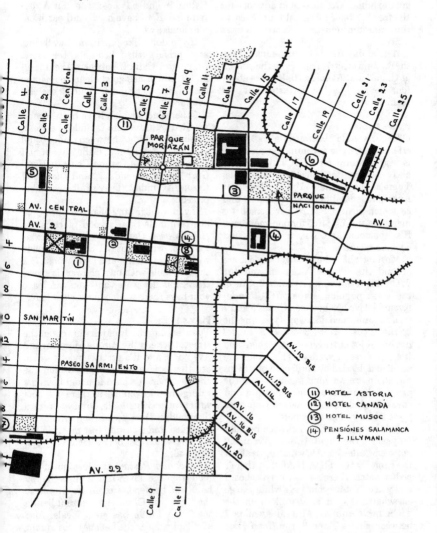

⑪ HOTEL ASTORIA
⑫ HOTEL CANADÀ
⑬ HOTEL MUSOC
⑭ PENSIÓNES SALAMANCA ⫶ ILLYMANI

Things to See

The underground **Museum of Gold**, beneath the Plaza de la Culture just north of the National Theatre, has an impressive display of pre-Colombian artefacts and gold exhibits. Get tickets in advance for the free 1½ hour bilingual tour. Next to the museum entrance is the tourist office.

A good day trip is to **Puntarenas**. Take the 6.30 am electric train from the station at Calle 2 and Avenida 20. It takes about four hours. The bus is faster but less scenic.

Places to Stay

OTEC, Avenida 3 between Calles 3 and 5, offers hostel-type accommodation which is very pleasant for US$1.25 per person and cooking facilities are available. There's also a new *Youth Hostel* at Avenida Central between Calles 29 and 33 which costs US$1.25 per person for members and US$1.65 for non-members. It's spacious and has a garden and cooking facilities.

Most of the other budget hotels are around the Parque Morazán and the *TICA* bus terminal on Avenida 2. One of the most popular is the *TICA Linda*, Avenida 2 No 553 between Calles 5 and 7 (it's an unmarked doorway – just ring the bell). It costs US$1.35/$2.50 a single/double. A lot of travellers stay there and it's often very crowded. The rooms are small and divided by hardboard partitions but there are washing facilities and the people who run it are very pleasant and speak English. You can store your bags there while you go elsewhere.

Another place which has been popular for years is the *Hotel Astoria*, Avenida 7 between Calles 7 and 9, which costs about the same as the TICA Linda but there's no hot water. There's a useful noticeboard and you can store your bags while you go elsewhere. It's an easy walk from the TICA bus terminal. Also on Avenida 7 between Calles 7 and 9, the *Hotel Poas* has been recommended. It has a good

atmosphere and a restaurant and bar. Singles cost US$3.

Other budget hotels in this area include the *Hotel Salamanca* and the *Hotel Illimani*, both on Avenida 2 between Calles 9 and 11 near the TICA bus terminal. Both have hardboard partitions and loud TVs.

If you don't like partitioned walls and semi-privacy then head for the *Hotel Managua*, Calle 8 between Avenidas 1 and 3, which has good clean rooms and costs US$2.35 a single. Doubles are also available.

Other places which have been recommended by travellers include the *Hotel Canada*, Avenida 5 between Calles 6 and 9; *Pension Americana*, Calle 2 about half a block from the Parque Central; *Hotel Gran Paris*, Avenida 1; and the *Hotel Coroci*, Avenida 1. They're all reasonably priced.

If you want to stay near the Coca Cola bus terminals then a good place is the *Hotel Musoc*, Calle 16 between Avenidas 1 and 3, which costs US$1.35 a single without own shower and US$2.05/$3.75 a single/double with own shower. It's very clean, has hot water and you can leave your bags there while you go elsewhere.

Places to Eat

There are hundreds of restaurants in the streets between the Parque Morazán and Avenida 2 and it's pretty obvious which are the expensive ones and which the cheaper ones. It's hard to avoid having a splurge in the evenings as there is such a variety of food available, but if you're on a tight budget then stick to *empanadas* for breakfast and a *casado* (set meal) in the evening which cost between US$0.75 and US$1.45.

La Fonda Restaurant just down the road from the TICA Linda has a 'happy hour' and the food is excellent. Similarly the *Kam Wak* Chinese restaurant beside the TICA Linda has good meals. Also excellent value is the Lebanese restaurant *Restaurante Beirut* near the Banco

Nacional which offers very reasonably priced specialities from that part of the world. It's open Monday to Saturday from 11.30 am to 11.30 pm.

There are, of course, all the usual fast-food places like McDonald's, Kentucky Fried Chicken, Pizza Hut and many others which offer American-style hamburgers and steak if you've forgotten what they taste like.

If you'd like to suck on a few beers after you've eaten, there are a number of places where you're likely to meet other travellers and ex-patriates doing the same. They include *Ye Pub*, Calle Central and Avenida 7 (decked out to look like an English country pub), which serves draught beer and is open from 4.30 pm to 2 am except on Sunday; *Arturo's Bar*, Calle 5 between Avenidas 1 and Central; and the *Key Largo*, Calle 7 between Avenidas 1 and 3. The last two are American-style bars. Another which is worth trying is the *Piano Bar*, Avenida 4.

On the corner of Calle Central and Avenida 2, the restaurant with no name but with 'La Perla' on the doormat, has been recommended. It's in an impressive old building across from Central Park and the three course lunch for US$2 is good value.

Quite a way from the centre in the San Pedro area is *La Fánega*, which is predominantly a student bar with folk music some nights.

Getting Around

The international airport (Juan Santamaria) is 16 km from San José along a freeway. A taxi there costs US$10. There are also colectivos which cost US$2 per person (eg *Taxis Unidos*) and minibuses from outside the San Juan de Dios Hospital as well as *Alajuela* buses from Calle 14 between Avenidas 1 and 3.

AROUND SAN JOSÉ

Probably the most interesting place to visit in the San José area is the **Volcan Irazu**. To get the best views from the edge of the crater you need to make a *very* early start because by late morning it gets covered with mist which often turns to drizzle. It might be best to stay overnight in Cartago in order to meet this deadline. Stay at the *Valencia* or the *Venecia*, both of which are close to the railway station. The latter is very clean, has friendly staff and is cheap.

From Cartago a bus leaves daily at 6 am (7 am on Saturdays) and goes to the top of the crater (about 2900 metres high) where it stays for about 20 minutes and then returns to Cartago. The fare is US$4 return. If you don't have the time to spare there are tourist mini-buses which do the trip from San José but they're fairly expensive.

Even though Cartago was founded in 1563 and was the former capital, it isn't that interesting as it has twice been completely destroyed by earthquakes.

El Salvador

One of the first things you'll notice coming into El Salvador is how intensively the land is farmed and how many people there seem to be. Villages crop up every kilometre or so along the road. In fact El Salvador, although the smallest of the Central American republics, is the second most densely populated country in the Americas (Haiti being the first). Three quarters of the land is under cultivation and 80% of this is devoted to coffee, making El Salvador the world's third largest coffee producer after Brazil and Colombia.

It wasn't always like this, however. Initially, the Spanish ignored El Salvador as it contained neither mineral wealth nor regions of intensive agriculture. The early Spanish colonists mingled with the Indians and as late as the mid-19th century, after the various attempts at federation with the other Central American republics had failed, there were only a few hundred thousand people living here. Then in the late 19th century, coffee was planted. The soil, composed mainly of a deep layer of porous volcanic ash and lava, and the climate proved ideal for the crop and since distances to the coast were relatively short, coffee-growing developed rapidly. Money poured into the country and the population increased by leaps and bounds until by 1981 it stood at 2.3 million. Cotton is also grown and the country has the largest industrial base in Central America.

The wealth which these developments generated was not evenly distributed of course. The usual oligarchy, here made up of a dozen or so ruling families, maintained a tight control on the coffee business and banking and ruled the country through one military dictator after another. The result was low wages, high unemployment and the emigration of several hundred thousand Salvadoreños to the United States and neighboring Latin republics, particularly Honduras. The latter reacted badly to this influx and it was the main cause of the 'Football War' fought between El Salvador and Honduras in 1969 (so called because it started as a riot at a football match between the two countries and quickly developed into a fully-fledged military conflict). Since that date there has been little trade or direct contact between the two and until recently their mutual land border was closed. It's now open again, but Salvadoreños going to Honduras need a visa and vice versa.

The wealth did, however, lead to the creation of Central America's best road system (nearly all roads are paved), good port facilities and a very modern and well-serviced capital, though out in the rural areas services leave much to be desired. Education is theoretically compulsory and free, but illiteracy remains at 50%.

Before the arrival of the Spanish, the

El Salvador

136

country was inhabited by the Pipil Indians who called their country 'Cuscatlán' (Land of Precious Things); and whose civilisation dated back to the 11th century. These people were farmers, potters, carpenters, masons, weavers and builders who had developed a system of hieroglyphics which have not yet been deciphered.

The ruins of their temples and ceremonial centres are scattered through-out the country and include the archaeological sites of Cihuatán, Tehuacán and Quelepa. Pyramids of a pre-Mayan civilisation which are 1400 years old have been discovered at San Andrés and Taxumal. The descendants of the Pipil – the Panchos Indians – live in Panchimalco not far from San Salvador. Only 10% of the present-day population are pure Indian, leaving a remainder of 80%

mestizo and 10% of unmixed white ancestry.

El Salvador was one of the first countries to declare its independence from Spain. In 1811, José Matías Delgado, a Creole priest and juror born in San Salvador, in conjunction with another priest Manuel José Arce, organised a revolt and removed the Spanish officials from office. The Audencia in Guatemala suppressed the revolt and took Delgado prisoner back to Guatemala, where he continued to agitate.

Independence finally came in 1821 following Iturbide's example in Mexico. Along with the other Central American republics, El Salvador originally joined the Mexican Empire of Iturbide but this soon collapsed and was followed by various attempts at federation between the five Central American countries. The mutual hostility between Conservatives and Liberals however, prevented anything coming of this. In fact at one time when federation was being discussed between representatives of the five countries meeting in San Salvador, war broke out between El Salvador and Guatemala!

These days, of course, El Salvador has become a household word as a result of the civil war which has wracked the country for well over 10 years now. Repression and brutality by one right-wing military junta after another and a complete absence of urgently needed land reform led to the left-wing opposition taking to arms. They were, and still are, supported by the majority of poor farmers who see little possibility of genuine reform ever taking place under the present regime.

Government forces quickly found themselves up against a formidable enemy who pushed them completely out of many rural areas and even out of some of the larger towns. Caught in a desperate situation, the government appealed for and was granted US military assistance, though not without considerable opposition from many members of the US Senate.

US accusations about Cuban and Nicaraguan military assistance to the guerrillas were bandied about and as the fighting continued both sides were guilty of committing atrocities.

When the government troops had regained some of their former lost ground, a US-sponsored election was eventually arranged in the hope of seeing a moderate, pro-western government installed but the guerrillas and many left-wing groups boycotted it. A centre-right government was installed as a result of the elections and for a while there was a lull in the fighting and a possibility that the two groups might discuss ways of sharing power and promoting land reform.

It didn't work out however and the civil war resumed. All this took place against a background of increasing belligerency on the part of the White House against the Sandinista government in Nicaragua. The US accused Nicaragua of being a Cuban stooge and of 'exporting its revolution' to neighbouring Central American republics. The White House began pouring troops and arms into Honduras, conducting huge and provocative manoeuvres both on land and at sea, and supporting the Nicaraguan *contras* with arms and training; all of which has led to the destabilisation of large areas of Nicaragua alongside the Honduran border. At the same time it granted huge new packages of military aid to the beleaguered Salvadorean armed forces, despite considerable Congressional objections. Memories of the Vietnam war were still very fresh in many people's minds and there was little enthusiasm for what might well become a similar conflict.

Despite all this aid, however, the Salvadorean armed forces have made little progress and large areas of the country are still in the hands of the rebels and likely to remain so. Not only that, but individual acts of sabotage and terrorism are becoming more and more common especially in San Salvador. A solution to the war is a long way off, especially while Nicaragua continues to be regarded by the White House as a staging post for Soviet and Cuban expansionism.

While the conflict continues it's probably best to avoid the country though quite a few travellers do continue to travel through it and on to Tegucigalpa in Honduras.

VISAS

Not required by anyone. Tourist Cards issued at El Salvador consular missions or at the border are supposed to be valid for 90 days but if you get them at the border the length of stay varies and is unlikely to be more than two weeks. There is a fee of US$2 for the Tourist Card.

MONEY

US$1 = 2.50 colónes (official)

The unit of currency is the colón = 100 centavos. The black market rate at the Guatemalan border where there are many dealers is US$1 = 3.15 colónes. In San Salvador it is US$1 = 3.95 to 4 colónes (cash only).

There is currently a 2 colónes entry tax and a 3 colónes exit tax. The departure tax for international flights is US$8.

GETTING THERE

To/From Guatemala

Many buses do the run from Guatemala City to San Salvador several times daily. The cost is US$8 one-way. Most of the buses depart from and arrive at the Terminal de Occidente on Boulevard Roosevelt. Bus companies include *Inter-Futuro Express*, *Melva*, *Ermex* and *Transportes Centro America*. The latter are the most expensive at US$10. The route these buses take goes through Santa Ana so you can get off there if you like. The fare from Guatemala City is US$5.

To/From Honduras

TICA bus have suspended services to Honduras, El Salvador, Nicaragua and Guatemala City so you will have to take a combination of local buses to get from El Salvador to Honduras. There are plenty of local buses daily from the Terminal de Occidente in San Salvador to San Miguel which take about four hours and cost US$2.40. From there you take another bus going to the Honduran border (Goascarán Bridge). This takes about 1½ hours and costs less than US$1. The bridge was actually blown up some time ago but otherwise the border is open normally. There are Honduran buses from the other side of the border to Tegucigalpa. This is the only way to get to Honduras at present.

To/From Nicaragua

The ferries from La Unión to Potosí across the Gulf of Fonseca have been suspended. Not only that, but La Unión is presently a dangerous place to visit because of the fighting so the only way of getting to Nicaragua is via Honduras.

SAN SALVADOR

As a result of the war, San Salvador is a changed city. People are reluctant to venture out onto the streets at night for fear of being shot or meeting with a bomb.

Information

The tourist office, at Calle Rubén Dario 619 (tel 217445/231845), has a free map of the country and of San Salvador and the staff are very helpful. More accurate maps are available from both Texaco and Esso filling stations.

The new central post office has a special exchange window where you can change money at much the same rate as on the street (US$1 = 3.95 colones).

Places to Stay

Hotels in the immediate vicinity of the old *TICA* bus terminal include the *Hotel Bruno*, Calle 1 Oriente, between Avenidas 8a and 10a. It was previously a very popular hotel with travellers and costs US$5 a single with own bathroom. Cheaper rooms without bathroom are available and the communal facilities are reported to be reasonably clean with hot water available all day.

Somewhat cheaper are the *Barletta Boarding House*, Av 8 Sur No 129, which is reasonably clean and costs US$2.40 per person without own bath; and the *Hospedaje Centro America*, Calle Concepción 658, which is clean and has large rooms without windows for US$2.40 a single.

Others which have been recommended include the *Hotel Pan Americano*, 8 Av Sur No 113, which costs US$4 per person; the *Hotel San Carlos*, Calle Concepción 121, for US$4 per person including own shower and toilet; and the *Casa de Huespedes Venvier* and *Boarding House Colonial*, both of which are on 6 Av Sur between 4 and 6 Calles Oriente. The Venvier is basic and costs US$4 a double while the Colonial is US$4 per person.

Going up-market, try the *Hotel Custodio*, 10 Av Sur No 109, which costs US$4/$8 a single/double.

San Salvador

KEY TO NUMBERING & NAMING OF AVENUES & STREETS.

Quadrant: Norte Poniente Odd Streets Odd Avenues	9a Av. Norte	7a	5a	3a	1a Av. Norte	AVENIDA ESPAÑA	2a Av. Norte	4a	6a	8a	Quadrant: Norte Oriente Odd Streets (Calles) Even Avenues (Avenidas)
9a Calle Poniente											9a Calle Oriente
7a " "											7a " "
5a " "											5a " "
3a " "											3a " "
1a Calle Poniente											1a Calle Oriente
CALLE ARCE											CALLE DELGADO
2a Calle Poniente											2a Calle Oriente
4a " "						AVENIDA CUSCATLÁN					4a " "
6a " "											6a " "
8a " "											8a " "
Quadrant: Sur Poniente Even Streets Odd Avenues	9a Av. Sur	7a	5a	3a	1a Av. Sur		2a Av. Sur	4a	6a	8a	Quadrant: Sur Oriente Even Streets Even Avenues

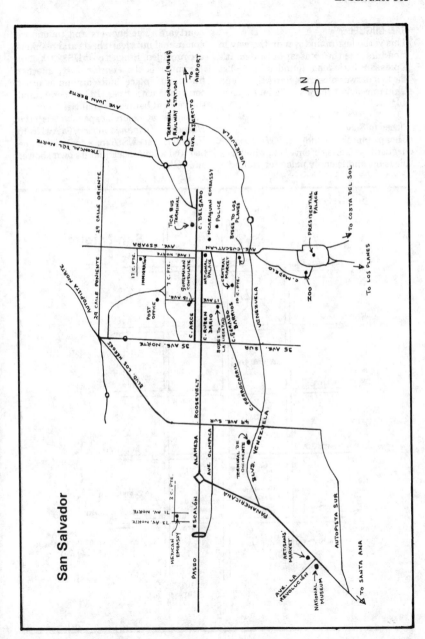

San Salvador

SAN MIGUEL

This is the last main town on the way to Honduras via the Goascarán Bridge. It's a pleasant little place founded in 1530 at the foot of two volcanoes, San Miguel and Chinameca, but there's not a lot to see or do.

Places to Stay

Cheap places include the *Hospedaje Argüeta*, 4a Calle Oriente 502, which is a pleasant and friendly place set around a courtyard. The showers and toilets are communal but clean sheets and blankets are provided. Singles cost US$2.80.

Similar is the *Pension Lux*, another traditional place built around a quiet courtyard with trees. It has communal shower and bathroom facilities.

Somewhat more expensive is the *Hospedaje Hispanoamerica*, 6a Av Norte B, which costs US$6 for a room with one bed and a hammock and its own shower and toilet.

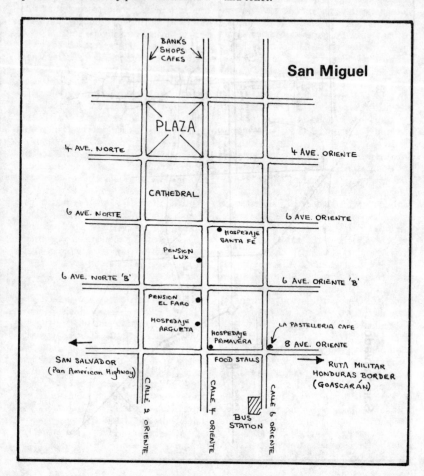

Guatemala

Guatemala is without doubt Central America's most fascinating country and a favourite among travellers. The reasons for this are apparent everywhere: from its volcanoes (some still active) and lakes to the lush jungles of the Petén with their spectacular Mayan ruins; and from the old colonial towns to the friendly Indian villages with their colourful markets and riotous fiestas. The country offers an endless variety of sights and sounds, rivalled only by parts of Mexico, and many travellers spend a lot of time here.

The early history of the country was moulded by the Mayan civilisation which took off around 100 AD but whose roots have been traced back to 2000 BC. It reached the peak of its first phase of development around 400 AD in the lowlands of Honduras, El Salvador, Belize, Guatemala and parts of southern Mexico when the great temple complexes of Copán (Honduras), Tikal (Guatemala) and Palenque (Mexico) were built. Although there are many others scattered throughout this area – many of them only accessible on foot – the above rank among the most impressive ruins you will find anywhere in the world and should not be missed on any account.

Even today, explorers still come across hitherto unknown sites from time to time, though the majority were discovered by Stephens and Catherwood during the revolution-torn 1830s, following independence from Spain. Their book *Incidents of Travel in Central America, Chiapas and Yucatán*, originally published in 1843 but now available in several paperback editions, makes fascinating reading.

The first phase of this civilisation came to a somewhat abrupt end around 900 AD when these large population centres were abandoned and there was a migration to the flat lands of the northern Yucatán. A cultural renaissance took place there, which involved the introduction of Toltec motifs (the Yucatán was part of the Toltec empire in the 10th century); a new style of architecture; religious rituals which included human sacrifice; and the construction of raised causeways linking the highlands with the coast. The cities of Chichén Itzá, Uxmal, Kabah and Tulum among others, were constructed at this time and continued to flourish until the arrival of the Spanish.

Unlike the highly centralised civilisations of the Aztec and Inca, the Maya were a collection of fiercely independent city-states and tribes who fought constantly with each other but who shared a common culture, religion and language and who traded extensively with one another. This lack of political union was one of the main reasons why the Spanish had to wage such a long and costly campaign in their efforts to subdue these people. Even though the bulk of the Mayan lands had been taken by 1527, it was not until 1697 that the last of the Mayan strongholds, centred on an island in Lake Petén Itzá, fell to the Spanish.

Despite the antagonism of the various states, the Maya created what might well be regarded as the most advanced pre-conquest civilisation ever to have existed in the Americas. Their arts and crafts, particularly pottery, weaving and sculpture, were all highly developed and their monumental ceremonial sites were constructed – incredibly as it may seem today – without the use of iron tools, the wheel or beasts of burden. They had invented a system of hieroglyphic writing, plotted the movements of the sun, moon and the nearest planets and invented two interlocking calendars (known as the Long and Short Counts by archaeologists) which were more accurate than either the Julian or Gregorian calendars.

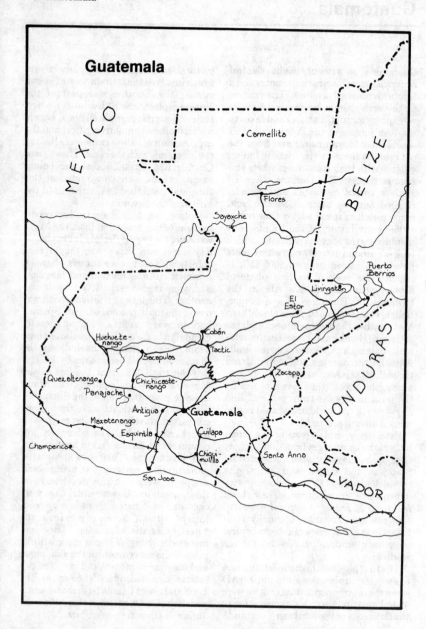

Guatemala

In common with other ancient civilisations, they had a highly mystical explanation of the universe and a pantheon of gods who were the guardians of natural events and human needs. The most important of these was Chac, the God of Rain, since water shortages were fairly common – not because rainfall was insufficient but because water was difficult to store in the porous rocks and soil of the area.

The Maya were fortunate in living in a fertile area with a rich variety of fauna and flora which provided them with much of what they needed in the way of food, clothing and medicines. Corn was the mainstay of their agriculture and the most important component of their diet. The various stages of its cultivation formed some of the most important events of the year and were intricately bound up with elaborate religious rituals aimed at propitiating the gods and assuring an abundant harvest. The climate was such that large surpluses of corn could often be grown. They also cultivated sweet potato, a variety of black bean, chili and cacao and collected honey from the nests of a certain variety of stinging bee which lived in hollow tree trunks. This honey was used for sweetening and making a fermented mead-like brew.

The Mayas were the only one of the three great American civilisations who traded extensively by sea and land. As a result, they had regular contact with peoples as far afield as Panama, the Caribbean islands and Mexico. The wealth which this trade generated, together with the large surpluses of corn, enabled them to support a non-productive social class of priests and nobles and to have time to construct their ceremonial centres, cities and roads. Land was held in common and each family assigned sufficient land on which to grow its food and pay 'taxes', which was usually a part of the harvest or a certain amount of labour on other projects. The building of houses, clearing of land and the planting and tending of crops were communal activities.

War between the various city-states was more or less continual though it took second place to the demands of agriculture and ceased entirely at planting and harvest time. The object of war was the capture of prisoners. The most important warriors captured in the war would be sacrificed to the gods and the rest enslaved. Wars were usually of very short duration and fought in a very ceremonial and ritualistic fashion with the headmen going into battle decked out in enormous quetzal-feathered headdresses. Even to this day the quetzal remains the national symbol of Guatemala though the bird is now very rare.

Many elements of the Mayan heritage remain intact despite 450 years of Spanish colonial and latterly *ladino* rule. Mayan Indians still make up about 50% of the population of Guatemala – the highest proportion of indigenous people in any Central American republic, including Mexico. The most obvious reminder of their ancestry is the very colourful and elaborately woven fabrics they wear, the patterns of which vary greatly from one village to the next. It's one of the most delightful aspects of Guatemala. Another example is the many different languages which they speak.

Other facets can be found by delving below the surface. Their religion, for example, is a composite of pagan image-worship and Catholicism. This stems from the days following the Conquest when the Spanish in their zeal for conversion, baptised as many Indians as they could lay their hands on. However, because of the numerical inferiority of the Spanish and the danger of insurrection, much of this was mere window-dressing and the Maya were allowed to continue practising their ancient rites as long as these could be acceptably incorporated into Catholicism.

Their attitude to commerce, too,

differs markedly from that of the *ladino*. The Indians, though industrious at a family and village level, have little interest in becoming affluent and making profits beyond their needs. All these various aspects come together to make the Maya a society within a society and although this has enabled them to remain a distinct entity, it has also fostered their exploitation at the hands of the ruling classes right up to the present day.

As in other parts of the Americas, the Conquest was initially a disaster for the Maya. With their lands taken from them, and distributed among the Conquistadores, the Indians were forced to work as unpaid labourers on the plantations which the Spanish established. A good deal of brutality was also employed to force acceptance of the new order. This, combined with the diseases which the Spanish brought with them (mainly smallpox, respiratory illnesses and syphilis), reduced the population of Central America (according to one estimate) from 14 million to two million in just 130 years. On the other hand, as little gold or silver was discovered in Guatemala, relatively few Spanish settled in the area. Antigua and then Guatemala City, after the former was destroyed by earthquake, served as the Audiencia for Central America throughout the colonial period.

Independence from Spain in 1821 ushered in a long period of tempestuous rivalry for power between the liberals and conservatives and between one Central American state and another. Though Guatemala was in many ways the most stable of the Central American republics, it was ruled throughout the 19th century and much of the 20th century by dictators who were supported by the armed forces, the *latifundista* (large land owners), the Church, and more recently, by the USA.

As in most other Central American republics, the plight of the landless grew steadily worse during this time so that by the 1950s statistics showed that the *latifundista* owned over 72% of the land and the *minifundista* (small land owners) owned only 14.3% with most of the holdings being insufficient to feed a family.

This was only one aspect of the imbalance; another was the cheap (and at times unpaid) labour requirements of the *latifundista*. In order to harvest the cotton, coffee and other crops which they grew on their estates they demanded large seasonal work forces. To ensure that enough labourers would be available for this work, those in power saw to it that the Indians were only allowed access to very small plots of land which would be insufficient to feed their families, thereby forcing them to look for work for part of the year. On occasion, when the labour force hasn't met requirements, the army has been called in to round up more workers, regardless of the circumstances.

Naturally, the Maya haven't taken all this lying down and there have been a number of revolts, notably in the 1830s during the attempted federation of the Central American republics; and again in 1898 and 1943. The last revolt, during the dictator Ubico's regime, prompted the abolition of debt-peonage (the system whereby a landowner would allow a landless peasant to cultivate a small patch of land in exchange for free labour on his plantation). The law which replaced it, however, was equally onerous.

In 1944, the Revolutionary Party led by Juan José Arévalo won a landslide victory in one of Guatemala's all too few free elections. Arévalo, supported by the liberals, intellectuals, teachers, and other professional groups, instituted a series of radical land reform acts aimed at redistributing the land among the peasants. These included the expropriation of land given to Ubico's generals and supporters; the redistribution of the National Fincas (150 large, state-owned farms, most of which had been confiscated from German settlers during WW II as a result of pressure from the USA); the setting up of agricultural cooperatives, labour unions, provision for education and medical care, a guaranteed minimum wage and the forced rental of uncultivated lands. It was a promising start to something which had been long overdue and a refreshing departure from the self-centred policies previously pursued by the dreary string of iron-fisted dictatorships which preceded it.

Arévaló's policies were continued with even more vigour by his elected successor, Jacobo Arbenz, who also began to make inroads into the power and privileges of corporate capital, particularly the United Fruit company which at the time owned more land than half the population of Guatemala. Unfortunately, the storm clouds were gathering. Both presidents were labelled 'communists' by the *latifundista*, the Church, the United Fruit company and the USA, and secret preparations were made to overthrow the government by providing an exiled Guatemalan officer, Colonel Castillo Armas, with money (US$18 million), arms and a training camp in Honduras. When Armas's forces were ready to attack, Arbenz strangely resigned though it's doubtful that the invasion would have succeeded.

Armas had himself declared president and among his first acts were the cancellation of the franchise of all illiterates (72% of the population), the banning of labour unions, the cancellation of the land reform programme and the return of all redistributed land to its former owners. In the upheaval which followed, many peasants, labour leaders and others were murdered, their houses burnt down and protesters shot or jailed. The familiar pattern of corrupt military dictatorships started all over again.

Since the eclipse of the Arbenz government, the repression of peasants and labour leaders has been growing steadily and the incidence of violence has increased alarmingly. Faced with this callous disregard for basic needs and human rights, a resistance movement sprang up in the Zacapa and Izabel provinces during Peralta's regime. The army reacted with increasing brutality. Wholesale arrests of 'suspects' were carried out – sometimes the entire population of a village – and many of those arrested were never seen again. No charges were ever announced and months later news would leak out that they had been murdered or a common grave would be discovered containing scores of bodies. No investigations of these murders were ever carried out and indeed Peralta's last act before resigning was to pass a law exonerating all those who were or might have been involved.

Even the re-election of the Revolutionary Party following Peralta's resignation didn't stop the rot, but then times had changed and with the army well entrenched, the new president found that he was little more than a puppet. With his options severely limited, Méndez turned to the only course of action which was open to him in his attempts to pursue land reform – the colonisation of the Petén jungles. This wasn't a new idea and had been tried before with disastrous results due to a lack of knowledge of the delicate ecological balance of the rainforests, insufficient finance, poor communications and the ravages of malaria. The new government's schemes met the same fate. As disenchantment grew, right-wing terrorist groups mushroomed and killings became an almost daily event, precipitating yet another army take-over. Nevertheless, the violence has continued and guerrilla activities have become bolder and more widespread.

Were it not for the events in nearby El Salvador and Nicaragua, which dominate media coverage and have done for some time, then probably much more would be heard about the situation in Guatemala. Unfortunately, the one thing that might head off what is fast becoming an inevitable confrontation – a genuine and radical land reform programme – is unlikely to be considered by the present rulers and Guatemala may well go the same way as El Salvador. Such an event would be an unmitigated disaster but in a country where the landless peasants are in much the same position as they have been for hundreds of years, and where the birth rate continues to add another 100,000 to the population every year, something has to give.

As a traveller you could go through this country without being too aware of the violence, especially if you stick to the main centres of population. This is not El Salvador. It would, however, be wise to check out the present situation, particularly in the rural areas, with other travellers coming from Guatemala; but don't be put off going here or you will miss something really fine.

VISAS

Required by all except nationals of Austria, Belgium, Denmark, Finland, Israel, Italy, Japan, Luxembourg, Netherlands, Norway, Spain, Sweden, Switzerland *and holders of Tourist Cards.* Tourist Cards are *officially* available to almost all nationalities (eg Australia, Canada, France, New Zealand and USA), cost US$1, are valid for a stay of 30 days extendable to 90, and can be obtained either at the border or from consular missions and airline offices. Getting a 30-day extension can soak up a whole day and you should expect to pay US$5 for it.

That is the official position, but in practice you'll come across travellers who have been charged US$4 for their Tourist Card and you'll very rarely meet an Australian or New Zealander who hasn't been told that he or she requires a visa (which costs US$10). So if you're travelling on one of those passports it's worth making an effort to get a Tourist Card before you arrive there though there's no guarantee that you'll get one! In addition some French travellers have

recently been told they need a visa because of President Mitterand's stand against US intervention in El Salvador (officially they only need a Tourist Card).

If you're one of those unfortunates (eg UK nationals) who need a visa, these cost US$10 and are valid for a stay of 30 days. It's very difficult to have a visa extended. UK nationals come in for special treatment because of the long-standing dispute between Guatemala and the UK over Belize – a situation which has grown worse since Belizean independence. The Poms not only have to pay US$10 but must supply three photos and their thumb prints for three separate copies of the visa application form! As if that were not enough, some UK travellers have also been required to buy a Tourist Card on arrival – for US$4!

There are no longer any Guatemalan consulates in Belize so if you're heading for Guatemala after Belize then make sure you get your visa beforehand. If you're coming from Mexico there is a Guatemalan embassy in Mexico City and consulates in Chetumal, Tapachula and Comitán (4 Avenida Poniente Norte 24). The consulate at Comitán will tell you to go to the border for a visa or Tourist Card (except British passport holders who must get a visa in Comitán, if they don't already have one).

There is an entry and exit tax of US$3 at both the El Salvador and Honduras borders but not at the Belize border (Belize is, after all, regarded as a province of Guatemala so you're not officially leaving the country when you go there!)

If you stay more than three months you need an Exit Permit which costs US$2.50.

MONEY

US$1 = 1 Quetzal (official rate)

The unit of currency is the Quetzal (Q) = 100 centavos. There are no import or export restrictions on local currency. The Quetzal is tied to the dollar but has been floated recently and is drifting very slowly upwards against the dollar. Because of this there is a blackmarket, but only in Guatemala City where you can get up to Q1.45 to the US dollar (for cheques or cash). Be careful of police. Elsewhere in the country the rate of exchange is only one for one.

It's possible to reconvert Quetzals back into US dollars at the Banco Central – up to a maximum of US$100 on a one to one basis. This means that if you bought your Quetzals on the blackmarket with US dollar cheques or cash then you make up to US$45 (depending on the exchange rate) on the reconversion. This may sound like a fairy story but it's not. All you have to do is go to the Banco Central and request permission to re-exchange Quetzals back to dollars. The transaction takes about 1½ hours and a stamp is put in your passport so you can't do it twice.

There is a 17% tax on all airline tickets sold in Guatemala but *SAM*, *Avianca* and a number of other airlines will accept quetzals for tickets so Guatemala is a good place to buy them, even with the high government tax. The airport tax for international flights is US$5.

BOOKS
If you'd like more detailed information on Guatemala refer to the recommended books in the general Facts for the Visitor chapter, or try the following:

Tikal W R Coe (University of Pennsylvania, 9th edn. 1977). History and maps, coloured plates and very useful on site. You can find it at bookshops in Guatemala City and at the Tikal Museum.

Guatemalan Guide, Glassman (Dallas, Texas, 1977). If you're going to spend a lot of time in Guatemala then this guidebook is a useful supplement to the information given in this book. It's on sale in bookshops and at the airport in Guatemala City.

300 Phrases in Common Use in Mayan, English & Spanish Antigua. A useful little phrase book you'll find for sale in the Yucatán and other parts of southern Mexico. If you can't find it the publishers are at Abelardo Fuente Vega, Calle 59 No 454, Mérida, Yucatán.

PRINCIPAL MARKETS

The main markets, market days and the specialties available at each is as follows:

Sunday

Chichicastenango; Huehuetenango (blankets); Momostenango; Nahualá; Panajachel (woven fabrics); Patzún (silk & wool, embroidered napkins, woven fabrics, striped red cotton cloth); San Lucas Tolimán (woven fabrics); Zunil; Palin (textiles); San Martín Jilotepeque (weaving and huipiles); Quiché (palm hats); San Cristóbal (textiles); San Juan Ostuncalco (sashes); Cantel (textiles); Sumpango (huipiles).

Monday

Antigua (silverware); Comalapa (Indian costumes).

Tuesday

San Pedro Carachá (pottery, textiles, wooden masks, silverware, woven fabrics); Sololá (woven fabrics); Patzún; San Lucas Tolimán; Sumpango.

Wednesday

Momostenango; Patzicía; Comalapa; Sumpango.

Thursday

Chichicastenango; Antigua; Patzún; Santa Cruz del Quiché; Totonicapán; Huehuetenango; Sumpango; San Martin Jilotepeque.

Friday

Sololá; San Lucas Tolimán; Santiago de Atitlán; San Francisco el Alto (woollen blankets, woven & embroidered fabrics); Sumpango; Comalapa.

Saturday

Patzicía; Santo Tomás Chiche; Sumpango; Antigua.

GETTING THERE

To/From Mexico

TICA bus have suspended their services to Mexico, Guatemala, El Salvador, Honduras and Nicaragua so if you need an international bus to Mexico City then you'll have to go with *Autopullman Galgos* (7 Avenidas, 19-44, Zona 1, Guatemala City), which has daily departures from Guatemala City via Talismán and Tapachula at 5.45 am, 10.15 am, 3.45 and 5.45 pm.

If you're heading north slowly, there are basically three routes into Mexico.

The first heads up into central Chiapas and is the route you must take if you want to go via San Cristóbal de las Casas. The other two follow the Pacific coastal route via Talismán and Tapachula:

Guatemala City-La Mesilla-Comitán-San Cristobal de las Casas. Both *El Condor* and *Rutas Lima* have several daily departures to La Mesilla (the border) where you must change buses for San Cristóbal. *El Condor* is the recommended line and cheaper than *Rutas Lima*.

Guatemala City-Quezaltenango-San Marcos-El Carmen-Talismán Along this route you change buses at the border (El Carmen) and take another local bus to Talismán and Tapachula.

Guatemala City-Escuintla-Mazatenango-Tecún Umán-Ciudad Hidalgo-Tapachula Along this route you change buses at the border (Tecún Umán) and take another bus to Ciudad Hidalgo and Tapachula.

The first two routes are serviced by *Unión Pacifico* which has daily departures at 6.30 am, 8.45 am and 12.45 pm. The journey to Tapachula takes about five hours along either route.

There is an alternative to the buses along the Pacific routes but it's strictly for railway buffs. A train departs Guatemala City for Tecún Umán at 7.30 am on Tuesdays, Thursdays and Saturdays (and returns from there at the same times). It costs a mere US$1.80 but takes about 10 hours. It connects with the Mexican Railways at Tecún Umán. Snacks and cold drinks are available on the train. If you like a modicum of comfort, take something soft to sit on!

To/From Belize

Bus departure times between Flores/Santa Elena and Melchor de Mencos (the border) are variable – they generally go when full – but there are two departures daily in either direction, from Melchor in the early morning and another at about 3.30 pm. The journey takes about three hours and costs US$1.50. There may also be direct buses from Melchor to Tikal but the schedule is irregular. It often depends on whether there are enough passengers. If one doesn't turn up then take a Flores/Santa Elena bus (preferably an early one) and get off at El Cruce where the road forks. Buses from Flores/Santa Elena pass through there, though you can also hitch. If you take a late bus from Melchor to El Cruce you'll be stranded for the night.

If you have to stay in Melchor overnight the *Hospedaje Zaculeu* is where most people stay but the *Hotel Mayalo* is reported to be cleaner and better value.

To/From El Salvador

Several international bus companies cover the route to San Salvador via Santa Ana. They are: *Mermex* (20 Calle 6-39, Zona 1, Guatemala City); *Transportes Centro-América* (9 Ave 15-06, Zona 1, Guatemala City); *Futuro Viaje* and *Transportes Melva*. They all charge US$5 to Santa Ana and US$8 to San Salvador except *Centroamerica* which charges US$10 to San Salvador. The journey time is about five hours to San Salvador.

To/From Honduras

The only direct route into Honduras is via the Mayan ruins of Copán. There is no direct bus from Guatemala City to Copán and you must change first at Chiquimula and then again at El Florido (the border).

The trip can be done in one day by catching the 7 am *Transportes Guerra* or *Transportes Rutas Orientales* (19 Calle, 8 Ave, Zona 1) buses from Guatemala City to Chiquimula. The fare is US$2.50. From Chiquimula there are *Volmi* buses to El Florido at 5.45 am and 11 am which cost US$2. *Volmi* also have buses at 2.30 pm and 5.30 pm but they only go as far as Jocotan. On the other hand, Jocotan is a better place to stay for the night than Chiquimula. You can stay at the *Pension*

Ramirez which costs US$1.50 per person and is run by a very friendly man. From El Florido (the border) there are mini-buses to Cópan for US$1 – this last stretch of road (about 14 km long) is pretty rough so expect delays after heavy rain. The journey from Guatemala City to Copán should take about six hours in the dry season.

If you need a Honduran visa they can be obtained at the border but note that if you intend to return to Guatemala after visiting Copán, you need a new Guatemalan visa or Tourist Card. There is no Guatemalan Consulate at Copán and the Guatemalan customs officials at the El Florido border are notorious for trying to extract money out of travellers by using various ploys (eg if you have a visa then you need a Tourist card – US$4; if you have a Tourist Card then you need a visa – US$10). All this in addition to the entry fee of US$1.50. The border is open from 8 am to 12 noon and 2 to 6 pm on the Guatemalan side and from 8 am to 3.30 pm on the Honduran side. If you want to go through the Guatemalan border at other times you will be up for an extra 'fee'.

It is sometimes possible to get lifts from Copán to Guatemala City in tourist agency mini-buses if they have spare seats. The price is negotiable but shouldn't be much more than the cost of public buses. Avoid the day-trips from Guatemala City to Copán offered by these agencies as they can cost up to US$70.

On the road from Guatemala City to Copán is the *Biotopo National Park*. This is cloud forest reserve and the only one where you can see the quetzal. The park rangers are very friendly and will let you leave your bags at the office while you explore the park. There are also camping facilities.

GETTING AROUND
Air

The main internal air service of interest

to travellers is the Guatemala City-Flores flight. Taking a flight over this section certainly saves a great deal of time and is more comfortable than the bus which takes at least 15 hours on a very rough road (see the section on buses). From Flores you go by bus to Tikal. There are also flights from Guatemala City direct to Tikal but they're much more expensive as it's a tourist run.

Both *Aviateca* and *TAM* fly from Guatemala City to Flores. The former has flights on Tuesday, Wednesday, Friday, Saturday and Sunday (at 4.45 pm from Flores) which cost US$41.75 one-way. *TAM* fly on Monday, Wednesday and Friday and cost US$30 one-way. Book tickets in advance if possible as there's often heavy demand for seats.

La Aurora airport in Guatemala City is eight km from the centre. Bus Nos 65 and 20 run from the centre, take about half an hour and cost US$0.50. You can catch them on Avenidas 8, Zona 1 or at the bus terminal on 4 Avenida, Calle 1, Zona 4. A taxi costs US$6.

Bus

There are a number of bus terminals in Guatemala City but nothing like the central terminals you find in Mexico. Most of the 1st class bus companies maintain their own terminals and these are scattered all over the city. Some of the main ones are:

Cobañerita 9 Calle 11-46, Zona 1
El Cóndor 19 Calle 2-01, Zona 1
Escobar 19 Calle 8-39, Zona 1
La Preciosa 15 Calle 3-37, Zona 1
Lineas América 18 Calle, 2 Avenida, Zona 1
Los Halcones 15 Calle 7-66, Zona 1
Rutus Orientales 19 Calle 8-18, Zona 1
Rutus Lima 8 Calle 3-63, Zona 1
Transportes Fuente del Norte 17 Calle 9-68, Zona 1
Transportes Galgos 7 Avenida 19-44, Zona 1
Transportes Higueros 17 Calle 6-25, Zona 1
Transportes Litegua 8 Avenida 15-42, Zona 1
Transportes Rebuli 20 Calle 3-42, Zona 1 (terminal at Zona 4)
Union Pacifico 9 Avenida 18-38, Zona 1
Union Pacifica y Las Patojas 9 Avenida, 19 Calle (terminal in Zona 4)

Most of the 2nd class bus companies are concentrated in two main terminals: the Zona 4 terminal between Avenidas 1 and 4 and Calles 7 and 9 serving mainly the western part of the country, the Pacific coast and El Salvador; and the Zona 1 terminal on 19 Calle between Avenidas 8 and 9 serving mainly the eastern and northern parts of the country and the Caribbean coast.

Details of some of the more popular routes are listed here but some bus schedules, notably in the Quiche area north of Quezaltenango and in Petén province, have been disrupted by guerrilla or government troop activities recently. You need to make enquiries if you're heading in those directions.

Guatemala City-Antigua Departures every half hour in either direction by many different companies (eg *La Preciosa*) from 15 Calle between Avenidas 3 and 4. The fare is US$0.50 and the journey takes one hour.

Guatemala City-Chichicastenango Many buses daily by *Transportes Rebuli* (US$1.50) and *Rutas Lima* (US$2).

Guatemala City – Cobán (not to be confused with Copán). Daily departures by either *Cobañerita* or *Escobar* at 6, 7, 8, 9.15 and 11 am and 1, 3.15 and 5 pm. The fare is US$3.50.

Guatemala City-Flores Departures daily by *Transportes Fuente del Norte* at 6, 7.30, 9 and 11 am and 12 midnight for US$8. There are also so-called 'Pullman' buses at 4.30 am for US$12. In the opposite direction there are the same number of daily departures but times vary depending on demand. If all goes well, this journey can take as little as 14 hours (no punctures or breakdowns) but it often takes 28 hours and has been known to take as long as 35 hours! After the turn-off for Puerto Barrios the road is atrocious.

There's also another company which does the run but they go via Cobán and this adds another six hours to the journey. The alternative is to fly – see the section on Air.

Flores/Santa Elena-Tikal From Flores (Santa Elena) there are usually two daily buses to Tikal though sometimes more if there is the demand. The first leaves Santa Elena at 6 am (from Tikal at 5 am). The journey takes two hours and costs US$2.

The road from Guatemala City to Flores has occasionally been cut in the past by guerilla activities so keep your eye on events in that part of the country.

Guatemala City-Huehuetenango Daily departures by *El Cóndor*, *Los Halcones* (7 am and 2 pm), *Rapídos Zaculeu* (6 am and 3 pm) and *Rutas Lima*. The fare is US$4.

Guatemala City-Puerto Barrios Daily departures by *Transportes Litegua* at 7 am, 4 and 6 pm which costs US$4; by *Transportes Fuente del Norte* at 6.30 am; and by *Unión Pacífica y Las Patojas* which has nine departures, the first at 5 am, and costs US$3.50.

Guatemala City-Puerto San José & Iztapa There are several daily buses from Guatemala City to Puerto San José and from there to the resort towns of Iztapa, Las Lisas and Monterrico. There are also direct buses from Guatemala City to Las Lisas.

Guatemala City-Panajachel daily departures by *Transportes Rebuli* every hour from 5 am to 6 pm which costs US$2; by *Transportes Higueros* at 4 am and 4 pm for US$2 (departs from Panajachel at 5.30 pm daily); and by *Rutas Lima* at 7.30 am which costs US$3 (departs Panajachel on Monday, Tuesday, Wednesday and Friday at 8 am and Thursday and Sunday at 8 am and 3 pm.). The journey by all companies takes about 3½ hours.

From Panajachel there are local buses to Santiago de Atitlán and many of the other villages around Lake Atitlán.

Guatemala City-Quezaltenango Daily departures by *El Cóndor* at 4.30, 9 and 11 am; *Rutas Lima* at 8 am, 3, 4 and 8.30 pm; *Líneas América* at 9 am and 2.30 pm; *Transportes Higueros* at 4 am and 4 pm via Panajachel; and by *Transportes Galgos* which has five buses. All these buses cost US$4 but not all are direct so make enquiries.

Huehuetenango-Quetzaltenango There are many departures daily; the fare is US$1.

Quezaltenango-Panajachel Many departures daily and the fare is US$2.

Train

Trains in Guatemala are really only for railway buffs as they're incredibly slow (the one from Guatemala City to San Salvador takes two days with an overnight stop in Zacapa!!) and very uncomfortable. Snacks and soft drinks are for sale on the trains but no meals are available.

The train from Guatemala City to Tecún Umán on the Mexican border has already been mentioned in the 'To/From Mexico' section. Probably the only other train which a traveller might consider using is the one from Guatemala City to Puerto Barrios. This departs at 6.30 am on Tuesdays and 7 am on Wednesdays, Fridays and Sundays. The fare is US$2 and the journey takes about 12½ hours. Take something soft to sit on!

Boat

All the regular boat services likely to interest travellers are in the Lake Izabal/Caribbean coast/southern Belize area. They include the following:

Puerto Barrios-Livingston-Punta Gorda (Belize) This ferry departs at 7 am on Tuesdays, Thursdays and Fridays and sometimes on Saturdays, all returning the same day. The fare is US$5 one-way and the journey takes about 2½ hours.

Puerto Barrios-Livingston There are two daily ferries in each direction, leaving Puerto Barrios at 10 am and 5 pm and Livingston at 5 am and 2 pm. The one-way fare is US$2.

There's also a ferry from Puerto Barrios to Río Dulce via Livingston on Saturdays and Sundays if there's enough demand. It costs US$5 one-way. It departs Puerto Barrios between 7 and 8 am and Río Dulce at around 2 pm.

Livingston-Río Dulce The mail boat between these places runs twice weekly and also stops at Castillo San Felipe (a ruined Spanish fort) en route. It departs Livingston on Tuesdays and Fridays around 11 am and the one-way fare is US$5. Some travellers have done it for less by asking around but this would be the exception rather than the rule. To travel between these two places at any other time generally requires renting a motorised dug-out which will cost around US$30.

Antigua

Antigua is in many ways Guatemala's cultural capital and the country's most delightful and interesting old colonial city. It's full of massively constructed old churches, monasteries and convents, many of which display moderate to severe earthquake damage – earthquakes are common in this area. It's very popular with travellers and has many language schools – there are few places where it would be more pleasant to stay and learn Spanish.

Founded in 1543, Antigua was the capital (site of the Audiencia) of Central America until 1773 when it was destroyed by earthquakes and the capital moved to Guatemala City. In its heyday, it was one of the most splendid cities in the Americas attracting artists, craftspeople and intellectuals from a wide area. Despite its early foundation, it was in fact the second capital – the first being at Ciudad Vieja about 5½ km from Antigua. Antigua was founded after the destruction of Ciudad Vieja by an enormous mud-slide in 1541.

Antigua is also noted for its amazing Holy Week celebrations when there are endless street processions and the city is a riot of colour. Intricately patterned carpets of flowers and sawdust are laid out on the streets down which the processions move. Naturally, they are destroyed by the end of the day but are remade all over again ready for the next procession the following day.

Each procession, which can take up to eight hours to go round town, includes floats carried on the shoulders of up to 100 men accompanied by a retinue of 1000 women carrying censers and other objects. It's not to be missed if you're in the area at the time.

Information

The tourist office is on the south-east corner of the Parque Central. It's open from 8 am to 12 noon and 2 to 5.30 pm though you'll often find it closed by 3 or 4 pm. The staff are very friendly and helpful.

Probably the best source of information about the city and the surrounding areas is Mike Shawcross's book *Antigua, Guatemala City and Area Guide* which can be bought in a number of bookshops around the town. It contains an excellent description of the two cities, nearby villages, markets and hiking trails in the surrounding area. Mike has lived in the area for a number of years and knows it like the back of his hand. He also rents out camping equipment and can arrange backpacking trips in the area between November and March.

The market is next to the bus terminal at the end of 4 Calle Poniente near the Alameda de Santa Lucia. It is open daily but is best on Mondays, Thursdays and Saturdays.

There is a laundromat opposite the tourist office on 5 Calle Poniente and another along the same street near the market. It costs US$1.50 per load plus US$1 for drying.

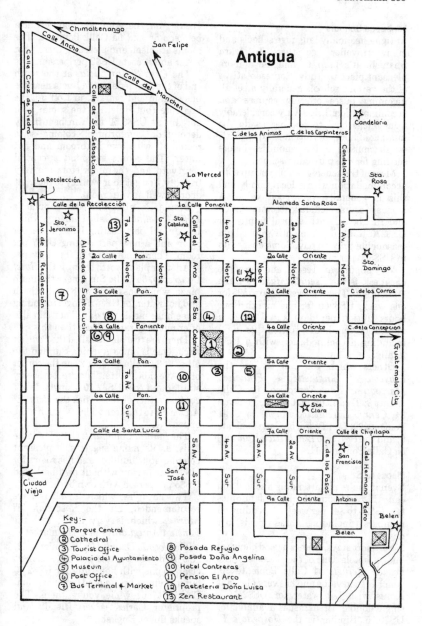

Antigua

Key:-
1. Parque Central
2. Cathedral
3. Tourist Office
4. Palacio del Ayuntamiento
5. Museum
6. Post Office
7. Bus Terminal & Market
8. Posada Refugio
9. Posada Doña Angelina
10. Hotel Contreras
11. Pension El Arco
12. Pasteleria Doña Luisa
13. Zen Restaurant

Language Schools

Antigua has many language schools and many travellers go there to learn Spanish. It's hard to imagine a more pleasant place to study. Representatives of the various schools generally meet all incoming buses offering courses and accommodation. Prices vary considerably from one school to another as do the number of hours of tuition per day so it's worth making a few enquiries before settling for one particular school.

Most of the schools can fix you up with accommodation with a local family and this is generally very good value. A language course including accommodation and full board with a local family for US$270 to $325 per month would be a reasonable price to pay. Some charge up to US$500 per month.

Very popular at present, and one of the cheapest, is the *Escuela Maya*, 5 Calle Poniente 20. They charge US$80 to $95 for one week, US$260 for one month (four hours tuition per day) and US$320 a month (seven hours tuition per day) including accommodation with a local family.

Others which you can try are the *Proyecto Lingüístico Francisco Marroquín*; *San Francisco*, 6a Calle Oriente 9; *Tecún Umán*, 6a Calle Poniente 34; *Centro Lingüístico Maya*, 5a Calle Poniente 20; *Don Pedro*, 5a Calle Poniente 6; and the *Proyecto Lingüístico Hunapu*, 5a Calle Poniente 11.

Places to Stay

Even if you're not attending a school you can still rent rooms locally with families for US$20 to $40 per week (depending on numbers) including three meals per day.

For short stays, there's a good choice of budget hotels. One of the cheapest is the *Posada Refugio*, 4 Calle Poniente 30, which is good value and has very pleasant rooms with hot water for US$2/$4 a single/double. Breakfast is available for US$0.75. Similar is the *Hospedaje El Pasaje*, on the Alameda Santa Lucía between 5a and 6a Calle Poniente. The rooms are clean and pleasant, there's hot water and it costs US$2 per person.

The *Casa Santa Lucía*, at the south end of the Alameda Santa Lucía near the bus station and market, just off 5 Calle Poniente (but quiet all the same), is a bargain at US$3.50 each in beautifully decorated, comfortable, colonial-style rooms all with own bathroom and hot water. The rooms surround a central courtyard and the proprietors are very friendly. You get your own key to the front door as well as your room.

Similar in price and also popular is *Doña Angelina*, 5a Calle Poniente, which has an old part costing US$3 to $4 per room and a new part costing US$7 per room. There's hot water in the showers.

Another place worth trying is the *Hotel Contreras*, 5a Calle Sur 8 near the main plaza, which has rooms with private bath and hot water for US$5 a single including three huge meals per day. They can also offer monthly rates at less than this.

There are two places called the *Pension Arco*. One is on 5a Avenida Sur and the other at 6a Calle Oriente 27 on the corner of 1 Avenida Morte. They're both very similar and cost US$2.20 a single. Don't confuse either of these with the *Hotel El Arco* next to the arch which is much more expensive.

The *Posada Colonial*, 2 Calle Poniente 2, is, as its name suggests, a pleasant colonial-style building and has rooms for US$4 per person without own bath and US$5 per person with own bath.

Two cheapies, which travellers have recommended, are the *Hospedaje El Marne*, which is very basic; and the *Pension Antigüañita* near the market.

The *Posada David*, 4 Calle Poniente 32, also used to be popular and has excellent clean rooms with hot water for US$2.50 but it's temporarily closed for renovation. Check it out while you're there. The proprietor, Carlos, is very friendly and speaks fluent English.

Places to Eat

Antigua is full of cheap *comedors*, for those not staying with families or who are not paying full board in a hotel, but it's difficult to recommend one over another. Many travellers patronise the *Pastelería Doña Luisa Xicotencatl* (usually known simply as Doña Luisa's), 4 Calle Oriente, one block east of the main plaza, which serves good breakfasts, chili con carne (US$1.25), cakes and teas. It's a very popular meeting place and has darts, chessboards and a noticeboard for travellers. If you'd like to speak to Mike Shawcross (the author of the guidebook we recommend) then you can often find him there.

Another popular place where people meet in the late afternoon and evenings is *La Galería* on the west side of the main plaza which serves draught beer and wine. Very popular at present is the *Restaurant Zen*, Calle del Arco 30A one block past the arch, which serves excellent cheap vegetarian food. There are always a lot of travellers in there.

AROUND ANTIGUA

The original capital of Guatemala, **Ciudad Vieja**, 5½ km from Antigua at the foot of the Agua volcano, is worth a visit. It's now only a very small village but ruins of the original colonial buildings can still be seen. It's best to combine a visit there with one to the market, which is busiest on Sundays. There are regular buses to and from Antigua for 10 centavos.

Beyond Ciudad Vieja is the village of **Santa María de Jesús** from where there are excellent views of Antigua itself. The main industry of the village is weaving and really beautiful *huipiles* can be bought from the houses of those who make them. There are frequent buses from Antigua on Santa María de Jesús' main market days (Monday, Thursday and Saturday).

Another place you might like to visit if you're interested in the local weaving is **San Antonio Aguas Calientes**, about nine km from Antigua. Lessons in the weaving technique are given there by Carmelo and Zoila Guarán for about US$1 per hour.

Volcano buffs have the choice of three to climb in the vicinity of Antigua. There is **Volcán de Agua** (3760 metres) the easiest of the three, which takes from four to five hours to climb starting from Santa María de Jesús, and even has a football field in the crater; **Volcán de Acantenango** (3976 metres), which takes up to nine hours to climb from the village of Acantenango (nearest bus from Antigua goes to La Soledad) but provides good views of the crater of Volcán Fuego; and **Volcán Fuego** (3763 metres), which is the hardest of them all and shouldn't be attempted by amateurs. Climbing it can take 12 hours and the going is very steep and rough. Fuego is the only one of the three which is currently active. The danger of eruptions and sulphurous fumes shouldn't be taken lightly. If you're thinking of doing any climbing first look at the file at the tourist office, and at Mike Shawcross's book.

CHICHICASTENANGO

Normally a quiet, uneventful town, Chichi comes alive on Thursdays and Sundays when thousands of Indians from the nearby mountain villages flock to town for the market. It's worth going just for the colourful spectacle but don't expect to find any bargains as it's very commercialised these days and local crafts, especially pottery and weaving, are very expensive.

Places to Stay & Eat

Cheapies include the *Posada Santa Marta, Cantina Claveles, Pensión Girón, Santa Marta* and rooms in the guest house run by Señora Jenny Taylor, an Englishwoman who lives in the town. Cheap rooms are also available in private houses – local boys will show you where they are for a small tip.

For food, try the *Pensión-Restaurant Katokok* and the *Cantina Claveles*.

CHIQUIMULA

For most people Chiquimula is just a town en route to Copán but it has an attractive colonial atmosphere and is worth a stopover.

Places to Stay & Eat

Cheap places to stay include the *Hotel Darío*, 8a Avenida 4-40, half a block from the main plaza; and the *Pension Hernández*, 3a Calle 7-41, which also offers good, cheap food.

POPTÚN

Halfway between Guatemala City and Flores, Poptún is a good place to relax. The farm *Finca Ixobel* has been recommended as an excellent place to stay with a family and enjoy some good cooking. Mike and Carol Devine are the hosts. Treehouses are US$1 and cabins US$4 per person. There are several walks to nearby caves and a three-day mule trek to a cave with Mayan art.

FLORES

The capital of El Petén department with a population of around 5000, Flores is an attractive colonial town built on an island in Lake Petén Itzá. Many people stay there en route to Tikal.

As a result of heavy rains in early 1981 the water of the lake, which has no natural outlet, rose four metres flooding much of the island, the causeway linking it to the mainland and many parts of the low-lying land bordering the lake. The causeway has been built up so that it's now passable by cars but buses and other heavy vehicles are not allowed across. All buses except those to Tikal now leave from San Benito on the mainland. Buses to Tikal leave from Santa Elena central market.

When the flooding was at its worst, many of the hotels and pensiónes in Flores were either partially or completely flooded and had to be closed. They are gradually being opened up again as the water recedes but this is a slow process and the ground floors of many are still flooded, as is the lakeside road which encircles the island. Unfortunately, the flooding has resulted in serious pollution of the lake so it's not recommended that you swim in it. Also tap water is considered unsafe to drink.

Places to Stay

Budget hotels which have managed to re-open, though in most cases only on the upper floor, include the *Pensión Universal* which is very popular with travellers and costs US$2 per person (note that the top two floors of this place get insufferably hot in summer as they're constructed of concrete and act like storage heaters at night); the *Pensión Casa Blanca* which costs US$2 a single (entry is via a plank-walk as the bottom floor is still flooded); the *Santana* which has rooms on the upper floor for US$4/$5/$6 a single/double/triple and is very popular (it also has boats for hire at 50 cents per hour); and the *Hotel Rey* which has rooms for US$3.

The *Hotel Peten* with rooms without bath for US$6 or with bath and lake view for US$10 and an excellent restaurant has been recommended.

On the mainland at Santa Elena there is the *Jade Hotel*, on the left immediately before the causeway, which costs US$1.50 a single and is basic but clean; and the *Hotel San Juan* which is also basic and costs US$3 a double. If you buy a ticket there for the bus to Guatemala City you can stay one night free.

There's also the *Bela Gautemala* which costs US$3 a double. It's opposite the bus station.

If you'd like to stay outside Flores on the northern shore of the lake, *El Gringo Perdido Camping* has been recommended by many travellers. They have small, open-sided thatched huts with space for two hammocks and grass areas for camping. The charges are US$1.10 for a tent and US$0.50 for a hammock (if you don't have your own). There are showers

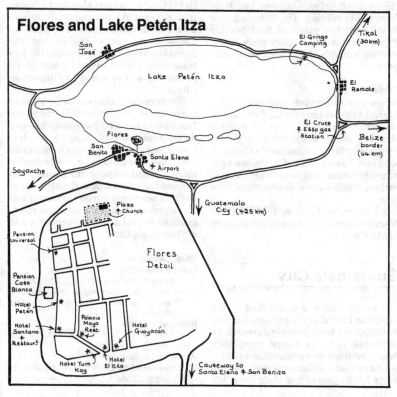

Flores and Lake Petén Itza

San José

Lake Petén Itza

El Gringo Camping

Tikal (30 km)

El Remote

El Cruce Esso gas Station

Belize border (64 km)

Flores

San Benito

Santa Elena Airport

Sayaxche

Guatemala City (425 km)

Flores Detail

Plaza Church

Pension Universal

Pension Casa Blanca

Hotel Petén

Hotel Santana Restaurs.

Palacio Maya Rest.

Hotel Guayacán

Hotel Yum Kay

Hotel El Itza

Causeway to Santa Elena & San Benito

and a dug-out for use by residents (free). The restaurant serves western-style food with dinner costing US$2.50 – large helpings. To get there from Flores, take a bus heading for Melchor and get off at El Cruce, from where it's a six km walk; or better still, take a bus going to Tikal and get off when you see the sign 'Gringo Perdido Camping' past the village of El Remate. It's a three km walk from there.

Places to Eat
The most popular places to eat are the *Santana* and the *Restaurant Mesa de las Mayas* but although the food is good it's expensive considering what you get. Another good place is the *El Gran Paro* on the corner of the first dry street, two doors from the Hotel Rey. The *Palacio Maya Restaurant* has excellent food but it's expensive and it's a strange place full of stuffed animals festooned with silly props.

Getting There
A new airport terminal and runway are nearing completion at Santa Elena on the mainland opposite Flores so it's possible that the chaos which used to attend getting on a flight to Guatemala City may soon end. Nevertheless, if you haven't got a confirmed seat you need to get there as early as possible as waiting lists tend to be long.

All buses to Tikal and Melchor de Mencos leave from the market place in Santa Elena.

Guatemala City

Guatemala City was established as the capital in 1776 after the previous capital, Antigua, had been severely damaged by earthquake. It was almost completely destroyed itself by earthquakes in 1917-18 and extensively damaged again in 1976 when 23,000 people lost their lives. It's not a very interesting city and indeed has few redeeming features but you'll probably find yourself staying there overnight at some point.

Information
Guatemala City sprawls over a large area and is divided up into 'zones' but almost everything of interest to travellers is either in Zona 1 or Zona 4. You can safely assume that anywhere with an address outside either of these two zones will be a long way from the centre. Addresses, on the other hand, are easy to find – 15 Calle 5-70, for example, indicates that a place is on 15 Calle between 5 and 6 Avenidas.

The tourist office (INGUAT), at Centro Civico Complex, 7 Avenida 1-17, Zona 4 (tel 311333/47) is open Monday to Friday from 8.30 am to 6 pm and on Saturdays from 8.30 am to 12 noon. The staff are pleasant and speak English but the literature they have is limited to bus timetables, a hotel list and a map of the country as well as a map of Guatemala City.

Better maps of Guatemala City and of other cities are obtainable from the Instituto Geográfico Nacional, Avenida de las Americas 5-76, Zona 13, which is open Monday to Friday from 8 am to 4.30 pm. They also stock a large selection of more detailed maps of the country but you need permission from the Ministry of Defence before you can buy some of these. If you arrive in Guatemala at the airport, Hertz have good maps of the country and of Guatemala City.

Useful Addresses
Central Post Office
    7 Avenida, 12 Calle, Zona 1. The *lista de correos* is kept there and is well organised. There's a small charge for each letter collected.
Immigration office
    8 Avenida, 12 Calle, Zona 1. For visa and Tourist Card extensions.
American Express
    Represented by *Clark Tours*, Edificio El Triángulo, Zona 4.

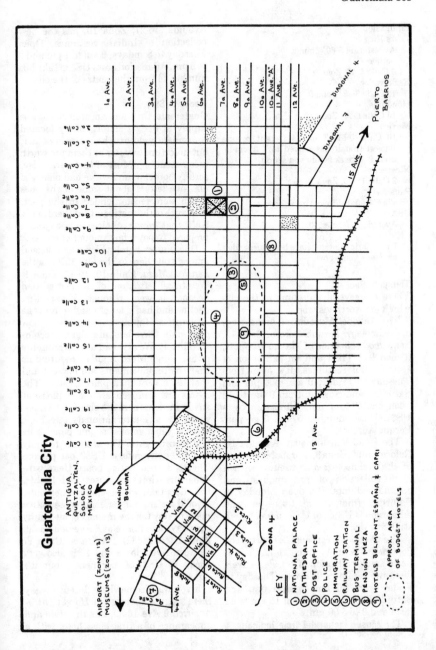

Guatemala City

KEY
① NATIONAL PALACE
② CATHEDRAL
③ POST OFFICE
④ POLICE
⑤ IMMIGRATION
⑥ RAILWAY STATION
⑦ BUS TERMINAL PENSIÓN MEZA
⑧ HOTELS BÉLMONT, ESPAÑA ¢ CAPRI
⑨ HOTELS BÉLMONT, ESPAÑA ¢ CAPRI
⌁ APPROX. AREA OF BUDGET MOTELS

ZONA 4

AIRPORT (ZONA 13)
MUSEUMS (ZONA 13)

ANTIGUA,
QUETZALTEN,
SOLOLA,
MEXICO

PUERTO BARRIOS

Embassies

Costa Rica
   Av Reforma 8-60, Zona 9
Colombia
   6 Calle 5-47, Zona 9
El Salvador
   12 Calle 5-43, Zona 9
Honduras
   15 Calle 6-23, Zona 10
Mexico
   16 Calle 0-51, Zona 14 (recent reports
   suggest that it has moved to 7 Avenida,
   Zona 9 – check before you set off).
Nicaragua
   2 Calle 15-95, Zona 13
Panama
   Via 5 4-50, Edificio Maya, Zona 4
USA
   Avenida Reforma 7-01, Zona 106
UK
   Diplomatic relations have been suspended
   for many years now.

Things to See

There are several museums in the city
which are worth visiting.

The **National Museum of Archaeology
and Ethnology**, Parque Aurora, Zona 13,
has a good collection of Mayan artefacts,
a model of Tikal and an exhibition of
Guatemalan costumes. It's open from
Tuesday to Friday, 9 am to 4 pm and
Saturday and Sunday from 9 am to 12
noon and 2 to 4 pm. Admission costs
US$1. Buses number 5 and 6 go past
Parque Aurora.

The **Popul Vuh Museum**, Avenida La
Reforma 8-60, Zona 9, is probably the best
of the archaeological museums with a
large collection of pre-conquest and
colonial exhibits. It's open Monday to
Saturday from 9 am to 5 pm and
admission is US$2, or US$1 if you have a
student card.

The **National Museum of Arts and
Popular Crafts**, 10 Avenida, 11-72, Zona 1,
has a small collection of textiles, silverware and ceramics. It's open Tuesday to
Friday from 10 am to 5.30 pm, and
Saturday and Sunday from 10 am to 12
noon and 2 to 5.30 pm.

The **Museo Ixchel del Traje Indígena**, 4
Avenida, 16-27, Zona 10, has the best
collection of Indian costumes. Open
Tuesday to Sundays, 9 am to 1 pm and 2
to 6 pm. Admission costs US$3. Take bus
number 14 from the centre of the city.

Places to Stay

Guatemala City has an almost endless
supply of budget hotels, many located
conveniently close to the centre in Zona 1,
but unfortunately few of them are worth
recommending. Most of them are noisy,
scruffy bordellos and we've had plenty of
abrasive letters about some of the ones
which were recommended in the past.
The truth of the matter is that there really
isn't that much choice unless you're
prepared to pay a fair amount of money.

One budget hotel which was a legend
among travellers in the late 1970s is the
Pension Meza, Calle 10, 10-17, Zona 1.
We almost left it out of the last edition
because it went through a period of
decline and had a lot of hassles from the
authorities. Happily those times are now
over and travellers are again recommending it. We also had a letter from the
owner, Jorge Meza Aguilar, assuring us
that the improvements are for real and
that it's a very good place to stay. The
rooms are arranged around a pleasant
shady garden, there are clean sheets, hot
showers, an international telephone
service, table games, a ping-pong table
and security gate. The staff are friendly
and the daily rate is US$3 per person.
There's a good notice board there with
departure times of buses and flights,
travellers mail and sale advertisements.
If you'd prefer a quieter, more conservative
place to stay (as the management put it)
they have an annexe at 8 Avenida 13-30,
Zona 1 (tel 24682). *Mi Hotel*, Calle 17
between Avenidas 9 and 10 is also very
cheap at US$1.65 per person but it's
dirty.

If you want somewhere decent to stay
there's a good choice. The *Hotel Centro-
América* 9 Ave 16-38, has the style and
appearance of a first-class hotel with a

patio and fountain, hot water all day, an excellent restaurant and bar (free ceviche de pescado with your beer), polite staff, brightly painted rooms, tiled bathrooms with fittings which work and yet it only costs US$6/$11 a single/double with own bath. That recommendation comes to you from a budget traveller with impeccable taste who poured derision on all others which were previously recommended.

Similar is the *Chalet Suizo*, 14 Calle 6-82, Zona 1, which has been popular for a number of years. It costs US$2.75/$5.50 a single/double without own bathroom and US$8.80 a double with own bathroom. There's hot water in the showers and the hotel is clean.

Also in this range is the *Calle 13 Inn*, Calle 13 near the junction with Avenida 9. It's clean and has hot showers and costs US$5/$7 a single/double with own bath. Also popular is the *Hotel Belmont*, 9 Avenida 15-30 and 15-46, which costs US$7.50 a double without own bath and US$11 a double with own bath.

Other good places which have been recommended in the past are the *Hotel Capri*, 9 Avenida 15-63; and the *Hotel Felix*, 7 Avenida 16-81. Both of these are similar to the Chalet Suizo.

Places to Eat
Zona 1 – and to some extent Zona 4 around the bus terminal – is full of cafés and *comedores* offering almuerzos and cenas for US$1 to $1.25. Just look for the blackboards propped up against the wall.

There are quite a few Chinese restaurants clustered together on Avenidas 6 and 8 around 12 Calle, Zona 1. In general, they're reasonably priced (around US$2), give you decent sized helpings and the food is good. One that is recommended is the *Fu Lu Sho*, 6 Avenida, 12-09. Another is the *Chao Mein*, 16 Calle 4-80, Zona 1, which is popular with local people and is very cheap – less than US$1 for a meal. There are others in Zonas 4, 9 and 10.

The *Maxipan*, 6 Avenida 15-22, which is a combined bakery and restaurant, has also been recommended as a cheap place to eat.

A nightclub which has been recommended is *La Quinta Restaurant*, 5 Avenida between Calles 14 and 15. Many local people go there for a night out. It has a disco and live music and our correspondent said he had two beers, several snacks and soup and the bill came to only US$2. It's a friendly place.

Getting Around
If arriving at La Aurora international airport, public buses Nos 6 and 20 will take you into the centre. They go down 7 Ave to the Palacio Nacional, which is on the main plaza.

Most first class bus companies have their own terminals in Zona 1 but if you arrive at the main bus terminal in Zona 4 and want to get into the centre from there, take public bus No 2, 5 or 6 from *El Triángulo* to 7 Ave in Zona 1. *El Triángulo* is a high-rise landmark a few minutes walk from Zona 4 bus terminal containing many airline offices, expensive boutiques and craft shops and American Express.

HUEHUETENANGO
Situated in beautiful mountainous countryside, this old lead and copper mining centre with a population of some 14,000 is of principal interest for its Indian market (daily but best on Thursday and Sundays) and for the nearby ruins of Zaculeu, the old capital of the Mam kingdom.

Information
There is no longer a tourist office here.

For Mexican visas and Tourist Cards, the Mexican consulate is at the *Farmacia El Cid*, 5 Avenida, 4 Calle.

Places to Stay
A good place is the *Hotel La Paz Anexo*, 4

Avenida, Zona 1. It's spotlessly clean and friendly and costs US$2 a single. The *Hotel Central*, 5 Avenida 1-33 north of the plaza, has been described as 'the best value in town'. It costs US$2/$4 a single/double. Washing facilities and excellent meals are available. Also reasonable value is the *Hotel Maya*, 3 Avenida 3-55, which costs US$2.20.

Other cheapies include the *Pensión San Ramón*, 4 Calle opposite the market which costs US$1.50 per person; the *Pensión Tikal*, 1 Avenida between Calles 4 and 5; and the *San Antonio* next door to the Tikal.

Avoid the *The Posada Español*, 4 Calle 4-13, near the main plaza. It's cheap at US$1.50 a single but it's dirty and dingy.

Places to Eat

The best place for a good, cheap meal is the *Hotel Central* but for breakfast you could try *La Pradera*, 3 Avenida 3-55, which has good dairy products – yoghurt, milk and ice-creams. There are a lot of cheap comedores on the east side of the market and on the west side of the plaza.

AROUND HUEHUETENANGO

The ruins of **Zaculeu** are about five km north-west of the city and include pyramids, a ball court and other structures. The yellow *Alex* buses go

there at 10.30 am, 1.30 and 3.30 pm. There are also slightly more expensive mini-buses which depart from 5 Calle and 4 Avenida.

LIVINGSTON

Livingston is a small town at the mouth of the Rio Dulce, with a population comprised mostly of black people of Jamaican origin. It's become a popular place for young travellers over the last few years and is a good place to break the journey from Flores to Guatemala City if you're not taking the plane.

To get there, leave the bus at Rio Dulce, stay there at the cheap riverside *Hospedaje Santa Isabel*, then take the twice weekly mail boat down the river to Livingston. You can also take a canoe to Castillo San Felipe, half-way between Rio Dulce and Livingston and stay there at the cheap hospedaje near the ruined fort. The mail boat calls there on its way down the river.

The beach closest to Livingston isn't one you're particularly likely to want to lie around on for any great length of time as it's pretty dirty, but there is a good one at Rio Blanco, some distance from the town.

The seven-tiered waterfalls (Los Siete Altares), about six km from town, are also worth visiting but the walk there involves fording a river which can reach waist height.

Places to Stay

There are plenty of cheap hospedajes as well as rooms in private houses. Cheapies include the *Pension Rio Dulce*, which is popular with travellers; and *Riki's Happy Haven*, on the main street. If you just want to sling a hammock ask for *Ramon's Place* where you can do this for US$1.

Places to Eat

The best places to eat are the *African Place* at the top of the hill which also has some good recorded music; and *Peter's New York Green House* where meals must be ordered a day in advance but it's well worth it as the food is excellent.

There are two lively bar-discos worth going to where the local blacks rock on to reggae – the *Maribu* and *Caribe*.

Panajachel

Panajachel, the main town on beautiful Lake Atitlán, is very popular with travellers as well as being a tourist resort – hence its nickname 'Gringotenango'. As you might expect, it caters for gringo tastes and those who come to Guatemala often have a tendency to knock it, preferring the more ethnic places. Personally, I think this kind of snobbery is unwarranted since despite the number of tourists, it's still a very pleasant place and prices are quite reasonable. Besides, the political violence in Guatemala has resulted in a considerable reduction in the number of tourists coming to Guatemala, particularly to Panajachel.

If you do find Panajachel too crowded for your tastes and would prefer somewhere quieter, it's very easy to take off to one of the small villages around the lake – there are plenty of ferries and buses.

Information

The tourist office is open weekdays from 8 am to noon and 2 to 6 pm, and Saturdays from 8 am to noon. Maps are available.

Panajachel is the only town on Lake Atitlán where you can change travellers' cheques. The Banco Agricola Mercantil is opposite the *Poco Loco* and is open Monday to Friday, 9 am to 12 noon and 2 to 4.30 pm.

Things to See & Do

The best time for the Indian market is on Sunday mornings though bargains are hard to find because of the number of tourists. If you're looking for examples of local weaving, it's probably better to spend some time visiting the various small villages around Lake Atitlán – each village produces its own characteristic weaving patterns.

For those interested in contemporary Indian art, a visit to **La Galería** (indicated on the map) is well worthwhile. There is also a gringo flea market at 7 pm on Saturdays where travellers sell and exchange various items, usually clothing and camping equipment.

Swimming in the lake is popular but be warned that hepatitis and amoebic dysentery are fairly common so avoid swimming near where rivers and streams enter.

Places to Stay

If you want a really cheap room with just basic facilities then ask around as soon as you get there rather than check into a hotel. Panajachel is full of cheap places though you may have difficulty finding a room in the high season (November and December). They range in price from US$20 per month to US$150 a month for a whole house.

Along the road which goes from the Shell station bar to the beach there are many places with rooms for US$1 to US$1.50 per night per person; hot showers are generally an extra US$0.25. Examples are *Rooms Santa Elena, Santander, Mario's Rooms, Chico's, Vista Hermosa*. Another good place is the *Casa Loma* opposite the Hotel del Lago, which also has a good restaurant.

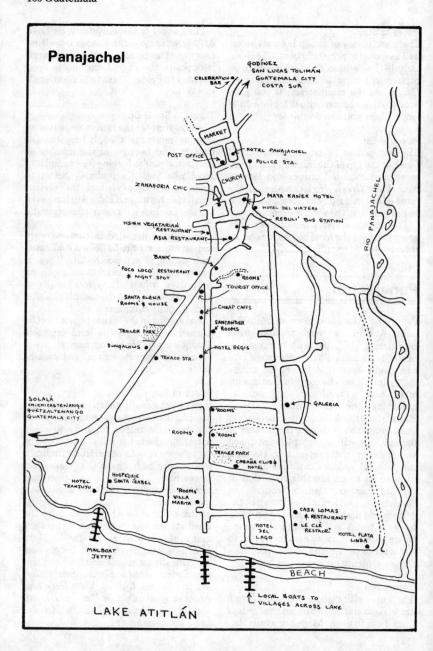

Panajachel

GODÍNEZ
SAN LUCAS TOLIMÁN
GUATEMALA CITY
COSTA SUR

CELEBRATION BAR

MARKET

HOTEL PANAJACHEL
POST OFFICE
POLICE STA.
CHURCH

ZANAHORIA CHIC

MAYA KANEK HOTEL
HOTEL DEL VIAJERO
'REBULI' BUS STATION

HSIEH VEGETARIAN RESTAURANT
ASIA RESTAURANT

BANK

POCO LOCO' RESTAURANT & NIGHT SPOT
'ROOMS'
TOURIST OFFICE

SANTA ELENA 'ROOMS' & HOUSE
CHEAP CAFES

SANTANDER ROOMS

TRAILER PARK
BUNGALOWS
TEXACO STA.
HOTEL REGIS

SOLALÁ
CHICHICASTENANGO
QUETZALTENANGO
GUATEMALA CITY

GALERIA

'ROOMS'

'ROOMS'
'ROOMS'

TRAILER PARK
CABAÑA CLUB & HOTEL

HOSPEDAJE SANTA ISABEL
HOTEL TEANJUYU

'ROOMS' VILLA MARITA

CASA LOMAS & RESTAURANT
LE CLÉ RESTAUR.
HOTEL PLAYA LINDA

HOTEL DEL LAGO

MAILBOAT JETTY

BEACH

LOCAL BOATS TO VILLAGES ACROSS LAKE

LAKE ATITLÁN

RIO PANAJACHEL

If you don't find what you want immediately, ask around where other travellers meet – more than likely someone will have a spare room or be about to leave a place. Camping is permitted at a certain spot on the beach and also at the *Trailer Park* near the Texaco station and tourist office, where it costs US$1 per person but water is only available at certain times.

If you won't be staying long or want the facilities of a hotel, then try one of the following which cost US$3 to $4 per person depending on the facilities.

Hotel Panajachel, close to the market, is a very pleasant, clean place with occasional hot water; it's quite popular with travellers. The *Naya Kanek Hotel* costs US$4 per person in rooms with tiled bathrooms and hot water all day. Rooms in both the annexe and the main block now cost the same though some rooms are better than others. *Hotel del Viajero* is basic, no-frills accommodation.

Places to Eat

Panajachel offers a whole spectrum of restaurants from simple Guatemalan comedores, to Chinese restaurants, health foods, juice bars and American-style hamburger joints. It might all sound like a transplant of the downtown areas of some North American cities but the resemblance is only superficial – there's too much local colour for it to be that way and the landscape is too exotic. Although some people avoid travellers' watering holes like the plague, I personally find them very entertaining in moderation – as do many other people it seems.

Without making an exhaustive list of the eating possibilities in Panajachel, the following are some of the best and most pleasant. It's difficult to recommend one place at the exclusion of another since the popularity of restaurants waxes and wanes from one season to the next – as they do in all places where travellers congregate.

Hsieh restaurant, is a very friendly place which serves excellent vegetarian food with a dinner currently costing US$1.50. *Fonda del Sol*, also near the Poco Loco, has a varied menu and reasonable prices. *Zanahoria Chic*, close to the market, serves good vegetarian food. *Blue Bird*, just off the market, offers daily 'specials' as well as good yoghurt and fruit salads. This restaurant is excellent value and portions are generous. *Maya Kanek* and *Brisas del Lago*, both on the main street going up to the market, offer meals at reasonable prices.

For breakfast try the *Restaurant Paradiso* which is up a small alley off the main road to the beach; or *The Last Resort* which has a huge buffet breakfast served till 12 noon which costs US$1.50. There's even a *Restaurant Sicodélico* near Mario's rooms and although it doesn't serve what its name suggests, it does have good meals and yoghurts. If you'd like some brown bread instead of puffed air go along to the *Panadería San Martín* around 3 pm.

For nightlife there are several places where travellers gather including the *Poco Loco* (films, chess boards, live music and bar); the *Lumiere Cine-Bar* (three different films per night at 6 and 8 pm); the *Celebration Bar* (good recorded music and bar); the *Posada del Pintor* (on a side street off the market, an English-owned bar and restaurant with cheap beer); and *Roger's Pub* (good music, bar).

If you want to work off some steam try *Le Cle*, a restaurant opposite the Hotel del Lago, which has a discotheque and bar in the evenings, though it is a little more expensive than the places already mentioned.

AROUND PANAJACHEL

Don't leave Panajachel before devoting at least a few days to the small villages around Lake Atitlán. You can get to most of them by ferry and/or bus, or if you prefer, you can walk to some of the nearest. Santa Catarina Palopó, for instance, is a two-hour walk on the road east out of Panajachel.

Santiago Atitlán

The mail boat from Panajachel departs daily from the Hotel Tzanjuyu pier and costs US$2.50 one-way and US$4 return. Departure time is variable but is usually at 10 am. Another boat leaves daily from the Hotel del Lago at 9.15 am and costs the same as the mail boat. There are also smaller boats which leave from the beach daily around 9 am, returning the same day at 11.45 am and cost US$2 one-way. There is a direct bus daily from Panajachel to Santiago Atitlán and return buses at 12 noon and 3 pm which cost US$1.25 and take about two hours. Another possibility is to take the ferry to San Lucas Tolimán and the bus from there to Santiago Atitlán (see the San Lucas section).

Probably the best place to stay in Santiago Atitlán is the *Hospedaje Chi-Num-Ya* which is very clean and costs US$2 per person. Others are the *Pensión Rosita*, near the church; and the *Brisas del Lago*, close to the market.

For places to eat, the *Santa Rita* offers good, cheap food; and the *Restaurant El Cayuco* is also good value.

If you're looking for handicrafts, particularly weaving, then it's worth visiting the Artexco cooperative but it's unlikely you'll find things cheaper there than in Panajachel because Santiago is on the tourist circuit.

San Lucas Tolimán

A ferry from Panajachel departs daily except Sunday at 7 am, takes about 1¼ hours and costs US$1.50. It returns between 9.30 and 10 am. This ferry stops at San Antonio Palopo if requested. There's also a direct bus at 7.30 am daily.

From San Lucas there are buses to Santiago Atitlán at 9 am, 12 noon and 3

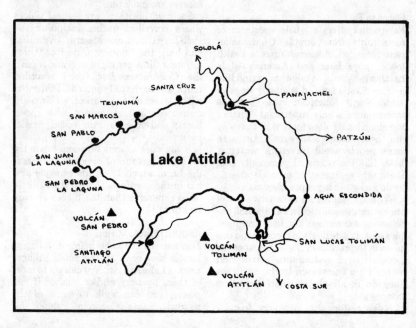

pm which take about one hour and cost US$0.50. They leave Santiago Atitlán for San Lucas at the same times.

Cheap places to stay include the *Café Tolimán* and *Jorge's Pensión*, both on the waterfront. Another cheapie is the *Santa Ana*.

For somewhere to eat, try *Jorge's*. If you're a volcano buff and are thinking of climbing either Volcán Tolimán or Volcán Atitlán nearby then enquire at American Pay as they have maps of the area.

San Pedro La Laguna

Ferries from Panajachel leave at 3 am and 3 pm on Tuesday, Friday and Sunday from the Hotel Tzanjuyu pier and cost US$1. They return on the same days at 4 am and 4 pm. These ferries go via San Juan La Laguna and San Pablo. There is a ferry from San Pedro La Laguna to Santiago Atitlán daily at 7 am for US$0.75, returning at 11 am.

Cheap pensiónes include the *Pensión Balneario*, *Pensión Chuasinahi*, *Hotel Felix* and *Hotel Felipe*, all of which are clean, basic and friendly. The Chuasinahi costs US$1 per person. Almost next to it on the beach is another hospedaje for just US$0.50 which is very good. On the other hand if you take a liking to this place you can find houses to rent on a weekly basis for as little as US$5.

There are simple cafés in the village where meals cost less than US$1. Otherwise, try the *Restaurant Chez Michel*, the *Piramides* or the *Casa Felipe*. The bakery in the village sells excellent spaghetti and cocoa for US$1. Also good is *La Ultima Cena* but it's painfully slow. Through a corn field is *Comedor Frances* which has very good food and 'the best papa fritas in the world'.

If you're interested in handicrafts, there's a rug-making cooperative on the beach.

San Antonio Polopó

This village is eight km beyond Santa Catarina Palopó which itself is about four km east of Panajachel. The gravel road connecting these villages is atrocious but there are mini-buses between all three. San Antonio itself has an excellent weaving cooperative, set up by Oxfam, where you can buy beautiful lengths of cloth. It also has one of the oldest churches in Guatemala with a superb carved-wood sanctuary. (Santiago also boasts a church dating from 1568.) Forget about Señor Feliks' hotel these days – he charges US$18 a single!

Should you want to stay at Sololá en route to Panajachel (I can't imagine why you might want to unless you're into early morning photography) then the place to stay is the *Hotel Letona*, 9 Calle, 5-41, just off 6 Avenida, which costs US$2/$4 a single/double. It has hot water, a restaurant and a pleasant garden.

PUERTO BARRIOS

This is the principal port on the Caribbean coast, but apart from the fact that it's the terminus for ferries to Livingston, Lake Izabal and Punta Gorda (Belize) and therefore okay as an overnight stop, there's no good reason why you would want to stay there.

Information

The post office is at 3 Avenida, 7 Calle.

Buses to Guatemala City by *Litegua* depart from 7 Calle between Avenidas 5 and 6.

Places to Stay

In contrast to other Guatemalan cities, Puerto Barrios is an expensive place and there are few budget hotels.

Hotel La Caribeña, 4 Avenida between Calles 10 and 11, costs US$2.50 per person or US$5.50/$6.50 a single/double in very pleasant private rooms with bathrooms. The hotel has its own very good restaurant. *El Dorado* 13 Calle between Avenidas 6 and 7, costs US$4/$8 a single/double. *Español* 13 Calle between Avenidas 5 and 6, is a friendly place with clean rooms and own bathroom but is a little on the expensive side.

If you don't mind spending a little over the odds then it's worth considering staying at the *Hotel del Norte*, 7 Calle, 2 Avenida on the sea front, which is as near as you're likely to get to the atmosphere of the Raffles Hotel in Singapore. It's a splendid, old-fashioned, colonial-style hotel full of 19th century charm. It's spotless, spacious and comfortable with charming – almost obsequious – staff. The dining rooms gleam with white linen. You can get a room for as little as US$5.50 without bath and US$7.50 with bath though it does also have more expensive air-con rooms.

Places to Eat

Most hotels have their own restaurants but if you're just on your way through then try the *Guana Chapi*, 9 Calle, close to the landing stage for the Livingston ferry, which is cheap and good.

QUEZALTENANGO

Quezaltenango is known locally by its old name of Xelajú which is often abbreviated on buses to Xela.

The largest city in western Guatemala, Quezaltenango (altitude 2335 metres) is also fairly modern. It was rebuilt after being destroyed in 1902 by the eruption of the nearby volcano, Santiaguito. The volcano is still active from time to time. The city has one of the most important markets in this part of Guatemala and Indians from all over the highlands go there to sell their wares.

Information

The tourist office on the plaza is open

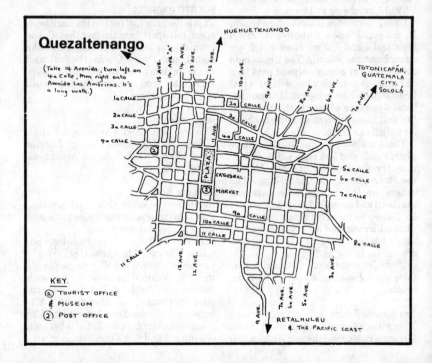

Quezaltenango

(Take 14 Avenida, turn left on 4a Calle, then right onto Avenida Las Américas. It's a long walk.)

HUEHUETENANGO

TOTONICAPÁN, GUATEMALA CITY, SOLOLÁ

CATHEDRAL

PLAZA

MARKET

RETALHULEU & THE PACIFIC COAST

KEY.
① TOURIST OFFICE
& MUSEUM
② POST OFFICE

Monday to Friday from 9 am to 12 noon and 2.30 to 5 pm and the staff are friendly and helpful. They have free maps of the city and information on nearby villages and their markets.

Like Antigua, Quezaltenango is a popular language school city where many people go to learn Spanish. One recommended school is the *Instituto Cooperativo Azumanche*. Classes cost US$90 per week for five hours daily tuition and full board with a local family.

Mexican Tourist Cards are obtainable from the consulate which is in a suite in the *Hotel Bonifaz*, 4 Calle, 10-50.

Places to Stay

Accommodation in Xelajú tends to be a little on the expensive side. Two of the cheapest places are the *Hotel Radar 99*, 13 Avenida 3-27, which costs US$1.75 per person and has hot water; and the *Floriani Hotel*, 12 Avenida near Calle 2, which is US$2.50 for a room with a double bed.

Other cheapies are the *Pensión Altense*, 9 Calle and 9 Avenida, which is clean and serves good meals (hot water extra); *Pensión San Nicolás*, near the main plaza; and the *Pensión Casa Linda*, 9 Avenida 10-17.

For something slightly up-market, try the *Hotel Casa Suiza*, 14 Avenida 'A', 2-36, a good place where rooms cost US$5/$6 a single/double including own bathroom; or the *Canadá*, 4 Calle, 12-22, a pleasant hotel with a good restaurant but somewhat overpriced at US$5/$9 a single/double with own bathroom.

Places to Eat

Two good, cheap places near the centre are the *Párajo Azul*, on the east side of the plaza; and the *Restaurant Capri*, next to the Hotel Capri, 8 Calle.

Others are the *Acurio Zurich*, 14 Avenida, 3-11; and the *Los Arcos*, 12 Avenida, both of which have daily specials and are good value.

Two places which serve European-style food for around US$2 are the *Delicadezas la Polonesa*, 14 Avenida 'A', 4-71 (sausages and pastries); and the *Aquarine Suiza*.

TIKAL

The ruins of Tikal rank among the world's greatest archaeological treasures and shouldn't be missed. Set in the luxuriant jungles of the Petén, these vast Mayan ruins of temples and public buildings date from between the 4th and 10th centuries AD and are little short of magical.

The site is a large one so be sure to spend at least two days there, particularly if you don't want to miss the more distant places such as the Temple of the Inscriptions. Allow even more time if you'd like to see something of the jungle which holds its own fascinations. A new paved road has been completed from Flores (Santa Elena) to Tikal so access by bus no longer involves a bone-shattering journey.

Information

There are no facilities here for changing travellers' cheques so bring along sufficient cash. The hotels will accept cheques if you're paying for your stay. There's also often a serious lack of change in the village so take along plenty of small bills if you're planning on eating there. Don't forget to bring your passport with you as this will be checked on entering Tikal village.

The ruins are open from 6 am to 5.30 pm. The best time to visit them is before 10 am and after 4 pm; at other times certain parts of the ruins can be very crowded with tourists on day trips. It's worth going to the trouble of getting a special pass at sunrise or sunset. Entry to the ruins costs US$1.

Places to Stay

The only way to visit Tikal cheaply is either to camp at the *Jungle Lodge* for US$1 per night or sling up a hammock in the open-sided thatched shelters near the airstrip. The washing facilities and toilets at the latter have been improved so you shouldn't have to rely on the facilities at the hotels. What you do need, however, is plenty of mosquito repellent and preferably a mosquito net.

Other accommodation in Tikal is expensive. The *Jungle Lodge* costs US$10 a double with own shower or US$20 with shower and toilet. The hotel has a large lounge with comfortable chairs. They don't seem to object to non-residents going there.

There is also the *Tikal Inn* at US$15 a double with private bath and toilet, and the *Jaguar Inn* which costs US$12 a double with private bath and toilet.

Places to Eat
As with accommodation, there isn't much choice. Unless you've brought your own food along with you then it's probably best to pay for a set meal at one of the hotels – this should cost around US$3 for dinner.

There are two comedores in Tikal village, the *Comedor Tikal* and the *Comedor Corazón de Jesus*, where you can buy cheaper meals but the food is nothing special. The former offers meals for US$2 and the latter for US$1.75. Their soft drinks and beer, on the other hand, are cheaper than at the hotels. Fresh fruit

and vegetables are almost impossible to buy.

THE PACIFIC BEACHES
Guatemala's Pacific beaches don't really compare with those of Mexico but if you're in need of some sun and sand after the markets and mountains, catch a bus to the Pacific port of San José and head off from there to Iztapa, Monterrico, Hawaii or Las Lisas. There are long stretches of black volcanic sand, white sand and a coastal canal which runs from Iztapa almost as far as Lisas.

At **Iztapa** there are cheap cabañas to rent as well as hotels. If you're coming from Guatemala City, take a bus to San José via Escuintla, or if coming from Lake Atitlán, there are buses from San Lucas Tolimán.

Hawaii is a small, laid-back village with sand dunes and bamboo cabañas for rent. It's about three km along the Chiquimula canal from Monterrico by boat. There are plenty of daily buses from Guatemala City to Monterrico.

Las Lisas is another laid-back beach resort between the canal and the sea about 25 km from the El Salvador border. It has cabañas for rent and a number of good seafood restaurants. Plenty of daily buses run from Guatemala city to Las Lisas and from there to the beach you go by boat along the canal.

Honduras

Honduras is a mountainous country of banana, cotton, sugar and coffee plantations. It also has extensive forest regions which cover just under half the total land area and supply a large proportion of the world's demand for fine timber, especially mahogany. The country also has rich mineral resources.

Although it's the second largest of the Central American republics, Honduras has a population of only 2½ million, most of whom live in the western part of the country. The majority (about 90%) are *mestizos*. There's now only a small minority (about one per cent of the population) of pure blooded Indians, concentrated in the area west of Santa Rosa de Copán along the Guatemalan border and along the Misquito coast east of Trujillo down to the Nicaraguan border. A large, black, English-speaking group predominates along the Caribbean coast and in the Bay Islands.

Honduras is one of the world's poorest and most exploited countries though recently, of course, it has been receiving vast amounts of American arms and money in a bid to turn it into an American bridgehead against the Sandinista government in Nicaragua. Meanwhile, although the Constitution (most of which is suspended under the military government) declares that primary education is compulsory, there are so few schools that 60% of the population remain illiterate. The majority of peasants live a hand-to-mouth existence on small plots of land, or work as agricultural labourers on the estates of the big landowners. Corruption rivals that found anywhere else in Latin America.

Like Guatemala and Belize, Honduras formed part of the lands occupied by the Mayas and the ruins of one of their major cultural centres can be seen at Copán in the extreme west of the country near the Guatemalan border. The ruins were discovered by Stephens and Catherwood in 1839 in thick jungle and were subsequently restored by the Carnegie Institute in the 1930s. Spread over many hectares and built on two levels (one of them overlooking the river), they include courts, temples, the 'Hieroglyphic Stairway', ballcourts and stelae. The stone carving is magnificent and includes some of the best Mayan art to be seen anywhere in Central America.

Columbus first landed on the mainland here in 1502 and named the country after the deep waters off the north coast – *honduras* is Spanish for 'depths'. Following the conquest of Mexico by Cortés, attempts were made to conquer and settle this area but the Spaniards quarrelled among themselves and the settlements got off to a poor start. There was also little gold and silver to make life interesting for them. The Indians were not subdued until the late 1530s when the Indian chief Lempira, who had fought the Spanish with 30,000 of his followers, was treacherously assassinated at a peace parley arranged with the Spanish.

Comayagua was founded in 1537 as the provincial capital and it remained the capital until 1880 when Tegucigalpa took over. It was home to the first university in Central America and is still an unspoiled, though run-down, colonial town of cobbled streets and white-washed houses.

Later in the 16th century, silver was discovered in the hills around Tegucigalpa. The growing economic importance of Honduras began to attract the attention of French, English and Dutch buccaneers who frequently raided the northern coast during the 16th and 17th centuries from their bases on the Bay Islands. These islands eventually passed into British hands, and along with the Misquito coast, remained so for over a century.

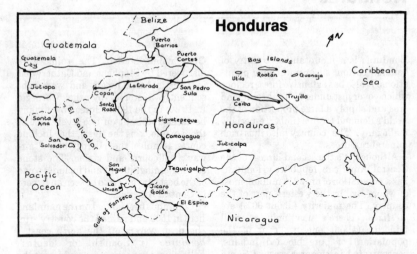

Following an appeal by the chiefs of the Misquito Indians, a British Protectorate was declared over the lands occupied by these Indians, a region which stretched east along the Honduran coast all the way down to the border with Costa Rica. During this period settlements of English and black Caribbeans were established at various points and their legacy is still very much in evidence today, particularly in the Bay Islands, Bluefields, the Corn Islands (Islas Maíz) and San Juan del Norte (formerly Greytown). The 'Kings' of the Misquito Coast were crowned in the Protestant cathedral in Bluefields.

The protectorate came to an end in 1859 when Britain signed a treaty with Honduras relinquishing control of the Bay Islands and the Honduran section of the Misquito coast, although they held the Nicaraguan section until 1889.

On 15 September 1821, following the success of Iturbide in Mexico, Honduras joined the other four Central American provinces in declaring independence from Spain. All were annexed to the Mexican Empire of Iturbide between 1822 and 1823. When the empire fell apart, Honduras joined the federation known as the United Provinces of Central America whose first president was José Arce. Social and economic reform was attempted some seven years later under the presidency of Francisco Morazán (Honduras' national hero) but it didn't get too far because of the fierce rivalry between the liberals and conservatives which led to the disintegration of the federation in 1838. Since that time political control of the country has passed back and forth between the liberals and the conservatives – the latter generally in the form of a military dictatorship.

The last liberal government was voted into power following free elections in 1957 but it was ousted six years later in a military coup. The head of the junta, General López Arellano, took over as president and remained there until 1971 when he was replaced by a civilian president. In typical Latin American style, this civilian president didn't last too long and was soon ousted by Arellano. He in turn was forced to resign some two years later following a scandal in which he was accused of accepting US$1¼ million in bribes from the US company United Brands, in return for substantial tax 'allowances'. He settled for a comfortable life of exile in Miami.

Despite – or perhaps because of – the presence of large numbers of American troops in the country and substantial military aid from the USA, Honduras' system of land ownership is still as feudal as it was when the Spanish left. A tiny percentage of the population owns almost 30% of the cultivable land while most peasants are virtually landless. There have been spontaneous peasant uprisings in the past and there is some guerrilla activity in various parts of the country, especially in the Juticalpa region. The military regime naturally sides with the landowners though in an unprecedented move in 1975 some 32,000 hectares belonging to Standard Fruit, United Brands and several other landowners was expropriated and distributed among the peasants. It remains to be seen whether the government will attempt to head off a Sandinista-style revolution by trying major economic and social reform.

VISAS

These are required by all except nationals of Japan and most West European countries, excluding Austria, France, Irish Republic, Luxembourg and Portugal. Visas valid for a maximum stay of 90 days generally cost US$3 (free to Canadians for a 30-day stay). In most cases you can buy a visa at the border for US$5.

Even if you don't need a visa you have to buy a Tourist Card at the border for US$3, valid for 30 days and renewable at immigration offices in large towns at a cost of US$5.50 for each extra 30 days. No onward ticket is required and you'll rarely be asked to show sufficient funds.

There is an entry tax of US$2 and an exit tax of US$1.

Nicaraguan visas The consulate at Choluteca has closed so if you need a visa for Nicaragua then make sure you get it elsewhere (eg Tegucigalpa).

MONEY

US$1 = 2 lempira (official rate)

The unit of currency is the lempira = 100 centavos. Honduran names for fractional amounts are: 5 centavos = *conquinto*; 10 centavos = *bufalo*; 20 centavos = *daime*; 50 centavos = *toston*.

There is a blackmarket, on which you can get up to US$1 = 3 lempira (cash) but this is only available in certain places. The normal street rate is 2.30 lempira (at Copán) to 2.60 lempira (at the border). You can also change travellers' cheques on the blackmarket. The usual rate is US$1 = 2.40 lempira.

If you're going to Nicaragua then make sure you take in as many córdobas as you're allowed to. The maximum is 5,000 córdobas but as you will have to change US$60 at the border on arrival, at the official exchange rate, make sure that this plus what you buy elsewhere doesn't exceed 5,000 córdobas as any excess will be confiscated.

You can pay for internal and international flight tickets with lempira.

GETTING THERE

TICA bus, which used to connect Guatemala City with Panama City via San Salvador, Tegucigalpa, Managua and San José has suspended its services except from San José to Panama so there are now no international buses.

To/From Guatemala

The usual crossing is via Copán where the famous Mayan ruins are situated. There are local buses from the border to Copán for US$1 and buses from there to Santa Rosa de Copán for US$2.50. The latter bus takes 3½ hours. Roads are quite rough in this part of the country.

To/From Nicaragua

Despite all the military manoeuvres and the activities of the *contras*, the border between Honduras and Nicaragua is open more or less normally although there is now only one possible crossing – via Choluteca, El Espino, Somoto and Esteli. The crossing via Danlí, Ocotal and

Somoto is closed at present.

There are buses from Choluteca to San Marcos de Colón, 15 km from El Espino, by *Mi Esperanza* 12 times daily in either direction for US$1.25 which take 1½ hours. From San Marcos there are colectivos to El Espino for US$0.50 per person. Between the Honduran customs/passport control and the Nicaraguan checkpost it is about 5½ km and you'll probably have to walk this as there are no buses and trucks rarely give lifts.

From the checkpoint to Somoto where Nicaraguan customs/passport control is situated is a further 20 km. There are occasional buses over this stretch (for a few cents – at the free market rate of exchange) or you can hitch with trucks (again, these cost a few cents).

From Somoto to Esteli there are regular buses. Border officials on both sides are friendly. Because of the amount of time it takes to cross the border and the changes involved you can no longer get from Tegucigalpa to Managua in one day.

GETTING AROUND
Bus
Copán-La Entrada-San Pedro Sula There are only direct buses between Copán and San Pedro Sula before 5 am which cost US$4 and take about five hours. After 5 am there are only minibuses as far as La Entrada and you'll have to change there for a bus to San Pedro Sula. The road between Copán and La Entrada is now surfaced.

Copán-Santa Rosa de Copán The bus costs US$2.50 and takes about 3½ hours.

Santa Rosa de Copán-Gracias-La Esperanza-Siguatepeque There are regular buses between all these towns. The total cost will be about US$7.

San Pedro Sula-Tegucigalpa The bus costs US$3.50 and takes about four hours.

Comayagua-Tegucigalpa There are buses every hour by *Catrachis* which cost US$1.50.

Tegucigalpa-Choluteca There are buses by

Mi Esperanza every three hours which cost US$2.50 and the road is surfaced.

Boat
There are ferries connecting the Honduran mainland with the Bay Islands. The *Caribbean Pearl* covers the La Ceiba-Utila-Puerto Cortés route departing La Ceiba on Mondays and Tuesdays. The fare to Utila is US$4 and the journey takes three hours. It sails from Utila to Puerto Cortés at night. This leg of the journey costs US$5. Bunks are available though they cost extra.

The *Caribbean Pearl* also sails irregularly from Puerto Cortés to Roatán via Utila. The fare is US$10. It's also possible to get rides on fishing boats for around US$10 per person.

There is also the *Suyapa* which sails between Guanaja, La Ceiba and Puerto Cortés; and the *Miss Sheila* which sails the same route and then goes on to George Town on Grand Cayman island. There are also occasional boats from Trujillo to the Bay Islands.

CHOLUTECA
You will pass through Choluteca on your way to Nicaragua and if it's getting late in the day when you get here, it would be better to stay rather than press on to Somoto, the first town in Nicaragua, as there's only one place to stay there.

Places to Stay
Most of the cheapies are around the market in the centre of town (don't confuse this market with the vegetable market south of the town centre). Most cost around US$4 a single.

The *Hotel Hibuezas* costs US$7 a double for two beds with own bathroom and fan; there are cheaper rooms without own bath. It's fairly clean, and purified iced water is available. There's a good, clean restaurant attached where you can eat for about US$1.

Cheaper are the *Hospedaje El Cedro*, which is good value at US$2.50/$4 a single/double; and the *Hotel San Carlos*, which is basic and friendly and costs US$2.50.

COMAYAGUA

Comayagua was the former capital of Honduras and until recently a completely unspoilt colonial town of cobbled streets and one-storied, white-washed houses. Sadly it's been allowed to deteriorate and these days is in need of considerable restoration.

The cathedral is one of the country's most interesting and contains some of the best examples of religious art in Honduras. There's also an anthropological museum with displays of Indian artefacts. You'll probably meet a lot of American GIs there on R&R.

Places to Stay

The cheapest place is the *Hospedaje Miramar* near the market which is very basic but costs only US$2 a single. Better is the *Hotel Libertad* on the main square (Parque Central). It's clean and has a pleasant patio and a choice of rooms. The cheaper ones are only divided by hardboard partitions and cost US$2.60/$3.70 a single/double without own bathroom. They also have larger rooms with proper walls and private shower and toilet for up to US$12.50.

These prices will probably not hold for very much longer as hotel owners are not likely to miss an opportunity and GIs generally have considerably more money to spend than budget travellers.

Places to Eat

Most restaurants in Comayagua have menus printed in both Spanish and English. The prices quoted on the English menu (in US dollars) are twice what are quoted on the Spanish menu (in lempira) so make sure you ask for the latter.

The *Restaurant China*, one block behind the market, offers good, cheap meals. The *Red Bird Restaurant* has been recommended for a minor splurge.

COPÁN

Copán is the site of some of the most magnificent Mayan ruins in Central America. Situated about one km from the town along the banks of the Río Copán, they were discovered by Stephens and Catherwood in 1839. At the time of their discovery they were covered in thick jungle but this was cleared away and the main features reconstructed by the Carnegie Institute in the 1930s. They have since been maintained by the Honduran government. Entrance to the ruins costs US$1.50 plus US$0.50 if you also want to visit the museum in town, which is open from 8 am to 12 noon and 1 to 5 pm. Guide books to the ruins are on sale for US$2.50 and US$5.

There is now a bank in Copán (open every morning except on Sundays) but reports suggest they will only change a maximum of US$20 in travellers' cheques per person per day. If you have quetzals left over from Guatemala these can be used to pay for things in Copán.

Places to Stay

A long time favourite and one which is excellent value is the *Pension Los Gemelos* which costs US$2/$4 a single/double. Similar in price is the *Hotel & Restaurant Paty* which is reasonably good value and offers *comida corriente* for US$1.50 plus other dishes ranging up to US$3.50.

Another place which has been recommended is the *Hotel Marina Anexo* near the plaza which has cheap rooms. The ones in the main part of the hotel are more expensive.

It's suggested you avoid the *Hospedaje Hernandez* because although the staff are friendly and at US$1 per person it is very cheap, it has a very noisy juke box which rocks on till 2 am.

Places to Eat

You can eat at both the Paty and the Marino but apart from these you should try the *Comedor Isabel* opposite the market which has set meals for US$1; or the *El Bosque* near the plaza, which has a pleasant verandah at the rear.

GRACIAS

Like Comayagua, though much smaller, Gracias is another of Honduras' time-warp towns where you can easily imagine yourself back in the 18th or 19th century. It's an old, unspoilt town and a regional capital. There are hot springs about 1½ hours walk from town.

Places to Stay

Two cheap places are the *Pension Giron* which has rooms for US$1.50 to $2 per person and its own restaurant where you can get a good meal for US$1.25; and the *Pension Herrera* which costs US$1.50 a single. Both are basic and close to the market.

LA CEIBA

This is one of Honduras' busiest ports but otherwise is an expensive and uninteresting town. If you're heading for the Bay Islands then you'll probably have to spend a night there.

Places to Stay

Most of the cheapies cost at least US$5 a double. Recommended are the *Los Angeles*, *El Paso* and the *Royal* all on the Avenida de la Republica; and the *Principe* on Calle 7.

SAN PEDRO SULA

This is Honduras' second largest city and although it was founded in 1536, nothing of the old town remains. There's little of interest for the traveller.

Places to Stay

Try the *Hotel Colombia Anexo*, Calle 3 between Avenidas 5 and 6, which costs US$2 to $3 a single. More expensive is the *Hotel Paris* which costs US$3 a single without private bath. Also worth trying is the *Hotel San Pedro*, Calle 3 and Avenida 2, which has rooms for US$3. The hotel has its own restaurant.

SANTA ROSA DE COPÁN

Santa Rosa is another of Honduras' colonial towns with narrow cobbled streets and a colourful festival which is held during the last 10 days of August every year. There are some good hiking possibilities in the surrounding area.

The bus station is about one km from the centre of town at the foot of the hill. There are buses every hour to San Pedro Sula.

Places to Stay

Cheap places include the *Pension Rivera*, 2a Avenida No 131, which costs US$1 a single but there are no showers; and the *Hotel Evir*, on the corner of Calle Real Centenario and Avenida 2a, which is somewhat more expensive as all the rooms have their own bathroom but it does have the best restaurant in town (though the *comida corriente* is expensive at US$2.25).

Tegucigalpa

Tegucigalpa has been the capital of Honduras since the late 19th century. It's actually an amalgam of two cities – Comayagüela, built on relatively flat land to the west of the Río Choluteca, and Tegucigalpa proper which is built on the slopes of Mt Picacho which overlooks the city to the north.

A good trip to make from Tegucigalpa is to the beautiful old mining villages of Santa Lucía, Valle de Angeles, San Juancito and El Rosario. The latter is now a ghost town in La Tigra National Park (a cloud forest). The park is Honduras' first, and so far, only national park. The terminal for the buses to the these villages is in front of the Cine Presidente, Calle 6 and Avenida 73. They leave every hour and cost US$0.50.

Information

The tourist office is at Edificio Soto,

Avenida 7a between Calles 2 and 3 opposite the Central Bank of Honduras at the rear of the Parque La Merced. The helpful staff can provide a list of hotels and a good map of Tegucigalpa.

Good maps of the country are available from the Instituto Nacional de Geográfia but getting hold of them is a long process involving form filling and passport production.

The Central Post Office is at 2a Avenida between Calles 4 and 5 in Tegucigalpa. Letters collected from the *lista de correos* cost a few cents and the service is very inefficient.

Buses to Choluteca leave from Calle 23 and Avenida 6.

Embassies
Belize
   Edificio Banco Municipal, Terminales de Cortés
Costa Rica
   1a Calle near the intersection with Av La Paz
El Salvador
   Calle San Carlos, Colonia Palmira
Guatemala
   Calle Juan Lindo (south end), Colonia Palmira. Open Monday to Friday from 9 am to 1 pm
Nicaragua
   Calle Juan Lindo 306, Colonia Palmira. Open Monday to Friday from 8 am to 12 noon. Visas take 24 hours. One traveller reported recently that the embassy has moved to the Alameda area (bus No 10) so check with the tourist office before you set off.

Places to Stay
Most of the cheapies are in Comayagüela rather than in Tegucigalpa itself. The *Hotel El Nilo Anexo*, 4a Calle between Avenidas 6 and 7 opposite the Hotel Richard 3, is one of the cheapest at US$2.50 a double. The hotel is part brothel. Similar is the *Pension Jalisco*, 3a Calle between Avenidas 3 and 4, which is also a brothel but costs US$1.50 a single.

Better is the *Hotel San Pedro*, Avenida 6a between Calles 8 and 9. It is clean and has older rooms which cost US$3.75 for a small bed and no private bathroom; and newer rooms for US$6 a double or US$7 for a room with two beds. Both of the latter have their own private shower and toilet.

Others which have been recommended in the past are the *Hospedaje Familiar*, Casa 801, Avenida 6a, which has rooms for US$2.50/$4 a single/double; and the *Hotel Alcázar*, Calle 5 between Avenidas 4 and 5, which has rooms for US$5 to $6 a double.

There are many other cheapies behind the large church on Calle 7a.

There are five hotels called the *Hotel Richard* but they each have a distinguishing number (1 to 5). No 1 is on 4a Calle between Avenidas 6 and 7 and the rest are on 5a Calle between Avenidas 6 and 7. They are all more or less mid-range hotels where you can expect to pay at least US$7 a double.

In Tegucigalpa itself try the *Hotel Granada*, 6a Calle No 1330, which charges US$6 a single; and the *Hotel McArthur*, 7a Avenida No 511, which costs US$6/$9 a single/double.

Places to Eat
Tegucigalpa has two excellent vegetarian restaurants – the *Restaurant Vegetariano*, Todo Rico 3C/4A, which is good and cheap; and the *Comedor Vegetariano*, 3a Avenida No 316.

THE BAY ISLANDS
These beautiful islands off the north coast of Honduras were once the haunt of buccaneers from England, France and Holland and were visited by Colombus in 1502 on his fourth voyage of discovery. From west to east the three main islands are Utila, Roatán and Guanaja with three smaller islands off the eastern end of Roatán.

The population of just under 9,000 is composed mainly of fair-skinned people

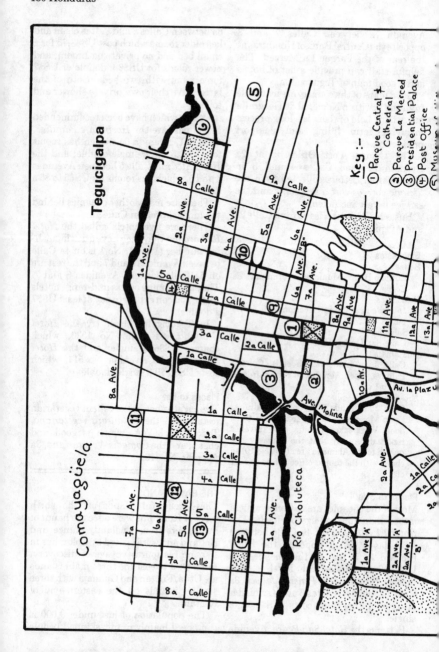

Tegucigalpa

Comayagüela

Río Choluteca

Key:-
① Parque Central ≠ Cathedral
② Parque La Merced
③ Presidential Palace
④ Post Office
⑥ Museum of ...

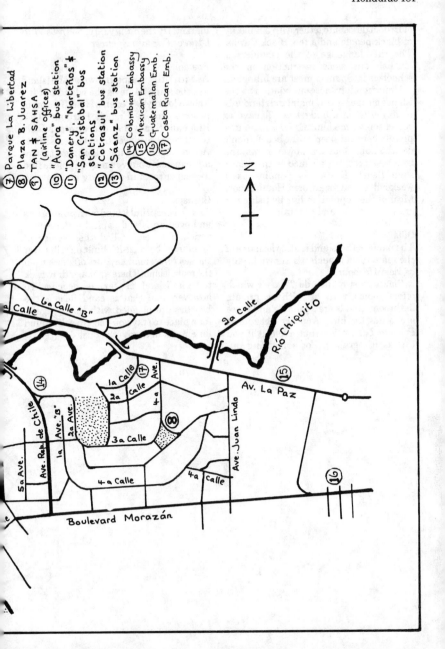

⑦ Parque La Libertad
⑧ Plaza B. Juárez
⑨ TAN ‡ SAHSA
    (airline offices)
⑩ "Aurora" bus station
⑪ "Daney", "Norteños" ‡
    "San Cristóbal" bus
    stations
⑫ "Cotrasul" bus station
⑬ "Sáenz" bus station
⑭ Colombian Embassy
⑮ Mexican Embassy
⑯ Guatemalan Emb.
⑰ Costa Rican Emb.

N
↑

6a Calle "B"
6a Calle
3a Calle
Río Chiquito

⑭
1a Calle
⑰ Ave.
2a Calle
4a Calle
Ave. Rep. de Chile
Ave. "a"
1a Ave.
2a Ave.
3a Calle
⑧
Av. La Paz
⑮

5a Ave.
4a Calle
Ave. Juan Lindo
4a Calle
⑯

Boulevard Morazán

of British descent together with a minority of black people and a few Black Caribs. The first language of the islanders is English but since instruction in the schools is in Spanish most are bilingual.

Unfortunately, accommodation on the islands is expensive by mainland standards so if you're on a budget you'll have to spend some time hunting for a room in a private house or sleep on the beach (don't do this on Guanaja however, as the beaches there are plagued with vicious sand fleas). Roatán is popular as a weekend retreat for affluent Hondureños. Most of the population live by fishing or growing coconut and plantain.

Utila

The name of the island is also the name of the main town though it's known locally as East Harbour.

Places to stay include *Trudy's* which offers rooms with or without private bathroom. Meals are available and there are boats for hire. Another cheapie is *Pension Las Palmas* but avoid it if you can as it's grubby. For something up-market, try the *Sandy Bay*, *Sonny's Villa Utila* or *Captain Spencer*.

Roatán

As with Utila the main town on the island has the same name as the island but it's known locally as Coxen's Hole. The main beaches are at French Harbour, Oak Ridge and Sandy Bay. Jeeps are available to get to these places from Coxen's Hole. Accommodation on this island is exceptionally expensive but you may be able to find a cheaper room in a private house.

Guanaja

This is a beautiful island with pine forests and even an island capital – Bonacca – which has been called the 'Venice of Honduras' because it's built on stilts over the sea on a small cay just offshore from the main island. There's a major drawback to this island as far as beaches go however, and that is sand fleas – the beaches are plagued with them. Again, for a place to stay you need to ask around for a room in a private house.

Nicaragua

Nicaragua is a hot, fertile, tropical country of sparsely populated rainforests, spectacular volcanoes (some of which are still active), and the two largest lakes in Central America – Lakes Managua and Nicaragua. The latter was, until fairly recent geological times, part of the Caribbean Sea but became isolated by earth movements and volcanic activity, so that over the course of many centuries it became a freshwater lake. Many of the different species of marine life which were trapped when access to the sea was cut off, adjusted to the gradual change in salinity and today the lake boasts, among other things, the only fresh-water sharks in the world.

Earthquakes are an ever-present threat in this country, the most recent and devastating one occurred in December 1972 when the capital, Managua, was almost completely destroyed. The city is still being rebuilt though mostly away from the old centre.

Until the late 1970s when the revolution and subsequent events here made world headlines and pushed the country into the forefront of Latin American politics, Nicaragua was in many ways a sleepy, Central American backwater. When first explored in 1522 by the Spaniards Andrés Niño and Gonzales Dávilla, from their base in Panama, the country was populated by two nomadic tribes of Indians in the north, the Suma and Misquito, and a settled tribe of agriculturalists in the south on the shores of Lakes Managua and Nicaragua. The latter had established a civilisation of sorts and lavished gold ornaments on the Spaniards, which excited their avarice and brought them scurrying back several years later in search of more. León and Granada were founded shortly afterwards but the supply of gold quickly ran out and most of the Spanish moved elsewhere.

Even today the bulk of the population, nearly half of which is urban, still lives in the narrow strip between the Pacific Ocean and the two lakes. The northern rain forests, between the lakes, the Caribbean Sea and the Honduran border, were ignored for centuries except by small bands of mainly British wood-cutters who came here in the 17th and 18th centuries in search of logwood (a source of textile dyes), rosewood and mahogany. (The wasteful logging caused serious environmental problems; in many places the soil has been washed away and the underlying subsoil and rock has baked into an infertile laterite on which almost nothing will grow – a process which is extremely difficult to reverse).

The failure on the part of the Spanish to settle the northern forests has led to Nicaragua having one of the most unusual and colourful histories of any Central American country.

Though nominally Spanish until independence, the whole of the Caribbean coastal area, together with a large slice of the coast of Honduras and the Bay Islands, was in practice controlled by the British. As early as 1678 the Governor of Jamaica had attempted to declare the coastal region a protectorate and although the idea was scotched at the time, it became a reality in 1780.

From that date until 1885 the area became the British Protectorate of Misquito, named after the Indian tribe inhabiting the region. During this time the 'kings' of Misquito were 'crowned' in Bluefields cathedral and the British settled several colonies of Jamaicans – both black and white – along the coast, particularly at Bluefields and San Juan del Norte (formerly Greytown). Black settlement there was augmented earlier this century following the establishment of banana plantations by the US-based

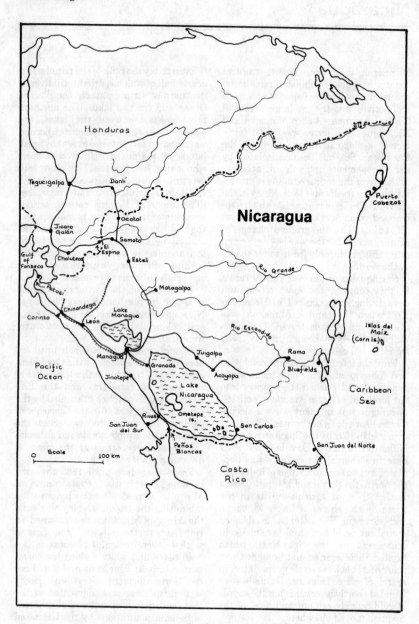

United Fruit Company in the area around Puerto Cabezas.

As a result of these movements of population from the Caribbean Islands, there is today a predominance of African blood along the coast. These people still retain their laid-back lifestyle, remain – at least nominally – Protestant, and still speak English although since instruction in the schools is in Spanish, most are bilingual. They make up some 9% of the population of Nicaragua.

While all this was going on along the coast, the Latin heartland became an independent republic in 1838, in line with other the Central American states. The first 20 years or so of independence saw constant rivalry between the liberals of León and the conservatives of Granada. It also experienced temporary annexation to the Mexican Empire of Iturbide and various attempts at federation with some or all of the other Central American republics.

The idea of federation has had a long but abortive history in this part of the world. It has ranged from its military imposition by the dictator José Santos Delaya in the early 20th century, which ended after US and Mexican intervention, to the most recent attempt in 1960 when the Central American Common Market was set up. This initially went well but eventually came to grief following a growing feeling in both Nicaragua and Honduras that the economic sacrifices outweighed the benefits. It also took a body-blow when the 'Football War' broke out between El Salvador and Honduras. Nevertheless, the idea lives on.

One of the most bizarre periods of Nicaraguan history occurred during the 19th century. Not only was the Caribbean coastal area alienated by British designs but in the middle of the century William Walker, a doctor and lawyer born in Nashville, USA, invaded the country at the head of a band of mercenaries – with the tacit support of the US government and the banking firm Morgan & Garrison.

Walker seized a steamer on Lake Nicaragua, which belonged to Cornelius Vanderbilt's 'Accessory Transit Company' and provided a link between the eastern US seaboard and the Pacific coast during the Californian gold rush, and then attacked and partially sacked Granada. The authorities were forced to capitulate and Rivas was installed as a puppet ruler with Walker as Commander of the Armed Forces. Vanderbilt's company was confiscated and its assets distributed among Walker's friends and collaborators. Shortly afterwards, Walker declared himself president and on the pretext of economic necessity and to gain the support of the southern US slave states, suspended the Nicaraguan laws against slavery. His government was formally recognised by the US in 1856 but a coalition of Central American states, backed by Vanderbilt, eventually drove Walker out of Nicaragua. He surrendered to the US Navy in order to avoid capture.

Undaunted, Walker was back again a few months later with another expedition, only to be arrested shortly after landing at Greytown by the US Navy, which returned him to the States. Most people would perhaps have been ready to abandon such grandiose schemes by then, but not Walker. Three years later he mounted yet another expedition, but this time it was to be his last. He was arrested by the British Navy and handed over to the Honduran authorities who shot him after a summary trial at Trujillo. Though undoubtedly a rogue in many ways, Walker's own account of his adventures, *The War in Nicaragua*, is worth reading if you'd like to follow up this period in Nicaraguan history.

Private intervention in the affairs of Nicaragua by US citizens was soon to be followed by direct US government intervention. In 1912 US Marines invaded the country to enforce the collection of customs dues which had been offered as collateral for a US loan the previous year. They stayed until 1933, leaving their groomed puppet, Anastasio Somoza, in control. From that day until mid-1979, Nicaraguan affairs were completely dominated by the Somoza family – from the presidential seat to the very paving stones on the street. With a totally cynical disregard for anything and anyone other than their own cronies and those whose support they bought, the Somozas ruled Nicaragua as though it were not only their God-given right but their own feudal backyard.

As a result of being either principal stockholders or outright owners of virtually every industrial installation, distribution and transport facility, communications medium, agricultural product, and bank or finance house they amassed a vast fortune estimated at over US$200 million. With an avarice which made the *conquistadores* look like philanthropists at a vicarage tea party, they even creamed off a large part of the disaster funds which flowed into the country from all over the world following the 1972 earthquake which destroyed Managua. Years after the quake the family was still charging rent on properties which no longer existed.

Obviously, they didn't maintain a private empire like that without violence and repression on a grand scale. By the 1970s the regime had become an embarrassment not only to their US backers but to almost every other Latin American country. Its days were numbered.

Opposition to the Somozas had first surfaced soon after the US invasion, in the form of Augusto César Sandino and a small band of guerrillas. They fought the National Guard (Somoza's bodyguard) and the US Marines with whatever weapons were available until Sandino was assassinated on his way to arranged talks with Somoza in Managua. Somoza claimed at the time that the assassination had been ordered by the then American Ambassador, Arthur Bliss Lane, but the guerrilla movement survived, naming

itself the Sandinistas after their leader. The final reckoning came in 1978 as support for the Somozas dried up. In that year a series of daring raids by the Sandinistas gave them control of a substantial part of the country, including the National Palace, and although they were temporarily driven back, their successes prompted the last of the Somozas to take to his heels in mid-'79 – to what he fondly imagined would be a luxurious retirement in Miami.

A new regime was set up in which power was shared between prominent members of the guerilla movement and civilians opposed to Somoza. Wide-ranging reforms – particularly in the areas of land distribution, wealth and education – were put into motion with assistance from other Latin American countries, Cuba in particular.

For a while things went along very smoothly and the revolutionary government acted with remarkable restraint. Unfortunately, just at that point, the political climate in the USA took a sharp turn to the right with the election of Reagan as president and suddenly the screws were on. The Nicaraguan government was accused of 'exporting' its revolution to neighbouring El Salvador and providing training camps for guerrillas from that country. The presence of many thousands of Cuban volunteers in the country naturally completed the picture as far as the American administration was concerned.

So almost overnight Nicaragua was cast in the role of a Cuban – and therefore Soviet – surrogate. The unthinkable was about to happen right on the USA's doorstep. The fact that what was being done in Nicaragua was already 50 years overdue, that something equally radical ought to be taking place in several other Central American republics if blood baths were to be avoided, and that the Nicaraguans were desperately in need of aid and assistance (denied to them by the USA) seems to have escaped the attention of the White House (though not necessarily those in Congress).

The *contras*, who were initially a ragbag collection of former Somozista national guards who fled the country following the overthrow of Somoza, have since been joined by others opposed to the Sandinista government including a number of former Sandinistas themselves. And Reagan has been fighting a running battle with Congress in order to provide the *contras* with money, arms and advisers.

The idea was to destabilise Nicaragua both economically and politically. It certainly achieved its economic objectives and led to a lot of bloodshed along the country's border with Honduras, but when it didn't bring the Sandinista government to its knees American troops and arms were poured into Honduras. Huge provocative military manoeuvres were staged both along the Honduran-Nicaraguan border and at sea, off the Caribbean and Pacific coasts of Nicaragua, and CIA saboteurs went to work in Nicaraguan ports.

The Sandinista government reacted by preparing (perhaps with good reason) for an American invasion of the country. Peasant farmers were moved away from the border region and a peoples' militia trained in the use of arms. The invasion didn't come but fear of it continues to plague the country and the diversion of scarce funds away from much needed investment in agriculture and industry into military purposes has had a devastating effect at many levels.

Unfortunately, it doesn't look like the pressure will ease in the near future. Certainly the Sandinista government has made mistakes (such as its treatment of the Misquito Indians on the north-east coast) but when it comes down to it, Nicaragua is simply too convenient a pawn with which Reagan can play propaganda games with the Russians, however far off the mark his assessment of the country might be.

Meanwhile, volunteers from all over the world are going to Nicaragua to help out with the harvesting and planting of crops and to develop educational programmes. They're also going there to demonstrate solidarity with a people and a government trying their best to put into effect changes which will result in a society that enjoys the same kind of rights and freedoms which Reagan vowed to defend when he took the oath of office.

Anyone who knew Nicaragua in the days of the Somozas will be amazed at the progress which has been made. Immunisation campaigns against polio in the children are well on the way to completion and illiteracy has been reduced from 50% to less than 10%. Everyone is now guaranteed a ration of such staples as rice, beans and kerosene at subsidised rates. Thousands of peasants who used to eke out a desperate living on the properties of the big landowners have been given small plots and formed co-operatives. Free schooling, health care and a minimum wage are now an integral part of a society which had previously never known such things. Each suburb and village is organised into a network of civil defence groups that organise everything from the voluntary paving of the roads to vigilance committees which keep an eye out for *contra* activities.

Naturally this hasn't all taken place without certain sections of the population opposing its loss of power and privilege, (would it in any country?), yet if Reagan and his supporters lack the imagination to see that most of the changes are constructive, then one day their myopia will rebound on them. What would they prefer – another El Salvador?

VISAS

Required by all except nationals of Belgium, Denmark, Luxembourg, Netherlands, Norway, Spain, Sweden, Switzerland and the UK. The visa situation for those who need them varies depending on where you apply. The usual charge is US$11. Most people get a 30-day visa, others get 90 days, but for some strange reason some people have only been given three days. It's possible to renew your visa once, at *Migración* in Managua, but a second renewal is difficult to come by unless you're a volunteer worker, an accredited press agent or something similar.

Avoid turning up at the border without a visa if one is necessary. Some people are issued with three-day transit visas but others are refused entry.

Before you're allowed into the country you must change US$60 into córdobas (US$15 if you're only staying three days or less). This applies whether you enter by air or land. It's not universally applied – we do get letters from people who have not been asked to do this – but it's safe to assume that most people will have to do so. You may also be asked for an onward ticket but if you tell them you're leaving by bus that's generally the end of the matter.

MONEY

US$1 = Cord 28 (official)
US$1 = Cord 50 (usual casa de cambio rate)
US$1 = Cord 625-630 (blackmarket rate)

The unit of currency is the córdoba (cord) = 100 centavos. Import of local currency is limited to Cord 5000 in total. Excess is confiscated so make sure that the amount you take in plus the Cord 1800 or so that you will end up with after changing your US$60 doesn't exceed this amount.

Because of the pressure from the United States, Nicaragua's economy is in really bad shape. There is a blackmarket on which you can get up to US$1 = Cord 630 inside the country but it's illegal, of course, so you must be discreet. If you're caught, you'll be roasted. The latest news, however (on the basis of one letter – so far unconfirmed), is that you can change US cash dollars and travellers' cheques legally for US$1 = Cord 630 at a casa de cambio in the centre of Managua. The writer didn't specify which casa de cambio. It might be he was mistaken.

You cannot buy airline tickets with either travellers' cheques or local currency. You must pay for them with cash US dollars. Enquire at the *Bank of America* about changing US dollar travellers' cheques into cash dollars. It may still be possible.

Most hotels in Managua demand payment in US dollars though this is not universally true. It largely depends on what the room rates are. Food and drink at restaurants are paid for in Córdobas.

Airport tax for international flights is US$10. There is a sales tax of 12% on all airline tickets bought in Nicaragua.

Prices quoted in this chapter are at the official exchange rate.

VOLUNTEER WORK

Nicaragua is suffering from a chronic shortage of seasonal workers because so much time has to be spent keeping watch for *contras*. A lot of young people from other countries are now lending a hand so you'll probably meet a lot of them. If you're interested, get in touch with the Central Sandinista Trabajar in Managua. The majority of help is needed between November and February/March (coffee), January to March (cotton) and in February (sugar cane). Help is very much appreciated, however, at any time of year. Come and find out for yourself what this revolution is all about.

GETTING THERE

Despite the activities of the *contras* and American pressure, Nicaragua's land borders are open to Honduras and Costa Rica more or less normally. There's no danger in crossing them. Ferries across the Gulf of Fonseca from Potosí to La Unión (El Salvador) have been discontinued so you cannot get between Nicaragua and El Salvador directly.

TICA buses between Managua and San José and Managua and Tegucigalpa have been suspended. *Sirca* still do the Managua-San José run and charge US$6.65 one-way.

To/From Honduras

Because of all the military activity along the border with Honduras, the two border posts are now separated by a 25 km strip and there are no longer any international buses between Tegucigalpa and Managua or vice versa.

Coming from Tegucigalpa you must first get to El Espino by bus or a combination of bus and taxi. From El Espino to the Honduran customs/passport control you need to take a taxi (share it with others going that way). From the Honduran post to the first Nicaraguan checkpoint it's a 5½ km walk and although trucks cross regularly they won't give lifts. There is no other form of transport. From this checkpoint it's another 20 km or so to Somoto where your luggage is searched and currency regulations enforced. Hitch with trucks over this stretch – there's a standard charge of a few cents. There is sometimes a public bus costing about US$1 including backpack, but don't count on it as local buses are in short supply.

By the time you reach Somoto you'll probably have to spend the night there. Check out the *Hotel Panamericano* on the plaza. It costs US$3.30 and is friendly though facilities are basic. The only restaurant is the *Zeteponat* but it's good value. There are buses to Managua in the morning. You cannot get from Tegucigalpa to Managua or vice versa in one day.

To/From Costa Rica

The normal crossing point between Nicaragua and Costa Rica is at Peñas Blancas on the main road between Managua and San José. There's a four km gap between the border posts but hitching between them is easy. If you want to get from Managua to San José in one day then you must catch the 5.20 am bus which leaves from the *Israel Lewitas Market* in Managua and if you want a seat, you must be there by 4.30 am. This is one of the few buses which go to the border from Rivas. Avoid *Sirca* buses if possible as they often get caught up at the border for hours. Expect heavy searches at this border (mainly looking for drugs). Remember that you need an onward ticket to get into Costa Rica – a bus ticket is sufficient.

GETTING AROUND
Bus

Because of Nicaragua's almost non-existent foreign currency reserves, local buses are in short supply as companies cannot afford the spares to keep their buses running. Bear this in mind when you need to take a bus and don't expect the companies to keep to their schedules. There's hardly any point in quoting bus fares since at the rate of exchange available on the street, this will rarely amount to much more than a few cents.

The different companies generally have their own terminals though they occasionally share the same one. The main terminals of interest to travellers in Managua are the ones at the Mercado Israel Lewitas (for buses to Rivas, Chinandega and León) and the Mercado Eduardo Contreras (for buses to Masaya and Granada). Buses to Rama go from the Contrán terminal east of the centre on the Carretera Panaméricana. Since all these terminals are quite a way from the centre you'll need to take either a colectivo or a bus to get to them. Colectivos are probably the most convenient but many have set routes so don't be too surprised if you hail one or two which refuse you. Agree on the fare before you get in. Local bus number 118 goes from the Intercontinental Hotel to the Mercado Israel Lewitas and bus number 109 goes from the same hotel to the Mercado Eduardo Contreras.

There are generally sufficient buses between the main centres and Esteli (for Honduras) and Rivas (for Costa Rica) though they may well be very crowded. To towns outside this main area you should be prepared to wait a while. Some journey times are as follows: Chinandega-Leon, one hour; Chinandega-Managua, three hours; Managua-Granada, 1½ hours; Managua-Rivas-Peñas Blanca, 2½ hours.

Both Bluefields and the Corn Islands (Islas Maíz) are no-go areas for tourists at present but you can still get as far as Rama. There seems little point in doing this though as there's nothing of great interest in Rama. If you do want to go, however, there are several companies, such as *TRANSICA* and *Transportes*

Nicaraguense, which do the 300-km run. They depart from the Contrán Terminal and take about five hours.

Train
There are a number of railways in Nicaragua but the ones of most interest to travellers are from León to Managua and Managua to Granada. Fares are generally about half the price of the buses but the journey times are about twice as long.

From León to Managua there are daily trains at 1 pm which take about 3½ hours and cost a few cents.

Boat
Rama-Bluefields Bluefields is off limits to foreigners at present but even if it wasn't you'd need to make enquiries about transport from Rama to Bluefields before you set off. There is no road between the two towns and planes and boats are the only means of transport. The *contras* blew up the *Bluefields Express* boat early in 1985 and it may not have been replaced yet. You can thank Reagan for that. Cargo boats may be the only form of river transport available.

Lake Nicaragua There are a number of ferry services on this huge lake which connect Granada with other lakeside towns and with the volcanic islands of Isla Zapatera and Isla Ometepe, but few of them have well-defined schedules and they generally depart when full. A selection of the services include:
Granada-Isla Ometepe There is a boat on Tuesdays at 12 noon which takes about four hours. The schedule is fairly reliable. The ferry goes to Moyogalpa, the largest of the two towns on the island. If this boat isn't running then try taking a ferry from San Jorge on the lakeshore south of the island. At Moyogalpa try the *Pension Jade* which is pleasant and clean and costs US$1. The pension has its own restaurant. At Alta Gracia you can also find accommodation at the same price.
San Jorge-Isla Ometepe One ferry daily in

either direction departing San Jorge around 1 pm and Moyogalpa around 7.30 am.

Granada-San Carlos There is an express boat on Mondays and Thursdays which takes five hours, otherwise there are much slower boats which depart on the same days around 4 pm and take about 15 hours. These slower boats return from San Carlos on Tuesdays and Fridays around 6 am and if you go on them, take a hammock and your own food and drink.

There are occasional boats from San Carlos to Los Chiles (Costa Rica) and from San Carlos to San Juan del Norte which are well worth the effort to find if you have plenty of time. If you're planning on entering Costa Rica this way you'll be in for intense negotiations for an exit stamp either at San Carlos or San Juan del Norte despite assurances by the tourist office in Managua that there shouldn't be any problems. Neither of the two places are official exit points for foreigners but some travellers continue to make it.

BLUEFIELDS

It's with great regret that we delete the sections on Bluefields and the Corn Islands (Islas Maíz). They are presently off-limits to foreigners and have been for some time since they are considered to be a 'war zone'. Once again, to a large extent, you have Ronald Reagan to thank for that. It used to be possible to get special permits to visit these places from 'Migración' in Managua (office open 8 am to 12 noon and 2 to 4 pm) but the fear of an American invasion still runs high so naturally they're not keen to have unvetted foreigners wandering around at will in the coastal areas.

By the time it opens up again, the area will have changed considerably. When it does, please let us have some details.

ESTELI

If you're heading to or from Honduras you may have to stay in Esteli overnight.

Places to Stay

Most of the cheapies are on Av Bolívar. They include the *Hospedaje La Florida*, which is reasonable at US$1 a single and US$1.80 a double; the *Hospedaje Juárez*, which is basic but OK and costs US$3.60 per person; and the *Hospedaje San Francisco* which costs US$1 per person.

GRANADA

Granada was one of the two original settlements founded in Nicaragua by the Spanish in 1524 and still retains a very Castillian atmosphere. In the buccaneering days it was attacked by both British and French pirates, who sailed all the way up the San Juan River and across Lake Nicaragua in search of plunder. It was burnt again by Walker's forces in 1856 and, more recently, it was damaged in the fighting between the Sandinistas and Somoza's forces.

Places to Stay

There are very few places to stay in Granada, but two cheapies which have been recommended are the *Pensión Cabrera*, Calle Calzada 308, (the street which goes from the Cathedral down to the lake), which is pleasant and clean and costs US$4.30 a double without own bathroom and US$4.30 per person in a room with own shower; and the *Pensión Vargas* which costs US$2.50 per person, but the management can be pretty surly.

There are very few places in Granada to eat in the evenings. Try to pick up a meal before 4 pm in the afternoon.

Managua

Capital of the country since 1858, Managua has had a sad history. It has been destroyed twice by devastating earthquakes – in 1931 and 1972 – and after the last one, the city centre was more or less abandoned except for a number of

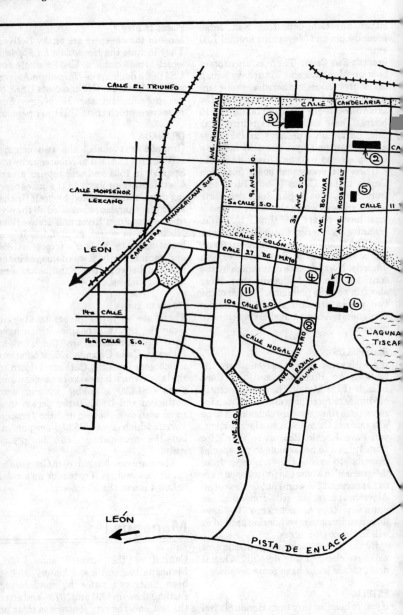

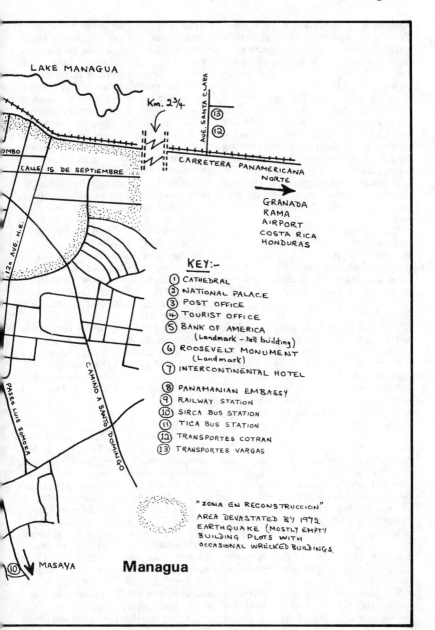

LAKE MANAGUA

Km. 2¾

AVE. SANTA CLARA

⑬
⑫

CARRETERA PANAMERICANA
NORTE

GRANADA
RAMA
AIRPORT
COSTA RICA
HONDURAS

OMBO

CALLE 15 DE SEPTIEMBRE

12a AVE. N.E.

CAMINO A SANTO DOMINGO

PASEO LUIS SOMOZA

⑩ ➘ MASAYA

KEY:-
① CATHEDRAL
② NATIONAL PALACE
③ POST OFFICE
④ TOURIST OFFICE
⑤ BANK OF AMERICA
    (Landmark - tall building)
⑥ ROOSEVELT MONUMENT
    (Landmark)
⑦ INTERCONTINENTAL HOTEL

⑧ PANAMANIAN EMBASSY
⑨ RAILWAY STATION
⑩ SIRCA BUS STATION
⑪ TICA BUS STATION
⑫ TRANSPORTES COTRAN
⑬ TRANSPORTES VARGAS

"ZONA EN RECONSTRUCCION"
AREA DEVASTATED BY 1972
EARTHQUAKE (MOSTLY EMPTY
BUILDING PLOTS WITH
OCCASIONAL WRECKED BUILDINGS.

Managua

large buildings which survived the quake. The city was rebuilt as a series of satellite towns spread over the surrounding hills, which gives it a very strange but pleasant feel, with large areas of unplanned parkland right in the centre.

On the other hand, things are very spread out and it can take a long time to get from one place to the next. Make sure you get hold of a map of the city from the tourist office if you're planning on staying for a few stays or want to get something done, otherwise it's easy to get lost. The new Sandinista government is planning on rebuilding the centre so things may change quite radically over the next few years.

You'll probably enjoy Managua a lot and may find yourself staying longer than you thought. It's full of an amazing number of journalists, left-wingers who come to support the Sandinista government, and curious travellers.

Information

The tourist office is in the Parque L A Velasquez near the Bank of America. It's open from 9 am to 5 pm. They have good maps of Managua and of Nicaragua for sale for US$2.

The Costa Rican embassy is at Centro Comercial, Camino Oriente. To get there from the centre of Managua take bus No 117 or 119.

Places to Stay

Most of the cheap places where travellers stay are around the former *TICA* bus terminal which is close to the Intercontinental Hotel on the top side of the city centre. Most of these will probably be full so if you want any chance of getting a room you'll have to be there first thing in the morning. Most hotels in Managua have to be paid for in cash dollars though there are still a few places where you can pay in córdobas.

For many years the most popular place has been the *Pensión Mesolito*, one block on the left-hand side from the former

TICA bus terminal towards the Intercontinental. It costs US$2/$3 a single/ double. There's no sign for the place but it's on the corner. It's clean and friendly but no longer serves meals and one traveller reported recently that 'the only hot part of the shower is when you touch the live wires dangling from the ceiling.'

Similar is the *Casa de Huespedes Santos*, a pleasant wooden house with basic facilities at US$2 to $3 per person; the *Pension Dorado*, another wooden house which is basic but clean and costs US$3 to $4 per person; the *Pension Mesa*, which costs US$3 per person; and the *El Almendra Hospedaje* (Almond Tree Lodge, one block from the former *TICA* bus terminal), which costs US$2/$3 a single/double.

Other cheap places include the *El Colibri* near the Cine Dorado which has good rooms with own shower and toilet; the *Hotel Royal*, near the centre; and the *Hotel Chapito*. These last two can be paid for in córdobas.

If you'd like to stay with a family, ask for Norma García, whose house is one block south of the *TICA* bus terminal and then one block west. The family is very friendly and the accommodation they provide is as good and cheap as you'll find anywhere.

Places to Eat

There are several small, cheap cafés on the same street as the former *TICA* bus terminal which offer breakfasts and dinner (rice, beans, *carne asada*, salad and plantain) at very reasonable prices. None of them are particularly special.

Quite a few travellers take advantage of the buffet breakfasts and lunches (12 noon to 3 pm) at the *Intercontinental Hotel* where you can eat as much as you want for what amounts to less than US$1 at the street rate of exchange. Nearby is the *Green House* (because that's what colour it is) which is popular and offers good beans, rice and egg.

For first class seafood go to the *Costa*

Brava, 200 metres south of the Cine Eldorado. Two popular meeting places for travellers are the *Café Libro La Yerba Buena* (snacks, coffee, beer) and the *Comedor Sara*. For late night get-togethers try the *Antojitos Restaurant*. This is an up-market restaurant but a good place for late drinks.

The *Grand Hotel Ruins* is also worth visiting. It houses a coffee bar, modern art gallery and an experimental theatre and dance group.

Getting Around

Buses between the city centre and the airport include Nos 104, 112 and 114. A taxi will cost about US$11.

To get to the Mercado Israel Lewitas (for buses to Rivas, León and Chinandega) take bus No 118 from the Intercontinental Hotel. To get to the Mercado Eduardo Contreras (for buses to Masaya and Granada) take bus No 109 from the same hotel.

AROUND MANAGUA

Managua is a convenient place from which to climb one or more of the volcanoes which dominate the city's skyline. The most accessible is **Volcan Santiago** in the Masaya National Park about 23 km from Managua. A road has been constructed right up to the crater; you can get a small group of people together and share a taxi. The volcano is double-crested, one half being dormant and the other still active. The views across Laka Managua to Momotombo are superb at any time of day, but the active part of the volcano is best seen at dawn or dusk when you can watch red-hot fissures open up in the lava plug and release clouds of steam and sulphurous gases. The national park is open Tuesday to Friday from 8.30 am to 4.30 pm and on Saturday and Sunday from 9 am to 5 pm. It's closed on Mondays. Bags can be left at the entrance lodge.

The other main volcano in the area is **Momotombo** at the western end of Lake Managua. You should only really consider climbing this volcano if you have suitable gear as the access road goes only halfway up the mountain. After that it's a strenuous three-hour trek to the top over rough terrain. A permit, from the Empresa Nacional de Luz y Fuerza in Managua, is needed to climb Momotombo because geothermal plants are being constructed on the slopes to tap the energy of the geysers. This permit is sometimes available from the police at León Viejo. The starting point for Momotombo is generally the village of La Paz Centro, about 60 km from Managua heading towards León.

MASAYA

Masaya is very close to Managua and visited by quite a few travellers. There is a good artisans market where you can find shoes, carved wooden objects, guitars, hats and bags. There's also a Centro de Artisans which is worth visiting (chess sets and hammocks are two of their products) but it tends to be expensive because it's quality stuff.

Places to Stay

The *Hospedaje Rex* is used by a lot of travellers but it's very poor value. It costs US$1.80 per person in rooms with two beds. If you don't fancy it then try the *Hospedaje Josephina* (no sign) opposite the train station which costs US$3.60 per room.

LEÓN

Along with Granada, León was one the two original Spanish settlements founded in Nicaragua by Hernández de Córdoba in 1524. It was actually first sited at León Viejo, 32 km from the present city at the foot of Momotombo, but the original city was destroyed by earthquake in 1609. Excavations are now in progress there.

León prides itself on being the intellectual centre of Nicaragua and has many schools and a university. It still retains a

Castillian atmosphere but it suffered greatly during the final struggle to oust Somoza. Few travellers, it seems, have been going there of late and information on the city is very sketchy.

Places to Stay

One of the best places is the *Hotel América*, 2a Avenida between Calles 12 Sur and Central (also known as Calle Rubén Dario). Rooms have their own toilet, shower and fan and are arranged around a leafy colonial courtyard. The management is very friendly and the rooms cost US$4.65 per person. If it's full then try the *Hotel Europa*, 4a Avenida Oriente and 3a Calle Norte. It's a very clean hotel and costs the same as the América.

RAMA

On the banks of the Río Escondido, Rama is where the road ends and further travel east can only be made by boat. It's quite an interesting little place and worth an overnight stay if you like watching the activity in a small jungle town. If you need to change money (travellers' cheques)

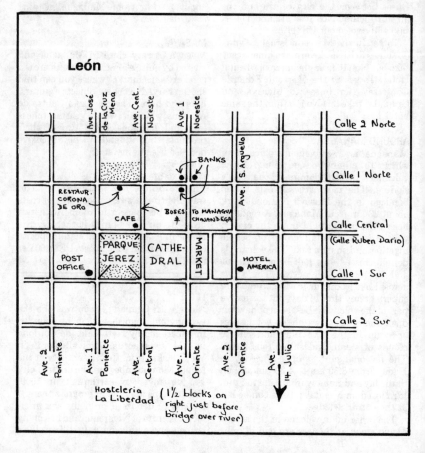

there is a branch of the Bank of Nicaragua.

Places to Stay

Almost all travellers stay at the *Hotel Amy* next to the Bluefields Express jetty. It's a big old hotel with basic facilities. The rooms contain a bed and table in an otherwise bare room with torn netting at the windows. Washing facilities are communal and frequently awash. Reasonably good meals are served downstairs in the big hall. Many local people go there in the evenings to talk or discuss business and drink beer or spirits.

Two other places which are cheaper than the Amy and just as good are the *Hotel Lee* and the *Hotel San José*. There are a few other cheap places in town but they're all in an advanced state of decrepitude and can't really be recommended.

SAN JUAN DEL SUR

San Juan del Sur is a pleasant fishing village on the Pacific coast (at least it's pleasant when it's not being attacked by the *contras*). There's a small but beautiful beach about three km north of town. It's well worth a visit if you have the time and if transport is available.

Places to Stay & Eat

There are two good places: the first is the *Hotel Estrella* which costs US$2.75/$5 a single/double; the other is the *Hospedaje Casa No 28* on the first street parallel to the one which runs along the beach. It's run by Edgar Masis Martinez who is very friendly. It has clean showers and toilets, you can use the cooking facilities and refrigerator and it's US$3.60 per person.

For a place to eat, try the fish restaurant along the beach – the garlic prawns are excellent.

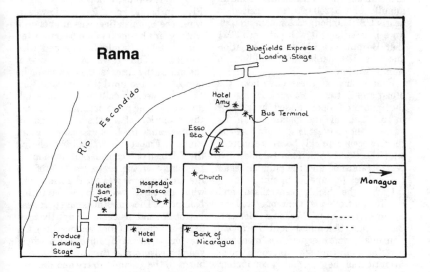

Panama

Although it was isolated geographically by the Darién jungle, Panama was a province of Colombia until 1903. In that year the Colombian Congress at Bogotá had refused to lease to the United States a strip of territory across the isthmus for the construction of what was to become the Panama Canal – a project deemed vital to US interests by President Roosevelt. In order to force the issue, an insurrection was engineered in Panama City and when Colombian troops were dispatched to suppress it, US warships were sent to stop them landing. An independent republic was proclaimed – immediately recognised by Washington – and a treaty signed with the new government whereby the US was granted partial sovereignty over a coast-to-coast corridor in return for US$10 million in gold and an annuity of US$250,000 (later raised to nearly US$2 million). Colombian protests were ignored and it was not until 1921 that Bogotá recognised the separation and the US paid US$25 million in 'compensation'.

Events such as these have been the bread and butter of Panama ever since the Spaniard Balboa crossed the isthmus in 1513 and saw the Pacific Ocean. Its value as the shortest land route between the two oceans quickly became apparent once the South American colonies had been established and the plunder began to flow back to imperial Spain.

Under the highly centralised and rigidly controlled system operated by Spain, certain ports – Veracruz (Mexico), Cartagena (Colombia) and Portobelo (Panama) – were designated as 'monopoly ports' and only through these could trans-Atlantic trade be legitimately conducted. The system was designed to maximise tax collection and prevent the development of local industries and trade between the various colonies as well as trade between the colonies and other European nations. It was to become one of the major sources of discontent among the *criollos* in the 18th and 19th centuries and eventually led to the break-up of the empire.

For the vast Viceroyalty of Peru – which then included Peru, Bolivia, Paraguay and Argentina – Portobelo was the designated 'monopoly port'. Once a year a convoy of galleons, accompanied by a naval escort, would set sail from Seville bringing European manufactures and taking back Peruvian gold, silver and agricultural products. These goods were initially collected at Callao, transported by sea to Panama City and then taken by mule train across the isthmus to Portobelo on the Caribbean coast. The more bulky goods such as cacao, quinine and vicuña wool were brought down the Chagres River in boats. For a few hectic weeks, while the Spanish fleet was at anchor, a whole year's business would be transacted and Portobelo would be crowded with merchants. Once it was over, because of the unhealthy climate, the port would be almost deserted until the next year.

All this wealth collected in one small and vulnerable place naturally attracted the attention of a constant stream of pirates and freebooters mainly from England, France and Holland who relieved the Spanish of a considerable amount of treasure over the centuries. One of the first on the scene was Sir Francis Drake who attacked twice, once capturing Nombre de Dios (another small port near Portobelo) and Cruces (a town on the road between Portobelo and Panama City). On that occasion the Spanish lost a whole year's treasure and the two towns were burnt to the ground. To try and prevent these attacks the Spanish built large and costly forts, some of which stand today, but they were only partially effective and certainly didn't deter Henry Morgan.

In 1671, Morgan took the fort of San Lorenzo at the mouth of the Chagres River, continued upstream and across to Panama City, which he razed completely. A month later he was back on the Caribbean coast accompanied by 200 mule-loads of treasure. Panama City was rebuilt on a new site and what remains of the old city (Panama Viejo) can still be visited a few km to the east of the present city. There were many more such forays, one of the more notable being the capture of Portobelo and San Lorenzo by Admiral Vernon in the 1730s when Spain and Britain were at war.

The vulnerability of Panama as a collection point eventually persuaded the Spanish to abandon the route and begin sailing around Cape Horn; so for a while Panama declined in importance. The buccaneers and foreign navies, on the other hand, were not the only factor which prevented the Spanish authorities from having things all their own way. Since European imports into the South American colonies had to take such a circuitous route to get to their destination, resulting in outrageously exaggerated prices and usually insufficient quantities, a lively contraband trade grew up around the fringe of the 'legitimate' trade. It's a tradition which survives to this day.

Panama's importance as the shortest land route between the two oceans came back into its own again in the late 1840s as a result of the Californian gold rush. At the time, the quickest – and often the safest – route between the eastern US seaboard and the Pacific coast was via Central America, and thousands of adventurers made the overland trek either through the Panamanian jungles or across Nicaragua to the Pacific coast and from there by sea to California. The gold rush prompted the construction of the first railway across the isthmus from

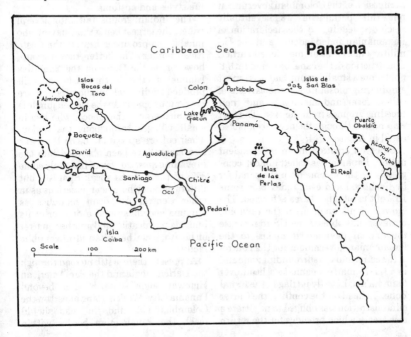

Colón to Panama City. The line took four years to build and cost the lives of many thousands of workers, mainly through yellow fever, only to be abandoned following the opening of the first trans-continental railway across the USA. Events were soon to revolve around the construction of a canal.

As early as the 16th century the Spanish had considered the possibility of constructing a canal across the isthmus but it was not until the 1880s that a concerted effort was made to make it a reality. The first attempt was made by Ferdinand de Lesseps following his successful completion of the Suez Canal. A company was formed in 1882 with capital of US$100 million and work went ahead for the next 11 years only to be abandoned after thousands of workers had died of yellow fever and other diseases. A few years later, the US government took up the project with the permission of the Colombian government but this permission was eventually rescinded leading to the declaration of Panamanian independence and the US military intervention mentioned earlier. Construction of the canal began again but not before a small fortune had been spent eliminating mosquitoes – the carriers of yellow fever and malaria – and their breeding grounds from the area. The first ship passed through the newly-completed canal in August 1914.

Since its creation as an independent nation, Panama has relied almost completely on the income from the canal for its livelihood and even today only some 16% of the total land area is farmed. The growth of nationalism in the republic, however, has obliged the US to increase the annual payment it makes to the Panamanian government for the control of the canal and the surrounding zone and in 1977-78 matters came to a head over Panama's right to fly its flag in the Canal Zone. To head off the conflict, the Carter administration was obliged to negotiate a new treaty which provides for the return of the Canal Zone to Panamanian sovereignty by the year 2000. Despite considerable opposition from the Senate and a lot of sabre-rattling among the US military establishment, it was ratified by a slim majority.

The population of Panama – around 1½ million – is quite a hotch-potch of racial mixes. Most are *mestizos* but there are sizeable communities of black people along the Caribbean coast and Indians in the provinces closest to Colombia and Costa Rica as well as the San Blas archipelago. There are also minorities of Asians and *blancos* of European and North American origin. The black people are descended from British West Indians brought in to construct the Colón-Panama City railway in the mid-19th century and later for the canal. As in similar communities in Costa Rica, Nicaragua, Honduras and Belize, they still speak English and retain their own life styles and customs.

The Indian groups fall into several tribes, the largest being the Guaymí who inhabit the provinces nearest the Costa Rican border. The better known group, however, is the Cuna on the San Blas Islands off the north coast who still produce traditional handicrafts and are semi-autonomous. In the Darién jungle is the third group, the Chocó, who live in small villages throughout the region. Their culture appears to be on the wane and many have been absorbed into the prevailing *mestizo* way of life. Only some 35% of the Indians speak Spanish, but illiteracy is nowhere near as serious as in other Central American republics as Panama spends around a quarter of its budget on education and another quarter on health, social benefits and other public facilities.

At present there is still no road through the Darién jungle and the Pan American Highway ends some 80 km beyond Panama City. Work is going ahead on the Colombian side and the road should reach the Panamanian border within about three years. Little is happening on the Panamanian side, however, and there's a good deal of discussion going on about the environmental issues and the increased ease with which plant and cattle diseases might spread from South America should the road be completed. It is quite possible that it will never be finished.

VISAS

Required by all except nationals of West Germany, Spain, Switzerland and the UK and holders of Tourist Cards. The fee for a visa is US$10 (free to Dutch nationals). Tourist Cards, which cost US$2 and are valid for a 30-day stay (extendable to 90 days), can be issued to all nationals except those from communist countries, Chile, El Salvador, Guatemala, India, Jamaica, Nicaragua, Pakistan, South Africa and Sri Lanka. To avoid delays at the border, get hold of one beforehand from an airline office, international bus office or consulate.

You must have an onward ticket before you will be allowed into Panama but this isn't always as simple as it sounds. If you're coming overland from Costa Rica a return bus ticket is sufficient (TICA bus will, in fact, only sell you a one-way ticket to Panama if you have a suitable airline ticket out). The cheapest of these bus tickets is a David-San José ticket (TICA or Tracopa) rather than a Panama City-San José ticket (US$16). In theory, the return half of these tickets is refundable, but in practice, they are only refundable at the office of issue and then usually only with 30 days notice and subject to a cancellation fee of 15%. This means that you can kiss goodbye to up to US$16 unless you're returning to Panama. There is, of course, the off-chance that you might find a traveller in South America who will buy it from you.

If you're flying into Panama then the situation is more complicated. Not only will immigration officials *not* accept a TICA bus ticket to Costa Rica, but they won't accept an airline ticket to Colombia either. The only one they will accept is one to your country of origin though it doesn't have to be from Panama (one from Mexico to your country of origin would be acceptable, for instance). The most extreme example was from an Australian who had a TICA bus ticket to Costa Rica, an airline ticket from Panama to Colombia and cash in excess of US$1000 and it still wasn't good enough! He was tidily dressed as was his companion but they were both refused.

You can expect baggage and body searches on arrival in Panama.

MONEY

The unit of currency is the US dollar known in Panama as the Balboa. Panama prints no paper currency of its own. It does mint its own coins but these are exactly the same as US coins except for the face design. Banking hours are Monday-Friday from 8 am to 1 pm.

Not all banks will change travellers' cheques. The Chase Manhattan Bank will change them but charges US$0.65 commission on *each* cheque.

The airport departure tax for international flights is US$15 and there is a US$4 government tax on airline tickets bought in the country.

Panama is an expensive country so if you're on a tight budget plan on spending as little time there as possible.

GETTING THERE
To/From Costa Rica

TICA bus (terminal at Hotel Ideal, ground floor, Panama City; and at Calle K, David) have daily buses from Panama City to San José, Costa Rica. They have suspended their services further north to Nicaragua, Honduras, El Salvador and Guatemala. Buses depart at 7 am, 11 am, 8 and 10 pm and the journey time on the first leg to San José takes between 15 and 18 hours depending on the delays at the border. The fare is US$16. *Sirca* also runs buses to San José and Managua from

Panama City and are somewhat cheaper than *TICA*. It's advisable to book in advance on any of these bus lines as there's a heavy demand for tickets.

You can travel between Panama City and San José somewhat cheaper by making the journey in stages. There are two express buses daily between Panama and David which take 5½ hours and 10 ordinary buses per day which take longer. There are frequent minibuses between David and the border which cost US$1.25.

To/From South America

You must have an onward ticket to get into Colombia whether you fly, go by boat, or go overland through the Darién. Because of this requirement, no airline company in Panama (or Costa Rica) will sell you a one-way ticket to that country unless you already have an onward ticket or are willing to buy one (if you're refused entry they have to fly you back at their own expense). Not only that, but if you need a visa for Colombia they won't give you one unless you first produce an onward ticket. Venezuela also demands an onward ticket.

The only way of getting around this is to fly to Ecuador or Peru.

Air

Most travellers choose this method of getting to South America as it's probably just as cheap as going overland through the Darién Gap (*pero sin adventura!*) as well as being quick and convenient. Also most airlines go via the beautiful and partially duty-free island of San Andrés so you can stop off at no extra charge. *SAM* (Sociedad Aeronautica de Medellín) and *COPA* (Compañia Panameña de Aviacion) both have flights to Cartagena, Barranquilla and Medellín (the first two via San Andrés) and generally offer the cheapest flights to these places and elsewhere in the region. *SAHSA* are also worth checking out.

Don't forget that *COPA* is not a member of IATA, to which most airlines belong, so its tickets are not transferable to another airline belonging to that association. This is really no problem since *COPA* has offices in Cartagena, Barranquilla and Medellín where refunds are available on the return halves of tickets but check when you buy one of their tickets that there are no special conditions attached to getting a refund. Refunds are best applied for in Barranquilla because if you apply in Cartagena it has to be referred to Barranquilla anyway. The office in Cartagena is at Calle Santos de Piedra 3466 near the Plaza Bolívar. Refunds take up to four days and you only get the money in pesos. At present, a Panama City-Medellín ticket with *SAM* or *COPA* costs about US$190 return. The flight takes about 45 minutes. Other airlines may offer comparable prices so it's a good idea to do some foot-work before you buy a ticket.

Some examples of present prices with *COPA* are: Panama City-Cartagena (US$98 one-way plus US$4 tax, and US$196 return plus US$8 tax); Panama City-Quito (US$212 plus US$9 tax one-way).

Flights to South American cities from Costa Rica are only marginally more expensive than those from Panama City and if you are trying to conserve as much money as possible there are definite advantages in flying from Costa Rica rather than Panama. The first is the existence of the student organisation *OTEC* in San José (see the Costa Rica section for details) which offers some excellent deals on cheap tickets. There's no such organisation in Panama. The second consideration is that you need an onward ticket to get into Panama in the first place. Unless you will be returning to Panama on the way back, the return half of your bus ticket (which is what you will probably have as an acceptable onward ticket) will be a waste of money since, in practice, they're not refundable. This means you will lose up to US$16. The third consideration is the high cost of living in Panama. The longer you spend looking for a ticket, the more you will spend.

The international airport in Panama City is at Tocumen, about 27 km from the city. The cheapest way to get there is by bus marked 'Tocumen' from the Plaza 5 de Mayo. They depart every 15 minutes, cost US$0.50 and take about one hour. A taxi there will cost US$14 if there are one or two of you and up to US$20 if there are four of you. Remember that the departure tax for international flights is US$15.

If you don't want to fly direct to Colombia and would like to go at least part of the way through the Darién Gap, there are internal flights to Puerto Obaldía near the Colombian border with *COPA* and *ADSA* and flights to the San Blas Islands off the north coast with *Transportes Aeros Interioranos*. These flights depart from the domestic airport at La Paitilla near Panama City. If you're heading north from Colombia via the Darién Gap these flights are a useful alternative if you can't find a boat between those places and Colón. For further details enquire at the airline offices in Panama City.

GETTING AROUND
Bus
Panama City-David Buses every hour by *Transportes Unidos Transchiri* (terminal on Plaza Herrera) which cost US$10.60 and take five to six hours.

David-Santiago Regular buses which cost US$6 and take about two hours.

Panama City-Colón This is the bus you need to take if you want to watch the ships pass through the Gatún and Miraflores locks on the Panama Canal. The *Paraiso Express* departs every hour in either direction (terminal on Plaza 5 de Mayo in Panama City). The fare is 35c each way.

Panama City-Chepo This is the first leg of the journey into Darién. There are regular buses costing US$1.20.

Other buses are included under the relevant city sections.

Train
The only railway likely to be of interest is the line between Panama City and Colón which runs more or less parallel to the canal and offers excellent views of Gatún Lake. There are several trains daily in either direction at 5, 6.45 and 9.50 am and 3.20 and 5.35 pm (Monday to Friday), and 8.30 am, 12.35, 5.50 and 10.50 pm (Saturday and Sunday) from Panama City; and at 4.50, 6.55 and 9.40 am and 3.35 and 5.25 pm (Monday to Friday), and 6.40 and 10.45 am, 4 and 9 pm (weekends) from Colón. Return fares are US$2.50 in 2nd class and US$4 in 1st class (air-con); one-way costs US$1.25 in 2nd class. The trip takes 1½ hours.

Overland through the Darién Gap

There are basically two ways through the Darién Gap: the first skirts the northern coast via the San Blas Islands and Puerto Obaldía making use of boat services and involves the minimum of walking, while the second heads off through the jungle from Yaviza to the Río Atrato and involves the maximum amount of walking. Either of these routes can be done in as little as eight days but it's probably safer to assume it might take up to two weeks. Remember that regardless of whether you're heading north or south, both Panama and Colombia demand onward tickets, so get them – and any visas necessary – fixed up before you set off. You may be able to get away with not having an onward ticket into Colombia at Turbo as long as you have an impressive collection of travellers' cheques.

Take dried food with you especially on the jungle route. There are very few places where you can buy food.

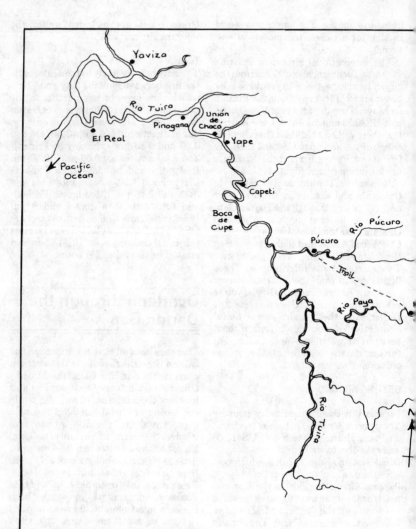

The Darien Gap Trail

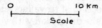

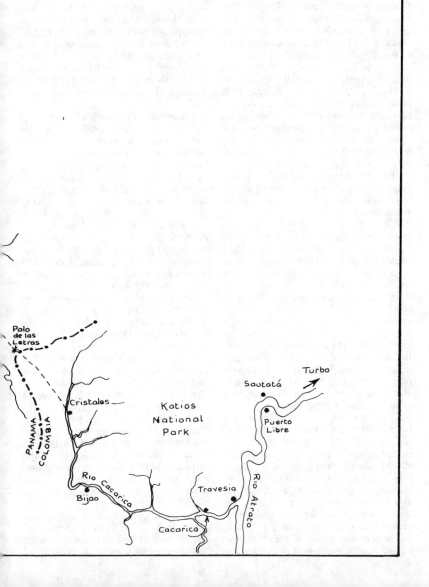

Along the northern coast

Thanks to Carlton Lee (USA) for providing us with information on this route. The route is: Colón-San Blas Islands-Puerto Obaldía-Acandí-Titumane-Turbo. The first leg of the journey involves finding a cargo boat which is going to Puerto Obaldía via the San Blas Islands from Colón. They're not that difficult to find as long as you're willing to pay their price – usually around US$25 including meals. Try *Guardia Nacional* cargo ships which often take a few passengers. The journey takes about three days and two nights and often involves an overnight stop at a Cuna village. Make your own sleeping arrangements on the deck (a hammock is very useful). It's an interesting trip and the boat is rarely out of sight of land. The only alternative is to fly but the flights are often booked up a long way in advance in either direction.

Puerto Obaldía is a small, pleasant tropical way-station for traffic between Colombia and Panama. It has good beaches, palms and blue sea and if you're on a tight budget you can sleep on the beach south of the town, though there are a few hotels if you'd prefer. If heading south you need to check with the immigration inspector there for an exit stamp or, if you're heading north, an entry stamp. The immigration inspector isn't noted for his laxity or friendliness so make sure you have all the necessary papers, visas and onward tickets. He'll also want to see how much money you have if you're entering Panama.

There are occasional launches and boats from Puerto Obaldía to Acandí in Colombia but they're infrequent and quite expensive. It's best to walk. This should take the best part of a day if the trail is in good shape and you don't have too much luggage. It's a well-defined trail and you shouldn't get lost – usually the largest path through the grasslands or the only cut through the jungle. If in doubt, ask someone en route. It nearly always follows an east-south-east direction. The first part of the trail goes through hilly, thick, sweltering jungle which is fairly steep in some places. This gives way to pleasant pasture land (where it's possible to buy dairy products from farmhouses along the way) and finally goes back down into the jungle before reaching Acandí. The latter part of the trail is nearly always very muddy as it's swampland and has often been churned up by the passage of horses (it's an idea to wear a pair of old sneakers which you can throw away at the end).

Acandí is a fair-sized village with a church, two or three hotels, a few cafés and several very small *tiendas* selling mostly bottled and canned goods of limited variety and quantity. It's a peaceful, interesting place where you can watch boats being made by hand. From Acandí there are a number of daily launches to Turbo via Titumane which cost about about US$11. Most of them leave by mid-morning as strong winds whip up the waters of the Gulf of Urubá in the afternoon. All the same, it's a pretty rough journey and you should expect to get soaked through unless you have waterproof clothing. Wrap up anything you want to keep dry in plastic and if possible, try to get one of the seats in the rear of the boat. The journey takes about four hours.

Turbo is a small port in the Gulf of Urubá for fishing boats and small time traders though otherwise it's uninteresting. There's a good variety of fresh and canned foods available, so if you're heading north then this is a good place to stock up. Whether you're heading north or south, you need to call at the Policia Distrito Especial two blocks down from the harbour to obtain an exit or entry stamp (there is no DAS office here). It's very informal and quick as long as your papers are in order.

The bank in Turbo may not change either cash US dollars or travellers' cheques so make sure you bring enough Colombian pesos with you to take care of expenses from Puerto Obaldía to either Medellín or Cartagena. There are daily buses from Turbo to Cartagena and Medellín. To Medellín they cost US$7.75 and take 14 hours. There is no Panamanian Consulate in Turbo so, if heading north, get your Tourist Card or visa elsewhere.

The whole journey should take between 10 and 12 days but could take longer if you have to wait around for boats between Puerto Obaldía and Colón. It shouldn't cost more than US$75 excluding the cost of any hotels you stay in en route. The only place you're likely to meet other travellers along the way is at Turbo.

Through the Jungle

Much of the current information about this trail comes to you from Lilian Wordell (Ireland) who set off from Panama City with seven other people intent on getting to Turbo and ended up there with just one other companion! It took them eight days in all (one day by bus, four by foot, one by canoe, one by a combination of three different boats and one day's rest) and cost US$83 in total which included bus, boats, accommodation and food.

This trip should only be undertaken in the 'dry' season (between December and March or possibly in July and August if little rain has fallen) and never without preparation. The rest of the time the trails are almost impossibly waterlogged and the rivers are raging torrents full of broken trees and the like. On the other hand, towards the end of the 'dry' season rivers get low and it's often difficult to find boats. Ideally you need camping gear and decent hiking boots but otherwise keep your baggage to a minimum. (Lilian did it entirely in a pair of old rubber thongs, with a small stove for making tea and soup, and no tent.) You might also, like Lilian make it in eight days but it's best to plan for a longer trek. A tent isn't necessary according to quite a few travellers who have done the trek. What is necessary is a light pack. The

total cost won't be much less than flying from Panama to Colombia but the sense of achievement will be incomparable.

The starting point for the trek is Yaviza or El Real which you can get to from Panama City either by plane or banana boat. The latter depart from the Muelle Fiscal, cost about US$10 and take between 12 and 36 hours to do the trip. There's no fixed schedule for these boats but, if possible, try to get a passage on the *Malagro* which is the largest and most comfortable. Simple meals are provided on board.

If you can't find a boat to Yaviza or El Real then get a boat to Canglun (they leave Panama daily at 8 am, cost US$11 and take about eight hours). Stay at the Evangelist Church in Canglun (about US$0.20 each). From Canglun there are minibuses to Yaviza (26 km) for about US$1. Although the Pan American Highway has been completed as far as Yaviza it has not been officially opened so there are no buses. Hitching along it is almost impossible.

If you end up at Yaviza then you first have to trek to Pinogana on the Río Tuira which will take about a day. To get there, first cross the river by canoe (10 cents) and then walk the 1½ hours to Pinogana. Wade through the river there and then walk three to four hours along a jeep track to Aruza. There are plenty of friendly Choco Indians along the way. Cross the river at Aruza by wading through it again and then walk about 45 minutes to Unión de Choco.

It may be more convenient, however, to get to El Real by boat from Panama City though these are unreliable. The port is about five km away from the town itself so you first have to get to the Mercadero where you're most likely to pick up a boat going to Boca de Cupe. The best place to enquire about these is the general store run by a man called Don Rico. Most of his provisions arrive by boat so he's generally well clued-up about what's going on. Avoid staying at Don Rico's as he charges

US$10 a double. His food is also expensive. You can camp either at the port or at the Mercadero. Prices on the boats are negotiable – as are all boat trips along this trail – but the journey to Boca de Cupe takes about four hours.

If you find yourself at Unión de Choco, take the same side of the river and head for Yape and Capeti and finally to Boca de Cupe, which will take about five hours. It's a very pleasant walk. Cross the river to Boca at the end for 10 cents.

Boca de Cupe is the last town of any size you'll see until you're near the end of the trail. It is there you must get your exit stamp from Don Antonio who runs a shop alongside the river (no problems). Just ask, everyone knows him. For a place to stay and a meal, ask for Maria whose house is down river just before you get to the church. The accommodation there is very primitive and dirty and you'll be charged US$1 per person plus US$1 for supper. She's also a bit crazy and will constantly change her mind about the prices of things.

From Boca de Cupe you must find a boat going to Púcuro which is the first Cuna village you encounter. You may have to wait two or three days for a boat but, once found, it's only a five or six hour trip to Púcuro. If you can't find a boat, ask Maria if her son can help.

When the river is high you'll land right at the village but at other times it's about half an hour's walk to Púcuro. Ask someone to direct you to the village chief – he speaks Spanish and is very friendly – and enquire where you can stay for the night. He may let you sleep in the meeting hall for US$1 each (with all the village gawping at you), but there are other possibilities. If you want to keep moving, however, ask someone where the trail to Paya starts.

The 18 km walk to Paya, the next village, can be done in a day and involves four river crossings, all of them fordable. You need to look hard for the trail after the third crossing. There are good camping sites just before the third crossing and just after the last. Guides can be hired in Púcuro for this section of the trail for about US$10. The walk should take you about six hours. When you get to Paya you will probably meet the chief's son, Alberto, who will have you taken either to the barracks about two km away where you can stay for the night and buy cheap meals, or to the house of any gringo who is staying there on a study programme. Some travellers have also been offered (free) accommodation on his floor.

Paya was once the site of the Cuna 'university' to which Cunas from all over the area came to study the traditional arts of magic, medicine and history. It fell on hard times about 100 years ago as the white man's technology and diseases gradually penetrated the area but it's still a very interesting place. Be discreet with a camera if you have one and ask permission before you take photographs. In Paya there's a foot-and-mouth disease control station where, if you're coming up from Colombia, your baggage will be inspected and anything made of leather – or even vaguely resembling leather – will be dipped in mild antiseptic to kill any pathogens.

The next part of the trail to Cristales via Palo de las Letras (the border marker between Panama and Colombia) is the most difficult and usually takes one to two days though you can do it in 10 hours under the right conditions. It's also the part where you're most likely to get lost so if in doubt, take a guide. Guides will charge about US$7 per person per day (that's US$14 per day because they'll charge you for the time it takes them to get back to the starting point, naturally!).

The first part of the trail to Palo de las Letras is uphill and well-marked; a British Army expedition went through there in 1972 and cut a trail which is still about three metres wide. Local Indians use it constantly so you'll have no difficulty following it. From the border marker it's downhill about 30 km to

Cristales and there are several river crossings involved where the trail often becomes indistinct or confusing. After the last crossing you come into cultivated areas and must keep to the left whenever the trail forks. Quite a few travellers, near the end of this leg of the journey, had adventures – though some would call them freak-outs – when they got lost at night and had to wade down the river for an hour to Cristales.

Cristales is the next stop but you're advised to carry on another half hour downstream to the National Park HQ where bed and board is available at very reasonable rates – the Katios National Park is across the river. The staff at the HQ are very friendly and helpful. They may let you sleep on the porch free of charge.

The last part of the trip from Cristales to Turbo is by a combination of motorised dug-out and banana boats which shouldn't cost more than US$20 in total. If the park workers are going for supplies in Turbo then it can be done in one haul but if not, then you'll first have to find a boat to Bijao and then, possibly, another to Travesia on the Rio Atrato. A motor dug-out from Cristales to Bijao will cost about US$10 (a rip-off but what can you do about it?) and take 2½ hours. The best person to ask about boats in Bijao is the store owner. You may have to wait a few days before a boat turns up. Bijao to Travesia may cost you US$10 in a motor dug-out and take about three hours. There is a shop in Travesia with expensive food, soft drinks and beer.

Once at Travesia you'll have no difficulty finding transport to Turbo. The *Lancha* to Turbo will cost about US$7.25 (cheaper to locals) and should take about 10 hours but it may stop en route and wait for calmer weather conditions, so assume it's going to take longer. Don't forget to visit the Policia Distrito Especial, two blocks down from the harbour in Turbo, for your Colombian entry stamp. Lilian didn't have an onward ticket but was let in without fuss anyway. Remember the bank there may not change either cash US dollars or travellers' cheques so bring enough Colombian currency with you to get you as far as Cartagena or Medellín. There are daily buses to both these places from Turbo.

For somewhere to stay in Turbo try the *Residencias El Viajero* which is good and clean with pleasant staff and costs US$2.20/$3.70 a single/double.

If you decide to take this route through the Daríen Gap then we strongly recommend you take with you a copy of *Backpacking in Mexico & Central America* by Hilary & George Bradt.

COLÓN

Colón is Panama's second largest city with some of Latin America's worst slums. It's a hustler's mecca and muggings are common so keep valuables out of sight and don't carry bags. It has a duty-free section (Zona Libre) like Panama City but the prices of goods are generally higher than the equivalent duty-free prices in the USA.

Most travellers only come to Colón en route to somewhere else. There are supposed to be boats to San Andrés island and connections from there to mainland Colombia but we haven't heard of any travellers who have found one for over four years. There are also supposed to be irregular contraband boats to Barranquilla from Dock 3 at the end of Calle 5 which cost US$25 and take about three days but the captains are, naturally, reluctant to take passengers. On the other hand, if you've decided to get to Colombia along the northern coast, boats going to Puerto Obaldía, via the San Blas Islands, leave from the Fox River Dock.

One place, 48 km north-east of Colón, that is worth visiting is the old port and Spanish garrison town of Portobelo, with its three large stone forts. It was from there that a flotilla of galleons used to sail for Spain once a year, loaded with

Peruvian gold, silver and other products. A festival is held on 21 October when the statue of the Black Christ is carried through the streets and there is feasting and dancing till dawn. There are frequent buses from Colón which depart from Calle 11.

Another excursion which can be made from Colón is to the San Blas Islands off the north coast about half way to Puerto Obaldía. They are inhabited by the Cuna Indians who run the islands on a semi-autonomous basis. It's an interesting place but accommodation tends to be very expensive and you'll even be charged a fee for photographs. Probably the best way to see something of them, if you're on a tight budget, is en route to Puerto Obaldía on the northern coast route to Colombia. Further information can be had from *SASA*, the airline which serves the islands.

Places to Stay

Colón is not a good place to stay, but if you have to, then try the *Pensión Acropolis* or the *Pensión Andros Annexo*, both of which are clean, comfortable and safe.

You can get a very good meal at the *Salty Restaurant* on the main street near the post office.

DAVID

David is the first main Panamanian town you come to after leaving Costa Rica. It's a pleasant combination of colonial and modern with a population of some 45,000. The main reason you would stop there would be to visit the mountain village of **Boquete** and the nearby extinct volcano of Barú which offers excellent hiking possibilities.

Places to Stay

The best places are the *Pensión Costa*

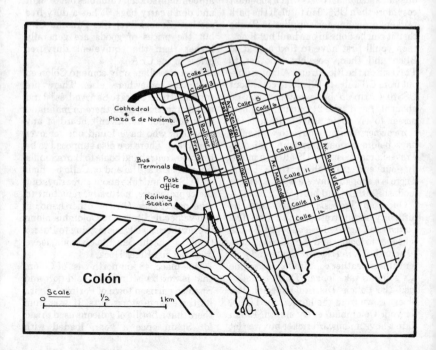

Colón

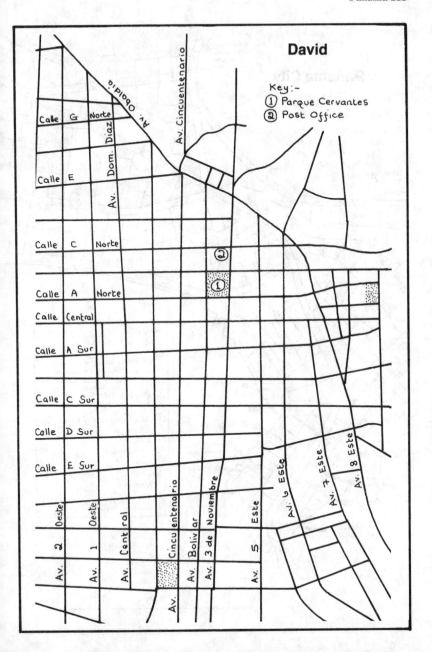

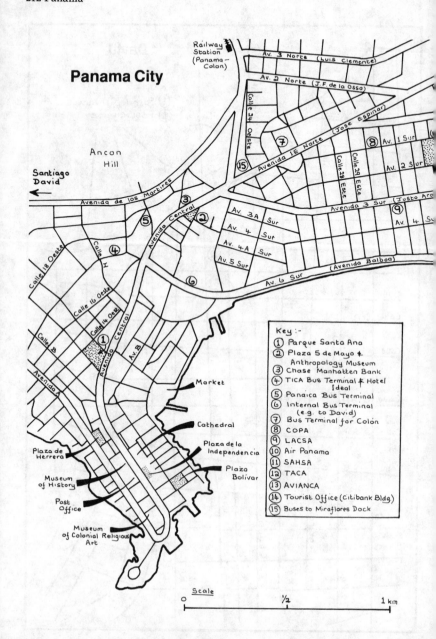

Panama City

Key:-
1. Parque Santa Ana
2. Plaza 5 de Mayo & Anthropology Museum
3. Chase Manhattan Bank
4. TICA Bus Terminal & Hotel Ideal
5. Panaica Bus Terminal
6. Internal Bus Terminal (e.g. to David)
7. Bus Terminal for Colón
8. COPA
9. LACSA
10. Air Panama
11. SAHSA
12. TACA
13. AVIANCA
14. Tourist Office (Citibank Bldg.)
15. Buses to Miraflores Dock

Railway Station (Panama–Colon)

Ancon Hill

Santiago David ←

Av. 3 Norte (Luis Clemente)
Av. 2 Norte (J.F. de la Ossa)
Calle 34 Oeste
(Jose Espinar)
Avenida 1E Norte
Calle 38 Este
Calle 39 Este
Av. 1 Sur
Av. 2 Sur
Avenida de los Martires
Avenida 3 Sur (Justo Aro)
Av. 3A Sur
Av. 4 Sur
Av. 4A Sur
Av. 5 Sur
Av. 4 Sur
Avenida Central
Av. 6 Sur (Avenida Balboa)

Calle 18 Oeste
Calle H
Calle 16 Oeste
Calle 14 Oeste
Calle B
Avenida Central
Av. B
Avenida A

Market
Cathedral
Plaza de la Independencia
Plaza Bolívar
Plaza de Herrera
Museum of History
Post Office
Museum of Colonial Religious Art

Scale
0   ½   1 km

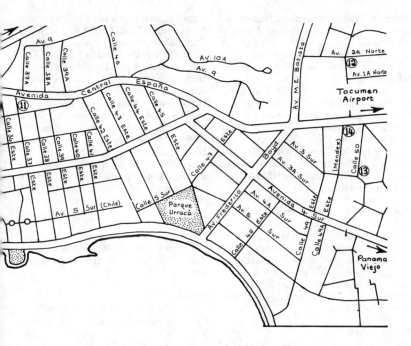

Rica, near the TICA bus terminal, which costs US$2.50 per person; and the *Pensión Chiriqui*, Avenida 4 Este (west of Calle Central), which is clean but noisy and costs US$4.50/$6 a single/double. There are cheap places to eat around the bus station.

BOQUETE
The main place of interest around David is the village of Boquete, set in beautiful forested mountain country which contains a great variety of wildlife. It has a cool climate the year round. Flower gardens and orange groves as well as coffee plantations are features of the area.

Places to Stay
The best places are the *Pensión Marilos* which is very clean, has its own excellent restaurant and costs US$5.50 a double; and the *Pensión Virginia* which has a range of rooms, is also very clean and friendly and has its own good, cheap restaurant. English is spoken in both pensiones. There is a small bank in the plaza which will change travellers' cheques.

Panama City

The capital of the republic with a population approaching half a million, Panama City is a brash combination of colonial Spain, modern North American pretension, glittering consumerism and some of the most squalid slums on the continent. In keeping with its position as a crossroads of the world, it contains elements of just about every race on the face of the globe. The present city was founded in 1673 after the buccaneer,

Henry Morgan, captured and burned the original city, known today as Panama Viejo. It's an expensive place so if you're on a tight budget, don't stay too long.

Information

The tourist office (tel 64 5203) is in the Citibank Building (5th floor), Avenida Central España on the corner of Calle 49a Mendez opposite the Hilton-Panama Hotel, Panama City. They have free maps of Panama City but better ones can be found at the British Consulate, Chase Manhattan Bank Building (5th floor), Via España 120.

American Express are represented at Boyal Bros Inc, Avenida de los Martires (tel 62 0300).

If you're thinking of trekking through the Darién Gap then a good place to buy supplies (jungle boots, hammocks, mosquito nets, etc) is the Army & Navy Store just off Plaza 5 de Mayo.

The COPA office is at Avenida 3 Sur and Calle 39 Este.

Things to See

The **Natural History Museum**, Avenida Cuba between Calles 29 and 30, is small but interesting and worth a visit. Entry costs 25c. The **National Anthropology and Archaeology Museum**, Plaza 4 de Mayo, has some excellent sections on all the various ethnic groups in Panama. Entry costs 50c. Both museums are open daily from 9 am to 12 noon and from 3 to 6 pm daily except Sundays.

Places to Stay

Many people stay at the *Hotel Ideal* which is above the *TICA* bus terminal but it's certainly not the cheapest with rooms going for US$12 a single even in the annexe.

Cheaper places include the *Pensión Herrera*, Plaza Herrera close to Calle 9a and Avenida Central, which is clean but noisy and costs US$8 a double and has its own good restaurant downstairs; the *Pensión Foyo*, Calle 6 near the Plaza

Catedral, which is clean and friendly with fans and costs US$5.50/$7 a single/double (but make sure you get a room away from the TV!); and the *Pensión Panama*, Call 6 No 8-40 opposite the Foyo, which is tatty and noisy, but clean and friendly and costs US$4/$6/$11 a single/double/triple (two double beds). Leave your valuables with the management.

If you want something really cheap, try the *Pensión Catedral*, Calle 6 3-48, which is scruffy, has no locks on the doors, but costs only US$2 per person. There are many others to choose from if these are full. The *Hotel Colonial*, Plaza Bolivar, which costs US$5/$7/$9 a single/double/triple, and the *Hotel Central*, close to the Colonial, which costs US$5 a single, are both popular with travellers. Another worth trying is the *Pensión America*, Av Justo Arosemena, which costs US$9/$14 a single/double.

Places to Eat

The *Restaurant Foyo* close to the hotel of the same name is recommended as good and cheap though nothing special (breakfast costs US$1 and lunch/dinner US$1.50). Others include *La Viña*, Calle 6 close to the Central Post Office; *La Cresta*, Via España and Calle 45, which has good meals for US$1 upwards; and the *Restaurant Fontana*, Avenida Central (Santa Ana), which has good meals for US$2.

There's also a place known simply by the name *Café* on the Plaza Santa Ana which offers excellent, reasonably priced meals at just US$2. It's been recommended by many travellers.

AROUND PANAMA CITY
Panama Canal

The Panama Canal is, of course, most people's number one place to visit. There are several choices here which include the train or bus to Colón, both of which run more or less parallel to the canal for much of its length and go across causeways on Gatún Lake. If you'd like to take a closer look, take the bus marked 'Paraiso' from the Zone bus station to Miraflores Lock and watch the ships go through. The bus costs 35c. You can also catch this bus at Pier 18.

Panama Viejo

Another place worth seeing is Panama Viejo, the original site of the city founded in 1519 which was destroyed by Henry Morgan in 1671. It's worth spending a few hours wandering through the ruins. The area has been landscaped (and floodlit) by the government. To get there you take bus No 1 or 2 from the bottom of Calle 12 or from several points along Via España. The one-way fare is 15c.

Taboga Island

If you've got time to kill you could make a trip to Taboga Island about 20 km offshore. It's a popular resort area for Panameños with the second oldest church in the western hemisphere but the sea is pretty polluted and swimming isn't advised. Probably the best part of a trip to Taboga is the journey out there. If you'd like to stay overnight the *Hotel Chu* is recommended. It costs US$10/$15 a single/double. It's clean and has its own restaurant though prices are a little high.

AZUERO PENINSULA

Most travellers don't stop long in Panama so memories of the place usually start and finish with the hustle and bustle of the two main cities. There's another, completely different side to this country however and if you have time it's worth visiting some of the small towns on the Azuero Peninsula.

Los Santos, for instance, is an old colonial town with cobbled streets and an attractive 18th century church with an interior made entirely of wood. There's also a small history museum on the plaza which is well laid out. A good place to stay is the *Pensión Deportiva* which costs US$5/$6.50 a single/double with own shower. There's only one restaurant in town but it serves good, cheap food.

There are regular buses to **Chitré** (20c) and to **Las Tablas** (90c) from Chitré. The latter takes one hour. West of Chitré in the mountains is another old colonial town, **Ocú**. There's one bus per day in either direction between Chitré and Ocú or take a colectivo. Stay at the *Posada San Sebastián* at Ocú.

At the end of the peninsula is the small village of **Pedasí** where there's a beautiful empty beach with crystal clear warm sea about half an hours walk from the village. For accommodation, ask around for the old man who rents out rooms, (with showers and toilets). He can also arrange meals for about US$1. Colectivos leave from Pedasí to Las Tablas when full, cost US$2 and take 1½ hours.

South America

Argentina

Despite being the second largest country in South America and the eighth largest in the world, Argentina has always fallen short of being able to establish itself as the major power which its size, range of industries and enormous capacity for stock-raising suggest that it could be. There are many reasons for this but the major ones are a string of corrupt military governments, bad economic management, and the fact that, unlike North America which was settled by millions of small landowners with their associated demands for a range of services and a voice in the political life of the nation, land in Argentina was owned by only a small section of the population in the form of huge estates.

Even when immigration from Europe began in earnest after 1857, landowners would only permit the newcomers to rent plots of land for four or five years on the understanding that they would move on to fresh plots when their leases expired and then only after the ground had been planted out with alfalfa in the final year. The system was thus totally loaded in favour of the estate owners and failed to create that middle stratum of skilled and semi-skilled workers and small landowners which might have resulted in a more balanced economy and political life. Today, Argentina shoulders an enormous foreign debt which can only be serviced by more loans and the re-scheduling of existing debts.

Argentina was a long time in being settled and wasn't regarded by the Spanish as a particularly important part of their colonial empire. That distinction went to Asunción in what is today Paraguay. The first attempt to settle the south bank of the La Plata was made by Juan de Solís in 1516, but after he was killed by the Indians the expedition was abandoned.

Another attempt in 1536 by Pedro de Mendoza met much the same fate but not before part of the expedition had been despatched north, resulting in the

foundation of Asunción, where the Spanish found the Indians were friendly. There were no further attempts to settle the La Plata area until 1580 and it was not until the turn of the 17th century that Buenos Aires became secure from Indian attack. Meanwhile, other expeditions launched from Peru and Chile led to the foundation of Argentina's oldest cities such as Jujuy, Salta, Tucumán and, further south, Mendoza and Córdoba.

For much of the colonial period Buenos Aires remained a small, unimportant town whose main function was to serve as a military outpost to rival its Portuguese counterpart across the La Plata estuary at Colonia. Argentina at this time was part of the vast Viceroyalty of Peru and only in 1776 did Buenos Aires become the capital of the newly created Viceroyalty of the Rio de La Plata which included Argentina, Bolivia, Paraguay and Uruguay. The whole of Patagonia and a good slice of the Pampas remained firmly under Indian control throughout this time and continued to be so right up until the middle of the 19th century.

The development of a national consciousness came about not so much as a result of disaffection with restrictive colonial policy but more as a result of British military and commercial intervention during the Napoleonic Wars in Europe. In 1806, a British naval squadron, which had just taken part in the annexation of the Cape of Good Hope, sailed for Buenos Aires and took the city. The occupation didn't last long and several months later the porteños (as inhabitants of BA are known) threw the British out. British reinforcements which arrived shortly after this event were insufficient to attempt a recapture and had to be content with taking Montevideo instead. When more reinforcements arrived the following year another attempt was made to take Buenos Aires. Again it failed and the British were forced to evacuate not only Buenos Aires but Montevideo as well.

These victories over a major power gave the porteños a great deal of confidence in their ability to govern themselves, so in 1816 independence from Spain was declared. The Spanish Viceroy had already fled the city in disgrace when it was first occupied by the British.

With the end of the Napoleonic Wars in Europe, Spain attempted to retake Argentina by blockading the La Plata estuary and sending in an army from Peru. The Royalist forces were soundly beaten by the republicans and from these battles emerged one of South America's greatest cult figures – General José de San Martín.

San Martín, who ranks along with Bolívar and Sucre as one of the liberators of Spanish America, went on from these victories to liberate Chile and begin the same process in Peru. In 1821 however, having occupied Lima and declared the independence of Peru, San Martín sailed to Guayaquil to solicit help or reinforcements from Bolívar whose armies were on their way down the Andes after having liberated Venezuela, Colombia and Ecuador. Just what happened when the two leaders met isn't known – it's said Bolívar had no stomach for his counterpart's monarchical ideas – but after their meeting San Martín took no further part in the wars of liberation and went into self-imposed exile in Europe.

Bitter internal conflicts arose shortly after Argentina's independence between those in Buenos Aires who wanted power to be centralised in the new republic, and the caudillos, landowners and gauchos on the other hand who stood for regional autonomy. A leader of the latter group, Rosas, took control of the country in 1829 and ushered in a reign of terror which was to last until his overthrow in 1851 by Urquiza with heavy Brazilian army support.

Though Rosas was far from popular, he did place tariff restrictions on the import of foreign goods which for a time gave Argentinian factories and workshops the

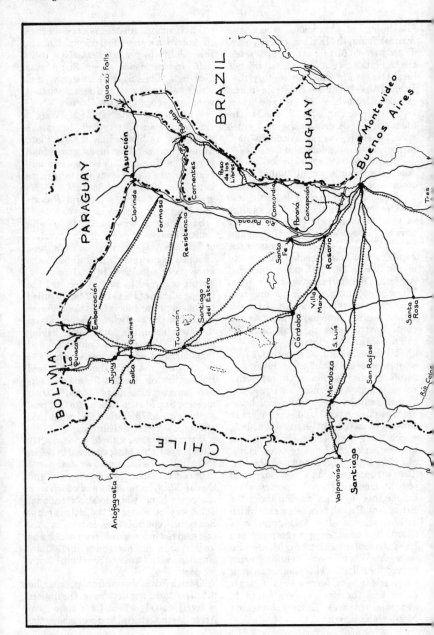

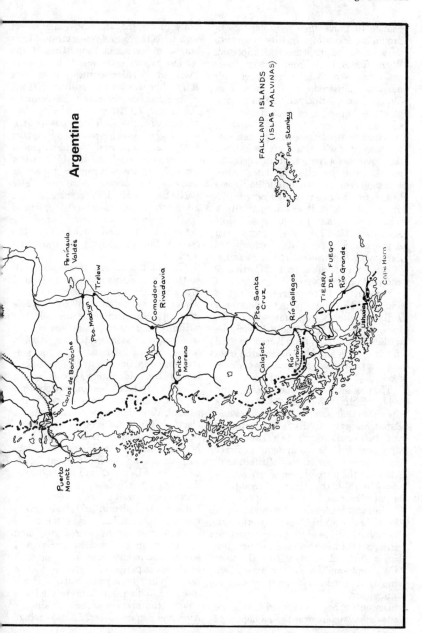

chance to prove they were capable of producing goods of a quality similar to those which had previously been imported. With Rosas' fall from power these restrictions were abolished and Argentina's nascent industrialisation collapsed as foreign goods, principally British manufactures, once more poured into the country.

With Urquiza in power, civil war once again erupted with Buenos Aires fighting the provinces for control. Though defeated in the early battles, Buenos Aires eventually came out on top and Bartolomé Mitre was installed as the first constitutional president. It was during Mitre's term of office that the War of the Triple Alliance (1865-70) was fought and Argentina expanded its territory (at Paraguay's expense) with the annexation of Misiones province, part of Corrientes and part of the Chaco.

Later in the 19th century the economic and social picture of Argentina was radically altered by immigration from Europe (between 1860 and 1930 some six million immigrants from Europe settled in the country) and by the demand from that part of the world for sources of cheap food.

The pressure for space and grazing land led to the Indian Wars of 1878-83 in which the tribes that occupied the Pampas and Patagonia were ruthlessly exterminated and their lands taken over by the officers who had led the campaign. Pedigree cattle were imported from Britain and, following the introduction of refrigerator ships in 1877, the export of fresh beef began in earnest.

The meat trade made Argentina one of the richest countries in the world and Buenos Aires one of its most important cities, but the wealth passed into very few hands. Not only that, but by the time WW II broke out there were more workers employed in industry than there were in agriculture.

Discontent began to spread among the industrial workers over the monopoly of power held by the conservative landowners and in 1943 a group of young army officers staged a successful coup. One of the leaders of this coup was Colonel Juan Perón, who'd had experience of Mussolini's Italy while serving as a military attaché at the Argentine embassy in that country. Perón saw, probably more clearly than anyone else, the need for a new type of leader who based his power and support on trade unions and the provision of industrial workers' facilities. He chose for himself the then-unimportant post of Secretary for Labour – a job no-one else particularly wanted. From there he went all-out to encourage the development of trade unions, collective bargaining between workers and employers and the construction of housing for industrial workers.

The widest possible publicity was given to these developments with the help of Eva Duarte, a glamourous radio actress whom he was later to marry. Perón's growing political influence was looked on with envy and alarm by his fellow officers who two years later arrested him. It was a serious miscalculation. Mass demonstrations were immediately organised by trade union leaders ably assisted by Eva Duarte and when it became obvious that the demonstrators were in control of the capital, Perón had to be released. In the elections which followed – by common consent, the cleanest that had ever been held in Argentina – Perón swept to victory with almost two-thirds of the seats in the Chamber of Deputies and all but two of the seats in the Senate.

Perón carried all before him for a while, but when Eva died in 1952 the euphoria began to wear off. The rising cost of living sparked widespread discontent, and corruption in government circles and state-owned industries began to approach levels not experienced since the days of Rosas. When it was rumoured that Perón intended to distribute arms to the trade unions, the army marched on Buenos Aires and Perón was forced to take refuge on board a Paraguayan gunboat which was in the harbour at the time. A fortnight later he was granted political asylum and allowed to travel into exile in Spain. A massive purge of Perónistas followed, from the top levels of government and the armed forces right down to the shop floor, and the military was placed in charge of the trade unions.

Nevertheless, Perón's influence as a political force was not spent and after a period of weak civilian government under Illia who was deposed by a right-wing military coup, the 1973 elections were won by the Perónista candidate. The new president promptly resigned and paved the way for Perón's return from exile. In the elections which followed, Perón again became the president but he died the following year and left the presidency in the hands of his second wife, Maria Estela Martínez de Perón.

It was a foolish arrangement in many ways. Maria Estela didn't have the same charisma as Perón himself and the opposition slowly got into its stride. Two years of violence, kidnapping and assassination followed in which thousands lost their lives. In the end the army took over again but the killings didn't stop. Over the next few years, assassination squads of both groups stalked the streets in search of their opponents.

During those years thousands of trade union activists 'disappeared' at the hands of right-wing assassination squads. Only recently have mass graves been unearthed and some light cast on what happened to all those people. In the meantime, inflation hit the roof. In 1976 it was a staggering 347% and over the next few years it hovered around 160 to 170%. More recently it's been brought under some degree of control and it seems that Alfonsin's government is prepared to take the necessary measures to bring it down to what would be acceptable in the industrialised nations of the northern hemisphere.

Faced with such an economic calamity and widespread censure abroad for its abuses of human rights, the military government desperately needed an external issue with which to divert attention. A war over the result of an arbitration decision which awarded three tiny islands off the southern end of Tierra del Fuego to Chile was the first option. But personal intervention by the Pope killed that one.

The next choice was perhaps obvious – the Falklands, or Islas Malvinas as they are known in Argentina. Just which government ought to bear the brunt of the responsibility for cranking this issue up into a full-scale war is open to question. Certainly both the British prime minister, Margaret Thatcher, and the head of the Argentinian junta, General Galtieri, were equally uncompromising and both needed a boost to their declining political fortunes.

Given Thatcher's determination to re-assert sovereignty and the high-tech armada which the British proved they are still capable of mounting, the outcome was probably a foregone conclusion but it wasn't as easy as they anticipated. In total, well over a thousand people had to die for a bunch of inhospitable, kelp-laced islands stuck in the howling vastness of the South Atlantic. Hundreds of Argentinian and British families mourn the death of their sons. A more cynical waste of human and financial resources is hard to imagine, while the almost criminal bellicosity of the gutter press on both sides needs no further comment. The whole exercise has also had a very negative effect on the British community in Argentina which, with the exception of South Africa, is the largest outside the Commonwealth.

In the meantime, orders for French Exocet missiles and British Harrier jump-jets came pouring in. Margaret Thatcher romped back into power for a second term as the reincarnation of Bodicea, while the Argentinian military rulers were swept from power in disgrace.

In December 1985 most of them were found guilty, by a civilian court, for their part in the murder and torture of detainees during their reign of terror, and were jailed for periods ranging from 4½ to 17 years. Three of the four who were cleared still face charges before a military court for Argentina's defeat in the Falklands conflict.

The war aside, Argentina's claim over the islands is a tenuous one. They have been settled and farmed by British people since 1833 and indeed the islands were first discovered by the English navigator, John Davis in 1592. In between times they were occupied briefly by the British in 1690, by the French in the early 1700s and again in 1764, by the Spanish in 1766, by the British again in 1767, by the Spanish again in 1770 and by the Britain yet again in 1771. The British abandoned the islands in 1774 and they were next occupied by the United Provinces of South America in 1820. The USA broke this settlement up in 1831 as a result of the illegal imprisonment of a group of American sealers and, finally, the British again took possession in 1833.

Britain has since spent millions of dollars on garrisoning the islands and constructing a runway which will take the largest of warplanes, while back home it sports the highest unemployment rate in Europe and its industrial base contracts by the hour.

Someone once announced (perhaps naively) over a microphone at a rock festival that, 'There's always a little heaven in a disaster area' and if anything positive can be said about the Falklands War, as far as Argentina is concerned, it is that it was the end of the line for the military junta. Since then, a democratically elected civilian government headed by Raul Alfonsin has taken over and enjoys overwhelming support from the people. It has also gained considerable respect abroad not only for its honesty and its determination to bring to trial anyone connected with the 'disappearances' during the 1970s and early 1980s but for its drastic yet realistic measures to get the economy back on its feet and inflation under control. Alfonsin has announced that the government will no longer print money to pay off its deficits and has established price controls on everything. This includes public services like electricity, gas and telephones as well as wages. The interest payable on bank deposits were likewise slashed to 6% from 40% to discourage speculation. Everyone hopes he will succeed – including, so far, the people of Argentina.

Politics aside, Argentina, along with Chile and Uruguay, has a very different population mix from the rest of Spanish America. All three countries have an almost exclusively European population as most of the Indians were wiped out in the 19th century in genocidal wars. That being so, you're not going to find those colourful Indian markets and fiestas which make Colombia, Ecuador, Peru and Bolivia so interesting. That's not to say you won't find these countries interesting – you will – and you'll find most people very friendly, eager to help and keen to talk to you about where you come from and what life is like there.

Argentina also offers some of the continent's most spectacular natural attractions. Some examples are Iguazú Falls, the Andean Lake District around Bariloche, the Moreno Glacier near Calafate and the world's most southerly, permanently inhabited town, Ushuaia, as well as Tierra del Fuego. There are the ruins of the old Jesuit reducciones in Misiones province between Posadas and the Iguazú Falls; as you head south, there is a huge wildlife sanctuary on the Valdés Peninsula where you can see colonies of penguins, sea elephants and sea lions; and only 30 km south of that, between Puerto Madryn and Comodoro Rivadavia, is the largest penguin colony outside of Antarctica.

VISAS
Visas are required by all except nationals of Western Europe, Canada, Japan and most Latin American countries.

British and New Zealand passport holders are still on what might be called the 'undesirable tourists' list and should expect major problems when applying for visas. These problems differ from place to place but it's generally true to say that the nearer you are to the Argentine border and the busier the border crossing, the easier it is.

In San Francisco, for instance, the Argentine consulate is barely even civil and will tell you that visas are not available except to businessmen and then

only after a two or three month wait. In Santiago, Chile, you'll be told it takes two months (but no problems otherwise). In Montevideo, Uruguay, it will take about two weeks but you have to pay for a telex to Buenos Aires (about US$8 to $9). In Puerto Montt, Chile, the consul is not only a very intelligent and sympathetic man who understands that not all Brits support their government's absurd stand on the Malvinas but he'll do his best to get you a visa. He'll tell you that officially it takes 15 days but that he can't guarantee it in less than three weeks. He also speaks perfect English.

Some travellers have reported that it's best to avoid leaving Argentina via La Quiaca on Sundays otherwise you'll be charged a 'baggage search fee' of US$3.50.

MONEY
US$1 = 83 australs.

The unit of currency is the Austral which replaced the peso in mid-1985 as part of an economic package designed to stabilise the economy and get inflation under control. As of November 1985, Australs could not officially be changed into any other currency. Airport departure tax is US$4 for international flights; US$1.40 for internal flights.

Hotels and travel agents usually give the best rates of exchange.

GETTING THERE
To/From Bolivia
The main road and rail route to Bolivia passes through the northern Argentine towns of Salta and Jujuy and crosses the border at La Quiaca/Villazón. Two other less-used routes further to the east are Salta-Orán-Agua Blanca/Bermejo (the border)-Tarija and Salta-Embarcación-Yacuiba (border)-Santa Cruz.

Via La Quiaca/Villazón There are two to three daily buses in either direction between Salta and La Quiaca. From La Quiaca they depart at 10 am, 3 and 9.30

pm from the Hotel Cristal, take about 11 hours and cost US$9. Between Jujuy and La Quiaca there are several daily buses in either direction with a number of different bus companies. From La Quiaca, both *Atahualpa* and *Panamericana* have four daily departures at 10 am, 12.30, 3, and 9 pm which take about eight hours and cost US$7. There are also a number of cheaper buses but they take 12 hours.

The trains are considerably cheaper but they take much longer. If you're in Salta, the train must be taken from the railway junction at Güemes east of Salta. From Güemes to La Quiaca there are trains on Monday and Friday at 4.30 pm which take 16 hours and cost US$8 (1st class) and US$6 (2nd class). These trains get very crowded because they originate from Buenos Aires. There are also local trains at 6 am on Monday, Thursday and Saturday which cost US$2 (1st class).

The border at La Quiaca is open weekdays from 7.30 am to 12 noon and 3 to 6 pm. On Saturdays, Sundays and holidays it is open from 9 to 11 am only. Trains do not cross the border so you have to get off at La Quiaca and either take a taxi to Villazón or walk the one km between the two stations. If you need to change money, note that the Banco de la Nación is only open until 1 pm. After that you can only change travellers' cheques at the *Casa León* next to the Hotel Cristal, but at 10% commission, so it's best to have cash. The Banco del Estado in Villazón has very short opening hours.

If you're heading for Bolivia and need a visa, avoid getting it in La Quiaca, as the consular staff there have a habit of demanding US$15 for it. Get it at Salta, Jujuy or elsewhere.

Via Aguas Blancas/Bermejo There are daily buses in either direction between Salta and Orán which take about six hours. From there you need to take another bus to Aguas Blancas on the border. Alternatively, there's usually one bus per day from Salta to Aguas Blancas (at 10 pm) which takes about 8½ hours – so you arrive before daybreak (have warm clothes handy). From Aguas Blancas you have to take a ferry across the river to Bermejo on the Bolivian side and then a bus from there to Tarija which takes about six hours. There's only one bus a day and it's often full so you may have to spend the night in Bermejo.

Via Yacuiba This is the route to take if you're heading to or from Santa Cruz. There are buses and trains from Salta to Aguaray. From there you must take a taxi across the border to Yacuiba. From Yacuiba you can pick up the *tren rapido* to Santa Cruz. It leaves once daily Monday to Friday and costs US$4.30 (Pullman), US$2.70 (1st class) and US$1.70 (2nd class). The *ferrobus* along this line has been discontinued.

To/From Chile

Salta-Antofagasta There are two buses per week in either direction by *Andino Geminis* and *Atahualpa* but the former is the better of the two. It leaves Salta on Wednesdays at 4 pm, takes about 29 hours and costs US$20. You can only buy tickets from the *Residencial Balcarce*, Ave Balcarce 460. It gets very cold over the passes so take plenty of warm clothing with you.

There is no longer any international train along this route, though Argentine railways still runs a service to Socompa near the border.

Mendoza-Santiago This is one of the main routes to/from Chile. There are no longer any trains along the route so the journey must be done by bus. The route is open all year – there is now a tunnel under the pass. There are frequent daily departures in either direction by a number of companies including *Fenix Pullman Norte*, *Tas Choapa* and *Pluma*, usually in the early morning between 8 and 9 am. They take between eight and 10 hours and cost US$14.70. There are also colectivos (like *Colectivos Coitram*) which take about the same time as the buses but cost US$18.

San Carlos de Bariloche-Puerto Montt This is also a very popular route since it goes through the Argentinian and Chilean Lake District. There are also buses between Bariloche and Valdivia. Full details of these routes are given in the chapter on Chile under the section headed 'The Lake District.'

Comodoro Rivadavia-Coyhaique *La Puntual* operate buses three times a week in winter and four times a week in summer which cost US$45 and take about 12 hours.

Río Gallegos-Río Turbio-Puerto Natales *Expreso Pingüino* run a daily bus to Río Turbio at 11.30 am and one bus a week to Puerto Natales on Saturdays at 8.30 am. The fare to Río Turbio is US$8 and to Puerto Natales US$10.

Río Gallegos-Punta Arenas There is one bus daily from Tuesdays to Sundays at 9 am and a bus on Mondays at 12 noon by *Expreso Pingüino*. The journey takes about eight to 10 hours depending on delays at the border and costs US$10. The booking office is at Zapiola 455 and is open from 9 am to 12.30 pm and 3 to 7.30 pm. Before you buy your ticket you must obtain a permit from the police. Get this from the Anexo Judicial, Zapiola 715 (open 1 to 5 pm – permit costs US$0.80). From Punta Arenas the bus departs daily at 9 am except on Mondays, when it leaves at 11 am.

Ushuaia/Río Grande-Porvenir *Sencovich* operate a bus twice weekly on Wednesdays and Saturdays at 6 am from Río Grande which takes about seven hours and costs US$8. The booking office is at Av San Martín 959, Río Grande. These buses from Río Grande to Porvenir connect with the ferries from Porvenir to Punta Arenas. Avoid *Transportes Turicisne* which also covers this route.

There are no direct buses between Río Grande and Río Gallegos although there is another ferry crossing between Punta Delgada and Primera Angostura. The ferries there are operated by *ENAP* (Chilean oil boats) and generally leave every two hours between 8 am and 9 pm daily, except between noon and 2 pm and whenever it's too rough to cross. The ferry is free to passengers. There are no buses along this route so you have to hitch.

If you've come down through Chile via Punta Arenas and Porvenir and continued on to Ushuaia by road and then want to head back up to Río Gallegos, it works out cheaper to try and get on a flight at either Ushuaia or Río Grande to Río Gallegos. Only *LADE* cover these routes (office on Av San Martín, Ushuaia, open Monday to Friday from 9 am to 12 noon and 2.30 to 6.30 pm). Ushuaia to Río Gallegos costs US$18. The flights are daily but are heavily booked.

To/From Paraguay
You can cross into Paraguay from Argentina either by bridge across the Río Paraguay or by ferry across the Río Paraná.

There are two buses daily from Monday to Friday and one bus daily on Saturday and Sunday in either direction between Formosa and Asunción which cost US$3.70. The companies which do this run are *Brujula*, *Godoy* and *La Internacional*. The ferry across the Río Paraná plies between Posadas and Encarnación (it takes railway carriages and vehicles). There are frequent daily crossing in either direction between 7 and 11 am and 2 and 6 pm. The fare is US$2.20. From Encarnación there are two trains per week and numerous daily buses to Asunción, and from Posadas there are frequent daily trains and buses to Buenos Aires.

To/From Uruguay
The various bridge and ferry crossings

between Argentina and Uruguay are described in the chapter on Uruguay.

To/From Brazil

Almost all travellers make the crossing between Argentina and Brazil (or vice versa) via the Iguazú Falls, one of South America's most spectacular sights. The road and rail connections between Buenos Aires and the falls, and from there east into Brazil are covered in the section on the Iguazú Falls.

GETTING AROUND
Air

Líneas Aéreas de Estado (LADE) and *Austral Líneas* both have extensive networks covering Tierra del Fuego and the southern half of Patagonia and their fares are often the same or, in some cases, even cheaper than the bus fare. The only snag with these flights, as you might well imagine, is that there's heavy demand for tickets and they are often booked out up to two weeks in advance. If so, get yourself on the waiting list as there are always cancellations. While you're in Buenos Aires, get hold of a copy of their schedules and fares. Their addresses are *LADE*, Calle Peru 710 (tel 34-7071); *Austral Líneas*, Av R S Peña 701 (tel 46-8841). *Austral* do not sell tickets at their head office nor will they accept credit cards.

Bus

Most of the buses in Argentina are modern, comfortable and fast but they are not particularly cheap, especially in Patagonia and Tierra del Fuego. Most large towns and cities have a central bus terminal though this isn't always the case. Examples of fares and journey times are as follows:

La Quiaca-Salta With *Atahualpa* or *Panamericana* the fare is US$9 and the journey takes 12 hours.

Salta-Tucumán Many companies cover the route. The fare is US$6 and the journey takes 5½ hours.

Tucumán-Córdoba Costs US$12 to $13 depending on the route and takes 11 hours.

Córdoba-Buenos Aires Costs US$13.60 with either *Costera Criolla* or *Cacorba* and the journey takes 13 hours.

Córdoba-Mendoza Costs US$10 and takes 10 hours.

Buenos Aires-Resistencia Three buses daily. The fare is US$22 and the journey takes 10 hours.

Resistencia-Salta There is one direct bus daily at 5 pm from Resistencia which costs US$25 and takes 14 to 16 hours. Buses often get stuck in the mud during the rainy season.

Buenos Aires-Posadas There are three buses daily by *Expreso Singer* (at 10.30 am, 3 and 4 pm from Posadas) which cost US$13 and take about 16½ hours.

Posadas-Iguazú Falls There are express buses daily at 5 am and 9 am which cost US$6.50 and take 4½ hours. The buses go via San Ignacio Miní where they stop for a while.

Buenos Aires-Bariloche Three buses daily with *Chevalier* which cost US$36 and take 24 hours. A good service which includes after-dinner brandies!

Train

There is an extensive network of railways in Argentina with frequent service between towns. A comprehensive timetable of the services available is beyond the scope of a book of this size and probably unnecessary since most travellers take a number of well-defined routes. Journey times are generally longer than they are by bus – but often much more pleasant if only because you can move around or visit the dining car. Fares in first class are generally about the same as the buses but second class (tourist class) is quite a bit cheaper.

Altogether there are six different networks of tracks, three of which share the same terminus in Buenos Aires (Retiro Station) with the remainder having their own terminals (Constitución,

Destination	Station	No per week	Journey time (hrs)	Fares Tourist	(US$) 1st	Pullman	Sleep
Bahía Blanca	Constitución	17	10-12	7.00	9.00	12.00	17.50
Bariloche	Constitución	3	32	17.00	22.00	32.00	37.75
Concordia	Lacroze	15	8½	7.00	9.00	12.00	16.00
Córdoba	Retiro	9	10-12	8.00	10.00	14.00	18.00
Corrientes	Lacroze	5	20½	11.00	14.00	18.00	22.00
Mendoza	Retiro	14	13-16	10.00	14.00	21.00	27.00
Posadas	Lacroze	7	20	11.00	16.00	22.00	27.00
Rosario	Retiro	63	4	3.00	4.00	6.50	
Tucumán	Retiro	11	17-22	11.00	15.00	23.00	27.00

Once and Lacroze Stations). You can get tickets and information on all of them at the Galerias Pacífico, Florida 729 (tel 311 6411/12/13/14) in Buenos Aires. It's open Monday to Saturday from 7 am to 9 pm and on Sundays from 7 am to 1 pm. Some of the services and their journey times and fares are given in the table above.

Hitching
Hitch-hiking is fairly easy in Argentina and you'll rarely be asked to pay for a lift. This applies as much in Patagonia and Tierra de Fuego as in the more developed northern part of the country, though in the former areas you may well have to wait longer for a lift as fewer people live there. Whether you're hitch-hiking or not, it's worth considering flying over short distances in the southern half of Patagonia and in Tierra del Fuego.

BARILOCHE (San Carlos de Bariloche)
Bariloche is the centre of the Argentinian Lake District and one of the major centres of population in the area. Set amid deep blue lakes, towering mountains, glaciers and pine forests it has an almost Bavarian alpine appearance.

Any Argentinian with the time and money visits Bariloche during the summer (December to March) when the meadows are ablaze with wild flowers. Recreation activities include fishing, skiing, climbing and hiking.

Information
The tourist office is in the Centro Civico and is open Monday to Saturday during winter (the ski season) from 8 am to 8 pm and everyday between those times in the summer. Between March-April and August-November it is often closed at the weekends. The office has a full list of all accommodation in the town and will ring ahead for you to make sure a place has a room.

The National Parks office, San Martín 24, is open daily from 8 am to 8 pm but doesn't have much information.

The *Cambio Velox*, Calle Moreno, (open Monday to Saturday) gives the best rate of exchange. When it's closed you can change cash dollars at the small kiosk at the end of the galeria 'Arrayanes'. They pay just as much as the casas de cambio.

The railway station is 5 km from the centre of town. Local buses run between the two and cost a few cents.

Things to See & Do
Bariloche is the Zermatt of Argentina and many people go there for the skiing during winter though, as you might imagine, it's a pretty ritzy scene and outside the budget of a shoestring traveller. Most travellers spend their time going on long walks – the lakes and mountains are among the most beautiful in the world. Information on easy treks into the mountains which don't require

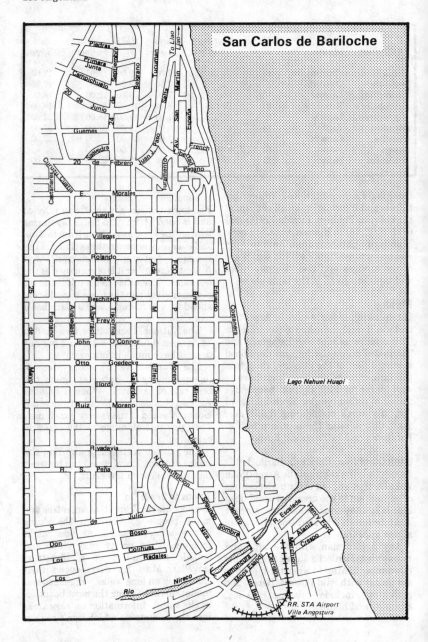

San Carlos de Bariloche

Lago Nahuel Huapi

RR. STA Airport
Villa Angostura

equipment is obtainable from the Club Andino Bariloche, 20 de Febrero 30. It's open 9 am to 12 noon and 3 to 8 pm Monday to Friday and 9 am to 12 noon on Saturday.

The **Nahuel Huapí Museum** is worth visiting if you're interested in Indian artefacts. It's open from 2 to 6 pm Tuesday to Friday in the summer months and 9 am to 1.30 pm and 3 to 7 pm in the winter.

Places to Stay

As with many of the places in the Chilean part of the Lake District, the best deals in accommodation are found in private houses. In the high season however, cheap accommodation can be difficult to find. The best thing to do is first contact the tourist office as it has a complete list of all accommodation available. If you have no luck there try the apartments behind Angel Gallarde.

The Club Andino offers very cheap accommodation in the off-season, but is only open to members during the ski season. In the off season you should try the *Hotel El Mirador*; at that time of year it's even cheaper than the refugios of the Club Andino. It costs US$2/$4, has hot water and is comfortable, though the woman who runs it has been described as 'a bit weird'.

There is also a *Youth Hostel* on the Llao Llao road about five km from the town which is open from 1 July to 15 August and 1 December to 31 March. It offers bed and breakfast and full board.

The *Residencial Adguinte* has singles/doubles for US$9/$11.

Places to Eat

La Cosa Nostra, B Mitre 357, is one of the cheapest places and has very good pizzas. Another cheap restaurant is *La Venida*, Palacios 153. *La Andina*, Elflein, has also been recommended as having very good cheap food. It's popular with local people and the empanadas are terrific.

Buenos Aires

The capital of Argentina and during colonial days, the seat of the Viceroyalty of La Plata, Buenos Aires is today a huge city of some nine million people. Until the meat export boom began in the mid-1880s it was a small city but since then it has expanded by leaps and bounds and there are now very few old buildings left.

Like other cities of its size, Buenos Aires has an endless variety of things to do and see if you have the time and/or the money. Yet, despite its size, it's a fairly pleasant place with some of the widest boulevards of any city in the world and it's very easy to get around using the underground railways, or *subte*, as local people know them.

Information

The main tourist office is at Santa Fe 883 (tel 31-2300/31-2089/31-6800) and there are branch offices at either end of Calle Florida. It's open Monday to Friday from 9 am to 5 pm. The staff are very friendly and helpful and they have a whole range of maps and literature.

In addition to the national tourist information office, most of the provinces also maintain their own information offices in Buenos Aires. They are known as Casas de Turismo and are open from Monday to Friday from noon to 7 pm though some of them may be closed in the winter. Many are located on Callao at the following numbers: Buenos Aires (No 237); Córdoba (No 332); Chaco (No 322); La Rioja (No 745); Mendoza (No 445).

The addresses of the others are:

Río Negro Tucumán 1916
Chubut San Martín 785
Entre Ríos Cangallo 451
Formosa Irigoyen 1429
Jujuy Santa Fe 967
Misiones Santa Fe 989
Neuquén Cangallo 687
Salta Maipú 663
Santa Cruz Córdoba 1345

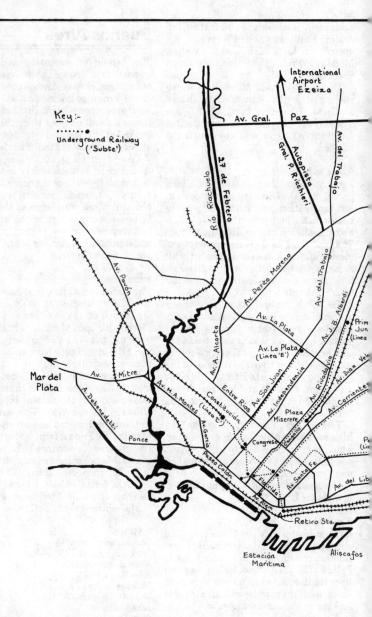

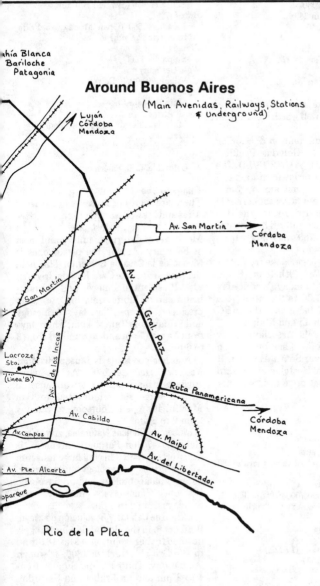

Around Buenos Aires

(Main Avenidas, Railways, Stations
& Underground)

ahía Blanca
Bariloche
Patagonia

Luján
Córdoba
Mendoza

Av. San Martín →   Córdoba
Mendoza

Av. San Martín

Av. Gral. Paz

Av. de los Incas

Lacroze
Sta.

(Linea 'B')

Ruta Panamericana →   Córdoba
Mendoza

Av. Cabildo

Av. Campos

Av. Maipú

Av. del Libertador

Av. Pte. Alcorta

oparque

Rio de la Plata

Catamarca Córdoba 2080
Corrientes San Martín 333
La Pampa Suipacha 346
San Juan Maipú 331
Santa Fe 25 de Mayo 358
Santiago del Estero Florida 274
Tucumán Mitre 836
Tierra del Fuego Esmeralda 355.

The National Parks Information Service, at Santa Fe 680, is well worth visiting and is very helpful.

The Railways Information & Booking Office is located at Galerias Pacífico, Florida 729 (tel 311 6411/12/13/14). It's open Monday to Saturday from 7 am to 7 pm and on Sunday from 7 am to 1 pm.

There is a good cambio on the corner of Lavalle and San Martín. You may need to bargain for the best rate. The sweater shop at Florida 780 has also been recommended.

For English language books try *Lottes Corner*, Córdoba 785 (9th floor, Room 18), which is open Monday, Wednesday and Friday from 1.30 to 6 pm and the owner speaks English; and the *ABC Libreria*, Av Tucumán and Maipú.

The Youth Hostels Association, Av Corrientes 1373 (1st floor) has information about hostels all over South America. If you need a Youth Hostel membership card it's the normal price of US$12 per annum.

Useful Addresses
Thomas Cook
    Av Córdoba 746
American Express Agents
    City Service Travel Agency, Florida 890 (tel 32-8416)
Aerolíneas Argentinas
    Peru 2 (tel 362-5008/6008/7008). There's also a branch office next to Exprinter on Santa Fe.
Austral Líneas Aéreas
    Florida 429
Líneas Aéreas del Estado (LADE)
    Peru 710 (tel 34-7071)

Embassies
Australia
    Santa Fe 846 (Swissair Building)
Brazil
    Paraguay 580 (Open Monday to Friday from 1.15 to 6 pm)
Canada
    Suipacha 1111
West Germany
    Villanueva 1055, Belgrano
Paraguay
    Maipú 464 (3rd floor)
South Africa
    Marcelo T de Alvear 590 (8th floor)
Switzerland
    Santa Fe 846 (12th floor)
USA
    Colombia 4300, Palermo

Things to See
There are scores of museums in Buenos Aires and it's well worth going along to see a few of them. Most are closed on Mondays, and during January and most of February. Among the better ones is **Museo de la Casa de Gobierno**. This is in the basement of the Casa Rosada, Irigoyen 218 (Presidential Palace) and contains historical exhibits relating to past presidents. It's open Tuesday, Wednesday and Friday from 9 am to 4 pm, Thursdays from 9 am to 7 pm and on Sundays from 3 to 6 pm.

Another good one is **Museo Histórico Nacional**, Defensa 1600. As its name suggests, this is an historical museum with a large section devoted to San Martín. It's open Thursday to Sunday from 2 to 6 pm.

Museo de Ciencas Naturales, Av Angell Gallardo 470 on Parque Centenario, is also worth a visit. This is a large museum with sections on zoology, mineralogy, botany, palaeontology and archaeology. It's open Tuesdays, Thursdays and Sundays from 2 to 6 pm.

Museo de Cabildo y Revolución de Mayo, Bolivar 65, in the old Cabildo building, is devoted to the revolution of May 1810 and to the British attack of 1806. It's open Wednesday, Thursday and Sunday from 4 to 8 pm and on Friday and Saturday from 6 to 10 pm.

One of the best museums in Buenos

Aires is the **Museo de Arte Hispano-Americano Isaac Fernández Blanco** on Suipacha 1422. It has an excellent collection of colonial art and silverware but the building itself is worth the visit – it's a beautiful old colonial mansion. The museum is open Thursday to Sunday from 2 to 6 pm. Admission is US$0.35.

Museo y Biblioteca Ricardo Rojas, Charcas 2837, is the former house of the Argentinian writer, Rojas. Apart from the displays, the house itself is worth a visit. It's open Wednesdays and Fridays from 3 to 6 pm. Entry is free.

One other place worth a visit if you're interested in Antarctica is the **Museo de la Dirección Nacional del Antartico**, Angel Gallardo 470. It's open on Tuesdays, Thursdays and Sundays from 2 to 6 pm.

For a completely different type of 'museum' try the *Presidente Sarmiento*, a sailing vessel built some 80 years ago and used as a training ship for a while. It's now a museum and moored at Dársena Norte. It's open in the afternoons at weekends. Another sailing ship, the *Uruguay*, moored at Boca Bridge, is due to be made into a museum.

Places to Stay

Buenos Aires can be a very expensive place and there are very few places to stay under US$10 per night. Also, the quoted price of a room isn't the only thing you have to think about. On top of the basic charge, there will be a service charge (*laudo*) of 14 to 30% plus a value added tax (*IVA*) of 16%.

If you're trying to keep costs down, try the *Youth Hostel*, Calle José Mármol 1555 (tel 92-0774), which costs US$2 per person per night. You must be a member of the Youth Hostels Association. To get to the hostel take Linea E subway to Estación Avenida La Plata or bus No 7 to the same place.

If you don't want to go that far then try the *Hotel Central Córdoba*, San Martín 1021/23 (tel 311 1175), which is only four or five blocks from the bus terminal and one block from Florida. It's a good, clean place and there are laundry facilities on the roof. Rooms cost US$5 a single with own bath and hot water.

In the past a lot of travellers used the *Hotel Torino*, 25 de Mayo 724, but it gets contradictory reports these days. One traveller described it as, 'a hole, no water most of the time, filthy, cheap but stuff goes missing', while another said it was 'still the best'. One thing is for sure – it's very cheap at US$2. Another of a similar standard is the *Hotel Mendoza*, or try the *Hotel Ocean*, Maipú 907.

The *Hotel O Rei*, Calle Lavalle 733, has also been suggested. Singles/doubles cost US$2.50/$4 without bath and US$4/$6 with bath. It's clean, basic and central but watch the locks on the doors.

For something a bit up-market there's the *Hotel Orly* at US$5.50/$9 for singles/doubles; the *Camino Red Hotel*, Calles Maipu 572, with singles/doubles for US$10/$16; or the *Hotel Waldorf*, Calle Paraguay, which charges US$7/$10 for singles/doubles, is very clean and central and has a baggage safe.

Places to Eat

The cheapest places to eat at lunchtime are a series of restaurants called *Supercoop* which are open between 11 am and 3 pm where you can get a complete lunch for just US$0.60. There are branches at Lavalle 2530, Sarmiento 1431, Piedras at the corner with Rivadavia, and Rivadavia 5708. Don't be put off by the often long queues – they move quickly.

The *Santa Generosa*, Florida 570, is also worth a visit. It's a self-service cafeteria and tea room where you can get a large steak (US$1.25), salad (US$0.80), grilled ham with melon (US$0.40) as well as vegetables.

For action in the evenings try the *Bar Sur* on the corner of Estados Unidos and Balcarce. Tango away the night. There's also an excellent Italian restaurant on this same street corner.

Buenos Aires

Getting Around

Airports The international airport is at Ezeiza, 35 km from the centre of the city. If you have no luggage catch local bus No 86 from the corner of Peru and Av de Mayo, but make sure it has 'Aeropuerto' in the window, as many 86s stop short of the airport. There are also *remise* taxis between the airport and the city centre which cost US$12 and take about 45 minutes. Buy a ticket before you leave the terminal at the Manuel Tienda León counter.

The airport for domestic flights and also for Montevideo as well as some flights to Asunción, Santiago, Rio de Janeiro, São Paulo, and Santa Cruz (Bolivia) is known as the Aeroparque and is four km from the centre at the end of the new port. To get there take local bus No 33 or 56 from Retiro Station. A taxi will cost about US$12.

Bus Terminals Most long-distance buses now run from the new terminal, Estación Terminal de Omnibus, behind Retiro Station (Línea C on the *subte*), though there may still be some running from the old terminals at Plaza Constitución and Once Station. To get to the latter, take *subte* Línea A to Plaza Miserere station.

Subways There are five different lines which link the city centre to the suburbs. Línea A runs from the Plaza de Mayo to Primera Junta under Calle Rivadavia. Línea B runs from the Central Post Office on Av L N Alem to Lacroze Station under Av Corrientes. Línea C runs from Plaza Constitución to Retiro Station and links all the other lines. Línea D runs from Plaza de Mayo to Palermo via the North Diagonal, Córdoba and Santa Fe. Línea E runs from Plaza de Mayo to Avenidas Directorio and J M Moreno via San Juan.

The fare is US$0.10 per trip, any distance. Buying a few tickets in advance will save a lot of time if you're going to be using the subway a lot. The lines are open from 5 am to 1 am daily. There are no problems with rucksacks and bags on the subways.

CALAFATE

If you've made it to this part of the world, then a trip to Calafate on the shores of Lago Argentino is a must. It is there, in the Parque Nacional de los Glaciares, you will find the spectacular Moreno glacier. The glacier, which is one km wide and 50 metres high, descends to the surface of the lake. It's a tremendous sight! Huge pieces of ice break off occasionally and thunder into the water to float off as icebergs, often creating large waves in the process. The glacier has almost cut the lake in two and has blocked off the outlets with a wall of ice. There's also another glacier – the Upsala glacier – at the end of the lake which can be visited by motorboat.

In addition to the glaciers, there are many walking possibilities in the mountains. For details contact the National Parks office.

Information

There is a tourist office (Av San Martín) and a National Parks office (opposite the ACA Motel) in Calafate.

Travellers' cheques and cash can be changed at the Banco de la Provincia de Santa Cruz but commission is charged.

Good maps of the area are available from the National Parks office.

Tents (US$2 – sleep four people) and four-berth cabañas (US$3 per person) can be hired from the tourist office.

The airport is about five minutes walk from the centre.

Places to Stay

The cheapest accommodation apart from camping, is a room in a private house. Try the one at San Martín 989. Apart from this there are 12 hotels to choose from in Calafate but most of them are quite

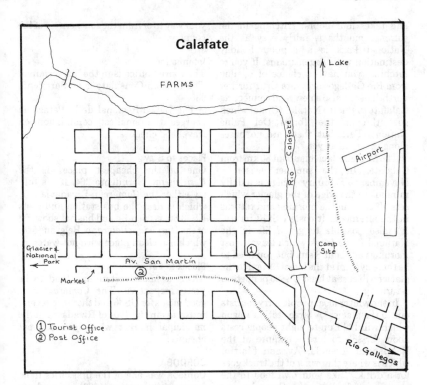

Calafate

Lake ↑

FARMS

Río Calafate

Airport

Glacier & National Park ←

Av. San Martín

Market

Camp Site

① Tourist Office
② Post Office

Río Gallegos →

expensive. The only one which falls into the budget category is the *Amado*, San Martín.

There's a municipal camp-site in Calafate which costs US$1 plus US$0.15 for a hot shower. There are two others, one about five km from town in the National Park and another eight km from the Moreno glacier. Before you can use these last two you need a permit from the *guardaparques* hut at the park entrance. There are also a number of *refugios* in the park which are free and generally provide firewood and heating. For details about these enquire at the National Parks office in Calafate.

If you'd like to stay at the Moreno glacier itself, the *Motel ACA* has a number of bungalows there which cost US$5 per day and will sleep four people, but they're often booked up at certain times in summer. Note that cooking isn't allowed in the cabins and there's often no food for sale so take your own supplies.

Places to Eat

There's not much choice in restaurants in Calafate and very few could be described as cheap. If you stay with a family it would be best to eat there. Otherwise try the *Pizzería OK*.

Getting There & Around

In the summer months there is a bus once a week in either direction between Río Gallegos and Calafate. It leaves Río Gallegos on Thursdays and Calafate on Saturdays (from Hotel El Quijote). The journey takes about six hours and costs US$13. A taxi costs US$30 (for the car) and takes four hours. Hitching in the summer months is fairly easy as the National Park is a popular holiday destination with Argentinians. If you're hitching, you have a choice of coming from Río Gallegos or Santa Cruz further north. There's also a new road connecting Calafate to Puerto Natales (Chile) which goes through the Torres Del Paine National Park but there are no buses along this road as yet.

The Moreno glacier is about 80 km from Calafate. In the summer season – November to February – there is a daily minibus to the edge of the glacier which sets off early in the morning and returns in the afternoon. It costs US$13 return. It's also possible to get a lift in the National Parks truck which leaves most mornings at about 8 am, but you need to be there by 5 am at the latest. A taxi to the glacier will cost at least US$25 per person return.

In the winter local people ferry tourists out to the glacier. A large station wagon which will hold up to eight people costs about US$65 to hire – enquire at the Residencial Avenida, Av San Martin, which is where the owner of the truck goes for a drink. Take your own food to the glacier, as food bought there is very expensive, when it's available.

In the summer months it's also possible to visit the Upsala glacier by motor boat. The boats go from Punta Bandera, 45 km from Calafate, at 8 am and return at 4 pm. A bus to Punta Bandera from Calafate costs US$8. The travel agents, *Turista Lacustre*, also offer the complete trip (to Punta Bandera by bus and the boat trip to the glacier) for US$19 return. The Upsala glacier is 30 metres high.

COMODORO RIVADAVIA

This oil and petro-chemical town is one of the largest in Patagonia, and the oil wells to the west and south supply around 30% of Argentina's crude. For travellers there isn't anything of great interest but you may find yourself staying overnight on your way to or from the southern tip of the country.

Information

The tourist office is in the bus terminal. The Chilean Consulate is on Sarmiento 936.

The Banco Regional de la Patagonia charges the smallest commission on travellers' cheques.

Places to Stay

One of the cheapest places is the *Residencial*, Sarmiento 264. If it's full, try either the *Comercio*, Rivadavia 341, which is near the bus station and costs US$3.80, is friendly and has hot showers; or the *Hospedaje Belgrano*, Belgrano 546, which is a clean place with hot water.

Places to Eat

Meals at most restaurants tend to be pretty expensive. The *Comercio* does good meals for US$6 and there are several *rotiserías* in the 400s of Rivadavia in the municipal market where you can eat cheaply.

CÓRDOBA

Córdoba was one of the first cities to be founded in Argentina (1573) and predates the first permanent settlement at Buenos Aires. These days it is the second largest city in the republic with over one million inhabitants.

Until a few years ago its many old buildings gave it a colonial feel, but with numerous new buildings going up the character of the city is changing. The mountains around Córdoba are very popular with walkers and there are a number of old villages worth visiting, though finding cheap accommodation is a problem if you don't have camping equipment.

Information

The tourist office is at the bus station, a huge modern building with restaurants, shops, a bank, post office and showers.

There are two railway stations, one for the Mitre Railway and the other for the Belgrano Railway.

Places to Stay

Three of the cheapest places are the *Hotel Lady*, Balcarce 324, which is friendly and has hot showers; the *Central*, about 100 metres from the bus station; and the *Hotel Entre Ríos*, Entre Rios, also close to the bus station which is reasonably clean and has hot water.

On the same street as the Entre Rios is the *Berlin*, a small hotel which is also cheap and clean. Also worth trying are the *Pasajeros*, Corrientes 564; and the *Florida*, Rosario de Santa Fe 459.

Places to Eat

Fairly good, cheap snacks can be bought from the cafés in the bus terminal. Try also the *Romagnolo* opposite the Mitre Railway station and the *Comedor Albéniz* opposite the Alto Córdoba (Belgrano) railway station. Both of them offer good cheap food.

IGUAZÚ FALLS

These magnificent falls are fully described in the chapter on Brazil.

Places to Stay

It's probably best to stay in Foz do Iguaçu on the Brazilian side, which is what most travellers do, as there's a much better choice of cheap hotels there. However, if you want to stay on the Argentine side there a few places in Puerto Iguazú.

A good place to try is the *Hospedaje Familiar Misiones*, opposite the back entrance of the bus station. It's clean, has friendly staff and you can use the kitchen and laundry facilities. It costs US$6/$9 for singles/doubles. Other places you might like to try are the *Turista* (a pleasant old building set high above the river); *Tres Fronteras*; *Marilyn*; *Oriente* and the *Residencial Arco Iris*.

Camping isn't allowed inside the National Park. The nearest site to the park entrance is *Ñandú*, which is five km away, and the facilities there are run-down so it's worth thinking about staying elsewhere. Just outside Puerto Iguazú is the *Camping Pindó* site but although the staff are friendly, it's very shoddy and hardly worth the US$2.75 they charge.

JUJUY

Jujuy is one of Argentina's oldest cities. Like Córdoba and Salta, it was founded in the early years following the Conquest. Jujuy and Salta were established by expeditions from Peru, and Córdoba and Mendoza by expeditions from Chile. It's a pleasant city with streets lined with orange trees and it's surrounded by wooded mountains. Many travellers use Jujuy as a base from which to explore the many interesting villages in the nearby mountains.

Information

The tourist office is on Belgrano 690 on the corner of Lavalle. The Bolivian Consulate is on Araoz 697, Ciudad de Nieva.

Travellers' cheques can be changed at *Horus* on Güemes close to the tourist office as well as at certain places on Belgrano.

Places to Stay

The *Italia*, Alvear 573, is a good place to stay and although it doubles as a brothel, it's cheap, clean and has hot showers. Similar is the *Residencial Belgrano*, Belgrano 627, which is an old building but it's cheap and clean. The un-named *pension* at Calle Otero 445 close to the railway station is also worth trying for a basic but clean room.

If all the above are full then you could try the *Chung King*, Alvear 627, which is run by a friendly family but tends to be noisy.

For something slightly up-market, try either the *Residencial Ledesma*, Lavalle 464, or the *Residencial Lavalle*, Lavalle 372.

Places to Eat
Los Dos Gorditos, on Alvear near the railway station, serves good cheap meals – it's sometimes known as *Los Obreros*. Similar is the *Bar-Restaurant Sociedad Obrera*, Gen Balcarce 357.

LA QUIACA
La Quiaca is on the main border crossing between Argentina and Bolivia. It's connected to the first Bolivian town, Villazón, by a road bridge. The distance between the two is about one km and taxis are available if you don't want to walk. Also, La Quiaca is at an altitude of 3442 metres, so you will need warm clothing.

It's been suggested that you cross into Bolivia and change money at a casa de cambio rather than use the street changers in La Quiaca.

There is a Bolivian Consulate in La Quiaca if you need a visa but it's suggested you obtain it elsewhere as they often demand US$15! There are other consulates in Salta and Jujuy. If you're coming from Bolivia, the Argentine border is open from 7.30 am to noon and 3 to 6 pm on weekdays, and 9 to 11 am on Saturdays, Sundays and holidays.

Things to See
Since there's precious little to see in La Quiaca, most travellers pass straight through. Should you have a few hours to spare however, it's worth visiting the Indian village of **Yavi**, 16 km from La Quiaca. The major attraction is the church of San Francisco with its magnificent interior decorated in gold, and windows made of onyx – have you ever seen onyx windows? To get into the church you need to locate the caretaker. She will show you round on Tuesday to Sunday from 9 am to 12 noon and Tuesday to Friday from 3 to 6 pm.

Places to Stay & Eat
Probably the best of the cheapies here is the *Hotel Cristal*, opposite the bus office about one km from the railway station.

It's comfortable and clean. If you don't want to walk the one km then try the *Grand* opposite the railway station; the *Pequeño*, Bolívar 236, which is clean and friendly; or the *Residencial Victoria* which is clean and has hot water. For meals, one of the best places is the *Café Escorpion* on 9 de Julio at the junction of Sarmiento.

MENDOZA
Standing at the foot of the Andes, Mendoza was founded in 1561 but completely destroyed in 1861 by earthquake and fire, so little of its colonial past remains. It was from Mendoza that San Martín set out across the Andes to liberate Chile in the early 1800s. The city is famous for its vineyards, and if you're in the area in March it is worth going there for the grape harvest festival – the *Fiesta de la Vendimia*.

Information
The tourist office at Av San Martín 1143 has very helpful staff and maps of the city are available. They also have a list of cheap places to stay in private houses. There are branch offices at the bus station and the airport.

There's also a Chilean tourist office in the Centro Comercial Caracol, Av San Martín (12th block), which has masses of information, maps, etc.

The Bolivian consulate is at 9 de Julio 1357 (2nd floor).

The only place you can change travellers' cheques at the weekend is at the cambio in Galería Tonsa, Av San Martín (1100 block), which is open till 8 pm on Saturdays. During the week check out the cambio opposite the LAN-Chile office on San Martin. *Maguitur*, Sarmiento 26, has also been recommended.

Like Córdoba, Mendoza has a large new bus terminal with many facilities.

Things to See
Most travellers to Mendoza pay at least one visit to the summit of Cerro de la

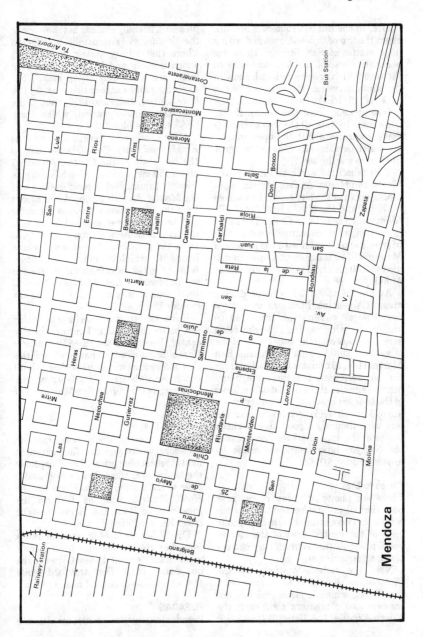

Mendoza

Gloria, in the huge Parque San Martín. From the top of this hill, crowned with a huge statue of San Martín, there are beautiful views of the Andean peaks to the west which are covered with snow in the winter months. The entrance to the park is 10 blocks west of the Plaza Independencia (local bus No 3). If you don't want to walk all the way to the top make enquiries about the open-topped bus which occasionally runs to the top of Rio Negro via the zoo.

Two museums worth visiting are the **Museo San Martín**, Av San Martín, eight blocks north of the city centre in a school building, and the **Museo Histórico**, Calle Montevideo near Calle Chile. The latter is principally concerned with San Martín's exploits and with the history of Mendoza. The museums are open from 9 am to 12.30 pm and 5 to 8 pm daily except Monday.

As one of the chief wine-producing areas of Argentina, Mendoza has quite a few *bodegas* outside the city open to visitors for wine tasting (They're often very generous with the wine). One of the largest is the Bodega de Arizú, San Martín 1149, 10 minutes by local bus from the bus terminal, but there are many others – enquire at the tourist office. Most of the *bodegas* are open for visiting from 8 am to 3 pm on weekdays. If you intend to buy wine then it's a good idea to check prices in the supermarkets first because the *bodegas* often mark up prices by anything up to 100%.

Places to Stay

There are plenty of cheap places near both the railway station and the new bus terminal. These terminals are at opposite ends of the central area of the city so you'll probably find yourself staying near the one you arrive at.

Near the railway station, try the *Victoria*, on the corner of Belgrano and Las Heras, which is clean and has hot showers and a pleasant courtyard; the *Nueva España*, Las Heras 774, which is pleasant, friendly and has hot showers; or the *Nevada*, Av Peru (parallel to Belgrano where the railway station is located), which is clean and has hot water. This last place also offers cheap meals. For something mid-range in this area, try the *Hotel Savoy*, Belgrano 1377, two blocks from the railway station, which costs US$5.45 a double.

Near the bus terminal, try the *Residencial Betty*, Calle Güemes, next to the bus station; the *Center*, Alem 547 about 150 metres away, which is run by a friendly family and is comfortable; and the *Maxim*, Lavalle 32 about four blocks from the bus station which has hot water and has been recommended by quite a few travellers. Another you might like to try is the *Residencial Ledesma*, Vicente López 511, which is similar to the above. A little further away from the bus station is *Residencial Las Mellizas*, Moreno 1819, which is also cheap and prices include breakfast.

If you want to camp you have to do this at Challao, about eight km from the city centre. The best of the three sites here is *Camping Suizo* which has good facilities (hot showers, a swimming pool and shop) but it isn't cheap at US$4 per person. Camping in the Parque San Martín is not permitted.

Places to Eat

There's a good choice of restaurants in Mendoza where you can find excellent food at reasonable prices. The cheapest of the lot are near the railway station. Also close to the station on Las Heras are the *Hotel Francia* and the *Pizzería del Rincón de la Boca*, Las Heras 485. The latter has good cheap pizzas.

The *El Rey de la Milanesa*, one block from Las Heras, has also been recommended for its meat dishes. Closer to the bus station is the *Don Angelo*, Lavalle 148, which also does good cheap meals.

POSADAS

Posadas is a way station en route either to

Paraguay via the ferry to Encarnación across the Río Paraná, or to the Iguazú Falls. There's nothing much to see in the town itself, but only an hour's bus ride away are the partially restored ruins of the once prosperous *reducciónes* of San Ignacio Mirí which flourished until the Jesuits were expelled from Spanish America in 1767. If you are going into Paraguay you can see similar ruins at Trinidad, near Encarnación.

Information
The tourist office is at Colón 1985. Maps of the town are available and the staff are friendly.

You can only change travellers' cheques at the Banco de la Nación, which is open from 6.15 am to 12.15 pm. The *casa de cambio* at Bolívar 443 will only change cash.

Things to See
If you're heading to Iguazú Falls you should not miss the ruins at **San Ignacio Mirí**. Buses go there from Posadas every two to three hours but the buses to Iguazú often stop there long enough for you to have a quick look if you don't want to make a separate journey. Entrance to the site is free.

San Ignacio is one of the most substantial of the Jesuit missions to be found in Argentina, Paraguay or Brazil. It consists of a huge plaza surrounded by many blocks of stone buildings which were once living quarters, as well as workshops, storerooms, a dining hall and a church. Many of the buildings are decorated with bas-relief sculpture. The ruins of the mission were rediscovered in 1897 and in 1943 were taken over by the Argentine government who set about restoring them.

The Jesuit missions among the Guaraní Indians resulted in one of the most interesting and tempestuous sagas in the history of the southern half of the continent. The first of the missions were set up in 1609 Guaíra region, which is now

a Brazilian province. The missions flourished and the one known as San Ignacio Mirí, built at the confluence of the Paranapanema and Pirapo rivers had, by 1614, collected some 2000 Indians. In 1627 slavers from São Paulo, in Brazil, attacked and the raids continued for several years, eventually making the settlements untenable.

A more secure place was obviously needed so in 1632 the Jesuits gathered together 12,000 of their Indian converts and floated down the Paraná on 700 rafts as far as the Guaíra Falls. They were forced to abandon the rafts there and trek through the virgin forest for eight days until they reached a place where the river was once again navigable. New rafts were built and the journey downriver resumed. New settlements were eventually established over 700 km from the original missions, in the area where the borders of present-day Argentina, Paraguay and Brazil meet.

By the early 18th century there were at least 30 different missions with a combined population of over 100,000. The end came shortly after 1767 when Charles III of Spain expelled the Jesuits from the colonies. Their prosperity declined rapidly, slavers raided them for the coffee plantations of São Paulo and their inhabitants began to drift off to the relative safety of the forest. In 1817 the missions which remained were closed down by the Paraguayan dictator Francia and the settlements burnt. These days only four of the missions display much of their former prosperity. San Ignacio Mirí is one of these. Two others on the other side of the Paraná in Paraguay are Trinidad and Jesús.

Places to Stay
The price of hotels in Posadas and in fact everywhere in Misiones province tends to be higher than anywhere else in Argentina – except Patagonia. Among the cheaper ones are the *Hotel Silvia*, Libano 885; the *Tía Julia*, Junín 880 (hot showers); and

the *Residencial Nagel*, Pedro de Mendoza 211. All are near the bus terminal.

If you'd like to stay near the ruins of San Ignacio Miní, you can camp free just outside the site where there are toilets and cold showers. It often rains heavily in this area so make arrangements accordingly. If you have no tent try the *Residencial San Martín* near the police station.

Places to Eat

Two good places to eat are *El Litoral*, Av Arrechea 35, opposite the bus station; and the *El Tropezón*, San Martín 187, which is good and inexpensive.

PUERTO MADRYN

Puerto Madryn was founded by Welsh colonists in 1865 and continued to attract immigrants from that country until 1911. They not only settled this area but pushed on inland to the Chubut Valley where their descendants remain to this day. In recent years the area has become a popular holiday destination.

Its main interest for travellers is the nearby Valdés Peninsula where you can see colonies of sea-lions and birds and even killer whales at certain times of the year (September to October). The peninsula is private property (it's used for sheep grazing) so you need to take an organised tour from Puerto Madryn.

If you find these tours too expensive then hitch-hike to Punta Loma, a little further down the bay from Puerto Madryn, where there are also seal and sea-lion colonies. The reserve here is open from 9 am to 12 noon and 2.30 to 5.30 pm. September and October are the best months to visit. Further south beyond Trelew at Punta Tombo there is a huge penguin colony which you can visit from September/October to February/March. They migrate further south during the rest of the year.

Information

The tourist office is at Sarmiento 386 (tel 71514) and is worth visiting since it has information about the various reserves as well as regional maps and maps of the nearby towns.

Things to See

The main wildlife reserves are at Punta Norte and Punta Piramides on the Valdés Peninsula, at Punta Loma on the bay just south-east of Puerto Madryn, and at Punta Tombo about 120 km south of Trelew. You can easily hitch-hike to Punta Loma from Puerto Madryn but to visit the other reserves you'll probably have to go on a tour or hire a taxi if there is a group of you. The latter is preferable since you get to stay longer at the reserves; the tour companies only stay about 60 minutes at each place which may not be long enough to see much.

For organised tours contact either *Tur-Mar*, 25 de Mayo 147 (tel 71104), or *Pu-Mar*, 28 de Julio 40 (tel 71766), both in Puerto Madryn. Full-day tours should cost about US$11 per person.

Places to Stay

Because it has been developed as a holiday resort, hotels in Puerto Madryn are on the expensive side - expect to pay around US$12 to $15. Three of the cheapest places are the *Paris*, on the corner of Roque Sáenz Peña and 25 de Mayo; the *El Antiguo*, 28 de Julio 147 (clean with cooking facilities); and the *Vaskonia*, 25 de Mayo 43 (hot showers available).

If you prefer to camp you can do this on the beach (many people do). There's also a site with good facilities at Ribera Sur, about two km from town on the beach but it gets very crowded in the tourist season.

RÍO GALLEGOS

Close to the southern tip of the Patagonian peninsula, Río Gallegos is the jumping-off point for trips both to Calafate and to Ushuaia (Tierra del Fuego). There is nothing much to see there and it's an

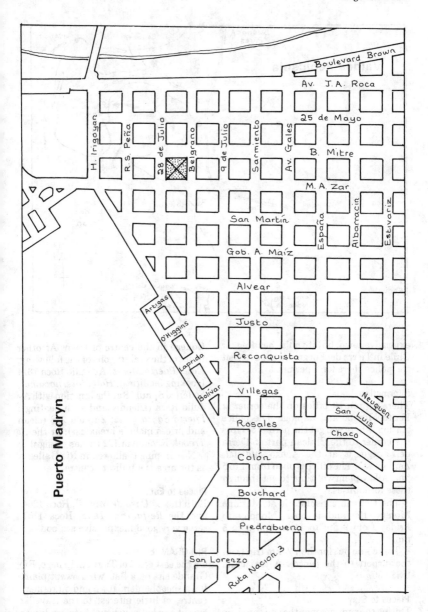

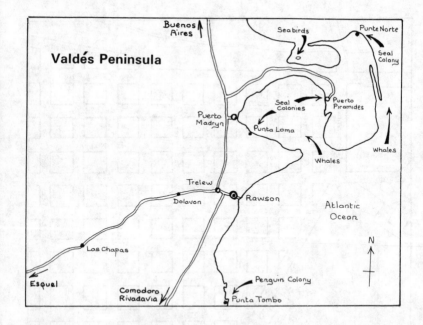

Valdés Peninsula

expensive town, but if you're heading for Chilean Tierra del Fuego you need to visit the police there for a permit.

Information

There's a tourist office on the corner of Perito Moreno and Zapiola. The police station, where you get the permit to cross the border to the Chilean part of Tierra del Fuego, is at the Anexo Judicial, Zapiola 715. The office is open from 1 to 5 pm. Allow plenty of time to get through these formalities.

The Chilean consulate is at Mariano Moreno 155 and is open Monday to Friday from 9 am to 1 pm and 3 to 5 pm.

There's no bus for the 7½ km trip from the airport to the centre. A taxi costs US$2.50.

Places to Stay

During the summer months you can sleep for free in the classrooms at the Salesian College in the centre of town. At other times of the year, try one of the following: *Hotel Puerto Montt*, Av Julio Roca 1614 (cooking facilities); *Hotel Internacional*, Federico Sphur 78 at the junction with Av Julio Roca (friendly and with heating); *Puerto Santa Cruz*, Zapiola 238 (clean and prices include breakfast); or the *El Trébol*, Rivadavia 122 (it has no sign).

No camping is allowed in Río Gallegos as the area is a military centre.

Places to Eat

Both the *La Casa de Miguel*, Roca 1284, and the *Restaurant Díaz*, Roca 1157, serve very good inexpensive seafood.

RÍO GRANDE

On the east coast of Tierra del Fuego, Río Grande sits on a flat, wind-swept plain. It's a sheepherders' town and oil refinery centre, of little interest to the traveller except as a halfway house between Punta Arenas or Río Gallegos and Ushuaia.

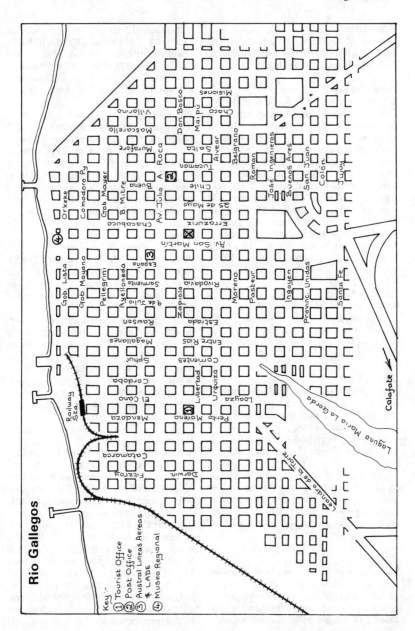

Rio Gallegos

Key:-
① Tourist Office
② Post Office
③ Austral Lineas Aereas
✈ LADE
④ Museo Regional

Information

Tourist information can be found at the Municipalidad, Calle Sebastián El Cano. It's open Monday to Friday.

Places to Stay

It's not always easy to find a room in Río Grande because most of the cheapies are occupied by men working on the oil installations. You may have to check quite a few before you find something.

Try the following: *Shelkman*, San Martín 236; *Albergue*, on the corner of Alberdi and Piedrabuena; *Hospedaje Irmary*, Estrada 743 (very clean and pleasant and two blocks from the *Senkovic* bus office); and the *Penion Río Bueno*, Alberdi 616 (basic but clean and friendly). The *Residencial Rawson* has also been recommended though it does cost US$8 per bed.

Places to Eat

The *Confitería Roca*, Roca 629, is open 24 hours a day and serves reasonably priced food. There's also a bar there. Another popular place which serves excellent food is *La Gaviota*.

Getting There

Sencovich buses leave for Porvenir at 6 am on Wednesday and Saturday. The trip costs US$6 and connects with the ferry to Punta Arenas.

There are daily buses to Ushuaia at 6 am and 12.30 pm during the summer months and once a day on Monday, Wednesday and Friday during the winter by *Los Carlos* which take up to five hours and cost US$7. Tickets should be bought from the Hotel Antártida. The buses leave from one block away from the Hotel Miramar.

SALTA

Like Jujuy and Córdoba, Salta is one of Argentina's oldest cities. It was founded in 1582 and has managed to preserve its colonial atmosphere. The streets are lined with fine old buildings and there are a number of very interesting churches including the cathedral, which has a beautiful interior; the Convent of San Bernardo; and the church of San Francisco, which is said to have the tallest tower of any church in South America.

Information

The tourist office is at Buenos Aires 93, one block from the main plaza. The staff are very helpful and they have a list of accommodation offered in private houses.

You'll find the Bolivian consulate at Santiago del estero 179. It's open Monday to Friday from 9 am to 1 pm. The Chilean consulate is at Zuviría 118.

Things to See

Several museums in Salta are worth visiting. The **Cabildo Histórico**, Caseros 549, is one of the best museums in Argentina and shouldn't be missed. It's open from Wednesday to Sunday from 3 to 8 pm.

Another museum which has a very good display of Indian crafts – particularly tapestry – is the **Museo de Arte Nativo**, Alverado 551 behind the Guémes statue. The **Museo Colonial Histórico y de Bellas Artes**, Caseros 575, is also worth a visit. It's open daily from 4 to 7 pm and from Wednesday to Sunday from 9 am to 12 noon.

Places to Stay

A good place to stay is the *Residencial San Jorge* which is difficult to find and there's no sign so you must ask directions. It has a friendly and helpful owner who is well-informed about Argentina and charges just US$2 per person.

If you can't find it then try the *Florida*, Urquiza 722 on the corner of Florida, which is very clean and friendly and has hot showers. Close by is the *Residenciales Viena*, Florida 184, which is similar.

Two others worth trying are the *Centro*, Belgrano 657; and the *Residencial Royal*, on the corner of Lavalle and Alvarado five blocks from the bus station, which is basic

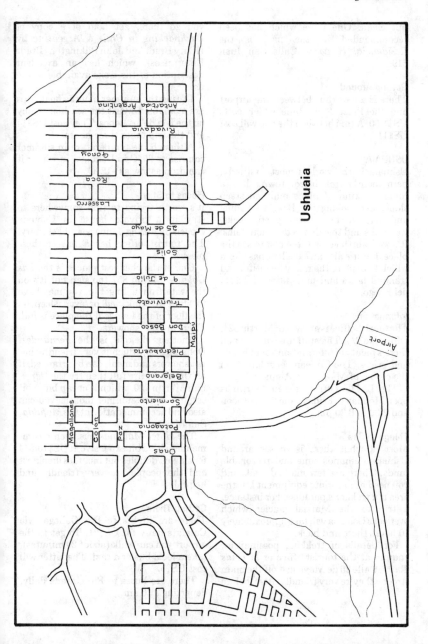

but clean. One more which has been recommended in the past is the *Residencial Hispano*, Calle San Juan 619.

Getting Around

There is a local bus between the airport and the Plaza 9 de Julio which costs US$1.50. A taxi between the two will cost US$11.

USHUAIA

Ushuaia is the world's most southerly, permanently inhabited town. It's a romantic kind of place built on steep slopes overlooking the Beagle Channel and backed by snow-capped peaks, waterfalls and thickly wooded mountains. It's well worth going there just to see the place, but it's also an excellent base from which to explore the many beautiful and tranquil lakes and mountains of Tierra del Fuego.

Information

The tourist office is at Av San Martín 524, Office No 2/3. The staff are friendly and there's plenty of information about hotels and prices. The Chilean consulate is on the corner of Maipú and Alapa.

The LADE Office at San Martín is open Monday to Friday from 9 am to noon and 2.30 to 6.30 pm.

Things to See

Most of what there is to see around Ushuaia demands time and reasonable funds. There are few marked trails and you need appropriate equipment but the area is a trekker's paradise. For instance, a trip to the Martial glacier which overlooks Ushuaia will take approximately 10 hours there and back.

For details of trekking possibilities, enquire at the tourist office or at *Onas Tours*, Calle 25 de Mayo just off the main street – they're very friendly. Also, before

you go there, get hold of a copy of *Backpacking in Chile & Argentina* by Hilary Bradt and John Pilkington (Bradt Enterprises), which has an excellent description of the treks available in the area.

During the summer months boat trips are available to visit the sea-lion colony on the Isla de los Lobos. They cost US$14 and the trip takes three hours.

Although the temperature in summer can rise to 25°C in Ushuaia, in winter it can drop as low as –12°C.

Places to Stay

It's worth trying to find somewhere to stay in a private house in Ushuaia especially during January and February. The tourist office has a list of these places.

One of the cheapest places is the *Las Goletas*, Maipú 857 (no sign but it's on the waterfront). To get in, you may have to share a bunk bed or even sleep on the floor of the lounge if the place is full. There are hot showers.

Another cheapie is the *Fernández*, Ochanaga 68, which is very friendly, has hot showers and meals can be arranged. If all the above are full then try the *Capri*, San Martín 720, which is cheap but a bit scruffy. In the summer months you can also find accommodation at the *Mafalda*, San Martín 5.

The *Hotel Malvinas* has been recommended. It's a bit expensive at US$10/$14 for singles/doubles but includes breakfast and the people are very friendly and helpful.

Getting There

There are flights to Río Gallegos via Calafate daily for US$21. To get to the airport you can walk (about 20 minutes), take a local bus or a taxi. The latter will cost US$5.

There are buses to Río Grande daily, departing at 6 am.

Bolivia

Geographically, Bolivia is the Tibet of the Americas. It's the most remote and isolated republic in the whole of Latin America and has a mystique about it which attracts many travellers. Though 70% of the country's total land area lies in the sparsely populated and undeveloped lowlands of the Amazon basin, the majority of the population live on the altiplano – a dry, barren and almost treeless plateau which varies in height from 3000 to 4000 metres. It has a vast, eerie sort of beauty which you're not likely to forget in a hurry. The plateau is surrounded by snow-capped mountains which in some cases rise to a height of 7000 metres and dictate the pattern of communications. Also on this plateau is the world's highest capital city – La Paz – at 3600 metres, and South America's highest and largest fresh-water lakes – Titicaca and Poopó.

Bolivia is the most Indian nation on the whole continent – some 70% of the population are pure-blood Indian. They're a rugged, sun-baked and severe people with a history of oppression and exploitation you'd be hard-pressed to find the equal of anywhere else in the world. Even the characteristic bowler hats and voluminous skirts worn by the women were imposed on them towards the end of the 18th century by the Spanish King, Carlos III. The style was modelled on the clothes worn by the peasant women of Estremadura, Andalusia and the Basque provinces. The centre parting of the hair was the result of a decree made by the Viceroy Toledo.

Following the collapse of the Inca Empire, the Spanish herded millions of these people to their deaths as slave-labourers in the silver mines of Potosí, and when the silver finally ran out and tin became a valuable commodity in post-independence days, the whole sad story was repeated. Today, although the mines have been nationalised, the miners at the face earn a wage insufficient to provide for the most basic of human needs. Life expectancy for them is a mere 35 years, by which time most have died of silicosis-pneumonia, a well-known occupational disease associated with working in high silica dust environments.

Short life expectancy isn't their only worry. The state mining company owns the houses in which the miners and their families live and when a miner dies, his family is forced to leave the house unless there are other members of the family still working in the mines. If his dependants can't find relatives willing – or even able – to help them, they are left destitute, and are then forced to migrate to the cities in search of work or to attempt to scratch a living from the soil. And scratch is certainly the word for it – the altiplano must have one of the world's most inhospitable climates for growing food. Rain rarely falls and when it does, usually causes flash floods. Temperatures drop to near freezing at night but can climb to 20°C during the day.

To compound their problems, most of the people are illiterate, speaking only one or other of the Indian languages, Aymara or Quechua, and until 1952, none of these people had the vote – for what it's worth in a country that's been ruled by one military dictatorship after another, and which has had more coups than most people have had hot dinners.

To make life bearable – especially in the mines – the Indians constantly chew coca leaves and in the evenings they blot out their pain and hunger with *aguardiente*, the local fire-water, which is almost pure alcohol.

The use of coca leaves goes back to the days of the Incas and earlier, when it was used for ritual purposes. The Spanish found it a useful stimulant and energetically promoted its use. It was good for business. Every year, a million kilograms of coca leaves were consumed in the Potosí mines. By levying a tax on these wages of misery the Church was able to finance the entire budget for the Cuzco bishopric out of it.

Today, much of the leaf is refined into cocaine either inside the country or in neighbouring Brazil, after which it is smuggled to the USA, Europe and Australia. Cocaine is one of Bolivia's major 'invisible' exports and because of the amounts involved, little of the activity takes place without the knowledge of high government officials, all of whom, naturally, have to be paid off.

It was silver however, which first brought Bolivia to the attention of the world. It was discovered by the Spanish in the Cerro Rico outside the town of Potosí in 1545.

So rich was that vein of ore, that this mine alone accounted for 99% of the mineral exports from Spanish America until other mines were opened in Mexico. According to the records of Spain's Casa de Contratación in Seville, 185,000 kg of gold and 16 million kg of silver were sent to Europe between 1545 and 1660 – an amount which was 3½ times the total European reserves at the time! Since a great deal of smuggling took place, the actual amounts must have been considerably more. In its heyday, Potosí rivalled in affluence and extravagant living, anything which Europe could offer at the time.

Little of this incredible amount of wealth ever saw the light of day in Spain since the monarchy was mortgaged to the hilt and precious-metal shipments were spoken for before they arrived. Extravagance by the monarchy and the Church, and the cost of financing the numerous wars which Spain waged in its bid for European hegemony, ensured that virtually all the silver and gold was immediately passed on to German,

Genoese and Flemish bankers to cover loans which they had advanced. One of the results of all this easy money was Spain's industrial and agricultural underdevelopment. It explains, in part, why Spain today is one of Europe's poorest countries.

Bolivia's main export today is tin, mined at Potosí and Oruro; closely followed by copper, extracted from the mines at Corocoro. Very little of the wealth these exports generate ever reaches the general populace, nor is it used to increase standards of living, or invested in development. It's creamed off by a small clique of top military officers and the very rich. Also, despite the fact that the mines have been nationalised, foreign companies are still involved in mining operations. One of the most unbelievable franchises handed out went to the Dutch conglomerate, Philips Industries, in 1964. Under the terms of the agreement, Philips was allowed to mine silver, lead and zinc from one of the Oruro mines for a return to the state of just 1.5% of the sale value of the ore!

Bolivia has had its share of political misfortunes too. Up until the late 19th century, Bolivian territory extended down to the Pacific Ocean around the town of Antofagasta. This littoral was annexed by Chile following the War of the Pacific (1879-1883) between Peru and Bolivia on the one hand and Chile on the other.

The reason for the conflict lay in the presence of vast deposits of nitrates in the Atacama Desert, most of which, until 1879, belonged to Peru and Bolivia. Although the Spanish had been aware of these deposits for centuries and utilised them to make gunpowder, they were not regarded as having any substantial value until it was discovered in the 19th century that nitrates were an excellent fertiliser.

Mining of the nitrates began in earnest around Antofagasta and further north in the Peruvian section using Chilean and, to a far lesser extent, Peruvian capital.

When the Bolivian government proposed a tax on the mineral, the Chilean navy attacked and after a lightning campaign, took the whole of the desert up to Tacna in Peru. Bolivia was 'compensated' with a railway from Antofagasta to Oruro with duty-free facilities at the port for the export of Bolivian commodities.

Bolivia has never accepted the loss and when national attention needs to be focused abroad, the government uses the Antofagasta issue to threaten war with Chile. As recently as 1978 the issue was stirred up to a point just short of a declaration of war, with Argentina lending support because it was dissatisfied with

the results of arbitration concerning three tiny islands in the Beagle Channel off Tierra del Fuego.

The tragedy of losing Antofagasta was compounded a few years later by the discovery of one of the world's largest and richest copper ore deposits in the area. However the Chileans didn't reap the benefits of their newly acquired territory for quite some time, either, as they had relied on British capital to finance the war.

Bolivia's next loss of territory was in 1903 when Brazil annexed the Acre Territory which stretched from Bolivia's present Amazonian borders to about halfway up Peru's eastern border. The reason this time was rubber. Centred on Manaus, the rubber boom took off in the latter part of the 19th century and by 1890 accounted for one-tenth of Brazil's export earnings. Initially, Bolivia participated in the boom by ransacking the forests of the Acre, but so rich was the area in

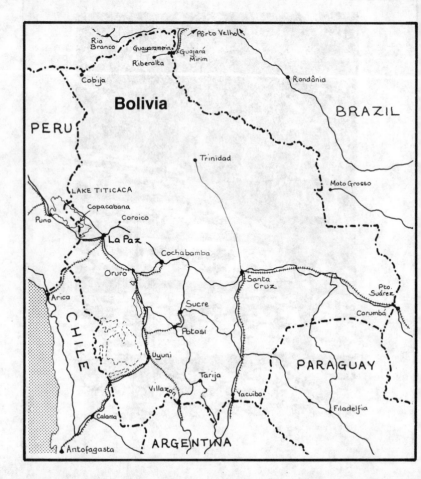

rubber trees that a dispute over sovereignty was eventually engineered and the Brazilian army was sent in. Bolivia was in no position to do anything about the annexation. It had neglected its Amazonian territories for centuries and communications were virtually non-existent. Only in very recent years has this situation begun to change. This time Bolivia was 'compensated' by a totally useless railway running from Pôrto Velho to Riberalta but it was never completed and fell into disuse not long afterwards.

In 1932 a dispute arose between Bolivia and Paraguay over sovereignty of the Chaco. The area had previously been of little interest to either country, being of very limited agricultural potential and inhabited only by a few tribes of Indians. The trouble started when various North American and European oil companies began to speculate about the possibility of finding oil deposits in the area. In a bid to secure favourable franchises, a quarrel was engineered with Standard Oil supporting Bolivia and Shell supporting Paraguay. In the ensuing war hundreds of thousands of people lost their lives. When peace was finally negotiated Paraguay came out on top and Bolivia lost a huge slice of its former territory.

It didn't lose as much as it might have thought if an agent of Standard Oil had not chaired the peace negotiations and secured continued Bolivian ownership over thousands of square km claimed by Paraguay, with an eye to future concessions for his company. This was only the start of the oil companies' interference in the affairs of the two nations and in the years which followed some incredibly one-sided concessions were handed out.

It might seem from the above account that Bolivia has accepted almost any kind of iniquity meted out. This isn't the case. Resistance to Spanish rule began here before anywhere else. There were mestizo revolts in La Paz in 1661, and in 1780 in Cochabamba, followed by Indian revolts in Cochabamba, La Paz, Oruro

and Sucre between 1776 and 1780. Independence from Spain came finally in 1825 following Sucre's victories at the battles of Ayacucho and Tumusla.

After a short-lived attempt at union with Peru, Bolivia was ruled by one military junta after another. Few governments have lasted for more than a year and many have lasted only a matter of weeks. Generally the coups involve few people outside the main plaza in La Paz, and are essentially a reshuffling of white military officers – power is held exclusively by the tiny *blanco* minority which represents no more than 5% of the population.

Defeat at the hands of Paraguay in the Chaco War, however, had revolutionary repercussions. Radicals gathered together under the banner of the Movimiento Nacionalista Revolucionario (MNR), led by Victor Paz Estenssoro, and won the elections of 1951. A military coup prevented them from taking office and led to an armed revolt by the miners. After heavy fighting the military was defeated, and Paz Estenssoro was brought back from exile in Buenos Aires to head the new government, which pressed ahead with a programme of reform.

The reforms – which included the granting of the franchise to illiterates (the majority of Indians), nationalisation of the tin mines and redistribution of land – had the effect of making the peasants and miners feel that they were part of the nation, and that the government was trying to do something for them. Even with US support, the MNR was unable to substantially raise the standard of living or increase food production. Dissension began to grow, forcing Estenssoro to become more and more autocratic. When he finally alienated even his former supporters, he was overthrown in a military coup headed by Gen Barrientos. One of Barrientos' first actions was to attack the miners, as they were the principal support behind the MNR. After much bloodshed, the leaders were arrested and either jailed or deported. The 1952 revolution was the country's 179th change of government! – and the only one which produced any discernible change in the status quo.

Throughout the late 1960s the familiar pattern of coups replaced one military officer with another until the right-wing Gen Hugo Banzer seized power in 1971. He became one of Latin America's longest-reigning dictators and ruled until 1978, when elections were held for a constituent assembly. They were denounced however, both inside the country and abroad, as blatantly fraudulent and were annulled. Two further attempts at electing an assembly were short-circuited by another coup, which led to the suspension of military and economic aid by the USA, the EEC and other countries.

One of Bolivia's greatest weaknesses has been the failure to settle and develop the lowlands on the east side of the Andes. Although things are beginning to happen there, the area is still only sparsely populated and then only by blancos and mestizos. For the most part, the Indians refuse to move from the *altiplano* despite its barrenness and harsh climate. Their roots lie in the highlands. They are physically adapted to it and fear that if they move to the lowlands they will succumb to the diseases prevalent there. Agrarian reform is seen by them largely as a means of preserving and reviving an old way of life which the Spanish almost destroyed and which others have since treated with contempt.

Nevertheless, the lowlands are being slowly colonised, though often by people from other countries. Mennonite farmers have set up a dairy industry and Santa Cruz has become a very cosmopolitan city with many immigrants from Japan, Germany and the United States. Naturalisation is available to all foreigners after three years' residence. The irony is that it was a very prosperous area during colonial times as a result of the activities of Jesuit missionaries who set up *reducciónes*, as they had done in neighbouring Paraguay. When they were expelled by the Spanish Crown, the settlements fell apart and were looted. Nothing remains of them today.

VISAS

These are required by everyone other than the nationals of Austria, Belgium, Canada, Denmark, Germany (West), Greece, Irish Republic, Israel, Italy, Luxembourg, Netherlands, Norway, Portugal, Spain, Sweden, Switzerland, UK and USA. The length of stay you get on entry depends on the political situation in the country at the time. If things are calm then it's usually 90 days; if not, it's often reduced to 30 days. You might have to pay a small (unofficial) 'fee' on entry which you'll be told is for the entry stamp or in lieu of a baggage search. It's all nonsense but it's better to pay if you don't want delays and hassles.

As long as you have a visa (where required) there are no special conditions about entry at most borders. The only exception is at Guayaramerín near Riberalta in the extreme north-east of the country. Details about this are given in the section on Guayaramerín.

It's no longer necessary to get an exit stamp from the immigration department in a large city before turning up at the border. All formalities are now taken care of at the border itself.

Carry your passport with you at all times in Bolivia. If you get stopped by the police and can't produce one then you'll be arrested. Every so often the police decide to comb hotels, bars and restaurants asking foreigners for their passports. It doesn't happen very often but if you are caught out you could waste two or three days staring at the blank walls of a prison cell.

If arriving or leaving via La Paz international airport expect heavy baggage and body searches. They're looking for drugs mainly. The same can be expected flying from Bolivia into Brazil or Chile or when crossing any of the land borders into those two countries.

The Immigration Office in La Paz is at Av Gozalvez 240, off Av Arce. Microbus Nos A, N and 130 pass nearby.

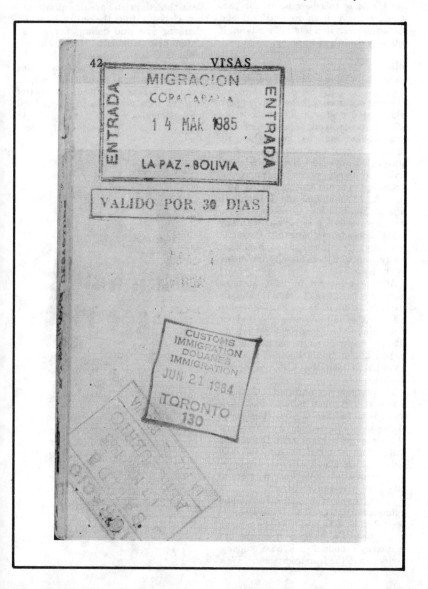

Depending on the political system there may be a curfew in La Paz (and other cities). It's wise to be aware of anything like this because in the past offenders have been rounded up and spent the night in a football stadium. It gets very cold there at night!

MONEY

Rates unquotable because of inflation.

The unit of currency is the Bolivian peso (B$) = 100 centavos. Throughout the 1970s the peso was one of South America's most stable currencies but in the early 1980s it began a catastrophic decline unequalled anywhere else in the world (even by such prime examples as Argentina in South America and Ghana, Uganda, Mozambique and Tanzania in Africa). The inflation rate now stands at a staggering 8000% p a. No-one with any sense in Bolivia now hangs on to pesos for any longer than they have to since what you can buy with them literally diminishes by the hour.

Austere measures in 1985, such as increasing the price of petrol tenfold, by the government of Victor Paz Estorrenso have resulted in price rises on just about everything. The rates for US$ haven't changed however, as the banks now buy and sell US$ at the blackmarket rate in an attempt to take the US$ out of the blackmarket.

The situation is reminiscent of Germany before WW II when workers took their wages home in wheel barrows. There is an almost desperate demand for US dollars. No-one seems to know when the decline will bottom out but Bolivians, especially street traders whose earnings are never more than a few dollars a day, seem to take it all with a pinch of salt.

Counting money has become a national but necessary occupation. It has replaced worry-beads. 500 and 1000 peso bank notes, (worth a fraction of a cent but printed by Thomas de la Rue & Company, London, and the Bundesdruckerei, West Germany) litter the gutters of the capital and are eagerly scooped up by the beggars. Indeed, any note over 100,000 pesos these days isn't a real bank note but just a 'cheque' from the central bank. By changing just one dollar, you are an instant peso millionaire. Hardly anyone, it seems, changes money in banks as the official exchange rate is totally unrealistic, yet to do otherwise is officially illegal. Even travellers' cheques are better changed privately (in shops or with local businessmen).

Until the Bolivian peso reaches a ceiling or the economy collapses there is little point in quoting exchange rates; and just when that will happen is anyone's guess. The prices quoted, even in US dollars, in this chapter should also be taken as a guide only. They may stay the same in relative terms; they may alter substantially. Whatever else you do, don't change more money than you need to get you through one or two days, as the exchange rate will have increased by then. And don't take pesos out of the country – no-one wants them (except travellers intending to go to Bolivia) and exchange rates are generally poor at the border.

There is a government tax of 13% on airline tickets bought in the country but it's payable in pesos. Airport departure tax for domestic flights is US$1. For international departures it is US$15. You can still pay for domestic airline tickets in pesos without bank receipts – this makes them some of the cheapest in the world.

GETTING THERE

Bolivia has road and rail connections with Peru, Chile, Brazil and Argentina. The road to Corumbá, Brazil from Santa Cruz isn't up to much though and it's much better and more reliable to take the train. Also the roads, or rather tracks, through the Chaco into Paraguay can be dismissed completely unless you have either plenty of time and stamina or your own very robust, four-wheel-drive vehicle. Occasionally there are trucks which cover this route but they don't go in the wet season as the route is impassable. At those times the only way you can get into Paraguay is via Brazil or Argentina.

To/From Peru

There are several ways to get to Peru from La Paz, all of them ending in Puno. The pleasantest route is via the Straits of Tiquina on Lake Titicaca to Copacabana and on to Yunguyo and Puno. *Transportes 2 de Febrero*, Av Manco Kapac 464 , La Paz, have two departures per day for Copacabana at 8 am and 3 pm; *Flota Copacabana* (at the main bus terminal) have three per week at 7.30 am on Tuesday, Thursday and Saturday; and *Transportes Riveros Herrera*, Av Montes 660, leave at 7.30 am on Thursdays and Saturdays.

Expreso Manco Kapac, Tumusla 506, also go daily at 7.30 am and 2 pm but many travellers complain about their service so you're advised to give them a miss if possible.

All the companies charge US$2.50 and take about 3½ hours. The ferry across the Straits of Tiquina costs US$0.15. There's no need to change buses as the ferries take the buses as well as the passengers.

From Copacabana there are frequent daily buses and trucks to Yunguyo (Peru). The buses cost B$10 or 200 soles; trucks are generally cheaper but you have to haggle with the drivers. From Yungayo there are daily buses by *Morales Moralitos*, *Transportes La Perla* and *Empresa 4 de Noviembre* to Puno which cost US$2.50 and take about four to five hours. The journey from La Paz to Puno can be done in one day if you don't want to stay in Copacabana.

The other route to Puno goes via Desaguadero and Guaqui via the southern edge of Lake Titicaca. The best company to travel with is *Panamericana* from the bus terminal in La Paz. They leave daily at 8 am stopping at Tiahuanaco for half an hour to give you time to visit the pre-Inca ruins. At the border (Guaqui) you change onto minibuses for the run into Puno. The entire journey takes about eight hours and costs US$6 (this is the through fare; you don't pay again when you change at Guaqui). The road between La Paz and Guaqui is very rough but from Guaqui to Puno it's surfaced all the way.

Many hotels and travel agencies in La Paz will offer to fix you up with tickets for this run but not one of them will charge you less than US$10. Since they use exactly the same buses you should avoid buying tickets from them unless you want to throw away US$4 or more.

It's also possible to get between La Paz and Puno by means of a luxury bus/Lake Titicaca steamer combination but this is much more expensive. Details can be found later.

To/From Chile

You have a choice here of rail or bus. On the railways you can either go to Arica or Calama. Passenger trains no longer go all the way to Antofagasta – they stop at Calama – so you have to complete the journey from Calama to the coast by bus. There are two trains per month to Arica but the *ferrobus* has been withdrawn so there's now only the ordinary train and you must change at the border. You also need plenty of warm clothes as the line is one of the highest in the world and it gets bitterly cold at night (-15°C isn't unusual). Expect long delays at the border as there's a lot of smuggling going on and Chilean customs are very thorough. The journey will take at least 22 hours. Because of the inflation rate, fares are changed frequently so there's no point in quoting them, but since you pay in pesos it's very cheap.

To Calama, the train leaves once weekly on Friday at 2 pm (in the opposite direction on Wednesday at 2.55 pm). Only one class is available and you must change trains at Ollague. The Bolivian carriages are in good shape but the Chilean ones are very rough (you'd think it would be the other way round!). As with the Arica train, you need plenty of warm clothing. The journey takes at least 24 hours including a four-hour thorough customs check at the border. Again, because of the inflation rate, fares are changed frequently but they're still very cheap. This train is very popular with travellers and offers spectacular views over the dry salt lakes and volcanos along the border region. Book your tickets for this train in La Paz at least two days in advance. The ticket office is open Monday to Friday from 8 am to 12 noon and from 2 to 6 pm. On Saturdays and Sundays the hours are 8 to 11 am. Be at the station at least three hours before the train is due if you want to be sure of a seat.

You can pick up this train at Oruro or Uyuni if you don't happen to be in La Paz. If you're coming in from Calama you can make connections to Potosí at Río Mulatos but you have to be very quick getting off the train at this junction as it sometimes only stops for one minute. Many passengers coming up from Chile get off the train at Oruro and take the bus from there as it's much quicker. Drinks and food are available on the train. If you're coming up from Chile, money changers get on the train at Ollague but they offer a worse rate than the Bolivian money changers who get on later and who will change both US dollars and Chilean pesos. Like the La Paz-Arica train, this one is full of smugglers too so expect thorough searches by Chilean customs.

The only international bus connection between Bolivia and Chile is La Paz-Arica. *Pullman Martinez* (from the bus terminal in La Paz) depart twice a week on Tuesdays and Fridays at 6 am taking 16 hours and costing US$10.

To/From Brazil

The most popular route to Brazil is via the Santa Cruz-Corumbá railway line. A rough sort of road also connects the two places but there's no scheduled transport.

There is a choice of *ferrobus*, *tren rapido* and even *tren mixto* on this line but most people take the *ferrobus* since it's much quicker and more comfortable. It departs Santa Cruz on Monday, Wednesday and Friday at 6 pm and costs US$11.80 (Pullman) and US$7.90 (Especial). Meals are served on the train and are usually pretty good but food is also available at one or two stops along the way. It usually takes 12 hours but can sometimes take longer. Buy tickets in advance from the railway station.

The *tren rapido* usually departs daily at 11.30 am and 3.45 pm but it can take 24 hours and it's invariably packed. Conditions are primitive in first and second class so you need a strong constitution if you're thinking of taking this train. The fares are US$5.25 (Pullman), US$3.30 (1st) and US$2.05 (2nd). Neither type of train actually goes over the border to Corumbá. The last station is Quijarro on the Bolivia/Brazil border. From there you must take a bus to Corumbá. These run daily every 45 minutes from 7 am to 5 pm. The Brazilian border post is open Monday to Friday from 6.30 to 11.30 am, 1 to 4 pm and 8.30 to 9 pm. At weekends it's open from 6.30 to 8 am, 10.30 to 11.30 am and 7.30 to 9 pm. There are daily trains from Corumbá to Campo Grande and São Paulo. Expect to be thoroughly searched by Brazilian police on Corumbá station (they're looking for cocaine).

There's only one hotel near the station in Quijarro – and they know it! It's across the tracks and up the dirt road on the far side, about 400 metres from the station. There are a couple of cheap places where you can buy food at the station.

The other border crossing from Bolivia to Brazil is from Guayaramerín to Guajará Mirim in the extreme north-east of the country. This route isn't anywhere near as popular as the above but more and more travellers are using it as a back door to the Amazon and Manaus. The difficulty is getting there as there are no roads connecting this part of Bolivia to the main cities. The only way to do it is to fly either to Guayaramerín itself (with *TAM*) or to Riberalta (with either *LAB* or *TAM*) or to get a riverboat. There are many possibilities for doing the latter; it's simply a question of deciding which river in the Beni you want to float down. These boats are primitive and often take a long time so it's worth considering the flights and since you can pay for domestic flights in pesos they're very cheap indeed – US$18 from Santa Cruz to Riberalta and half that from Trinidad to Riberalta.

Details about border crossing formalities on this route are given in the section on Guayaramerín.

To/From Argentina

You can get to northern Argentina from Bolivia either by train or bus along two routes – Potosí-Villazon-La Quiaca-Jujuy, and Santa Cruz-Yacuiba-Embarcación. There's also a minor route from Tarija to Embarcación via Oran along which there are occasional buses.

Via Villazon/La Quiaca This is the most popular route with both rail and road connections. There are no longer any trains which cross the border so you must get off at Villazon, walk or take a taxi across the border, and take another train from La Quiaca. Trains depart La Paz on Mondays, Thursdays and Fridays at 11.30 am and go via Oruro. There are also trains from Sucre via Potosí to Tupiza (just north of Villazon) which depart Potosí on Thursday and Sunday at 2.15 pm. All these trains are *tren mixto* – there are no longer any *ferrobuses*. There's even a rumour that the railway authorities are going to stop running to Villazon and go only as far as Tupiza. There doesn't seem any rhyme or reason for that so enquire about it.

As far as buses go, *Panamericana* operate an international connection from La Paz to Jujuy and Salta in Argentina. From Potosí there are four departures per day for Villazon by *Boqueron, 10 de Noviembre, Transportes Tupiza* and *Chicheño*. They all leave at 5 pm and cost US$2.30. From Sucre there is one departure per day to Villazon with *Pullman 10 de Noviembre*. You can also get to Villazon from Tarija.

Via Yacuiba From Santa Cruz the *tren rapido* departs for Yacuiba on the Argentinian border everyday from Monday to Friday at 1.30 pm. Fares are US$4.30 (Pullman), US$2.70 (1st) and US$1.70 (2nd). The journey takes about

12 hours. There are no *ferrobuses* along this line any more. From Yacuiba you must either walk or take a taxi across the border and then pick up another train or bus from there to Embarcación.

GETTING AROUND
Air
Lloyd Aero Boliviano (LAB) and *Transportes Aereas Militares (TAM)*, the Bolivian military airline, cover both international and internal routes and are well worth considering if your time is limited or the bus journey is a particularly rough and long one. Get hold of a copy of their schedules and fares as soon as you reach a large city.

Fares are cheap by any standards but since you can pay for domestic fares in pesos this makes them some of the cheapest in the world. For instance, you can fly from Santa Cruz to Riberalta for just US$19 including taxes or Santa Cruz to Sucre is just US$7.50! There's not much difference between *LAB* and *TAM* as far as fares go but the latter tends to be cheaper. On the other hand, *LAB* are notorious for cancellations so don't cut things too fine if you have to be somewhere on a certain date to catch an international flight. They'll cancel because of bad weather or even because the plane isn't fully booked. This is especially true down in the Beni lowlands.

For cheap international flight tickets, *Shima Tours*, Calle Potosí 1310, La Paz (tel 372001-5), has been highly recommended. It's run by Japanese people.

Bus
The bus network in Bolivia is well-developed and buses tend to be fairly good though some companies run decidedly better buses than others. Roads vary from good surfaced highways to rough, pot-holed, gravel tracks. Some of the worst roads are between Sucre and Cochabamba and Sucre and Santa Cruz. The one between Oruro and Cochabamba is very dusty but otherwise is in good shape. Where roads are rough it's best to take the *ferrobus* if there is one.

A few years ago, very few Bolivian cities had central bus terminals and the various companies' offices were scattered all over a certain section of each city. More and more cities now have a central terminal – La Paz, Oruro, Potosí, Santa Cruz, Sucre and Tarija for instance, and there are plans for one in Cochabamba.

Most long-distance bus journeys are done at night though there are generally a few daytime departures. If you don't want to travel at night then either get a ride on a truck or look around for a minibus. The latter often don't leave from the central bus terminal but tend to hang around the Indian markets and go when full – there's no regular departure schedule. They're just as good as buses and no more expensive. You'll hear the drivers shouting out their destinations as soon as you're in the right area. Riding on trucks can be rough or just as good as a bus depending on the cargo and how many people are on board. They're certainly the best for views.

La Paz-Copacabana These buses have already been covered under the section 'To/From Peru' where international connections are detailed.

La Paz-Coroico *Flota Yungeña*, Av de las Americas 344 (tel 312344), Villa Fatima, cover this route and like the buses to Copacabana, don't leave from the central bus terminal but from the above address which is a suburb of La Paz. To get there from the centre take microbus B or any bus with 'Villa Fatima' in the front window. These buses go up to the top of Av Busch, turn left and shortly afterwards go past a petrol station at a V-shaped junction. Get off there.

There are supposedly buses to Coroico daily from Monday to Friday at 9 am and on Saturday at 8.30 am but they don't always go so it's best to confirm the day before that one is going. This company also runs buses to Chulumani, Caranavi and Irupana. The journey takes about five hours. From Coroico the buses depart at 7 am daily except Sunday but are often booked up in advance.

La Paz-Desaguadero, Guaqui and Tiahuanaco *Transportes Autolineas Ingavi*, on the corner of José Assin and Eyzaguirre, run nine daily buses to these places, the first at 7 am and the last at 5.30 pm. If you just want to see Tiahuanaco, however, and you are going to be heading for Puno via Guaqui then it isn't worth making a separate journey from La Paz and back unless you want to spend all day at Tiahuanaco (half an hour is adequate for most people). Instead, see the ruins en route to Puno by taking a *Panamericana* bus from La Paz to Puno. The buses of this company stop there for half an hour to give you time to see the ruins.

La Paz-Oruro Many daily services by many different companies from early in the morning until late at night. The journey takes about three to 3½ hours on a good surfaced road.

La Paz-Cochabamba Many departures daily by many different companies. Most departures are at night which is a pity since it's a very picturesque journey. *Nobleza* is the only one with a daytime departure (9.30 am) from La Paz, and *Transportes 6 de Agosto* is the only one from Cochabamba (also at 9.30 am). The journey takes about 9 hours and costs US$3.50. There are also many daily departures by many different companies between Oruro and Cochabamba and as most of them go during daylight hours, it's preferable to start from Oruro rather than La Paz. From Oruro the journey takes five hours and costs US$2. The road is very dusty but otherwise in good shape.

La Paz-Potosí One bus daily in either direction by *Pullman Andino, Autobuses Potosí, Relampago, Transportes La Paz* and *Transportes 10 de Noviembre*. All the departures are at night from 5.30 to 6.30 pm depending on the company. The journey takes about 12 hours and costs US$3.50. The road can be rough in parts.

There are also several departures daily in either direction between Oruro and Potosí. From Oruro *Flota Alianza* (daily at 6.30 pm) and *Flota Universo* (daily at 7.15 am and 8.15 pm) go to Potosí. From Potosí *Flota Alianza* and *Flota Universo* (both daily at 6.30 pm) and *Boqueron* (daily at 5 pm) go to Oruro. The journey takes about 14 hours and the fare is US$2.40. Most of these buses from La Paz continue on to Sucre at around 8.30 am.

Potosí-Villazon Four departures daily in total, one each by *Boqueron, Transportes 10 de Noviembre, Transportes Tupiza* and *Chicheño* and all at 5 pm. The fare is US$2.30 and the journey takes about 12 hours.

Potosí-Sucre One departure daily in either direction by *Autobuses Potosí* (at 8.30 am from Potosí), *Transportes La Paz* (at 8.30 am from Potosí and 9.30 am from Sucre) and *Transportes 10 de Noviembre* (at 9.30 am from Potosí). The journey takes about five hours and costs US$5. Buses may be cancelled if there are insufficient passengers.

Sucre-Cochabamba *Transportes Condor, Cisne, Pullman Minera* and *Pullman Unificado* all operate one bus daily in either direction. From Sucre they all leave between 5.45 and 6.30 pm and from Cochabamba at 6 pm. The journey takes about 12 hours, costs US$15 and it's a very rough road.

Sucre-Santa Cruz There are no direct buses between Sucre and Santa Cruz. What you have to do is take a bus for Cochabamba and change where the Sucre-Cochabamba road meets the Cochabamba-Santa Cruz road. Connections are arranged so that you don't have to spend too much time waiting around at the change-over, but it's a very rough road. Similarly, if you're coming from Santa Cruz you have to take a Cochabamba bus and change at the crossroads. The buses which operate this scheme are the same ones which offer services between Sucre and Cochabamba.

The journey takes about 21 hours in total. It's worth thinking about taking a flight instead (about US$9).

Cochabamba-Santa Cruz Daily departures in either direction by many different companies. All the buses go at night and leave Cochabamba between 4 and 6 pm.

Train

There are a number of *ferrobus* services which are well worth considering if you'd like to see something of the countryside but don't plan on using trucks to get from one place to another. (As many long-distance buses travel at night they're not much good for seeing anything.)

La Paz-Cochabamba This is a superb journey with some beautiful countryside along the way. There's a *ferrobus* three times a week in either direction (on Monday, Wednesday and Friday from Cochabamba) at 8 am, though it sometimes goes earlier. Journey time is nine hours and the fares are US$3.10 (Pullman) and US$2.07 (Especial). Excellent meals (either steak or chicken) are available on board for about US$1.50 as well as soft drinks and beer. There is also a *tren expreso* three times a week in either direction (on Tuesday, Thursday and Sunday from Cochabamba) at 7.50 am. The fares are US$2.22 (Pullman) and US$1.48 (Especial). You need to ring the railway enquiries office in La Paz (tel 353510) for departure days and times for both the *ferrobuses* and the *tren expreso* as they're always changing them. Buy tickets for the trains the day before from 6 am onwards in Cochabamba and from 7 to 11.30 am and 2 to 5.30 pm in La Paz.

The *ferrobuses* don't go via Oruro so you can't use these trains to get to that city. There are, however, other *ferrobuses* and *tren expreso* between Cochabamba and Oruro and between La Paz and Oruro. You can also use trains running between La Paz and Potosí, La Paz and Sucre and La Paz and Villazon to get to Oruro.

Cochabamba-Oruro There are daily *ferrobuses* in either direction twice daily (at 7.25 am and 2 pm from Cochabamba) and a *tren expreso* once a week (on Tuesday at 8.30 am from Cochabamba). The fares are US$1.67 (Pullman) and US$1.12 (Especial) on the *ferrobus* and US$1.20 (Pullman) and US$0.80 (Especial) on the *tren expreso*.

La Paz-Potosí There are three *ferrobuses* and two *tren expreso* per week in either direction between the two cities but the timetable is erratic so you must make enquiries at the station. The weekly frequency, however, is generally maintained. From Potosí the *ferrobuses* are supposed to depart on Tuesday, Thursday and Sunday at 11 am arriving about 5 pm in Oruro and 8.30 pm in La Paz. The fares are US$4.17 (Pullman) and US$2.78 (Especial). Buy your tickets the day before at the station. The *tren expreso* is supposed to depart Potosí on Monday and Thursday at 8.55 pm. This train begins its journey in Sucre. The fares are US$2.98 (Pullman) and US$1.97 (Especial). Good meals are available on the *ferrobus* for around US$1.50.

La Paz-Sucre There are two *tren expreso* per week (on Monday and Thursday at 3 pm from Sucre) and two *tren mixto* per week in either direction. Timetables are erratic so make enquiries before you plan a journey. There is no *ferrobus* all the way between La Paz and Sucre but they do run between La Paz and Potosí so it's best to break your journey at Potosí.

Potosí-Sucre There are no longer any *ferrobuses* between Sucre and Potosí. The *tren expreso* departs Sucre on Monday and Thursday at 3 pm and from Potosí on the same days at 7.30 am. The journey takes five hours and costs US$1.20 (Pullman) and US$0.75 (Especial). Buying tickets for this train in Sucre can be a pain in the neck if you want to travel Especial class as you must queue up at 6.30 am and you'll be lucky to get away by 9.30 am. It's better to travel Pullman class in which case there's no point in going for your ticket until around 10 am. You won't have to queue at all then (the earlier queue is mainly for hopefuls who want Especial all the way to Oruro and La Paz).

Cochabamba

Founded in 1542, Cochabamba is one of Bolivia's most pleasant cities as far as climate goes, and is the country's third largest. It's at an altitude of 2500 metres amid rolling hills in an important agricultural area. Many old colonial houses and churches remain and the city is noted for its fiestas and its large and interesting market. It used to be the second city of Bolivia and it still has an influential financial district but these days the focus of development has moved to Santa Cruz.

If you're on a tight budget you should also beware of going there when a fiesta is due. Fiestas are certainly good fun but several days before they begin, hotel prices double and stay that way until they're over. Likewise, the price of other things such as food and drink can double.

Information

The tourist office has a kiosk on Gral Acha, half a block from the main plaza (14 de Septiembre) in front of the post office. The main office is in the Edificio Prefectual on the top side of the same plaza. Neither is of much use, though they do have a list of hotels and prices. They have no maps of the city. If you want one of those you'll have to buy the *Guiá para conocer Cochabamba*, by Alfredo Medrano, which is mostly rubbish and expensive at US$3. The only other thing of any use which it contains is a complete list of the microbus routes.

If you have cash to change then go to the Plaza Colón where there are plenty of touts. For cheques go to the *Libraria La Juventud* on the main plaza where you

can change legally and get the best exchange rate in town. Other travellers have recommended *Turismo Harasic*, Heroinas (otherwise known as Av Perú) near the junction with 25 de Mayo. There are also two cambios on the same side of the main plaza as the Libraria La Juventud and another on España half a block from the main plaza towards Heroinas. Some travellers have reported that *Exprinter*, also on the main plaza, won't change travellers' cheques.

Turismo Hurasic, Heroinas, has been recommended as a good travel agent.

There is a good selection of English language books and a small selection of German and French ones at the *Los Amigos del Libro*, 25 de Mayo 5829 under the Boston Hotel.

There is a swimming pool at Club Social on Mexico near the Plaza Colon, but it's empty in winter.

Things to See

The **Archaeology Museum**, Oquendo near the junction with Sucre, is part of the University of San Simon and well worth a visit. It contains exhibits from Tiahuanaco and Incallacta. It's open from 8.30 am to noon and 2 to 6 pm. Another group of local museums is housed in the **Casa de la Cultura** at the junction of Peru and 25 de Mayo. Entry is free.

It's also worth visiting the **Palacio de Portales** across the river between Av Portales and Buenos Aires near the junction with Potosí. It's open weekdays from 5 to 6 pm, Saturdays from 10 to 11 am, and Sundays from 11 am to noon.

Cochabamba's market – the **Mercado de Ferias** – takes place next to the railway station everyday. These days, sweaters, blankets, *mantas* and other similar articles are mainly found in one corner of the market, the *Galería Artesanal Incallacta*, on the left hand side as you walk towards the station. The rest of the market is like any other around the third world – pots and pans, plastic products, toiletries, etc.

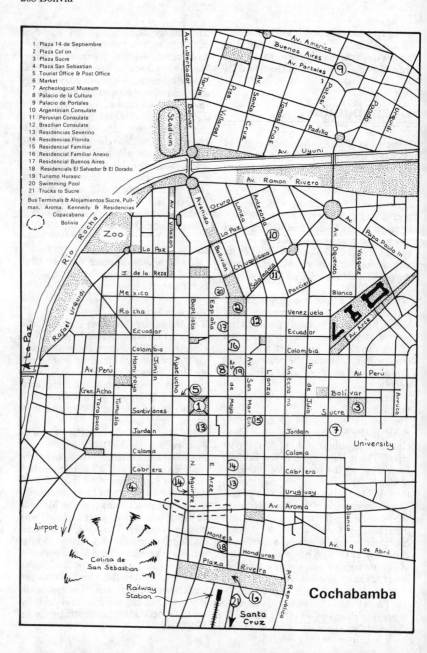

1 Plaza 14 de Septiembre
2 Plaza Col'on
3 Plaza Sucre
4 Plaza San Sebastian
5 Tourist Office & Post Office
6 Market
7 Archeological Museum
8 Palacio de la Cultura
9 Palacio de Portales
10 Argentinian Consulate
11 Peruvian Consulate
12 Brazilian Consulate
13 Residencias Severino
14 Residencias Florida
15 Residencial Familiar
16 Residencial Familiar Anexo
17 Residencial Buenos Aires
18 Residencials El Salvador & El Dorado
19 Turismo Hurasic
20 Swimming Pool
21 Trucks to Sucre
Bus Terminals & Alojamientos Sucre, Pullman. Aroma. Kennedy & Residencias Copacabana Bolivia

Cochabamba

If you're a ruins buff, it's worth visiting the Inca ruins at **Incarakay**, a three hour walk uphill from the village of Sipe-Sipe. You can get as far as Sipe-Sipe by bus from Cochabamba. They leave in the early morning and go via Quillacollo. From Sipe-Sipe you can either walk or take one of the occasional trucks which will drop you within 200 metres of the ruins.

Places to Stay

The most popular of the budget hotels is the *Residencial Familiar*, Sucre 0554, and its extension, the *Residencial Familiar Anexo*, 25 de Mayo 0234. Both are very pleasant, very clean and have rooms arranged around a central courtyard. There is hot water in the showers. They cost US$2.80 per person. Try to get there early in the day as they're often full by late afternoon.

Also good value in this price bracket is the *Residencial Florida*, 25 de Mayo between Calama and Cabrera, and the *Residencial San Severino*, 25 de Mayo 0621. Both are clean, pleasant, have hot water in the bathrooms and cost US$2.50 per person without own bath.

Perhaps even better value is the *Residencial El Salvador*, Montes 0420 at 25 de Mayo, close to the market area. It costs the same as the above but it's a new building with rooms facing out onto the street. The bathrooms have hot water. Opposite is the *Residencial El Dorado*, 25 de Mayo 1034. This is a slightly older place with rooms around a central courtyard. It's clean, friendly, has hot water and costs US$2.60 per person.

There are plenty of other places to stay either on or just off the Av Aroma but it's a noisy street because of the buses and not that pleasant. Surprisingly, a lot of hotels aren't as cheap as you might expect. They include the *Alojamiento Sucre*, *Residencial Pull-man*, *Alojamiento Aroma*, *Alojamiento Kennedy* (a rip-off at US$3.50 per person), and the *Residencial Bolivia* (at US$2.60 per person). Most of them cater for one-night stands and are nothing special.

Similar to these are the cheapies on the first block of Junín from Av Aroma (*Alojamientos Oruro*, *Andino* and *San Pablo*). One place which is reasonably good value in this area is the *Alojamiento Escobar*, Aguirre near the junction with Uruguay. This place is used by quite a few travellers and costs US$1.80 per person but the toilets (two only) and the shower (one only) are reported to be totally inadequate.

The *Residencia Urcupina* on E Arze is cheap, clean and has hot showers. Doubles are US$3.40.

If you're looking for something up-market then try the *Hotel Boston*, 25 de Mayo 5829 near the junction with Heroínas (otherwise known as Av Perú). This is definitely middle-range at US$5.80/$8.20 a single/double without bath (!!) and US$7.75/$12.30 a single/double with own bath. There is no longer a restaurant there.

The *Residencial Buenos Aires*, 25 de Mayo 0329, at US$3.80/$6.30 a single/double without own bath and US$5.50/$9.25 a single/double with own bath is definitely over-priced. The rooms surround a somewhat dark, covered courtyard which doubles as a popular public restaurant.

Places to Eat

The cheapest place to find a meal is in the market area along 25 de Mayo between Sucre and Jordan. In the evening in the same block there are street stalls selling hamburgers, shish kebabs and the like and there's a very cheap barbecued-chicken shop.

The *Restaurant Dragon de Oro*, Plaza 14 de Septiembre (the main plaza), serves excellent Chinese food when the staff is on form but when they're not (and this can happen without warning) then it's very disappointing. Most dishes cost US$2 to $3.50 but you can also get omelettes and various fried rice dishes for

US$1.70. The toilets there seem to have borne the brunt of an English soccer team's hooliganism.

Also in the same plaza is the *Restaurant Mar del Plata* which is basically a chicken and chips/steak house. Normally the food is OK but if you complain that your chicken isn't cooked, then you can expect both abuse and insolence from the staff. I virtually had to stuff my chicken and chips into the manager's face before he agreed to put it back under the grill where it should have been for at least 20 minutes longer before it met my knife and fork.

One very popular place with gringos is *Maggy's*, 25 de Mayo on the corner with Sucre. The only trouble with this place is that it doesn't open until late in the morning so it's not much use for breakfast. For very good hamburgers go to the *Manantial Snack/Cafeteria* on the Plaza 14 de Septiembre. This is mostly a beer bar but their hamburgers are excellent.

Whatever else you do, *don't* go to *Burger Plaza*, also on the same plaza, for a hamburger. Someone with a lot of money, no experience and absolutely no suss must be behind this place because it's an unmitigated disaster in every way. It's also very expensive. Don't be seduced by the bright lights and the tasty conversion job.

If you want a splurge without angst then head up to the start of Av Balliavian where there are several partially open-air mid-range restaurants. Although the food is relatively expensive (expect to pay around US$3 for a full meal) it is very good.

If you're looking for fish, a number of travellers have recommended *Snack 6 de Agosto*, 6 de Agosto, which serves trout for about US$3.

Avoid the *Café Paula*, 25 de Mayo y Bolívar – the food is lousy.

Cochabamba has some good ice-cream parlours and although everyone has their own favourite, two of the best are the *Heladería España*, España; and the *Kivon Ice Cream Parlour*, Peru between España and 25 de Mayo.

Getting There

Cochabamba is one of the few Bolivian cities which still has no central bus terminal. There are rumours of a new one being built but for the moment the bus offices and their depots are strung out along Av Aroma.

Buses to Puerto Villaroel depart from Lanza 7065 (*Sacaba*) and Lanza 6901 (*Chapare*). Trucks to Puerto Villaroel go from Av República and to Sucre from Av Aguirre.

COPACABANA

This interesting little red-roofed town on the shores of Lake Titicaca is well worth visiting en route from Puno to La Paz, especially when there is a fiesta. There's actually a small fiesta every Saturday, but the two big ones are on Good Friday and Independence Day. The latter goes on for a whole week (August 3 to 10) and is one of the liveliest and most colourful you're ever likely to come across. It includes lantern processions, parades, brass bands, groups of Indian flautists, amazing fireworks displays and plenty of *chicha*. People rage night and day for a whole week. For the rest of the year it's a quiet little town and convenient for visiting the Island of the Sun in Lake Titicaca, the legendary site of the Inca's creation.

Information

There is a bank in Copacabana which will change travellers' cheques, but it's often only open from Wednesdays to Sundays so if you're coming in from Peru bring some Bolivian pesos with you.

Buses *2nd Novembre* and *Maksa* to La Paz both have offices in the plaza.

Things to See

Obviously the main thing to catch in this town is a fiesta if there happens to be one about the time you're passing through. At other times the shrines on top of the hill which overlook the town are well worth visiting, if only for the superb views across Lake Titicaca. To get there follow the stone steps out of town which start behind the Hotel Embassador.

The **Island of the Sun** is worth a visit but getting to it can be expensive. On the Island is a flight of Inca steps leading down to the shores of the lake. There's also a more substantial ruin known as *Pilko Caima*. The **Island of the Moon** is sometimes closed and is not as interesting.

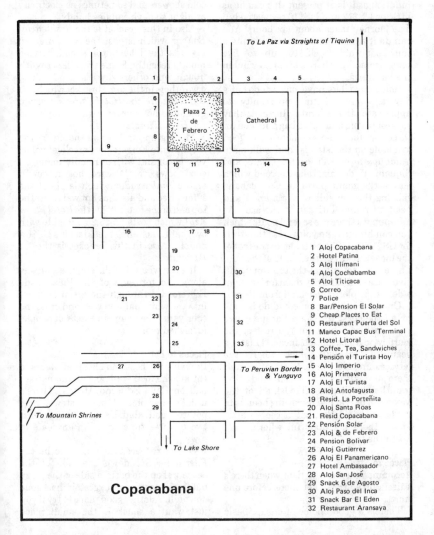

To La Paz via Straights of Tiquina

Plaza 2 de Febrero

Cathedral

To Peruvian Border & Yunguyo

To Mountain Shrines

To Lake Shore

1 Aloj Copacabana
2 Hotel Patina
3 Aloj Illimani
4 Aloj Cochabamba
5 Aloj Titicaca
6 Correo
7 Police
8 Bar/Pension El Solar
9 Cheap Places to Eat
10 Restaurant Puerta del Sol
11 Manco Capac Bus Terminal
12 Hotel Litoral
13 Coffee, Tea, Sandwiches
14 Pensión el Turista Hoy
15 Aloj Imperio
16 Aloj Primavera
17 Aloj El Turista
18 Aloj Antofagusta
19 Resid. La Porteñita
20 Aloj Santa Roas
21 Resid Copacabana
22 Pensión Solar
23 Aloj & de Febrero
24 Pension Bolivar
25 Aloj Gutierrez
26 Aloj El Panamericano
27 Hotel Ambassador
28 Aloj San José
29 Snack 6 de Agosto
30 Aloj Paso del Inca
31 Snack Bar El Eden
32 Restaurant Aransaya

Copacabana

If you can get there it has the ruins of an Inca temple.

Boats going to the islands can be found down at the lake shore. Motorboats cost up to US$30 per boat (up to 10 people) if you just want to visit the Island of the Sun or US$40 if going to both (but with inflation as it is at present this can be as little as US$12 and US$16 respectively). The journey takes about six hours. You can do it somewhat cheaper by hiring a sail boat (about US$16, up to five passengers), but there's often no wind in the mornings.

Some travellers have suggested that a day trip gives little opportunity to appreciate the islands. Instead they suggest taking a sleeping bag and food for three or four days (there's no food available on the islands) and walking to Yampupata via Titicachi, Chani and Siquani. To do this, take the road which leaves the main plaza in Copacabana skirting the top side of the market and head off round Titicaca to the east. At Yampupata there are several boats which you can hire to take you across the strait for US$1.50. Ask to be taken to the foot of the Inca stairway on the Island of the Sun. There is a hacienda at the top which will give you a clean and dry room for less than a dollar. Explore the island from there.

One of the things you could do is walk round the coast to Khasa Parque where you can hire a boat for the rest of the journey to Roca de los Incas. This is a beautiful, tranquil place where the terraces are still under cultivation and there are flocks of sheep and tiny traditional villages. The Island of the Moon can be reached by rowing boat from the Island of the Sun but as there's little to see there it's doubtful whether it's worth the trip.

Places to Stay
Accommodation is very tight when there's a fiesta on so try to get there before one starts.

There's a good choice of cheap, basic accommodation in Copacabana, but prices may double at fiesta times. One of the best is the *Alojamiento Gutierrez*. It's friendly and has clean sheets and cold showers. Two others which are similar are the *Residencial Copacabana* and the *Alojamiento Illimani*. Both have only cold showers and sometimes no electricity at night so have candles handy.

Also in this bracket is the *Residencial Bolívar* which is past the San Jose and towards the lake but it's had varying reports recently. Some travellers say it's 'rough' and others say it's 'good value'. Two others in the same bracket which you could try are the *Hotel Turista* ('clean, quiet and hot showers twice a day') and the *Hotel Tunari*.

Moving up-market you should try the *Alojamiento Emperador* ('excellent value, very clean and with a friendly manager, good views over Titicaca, hot showers'); or the *Ambassador* which is about the same price and also has hot water. At the top end of the market, try the *Hotel Playa Azul* which costs US$3.25 a double with own bath. Including breakfast it's US$6 a double. Also in this bracket is the *La Porteñita*.

If everywhere is full, enquire halfway along the top side of the Plaza 2 de Febrero. Go through the green door set into the white painted wall and cross the courtyard. They sometimes let-out simple, furnished rooms.

Places to Eat
Probably the best and cheapest places to eat are the food stalls inside the market hall on Calle Eduardo Aboroa. There's usually a choice of meat, stews, rice, potatoes and salad. Expect to pay at least two to three times more in any café in town.

One of the best cafés used to be the *Puerto de Sol* down the side of the cathedral on the bottom side of the plaza but recent reports suggest it has gone downhill. Another good place to try if you just want a snack is the small place marked on the street plan as 'coffee, tea and sandwiches'. For *salteñas* in the morning go to *El Tigre Restaurant*.

Avoid the restaurant at *El Turista*. The meals are poor.

COROICO

Coroico is very popular with travellers for its friendly people and beautiful mountain scenery – snow-capped peaks and tropical, forested valleys surround the town. Because the town is at a height of only 1525 metres, the climate there is much warmer than on the *altiplano*. The best way to get to the town if you have four or five days to spare is via the magnificent paved Inca road which starts from La Cumbre – the highest point on the La Paz-Coroico road – and heads over a 4850-metre-high pass and then down the valley of the Huarinilla to Chairo, about 19 km from Coroico. In many ways this trail is in a much better state of preservation than the Inca Trail to Macchu Picchu. There are superb views the whole way.

The trek takes most people four days at a relatively comfortable pace (about six hours of walking per day). It's not difficult and needs no special equipment though the climb up to the pass above La Cumbre can be exhausting. After that, however, it's all downhill. You need to bring plenty of warm clothes for the climb over the pass – snow sometimes falls – but after that it gets increasingly warm and the last two days are through humid jungle. You can expect rain every day during the wet season (December to February) and even during the dry season there are frequent showers. There are two villages along the way but don't count on being able to buy any supplies in them. Bring with you all the food you'll need. It's also a good idea to bring a water container with you as camp sites – especially on the last two days of the trek – don't always coincide with streams.

The *Flota Yungeña* (the line which runs between La Paz and Coroico) buses out of Coroico can often be booked up two days in advance so if you don't want to spend more time there than you have to, book a ticket as soon as you arrive.

Places to Stay

The most popular place with travellers is the *Lluvia de Oro* which has a swimming pool and offers good meals. If it's full, the *La Plaza* is clean and hospitable, or try the *Alojamiento Coroica*.

If you'd like to stay in Coroico for a while ask about renting a house but remember that they're very much in demand so check with other travellers. The bar on the main plaza is good for snacks and drinks and is a popular meeting place for travellers.

Other travellers have suggested eating at the German-run *La Casca* on the plaza, or at the *Restaurant Kory*.

La Paz

At 3600 metres, La Paz is the world's highest capital city. It sits at the bottom of a natural canyon several hundred metres below the level of the *altiplano*, with snow-capped Mt Illimani (6462 metres) towering over it. The first sight you get of the city from the rim of the canyon is magnificent. The sky-scrapers of the banks and business houses down in the centre resemble scale models and are surrounded on all sides by houses which climb up the steep slopes of the canyon.

La Paz was founded in 1548, 10 years after Sucre, following the discovery of gold by the Spanish in the Río Choqueyapu, which runs through the centre of the city. Despite the many sky-scrapers that have been built between the bottom side of the Plaza Murillo (the main plaza) and the Av 16 de Julio, the old part of the city has managed to retain a colonial flavour, and the houses of the Indian section which climb up the steep canyon sides are reminiscent of the cobbled streets and markets of old Quito.

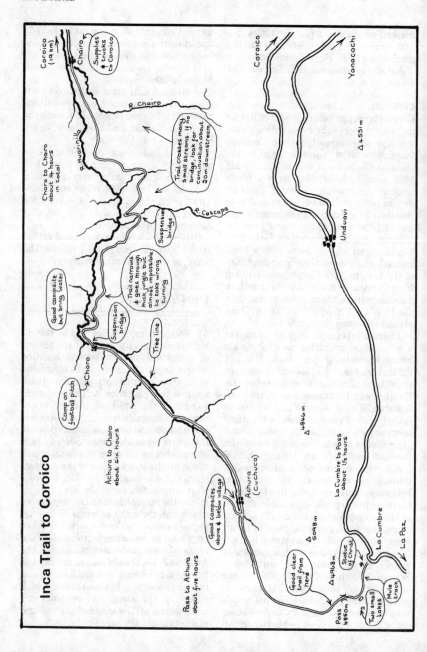

Information

The tourist office is in a kiosk on the central island of the Av 16 de Julio between Loayza and Bueno. It has lists of hotels, bus and train timetables, a map of La Paz and two sketch maps of Inca trails which can be explored in the area (the Yunga Cruz and the Choro). The staff there are very friendly and helpful and can speak English if your Spanish isn't up to much.

If you're going trekking and need detailed maps of certain areas you can get these from the Instituto Geografico Militar, on the corner of Saavedra and Rafael Subrieta. Take your passport with you when buying maps.

It's supposed to be illegal to change money on the streets instead of at a bank or casa de cambio but you wouldn't know it judging from the number of touts that hang around all the way along Camacho and Loayza. That is the place to change if you have cash. You must change cheques at a casa de cambio unless you can find someone with a foreign currency account who is willing to change.

A taxi between the city and centre and the International Airport will cost about US$5 for the car. If you're arriving in La Paz taxi drivers will naturally quote you much more. For a cheap trip into town from the airport – walk one km to the main road. Large new buses going to Plaza San Francisci shops stop under the overpass.

There's an immigration office at Av Gabriel Gozalvez 240, off Av Arce. Microbus numbers A, N and 130 pass nearby.

There is a possibility of hiring camping equipment for use on the Inca trails from Club Andino, Calle Mexico 1638, but it is only a possibility; there's nowhere else in La Paz.

American Express is located at Magri Tours, Edificio Avenida (5th Floor), Av 16 de Julio 1490.

Embassies

Argentina
Edificio Banco de la Nacion Argentina (2nd Floor), Av 6 de Agosto, opposite the tourist office. Open 9 am to 12 noon and 2 to 4 pm.

Brazil
Calle Fernando Guachalla 494. Open 10 am to 12 noon and 2 to 4 pm.

Chile
Av 6 de Agosto 2932 on the corner of Pedro Zalazar. Open 8.30 am to 1.30 pm.

Paraguay
Edificio Venus (7th Floor), Av Arce on the corner of Montevideo. Open 8 am to 12.15 pm. Visas issued on the spot, no photos required.

Peru
Av Mariscal Santa Cruz, Edificio Bolívar. Open 9 am to 12 noon and 2.30 to 6 pm.

Airline Offices All the main airline offices are on Av 16 de Julio, Loayza or Av Camacho – *Lloyd Aereo Boliviano*, *Ecuatoriana*, *Aerolineas Argentinas*, *Avianca*, *Varig*, *AeroPeru* and *LAN Chile*. *TAM* is on the corner of Montes and José Maria Serrano near the Plaza Mendoza.

TAWA and *Point Air Mulhouse* (the French charter companies) are above the *Peña Naira* on Sagarnaga by the side of San Francisco church.

Foreign Language Books There is a good selection of English, French and German novels (though nothing madly intellectual) at *Los Amigos del Libro*, Calle Mercado. Most of it is escapist trash along with the current best-selling novels. They also stock a number of travel guides and the Bradt trekking guides.

Things to See

Of La Paz's religious buildings the one which is most worth seeing is the **Church and Monastery of San Francisco** facing the Plaza San Francisco. If you go down there on Saturday mornings you may see a number of Indian weddings.

La Paz has several museums which are worth visiting, many of them housed in

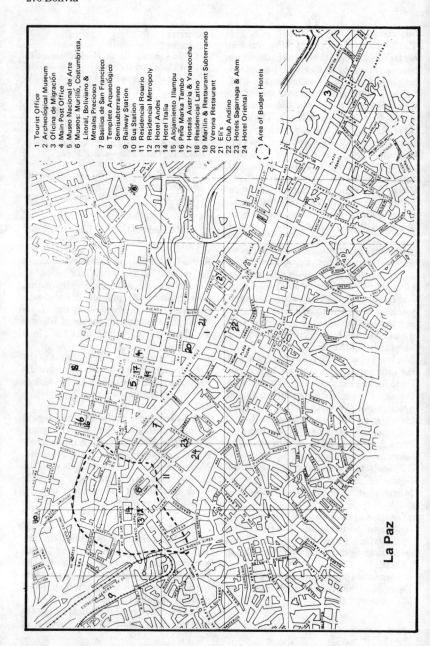

La Paz

1 Tourist Office
2 Archeological Museum
3 Oficina de Migración
4 Main Post Office
5 Museos: Murillo, Costumbrista,
   Litoral, Boliviano &
   Metales Preciosos
6 Museos Nacional de Arte
7 Basilica de San Francisco
8 Templete Arqueológico
   Semisubterraneo
9 Railway Station
10 Bus Station
11 Residencial Rosario
12 Residencial Metropoly
13 Hotel Andes
14 Hotel Italia
15 Alojamiento Illampu
16 Peña Marka Tambo
17 Hostals Austria & Yanacocha
18 Residencial Latino
19 Marilín & Restaurant Subterraneo
20 Verona Restaurant
21 Eli's
22 Club Andino
23 Hotels Sagarnaga & Alem
24 Hotel Oriental
---- Area of Budget Hotels

beautiful old colonial mansions. Two which you shouldn't miss are the **Museo Nacional de Arte** and the **Museo Nacional de Etnografía y Folklorico**. The former is housed in the 18th-century palace of the Condes de Arana on Calle Socabaya opposite the cathedral. It's open weekdays from 10.30 am to 6.30 pm and on Saturdays from 10.30 am to 1 pm. Entry is US$0.25. The Ethnology Museum is at Calle Ingavi 916 in the former house of the Marqueses de Villaverde. It has a good collection of craftwork, weavings and musical instruments as well as other things and is open Tuesdays to Saturdays from 10 am to 1 pm and 3 to 7 pm.

Much of Calle Jaén is taken up by four museums – the **Casa Murillo**; the **Museo de Metales Preciosos**, Jaén 777; the **Museo del Litoral Boliviano**, Jaén 789; and the **Museo Costumbrista Juan de Vargas**, on the corner of Jaén and Sucre. All these museums are open from 9 am to 12 noon and 2.30 to 6.30 pm from Tuesday to Sunday. There is a small entrance charge to each.

Those with an interest in minerals would also be advised to visit the **Museo Mineralogico**, 3rd floor, Banco Minero de Bolivia, Comercio 1290, on the corner of Colón. It's open Monday to Friday from 9 am to 1 pm and 2 to 4.30 pm.

The **Museo Tiahuanaco** (Museo Nacional de Arqueología), on the corner of Frederico Zuazo and Tiwanaku, opened again in 1985 after a complete re-fit and is a must. It's open Tuesday to Friday from 9.30 to 11.30 am and 2 to 5.30 pm and on Saturdays from 9 am to 12.30 pm and 2 to 6 pm. Entry costs US$0.20.

Many people make the trip to the **Valley of the Moon**, an eerie sort of place with an apt name. It's further down the canyon from the centre of La Paz. To get there, you take microbus No 130, marked *Aranjuez*, from the Av 16 de Julio and then walk 15 minutes from where they put you down. Alternatively you can take a taxi since they only cost US$1.50 one-way.

The most well-known and popular excursion outside of La Paz is to the famous pre-Inca ruins at **Tiahuanaco** (Tiwanaku) near the southern end of Lake Titicaca. Very little is known about the people who constructed them, but links have been established with the coastal cultures which flourished at the time, around 800 BC. Reconstruction and excavation is still going on there. Entry to the ruins costs US$0.50.

Tiahuanaco isn't really anything to get too steamed up about unless you're an archaeology buff; they don't amount to much and many of the statues which were found there are now in La Paz. An hour, or even half an hour, would satisfy most people. That being the case, it makes sense to see them en route to Puno rather than making a special trip which is going to take up most of the day. *Panamericana* enable you to do just this. Their buses/minibuses run between La Paz and Puno daily taking about eight hours and allow a half-hour stop at Tiahuanaco. The cost is US$6. If you're going there on a day trip from La Paz, get there early and leave early as the buses going back get very crowded.

Want to know what makes mountaineers tick? The Club Andino, Calle Mexico 1638, offers a trip to the summit of Chacalteya (5500 metres) on Sundays at 9.30 am. Anyone can go (assuming they can take the altitude) and there's a minibus laid on to take you to where you have to start walking. If you want to go, make sure you book ahead. There are incredible views from the top.

Places to Stay

There are two main streets on which you will find most of the budget hotels. They are the Av de las Americas just below the railway station; and Manco Capac, parallel to it. The ones on las Americas are mostly basic, though clean, concrete boxes which are all right for one night but not somewhere you would particularly want to stay for a week or so. They include the *Alojamientos Mexico, Internacional, Rex, Liberty* and *Pasajero*.

For a longer stay in this bracket one of the best is the *Hotel Los Andes*, Manco Capac 364. It offers clean, airy rooms with good beds, the management are eager to please and it has its own restaurant. Rooms cost US$1.80 per person without own bath and US$2.50 per person with own bathroom. If it's full there is the *Alojamiento Metropoly*, Manco Capac 300, just down the road. It's of a similar standard, the management are friendly and it costs US$1.80/$2.60 a single/double and US$1.20 per person in rooms with more than two beds. Both hotels have hot water.

Outside this area but deserving the same recommendation is the *Hostal Austria*, Yanacocha 531, which is very popular with budget travellers. It's a pleasant place to stay, has cooking facilities, hot showers, a TV lounge and a useful (free) noticeboard. It costs US$2.40 a double without own bath. There are no single rooms.

The *Hotel Italia*, Manco Capac 303, is still popular with Italian travellers (perhaps because of the name) but some others who have stayed there recently report it to be somewhat run-down and not really worth the US$3.50 a double without own bath. It looked clean enough to me and people I spoke to confirmed that there was plenty of hot water.

One of the real cheapies in this range is the *Alojamiento Illampu*, Illampu 635. It's very basic but clean and friendly with hot water and a TV lounge (of sorts). It costs US$1.60/$2.60 a single/double without own bath.

On Calle Colombia 222, the *Residencial Don Guillermo* has been recommended. It is a colonial style building, singles/doubles are US$3/$5 and it's clean and friendly.

Also on Illampu at 1070, the *Hostal Alborada* has been described as a bargain at US$4 a double. It's a new, clean place run by friendly, English-speaking people.

Moving up-market there are a number of places which are very popular with travellers. The best is probably the *Residencial Rosario*, Illampu 704 (tel 325348). This is a beautifully restored hotel with cobbled patios and balconies and tastefully furnished rooms to match. It's not surprising that it's often full during July, August and September. Nevertheless, it's worth making enquiries to see if they have a spare room. There are 30 rooms with common bath at US$4.10/$5.10/$6.70 a single/double/triple and 10 rooms with own bath at US$6.65/$8.40/$11.55 a single/double/triple. There's hot water, a cafeteria, laundry service and a baggage store.

Next best is probably the *Hotel Sagárnaga*, Sagárnaga 326, another very popular mid-range hotel. Like the Rosario it often has group block-bookings during the northern hemisphere holiday period. It has friendly staff, pleasant, well-furnished rooms which are cleaned daily, a video/TV lounge and a restaurant (not always open). It costs US$4/$6.10 a single/double without own bath and US$8.50/$14 a single/double with own bath.

Cheaper and almost as good as the Sagárnaga is the *Hotel Alem*, Sagárnaga 336 right next door. It's a clean modern place with a TV lounge and its own restaurant; rooms there cost US$3.50/$5 a single/double without own bath and US$9.80 a double with own bath. The showers naturally have hot water.

Two others at about the same price but on the other side of town near the Plaza Murillo are the *Hostal Yanacocha*, Yanacocha 540 (opposite the Austria); and the *Residencial Latino*, Junín 857. The Yanacocha is a supposedly two-star hotel (it doesn't look like it!) with large, clean, airy rooms and good beds which costs US$4/$6.80 a single/double with common bath and hot water. The Latino is perhaps the better deal of the two. Again, it's supposedly two-star but it's a lot brighter and costs US$4.50/$6.13 a single/double without own bath and US$8.50/$10.10 a single/double with own bath. They also have cheaper rooms available.

The *Hotel Milton* has also been recommended and costs US$4.40/$7.20/$10.20 for singles/doubles/triples. It is in a great location to view the markets, as the streets around it fill up with stalls, particularly on weekends.

Places to Eat

La Paz is full of places where you can buy *empanadas* in the morning, which is what most people start off their day with. Some of the best are still to be found at *Los Laureles*, Evaristo Valle 167.

For lunch you probably can't beat the well-known and immensely popular *Marilin*, on the corner of Potosí and Socabaya, where for just US$0.60 you can get a tasty four-course lunch (salad starter, soup, main course and dessert). It's very popular with local office workers. Their evening meals are quite expensive though and (surprisingly) their *empanadas* are nothing special.

If you can't get a table there at lunch time then go next door to the *Restaurant Subterraneo*, Potosí 1120. Their meals aren't quite as good (with the exception of the soups) but they're certainly very acceptable and the prices are the same.

The *Cafeteria Verona*, on the corner of 16 de Julio and Colón, has been described by many travellers as 'the best café in Bolivia' and if the clientele is anything to go by then a lot of Bolivians would appear to agree with them. This restaurant is packed night and day and with good reason. The food and the size of the portions are top value. The cuisine is Bolivian and international. You'll probably have to join the queue for a table if you go there in the evening. It's highly recommended.

Another very popular place, especially with gringos, is *Eli's*, on the corner of 16 de Julio and Bueno (diagonally opposite the tourist office), open from 8 am to 10.30 pm. They offer cheap Continental and American breakfasts (US$0.50 to $1.20) and pancakes, soups, omelettes, hamburgers and a *plato del dia* which could be goulash, pique a la macho, lasagna or barbecued chicken for US$1.40. Their prices include taxes which is unusual in La Paz.

Other local restaurants which are worth trying are the *Restaurant Ballivian*, Sagárnaga about half a block from Av Santa Cruz on the first floor, which is friendly and has cheap beef and chicken dishes; *Dino's*, Evaristo Valle, which has good barbecued chicken, although one traveller said that it was dirty and not so good; *La Rueda*, Evaristo Valle, which offers mixed grill at about US$3 and cheap Argentinian wine; and the Chinese restaurant on the corner of Calles Illampu and Graneros which offers very good food for US$0.80 to $1.50 per dish.

Los Escudos on the upper part of the Avenida Mariscal Santa Cruz has been recommended for its four-course businessmens' lunch for US$0.60 including bread, tea and tax in attractive surroundings.

If you'd like to be close to where the decisions are made in Bolivian political circles you could sit and eavesdrop over a coffee in the *Confiteria Club de la Paz*, on the corner of Camacho and Ayacucho. This is where the politicians go to relax after doing their bit in the Chamber of Deputies.

Entertainment

Like Cuzco and Arequipa, La Paz has its spread of *peñas* – folklore music venues. The most famous of them is probably the *Peña Naira*, Sagárnaga, next to the San Francisco church. The quality of music there is excellent and the musicians are drawn from all over Bolivia but the atmosphere is sterile. This is entirely because of the way the place is run and in no way a reflection on the musicians. You are assigned a seat and you have to stay there. You can't dance; you can't even move around and it's either very smokey and warm, or fresh and cold as hell. Compare it with the *Qhatuchay* in Cuzco. There's also too much talk from the man who introduces the various bands. However, try it for yourself – you may disagree. The peña is open nightly from 10 pm during August, and on Thursday, Friday and Saturday nights during the rest of the year. Entry costs US$4 per person including one drink (a Pepsi-Cola or a small glass of red wine). Subsequent drinks all cost US$1 each. It's clearly not a cheap night out! Across the yard from the peña is the Naira Restaurant which offers very good but expensive food.

Similar in a lot of ways but somewhat better in terms of audience participation is *Los Escudos Restaurant & Peña*, Av Mariscal Santa Cruz between Ayacucho and Colón. This is a much larger place – actually a restaurant with bar and stage. It's open every evening from Monday to Saturday and costs US$2 each.

Perhaps the best two places are the *Peña Wara*, Sagárnaga 229 (one block up from the Naira), which is open Thursday, Friday and Saturday from 10 pm; and the *Peña Marka Tambo*, Jaén 710, near the corner of Jaén and Indaburu. It's a combination of an up-market restaurant and peña.

Depending on what you're looking for you might also want to check out *El Lagar del Virrey*, Murillo 947 near the junction with Sagárnaga. This is a restaurant, café and theatre. There are folklore shows on Monday, Tuesday and Wednesday and pantomime comedies on other days. It's open from 12.15 to 2.30 pm and 7.30 pm to 1 am Monday to Saturday.

As for bars where you might meet other travellers, there's not too much choice. Some correspondents have suggested *Charlie's Bar*, Av 6 de Agosto near the junction with Guachalla (it's in the bottom of the high-rise there). Others have suggested *Giorgissimo* on Loayza but this latter isn't a travellers bar by any stretch of the imagination. A good sawdust and swill place where you can drink beers cheaply until the wee hours can be found on the corner of Evaristo Valle and the Plaza Velasco (there's a huge neon La Paz brewery Bacchus straddling a barrel on the front wall).

Folklore shows can be seen at both the *Coloseo Cerrado* and the *Teatro al Avenida Libre* near the university on Sundays.

Getting There & Around

All buses to other cities in Bolivia (and to Puno, Peru, and Arica, Chile) except those to Coroico and Copacabana, now leave from the Terminal Terrestre, Plaza Antofagasta at the end of Av Armentia. Most departures are at night.

Flota Yungeña (to Coroico, Chulumani, Caranavi and Irupana) leave from Av de los Americanos 344 (tel 312344), Villa Fatima suburb. Microbus B or any with 'Villa Fatima' in the front window will take you there. Wait till the microbus gets to the top of Av Busch, takes a left and passes a petrol station, then get off.

There are three companies which service the route to Copacabana. They are *Transportes 2 de Febrero*, Av Manco Capac 464; *Transportes Riveros Herrera*, Av Montes 660, and *Expreso Manco Capac*, Tumusla 506. None of these companies have signs outside their offices.

If you are travelling by train from La Paz and want to book a ticket, get to the station by 7 am the day before – by 9 am all the tickets are gone. Tickets are not sold more than one day in advance.

ORURO

Oruro is a typical *altiplano* town near the shores of Lakes Uru Uru and Poopó and an important mining centre for silver, tin and tungsten. Most of its population of 160,000 are Indian. Except for the area around the plaza it's an ugly town and there's very little there for the traveller unless you're fortunate enough to be going through on the Saturday before

Ash Wednesday. This is when the *fiesta* of La Diablada takes place – one of the most spectacular of all the *fiestas* in Bolivia. If you'll be in the area at that time then try to get there several days before it starts otherwise it's unlikely you will find anywhere to stay. For the rest of the year Oruro is probably only going to be an overnight stop on the way to somewhere else.

Information

The tourist office can be found at Calle Quijarro and Plaza 10 de Noviembre. They give out a free booklet about the town and a street map.

Oruro now has a new, purpose-built bus terminal with cafés, shops and even a multi-star hotel. Buses fully booked up days in advance are now a thing of the past.

Things to See

There's very little to see here. The zoo (see the street plan) has a moth-eaten and very sad-looking collection of Bolivian animals and birds and a few from elsewhere. The museum next to the zoo has a good, though small, exhibition of paintings, masks, Inca stone sculpture, pre-Columbian axe-heads, mummies, various trepanned skulls, stuffed animals and butterflies. There's a small entry charge to both places.

Places to Stay

There's only a limited selection of cheapies in Oruro and they are indicated on the street map. While they're certainly cheap none of them have hot water and some don't even have showers! You may also find that many of them are full by late afternoon.

There's not much to choose between them but the best of the bunch are the *Alojamiento Central*, Potosí 5921; the *Alojamiento Pagador*, Ayacucho 319, clean and friendly but no showers and US$0.80 per person; *Alojamiento Ayacucho*, Ayacucho 339, very popular since it only costs US$0.50 per person; and the *Alojamiento Scala*, Ayacucho opposite the Pagador, also very cheap and often full.

Even more basic is the *Alojamiento Derby*, Ayacucho 298. In the same general area but closer to the bus terminal is the *Pension Sucre*, 6 de Agosto between Ayacucho and Cochabamba facing the railway tracks.

If you'd prefer better facilities then head for the *Hotel Lipton*, 6 de Agosto, 1½ blocks from the bus terminal. This place is good value and has hot showers in the mornings. It costs US$2.50 per person.

Places to Eat

One of the best places is the *Restaurant Pigalle*, Plaza 10 de Febrero next to the cinema. It's a little more expensive than other places but only marginally so and if you choose wisely you can have soup and an omelette for about US$1. There is heating in the evenings. Also very good is the *Centro Español*, Adolfo Mitre three blocks west of the Plaza 10 de Febrero. The food is excellent.

Two others which travellers have recommended are the *Restaurant Fuente Suiza*, Bolívar 498/6 de Octobre 1599, which has very good soups and is cheap 'despite the ritzy clientele'; and the *Confiteria Dallas*, Bolívar 689.

The *Huari Bar*, on the corner of Junín and Galvarro, is another rustic possibility. The *Pension Cochabamba*, on the corner of Potosí and Ayacucho is a lively bar in the evenings if you're looking for somewhere to have a beer.

Potosí

Potosí was once the most glittering town in South America. Shortly after the Conquest, the Spanish discovered silver in the Cerro Rico, the hill which overlooks the town, and the mine quickly became

Oruro

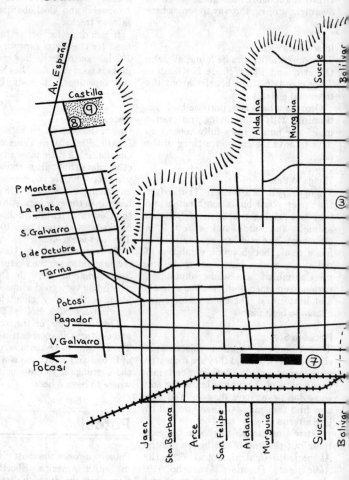

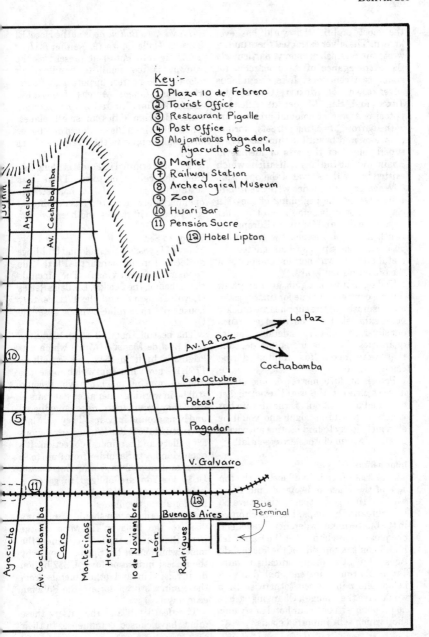

Key:-
1. Plaza 10 de Febrero
2. Tourist Office
3. Restaurant Pigalle
4. Post Office
5. Alojamientos Pagador, Ayacucho & Scala.
6. Market
7. Railway Station
8. Archeological Museum
9. Zoo
10. Huari Bar
11. Pensión Sucre
12. Hotel Lipton

the most prolific the world has ever known. The silver extracted there underwrote the Spanish economy, particularly the extravagance of its monarchy, for about two centuries. Like the famous silver towns of Mexico (Guanajuato, Taxco and San Miguel de Allende), Potosí is a gem of colonial architecture with narrow, twisting streets, former mansions and beautiful churches. It's a superb blend of the arts of mediaeval Spain and the Indian civilisations which existed before the arrival of the Spanish.

When the silver lodes were eventually exhausted at the beginning of the 19th century, Potosí became almost a ghost town. The demand for tin, in Europe and North America, rescued the town from obscurity; the Spanish had ignored the metal and thrown enormous amounts of the ore onto spoil heaps.

Today, Potosí is again an important mining centre, this time for tin, tungsten and bismuth but the supplies are quickly being exhausted. It even manages to turn out silver, though in considerably smaller quantities than the incredible deposits that were taken for granted during colonial times.

Potosí, at 4070 metres, is one of the highest cities in the world (even higher than La Paz). Not only is the air thin but it gets very cold at night and you'll be extremely lucky to find heating anywhere. Plenty of warm clothes are essential!

Information
The tourist office is in a kiosk at the top side of the Plaza 6 de Agosto but it's a waste of time going there - they have no brochures and no maps. The branch office in the bus terminal is derelict. Travellers' cheques can be changed at the Banco del Estado on the top side of the Plaza 6 de Agosto but at a totally unrealistic rate. Try a pharmacy instead, but don't go before the banks open (otherwise they won't have the change). Changing cash is no problem - ask at your hotel or try any shop which sells imported goods.

Lloyd Aero Boliviano is at the Hotel El Turista, Calle Lanza 19. Neither *LAB* or *TAM* fly into Potosí at present as the runway is too small to handle their planes. The nearest airport is at Sucre. However, *Lineas Aereas Imperiales, (LAI)*, do offer a limited service to certain other Bolivian cities in small planes. Their office is on Plaza Alonzo de Ybanez diagonally opposite the Restaurant Las Vegas.

The bus terminal in Potosí is a long way from the centre of town. There is a restaurant there but it has strange opening hours and often has nothing for sale except soft drinks and beer.

Things to See
Many of Potosí's finest colonial buildings are located around or near the Plaza 10 de Noviembre (main plaza). They include the **cathedral**, the **Cabildo, Las Cajas Reales** (Royal Treasury) and the 17th century house of the mine-owner, José de Quiroz.

The best of them all is probably the **Casa Real de Moneda** (Mint) which was originally built in 1542 and re-built in 1759. It's now a museum which houses the wooden minting machines which could still be in working order after 400 years of use if they weren't partially dismembered and lying around in heaps. They were last operated in 1951! It also houses a religious art gallery and a mineral collection. It's open Monday to Saturday from 9 am to 12 noon and from 2 to 5 pm. Entry costs US$0.25. You are obliged to go on a guided tour (no further charge) and these last for about two hours.

One experience you shouldn't miss is a visit to the **Pailaviri Tin Mine** in the Cerro Rico outside town. This is one of the mines which made the Spanish monarchy the richest in Europe (over US$2 billion in silver). Tin and other metals from these mines still underpins the Bolivian economy.

The death toll and the misery these mines have caused is immense. In their quest to extract the silver as quickly as possible, and because the miners died so fast in the deadly working conditions, the Spanish had to import over 2500 Indian slaves (taken from over a 600-km radius), with twice that number of dependants and 30,000 pack animals – *per year*. Eight million people died in the three centuries following the discovery of tin there.

The working conditions are still outrageous. Miners die of silicosis-pneumonia within 10 years of entering the mines. The temperature goes from the freezing cold of the *altiplano* to sauna heat in the deeper reaches of the mines. It's a very sobering experience going into these mines, though you won't actually get to see the miners at work – they understandably feel that having tourists gawping at them is demeaning.

To get there take microbus A or B from the main plaza (or go up with the miners in their truck at 7.30 am from either the main plaza or the Plaza 25 de Mayo). If you take the bus, make sure you get to the mine entrance before 9 am as they only take a maximum of 20 people on a tour at one time – tours last for about three hours. The entrance fee is about US$1.50 which goes to the miners' benevolent fund.

It's also possible to visit private mines in the Cerro Rico but this isn't easy to arrange on your own and the safety of them is sometimes questionable. There are agencies in Potosí which can arrange visits.

Mining conditions are a sensitive issue in Bolivia and the mines are frequently closed to visitors. Before you go up there, enquire at the tourist office to see if they're open.

Places to Stay

The local authorities in Potosí classify the hotels into four different categories but there's almost no difference between the first and second (the cheapies). As far as the cheapies go, Potosí has nothing exceptional to offer the budget traveller. They're all very basic concrete boxes with

no heating (though plenty of blankets) and there's usually a hot shower. There's also a two-tier price system, a higher one for foreigners and a lower one for Bolivians but in most places you should have no problem securing the lower price.

The best in the lower range is the *Alojamiento La Paz*, Oruro 262, which is very clean, secure, has a sunny courtyard, clothes-washing facilities and a hot shower (electric – so you can use it at anytime). It costs US$1/$1.60 a single/double (or US$1.50 and US$2.40 respectively if you pay 'foreigners' prices). Hot showers cost US$0.20 extra. If it's full you can stay for the same price at the *Alojamiento Oruro*, Oruro 292, next door to the La Paz; the *Posada San José*, Oruro 173; or the *Pension Sucre*, also on Oruro opposite the San José.

In the next category the *Alojamiento Ferrocarril*, Villazon 159, is still popular with many travellers though these days it gets a variable press. It is very convenient for the railway station but a long walk from the centre of town. It costs US$1.20/$2 a single/double (or US$1.80/$3 'foreigners' prices). Hot showers are extra. Other places in this range are the *Alojamiento Villa Imperial*, Serrudo 296 (clean and good value); *Residencial 10 de Noviembre*, Serrudo 181; *Alojamiento Tarija*, Serrudo 262 (a huge place); and the *Hostal Santa Maria*, Serrudo 244.

The next category is priced at US$1.40/$2.40 a single/double (or US$2.10/$3.60 'foreigners' prices). There are three good places: the *Hotel Central*, Bustillo 1230, which is a very pleasant, old, wooden building with rooms surrounding a quiet courtyard and close to the centre of town; the *Residencial Copacabana*, Serrudo 319, a huge green building that is good value and has its own cheap restaurant.

Third is the *Residencial Sumaj*, at Gumiel 12 opposite the Hotel IV Centenario. A traveller once wrote describing the decor in the rooms of the latter as 'punk rock'! We can confirm that they're still that way and the place is still

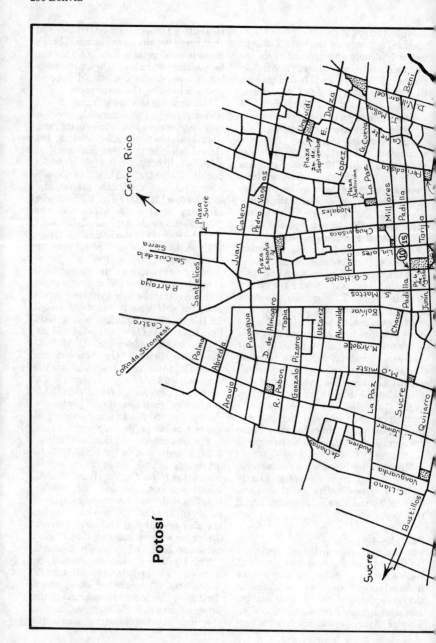

Potosí

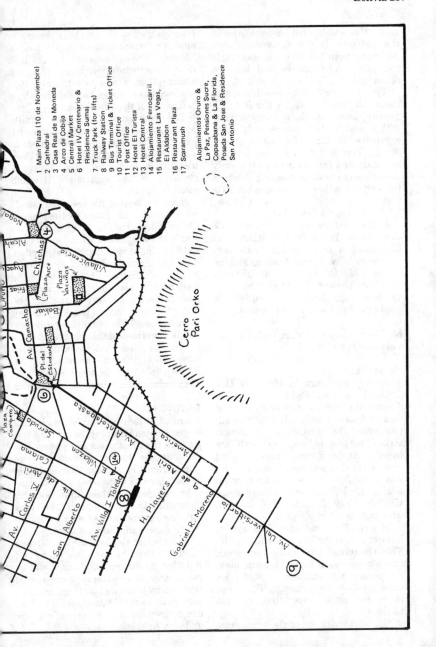

1 Main Plaza (10 de Noviembre)
2 Cathedral
3 Casa Real de la Moneda
4 Arco de Cobija
5 Central Market
6 Hotel IV Centenario & Residencia Sumaj
7 Truck Park (for lifts)
8 Railway Station
9 Bus Terminal & Ticket Office
10 Tourist Office
11 Post Office
12 Hotel El Turista
13 Hotel Central
14 Alojamiento Ferrocarril
15 Restaurant Las Vegas, El Aldabon
16 Restaurant Plaza
17 Scaramush

Alojamientos Oruro & La Paz, Pensiones Sucre, Copacabana & La Florida, Posada San Jose & Residence San Antonio good value and has hot showers. Also in this category is the *Residencial San Antonio*, Oruro 136, which is reasonable value, has hot showers and its own restaurant.

If you want better facilities than any of these can provide then try the *Hotel El Turista*, Lanza 19, which is very popular with travellers but considerably more expensive at US$3.12/$5.20 a single/double. They only have hot water in the mornings and for one hour in the early evening and there's no heating either in the rooms or in the common areas. A little over-priced considering what it offers. The *LAB* office is located there.

At the top of the range are the *Hotel IV Centenario*, Plaza de Estudiantes, at US$10/$12 a single/double with own bathroom, hot water and heating; and the *Hostal Colonial*, Hoyos 8, at US$16 a double for the same facilities. The latter will also change travellers' cheques at a good rate if you are staying there.

NB There's an active drug squad in this town so be careful.

Places to Eat

The best restaurant in Potosí is *Don Lucho*, Linares and Padilla (on Padilla). The food there is some of the best you'll find find in South America. It's tasty, well-presented, the servings are generous, service is prompt and the staff are friendly. At lunch times they offer what must be the cheapest *almuerzo* in Potosí – just US$0.30! In the evenings, main courses are US$1.20 to $1.40 and soups US$0.50. They also stock good Bolivian wine from the Tarija region.

Of a similar standard is *El Aldabón*, Linares 35 near the junction with Padilla. This restaurant also has a very good, cheap *almuerzo* at US$0.30 (soup, meat and potato salad and dessert) with a-la-carte meals in the evenings. The soups there are much better than at Don Lucho's.

Also worth visiting, in the same price range, is the *Restaurant Plaza*, Ayacucho opposite the entrance to the Casa de la Moneda. The restaurant is on the first floor, has a rustic atmosphere and a good sound system. They also open early in the morning (for coffee and sandwiches) long before any of the other places.

The *Restaurant Las Vegas*, Padilla opposite Don Lucho, is very popular with local people especially in the evenings as a meeting place and to drink beer. They also offer a limited selection of meals – steak or chicken with mixed rice and salad for US$1.

If you're looking for fast food, sandwiches and/or coffee then try the popular *Coffee Shop*, Padilla 11 near the Las Vegas, but remember that it doesn't open until late in the morning. Some travellers have recommended the *Restaurant Scaramush*, Bolívar 814, and while the food may be very good and the prices reasonable, I'm not sure what effect the decor will have on your brain if you stay there too long. If the Sumaj has punk rock rooms then this is definitely post-punk.

One last place that's good value for *almuerzo* is the café attached to the *Residencial Copacabana* – US$0.25.

SANTA CRUZ

Founded in 1561 by Spaniards who had migrated from Paraguay, Santa Cruz was isolated from just about everywhere else for centuries due to the lack of communications. Then in the 1960s and early 1970s it became a boom town, prospering from the profits gained from cocaine, agriculture and cattle ranching, and took on the characteristics of a 19th-century North American wild-west town.

It seemed for a while in the late '70s and early '80s that the city's low adobe and red-tiled traditional buildings would be swept away, in the name of progress, to be replaced by high-rise buildings, but that only went so far. Instead, conservation and renovation are the order of the day and very successfully so.

Nevertheless, there's no other city in Bolivia where you will see so many brand new four-wheel drive Ford and Toyota cars and trucks and such a cosmopolitan population ranging from Mennonite farmers to Japanese and American businessmen and agriculturalists to South African cattlemen and English timber prospectors. As you might expect, it's a relatively expensive city but still fairly pleasant.

Information
The tourist office, on the corner of Chuquisaca and Nuflo de Chavez, is just a nonsense place and not worth even a passing thought. They have no information, no maps, not even a telephone directory!

Large-scale coloured street maps of Santa Cruz can be bought from many bookshops in the centre of town but they're expensive at US$3.

There are two casas de cambio on the 24 de Septiembre side of the main plaza for changing travellers' cheques. For cash, the money changers hang out in force at the Junín-Libertad corner of the main plaza and outside the bus terminal. Changing money on the street is supposed to be illegal but you wouldn't know it from the blasé way they conduct their business.

There's a laundromat, *Romi*, at Arenales 222 between Murillo and Aroma. It costs US$0.80 per load including drying. Get there early as it's busy.

If you're heading for Corimbá (Brazil), get an 'exit stamp' from the immigration office in Santa Cruz first, or you'll be prevented from getting on the train and forced by the police to go back into town for it, or pay a fine, and miss your train. You'll also have to pay for your exit stamp at the border.

Consulates
Argentina
  Banco de la Nacion Argentina building, Plaza 24 de Septiembre. Open 8 am to 12 noon Monday to Friday.

Brazil
  Calle Figueroa 145. Open 9 am to 12 noon Monday to Friday.
Paraguay
  Calle Sucre 617.

Places to Stay
Like one or two other places in Bolivia, hotel receptionists in Santa Cruz will show you a list of prices for tourists (in US dollars) and prices for Bolivian nationals (in pesos), the former being considerably more than the latter. They'll tell you it's 'police regulations'. Even so, it doesn't mean you have to pay in hard currency. You pay in pesos but at the blackmarket rate of exchange.

The best value for money if the prices hold is the *Residencial Bolívar*, Calle Sucre 131. It's clean, has hot water, a shady courtyard and is a bargain at US$1.25 per person without own bath. In the same price bracket but not such good value are the *Posada Sucre*, Vallegrande 93, at US$1.50 per person without bath or hot water; the *Alojamiento Boston*, Florida 418 (there's no sign), used by Mennonites when they're in town; and the *Alojamiento Tupiza*, Buenos Aires 138. The Posada Sucre is very basic but friendly and like the Boston, often full.

Going up in price, the *Residencial Copacabana*, Calle Junín 217, has been popular for years and is often used by workers on expatriate projects when they're in town. It's a large place built on the 'gallery' system, it's kept clean and tidy, has hot water, a TV lounge and an attached restaurant. The charges are US$5/$7 a single/double without own bath and US$6/$8 a single/double with own bath.

If you're looking for something smaller and more traditional then the *Alojamiento Santa Barbara*, Calle Santa Barbara 151, is excellent value and very popular with travellers. It's clean, friendly and the rooms, which surround a leafy courtyard, cost US$3.70/$5.30/$8 for singles/doubles/triples, all without own bath. They also offer dormitory-style beds for US$2.65

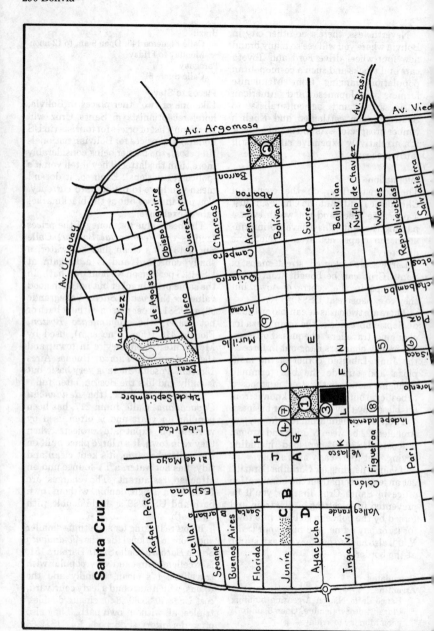

Santa Cruz

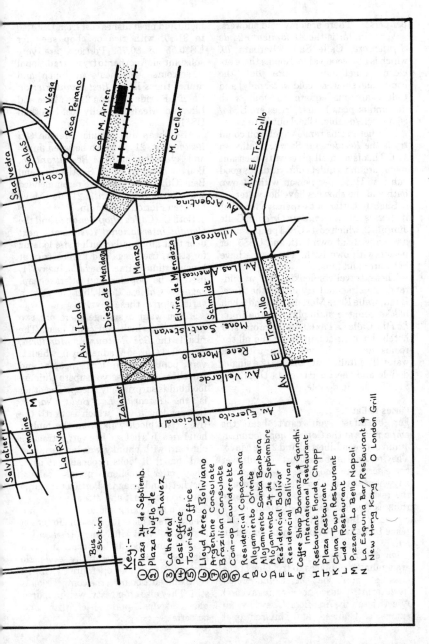

Key:-
1. Plaza 24 de Septiemb.
2. Plaza Ñuflo de Chavez
3. Cathedral
4. Post Office
5. Tourist Office
6. Lloyd Aereo Boliviano
7. Argentine Consulate
8. Brazilian Consulate
9. Coin-op Launderette
A. Residencial Copacabana
B. Alojamiento Oriente
C. Alojamiento Santa Barbara
D. Alojamiento 24 de Septiembre
E. Residencial Bolívar
F. Residencial Ballivian
G. Coffee Shop Bonanza & Gandhi
   International Restaurant
H. Restaurant Florida Chopp
J. Plaza Restaurant
K. China Town Restaurant
L. Lido Restaurant
M. Pizzaria Lo Bella Napoli
N. La Esquina Bar/Restaurant
   New Hong Kong   O London Grill

per person. There are only cold showers.

Very similar is the *Alojamiento 24 de Septiembre*, Calle Santa Barbara 79, which is also good value. Rooms there are clean, quiet and secure but the communal showers (cold water only) and toilets are inadequate to cope with demand at peak hours. Prices are US$4/ $6 a single/double. Checkout is 10 am.

Another in this range which you could try is the *Residencial Suarez*, Ballivian 149. This is a small place with pleasant rooms around a quiet courtyard. It's good value at US$3 per person without own bath and the showers have hot water.

Slightly better but expensive for what it offers is the *Alojamiento Oriente*, Calle Junín 362, which costs US$3 per person in a room without own bath and US$5 per person with own bath. The rooms have hot water and fans.

Those travellers looking for a mid-range hotel should try either the *Hotel Italia*, Calle Rene Moreno, one and a half blocks from the main plaza; or the *Hotel La Paz*, Calle La Paz 69. Both are one-star hotels, have air-conditioning and all the rooms have their own bath with hot water. The Italia costs US$8/$12 a single/ double and the La Paz costs US$10.20/ $13.20 a single/double.

Places to Eat

For breakfast you can't beat the *empanadas* at the *Coffee Shop Bonanza*, Junín between Libertad and 21 de Mayo. They're some of the tastiest you will ever come across and no more expensive than anywhere else despite the appearance of the restaurant. Also good for the same thing is the *Restaurant España*, on the corner of Junín and España, but this place tends not to open until around 10 am.

For cheap lunches and dinners there are a number of places to try. One of the cheapest must be the *China Town Restaurant*, Velasco between Ingavi and Ayacucho on the first floor. They have an extensive Chinese and international menu and most dishes cost from US$1.40 to $1.80, with rice or chop suey for US$0.55 to $0.75. Portions are very substantial. Another to try for traditional three-course set meals at lunch and dinner times is the *Restaurant Florida Chopp*, Florida between 21 de Mayo and Libertad. Meals generally cost less than US$1.

Also cheap and popular are the *Oki Restaurant*, 21 de Mayo between Junín and Ayacucho; and the *Restaurant 85*, Bolivar between 24 de Septiembre and Beni. Other travellers have recommended the *Plaza Restaurant*, 21 de Mayo between Florida and Junín.

Both the *Coffee Shop Bonanza* and the *Gandhi International Restaurant* next door to it are popular with those looking for steak, fried eggs and French fries at lunch or dinner time. The *Lido*, Ingavi 71, used to be popular and offers cheap, vaguely Chinese food but it gets a variable press these days.

If you want a splurge there are two restaurants which you can't beat. The first is the *Bar Restaurant Mandarin*, Sucre 209 (closed Wednesdays), which is very popular with local people and travellers alike. It serves superb Chinese food but is surprisingly cheap. The other is the *Pizzaria La Bella Napoli*, Independencia 635, which is worth the five or six block walk from the budget hotel area. It's housed in a very attractive old barn with chunky wooden furniture and though it looks expensive, it isn't. They offer excellent pizzas, salads, spaghetti and lasagna. Portions are large and service is fast and attentive.

If you're looking for an English pub then you're in luck! Run by John Robinson and his Bolivian wife Nancy, the *London Grill*, Bolivar 85, is just that. It has a friendly, boozy, delightfully eccentric atmosphere with an open fire (when it's cold) and dart board – the competition is stiff. They also offer tasty, well-prepared meals (soups, pork, beef, fish and desserts).

Diagonally opposite the London Grill on the corner of Bolivar and Beni is another lively local bar generally packed with people from early afternoon till late at night.

The best real coffee in Santa Cruz is to be found on the corner of Libertad and Junín on the plaza.

There are quite a few discotheques in Santa Cruz which are popular with the more affluent younger set. The best of them are outside the central area so you're going to need a taxi to get there. Entry generally costs around US$1 but if you want to conserve your funds after that then you'll have to stay with soft drinks. Beers are rarely less than US$1 (small bottle) and spirits can be as much at US$3.00. They usually open at 9 pm and go till 3 am but don't fill up until 11 pm.

Getting There

There is a new international airport, Viru-Viru, about 16 km from the centre of town which is the most modern in the country. It handles all domestic flights as well as international flights to Asunción, Caracas, Campo Grande, Manaus, Miami and Sáo Paulo. There are frequent minibus services between the airport and the bus terminal which cost US$0.50 and take about 20 minutes. A taxi will cost US$3 to $5.

The long-distance bus terminal is at the junction of Av Cañoto and Av Irala.

Sucre

In colonial times Sucre was the seat of the Audiencia of the Charcas and although it is still the official capital of Bolivia, only the Supreme Court still meets here as the other functions of government have been lost to La Paz. Founded in 1538, it's a beautiful, quiet, white-washed city with a mild climate – the altitude is 2790 metres. It was here that the country's Declaration of Independence was signed.

Information

The tourist office is at Calle Potosi 102 on the corner of San Alberto. There's also a very helpful branch office at the airport which has free maps of the city.

You might experience difficulty changing travellers' cheques in Sucre as most of the banks won't take them. If so, try Calle Colón 423.

Things to See

Of the many old churches in Sucre be sure to visit the **cathedral**, on Calle Ortiz. It was built in the 17th century, contains the **Museo de la Iglesia** and is open Monday to Friday from 10 am to 12 noon and 3 to 5 pm and on Saturdays from 2 to 6 pm. Another must is the church of **San Miguel**, which has been beautifully restored after being closed for 120 years, and is the oldest church still in use in South America. It's open between 6.30 and 8 pm.

It's worth trekking up the hillside to see the **Monasterio y Museo de la Recoleta**. It's open Monday to Fridays from 9 to 11.30 am and 2 to 5.30 pm. There are superb views over the city from the edge of the plaza which faces this church and an Indian market lining the road up to it. The **Museo de Santa Clara**, Calle Calvo 212, is also worth a visit if you are interested in sacred art. It's open Monday to Friday from 10 am to noon and 3 to 5 pm, and Saturday from 10 am to noon.

On the bottom side of the Plaza 24 de Mayo is the **Casa de la Libertad**, which is where Sucre and the other generals who fought the independence war came to work out a constitution for the newly independent country. The historical relics are worth seeing, but of major interest is the building itself, which has been beautifully restored. It's open from 9 am to 12 noon and 2 to 5 pm Monday to Friday, and 10 am to 12 noon on Saturdays. Entry costs US$0.10 plus US$0.20 camera fee if you intend to use one. Guided tours are available in Spanish.

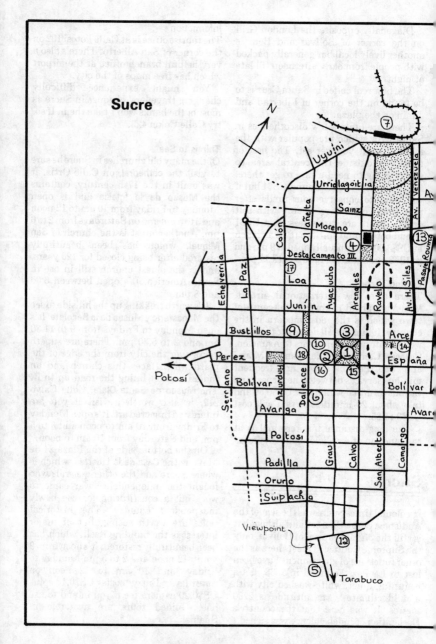

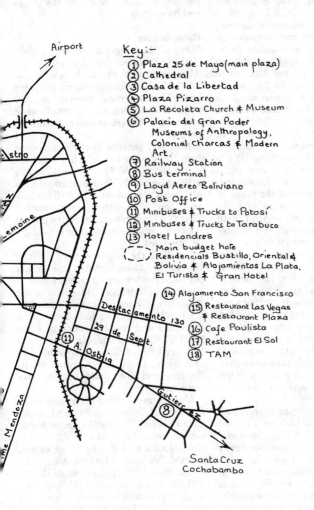

Key:-
1. Plaza 25 de Mayo (main plaza)
2. Cathedral
3. Casa de la Libertad
4. Plaza Pizarro
5. La Recoleta Church & Museum
6. Palacio del Gran Poder
   Museums of Anthropology,
   Colonial Charcas & Modern
   Art
7. Railway Station
8. Bus terminal
9. Lloyd Aereo Boliviano
10. Post Office
11. Minibuses & Trucks to Potosí
12. Minibuses & Trucks to Tarabuco
13. Hotel Londres
   Main budget hote
   Residencials Bustillo, Oriental &
   Bolivia & Alojamientos La Plata,
   El Turista & Gran Hotel
14. Alojamiento San Francisco
15. Restaurant Las Vegas
   & Restaurant Plaza
16. Cafe Paulista
17. Restaurant El Sol
18. TAM

Airport

Santa Cruz
Cochabamba

Another excellent museum is the **Museo Universitarios**, Calle Bolívar 698 which, like the Casa de la Libertad, is housed in a tastefully restored old mansion. This is actually a combined anthropology, colonial and modern art museum. Entry is just US$0.05 and it's open from 8.30 am to 12 noon and 2 to 6 pm Monday to Friday, and from 9 am to 12 noon on Saturday. Another museum which is worth getting to is the **Museo de Santa Clara**, Calle Calvo 204.

About 60 km from Sucre is the small town of **Tarabuco**, famous for its Sunday market and colourful weaving. It's a predominantly Indian town and you'll come across many of its inhabitants selling their wares around the plaza in Sucre. In the tourist season (July to September) it can get overrun with tourists and prices naturally rise at those times but it's still worth visiting.

The cheapest way to get there is by public bus or minibus from the top of Calle Calvo and just below La Recoleta church, between 6 and 8 am (they go when full). It's sometimes possible to find a bus as late as 9 am if demand warrants it but usually it's trucks only after 8 am and they won't go until they're overflowing. It costs about US$0.30 and though journey times differ it shouldn't take more than 2½ hours. There are no problems about getting back to Sucre in the late afternoon.

If you prefer something more organised you can go there and back on a luxury tourist bus with *Solarsa Tours*, Arenales 212 (tel 25386). It leaves every Sunday at 8 am and returns at 3 pm and costs US$3.35 per person. If you want to stay in Tarabuco for the night the *Prefectural* at the bottom end of the plaza is good value. If you find Tarabuco too touristy then try **Betanzes** on the road between Sucre and Potosí. It also has a Sunday market, just as colourful, with hundreds of stalls and not a tourist in sight.

There are two simple hotels if you want to stay overnight: the *Hotel Betanzes* and *Hotel Sucre*, almost next to each other in the centre of town where all the trucks and buses stop.

Places to Stay

Many of the budget hotels are on Calle Ravelo. Perhaps the cheapest is the *Alojamiento La Plata*, Ravelo 32, at US$1/$1.40 a single/double without own bath. The communal showers have hot water. It's basic but popular with those on a very tight budget as well as with local people.

Also very popular is the *Residencias Bustillo*, Ravelo 158, which is excellent value at US$1.50/$2.40 a single/double without own bath. The rooms are spotless with crisp, clean sheets, the staff friendly and there's hot water in the showers. There's a basic restaurant on the ground floor but it often opens too late to be of use for breakfast.

Similar is the *Alojamiento El Turista*, Ravelo 118. Rooms here cost US$1.40 per person. Another cheap place which is popular with budget travellers is the *Alojamiento San Francisco*, Arce 191. It's much the same as the above with a courtyard and friendly staff and costs US$1/$1.80 a single/double without own bath and US$1.20/$2 a single/double with own bath. There is hot water in the showers and the hotel has its own restaurant.

Moving up-market a little there is the *Residencial Oriental*, Alberto 43, which has rooms for US$1.70/$3 a single/double without own bath and US$2/$3.50 a single/double with own bath (hot water); and the *Residencial Bolivia*, Alberto 42, which costs US$3/$4.20 a single/double without own bath and US$3.50/$4.80 a single/double with own bath. There is hot water all day. There's no obvious reason why the Bolivia should be almost twice as expensive as the Oriental.

Similar in price is the *Grand Hotel*, Aniceto Arce 61, which is very popular and often full. It costs US$2.50/$3.80 a single/double with own bath and hot water. The hotel has its own restaurant.

In the same category is the *Hotel Londres*, Av Hernan Siles 6, which looks like it should be expensive but isn't. It offers very large, clean rooms for US$2/$3 a single/double without bath and US$3/$4 a single/double with own bath. There is hot water all day. The hotel has its own restaurant and there is often entertainment (a rock bank or a peña) on Saturday nights.

Places to Eat

For a good, cheap, traditional lunch it's hard to beat the *El Sol*, Colón 423 (no sign – just walk through into the courtyard). They don't normally offer breakfasts or dinners, however.

Many people use the two restaurants next to each other on the top side of the main plaza – the *Restaurant Plaza* and the *Restaurant Las Vegas*. The Vegas has been popular for years for lunches and dinners (it's closed in the morning and on Tuesdays) and produces reasonable, but not exceptional food. You can get a main course there for about US$1.50. It also offers good ice cream, milk shakes and juices. The Plaza was more recently established and is considerably larger than the Las Vegas. It also has a small balcony overlooking the plaza. The meals are excellent and sufficiently large that you could easily get by on only one a day. Especially good are their soups and the *milanesa napolitana* with French fries, vegetables and separate salad. The latter will cost you just US$2 plus 10%. It's closed on Thursdays.

There is supposed to be a vegetarian restaurant operated by the Hare Krishna people called *Govinda* at Av Hernan Siles 948 (more or less opposite the Hotel Londres but no sign) which several travellers reported was excellent but I tried that address four times and it was never open for anything remotely resembling a restaurant. Let us know if you get in.

There are very few *salteña* places in

Sucre to take care of breakfast but the best is the (un-named) café almost next door to the Café Paulista, Calle Ortiz between Audiencia and Dalence. You'll recognise the place from the blackboard hanging from the door with 'salteñas' chalked on it. They also serve coffee and juices. It's cheap and friendly. If you're staying at the Oriental or the Bolivia then try the little café two doors down from the Bolivia.

Surprisingly, for a town with so many students, there are few places to go in the evening except the cinemas. At weekends, but not often on weekdays, it's worth checking out the following *peñas* to see if there's anything scheduled: *Misk'i Huasi*, San Alberto 290 and *Jakañani*, L Cabrera 350.

As for discotheques there are the *Viva Maria*, Plaza San Francisco 10 (daily); *El Cuerno*, España 162 (closed Mondays); and the *El Sotano*, Parque Bolívar (closed Mondays). There's also a very popular disco at Ravelo 254 which caters for the younger end of the market and often seems to be open in the afternoon as well as the evening. The *Hotel Londres* sometimes has a rock band playing on a Saturday night (small entrance charge) but it's nothing like a Santa Cruz disco and the dancing is very restrained.

There are supposed to be two *whiskerias*: *El Pub*, España 13; and *La Oficina*, España 34, but they appear to have strange opening hours. Check them out if you're interested.

Getting There

The long-distance bus terminal is a long way from the centre of town on Gutierrez. A colectivo there costs US$0.10 per person. If your bus is cancelled or you can't get a bus on the day you want one, then it's worth checking the minibuses which congregate alongside the railway tracks halfway between the bus station and the centre of town. There's an Indian market alongside the tracks too. These minibuses are often much less fuss and just as fast and cheap as the regular buses but they only go when full.

There are microbuses between the airport and the centre of town which cost about US$0.10. A taxi will cost around US$2.50 for the car.

TARIJA

The largest town in southern Bolivia and close to the Argentine border, Tarija was founded in 1574 and sits in a very fertile valley where grapes are grown. It declared its independence from Spain in 1807 and formed what was, for a time, a separate republic. It's famous for its fiestas, wine and local colour.

Information

The tourist office is at Calle Bolívar 734, and has very helpful staff. Close by are the *LAB* and *TAM* offices.

The new bus terminal is on the outskirts of town on Av de las Americas.

Things to See

Tarija still retains a strong colonial atmosphere and it's worth spending some time strolling round the centre of town. The main attraction of the place is its fiestas. The most important are the **Fiesta de la Uva** when there is an exhibition of grapes, wines, liqueurs and colourful parades and folklore performances which go on for three days; and the **Fiesta de San Roque**, which takes place on the first three Sundays of September and includes some very colourful and often boisterous parades. One of the most popular of these takes place on the first Sunday of the month and includes *chunchas*, a Chaco tribe who dress up as Red Indians, and parade through the streets with the images of the saints. If you're in the area at the time it's well worth making the effort to be there.

Places to Stay

All the cheap hotels are on Calle Sucre. Very popular is the *Alojamiento Los 8 Hermanos*, Calle Sucre 782, close to the Hotel Sucre, which is clean, has hot showers and costs US$2. Not quite as good but with the same prices is the *Hostal Familiar*, Calle Sucre 656.

Slightly more expensive at US$2.50 is the *Residencial Miraflores*, Sucre 920. It has hot showers 24 hours a day and the rooms look out onto a bright, pleasant courtyard where you can wash clothes. If it's full, try the *Residencial Zeballos* five doors up the same street.

The *Hotel Sucre*, Calle Sucre 760, is the place to go if you want something a little up-market. It's very clean, has good beds and hot water all day.

Places to Eat

For really cheap but very good food go to the market which is one of the most hygienic you're likely to come across in South America. You can get a traditional stew of noodles, lentils and minced meat with salad and hot sauce for just US$0.20 (or US$0.40 if you also want soup).

Good three-course meals are available at the *El Rinconcito*, Calle Sucre 556, for US$0.50. Very good *lomo* and *churrasco* can be found for US$1 at an unnamed restaurant at Calle Ingavi 363. More expensive are the meals at the *Hotel Sucre*, Calle Sucre 760.

In the mornings you can find tasty salteñas at *El Opera*, Calle Sucre 496.

UYUNI

Uyuni lies on the bleak and bitterly cold *altiplano* near the shores of the immense salt lake Salar de Uyuni, which is really the only thing of interest here. When it's dry, it's a blinding-white, featureless salt desert (ever seen Lake Eyre in South Australia?), but when rain falls it can collect up to 15 cm of water. At times like these it's an eerie sight as the blue of the water merges with the blue of the sky and there appears to be no horizon. The only reason you'd come through Uyuni would be if you were heading to or from Antofagasta on the train.

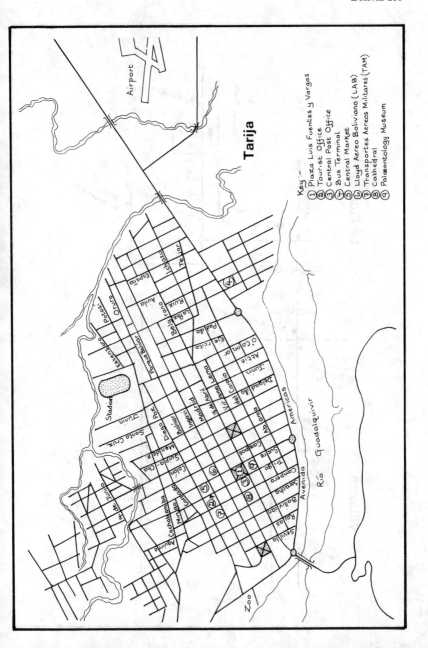

Tarija

Key:-
① Plaza Luis Fuentes y Vargas
② Tourist Office
③ Central Post Office
④ Bus Terminal
⑤ Central Market
⑥ Lloyd Aereo Boliviano (LAB)
⑦ Transportes Aereos Militares (TAM)
⑧ Cathedral
⑨ Palaeontology Museum

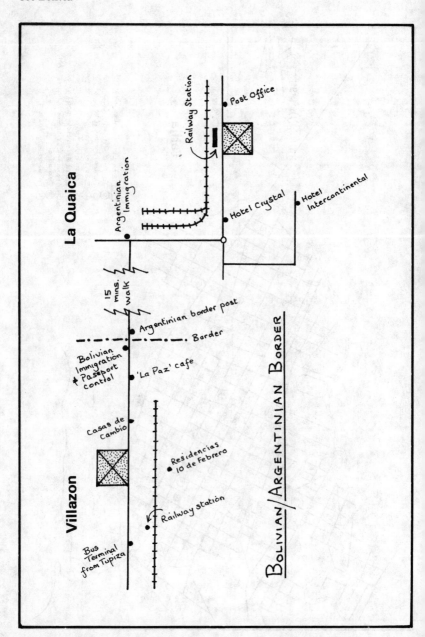

Places to Stay

It's possible to sleep in the waiting room at the station but it gets crowded. Better to stay at the *Hotel Avenida*, a basic hotel but one which has its own restaurant.

GUAYARAMERÍN

In the north-east corner of Bolivia on the banks of the Mamore river, Guayaramerín is Bolivia's back door to Brazilian Amazonia. It faces the Brazilian town of Guajará Mirim but unlike that sprawling modern town, Guayaramerín remains a typical red-dust frontier village of the Beni, isolated from the rest of Bolivia and accessible only by plane or riverboat. Apart from seasonal tracks through the bush, the only road connection is to nearby Riberalta.

Information/Border Formalities

There are no restrictions on passage between the two towns regardless of nationality but if you intend to go further into Brazil then you must follow a certain procedure. First go to the Brazilian consulate in Guayaramerín for a visa (where required). Next, visit Bolivian Immigration on the waterfront to obtain your exit stamp (free) and then take a boat across the river. Just above where the boats land in Guajará Mirim is the police office where you must get your **Brazilian entry stamp and go through customs. Expect a thorough drug search.**

There are frequent launches (US$0.40) and speed boats (US$0.60) across the river day and night but expect to pay more in the small hours. There is also a flat-top barge which serves as a car ferry and is free to pedestrians but it only goes when there are cars to take across.

There is an airport in both the Bolivian town (served by *LAB and TAM*) and the Brazilian town (*Varig/Cruzeiro*).

Places to Stay and Eat

The *Hotel Plaza* and the *Hotel Plaza Anexe*, both on the main plaza, offer very basic but cheap accommodation. Similarly, there are one or two simple cafés and *fuentes de soda* where you can find a meal. If you want more choice or a higher standard of accommodation and food, then it would be better to stay in Guajará Mirim, though it would cost a lot more.

Getting There

Bus There is a surprisingly good road (part paved, part gravel) between Guayaramerín and Riberalta with a bus twice a day in either direction at about 9.30 am and 4 pm. The journey takes about 2½ hours. At other times it's more convenient to take a pick-up truck. These congregate about six blocks up the road from the main plaza going away from the river but they always drive around town looking for more passengers before taking off so you can wave them down in the main plaza too. The going price for foreigners is about US$2; locals pay US$1.

Boat Guayaramerín can be the starting point for an interesting riverboat trip into the Beni lowlands. There is a blackboard outside the Port Captain's office next to Immigration with a full list of the day's departures on it and you'll never have to wait more than a day or two to find a boat heading in your intended direction. This is especially true of Puerto Villaroel south of Trinidad. For boats going up the Beni river itself it's probably best to go first to Riberalta and take one from there.

VILLAZON

Villazon is on the main border crossing between Bolivia and Argentina, and is connected to the first Argentinian town, La Quiaca, by road bridge. It's only about one km between the two, and taxis are available.

If you're heading into Argentina, the border is open from 7.30 am to noon and 3 to 6 pm on weekdays; and 9 to 11 am on weekends and holidays.

RIBERALTA

Built on a bluff overlooking a wide sweep

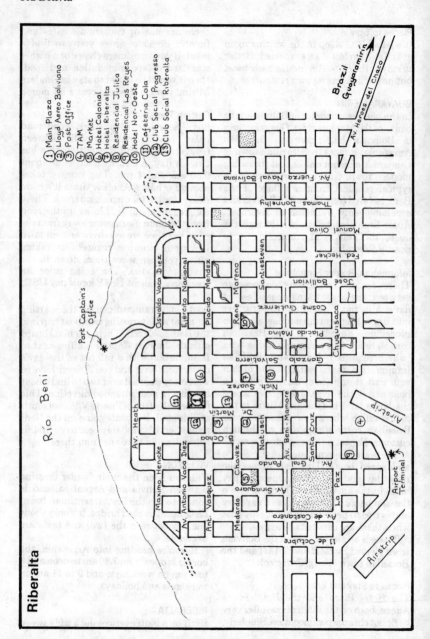

Riberalta

Río Beni

Port Captain's Office

① Main Plaza
② Lloyd Aereo Boliviano
③ Post Office
④ TAM
⑤ Market
⑥ Hotel Colonial
⑦ Hotel Riberalta
⑧ Residencial Julita
⑨ Residencial Los Reyes
⑩ Hotel Nor-Oeste
⑪ Cafeteria Cola
⑫ Club Social Progresso
⑬ Club Social Riberalta

Brazil Guayaramirín

Av. Heroes del Chaco

Av. Fuerza Naval Boliviana
Thomas Donnelly
Manuel Oliva
Fed. Hecker
José Ballivian
Cosme Gutierrez
Chuquisaca
Santiesteven
Rene Moreno
Placido Molina
Gonzalo Salvatierra
Nich. Suarez
Dr. Martin
Natusch
Av. Beni-Manore
Santa Cruz
Oswaldo Vaca Diez
Ejercito Nacional
Placido Mendez
B. Ochoa
Chavez
Pando
Av. Siminguaro
Medarda
Av. de Castañero
Maximo Hencke
Av. Antonio Vaca Diez
Ant. Vasquez
11 de Octubre
Av. La Paz
Av. Gral. Manore
Av. Heath

Airstrip
Airport Terminal
Airstrip

of the Rio Beni, Riberalta is the second largest centre of population in the Beni province. It was once the projected terminus of the Mamore railway which was intended to link it to Pôrto Velho in Brazil but the line was never completed. Even today, Riberalta remains cut off from the rest of Bolivia in terms of both roads and development capital.

For most of the day it's a hot, sleepy, red-dust town surrounded by thick bush. Hardly anything moves except the overhead fans. Then in the evening it bursts into life as hundreds of young people mount their low-powered Japanese motorbikes and drive endlessly around the plaza casting longing glances at those sitting expectantly on the benches. The rest of the population takes to the pavement cafés, the bars, the social clubs (open to all) and the cinemas (there are three of them). Local musicians often put on an impromptu performance from the back of a truck.

If you need to change money here then first enquire at *Maxi Turismo*, Dr Martin just off the main plaza. They'll put you in touch with someone who will change at a good rate.

Places to Stay

Undoubtedly the best place is the *Residencial Los Reyes*, Av Gral Pando (tel 615) close to the airport. It's run by a very friendly and helpful family, who offer spotlessly clean, pleasantly decorated and furnished rooms with clean sheets, fans and even toilet paper. There's a choice of rooms without own bath for US$2.20 per person and rooms with own bath for US$2.70 per person. There's no hot water but then who needs it in this climate? No mosquitoes either. There's an attached *tienda* and a restaurant is being constructed. Similar in price is the *Hotel Nor Oeste*, Av Rene Moreno 597. It's a two-storey hotel but not as pleasant as the Los Reyes and has no shady courtyard.

More basic than these is the *Residencial* *Julita*, Santiesteven. The rooms surround a shady courtyard but it's over-priced at US$2.20 per person. Even more basic is the *Hotel Riberalta*, on the corner of Rene Moreno and Nich Suarez.

If at all possible avoid the *Hotel Colonial*, Placido Mendez just off the main plaza. From the outside this place gives the appearance of being a high-class hotel but on the inside all it offers are dingy, stuffy and scruffy rooms without even a fan (unless you complain vigorously). It isn't just a rip-off, it's outright banditry at US$3.30/$7.70 a single/double with own bathroom. There's no hot water, no toilet paper, no breakfast included in the price, plenty of mosquitos and a surly receptionist.

Places to Eat

The best place for breakfast and one which is popular with local people is the *Cafeteria Cola* on the main plaza. It offers coffee (10 cents), egg sandwiches (25 cents) and complete breakfasts for 35 cents. It's good for soft or hot drinks at other times of the day (no beer).

Probably the best place for lunch or dinner is the *Club Social Riberalta*, on the corner of Dr Martin and Medardo Chavez. It's a huge place with internal rooms and an open-air courtyard with a stage and dancing area. The staff are friendly and it offers good, tasty meals for US$1 to $1.50 (usually beef or chicken with mixed salad, rice and mashed potatoes). Very similar is the *Club Social Progresso* on the main plaza though they're not keen on preparing lunches.

Getting There

Air Both *LAB* and *TAM* fly into Riberalta. There's very little price difference between the two. Flights are often cancelled, sometimes for several consecutive days, because of either bad weather or insufficient passengers so don't check out of your hotel or hump your bags up to the terminal until you're absolutely certain there is a plane waiting.

LAB is scheduled to fly Riberalta-Trinidad-Santa Cruz on Monday, Wednesday and Sunday. *TAM* is scheduled to fly Riberalta-Guayaramerín-Trinidad-Cochabamba on Monday; Riberalta-La Paz on Tuesday; Riberalta-Trinidad-Cochabamba on Wednesday; Riberalta-Trinidad-La Paz on Thursday; Riberalta-Reyes-La Paz on Friday; Riberalta-Cobija-La Paz and Riberalta-Santa Cruz on Saturdays. The *LAB* office is in the centre of town. You should buy *TAM* tickets either from a travel agent or direct from their terminal which is about 100 metres to the left of the main terminal building.

Bus The only road out of Riberalta goes to the Bolivian border town of Guayaramerín and there are two buses a day in either direction. There is no road to Trinidad or to anywhere else further south – you must either go by riverboat or by air.

Boat The Port Captain's office has a blackboard listing the day's departures but you'd need a strong constitution to want to go on most of the riverboats which you're likely to come across here. They're very small and primitive but, unlike most of the boats which ply various stretches of the Amazon, they're never crowded.

TRINIDAD

Founded in the late 17th century, Trinidad is the capital of the Beni province and a town of some 40,000 people. Like Santa Cruz to the south, it is expanding rapidly as the surrounding region is developed for agriculture and cattle ranching. Also like Santa Cruz, it has a distinctly different atmosphere from the towns and cities of the Bolivian highlands and a relatively cosmopolitan population.

Information

The tourist office is in the Edificio Prefectural, Plaza José Ballivian.

Places to Stay

One of the best places is the *Hotel Yacuma*, on the corner of Calle La Paz and Santa Cruz (a large white building). If offers clean, pleasant rooms for US$1.50/$3.50 a single/double without own bath. If it's full, try the *Hotel Loreto* further up Calle La Paz which is of a similar standard and costs US$1.50 per person.

Places to Eat

One of the best and most popular places is the *Chifa Hong Kong* on the main plaza (Plaza José Ballivián).

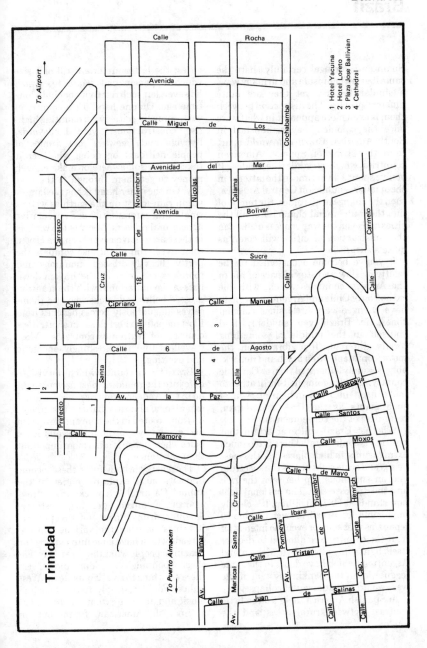

Trinidad

1 Hotel Yacuina
2 Hotel Loreto
3 Plaza Jose Ballivian
4 Cathedral

Brazil

Spain and Portugal certainly share the same Iberian peninsula and in many ways a similar history, yet they are quite different peoples. The distinction between them is even more apparent in what were once the colonies they established in South America. Brazil is a world apart from the string of Spanish American countries which straddle the Andes. If you've spent a lot of time in the latter or in the smaller republics of Central America, then the change in attitudes, the tempo of life, the multi-racial character of all the cities and even the way space is utilised in the construction of cities will come as quite a surprise.

If you've become accustomed to the relatively slow and stoical pace of life in the Andean countries which, with the exception of Chile and Argentina, seem to have changed very little since colonial times, in Brazil you suddenly find yourself in the middle of something totally different. It's vibrant, on the move, confident, often brash and remarkably sexually liberated for a Catholic country. It's also going hell-for-leather to make itself into the industrial rival of such giants as the USA and Japan, regardless of the consequences.

Whether Brazil will ever attain that position is conjectural. There is too much extravagance in high places, recklessness on a grand scale right across the spectrum and an enormous gap between the rich and the dispossessed. The national debt now stands at US$100 billion. It's clearly impossible for Brazil to ever be able to repay this vast sum, or even the interest on it. If the country was allowed to declare itself bankrupt, along with Mexico and Argentina (which have debts in the same league), then the banking system of the west would be in danger of collapse.

In Spanish America there's often little contrast between rural areas and the cities; the latter are often still of a size which a person can relate to. Brazil however, left such relativity behind a long time ago. On one hand it's a country of vast, sprawling cities with daunting high-rise constructions, wide boulevards, flyovers and freeways and armies of people hell-bent on doing whatever it takes to get somewhere or make enough money to get them through to the next day. On the other hand it has the largest virgin rain-forest on the earth as well as small rural communities and speculative agricultural projects. Many of the workers in these areas have never been to a city in their lives. You might also compare the portly, heavily-dressed, mammas and toothless old men in the broken-down bars of the hinterland, with the scantily-dressed belles and bucks who lord themselves languorously across beaches from Florianopolis to Fortaleza. In short, it's a country of extreme contrasts. Most travellers find it refreshingly energetic and exciting.

Brazil isn't a country which you visit to dive into the romantic past as you might do in the Andean countries. It's a sensual experience, almost sybaritic. It's urgent, up front, rooted in the here and now, with perhaps an eye to the future, and it's a place where image is often more important than substance.

The energy which fuels these people finds its most explosive outlet in the annual Carnival – a week-long extravaganza of music, dancing, costume, laughter, drunkenness and street crime. It brings together the various cultural threads which have gone into making the Brazilian people what they are today. For sheer spontaneity, colour and excess there's nothing to rival it outside the West Indies. You'll certainly find colour and music and, to some extent, excitement at a Spanish American fiesta but in

comparison with a Brazilian Carnival it may well feel like a vicarage tea party. One of the reasons for this is that there is no other country in the world which has such a mix of different races with their various cultural traditions. Ritual plays second fiddle to spontaneity in Brazil.

African, Portuguese and Amerindian have intermarried freely here since the Portuguese first arrived around 1500 AD and although there is some racial discrimination there's no other country on the continent where the various races are so thoroughly mixed. Apart from the few remaining tribes who inhabit the Amazon forest, Brazil has no parallel to the kind of dual culture which exists in those Spanish-American republics that have large populations of pure Indians, such as Guatemala, Ecuador, Peru or Bolivia.

Immigration, either forced or voluntary, has naturally left its mark on this vast country. Black people are still predominant in the coastal region north of Rio de Janeiro while white people – mainly descendants of immigrants from Italy, Portugal, Spain and Germany – live to the south. In the 70 years up to 1950 Brazil took in over 4½ million immigrants from Europe and has averaged around 50,000 per year since then. There's also a sizeable Japanese community which owns large chunks of the coffee and market gardening agri-business.

However the beaches, the pockets of affluence and even the Carnival are just one facet of Brazil. Another is the poverty and devastation. Behind the glitter of the city centres, the skyscrapers, the super-highways and the extravagance of the wealthy, there are millions of industrial and agricultural workers whose wages don't cover the bare necessities of life. They are forced to live in the squalid *favelas* which encircle every Brazilian city. For the most part these are without such basic amenities as water, sanitation, power or medical facilities – things which other industrialised nations take for granted.

While the military ruled Brazil, for the 20 years until 1985, trade unions were prohibited and political expression was rigidly controlled. Torture during interrogation and the 'disappearance' of opponents of the regime, though officially denied, were commonplace. Until fairly recently 'death squads' of off-duty policemen methodically gunned down so-called subversives in the cities under the pretext of putting a squeeze on drug, gambling and prostitution rackets.

Since the restoration of civilian government things are changing for the better but the effects of 20 years of repression can't be dealt with in a matter of months whatever the expectations of the population. This is particularly true in a cataclysmic economic climate in which the International Monetary Fund (IMF) is demanding major cuts in spending on social projects and a freeze on wage increases, despite three figure inflation.

Yet another facet of Brazil is the rape of the Amazon forest. While it's true that much of the responsibility for this lies squarely on the shoulders of rapacious multinational companies and foreign entrepreneurs, it could not have taken place without the collusion of the military government which was riddled with corruption.

The forest is enormous; the last of its size in the world. It contains one third of the world's trees and covers five million square km – an area larger than the whole of Europe. Yet its very size is its Achilles' heel, as Brazilians and others have always assumed that there's no end to it.

Previously unknown Indian tribes each with their own completely self-sufficient cultures are still occasionally found by explorers and road construction teams. However, of the thousands of tribes which lived there more or less undisturbed until the middle of the last century, only some 100 remain with a total population numbering no more than 40,000. They've been reduced to their present levels by outright murder (by planters, trappers, ranchers, road construction teams and the army), by European diseases to which they have no immunity, and by the loss of forest cover. These are forest cultures – when the forest goes, so do the cultures.

By a strange irony this forest, though one of the world's most lush, is also potentially a desert. This is something which is hard to believe when you're in the middle of it. Left alone it is self-perpetuating. The trees live almost entirely by recycling whatever drops to the forest floor and also recycle about half of the rain which falls. But they're rooted in only the shallowest of soils covering a laterite bedrock so when the tree cover is removed there is nothing to soak up the rain. Flooding, erosion and leaching take place. In as little as two years, what little soil there was gets washed away and the sun begins to oxidise the laterite. Unless this process is reversed, which is none too easy, the end result is a desert.

You'll see patches of this kind of desert and others well on the way to it if you take the road through the jungle from Pôrto Velho to Manaus. Many of them date from the attempts to resettle destitute Sertão peasants in Amazonia. Even selective forestry has proved to be virtually impossible or at best, uneconomic because of the high degree of biological co-operation between the various plants and animals which live in the forest. If this balance is seriously disturbed the forest suffers. Many trees, valued for their wood, will not grow if there are too few or too many of the same type growing in the same area. Others will not grow unless there are certain types of insects or vertebrates present.

It's only in recent years that researchers have begun to piece together the extremely complex pattern of relationships which holds this type of forest together. Not only that, but the majority of drugs used to cure human illnesses have their basis in plant products. There are probably thousands of remedies waiting to be discovered yet many species of plant are rapidly heading for the endangered species category as a result of the incursions on the forest.

But who cares when (at least potentially) there's money to be made by burning it down? There is a lingering belief that the area can be made into the larder of Brazil, so every year millions of hectares of the forest are burnt down in the vain hope that it can be made productive.

In the last 60 years one quarter of the forest has been destroyed and every year another 4% is burnt down. At that rate it will be gone by 2000 AD. It's difficult to appreciate, without going there, the amount of burning which is being done. In the 2400-km journey from Campo Grande to Manaus you will rarely be out of sight of huge forest fires on either side of the road or the charred remains of a previous one. From the air it's even more catastrophic.

This isn't going entirely unnoticed however and Brazil has a very active conservation movement. There are also laws governing forest clearance but with only some 100 inspectors to cover an area for which 20,000 would be too few, these are either evaded or ignored entirely. Even the government department set up to manage and protect this asset has been known to put in motion secret deals which involve the selling-off and clearance of areas of the forest as large as some European countries.

Concern for this forest is not confined just to conservation activists. It's been estimated that this forest supplies a large proportion of the world's oxygen. If it goes, your vegie garden isn't going to offer much in the way of compensation. Already, major climatic changes are being reported all the way from Ecuador to Bolivia. The level of the Amazon has risen significantly over the last 10 years and annually threatens many riverside ports and villages which previously rarely had to think about such things.

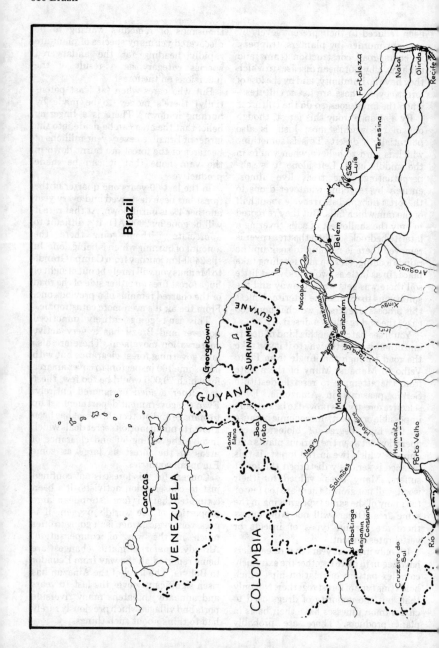

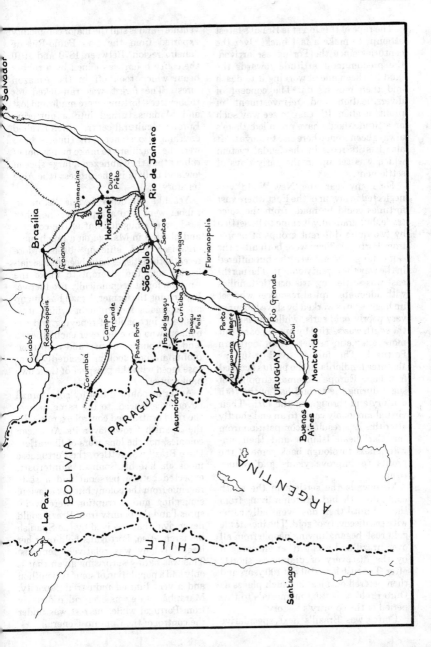

The rape of this forest is Brazil's latest attempt to make a fast buck. Over the centuries since the Portuguese arrived, the predominant attitude towards the land has been one of working it to death and then moving on. The concept of diversification and re-investment of profits is alien. It's easy to see why such an attitude should have prevailed: there's always been somewhere else to move to. It also has its roots in the feudal system which was set up in the early days of settlement.

For many years the 'New World' was neglected in favour of the East where vast fortunes could be made from the spice trade, but gradually it came to be settled by two quite different groups of people from Portugal. They were both after the same thing – instant wealth – but differed in the way they went about it. The north-east was settled by aristocratic families with adequate capital resources who set up huge estates worked by slave labour or very poorly paid serfs, while the land to the south was settled by much poorer but more energetic settlers from northern Portugal. The former lived it up as absentee landlords on the profits accrued from being Europe's foremost suppliers of sugar during the second half of the 16th century and throughout the 17th. Their virtual monopoly came to an end shortly after this as a result of competition from the Caribbean Islands and their unwillingness to plough back some of the profits to improve yields and reduce costs.

Meanwhile the settlers in the south could do little but scratch a living from the soil until their day eventually came with the discovery of gold. The inevitable gold rush began drawing people from all over Brazil and was further encouraged by the discovery of diamonds shortly after. The rush lasted about 100 years and then petered out, leaving such places as Ouro Prêto as lasting memorials to this period of the country's history.

Coffee was Brazil's next speculative venture – and is still the major commodity exported from the São Paulo-Rio de Janeiro region. Between 1870 and 1910 the coffee boom was joined by a rubber boom which took off in the Amazon forest. The forest was ransacked for rubber trees, fortunes were made and lost and Manaus turned into a glittering European cultural centre which rivalled anything in existence at the time. So keen were the Brazilians to make money out of rubber that they annexed a large slice of lowland Bolivia in the process (the Acre territory).

Yet like all other booms before it, rubber went into a rapid decline when seeds were smuggled out of the country and planted in Malaya on a much more organised and efficient basis. More recently the fetishes have been industrialisation and the attempt to make the Amazon forest economically productive. In pursuing the former, Brazil has run up an enormous foreign debt which it is basically incapable of repaying and the bankers who once fell over each other to lend the country money and reap their profits are now looking decidedly ill at ease faced with the prospect of their own bankruptcy.

As far as political history goes, Brazil never experienced, to the same degree, the rigid centralised control exercised by the Spanish Crown over its American colonies, nor the long wars of liberation. Once Brazil was settled, the Portuguese monarch, like his Spanish counterpart, expected both a personal and a state revenue from the colony but tax evasion, smuggling and corruption were widespread and the bounty from Brazil could never rival that received by the Spanish monarch. Also, Portugal's hold over her largest colony was relatively tenuous. This was hardly surprising given that it only had a population of some two million and a very limited industrial capacity. Maranhão state was even ruled directly from Portugal while the rest was under the control of the Captain-General.

The break with the mother country came relatively easily and the process was initiated by the Napoleonic Wars in Europe. Following the conquest of Portugal by the French, the Portuguese royal family was shipped to Brazil by the British Navy in 1808 along with a British ambassador, who was charged with the task of opening up Brazil to British manufactures and as a source of raw materials. British capital had already made inroads into the Brazilian economy before this time but was to become even more intrusive over the next century or so until replaced by American, Japanese and German finance. With the end of the wars in Europe, King João VI returned to Portugal in 1821 leaving his son Pedro in charge of the colony. The Portuguese parliament mistrusted this arrangement and demanded that Pedro return. The colonists refused to accede to this demand and independence was declared in December of that year with Pedro crowned as emperor. The Portuguese were in no position to oppose the move.

Dom Pedro didn't fare too well. There were secessionist movements in the north, he lost the Banda Oriental which subsequently became independent Uruguay, and he had serious marital problems. After a military revolt in 1831 he abdicated in favour of his son, at that time only five years old. At the age of 15, Dom Pedro II assumed the title of emperor and ruled until the monarchy was abolished in 1889. His reign was one of peace and relative prosperity for Brazil and being an enlightened liberal he did his best to reform the social and political structures. Communications were improved, agriculture encouraged and corruption checked.

It was also during Dom Pedro II's reign that Brazil was instrumental in toppling the Argentinian dictator Rosas and defeating the Paraguayan dictator López. Dom Pedro II finally lost his crown a year after slavery was abolished in 1888, because of the opposition of the land-owners, and was forced into exile in France where he died a pauper's death two years later.

Following the departure of Dom Pedro II a republic was declared and continued somewhat uneventfully until 1930 when the old power structure was overthrown in a revolution headed by Getulio Vargas, the Governor of Rio Grande do Sul. Vargas quickly assumed the powers of a dictator and ruled for 15 years, after which a liberal republic was restored.

Corruption, instability and the increasing control of the economy by foreign capital eventually culminated in a military coup in 1964. The country was set for 20 years of military dictatorship.

By 1984 it was becoming obvious that the army could no longer hold on in the face of increasing civilian militancy and a date was set for elections. In those elections the respected and very popular elder statesman, Tancredo Neves, captured the presidency but died before he could take office. His Vice-President, Jose Sarney took his place and although his base of support was considerably less than Neves', he seems to be taking some bold stands especially regarding IMF demands relating to the country's massive foreign debt. It won't be an easy job.

Like many of the ex-Spanish colonies, Brazil is still haunted by the legacy of its colonial past. Unlike North America which was settled by the *Mayflower* pilgrims who crossed to America as pioneers and free workers on their own farms, Latin America was founded on Spain and Portugal's abundance of subjugated labour. Enslavement of the Indians was followed by wholesale transportation of Africans. Through the centuries, a legion of unemployed peasants has always been available for relocation to new production centres, be they mineral or agricultural. This structure persists today and frustrates the growth of an internal consumer market as well as ensuring that wages remain low.

The internal economic development of the Latin American colonies was never the goal of the ruling class. They were seen instead merely as a source of gold, silver and food for Europe. Wealth moved in one direction only and that was to Europe. By contrast, the centre of gravity in North America from the outset was the farms and workshops of New England. Profits were re-invested and a healthy internal economy developed. In Latin America, profits were squandered in high living and on faraway wars. It remains to be seen whether Brazil will achieve the desired transformation before it destroys the assets it still has.

VISAS

Required by all except nationals of Western European countries, Canada, and many – though not all – of the countries of the West Indies, Central and South America. Visas are valid for a stay of three months and are renewable. You may be asked for an onward ticket when applying for a visa but this isn't usually the case. If so, they generally accept an airline ticket out of any country in South America back to the USA or Europe for instance. Alternatively, a long-distance return bus ticket is sufficient (eg Montevideo-Pôrto Alegre). If you don't need a visa for Brazil it's a breeze getting into the country. Simply turn up at the border and get a stamp in your passport – no questions, no fuss, nothing to show.

Renewing visas, on the other hand, can be problematical. In this case they certainly want to see an onward ticket and 'sufficient funds'. Renewing visas is best done inside the country. Don't go into a neighbouring country and start all over again if at all possible. If you do this (eg in Montevideo) they'll not only demand an onward ticket and 'sufficient funds' but tell you that they have to telex Brasilia and it could be anything up to 15 days before they get a reply. You'll come across people who've been caught out this way if you go to Montevideo.

There are a number of border crossing points between Brazil and neighbouring countries (Guajará Mirim and Guayaramerín on the Bolivian border and over the Friendship Bridge between Foz do Iguaçu and Puerto Pte Stroessner on the Paraguayan border, for instance) where there is unrestricted passage between the two sides. You can go back and forth as many times as you like without a visa or even passport formalities but if you intend to go further into Brazil then make sure you get stamped in, otherwise you'll have problems later.

At most Brazilian border posts (but not Foz do Iguaçu where they couldn't care less) you can expect a cursory baggage search. If you're coming from Bolivia, however, it can be very thorough because of the cocaine trade. Corumbá is the worst place for this and even though you've been checked out once at the border you may well be hauled in again for another thorough search at Corumbá railway station.

MONEY

US$1 = Cz 7495 (official floating rate – rising steadily)

The unit of currency is the cruzeiro (Cz) = 100 centavos. In Brazil there is both an official bank rate vis-a-vis the US dollar and what is called the *mercado paralelo* or open market rate. The difference between the two is usually about 20%, the latter being higher. It's entirely legal to change money anywhere you like and so naturally you will do it at the *mercado paralelo* rate with a hotel manager, travel agent, shopkeeper or even on the street. There is no such thing as a black market. You can find out what both rates are any day by picking up a national newspaper and looking in the financial section. Even banks display the two rates in their front window.

The idea behind this is an attempt to control the money supply and get to grips with Brazil's massive foreign debt. Anyone who needs US dollars to keep their business going is free to buy them anywhere they please but the supply is restricted. If you buy them at a bank you pay through the nose for them. Both cash and travellers' cheques are acceptable on the *mercado paralelo* but cash is much more versatile. It's not always possible to find someone who will accept travellers' cheques and it's almost impossible in small towns. Naturally the rate for cash is higher than for travellers' cheques. Bring lots of green-backs with you – as many as you dare carry! It makes life in Brazil a lot cheaper.

Inflation in this country is fierce. Exchange rates escalate daily so don't change more money than you need to get you through the next few days unless you're going to areas where you will have little or no opportunity to change money (like parts of the Amazon basin). Exchange rates are generally best in São Paulo and Rio but this isn't always the case. I changed money in Pôrto Velho at the best rate I'd ever been offered but it is generally true that the best rates are to be found in the large cities of the east coast.

By the time you read this, the rates quoted here will be wildly out of date so you need to do some homework before you get to Brazil. Find a traveller who has just come from there and get a line on what the *mercado paralelo* rate currently stands at. Most Brazilians who want dollars are usually fairly straight about what they are worth but if you cross a border blind then you're a sitting duck.

Don't have money sent to Brazil while you're away from home. You can only collect it in cruzeiros and when you leave, reconversion into US dollars is restricted to 30% of the original amount – and that's only if you leave from a place where dollars are available (like large international airports). Forget about reconversion entirely at land borders. If you need money sent to you then do it in Uruguay or Paraguay where you can pick it up in dollars.

GETTING THERE
To/From Uruguay
The main route to Uruguay is the coast road from Montevideo to Pôrto Alegre via Chuy (the Brazilian/Uruguayan border town) and Pelotas. This is the preferred route these days as it's a very good, surfaced road. You can either do the journey in stages by local buses which is cheaper (by about US$10) or take one of the direct international buses between either Pôrto Alegre or Pelotas and Montevideo.

Both *ONDA* and *TTL* operate international buses daily in either direction. In Pôrto Alegre buy your ticket at the Rodoviaria (bus terminal). For the schedules and terminal addresses in Montevideo refer to the chapter on Uruguay. Both companies charge the same – US$20 Montevideo-Pelotas and US$24.50 Montevideo-Pôrto Alegre. The journey takes about 12½ hours.

The other main highway is from Treinta y Tres or Melo to Pelotas via the Mauá bridge and the border towns of Río Branco (Uruguay) and Jaguarão (Brazil) but it isn't used as much as the coastal highway these days.

To/From Argentina

The only place you're likely to cross the border between Brazil and Argentina is at the Iguazú Falls. *Sulamericana* operate buses 10 times daily (plus two *leitos*) in either direction. There are six daily buses in either direction between Curitiba and Foz do Iguaçu which take 12 hours.

From Curitiba the first leaves at 7 am and the last at 11.30 pm. From Foz the first leaves at 6.30 am and the last at 9.30 pm. From Foz you take one of the hourly local buses to Pôrto Meira (a few cents) and the ferry from there to Puerto Iguazú (Argentina). The ferry operates between 8 am and 6 pm daily except between noon and 2 pm and sometimes in February when the river is in flood. The ferry costs about US$0.50 except on weekends and holidays when it's double.

From Puerto Iguazú there are buses approximately every hour with several companies to Posadas which take seven hours. From Posadas you can either cross the river by ferry to Encarnación (Paraguay) or take a train to Buenos Aires (seven per week).

To/From Paraguay

The most convenient direct crossing between Paraguay and Brazil is over the 'Friendship Bridge' between Foz do Iguaçu and Puerto Pte Stroessner. There are local buses from very early in the morning until late at night in either direction which cost about US$0.25 and take 15 to 20 minutes but if you need to go through passport control you cannot use them because they won't wait for you. Movement between the two towns is unrestricted – you can cross the bridge as many times as you like without going through passport control but if you intend going further into either country then you must go through passport control and get the necessary stamps.

Actually, if you're leaving Paraguay and going to Brazil the Paraguayans couldn't care less about stamping your passport so you could go there without passing through passport control, spend as much time as you like in Paraguay and then go back to Brazil, again without passing through passport control as long as you either walked across the bridge or took a local bus. It's probably not advisable to do this and you certainly shouldn't do it in the opposite direction unless you intend to leave the same way. Backpackers tend to be conspicuous so it's advisable to go through official channels.

If you're going between Foz and Asunción, on the other hand, it isn't worth the US$0.50 'saving' to take a local bus to Puerto Stroessner and then another from there to Asunción because the local buses won't wait at passport control. You'll end up walking across the bridge and then having to find another on the other side. It's much better to take a direct international bus since these cater for the time necessary to go through passport control. *Rapido Yguazú* (daily at 1.30 pm from Foz), *Unesul*, *Pluma* (daily at 6.30 am and 10.15 am from Foz) and *Nossa Senhora de la Asunción* (daily at 5.30 and 8 pm (leito) from Foz) cover the route. The fare is US$3.50 and the journey takes about 5½ to 6 hours. If you're going into Paraguay you have to buy a Tourist Card for about US$1.50 at passport control regardless of nationality.

Another crossing point is further north

between Pedro Juan Caballero (Paraguay) and Ponta Porã (Brazil). There are five daily buses in either direction between Campo Grande and Ponta Porã which take six to seven hours and cost US$7. Alternatively you can take the train. These depart Campo Grande daily at 9 am (slow train: takes eight hours and costs US$3 in 1st class and US$2 in 2nd class) and 4.45 pm (express: takes six hours and costs US$5). They depart Ponta Porã daily at 6.40 am (express) and 8.45 am (slow train).

Ponta Porã and Pedro Juan Caballero are actually the same town – the border merely divides it in half. To cross the border simply walk down the road. There is a Paraguayan consulate in Ponta Porã and a Brazilian consulate in P J Caballero for those who need visas. There are three buses daily in either direction between P J Caballero and Concepción or Asunción by *Amambay* (at 10 am, 5.30 and 7.30 pm from Asunción). Expect long delays on this road as work is going on.

To/From Bolivia

The main crossing point between Bolivia and Brazil is at Corumbá on the Río Paraguai. There are two daily trains in either direction between Campo Grande and Corumbá. From Corumbá they depart at 8 am (slow train: takes 11 hours and costs US$4 in 1st class and US$2.50 in 2nd class) and 9 pm (express: takes 9¾ hours and costs US$7 – no 2nd class available). From Campo Grande they leave at 8.17 am (slow train) and 9 pm (express).

The alternative is to take the bus but there's only one per day in either direction. There is a Bolivian consulate in Corumbá for those who need visas. Between Corumbá and the Bolivian border town of Quijarro you must take either a bus or a taxi. From Quijarro there is a *ferrobus* to Santa Cruz three times per week and a *tren rapido* usually once, but sometimes twice a day. By *ferrobus* the journey takes about 12 hours and costs US$11.80

(Pullman) and US$7.90 (Especial). The *tren rapido* costs US$5.25 (Pullman), US$3.30 (1st class) and US$2.05 (2nd class) and takes about 24 hours. If you want something approaching comfort, don't go 2nd class.

The other crossing point is via Guayaramerín/Guajará Mirim on the Río Mamoré south-west of Pôrto Velho. The railway between Pôrto Velho and Guajará Mirim was closed many years ago but there are buses between the two places via Abuña daily by *Novo Estado* and *Rondonia*. From Pôrto Velho, *Novo Estado* have buses at 7 am and 10 pm and *Rondonia* have buses at 2 pm, 7 pm (leito) and 12 midnight. The fare is US$8.10 and the journey takes about 14 hours. Buy your ticket as far in advance as possible because there's a gold rush happening just south of Abuña so there's a lot of competition for tickets. If you can't get one on the day you want to leave try going to the bus terminal around 9 pm. There are often people trying to sell tickets which they can't use for some reason. Some sections of this road are unbelievably bad even in the dry season. I dread to think what it's like in the wet. It certainly demonstrates the monumental stupidity and short-sightedness of ripping up a perfectly functional, though slow and antiquated railway and replacing it with a dirt track through the jungle.

At Guajará Mirim you simply take a boat across the river to Guayaramerín in Bolivia but make sure you go about passport formalities in the right sequence otherwise you'll waste a lot of time – full details under Guajará Mirim (in this chapter) and under Guayaramerín (in the Bolivia chapter). There are daily buses and pick-up trucks between Guayaramerín and Riberalta and flights from Riberalta to both Santa Cruz and Cochabamba several times per week. It's an interesting trip this way.

To/From Peru

The only way you can get between Brazil

and Peru is either by flying or by riverboat down the Amazon. The usual route for either is between Manaus and Iquitos via Tabatinga, Benjamin Constant (both in Brazil), Leticia (Colombia) or Ramón Castilla (Peru). The latter four towns are all very close to each other at the tri-borders of Peru, Colombia and Brazil on the Amazon River. Riverboats are easy to find from Manaus to either Tabatinga or Benjamin Constant (the average fare is US$40 including food and the journey takes about 7 days), but they are much less frequent from there to Iquitos. You may have more luck in Leticia. More details about these riverboats between the three countries can be found in both the Colombia and Peru chapters.

If you don't want to take riverboats, the air fare from Manaus to Iquitos is US$230 if you pay for the ticket entirely in Manaus but there is a cheaper way to do it. First buy a ticket to Tabatinga (US$80) then at Tabatinga get off the plane and go into the airport terminal and buy another ticket to Iquitos (US$74). After that you re-board the same flight! The plane stops long enough at Tabatinga to allow you to do this. Details of Amazonian riverboats within Brazil are given in the 'Getting Around' section.

To/From Colombia

The only point of entry into Colombia from Brazil is via Leticia on the Amazon. (See the 'To/From Peru' section).

To/From Venezuela

There is only one route between Brazil and Venezuela. This is the road from Boa Vista to Ciudad Bolívar via the Venezuelan border town of Santa Elena. There is one bus per day in either direction between Boa Vista and Santa Elena which costs US$2.50 and takes about seven hours, though it can take longer depending on the state of the road. It's operated by *União Cascavel* and leaves Boa Vista at 8 am and Santa Elena

at 7 am. Expect border formalities to take around two hours – very thorough searches. Between Santa Elena and Km 88 (south of El Dorado) there are no buses so you must either hitch-hike, take a jeep or fly.

Flights between Santa Elena and Ciudad Bolívar are US$25 one-way. There are daily jeeps between Santa Elena and Tumeremo via Km 88 which cost about US$9 per person (six passengers) or US$11.25 (five passengers) and take 9 to 10 hours. From Km 88 and El Dorado there are daily buses to Ciudad Bolívar which cost US$4 and take about 7½ hours. Likewise, from Ciudad Bolívar there are daily buses to Caracas for about US$5.40 which take nine hours. The road is surfaced as far south as El Dorado. After that it's a gravel road, sections of which are in disrepair.

There is a Venezuelan consulate in Boa Vista.

These days quite a few travellers stop off at Km 85, also known as Las Claritas. Luis and Jorge Gonzalez have a camp site in their grounds just outside the village. They're very friendly people.

To/From Guyana

As with Venezuela, there is only one crossing point into Guyana. This is the road from Boa Vista to Lethem via Bomfim. There is one daily bus in either direction between Boa Vista and Bomfim as well as colectivos. The bus departs Boa Vista at 8 am and from Bomfim at 2 and 3 pm. It takes about three hours and costs US$4.50. At Bomfim you must get your Brazilian exit stamp and then walk the five km to the River Tacutu (border), where you hire a row boat to take you across the river to Lethem. There are no roads north from Lethem to the rest of Guyana so you must fly.

GETTING AROUND
Flights

Unlike in the Andean republics, short

plane hops in Brazil are not all that cheap, though with the current exchange rate of the cruzeiro against the US dollar they're not that expensive either. Distances in Brazil are enormous so you may consider taking the occasional flight here and there, particularly in Amazonia where the roads are rough and bus journeys long (and often hazardous). It's sometimes possible to find free flights with the armed forces *(FAB)* by asking around at the smaller airports but don't get too excited about the possibility because we've had no reports lately from travellers who've made it.

What is worth considering, especially if your time is limited, is the Brazil Air Pass. This is offered by all three of the airlines which cover the internal routes though *Varig/Cruzeiro* have the more extensive schedule. The Pass costs US$250 for 14 days (limited to five trips) or US$330 for 21 days (unlimited trips) and must be bought outside Brazil. You'll be issued with an MCO stamped 'Brazil Air Pass' and when you get there you simply go to any office of the airline and they'll help you work out an itinerary. You can start from any point you like and finish at any point you like. Think carefully about where and when you're going to use the ticket for the first time otherwise you could find yourself doing precious little but getting on and off planes for 21 days.

Buses

Bus transport in Brazil anywhere south of Amazonia is excellent. The buses are modern, comfortable and much faster than the trains. Not only that, but because of the exchange rate of the cruzeiro, they're surprisingly cheap too. In addition there's usually a choice of ordinary buses and *leito*. The latter are essentially sleepers and travel at night, have reclining seats, foot rests, a toilet and on-board refreshments but they are about double the price of the others.

All the main cities and many of the smaller ones have modern centralised bus terminals known as *Rodoviárias*. When they are combined with the railway station they are known as *Rodoferroviária*. Some of these places are like cities within a city and have virtually every facility the traveller is ever likely to need – cafés, news-stands, washrooms, toilets, bookshops, information kiosks – and above all they're convenient since they bring together all the various bus companies. Catching a bus is simplicity itself.

The only difficulty you might have is choosing which company to go with as on some routes there can be up to 10 companies operating. At some terminals all the bus companies clearly display their schedules or have a leaflet which they hand out. At others (São Paulo and Salvador are two prime examples) no schedules as displayed so if your Portuguese isn't up to much it can be frustrating.

It's usually advisable to book in advance on main routes (a few hours is generally sufficient) though you'll rarely have any difficulty getting a seat on the day you want to travel – if one company's buses are full, try another. There's little to choose in quality between one company and the next.

Highways in Brazil are generally excellent and a lot of progress has been made in recent years, even in the Amazon region. For instance, there is now a good, surfaced road between Cuiabá and Pôrto Velho. Elsewhere in Amazonia, however, there are few surfaced roads and most are not even gravelled. In the dry season those reassuring thick red lines on maps of this area are often little more than vast seas of red dust and you and your baggage will end up covered in the stuff. (To minimise the effects on your baggage, get hold of a large fertiliser bag or some other suitably large plastic bag and put your pack inside it before you stow it away in the luggage compartment.) In the rainy season those same *roads* are just yawning oceans of thick mud. At these times buses often travel in pairs so that they can haul each other out of the mire.

If you're hitching on top of a lumber truck, be prepared for km after km of duststorms as your truck jockeys to overtake the bus or truck in front. Neither will be prepared to give a centimetre in conditions where visibility rarely exceeds a few metres and where there are other unseen trucks with megatonnes of lumber hurtling towards you in the opposite direction. If you think danger is fun, try this one for a laugh! I fondly hoped and eventually came to believe that the Brazilians had some mysterious sixth sense about these things. You'd better do the same.

Much of the Transamazonian system of highways has been completed but very little of it has been surfaced, so every time it rains half the bank gets washed away and pot-holes appear. Add to this the fact that the forest on either side of the road for hundreds and hundreds of km has been burnt to the ground so there's nothing to hold and absorb the water which comes down in sheets. As a result, the quality of the highway along any particular section depends largely on how long ago it was constructed.

In a country the size of Brazil it's obviously impossible to provide a complete schedule of services, fares and journey times nor would this be particularly viable since the first two change constantly. If you need this sort of information there's a very useful little publication called, *Guia de Viagens*, which is on sale at most newsagents in any bus terminal in Brazil. It costs about US$0.70 and has the schedules of all buses throughout Brazil, except for the more remote places.

Some examples of bus services, fares and journey times along the more popular routes however, are:

Pôrto Alegre-Florianopolis Two direct and several indirect buses daily by *São Cristovão*. The direct buses take seven hours and the indirect buses about eight hours. The fare is US$5.50.

Pôrto Alegre-Curitiba Six buses daily, three via the coast and three via Caxias do Sul. The fare is US$7.95.

São Paulo-Foz do Iguaçu Several direct buses daily which cost US$10 and take about 18 hours along good surfaced roads.

São Paulo-Cuiabá Direct buses which cost US$16 and take 26 hours along good surfaced roads.

São Paulo-Rio Departures by *Itapemirim*, *Expreso Brasileiro* and *Cometa* at least every hour in either direction 24 hours a day. They all cost the same (US$4.20) and take about six hours. There is a meal stop en route.

Rio-Belo Horizonte The journey takes seven hours and costs US$6. There are buses every half hour from 8.30 am to 12 midnight.

Belo Horizonte-Brasília Nine departures daily by *Itapemirim* and *Penha*, most of them in the evening. The fare is US$8 and the journey time 12 hours.

Brasília-Salvador One bus daily in either direction which costs US$17 and takes 24 hours.

Salvador-Recife The journey takes 12 hours and costs US$8 to $10.

Fortaleza-Belém Two daily departures each by *Ipu Basília* and *Expreso Timbira* which cost US$15.

Fortaleza-São Luís Several departures daily which cost US$13 and take 19 hours.

São Luis-Belém Two buses daily in either direction by *Transbrasiliana* which take 24 hours and cost US$7.80.

Trains

South of a line stretching roughly from Corumbá through Brasília to Recife there is a good system of railways. They're significantly cheaper (in 2nd class) than the buses though they are somewhat slower. Second class is more than adequate and rarely crowded. Trains are kept clean and meals can be bought either in the dining car or brought to your seat. Other refreshments (coffee, mineral waters, beer and wine, etc) are brought round periodically. Sleeping cars are available on the long-haul routes. If you plan on using the railways very much in Brazil it's a good idea to get hold of the railway timetable – free from tourist offices. Examples of railway fares and travelling times are as follows:

São Paulo-Rio de Janeiro There are two trains daily in either direction. The express train departs São Paulo (Luz Station) at 11.20 pm and Rio (Dom Pedro II Station) at 11 pm. The journey takes eight hours and costs US$8.50 (*leito superior* – upper bunk), US$10.20 (*leito inferior* – lower bunk), US$11 (single cabin) and US$18.70 (double cabin). There's also a daily non-express train in either direction at 8 am which takes 9¼ hours. Second class is available on this train.

The buses between São Paulo and Rio are cheaper, faster and far more frequent.

São Paulo-Brasília There are two trains per week in either direction at 8.50 pm on Fridays and 10.05 am on Sundays. The journey takes 22½ hours and the fares are US$4.30 (ordinary seat), US$7.13 (reclining seat), US$8.60 (*leito superior* – upper bunk), US$9.25 (*leito inferior* – lower bunk) and US$17.85 (cabin).

Corumbá-Campo Grande-São Paulo There are two trains daily in either direction but only the 9 am train from São Paulo does not involve a change at Bauru. It arrives in Campo Grande at 8.17 am the next day and at Corumbá at 7.17 pm. The second train leaves São Paulo at 10.25 pm, arriving at Campo Grande at 11 pm the next day and at Corumbá at 6.40 am on the second morning.

In the opposite direction, the first train leaves Corumbá at 8 am, getting to Campo Grande at 7 pm that night and São Paulo at 10 pm the next night. The second train leaves at 9 pm, gets to Campo Grande at 6.40 am the following day and São Paulo at 6 am the day after that.

Campo Grande-Punta Porã Some people use this link to get into Paraguay. There are daily trains in either direction, at 9 am (arrives 4.12 pm) and 4.45 pm (arrives 10.34 pm) from Campo Grande and 6.38 am (arrives 12.28 pm) and 8.46 am (arrives 3.59 pm) from Punta Porã.

Fortaleza-Teresina There is a train once a week between these two state capitals on Fridays at 7 pm. The fares are US$5.95 (1st class) and US$2.30 (2nd class).

Riverboats

Most of the riverboats of interest to travellers are, naturally, on the Amazon river, though refer to the 'Corumbá' section for details of riverboats from there through the Pantanal to ports close to Cuiabá.

Manaus-Santarém-Belém The largest boats along the Amazon are operated by *ENASA* (offices: Av Pres Vargas 41, Belém (tel 223 3572); and Rua Marechal Deodoro, Manaus). They have a number of boats, some of which have cabins and others which don't. First class tends to be somewhat outside the pockets of budget travellers so if you want to keep costs to a minimum go 2nd class and take a hammock with you (or buy one in Belém or elsewhere). Third class isn't recommended as it gets very crowded and meal arrangements are primitive (you queue at the cookhouse door with your own plate, cup, knife and fork). Also, it's sometimes impossible to buy a 3rd class ticket (unless you're Brazilian) without a waiver from the police or a letter from your consulate (British consulates won't co-operate here). If you're going 1st or 2nd class then try to book your tickets a week in advance.

The boats generally leave Belém, Santarém and Manaus once a week in either direction but the days change so you need to make enquiries. Between

Belém and Manaus the journey takes five to six days and costs US$50 (1st class) and US$25 (2nd class). These fares are more than likely to change as transport companies adjust their fares to keep pace with Brazil's raging inflation.

Most travellers, however, don't take the *ENASA* boats. Instead they go down to the smaller docks where the wooden boats leave from. These boats are generally in fairly good condition but they do take on as many people as they can get so hammock space is limited and by the time you reach your destination you'll know everybody and their personal habits intimately.

Usually there are two decks, the upper being the better of the two and somewhat more expensive. There are cabins on some boats but they get stuffy especially at night so a hammock is preferable. No need to worry about mosquitos at night – there are very few of these on the large rivers and generally there's too much wind. The food can be monotonous (beans and rice with the occasional piece of fried fish – often piranha). Water is taken from the river.

In Manaus, Santarém or Belém there are generally boats leaving everyday going up or down stream (depending on where you are) so there's no worries about finding one. Between Manaus and Santarém or Santarém and Belém the journey takes about 2½ to three days and costs US$20 (upper deck) and US$17 (lower deck). Again, these prices will change so that the fares keep up with inflation.

Manaus-Tabatinga/Benjamin Constant
ENASA don't cover this route so you have to find a wooden passenger or cargo-boat to take you there. They dock in Manaus at the same place as the other small boats. Unlike going down to Santarém and Belém, you may have to wait a few days to find a boat but there are at least one or two per week. The journey can take as little as four days but you should reckon on six to be safe. If there are problems (breakdowns,

running out of fuel, navigation balls-ups) then it can take considerably longer. Fares are negotiable but shouldn't be more than US$40 per person including food. Most of the boats call at Coari and Tefé en route.

For details about riverboats further up-river from Tabatinga/Benjamin Constant/ Ramón Castilla/Leticia, see under 'Colombian Amazonia' in the Colombia chapter and 'Iquitos' in the Peru chapter.

Belém

Exactly 150 km from the Atlantic Ocean, Belém is the largest port on the Amazon with a population approaching 800,000. It exports the products of the Amazon basin – rubber, Brazil nuts, jute, hard woods and rice – and like Manaus, it has a steamy, run-down sort of elegance to it. At least this is true of the centre, where the streets are shaded by old mango trees, and the area around the Portuguese-built fort and the old cathedral. The suburbs are relatively modern and even around the main Praça da Republica, plush high-rise hotels have been built.

Belém's early history was one of chop and change between the Portuguese, Dutch and French as these nations wrestled for control of the Amazon delta and the Guianas. It's well worth spending two or three days here before you take a riverboat up the Amazon or a bus going south. Indeed, some travellers say that they prefer Belém to Manaus.

Information
The main tourist information office is at *DETUR*, Av Nazaré 231 (tel 223 5802) but it's hardly worth visiting. They don't appear to know very much and they only have a poor quality map of the city with a few points of interest marked on it for US$0.50. The map sold at most news-stands is worse.

Airline offices
VASP
Av Pres Vargas 620 (tel 222 9611/7830).
VARIG/Cruzeiro
Av Pres Vargas 768 (tel 224 3344).
Surinam Airways
Rua Senador Manoel Barata 704 (14th Floor, Room 1401) (tel 222 5304).
TABA
Rua Ó de Almeida 498 (tel 226 4111).

Things to See

It's worth spending a morning or afternoon wandering around down by the waterfront in the old part of town where you'll find the famous **Ver-o-Peso** open-air market and a small, garbage-strewn dock for small fishing boats. The market used to sell all manner of things but has contracted in recent years and is now really only of interest if you're looking for a hammock (for the boat journey up the Amazon). Nearby is the **Forte do Castelo**, the old Portuguese fort, which costs US\$0.10 entry and has good views over Guajara Bay and the dock where the small fishing boats tie-up.

In the shady square just outside the entrance to the fort are the **Santo Alexandre church**, built by the Jesuits and being converted into a museum of religious art; and the **Catedral da Sé**, the cathedral church of Belém. Walking further away from Ver-o-Peso, you come to Largo do Carmo and **Our Lady of Carmo church**.

Close by are the **Palacete Pihno**, decorated with beautiful tiles popular in colonial days; the palaces of **Lauro Sodré** and **Antonio Lemos**, now used by the state and municipal governments; and the **São João Batista church**, formerly the cathedral. The **Pôrto do Sal**, round the headland from the fort, may also be worth a visit if there are small boats tied up there.

Most travellers also visit the **Emilio Goeldi Museum**, Av Alcindo Cacela between Av Magalhaes Barata and Av Gentil Bittencurt (entrance on Cacela), which is a zoo taking up a whole block and containing some enormous Amazonian rain-forest trees. It also houses the Amazonian National Research Institute. Personally, I was disgusted with the cruel conditions in which many of the animals and birds are kept. Large cats, such as pumas, are condemned to solitary confinement in concrete cages, two metres square, with nothing to do but pace neurotically to and fro all their lives. Huge birds with metre-wide wing spans fare no better. This sort of degrading nonsense went out with the 19th century in most places. The concentration camp is open Tuesdays to Fridays and on Sundays from 8 am to noon and 2 to 6 pm. On Saturdays it's open from 8 am to 1 pm. Entry costs US\$0.10.

Near the Goeldi Museum the **Basilica of Nossa Senhora de Nazaré** is worth a visit for its beautiful marble and stained-glass work.

Further down Av Almirante Barroso from the bus terminal at the junction of Barroso and Rua do Chaco is a **Turtle Farm** which is open to visitor's daily from 8 am to 12 noon and 2 to 6 pm.

At the northern end of the Amazon delta is **Macapá**, the capital of the Territory of Macapá, which is worth visiting if you have the time – as much for the ride through the delta as for the huge, restored Portuguese fort which is open to the public. Ferries to Macapá from Belém are sporadic so you need to make enquiries at *POSTO SÃO BENEDITO*. It's a 48-hour trip and should cost about US\$10. You can also get there by taking a ferry to Pôrto Santana and then a bus (frequent) or taxi from there to Macapá (30 km).

Between Belém and Macapá is the island of Marajó which sports large herds of wild buffalo. If you want to visit ask *ENASA* when the ferry is going. There's usually one every five to seven days and the trip takes about four hours. Tours can be arranged in Belém either with the *Grão Pará Hotel* or with travel agents.

Places to Stay

The real cheapies are all on Blvd Castillo Franca facing the docks. They are: the

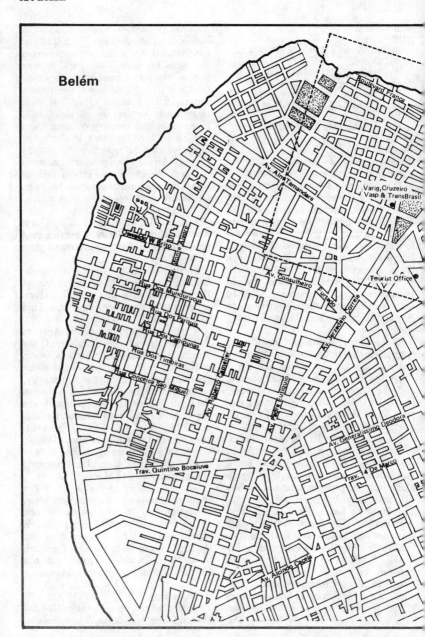

Belém

See Enlargement

Av. Harechal Hermes

Rais Vasconcelos

Trav. Benjamin Constant

Visconde De Souza Franco

Av. Senador Lemos

Rua Jeronimo Pimentel

Dom Romualdo De Seixas

Av. Alcindo Cacela

Goeldi Museum / 200

Trav. 3 De Janeiro

Trav. 3 De Maio

Trav. 14 De Abril

Francisco Caldera Castelo Branco

Avenida Jose Bonitacio

Bus Terminal

Av. Almirante

Turtle Farm

Hotel Grajau, Blvd Franca 566, which is basic and very friendly but has no hot water and costs US$3.35/$5.83 a single/double without own bathroom but including breakfast; the *Hotel Canto do Rio*, Blvd Franca 545, which is similar to the Grajau and costs US$2.50/$5 a single/double without own bathroom but including breakfast; and the *Hotel São Jorge*, Blvd Franca 506, again similar to the above two which costs US$1.65/$3.35 a single/double excluding breakfast. They also have a dormitory for US$0.65 per person.

Just off this same street but with its sign actually on the street is the slightly better *Hotel Transamazonica*. This costs US$2/$3 a single/double without own bathroom and without breakfast.

Also in this category is the *Hotel Fortaleza*, Rua Frutuoso Guimarães 276, an old place with a second floor which has been partially cut in half to create two floors with hardboard partitions. It's a bit grubby and dingy and few of the rooms have windows but it is cheap at US$1.50 a double without breakfast or US$2.15 a double with coffee (only) in the morning.

Similar is the *Hotel Manaus*, 13 de Maio 150. It's a friendly place and costs US$2/$3 a single/double without own bath and US$2.15/$4.15 a single/double with own bathroom without breakfast. If you want breakfast it's another US$1 per person.

Many travellers, however, rate the *Hotel Central*, Av Pres Vargas 290, as the best value in Belém and I agree with them. It's a huge place, centrally located and the staff are very friendly. The rooms are spotless, the sheets crisp and clean and there are hot showers. It costs US$4.15/$5 a single/double without own bath but with fan and handbasin. Rooms with their own bath cost US$6.15/$7 a single/double. There are also more expensive rooms with air-conditioning. All these prices include a very good breakfast. The restaurant on the roof

offers good food but it's rather expensive at US$2 for a *prato do dia*.

Also on Av Pres Vargas, the *Hotel Avinda* with rooms for US$3 has been recommended.

Very similar are the *Hotel Vitoria Regia*, Rua Frutuoso Guimarães 260, which costs US$3/$5/$7.15 a single/double/triple without own bathroom and US$3.75/$5.85/$8 with own bath; the *Hotel S Geraldo*, Travessa Padre Prudencio 56 at the junction with 13 de Miao, which costs US$3.33/$5.85 a single/double without own bath and US$4.15/$6.66 a single/double with own bath; and the *Hotel Lis*, Praça Saldanha Marinho at Rua João Diogó 504. The Lis has doubles with fan for US$3.50 and small air-conditioned doubles with own bathroom and fridge for US$6. There's a good, cheap restaurant upstairs. The owner will change money (cash only). All the prices in this section include breakfast.

Another hotel which has been warmly recommended is the *Sete Sete*, Rua 1 de Março 77 behind the Praça da Republica, which costs US$5 a double including breakfast.

Places to Eat

Other than a *prato do dia* available at many restaurants or a similar meal at the *Hotel Central* (plus the choice of an a-la-carte meal for around US$2.50) try the *Hakata*, 13 de Mayo 177 at the junction with Av Pres Vargas 177. This is very popular with office workers at lunchtime and with others in the evening. They have a range of 'international food' – stews, steaks, fish, salads, rice and barbecued meat – for around US$1.50 per dish with trimmings. They also have hamburgers and pizzas. It's run by Japanese people but they cater to local tastes. They have a more exotic branch (same name) partially surrounded by Japanese gardens at Av Dr Morães 294.

For a splurge go to the *Circulo Militar* restaurant inside the old fort. The food and the atmosphere are very good and there are excellent views across the river. Expect to pay around US$3 per head.

The most colourful of the bars in Belém are to be found in the street behind the Blvd Castillo Franca close to the junction with Av Pres Vargas. These are real waterfront dives full of whores, sea dogs, smugglers, adventurers and criminals. It's bare boards, bare tables, bare bottoms and heaps of atmosphere. Don't miss it.

Local young people hang out at the *Café do Parque* on the Praça da Republica so this is a good place to meet people. Another traveller recommended the *Casa de Sucos* in the Praça da Republica near the Teatro da Paz for its 'excellent sucos and 1950s American teeny-bopper decor that could be right out of Buddy Holly's Lubbock, Texas.'

Getting There
There are regular buses to the airport every 15 minutes or so from the Prefeitura which are marked, *Perpétuo Socorro*. The fare is US$0.10. A taxi will cost about US$3.60 though it's sometimes possible to bargain down to US$3. They will refuse to use the meters.

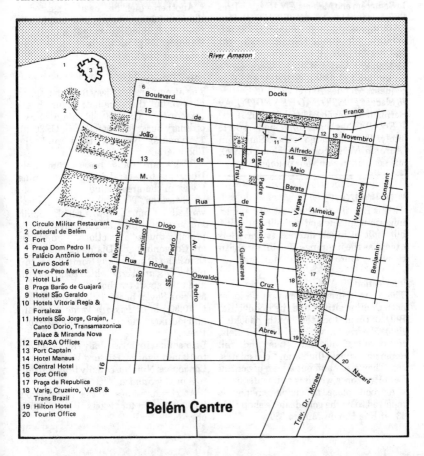

1 Circulo Militar Restaurant
2 Catedral de Belém
3 Fort
4 Praça Dom Pedro II
5 Palácio Antônio Lemos e Lavro Sodré
6 Ver-o-Peso Market
7 Hotel Lis
8 Praça Barão de Guajará
9 Hotel São Geraldo
10 Hotels Vitoria Regia & Fortaleza
11 Hotels São Jorge, Grajan, Canto Dorio, Transamazonica Palace & Miranda Nova
12 ENASA Offices
13 Port Captain
14 Hotel Manaus
15 Central Hotel
16 Post Office
17 Praça de Republica
18 Varig, Cruzeiro, VASP & Trans Brazil
19 Hilton Hotel
20 Tourist Office

Belém Centre

The bus station (Rodoviária) is at the junction of Av Almirante Barroso and Av Gov Malcher. To get there from the centre take any bus marked 'Aero Club' from along Av Pres Vargas, the Praça da Republica or along Rua Bittencurt. The fare is 10 cents. These buses also pass the Goeldi Museum.

There are buses to Fortaleza (US$14), Brasília (US$18), Rio (US$27), Belo Horizonte (US$23), Recife (US$18, 36 hours), and Salvador (US$18, 36 hours).

River Transportation
To Santarém and Manaus *ENASA*, Av Pres Vargas 41 (tel 223 3572); *TENAVE*, Rua São Boaventura 86 (tel 222 4576); *JONASA*, Rua Prof Nelson Ribeiro 161 (tel 224 6811/6012).

To Marajó *ENASA*, Galpão Mosqueiro e Soure (tel 222 3364); *RODOMAR*, Rua Siqueira Mendes 10 (tel 224 3107).

To Macapá *POSTO SÃO BENEDITO*, Av Bernado do Sayão 868 (tel 222 6025).

ENASA has had some bad reports lately. There are cargo boats to Santarém (*Antonio Nery* is one) for about US$20, but keep an eye on your belongings.

BELO HORIZONTE
This is Brazil's third largest city and an important mining and agricultural centre but isn't of much interest to travellers except as the jumping-off point for a visit to nearby Ouro Prêto and Mariana.

Information
There are tourist information desks at both Confins airport and the Rodoviária. Both of them stock the monthly booklet, *Belo Horizonte*, which lists all hotels, restaurants, museums, bus and rail departure times, flights and consulates, etc. They also hand out a map of central Belo Horizonte which is quite adequate.

A good place to change money is reported to be the gold dealer's shop Loja 43, at Rua Rio de Janiero 630.

Places to Stay
One of the cheapest places and one which many travellers recommend is the *Hotel Magalhães*, Rua Espírito Santo 237. It's excellent value at US$2.50 a double. Otherwise try the *Hotel Madrid*, Rua Curitiba directly opposite the front of the Rodoviária. It's a little bit noisy but perfectly adequate for a night and costs US$3.40/$5 a single/double without own bath and US$5/$6.80 a single/double with own bath. The bathrooms and toilets are clean and there's hot water in the showers.

Another which has been suggested is the *Hotel Magnata* which is two blocks from the Rodoviária along Rua Guarani. It costs US$2 a single including an excellent breakfast.

Getting There
The airport is a long way from the centre of town but there are both luxury buses (*executivo* – US$1.50, 40 minutes) and ordinary buses (*convencional* – US$0.40, 1½ hours) between there and the Rodoviária.

There are daily buses from Belo Horizonte to several famous old mining towns in the area including Ouro Prêto and Mariana. The mines are more or less worked out but the towns which remain are very beautiful and among Brazil's premier tourist attractions. Two others are Congonhas and Diamantina.

Ouro Prêto 12 buses daily from 6.45 am to 9 pm by *Pássaro Verde* which cost US$1.15 and take about two hours.

Mariana Seven buses daily from 6.30 am to 10.30 pm by *Pássaro Verde*. The fare and journey time are the same as to Ouro Preto.

Diamantina Six buses daily from 5.30 am to 12 midnight by *Pássaro Verde*.

Congonhas Nine buses daily from 6.15 am to 8 pm by *Sandra*.

At certain times of the year there's heavy demand for tickets so try to book ahead.

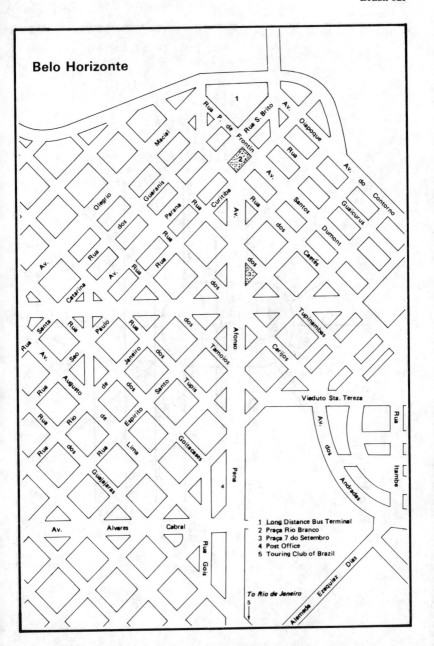

Belo Horizonte

1 Long Distance Bus Terminal
2 Praça Rio Branco
3 Praça 7 do Setembro
4 Post Office
5 Touring Club of Brazil

To Rio de Janeiro

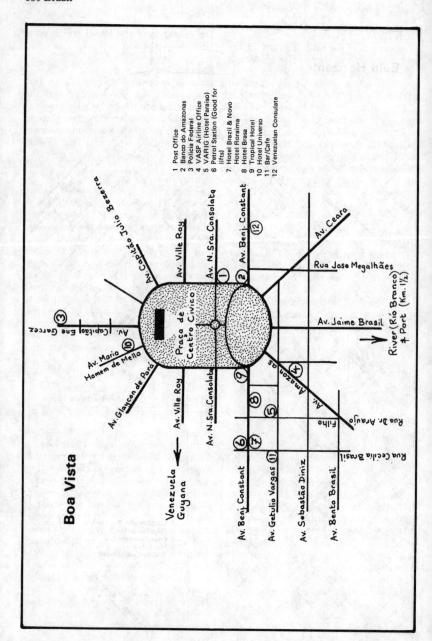

Boa Vista

1 Post Office
2 Banco do Amazonas
3 Policia Federal
4 VASP Airline Office
5 VARIG (Hotel Paraiso)
6 Petrol Station (Good for lifts)
7 Hotel Brazil & Novo
8 Hotel Roraima
9 Hotel Brasa
10 Tropical Hotel
11 Bar/Cafe
12 Venezuelan Consulate

BOA VISTA

The capital of Roraima territory in the extreme north of Brazil, Boa Vista is a modern boom town which over the last few years has grown to an estimated 80,000 people. The city centre itself is fairly pleasant with wide avenues radiating out from the huge Praça de Centro Civico. Much of this area of Brazil is natural grassland and the principal activity is cattle raising. For most travellers, Boa Vista is simply an overnight stop on the way to or from Venezuela.

Information

The Venezuelan Consulate is on Av Benjamin Constant next to Hotel Lua Nova. It's open from 8 am to 1 pm. When applying for your visa you need a valid yellow fever vaccination certificate but onward tickets are not asked for these days. The consul is friendly and helpful.

The best place to change money is at the pharmacy on the Praça do Centro Civico or at the *Drogafarma* near the Hotel Tropical. They will change Venezuelan bolivars as well as US-dollar notes.

Places to Stay

One of the best places is the *Hotel Lua Nova*, Av Benjamin Constant 591. It's a friendly place and is good value at US$2.50 a double without bath and US$4.50 a double with own bath. If it's full then try the *Hotel Brasa* Av Benjamin Constant, which is reasonable value at US$3.50 a double without own bath.

Last on the list is the *Hotel Brasil*, Av Benjamin Constant, which costs the same as the Brasa but isn't anywhere near such good value since it has deteriorated over the last couple of years. It's now dirty and the toilets are broken. The proprietor is a bible basher so if you're an unmarried couple or mixed group expect some initial vagueness about vacancies.

If you don't mind paying slightly more then try the *Nova Hotel Roraima* round

the corner from the Brasil which costs US$3.50 per person.

Places to Eat

Food is expensive everywhere in Boa Vista. Both the *Hotel Brasil* and the *Nova Hotel Roraima* offer good meals at reasonable prices. Another good place to try is the *café/bar* (no name) on the corner of Av Getulio Vargas and Rua Cecilia Brasil.

Getting There

The Rodoviária is on the outskirts of town about a half hour walk down Av Ville Roy. If you don't want to walk, there are public buses available between the centre and the terminal.

If you're looking for a lift to either Venezuela or Guyana one of the best places to check out is the petrol station opposite the Hotel Brasil. Trucks don't come in that frequently so it's best to hang around on the patio of the hotel where it's shady, and every time a truck pulls up, walk across to the garage and ask. The lifts are often free. If you can't get one, there are daily buses.

Brasília

Brasília is a vast architectural wank. It's both an enormous, almost criminally expensive monument to the vanity of architects and military dictators and an altar to the internal combustion engine. Without a car and a full tank of petrol it takes forever to get from one point to another. Certainly there are some magnificent and imaginative buildings and sculptures but as a place where human beings can live and create some sort of community it's a dead loss.

Every weekend, as soon as work is over, those who can afford it pull out of their glorified workers' barracks and head off in droves to Rio and other places where there is life on the streets and laughter in

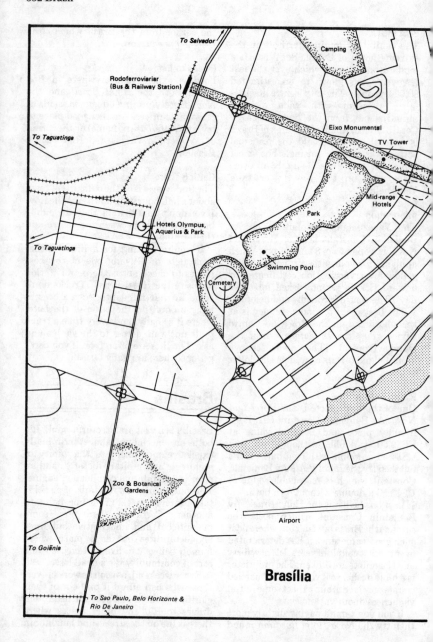

To Salvador

Camping

Rodoferroviariar
(Bus & Railway Station)

Eixo Monumental

TV Tower

To Taguatinga

Mid-range
Hotels

Hotels Olympus,
Aquarius & Park

Park

To Taguatinga

Swimming Pool

Cemetery

Zoo & Botanical
Gardens

Airport

To Goiânia

Brasília

To Sao Paulo, Belo Horizonte &
Rio De Janeiro

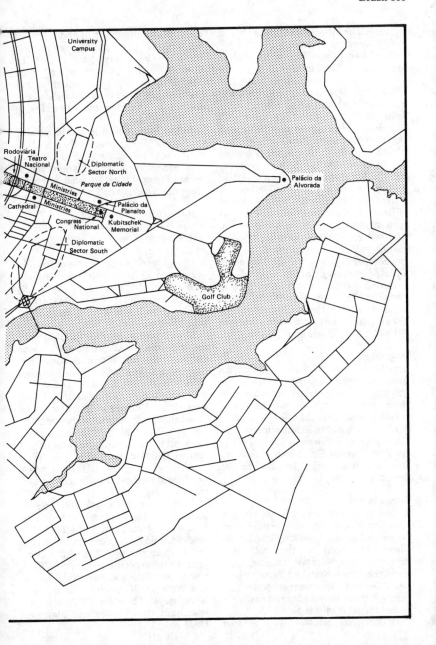

the cafés. Brasília dies at the weekend. It hardly seems surprising.

Considering the rich diversity of plant and animal life in Brazil and the spontaneity of its people, Brasília appears to have been conceived by philistines who have banished all this untidy nonsense from their manicured creation. It's illuminating to discover that those with the cash to escape Prof Lucio Costa's 'vision' have built themselves places on the other side of the lake in typically 'untidy' but gregarious human huddles.

However, it is there, and no-one is going to pull it down and it is the capital of Brazil. If you're just visiting, it's sheer scale does give it a certain magnetism. You will undoubtedly have seen photographs in glossy magazines of the dual sky-scraper at the end of the Parque da Cidade, of the cathedral and of the Congress buildings and palaces. They're certainly photogenic (though often not as large as a photograph would suggest) but once you have seen them there's precious little else to hold you here.

Information

Brasília appears to have closed down its tourist information service. There is now only a private tour agency in the Rodoviária (local buses) but they will telephone hotels to make sure there is a vacancy.

All poste restante letters addressed to the main post office go to Agencia No 7, Av W-3, Quadra 508, which is four km from the Rodoviária. The bus to the airport passes it.

Things to See

If you have the time it's well worth spending a whole morning or afternoon (even a whole day) walking around the main attractions – the cathedral, ministries, the National Theatre, Congress, the palaces and the TV tower which has a 75-metre-high observation platform (entry is free). By walking you really get to feel the scale of this place.

Of course you can also take a bus tour

but it's not quite the same and if you are into taking photographs, you'll have difficulty doing it without having the foreground clogged with others doing exactly the same thing. Book bus tours at the travel agency in the Rodoviária or at the hotels in the downtown area close to the Rodoviária.

In the Park, which is within walking distance of the hotel sector, there is a lake with boats for hire, plenty of places to sit and sunbathe, a model train and a swimming pool with artificial waves for five minutes every half hour.

Places to Stay

There is a *Youth Hostel* at A W Quadra 704, Bloco M, Casa 35 (tel 0612 259 229), but it's often full.

Cheap hotels in the centre of Brasília (eg around the Rodoviária) are not easy to find though there certainly are hotels there. If you can afford a more expensive one then you'll save a lot of time getting on and off buses.

Most travellers head for the SIA (Setor de Indústria e Abastecimento) about halfway between the Rodoviária and Taguatinga. The yellow Pioneira buses (Nos 301, 306, 310, 311, 335, 336 and 337) all go that way but you need to keep your eyes skinned otherwise you'll miss the small cluster of hotels since they're about 200 to 300 metres from the main road. Look out for a car sales agency for Honda (called 'OK Motovéis') with 'OK . . . OK . . . OK' all along the wall in red, white and blue alongside the main road. Get off there.

At SIA there are three hotels all next to each other. The cheapest is the *Hotel Olympus* which costs US$4.20/$5.25 a single/double with own bathroom and hot water, clean sheets and breakfast (fruit juice, fruit, bread, margarine and coffee). It's supposedly a one-star establishment and it's actually not bad but it's seen better days. There's a TV lounge and restaurant (for lunches and dinners – US$1.25 to $1.50).

More expensive is the *Hotel Aquarius*, a two-star establishment, which costs US$8.80 a single or double for a 'standard' room and US$10 for a 'luxo' double bed or US$11.35 a double. There are discount rates of US$7 and US$8 respectively at the weekends. The hotel has its own restaurant.

Next to these two hotels is the considerably more expensive *SIA Park Hotel* (three-star).

Closer to the centre of town, the *Mirage Hotel* in the N Hotel Sector has been recommended. It costs US$4 per person.

It's worth asking for a discount at the hotels as they are often desperate for custom. A four-star hotel with discount can be cheaper than a two-star.

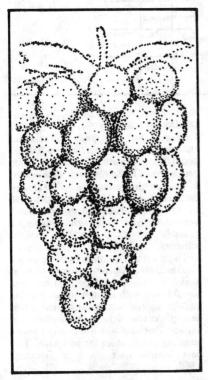

Places to Eat
There are plenty of cheap places to eat on the top level of the Rodoviária (they're mostly snack bars rather than restaurants). There are also several cheap restaurants in the large shopping complex next to the Rodoviária, facing the National Theatre.

There are also cheap eating places in the Banking Sector, but avoid *King Burger* like the plague – it's disgusting.

Getting Around
There are two buses which go between the Rodoviária (local buses) and the airport every 15 minutes or so. They are No 102, marked 'Aeroporto', which goes across the lake bridge and through the more exclusive suburbs; and No 118, marked 'Aeroporto/Velhacap', which goes a shorter way. The journey takes about 30 minutes and costs US$0.25.

Between the Rodoferroviária (long-distance buses and trains) and the Rodoviária (local buses) take bus No 131 which goes up and down the main drag every 15 minutes and costs US$0.10.

CAMPO GRANDE
You may have to stay overnight here if you're heading to or from Bolivia via Corumbá or heading to northern Brazil via Cuiabá. It's a typical, bustling, sprawling, industrialised Brazilian city and the capital of Mato Grosso do Sul, but otherwise is of little interest to travellers.

Information
There's no tourist office as such but you can get information and maps from MSTUR, Rua 15 de Novembro 851.

Places to Stay
There are many cheap places around both the railway station and the bus terminal. There isn't a great deal to choose from among most of them as far as quality goes. It's more a question of whether they are full or not.

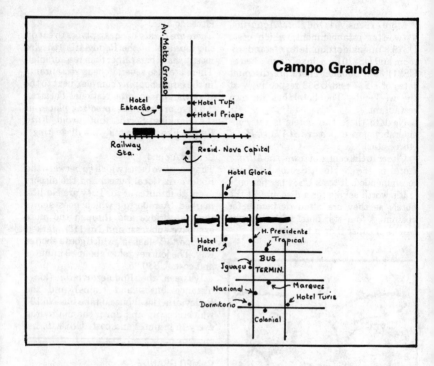

Among the best are *Hotel Turis*, which is quiet and friendly with constant hot water and clean sheets (if they're not, they'll uncomplainingly change them); *Hotel Nacional*; *Hotel Tropical*, a little scruffier than the others; and the *Hotel Presidente*.

If you're looking for something mid-range in this area then try the *Hotel Iguaçu* which is about twice the price but with better facilities. For something really cheap try the *Dormitorio Marques* or the other dormitorio (no name) marked on the map above the Hotel Nacional.

Getting There
The bus terminal is a huge modern building three stories high. Buses leave night and day for virtually everywhere in Brazil. Most of the ticket offices are on the top floor.

CAXIAS DO SUL
Caxias do Sul is a quiet and relaxing though fairly large town (around 300,000 population) in an attractive, mountainous area north of Pôrto Alegre. It's the centre of the wine-producing area of Rio Grande do Sul and is a good jumping off point for visits to the smaller towns of Bento Gonçalves and Garibaldi where it's possible to arrange visits to various wineries.

There isn't very much to do or see in Caxias itself (though the journey there is very beautiful and interesting) and you should take with a pinch of salt the so-called 'tourist attractions', but once every three years it hosts the *Festa da Uva* (Grape Festival) which is a major event drawing people from far and wide. The last festival took place in February 1986.

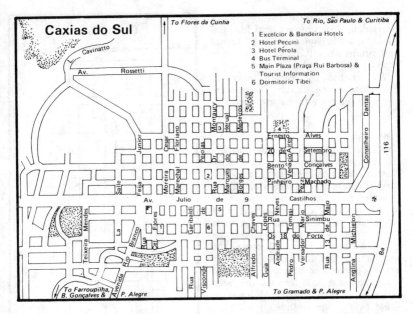

Caxias do Sul

Key to map:
1 Excelcior & Bandeira Hotels
2 Hotel Peccini
3 Hotel Pérola
4 Bus Terminal
5 Main Plaza (Praça Rui Barbosa) & Tourist Information
6 Dormitorio Tibei

Information

There is a tourist information kiosk in the main square (Praça Rui Barbosa) which is friendly and has a range of leaflets including good maps (in Portuguese) about Caxias and nearby towns and wineries.

Places to Stay

The cheapest place in town is the *Dormitorio Tibeo*, Rua Sinimbu 1900 (just off the Praça Rui Barbosa). It's very basic but acceptable for a night. Very good value, however, is the *Hotel Pérola*, Rua Marques do Herval 237 (tel 221 1861), which is spotless, very friendly, has polished wooden floors and hot showers. Rooms without their own toilets and showers cost US$2.10/$3.50 a single/double. Rooms with their own bath cost US$2.65/$4.40 a single/double. It's highly recommended and the prices include breakfast.

If that's full then try the *Excelsior Hotel*, Rua Sinimbu 2421. Rooms here cost US$2.15/$3.85 a single/double without own bath and US$2.80/$5 a single/double with own bath. They also have triple rooms.

Moving up-market somewhat there is the *Hotel Peccini*, Rua Pinheiro Machado, which costs US$3.15/$6.30 a single/double without own bath and US$8 a double with own bath including coffee in the morning; and the *Bandeira Hotel*, Rua Sinimbu 2435, almost next door to the Excelsior, which costs US$3.50/$5.25 a single/double including own bath and breakfast.

Getting There

Expreso Caxiense has many buses daily in either direction, both direct and semi-direct. From Caxias to Pôrto Alegre there are seven direct buses daily from 7 am to 6.30 pm. The fare is about US$2 and the journey takes about two hours.

Likewise there are many daily buses to Bento Gonçalves and Garibaldi from Caxias.

From Caxias *Pluma* has two direct buses daily (one conventional bus and one *leito*) to São Paulo (2 pm and 6.15 pm) and Blumenau (10.20 pm). They also have buses to Curitiba.

You cannot get direct buses to Florianópolis from Caxias. To get there you must go via either Pôrto Alegre or Curitiba.

CORUMBÁ
On the banks of the Rio Paraguai opposite the Bolivian border town of Puerto Suárez, Corumbá is an important commercial centre and a place which many travellers pass through on their way to or from Bolivia. It's also the starting point for a trip into the Pantanal, a vast, swampy area which stretches all the way from here to Cuiabá and is one of the world's largest wildlife reserves. If you're heading north from here it's well worth trying to get a boat through this area rather than taking trains or buses to Cuiabá via Campo Grande.

Information
There is no tourist office in Corumbá.

It's possible to change money at the taxi rank near the waterfront.

The Bolivian Consulate is at Rua Antonio Joao 131, on the opposite side of the bus terminal from the museum. It's open Monday to Friday from 8 am to noon and 3 to 6 pm, and on Saturdays from 8 am to noon. You must get your Brazilian exit stamp before applying.

There's also a Paraguayan consulate in Corumbá.

Things to See
The **Museu Regional do Pantanal**, Rua Delamaré 939, is well worth a visit if you're heading up to that part of Brazil. It's open 8 to 11 am and 2 to 6 pm Mondays to Fridays, and 8 am to noon on Saturdays, closed Sundays. If the barrier is across the bottom of the stairs, ask for it to be removed so you can see the more extensive part upstairs.

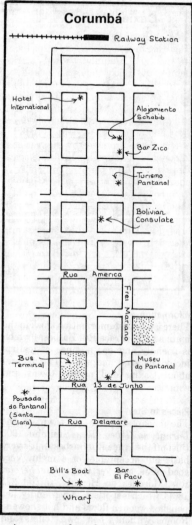

An arts and crafts centre has been opened in the old jail a little way from the centre of town on Rua Dom Aquino Correo.

Visiting the Pantanal
This area is chock-a-block with a diverse

range of wildlife and because the vegetation isn't as dense as that in the Amazon basin it's much easier to see. There are over 600 species of birds living in this area, mainly waders, storks, herons and ducks but also quail and parrots. There's also ocelot deer, pumas, boars, anteaters, tapir and rhea as well as a variety of giant water guinea pig. You will also see hundreds of alligators lining rivers and water holes.

The area is protected by the National Parks authority, though only the Biological Reserve of Cará-Cará is officially a national park. Hunting is strictly prohibited though fishing is allowed. The best time to see the area is in the dry season from September to January when the birds especially are at their noisiest and busiest. In the wet season it floods and the animals and birds are forced to retreat into the interior so there's very little to be seen within 100km of Corumbá.

In the dry season contact Bill Seffusatti, Rua Tiradente 962 (tel 231 4834), or at the El Pacu bar on the Corumbá waterfront. Bill has two boats and can provide fishing bait and tackle. He offers some of the best and cheapest trips into the Pantanal. Many travellers have recommended him and indeed he's written to us himself to point out a couple of previous errors we had in the book and to say that he only does these trips in the dry season. Bill speaks English, French, Italian and Spanish as well as Portuguese.

Another outfit which can organise trips into the Pantanal is Empresa de Turismo Pantanal, Rua Frei Mariano (tel 231 4788), which offers a jeep trip, but to make this economical you must have a group of eight to 10 people.

You can also make enquiries with Herman, the owner of the El Pacu bar. He can arrange boat trips or day-trips by jeep.

It's no longer possible to take boats south from Corumbá as a means of getting into Paraguay, as they've been stopped due to smuggling.

Places to Stay

Probably the most popular place is the Schabib Hotel, Rua Frei Mariano 1153, run by a very friendly and helpful multilingual owner. It's basic but clean and costs US$5 a double. Meals here tend to be a little on the expensive side.

Another place which you can try is the Internacional opposite the railway station. It's very basic but clean and friendly and costs US$2.50 a double. The mosquitos here are voracious. Also near the railway station, the Hotel Esplanada has been recommended.

Outside Corumbá the Pousada Santa Clara ranch is a popular place to stay. Horse riding and boats can be hired but just how much you'll see of the wildlife is another matter.

Places to Eat

The Hotel Schabib offers meals for around US$2. Meals at the El Pacu bar cost about US$3. This is also the place to head for if you want some local colour. It's run by a German man called Herman and his Brazilian wife.

Another bar which is worth trying is the Bar Zico near the top of Rua Frei Mariano fairly close to the Hotel Schabib. The latter serves strong, locally brewed beer (caracu).

Getting There

Trains to Campo Grande leave at 7 am and 9 pm daily, take 11 hours and cost US$35.

Crossing the Bolivian Border If you don't need a visa for Bolivia then go straight to the border after you've got your Brazilian exit stamp from the police at the railway station. The police are open Monday to Friday from 6.30 to 11.30 am, 1 to 4 pm and 8.30 to 9 pm. At weekends they're open from 6.30 to 8 am, 10.30 to 11.30 am and 7.30 to 9 pm. There are no charges. There are buses every 45 minutes to the border from Corumbá between 7 am and 5 pm.

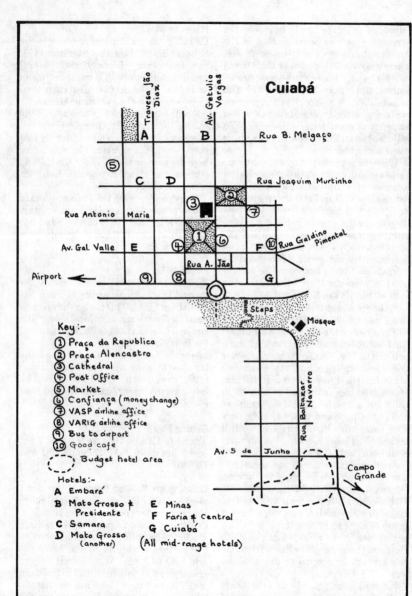

Cuiabá

Key:-
1. Praça da Republica
2. Praça Alencastro
3. Cathedral
4. Post Office
5. Market
6. Confiança (money change)
7. VASP airline office
8. VARIG airline office
9. Bus to airport
10. Good cafe
- - - Budget hotel area

Hotels:-
A Embaré
B Mato Grosso & Presidente
C Samara
D Mato Grosso (another)
E Minas
F Faria & Central
G Cuiabá
(All mid-range hotels)

CUIABÁ

The capital of Mato Grosso state with a population of some 100,000, Cuiabá is a pleasant city with friendly people, plenty of trees and a mixture of old and modern buildings. There isn't a great deal to see as such but it's sometimes possible to get on a free *FAB* flight from here to Pôrto Velho or Manaus – the alternative is to go by bus.

Information

The tourist office, *Turimat*, is at Palacio Alencastro (4th floor). They have good maps of the city. There's also a counter at the airport but there's often no-one there.

If you're heading for Corumbá from Cuiabá it's worth making enquiries to see if the ship still sails from Pôrto Jofre through the Pantanal. It used to sail on Saturdays and take two days.

Transport from Cuiabá is easy to find. The *Hotel Santa Rosa* at the changeover place is beautiful but very expensive. In the opposite direction the boat used to leave Corumbá on Thursdays.

Places to Stay

There are many hotels around the new bus terminal but they're all very expensive. If you are looking for a cheaper place then you'll have to take a bus into the centre of town and check out the ones there. There are plenty of budget hotels around where the bus terminal used to be at the end of Rua Baltazar Navarro.

One of the best is the *Hotel Santa Luzia* which is clean and tidy and has cleaners who sing, a TV and a fridge for guests to use. Other cheapies on the same street and on Av 5 de Juho parallel to it are the *Ideal Dormitorio Cezar*, *Alvorado Motel* and *Dormitorio Ideal*. Avoid the *Hotel Miranda* which is scruffy and dirty; you'll need a gas mask just to visit the toilet.

In the centre of town there are a number of mid-range hotels which are worth checking out if you don't want to walk as far as the old bus terminal. The best are the *Hotel Mato Grosso* (there are two hotels with this name – take your pick, they're both about the same standard); and the *Minas Hotel*.

Places to Eat

You can find good, relatively cheap meals at most of the *lanches* places along Av Gal Valle. These are places which serve set-menu business lunches and dinners. There's also another very good place round the corner from the Hotel Central (itself on Rua Gal Pimental) that is marked on the street plan. If you want to put your own food together there is a wide range available at the market.

Getting There

A new long-distance bus terminal has been constructed on the outskirts of town. It's a huge place with many facilities. There are many local buses from there into the centre of town (US$0.15).

Curitiba

Curitiba is a modern city of 1½ million people, mainly descendants of German, Italian and East European settlers. It has one or two interesting areas which are worth exploring but its main interest as far as travellers is concerned is the railway journey from here to Paranaguá over the escarpment and down to the coast. This is one of the most interesting rail journeys you can make in Brazil. The line passes through many tunnels and over several hair-raising bridges high up above deep gorges. There are many waterfalls and interesting rock formations and the views down to the coast over the lush rainforest are superb. Details of this trip can be found under the Paranaguá section.

Information

There are no less than four information

tourist kiosks at the Rodoferroviária and they are all an absolute waste of time. They don't even have a sketch map of Curitiba and suggest you go to a bookshop and buy the *Guia Turístico do Curitiba e Paraná* which is published yearly and costs US$2.50. And this, other than the map of Curitiba and Paraná state which it contains, is a waste of money. It has hardly any useful information in it. If you do buy any guide then make it the *Guia Sul* which covers the whole of the south and even has information on Uruguay and Argentina. It costs US$3.

The main post office is at Rua 15 de Novembro 700. There's another large post office at Rua Mal Deodoro 298. International telephone calls can be made at *TELEPAR*, Rua Visconde de Nácar 1415. Efficient service but somewhat expensive. A call to Montevideo alone will cost US$10!

Consulates

Bolivia
  Rua Bruno Filgueira 1662 (tel 232 5698). Open Monday to Friday from 1 to 5 pm.
Chile
  Rua Mal Deodoro 235 (1st floor, Room 101) (tel 232 4743). Open Monday to Friday from 8 am to 12 noon.
Paraguay
  Rua Comendador Araujo 143 (12th floor) (tel 222 9226). Open Monday to Friday from 8.30 am to 12 noon.
Peru
  Alameda Dr Muricy 926 (tel 233 4711).
Uruguay
  Rua Mal Deodoro 503 (Room 303) (tel 223 4161). Open Monday to Friday from 8 am to 1 pm.

Bookshops For a reasonable selection of English-language books check out the *Livraria Curitiba*, Rua Vol da Pátria 205 (Praça Santos Andrade), also at Rua 15 de Novembro 870 and Rua Mal Deodoro 275; or the *Livraria Ghignone*, Rua 15 de Novembro 409.

Things to See
Much of Curitiba is now a typical modern city – though it's pleasant enough. Have a walk along the Rua 15 de Novembro, the city's principal shopping street which is now a pedestrian area. It's full of clothing and footwear shops, bookshops, travel agents, bars and restaurants.

Close by, behind the cathedral, is the **Largo da Ordem**, a superbly restored section of old Curitiba with cobbled pedestrian areas, interesting churches and a number of bars and restaurants each with their own distinct theme.

There are three museums which are worth a visit. The **Museu Paranaense** housed in the large mid-European-style old building on Praça Generoso Marques catalogues the history of Paraná state and also has one of the best displays of the development of the typewriter you're likely to come across, ranging from some of the very first models ever produced to the computers of today. It's open Monday to Friday from 12 noon to 6 pm and on weekends from 1 to 6 pm.

Also worth a visit is the **Museu do Arte Sacra** in the Igreja da Ordem (Largo da Ordem), open Tuesday to Friday from 2 to 8 pm and on Sunday from 10 am to 1 pm; and the **Museu de Arte Contemporanea**, Rua Westphalen 16, which is open Monday to Friday from 9 am to 6 pm and on Sunday from 2 to 6 pm.

Places to Stay
There's a good choice of places right opposite the Rodoferroviária on Av Afonso Camargo and this is where most travellers stay. The best value is the *Hotel Wang*, Av Afonso Camargo 549, which is spotlessly clean, run by a very friendly Chinese family and costs US$1.75/$3.15 a single/double without own bath and US$2.65/$4 a single/double with own bath. The communal showers and toilets are the cleanest I've seen in Brazil and they have hot water. The rooms are secure and there's a TV lounge. The best rooms are upstairs although the front ones are a little noisy because of the main road in front of the hotel.

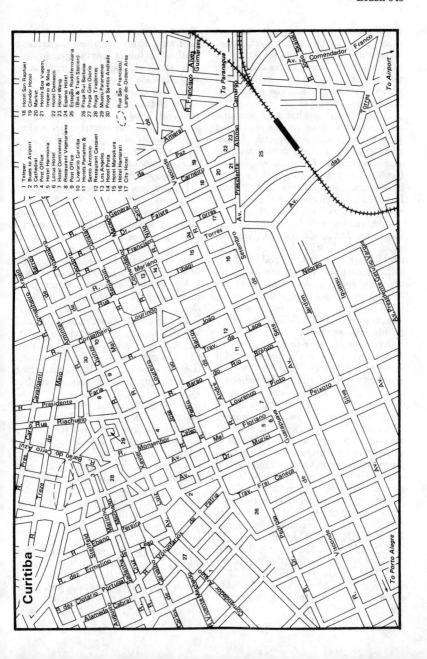

Curitiba

1 Telepar
2 Buses to Airport
3 Cathedral
4 Post Office
5 Hotel Harmonia
6 Lotus Hotel
7 Hotel Continental
8 Restaurant Vegetariano
9 Post Office
10 Livraria Curitiba
11 Hoteis Palmetur & Santo Antonio
12 Restaurant Cascavel
13 Los Angeles
14 Hotel Prata
15 Hotel Matsukura
16 Hotel Hamarati
17 City Hotel
18 Hotel San Raphael
19 Condor Hotel
20 Market
21 Hotel Bela Viagem, Imperio & Maia
22 Hotel Damasco
23 Hotel Wang
24 Espana Hotel
25 Estação Rodoferroviaria (Bus & Train Station)
26 Praça Rui Barbosa
27 Praça Gen Osorio
28 Museu Paranaense
29 Praça Tiradentes
30 Praça Santos Andrade

--- Rua São Francisco/ Largo do Ordem Area

The other place which is excellent value and, unlike the others, quiet because it's off the main street is the *City Hotel*, Rua Francisco Torres 806, which costs US$1.75/$2.65 a single/double without bath and US$3.35/$4.40 a single/double with own bath.

Cheaper than these but more basic and not such good value are the *Hotel Bon Viagem*, Av Afonso Camargo, which costs US$1.20/$1.75 a single/double without own bath; and the *Hotel Maceío*, Rua da Paz 665 near the junction with Camargo (the large sign outside says 'Hotel Damasco'), which costs US$1.20/$2.10 a single/double without own bath.

Others opposite the bus station include the *Hotel Maia*, Av Afonso Camargo, which costs US$2.65/$4.40 a single/double without own bath and US$3.50/$5.25 a single/double with own bath; and the *Hotel Imperio*, Av Afonso Camargo 367, which is a mid-range hotel costing US$4.75/$6.90 a single/double without own bath and US$7.75/$8.60 a single/double with own bath.

If you would prefer to stay in the city centre then the *Hotel Lotus*, Rua Mal Floriano Peixoto 742 (tel 224 8069), is excellent value. It's run by a very friendly Japanese man called Nobuo ('Jorge') Chiba who's been in Brazil for some 15 years. He offers spotless, very pleasant rooms for US$2.30/$3.50 a single/double without own bath and US$3/$4.20 a single/double with own bath. This hotel is much quieter than those around the bus station and far more convenient for the centre. Highly recommended.

None of the other hotels in this area compare with the Lotus though they are cheaper. They include the *Hotel Harmonia*, Rua Mal Floriano Peixoto 722 (scruffy and US$1.75 per person); *Hotel Continental*, Rua Visconde de Guarapuava 2814 (very basic and US$1.40/$1.75 a single/double without own bath – probably a whorehouse); and the *Hotel Palmares* and *Hotel Santo Antonio*.

Places to Eat

Like most Brazilian cities, the centre of Curitiba is full of *lanches* places where you can get a cheap meal at lunch times. In the bus station area, the best value by far is the *Dragão de Ouro*, Av Afonso Camargo 451 (1st floor) right opposite the terminal. The food is excellent, the servings huge, the service quick and the staff friendly. Buy yourself a feast for US$1 to $1.50. They have set meals of the day (a choice of up to 10 different dishes) so it's easy to order.

For a splurge in the evening go up to the Largo da Ordem/Rua São Francisco. There are quite a few pleasant restaurants all with a different theme but you need to have a good look at the menus as some are considerably more expensive than others. They include the *Lancelot/London Pub*, Rua São Francisco 340 (expensive, slow, indifferent but interesting decor and a nice place for a drink); *Bebedouro Bar & Restaurant*, Rua São Francisco 337 (a large place with a mezzanine, live rock bands, dancing, very popular); and the *Schwarzwald*, Rua Claudino dos Santos 63 – the continuation of São Francisco (German food in mock Bavarian setting, clichéd oompah band tapes, quiet place for a drink, attentive service).

If you can't afford a meal at these places then there is the *Pig Burger* round the corner at Rua Barão do Cerro Azul 85-A. Here you can eat American-style hamburgers and other fast food at very reasonable prices. A large hamburger with cheese and bacon will cost 60 to 70 cents. The pizzeria opposite the bus station gives large portions, especially for the meal of the day.

Getting There

The bus terminal and railway station both share the same terminal (Rodoferroviária). It's a huge place with snack bars, bookshops and a restaurant. Bus companies display their schedules so it's easy to find the right one. Short-distance buses still go from the old terminal on Rua João Negrão 350. Buses run from Curitiba to Rio every 15 minutes with *Penha*. The fare is US$6. Trains to Paranaguá run at 12.30pm.

Alfonso Pena Airport is 15 km from the city centre; taxis there cost about US$6. There are also public buses from Rua Westphalen opposite the Hotel Presidente which go about once an hour and are marked 'Aeroporto'. The fare is about US$0.15. These buses pass the junction of Av Presidente A Camargo and Av Das Torres so you can also pick them up from there.

DIAMANTINA

Diamantina, a six-hour bus ride north of Belo Horizonte, is one of Brazil's unspoilt colonial gems. It was founded in 1729 soon after diamonds were discovered in the area and continued to prosper until about 100 years ago when the diamonds petered out. It has some beautiful old mansions with overhanging roofs and it's a very peaceful and interesting area to walk around.

Places to Stay
A good place is the *Nosson Hotel* opposite the bus terminal. It's run by friendly people and has hot showers.

Places to Eat
Go down the Rua Campos Carvalo from the cathedral and try the *churrascaría* on the left-hand side. Another good place is the *Restaurant Confinca* which serves excellent but expensive food, at Rua da Quitanda 39, on the right-hand side of the post office.

Getting There
There are buses six times daily from Belo Horizonte by *Pássaro Verde*, the first at 5.30 am and the last at 12 midnight.

FLORIANÓPOLIS

The state capital of Santa Catarina, Florianópolis is on the island of Santa Catarina which is joined to the mainland by two bridges, one of them a steel suspension bridge (now closed to both traffic and pedestrians) and a modern concrete bridge.

It's a very clean and prosperous-looking city and although there are a lot of gleaming white and pastel coloured high-rise buildings it retains a relaxed Mediterranean atmosphere. The industrial sector is across on the mainland at Estreito and Coqeiros.

Most travellers, of course, come here in search of beaches and there are scores of them all the way around the island. It's just a question of finding one which suits your pocket and taste.

Information

There is a tourist information centre on the Praça 18 de Novembro but it apparently closes during the winter months. The kiosk at the Rodoviária, however, stays open until late in the evening all year round. It is very helpful and has good free maps of Florianópolis and of the Ilha de Santa Catarina. Only Portuguese is spoken.

Things to See

Since there are so many beaches around the island it's a good idea to take one of the bus tours offered by *Ilha Tur*, Rua Felipe Schmidt 27 (Edificio Dias Velho) (tel 22 6333), and get an idea of what is available. The tours cost US$5.25 per person. If you can't afford that there are plenty of far cheaper local buses which go to various parts of the island from the Terminal Urbano in front of the Rodoviária.

For a tour of a different kind you really ought to consider going off for the day in a sailing boat. *Scuna-Sul*, Terminal Marítimo, Av Beira Mar (between the two bridges) (tel 22 1806), offers four different cruises, the cheaper ones lasting five hours (visiting the northern part of the bay up as far as the Ilha de Anhatomirim) and eight hours (visiting the southern part of the bay down as far as the fort on the Ilha de Araçatuba). These tours are remarkably cheap – US$5.25 per person for the northern bay and US$7.90 for the southern bay. Get a group together and you'll have the boat to yourselves. There's also a 48-hour trip that takes you right around the island.

Places to Stay

Two of the cheapest places are the *Dormitorio Estrela* and the *Dormitorio Tropical* which are both on Rua Mafra close to the junction with Rua Bento Gonçalves. The former is clean and well-run; the latter is grubby.

Slightly more expensive is the *Hotel Cruzeiro*, Rua Mafra 68, which is very basic and grubby but is friendly and has hot water. It costs US$1/$2 a single/double without own bathroom.

The *Hotel Colonial* at Rua Mafra 45 is of a similar standard, costs the same and also has hot water. The staff are very indifferent – they've probably seen too many whores and their clients for one more traveller to prod them into life.

The *Hotel Regencia*, Rua Mafra 70, which is very good value at US$1.25/$2.50 a single/double both with own bathroom (!) and hot water. Definitely worth that little bit extra.

Moving somewhat up-market, the best place to stay is the *Hotel Sumaré*, Rua Felipe Schmidt 53, which is excellent value at US$2.65/$5.25/$7.90 a single/double/triple all without own bath but there's hot water in the showers. The rooms and communal areas are spotless, pleasantly decorated and there are clean sheets and towels. The staff are friendly, the rooms secure and there's a TV lounge.

Not quite such good value but cheaper is the *Hotel Majestic*, Rua Trajano 4, which costs US$2.10/$4.10/$6.30 a single/double/triple without breakfast. The

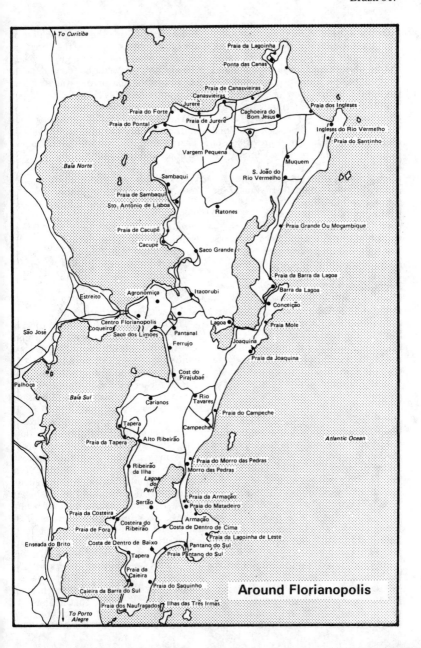

Around Florianopolis

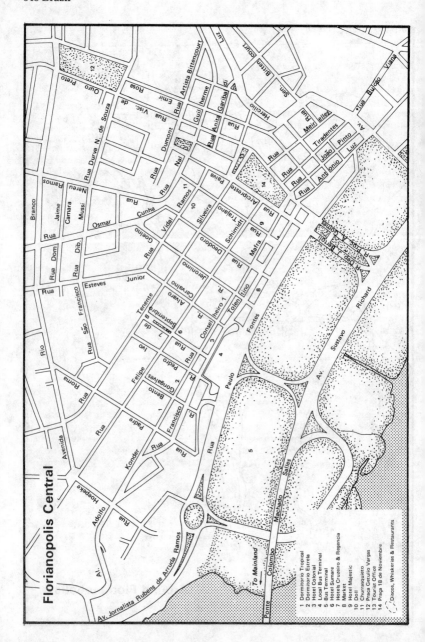

Florianopolis Central

1 Dormitorio Tropical
2 Dormitorio Estrella
3 Hotel Colonial
4 Local Bus Terminal
5 Bus Terminal
6 Hotel Sumare
7 Hotels Cruzeiro & Regencia
8 Market
9 Hotel Majestic
10 Poll
11 Churrasqueito
12 Praça Getulio Vargas
13 Tourist Office
14 Praça 18 de Noviembre
⌐ ⌐ Discos, Whiskerias & Restaurants

staff are indifferent and the rooms are somewhat gloomy.

Places to Eat

As elsewhere, there are plenty of *lanches* places but if you want something different then give the *Churrasquieto*, Rua Vidal Ramos, a try. It's popular with local people especially at lunch times. Kebabs will cost you around US$1.60 but there are cheaper meals available.

Close to the above is *Doll - Produtos Natural*, Rua Vidal Ramos. This is just the ticket for health-food seekers and is very popular - all the usual food plus a wide variety of juices.

For somewhere to relax in the evening and to meet other singles try the *Champagne Bar*, Rua Mafra 123. It's a kind of *wiskeria* which is open from 6 pm to 4 am. It isn't particularly cheap. Cheaper *wiskerias* and discotheques popular with local young people can be found on Rua Anita Garibaldi one street up from the top of the main Praça 18 de Novembro.

Fortaleza

The principal city of the north-east Atlantic coast and capital of Ceará state, Fortaleza is well known for its many good beaches and is very popular with Brazilian holiday makers. It also hosts the famous *Regata de Jangada Dragão do Mar* around the middle of July each year.

This festival had its origins in the annual race between the traditional fishing rafts which can still be seen on this part of the coast, though rarely in Fortaleza itself. It's almost become the 'Americas Cup' of South America's north-east coast since there's a lot of prize money and advertising involved. You'd be lucky to find a sail which didn't resemble an advertising hoarding. Nevertheless, it attracts huge crowds and there's a lot of excitement around the

place at this time. Do go and see it if you're in the area.

Fortaleza is also the jumping off point for a visit to the **Ubajará National Park**, and its caves, which is about halfway to Teresina.

Information

The main tourist office, *Emcetur*, is in the Centro de Turismo which takes up a whole block between Ruas Sampaio and Pompeu and Ruas Jaguaribe and Moreira next to the railway station. The staff are very friendly and helpful and have a range of literature including good free maps of Fortaleza. There is a branch of the tourist office at the airport with the same range of literature.

One good place to change money is the Hotel Oberon Palace at the Fortaleza end of Av Pres Kennedy. It's not always easy to find someone willing to change money in Fortaleza. If you have problems at the weekend then ask at *O Quixadá*, a shop selling clothes and other tourist curios in the Tourist Centre.

Things to See

To get to the best beaches south-east of the city, take bus *P Futuro* from the Praça José de Alencar. The Praia do Futuro, 8 km from Fortaleza is recommended. Heading north-west, try Praia Icarai, 22 km from Fortaleza. At most of these beaches you can see the traditional *jangadas* coming in with their catch just before sundown. If you're just passing through then join the throngs to the east of the town centre along Praias Iracema, Meireles and Mucuripe. They're often very crowded.

There are literally hundreds of undiscovered yet magnificent beaches between Fortaleza and Natal but if you're looking for other gringos then you'll find quite a few at the famous Canoa Quebrada.

The **Centro de Turismo** is certainly worth a visit despite the connotations its name might imply. The complex was

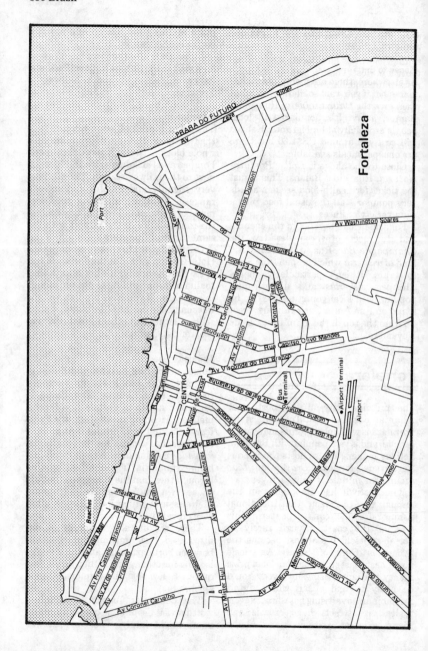

Fortaleza

once the city's prison but has been refurbished and now has many shops selling clothes, lace work and other tourist curios. There's also an outdoor restaurant and bar, under shady trees, which often has live music in the evenings. Prices are reasonable (about US$2 to $2.50) but if you want to spend the absolute minimum then you're quite welcome to sit there with a coconut milk drink which costs just a few cents.

The upstairs of the main building is given over to a museum which is well worth a visit (free). It has interesting exhibits of Cearense folk art, painting and a genuine old *jangada*. There's also a hilarious but imaginative collection of models of people and animals made by welding together old car and truck parts. I've seen this before elsewhere but whoever is responsible for these deserves wider recognition. There's even one of a bull and cow copulating which moves on truck springs!

The old fort here, first constructed by the Dutch, is not open to the public as it's used by the army.

The **Ubajará National Park** is well worth visiting if you have the time. A few travellers have suggested that the caves themselves are not that impressive but that the village is. If you need to stay overnight or longer then go to the *Hotel Gruta* which is cheap. The *Pousada Nebliza* is also good value but considerably more expensive. The caves are about 18 km off the main surfaced road between Fortaleza and Teresina near the Piauí state border.

Prainha is a local fishing village with a beach. Buses leave from Escola Normal at 10.30 am and take one hour.

Places to Stay

Budget accommodation in Fortaleza is at a premium. Most of the real cheapies are down the Rua Senador Pompeu at the waterfront end but the vast majority are revolting hovels you wouldn't kennel a scrofulous dog in. Avoid the *Roraima*

Hotel (No 757), the *Hotel Tio Patinha* (No 725) and the *Hotel Maravilha* (No 557).

One which doesn't fit into this category and is reasonable value is the *Hotel Savoy*, Rua Pompeu 492, which offers rooms without own bath for US$2.15/$3.65 a single/double and rooms with own bathroom for US$3.35/$5.35 a single/double all including breakfast. Similar but not quite as good is the *Hotel Moreira*, Rua Pompeu 562.

Apart from these you have mid-range hotels to look at. Recommended is the *Hotel Real Grandier*, Rua Major Facundo 160, which is fairly small, so it's often full, and costs US$5.65 for a double with own bath and breakfast (they also have singles); and the *Hotel Passeio*, Rua João Moreira 221 opposite the Praça dos Martires, which is friendly, quiet and has rooms with their own shower and toilet for US$8.35 a double with fan and US$9.85 a double with air-conditioning. The rooms are very clean and secure, there's room service, and breakfast (included in the room price) is brought to your room in the morning!

If you're thinking in terms of mid-range hotels then at all costs avoid the *Hotel Excelcior*, junction of Rua G Rocha and Praça do Ferreira. It cracks itself up to be three-star but it's the biggest rip-off in South America.

Places to Eat

A lot of tourists eat at the *Centro de Turismo* but it isn't anything special though the prices are reasonable at around US$2 to $2.50 a meal. For a really good meal at about twice what you would pay for a *lanch*, go to the *Restaurante Belas Artes*, rua Barão de Rio Branco. This is a large, clean place.

Restaurant Lanches Amarantes on Gen Sampio has been recommended for anything from hamburgers to full meals.

If you spend your day on the beaches just to the east of the city centre then there are many restaurants to choose from along the Av Pres Kennedy facing the beaches. Don't hesitate to try them out. They may look expensive but prices are surprisingly reasonable for the amount of food you get. A very generous and tasty meal of fried fish, chips, rice, salad and dressing will cost about US$3. Eat a meal here and it will last you all day. One that has been recommended is *Peixada de Meio*.

Lobsters are also a favourite here but they're not particularly cheap. If you want to try one but don't want to spend a lot of money, check out *Sandras*, Av Perimetral, Praia do Futuro (8 km south of the city).

Getting Around

The Rodoviária is quite a long way from the centre on Av Borges de Melo near the junction with the Av Luciano Carneiro. To get between the centre and the terminal take bus marked 'Praça de Alencar/Rodoviária'. Other buses may go there but ask before you get on. It costs a few cents and takes about 25 minutes via a circuitous route.

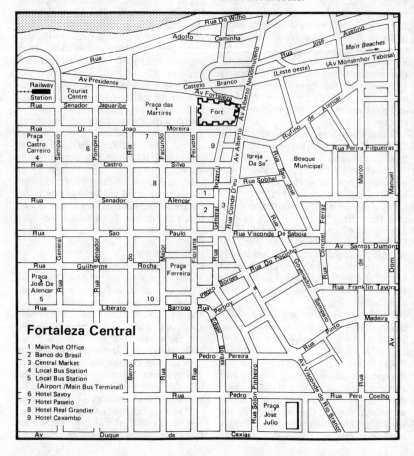

Fortaleza Central

1 Main Post Office
2 Banco do Brasil
3 Central Market
4 Local Bus Station
5 Local Bus Station
  (Airport /Main Bus Terminal)
6 Hotel Savoy
7 Hotel Passeio
8 Hotel Real Grandier
9 Hotel Caxambp

Buses between the centre of town and the airport also start from the Praça de Alencar and are marked 'Aeroporto'. They go every half hour, take about 20 minutes and cost US$0.15. These buses follow much the same route as those to the bus terminal but don't actually go to the latter.

Foz do Iguaçu

From being just a relatively small, dusty town only a decade ago, Foz do Iguaçu has mushroomed into an important centre. The transformation has come about as a result of tourism (the Iguaçu Falls) and more importantly, the Itaipú Dam across the Rio Paraná. Itaipú, jointly constructed by Brazil and Paraguay, is one of the largest hydroelectric schemes in the world. When completed it will have a capacity of 12.6 million kilowatts.

The town stands on the banks of the Paraná river close to the junction of the Brazilian, Argentinian and Paraguayan borders opposite the Paraguayan town and port of Puerto Stroessner.

Information
The tourist office is at Rua Brasil between Rua Jorge Sanways and Rua Quintino Bocaiuva. It's a kiosk on the street but has only maps of Foz to hand out.

There are usually street changers hanging around on the Rua Brasil outside the Rodoviária. Otherwise try one of the more expensive hotels opposite the same bus terminal. *Turismo Dick*, also opposite the terminal; and the 'tourist' agency opposite the cinema on the corner of Avenida Brazil have been recommended.

The Argentinian Consulate is at Rua Eduardo Ramon Bianchi 26 (tel 74 2877) and the Paraguayan Consulate is at Av Republica Argentina 666 (1st floor) (tel 73 4057).

There is free passage between Foz do Iguaçu and Puerto Stroessner (Paraguay).

You can cross the Friendship Bridge as many times as you like without a visa and without going through passport control but if you're going further into either country you should go through passport control in the normal way (these controls are at either end of the bridge).

Puerto Stroessner is a duty-free area whereas Foz is not. The possibility exists of supplementing a tight budget by purchasing duty-free spirits in Paraguay and taking them to Brazil for sale. Whisky and other spirits go for high prices in Brazil (at least they do in most places in Brazil but Foz is probably inundated with the stuff).

Things to See
Most travellers come to Foz to see the **Iguaçu Falls** (spelt Iguazú in Spanish). They are one of the natural wonders of the world and at least the equal in grandeur of Niagara and Victoria Falls. They're magnificent at any time of year but perhaps best seen between August and November because at that time you can get right to the edge of the drop from the Argentine side by means of a catwalk. You can get right up to them at any time of year from the Brazilian side.

Naturally, when the river is in flood between May and July there's a tremendous increase in the volume of water. Most of the catwalks on the Argentine side were destroyed in unusually heavy flooding several years ago.

Above the main falls, the Iguaçu River, studded with many small forested islands, gradually spreads out to a width of about four km and then thunders over a 60-metre high precipice in a wall of water nearly 2½ km wide. Other smaller falls, some of them broken by ledges of rock, make up the rest of the four km.

Hanging over the throat of the falls (known appropriately as the *Garganta do Diablo* – Devil's Throat) is a perpetual cloud of spray in which rainbows are visible whenever the sun shines. Darting

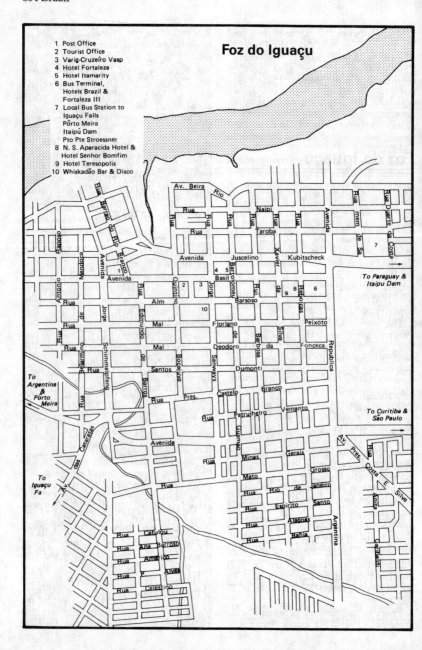

Foz do Iguaçu

1 Post Office
2 Tourist Office
3 Varig-Cruzeíro Vasp
4 Hotel Fortaleza
5 Hotel Itamarity
6 Bus Terminal,
  Hotels Brazil &
  Fortaleza III
7 Local Bus Station to
  Iguaçu Falls
  Pôrto Meira
  Itaipú Dam
  Pto Pte Stroessner
8 N. S. Aparacida Hotel &
  Hotel Senhor Bomfim
9 Hotel Teresopolis
10 Whiskadão Bar & Disco

To Paraguay &
Itaipu Dam

To Curitiba &
São Paulo

To Argentina &
Porto Meira

To Iguaçu Fa

in and out of this from rock ledges actually behind the wall of water where they nest, are huge numbers of swifts which feed on the insects (especially dragonflies and butterflies) around here.

All around the falls there is lush jungle and both the Brazilian and Argentine governments have made their respective sides into National Parks. On no account should you miss out on this tremendous sight.

The falls are naturally a photographer's paradise but make sure you have either a plastic bag or an overcoat if you want to take pictures from the edge of the catwalks on either side as there's a lot of spray. You can hire waterproof coats on the Brazilian side for a few cents. The Brazilian side is perhaps the best for over-all views though it's worth visiting both.

To get to the falls from Foz, take one of the *Transbalan* buses marked 'Cataratas', from the local bus terminal. From Monday to Saturday there are buses at 6, 8 and 10 am, 12 noon and 2, 4, 6, 8 and 10 pm. On Sundays they leave every hour from 6 am until 10 pm (but no bus at 9 pm). The fare is US$0.40 one-way and takes 35 to 40 minutes (they'll take cruzeiros or guaraní). Halfway to the falls you have to pay the National Park entrance fee of US$0.45.

The bus drops you outside the Hotel das Cataratas and you then take a well-constructed path through the rain-forest along the side of the canyon, right up to the edge of the falls. There are several viewing points along the way.

The return buses can not be caught outside the hotel. Instead you have to pick them up about 300 metres further down the road opposite the small café, or down at the terminus above the elevator. Tour buses are also available but they're a waste of money.

Post cards and photographic slides are for sale at the falls and there's even a post office there.

If you have the money there are helicopter flights over the falls which leave from opposite the Hotel das Cataratas. They cost US$26 and last about eight minutes.

To get to the Argentinian side of the falls from Foz you have to take a *Transbalan* bus marked 'Pôrto Meira' from the local bus terminal to Pôrto Meira, (a 10 to 15 minute journey costing a few cents), followed by the ferry across the Iguaçu River to Puerto Iguazú and then another bus from there to the falls (about 22 km). The ferries run frequently and from where they tie up in Puerto Iguazú you'll find the *Güembé Tours* minibus to the falls. It leaves at 7 am, 11 am, 2 and 5.30 pm and returns at 8.15 am, 1, 3 and 6.15 pm. The journey takes about 30 minutes. Have some Argentine australs ready to pay for this and the park entry fee. The walk along the top of falls on this side is much longer and ends in a catwalk which overlooks the Devil's Throat.

You do not need a visa for Argentina if you intend to return the same day. This does not apply to British passport holders who are not admitted without a visa.

If getting to the Argentine side of the falls by public transport seems like a lot of hassle then tours are available from Foz. These generally leave daily at 9 am and return five hours later giving you time to walk to the end of the catwalk. They vary in price between US$7 and US$9.50. Check out *Venson Turismo Ltd*, Av Brasil 93 (tel 73 2039) or *Caribe Turismo*, Rua Jorge Sanways 679 (tel 72 2042).

The other major sight at Foz is the Itaipú Dam, construction of which is still going on. A number of tourist development projects are on the drawing board for the lake but no work has been started as yet. The public relations department at the dam offers free films and visits to the dam in their own coaches. These happen daily at 8.30 am, 10 am, 2.30 and 4 pm. First you see a 15 minute film about the history of the dam in either Portuguese or English (take your pick) and then you go on a half-hour tour of the site. The coaches stop twice so you can take

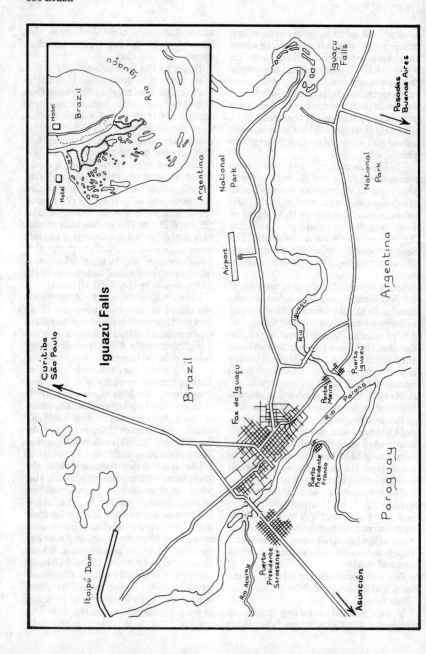

Iguazú Falls

photographs (much better in the morning). The scale of the undertaking is massive and well worth a visit.

To get to the public relations office, take an *Itaipú* bus marked 'Canteira da Obra' from the local bus station in Foz and get off at the control point (you can't miss it – it looks like a highway tollgate). The bus takes about 10 minutes and costs a few cents. They're frequent throughout the day.

Places to Stay

Don't arrive in Foz at the weekend as all the cheap hotels will be full. The cheapest place is the *Dormitorio Apolo*, Rua Barroso between Eng Rebouças and Xavier da Silva. It costs about US$1 but is often full. Somewhat better is the *Hotel Senhor Bomfin*, off the Rua Barroso between Eng Rebouças and Xavier da Silva. It's pretty basic but good value at US$1.75 per person in a room without its own bath, but because it's only a small place it's often full. Similar, but overpriced, is the *Hotel Teresopolis*, Rua Barroso 268, which costs US$2.10/$3.50 a single/double. Also in this category is the *Hotel N S Aparecida* next door to the Bomfin.

Many travellers stay at the *Hotel Brasil* right next to the Rodoviária. The rooms here are tiny and somewhat stuffy and only one clean sheet is provided. The communal showers and toilets can be very smelly and in urgent need of liberal quantities of 'Ajax' and 'Harpic'. It costs US$2.65 per person. Other than its location I honestly can't see why it's so popular.

Better value is the *Hotel Itamaraty*, Rua Xavier da Silva between Brasil and Kubitschek. This offers clean rooms with polished wooden floors and communal showers with hot water for US$2.10/$3.50 a single/double. They also have rooms with their own showers and toilets for US$4.20 a double. The staff are friendly and the rooms are secure (even though they might not look it). Similar is the

Hotel Fortaleza, Rua Rui Barbosa 457. This is a quiet, old building which offers rooms without their own shower for US$3.50/$5.25 a single/double.

If you want to splurge and stay at the *Hotel das Cataratas* then the charges are US$41/$46 a single/double for a 'standard' room and US$58.50/$65 a single/double for a 'superior' room.

Camping is possible at the entrance to the National Park.

Places to Eat

If you're on a budget then there's not a lot of choice and you'll be more or less limited to the restaurants around the Rodoviária. No matter – they're good value and offer very filling set meals. Very popular are the *Restaurant Italia* and the *Comercial*. The restaurant on Barroso at the junction of Rebouças on the Rodoviária side of the road offers excellent fish meals.

Unless you want to splurge, avoid the restaurants along Kubitschek such as the *Bier Haus* and the *Bambu*. They have very little under US$2.25 and most things are priced between US$3.50 and $7. Their beers are expensive too.

Getting There

There are two bus stations in Foz. Long-distance buses leave from the Rodoviária, Av Brasil. Construction work is going on to extend this terminal so it will soon be much larger. Local buses (to the Iguaçu Falls, Pôrto Meira (for the ferry across to Argentina), Puerto Stroessner, the airport and the Itaipú Dam) leave from the other terminal on Av Kubitschek opposite the Hotel Impala.

Between the airport and the Rodoviária there are local *Transbalan* buses once every hour in either direction which cost about US$0.20. 'Executive' buses are also available for just less than US$1. Taxis will cost US$4.50 to $5.50. Flights to Brasília cost US$103 via São Paulo – saving a two day bus ride.

GUAJARÁ MIRIM

This is the Brazilian border town on the Mamoré River facing the Bolivian border town of Guayaramerín. In stark contrast to its Bolivian counterpart, it boasts wide metalled streets, shops full of consumer goods, quite a few very reasonable hotels and a huge civic centre surrounded by acres of manicured lawns.

Information

Passage between the Brazilian and Bolivian towns is unrestricted – you can go cross the river as much as you like without going through passport control but if you intend going further into either country, then you must go through the appropriate controls *and you must do it in the right sequence* otherwise you'll waste a lot of time getting sent back.

To leave Brazil and go to Bolivia, first go to the Bolivian consulate, Av 15 de Novembro, and get a visa. *You must do this regardless of whether you normally need one*. The consul is a very friendly man. The visas are free and no photos are required. The consulate is open Monday to Friday from 8 am to 12 noon. Next go to the Brazilian Federal Police HQ, Av Dr Antonio da Costa 842, and get your exit stamp. After this go down to the river and take either a launch (US$0.40) or a speedboat (US$0.65) across the river to Guayaramerín (they're frequent throughout the night and day). When you get there, go to Bolivian immigration – it's right in front of where you land. Formalities take a few minutes and there are no charges or hassles.

Things to See

Guajará Mirim was the other terminal of the Mamoré-Madeira railway and like Pôrto Velho, it has a number of old steam engines, rolling stock and sections of track which will be of interest to railway buffs. Next to these is a natural history museum which is housed in the old railway station.

Places to Stay

There's not a lot of choice of places to stay and if you arrive late (as you will if you take an afternoon bus from Pôrto Velho) then most hotels will be full.

One of the cheapest is the *Hotel Mamoré*, Av Benjamin Constant near the Cathedral. It costs US$5/$6.65 a single/double for a room without its own bath or fan but with clean sheets, no mosquitoes and including breakfast in the morning. If it's full they may let you sleep on a mattress on the floor in the patio for about half the cost of the rooms (but, if you're a couple, they'll offer you the kitchen and demand the same price!). The owner is friendly enough however.

Somewhat more expensive is the *Fenix Palace Hotel*, Av 15 de Novembro 459, which costs US$5/$8.35 a single/double for a room without its own bath but with a fan, and US$8.35/$13.35 a single/double with own bath. Across the road is the *Hotel Mini-Estrella Palace* which has similar prices.

If you're really short of money you could probably sleep out on the lawns of the civic centre – they're vast! There's also a very basic *pensão* one block down from the Federal Police HQ on Av Dr Antonio da Costa which would be worth a try but don't expect any comforts or running water.

Getting There

There are boats to Trinidad and Puerto Villaroel, the port which serves Cochabamba and Santa Cruz. It takes between 10 and 20 days depending on whether you're going up or downstream. It costs about US$10 to Trinidad and US$15 to Santa Cruz.

Manaus

Manaus is a city of legends. It's set in the middle of the Amazon jungle 1600 km from the sea and until recently was only

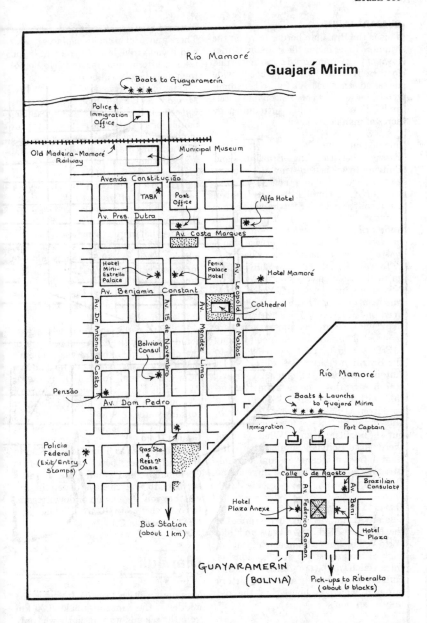

Guajará Mirim

Río Mamoré

Boats to Guayaramerín

Police & Immigration Office

Old Madeira-Mamoré Railway

Municipal Museum

Avenida Constituição

TABA

Post Office

Alfa Hotel

Av. Pres. Dutra

Av. Costa Marques

Hotel Mini-Estrella Palace

Fenix Palace Hotel

Hotel Mamoré

Av. Benjamin Constant

Cathedral

Av. Leopoldo de Mattos

Av. Dr. Antonio de Costa

Av. 15 de Novembro

Av. Mendez Lima

Bolivian Consul

Pensão

Av. Dom Pedro

Policia Federal (Exit/Entry Stamps)

Gas Sta. & Rest.nt Oasis

Bus Station (about 1 km)

Río Mamoré

Boats & Launchs to Guajará Mirim

Immigration

Port Captain

Calle 6 de Agosto

Av. Federico Roman

Av. Beni

Brazilian Consulate

Hotel Plaza Anexe

Hotel Plaza

GUAYARAMERÍN (BOLIVIA)

Pick-ups to Riberalto (about 6 blocks)

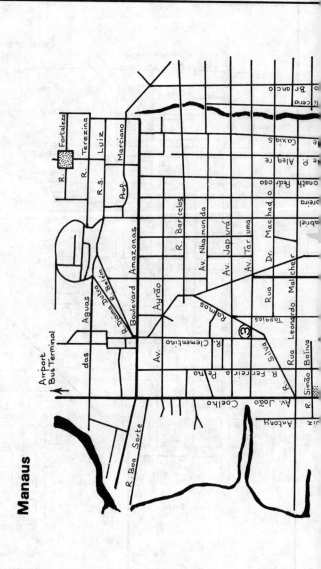

Manaus

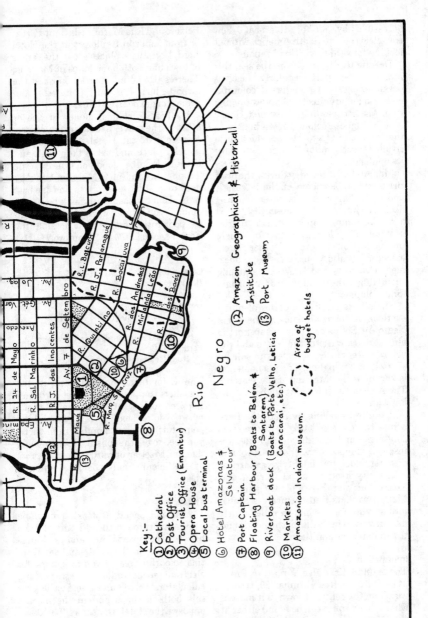

Key:-
1. Cathedral
2. Post Office
3. Tourist Office (Emantur)
4. Opera House
5. Local bus terminal
6. Hotel Amazonas & Selvatour
7. Port Captain.
8. Floating Harbour (Boats to Belém & Santarem)
9. Riverboat dock (Boats to Pôrto Velho, Leticia, Caracarai, etc)
10. Markets
11. Amazonian Indian museum.
12. Amazon Geographical & Historical Institute
13. Port Museum

◯ Area of budget hotels

Rio Negro

accessible by air or riverboat. Few travellers come to South America without looking forward to visiting Manaus.

Despite its distance from the sea, this remote river port regularly receives ocean-going ships and has a colourful collection of architectural styles ranging from the British-built Customs House and Portuguese colonial town houses to the Italianate Opera House which once rivalled those of many European cities for its opulence.

Manaus had its heyday during the brief Brazilian rubber boom of the late 19th and early 20th centuries, after which it declined into relative obscurity. It is again becoming important as a tourist centre and collection point for jungle products (timber, jute and other fibres, essences, palm oils, resins, dyes, medicinal roots and Brazil nuts among them) due to the opening up of Amazonia for development.

The city is built on a series of bluffs overlooking the confluence of the rivers Negro and Solimões. For about six km the almost black water of the Negro and the yellow water of the Solimões run side by side without mingling. The phenomenon is known as the 'Meeting of the Waters'. The Amazon at this point is about eight km wide.

If you're travelling by road, the ferry across the river will take you over this confluence and provide you with an awe-inspiring glimpse of the enormous volume of water which this mighty river carries.

The city itself is full of interest and local colour and there's plenty going on. Many travellers find themselves drawn into staying for a while in order to get more involved in the life of the jungle and the Indian communities.

Information

The main tourist office, *Emantur*, Praça 24 de Outubro, Rua Taruma 329, is some way from the centre of town, but most of what it has to offer can be found either at the Hotel Amazonas, at the junction of Peixoto and Rua Marques da Santa Cruz; or from Amazon Explorers at the Hotel Lord. Both these places are in the centre of town and both have maps of Manaus. There's also an information kiosk at the airport but it's only interested in promoting expensive tours.

It's best to change money at one or other of the travel agents in the centre. *Selvatour* at the Hotel Amazonas is a popular place and takes both cash and cheques. Another good one is next to the Telamazona on Rua G Moreira. You may need to do some leg-work to find the best rate. Don't accept stories about the amount you want to change being 'small' (= poor rate) and avoid if possible the 'travel agents' at 7 de Setembro 711 (1st floor).

Consulates

Bolivia
    Fortaleza 80
Colombia
    Av Eduardo Albeiro 436 (Sala 31)
Ecuador
    Conj Belo Horizonte, Casa 6, Parque 10
Peru
    Rua Rocha dos Santos 85

The Colombian consul is apt to tell travellers that a visa or tourist card isn't required for a visit to Leticia. If that's where you're heading and you intend going further into Colombia from there, you need to tell the consul. He'll probably demand to see an onward ticket and proof of 'sufficient funds' before issuing a visa.

Things to See

You should spend at least a morning wandering through the old part of town between the Opera House and the waterfront to take in the sights and smells of this colourful area. If you're looking for electronic goods (radios, cassette players, calculators) there's an endless variety for sale both in shops and in the market opposite the Hotel Amazonas. The **Opera House** itself was first built in 1896, rebuilt

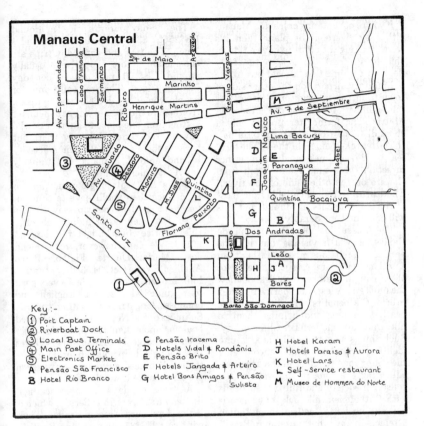

Manaus Central

Key:-
① Port Captain
② Riverboat Dock
③ Local Bus Terminals
④ Main Post Office
⑤ Electronics Market
A Pensão São Francisco
B Hotel Rio Branco
C Pensão Iracema
D Hotels Vidal & Rondônia
E Pensão Brito
F Hotels Jangada & Arteiro
G Hotel Bons Amigos & Pensão Sulista
H Hotel Karam
J Hotels Paraiso & Aurora
K Hotel Lars
L Self-Service restaurant
M Museo de Hommen do Norte

in 1929 and fully restored again in recent years. It's open Monday to Saturday from 11 am to 5 pm and entry is US$0.50.

The barrios clinging to the sides of the *guarapés* are worth a wander around as long as you're not displaying conspicuous signs of wealth such as cameras. Even then, it's probably safe as long as there are a few of you and it's daylight. The contrasts have to be seen to be believed. Many of the old wooden houses look like they're about to collapse at any time, yet as often as not, there will be a colour TV blaring away inside and a shiny car parked outside on the litter-strewn street.

The meeting of the rivers Negro and Solimões is well worth seeing. If you're coming up by bus from Pôrto Velho or heading in that direction you'll see this remarkable sight on the ferry across the river without having to make a separate trip. At the point where the two rivers meet there's a sharply defined colour change from the muddy yellow of the Solimões to the clearer dark brown verging on black of the Negro. As you cross the eight km wide river you'll see huge logs floating past which support their own mini-jungles on the surface, as well as ocean-going liners which tie up in mid-stream. It's quite a sight.

If you're not entering or leaving Manaus either by riverboat or plane then it's worth making the effort to have a ride on this ferry (free). To get to the ferry departure point, take a local bus to the old military airport (on the other side of town from the international airport) or bus number 407 from the Praça da Matriz. The former terminates only a short distance from the ferry terminal; the latter takes you right there. The ferry leaves three times a day in either direction (at 9 am, 1 and 5 pm from Careiro on the other side of the river). There are also tours available from most of the travel agents in Manaus but this will cost you considerably more.

The **Museu do Indio**, Rua Duque de Caxias, is worth visiting but it's the annexe of a religious mission rather than a national museum. As such there's a lot of self-congratulatory eyewash about how the nuns and priests are sparing no effort to bring the 'benefits' of civilisation to the heathen Indians and helping them to 'integrate' into modern Brazilian society. Such things as getting all the kids into identical school uniforms, encouraging the young men to enlist in the army, re-educating everyone in the ways of the consumer society and filling their heads with Catholicism all suck, but there is perhaps no better collection of Indian artefacts in any other museum in Brazil. Entry costs about US$0.15.

The **Museu do Homendo Norte** on Avenida 7 September near the corner of Avenida Joaquim Nabuco is worth a visit, as is the **Handicraft Institute** on Rua Recife, a bus ride out of the centre.

There is an interesting but rather run-down zoo at CIGS, also known as Casac. Catch a 218 bus to Ponta Negra from the side of the Bank of Brazil and tell the driver where you want to get off.

There are many river tours available from travel agents and individuals in Manaus. These last from one to three days and involve overnight stays either on riverbank or floating lodges.

The one-day tours are priced at around US$25 to $35 which usually includes lunch. The two and three day trips are considerably more expensive – usually around US$100 per person per day including food. They're really only for people who either don't intend to take a riverboat in the normal way as a means of getting from one place to another or who haven't the time. Not only that, but because there's so much human activity in and around Manaus, it's unlikely you'll see much wild life.

If it's the real jungle you want to experience then you'll have to think in terms of a much longer trip – say, 10 days or so. Few agencies or individuals offer this at a price which budget travellers can afford. We can, however, recommend José Maria Duarte Fialho, Praça Adalbento Valle (tel 234 5388) (or contact him through *Selvatour*. He's a very good tour guide who speaks English and organises long trips up either the Rio Solimões or Rio Negro by motor-powered boat for about half the price the other agencies charge. He'll take you to villages in the jungle, help you fish for piranha – the lot. You need a group of six to seven people to make it worthwhile.

As far as one-day trips are concerned, *Amazon Explorers Tour Service* which is in the Hotel Lord is recommended. Their trips cost US$35, and include English-speaking guides, excellent food on board and free local spirits (the alcoholic variety). These people will go out of their way to show you something of the life of the Amazonian river people and stop several times to enable you to see rubber plantations and unusual flora. They're even willing to stop the boat if you want to swim for a while.

Places to Stay

Most of the budget hotels are located along Av Joaquim Nabuco between Av 7 de Setembro and the waterfront.

The cheapest of the hotels in this area is the *Pensão São Francisco*, Rua Leão 432.

It's very basic and a little grubby but otherwise good value at just US$1.65/$2.30 a single/double without own bathroom. There are clothes washing/drying facilities. Many travellers stay here.

Almost as cheap but three blocks towards the centre of town is the *Hotel Lars*, Rua dos Andradas 196, which is basic and clean and quite popular with travellers. It costs US$1.85 per person and includes coffee in the morning.

Another cheap one is the *Hotel Rondoñia* with tiny rooms for US$2.

Slightly more expensive is the *Hotel Paraiso* (formerly the Hospedaria Paulista), Rua J Nabuco 154. This costs US$2.50/$4.15 a single/double without own bath and US$5 a double with own shower and toilet. It's basic but clean and secure and the staff are very friendly. Prices include breakfast and there are fans in the rooms.

Also good value is the *Pensão Sulista*, Rua J Nabuco 347, which is very clean, has hot showers, a TV lounge and fans in the rooms. It costs US$3.35/$5 a single/double both with own bathroom and including coffee in the morning. Similar is the *Hotel Rio Branco*, Rua dos Andradas, which is very pleasant and clean and has a relaxing, leafy courtyard. It's a bargain at US$2.50/$3.35 a single/double without own bath and US$5.85 a double with own bathroom and air-conditioning. Morning coffee is included in the room prices.

Other similar hotels which you could try if those already mentioned are full, are the *Hotel Rondonia*, Rua J Nabuco 703, which is fairly clean and costs US$2.35 a single and US$2 per person in other rooms without own bath or breakfast; *Hotel Vidal*, Rua J Nabuco, which costs US$1.65/$2.85 a single/double without own bath or breakfast; and the *Hotel Jangada*, Rua J Nabuco 391, which costs the same as the Rondonia.

Going up-market, try the *Hotel Aurora*, Rua J Nabuco, which has a few rooms without own bath for US$2.35/$4.65 a single/double but they're usually full.

Most of the rooms have their own bath and cost US$5.15/$8 a single/double including coffee in the morning. The staff are very friendly and you can change money at a good rate. Similar is the *Hotel Karam*, Rua J Nabuco 129. All the rooms here have their own bath and cost US$5.85/$7/$9 a single/double/triple with air-conditioning, refrigerator and including a very good breakfast. The *Hotel Arteiro*, Rua J Nabuco 471, is similar to these two.

Avoid the *Pensão Universal*, Rua J Nabuco 508. It's as rough as guts.

Places to Eat

Many travellers eat at the restaurants on or off Rua J Nabuco. Perhaps the best is the *O Bem Amado*, Rua J Nabuco 497. It's run by young people who are eager to please and serve delicious food. It's very popular in the evenings and prices are very reasonable. Next door is the *Restaurant Rio Branco* which offers reasonable meals for US$1. The man who runs it is very keen for custom but the food, as yet, isn't anything special and there are no fans in the place so it can be very stuffy. Perhaps he'll remedy this in future?

The café next to the Pensão São Francisco is also popular though mainly as a drinking spot. People looking for riverboats often come here after wandering around at the dock.

For a minor splurge you must go to the *Xamego*, Rua dos Andradas 196 next door to the Hotel Lar. The food here is excellent. Absolutely delicious! And, for the price you pay – US$2 to $2.50 – great value. It's very, very clean, has a pleasant atmosphere and taped music.

The fish restaurant *Sao Francisco* on Avenida Rio Branco has been recommended, as has the *Panorama* next door. There's a good Chinese restaurant, *China*, at 1127 Av Getulio Vargas.

For self-service food there are several restaurants in the streets round the back of the Hotel Amazonas which are popular at lunch times. One of the best is the *Sirve-sé*, Rua Dr Moreira 128. Eat a good lunch here for around US$1 (set menu). The owner is keen to please. It's closed in the evenings and on Sundays, as are most of these sort of places.

Vegetarians should try the *O Vegetariano*, Av 7 de Setembro 874 (6th floor). It's open Monday to Friday from 11 am to 2.30 pm and offers reasonably priced salad buffets with juice, bread and dessert.

Getting There

Bus *União Cascavel* and *Marlin* are the two main bus companies. The former have buses to Boa Vista at 8 am and 9 pm daily which cost US$10 and take about 19 to 26 hours along an unsurfaced road (in the wet season the road can be cut for days); and to Pôrto Velho at 9.30 am and 2 pm daily which take about 30 hours (again, this road may be closed at times from November to February even though it is surfaced).

Riverboat Manaus is a very busy port and you can find riverboats to just about anywhere on the Amazonian river system. Most of them dock along the *guarapé* at the end of Rua Leão (see the street plan) though there are a few which dock on the other side in which case you'll have to go down Rua Bocaiuva and over the new concrete bridge. All these boats have signs up advising where they go so you simply have to walk around until you find the one (or several) which you want.

Along the main river courses you'll have no problem finding a boat within a day or so but to the more obscure places such as Caracarai on the Rio Branco south of Boa Vista, it may be a week or even more before you find anything.

Regular boats to Benjamin Constant and Tabatinga include the *Marcia Maria, Cap Pinheiro II, Cap Nunes II, Avelino Seal* and the *Paulo Moises IV*. The journey to Tabatinga should take about two days and two nights and cost about US$10. Regular boats to Santarém include the *Rio Guana, Miranda de Dios, Ayapua* and *11 de Mayo*. These also take about two days and two nights and cost about US$18 including food.

If you can't find what you want go down to the Capitania do Pôrto (Port Captain), Rua Santa Cruz. This office has a list of all ships and boats currently sailing.

The much larger steamers down to Santarém and Belém are operated by *ENASA*, Rua Marechal Deodoro 61 – look for the *Transnave* sign. These depart once a week in either direction. To Belém it takes five days and cost US$50 and to Santarém it's US$30. Because of the constantly decreasing value of the cruzeiro these fares will undoubtedly increase before long so use them as a guide only.

Getting Around

The Rodoviária (for buses to Boa Vista, Pôrto Velho, Cuiabá, etc) is a long way from the centre of town, on the same road as the airport. To get there from the centre of town take bus Nos 9002 (marked 'Inter-Barrios'), 505 (marked 'Vista Bela'), 2 (marked 'Cidade Nova'), 613 (marked 'Hileia') or the bus simply marked 'Aeroporto'. Most of these go down Epaminondas from the Praça do Matriz. Once you're over the top of the hill and going down the other side, watch out for the Conjuntos dos Jornalistas (a housing estate) and the huge stadium on the left hand side. Then you'll see the *Antarctica* beer factory, again on the left. Get off here where two major roads merge and there's a Shell petrol station on the corner. The Rodoviária is opposite the petrol station.

Between the airport and the city centre take the bus marked 'Aeroporto'. It runs every half an hour, costs US$0.10 and takes about 25 to 30 minutes passing the Rodoviária en route. A taxi will cost US$5 but if you're waiting for the local bus, empty taxis may stop and offer you the ride for considerably less (US$2 to $2.50, for instance).

Ouro Prêto

Ouro Prêto is Brazil's most magnificent colonial gem and shouldn't be missed on any account. Founded in 1711 in the wake of the gold rush, it still retains its 18th-century atmosphere and was once the capital of Minas Gerais state. It was declared a national monument in 1933 and for one day a year (24th June) it once again becomes the state capital. Like the gold and silver towns of Guanajuato and Taxco in Mexico, it's a living museum of steep cobbled streets, beautiful colonial mansions, baroque churches and shady gardens. Many of the churches display the wood and soapstone work of one of Brazil's most famous sculptors, Aleijadinho. São Francisco de Assis and Carmo are two notable examples.

It's naturally a tourist town these days with prices to match yet somehow it doesn't seem to matter because it's so interesting. There's also a large student population who attend the famous School of Mines here so there are ways of enjoying yourself without spending a fortune. You need at least two days to see the town properly and more if you want to soak up the atmosphere of the place.

Twelve km away is a similar colonial town – Mariana. This isn't as commercialised as Ouro Prêto and prices tend to be lower. Similar but much further away are Congonhas and Diamantina. Halfway between Ouro Prêto and Mariana is a village with a working goldmine which you can visit for US$3.

Information

The tourist office is on Praça Tiradentes 41. Although this office shows films about the town (at 9 am, noon and 4 pm on weekdays, and 9 am, 10.30 am, 1, 3 and 4 pm on weekends and holidays) it's otherwise pretty uninformative. They do have maps of the town for sale for US$0.50 and guide books (all in Portuguese) at various prices. They also have a leaflet with details of the church and museum opening times (essential if you don't want to waste a lot of time). No English is spoken.

Things to See

Obviously the first thing to do here is to get hold of the tourist office leaflet on the museums and churches and then stroll around. Almost all the churches have an entry charge (US$0.25 on average). Many of them are divided up into the church proper (free) and a museum (which you pay to get into to). I personally felt that some of the museum sections were hardly worth seeing. You may disagree.

One which is worth visiting is the **Museu da Inconfidencia** on the Praça Tiradentes which contains the bulk of Aleijadinho's work. You may not wear shorts in any of these places and you may not take photographs. Not only that, but in the Museu da Inconfidencia you have to leave all cameras (whether they're in a case or not) at reception and woe betide the foreigner who voices objections. There's a 'security guard' in reception there who is the re-incarnation of Rosa Cleb (remember 'From Russia with Love'?) – she's abusive, ugly and arrogant.

Whatever you do, don't miss the **Minerology Museum** in the School of Mines (the old Governor's Palace at the top end of the Praça Tiradentes). It surely must have the most beautiful and colourful collection of mineral specimens in the world. Absolutely superb! Entry costs US$0.25. Photography is prohibited.

If you have the time it's worth visiting the **Minas de Passagem**. There are functioning gold mines here about 5 km from Ouro Prêto on the road to Mariana. The entry fee is a bit steep but they will show you how to wash out gold.

Places to Stay

Because it's a tourist town there's very little choice in budget accommodation in Ouro Prêto. There is, however, a chance

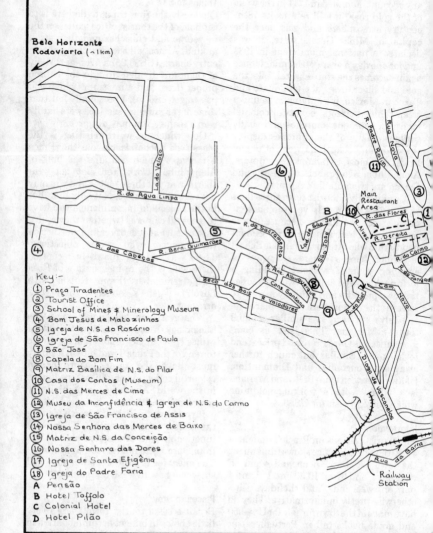

Ouro Prêto

Belo Horizonte
Rodoviaria (~1km)

R. do Agua Limpa

R. das Cabeças

R. Bern. Guimarães

Ldo Velaso

Beco dos Bois

R. do Sacramento

Ldo de São José

R. São José

R. Ant. Albuquerque

R. Cons. Santana

R. Valadares

Main
Restaurant
Area

R. das Flores

R. Alvar

R. Direita

R. do Carmo

R. do Jangad

Cam Nova

R. do Pilar

R. Diogo de Vasconcelos

Rua da Barra

Rua Nova

R. Padre Rolo

Railway
Station

Key:-
① Praça Tiradentes
② Tourist Office
③ School of Mines & Minerology Museum
④ Bom Jesus de Matozinhos
⑤ Igreja de N.S. do Rosário
⑥ Igreja de São Francisco de Paula
⑦ São José
⑧ Capela do Bom Fim
⑨ Matriz Basilica de N.S. do Pilar
⑩ Casa dos Contos (Museum)
⑪ N.S. das Merces de Cima
⑫ Museu da Inconfidência & Igreja de N.S. do Carmo
⑬ Igreja de São Francisco de Assis
⑭ Nossa Senhora das Merces de Baixo
⑮ Matriz de N.S. da Conceição
⑯ Nossa Senhora das Dores
⑰ Igreja de Santa Efigênia
⑱ Igreja do Padre Faria
A Pensão
B Hotel Toffolo
C Colonial Hotel
D Hotel Pilão

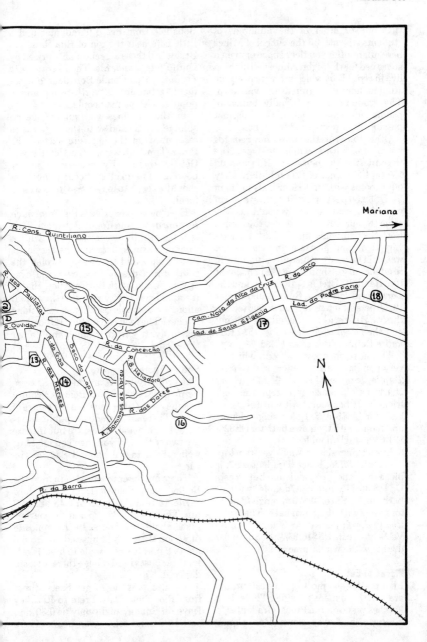

that one or other of the hundreds of students who attend the School of Mines here might offer you floor space or even a spare bed for the night. Almost all of them live in *republicas* which are self-governing student houses scattered all over town. The students are a friendly bunch of people in general so it's a distinct possibility, especially at weekends.

Other than this there are a few *pensãos* not all of which are signposted. One of the friendliest is the *pensão* at Rua Paraná 137 on the corner of Rua do Pilar. They offer rooms with up to four beds in them for US$2.50 per person (if there are two of you it's more than likely you'll get the room to yourself and the key to the room). Both the bedrooms and the bathroom are very clean and pleasant and there's hot water. There are generally students in residence also. Similar are the *pensãos* at Rua Randolfo Bretas 11 (no sign); and the *Dormitorio Jotu Jotu*, Rua Getulio Vargas 10. Others which have been suggested are the *N S Aparecida* at the railway station; and the *Dormitoria Sereno* at 1510 Rua Padre Rolim which costs US$2.

The next cheapest and one which is very popular with travellers is the *Hotel Toffolo*, Rua São José 76. This is a very charming old place, well kept and very friendly. It has rooms without their own bath for US$6.70/$11.65 a single/double and rooms with their own bath for US$20/$21.65 a single/double.

Everything else is way over the top. The *Hotel Pilão*, Praça Tiradentes 57, is pleasant and convenient but costs US$13.35/$15 a single/double without bath and US$16.70/$20 a single/double for rooms with their own bath. The *Hotel Colonial*, Travessa do Padre Camilo Veloso 26, costs US$16.65/$21.65 a single/double with own bathroom.

Places to Eat

Like the hotels, most of the restaurants are on the expensive side. There is a *lanches* place on the Praça Tiradentes, a *Hosteria* half way down Rua Conde Bobadela from Praça Tiradentes and a little café near the top of Rua Randolfo Bretos. All these are reasonably priced by Ouro Prêto standards. The *Restaurante La Luna*, Rua Conde Bobadela, a basement restaurant, is worth trying and is popular with young people.

In the evenings you might like to splurge a little and go to the large rustic restaurant on the opposite side of the Praça Tiradentes from the Hotel Pilão. Get in there early because it's very popular. The food is excellent but you should expect to pay US$3 to $4 for a meal.

Even more expensive is the *Calabouço Restaurante*, Rua Conde Bobadela. This is a beautifully decorated place with a romantic atmosphere but the service is deadly slow and they seem to play the same dirgy, dreary tape over and over again. Surely at the prices they charge (around US$4 to $5 for a meal) they could afford a reasonable selection of something livelier? The food is good but the portions niggardly. It's open at lunch and dinner times only.

Getting There

The ordinary bus terminal (for *Pássaro Verde* buses to and from Belo Horizonte) is some two to three km from the centre of town. There are infrequent public buses between here and the centre but if there are two or three of you then you might as well take a taxi – about US$1 for the car.

There are buses to Ouro Prêto from the Rodoviária in Belo Horizonte by *Pássaro Verde* 12 times daily from 6.45 am to 9 pm. The fare is US$1.25 and the journey takes about two hours. In the opposite direction there are 11 buses daily from 6 am to 8 pm. It's advisable to buy tickets for these buses in advance – there's a lot of demand.

It's also possible to get buses direct from Rio. From Ouro Prêto to Rio they leave on Sunday night only at 9.30 pm, cost US$4 and take seven hours. There are buses every half hour or so from the Praça Tiradentes in Ouro Prêto to Mariana.

PARANAGUÁ

Paranaguá is a delightful mixture of semi-tropical seediness (rapidly undergoing extensive renovation) and modern port city. Although founded in 1585, it's still a relatively small city of around 135,000 inhabitants but it has a lot of atmosphere and some interesting waterfront cafés. The old part of town is quite small, peppered with 18th century churches and easily seen in a day though you may well consider staying overnight. The railway from Curitiba to Paranaguá, completed in 1880, is justly famous as one of the most spectacular in all Brazil and you should try to make this journey if at all possible.

Information

There is a tourist information kiosk opposite the railway station which is very helpful and provides free maps of the town as well as descriptive leaflets in various languages (including English).

Things to See

All the old churches here are worth visiting and a lot of effort has gone into renovating them. They're in stark contrast to the usual baroque gold-encrusted gaudiness of most Brazilian churches. These are all delightfully simple though there are some superb examples of stained-glass in one or two. They include the **Igreja de São Benedito** (1784), **Igreja de Nossa Senhora Rosario** (the cathedral church built in 1578 and the oldest in the city), **Igreja São Francisco das Chagas** (1741) and the **Igreja de Nossa Senhora de Rosio** (1813).

Don't miss the **Museu Historico** and the **Museu Arqueologia e Artes Populares** which are excellent. They're both housed in the same restored former Jesuit College on the waterfront which was built between 1736 and 1755. The building itself is worth visiting. In the museums there's everything from enormous wooden machines to dug-outs and Indian pottery but the labelling is entirely in Portuguese and sometimes excessively brief. Entry costs US$0.10 and the museums are open Tuesday to Friday from 10 am to 5 pm and Saturday to Monday from 12 noon to 5 pm.

The old and the new municipal markets on the waterfront can be very interesting depending on which day you visit – live fish, shrimps, lobster, fruit, vegetables and flowers.

Boat trips are available along the waterfront and up to the modern Dom Pedro II docks. They're operated by *Transturmar* and leave daily at 10.30 am, 12 noon, 2 and 4 pm and last for one to 1½ hours. Pick them up at the end of the Av Arthur de Abreu.

It's also possible to find a boat to take you to **Fortaleza da Ilha do Mel**, the old Portuguese fort on Mel Island, but you can't visit all of the above and the fort in one day.

Places to Stay

You can get an interesting and basic room overlooking the waterfront at the *Pensão Bela Vista*, Rua Gen Carheiro, for US$1/$2 a single/double. Very similar is the *Hotel Mar de Roses* a few doors along the same street.

For something a little more expensive try the *Hotel Impala*, Rua Mestre Leopoldo. There are many other hotels in Paranaguá but they're all considerably more expensive.

Places to Eat

There are a lot of restaurants in Paranaguá but for quality and quantity it's unlikely you'll beat the *comercio* at the *Pensão Bela Vista*, Rua Gen Carheiro on the waterfront. For US$2.80 you'll be served a delicious feast which will easily feed three people. It includes baked fish, potato/mayonnaise salad, tomato/onion/lettuce

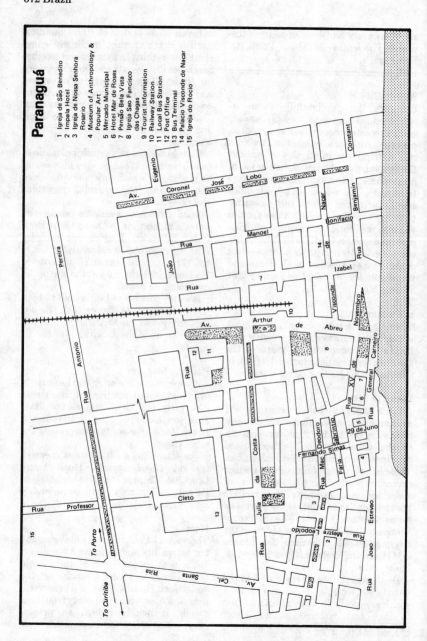

Paranaguá

1 Igreja de São Benedito
2 Impala Hotel
3 Igreja de Nossa Senhora Rosario
4 Museum of Anthropology & Popular Art
5 Mercado Municipal
6 Hotel Mar de Roses
7 Pensão Bela Vista
8 Igreja São Francisco das Chagas
9 Tourist Information
10 Railway Station
11 Local Bus Station
12 Post Office
13 Bus Terminal
14 Palácio Visconde de Nacar
15 Igreja do Rocio

salad, a meat dish in rich, tasty sauce, prawns, *feijoa*, fried rice, spaghetti, bread and coffee. Incredible! One of the best meals you'll find in the whole of Brazil. Not only that but the staff are very friendly and there are tables and chairs out on the footpath as well as inside.

The restaurant inside the old municipal market also does a good spread and is popular with day-trippers.

Getting There

The train is the most popular form of transport and there is a choice of *automotriz* (rail car) and ordinary passenger train. From Curitiba to Paranaguá there is an *automotriz* daily at 8.30 am and a passenger train daily at 7 am (with an additional one on Sundays only at 1.30 pm). In the opposite direction, the *automotriz* leaves Paranaguá daily at 3.30 pm. The *automotriz* takes two hours 50 minutes on the down journey and 2½ hours coming back. The passenger trains take longer.

The fares for the *automotriz* are US$4.40 one-way and US$6.15 return. On the passenger train the fares are US$1.75 (1st class) and US$1.40 (2nd class) one-way (double that return). Buy tickets for the *automotriz* a day in advance.

You can also go by bus but the road journey isn't as spectacular. *Viacão Graciosa* run 12 direct buses daily in either direction from 6.30 am to 10 pm and four other buses daily which call at other places en route. Some of these buses are luxury class (four per day in either direction) and the others conventional. The fare is US$1.35 and the journey takes 1½ to two hours.

Some travellers prefer to take the train down and a bus back as this allows you to stay longer in Paranaguá.

PÔRTO ALEGRE

Pôrto Alegre is one of the largest commercial and industrial cities in the south of Brazil with a population well in excess of a million. Coming in by bus, you'll see its high-rise sky-line come into view from far away. It's also a fresh-water port which lies at the northern end of the Largoa dos Patos, 275 km from the open sea. It isn't of great interest to travellers except as an overnight stop en route to or from Uruguay/Argentina but it is a pleasant enough place.

Information

Setur's main tourist office is at Rua dos Andradas 1234 (18th floor). There is a branch office (a kiosk) at the Rodoviária which stocks the monthly booklet, *Programa* (usually free), which contains all you'll probably need to know and lots more (massage parlours, strip shows, etc) as well as a good map of the city. You can also pick this booklet up at the airport.

Consulates

Argentina
  Rua Prof Annes Dias 112 (1st floor) (tel 24 6799).
Paraguay
  Praça Dom Feliciano 39 (6th floor) (tel 25 0582).
Uruguay
  Rua dos Andradas 1237 (tel 21 2866).

Places to Stay

One of the cheapest places is the *Hotel Vitória* (previously the Hotel Colonial), Voluntários do Pátria 459, but I wouldn't kennel a mongrel with psoriasis here. It's filthy and dirt cheap. If you're absolutely broke then stay instead at the *Hotel Viaducto*, Rua Duque de Caxias 1454, which has catatonic staff but only costs US$1 per person.

In the centre of town there are three hotels which are reasonable value and well maintained. The cheapest is the *Pensão San Jeronimo*, Independencia 116, which costs US$1.75/$3.50 a single/double without own bath. Better are the *Hotel Henrique*, Rua Gen Vitorino 182 on the corner of Rua Dr Flores (tel 26 4919), which is friendly and costs US$2.65/$4.40 a single/double without own bath and US$5.25 a double with own bath (hot

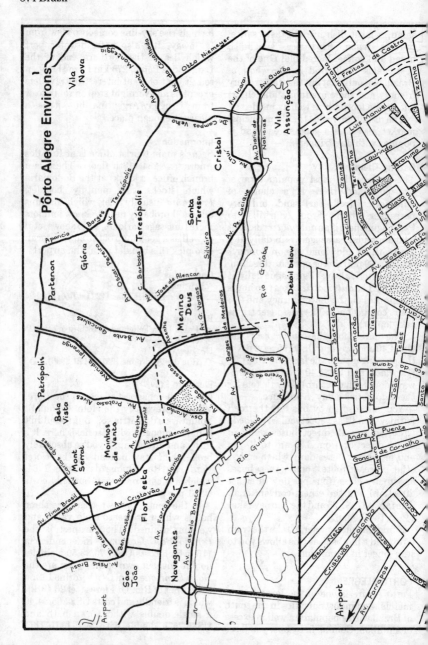

Pôrto Alegre Environs

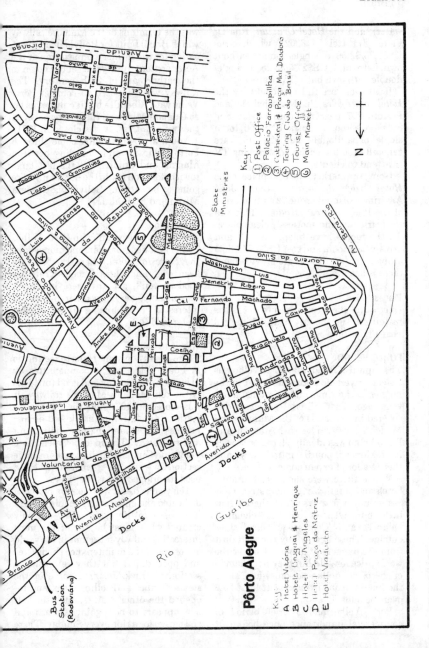

Pôrto Alegre

Key:
A Hotel Vitória
B Hotels Uruguai & Henrique
C Hotel Los Angeles
D Hotel Praça da Matriz
E Hotel Viaducto

Key:
① Post Office
② Palacio Farroupilha
③ Cathedral ≠ Praça Mal Deodoro
④ Touring Club do Brasil
⑤ Tourist Office
⑥ Main Market

water); and the *Hotel Uruguai*, Rua Dr Flores 371 (tel 25 6302), which costs US$1.75/$3.50 a single/double without own bath and US$2.65/$5.25 a single/double with own bath (hot water).

If all these are full you could try the *Hotel Los Angeles*, Rua Marechal Floriano Peixoto 277 near the corner with Sen Salgado Filho. It costs US$3.50 for a single or a double but the staff are generally too pre-occupied watching TV to attend to clients.

Going up-market, the best place is the *Hotel Praça da Matriz*, Largo Joáo Amorim de Albuquerque 72 on the corner of the Praça Marcel Deodoro. This is a really friendly and spotlessly clean place. All the rooms have telephone, TV and private bathroom and cost US$5.75/$8.25 a single/double. Towels are provided and there is hot water.

Places to Eat
One of the cheapest places to eat is the *restaurant* in the Mercado Municipal near Praça 15.

PÔRTO VELHO
The capital of Rondonia, Pôrto Velho was a sleepy riverside port almost lost in the jungles of the Amazon basin until a few years ago. Then alluvial gold was discovered in the sands of the Mamoré and Madeira rivers. The rush was on and Pôrto Velho was ideally placed to service it all. Money is pouring into the town and there's a lot of expansion going on.

Where there were shops, restaurants, hotels and bars down the main street (7 de Setembro) a few years ago there's now little but agencies sporting chemical balances and 'Compra-se Ouro' signs outside. These agents buy the gold dust from the panners at about 5% below the world price for gold but they pay them in cruzeiros not dollars so somewhere along the line someone is making at least 20% over the odds.

Pôrto Velho had a brief period of commercial importance once before. It was the terminus of the Mamoré railway which Brazil built for Bolivia in compensation for the former's annexation of the Acre territory during the rubber boom in the early years of 20th century. The railway was supposed to connect Pôrto Velho with Riberalta but it only got as far as Guajará Mirim on the border between the two countries. It was closed in 1971.

You'll almost certainly come through Pôrto Velho if you're heading between Manaus and Cuiabá. It's the last large town before you get to the border if you're going to be entering Bolivia via Guajará Mirim and Riberalta.

Information
There is no tourist office in Pôrto Velho.

The best deal for changing money is at the *Floresta Hotel* where they're very keen to buy and offer an excellent rate – as good as you'll get anywhere in Brazil. Inexplicably, very few other places are interested in changing (maybe they prefer gold?).

Things to See
There's really only one thing to see and do in Pôrto Velho but it compensates by being very interesting and good fun. This is the old Madeira-Mamoré railway. It was closed in 1971 and the facilities – stations, track, rolling stock and almost priceless old steam engines – left to rot and rust away. The road between Pôrto Velho and Guajará Mirim ran along large sections of where the track used to be and used its bridges across the rivers.

Ten years after it was closed a bunch of dedicated and enterprising people brought it all back to life again. They not only created what must be one of the most interesting railway museums in the world out of one of the maintenance sheds (free and open daily) but they re-opened a section of track, restored some of the steam engines and rolling stock and re-opened the other maintenance shed. It now appears to be a going concern and you can go for a ride every Sunday. There

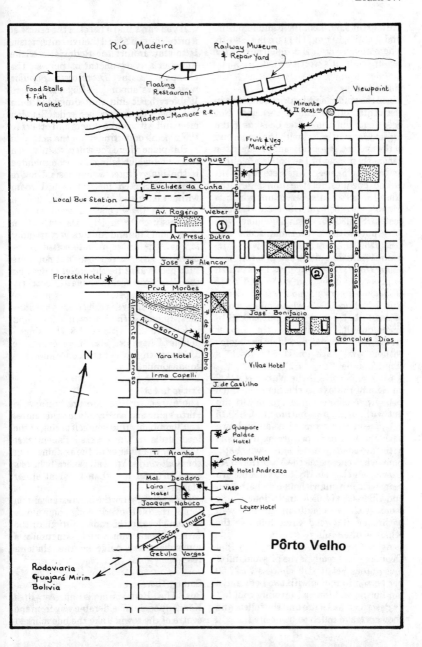

Pôrto Velho

are trips at 8.30, 9.35, 10.35 and 11.35 am, and 2 and 3.10 pm. The fare is US$0.15. There's even a craft shop open next to the repair sheds. It's worth a visit!

Places to Stay

Since the gold rush, the prices of hotels in the centre of town have rocketed. Not only that, but the better ones are often full so you may be left with the rough end of the market. If you do want to stay in the centre then most of the hotels are either on or just off the Av 7 de Setembro.

The cheapest of the bunch are the *Hotel Sonora*, 7 de Setembro, which is friendly and good value but often full and costs US$3.30/$5.30 single/double with fans but without own bathroom and US$5/$8.30 a single/double with air-conditioning but also without bathroom; *Villas Hotel*, Rua Gonçalves Dias, which is pleasant, fresh and clean and costs US$3.30 per person; and the *Hotel Laira*, Rua J Nabuco 2005, which offers rooms without bathroom for US$3.50/$6 a single/double. Similar is the *Leyzer Hotel*, Rua J Nabuco, which has rooms without own bath for US$2.50/$4.15 a single/double.

More expensive is the *Nunes Hotel*, 7 de Setembro next to the Sonora, which costs US$5 per person in a room with fan but without its own bathroom, US$9.15 per person in a room with fan and own bath and US$10.85 per person in a room with air-conditioning and own bath. Somewhat cheaper is the *Yara Hotel*, Av Osorio, which costs US$6.60 a double in a room with fan but without own bathroom and US$6.65/$11.65 a single/double for a room with air-conditioning and own bathroom. It's good value but like the others is often full.

Avoid the *Hotel Andrezza*, Rua Mal Deodoro. This really is the pits and full of mosquitoes yet it still charges US$2.50 per person in rooms with two beds and a fan but no window. It certainly couldn't be described as secure and the toilets and showers leave much to be desired.

If you can't find a hotel in the centre at a price you can afford then the alternative is to stay around the Rodoviária where there is a good choice of places. The cheapest is the *Dormitorio Popular* which costs about US$1.50 per person. It's very basic and a bit dingy but each room does have a shower and toilet. It's often full with gold panners and others in the process of getting in on the act.

One place where you will certainly get a room and which is highly recommended is the *Lider Hotel* which costs US$5 a double, US$6.65 for a four-bed room without bath and US$6.65 a double for a room with its own bath. It's a new place, spotlessly clean, good beds with clean sheets and fans and run by a very friendly family. The prices include coffee in the morning. At a similar price but not quite such good value are the *Hotel Dulce* and the *Hotel Barroso*. In the latter hotel try to get a room upstairs.

More expensive is the *Hotel Angradus Reis*. Rooms with their own shower and toilet here cost US$6.65/$8.30 a single/double. There are also more expensive rooms with own bathroom and air-conditioning.

Places to Eat

There are surprisingly few restaurants in Pôrto Velho and hardly any *lanches* cafés. You'll probably find yourself eating at the food stalls in the covered fish market down by the river or at the restaurant in the Rodoviária. You can generally have a good meal for less than US$1 at either place.

For a splurge, try the bar/restaurant on top of the bluff overlooking the railway station close to the radar station, or the floating restaurant which is actually a somewhat ritzy barge on the Madeira river.

Getting There

Bus The Rodoviária is on Av Pres Kennedy some considerable way from the centre of the town. Take the bus marked

'Hospital do Base' to get to or from the centre (US$0.15, about 10 minutes). This bus goes up 7 de Setembro and then along Av Nacões Unidas before going onto Av Pres Kennedy.

The bus to and from the airport is marked, 'Aeroporto'. You can pick it up either along 7 de Setembro or at the Rodoviária. It costs US$0.15 and takes about 20 minutes.

Riverboat There are riverboats from Pôrto Velho to Manaus and to Manicoré and Humaita but they're not very frequent. To Manaus there are generally two boats a week on Thursday and Saturday at around 6 pm. On the Saturday boat you must change at Manicoré. The journey takes three to four days downstream and more upstream. The fares are US$27.50 (1st class) and US$22.50 (2nd class). 2nd class is not recommended. The *Brotinho* goes to Borba, Aripuana, Manicoré and Humaita. You'll be very lucky indeed to find a boat to Guajará Mirim.

Recife & Olinda

Facing each other across what was previously a stretch of swamp, sand bars and estuary are Olinda and Recife. The former, once the capital of Brazil, is a beautifully preserved colonial enclave and the latter is a huge modern city (Brazil's fourth largest) which sprawls for miles down the coast. Both of them sport interesting and colourful artists' colonies and both are well worth visiting. The whole area saw a great deal of competition and confrontation between the Portuguese and the Dutch during the 16th and 17th centuries and both left their fortresses which survive today.

Recife was originally built on little more than a sandbar but drainage and landfill of the low-lying land over the centuries gradually led to its expansion. More recently, high-rise development catering largely to the holiday industry has converted Boa Viagem beach into a sort of Copacabana of the north. Nevertheless, the old centre still retains a degree of charm with its winding, narrow streets, old churches, markets and leafy squares. This is especially true of the artists' quarter centred around the Pátio de São Pedro.

Olinda is another world. Apart from the T-shirt and lace tablecloth sellers and the Adidas and Nike-clad youths playing football in front of the São Bento monastery, you could be back in 16th century Brazil.

Founded in 1537 and only six km from Recife, Olinda was the first capital of Brazil. Built on a forested rise overlooking the ocean, it's awash with mildewed colonial churches, monasteries, palaces and old houses with latticed balconies. A lot of restoration work has been going on here for years (it's been declared a national monument) and there's now a large artists' colony which turns out some really fine wood carvings and paintings. Further up the coast a lot of housing development has taken place, though not on the scale of Boa Viagem beach south of Recife, and there's also a beach popular with surfers and other young people.

Both Recife and Olinda have their respective carnivals which tend to be less commercialised than those of Rio and Salvador.

Information

There are many branches of the tourist office but the most useful are those at the Rodoviária (the woman who staffs this office is very helpful); the Pátio de São Pedro, Loja 17; and at the airport. The latter rates as the best in Brazil – the man who staffs it is very keen and will fall over backwards to help you plus he has excellent free maps. The opening times of the churches, art galleries and museums are published in the daily newspaper, *Diário de Pernambuco*.

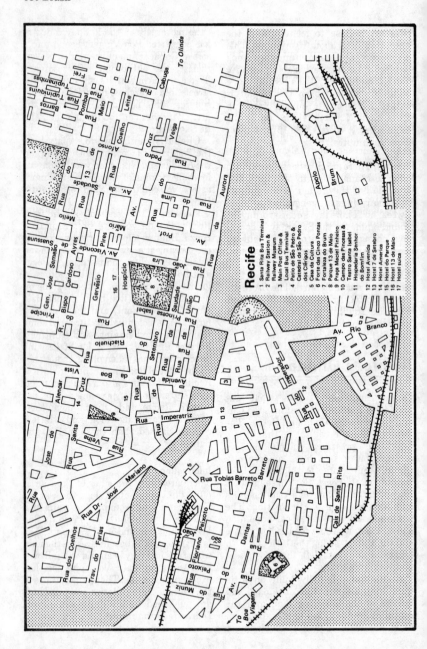

Recife

1 Santa Rita Bus Terminal
2 Railway Station &
  Railway Museum
3 Main Post Office &
  Local Bus Terminal
4 Patio de São Pedro &
  Catedral de São Pedro
  dos Clérigos
5 Casa da Cultura
6 Forte das Cinco Pontas
7 Fortaleza do Brum
8 Parque 13 de Maio
9 Praça Maciel Pinheiro
10 Campo das Princesas &
  Teatro Santa Isabel
11 Hospedaria Senhor
  do Bomfim
12 Hotel Avenida
13 Hotel 7 de Setembro
14 Hotel América
15 Hotel do Parque
16 Hotel 13 de Maio
17 Hotel Suica

Things to See

Some of the old churches in the centre of Recife are worth visiting but you need to find out what their opening times are before you set off. One of the best, **São Pedro dos Clerigos**, is conveniently located on the Patio de São Pedro, which is the centre of the artists' district. This square has lots of other shops, galleries, bars and mellow little restaurants which are ideal for hanging out and talking to local people. There are often music and/or poetry gigs here on Friday, Saturday and Sunday evenings. It's a very colourful and interesting area.

You should also visit the **Forte das Cinco Pontas** opposite the Rodoviária. Built by the Portuguese in 1677, it is open to the public on weekdays from 9 to 11 am and 1 to 5 pm. It contains a cartographic and photographic history of Recife which gives you a good idea of how much the city has changed over the years – and how much effort has gone into those changes! Unfortunately, you can't see the sea from the fort any longer because of a fly-over which obstructs the view! There's a small entry charge.

The **Casa da Cultura de Pernambuco**, Rua Floriano Peixoto, a huge colonial-style building overlooking the Rio Capibaribe and formerly a jail, is also worth checking out. It houses shops selling local hand-made crafts, a theatre, snack bars and museum (ceramics, folklore and musical instruments). You can also pick up tourist information here. It's open Monday to Saturday from 9 am to 8 pm and on Sundays from 2 to 8 pm.

If you like museums then there's another bunch along Av 17 de Agosto. They include the **Museu do Açúcar** which has models of colonial mills, instruments of torture and much else; the **Museu do Homem do Nordeste**, an anthropology museum about the peoples and history of the north-east; and the **Museu do Farmacopeia Popular**, which will delight anyone interested in herbalism.

Olinda is a place which you set off for in the early morning and spend all day strolling around, going wherever your interest takes you and having lunch at one of the restaurants. Some of the most interesting monuments here are the **Convento de Nossa Senhora das Neves** (1585), much photographed and open daily from 8 to 11.30 am and 2 to 4.30 pm; the **Seminário de Olinda** (1584), open whenever there's someone around to let you in; the **Convento de Conceicão** (1585), no fixed hours – ask at the entrance; and the **Mosteiro de São Bento** (1582), open daily from 8 to 11 am and 1 to 5 pm. The latter is a huge, rambling building and is absolutely fascinating. It has cloisters, galleries, a library and endless dark passageways to explore but the only way to see most of it is to go up the stone steps to the left as you enter. There's a wooden gate here which is usually locked. It wasn't when I went in so I (presumptuously?) hopped upstairs before anyone could see me and spent a long time wandering around. I received some curious glances when I finally came down (nothing suggesting I'd offended) but it might be best to ask permission first – I'm sure they wouldn't object if you expressed genuine interest.

The **Museum of Sacred Art**, housed in the former Episcopal Palace (1696), is also worth a visit, open Tuesday to Friday from 8 am to 12 noon and 2 to 6 pm and on weekends from 2 to 6 pm, small entry charge; as is the **Museum of Contemporary Art** – to bring you back into the 20th century. The latter is housed in the prison of the Inquisition which was built in the 18th century and has a large collection of national and foreign art. It's open Monday, Wednesday, Thursday and Friday from 8 am to 5 pm and on weekends from 2 to 5.30 pm.

Boa Viagem is really a beach for the well-heeled and lit up at night but is pleasant nevertheless. It's best to go up the coast past the old part of Olinda. The beaches here are thronged with young people and there are a lot of restaurants and clubs. Beaches to try north of Olinda are Rio Doce, Janga, Pau Amarelo and Maria Farinha.

Places to Stay

Recife isn't an easy place to find budget accommodation in, especially around the Rodoviária. Many, perhaps even most of the cheapies in this area, are for whores and their clients. We got into one lift to check a place out just as a couple – the woman with her skirt pulled up over her head and no underwear – got out. These insights into local customs don't faze me but it gives you some idea of what you're in for if you're on a very tight budget.

One place which won't give you high blood pressure in this respect and also one of the cheapest places to stay in Recife is the *Hospedária Senhor do Bonfim*, Rua dos Pescadores 8 just round the back of the Rodoviária. It's a fairly small place (32 rooms) which is well-maintained and clean and costs US$2.50/$4.15 a single/double without own bath.

Another which is good value but quite a way from the bus station is the *Hotel 7 de Setembro*, Rua Matias de Albuquerque 318 near the junction with Rua do Sol (which runs along the bank of the Rio Capibaribe). This is a very pleasant place, the management is friendly and rooms cost US$4/$5 a single/double without own bath.

Also excellent value is the *Hotel Avenida*, Av Martins de Barros at the junction of Rua Siqueira Campos, which faces onto the river and enjoys good sea breezes. Rooms without own bath cost US$4.20/$5.25 a single/double. Rooms with own bathroom cost US$5.25/$6.30 a single/double.

For the next batch of possibilities you have to move across the river to the Bela Vista area. Three popular places are the *Hotel do Parque*, Rua do Hospicio 51; the *Hotel 13 de Maio*, Rua do Hospicio 659; and the *Suiça Hotel*, Rua do Hospicio 657.

The 13 de Maio and the Suiça, both on the top side of the Parque 13 de Maio, are probably the better value. The 13 de Maio costs US$4.65/$5.15 a single/double without own bathroom and US$6.35/$7 a single/double with own bathroom both including breakfast. The hotel also has its own restaurant. The Suiça costs US$3.35 to US$3.65 per person in rooms with fan but without bathroom and US$4.15/$5.35 a single/double with bathroom. All prices include breakfast. Like the 13 de Maio, the Suiça also has its own restaurant.

The Hotel do Parque is perhaps a little overpriced at US$4.35 a single for a room without its own bath and US$6.35/$7.35 a single/double with own bath including breakfast. It's often full with Brazilian small businessmen.

You may also like to consider the *Hotel América*, Praça Maciel Pinheiro 48 (tel 221 1300/1389). This is a mid-range hotel but not as expensive as it appears. It has good facilities, the rooms are pleasant with fan and refrigerator and many of them have a balcony overlooking the square, but the breakfasts are substandard. It costs US$4.90/$5.45 a single/double without own bathroom and US$8.10/$9 a single/double with own bathroom.

If you want to stay close to the beach then there are a few fairly reasonably priced possibilities along Boa Viagem but two of them are hostel-type accommodation popular with young Brazilians. Closest to the beach is the *Albergue Arrecife*, Rua Padre Carapuceiro 132 on the corner of Rua de Navegantes (tel 326 7549), one block back from the beach. The people here are very friendly and the charge is US$4.50 per person in dormitory rooms. Men and women are separated. There's a cafeteria and TV lounge. The hostel advertises itself as 'created to lodge young spirited persons who travel in a practical and economical way'.

The other hostel is several blocks away from the beach and further to the south. It's the *Albergue do Mar*, Rua Antonio

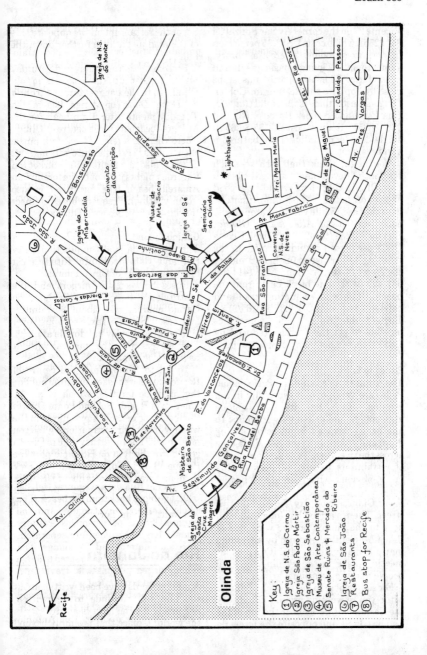

Olinda

Key:
① Igreja de N.S. do Carmo
② Igreja São Pedro Mártir
③ Igreja de São Sebastião
④ Museu de Arte Contemporânea
⑤ Senate Ruins ✳ Mercado do Ribeira
⑥ Igreja de São João
⑦ Restaurants
⑧ Bus stop for Recife

Vicente 27 on the corner Av Sáe Souza(tel 341 6255), which costs US$3.35 per person in dormitory rooms. There's a library, games room, TV lounge, baggage safe and a cafeteria. The 'Aeroporto' bus stops close by opposite the Restaurant Golden Dragon. Lastly there is the *Hotel Gaivota*, Rua Fernando Simões Barbosa 632 (tel 326 3685). Rooms cost US$5/$6.65 a single/double including own bathroom and breakfast.

You might think that with so much residential development along the beach past Olinda that there would be a good choice of hotels. This, unfortunately, isn't the case. While you hunt around you could stay at the *Albergue de Olinda*, Rua do Sol 233 (tel 429 0413), which costs US$3 per person including coffee in the morning. Otherwise go further up and try the *Hotel 14-Bis*, Av Beira Mar 1414 (tel 081 429 0409), one block back from the beach. It has a swimming pool and cafeteria and costs US$8.35/$11.65/$15 a single/double/triple. It's sometimes possible to get these prices reduced by US$1 if there's not many people staying.

Places to Eat

The restaurants around the Pátio de São Pedro are very popular especially in the evening. Each has its own unique atmosphere and prices vary from one to another so check a few out before sitting down and ordering. In the Boa Vista area across the river there's an excellent choice of restaurants to suit all pockets. It's fairly obvious which are the cheaper ones.

For Chinese food, try the *Fuji* on this street. There's a good bar (open till late) next to the church on the wide end of Praça Maciel Pinheiro run by a German man and his Brazilian wife. It's a popular meeting place in the evening for local people and the occasional gringo.

For somewhere to have lunch or dinner while you're walking around Olinda try the *Restaurant da Sé* near the top of the Ladeira da Sé and opposite the Igreja da Sé, or the restaurant on the opposite side of the road just a little further down the hill.

For some action on Friday and Saturday nights further up the coast from old Olinda go to the bar-restaurant *Ciranda de Dona Duda* on Janga beach. On Tuesday nights after 9 pm head for the Milagres beach near the centre of Olinda where there is a *feira* – local folk music show – and a vegetable and crafts market. There's also a small craft market on Saturday nights in front of the fort on Pau Amarelo beach (the fort itself is also worth visiting). Frequent buses connect the various beaches with Olinda.

Getting Around

The Rodoviária is at the junction of Av Sul and Cais de Santa Rita almost opposite the fort of Cinco Pontas.

Buses between the airport and the centre leave from Nosso Senhora do Carmo church, take about 30 minutes and cost US$0.35. Taxis cost just over US$2 during the day but double at night. The drivers use the meters without having to be reminded.

To get to Olinda from the centre of Recife you need to take a bus from outside the main post office, which is at the junction of Rua do Sol and Ponte Duarte Coelho. None of them have Olinda in the window or on their destination sign so you need to ask. The route they take to Olinda goes down the Rua do Hospicio past the Parque 13 de Maio so you can also pick them up here. The fare is about US$0.15. Ask other passengers where to get off because it's not very obvious (tell them you want 'Olinda Turistico').

Rio de Janeiro

A million words have been written about Rio and will continue to be written. Scenically it's the most beautiful city in the world; a place that is simply beyond compare. Who has not seen pictures of the Sugar Loaf mountain rising out of Guanabara Bay flanked by curving white-sand beaches? Who has never heard of Copacabana or the Girl from Ipanema? Even famous bank robbers come here to spend their ill-gotten gains. And who has not dreamed of looking out from the summit of Corcovado at night over the billions of twinkling lights some 700 metres below? It is magnificent!

Even the pollution (which can be bad at times) and the ever-present threat of having your towel (and everything else) stolen from under you while you lie on the beach still somehow doesn't seem to matter too much. Rio really is the icing on the cake of any visit to Brazil.

Rio is one of the most densely populated areas in the world. All those skyscrapers which sprawl for over 20 km along the waterfront are crammed into a narrow strip between the island-studded waters of Guanabara Bay or the Atlantic Ocean and the lush green mountains which rise up abruptly behind them. Yet there always seems to be space for shady plazas, palm-lined promenades and delightful, carefully preserved old colonial buildings and churches. Of course, the number of restaurants, bars, discotheques and clubs are legion. Rio never stops – it throbs night and day. Indeed it's like an endless carnival. You'll love it!

Guanabara Bay was discovered by the Portuguese navigator, Gonçalo Coelho, in 1502, but was first settled by the French in 1555. Twelve years of rivalry ensued between the two nations until the French were finally thrown out in 1567 by Estácio de Sá and his uncle, Mem de Sá. The new city which was founded grew rapidly despite Indian opposition and was chosen as the capital of the southern provinces when Brazil was divided in two by the Portuguese king, Sebastião. Except for a short period from 1576 to 1608 when Salvador was the sole capital, Rio remained the southern capital until 1763 when it became the seat of the viceroy. After independence was declared in 1834, Rio was declared the nation's capital, a position it maintained until 1960 when Brasília was completed. Its present population verges on seven million, making it the second largest city in Brazil, topped only by São Paulo.

Information

The State Tourist Office (tel 221 8422), the Municipal Tourist Office (tel 232 4320), *Riotur* (tel 232 4320) and *Cebitur* (tel 273 9592) are all at Rua da Assembléia 10 on the 7th, 8th and 9th floors. In addition there is *Embratur*, Rua Matriz e Barros 13 (9th floor) (tel 273 2212). From all these places you can obtain information and maps. Make sure you pick up a free copy of that particular month's *Riotur* booklet which is in Portuguese and English and represents the combined efforts of all the above agencies.

There is also a branch tourist office at the Novo Rio Rodoviária but it's not much use because all they have is a very basic *Visitor's Guide and Tourist Map* on which are marked only the main roads and the location of the ritziest hotels.

The Touring Club do Brasil is at Rua Gen Severiano 201, Botafogo (tel 295 7440 ext 331). There's a good range of information and English is spoken.

The *Riotur* booklet probably contains all the information you're likely to need for a short stay but if you contemplate staying for two or more weeks it's worth thinking about buying one of the more detailed guides available. The best of these are *The Insider's Guide to Rio de Janeiro* by Christopher Pickard (in English, about US$6.75) and/or the *Guia Rio* (mainly in Portuguese with an English section, about US$3). The latter is published annually by Guia Quatro Rodas who also publish guides to the whole of Brazil, São Paulo, the southern states and a camping guide. The *Guia Rio* contains a comprehensive A to Z street guide with index.

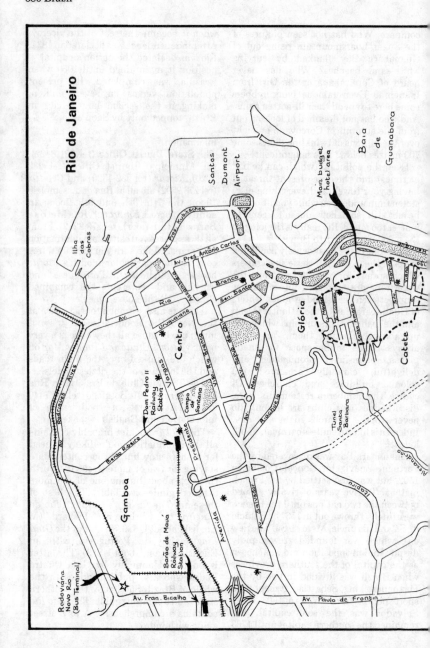

Rio de Janeiro

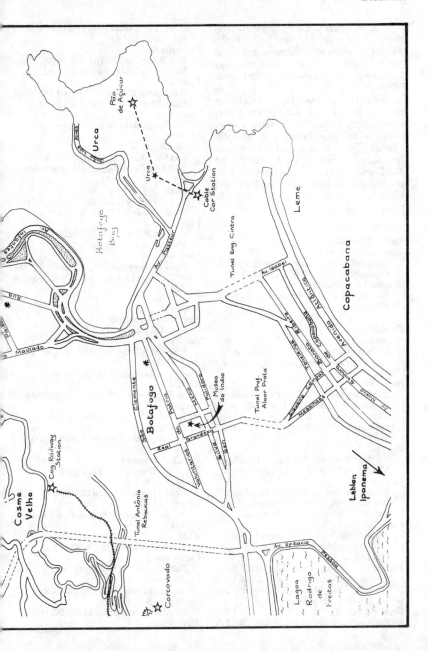

To know where you are going in Rio you need a good map. The best by far is the *Plano da Cidade Rio de Janeiro* published by Schaeffer. It's available at most bookshops and news-stands and costs US$0.40.

Probably the best place to change money is at one or other of the travel agents along Av Rio Branco. Rates vary so check a few out before you actually change. The cambio at Av Rio Branco 33 has been recommended. *Exprinter*, Av Rio Branco 57, is said to be the best place to change travellers' cheques. Also good rates at *Inta Turismo*, Avenida Copacabana 226.

Useful Addresses
American Express
    Kontik-Franstur, Av Atlantica 2316, Copacabana (tel 237 7778/257 7891).
Wagons-Lits Cooks
    Exprinter, Av Rio Branco 57 (tel 253 2552).

Consulates
Argentina
    Praia de Botafogo 242 (6th floor) (tel 551 5498). Open Monday to Friday 12 noon to 5 pm.
Australia
    Rua Voluntários da Pátria 45 (5th floor), Botafogo (tel 286 7922). Open Monday to Thursday 8 am to 12.30 pm and 1.30 to 4.30 pm and on Fridays from 8 am to 1 pm and 2 to 3.45 pm.
Bolivia
    Av Rui Barbosa 664 (tel 551 1796). Open Monday to Friday from 8 am to 1 pm.
Canada
    Edificio Argentina, Praia de Botafogo 228 (tel 551 2542). Open Monday to Friday from 8 to 10.30 am and 1.30 to 4 pm.
Chile
    Praia do Flamengo 382 (Room 401) (tel 205 2496). Open Monday to Friday 8.30 am to 2.30 pm.
France
    Av Pres Antonio Carlos 58 (6th floor) (tel 210 1272). Open Monday to Friday 8.30 am to 1 pm and 2.30 to 5 pm.
Great Britain
    Praia do Flamengo 284 (2nd floor) (tel 225

7252). Open Monday to Friday 9 am to 12 noon and 2 to 4 pm.
Netherlands
    Rua Sorocaba 570 (tel 246 4050). Open Monday to Friday 9 am to 12 noon.
Paraguay
    Rua Carmo 20 (Room 1208) (tel 242 6296). Open Monday to Friday 9 am to 1 pm.
Peru
    Av Rui Barbosa 314 (2nd floor) (tel 551 6296).
South Africa
    Rua Voluntários da Pátria 45 (6th floor) (tel 266 6246). Open Monday to Friday 9 am to 4 pm.
Uruguay
    Rua Arthur Bernardes 30 (tel 225 00089). Open Monday to Friday 9 am to 1 pm.
USA
    Av Pres Wilson 147 (tel 292 7117). Open Monday to Friday 8 am to 5 pm.
Venezuela
    Praia de Botafogo 242 (5th floor) (tel 551 5097). Open Monday to Friday 8.30 am to 1.30 pm.

Airlines
Aerolíneas Argentinas
    Rua São José 40 (tel 224 9242).
AeroPeru
    Praça Mahatma Gandhi 2 (tel 240 0722).
Air France
    Av Rio Branco 257 (tel 220 3666).
Alitalia
    Av Pres Antonio Carlos 40 (tel 240 1005).
Avianca
    Rua Mexico 11/C (tel 240 4413).
British Airways
    Av Almirante Barroso 6 s/2006 (tel 220 1014).
British Caledonian
    Av Rio Branco 251-B (tel 221 0922).
Cruzeiro do Sul
    Av Rio Branco 128 (tel 224 0522).
Japan Air Lines
    Av Rio Branco 108 (9th floor) (tel 262 4366).
KLM
    Av Rio Branco 311/A (tel 210 1342).
LAN-Chile
    Rua São José 70 (8th floor) (tel 221 2882).
Lufthansa
    Av Rio Branco 156/D (tel 262 1022).
South African Airways
    Av Almirante Barroso 22 (tel 262 6002).
Transbrasil

Av Calógeras 30/C (tel 240 8722).

Varig

Av Rio Branco 277 (tel 292 6600).

Vasp

Rua Santa Luzia 735 (tel 292 2080).

Viasa

Rua do Carmo 7 (4th floor) (tel 224 5345).

Things to See

Two of Rio's biggest attractions are, of course, visits to the top of Pão de Açúcar (Sugar Loaf) and Corcovado. The view from the summit of either is an unforgettable experience whether by day or night.

To get to the top of **Pão de Açúcar** you must take the cable car (there's no road) from Av Pasteur 520. To get there from the city centre or Flamengo take bus No 107. From Copacabana, Ipanema or Leblon take bus No 511. Cable cars go up every 30 minutes from 8 am until 9.30 pm. The last car down is at 10 pm. The return fare is US$2.45. The journey up to the top is in two stages with a change at Urca, where there's a restaurant with million dollar views, rip-off prices and niggardly servings, so bite back the temptation to eat there. Do, however, check out if there's a rock band playing in the auditorium next to the restaurant. There's usually entertainment there on Friday, Saturday and Sunday nights though the music doesn't usually start until 10 pm. What a great place to dance all night! There is also a samba show on Monday nights from 9 pm to 1 am. It costs US$6 including the cable car fare. Right at the top of Sugar Loaf there's only a snack bar.

To the top of **Corcovado** you have a choice of the cog railway or taxi. The cog railway station is at Rua Cosme Velho 513 and there are trains up to the summit every half hour or hour depending on demand. It's a beautiful 20 minute journey through lush forest and is very steep in parts – definitely not to be missed. The fare is US$1.85 return. Outside the cog railway station the taxi drivers will besiege you with offers of hiring the car 'for the day' for about US$2.05. This is pretty good value if there is a group of you but remember that each vehicle which goes up to the top is also charged US$1.70 entry fee so you must add this to the bill. Resist the temptation to walk to the top as there's a very good chance you'll be robbed. There are restaurants and snack bars at the summit.

Corcovado, like Sugar Loaf, is a photographer's paradise but if you don't want Niteroi on the other side of Guanabara Bay and the incredible 14 km long Costa e Silva Bridge to disappear in the smog which regularly shrouds Rio then choose a clear day. The transparencies which you can buy on Sugar Loaf and Corcovado are not cheap and the colour is poor.

To get to the cog railway station from other parts of Rio you can take local bus Nos 108, 422, 497, 498, 569, 583 and 584. All these should be labelled 'C Velho' though this is sometimes combined with another destination such as 'C Velho/ Leblon' (No 583/584) or 'Machado/Leblon' (No 569). If you're staying in the budget hotel area a lot of these buses can be picked up along Av Rio Branco/Rua Da Glória/Rua do Catete/Largo do Machado/ Rua das Laranjeiras.

Rio, of course, is the playground of Brazil and its **beaches** are world famous. Sweeping round south-east from the city centre there are Flamengo, Botafogo, Leme, Copacabana, Ipanema and Leblon with the latter two being the quieter and less crowded of them. Theft and robbery, however, is a big problem. Don't go to any of these beaches with anything you want to see again. Don't go alone and never take valuables or cameras with you – you'll just be inviting trouble. Gangs of children and youths work these beaches everyday and you'll come across other travellers who have rocked down there without a care in the world and literally been stripped down to their bathers. You

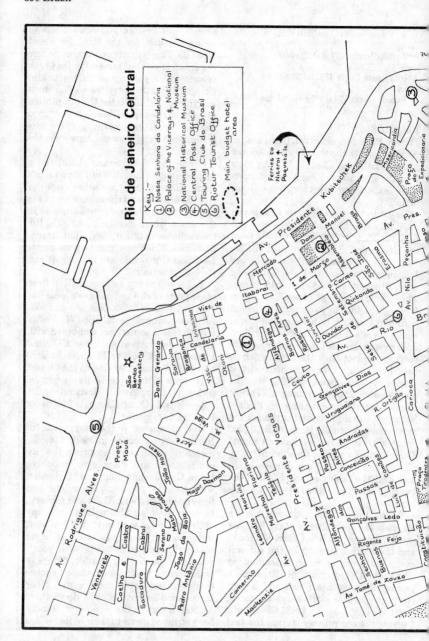

Rio de Janeiro Central

Key:-
① Nossa Senhora da Candelária
② Palace of the Viceroys & National Museum
③ National Historical Museum
✝ Central Post Office
⑤ Touring Club do Brasil
⑥ Riotur Tourist Office
⑥ Main budget hotel area

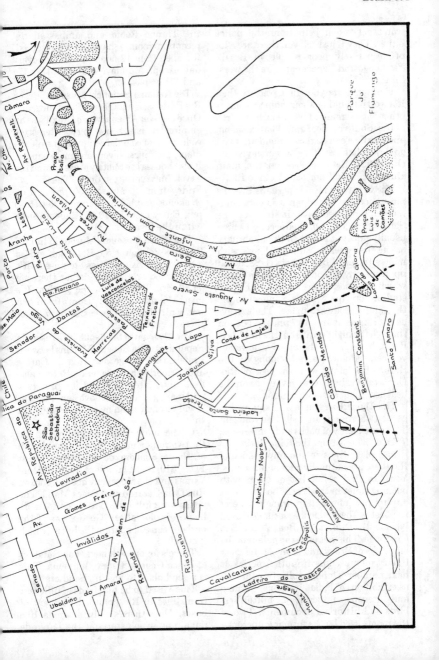

won't get much help from the police either. They'll just tell you there are a lot of desperately poor people in Brazil. Flamengo and Copacabana are the worst for this.

If beaches are your first priority then it's worth thinking about going to one or other of the smaller towns south or north of Rio. South of Rio, **Parati, Ilha Jaguanum** and **Ilha Bela** can be recommended. If you go down that way it's also worth visiting the **Itatiaia National Park** on the main Dutra highway from São Paulo to Rio.

The **Carnaval** in Rio is perhaps Brazil's most spectacular though it is very commercialised these days. It starts on the Saturday before Ash Wednesday (which usually falls in the last week of February or the first week of March). Those with money to spend buy tickets (US$20 and up from any branch of *Banerij* bank) which entitle them to entry to the stadium on Rua Maquis Sapucai to see the samba groups compete. The extravaganza starts at around 7 pm and goes on through the night until 9 am the next day. If you haven't got the money, however, you can watch the parades along Av Rio Branco free along with the rest of Rio. Don't take valuables with you – as on the beaches, robberies are common.

The **Tijuca Forest** is a 120 square km garden where you can easily lose yourself. There are plenty of paths and some roads. Take a 233 bus from the Rodoviaria.

In a place the size and importance of Rio there are naturally a lot of museums. You can find a full list of them with opening times in the *Riotur* booklet or at any tourist information branch. One of the best is **The National Museum** (Museu Nacional), Ouinta da Boa Vista, São Cristóvão. This was once the palace of the emperors of Brazil and is one of the most important museums in South America. It has a number of foreign collections as well as exhibitions of Indian weapons, clothing and utensils, mineralogy, butterflies, birds and historical documents. Two of the rooms used by the former emperors –

the Throne Room and ambassadorial reception room – have been preserved. It's open from 12 noon to 4.45 pm every day except Monday. Bus Nos 472, 474 and 475 go past it.

The **National Historical Museum**, Praça Rui Barbosa, is another excellent museum. Once the War Arsenal when Brazil was an empire, it has some very interesting collections of colonial sculpture, furniture, maps, paintings, silverware and weapons. It also houses the **Military Museum** and the **Naval Museum**. It's open Tuesday to Friday from 10 am to 5.30 pm and on weekends and holidays from 2.30 to 5.30 pm. Entry costs US$0.10. Bags must be left in the foyer.

The **Indian Museum** (Museu do Indio), Rua das Palmeiras 55, Botafogo, is also well worth a visit. It's easy to miss as it's not marked on the outside but there's a small Brazilian flag in the garden. It's open Monday to Friday from 10 am to 5 pm. Entry is free. The easiest way to get there is via the metro.

The **Museum of the Republic** (Museu da Republica), Rua Silveira Martins between Praia do Flamengo and Rua do Catete and formerly the Palacio do Catete also used to be interesting but it's presently undergoing compete renovation. Perhaps it will be open again by the time you read this.

Of the many religious buildings in Rio the two you shouldn't miss are the church of **Nossa Senhora da Candelária** (built 1775-1810) in the middle of Av Presidente Vargas and the **Monastery of São Bento** on Rua Dom Gerardo near Praça Mauá. The latter was built in 1641 and is a treasure house of colonial art. Good views of the harbour can be had from the hill on which it stands.

There's an **open-air market** on Sundays at Praça General Osorio, Ipanema. This is a good place to pick up handicrafts.

There used to be hundreds of different tram lines in Rio before the advent of buses. Now there's only a single line remaining which starts at the Largo de

Carioca and goes to either Dois Irmãos or Santa Teresa. It's a colourful trip and worth the effort.

Football fans should check out the Maracama Stadium. Match day is expensive at US$8 but there are usually two or three matches. There's also a (free) sport museum here.

Places to Stay

There are quite a few cheap places between the main Dom Pedro II railway station and the old aqueduct which crosses Rua da Lapa and Av Mém de Sá in the Lapa district between the centre and

Rio de Janeiro Metro

Linha 2

Linha 1

Irajá
Inhaúma
Del Castilho
Saens Peña
S.F. Xavier
Alfonso Pena
Mª da Graça
Maracaná
São Cristovão
Estacão
Praça Onze
Central
Pres. Vargas
Uruguaiana
Carioca
Cinelândia
Glória
Catete
Largo do Machado
Morro Azul
Botafogo

Glória but they're very run-down, the area is pretty rough, and you won't meet many other travellers there. They're also not much cheaper (if at all) than the area further south.

Most travellers stay in the Glória/Catete/Flamengo area between the centre of the city and Botafogo. Naturally everyone has their own favourite but there's definitely a consensus of opinion (including my own) which rates the *Hotel Turístico*, Ladeira da Glória 30 (tel 225 9388), as the best in Rio. It's right opposite the beach-side entrance/exit of Glória metro station slightly up the hill between two restaurants whose tables and chairs spill out onto the sidewalk. It's excellent value, very friendly indeed, totally secure, spotlessly clean and housed in a charming old building with small balconies. It costs US$2.70/$4.25 a single/double without own bathroom and US$3.35/$5.60 a single/double with own bathroom. There's hot water in all the showers. Prices include breakfast. The owner is Senhor Antonio – a former Galician from Spain who (naturally) speaks Spanish as well as Portuguese. If it's full, make a reservation for later in the week. It's very popular with travellers and Brazilians alike.

Coming out of the other side of Glória metro station and walking one block down towards the city is Rua Candido Mendes where there are two other very popular travellers' hotels. The first is the *Hotel Monte Castelo*, Rua Candido Mendes 201. This costs US$2.90/$3.20 a single/double without own bath and US$3.45/$3.85/$4.60 a single/double/triple with own bathroom. The staff are very friendly and prices include coffee in the morning.

A few doors down the street is the *Hotel Candido Mendes*, Rua Candido Mendes 117. This is a very clean, modern place and rooms cost US$3.40/$5.10 a single/double with own bathroom. Most of the rooms are air-conditioned. It's often full so get there early. On the same street is

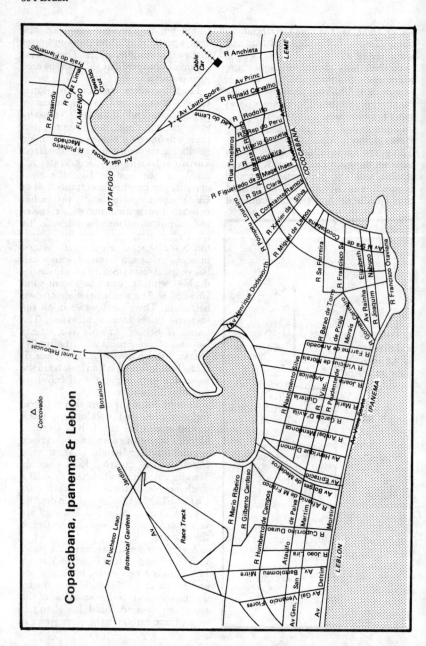

Copacabana, Ipanema & Leblon

the *Hotel Ve Mar*, Rua Candido Mendes 44. This isn't such good value as the rooms tend to be on the gloomy side. There are no singles and doubles cost US$5.95 with air-conditioning.

If you're looking for something considerably cheaper in this area then right outside the Glória metro station is the *Hotel Benjamin Constant*, Rua Benjamin Constant 10. It's very basic and has a 10 am checkout time (most places are 11 am or 12 noon) but it does cost just US$1.35 per person without coffee in the morning.

Further down towards Botafogo either on or off Rua do Catete and close to Catete metro station there are many more hotels popular with travellers (and with overland tour companies). Three of the cheaper ones are: *Hotel Hispano Brasileiro*, Rua Silveira Martins 135, a pleasant place but with no single rooms, doubles without bath are US$4.30 plus there are doubles with own bath for US$4.25 to $5.35 all including breakfast; *Hotel Mengo*, Rua Correa Dutra 31, good value at US$3.40/$4.75 a single/double without own bath and US$5.10/$6.80 a single/double with own bath and air-conditioning all including breakfast; *Hotel Ferreira Viana*, Rua Ferreira Viana 58, which is very good value, clean and modern with singles/doubles for US$3.50/$4.70 without own bath and US$5.45 a double with own bath. All prices include breakfast.

Somewhat more expensive but in the same area is the *Unico Hotel*, Rua Buarque de Macedo 54 (tel 205 9932). This is a clean modern place and the management are friendly and eager to please. All the rooms have their own hot showers, TV, piped music and air-conditioning and cost US$6.50 a double. The prices include breakfast. There are no single rooms.

Others you might like to try in this area are the *Hotel Caxambo*, Rua Correa Dutra 22, an old hotel with doubles for US$3.15 without own bath (no singles without bath) and rooms with own bath

for US$3.15/$4.50 to $6.80 a single/double all including breakfast; *Hotel Cambuquira*, Rua Correa Dutra 31, a very modern hotel where all rooms have their own bath and cost US$5.95/$8.90 a single/double including breakfast; and the *Rondonia Hotel*, Rua Buarque de Macedo 58, which has rooms without own bath for US$5.10/$6.30 a single/double and rooms with own bath for US$6.80 a double. All the rooms in the last hotel have air-conditioning, TV and the prices include coffee in the morning.

On the Rua do Catete itself try the *Hotel Victoria*, Rua do Catete 172. This is an old place which has increased its prices by doing little more than putting carpets down on the floor but it's reasonable value at US$3.40 a single without own bath and US$3.90 a single, US$4.75 to US$5.45 a double and US$7.65 a triple all with own bath. There's hot water in the bathrooms. In the same block is the more expensive *Hotel Monte Blanco*, Rua do Catete 160 (tel 225 0121). This hotel has been completely refurbished and all the rooms have their own bath and air-conditioning. It costs US$5.10/$5.95/$6.40 a single/double/triple. There's a garage for those with their own transport.

In Copacabana, the *Copalinda* at Copacabana 956, has been recommended. The cost is US$9 per night which includes a substantial breakfast. It's only one block from the beach. The staff are friendly and there's hot water 24 hours a day. Each room has a safe inside the cupboard so you can lock up your valuables.

Outside the ones already covered there are a few places which have been recommended in the past but which we haven't had any news about for some time. They may be worth checking out. They include the *Casa de Estudante Universitário*, Av Rui Barbosa 762, Botafogo, (take your own bedding); and the house at Rua Almirante Gomes Ferreira 86, Urca, at the bottom of the Sugar Loaf mountain. The latter is for women only and it's only open to visitors in January, February and July.

If you'd like somewhere really special to stay outside the city then head for the unusual and interesting hotel *Fazenda São João*, outside Novo Friburgo (tel 0245 42 1304). Look for the sign on the right as you reach Km 29 after Cachoeira de Macacu. From there it is another 11 km along a winding laterite mountain road. Cars with careful drivers just about make it; otherwise you can hire horses from the Garlipp Hotel or walk and hitch. The Fazenda is run by Elizabeth and Horst Garlipp. It's a Hansel-and-Gretel house where 18 kinds of hummingbird visit the gardens. Elizabeth grows orchids and there's free riding, swimming, sauna and tennis.

Places to Eat

As in most Brazilian cities, lunch time is *lanch* time and there are thousands of places which do these set meals. In the centre itself head for Cinelandia (close to the metro station of the same name) or anywhere along Uruguaiana. There are also many restaurants in the streets between Uruguaiana and Av Rio Branco. Get there earlier rather than later because they get incredibly busy. Vegetarians should try the restaurant on the corner of Rua Santa Luzia and Mexico – it's only open for food at lunch times, at weekends it's a gay disco. Another recommended vegetarian restaurant is the *Superbom* at Largo São Francisco 34.

Along the Rio do Catete close to the junction with Rua Correa Dutra try the *KTT*, Rua do Catete 202A. You either like this place or you don't (it gets a very varied response from travellers). It's a bit grubby but is good value. They also have special *churrasquinho* with chips and two fried eggs for US$1 which is excellent value. If you don't like the place then try the *Rio Galicia* also on Rua do Catete near the Hotel Victoria. It's been recommended by several travellers. In the Glória area try *Hobbies* between Rua Candido Mendes and Rua Benjamin Constant.

If you're trying to economise, *Rics* fast food chain has been recommended. There's one on Av Alvarino and you can get steak, egg and chips for US$1.

In the evenings for those staying in the Glória area, the restaurant at the junction of Rua Candido Mendes and Rua da Glória is popular. The food is excellent, the service quick and the waiters friendly. Meals cost about twice the price of a *lanch*. The two restaurants on either side of the Ladeira da Glória at the beginning of Rua do Catete and right next to the Glória metro entrance are somewhat more expensive but they are very popular especially for drinks until midnight.

If you're in the Copacabana area at night there is plenty of choice in the streets between the Av Atlantica (the road which goes along the beach) and Av Nossa Senhora de Copacabana. Obviously, the restaurants on the beach front itself tend to be more expensive since you're paying for the real estate and the views but at the back you can find some surprisingly cheap restaurants as well as some very expensive ones.

Nightlife

There are a thousand and one things to do in the evenings but much will depend on your budget. The Cinelandia area (near the metro station of the same name) rages all night. Here there are hundreds of bars, some of them with music or some sort of show. It's especially of interest to gay people. A gay men's bar which has been recommended is *La Bohemia* which has excellent drag shows at 2 am on Saturdays nights. Entry costs about US$1. There's also a good choice of movie houses in this area which generally have the latest releases from North America and Europe. Prices are very reasonable.

Over in Copacabana the Av Atlantica comes alive in the evening with hawkers selling all manner of things from T-shirts to jewellery to roasted peanuts. Without doubt the most popular of the discotheques here is *HELP*, Av Atlantica 3432. There are live bands every night from 10 pm until dawn. Entry costs about US$4.25. You better turn out your best jeans and shirt if you're thinking of going – there are some very ritzy people gliding into this place.

Another disco which is very popular is *Regine's* underneath the Meridien Hotel, Av Atlantica 1020. It's also worth checking if there are bands playing at the halfway cable car station on Morro da Urca at weekends.

A gay womens' bar which has been recommended is *Zig Zooq*, Rua Bartholomew Mitre in Leblon. It's actually a mixed men and womens' bar but there are far more women than men there. It's very friendly and worth visiting even by straight people.

The English pub *Lord Jim's* in Copacabana has also been recommended.

Getting There & Around

Airports Santos Dumont Airport adjacent to the centre of the city is used exclusively for the Rio-São Paulo shuttle service. All other internal and international flights use Galeão International Airport on Governador Island about 16 km from the city centre. There is a C-5 bus (with 'Galeão on the direction sign) every half hour between Santos Dumont Airport and the International Airport. It costs US$0.60 and takes about 30 minutes. You can also pick up this bus outside the front of the Novo Rio Rodoviária.

Bus All long-distance buses arrive and depart from Novo Rio Rodoviária, Av Francisco Bicalho. This is quite a way from the centre of town in the Novo Cristo area so you'll need to get a local bus or taxi to wherever it is you want to go.

The local buses depart from their own terminus at the back of the Rodoviário on Rua Ecuador. At each bus stop there's a map of the route which the bus takes so it's easy to find the one you want.

If you're heading for Copacabana, Ipanema or Leblon then (depending on where exactly you want to go) you need Nos 126 (Pinheiro Machado/Praça de Botafogo/da Passagen/Princesa Isabel/ Barata Ribeira/Raul Pompéia); 127 (Praça Mauá/Rio Branco/Parque do Flamengo/Tonelero/Epit Pessoa/Gen San Martín); 136 (Pres Vargas/Tiradentes/ Praia do Flamengo/Tunel Velho/ Copacabana Poto 5); 172 (Praça Mauá/ Rio Branco/Praia do Flamengo/Praça de Botafogo/Jardim Botanico/Visc de Albuquerque); or 173 (Tunel Santa Barbara/Pinheiro Machado/Jardim Botanico/Jockey Club/Visc de Albuquerque). There's also a luxury air-conditioned bus which goes direct to Copacabana, Ipanema and Leblon (without stopping at intermediate places) from immediately outside the back of the Rodoviária.

If you're heading for the budget hotel area (Glória/Catete) then you can only take the No 170 (Praça Mauá/Rio Branco/ Glória/Largo do Machado, Sáo Clemente/ Jardim Botanico/Jockey Club). This is the only one which will take you down the Rua do Catete via Glória. You can also use any of the buses mentioned which go via the Av Rio Branco *but you must get off at the end of Rio Branco* and then take the Metro either one station (Glória), two stations (Catete) or three stations (Largo do Machado). If you don't get off at the end of Rio Branco on these buses then they go all the way down the Praia do Flamengo to Praça de Botafogo before stopping again. If you get caught out this way, take the Metro back and get off where you want to be along Rua do Catete.

Rio is a big place and using public buses is very time-consuming. Where possible, use the Metro instead. In the evenings, if you're staying in the Glória area and want to go to Copacabana/Ipanema/Leblon, think seriously about taking a taxi. You'll save heaps of time and hassle.

Metro Rio has an excellent underground railway (Metro) with two lines which meet at *Estação*. It's a pity it's not more extensive. It runs Mondays to Saturdays from 6 am to 11 pm but is closed on Sundays. Tickets are a bargain at US$0.10 per journey (any number of stops) or US$1.10 for a book of 12 tickets.

Train The main railway station in Rio is Estação Dom Pedro II on the Av Pres Vargas. On the Metro line you need 'Central' station. You'll probably only use this station if you are going to or coming from São Paulo on the train.

Boat The ferry station (*Estação das Barcas*) is at the back of the Av Pres Kubitschek flyover at the junction with Rua 7 de Setembro. There are ferries to both Niteroi (across the other side of Guanabara Bay) and to Paqueta Island. To Paqueta Island there is a choice of ordinary boat and jet boat (like the ones between Hong Kong and Macau).

The jet boats (*Aerobarcos*) only operate on Saturdays, Sundays and public holidays and costs US$1.35 one-way. They leave Rio every half hour (except at 12.30 and 1 pm) from 9.30 am to 4.30 pm. In the opposite direction they leave Paqueta every half hour (except at 12 noon and 12.30 pm) between 9 am and 4.30 pm.

The ordinary ferries run everyday. They depart Rio eight times daily between 5.30 am and 11 pm and Paqueta between 5.30 am and 8.30 pm. On Sundays there is no ferry at 5.30 am from either end. On this day the first ferry from Rio is at 7.10 am and from Paqueta at 7 am. The fare is a few cents and the journey takes 70 to 90 minutes.

There is no fixed schedule as such for the ordinary ferries to Niteroi – they leave when full. This is no problem, however, as there are at least 100 sailings in each 24 hour period (the ferries go all night and all day). The fare is a few cents and the journey takes about 30 minutes.

Salvador

A traveller once wrote-in describing Salvador as 'a slum without Rio's scenic grandeur'. Slums there certainly are, as well as heaps of rotting refuse and an ever-changing pastiche of odours both revolting and exquisite, but most travellers would probably agree that 'faded tropical elegance' is a kinder and more accurate description of this city. And 'slum' certainly doesn't describe the ritzy suburbs which stretch for miles all along the Atlantic coast or the beautiful beaches you'll find both here and on the island of Itaparica. Whichever description you prefer, Salvador is still one of Brazil's most interesting cities.

It's interesting partly because of its very mixed population. Here you'll see every shape, size and colour of people imaginable with a large proportion of black and *mestiço*. The cultural mix shows in the flowery white lace dresses of the Bahian women, the black youths in their Rasta colours, the music coming from the bars, the heavily pagan-influenced religious ceremonies and the colourful and riotous fiestas. It's also interesting because until 1763 it was the capital of Brazil and the old part of the city is full of fascinating old churches and monasteries, mansions, elegant townhouses and leafy squares connected by narrow cobbled streets. Some areas definitely have an air of prolonged neglect but others have been restored and are home to a wide variety of lively and rustic bars and restaurants.

The old part of town is divided into two parts – the Baixa, or lower part alongside the bay, which contains the commercial district and the docks; and the Alta, or upper part, which is built on a small plateau some 70 metres high overlooking the lower part of the city and the bay. It's on this plateau that most of the colonial buildings are to be found. The modern city spreads out to the east over the rest of the peninsula and has excellent roads linking its various parts. The population is about 1.5 million making it the fifth largest city in Brazil.

Information

The main tourist office is in the Belvedere da Sé next to the Praça da Sé. It's one of the best in Brazil, open daily from 8 am to 6.30 pm and the staff are very helpful. They have excellent maps of Salvador which cover the whole of the city and cost US$1.

Also make sure you get hold of their leaflets (in English or Portuguese): 'Bahia Tours', 'Bahia Praias e Ilhas' and the twice weekly 'Bahia Eventos'. The first has well thought-out itineraries for two-day, four-day and six-day tours of the main tourist areas of Salvador and nearby beaches and islands. The second specialises in describing the island of Itaparica and its beaches as well as the beaches of the Atlantic coast. The last publication is self-explanatory.

There are branches of the tourist office at the Rodoviária (also very good and open daily from 9 am to 9 pm), at the airport (open 9 am to 11 pm or later if there are still flights arriving after that), and at the Pôrto da Barra, Praça Anchieta (open Monday and Wednesday to Saturday from 8.30 to 11 am and 2 to 5.30 pm).

Salomão Fainstein, Av Estados Unidos 379, is one of the best places to change cash and travellers' cheques – better rates than the banks, or try the furniture shop on the same street.

If you arrive in Salvador (by bus or air) late at night it's worth considering taking a taxi to a specific hotel. The Praça da Sé and surrounding area is not a place to be wandering around late at night encumbered with a rucksack. Policing has been stepped up lately but you never know.

The Elevator & the Plano Inclinado Between the Baixa and the Alta of the old town there is both an elevator (on the Praça Municipal) and two steel cable operated cars (one behind the Cathedral on the Praça da Sé and the other further along). The elevator seems to be open at all hours everyday. The Planos Inclinados are only open Monday to Friday from 6 am to 8 am and on Saturdays from 6 am to 1 pm. The fare on either the elevator or the Plano Inclinado is just half a cent! It is not advisable to walk down the steep roads between the two parts of the city especially at night. You'll probably be robbed. Even during the day Brazilians will stop and warn you if they see you doing this.

Things to See

You need to spend some time in Salvador if you want to see it properly – several days at least plus however long you have in mind for spending on the beaches.

The main colonial part of town with its old churches, monasteries and museums stretches from the **Museum of Sacred Art** close to the Praça Castro Alves, along the Rua Chile and Rua da Misericórdia to the Praça da Sé and the Praça 15 de Novembro then down the Rua Alfredo de Brito, through the Praça Pelourinho and up the Rua Luiz Vianna Filho on the far side to the Largo do Carmo. Apart from one or two old churches at Boa Viagem and Ribeira you will see just about everything if you spend a couple of days strolling around this area.

The **Museu de Arte Sacra da Bahia** (housed in the 17th century Convent of Santa Teresa), at the junction of Ladeira de Santa Teresa and Rua do Sodré, is excellent both for its contents and the building itself and shouldn't be missed. It's been completely and very carefully restored and the exhibits are excellently displayed. It's open Monday to Saturday from 10 am to 12 noon and 2 to 5.30 pm and the entry fee is US$0.30.

Further along on the Praça Anchieta, which is a continuation slightly downhill of the Praça 15 de Novembro, you should visit the **Igreja de São Francisco** to see a prime example of golden baroque excess (open Monday to Saturday from 8 to

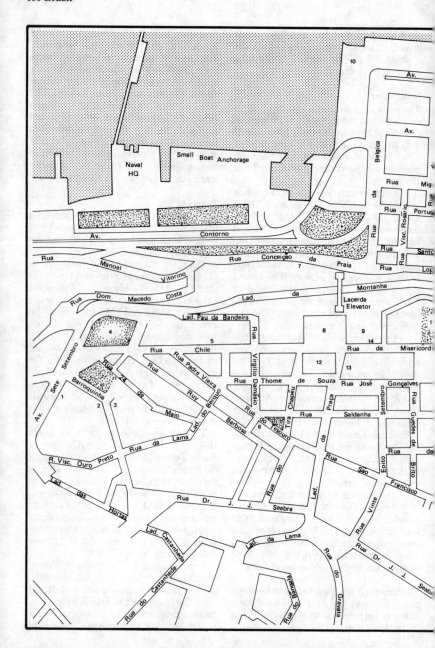

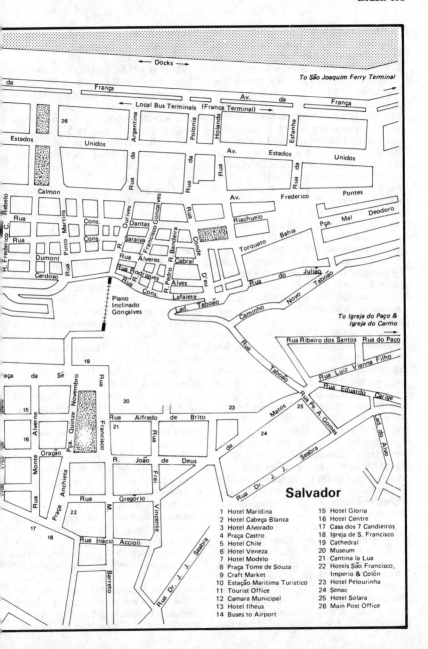

Salvador

1 Hotel Maridina
2 Hotel Cabeça Blanca
3 Hotel Alvorado
4 Praça Castro
5 Hotel Chile
6 Hotel Veneza
7 Hotel Modelo
8 Praça Tome de Souza
9 Craft Market
10 Estação Marítima Turístico
11 Tourist Office
12 Camara Municipal
13 Hotel Ilheus
14 Buses to Airport
15 Hotel Gloria
16 Hotel Centre
17 Casa dos 7 Candieiros
18 Igreja de S. Francisco
19 Cathedral
20 Museum
21 Cantina la Lua
22 Hotels São Francisco,
   Imperio & Colón
23 Hotel Pelourinha
24 Senac
25 Hotel Solara
26 Main Post Office

11.30 am and 2 to 5.30 pm and all day on Tuesday); and the **Igreja da Venerável Ordem Terceira de São Francisco** next door to it, which is open the same hours except on Saturdays when it's only open in the mornings.

Up on Largo do Carmo you shouldn't miss the **Igreja e Museu do Carmo** part of which is a hotel these days. The museum itself isn't particularly well organised. It's insufficiently lit and there's rather too many Mother Mary and Baby Jesus dolls littering the place but the building itself is interesting even if it is in a bad state of repair. There's a small entry charge. On the Praça 15 de Novembro there are also two museums which are worth visiting – the **Museu da Cidade** and the **Museu Abelardo Rodrigues**.

For crafts, curios and Bahian clothing (especially the white lace dresses) browse around the shops along Rua Alfredo de Brito and the Praça Pelourinho. There are some excellent things to be found along here.

Quite a few of the tourist leaflets recommend a visit to the **Mercado Modelo** in the Baixa opposite the Lacerdo elevator. Personally I wouldn't go near it. It's simply too much hassle (it's seen too many tourists) and there's too much gratuitous weirdness being dished out in an attempt to distract your attention and relieve you of your cash.

A market which is worth spending some time in is that at São Joaquim about three km up the coast past the docks and near the São Joaquim ferryboat terminal. It happens every day except Sunday though Saturdays tend to be the best. It has the lot and is one of the cheapest places to buy things in Salvador. Photographers will love this place.

There are scores of excellent beaches and coves all along the Atlantic coast from Barra Point to Itapuã and way beyond. Most of them are lined with restaurants, bars and the houses of the rich. There are surprisingly few hotels and cheap places. You'd either have to ask around, rent a house and share it with other people or commute there from central Salvador.

Check out these beaches by taking the airport bus from the Praça da Sé and get off wherever you like. If you want to camp-out then you'll have to go up to Arembepe or beyond. This last beach had the glitter spread on it by Mick Jagger, Janis Joplin and others. In addition to the Atlantic beaches there are also beaches on the bay side of the peninsula at Boa Viagem and Ribeira.

Outside Salvador it's well worth visiting **Itaparica** island – and possibly staying there. There are some superb beaches around the town of Itaparica and at many other spots on the island. During the week there are very few people on the beaches but at weekends it can get crowded. To get to the island take a local 'S Joaquim' or 'Agua de Meminos' bus from the Av da França terminal to the São Joaquim ferryboat terminal. There are ferries from there, every hour on the hour from 6 am to 10 pm daily, to Bom Despacio on Itaparica. The ferry takes 40 minutes to one hour and costs US$0.25. It's a very pleasant trip. At Bom Despacio you can take either a VW Combi (US$0.25) or a local bus (cheaper) to the town of Itaparica, 15 to 20 minutes. There are also Combis to Mar Grande and other places where there are beaches. Taxis are also available.

The town of Itaparica is a weekend cottage place for rich Salvadorans so there's generally nothing much going on there during the week. The old churches and the fort of São Lourenço are impressive and worth visiting if you can get in but they're usually closed.

As far as places to eat goes it's probably best to go to the basic restaurant in the same plaza as the Cathedral (Matriz do Santissimo Sacramento). The other restaurant, the *Restaurante Balneario*, next to the fort is rosily described in tourist literature as some sort of cordon bleu establishment. It's nothing of the sort.

It's also very expensive and the building is decidedly lacking in imagination. Who in their right mind would build a restaurant right on the beach but without a beach view!? (It's partially sunken).

There is no obvious cheap accommodation in Itaparica. There is, however, the *Hotel Icarei* close to the fort which is very pleasant, has a shady courtyard and its own restaurant. Sited in an old villa it costs US$12.50 a double with own bathroom and including breakfast. Checkout time is 1 pm.

Todos os Santos Bay with its many islands, including Itaparica, is an excellent place to go sailing. If you'd like to do this *Kontik-Franstur* down at the Estação Maritima Turistico (in front of the Mercado Modelo) have several schooners which set off daily at 9 am (according to demand) and return between 5 and 6 pm. They sail first to the Ilha Frades (Ponta de Nossa Senhora) where they stay until 1 pm to allow time for swimming and the like and then cross to Itaparica where they stop for lunch. They leave here at about 5 pm. The cost is US$11.65 per person or US$8.35 if there are more than 15 people on board. Drinks on board are included in the price.

Festivals
As far as festivals go, the **carnival** is obviously the biggest and most boisterous of the lot. It takes place on the Sunday before Lent and ends at midnight (for some) before Ash Wednesday. It's certainly one of the best in Brazil and a lot less commercialised than Rio's, but unfortunately this is becoming less and less true as the years go by.

But the carnival isn't the only festival. There are quite a few others which are just as wild. In the first week of February there is the Festas de Yemanjá, which is of pagan origin honouring the Goddess of the Sea. People take gifts down to the beach at Rio Vermelho and float them out to sea to the accompaniment of much ritual, music and dancing. Another

which is worth seeing if you're in the area at the time is the festival of São João in the third week of June. Bonfires are lit in the streets and people entertain each other in their homes with food and a local liqueur known as *ginepapo*. The festival of Nossa Senhora de Concessão between December 4th and 8th has also been recommended.

Places to Stay
The majority of budget hotels are either on the Praça Anchieta or the streets which lead into this square, and the Praça da Sé. There are a few others down near the bottom of Rua Alfredo de Brito (which there becomes the Rua José de Alencar/Praça Pelourinho) and one or two more in the streets close to the Praça Castro Alves.

One of the most popular is the *Hotel Solar São Francisco*, Praça Anchieta 16A. This is a small place and is excellent value. It's quiet, friendly and secure and costs US$1.65/$3.35 a single/double without own bathroom. Similar, but not quite such good value, is the *Hotel Colon*, Praça Anchieta 20, which costs US$2.50 a single and US$4 to US$5 a double without own bathroom or coffee in the morning.

If both are full you could try the *Hotel Imperio*, Praça Anchieta 14, which costs US$1.65/$2.50 a single/double without own bathroom but note that it has a 9 am checkout (very early!).

Moving off the square itself, there is the *Hotel Glória*, Rua Monte Alverne 11, a very large place where you'll almost certainly get a room. The staff are friendly and it's good value at US$1.65/$2.50 a single/double without own bath and US$2.50/$3.35 a single/double with own bath. Prices include coffee in the morning. Further down the street is the *Hotel Benfica*, Rua Monte Alverne 6, which is about the same standard. It costs US$1.65/$2.50 a single/double without own bath and US$2.15/$3.35 a single/double with own bath; checkout time is 10 am.

The *Pensão Moderna*, Rua Monte Alverne 9, and the *Hotel Jequié*, Rua Saldanha da Gama 14 (US$2.50 a double with own bathroom but no coffee in the morning), can't really be recommended though the latter is probably all right for a night.

Moving to the Praça Castro Alves area, the *Hotel Alvorado*, Ladeira de Barroquinha, is one of the cheapest. It's an old building and very basic but has friendly staff and costs US$1.65 a double without own bathroom. Opposite is the *Hotel Cabeça Blanca*, Ladeira de Barroquinha 15. This is a fairly modern building and clean but it appears to cater mainly for whores and their clients. It costs US$5 a double with own bathroom. There are no singles.

Somewhat more expensive but very good value is the *Hotel Maridina*, 7 de Setembro 6 just off the Praça Castro Alves. It's very clean and well run and costs US$4.15/$5 a single/double without own bathroom and US$6.65/$10 a single/double with own bathroom. All prices include breakfast and checkout time is 10 am.

Around the Praça Tomé de Souza (otherwise known as the Praça Municipal) there are a few other good hotels. Cheapest is the *Hotel Veneza*, Rua do Tesouro 27 facing the small triangular shaped square. It's clean and well-run and costs US$2.50 a double without own bathroom and US$4.15 a double with own bathroom. There are no singles. The *Hotel Ilheus*, Ladeira da Praça 4 very close to the Cámara Municipal (the old palace which faces the Praça Municipal), is fairly priced and the staff are friendly. It costs US$3.35 for a couple (double bed) and US$5 a double (two beds) without own bathroom and US$5 for a couple with own bathroom including breakfast. Checkout time is 10 am.

For a mid-range hotel in the same area try the *Hotel Chile*, Rua Chile 7. This is a large place with some pretensions to being better than it is but quite a few travellers stay here. It costs US$3.65/$6.65 a single/double without own bathroom, US$8.35 a single with own bathroom but without air-conditioning and US$12.50/$14.15 a single/double with own bathroom and air-conditioning. All prices include breakfast.

Down near the bottom of Rua Alfredo de Brito there is the *Hotel Solara*, Rua José de Alencar 25, which is clean and good value at US$4.25 a double without own bathroom but including breakfast. Close by is the *Hotel Pelourinho*, Rua Alfredo de Brito 20. This is a very pleasant two-star hotel created by modernising what was previously a small mansion. For the price it's considerably better value than the Hotel Chile. Rooms, all of which have their own bath, cost US$9.15 a single and US$11 to $12.50 a double including breakfast. You must add tax to all these prices. The hotel has its own restaurant, bar and craft shop, which is very expensive but they're works of art!

There's one other place which is definitely worth considering since it's excellent value. It's a question of whether you can handle living in the red light district in the Baixa. Before you make it the last on your list you should know that it's only a few doors away from the Lacerdo elevator and so no worries even late at night. It's the *Hotel Modelo*, Conceição da Praia 16, on the second and third floors (the stairs are at the end of a short corridor with clothing stores on both sides). It's very clean and secure, towels and soap are provided, there are hot showers and the rooms at the front overlooking the bay are an absolute bargain. It costs US$1.35/$2.50 a single/double without own bath and US$3.35 a double (rear rooms) and US$5.15 a double (front rooms) with own bath. Prices include breakfast but the bread is generally inedible.

If you need to stay close to the Rodoviária the *Casa de Hospedajem*, Rua Banco dos Ingleses 39, Campo

Grande (tel 235 4423), has been recommended. It costs US$2 per person in dormitory-style rooms including breakfast. It's run by a friendly woman, has a very pleasant atmosphere and is just five minutes walk from the bus terminal.

Another hotel which has been recommended in the past is the *Hotel Anglo-Americana*, Av 7 de Setembro 1838, which has large rooms with showers and is very clean.

Places to Eat

Bahian food can be really excellent but isn't easy to find unless you want to splurge. It's hot and spicy and a treat if you've been living off *lanches* for a while. Give *vatapá* a try – it's made from fish, rice, cashew nuts, ginger, mint and parsley – but choose a reasonably good restaurant.

There are surprisingly few restaurants as such in the Praça da Sé area – most would be better described as snack bars. There is, however, the *Cantina La Lua*, Praça 15 de Novembro on the corner of Rua Alfredo de Brito. This is very popular with local people and travellers alike. Downstairs and spilling out onto the pavement, is a bar full of colourful characters, cultivated weirdos, husslers, dealers and bewildered tourists – a great place for hanging out. Upstairs is the restaurant which offers good food at reasonable prices. Get there early if you want a table. Round the corner on Rua Alfredo de Brito there are two or three other restaurants including a vegetarian restaurant/juice bar.

For a splurge you should go down to *SENAC*, Largo do Pelourinho/Rua José de Alencar. This is a restaurant/artisan display shop/juice bar/folklore complex set up to encourage and market the many facets of Bahian culture. A meal costs US$5 per person but this gives you a choice of some 30 regional dishes and you can eat as much as you like. It's not cheap but it is excellent. It's open everyday except Sunday. In addition to the rest-aurant there is a nightly folklore show starting at 8 pm (dance and music) entry to which costs US$1.65.

Another place for a good meal in the evening is *Ibeza Bar* on Rua Alf Brito, where there's excellent food, murals, a good atmosphere and it's cheaper than SENAC.

At lunch times it's probably best to go down into the commercial district in the Baixa and eat a *lanch*. There are scores of these places in the narrow streets up against the bottom of the hill.

For a place to hang out go to the *Cantina La Lua* mentioned previously. For waterfront life in a major port (whores, merchant seamen, husslers, dancers on the thin wire, etc) try the *Bar Damasco*, Rua Conceição da Praia close to the Hotel Modelo – good juke box, cheap beers, friendly people.

For no-nonsense drinkers who like loud music, bare boards and precious little else, try the *Bu San Bar & Restaurant* between the Hotel Modelo and the Lacerdo elevator. It's run by a black-belt Tai Kwon Do Korean expatriate married to a Brazilian woman. No nonsense as far as violence is concerned here – he throws out guys three times his size. These last two bars are good places for changing cash.

Getting Around

The Rodoviária (bus terminal) is five km from the centre of town. To get to the Praca da Sé (the main budget hotel area), take a bus Campo Grande and change there.

Many buses marked 'Rodoviária' go all over the city before they get to the Praça da Sé and so take a long time. Try to get one marked 'Rodoviária/Sé' or 'Rodoviária/ T França'. The latter can take a long time and terminates at the local bus station on Av da França between the commercial district and the dock warehouses. If you take this then you'll have to walk about 200 metres past the Mercado Modelo to the Lacerdo elevator, go up this, turn left at the top and walk another 200 metres or so to get to the Praça da Sé. Bus fares are about 10 cents. The bus from the Rodoviária to the Praça da Sé can take up to an hour in the rush-hour; less at other times.

Local buses to the ferry terminal at São Joaquim (for Itaparica) leave from the Av da França terminal. They take about 10 minutes and cost 10 cents.

Between the airport and the Praça da Sé there are 'executive' buses (there's a stop on the corner of Praça Municipal) which go all along the Atlantic coast from Barra to Itapua and then along the 7 de Setembro/Carlos Gomes. They cost about US$0.55 and take an hour. A taxi will cost about US$6.50 (at the airport you must buy tickets for the taxis before you take one.

SANTARÉM

Built on the southern bank of the Amazon River half way between Belém and Manaus where the River Tapajós joins it, Santarém is a pleasant little place with a busy and interesting waterfront. Founded in 1661, the old part of town still has many narrow streets and traditional houses. It's a very relaxing place and you may find you like it at least as much as Belém or Manaus. Like Manaus it offers the spectacle of the 'Meeting of the Waters' (the Amazon and Tapajós). Bauxite and gold have been discovered nearby so there's a lot of expansion going on at present.

Information

There is no tourist office. Travellers' cheques can be changed at the Banco do Brasil. Avoid changing cheques at the Hotel Tropical as the exchange rates there are lousy. Many hotels in the centre won't change cheques even if you're staying there.

Things to See

The big attraction here is the 'Meeting of the Waters' where the light brown Amazon meets the green-blue waters of the Tapajós. You can actually see this from the shore but it's worth hiring a boat and going out there. A two to three hour trip on a boat should cost around US$25 shared between as many people as you can round up. You don't have to go for this long if there are not enough for a group. If you just want to see the 'Meeting of the Waters' it doesn't take more than half an hour and is obviously a lot cheaper. Ask around among the boats tied up along the Rua Bittencourt (waterfront).

Places to Stay

The *Hotel Camino*, Praça Rodrigues dos Santos 877, is one of the best places both in terms of its position overlooking the main square and for its prices. It's an excellent hotel, clean and well maintained and has a verandah at the front where you can sit and watch the market and the river. It costs US$3.35/$4.15 a single/double with own bathroom and including breakfast. It's very popular and often full.

Next best is probably the *Equatorial Hotel*, Av Rui Barbosa near the junction with Travessa S Lemos. It's clean and quiet and the staff are friendly. Rooms cost US$3.35/$5 a single/double with fan but without own bath, and US$5/$6.65 a single/double with own bathroom. There are also more expensive rooms with air-conditioning. All prices include breakfast. Similar are the *Hotel Alvorado*; and the *Horizonte Hotel*, Travessa S Lemos, which is brand new and should be good if you're looking for something up-market.

Another place which is worth trying is the *Drink Hotel* (yes, that's what it's called!) right on the waterfront. It's a fairly new hotel with a balcony restaurant overlooking the river and has a good music system. Rooms cost US$5 a double with own bathroom. The staff will change cash but the rate isn't too good.

One of the cheapest places is the *Hotel São Luis*, Travessa S Lemos. It's basic

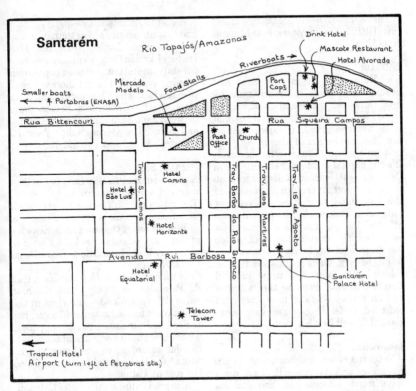

Santarém

Rio Tapajós/Amazonas

Drink Hotel
Mascote Restaurant
Hotel Alvorada

Riverboats →

Smaller boats
← ✳ Portobras (ENASA)

Mercado Modelo

Food Stalls

Port Capt

Rua Bittencourt

Post Office

Church

Rua Siqueira Campos

Hotel Camino

Hotel São Luis

Trav. S. Lemos

Trav. Barão do Rio Branco

Trav. dos Martires

Trav. 15 de Agosto

Hotel Horizonte

Avenida Rui Barbosa

Hotel Equatorial

Santarém Palace Hotel

Telecom Tower

← Tropical Hotel
Airport (turn left at Petrobras sta)

but all right and has its own restaurant. Rooms cost US$2.50/$4.15 a single/double without own bathroom.

For something up-market, try the *Santarem Palace Hotel*, Av Rui Barbosa 226. Rooms cost US$8.65/$12.30 a single/double plus 10% service charge. The rooms have their own shower, toilet and air-conditioning but the staff aren't particularly friendly.

Places to Eat

There are *lanch* restaurants here as elsewhere at the usual prices but first consider eating down at the waterfront next to the market. There are a lot of stalls down there offering many varieties of excellent barbecued fish.

For a splurge go to the *Mascote*

Restaurant where you can eat either inside or outside. It's a popular restaurant, the food is excellent and the portions generous. Expect to pay around US$2.50 to US$3 per dish.

Beer drinkers should be aware that the price of the amber nectar in Santarém is almost double what is charged elsewhere in Brazil.

Getting There

There are no public buses between the airport and the centre of town which means you have to take a taxi and it's a closed shop. The standard fare is US$8.35 for the car for the 14 km journey. Attempts at bargaining are a waste of time.

Buses to Maraba cost US$19.

The boat *Rio Guama* goes to Belém and costs US$20. The *7 Septembre* to Manaus costs US$16.

SÃO LUÍS

São Luís is a steamy, tropical and beautiful old colonial town surrounded by mud flats and the estuaries of various rivers. Indeed, as far as coastal colonial relics are concerned, it might well be considered to be Brazil's best.

It isn't just a colonial relic, however. It's the capital of Maranhão state up in the north-east corner of Brazil and an important port for the rice plantations in the hinterland as well as a developing industrial centre. Little of this has affected the old centre itself except for some sensitive restoration work which has given back to the main plazas their former beauty. There are thousands of old colonial-style houses, narrow cobbled streets plunging down to the estuaries and an endless vista of moss-encrusted red-tiled roofs. People are very easy-going. It's well worth a visit.

Information

The tourist office, *Maratur*, is at Av dos Franceses and Av Pedro II. They don't have much information. You can get good, large scale maps of the town from the Hotel Central, Praça Benedito Leite, and sometimes at the Hotel Aliança. The so-called tourist office at the airport is a joke.

You can only change travellers' cheques at the *Banco do Brasil*.

Things to See

São Luís is the ideal place to simply wander around all day. There are endless points of interest in the narrow, cobbled streets and very little has changed since the 17th century. The **Museu do Estado**, Rua do Sol 302, is well worth a visit. Entry costs US$0.15 and it's open Tuesday to Friday from 8 am to 12 noon and 2 to 6.30 pm as well as on weekends from 3 to 6 pm.

A visit to **Alcantara**, a desperately poor and half-ruined city across the bay, is also recommended. Dating from the 17th century like São Luís, Alcantara was once the state capital but now has a population of only around 2000. To get there you need to take a boat which leaves São Luís from close to the Governor's Palace daily between 7 and 8 am and returns between 1 and 2 pm. The journey takes about 80 minutes and the fare is US$1.75.

Places to Stay

Accommodation in São Luís is a sellers market because there are so few hotels. The situation isn't going to get much better for a while because Texaco is drilling for oil off the coast so there's a lot of personnel lodged in São Luís. Flea-pits you'd pay US$1 for in Rio or Salvador go for US$5 here.

Of the cheapies the *Hotel Grande*, Rua da Palma 66, probably offers the best value. It's very friendly and right in the centre but it has no hot water (it's very hot in São Luís!). It costs US$1.65 per person without own bath and without breakfast. Similar according to one traveller who wrote to us is the *Hotel Lusitano* also on the Rua da Palma.

Also good value are the *Hotel Colonial*, Rua Afogados 84, which costs US$1.65/ $3.35 a single/double without own bath but including coffee in the morning; and the *Hotel Ribamar*, at the junction of Rua João Victal and Praça João Lisboa, which costs US$2.50 per person without own bath (no hot water) but including coffee in the morning.

All the above are no-frills hotels which are fine for a couple of days. If you want something better then try to get into the *Hotel Aliança*, Rua da Palma 20. It costs US$5 a single and US$5.85 to $6.65 a double without own bathroom and US$6.65/$8.30 a single/double with own bathroom. Get there early if you want a room as it's very popular.

Almost everything else is either relatively expensive or very expensive. If

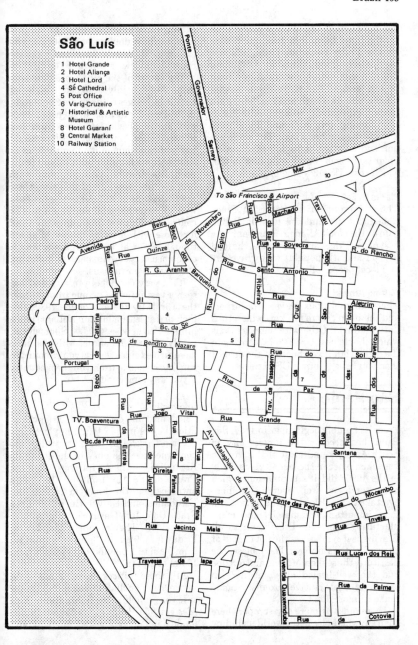

São Luís

1 Hotel Grande
2 Hotel Aliança
3 Hotel Lord
4 Sé Cathedral
5 Post Office
6 Varig-Cruzeiro
7 Historical & Artistic
   Museum
8 Hotel Guaraní
9 Central Market
10 Railway Station

you have to take one of these places then try the *Hotel Lord*, Rua Joaquim Távora on the Praça Benedito Leite. It's not particularly good value at US$10.40/$12.15 a single/double without own bath or fan and US$12.40/$14.70 a single/double with own bath and fan. There are more expensive rooms with air-conditioning, own bath and TV. Prices include a poor breakfast. The staff are unfriendly. Better, perhaps, is the *Pousada Solar do Carmo*, Praça João Lisboa 400, which costs US$13 a single.

Places to Eat

The restaurant on the corner of Praça Benedito Leite and the Rua da Palma (run by the Hotel Aliança) is probably the best place. Prices are reasonable, the food is good and it's popular with travellers and local people alike.

Getting Around

There is a public bus between the airport and the town centre (15 km) which runs until midnight. Otherwise there are taxis which should cost US$3.30 (according to the meter) but if you board at the airport then you have to buy a US$5 ticket.

São Paulo

From its humble beginnings in 1554, São Paulo has become the largest city in South America and most of this growth has taken place in the last 40 years. Only in the 1960s did it's population, which now stands at well over 13 million, overtake that of Rio's. It's the largest and most important commercial and manufacturing centre in Brazil and to all Brazilians it symbolises the pot of gold at the end of the rainbow. The jobless, the destitute, the seekers of fame and fortune and the well-heeled all come here in search of that elusive promise. Some make it; most don't.

There must be more sky-scrapers here than anywhere else in the world including Manhattan and you wouldn't be the first person to have doubts about your survival rating as the city's formidable skyline comes into view as you near the city.

The centre of the city is an incredible maze of boldly-designed high-rise buildings, bridges between different levels, multi-lane highways, immense crowds and shady plazas left over from less frenetic times. You either love it or hate it but you can't ignore it. To love it, or at least become familiar with it, you really need friends who you can stay with because, like any city of this size, there are thousands of different suburbs each with its own character and interest. The centre is really only for businessmen and for those with a lot of money to spend though as far as eating and sleeping is concerned, it isn't too expensive. Pollution, of course, is outrageous.

It's a very cosmopolitan city and has seen a vast influx of people from all over the world. By the end of the 1930s this included at least a million Italians, half a million Portuguese, 400,000 Spanish and nearly 200,000 Japanese. Millions more have arrived since then so you're bound to run into someone from your own country if you stay long enough.

Information

There are nine different tourist information kiosks in São Paulo but probably the most useful as far as travellers are concerned are the ones in the Praça Republica (on the Av Ipiranga side); the Praça da Sé (in front of the metro entrance); at the junction of Rua dos Estudantes and Galvão Bueno; and the Praça Dom José Gaspar (on the Av São Luis side). They're open Monday to Friday from 9 am to 7 pm, on Saturdays from 9 am to 1 pm and on Sundays from 10 am to 2 pm.

All these offices have some good information including maps but make sure you get hold of the publications, *Este Mes em São Paulo* (This Month in São Paulo – in Portuguese and English), and

Guia Hoteis e Turismo (Hotel & Travel Guide – also in Portuguese and English). Both are published monthly and include good maps of the centre of the city. They should be free though sometimes you may be asked to pay for the former. Many hotels stock one or other of the these publications.

If you'll be staying some time in São Paulo then buy a copy (about US$3) of the Guia Quatro Rodas guide, *Guia S Paulo*, as it contains an excellent A to Z of all the streets (entirely in Portuguese).

The main post office is on the corner of Av São João and the Parque Anhangabaú. The poste restante is also here.

For changing money, ask at your hotel – they'll undoubtedly know someone even if they don't do it themselves, or try *Exprinter* on Rua Barao Itapetininga.

American Express is represented at *Kontik-Franstur*, Rua Marconi (2nd and 4th floors) (tel 259 4211). Go down Barão de Itapetininga (opposite the Av Ipiranga side of the Praça da Republica) and turn left two blocks down. It's closed for clients' mail between 12 noon and 2 pm. Wagons Lits-Cooks are at Av São Luís 258 (tel 256 3811).

Almost all the major airlines can be found on Av São Luís. *Varig-Cruzeiro* is at Rua da Consolação 362/372 (tel 258 2233); *Transbrasil* is at Av São Luís 250 (tel 259 7066), and *VASP* is at Av São Luís 91 (tel 257 6370).

Consulates

Argentina
Rua Araujo 216 (8th floor) (tel 256 8555).
Australia
Rua Vol da Pátria 45 (5th floor) (tel 286 0544).
Bolivia
Rua Quirino de Andrade 219 (3rd floor) (tel 255 3555).
Canada
Av Paulista 854 (5th floor) (tel 287 2122).
Chile
Av Paulista 1009 (10th floor) (tel 284 2185).
Colombia
Rua Marconi 94 (7th floor) (tel 255 4056).

Ecuador
Av Paulista 807 (2nd floor) (tel 289 9708).
France
Av Paulista 2073 (17th floor) (tel 287 9522).
Great Britain
Av Paulista 1938 (17th floor) (tel 287 7722).
Japan
Av Paulista 475 (7th floor) (tel 287 0100).
Netherlands
Av Brig Faria Lima 1698 (3rd floor) (tel 813 0522).
Paraguay
Av São Luís 112 (10th floor) (tel 255 7818).
Peru
Rua Suécia 114 (tel 853 9372).
Uruguay
Rua Gal Jardim 770 (7th floor) (tel 259 5882).
USA
Rua Padre João Manoel 933 (tel 881 6511).
Venezuela
Av Brig Faria Lima 1084 (6th floor) (tel 813 9966).

Things to See

As we said before, to enjoy São Paulo you really need to stay with friends who know it well. It isn't really a place for people on a tight budget. Not only that, but distances can be enormous and as there's only one metro line you'll have to resort to buses a lot of the time to get anywhere. To do this successfully you'll need a very good working knowledge of Portuguese, which few travellers seem to have.

The **Praça da Republica** is worth wandering around in the afternoon or the evening as there always seems to be a craft market there and you may well meet local young people who can turn you on to places where you can enjoy yourself without spending a fortune. The Praça da Sé is similar.

Another place to catch an artisan/antique market is on Sundays in the Bixiga district at the junction of 25 de **Mayo** and **Av Brig Luíz Antonio**. It's a popular area for evening entertainment with its bars, restaurants and theatres.

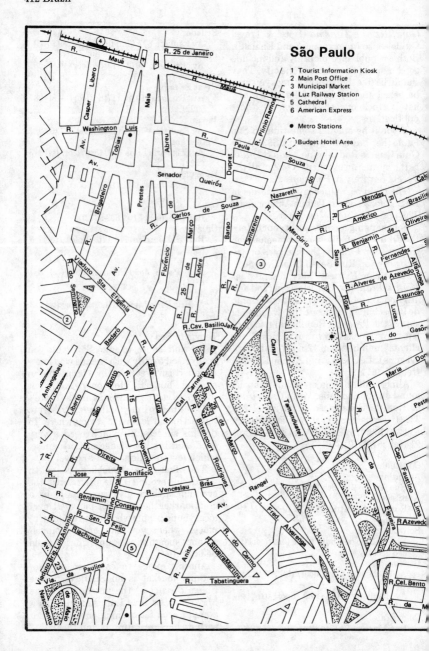

São Paulo

1 Tourist Information Kiosk
2 Main Post Office
3 Municipal Market
4 Luz Railway Station
5 Cathedral
6 American Express

● Metro Stations
◌ Budget Hotel Area

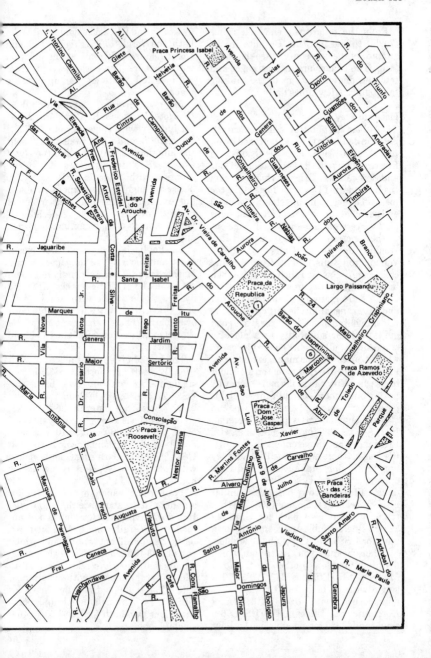

From the square you can take a bus (702U) to the Institute Butanta in the grounds of the university to see the snake farm. The snakes are in glass cages and pits and demonstrations of the milking takes place a few times daily.

Places to Stay

The bulk of the budget hotels are near the Estação da Luz in the area bounded by Av Rio Branco, Av Duque de Caxias, Av Prestes Maia and the two stations of Luz and Sorocabana. To get to this area from the Rodoviária (Terminal Tieté) take the metro (Tieté station – direction Jabaquara) and get off at Luz station. Follow the signs for Av Prestes Maia and you'll come out at the junction of that avenue and Rua Washington Luís. Carry on down Washington Luís (slightly uphill) and cross the Av Caspar Libero. You are then in the budget hotel area.

There are many hotels in this district and they range from the dirt cheap to the mid-range but price isn't always a good guide to their suitability as a place to stay. Almost all the dirt cheap places are whore houses and the managements may not be too keen to rent rooms on a 24-hour basis when they can make more money by letting out a room several times a night.

One very cheap place where you can stay without problems is the Sta Terezinha, Rua Aurora 205 at the junction with Efigenia. The management is friendly, it's basic, there are no frills and they apparently don't take whores and their clients. It costs US$1.20/$2 a single/double all without own bath. Very similar is the Hotel Braga, Efigenia 493. This has rooms without own bath for US$1.50/$2.55 a single/double and rooms with own bath for US$3.10/$3.25 a single/double.

Other cheapies you can try but which definitely double as brothels are the Hotel Monaco, Sta Efigenia 143, US$1.70 a single without bath and US$3.40 for a double bed with own bath; Hotel Horizonte, Sta Efigenia 375, US$1.70 a single and US$2 for a double bed without own bath and US$2.55 a double with own bath; the Hotel Albion, Efigenia 506; and Hotel Londres, Efigenia at the junction with Gusmões. There are always plenty of mini-skirted loiterers around these places.

My own recommendations would be the Hotel Pauliceía, Rua Timbiras 216 at the junction with Efigenia (tel 220 9733); the Hotel Luanda, Sta Efigenia 348 near the junction with Aurora; and the Hotel Galeão, Rua dos Gusmões 394 at the junction with Efigenia (tel 220 8211). These are slightly more expensive places but excellent value and well within a budget travellers reach, especially if you're happy with communal showers and toilets.

The Pauliceía is very good value, clean, quiet and secure. The management are neither friendly nor unfriendly but there are no hassles at all. Rooms cost US$2.55/$3.70 a single/double without own bath and US$3.70/$5.10 a single/double with own bath. There's hot water in the showers and the price includes a simple breakfast.

The Luanda is an older place but with friendly staff. It costs US$3/$5.75 a single/double without own bath and US$4.25/$7.65 a single/double with own bath. There's hot water in the showers.

The Galeão is also very good value and clean at US$2.90/$4.75/$6.10 a single/double/triple without own bath and US$4.25/$6.80/$8.65 a single/double/triple with own bath. A laundry service is available.

Two others which are of a similar standard to the above are the Hotel Ofir, Rua dos Timbiras 258, which is a clean, modern place, all rooms having their own bathroom (with hot water) and which costs US$3.40/$5.95/$8.50 a single/double/triple; and the Hotel San Remo, Sta Efigenia at the junction with Av Ipiranga, which has rooms without own bath for US$2.90/$4.75 a single/double and rooms with their own bath for US$3.40/$5.45 a single/double.

Other hotels in this area are generally considerably more expensive. The *Hotel Paramount*, Efigenia 121, has rooms without own bath for US$6.30/$7 a single/double and rooms with own bath for US$7.90/$8.75 a single/double. The *Hotel Copacabana*, Rua Aurora 264, has rooms without own bath for US$4.25/$7.45/$10.15 a single/double/triple and rooms with their own bath for US$5.10/$9.15/$11.70 a single/double/triple. Prices include breakfast.

The *Hotel Minho*, Av Duque de Caxias at the junction with Efigenia (tel 222 7633), looks like a cheapie but is far from it. It costs US$5.75/$8.15/$9.45 a single/double/triple without own bath and US$7.45/$9.65/$11.90 a single/double/triple with bath. Prices include coffee in the morning. The *Hotel Cometa*, Av Duque de Caxias 907, is somewhat cheaper. It costs US$5.25/$7.45 a single/double without own bath and US$6.45/$9.50 a single/double with bath.

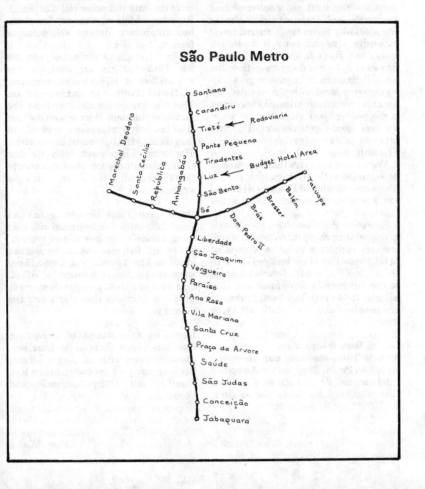

São Paulo Metro

Lastly there is the *Aliança Hotel*, Rua Gen Osório 235 at the junction with Efigenia (tel 220 4244). This has carpeted rooms with telephone for US$3.40/$6.60/$9.85 a single/double/triple without own bath and US$5.95/$8.50/$12.70 a single/double/triple with own bath. The price includes coffee in the morning.

Places to Eat

There are a million restaurants in São Paulo and because of the cosmopolitan population, at least half a dozen offering every conceivable type of cuisine. Most of the speciality restaurants are relatively expensive. One that is not is the Italian restaurant, *Bar e Restaurante Leão*, Av São João 320 a few doors away from the Hotel Britannica. Here you can get an all-you-can-eat meal with a good salad bar for a very reasonable price. Skewered and barbecued beef, pork, chicken and sausage; a range of good vegetables and all manner of pizzas, pastas and ravioli are available. The staff are pleasant.

Vegetarians could try the *Superbom*, 9 de Julho 180 at the junction with Toledo. There are branches at Praça da Sé 62 and the Praça da Republica 128 (lunches only).

Like other Brazilian cities, São Paulo is peppered with cheap *lanch* houses which are very popular with office workers at lunch times. One of the best you'll find in the whole of Brazil is the *Lanches Aliados* at the corner of Av Rio Branco and Rua Vitoria. It has excellent food, prices are competitive and the staff are very friendly.

Getting There & Around

Airports There are three airports which serve São Paulo. They are the Aeroporto Internacional de São Paulo, Cumbica, Guarulhos (19 km from the centre);

Congonhas, Av Washington Luís (close to the centre and for local flights) and the Aeroporto Viracopos near Campinas some 97 km from São Paulo. If you are going to fly into or out of São Paulo then make sure you'll be routed through the first or second of these airports. If it's the last, give it a miss as taxis cost at least US$45.

Bus The *Terminal Tieté* is the main bus terminal and caters for buses to all the state capitals and major cities of Brazil. It's a huge building and very few of the bus companies display schedules or fares.

The ticket offices and bus bays for the São Paulo-Rio run are down on the ground floor at the back of the terminal. All the other offices are on the first floor. There is an information desk in the middle of the main concourse on the first floor but only Portuguese is spoken and they do not hand out tourist information. The terminal is connected directly with the Tieté metro station which you need to take to get down to the centre – follow the signs.

Metro Like Rio, São Paulo has an excellent metro (underground railway) though there's only one line at present. There are frequent trains, no worries about backpacks and it costs US$0.15 per journey (regardless of distance) or US$1.25 for a book of 10 tickets. Use this metro to get to or from the Rodoviária and the budget hotel area.

Train The only station of interest to travellers is the Estação da Luz, Rua Mauá junction with Av Caspar Libero. It's here you pick up the trains to Rio, Brasília and Campo Grande and Corumbá.

Chile

Encompassing only the narrow strip of land between the Pacific Ocean and the high peaks of the Andes – never more than 180 km wide – but with a coastline of over 4500 km, Chile must be one of the most geographically unusual countries in the world. Few other countries can boast five distinct climatic regions which range from the Atacama Desert – one of the hottest and driest areas in the world – to the snow-covered volcanoes, forests and tranquil lakes of Valdivia and the wild and windswept glaciers and fjords of Tierra del Fuego.

It was only relatively recently however, that Chile attained its present size. Not until late in the 19th century were the proud and warlike Araucanian Indians south of the Bío Bío finally subdued and the land opened to settlement. At the same time, Chile's victory over Bolivia and Peru in the War of the Pacific (1879-1883) left it in possession of the mineral-rich Atacama Desert up as far as Arica. Neither of the two losers in that war – especially Bolivia, which lost its main outlet to the sea at Antofagasta – have ever fully accepted Chile's annexations and resentment continues to smoulder below the surface. Other far-flung Chilean possessions include the islands of Juan Fernandez (of Robinson Crusoe fame), and Easter Island where the world-famous red-capped *ahus* stand as mute testimony to a lost Polynesian civilisation.

Not only that but the population of Chile is quite different from that of Bolivia, Peru and Ecuador. Intermarriage here was much more common than in the republics to the north and Chile also took in large numbers of immigrants from Europe, especially from Germany and Switzerland. The result is that today, like Argentina and Uruguay, it bears more resemblance to the USA and Canada than it does to the Spanish-speaking republics to the north and north-east. There are still descendants of middle-European immigrants who are bilingual in Spanish and German, and the building styles in certain areas of the south resemble those found in the alpine areas of Europe.

The area's first contact with Europeans came in 1535 in the form of an expedition led by Almagro, one of Pizarro's principal lieutenants. By following the Inca road down as far as Salta and then crossing the Andes, they reached the Chilean heartland but were bitterly disappointed at finding no gold and returned to Peru to squabble over what remained of the spoils of the Inca empire. A more determined band of settlers arrived a few years later under the leadership of Pedro de Valdivia. They founded the cities of Santiago and Valdivia but were unable to push any further south because of the fierce resistance put up by the Araucanian Indians. The struggle between the two groups was to continue into the 19th century despite a treaty in the mid-17th century which allocated all land south of the Bío Bío to the Indians.

Shortly after Valdivia's arrival, the land was divided up into enormous estates worked – despite strident objections from the Church – by Indian serfs. The system remained intact until the 17th century when a number of cosmetic reforms were made which in theory freed the Indians. In practice, however, all that happened was the substitution of one form of bondage for another. Under the new *inquilino* system, a worker who left his home and job in search of another, found all other estates closed to him. Very little happened to change all this until the War of the Pacific, after which many of the ex-servicemen refused to return to their wretched lives on the estates. Instead, they flocked either to the cities in search of work or to the newly opened lands south of the Bío Bío. It was the descendants of these people who eventually elected to power Chile's first socialist president, Aguirre Cerda, in 1938.

Throughout the colonial period Chile remained part of the viceroyalty of Peru and right up until 1778 all trade between Chile and anywhere else had to pass through Lima. The resultant high cost of living led to widespread smuggling, particularly by French and British pirates, and to discontent among those footing the bill.

It was during this period that the settlement of Punta Arenas was established in the Straits of Magellan to try and prevent French ships from passing through. Eventually, in 1810 discontent with being ruled from Lima and Spain led to a revolt which was, to all intents, a declaration of independence. It was followed by seven years of war against a Spanish army of occupation which was only defeated when San Martín, fresh from the liberation of Argentina, crossed the Andes and gained a decisive victory over the Royalist troops.

One of the leaders of the Chilean insurrection, Bernardo O'Higgins – the son of an Irish-born Viceroy of Peru and a Chilean mother – became the first president of the new republic but made the mistake of tampering with the priorities and privileges of the estate owners and was deposed in 1823. Civil war broke out and was to last until the conservation forces of Portales restored order in 1830. From that date until the early part of the 20th century, Chile was ruled by a small oligarchy of landowners.

The power of the landowners was finally challenged in the 1920s under the liberal regime of President Alessandri but it wasn't until the election of Aguirre Cerda in 1938 that anything very radical was attempted. He was the first president

to come from the ranks of the working classes, and his programme of reform included major changes to the education and health services as well as land redistribution. Further reforms were attempted by Eduardo Frei, who was elected president in 1964, but they generally succeeded only in raising expectations which couldn't be satisfied. Then came the election to the presidency of Dr Salvador Allende in 1970.

Allende was the leader of the Unidad Popular, an alliance of several political parties including the Acción Popular Independiente and MAPU, a left-wing splinter group from the Christian Democrats. In order to push through its programme of nationalising foreign-owned resources, extension of the state sector of the economy and radical agrarian reform, the UP was forced to enter into a coalition with the Christian Democrats. The latter were entirely on the side of big business and the landowners and therefore had little or no intention of supporting the UP's intended reforms. However, this proved to be only one of the UP's problems. Not only did it get itself into strife by its constant though futile attempts to appease the Christian Democrats, but it seemed incapable of keeping up with and encouraging the advances which the workers had made for themselves. One of the reasons for this was that the UP leadership was firmly committed to the idea of 'revolution in stages' via legal methods according to the Constitution, and so often found itself at odds with the workers.

Against a background of mounting independent action by factory and agricultural workers, a soaring inflation rate which eventually hit 150% and stayed at that level for two years (very high by the standards of those days), and the increasing polarisation of the country into left and right-wing camps, the Christian democrats encouraged the **truck drivers to go out on strike in an attempt to overthrow the UP. They were**

Chile

shortly joined by the professional classes, shopkeepers, bank employees, technicians and upper-class school pupils. In response, the factory and agricultural workers formed self-defence committees, occupied factories and commandeered trucks to keep goods moving and shops forcibly opened to ensure that people were fed.

North American business interests soon entered the fray under the umbrella of the Kennecot Copper Corporation which owned the Atacama mines – one of the mainstays of the Chilean economy. The company announced that it would seize exported copper to 'defend its rights' and though this caused some considerable degree of concern in the government, the strike collapsed some three months later in the face of the concerted effort put up by the factory and agricultural workers. The victory, however, had its costs. One of these was a demand by Communist elements within the UP to have three generals brought into the government.

In March 1973, elections were again called but not before the Communists, worried that the UP would lose the elections unless it appeased the middle classes, attempted to have all property which was taken over during the strike returned to its former owners. The attempt caused internal dissension within the UP and led to another spontaneous mobilisation by the workers to protect the gains they had made. The proposed measure had to be dropped. In the elections the UP secured 44% of the vote, giving it a mandate for another term in office, but its weaknesses remained, particularly its inability to rely on its own popular base of support – the miners, factory workers, agricultural workers and the urban poor. Allende and various other factions within the UP continued to be obsessed with alliances with the Christian Democrats, who nevertheless continued to support attempts to discredit the UP. As the national debt increased, the price of copper on the world market plummeted,

foreign aid and investment dried up, inflation hit record levels, major imbalances between the various sectors of the economy began to cause problems, and what had been feared all along eventually happened – the army took over.

In the fighting which followed, many thousands of people lost their lives – including Allende, who was gunned down in the presidential palace. Thousands of others were executed, tortured, imprisoned or simply 'disappeared.' The torture, brutality and total disregard for basic human values, let alone human rights, which Pinochet's junta employed to eliminate or subdue those who had supported the UP or been involved in the factory or farm occupations, caused an international outcry. Chile was ostracised and isolated politically and economically for many years afterwards not just by the industrialised west but by many other countries too.

None of these sanctions appear to have induced Pinochet to either moderate his stand or to make amends. Ever since that bloodbath, Congress has been closed, the Chilean people have been forced to adjust to an iron-fisted dictatorship however onerous, to curfews, arbitrary arrest, conspicuous armed police and army patrols and a deteriorating economy. It seems incredible that it has gone on so long.

But it can't last for much longer, that is now patently obvious even to those who opposed Allende in the days of the UP government. Opposition to the incompetent management and direction of the economy by Pinochet and his supporters, and the suppression of comment and action of a well-educated and intelligent population, is getting more and more vocal. Even the newspapers and weekly magazines now openly criticise the military regime. Go into any bar and you'll hear people stridently denouncing the regime where only a few years ago, such comments were being made in whispers and with glances over the shoulder. Something has to give, though it doesn't look like Pinochet is going to do anything voluntarily.

Those are the politics of the country and few people will not be acquainted with them. The other side of the country is the people themselves. You'd be hard-pressed to find a friendlier, more hospitable and endearing bunch of people anywhere in Latin America. Don't be put off this country by the politics. Come and meet the people, live with them and talk to them. For many years after Pinochet took over, foreigners shunned the country and Chileans saw very few travellers. They obviously missed the opportunity to talk with others about what life and conditions were like elsewhere. They missed that essential contact badly. By coming here you're not endorsing Pinochet's regime and everyone in Chile knows it. Come here and spend some time. You might help them regain their self-respect and confidence but don't take hospitality for granted. Wages have had the lid on them for years and the average earnings for office workers, for example, are around US$60 a month. They don't know how they make ends meet and neither do I.

VISAS
Visas are required by very few people (Australian and New Zealand nationals are exceptions). Most people are given an entry stamp which allows them to stay for up to 90 days. The fee for a visa varies but is usually about US$8.

Argentine visas The embassy is at Calle Vicuna McKenna 41, Santiago (tel 222 8977). It's open Monday to Friday from 9 am to 2 pm. There's no longer any problem with visas for New Zealanders but British nationals still have problems. As far as the latter are concerned, the embassy in Santiago is virtually a waste of time – they'll tell you it takes at least a month to get a visa. Instead, go to Puerto

Montt where the consulate is much more sympathetic and can generally get you a visa in about 15 days.

Bolivian visas The embassy is at Av Sta Maria 2796, Santiago (tel 222 5690) and is open Monday to Friday from 9 am to 1 pm.

Peruvian visas The embassy is at Andres Bello 1751, Santiago (tel 490 045) and is open Monday to Friday from 10 am to 3 pm.

MONEY
US$1 = Ch$178 (official)

The peso is presently floating against the US dollar and the exchange rate is gradually rising so use this rate as a guide only.

The unit of currency is the Chilean peso (Ch$). There is no limit on the export or import of local currency. There is a blackmarket of sorts for cash dollars but it's very open, especially in Santiago where you'll be approached by dealers particularly along Huerfanos, Agustinas and Ahumada in the centre of the city. The blackmarket rate is about 12.5% above the official rate. The street changers will probably take you to seemingly obscure offices on the main streets in this area. Don't worry about this as it's quite normal and safer for the both of you.

If you have US-dollar travellers' cheques then it's better to convert these first into cash dollars and then change. If you have American Express cheques then this is simplicity itself. Just go down to American Express Banking Corporation, Agustinas 1360, and cash in the cheques for US dollars at about 1% commission (you can pay the commission in Chilean pesos). After this just go and change the cash on the street.

You can buy international flight tickets in Chile using Chilean pesos and without having to provide a bank receipt showing that you bought the pesos at a bank. This reduces the cost of these flights by around 11.5%.

The airport departure tax for international flights is US$5. For domestic flights it is Ch$100.

GETTING THERE
To/From Peru

The only crossing point between Peru and Chile is via Tacna and Arica in the extreme north of the country. There is a choice of train, colectivo or bus. The colectivos are the most convenient and the fastest. There are several companies and they leave from Calle Mendoza in Tacna and from Chacabuco between Baquedano and Colón in Arica. They cost US$1.75 to US$2 depending on whether you pay in Peruvian soles or Chilean pesos and take about one hour. The taxi driver handles all the passport formalities but there's a cursory baggage search at the Chilean frontier. Both borders are a breeze to get through. The taxi drivers will take both foreigners and locals – no worries.

There are daily departures in either direction by train at 11 am and 2 pm which take about 1½ hours and costs US$1. Exit stamps are available at the station but you must be there half an hour before departure.

The buses cost about the same as the trains but they're not as convenient or as fast as the colectivos.

To/From Bolivia

Arica-La Paz There is a choice of train or bus along this route. The *ferrobuses* have been discontinued and there is now only an ordinary train in either direction twice a month but the actual dates vary each month so you need to make enquiries either at the station or at the tourist office. You must change trains at the border and this can take hours because there's a lot of smuggling going on. It's very cold at the changeover station (it's at about 4000 metres). The fares from Arica are US$13 (1st class) and US$10.50 (2nd class). From La Paz they are unquotable because of inflation in Bolivia. For somewhere to stay at the border, ask in the houses. You can sleep in the barns for a few soles and they give you blankets.

It's probably best to take the bus between the two places. There are two companies which cover the route: *Pullman Martinez* (at the Terminal de Buses in La Paz and at Pedro Montt 620 in Arica); and *Litoral* (at the Terminal de Buses in La Paz and Chacabuco 454 in Arica). They both depart at 6 am on Tuesday and Friday in either direction and take between 16 and 20 hours. The fares vary depending on whether you're going from Arica to La Paz or vice versa and on whether the bus is *directo* or you need to change at the border. In La Paz they generally quote US$10. In Arica they quote US$13.30 (directo) and US$7.35 (change at the border). It's a rough road in parts.

Antofagasta-La Paz You can only do this journey by train and the passenger trains only start from Calama – not from Antofagasta – so you must first go to Calama from Antofagasta by bus. The train departs once weekly in either direction on Wednesday at 2.55 pm from Calama and on Fridays at 2 pm from La Paz and takes about 36 hours. The fares depend on which end you buy your ticket. In Calama they cost US$16.45 (1st class) and you should buy your ticket on Tuesdays between 3 and 4.30 pm or on Wednesdays between 8.30 am and 12.45 pm. In La Paz the prices are unquotable due to inflation. Take your passport with you when buying tickets and make sure you have a visa if one is needed.

As on the Arica-La Paz line, you must change trains at the border (Ollague) and this can take some time (three to four hours is not unusual). It's very cold at the frontier – temperatures can drop to –15°C (this is one of the highest railway lines in the world and the area is one of the world's most barren). Temperatures are often well below freezing so don't go on this train without warm clothing. The Bolivian trains are in reasonable condition. The Chilean trains are like cattle trucks.

There is a Bolivian consulate in Antofagasta, Av Grecia 563, office No 23

(tel 22 1403), open Monday to Friday from 9.30 am to 1 pm and 3 to 6 pm, and in Calama (Calle MacKenna 1976), open Monday to Friday from 9.30 am to 12 noon and 4 to 5.30 pm.

You can generally change money on the train at Ollague but the rates are not always very good. Make sure you know exactly what the current rates are before changing money.

To/From Argentina
All train services to Argentina have been suspended so the only way to get there is by road or air. The two main crossing points into Argentina are:

Santiago-Mendoza There are several companies which cover this route and you can book at either the Terminal de Buses Norte, Calle Gen MacKenna; or at the Terminal de Buses Sur, Alameda Bernardo

O'Higgins 3800 ('Universidad Technica' metro station).

The main companies with their departure times from Santiago are: *Fenix Pullman Norte*, daily at 9 am, US$16.65; *Chile Bus*, daily at 7.30 am, US$14.65; *Pluma*, daily at 8 and 8.40 am, US$14.65. All these buses take six to seven hours. There are also colectivos which cover the route which you can find at the Terminal de Buses Sur but they cost US$18 (eg *Colectivos Coitram* daily at 7 am).

Many of these companies also operate buses to Buenos Aires, daily, about 24 hours, US$41.50; and to Rio de Janeiro, three times per week, about 72 hours, US$83; and São Paulo same frequency, about 63 hours.

Through the Lake District - Valdivia/Osorno/Pto Montt-Bariloche Full details of these routes are included in the lake district section of this chapter.

Routes further south

There are a number of border crossing points south of Puerto Montt which are useful if you are visiting the National Parks of Chile and Argentina or if you get down to Tierra del Fuego.

Puerto Aysen-Coyhaique-Comodoro Rivadavia
There are *La Puntual* buses in either direction three times a week in the winter and four times a week in summer, which cost US$45 and take about 12 hours.

Torres del Paine National Park-Calafate This border crossing is closed at present due to a border dispute between the two countries. You must go further south to Puerto Natales to cross the border.

Puerto Natales-Río Turbio/Río Gallegos There are buses once a week in either direction between Puerto Natales and Río Gallegos and twice a day between Puerto Natales and Río Turbio (the latter takes about two hours). Many Chileans work in the coal mines at Río Turbio. You can also cross this border by foot if you like.

Punta Arenas-Río Gallegos There are daily buses in either direction from Monday to Friday (at 9 am and 2 pm from Río Gallegos) by *Expreso Pingüino* which cost US$11 and take about eight to 10 hours.

Porvenir-Río Grande There are weekly *Sencovi* buses in either direction. They leave on Wednesdays and Saturdays at 6 am from Río Grande which connect with the ferries to Punta Arenas, and on the same days at 2 pm from Porvenir. The trip takes about seven hours and costs US$8. Avoid *Transportes Turicisne* buses which also cover this route.

Punta Arenas-Río Gallegos There is a bus at 9 am daily except Mondays (when it leaves at 11 am) from Punta Arenas to Río Gallegos which takes about six hours and costs US$15. It's also possible to get direct from Porvenir to Río Gallegos without crossing over to Punta Arenas but it isn't easy and you may get stuck.

If you want to try this then you must first hitch to Punta Delgada where there is a ferry to Primera Angostura. The ferries there are operated by *ENAP*

aerovías DAP

Twin Otter

PUNTA ARENAS-XII REGION-CHILE

(Chilean oil boats) and generally leave every two hours between 8 am and 9 pm daily except between noon and 2 pm or whenever it's too rough to cross. The ferry costs about US$1. There is nowhere to stay at either Punta Delgada or Primera Angostura if the ferry isn't operating, and there is no bus service between either Primera Angostura and the main Punta Arenas-Río Gallegos road (16 km) or between Punta Delgada and Río Grande. Again, you must hitch. If you're trying to get from Río Grande to Río Gallegos it's often more convenient and can be cheaper to fly – about $US30.

NB On all the southern routes you must report to Inventigaciones at Puerto Aysen, Puerto Natales, Punta Arenas or Porvenir before turning up at the Argentinian border. The same goes if you are crossing from Argentina to Chile in which case you need a permit from the police. Travellers have been sent back for failing to do this.

If you hold a British passport and you either can't get a visa or don't have the time to wait for one but want to get to Brazil then you must either go via Bolivia (by bus and/or train) or fly from Santiago to either Uruguay or Brazil. The cheapest flights are from Santiago to Montevideo, Uruguay. Both *LAN-CHILE* and *Ladeco* cover the route and the fares are the same – US$185 one-way, payable in Chilean pesos (equivalent to about US$162 if you changed your money on the street).

GETTING AROUND

Except for the occasional journey in second class on the railways in winter (when the heating sometimes doesn't work), travel in Chile is a dream come true. All the main roads are surfaced and only rarely will you come across a gravel track and only then in remote rural areas. All the buses are comfortable (some of them luxurious), well-maintained, fast and punctual. They generally have a toilet and coffee/tea on board. In com-

parison to the Andean countries they work out more expensive but when you consider the distances from one city to another they're a bargain. The trains are even cheaper.

Only rarely need you book a ticket more than a few hours in advance. Both the train stations and the bus terminals are well organised and even if your Spanish isn't up to much it's a breeze finding the right ticket office. Schedules and fares are always prominently displayed – unlike in many Brazilian bus terminals. Not only that, but there are no worries in Chile about theft. You don't have to watch your belongings like a hawk. You can fall asleep, get off the bus for a snack, or whatever, and they'll still be there when you get back. You can't, of course, be as nonchalant as this in the bus terminals themselves but even there they are a long chalk from the bus terminals in the Andean countries to the north where you must be constantly alert.

Air

Like Brazil, Chile offers 21-day air passes known as the 'Visit Chile Pass' with *LAN-Chile*. The cities that you can fly to include Arica, Iquique, Antofagasta, Santiago, Puerto Montt, Coyhaique, Punta Arenas and Easter Island. Depending on the routing you choose the passes cost US$249, US$288, US$449 or US$488 (the latter two include Easter Island). The passes must be bought outside Chile.

Because of the enormous distances in Chile, you may want to take the occasional flight if your time is limited. Flights can be paid for in Chilean pesos without having to produce bank receipts. Both *LADECO* and *LAN-Chile* service the internal routes. It's generally thought that *Ladeco* is cheaper than *LAN-Chile* but this isn't true. The only difference is that *Ladeco* services more cities than *LAN-Chile*, which only flies to the larger cities.

LAN-Chile fly from Santiago to: Antofagasta – daily except Saturday at 8 am, US$79; Iquique – daily at 8 am, US$90; Arica – daily at 8 am, US$92; Puerto Montt – daily at 9 am, US$64; Punta Arenas – daily at 9 am, US$119.

Ladeco fly from Santiago to: El Salvador – three times weekly; Antofagasta – nine times weekly, US$79; Calama – six weekly; Iquique – daily, US$90; Arica – eight weekly, US$92; Concepcion – nine weekly; Temuco – four weekly; Osorno – three weekly; Valdivia – three weekly; Puerto Montt – daily, US$64; Coyhaique – three weekly, US$87; Punta Arenas – daily, US$119.

From Arica to Antofagasta the one-way fare is US$35 and to Iquique US$16. From Puerto Montt to Punta Arenas costs US$90.

Bus

Most Chilean cities have a central bus terminal where all the various bus companies are collected together. Schedules and fares are prominently displayed so it's very easy to find the bus you want. Fares do vary from one company to the next and there are often *ofertas*, or fare promotion deals, which can sometimes be as little as half the normal fare, so it's worth comparing prices if you want to save money. On a long haul you can save up to US$5.

As in Brazil, there are ordinary buses and sleeper buses. The latter have reclining seats and foot rests similar to those in first class on planes and cost about twice the price of the ordinary buses. There's usually a choice of several companies on the main routes so you don't normally have to book more than a few hours in advance. For minor rural destinations (in the Lake District, for instance) there may only be one bus company which covers a particular route, in which case it's wise to book ahead.

Student reductions are sometimes possible on the buses so it's worth enquiring when you buy your ticket. The discount is usually about 25%. You may not have much success getting them in the north of Chile but they're quite common in the Lake District. Naturally, you won't get a student discount on top of a special fare deal (an *oferta*).

There are two bus terminals in Santiago, one for buses going north (Terminal de Buses Norte, Gen MacKenna on the corner of Amunategui) and one for buses going south and to Valparaiso (Terminal de Buses Sur, Av O'Higgins 3800). The Terminal Sur is actually two separate buildings – the main terminal and another smaller one called Alameda. The latter handles only two companies, the main one being *Tur-Bus* which is a luxury bus company operating buses to Valparaiso and to many places in the Chilean Lake District.

Some examples of journey times and fares are:

North of Santiago

Destination	Journey Time	Fare
Arica	27-28 hours	US$31
Iquique	25 hours	US$26-28
Antofagasta	15-18 hours	US$16-21

Bus companies which cover the Santiago-Iquique/Antofagasta/Arica route include *Pullman Fichtur, Flota Barrios, Tramaca, Buses Evans, Fenix Pullman Norte, Chile Bus, Flecha Norte, Buses Carmelita* and *Tarapaca*.

Santiago-Valparaiso/Viña del Mar

The most convenient bus company for Valparaiso and Viña del Mar is *Tur-Bus* which has frequent daily departures in either direction (from 6.30 am to 10 pm from Santiago and from 6.10 am to 8.45 pm from Valparaiso/Viña del Mar). Some of the buses to Viña del Mar go via Valparaiso but others go direct. The two cities are only a few km apart in any case so it's easy to take a local bus between the two. Santiago to Valparaiso takes 1¾ hours and to Viña del Mar about two hours. The fare is the same to either – US$2 one-way and US$3.35 return.

South of Santiago

Destination	Journey Time	Fare
Concepción	7-9 hours	US$6.50-$9
Temuco	10-11 hours	US$8
Valdivia	13-14 hours	US$9.50
Osorno	14 hours	US$9.50-$10.50
Puerto Montt	16 hours	US$11.50-$12

Bus companies which cover the southern routes include *Buses Norte, Tas Choapa, Tus-Bus, Cruz del Sur, ETC, Transbus, Igi Llama, Turibus, Pullman Lit, Via-Tur* and *Nuevo Longitudinal Sur*.

Train

With the exception of the Arica-La Paz and Calama-La Paz lines, there are no passenger services on the railways north of Santiago. The only trains of interest to travellers are those from Santiago to Valparaiso and Santiago to Puerto Montt via Concepción and Osorno.

Santiago-Valparaiso These trains leave from Estación Mapocha in Santiago. The trip takes three hours and costs US$1.60. There are the following services:

To Valparaiso: 8.35 am (daily); 12.40 pm (Monday to Saturday); 4.40 pm (daily), and 7.25 pm (daily).

From Valparaiso: 7.25 am (daily); 11.30 am (daily); 2.30 pm (daily), and 6.40 pm (daily).

Refer to the table below for services running south from Santiago to Puerto Montt.

Rapido trains have only Salon class available. Expresso trains have both Salon and Economy classes.

In addition to the Salon and Economy classes there are more expensive compartments on some trains (eg to Concepcion, Valdivia and Puerto Montt). A shared compartment to Valdivia would cost US$22.35 (lower bunk) and US$16.65 (upper bunk). To Puerto Montt they would cost US$24 (lower bunk) and US$18.35 (upper bunk). It's worth considering getting a bunk in a compartment on long overnight journeys. Santiago to Valdivia, for instance, takes 20 hours.

If you do go in the ordinary cars then think seriously about spending that little extra and going Salon class rather than Economy. In the winter time the heating doesn't always work in Economy class so it can get very cold indeed. This doesn't happen in Salon class.

All trains going south from Santiago

Train	Destination	Departure	Fare US$ Salon	Economy
Salon	Temuco/Concep	8.15 am daily	$9.60	$5.60
Automotor	Concepcion	8.30 am daily	$7.35	$5.00
Automotor	Linares	12.00 noon daily		
Salon	Concepcion	1.30 pm daily	$7.35	$5.00
Expreso	Chillan	4.00 pm daily		
Salon	Chillan/Concep	5.30 pm daily	$7.35	$5.00
Automotor	Linares	7.00 pm daily ex Fri/Sat		
Automotor	Chillan	7.00 pm Fri only		
Rapido	Valdivia	8.30 pm daily	$11.00	$6.65
Expreso	Pto Montt/Valdivia	9.15 pm daily	$11.65	$7.65
Super Salon	Concepcion	10.30 pm daily	$7.35	$5.00
Auto Expreso	Concepcion	11.00 pm daily	$7.35	$5.00

start from Estación Central. Tickets for trains going south can be bought either at Estación Central or in the centre of Santiago at the railways booking office ('Venta de Pasajes Informaciones' – a yellow sign) in the Galería Libertador, Alameda O'Higgins 851. This office is open Monday to Friday from 9 am to 6 pm and on Saturday from 9 am to 1 pm.

Boat

A road is being constructed south of Puerto Montt which will eventually extend as far as Punta Arenas but until it is completed the only way of getting further south is either to fly or take a ship. Depending on where you want to go, there is choice of three shipping lines.

Empresa Maritima del Estado (Empremar), Avenida Suiza 248, Santiago (tel 572650), and Av Portales 1450, Puerto Montt, operate the boats from Puerto Montt to Puerto Chacabuco (close to Puerto Aisen and Coyhaique) calling at Chaitén, Quellón, Melinka, Puyuhuapi, Puerto Cisnes and Puerto Aguirre, en route. The journey takes 48 hours. In the summer months (December to March) they continue on from Puerto Chacabuco down the fjord to Laguna San Rafael. The boats sail from Puerto Montt twice a week on Tuesdays at 8 pm and Thursdays at 8 am. Fares to Puerto Chacabuco are US$14.65 (seat only) and US$20 (berth). The charge for meals is US$4.65 (four daily).

Transmarchilay Ltda, Libertad 669, Ancud (tel 317), and 21 de Mayo 417 (2nd floor), Coyhaique (tel 21971), operate two ferries between Chiloé Island and the mainland. The *El Colono* sails between Quellón and Puerto Chacabuco. It departs Quellón on Tuesdays, Thursdays and Sundays at 12 noon and Puerto Chacabuco on Mondays, Wednesdays and Fridays at 3 pm. The fares are US$14 (Pullman) and US$8.90 (Tourist class). The *La Pincoya* sails between Chonchi and Chaitén. It departs Chonchi on Tuesdays, Thursdays and Fridays at 8 am and Chaitén on Tuesdays, Thursdays and Fridays at 3 pm. The fare is US$3.55.

Naviera Magallanes (Navimag), Angelmó, Puerto Montt (tel 3318), operate the long haul boats south to Puerto Natales. They depart Puerto Montt twice a month and take three days to get to Puerto Natales. The fares are US$473 to US$899 (single cabin), US$249 to US$473 (per person, double cabin) and US$83 (2nd class). The fares include all meals. It's sometimes possible to travel in the restaurant on the ship for half the 2nd class fare so make enquiries about this if you're interested.

The exact departure days at either end depend on what sort of cargo is being loaded so you need to check.

ANTOFAGASTA

Antofagasta is the largest port city on the coast of northern Chile with a population of about 250,000. Most of the nitrates and copper mined in the Atacama Desert are exported through this port and it's also an important import/export centre for Bolivia. In fact, until the War of the Pacific (1879-1883), Antofagasta was actually a part of Bolivia.

After it was annexed by Chile, Bolivia lost its outlet to the sea but was given duty-free facilities there for the export of its goods. It's quite a lively little city with a certain understated charm though there isn't a great deal to do or see. For many travellers it's the jumping off point for visits to the Atacama Desert and one of the possible routes into Bolivia.

Information

The tourist office is at Balmaceda 2786 on the corner of Bolívar on the sea front. It's a dirty, yellow building. The staff are enthusiastic and eager to help but you must be able to speak Spanish. They have free maps of the city, of Iquique and of the surrounding area as well as bus and train timetables. There's also a municipal tourist kiosk at the junction of Prat and Matta. They also have maps of the city.

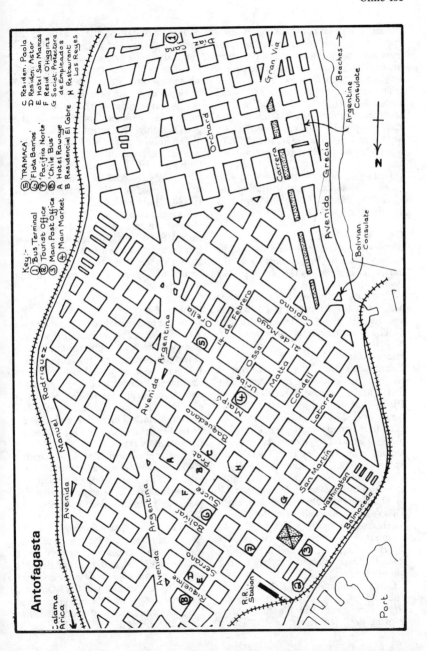

Antofagasta

Key:-
① Bus Terminal
② Tourist Office
③ Main Post Office
④ Main Market

⑤ TRAMACA'
⑥ Flota Barrios'
⑦ 'Pacifica Norte'
⑧ 'Chile Bus'

A Hotel Rawaye
B Residencial El Cobre

C Residen. Paola
D Residen. Astor
E Hotel San Marcos
F Resid. O'Higgins
G Societ. Protectora de Empleados
H Restaurant Los Reyes

There are street money changers down Prat but they don't offer any better rates than the casas de cambio. The *Banco do Brasil*, Prat, doesn't charge commission for changing travellers' cheques.

The Argentine consulate is at Manoel Verbal 1640 (tel 22 2854) and is open Monday to Friday from 9.30 am to 1 pm and 3 to 6 pm. The Bolivian consulate, on Av Grecia 563 (Office No 23) (tel 22 1403), is open Monday to Friday from 8 am to 2 pm.

There's a good photographic shop with cheap developing and printing at *Multifoto*, Matta 2558. The owner is friendly and speaks some English.

Things to See & Do

It's worth walking around down by the railway station (freight only) and the tourist office which is the oldest part of town.

There are a number of fairly pleasant beaches at the far end of the Av Grecia and further along on the Av Ejercito which are popular with young people.

Places to Stay

Two hotels stand out above the rest as offering the best value for money. The first, and the cheapest, is the *Residencial Paola*, Prat 766, which costs US\$2 per person or US\$3.65 a double if you stay for more than two nights. It's very clean and pleasant and all the rooms are arranged around a central lounge. There's hot water all day. The other is the *Hotel Rawaye*, Sucre 762, which is very friendly and clean and excellent value at US\$2.65/\$4.30 a single/double without own bath. There's hot water all day. Both these hotels are very popular with travellers. At a similar price but not such good value is the *Hotel Imperio*, Condell 2736, which costs US\$2 per person but has no hot water.

Going up in price, the *Residencial El Cobre*, Prat, just opposite the Paola, offers very clean and pleasant rooms fronting onto the street for US\$5.30 a double, with gallons of hot water in the communal showers. It's a huge place so you'll always find a room there. Similar is the *Residencial Astor*, Condell 2995, which is scruffy but otherwise clean and has a pleasant courtyard. It costs US\$3.30 per person in rooms with own toilet but communal showers (hot water in the evenings only). Breakfast is available.

The *Residencial O'Higgins*, Sucre 665, is another possibility. It's a large old building with high ceilings and costs US\$2.35/\$4.35/\$5.35 a single/double/triple. Breakfast (US\$0.30) and lunch (US\$0.80) are available.

You could also try the *Hotel San Marcos*, Lattore 2946 (tel 24124), which costs US\$4/\$4.80/\$5.60 a single/double/triple without own bathroom and US\$5.30/\$6.80/\$8 a single/double/triple with own bathroom. There is hot water in the mornings only.

Places to Eat

By far the best place to eat in Antofagasta is the *Sociedad Protectora de Empleados*, San Martín 2544 (opposite the Banco O'Higgins and just off the main plaza). It's very popular with local people at lunch time because it offers filling, tasty and economical meals. The service is excellent. For just US\$1.20 you get a starter, soup, main course and dessert. Wine, beer and soft drinks are available. It's spotlessly clean.

The *Bar Restaurant Los Reyes*, Condell 2540, is even cheaper at lunchtimes (about US\$1) but you don't get soup. In the evenings it's relatively expensive (fish, chips and salad will come to US\$2.30).

Other cheap places to try are the *Restaurant Sociedad Italiana*, Prat 730, which offers lunches for just over US\$1 (starter, soup, fish and salad and dessert) with more expensive meals in the evenings (US\$2 to \$2.75); and the *Café Oriente*, Baquedano 634, which has a mixture of European and Latin-style food, all dishes being under US\$1.

The popular *Apoquindo*, Prat 616, serves a good range of tasty food but you'll end up paying two to three times what a meal would cost elsewhere.

Getting There

Although there is a central bus terminal at the junction of Diaz Cana and Orchard to the south of the main part of town most bus companies appear to be shunning it and instead retain their own terminals in the centre of town. Companies which are doing this include: *Tramaca* (Uribe above the junction with 14 de Febrero); *Chile Bus* and *Flota Lila* (Riquelme 513); *Transportes Chile* (Latorre 2720); *Pacifico Norte* (Bolívar 458) and *Flota Barrios* (Condell between Sucre and Bolívar).

All these companies have buses to Santiago and Arica (and intermediate stations) but the best company for buses to Calama (and the Atacama Desert) is *Tramaca*. They operate 11 buses daily (13 on Saturdays and Sundays) to Calama and Chuquicamata which cost US$3.30 and take about 2½ hours.

Arica

Arica is a rapidly growing sea port and resort town at the extreme northern tip of Chile. It's a free port for Bolivian exports and almost half the goods which Bolivia produces flow out through Arica via the railway which links the town with La Paz.

Until the War of the Pacific (1879-1883), the town was a part of Peru, which stretched down to Iquique at that time. No rain ever falls in Arica and all water has to be piped in from the surrounding hills. It's an attractive place which nestles below a spectacular headland from the top of which are excellent views over the surrounding desert on one side and the ocean on the other.

Information

The tourist office, at Prat 375 (2nd Floor), is staffed by helpful people. Make sure you get hold of the useful booklet *Arica – Guía de Turismo y Compras*, which is free at the tourist office, many hotels and travel agencies.

Most of the street money changers are found at the junction of 21 de Mayo and Colón. They offer better rates than the banks.

The new bus terminal is on Av Diego Portales at the junction with Santa María. It's quite a long way from the centre so allow about 20 minutes if you are walking.

Consulates

Argentina
  Manuel Rodríguez 95 (tel 31322).
Bolivia
  Bolognesi 344 (tel 31030).
Peru
  Yungay 304 (tel 31020).

Airlines

Ladeco
  18 de Septiembre 370 (tel 32596).
LAN-Chile
  7 de Julio 148 (tel 31261).
Lloyd Aereo Boliviano
  Patricio Lynch 298 (tel 31124).

Things to See

Arica is a beach resort for rich Bolivians and it's one of the few places where you can catch some warm sea south of Ecuador. The best beaches are around the other side of the headland, the Morro de Arica, along the Av Costañera where there are a number of sheltered coves.

If you can get a group together and hire a colectivo, it's worth visiting the **Museo Archueologico San Miguel de Azapa** in the Azapa valley at Km 12. The museum has an excellent collection of exhibits which chronicle the various civilisations which have come and gone in the area from the 7th century BC until the arrival of the Spanish. It's open weekdays from 9 am to 5 pm and Saturdays from 1 to 6 pm.

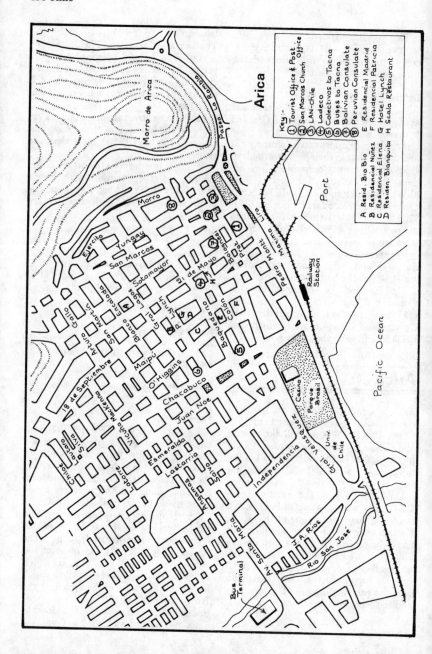

Arica

Key:-
1. Tourist Office & Post Office
2. San Marcos Church
3. LAN-chile
4. Ladeco
5. Colectivos to Tacna
6. Buses to Tacna
7. Bolivian Consulate
8. Peruvian Consulate

A Resid. Bio Bio
B Residencial Madrid
C Residencial Nuñez
D Residen. Blanquita
E Residencial Elena
F Residencial Patricia
G Hotel Lynch
H Scala Restaurant

Parque Nacional Lauca The Lauca National Park covers a large area north-east of Arica up against the Bolivian border at an altitude of between 3000 and 6300 metres. It's well worth visiting even if you only go for a day. The scenery is magnificent, especially around Lago Chungara which sits between two snow-capped volcanoes and is supposedly the highest lake in the world. There's a lot of wild-life in the park and you'll undoubtedly see vicuña, guanaco, vizcacha, condor and waterfowl even on a short visit.

The park is about 120 km from Arica and straddles the Arica-La Paz highway. The drive from Arica takes about four hours, the first 100 km over a surfaced road. The cheapest way of getting to the park is to take the Arica-La Paz bus and get off near Lago Chungara where there is an information centre with a few beds and a kitchen. Take food and warm clothing.

If your time is limited or you prefer something more organised then check the tourist agencies in Arica which organise tours. These include *Huasqui-Tour, Turismo Payachatas, Parina Tour* and *Jurasi*. *Payachatas*, Av Bolognesi, offer a one-day tour by VW Combi which leaves Arica at 7.30 am and returns at 8.30 pm. It costs US$10 and includes breakfast at the Inca ruins en route. They also visit the puna village of Parinacota where little has changed since the 16th century. Travellers who have taken this tour have recommended it highly.

Places to Stay

The cheapest place is the *Residencial Nuñez*, Maipú 516, which costs US$1.20 per person. It's basic, clean sheets are provided and there's hot water. Similar is the *Residencial Patricia*, Maipú 269, which is good value at US$1.65 per person. It's a little on the grubby side but otherwise pleasant and popular with travellers. Another cheapie is the *Residencial El Cobre*, Gen Lagos 672, which is clean and good value at US$1.80/$3 a single/double.

Moving up-market slightly, the *Residencial La Blanquita*, Maipú 472, is clean, has hot water 'when the pressure allows' and is good value at US$2.70/$4/$6 a single/double/triple. Similar and highly recommended by many travellers is the *Residencial Madrid*, Baquedana 685, which is clean, has hot water and costs US$2.40/$4 a single/double. Another is the *Residencial Sotomayor*, Sotomayor 442, which costs US$2.35 per person but has no hot water.

If you're looking for something mid-range then try the *Hotel Lynch*, Lynch 589, which costs US$4.40 to US$5.85 a single and US$7.30 a double without own bath and US$13.30 a double with own bath. There's a discount of 5% for those staying more than two days!!

Places to Eat

There are plenty of cafés along 21 de Mayo, 18 de Septiembre, Maipú, Bolognesi and Colón. Some of the cheapest places are along the latter two streets where you can get soup, a starter, hamburger and a juice for less than US$1. Elsewhere in town you can pay double this for just a hamburger. Try the *Rotiseria Colón*, Colón 325. There's also a menu at 18 de Septiembre 431.

A very popular meeting place with young people is the *Scala*, 21 de Mayo 201 at the junction with Colón. It does hamburgers, coffee and beer but is relatively expensive.

Getting There

There are daily buses (some during the day, others at night) to Iquique (US$4.50 to $5.30), Antofagasta (US$11 to $12.60, 10 hours) and Santiago (US$18.70 to $31, 27 to 28 hours). Book a day in advance if possible especially for the daytime buses. There are also international buses to La Paz (Bolivia), and to Tacna and Arequipa (Peru). Colectivos to Tacna (several companies) go from Chacabuco between Baquedano and Colón. The leave when full throughout the day.

If you're taking the train to Tacna in Peru you need to turn up about half an hour before departure to give the police time to get through exit formalities.

Calama

Calama sits on the high plain in the middle of the Atacama desert and is the commercial centre for the nearby open-cast copper mines of Chuquicamata, which are the largest in the world. Coming up from Antofagasta, you can see the smoke pouring out of the stacks at Chuquicamata for miles before you arrive in Calama. For travellers the town is a jumping off point for visits to the oasis villages of San Pedro de Atacama (on the edge of the Salar de Atacama), Toconao, Chiu Chiu and, of course, the copper mine at Chuquicamata. It's also the terminus of the Calama-La Paz railway which is used by many travellers as a way to and from Bolivia.

Information

The tourist office is on the corner of Vicuna MacKenna and Latorre. The staff are enthusiastic and friendly and have free maps of Calama and the surrounding region. No English is spoken.

The best place to change money is at the Tramaca bus terminal – just ask the ticket staff who offer good rates. The only other possibility is at the Banco de Credito and they only change cash. You cannot change travellers' cheques in Calama.

The Bolivian consulate, at MacKenna 1976, is open Monday to Friday from 9.30 am to 12 noon and 4 to 5.30 pm. If you are taking the train to Bolivia then make sure you come here first for a stamp in your passport before buying the train ticket. In the past we had reports that the consul demanded money for what should have been free stamps but that doesn't appear to be the case anymore.

Things to See

The **Chuquicamata Copper Mines** are the largest open-cast copper mines in the world and well worth a visit. They are about 12 km from Calama. Guided tours (in the company's buses) preceded by a video (in Spanish) take place on Mondays, Wednesdays and Thursdays at 1 pm from the Public Relations Office (*Relacciones Publicas*) in Chuquicamata. The tour lasts about two hours and may be free if there's a large group going on it; otherwise expect to pay about US$0.60.

The Public Relations Office is at Puerto Uno and to get there from Calama it's best to hire a colectivo which should cost US$0.65 per person. There are public buses from Calama but they don't go as far as the Public Relations Office and you may find yourself having to walk two km. It's a very interesting tour. Take your passport and camera with you. Although photography is officially prohibited inside the refinery building, control is very lax.

The mine's canteen is just opposite the Public Relations Office so if you go there around 12 noon you can have a very good, cheap meal; the service is excellent.

The Oasis Villages

The most important of the oasis villages is **San Pedro de Atacama**, about 120 km south-east of Calama. If you're in this area you really must put aside at least two or three days to visit this place. It's not only very relaxing but also very interesting and the landscapes are out of this world. The village sits at the edge of the Salar de Atacama, a completely flat and largely dried-up salt lake into which a stream still flows. On the eastern side of the Salar rise enormous volcanos as far as the eye can see; some of them snow capped, some of them still active (you can see them smoking at certain times of the day). This is the border region between Chile, Bolivia and Argentina. On the other side of the Salar, within walking distance of the village, is the famous Valley of the

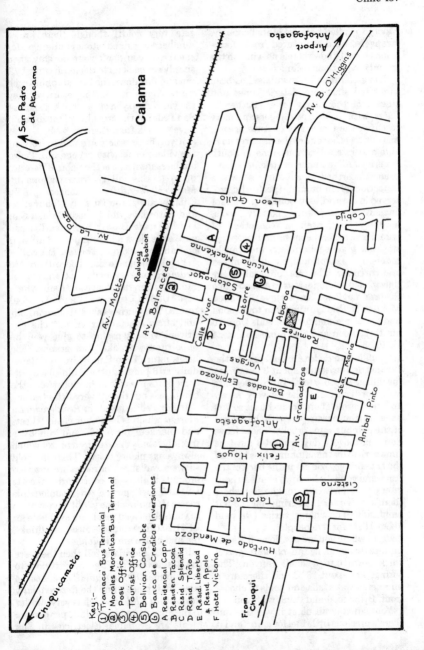

Moon, so-called because of its bone-dry, strangely wind-sculptured rock formations (yes, I know there's no wind on the moon!) in glorious technicolour.

The area around this village has been inhabited since pre-historic times and since 1955 the village priest, Father Le Paige, with the help of villagers and more recently, the University of Antofagasta, has put together one of the most remarkable and interesting museums in South America. All manner of artefacts have been unearthed, including a whole collection of mummies (perfectly preserved in the arid, salty soil), fragments of ancient woven fabrics, pottery, tools, jewellery and even a collection of paraphernalia for preparing and ingesting/smoking psychedelic plants and mushrooms. It's exceptionally well organised and cared for. The museum (called the **Universidad del Norte: Museo Arqueologico Gustavo Le Paige de Walque**) is open Monday to Friday from 8 am to 12 noon and 2 to 6 pm and on weekends from 10 am to 12 noon and 2 to 6 pm and costs US$0.35.

Outside San Pedro are hot springs, the Termas de Puritama, about 35 km from the village en route to El Tatio. These are well worth visiting (there's very rarely anyone there). There are no buses so you have to arrange transport with the drivers of the sulphur-mine trucks. These leave San Pedro every day around 8 am (the time varies) for the sulphur mines beyond the hot springs. You get in the back of the truck and you'll be let down about an hour later (it's a fairly cold, rough ride) where there's a sign for the springs on the left hand side. The charge varies (we paid about US$1 for five people).

From where you are put down it's a 20-minute walk along an obvious gravel track down into a small canyon. The springs are about 33°C and there are a number of waterfalls and pools to choose from. Bring food and drink with you.

You can stay all night if you like but there's precious little fuel for a fire (and it gets very cold!) though there are a number of ruined stone buildings for shelter. If you don't want to stay then simply get back up to the main track by 1 pm and flag down the first sulphur truck which comes by. On the return journey they may drop you off several km short of San Pedro at the crushing plant so you'll have to walk from there.

If you have time you should also visit the village of **Toconao** beyond San Pedro on the eastern side of the Salar. There are buses to this village from Calama by *Morales Moralito*, Balmaceda 1852, Calama, at 4 pm on Tuesdays, Thursdays and Saturdays which pass through San Pedro en route. Buses return from Toconao on Wednesdays and Fridays at 8 am and on Sundays at 6 pm. The fare is US$3.

From Calama to San Pedro there are *Tramaca* buses every day at 9 am, except Sunday when they leave at 11 am, which cost US$2.45 one-way and US$4.40 return. The journey takes about one hour and offers spectacular vistas. The bus drivers will often stop to give you the opportunity to take photographs. The buses return from San Pedro to Calama daily at 6 pm from the main plaza. It's sometimes possible to hitch between the two places but there's very little traffic.

In San Pedro stay at the *Residencial La Florida* which is basic but clean (sheets and blankets provided) and run by a friendly family assisted by a parrot which always has plenty to say. There are cold showers available. The rooms are arranged around a pleasant courtyard. It costs US$1.35 per person in double/triple rooms (if you're alone you'll have a room to yourself). Good meals are available for US$1.20 (three courses). Beer, soft drinks, tea and coffee are available.

If the La Florida is full then there are the *Residencial El Pukara*, next door to the Florida; *Residencial Cobre Loa* (a very small place); and the *Residencial y Restaurant Chiloe*, which is very similar to the Florida and costs US$2 per person. Meals are available. Electricity in San

Pedro is available only from dusk to around 9.30 pm.

For somewhere to eat other than the Florida try the *Restaurant Juanita* on the plaza.

There are a number of good tiendas in the village where you can buy bread, cheese, fruit, vegetables, wine, beer and canned goods so there's no need to bring these from Calama. Local *vino* at the bottle shop/bar just down the street from the Florida costs about US$0.80 per litre and is very palatable. You meet a lot of local people there in the evenings.

There is a good craft shop on the plaza in San Pedro where you can find excellent examples of cactus-wood carving.

There are other places of interest which you can visit from Calama including the village of **Chiu Chiu** (fine examples of cactus-wood carving) but there is no public bus so you'll have to hire private transport. This is going to work out expensive unless you can get a group together. Once you have a group, however, the best man to contact in Calama is Luis Gutierrez, Angamos 2687, Pob Santa Rosa, Calama. He organises tours to remote spots along the border region as well as to San Pedro, Toconao and the geysers. His vehicles will take up to eight people and cost around US$100 including food.

Places to Stay (In Calama)

The *Residencial Toño*, Vivar 1968, has been popular with travellers for years. It has clean sheets and adequate blankets and costs US$1.65 per person in double rooms. Hot showers cost US$0.35 extra. Similar is the *Residencial Capri*, Vivar 1639, which is friendly and very clean and costs US$2/$4 a single/double. There is hot water in the showers in the mornings.

Another worth trying in this category is the *Residencial Libertad*, Granaderos 2008, which is basic, has clean sheets, hot water all day and costs US$4 a double. There are no singles.

Somewhat more expensive is the

Residencial Splendid, Ramirez 1960, which is a very clean, homely and secure hotel popular with local salesmen and the like. It costs US$2/$4.65/$6.65 a single/double/triple without own bath and US$4/$7.30/$10 a single/double/triple with own bath. There's plenty of hot water in the mornings and evenings. Breakfast (two fried eggs, bread, coffee) is available for US$0.80 – good value.

Other cheapies include the *Pension Latorre*, Latorre 2091; the *Residencial Mi Casa*, Ramirez 2262, which are both basic but acceptable (no hot water) at US$1.35 per person; the *Residencial El Tatio*, Gallo 1987, which is clean and has hot water available all day and costs US$3.35/$4.65 a single/double with breakfast available; and the *Residencial Apolo XX*, Vargas 2206, which is similar to the Libertad.

Places to Eat

The best value in town is probably the *Hotel Restaurant Victoria*, Vargas 2102 on the corner of Abaroa. You can get very good two-course meals (soup, steak with rice) for US$1. They also have very cheap beer and Chilean wines for sale. Similar is the *Restaurant Osorno*, on the corner of Granaderos and Espinoza, which offers four-course meals for around US$1.10. For a splurge, try the *Club Yugoslavia* on the main plaza or the *Restaurant Chi Kang*, Espinoza between Latorre and Vivar. The *Restaurant La Florida* has also been recommended.

For some action in the evening try the *Postoyna Disco*, Latorre 2152. There are also a number of topless bars/discos in Calama. Most of them charge around US$4 which includes a bottle of wine.

Getting There

Trains to Bolivia depart once weekly on Wednesdays at 2.55 pm. Tickets are sold on Tuesdays between 3 and 4.30 pm and on Wednesdays between 8.30 am and 12.45 pm. There's one class only. You must change at Ollague and that often involves a four-hour wait. The Chilean carriages are bad news; the Bolivian ones are reasonably good. There are no passenger services to Antofagasta.

Tramaca bus company operates direct buses to Antofagasta, 11 times daily from 7.30 am to 9.30 pm, US$3.35; Arica, 9 pm daily, US$9.40; Iquique 10 pm daily, US$6.45; and Santiago, 12 noon and 3.30 pm daily, US$23.30.

CHILOÉ ISLAND

Just off the south coast of the Lake District lies Chile's largest island, some 250 km long and about 50 km wide. It has a romantic and brooding quality to it and in some ways is similar to the Scottish Hebrides. The difference is that here, instead of stone crofts, the houses are of clapboard with corrugated iron roofs. It's only sparsely populated and most people live within sight of the ocean. Inland are vast virgin forests. The major occupations are fishing and the growing of wheat and potatoes. For much of the winter months the island is enveloped in mists and rain is frequent.

Chiloé Island is a very relaxing place to visit and when the sun breaks through it can be spectacularly green and beautiful, with views across the gulf to the snow-capped, volcano-dotted mainland.

Ancud and Castro are the only towns of any size on the island. Two smaller centres of population, Chonchi and Quellón, are of interest because they're the ports for ferries to the mainland.

Getting There

There are daily buses from Puerto Montt to Ancud, Castro and Quellón which involve a ferry crossing between Pargua and Chacao. Buses go on the ferries so there's no need to change. Full details of the buses can be found under the section on Puerto Montt.

Ferries to the mainland at Chaiten and Puerto Chacabuco from Chonchi and Quellón respectively can be found under 'Getting Around – Boats' in the introductory section of this chapter.

Ancud

The largest centre of population on the island, Ancud is a picturesque fishing and agricultural town built on a series of small hills overlooking a bay to the north.

Information The tourist office is at Chorrillos at the junction with Ramirez at the corner of the Plaza de Armas. The office is part of the museum which is also worth visiting. Maps of the town and up-to-date information about all the hotels and residencias are available.

Cruz del Sur (buses to Puerto Montt, Castro and Quellón) has its terminal on Chacabuco 672. Local rural buses have their terminal at the junction of Prat and Libertad.

Transmarchilay (the company which operates the Chonchi-Chaiten and Quellón-Puerto Chacabuco ferries) has offices at Libertad 669 (tel 317) over-looking the Plaza de Armas. If heading further south, confirm ferry times there.

Things to See Ancud is a place for strolling around and relaxing, popping into cafés and talking with local people. In addition to the museum on the Plaza de Armas there is the restored fort of San Antonio (built by the Spanish) which you get to by following the coast road north.

Places to Stay For some reason, many of the owners and staff of the hospedajes and residencias here appear to have won a fortune on the national lottery and then lost it on the dogs. They can not only be hostile but appear to be hell-bent on extracting as much money out of you as possible. This is in stark contrast to the rest of the populace who are very friendly and helpful.

Probably the cheapest place available is the *Hospedaje Casa del Apostolado* which costs US$1 per person without breakfast and US$1.35 with breakfast.

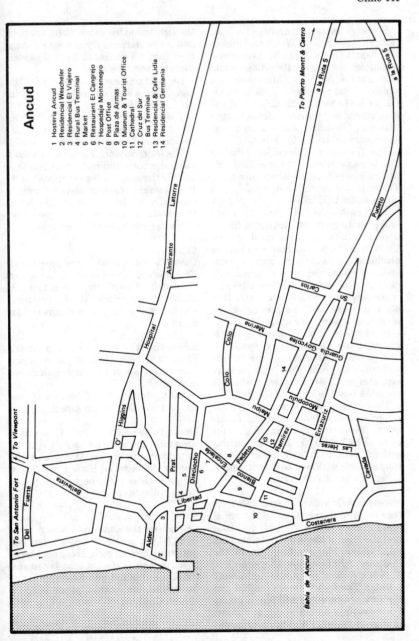

Ancud

1 Hosteria Ancud
2 Residencial Wescheler
3 Residencial El Viajero
4 Rural Bus Terminal
5 Market
6 Restaurant El Cangrejo
7 Hospedaje Montenegro
8 Post Office
9 Plaza de Armas
10 Museum & Tourist Office
11 Cathedral
12 Cruz del Sur Bus Terminal
13 Residencial & Cafe Lidia
14 Residencial Germania

To San Antonio Fort
To Viewpoint
To Puerto Montt & Castro
a la Ruta 5
a la Ruta 5

Del Fuerte
Bellavista
Alder
O'Higgins
Prat
Dieciocho
Encalada
Libertad
Blanco
Pedeto
Ramirez
Las Heras
Caveda
Costanera
Errazuriz
Mocopulu
Maipu
Guardia Govogolea
Marina
Colo
Colo
Hospital
Almirante
Latorre
Carlos
Su

Bahia de Ancud

Slightly more expensive are the *Alojamiento Elvira Navarro*, Pudeto 361, which costs US$2.35 per person including breakfast; the *Alojamiento José Santos Miranda*, Mocopulli 753, which is US$2 per person without breakfast or US$2.35 with breakfast and has hot showers; and the *Alojamiento Natalia Mendoza*, Errazíriz 430, which is the same price as the Santos Miranda.

The *Residencial Germania*, Pudeto 357, is also relatively cheap at US$2.65/$4.85 a single/double without own bath. There is hot water and breakfast is available for US$0.50.

The *Residencial El Viajero*, Bellavista 491, is a strange place. Not a soul smiled once and although the maid quoted US$2.65 per person without own bath or breakfast the owner subsequently demanded US$3.35 per person which only came down to the original price after a lot of nonsense and hostility. Even at that it's overpriced and the service in the hotel's restaurant is agonisingly slow.

Similarly, at the *Hospedaje Montenegro*, Blanco Encalada 541, you may first be quoted US$2/$4 a single/double without own bath but this quickly escalates to US$4 per person which is nonsense considering what you get.

The only place where a friendly reception was found was at the *Residencial Wescheler*, Cochrane 480. This costs US$2.65/$5.35 a single/double without own bath and US$5.35/$8 a single/double with own bath (hot water). Unfortunately it's often full.

Places to Eat One of the cheapest places is the *Cocineria Real* behind the Municipal Market. Good food is available for about half the price of the other restaurants in the market. For a splurge go to the *Restaurant El Cangrejo*, Dieciocho 155. This is a seafood restaurant and is very popular. The food there is excellent and the servings generous and judging from the scrawlings on the walls, it appears that every traveller who has ever passed through Ancud has eaten there. Try their *paltina de mariscos* if you want a change from fish; it's a meal in itself. The staff there are very friendly.

For good coffee and cakes try the *Café Lidia*, Chacabuco 650 next to the *Cruz del Sur* bus office.

There are discotheques at *Bar Macarracos*, Maipú 232, and at *Doscotheque Sorbo's* on Bellavista.

The *Hosteria Ancud* is the town's most expensive hotel and restaurant and so is outside the range of budget travellers. It is, however, a pleasant place for a drink especially in the winter months when there's always a log fire crackling away. The hotel overlooks the bay.

Castro

Castro is the capital of the province of Chiloé which also includes a portion of the mainland around the town of Chaiten. It's notable for the huge wooden cathedral on the main plaza which stands out for miles.

Information The tourist office is on the Plaza de Armas. Maps of the town and information about the surrounding area is available.

The bus terminal is off San Martín near the junction with Sergio Aldea.

Things to See Like Ancud, Castro is a town for strolling around but do visit the waterfront market on Montt and the **Regional Museum** on Blanco 261. There are good views over the town from the Cerro Millantuy.

Places to Stay A good place is the *Hotel Octavio* on the waterfront which costs US$1.50 per person. It's clean, has hot water and there's a good, cheap restaurant downstairs (breakfast of eggs, bread and coffee for US$0.50 and lunch/dinner of fish or fillet steak with chips and salad for around US$1.80).

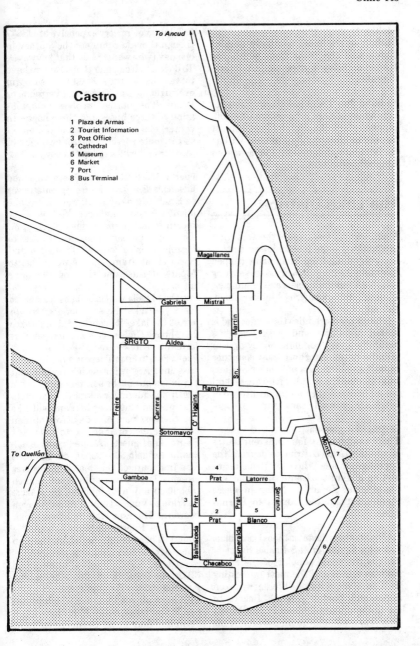

Castro

1 Plaza de Armas
2 Tourist Information
3 Post Office
4 Cathedral
5 Museum
6 Market
7 Port
8 Bus Terminal

To Ancud

To Quellón

Magallanes

Gabriela   Mistral

SRGTO   Aldea

Freire   Carrera   O'Higgins   Ramirez

Sotomayor

Gamboa   Prat   Latorre

Prat   Serrano

3   1

2   5

Prat   Blanco

Balmaceda   Esmeralda

Chacabco

San Martin

Sn.

Montt

Quellón

Quellón is the most southerly port of Chiloé and the town from which the *Transmarchilay* ferries sail to Puerto Chacabuco.

Places to Stay There is a *Youth Hostel* of sorts where you can get a bed for US$0.50. Otherwise try the *Hotel Playa*, Montt 255; or the *Hosteria La Pincoya*, La Paz 64. Both are cheap. The Playa has an attached restaurant.

The Lake District

There are very few areas of the world that can match this one for scenic grandeur. It has everything from high, snow-capped mountains to crystal-clear lakes, smoking volcanoes, forests, glaciers and in summer, a delightful northern Mediterranean climate.

The district straddles the Andes and is shared by Chile and Argentina. It's naturally a very popular holiday destination for nationals of both those countries as well as thousands of other travellers from all over the world. There are several passes between the two countries, two of which are open all year round.

Getting to Argentina

There are basically four different routes across the Lake District to or from the Argentinian side, three of them terminating at San Carlos de Bariloche and the other at Zapala or Neuquén where there are trains and buses to Buenos Aires.

(1) The Southern Route via Lagos Llanquihue, Todos los Santos, Frías & Nahuel Huapí

This is the most popular of the cross-Andean routes and the most interesting as it involves a lot of different trips on buses and boats. Through tickets to Bariloche are available in Puerto Montt from *Turismo Andina de Sur*, Av Varas 437, but they're very expensive at US$77 though they do complete the journey in one day (who wants to do that anyway!). To do it much cheaper than that you have to do the journey in stages with an overnight stop at Ensenada, Petrohué or Puella. The journey involves a combination of three buses and three boats. In winter, make enquiries before you set off as the route (description following), can sometimes be blocked with snow.

Puerto Montt-Petrohué via Puerto Varas and Ensenada *Empresa Fierro* operate buses to Ensenada daily at 10 am which take about 1½ hours and cost US$1.65. They return from Ensenada daily at 1.30 pm. The same company also operate buses to Petrohué on Tuesday, Thursday and Saturday at 10 am. They return to Puerto Montt at the same time on the same days.

Petrohué-Puella via Lago Todos los Santos Here you take the steamer *Esmeralda* across the lake. It costs US$11 and takes 2-1/2 hours. Chilean customs and passport formalities are cleared at Puella.

Puella-Puerto Frías There is a bus over the pass into Argentina which takes about 1½ hours but in the summer months it's worth considering walking this stretch. It's a pleasant but steep hike and will take you the best part of a day. Argentinian customs are cleared at Puerto Frías.

Puerto Frías-Puerto Alegre-Puerto Blest-Puerto Pañuelo-San Carlos de Bariloche The first part of this last hop involves crossing Lago Frías on a small launch (about 20 minutes) followed by a short bus ride to Puerto Blest. From there you board the *Modesta Victoria* lake steamer and go to Puerto Pañuelo (about 1½ hours). There is another short bus hop from there to San Carlos de Bariloche.

(2) Osorno-San Carlos de Bariloche via Lago Puyehue and the Puyehue Pass

This is an all-road journey which passes beside four lakes. *Buses Norte* have a bus between Osorno and Bariloche daily at

10.30 am which takes about 8½ hours and costs US$14.65. *Tas Choapa* also offer a similar bus. There are also buses to Zapala (US$14.65), Mendoza, Rosario and Buenos Aires by *Turismo Lanin* on Tuesday, Wednesday, Thursday, Friday and Sunday at 10 am. The route is open all year though snowfalls in winter may occasionally cause delays.

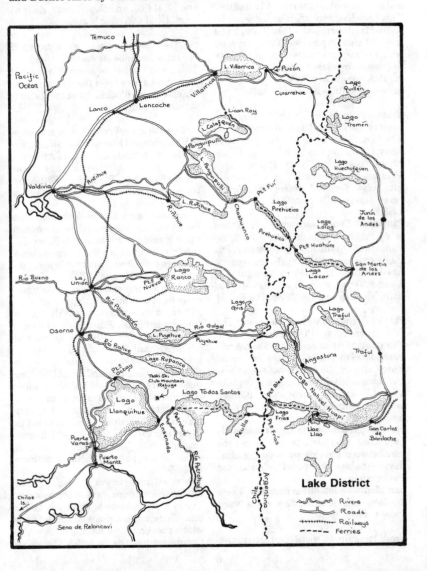

Lake District

〜〜〜 Rivers
Roads
++++++ Railways
‒ ‒ ‒ Ferries

(3) Valdivia-San Carlos de Bariloche via Lago Panguipulli, Lago Pirehueico and Lago Lacar and San Martín de los Andes

Along this route it used to be possible to go from Valdivia to Riñihue on Lago Riñihue and then by boat from there to Choshuenco. This is no longer possible as there are no regular boats across this lake (though you can still charter your own) and the road which skirts the southern end of the lake to Enco is now closed. The new route goes via Panguipulli. In winter, make enquiries as it's sometimes blocked by snow.

Valdivia-Panguipulli Four companies operate buses to Panguipulli from Valdivia. They are *Buses Chile Nuevo*, nine times daily from 7.55 am to 6.30 pm, US$2; *Buses Oriente*, daily at 4 pm; *Buses Valdivia*, six times daily from 6.45 am to 7 pm, US$1.65; and *Buses Pirehueico*, seven times daily from 8 am to 6 pm, US$2.

Panguipulli-Choshuenco and Pto Fuy There is no longer a launch service on Lago Panguipulli so you must go by road to Pto Fuy (sometimes spelt Fui). *Transpacar* has daily buses to Pto Fuy via Neltume at 3 and 3.30 pm. *Estrella* also has one bus daily Monday to Saturday to Pto Fuy at 2.45 pm.

Pto Fuy-Pirehueico via Lago Pirehueico The launch across Lago Pirehueico leaves Pto Fuy daily at 8 pm and takes 1½ hours.

Pirehueico-Pto Huahún There is a road which crosses the border between these two towns and you can either walk or take a local bus which leaves every morning except on Thursdays. Argentinian customs are cleared at Pto Huahún.

Pto Huahún-San Martín de los Andes via Lago Lacar There is a launch across the lake between the two towns on the same days as the buses between Pirehueico and Pto Huahún.

San Martín de los Andes-Bariloche There are daily buses in either direction between these towns.

From Panguipulli there is an alternative route into Argentina via Lago Calafquén and the Carrirriñe Pass.

If you want to do the Valdivia-Bariloche trip in one hop then both *Tas Choapa*, on Monday, Thursday and Saturday at 9.15 am, US$14.65; and *Buses Norte*, daily at 7 am, US$14.65 offer buses.

(4) The Northern Route via Villarrica & Puesco to Junín de los Andes

This road route between Chile and Argentina goes across the Tromen Pass which can be blocked by snow for four months in winter.

Valdivia-Villarrica/Pucón There are buses to Villarrica and Pucón on Lago Villarrica by *Buses Jac* daily at 7 am, 11 am and 4 pm except on Sunday when they leave at 7 and 11 am only. The fare is US$2.30. In the opposite direction they leave Villarrica at the same times.

You can also get to Villarrica and Pucón from Temuco and the service from there is much more frequent. *Buses Jac* run from Temuco to Villarrica and Pucón 18 times daily from 7 am to 8.35 pm, take two hours and cost US$1.45. In the opposite direction they leave 16 times daily from 6.45 am to 7.15 pm.

A third way of getting to Villarrica is from Panguipulli. *Buses Rurales Andes* leave Panguipulli daily at 3.30 pm and Villarrica daily at 7 am. The journey takes about 3½ hours and goes via Calafquén, Coñaripe and Lican Ray. The bus doubles as a school bus along some stretches and the road is rough in parts.

If you get off at Villarrica and stay there for a while then all you need do to get to Pucón is take one of the buses which come through from Valdivia or Temuco. It takes about half an hour and costs US$0.50.

Villarrica-Curarrehue-Pte Basa *Buses Regional Villarrica* have daily buses to Pucón and Curarrehue at 11 am and 5 pm. There's also a daily bus at 3.30 pm which goes on to Pte Basa.

Curarrehue-Junín de los Andes There's no

public transport between these two places so you'll have to hitch.

CHOSHUENCO
Places to Stay
Accommodation at Puerto Fuy is expensive so it's better to stay at Choshuenco at the eastern end of Lago Panguipulli if you're heading for Argentina. Stay at the *Hotel Ruca-Piura* which is a beautiful place and offers rooms for US$3. Good food is available at reasonable prices and there are boats for hire.

ENSENADA
Places to Stay
The cheapest places to stay are the *Youth Hostel* at the *Centro Juvenil* about one km out of town on the main road and the *Boy Scouts* who have a large lodge.

The *Teski Ski Club* has a mountain refuge outside of Ensenada, which has excellent views over the lake, and is a good base for climbing the Osorno volcano. It is worth making the effort to get there. Take the Ensenada-Puerto Octay road and turn off about three km from the town (signposted). From there it's another nine km up the side of the mountain (below the snow line). It's open all year, has a warden who looks after the place, a log fire and hot water. As far as hotels in the town go, one of the cheapest is the *Millantu*.

PANGUIPULLI
There is a tourist office in Panguipulli on the main plaza but it's often closed in winter.

Places to Stay
There are several hotels and residencias to choose from in Panguipulli but the best value is the *Residencial La Bomba*, on the corner of Rozas and Freire, which is friendly and pleasant and costs US$1.60 per person. There is hot water in the showers. Somewhat more expensive but very friendly and popular with travellers and hikers is the *Hospedaje El Ciervo*, Calle Valdivia between Carrera and Rozas, which costs US$2.50 per person. There's no hot water in the showers. Excellent, reasonably priced meals are available in the restaurant downstairs.

Other reasonably priced places to stay are the *Hotel Bellavista*, on the corner of Freire and Rozas, and the *Pension Central*, Rozas between Rodriguez and Freire (not to be confused with the Hotel Central).

For something vaguely mid-range, try either the *Hotel Central*, Calle Valdivia between Carrera and Rozas, or the *Hosteria Quetropillan*, on the corner of Garay and Freire. If you have money to burn then think about staying at the *Club de Yates* at the end of O'Higgins on a beautiful site with excellent views across the lake. It has very comfortable rooms with their own private shower and toilet and hot water and costs US$13.50 a double in winter and US$20 a double in summer including breakfast. In winter there's always an open log fire in the lounge bar (open to non-residents) and in summer they have discos.

Getting There
There are two bus stations in town, the main one on Valdivia for buses from Temuco, Valdivia and Santiago and down the lake to Choshuenco, Neltume and Pto Fuy (latter by *Transpacar* daily at 3 and 3.30 pm and by *Estrella* Monday to Saturday at 2.54 pm); and the smaller one on Freire for the *Buses Rurales Andes* services to Calafquén, Lican Ray and Villarrica (daily at 3.30 pm, 3½ hours).

PETROHUÉ
Places to Stay
There are very few cheap places but try the Küscher family's house as they may have a room to rent. They're on the other side of the river. The *refugio* above town is being renovated but this may be completed by the time you read this so make enquiries.

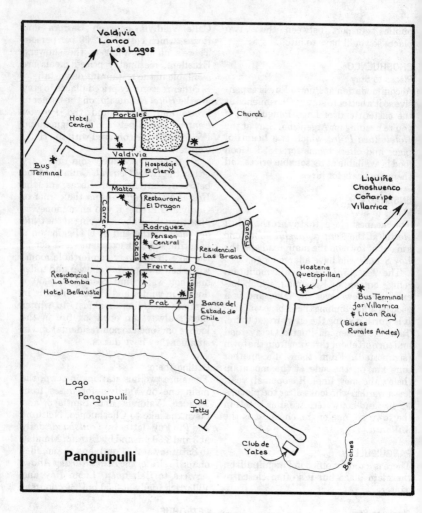

Panguipulli

PUCÓN

Pucón, at the far eastern end of Lago Villarrica, is a very beautiful place with a black volcanic sand beach but it caters largely to rich Chileans who pack the town during the summer months. At that time it can be very difficult to find cheap accommodation. In the winter there are very few visitors.

Information

There is a tourist office and handicraft centre on Brasil near the junction of Caupolicán but it's usually closed in winter.

Most of the bus companies have their offices near the junction of O'Higgins and Palguin.

Places to Stay

For accommodation try the house at Geronimo de Alderete 699 (painted yellow) which offers cheap beds. The *Residencial Lincoyan*, Calle Lincoyan, also has cheap rooms at US$2 per person. It's friendly and has hot showers.

PUELLA

Places to Stay

Accommodation at Puella is with various families who put travellers up for the night. It's a little on the expensive side but excellent value. Dinner, bed and breakfast in a warm, cosy bedroom with embroidered sheets and all essential amenities. You don't need to go looking for these places, they'll look for you. Food is hard to find so bring your own, although there's a tiny store at the rear of the Hotel Puella.

PUERTO VARAS

Puerto Varas is a large town with a

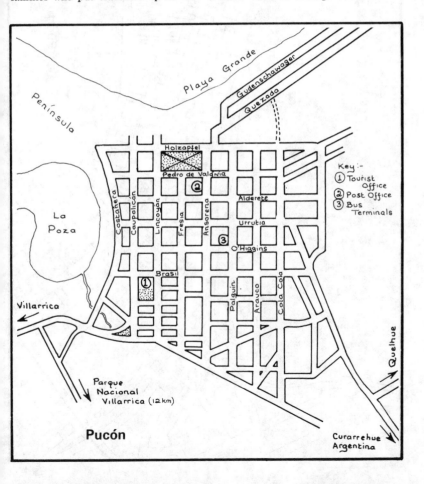

Pucón

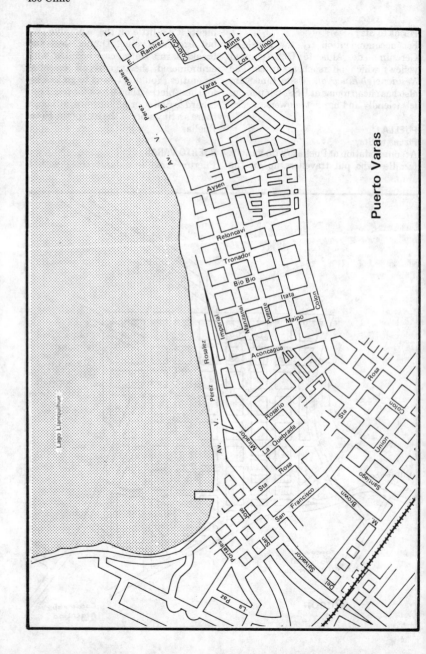

Puerto Varas

population of about 23,000, so there's no problem about finding accommodation.

Information
There is a tourist office at Santa Rosa 340 (tel 278) which has brochures about the entire area.

Places to Stay
As in Puerto Montt, many families offer relatively cheap accommodation, so if you want to stay, it's best to wander around town and keep an eye out for this kind of place. If you don't find anything immediately then try the *Residencial Unión*, San Francisco 669 opposite the bus terminal which is basic but clean and has hot showers.

VILLARRICA
This town is a popular place to stay and has superb views over Lago Villarrica and over to the Volcan Villarrica. The snow-covered volcano still smokes for most of the year and, if you're lucky, you may be there during an eruption. White-hot lava pouring out over snow is quite a sight. This happens relatively frequently.

Information
The tourist office is on Pedro de Valdivia close to the junction with Acevedo but it's often closed in winter.

Places to Stay & Eat
If you want somewhere free to stay and have your own bedding, carry on to Pucón and walk the eight-km gravel road out of Pucón to the Parque Nacional Villarrica entrance. At one km and three km from the park entrance are picnic areas with wooden huts, fireplaces and weatherproof walls where you can stay free. There are excellent views from these huts.

One of the cheapest places in Villarrica itself is the *Hotel Fuentes*, Reyes 665. It's very popular with travellers and hikers and costs US$2 per person in pleasant, comfortable rooms. There is hot water in the communal showers in the mornings (before 9 am). Downstairs is a bar and restaurant and they'll cook more or less anything for you if you tell them what you'd like in advance. There's usually an open log fire in the restaurant during winter and the staff are very friendly.

Also good value is the *Hospedaje*, Letelier 702, run by a local family which is very clean, has hot showers and costs US$2.60 per person. The rooms are pleasant and comfortable. Others in this category include the *Residencial Victoria*, Muñoz 530; *Residencial Puchy*, Valdivia 678; and the *Gran Hotel*, Henriquez 709.

For a splurge, try the *Hosteria Reyhuen*, Montt 668, which is a beautiful place with hot showers, heating in the rooms and its own restaurant. It costs US$4.60 per person in rooms with their own showers and toilet. It's run by Gualberto Lopez who speaks English.

For somewhere to eat other than the Hotel Fuentes try one or other of the restaurants along Henriquez near the junction with Letelier. For a splurge, try the excellent *Club Social Bar-Restaurant*, Valdivia 640. A fish meal will cost about US$2.20, with salads for around US$1 (generous portions). It's heated in winter.

There is a *peña* on Acevedo between Bilbao and Gallo which has a lot of atmosphere and reasonable prices. It's open even in winter but make enquiries to see whether there are any musicians playing on the night you choose to go.

Getting There
The main bus terminal is on Pedro de Valdivia at the junction with Muñoz. There are daily buses to Santiago (one per company usually around 8 pm) by *Pullman Lit*, *Fenix*, *Tur-Bus* and *Igi Llaima*.

You can also get buses to Argentina with *Buses Unión del Sud*, to Zapala and Neuquén on Tuesday, Wednesday, Thursday and Sunday at 2 pm; *Fenix*, to Mendoza daily, US$24.35; and *Igi Llaima*, to San Martín de los Andes (US$13.35)

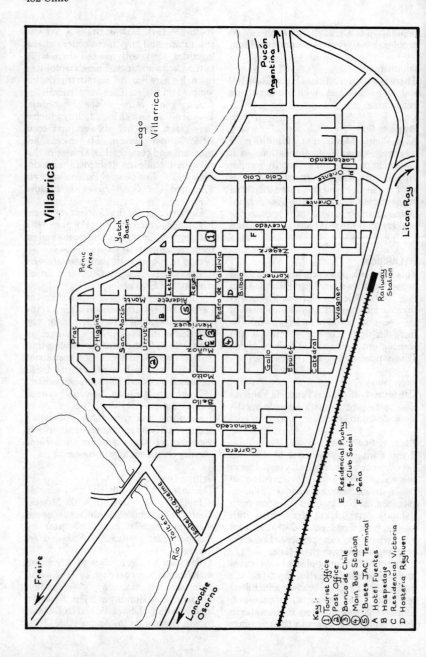

Villarrica

Key:-
① Tourist Office
② Post Office
③ Banco de Chile
④ 'Buses JAC' Terminal
⑤ Main Bus Station

A Hotel Fuentes
B Hospedaje
C Residencial Victoria
D Hosteria Rayhuen
E Residencial Puchy
+ Club Social
F Peña

and Neuquén (US$21.35) on Monday, Wednesday and Friday at 7.30 am.

Across the road from this terminal on Muñoz is the *Buses Regional Andes* terminal from which there is a daily bus to Panguipulli via Lican Ray at 7 am. They also go just to Lican Ray at 8.30 am and 3 pm.

Buses Jac have their terminal on Reyes between Muñoz and Henriquez and another office at the corner of Reyes and Montt. This company does the Temuco-Villarrica-Pucón and Valdivia-Villarrica-Pucón runs. There are 16 buses daily to Temuco from 6.45 am to 7.15 pm. Villarrica to Temuco takes about two hours and costs US$1.45. There are three buses daily to Valdivia at 7 am, 11 am and 4 pm.

Buses Regional Villarrica, Reyes next door to the Hotel Fuentes, runs buses to Pucón, Curarrehue and Pte Basa daily at 11 am, 3.30 and 5 pm.

OSORNO

Osorno is one of the largest towns of southern Chile. It has a population of over 100,000 and is a major transport centre for buses and trains to the Lake District especially to Lagos Puyehue and Rupanco and to the Parque Nacional Puyehue.

Osorno is inhabited mostly by the descendants of German immigrants to Chile, so many of the people there are bi-lingual.

Information

The tourist office is on the second floor of the bus terminal. The staff are very helpful and have a wide range of literature and maps (all of them free).

The quickest and most convenient way of changing money is to go to *Comercial Real*, Ramirez between Cochrane and Freire. It's an electrical and white-goods shop. There's no fuss and it's all done within a few minutes. They take both cheques and cash. Exchange rates are very favourable.

Places to Stay

Most of what you would expect to be cheapies in Osorno appear to be owned by hard-nosed, hard-faced sharks who quote the first figure that comes into their head. For the flea pits which most of them offer it's outright banditry.

A crumbling Dickensian hovel here commands no less than US$4 per person with coffee in the morning if you're lucky. In this respect it's very unlike the rest of the Lake District where you can generally find something decent for a reasonable price. Avoid the *Residencial Stop*, on the corner of Balbao and Freire, and the *Residencial Hein*, Cochrane between Balbao and Rodriguez. It's better to hang around the bus terminal and see what turns up – people will approach you with offers of accommodation. There are quite a few hotels around the bus station especially along Eduviges so if nothing better is offered try one of those.

One which can be recommended is the *Villa Eduviges Hotel*, Eduviges 856 (tel 5023). It's good value, friendly and clean with constant hot water and costs US$4.60/ $8.60 a single/double all with own bathroom. A little expensive for sure but it can be difficult to find anything cheaper.

Places to Eat

A very good place to eat is the *Club Social Ramirez*, Eduviges almost next door to the Villa Eduviges Hotel. For US$1.60 you can get an excellent meal. The portions are very generous and the food tasty.

Getting There

From the bus terminal in Osorno you can get buses to most of the larger towns in the Lake District – Temuco, Valdivia, Puerto Varas and Puerto Montt. Going north from Osorno there are buses to Valdivia (US$1.65 to $1.85) and Temuco (US$3.65) by *Pullman Lit*, *Cruz del Sur*, *Igi Llaima*, *Vaftur*, *ETC* and *Buses Norte*. Going south there are buses to Puerto Varas and Puerto Montt (both US$1.65 to $2) by

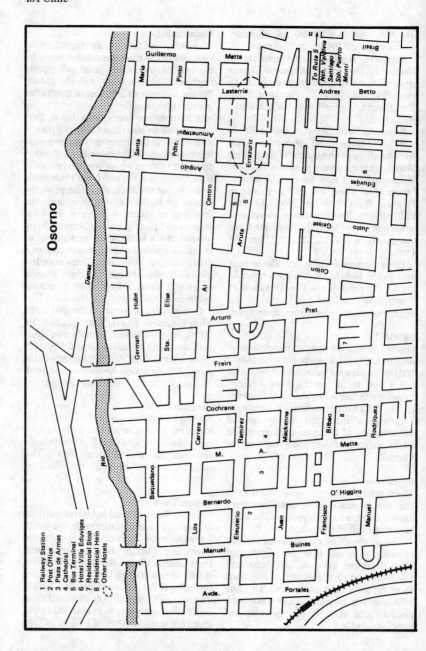

Osorno

1 Railway Station
2 Post Office
3 Plaza de Armas
4 Cathedral
5 Bus Terminal
6 Hotel Villa Eduviges
7 Residencial Stop
8 Residencial Hein
⊙ Other Hotels

To Ruta 5
Nth. Valdivia
Santiago
Sth. Puerto
Montt

Cruz del Sur, Igi Llaima, Buses Chiloe, ETC and *Varmont.*

You can also get buses to Bariloche, Mendoza, Rosario and Buenos Aires (Argentina) with *Turismo Lanin* (daily, except Saturday and Monday, at 10 am), *Buses Norte* (to Bariloche daily at 10.30 am) and *Tas Choapa.* The fare to Bariloche is US$14.65.

Most of these lines, plus *Turibus, Transbus, Via-Tur* and *Tur-Bus,* have daily departures to Santiago and Valparaiso.

PUERTO MONTT

Puerto Montt is the gateway to the southern end of the Lake District, to the island of Chiloé and to Chilean Patagonia. It's the transport hub for buses, trains, planes and boats going north, east and south from here. In itself it's a very lively and interesting little place with good markets and many reminders of its German-influenced past – the area was settled by German immigrants in the mid-19th century. Not only that, but it's a long way from discarding its 'pioneer' appearance. Weather-board houses are almost universal in this area.

Information

The tourist office is in a kiosk on Av Vargas in the large public square and gardens which face the sea front. The staff are very helpful and have a range of literature including a map of the town. There's also an office in the railway station but it only seems to open when trains arrive.

The Argentine consulate at Cauquenes 94 near the junction with Varas (2nd floor), is open Monday to Friday from 9 am to 2 pm. The consul is extremely pleasant and helpful and speaks perfect English. If you have a British passport and need a visa then this is the best place in South America to get it. This man will do his level best to get you one within 15 days (it's at least a month anywhere else).

Things to See

The biggest attraction is the picturesque fishing village of **Angelmo** about three km west of the town centre along the Av Portales. There are frequent local buses between the two which cost a few cents. Just before you get to Angelmo there is a row of craft shops selling goods ranging from sweaters and handmade boots to curios. There is also a row of seafood cafés along the front at Angelmo itself where you can eat very well for less than US$1.

In Pto Montt itself there is the **Museo Vicente Perez Rosales**, on the corner of Av Varas and Quillota, which chronicles the settlement of this area by the Germans during the latter half of the last century. There's also a private museum, the **Museo Pozuelo Caicumeo**, Manuel Rodriguez 240, which is concerned with the indigenous inhabitants of Chiloé Island.

Places to Stay

Most travellers to Pto Montt stay in rooms in private houses and the best of these places is Sn Raul Arroya's house at Concepción 136. Concepción is a very short street and this house is right at the end and round the corner, up against the bottom of the hill. Raul is very friendly and he and his family will make you very welcome. He'll probably find you before you find him since he often goes to meet incoming buses and checks out the tourist office for travellers. The rooms are very clean and pleasant and cost between US$1.65 to US$3.35 per person, the more expensive ones being double rooms with their own shower and toilet. There's hot water in the showers and breakfast is included in the price. Raul can arrange evening meals for you (very reasonable prices and excellent food) if you give him advance notice. Highly recommended and popular with travellers.

Another good place is at Vial 754 off Balmaceda on the left hand side. It's run by an old woman who is very friendly. The

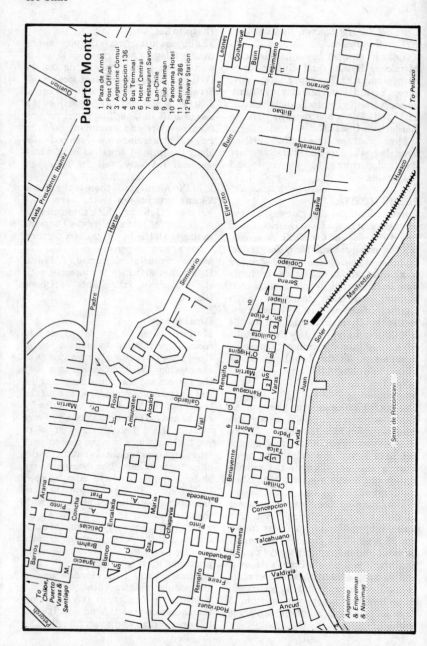

Puerto Montt

1 Plaza de Armas
2 Post Office
3 Argentine Consul
4 Concepcion 136
5 Bus Terminal
6 Hotel Central
7 Restaurant Savoy
8 Lan-Chile
9 Club Aleman
10 Panorama Hotel
11 Serrano 286
12 Railway Station

rooms have clean sheets and are good value at US$2 per person including breakfast. There are hot showers and home-baked bread is available.

The house at Anibel Pinto 328 has also been used by travellers for many years. Some people like it a lot saying it's warm, very clean, friendly and good value at US$4 a double. Others don't appear to be all that impressed. Check it out for yourself. There's hot water in the showers. The tourist office recommends Serrano 286 as being good value but it's some distance from the centre of town and costs US$2.50 including breakfast.

Other than private houses there is the *Hostal Panorama*, up on the hillside above the junction of Benavente and San Felipe. You can't miss it as there are huge signs. It looks expensive but it's surprisingly cheap at US$2.65 per person including breakfast but without own bath. Meals are relatively expensive (fish and chips will cost US$2.35).

The *Hotel Central*, Benavente 550, costs US$4 per person with own shower and toilet and hot water. It's very pleasant but if you don't want to pay that much then ask for the owner, Hans, who offers rooms in his own house for US$2.65 per person (hot water in the showers). He's a very friendly and interesting man who speaks German and some English as well as Spanish.

Places to Eat

Perhaps the best restaurant in Puerto Montt is the *Bar Restaurant Savoy*, Rancagua 256 on the junction with Rengipo. It's an excellent place with a very pleasant atmosphere and friendly staff. The food is tasty, the servings generous and the prices very reasonable. A fish or a vegetarian dish, both with separate salad, a bottle of wine and two hot drinks, will cost about US$5. *La Nave*, on the corner of Av Varas and Ancud, is also very good.

A restaurant which is popular with local people and which sometimes has live music in the evenings is the *Restaurant Bodegón*, Av Varas 931, but it tends to close early. The *Club Aleman*, Av Varas 264, is also popular especially as a drinking spot though they do offer meals too. It's somewhat more expensive than most places but you can often run into other travellers there.

Getting There

There's a huge central bus terminal in Pto Montt along the Av Portales. There are daily buses to Santiago by *Turibus, Cruz del Sur, Buses Lit, Via Tur, Bus Norte, Transbus, Varmont, Igi Llaima* and *Tas Choapa*. They all leave in the evening between 4.30 and 8 pm and cost between US$10 and US$12.

To Ancud, Castro and Quellón on Chiloé Island there is a choice of three companies: *Buses Chiloé*, to Ancud and Castro daily at 8.15 am and 9.45 am; *Cruz del Sur*, eight buses daily in either direction to Ancud and Castro, from 7.30 am to 7 pm from Pto Montt, and from 7 am to 5.15 pm from Castro (the 9 am and 1 pm buses from Pto Montt continue on to Quellón); *Transbus/Trans Chiloé* leave eight times daily in either direction to Ancud and Castro in the summer months but only once daily in either direction at 5 pm in the winter months. Buses to Quellón daily at 11.15 am and 12.30 pm. The fares and journey times are the same for all companies – Ancud US$2.35, two hours; Castro US$3.35, 3½ hours.

To Temuco and Valdivia the main companies are *Cruz del Sur*, daily at 11 am, 2 pm and 4.30 pm (US$2.65 and US$4.65 respectively); *ETC*, five times daily from 7 am to 6 pm; and *Transbus*, daily at 3.45, 5.30 and 8 pm.

Transport to the lakes is covered by *Tur-Bus*, who go to Villarrica and Pucón; and *Empresa Fierro*, to Ralún, Ensenada (daily at 10 am, returning at 1.30 pm, US$1.65, 1-1/12 hours), and to Petrohue on Tuesday, Thursday and Saturday at 10 am, returning at the same time, so you cannot go there and back in one day.

You can also get to Bariloche (Argentina) from Pto Montt with *Bus Norte*, daily at 8.30 am; and *Turismo Lanin*, on Tuesday, Wednesday, Thursday, Friday and Sunday at 8 am. The fare is US$14.65. All these buses go via Osorno and Puyehue.

If you want to go to Bariloche via Ensenada, Petrohue and Peulla (via Lago Todos los Santos and Lago Frias) then you either need to do it in stages or take a flight (daily from Puerto Montt at 3.40 pm, US$35) or take the 'Bus-Boat-Bus-Boat-Bus' trip offered by *Turismo Andina del Sur*, Av Varas 437, Pto Montt. This is a very expensive trip at US$77 but it includes all transport, two meals and an overnight stay in a hotel. They offer this trip throughout the year – it can be problematical getting to Argentina via Lago Todos los Santos in winter time by any other means.

Trains to Santiago from Pto Montt leave daily at 9 am (Expreso, arrives 8.10 am next day) and 4 pm (Rapido, arrives 11.20 am next day). There's also a daily *bus carril* to Osorno at 6 pm.

There is a local bus between the airport ('El Tepuel') and the bus terminal which connects with all outgoing and incoming flights.

Santiago

The capital of Chile and South America's fourth largest city, Santiago is a bustling modern metropolis, yet it still has quite a number of mansions, churches and other monuments dating back several centuries. The city was founded in 1541 by Pedro de Valdivia who followed the Inca road south from Cuzco to Jujuy and Salta and then crossed the Andes to reach the Chilean heartland. It's history is well-documented in the Casa Colorada (Museum of Santiago) on the corner of the Plaza de Armas.

Parts of the old centre, especially the budget hotel area with its roaring traffic and fumes, may make you wonder why you came to the city (it's no worse than Lima or Rio) but if you take the time to stroll around you'll find that it rapidly grows on you.

There are plenty of beautifully land-scaped parks and gardens, artists' colonies and superb views over the city and away to the snow-capped peaks of the Andes (when the pollution clears). People are very friendly and eager to talk to visitors from abroad, even in the cafés and bars of the commercial centre.

The pedestrian streets of Ahumada and Huerfanos are always thronged with shoppers and strollers and there are often impromptu performances by street-theatre groups and musicians, especially in the evenings. The police are very much in evidence as you might expect given the political circumstances yet no more so than in several other Latin American capital cities. Even demonstrators occasionally march through the streets these days.

Information

The tourist office, at Catedral 1159 (tel 60474) opposite the National Congress, is open Monday to Friday from 9 am to 5 pm and, in summer only, on Saturdays from 9 am to 1 pm. The staff are very friendly and helpful and have a range of literature, good maps and other information and English is spoken. If you arrive on a weekend when the office is closed there is a municipal information kiosk at the junction of Huerfanos and Ahumada which is open on Saturday mornings.

The easiest way to change money if you have cash dollars is to walk down Agustinas or Huerfanos in the city centre. There are heaps of money changers along these two streets. Once you've agreed on a rate they'll often take you to offices in nearby buildings where the transaction takes place.

There is no danger in doing all this and in fact it's much better for both parties. These people usually also accept travellers' cheques but the rate isn't too good, so the best thing to do with these is to cash them into dollars first at a bank (you can do this in Chile).

Take American Express cheques to the American Express International Banking Corporation, Agustinas 1360, where you can get cash dollars for 1% commission (pay the commission in Chilean pesos). After that, change the dollars on the street market.

For trekking information and details of *refugios* in the national parks go to the National Forests office – Corporación Nacional Forestal (CONAF), General Bulnes 285.

The Federación de Andinismo de Chile, Almirante Simpson 77, just off Av Vicuña MacKenna, caters for those interested in mountaineering in the Andes. The people are very friendly so if you are interested then come and speak to them.

The Secretaria Nacional de la Juventid, Estados Unidos 359 (also at Villavicencio 352, round the corner from the first) don't have much information on the youth hostels in Chile and will direct you to the Santiago youth hostel for this information (eg for the *Guía Turistica de los Albergues Juveniles*).

At the time of writing, the main post office on the Plaza de Armas was closed for renovation. The temporary central office is on Morandé facing the Plaza de la Constitución opposite the Hotel Carrera. If you are posting packages and parcels from this office, first make sure you read the instructions about how to go about it, otherwise you'll queue up in vain only to be told it's not acceptable (glued brown wrapping isn't acceptable – you must use Scotch tape).

The Lista de Correos is in a different office at Agustinas 1137 (2nd floor) – it's very well organised.

American Express is on Turismo Cocha, Agustinas 1360 and Thomas Cook is at Agustinas 1058.

Embassies

Argentina
Vicuña MacKenna 41 (tel 222 8977). Open Monday to Friday from 9 am to 2 pm.

Australia
Gertrudis Echenique 420 (tel 228 5065). Open Monday to Friday from 9 am to 12 noon and 2 to 3.30 pm.

Brazil
Antonio Varas 647 (tel 741959). Open Monday to Friday from 10 am to 2 pm.

Bolivia
Av Sta Maria 2796 (tel 222 5690). Open Monday to Friday from 9 am to 1 pm.

Canada
Ahumada 11 (10th floor) (tel 62256). Open Monday to Friday from 8.30 am to 1.30 pm.

France
Condell 65 (tel 225 1030). Open Monday to Friday from 9.30 am to 12 noon.

Germany (West)
Agustinas 785 (7th floor) (tel 35031). Open Monday to Friday from 9 am to 12 noon and 2 to 3.30 pm.

Paraguay
Burgos 245, Las Condes (metro station Alcantara). Open Monday to Friday from 9.30 am to 1.30 pm. This is a temporary address while their consular offices at Huerfanos 886 (Apt 514) (tel 394640) are being refurbished.

Peru
Andres Bello 1751 (tel 4900450). Open Monday to Friday from 10 am to 3 pm.

Uruguay
Pedro de Valdivia 711 (tel 223 8398). Open Monday to Friday from 10 am to 3 pm.

UK
La Concepción 177 (4th floor) (tel 223 9166). Open Monday to Friday from 9.30 am to 12.30 pm and 3 to 4 pm.

USA
Merced 230 (tel 710133 ext 255). Open Monday to Friday from 8.30 am to 10.50 am.

Airlines

Aerolineas Argentinas
Moneda 756 (tel 393922).

AeroPeru
Teatinos 335 (tel 715035/712380).

Avianca
Moneda 140 (tel 81919).

Air France
Agustinas 1136 (tel 725333).

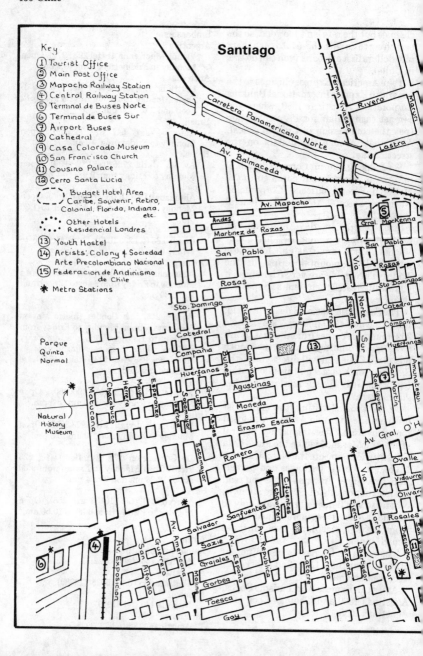

Key
① Tourist Office
② Main Post Office
③ Mapocho Railway Station
④ Central Railway Station
⑤ Terminal de Buses Norte
⑥ Terminal de Buses Sur
⑦ Airport Buses
⑧ Cathedral
⑨ Casa Colorado Museum
⑩ San Francisco Church
⑪ Cousiño Palace
⑫ Cerro Santa Lucia
⌒ Budget Hotel, Area
Caribe, Souvenir, Retiro,
Colonial, Florida, Indiana,
etc.
•••• Other Hotels
•••• Residencial Londres
⑬ Youth Hostel
⑭ Artists' Colony & Sociedad
Arte Precolombiano Nacional
⑮ Federacion de Andinismo
de Chile
✱ Metro Stations

Santiago

British Caledonian
  Agustinas 1243 (tel 87538).
Canadian Pacific
  Huerfanos 669 (tel 393058).
Ecuatoriana
  Huerfanos 1160 (tel 64251).
Iberia
  Agustinas 1115 (tel 714510).
KLM
  Agustinas 802 (tel 398001).
LAN-Chile
  Perez Valenzuela 099 (tel 225 5262). Also at the corner of Agustinas and Morandé.
Lufthansa
  Agustinas 1080 (tel 722686).
Lloyd Aereo Boliviano
  Moneda 1170.
Pan American
  Bernardo O'Higgins 949 (23rd floor) (tel 725484).
SAS
  Moneda 1160 (9th floor) (tel 82736).
Swissair
  Agustinas 1046 (tel 62324.
Varig
  Huerfanos 1201 (tel 716026).
Viasa
  Agustinas 1046 (tel 82401).
LAP
  Huerfanos 1160 (tel 721142).
Ladeco
  Huerfanos 1157 (tel 82233).

Things to See & Do

Two of the most interesting things to do in Santiago are visits to the summit of **Cerro Santa Lucia** and **Cerro San Cristóbal**. The former is the rocky, landscaped hill right in the centre of the city which is honeycombed with gardens, footpaths, plazuelas and fountains. It's crowned by the remains of a fortress from which there are superb views over the city and away to the snow-capped Andes (weather and pollution permitting). Local people will advise you not to go there after dark as muggings are not uncommon. It's perfectly safe during the day and entry is free.

Cerro San Cristóbal on the other side of the Mapocho River is much higher and crowned by a white statue of the Virgin (similar in some ways to Corcovado in Rio). There is a funicular railway to the summit which is very popular with local people. It was constructed in 1925 and takes you up 485 metres. The return fare is US$0.55 though you can also buy one-way tickets if you prefer to walk back down or take the minibus. It's in operation every day of the year from 10 am to 7 pm (up to 8 pm on Sundays). You board the railway at Plaza Caupolican (down Pio Nono which is across the river from the Plaza Baquedano at the junction of Alameda O'Higgins and Av Vicuña MacKenna). The views from the summit are spectacular.

There's also a cable car service to the summit from the Estación Oasis Teleferico on Av Pedro de Valdivia Norte (metro station Pedro de Valdivia) which is open the same hours as the funicular railway and costs US$1.35 return (one-way tickets also available); and a minibus service for about US$0.35 one-way which can be picked up at Plaza Caupolican, Av Pedro de Valdivia and just about anywhere else on the tortuous road to the summit.

The **Zoological Gardens** are close to the Plaza Caupolican funicular railway station (access via the railway); and about halfway down the mountain, alongside the road and cable car line, is the *Salon Bar Tupahue* which is open Monday to Friday from 3 pm to 12 midnight and on Saturdays, Sundays and holidays from 11 am to 12 midnight. As you might expect, drinks and food are somewhat expensive.

Down in the city itself there are number of museums and palaces which are well worth visiting. Two of the palaces are the **Palacio Alhambra**, Compañia 1340, which houses paintings and is open Monday to Friday only between 11 am and 1 pm and 5.30 to 8 pm; and the **Palacio Cousiño**, Dieciocho 438, which has been preserved as a stately home and is open Wednesdays to Saturdays from 10 am to 1 pm and 4 to 9 pm and on Sundays from 10 am to 1 pm.

One of the best museums in Santiago is the **Casa Colorada - Museo de Santiago**,

Merced 860 on the corner of the Plaza de Armas. This museum chronicles the history of the city of Santiago and a lot of effort has gone into creating the displays and dioramas. It's well worth a visit not just for the displays but for the building itself. It's open Tuesday to Saturday from 10 am to 1 pm and 2 to 6 pm and on Sundays, Mondays and holidays from 10 am to 1 pm. Entry costs US$0.25.

The **National History Museum**, Quinta Normal right at the far end of Calle Catedral, is also good value especially for its Easter Island exhibits. There are also zoological and botanical sections. It's open Tuesday to Saturday from 10 am to 1 pm and 2 to 6 pm, and on Sunday, Monday and holidays from 2.30 to 6 pm.

The prominent **Church of San Francisco** on the Alameda O'Higgins, one of Santiago's oldest buildings, is worth visiting and now houses the **Museo de Arte Colonial**. Not only does it have the usual collection of religious paintings but a fascinating display of old and exotic locks and keys. The church itself is a massive, austere building surrounding a leafy courtyard. It's open at the usual hours and costs US$0.25 entry.

The **Museo Precolombiano**, Bandera 361, catalogues 4500 years of civilisation before the arrival of the Spanish and is open Tuesdays to Saturdays from 10 am to 6 pm and on Sundays from 10 am to 1 pm.

Another museum which is worth checking out is the **Sociedad Arte Precolombiano Nacional** at the artists' colony on Victorino Lastarria 305-321 at the back of the Hostal del Parque. This museum is entirely dedicated to Easter Island and not only has some fine exhibits but also a video which runs continuously. It's free and open daily from 10 am to 1 pm and 3 to 8 pm and on Sundays from 10 am to 2 pm. The surrounding houses have all been renovated and are used as artists' studios. You can get a very good idea of the direction in which modern Chilean art is going by wandering around the studios there. Also in this complex is the *Pergola de la Plaza* bar and restaurant where you can rub shoulders with the glitterati. It isn't cheap (US$2 to $4 for a meal and expensive drinks).

Santiago has a lot of cinemas and if you shop around you can pick up some of the best films on the circuit. Tickets are only a fraction of what they would cost in America or Europe.

Places to Stay

The budget hotel area is mainly around the Terminal de Buses Norte, on the corner of Gral MacKenna and Amunategui. Most of the hotels are on Gral MacKenna, Amunategui, San Pablo and San Martín and are mostly pretty gloomy Dickensian relics in need of major structural repair and gasping for redecoration. Toilets and bathrooms leave much to be desired and you should avoid putting any undue pressure or weight on fixtures since they're likely to part company with the wall and end up smashed on the floor. Locks on doors are often a statement of intent only, but luckily this is Santiago and not Lima or Bogotá so baggage is relatively safe. Clean, crisp sheets are usually provided but you should enquire whether hot showers are included in the price because at some places they are not. If they're not, then this can push up the price by up to US$1.30 per person!

There are only a few which can be recommended. Probably the best is the *Hotel Caribe*, San Martín 851, which is clean, airy and good value at US$2.30 a single (downstairs), US$3 a single (upstairs) and US$4 a double without own bathroom but including hot showers. Food and drink is available and the manager is friendly. Some travellers have criticised this place but most agree that it is good value.

Similar is the *Hotel Indiana*, Rosas 1334, which costs US$2.60 per person in double rooms without bath and US$4.60 per person in doubles rooms with own bath. Hot water is included in the price and the hotel is clean and well-run but I thought it was somewhat overpriced for what it offered.

You could also check out the *Casa del Estudiates Americano*, Huerfanos 1891 near the junction with Cienfuegos, which costs US$2 per person including breakfast. It may be full but those who have stayed there say it's good value. It's officially Santiago's Youth Hostel and affiliated with the IYHA.

The only other cheapie in this area which can be suggested is the *Hotel Souvenir*, Amunategui 856. To like this place you need to be the sort of person who has a fascination for antedeluvian plumbing fixtures, 25-watt light bulbs and vast, irregular and undulating wooden stairs and corridors which attest to the carpenter's triumph over earthquakes, riot, civil commotion and Acts of God. It has clean sheets, hot showers all day (take matches with you to the bathroom to re-light the gas pilot light), it's secure despite the appearance of the doors and it costs US$1.60 to $2 a single and US$3.30 a double without own bathroom.

Others in this area, none of which can seriously be recommended, include the *MacKenna*, Mackenna 1471 (US$2.30/$4 a single/double without own bath and US$5.30 a double with own bath); *Retiro*, MacKenna 1264 (US$2.60/$5.30 a single/double excluding hot showers which cost another US$0.60 per person); *Colonial*, MacKenna 1414 (US$2 per person); *Florida*, MacKenna 1250 (US$2 per person – no hot water available); and the *San Felipe*, MacKenna 1248 (US$3.30/ $4.60 a single/double, with hot showers costing an extra US$1.30 per person – outright banditry).

Outside this area there is one place which can be wholeheartedly recommended and which is very popular with travellers. It is the *Residencial Londres*, Londres 54 (tel 382215), very close to the Church of San Francisco on Alameda O'Higgins (Calle Londres runs down the side of the church). This place is excellent value and well worth the walk. It costs US$2.60 per person in rooms without their own private bath and US$6.60 a double with own bath. There's hot water (no extra charge) all day. The rooms are very pleasant, spotlessly clean with polished floorboards, the staff are very pleasant and helpful, it's totally secure and there's even a pleasant lounge with TV. Get there as early as possible if you want a room – it's popular with local people too. This is the best hotel in Santiago for the price and the facilities offered.

Moving up-market, the *Hotel Londres*, Londres 61 (opposite the Residencial Londres), can be recommended at US$4 per person. The staff are friendly. Similar in value is the *Cervantes Hotel*, Morandé 631 (tel 67966). This hotel offers pleasant rooms with clean sheets and towels and even toilet paper for US$8.30 a double without own shower and toilet and US$6.30/$10.30 a single/double with own bathroom. There's hot water all day. The staff are friendly and the hotel has its own snackbar and restaurant.

Should you only be staying in Santiago for less than 12 hours overnight (you might, for instance, have been here previously and be on your way through again) then think about the *Vegas Hotel*, Londres 49 (tel 383225), if you're a couple. It's a high-class whorehouse so they have no single rooms – they're all doubles and they all have huge double beds with crisp, clean sheets, music and soft lighting. Not only that, but each room has beautiful and spotless showers, bidets and toilets (towels and toilet paper provided) and carpeted floors and walls (yes, even the walls!). It's a bargain at US$4 per person per 12 hour period if you've just suffered a long and tiring bus or train journey. There's even room service! Don't overstay the 12 hours or they'll hit you for another US$4 each!

Places to Eat

There are a thousand and one places to eat in Santiago especially around the bus stations, the pedestrian streets of Huerfanos and Ahumada, the Plaza de Armas and along the Alameda O'Higgins. One or another will offer everything from MacDonalds to seafood to *sukiyaki* to cheap businessmens' lunches. If you want a full run-down of most of the possibilities as well as what live bands and playing, discotheques, etc, then get hold of a copy of the weekly newspaper *Wilkén*.

Two cheap places which can be recommended are the *Pollo Montserrat*, Plaza de Armas, which offers cheap fried chicken; and the *El Paso*, San Martín opposite the Hotel Caribe, which offers cheap, fixed-menu meals for about US$1.

Many travellers have also recommended the *Bar Central*, San Pablo 1063, which offers seafood. The food is certainly good and the portions generous but I did think it was relatively expensive. It's also popular with local people.

Another traveller raved about the food, wine and freshly baked bread at *Chez Henri* in the Plaza del Armas. They also have ice-cream and show first run movies for US$1.20.

My own recommendation for seafood would be the *Los Alemanes*, Huerfanos close to the Sylvestre. You can get a huge portion of fish with trimmings for US$1 to $2 plus salads (US$0.50) and a litre of wine (about US$1). It's popular with young people so get here early if you want a table on the very popular mezzanine. They also offer chicken and steaks (equally good).

If you'd like excellent self-serve food then go to *Sylvestre*, Huerfanos 956. There's a large variety of different dishes and the portions are generous. You can eat enough to last you all day for less than US$2. They only serve this sort of food at lunch time. In the evenings it's cocktails and table service.

Getting There & Around

Airports The international airport (Arturo Merino Benítez) is at Pudahuel, 26 km from the city centre. The best way to get between the two is to take the *Tour Express* bus from the downtown terminal at Moneda 1523 near the junction with San Martín (tel 717380). They leave every half hour (on the hour and the half hour) from 6.30 am to 9 pm from the city centre and every half hour from the airport (at 15 minutes to and past the hour) from 7.15 am to 8.15 pm. At other times of the day they meet incoming flights as and when they arrive. The fare is US$0.90 and the journey takes about 30 minutes.

Bus There are two bus terminals in Santiago: Terminal de Buses Norte, at the corner of Gral MacKenna and Amunategui, for buses north of Santiago and to Mendoza (Argentina); and Terminal de Buses Sur, Alameda Gral O'Higgins 3800 (metro station 'Universidad Tecnica'), for buses south of Santiago and to Valparaiso and Mendoza (Argentina).

The latter terminal actually consists of two terminals on adjacent blocks – the larger main terminal and a smaller one known as 'Alameda', which deals with *Tur-Bus* services to Valparaiso, Viña del Mar and to various destinations in the Lake District such as Temuco, Valdivia, Osorno, Villarrica and Puerto Montt.

Train Trains south to Concepción, Temuco, Valdivia, Osorno and Puerto Montt leave from Estación Central, Alameda Gral O'Higgins (metro station Estación Central). Trains to Valparaiso leave from Estación Mapocho, Av Balmaceda at the junction with Morandé (no metro access).

For trains going south you don't need to go right out to Estación Central to book tickets. You can get them at 'Venta de Pasajes e Informaciones' (yellow sign) in the Galería Libertador, Alameda O'Higgins 851, Monday to Friday from 9 am to 6 pm and on Saturday from 9 am to 1 pm.

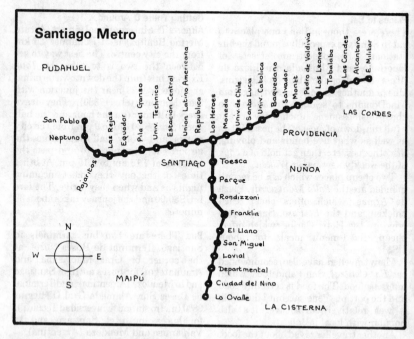

Santiago Metro

Metro Santiago has an excellent metro system with two lines presently in operation. It's the most convenient system of public transport to be used whenever possible (eg for the Terminal de Buses Sur, Estación Central and for the embassies, most of which are in Providencia or Las Condes). It operates Monday to Saturday from 6.30 am to 10.30 pm and on Sundays and public holidays from 8 am to 10.30 pm. There are trains at approximately three minute intervals and the fares are about US$0.15 per trip (any distance) or US$1.40 for a book of 10 tickets.

VALDIVIA

This was one of the very first settlements founded by the Spanish in Chile, though much of its present character is the result of German immigration in the mid-19th century. It was badly damaged in 1960 when an earthquake and tidal wave struck the town, but despite this disaster, it's still largely a town of weather-board houses with corrugated iron roofs. Modern concrete construction is beginning to intrude here and there though, especially on the island of Teja just across the river where the university is situated. Valdivia is a lively little town with a high percentage of students.

You shouldn't have much difficulty finding someone around here to talk to or take you to a party. It's also a major centre of the Lake District and there are buses to scores of small towns further inland.

Information

The tourist office, at Av Costanera (otherwise known as Av Prat) on the riverfront between Libertad and Maipú, is closed on weekends.

Things to See

There isn't a great deal to see in Valdivia itself except perhaps the old Spanish tower at the corner of Yungay and Yerbas Buenas and the **Museo Arqueologico** at the University on Teja Island (walk across the bridge, turn first left and it's about 200 metres on the left down that road).

Outside Valdivia where the Rio Valdivia and the Rio Tornagaleones join the Pacific Ocean, there are three 17th century Spanish forts at Puerto Corral, Niebla and on the island of Mancera. All but Niebla are accessible only by boat. There are buses to Niebla (from the bus terminal) daily at 8.30 and 10 am, 1, 2 and 6 pm. They return at 8.15 and 11 am, 1, 4.30 and 6 pm. The fare is about US$0.90.

There are many launches and ferries available down the estuary between Valdivia and Corral, Niebla and Mancera. The cheapest way to get to any of them is by one of the regular ferries which leave from the Muelle Fluvial next to the tourist office in Valdivia. The ferries are the *Sayonara, Panguipulli, Duby, Titania* and *Pillanco*. One or other of them leaves Valdivia daily at 7.30, 8, 8.45 and 11.30 am, 12.15, 1, 2, 4, 5, 6 and 9 pm and from Corral at 8, 9.15, 9.45 and 10.30 am, 1.30, 4, 5.30, 6, 7, 7.30 and 8 pm. The journey takes 1½ hours and costs US$0.90.

If you prefer a tour which will take you there and back via Corral and Mancera then it will cost considerably more. The *Motonave* boats, *Rio Calle Calle* and the *Neptuno* both offer similar half-day tours between 1.30 and 6.30 pm which include visits to Corral and Mancera. They cost US$7.75. For reservations on the *Rio Calle Calle* contact Hotel Villa del Rio, España 1025 (tel 6292); and for the *Neptuno* call 3235 or make arrangements down at the riverfront.

There are other launches but they're luxury trips which cater to idle minds and deep-sea fishermen (no connection implied).

Places to Stay

Valdivia isn't a particularly cheap town to stay in. Most of the private houses which offer rooms are full with students from Valdivia University for most of the year so there's little point in wasting good shoe leather by trying to find one. Not only that, but owners are very reluctant to let rooms to short-stay visitors though one traveller wrote to say that the *Casa de Estudiantes*, Camilo Enrique 792, will take short-stay visitors if there is room. It costs about US$2.50 per person including breakfast and is very clean and friendly. During the vacations you might have more luck so it may be worth strolling down Camilo Henriquez, Cochrane and Anibel Pinto where most of them are located. At these times try Cochrane 375 and Anibel Pinto 1335.

Other than these, one of the cheapest places to stay is the *hospedaje* at Baquedano 670 (tel 4549) run by Sn Edgardo Quiroz which costs US$3.20 per person (less in winter) and has hot water and central heating. Edgardo speaks English. The *hospedaje* at Carlos Anwanter 802 is a real gem. It's run by a very friendly old lady and is very popular with young people. It's as clean as a new pin, very pleasant, has hot water and heating in the rooms and costs US$3.35 per person either in dormitory-style rooms or doubles.

Another which is very pleasant is the *Hospedaje Pension Estudiante*, Casa 377 in a small alley off Chacabuco. It's very clean, has a homely lounge with an open fire and hot water but there's no heating in the rooms. It costs US$4.65 a double. The owners are very friendly. There's also a *Youth Hostel* of sorts at Escuela 21 near the junction with Av Picarte which costs US$0.75.

Just up above the bus terminal are the *Residencial Ainilebe*, Av Picarte 875, at US$3.35 per person with hot showers and meals available; and the *Residencial Germania*, Av Picarte 873, which costs US$5 a single, US$8.65 for a double bed

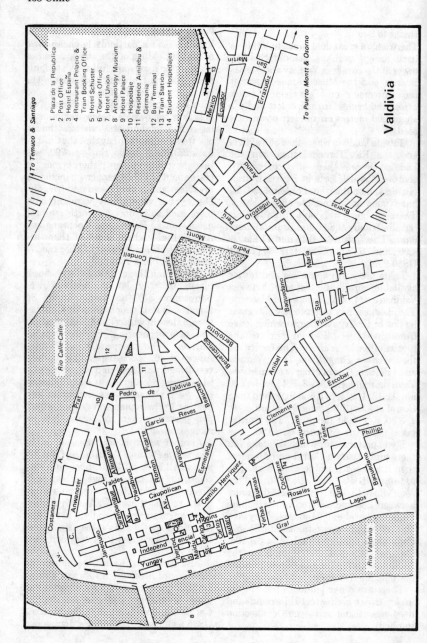

Valdivia

1 Plaza de la Republica
2 Post Office
3 Hotel España
4 Restaurant Palacio &
  Train Booking Office
5 Hotel Schuster
6 Tourist Office
7 Hotel Union
8 Archaeology Museum
9 Hotel Palace
10 Hospedaje
11 Residence Ainilebu &
  Germania
12 Bus Terminal
13 Train Station
14 Student Hospedajes

To Temuco & Santiago

To Puerto Montt & Osorno

Rio Calle-Calle

Rio Valdivia

and US$10 a double including breakfast. There's hot water in the showers, heating in the rooms and meals are available. The owners are friendly and speak German. It's a little overpriced considering what is offered elsewhere.

If you'd like to stay right on the riverfront then check out the *Hotel Union*, Av Prat 512 opposite the tourist office, which costs US$3.35 per person or US$6 a double. Breakfast costs US$0.50 and lunch or dinner US$1.65. 'Treat yourself to some olde worlde charm' as one traveller put it. Another place with heaps of olde worlde charm though somewhat more expensive is the *Hotel Schuster*, Maipú 60. It's a large, rambling old wooden hotel with very clean, airy rooms and the manager speaks both German and English. It costs US$5.60/$7 a single/double without own bath and US$10 a double with own bath. There is hot water all day in the showers and the rooms are heated. Breakfast is available but no other meals. There's an attached bar on the ground floor.

If you're looking for a mid-range hotel then try the *Hotel Palace*, Chacabuco 308, which costs US$9.20/$11.85/$14 a single/double/triple all with own bath, hot water and centrally heated. Breakfast costs US$1.15.

Places to Eat

There are hardly any cheap places to eat in Valdivia so it's worth asking at the place where you are staying if they can fix you up with a meal. If they can't do this then there are two good restaurants on Arauco between Caupolicán and García Reyes on the right hand side as you walk away from the river. They're popular with local people too and the food is very good.

For coffee and snacks check out the *Restaurant Palacio*, on the corner of O'Higgins and Arauco, which is very popular with young people especially on Saturday mornings – in fact you'll be lucky to squeeze in there at that time.

Getting There & Around

The train station is quite a long way from the centre of town on Ecuador next to the Rio Calle Calle and parallel to the Av Ramon Picarte. Get a local bus or taxi into the centre unless you want to stay near the central bus terminal, in which case you can walk there in about 10 minutes. To book tickets for the railway you don't have to go all the way to the station. There is a booking office in the centre of town at the junction of O'Higgins and Arauco.

The bus terminal is on A Muñoz below the junction of Anwanter and Av Picarte. All long-distance buses and buses to the Lake District depart from there. It's very well organised and there's a huge direction indicator in the entrance which lists destinations, journey times, distances and bus companies serving the small towns of the Lake District.

Buses to the large cities (Santiago, Temuco, Osorno and Puerto Montt) are covered by several large companies including *Tas Choapa, Buses Norte, Nuevo Longitudinal Sur, Turibus, Cruz del Sur, ETC, Transbus* and *Igi Llaima*. Departures to Santiago are all in the evenings. There are usually several departures daily from early morning to late at night to Puerto Montt, Osorno and Temuco by all the above companies. Enquire about student discounts on ticket prices (*Igi Llaima* certainly offers them). *Tas Choapa* and *Buses Norte* also have buses to Bariloche (Argentina), the former on Monday, Thursday and Saturday at 9.15 am (US$14.65) and the latter daily at 7 am (US$14.65).

To the smaller places in the Lake District there are the following services:

Buses Chile Nuevo: To San José (US$1), Lanco (US$1.65), Panguipulli (US$2) and Malalhue (US$1.80) nine times daily from 7.55 am to 6.30 pm.

Peila del Sur: To Mehuin (six times daily from 7.55 am to 5.10 pm) and Queule (at 12.30 and 5.10 pm Monday to Saturday and 1 pm on Sunday).

Buses Oriente: To Mafil and Huichaco (at 12 noon, 4 and 6 pm daily); Mafil and San Pedro (6 pm daily) and Mafil and Panguipulli (4 pm daily).

Buses Riñihue: To Los Lagos and Paillaco (eight times daily in either direction from 8.20 am to 6.30 pm).

Buses Futrono: To Futrono (Monday to Friday five times daily from 7.30 am to 5.55 pm; four times daily on Saturday from 7.30 am to 3.30 pm and on Sunday at 7.30 am and 6.30 pm).

Buses Linea Verde: To Mafil and Huichaco (Monday to Friday five times daily from 7 am to 6 pm; four times daily on Saturday from 7 am to 4.30 pm and on Sunday at 2 pm); and to Mafil and Quinco (daily at 3.40 and 4.30 pm).

Buses Valdivia: To Panguipulli via Lanco, Purulon, Malalhue, Melefquen and Huellahue (six times daily from 6.45 am to 7 pm; fare to Panguipulli, US$1.65).

Buses Jac: To San José, Lanco, Lancoche and Villarrica (daily at 7 am, 11 am and 4 pm except on Sunday when it's 7 and 11 am; fare to Villarrica, US$2.30).

Buses Pirehueco: To San José, Lanco, Malalhue and Panguipulli (seven times daily from 7 am to 6 pm; fare to Panguipulli, US$2).

VALPARAISO

A more unlikely place for the country's principal port and second largest city is hard to imagine. The commercial and industrial sector is crammed into a narrow strip of land along the sea front with steep mountains rising abruptly behind it. However steep they might be, they're all covered with housing suburbs and shanty towns connected by tortuous roads, incredibly long flights of steps and *ascensores* (funicular railways) similar to the ones in Salvador, Brazil. There's a lot of poverty in these shanty towns so if you go wandering around up there don't display conspicuous wealth of any sort (even local people will warn you about this).

The commercial centre, on the other hand, is quite safe and has a sort of cluttered charm with its narrow, winding, cobbled streets, attractive buildings and a thousand and one bars and clubs filled with sailors.

Information

Tourist information (maps of the city but little else) can be obtained from either the municipal building, Condell 1490, or from the kiosk on the quay next to the Customs House.

The railway to Santiago runs along the sea front and through Viña del Mar before climbing into the hills.

Things to See

Apart from strolling around the city there's not a great deal to do in Valparaiso. The main reason for this is that those with money to spend on pleasure and non-essentials go to Viña del Mar to empty their pockets. The contrast between the poverty of Valparaiso and the conspicuous wealth of Viña is like the difference between chalk and cheese.

The **Museo del Mar**, Calle Merlet, formerly Lord Cochrane's house, overlooks the harbour, but has been closed for some time now for restoration work and even the gates to the compound are locked. It seems, however, that it is still possible to visit the house if you get prior permission from the Dirección de Bibliotecas, Archivos y Museos in Santiago. At least, that's what the notice on the gate says. To get there you take the funicular railway (a few cents) opposite the Garden Hotel, carry on another 20 metres uphill when you get off and then turn left. The house is at the end of this street.

Places to Stay

The cheapest place is the *Youth Hostel* at Cuarto Norte 636 which costs US$2 per person but it's been described as a 'dump' by travellers who have stayed there.

There are very few hotels around the bus terminal itself. Most of them are along Serrano, Cochrane and Blanco close to the Plaza Sotomayor. Try the *Residencial Lily*, Blanco Encalada 866 next to the Bar Ingles or the *Hotel Reina Victoria*, Plaza Sotomayor 190. The latter costs US$4/$6 a single/double (2nd

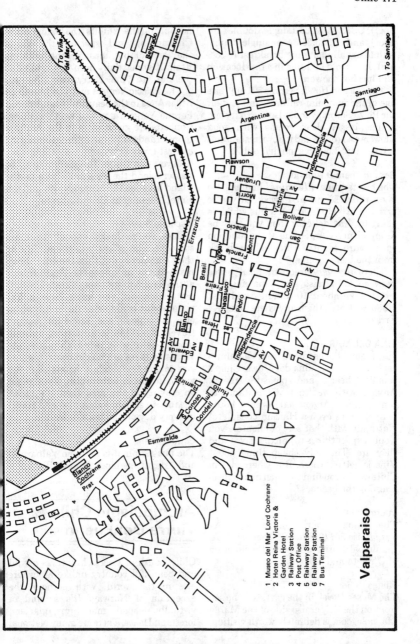

Valparaiso

1 Museo del Mar Lord Cochrane
2 Hotel Reina Victoria &
  Garden Hotel
3 Railway Station
4 Post Office
5 Railway Station
6 Railway Station
7 Bus Terminal

floor), US$3.35/$4.65 a single/double (3rd floor) and US$3.35/$4 a single/double (4th floor) all including breakfast (8 to 9 am). It's an old building in a fine location and has hot showers.

The *Garden Hotel*, Serrano 501 opposite one of the funicular railways and just off the Plaza Sotomayor, is also worth trying. It has large, clean rooms with good showers and toilets and it's own restaurant. It costs US$3.50/$5 a single/double.

Getting There & Around

The bus terminal (*Terminal Rodoviario*) is on Pedro Montt at Rawson. If you're arriving in Valparaiso on a bus which is going to Viña del Mar then you may be dropped on Av Argentina at the junction with Pedro Montt, which is one block from the bus terminal.

There are very frequent local buses between Valparaiso and Viña del Mar which take about 10 minutes and cost US$0.30. Catch them anywhere along Av Errazuriz.

VIÑA DEL MAR

Just around the headland from Valparaiso (about nine km), Viña del Mar is Chile's premier beach and pleasure resort. Anyone with wealth in Chile (and, to some extent, Argentina) owns a house here. There's even a Haitian consulate! Naturally with that sort of clientele you would expect things to be expensive – and they are. The only cheap thing about Viña is getting there. But where else in Chile would you find so much naked flesh roaming the beaches?

Information

The regional tourist office is at Av Valparaiso 507 (3rd floor). There is also a municipal tourist office near the junction of Quillota and Arlegui.

Things to See

The **Museo Naval**, in the castle on the sea front on the Valparaiso side of the Marga Marga lagoon, is definitely worth visiting,

not only for the exhibits (the history of the Chilean navy and especially the War of the Pacific) but also for the building itself. It's open daily from 10 am to 12.30 pm and 3 to 6 pm. Entry costs US$0.10.

The **Palacio Vergara** and the **Museo de Bellas Artes** in the beautifully landscaped Parque Vergara are also worth visiting. Concerts are given there in the summer months and there's an international song contest every February.

If you don't have the money to go to Easter Island there's a *moai* on a traffic island between the Museo Naval and the Hotel Miramar at Caleta Abarca.

Places to Stay

Unless you're lucky enough to meet someone who offers you hospitality at their summer home, then the only cheap place to stay in Viña is the *Youth Hostel* at the Sausalito stadium. It costs US$0.80 per person but you must have a YH membership card to stay there. Anywhere else is outside the scope of budget travellers – Viña is an almost entirely modern town with very high real estate values so there are no old centres where you might find budget hotels like you would almost anywhere else. If you're set on staying in the area then it's much cheaper to stay in Valparaiso and travel in every day on the train or bus.

Getting There

The bus terminal is between Valparaiso and Arlegui one block from Quillota.

Archipelagic Chile & Tierra Del Fuego

Chile, south of Puerto Montt, is a wild and beautiful country unlike anywhere else in the world, with perhaps the exception of Norway. It's a land of virtually unspoilt mountains, glaciers, forests and lakes. There are many National

Parks in the area. At the southern tip, of course, there is the lure of Tierra del Fuego, the most southerly land mass in the world outside of Antarctica itself. The island and the adjacent mainland were, until recently, important sheep-raising areas.

As the Germans settled in Valdivia, the British and Yugoslavs settled in Tierra del Fuego and there are still sizeable populations of their descendants in the area. Just south of Tierra del Fuego is Isla Navarino which supports the world's most southerly, permanently occupied settlement – Puerto Williams. It's difficult to get there these days though because the ferry from Ushuaia (Argentina) has been suspended due to a territorial dispute over the ownership of three small islands close by.

A road is being built to link Puerto Montt with Coyhaique and Villa O'Higgins but it is not yet complete (only the stretch from Chaitén to Coyhaique is presently open) so the only way of getting down to this area is either by boat or plane. Transport services to this area are covered under 'Getting Around' and under 'Chiloe Is' and 'Puerto Montt'.

CHAITÉN
The port of Chaitén is actually a part of the province of Chiloé and is connected to the island of Chiloé by *Transmarchilay* ferry from Chonchi (on Tuesday, Thursday and Friday at 8 am from Chonchi and on the same days at 3 pm from Chaitén; fare US$3.55). You can also get to Chaitén by the *Empremar* ferry from Puerto Montt.

Places to Stay
For somewhere to stay try either the *Hotel Mi Casa* or the *Hosteria Schilling*.

COYHAIQUE
With a population of some 30,000, Coyhaique (sometimes spelt Coihaique) is one of the largest towns south of Puerto Montt. It's a popular centre for hiking in the area and is connected to Puerto Aysen and Puerto Chacabuco by road (102 km).

Information
There is a tourist office on the corner of José de Moraleda and Condell.

Places to Stay
One of the cheapest places is the *residencia* at José Carrera 33. If that is full then try the *Residencia La Bomba*, Cochrane 532 (tel 22518), which costs US$2/$4/$6 a single/double/triple. There is hot water in the showers and heating is available in the rooms.

The *Residencia Puerto Varas*, Ignacio Serrano 168 (tel 21212), is also reasonable value at US$3.25/$6.50 a single/double. There's hot water and heating in the rooms and common areas. The hotel has its own restaurant and bar.

Similar in price is the *Hotel Español*, Baquedano 237 (tel 21150), which costs US$3.85/$7.75 a single/double. There are hot showers, and heating in the common areas. The hotel has its own restaurant.

Places to Eat
For good food and occasional live music try the *El Colonial*, Barroso 713. For snacks such as hamburgers go to the *Café Kalu*, Prat 402.

Getting There
Air *Ladeco* (Gral Parra 210, Coyhaique) fly between Puerto Montt and Balmaceda (55 km south of Coyhaique) on Tuesdays, Thursdays and Saturdays – at 12.45 pm from Puerto Montt and 6.15 from Balmaceda. The flight takes about an hour and costs US$30. There are buses between Balmaceda and Coyhaique which take about one hour. *TAC* (Eusebio Lillo 315, Coyhaique) have flights from Puerto Montt to Coyhaique daily at 11.15 am from Puerto Montt and 1.50 pm daily from Coyhaique. The fare is US$33. They also fly Coyhaique-Chile Chico-Cochrane on Monday, Wednesday and Friday at 1 pm.

Coyhaique

Key :-
1. Tourist Office
2. Post Office
3. Museum
4. Bus Terminal

Coyhaique Alto
Argentina

Chaiten (420 km)
Pto. Chacabuco (81 km)

Balmaceda
Pto. Ibañez

Bus There are two bus companies which connect Coyhaique with Puerto Aysen. *Transportes La Cascada*, Terminal de Buses, on the corner of Lautaro and Magallanes, Coyhaique, and also at Sargento Aldea 514, Pto Aysen, operate buses from Coyhaique at 8.30 am, 12.30 and 6 pm Monday to Saturdays and at 10 am, 6 and 8 pm on Sundays and from Pto Aysen at the same times on the appropriate days. *Transportes Don Tito*, on the corner of Bolívar and Lillo, Coyhaique, and Sargento Aldea 735, Pto Aysen, operate buses from Coyhaique at 8.30 am, 1 and 6.30 pm Monday to Saturday and at 1 and 6.30 pm on Sundays and from Pto Aysen at the same times on the appropriate days.

There are also buses to Pto Cisnes by *Viajes Iscar Muñoz*, Independencia 5, Coyhaique (Tuesday and Saturday at 2 pm from Coyhaique and Wednesday and Sunday at 2 pm from Pto Cisnes, US$7.75); to Chaitén by *Transportes Arte Tur*, Terminal de Buses, Coyhaique (on Monday and Thursday at 9 am, US$17.40); and to Comodoro Rivadavia (Argentina) by *Transportes Giobbi* (on Tuesday, Thursday and Saturday at 8 am and on Monday, Wednesday and Friday at 1 am, 10 hours, US$19.50).

Ferry There are *Transmarchilay* ferries to Puerto Chacabuco from Quellón on the island of Chiloé (on Tuesday, Thursday and Sunday at 12 noon from Quellón and on Monday, Wednesday and Friday at 3 pm from Pto Chacabuco), fare US$14.20 (Pullman) and US$8.90 (Tourist class). You can also get to Puerto Chacabuco by *Empremar* ferry from Puerto Montt (on Tuesday at 8 pm and Thursday at 8 am), journey time is 48 hours, fares US$20 (bunk) and US$14.65 (seat only) plus meals at US$4.65 per day (four meals daily).

PUNTA ARENAS
Punta Arenas is at the very end of the Chilean mainland looking across the Straits of Magellan to Porvenir and Tierra del Fuego. A city of some 80,000 people, it once resembled Puerto Montt and the towns of Chiloé Island with its wooden buildings but these have mostly been replaced with concrete and brick. Much of that redevelopment has been fuelled by the discovery of oil in the region.

Information
The tourist office is at Waldo Seguel 689 (tel 24435). The office is often closed in the afternoons.

There is an Argentinian consulate at Av 21 de Mayo 1878 which is open Monday to Friday from 10 am to 2 pm.

The *LAN-Chile* office is at Lautaro Navarro 999 (tel 23338) and *Ladeco* is at 21 de Mayo 1153 (tel 24927).

Things to See
Two museums worth seeing are the **Patagonian Museum**, Plaza de Armas, which has good small-scale models of the area, and the museum in the Colegio Salesiano, on the corner of Calles Bulnes and Sarmiento, which concentrates on natural history and the Indians who live in this area. Entry to both costs US$0.25.

Places to Stay
As with many places in southern Chile, the best deals in accommodation are offered in private houses. Three of those which have been recommended are at Calle Boliviano 238; Calle Boliviano 366; and Calle Angamos 320 (good value, clean and helpful). Another very cheap place to stay is at the school house during the holidays – enquire at the Secretaria de la Juventid.

One reasonably priced hotel which you can try if these are full is the *Residencia Roca*, Calle Roca near the main plaza.

If you're from the UK, get along to the *British Club*, Calle Roca 858, above the Chamber of Commerce. It has a homely pub atmosphere and good billiard tables.

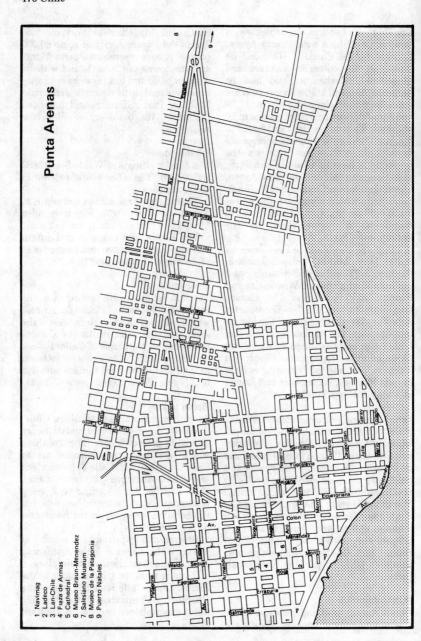

Punta Arenas

1 Navimag
2 Ladeco
3 Lan-Chile
4 Plaza de Armas
5 Cathedral
6 Museo Braun-Menendez
7 Salesiano Museum
8 Museo de la Patagonia
9 Puerto Natales

Getting There

Bus Buses to Puerto Natales are operated by *Expreso Fernández*, Chiloé 930; *Empresa Buses Cóndor*, Av Colón 615; *Puratic y Mancilla*, Chiloé 957; and *Bus Sur*, Menéndez. Expreso Fernández usually offers the cheapest tickets.

Buses to Rio Gallegos (Argentina) are operated by *Expreso Ghisoni Pingüino*, Lautaro Navarro 971. They generally leave daily at 9 am except on Monday when they leave at 11 am. The journey takes about six hours. Make sure you go to the police to go through the necessary formalities before boarding the bus.

Boat For shipping services north to Puerto Montt and intermediate ports enquire at *Empremar*, Lautaro Navarro 1336 (tel 21608), and at *Navimag*, Independencia 830 (tel 26600/21608). Both these companies *may* have passenger accommodation on their ships but you can't guarantee it. If you want assured passages on ships going north then you'll have to go to Puerto Natales from where *Navimag* have passenger/cargo ships twice a month to Puerto Montt.

There are regular ferries across the Straits of Magellan between Tres Puentes, five km from Punta Arenas, and Porvenir at 9 am daily from Punta Arenas (except Sunday when it leaves at 11 am) and 6 pm daily from Porvenir (except on Saturday when it leaves at 3 pm). The journey takes about 2¾ hours. There are buses from the town centre to the ferry wharfs at either end.

PUERTO NATALES

Near the tip of mainland Chile, Puerto Natales is the centre for exploring the spectacular Torres del Paine National Park. It's also the terminus of the *Navimag* passenger ships from Puerto Montt.

Information

Those who intend trekking in the Torres del Paine National Park should call in at the National Parks office, Av Tomás Rogers. You can pick up good maps of the area and find out where the *refugios* are located. (These are simple mountain huts, some of them with basic facilities, where you can find shelter for the night.) The *refugios* are free though you must pay the entrance fee to the National Park. A good map to get hold of is the *Conaf* (Corporacion Nacional Forestal) one titled 'Parque Nacional Torres del Paine'. This has all the *refugios*, roads, tracks, ranger stations and picnic areas marked on it.

In the summer months *Bus Sur*, Baquedano 534, operates a service from Puerto Natales to the National Park entrance on Wednesdays and Saturdays at 7 am. It returns from there on Wednesdays at 7 pm and and Sundays at 2 pm. The fare is US$8. It's also sometimes possible to get a lift in a Parks Administration vehicle to the entrance. During the rest of the year you'll have to hitch (very few vehicles). If there's a large group of you (up to eight) it's often cheaper and more convenient to hire a minibus to take you from Puerto Natales to the park entrance – about US$30 for the bus.

Places to Stay

One of the cheapest places during summer is the hostel at the *Secretaria de la Juventid*, Ramírez 856. Otherwise, try the *Pension El Busca*, Valdivia 845; or the *Pension Magallanes*, Magallanes, which is popular with mountaineers.

Getting There

Buses to Punta Arenas are operated by *Expreso Fernández*, Eberhard 599; *Puratic y Mancilla*, Bulnes 501; and *Bus Sur*, Baquedano 534.

PORVENIR

This is the only settlement of any size in Chilean Tierra del Fuego. It has a population of about 4500, mostly of Yugoslav extraction. The only reason you would go there would be because you were heading for Ushuaia (Argentina).

Places to Stay & Eat
There are a number of good, reasonably cheap *pensiones* including the *Residencia Cameron*. Ask around for others – it's a very small town. For somewhere to eat – most pensiones offer full board – try the *Yugoslav Club*, which does good lunches for around US$1.50. The *Restaurante Puerto Montt* is also good for seafood.

Getting There
If, because of rough weather, the ferries to Punta Arenas are cancelled then the alternative is to fly. Both *TAMA*, Mejicana 726, Punta Arenas, and *Aeropetrol* have flights. Both companies have free transport to and from each airport.

Easter Island (Isla de Pascua)

Easter Island is one of the world's most fascinating archaeological enigmas. Though no one can be absolutely certain, it's now generally agreed that the first people to come here in the early fifth century were Polynesian colonists from the Marquesas.

Shortly after this a unique civilisation arose, one facet of which was the carving of the giant stone heads – the *moai* – and their erection on long stone platforms – the *ahu*. It is these stone heads, some of them topped with a 10-tonne cap of red stone, which have made the island famous the world over. It's thought that their function was to protect the villages from evil spirits. As the culture continued to evolve, agricultural prosperity allowed the population to increase until at its height an estimated 45,000 lived on the tiny island.

The island obviously could not support a population density of 260 people per square km indefinitely and it's assumed that some sort of ecological crisis arose as natural resources were exhausted, woods turned into farming land and the delicate balance between flora and fauna destroyed. By the beginning of the mid-16th century it's thought that food shortages led to wars between various groups and a drastic reduction of the population.

Whatever happened, by the time the island was discovered by Jacob Roggeveen on Easter Day 1772 there were only a few thousand inhabitants left and they remembered very little about the civilisation which preceded them.

The last straw came in 1861 and 1862 when Peruvian slavers abducted more than 1500 of the survivors. Only a few ever returned but they brought smallpox back with them. It wasn't long before the population had hit the all-time low of 111. In 1888, Chile annexed the island and in 1935 declared it a national park. Since then the population has again been increasing and now stands at around 2500, though not all are of Polynesian origin. Thor Heyerdahl's book *Aku-Aku*, is worth reading before you go there.

HANGA ROA
Information
There is a tourist office at the airport and in the only town on the island – Hanga Roa (Tuu Maheke; tel 55). The airport information office has a list of local families who rent out rooms. As any other form of accommodation is going to cost you an arm and a leg it's best to check with them before being drawn off by the tour guides and hotel proprietors who come to the airport to meet incoming planes.

Places to Stay
The prices for accommodation on the island are more or less fixed, though you may have some leeway for bargaining if a place is half empty. If you want to keep costs to minimum you will have to stay away from the two hotels – the *Hotel*

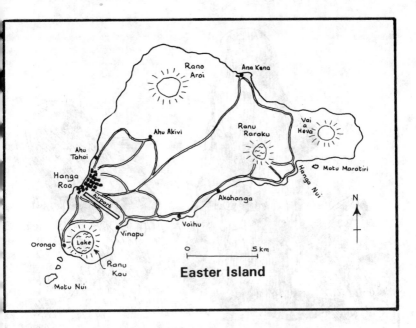

Easter Island

Hanga Roa and the *Hotel Hotu Matua* – and find a room in one of the many residencias or with a family.

Most residencias will charge US$14 to $16 a single and US$25 a double for bed and breakfast; US$22 to $30 a single, US$40 a double for half board, and US$37 to $45 a single and US$56 a double for full board. Some residencias are prepared to rent you a room only but there isn't any advantage in doing this unless you're going to put your own food together with what you can buy at Hanga Roa market. Food at the few restaurants on the island will cost you as much as it does at a residencia. (You can bring in canned food from outside but fresh fruit and vegetables are not allowed).

One place to stay which has been enthusiastically recommended is the *Pension Tahai*, run by Maria Hey, which costs US$20 per night per person for full board. You stay in a very clean bungalow with attached dining room, lounge and bathroom (cold water only), and the meals Maria cooks have been described as 'excellent'. She's not as aggressive as the other punters at the airport so she doesn't scoop up the clientele that she ought to.

Another place to try is the *Residencia Taheta One One* which will rent rooms for US$10 per person including hot showers. Some others to try are the *Residencia Orongo* or the *Toro Nui*, both on the main street of Hanga Roa, and the *Residencia Kai Poo*.

It's suggested you avoid the *Residencia Apina-Nui*. We had a long letter from an American and a Japanese traveller who had a very bad time there. The owners were described as exceptionally rude (once the deposit had been paid) and they refused to stick by the conditions which they had offered at the airport.

AROUND THE ISLAND

There are over 300 of the famous stone

heads scattered over the island, and an additional 276 in the quarry of Rano Raraku, 193 of which are almost complete. There is also the ceremonial site of Orongo (petroglyphs and bird man) on the slopes of Rana Kau. There is no charge to any of the sites except Oronga which costs US$2.

Most of the sites are within walking distance of Hanga Roa. A one-day walk, for instance, will take you to Vinapu, Vaihu, Akahanga and the quarry of Rano Raraku. A second day could take you to Ahu Akivi and back to Hanga Roa via Ahu Tahai. Orongo will only take up a few hours. If you like, you can camp at Rano Raraku but only near the Ranger's hut. If you want to go further to Ana Kena on the far side of the island where the *moai* were re-erected by Thor Heyerdahl's expedition, you need to think about hiring a horse (US$10 per day) or a motorbike (US$20 per day – ask at the Hotel Hotu Matua). There are also some very expensive organised tours (US$80 for a one-day tour) in VW buses, run by *Iorana Tour*.

Getting There

Unless you're flying across the Pacific and can fit in Easter Island as a stopover, it's very definitely off the budget traveller's beat. The island is one of the most remote in the world. It's 4050 km from Tahiti and 3800 km from mainland America. You could get there on a stop-over on a routing such as Sydney-Auckland-Tahiti-Easter Island-Santiago but this certainly isn't the cheapest way of getting from Australia/ New Zealand to the Americas and involves a change of flights at Tahiti. *LAN-Chile* fly Santiago-Tahiti on Wednesdays and Tahiti-Santiago on Saturdays both via Easter Island but the flights cost US$1079 one-way! A return flight to

Easter Island from Santiago by *LAN-Chile* will cost about US$350 but you can pay for this in Chilean pesos because it's an internal flight. The outward flights are on Wednesdays and the return flights on Saturdays.

Colombia

Colombia is one of the most quixotic of the Andean countries with a character and history as wild as its geography. It runs the whole gamut from the sparsely inhabited, jungle-covered lowlands to the cool, fertile, high valleys sandwiched between the three main cordilleras which fan out across the country from the Ecuadorian border. Racially, it resembles Brazil, and to a lesser extent Venezuela, in having a very mixed population. Most of the inhabitants are *trigueños* – various mixtures of white, black and Indian blood – though they are by no means equally distributed over the whole country. Many pure or almost pure Indian groups live in the remoter parts of the country such as the Pacific coast, the Santa Marta highlands and the Amazon jungle, while on the Caribbean coast black people predominate. The culture and music of the black people resembles that of their counterparts throughout the Caribbean.

With such a mixed population you would think the government would by now be mestizo-dominated like it is in Mexico. Not so. As in most other South American countries, political power and wealth remain the preserve of a small group of families, nearly always the descendants of the original conquistadores or more recent arrivals from the USA, Canada, Germany and Switzerland. The Jewish community also has a significant stake in this select group and its members have the dubious distinction of being the favoured kidnap targets of left-wing guerilla groups. The marijuana and cocaine trade to the United States also had a tremendous effect on the ranks of the *nouveau riche* and the political establishment.

Strongly influenced by their surroundings, the various groups tend to regard each other with suspicion or, at least, reserve. From the Bogoteño perspective, coastal people are a bunch of sybarites too much given to dancing, sexual adventurism and thievery. They regard themselves as cultured, dignified and industrious. Such stereotyping isn't always appropriate. Nonetheless, in Colombia the various racial and cultural groups occupy distinctly separate dimensions in the life of the nation, maintaining their own specific lifestyles, values, music, architecture and religious practices. It's one of the facets of this country which makes it so interesting to travellers. In effect, it's several countries rolled into one.

There is, however, a darker side to the Colombian character. More than any other South American country, Colombia still preserves some of the more astringent aspects of medieval Spanish *machismo*. This is a concept which defines male-to-male relationships in terms of constantly having to display one's courage and endurance by dicing with danger and death (in crime, war, cars or on horseback, for instance) and of male-to-female relationships which are characterised by male dominance, potency (generally equivalent to fathering as many children as possible) and sexual conquest along with chivalry, charm and attentiveness. The rules are rigidly defined and disregarded only with peril. Much of what goes on in this country can be seen in terms of *machismo*. It lies at the base of the violence, crime and sexual repression which permeate the Colombian way of life and it demands that, as a traveller, you keep your opinions – particularly political opinions – to yourself and your wits about you. Colombia is not a country for indulging in romantic reveries.

The violence which simmers below the surface and frequently bubbles over is reflected in the ubiquitous, machine-gun-toting police force – a grossly underpaid and corrupt poor-man's job – and in

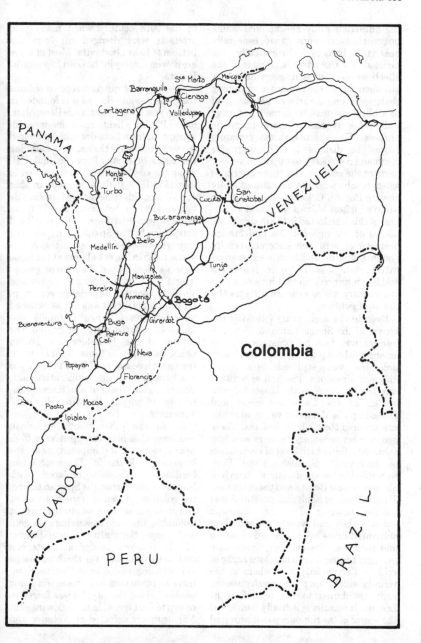

the numerous army checkpoints which punctuate every country road, especially near the borders. Theoretically the rationale for the latter is to restrict the effectiveness of left-wing guerrilla groups but when you see the amount of smuggling that goes on and the bribes which are paid so a blind eye may be turned, you may well think it has a more mundane purpose. The guerilla threat certainly cannot be dismissed. Certain groups command considerable support in various parts of the country and there are times when bomb incidents are almost daily news in Bogotá. Colombia has one of the world's highest kidnap rates and awareness of this is reflected in the design of the houses of the rich *blancos* and foreign businessmen with their elaborate security systems, guards and high walls topped with broken glass. The overt repression and fear is as predominant here as it is in any country where violence dictates the course of politics.

Even in the early years following the arrival of the Spanish around 1500, the country was torn by constant feuding among rival *conquistadores*. What is now Colombia was explored from three different directions. The first expedition was led by Jiménez de Quesada, who landed on the Caribbean coast and pushed up the Magdalen valley where he encountered the Chibcha Indians. These people were sedentary farmers who had achieved a fairly high level of civilisation by the time the Spanish arrived. They were ruled by two chiefs, one of whom had his capital near Bogotá and the other near Tunja. Their agricultural potential was limited, however. The only domestic animals they had were dogs and their cultivated crops were confined to maize and potatoes. Nevertheless, there were persistent rumours of a fabulous cache of gold in a secret city somewhere in the vicinity which kept the Spanish guessing and contributed to the legend of El Dorado. It was never actually found, but the source of the rumours was discovered

in the 20th century when many gold artefacts were dredged up from the bottom of Lake Guatavita. Most of these are now on display in the Gold Museum at Bogotá.

Quesada was quickly able to subdue the Chibchas and Bogotá was founded in 1538. A year later, Sebastian de Benalcázar, one of Pizarro's lieutenants, mounted an expedition from Ecuador and conquered the southern half of the country, founding the cities of Pasto, Popayán and Cali along the way. His expedition arrived in Bogotá in 1539. In the same year another expedition, this time led by Nicolaus de Federmann on behalf of the German Welsers who had been granted a land concession by the Spanish king, entered through Venezuela, crossed the Andes and arrived in Bogotá almost at the same time as Benalcázar. The three groups fought tooth and nail for supremacy and since the centre of imperial power was in faraway Lima, order was not established for many years. When it finally was imposed, Bogotá was designated the capital of the Presidency of Nueva Granada subject to Lima. In 1718, when the vast vice-royalty of Peru became too cumbersome as an administrative unit, Bogotá became the capital of its own vice-royalty which at the time included Venezuela.

As in the other South American countries, Colombia's independence from Spain received its impetus from the Napoleonic Wars in Europe. When Ferdinand VII was replaced with Napoleon's brother on the Spanish throne, the colonies refused to accept the move and rival juntas were set up throughout Colombia, the main ones being at Bogotá and Tunja. Soon after, Simon Bolívar ('El Libertador') landed at Cartagena and fought his way up the Magdalena valley to Bogotá and on to Cúcuta. From there he pushed on to Caracas but being unable to hold the city, he was forced to return to Cartagena. In the following year Napoleon was defeated at Waterloo and the Spanish Crown set about re-conquering its colonies. By the time this got underway, however, Bolívar had assembled an army of horsemen from the Venezuelan llanos and some 5000 British ex-Peninsular War veterans at Angostura (later renamed Ciudad Bolívar). With this army he marched across the Andes into Colombia and joined forces with Santander's liberation fighters. Together they defeated the Royalists, first at the battle of the Vargas in the lowlands and again at the battle of the Boyacá.

With Colombia free, a revolutionary congress was held at Cúcuta. Opposing factions quickly emerged. Bolívar stood for a centralised and unified republic made up of Venezuela, Colombia and Ecuador, whereas Santander favoured a looser federal arrangement of sovereign states. Initially, Bolívar's idea prevailed and the Republic of Gran Colombia came into being. It was short-lived, however, and even before Bolívar died, the Republic had split into its three constituent countries. Bolívar remains the most important national hero as a result of the wars for independence – witness the number of statues and streets named after him – but in many ways, the adulation given him is perhaps out of proportion to what he actually achieved. He certainly 'liberated' the upper classes and the *blancos* from the control of the Spanish throne, but he did precious little for the Indians, the blacks and the mestizos who continued to be exploited and denied access to power just as they had been in colonial days.

The factions which had come to the fore at the first revolutionary congress quickly coalesced into the rival political forces of the Liberals and Conservatives, and the two groups were to fight each other for power throughout the 19th century. Depending on their military fortunes, both parties took it in turn to impose their policies on the country without any concern for continuity. The activities of the church, which supported the Conservatives, further poisoned the political climate and in 1899 things came to a head in a full-scale civil war. The war was to last three years and during that time at least 100,000 men lost their lives. The Liberals, though militarily defeated, were by no means eclipsed as a political force and the rivalry simmered on.

It was in the aftermath of this war, with the country weak and in no position to put up effective resistance, that the United States encouraged a group of dissidents in Panama to declare the independence of what was, until then, a province of Colombia. In return the US wanted quasi-sovereign rights to a strip of territory through which they wanted to build a canal. Bogotá refused to accept the loss of its province and it was not until 1921 that the independence of Panama was finally acknowledged and the United States came up with a belated US$25 million as 'compensation.'

Colombia's troubles, on the other hand, were not over. In 1948 the simmering rivalry between the Liberals and Conservatives exploded yet again and led to 10 years of the worst violence the country had ever experienced. It began with the assassination of a progressive mayor of Bogotá and spread rapidly to the rest of the country, with encouragement from the major political figures in the capital. About 300,000 people are estimated to have died in this civil war, known as 'La Violencia,' and the memory of those terrible years, which had a devastating effect on the Colombian psyche, is still very much alive today.

The absurdity of all that killing was that the people were fighting for a largely unreal cause since there was little choice between the politicians of either side. Ever since independence, the presidents of Colombia have all been drawn from about five families and these same families are likely to continue to hog power until the next revolution comes around. La Violencia came to an end in the mid-1950s with a deal between the leaders of the two parties in which they both agreed to swap the administration of the country every four years until 1974 and to support the same presidential candidate. What prompted peace negotiations wasn't, however, just the lack of any clear victory in sight for either party but the leading families' fear of the growing power of the *campesinos*.

After years of guerilla-style fighting the *campesinos* had welded themselves into experienced peasant armies which had become a law unto themselves. At this stage of the fighting there had grown a strong 'power to the people' spirit among

the *campesinos* which began to lead to the expropriation and re-distribution of the *haciendas* of wealthy Bogotá barons and Medillín *mafiosi*. The deal between the two political parties narrowly averted what could easily have become a genuine agrarian revolution.

As a result of the sell-out, the *campesinos* had to painfully piece together the fabric of their peacetime lives, having achieved absolutely nothing, politically or in terms of land reform, during all those years of killing. Because nothing was settled or accomplished, the undercurrent of rivalry and violence

simmers on. Certainly it has been possible to hold elections since 1974 but the country still has a long way to go before before the threat of another civil war can be discounted.

As far as guerrilla organisations go, it seemed that with the election of Betancur, a compromise might have been reached. He was certainly willing to talk to them and go some way to meeting their demands. Indeed he set out pursuing a broadly reformist programme and even offered an amnesty to the guerrillas. But somewhere down the line something went wrong and at the beginning of November 1985 the 19 de Abril guerrillas (M-19) took over the Palace of Justice in the heart of Bogotá, taking at least 14 members of the Supreme Court hostage. What happened after that is hard to believe. Unwilling to negotiate, the army simply destroyed the building and killed every single person inside including between 40 to 50 guerrillas and all the Supreme Court hostages. Many soldiers also lost their lives in the assault. The repercussions of this are likely to go on for quite some time.

More recently, another factor which has riven Colombia to its roots is the drug trade in marijuana and cocaine. At the beginning of the 1970s *mafiosi* from North America moved into the country in force with billions of dollars at their disposal. They set up plantations, commandeered land from the Indians, built clandestine airstrips and set about corrupting the political establishment, the police and the army. Thousands of poverty-stricken peasants and unemployed men from the towns and villages flocked to work for the mafia either on the plantations or in allied transport services.

Fortunes were made and lost and billions of dollars were laundered through various forms of gambling. But the suppliers became greedy and began to mix the marijuana with rubbish – other dried plants, horse manure or anything else which was handy. The buyers wized-

up to this and responded with counterfeit dollars. Meanwhile the American coast guard stepped up its patrols. The end result was that the marijuana market collapsed, though the cocaine trade still continues.

With no more work available for those who had been sucked into the marijuana business, coupled with the unwillingness of those workers to return to their former desperate lives in the small villages and towns, the unemployed gravitated in large numbers to the cities. Wives and children were deserted in droves, thousands of women were driven to prostitution and the men took to eking out a living as best they could in the cities. Inevitably there was a lot of violence and this is one reason why the streets of many Colombian cities are not particularly safe places to be. Conspicuous wealth – a camera, a watch – is a magnet for thieves and muggers. You must be very careful in Colombia.

This long account of Colombia's violent past and present might make you hesitate to go there. Certainly you do need to be careful but it should be remembered that it's probably no worse than many other countries around the world and certainly no worse than the inner city areas of many North American and British cities. It is worth coming to Colombia as long as you keep your wits about you and don't do silly things. The country is stunningly beautiful with a great deal to offer – historic, colonial cities like Cartagena, Popayán and Antioquia; important archaeological sites such as those at San Agustín and in the Sierra Nevada de Santa Marta (which also contains the highest peaks in the country); spectacular gorges such as the one en route between Popayán and Pasto', and a whole variety of jungle trips and pioneer towns in the Amazon basin which are every bit as interesting as those possible in neighbouring republics.

WARNING

Columbia, like Peru, is notorious for rip-offs and muggings. If you don't want your belongings to disappear, you must keep your eye on them at all times. This applies particularly on long-distance bus journeys where your bags are in the luggage compartment or on the roof. Every time the bus stops, get off and watch your bags. If you don't, they won't be there when you arrive at your destination. Avoid dubious-looking areas of cities especially if you are alone and particularly at night. Certain barrios of Bogotá and Medellín should be considered completely off-limits in this respect if you don't want to be mugged.

One of the nastiest variations of the rip-off is becoming quite common in the Popayán/San Agustín area. The pattern is as follows: an apparently friendly local person will strike up a conversation with you on a bus or at a roadside café and offer to share his food and drink with you. Since you don't want to offend, you accept. A day or two later you wake up in some flea pit of a hotel minus everything except the clothes you stand in – if you're lucky. The food or drink is laced with a whacking dose of barbiturates – available freely without prescription at chemists. We've had letters from people to whom this has happened so it's no rumour. Even the tourist office in Popayán will warn you against this. The trick is spreading to other areas of the country and into neighbouring republics.

VISAS

Visas are required by all except nationals of Austria, Belgium, Denmark, Finland, France, Germany (West), Irish Republic, Israel, Italy, Japan, Luxembourg, Netherlands, Norway, Portugal, Spain, Sweden, Switzerland, UK, USA and holders of Tourist Cards. The normal length of stay given on arrival is 60 days but if your funds are limited, you may only be given 30 days (renewable for a further 30 days). Tourist Cards for those not exempted from the visa regulations – eg Australians, Canadians and New Zealanders – are issued free of charge by airlines and Colombian embassies.

In general it's safe to assume that an onward ticket and 'sufficient funds' will be required before you'll be allowed into the country though we have had reports that these are not demanded at San Andrés Island or Cucutá. Otherwise if you arrive by air, both money and onward ticket are likely to be carefully scrutinised. If you're one of those nationals who need a Tourist Card you must have your onward ticket before the card will be issued. There's not much point in trying to get around this requirement as no airline flying into Colombia will accept you as a passenger unless you have an onward ticket – and they'll want to see it. US$20 per day is regarded as 'sufficient funds' (US$10 for students). Officials at land crossings tend to be more lax than those at airports and rarely want to see money.

If you're coming to Colombia from Ecuador and need a visa, there is a Colombian Consulate at Tulcán.

If you're flying into Panama from Colombia, airlines won't accept a TICA bus ticket from Panama to Costa Rica as an onward ticket (onward tickets are obligatory for Panama). You must have an airline ticket.

Customs searches can be very thorough if you're arriving by air – including from the USA.

Exit stamps are now available at border posts. It's no longer necessary to visit a DAS office in the nearest town before turning up at the border. The only exception to this is if you're heading for Venezuela via Cúcuta where there are no facilities at the border.

MONEY

US$1 = 170 pesos (rising slowly)

The unit of currency is the peso (C$) = 100 centavos. Inflation is in double figures, so the rate quoted here will continue to rise against the US dollar.

There is a black market for currency, especially in the Caribbean ports, but the risks of being ripped-off in the exchange weigh heavily against its use.

Most banks won't even touch travellers' cheques and those which do, will often charge 8% commission. Avoid the *Banco Royal de Colombia* in this respect. The

Banco de la República will generally change them without commission and its exchange rates are usually pretty good. Casas de cambio are generally much less hassle than banks if you need to change money. Don't assume that bank tellers are honest – count the money you're handed carefully.

There are no restrictions on the import of local currency. Export is limited to C$500.

The airport departure tax for international flights varies. In most places it's US$10. In Bogotá it's US$15 and in Leticia it's US$7. On San Andrés Island it's often the first figure that comes into their head. Some travellers have been asked for US$20!! Airline tickets bought in the country attract a government tax of 12%!

MAIL
Don't have mail sent to *lista de correos* in Cali. They don't have such a thing and you'll never receive any letters sent there.

GETTING THERE
To/From Europe & North America
For many people, Colombia is the starting point of a trip to Latin America. There are many flights from various European and North American cities to Barranquilla, Bogotá, Cartagena and Medellín. Plenty of bargains are available, especially in London, New York, Miami, San Francisco and Los Angeles, and it pays to shop around before buying a ticket. More details of these flights are given in the Introductory chapter of this book.

To/From Central America
For those coming overland through Central America, several choices are available: fly from Costa Rica either direct or via San Andrés Island; fly from Panama; or travel overland through the Darién Gap – there are two routes to choose from. Full details of all these routes are given under the 'Getting There

& Getting Around' sections of the Costa Rica and Panama chapters. If you're heading north to Central America, then check out *COPA* (which flies Medellín-Panama City), *Avianca* (which flies Cali/Bogotá-San Andrés) and *SAHSA* (which flies San Andrés-Tegucigalpa). Remember that you will need an onward ticket to get into Panama or Costa Rica. A TICA bus ticket from Panama City to San José is generally acceptable for Panama though some travellers have experienced difficulties with immigration officials in Panama City even though they had such a ticket. You have problems with Costa Rica these days because TICA bus have suspended their services from San José to Managua so you can't keep such a ticket in reserve for when you're heading back north.

To/From Ecuador

By far the most common point of entry from Ecuador in the south is the Tulcán/Ipiales border. There are no direct buses between the two border towns so you'll have to take colectivos or taxis and change at the border.

You can now also get between Colombia and Ecuador via the Oriente lowlands on the eastern side of the Andes. From Puerto Asís on the Rio Putumayo east of Pasto, take the *Coop Transmayo* bus to San Miguel (daily at 7 am, 9 am, 11 am and 2 pm; US$3; five hours). It's a pretty rough road and there are a lot of checkpoints. From San Miguel you take a motorised canoe (plenty of them) to La Punta in Ecuador (costs US$2.50 though they initially ask for US$5; 25 minutes). The village of La Punta is just a few huts, stalls and a checkpoint. From here there are plenty of *busetas* to Lago Agrio (one hour, US$0.40). There are plenty of regular buses to other parts of Ecuador from Lago Agrio.

To/From Venezuela

You have the choice of the coastal route between Cartagena, Barranquilla and Santa Marta to Maracaibo or the highland route from Caracas and Mérida to Cúcuta via San Cristóbal.

To/From Brazil

The only viable point of entry is via Leticia on the Amazon close to Tabatinga, Benjamin Constant and Ramón Castilla at the tri-border of Colombia, Brazil and Peru. All these towns have airports and are connected either by road or frequent ferry services. Numerous flights are available from one or other of these towns to Bogotá, Manaus, Iquitos and many other places.

GETTING AROUND

Colombia's main centres of population lie in the upper valleys of the Cauca and Magdalena and along the Caribbean coast. As a result its transport networks tend to run almost entirely in a north-south direction except along the coast and from Cúcuta to Mérida and Caracas in Venezuela. Since both the Cordilleras Central and Oriente reach the permanent snow line, east-west cross-connections between the valleys are limited. Vast areas of the country, particularly the Pacific coast and the Orinoco and Amazon basins, are only sparsely populated and roads there are few or entirely absent.

If you're a jungle or a river-trip buff and are intent on visiting these areas, you'll have to rely on riverboats and/or short hops in small planes. Very few riverboats run on any regular schedule and as most are primarily cargo boats, living conditions are generally primitive and food, where provided, is monotonous. You need plenty of time if you're contemplating one of these trips. Finding a boat often involves waiting around for several days in a river town and talking to the captain or crews of boats. On the other hand, there are many small airlines, which operate over limited areas, that you can turn to if you get stuck or want to get moving. The fares are generally remarkably cheap, even cheaper if you're prepared to sit with the cargo (which can often be fish!) on a freight plane. Some of the smaller lines are *Aeropesca*, *Aerotal*, *Satena*, *Línea Aero Caribe* and *TANA*. Few of them maintain ticket offices in towns so a trip to the airport is usually necessary to find out when they leave and to fix up a seat.

Even in the populated areas, short plane hops are sometimes well worth the extra money, particularly where they cut out long, tedious bus journeys over rough roads. Internal flights rarely cost more than three times the bus fare over the same distance. The cheaper flights are, naturally, with the smaller airlines like *SAM* and *Satena*. *Avianca*, the national carrier, has a more extensive network of flights but its prices are generally higher than the others.

Some short hops you might consider are from the Caribbean ports of Cartagena or Barranquilla to Medellín and Bogotá and from Turbo to Medellín if you're coming from or heading to the Darién Gap. Flights into the Putumayo and Amazon river towns of Puerto Asís, Puerto Legiuzamo and Leticia are also becoming popular with travellers who want to see something of this part of the country but have limited time at their disposal.

Colombia does have a limited network of railways but few lines offer passenger service and they're only rarely used by travellers. The only line you're likely to use, if at all, is the one from Santa Marta to Bogotá. There are no longer any passenger services on the line from Medellín to Cali and Popayán. Trains take considerably longer to reach their destinations than buses.

Bus transport along the main roads is generally very good, fast and comfortable. Buses are usually of the pullman-type with plenty of leg room. Off the main routes, however, or along rough roads, older buses are generally used. These can be cramped, uncomfortable bone-shakers where you sit for hours with your knees pressed hard against your chest. On most main routes the alternative to a bus is either a 'buseta' (a mini-bus which costs slightly more than a regular bus but takes about the same time) or a colectivo (a shared taxi which leaves when it's full and costs about half as much again as a bus).

Many cities already have, or are in the process of building, a central bus terminal. Where there isn't one, the various bus company terminals tend to be concentrated along one or two adjacent streets. If there are only a few buses each day to a certain places it's a good idea to book one day in advance.

The Main Routes
The Caribbean Coast: Cartagena to Maracaibo (Venezuela)

There are no longer any direct buses from Cartagena or Barranquilla to Maracaibo. You must change at Maicao on the Colombian side of the border. If you don't already have a Venezuelan visa or Tourist Card, there are consulates in Cartagena and Maicao. Maicao is no place to have to spend the night so get your visa before you arrive there.

Cartagena-Barranquilla There are frequent daily buses in either direction, *Rapidos Ochoa* and *Transportes Cartagena*, which cost US$4.50 and take about three hours.

Cartagena-Santa Marta There are direct buses by *Expreso Brasilia* at 9 and 11 am which take 5½ hours (including a 1-1/2 hour stop in Barranquilla) and cost US$6.

Barranquilla-Maicao (via Santa Marta) There are frequent daily buses by *Rapidos Ochoa*, *Línea Dorada* and *Expreso Brasilia*. The fare is US$9.15 and the journey takes about six hours. If you don't want to stop off in Santa Marta make sure the bus you get on doesn't involve a change there. If you're entering Colombia from Venezuela along this route, the amount of smuggling which goes on – from TV sets to whiskey and everything else under the sun – is mind-boggling. So too are the number of police and army checkpoints. The bus will have to stop at all of these while a check is made and bribes paid. The journey, therefore, takes considerably longer in this direction.

Maicao-Maracaibo Direct local buses are now very irregular. You're most likely to find one in the early morning. The fare will be about US$5 and the journey takes about three hours. If you have no luck locating a through-bus, take one to the border and another from there to Maracaibo. Venezuelan border officials may want to see an onward ticket and money but this isn't always the case. The Colombian border officials, on the other hand, will definitely want to see an onward ticket if you're entering the country this way. If leaving Colombia, exit stamps are obtainable at the border – there's no need to visit the DAS office in Maicao.

The Highland Route to Venezuela: Bogotá to Caracas via Cúcuta

Bogotá-Tunja There are many buses daily by *Los Libertadores* and *Linea Gazela* among others which take two to three hours and cost US$2.30 to US$3.

Tunja-Bucaramanga There are daily buses by *Berlina del Ponce* which cost US$5.60 and take nine hours.

Bogotá-Cúcuta The same bus companies which run to Bucaramanga also run to Cúcuta. There are several departures every day in either direction. The fare on *Pullman* is US$17 and the journey takes about 18 hours. If you don't fancy the prospect of 18 hours on a bus, *Avianca* flies there on Monday, Wednesday and Friday for US$43.

Cúcuta-San Cristóbal (Venezuela) Buses and colectivos between these two towns cost the same (US$1.50) so you may as well take a colectivo. The journey takes about two hours.

There are no facilities for an exit stamp at the border here so you need to visit the DAS office in Cúcuta before turning up at

the border. Venezuelan officials will send you back to Cúcuta if you don't have a stamp. There are Venezuelan consulates in Bucaramanga and Cúcuta. You're advised not to get your visa or Tourist Card in Cúcuta unless you've checked out with other travellers beforehand that there are not going to be any hassles.

The Cauca Valley: Cartagena to Ecuador via Medellín, Cali, Popayán, Pasto and Ipiales

Cartagena-Medellín There are several buses daily with a number of companies such as *Rápido Ochoa* and *Expreso Brasilia*. The latter has departures at 2.30, 3.15, 7, 8.30 and 10.15 pm and 12.15 am. The journey takes between 13 and 15 hours and costs US$13. Buy your ticket in the morning on the day of departure. This route is notorious for rip-offs so keep a constant eye on your baggage. The road is now paved all the way. Both *Avianca* and *SAM* have daily flights in either direction but they cost US$60.

The same company also runs buses all the way to Bogotá but, although it's a good paved road, the journey takes 23 hours. That's a long time on a Colombian bus having to get off at each stop to keep an eye on your baggage – not recommended.

Medellín-Cali Buses run throughout the day and night by companies such as *Empresa Arauca, Flota Magdalena* and *Palmira* (all of which have pullman-type buses). The fare is US$13.60 and the journey takes about 10½ hours though it can sometimes take up to 13 hours. You're advised to travel by daylight, as the landscape is outstandingly beautiful. It's a good road except for one or two small stretches. There are occasional army/ police checkpoints along the way where baggage may be examined.

Cali-Popayán There are frequent buses to Popayán virtually 24 hours a day. Companies which do this run include *Empresa Palmira, Transportes Tejada, Flota Magdalena, Cootranar* and *Transportes Ipiales*. The ordinary buses cost

US$2 and the journey takes about 2½ hours. There are also a number of *busetas* which do this run that cost only slightly more than the buses but take less time.

Popayán-Pasto Frequent departures daily by *Transportes Ipiales, Cootranar, Flota Magdalena, Expreso Bolivariano* and *Coop de Nariño*. Buses cost between US$5.25 and US$6.40 and take 6½ hours. *Supertaxis del Sur* also cover this route. This is one of the most spectacular roads in Colombia so make sure you go during daylight. The road follows a vast canyon with tiny settlements clinging to the almost vertical sides.

Pasto-Ipiales Many departures daily by several companies, eg *Flota Magdalena* and *Expreso Bolivariano*. All the companies charge the same fare (US$2.30) and the journey takes a little under two hours.

If you don't particularly want to stop at Pasto, there are direct buses from Popayán to Ipiales by *Transportes Ipiales* every hour which cost US$5.25 and take about 10 hours.

Pasto-Tumaco Tumaco is a small port on the Pacific coast partially built out into the sea on stilts, with a Caribbean-style atmosphere. There are archaeological sites nearby. *Cootranar* has one bus per day in either direction. It leaves Pasto at 7 am. The fare is US$8.50 and the journey takes about nine hours.

Ipiales-Tulcán (Ecuador) There are no direct buses, colectivos or taxis between these two border towns so you must take transport to the border and change there. Probably the cheapest way of getting to the border is by mini-bus.

There is an Ecuadorian Consulate in Ipiales if you need a visa. It's no longer necessary to visit the DAS office in Ipiales for an exit stamp. All the paperwork is done at the frontier post on the Rumichaca bridge over the Carchi river.

The Magdalena Valley: Santa Marta to Popayán via Bucaramanga, Bogotá, Neiva and San Agustín

The road from Santa Marta to Bogotá goes via Valledupar and Bucaramanga and the road is now surfaced. *Expreso Tayrona* and *Expreso Brasilia* both operate buses along this stretch. They both cost US$23 but the former takes 26 hours and the latter 24 hours. There are plenty of army roadblocks en route where searches are carried out. Keep an eye on your baggage.

If you don't fancy a 24-26 hour bus journey then there are daily flights from Cartagena, Barranquilla and Santa Marta to both Bucaramanga and Bogotá. Cartagena to Bogotá costs US$48 with *Avianca*.

Bogotá-San Agustín Five buses daily in either direction with *Coomotor* which cost US$10 and take about 11 hours. The early buses from Bogotá are at 7 am and 9 am. If you're taking one of these direct buses from San Agustín to Bogotá, the bus office has a habit of selling you the more expensive pullman ticket and then putting you on an ordinary bus. Beware of this.

San Agustín marks the end of the Magdalena Valley. From here you can either head into the Amazon basin via Florencia or into Ecuador via Popayán, Pasto and Ipiales.

San Agustín-Popayán There are four buses daily in either direction with *Coomotor* and *Autobuses Unidos del Sur* which cost US$8.35 and take about 10 hours via the old (usual) route. A new road has opened up between these two towns but you virtually need 4WD to make it especially in wet weather. There are also weight limitations on the bridges. With the right vehicle, however, it cuts the journey time down to five or six hours. At present there are no buses along this road.

NB See the warning about drug-laced food and drink schemes which quite a few travellers have fallen victim to along this route. Don't accept offers of food or drink from anyone on this trip.

San Agustín-Florencia There are no direct buses from San Agustín (though there are from Neiva) so first take a bus to Altamira – *Coomotor* has several departures daily – and then another bus from there to Florencia which takes about four hours. It's a spectacular journey so make sure you do it in daylight. Many wild orchids can be seen along the way; sit on the left-hand side of the bus going to Florencia.

San Agustín-Mocoa The direct road is closed at present.

Cross-connections between the Cauca and Magdalena Valleys

Medellín-Bogotá There are daily buses every hour in either direction from early morning to midnight with several companies eg *Flota Magdalena, Flota Occidental* and *Rápido Tolima*. The fare is US$10.30 and the journey takes 10 to 12 hours depending on the season.

Cali-Bogotá Frequent daily buses in either direction with *Flota Magdalena* and *Empresa Palmira* which cost US$15.20. The journey takes 10 to 15 hours. Busetas and colectivos are also available, the former costing about 50% more than the buses and the latter about 2½ times more.

Popayán-Bogotá There are several daily buses by *Expreso Bolivariano* (Carrera 13 No 8-86, Bogotá) and *Flota Magdalena* (Carrera 22, Calle 13-20, Bogotá) which cost US$17.20 and take about 16 hours.

NB Transport and accommodation details for Colombian Amazonia (Leticia, Puerto Asís, Puerto Leguizamo, etc) are together in a separate section towards the end of this chapter. The same applies for details of the Caribbean island of San Andrés and Providencia.

BARRANQUILLA

This is a hot, seedy, Caribbean port with little to recommend it except perhaps a night's sleep on your way somewhere else. If time permits, it's well worth making the extra effort to get to Cartagena instead – three hours away by bus. There are lots of hustlers around the Plaza Bolívar – where the bus terminals are – who'll offer to show you a hotel. You're advised not to take up their offers as you'll end up paying their 'commission' as well as what the hotel wants for a room. Bag snatchers are notorious here so keep your eyes open.

Information

There is a tourist information desk in the Biblioteca Regional on Carrera 38 but it's hardly worth going there as they have no maps or timetables, etc. The main office is way out in the suburbs on Carrera 52 No 72-46.

There's a Venezuelan Consulate (shown on map), if you're heading that way.

Places to Stay

There are quite a few cheap dives around the bus terminals at Plaza Bolívar and along the Paseo Bolívar (Calle 34) but not many can be recommended. Some of the better ones are the hotels *Zhivago, Roxy* and *Real*. Hotel Zhivago is located about 20 metres down Carrera 44 from the Plaza Bolívar. You'll find the Hotel Real a few metres down Paseo Bolívar on the left-hand side from the Plaza Bolívar. It's a little more expensive than others nearby but the rooms have a hand basin, fan and clean communal showers and toilets. It's a haven of peace compared with the others. The management is friendly and one of the sons of the receptionist speaks English and German as well as his native Spanish. The hotel has its own restaurant but meals here are expensive compared with what's available outside. Highly recommended.

Residencias Amy, Calle 35 No 43-12, is also good value. It costs US$7 a double and is safe and noisy (a TV set blares away all evening in the lounge area). If you don't mind doing a little walking, the *Hotel Bolivia*, at the junction of Colombia 33 and Carrera 38, is worth trying.

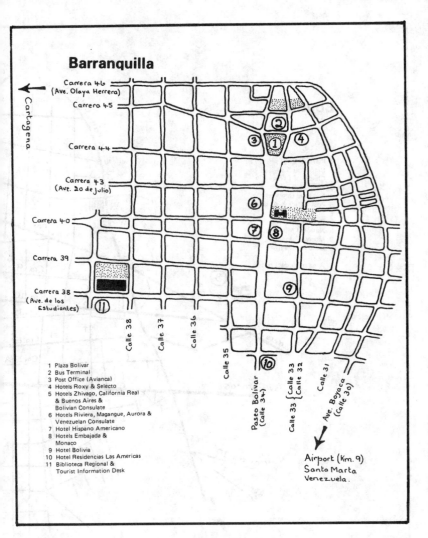

Barranquilla

1 Plaza Bolivar
2 Bus Terminal
3 Post Office (Avianca)
4 Hotels Roxy & Selecto
5 Hotels Zhivago, California Real
   & Buenos Aires &
   Bolivian Consulate
6 Hotels Riviera, Magangue, Aurora &
   Venezuelan Consulate
7 Hotel Hispano Americano
8 Hotels Embajada &
   Monaco
9 Hotel Bolivia
10 Hotel Residencias Las Americas
11 Biblioteca Regional &
   Tourist Information Desk

Places to Eat

The café on the corner of Carrera and the Paseo Bolívar serves excellent, tasty food. It's a little more expensive than similar cafés in the vicinity but the helpings are large. The staff are friendly and they have cheap ice-cold beers.

Getting There

A taxi to the airport now costs US$7 but the cheapest way to get there is by local bus which costs a few cents and takes three-quarters of an hour. Catch it near the Hotel Zhivago – it will be marked 'Malambo'.

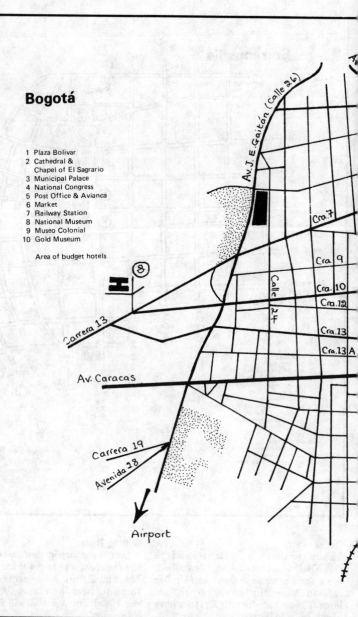

Bogotá

1 Plaza Bolivar
2 Cathedral &
  Chapel of El Sagrario
3 Municipal Palace
4 National Congress
5 Post Office & Avianca
6 Market
7 Railway Station
8 National Museum
9 Museo Colonial
10 Gold Museum

Area of budget hotels

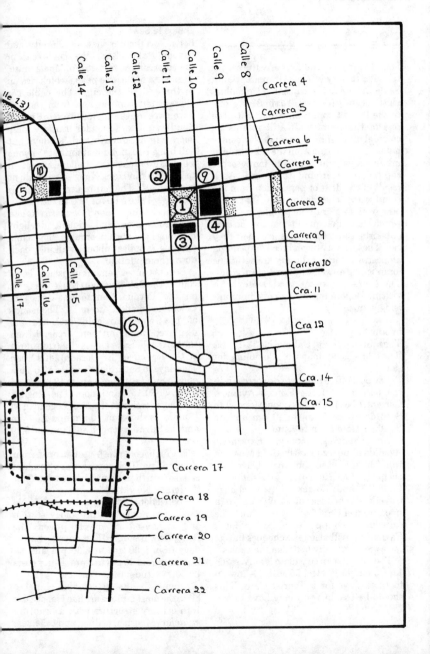

Bogotá

Founded in 1538 and formerly the seat of the vice-royalty of New Granada, Santa Fe de Bogotá is the capital of Colombia. Until recently it was still a small city, due to the lack of communications with the rest of the country. It still retains its colonial atmosphere around the centre but is now suffering from the same kind of urban blight which affects many other capital cities around the world. As a result of the drift of population from the countryside towards the cities, there are now over four million people, many of whom live in squalid barrios on the outskirts, scratching a living as best they can. These shanty towns breed desperation and certain parts of the city are notorious for mugging as well as guerrilla activities. There are plenty of good reasons for visiting Bogotá but beware of compromising your safety.

Information

The tourist office at Calle 28 No 13-15 (1st floor) has good maps of Colombia for sale.

The post office plus *lista de correos* is in the basement of the Edifico Avianca, Carrera 7 No 16-36. It's open Monday to Saturday from 7 am to 10 pm and on Sundays from 8 am to 1 pm.

For changing money, *Exprinter*, Avenida Jiménez near the Gold Museum will change cash but not travellers' cheques. The *Banco de la Republica*, Calle 15 and Carrera 7, will change travellers' cheques but only up to a maximum of US$50 at any one time. The casa de cambio opposite the Hilton Hotel, Carrera 13, will also take cheques but its rates are marginally less than the bank's.

The Venezuelan consulate is at Avenida 13, Colombia 103 (tel 56 3015). Allow up to three days for a Tourist Card. This should be free but you may have to pay US$5.

Things to See

For a spectacular view of the city and beyond, take either the cable car or funicular railway to the top of Montserrate, the lowest of the two peaks which rise up to the east of the city. The cable car operates four times an hour from 8 am to 6 pm on weekdays and from 5 am to 6 pm on Sundays. The funicular railway only operates on Sundays and holidays but will bring back fond memories to anyone who has ever taken the similar contraption to The Peak in Hong Kong – the gradient is about 80°! The return fare on either is US$1.50. Take a bus or taxi to the base of the mountain – *don't walk* as it's a dangerous area and violent daylight muggings are not uncommon. The same warning applies about walking back down the mountain.

Bogotás most famous museum is, of course, the **Gold Museum** (Museo de Oro), on the Parque Santander, corner of Colombia 16 and Carrera 6a. Thousands of pre-Colombian gold artefacts are displayed, many of them dredged from the bottom of Lake Guatavita (the source of the legend of El Dorado). It's open Tuesdays to Saturdays from 9 am to 4 pm and on Sundays from 9 am to 12 noon and costs US$0.15 admission. The English language version of the film 'Legend of El Dorado' is shown at 10 am and 2.30 pm and the Spanish version at 11 am and 3.30 pm.

The **Archaeological Museum**, open from 10 am to 5 pm Tuesdays through Sundays is also worth a visit. It's situated at Carrera 6, No 7-43.

The **National Museum**, Carerra 7, No 28-26, has a good anthropology section and is housed in an old prison, the Panóptico. It's open Tuesdays to Saturdays from 9.30 am to 6.30 pm and on Sundays from 10 am to 5 pm. Entry costs US$0.15 (students half price).

Among the many colonial churches here, the most famous are **San Francisco**, a 16th century structure with a beautiful *mudéjar* (Moorish) ceiling; and **La Tercera**

Orden, which is notable for its intricately-carved wooden altars and confessionals.

Outside Bogotá, be sure to pay a visit to the **Zipaquira Salt Mines** which are so huge that a cathedral capable of holding up to 10,000 people was carved out of one of the galleries in 1954; and it was all carved out of solid salt! Though the mines have been exploited for centuries, they still contain vast reserves. Entry costs US$0.25. To get there from Bogotá, take one of the frequent buses from Avenida Caracas which cost US$0.35 and take about 1¼ hours. Get off the bus at the entrance to the village. The mines are about 15 minutes walk up the hill to the left.

It's unlikely you'll pick up much of the romance surrounding the legend of El Dorado by visiting lake Guatavita these days since the old town has been submerged by a hydro-electric scheme. Some travellers have recommended a trip to Guatavita Nueva saying that the church there – and the town – are very interesting.

Places to Stay

The budget hotel area is roughly between Calles 13 and 17 and Carreras 15 and 17 near where the various bus terminals used to be. Hotels vary a great deal in quality.

There is a *Youth Hostel*, Carrera 16a, No 22A-16, and although it has hot showers, a lounge area and cooking facilities it costs US$4 if you have a membership card and US$5 if not.

The *Hotel Carmelia*, Calle 16 and Carrera 15, is good value at US$4.50 a double and very quiet. Similar is the *Residencias Buenos Aires*, Calle 16 No 15-84, which has very friendly staff and newly decorated rooms with own bath for US$4.50 a double; and the *Hotel Dorantes*, Calle 13 No 5-07, which also costs US$4.50 and is comfortable.

Slightly more expensive is the *Residencias Panama*, Carrera 16 No 16-18, at US$5 a small double. It has good hot showers but it isn't as clean as the others.

The *Hotel Internacional*, Carrera 5a No 14-45, is clean and comfortable and costs US$7 a double without own bath and US$8 a double with own bath.

Somewhat cheaper is the *Hotel Zaratoga*, Av Jiminez No 4-56, which is good value and secure and costs US$6.40/$8.80 a single/double with own bath and hot water. The *Residencias Alemanes* has been used by travellers for many years but it's now moved to Calle 20 No 16-34 and is more expensive than it used to be. These days it costs US$6.40 a double without own bath and US$7.20 a double with own bathroom but the rooms are large, clean and airy and there are hot showers. Sometimes you can get these prices reduced somewhat by negotiation.

Another place which travellers sometimes use in the same area is *El Buen Amigo*, Carrera 16, No 14-45. It costs around US$2.80 a single.

Places to Eat

Try the *Restaurant Lilia*, Carrera 15 just south of Av Caracas; the *Restaurant Santa Fe*, Av Jiminez, which has excellent cheap food and live music; or the very popular Chinese restaurant at the junction of Calle 17 and Carrera 4.

For vegetarian food the *El Vegetariano*, Calle 18 and Carrera 5 has been recommended. There's a branch at Calle 22 and Carrera 8. You can also find excellent food at *Doña Hertha's*, Calle 19 (also called Av Ciudad de Lima) No 8-61 between Carreras 8 and 9. You can get goulash and rice with bread here for just under US$2.

Getting There & Around

There is a new bus terminal on Carrera 68 near Calle 13 which is a long way from the centre of the city but it makes travelling a lot easier. Timetables and routes are well displayed so there are no problems about finding the right bus. There are plenty of local buses from the terminal to various parts of the city.

Local buses between the centre of the

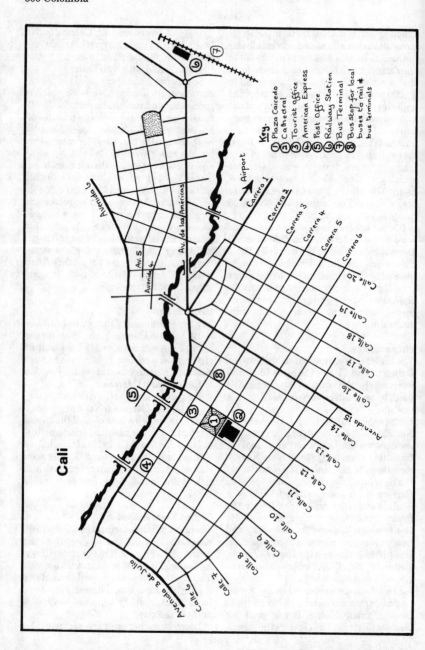

Cali

Key:
1. Plaza Caicedo
2. Cathedral
3. Tourist office
4. American Express
5. Post office
6. Railway Station
7. Bus Terminal
8. Bus stop for local buses to rail & bus terminals

city and the airport run from the west end of Av Caracas. They take about 40 minutes and cost about US$0.15.

CALI

Cali was a sleepy, little colonial town until 1900 but all that changed with the coming of the railway. Today it is Colombia's third largest city and a major industrial centre. Other than the cathedral and the church and monastery of San Francisco, very little of the old town remains so there's not much of interest for the traveller. It's unlikely you'd make more than an overnight stop here.

Information

The tourist office is at Av 6 opposite the post office just over the river.

The only bank which will change travellers' cheques here is the *Banco Royal* but they charge 8% commission. Neither the *Banco de la Republica* nor the casas de cambio will change cheques.

Cali has a purpose-built bus terminal from which all buses depart and arrive. It's well organised, so finding the bus you want poses no problems.

Places to Stay & Eat

The best of the cheapies is the *Hospedaje Bolívar*, Calle 25 and Carrera 4N, very close to the bus terminal. It's excellent value at US$4 a single and has a friendly staff. If this place is full, try the *Residencias Las Américas*, Calle 25, 2N-31. It costs US$5 a double with own bath and is adequate though noisy.

There are plenty of cheap cafés and *fuentes de soda* around the bus terminal though none stand out as being exceptional.

Cartagena

Cartagena is Colombia's most fascinating and beautiful city and is an absolute must. It was one of the first cities founded by the Spanish in South America and dates back to 1533. For many years it served as a major collection point for the plunder from the rest of the continent. To keep the treasure safe until the galleons could ship it back to Spain, the city was surrounded by massive walls and fortifications which the Spanish were fond of thinking were impregnable. They weren't, of course, and though Cartagena successfully withstood many sieges it did fall to Sir Francis Drake in 1586 and to Baron de Pointis and Ducasse in 1697, both of whom sacked the city.

Despite these setbacks, the old part within the walls is a living museum of 16th and 17th century Spanish architecture – narrow winding streets, numerous churches and monasteries, large mansions with overhanging balconies, shady patios, formal gardens and plazuelas, palaces, etc. The market on either side of the harbour is chaotic and lively, with plenty of bars and jukeboxes pounding out reggae.

Information

There's a tourist office at Plaza Bolívar opposite the Palace of the Inquisition. There's also a branch office on Calle Santo Domingo. Be sure to pick up a map of the city which indicates all the main places of interest.

Only the *Banco Royal* will change travellers' cheques and then only at 8% commission. You must produce the proof of purchase slips before they will entertain you. The *Banco de la Republica* won't change cheques.

The American Express office is at Carrera 4 No 7-196, Boca Grande.

The Venezuelan consulate is open Monday to Friday from 8.15 am but they're likely to tell you to get your

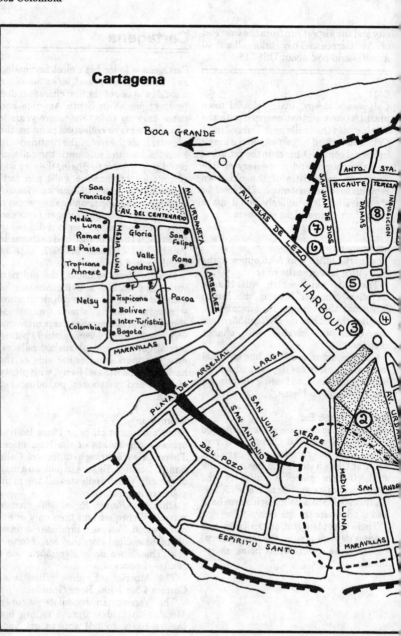

Cartagena

BOCA GRANDE

San Francisco
Media Luna
Remar
El Paisa
Tropicana Annexe
Nelsy
Colombia

AV. DEL CENTENARIO

Gloria
Valle
Londres
San Felipe
Roma

Tropicana
Bolivar
Inter-Turística
Bogotá

Pacoa

MARAVILLAS

AV. URDANETA

AV. BLAS DE LEZO

HARBOUR

SAN JUAN DE DIOS

ANTO.
RICAUTE
DAMAS
STA.
TERESA
INQUISICION

8

7

6

5

4

3

PLAYA DEL ARSENAL

LARGA

SAN JUAN

SAN ANTONIO

SIERPE

DEL POZO

ESPIRITU SANTO

2

AV. URDA

MEDIA LUNA

SAN ANDR

MARAVILLAS

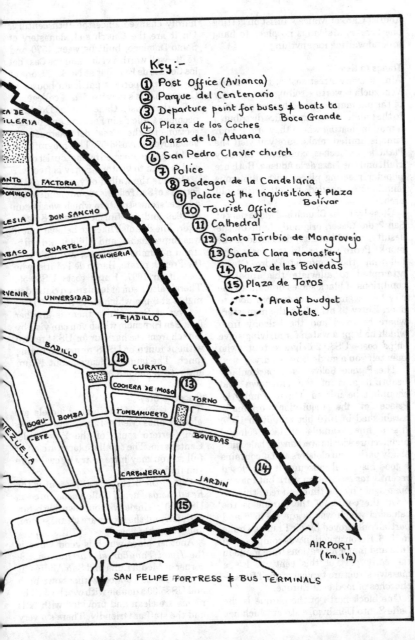

Key:-

1. Post Office (Avianca)
2. Parque del Centenario
3. Departure point for buses & boats to Boca Grande
4. Plaza de los Coches
5. Plaza de la Aduana
6. San Pedro Claver church
7. Police
8. Bodegon de la Candelaria
9. Palace of the Inquisition & Plaza Bolívar
10. Tourist Office
11. Cathedral
12. Santo Toribio de Mongrovejo
13. Santa Clara monastery
14. Plaza de las Bovedas
15. Plaza de Toros

- - - Area of budget hotels.

FACTORIA
DON SANCHO
QUARTEL
CHICHERIA
UNIVERSIDAD
TEJADILLO
BADILLO
CURATO
COCHERA DE MOSO
TORNO
TUMBAMUERTO
BOVEDAS
CARBONERIA
JARDIN

ANTO
DOMINGO
LESIA
BACO
RVENIR
BOQUI-ETE
BOMBA
VENEZUELA

RA DE
ILLERIA

AIRPORT (Km. 1½)

SAN FELIPE FORTRESS & BUS TERMINALS

Tourist Card at Maicao. Insist on getting one here as Maicao is no place to hang around waiting for anything.

Things to See

Almost every street east of the Avenida Venezuela is worth strolling down. Many of the old mansions and houses are open to the public – the tourist office distributes a map indicating where they are. If your time is limited, make sure you visit the **Plaza de los Coches**, containing the City Hall, and the **Plaza de la Aduana**. Both are popular meeting places with numerous small cafés shaded by attractive old arcades.

Close by is the **Church and Monastery of San Pedro Claver**, originally built by the Jesuits in 1603 but later dedicated to the monk, Pedro Claver. In the early days following the Conquest Pedro Claver attempted to alleviate the appalling conditions of black slaves brought to the city by begging for money from door to door. Entry to his cell in the monastery where he lived and the balcony from which he kept a watch for arriving slave ships costs US$0.25. Ignore touts who may tell you a guide is necessary.

The **Parque Bolívar** is a particularly beautiful area of the old town and shouldn't be missed. On it stands the **Palace of the Inquisition**, originally established in 1610 but rebuilt in 1706. It's a fine example of late colonial architecture with its overhanging balconies, shady patios and cloisters and it contains a good historical museum. It was closed recently for restoration work but may be open again by the time you read this.

On the corner of the parque is the **cathedral** which was begun in 1575 and partially destroyed by Sir Francis Drake in 1586. Reconstruction was completed in 1612 and major alterations were made in the early part of this century. It's a massive structure typical of the fortress-churches of medieval Europe.

One block north of the parque is the Calle Santo Domingo, a street which has hardly changed since the 16th century. On it are the **Church and Monastery of Santo Domingo**, built between 1570 and 1579 – well worth a visit – and the **Casa del los Condes de Pestagua** at No 33-29, one of the more important patrician houses in Cartagena. It's now used as a college.

Further east, Calle Santo Domingo becomes Calle de la Factoria and on this section is the **Casa del Marqués de Valdehoyos** at No 36-57. This magnificent building is now owned by the tourist office and is open to visitors. Entry is free.

Outside the walled city, a visit to the **Fortress of San Felipe** is recommended. It's a huge, stone structure which was begun in 1639 and not finished until 18 years later. The Spanish liked to believe that it was impregnable, and while it did withstand a number of sieges, it didn't stop the French pirate, Baron de Pointis, who took it in 1697. Entry costs US$0.55. There's also a son et lumiere on Saturday nights at 9 pm which costs US$ 1.50.

Over at Boca Chica there is another fort, **San Fernando**, which you can visit by launch from the harbour for US$4 return without lunch or US$8 return including lunch. The launches leave about 10 am and return about 3.30 pm.

Places to Stay

The majority of the budget hotels are along Calles Media Luna, San Andrés and Gerrero south of the Parque del Centenario. The smaller places are often full so you may have to try a few before you find a room.

One of the best deals at present is the *Residencias Pacoa*, Calle Pacoa. It costs US$2.80 a single without own bath but with fan and the rooms are clean, secure, and 'tolerably noisy'.

Another place which is good value is the *Hotel Familiar el Turista*, on the corner of Media Luna and San Andrés. It costs US$4.80 a double without own bath and US$5.60 a double with own bath. The rooms are clean and provided with fans and the staff are friendly. There's a very good cheap restaurant attached. It's popular with travellers and recommended as the 'best of the bunch'.

Similar is the *Hotel Romar*, Calle Media Luna 926, which is a nice place, with rooms arranged around a courtyard, that costs US$5.60/$7.20 a double/triple with own bath; and the *Residencias Valle*, San Andrés, which costs US$4.80 a double without own bath.

The *Hotel Roma*, Calle San Andrés, used to be *the* travellers hotel but the owners appear to have become very greedy these days and have raised their prices to US$9.60 a double without own bath. That's plainly a rip-off considering what you get for your money.

For the location of other cheapies, see the street map.

Places to Eat

There are any number of good, cheap cafés on the same streets as most of the budget hotels. The average price of a *comida corriente* is about US$1. For somewhere to hang around and watch the passers by, try one of the many cafés around the Plaza de los Coches or the Plaza de la Aduana.

The *Restaurant Las Muras* on Calle San Andres is popular with the locals.

Getting There & Around

All the long-distance bus terminals are located outside the old city walls in the suburb of Bosque. Public buses go there from the Parque del Centenario.

A taxi to the airport will cost US$3 – it's only a short distance. There are also public buses which cost a few pesos. If you're heading to the airport from town, these buses leave from Avenida Urdaneta Arbeláez.

CÚCUTA

Cúcuta is really only of interest because it lies on the main highland route from Colombia to Venezuela.

Information

The tourist office is at Calle 10, No 0-30. The staff are helpful and street maps are available.

The Venezuelan Consulate is at Avenida O, Calle 8, if you need a visa or Tourist Card. Try and get yourself fixed up with either of these before you get here, however, as travellers have had silly hassles here in the past, one of which included having a blood test for syphilis before the visa or tourist card was issued!

Colombian exit stamps are not available at the border, (unlike most other border crossings) so before you leave town call at the DAS office, Calle 17, No 2-60. It's open every day, except Sunday, from 8 am to noon and 2 to 5.30 pm.

Places to Stay

Two of the cheapest places are the *Hotel Su Nueva Residencia*, Avenida 8a, No 3-63, which is clean and has rooms with bath and fan; and the *Residencias Los Rosales*, Calle 2, No 8-39, of similar standard. Both are close to the bus terminal. Another which has been recommended is the *Hotel Ottawa*, also opposite the bus station, which costs US$7 a double and is clean though the front rooms are noisy.

If you have a choice, it's suggested that you stay at Pamplona rather than Cúcuta. It is a much more pleasant town, a few hours by bus along the road to Bucaramanga.

FLORENCIA

In the last 20 years, the area around Florencia has become an agricultural boom centre though it's sparsely populated. It's one of the gateways to Colombia's Orinoco and Amazon basins and many travellers pass through here en route to places like Puerto Asís, Puerto Leguizamo and Leticia. The road into town from San Agustín or Neiva via Altamira offers spectacular views but is best seen in the dry season from January to March when it's ablaze with tropical flowers.

Places to Stay

There are several cheap places, most of them near the central plaza. Try the *Residencia Bachue*, Carrera 11, No 16-41, near Don Pollo, which is reasonably good value. The rooms have fans. If full, the *Apartamentos Capri* is relatively cheap and has clean rooms with own bathroom.

Restaurants in Florencia tend to be more expensive than equivalent places elsewhere in the country as a lot of food is brought in by truck from outside the area. The *Tocarema* offers good, four-course comidas for around US$1.50.

Getting There & Around

Satena has flights to both Puerto Asís and Puerto Leguizamo three times weekly. *Aeropesca* no longer takes passengers.

The bus to the airport, marked 'Cootranscoqueta', leaves every hour from near the market and costs a few pesos.

IPIALES

Close to the Ecuadorian border on the Pan-American Highway, most travellers pass through Ipiales on their way to Ecuador. It's not a particularly attractive town, but is famous for the **Sanctuary of the Virgin of Las Lajas** and the very colourful Saturday morning Indian market. The Sanctuary – there are postcards of the building for sale everywhere – is well worth a detour to see. It's built over a bridge which spans a canyon and is a major pilgrimage centre. The easiest way to get there is to take a colectivo from Ipiales.

Information

If you need an Ecuadorian visa, there is a consulate at Carrera 6, No 16-47. Colombian exit stamps are available at the border – no need to visit the DAS office in town.

Places to Stay

Most of the budget hotels are marked on the street map but one which has been recommended is the *Hotel Boca Grande*, on the main plaza. This costs US$2 a

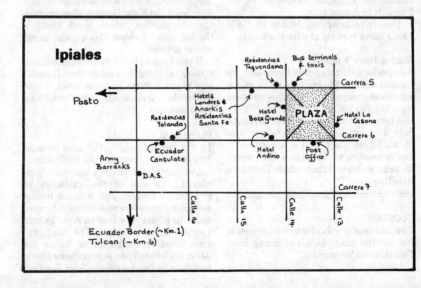

single. It's more than like that the police will come and check you out soon after you've booked into a hotel. Few travellers actually stay in Ipiales overnight – most push on to Tulcán across the border or further to Otavalo or Quito.

MEDELLÍN
Founded in 1616, Medellín is one of Colombia's fastest-growing cities with a population of over 1½ million. It's main industrial product is textiles and with four universities it's also an important educational centre. If you take the time to wander around one of the campuses, particularly that of the University of Antioquia, you may meet someone who will not only offer to show you the city but also accommodation.

On the other hand, it isn't an outstandingly interesting place unless you're introduced to one of the social circuits, and it has the drawback that it seems to have collected hustlers from the four corners of the earth. Certain areas, especially those around where the the bus terminals used to be and the market (where most of budget hotels are), seem to be full of hustlers, hookers and pimps and you're advised to keep night-time strolls in these areas to a minimum.

Information
The tourist office on the corner of Calle 58 and Carrera 49 has a good range of literature and maps of the city.

Things to See
Very few colonial buildings remain in Medellín – most have been demolished in the fever of reconstruction and modernisation. What has been left isn't particularly notable though you might like to visit the 17th century **cathedral** on the Parque Berrio.

Probably one of the most pleasant places to visit in Medellín is the **Botanical Gardens** opposite the University of Antioquia campus. Even if you only have a vague interest in plants, they're worth a

visit. Any bus going down Carrera 52 will take you there. Entry costs US$0.15 but avoid the expensive restaurants inside – even soft drinks are twice the price they are anywhere else.

Places to Stay
You should think twice about staying in any of the budget hotels in the immediate vicinity of where the old bus terminals used to be (between Carreras 46 and 50 and Calles 44 to 42). It's not a very safe area, especially at night. There's no way you can guarantee that your baggage will be in the room when you get back, however securely you lock the door. This is one place where it's better to pay a little extra and be sure.

Away from this area there are a number of places in the market area between Carreras 52 and 54 and Calles 45 and 50 which won't burn too big a hole in your pocket. Good value and popular with travellers for a number of years is the *Hotel Commercio*, on the corner of Calle 48 and Carrera 54, which costs US$8 a double with own bath and there's hot water 24 hours a day. It's very clean and secure and the receptionist speaks English. The best rooms are on the top floor. Good meals are available in the restaurant on the first floor.

Others which can be recommended are the *Hotel Nuevo*, Calle 48 No 53-69, which costs much the same as the Comercio but isn't quite as pleasant; and the *Hotel San Francisco*, Carrera 54 just round the corner from the Comercio.

Outside this area, the *Hotel Casa Blanca*, Calle 50 and Carrera 47 (not to be confused with the *Hotel Casa Blanca 70*, Carrera 45 and Calle 70), has been recommended. It costs US$9 a double. Also recommended is the *Pensión Estrella*, Carrera 48, which is US$2.20 per person and is clean and secure.

The *Hotel Rumania* on Calle 58 and Carrera 50A has been recommended. It's opposite the new Villanueva shopping centre and costs US$2.50.

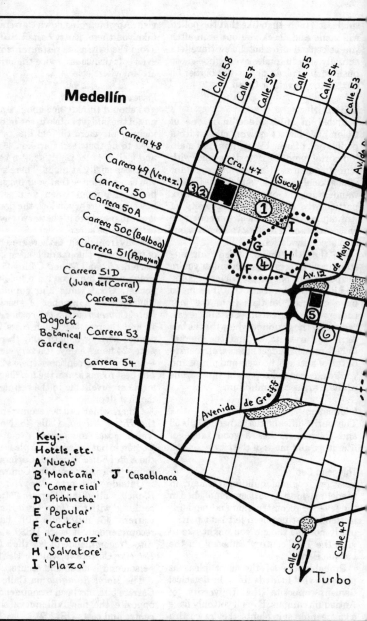

Medellín

Calle 58
Calle 57
Calle 56
Calle 55
Calle 54
Calle 53

Carrera 48
Carrera 49 (Venez.)
Carrera 50
Carrera 50A
Carrera 50C (Balboa)
Carrera 51 (Popayan)
Carrera 51D (Juan del Corral)
Carrera 52
Carrera 53
Carrera 54

Cra. 47 (Sucre)

Av. de Mayo

Av. 12

Avenida de Greiff

Bogotá
Botanical
Garden

Calle 50
Calle 49

Turbo

Key:-
Hotels, etc.
A 'Nuevo'
B 'Montaña'   J 'Casablanca'
C 'Comercial'
D 'Pichincha'
E 'Popular'
F 'Carter'
G 'Veracruz'
H 'Salvatore'
I 'Plaza'

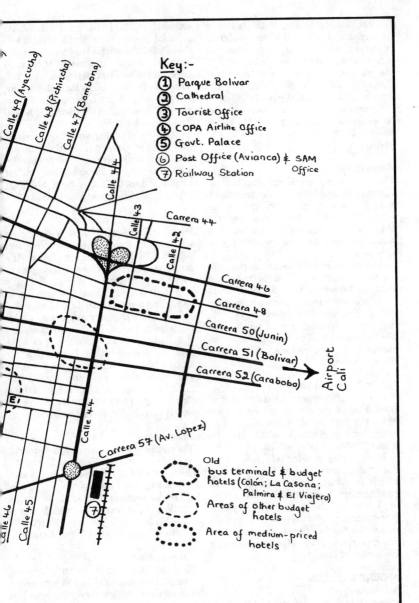

Key:-

① Parque Bolivar
② Cathedral
③ Tourist Office
④ COPA Airline Office
⑤ Govt. Palace
⑥ Post Office (Avianca) & SAM Office
⑦ Railway Station

Calle 49 (Ayacucho)
Calle 48 (Pichincha)
Calle 47 (Bombona)
Calle 44
Calle 43
Calle 42
Carrera 44
Carrera 46
Carrera 48
Carrera 50 (Junin)
Carrera 51 (Bolivar)
Carrera 52 (Carabobo)

Airport
Cali

Calle 44
Calle 46
Calle 45
E1
Carrera 57 (Av. Lopez)

⊙⊙⊙ Old bus terminals & budget hotels (Colón; La Casona; Palmira & El Viajero)

◯ Areas of other budget hotels

∴∴∴ Area of medium-priced hotels

If you'd prefer to stay in the centre of town around the Plaza Bolívar you should expect to pay at least twice what the hotels in the market area charge. Two of the cheaper ones here are the *Hotel Universo*, Calle 52, No 51-85; and the *Residencias Plaza*, Calle 54, No 49-27.

Up-market from these two are the *Hotel Salvatore*, Carrera 50, No 53-16; and the *Hotel Veracruz*, Carrera 50, No 54-18.

Places to Eat
There are many small cafés on Bolívar (Carrera 51) and in the market area which serve *comida corriente* and *cena* for less than US$1. Avoid the cafés around the old bus terminals unless you want to watch posted prices change before your very eyes!

Around the Plaza Bolívar, try the cafés on the pedestrian street between the Plaza and Avenida 12 de Mayo (Carrera 50) which is where many office workers go for their lunch. The prices are a little higher but the food is good and there's plenty of variety. The *La Estanza* in one corner of the plaza has been recommended.

Getting There & Around
There is a new central bus station out of the centre of the city so it's now much easier to find the bus you want. The easiest way to get into the centre is to take a taxi (US$1.60) or colectivo.

There's also a relatively new international airport 30 km from the city which is where you'll land if you're coming from somewhere like Costa Rica or Panama. The old Olaya Herrera International airport is now only used for domestic flights. There are minibuses and colectivos between both airports and the centre of the city.

AROUND MEDELLÍN
Antioquia
It's worth making a day-trip to Antioquia, 50 km north-west of Medellín, which was founded in 1541 and still retains its colonial atmosphere. Until 1826 it was the capital of the department of Antioquia, after which time the centre of regional government was transferred to Medellín. There are frequent buses there throughout the day with *Flota Urbara* and *Transportes Sierra* which take about 2½ hours. The fare is US$1.50.

If you're planning on going overland through the Darién – see the Panama chapter for full details – this is also the road you take to **Turbo** on the Gulf of Urabá. Buses to Turbo from Medellín take about 14 hours and cost US$8.40.

PASTO
Pasto was one of the first cities to be founded by the Spanish but very few colonial buildings remain today. It's largely an Indian town and the people are very conservative. When Bolívar's Republic of Gran Colombia split up in 1830, Pasto attempted to join Ecuador but was prevented from doing so by Colombian troops. It gets cold at night – the altitude is 2600 metres – so have something warm handy. It's worth a trip around the smoking volcano of **Galeras** if you have time and the weather is favourable (put aside half a day for this). Pasto is noted for its colourful, lacquered wooden bowls and its leatherwork.

Information
The tourist office, (*Turismo de Nariño*), on Calle 18 between Carreras 25 and 26, has quite a lot of information on the area and free maps of the city.

The Ecuadorian Consulate is on the 2nd floor of the Textiles Sabadell building, Calle 17, No 26-55. The consul is friendly and they have information on Ecuador.

Places to Stay
Most of the hotels around the bus terminal are about as basic as you can get and many rooms are very noisy – not just because of the buses but because of juke boxes in cafés which pound away till all

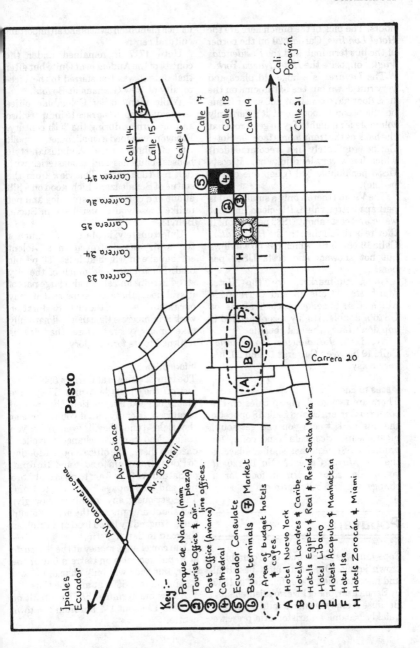

Pasto

Key:-
1. Parque de Nariño (main plaza)
2. Tourist Office & air-line offices.
3. Post Office (Avianca)
4. Cathedral
5. Ecuador Consulate
6. Bus terminals
7. Market
--- Area of budget hotels & cafes.

A Hotel Nuevo York
B Hotels Londres & Caribe
C Hotels Egipto & Real & Resid. Santa Maria
D Hotel Libano
E Hotels Acapulco & Manhattan
F Hotel Isa
H Hotels Zorocán & Miami

hours. The pick of the bunch here are the *Hotel Londres*, Carrera 20 on the corner of the bus terminal; and the *Residencias Viena*, opposite the *Hotel Nueva York*.

The *Londres* is a huge old place and very run-down but the bathrooms on the first floor have constant hot water (none on the second floor!) and it's certainly tolerable for a night. Try to get a room at the back as the front rooms face the Hotel Caribe (definitely not recommended) which has a very loud juke box. It costs US$3 per double bed (sleep one or two people).

The *Viena* (there's only a small sign) is perhaps better value. It's clean, has hot water and costs about US$2 per person. If they're both full then try the *Hotel Zulia*, Calle 19 No 19-61, which has no windows but hot showers and costs US$2 per person.

Going up-market, try the *Hotel Manhattan*, Calle 18 and Carrera 22, which offers huge, quiet, clean rooms for US$6 a double. Highly recommended if you don't fancy the real cheapies.

Avoid the *Residencias Magdellana*, Calle 19 between Carreras 19 and 20. It's very noisy.

Places to Eat

There are two good, cheap cafés on the corner of Carrera 20 and Calle 18 opposite the bus park where you can get soup, meat, beans, rice, salad and coffee for around US$1. Another similar place is the *Rio Mayo*, Calle 17, No 19-126. If you'd like some German food for a change, try *Erik's Restaurant*.

Popayán

Popayán was once one of Colombia's crown jewels. One of its most beautiful and historic cities, it was founded in 1536 by Benalcázar, one of Pizarro's lieutenants. Because it enjoyed such a mild climate it quickly became an aristocratic preserve for rich plantation owners and an important cultural centre.

Until 1717 it remained under the control of the Audencia at Quito but after that date it was transferred to the Vice-royalty of New Granada at Bogotá.

While many other Colombian cities were caught up in the race to industrialise and modernise during the 20th century, Popayán remained a small, quiet, unspoilt city of white-washed Andalusian-style houses, churches and monasteries with rich red-tiled roofs. The view from the statue of Benalcázar which stood on a hill at one end of town was stunning and not unlike those you can still see in Sucre, Bolivia.

Unfortunately, in March 1983, much of the town was destroyed in a violent earthquake in which at least 500 people died. For a long time much of the city stood in ruins and although a large part of it still does, there are signs that it may once again rise from the dust. Restoration work is in progress though it will naturally take many years before the city is returned to its former glory.

Information

The tourist office is at Carrera 6, No 3-64, just off the Plaza de Armas. They have plenty of good information, they're well organised, friendly and if you're there at the right time they'll even offer you coffee. You can also change travellers' cheques there. The office is open Monday to Friday from 8 am to noon and 2 to 6 pm, on Saturdays from 8 am to noon and 2 to 5 pm, and on Sundays from 9 am to 1 pm. Take seriously any warnings they give you about muggings in the area or about being drugged by laced food and drink on the road to San Agustín.

You can change money at the *Banco de la Republica*, also on Carrera 6 near the river, but they will only change up to a maximum of US$50 at any one time.

A new bus terminal has been built on Carrera 17 about 1½ km from the town centre.

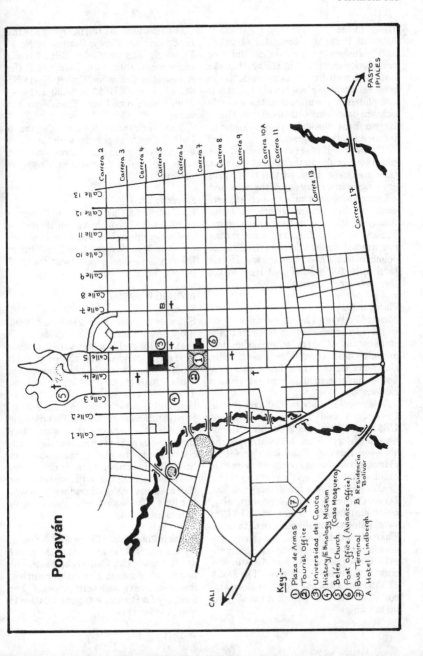

Popayán

Key:-
1. Plaza de Armas
2. Tourist Office
3. Universidad del Cauca
4. History/Ethnology Museum
5. Belén Church (Casa Mosquera)
6. Post Office (Avianca Office)
7. Bus Terminal
A. Hotel Lindbergh
B. Residencia Bolívar

CALI

PASTO
IPIALES

Things to See

Most of Popayán's beautiful churches and mansions were either partially or completely destroyed in the earthquake and although restoration work is in progress it will be a long time before this is completed. In the meantime there's little point in describing what used to be there. If you pass through, please keep us informed of the progress.

The famous Easter fiesta may still take place so if you're in the area at the time then make enquiries. At this time there are processions every day of the week and a festival of sacred music which attracts some of the best musicians in Latin America. It's also a time when many Indians come in from the surrounding countryside dressed in their traditional colourful skirts and black shawls. Hotels tend to be full around that time so get there earlier if you can.

Places to Stay

Most of Popayán's hotels were destroyed in the earthquake, which is a great pity since some of them offered the best accommodation available anywhere in Colombia for the price. Since then new hotels have opened but prices remain reasonable.

The *Hotel El Viajero*, Calle 8 between Carreras 4 and 5, is good value at US$3.20/$3.80 a single/double without own bath but with hot water in the showers. Similar is the *Residencial El Principe* on the same street which is quiet, clean and friendly.

Also good value is the *Residencial San Diego*, Carrera 6, which is clean and airy, quiet and friendly and costs US$3.75/$4.20 a single/double with own bathroom. There is no hot water but there are cooking and washing facilities. Similar in price is the *Residencial San Agustín* just outside town across the river. The *Hotel El Viti*, Calle 2 Norte No 78, is clean and costs US$3.20 a single but it usually has no hot water.

Others which are worth trying are the *La Casona del Virrey*, Carrera 5a No 4-72, which costs US$4.80 to US$6.40 for a huge room with own bath; and the *Residencial Colombia*, Calle 0 Norte No 44, which costs US$2.50/$3.30 a single/double with own bath. There's no hot water.

The *Residencial Bolívar*, Carrera 5 Calle 7, used to be popular with travellers but it has dropped from favour and isn't such good value anymore at US$3 per person.

Places to Eat

La Castellana, Carrera 6, No 6-47, serves excellent food though it's a little on the expensive side at US$2 for a meal. For an excellent breakfast go to the *Las Pitufos*. It's very cheap and popular with the local people. Try their empanadas.

AROUND POPAYÁN
Silvia

Silvia is a popular weekend haunt for people from Cali at certain times of the year. It's located in a high valley, at over 2750 metres, and though it's no longer an Indian village it does have an interesting Indian market on Tuesday mornings. There are two routes – both equally beautiful – which you can take from Popayán. The first through Piendamó is paved all the way but there's only one through-bus at 6 am on market days with *Sotracauca*. The journey takes about an hour. On days when there is no market you must take the bus to Piendamó on the Cali road and change there for a colectivo to Silvia. The second route goes through Totoró and is unpaved.

Places to Stay If you'd like to stay in Silvia, try the *Hotel Cali* next door to the *Hotel de Turismo*. The Cali occupies an old house and, although it's a little primitive, it's inexpensive and very pleasant. For food, try *La Parrilla* – accommodation is also possible there.

Puracé

Puracé is a small village at the base of the nearby volcano of the same name. The volcano itself still smokes but rarely erupts. Beyond the village is the **Puracé National Park** where geysers and high-altitude vegetation can be seen. The geysers are interesting because they are different colours according to which variety of algae they support, which in turn depends on the geyser's temperature. If you're planning on camping in the park expect to pay over US$1 for the privilege. There are hot springs at Pilimbala about 14 km from Puracé and hot sulphur springs 25 km from Puracé (hitch-hiking possible).

Places to Stay In the village you can rent small cabins with attached bathrooms for US$8. This includes firewood. The cabins will sleep six to eight people. *Señora Rosa* has been recommended for accommodation. She has rooms for US$1.60 per person and also offers enormous dinners for less than US$1.

Getting There There are about eight buses a day to Puracé from Popayán and the journey takes a little under two hours. Enquire at the tourist office for bus times as they vary.

SAN AGUSTÍN

The head of the Magdalena Valley in which San Agustín is situated is the site of a vanished culture which flourished between the 6th and 13th centuries. Almost nothing is known of these people though archaeologists have drawn parallels with the Tiahuanaco civilisation of northern Bolivia and the Mayans of the Yucatan. Perhaps, like many other local-ised civilisations of the Andean region, this one too fell victim to the Inca policy of suppressing all cultures other than their own – this area of Colombia was the northernmost point of the Inca empire.

What is certain is that these people left hundreds of large, free-standing, stone statues of men, animals and gods which are *the* attraction for all travellers to this region. There's nothing as magically evocative as far as ancient civilisations go as the statues at San Agustín until you get to the Mayan relics in Guatemala to the north, or the sites of the Peruvian cultures to the south. The area is also one of great natural beauty. Don't miss this place or the artificial burial caves constructed by the same people at nearby Tierradentro.

Information

The tourist office, near the restaurant Brahma on the road towards tha Parque Archeologico, has free maps of the area, information on buses and taxi fares, a leaflet (in English) about the archaeol-ogical sites and information about hiring jeeps and horses. (Jeeps cost roughly US$5 per person for six hours and take up to six people. Horses are cheaper.)

The same information is available from the Hotel Yalconia, just outside of town, and the maps are also available from the Motel Osoguaico, about 2½ km from town en route to the Parque Arqueologico.

Things to See

Rain shouldn't prevent you from visiting any of the sites around San Agustín as long as you're prepared to walk or go on horseback at certain times of the year. The rainy season is from June to September and during these months it may not be possible to get motorised transport to some of the remote sites like Alto de los Idolos. The dry season runs from December to February.

The closest sites to San Agustín are the **Bosque Arqueologico** where the statues have been left more or less where they were found, and the **Parque Arqueologico**, where the statues have been re-arranged and linked by gravel paths. These sites are adjacent to each other about four km from San Agustín. Entry to each costs US$0.15.

Further away is **Alto de los Idolos**. This

is 10 km by foot but it's a strenuous seven-hour round trip so it's better to go first by bus to San José, 27 km from San Agustín. The bus schedule is irregular (check with the tourist office in San Agustín). The site is only five km from San José by foot.

If you need somewhere to stay in San José then try the *Hospedaje San José* on the main square. It's basic and only has cold water but it's friendly and costs US$1.75/$2.25 a single/double. Eat at the *Restaurant Central* which offers excellent meals for about US$1.15.

Don't go off walking to these sites alone – robberies are not unknown.

If your time is limited, a number of excursions by jeep to all the main places of interest are on offer. Make sure you know what you are paying for, as itineraries differ. One of the best is offered by the Hotel Central which visits Alto de los Idolos, Alto de las Piedras and the two waterfalls of **Salto de Mortino** and **Salto de Bordones**. It costs US$4.65 per person.

If you'd like to know more about the people who created these statues then get hold of a copy of the booklet (in English and Spanish) produced by the Colombian Institute of Archaeology. This is available at the museums in San Agustín and San Andrés (near Tierradentro) for US$1.25. If you read Spanish well, the best books are *Exploraciones Arqueológicas en San Agustín* and *San Agustín, Reseña Arqueológica* by Luis Duque Gomez.

Places to Stay

There are a number of hotels here which are very popular with travellers. Everyone has their own favourite but they all cost much the same.

The *Residencias Luis Tello* (no sign), Calle 4, No 15-33, is very good value, has hot showers and costs US$1.60 per person, with good meals available for US$1.20. The *Mi Terruño Hotel*, Calle 4a No 15-85, is very friendly and popular though it only has cold water. It costs US$1.60 per person including coffee in the morning. Similar is the *Residencial Familiar*, Calle 3, No 11-37, which is clean and friendly and also costs US$1.60 per person. A laundry service is available.

Other people have recommended the *Residencias Eduardo Mitto* (no sign), Calle 4 No 15-71 which also costs US$1.60 per person but has no hot water. Up on the hill above town on the way to the Parque Arqueologico on the right hand side is a small sign saying 'Hotel'. You can find accommodation there for just US$0.80 per person. The *Hotel Colonial*, Calle 3 No 11-27, has also been recommended. It costs US$1.60 per person but has no hot water.

If you want to camp, head out to the *Motel Osoguaico* on the road to the Parque Arqueologico, where you can camp for about US$0.50 per night including the use of hot showers.

Places to Eat

Many people eat at the *Hotel Central* which offers good, cheap comidas for US$1.30. If you're looking for vegetarian food, try the *Restaurante Brahma*, Calle 5, No 15-11. It serves very tasty meals for around US$1.20 and excellent fruit salads.

SANTA MARTA

Santa Marta is very hot but less humid than Cartagena and the sea breezes make the heat a little easier to tolerate.

Information

The tourist office is on the corner of 2 and 16. The small farm where Simon Bolívar died is on the outskirts of town and is a national monument. Along the coast is the Parque Nacional de Tyrona.

Buses going along the coast have poor facilities for luggage, so either wrap your pack or insist on taking it inside.

Places to Stay & Eat

The *Hotel Miramar* (not the expensive Residencia Miramar) on Calle 10 half a block from the sea, costs US$2 and is popular with travellers.

At the Pueblito of Orrecifies you can hire a hammock or camp. Several local people offer food but it's not cheap. You can also rent small houses.

TIERRADENTRO

North of San Agustín and east of Popayán, near the village of San Andrés, is Tierradentro where there are a number of artificial burial caves constructed by the same people who left the stone statues at San Agustín. The largest are very impressive and are painted in geometric patterns. Nearby at El Tablón are more of the stone statues found at San Agustín.

You're advised to take one or more torches with you when visiting the caves as the guards don't have them. Only the four highest of the 20 tombs at Segovia are lit by electricity and then only till 11 am daily. There's also a museum near the site which is open from 7 to 11 am and 12 noon to 5 pm. As at San Agustín, horses can be hired to visit the various places of interest but note that the path to El Duende is too steep for horses beyond Segovia. It's also possible to walk around as the nearest site is only 15 minutes (uphill) from the museum and the second is a further 10 minutes.

Places to Stay & Eat

Over the last two or three years Tierradentro has become relatively expensive and you can expect to pay at least US$2 per person in all the *hospedajes* and at least US$1.60 for a meal in the cafés. Nevertheless, travellers still recommend a visit.

The best deals in accommodation are to be found in the private houses on either side of the museum, close to the turn-off for Segovia. No camping is allowed in the museum grounds.

One popular place is the house owned by Señora Marta del Angel (often referred to as Doña Maria). There you can find accommodation for US$2 per person and excellent meals for the usual price. There are superb views of the surrounding countryside from this house. The *Hospedaje El Bosque*, 500 metres from the museum, has also been recommended as being friendly and pleasant.

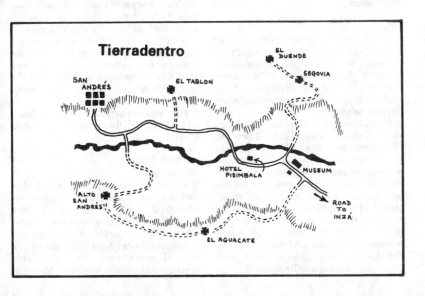

Tierradentro

EL DUENDE
SEGOVIA
SAN ANDRÉS
EL TABLON
HOTEL PISIMBALA
MUSEUM
ALTO SAN ANDRÉS
ROAD TO INZÁ
EL AGUACATE

If you want to stay in San Andrés itself then try the *Residencias Murujuy*. This is clean and serves very good meals.

It's more than likely you'll eat at the house where you stay, but if that isn't possible then try the *Fonda Antioqueña* in the village which has good, reasonably cheap food.

Getting There
Only on market days (Wednesday) can you get transport direct to San Andrés village. During the rest of the week you'll have to walk part of the way.

There are daily buses from Popayán to Cruce San Andrés (about two km from the museum) which cost US$4.50 and take about five hours. Coming from San Agustín, you must change at La Plata and it's quite likely that you will have to spend the night there. The bus from La Plata to Tierradentro leaves at 5 am, costs US$1.80 and takes about three hours. In the opposite direction, it leaves Tierradentro at about 3.30 pm. The La Plata-San Agustín bus departs at 8 am, costs US$4.45 (pullman) and takes about seven hours.

TUNJA
If you're coming up from Venezuela or heading in that direction from Bogotá it's well worth stopping off in Tunja en route. It's one of the oldest cities in the country and the site of a former capital of the Chibcha kings who held power long before the Spanish arrived.

Almost nothing is left of the Indian city except the rock throne of Zipa – one of the Chibcha kings – but much of the colonial architecture of the Spanish city, founded in 1539, remains. Like Cartagena, there are overhanging balconies, leafy little plazuelas, cloistered streets and many carved stone doorways complete with coats of arms. Some of the churches contain superb examples of the wood-butchers' art. Unlike Cartagena, however, it has a very cool climate. You'll need warm clothing, especially at night.

Information
The tourist office is on the main plaza.

Things to See
The most beautiful of the churches, and the one which contains the best woodwork, is **Santo Domingo**, begun in 1594. It's been closed for repairs for some years now but may soon be open again. Similarly, the church of **Santa Barbara** which is also full of colonial woodcarving is also closed for repairs.

The **Museo Don Juan de Vargas** is worth a visit. The former mansion has been converted into a museum of colonial Tunja.

Places to Stay & Eat
Good cheap places to stay around the centre of town include the *San Francisco* on the main plaza near the cathedral, which is clean and friendly but has no hot water. It costs US$4.50/$6 a single/double and has its own restaurant.

Similar is the *Hotel Americano* which is run by friendly people and has a pleasant patio and costs US$5.90 a double. Cheaper is the *Hotel Bocacanse* near the bus station which has hot water and costs US$2.40/$4 a single/double.

Avoid the *Pension Fundador* on the corner of Plaza Bolívar, which is dirty yet still costs US$3.60 a single; and the *Hotel Dux*, just off the Plaza Bolívar, where the management are about as bad as the plumbing.

For a place to eat, *La Fonda* is popular and offers good, filling meals for around US$1.50.

AROUND TUNJA
Villa de Leiva
The most interesting place nearby is **Villa de Leiva**, set in beautiful olive-growing countryside, which was used by the Spanish viceroys as a summer retreat. Unlike Tunja, where modern offices and apartment blocks have intruded on the colonial atmosphere, Villa de Leiva remains completely unspoilt. Many of

the historic mansions here are open to the public, including the one used by the viceroys for the first congress of Gran Colombia, and the house in which Antonio Nariño lived.

In addition, the **Monasterio de las Carmelitas** houses one of the best museums of religious art in the country. It's open only on Saturdays and Sundays from 2 to 5 pm.

The Saturday market is well worth visiting – prices for handicrafts are generally lower than elsewhere in the country. There is a tourist office just north of the main plaza if you need information.

Places to Stay For somewhere to stay try either the *Hotel Colonial* just off the main square, or the *Hospedaria La Villa* which both cost US$2.40 a single. The *Hospedaje Los Olivos* is similar. There are also really good rooms available at the *Bar La Roca* in the main plaza. They're very clean and pleasant, and many have balconies overlooking the plaza. Hot water is available and it costs US$4 a single.

Getting There To get to Villa de Leiva from Tunja, catch a *Valle de Tenza* bus which takes about 1¾ hours and costs US$1.20. There are also colectivos from the bus terminal in Tunja which leave more or less every hour.

TURBO

If you're going to or from the Darién Gap in Panama then you'll have to pass through Turbo on the Gulf of Urabá. It lies at the centre of Colombian banana-land but is otherwise uninteresting. Note that if you are heading for Panama, there is no Panamanian Consulate here. For accommodation try the *Residencial El Viajero* which is clean and has pleasant staff and costs US$2.40/$4 a single/double.

The buses from Turbo to Medellín take about 14 hours and cost US$8.40.

The Colombian Caribbean Islands – San Andrés & Providencia

These two beautiful coral islands, about 220 km off the coast of Nicaragua, provide an ideal opportunity to experience the ambience of the Caribbean while en route to Colombia from either Central America or the USA. Getting there generally involves no extra cost, in terms of transport, as many of the airlines which fly to Colombia call at San Andrés. Despite the fact that the island is a popular destination for Colombian holiday-makers and a duty-free zone, it remains largely unspoilt. Providencia, being more remote, is completely unspoilt.

Both islands are covered with coconut palms, have white coral beaches and clear, turquoise-blue sea. They're everything you might expect of an archetypal Caribbean island. The population consists largely of black, English-speaking people of Jamaican origin – the islands were once a British colony – who are very friendly and easy-going. Wildlife – particularly birds and iridescent green and blue lizards – abounds in the palm forests and there are good opportunities for snorkelling and scuba diving off the small cays.

Getting There
Air You can fly into San Andrés from most Central American capitals – Belize, San Salvador, Tegucigalpa, San José and Panama – and from Miami. The main airlines that stop off here are *Avianca*, *SAM*, *SAHSA*, *LACSA* and the *Costa Rican* airlines. Most of them offer stop-overs en route to the Colombian mainland at no extra cost. If you're heading north from South America, *Avianca*, *SAM*, *LACSA* and *SAHSA* fly in from Barranquilla and *SAM* flies in from Cartagena. Discounts are sometimes offered when there is a tourist promotion campaign going on.

It is not always cheaper to fly all the way from the Colombian mainland to Miami via San Andrés with the same airline. You could, for instance, find that it's cheaper overall to fly with *SAM* to San Andrés and then continue north with *SAHSA*. To give you some idea of the costs involved, there are flights from Cali or Bogotá with *Avianca* for US$80 and flights from San Andrés to Tegucigalpa in Honduras, with *SAHSA* for US$130.

There are daily flights from San Andrés to Providencia with *Satena* for US$30. Buy your ticket at the airport terminal.

Boat There are occasional cargo boats from Cartagena (eg the *Johnny Cay* – enquire at the Muelle de Pegasos or the Maritima San Andrés office) which cost US$35 and take three days. They're not worth waiting around for unless they're going within a day or two of when you enquire. Food is included in the fare but you need your own hammock as there are no cabins available. There are also cargo boats from Colón (Panama) which leave about twice weekly, cost US$28 and take about 30 hours. There are no boats at present from Bluefields or the Corn Islands (Nicaragua). There are occasional cargo boats from San Andrés to Providencia but they're hard to track down.

SAN ANDRÉS
Information
There are banks on the island where you can change travellers' cheques, but it's a lot less hassle and often to your financial advantage to change at *La Opera Washington* sports shop.

The post office is, as usual, in the *Avianca* office which is on Av Duarte Blum.

Most of the airline offices are also on Av Duarte Blum.

Things to See
There are a number of small cays (coral islets) just off the coast which are worth visiting especially with snorkelling gear.

This can be rented on San Andrés for US$4 to $5 per day. The most popular, and therefore at times the most crowded, is the **Johnny Cay**. Boat trips there cost US$3 return, but if you're a strong swimmer, you could swim out. The boats leave from the beach between Av 20 de Julio and Av Duarte Blum.

El Cliff is a high point close to the runway which offers excellent views over the town and the rest of the island. Follow the road which winds up there from the airport terminal – the walk takes about 20 minutes.

Morgan's Cave (La Cueva de Morgan) is a natural cave in the centre of the island which was supposedly used by the Welsh pirate Henry Morgan as a base during the 1600s. If you don't mind walking – it will take you all day there and back – then follow the coast road round the west side of the island and branch off at **El Cove**, a tiny anchorage. Otherwise hire a bicycle in town. Mini-mokes can also be hired but you need to get a group together as they're not cheap. It's a really beautiful coast road and there are occasional bars/cafés where you can find ice-cold beers and mineral waters.

Despite its proximity to town, the beach opposite the Johnny Cay is perhaps the best on the island. There are others like **San Luis** (bus from the centre of town), but this one is a shell beach and at times is heavily polluted with oil and garbage unlike the beaches at the north end of the island.

At the southernmost tip of the island is the **Hoyo Soplador**, an underground channel with an outlet at the far end carved out of the coral by the sea. When the wind is in the right direction the sea spurts out of the opening like a geyser. It's said to reach the height of the coconut palms when the current is really strong.

Places to Stay
By far the most popular place with travellers, and also one of the cheapest, friendliest and most pleasant is the *Hotel*

Restrepo. It's on the opposite side of the runway from the airport terminal. It costs US$2.40 per person regardless of what room you get – some rooms have their own shower and toilet; others don't. All the rooms are clean and have fans. There's a common room/dining room downstairs where you can get breakfast (two fried eggs, home-made bread, coffee), lunch and dinner (rice, beans, fish or meat, salad, sweet and coffee). All meals cost US$1.20. Some of the men who belong to the fishing cooperative live there. They're very friendly and will often offer you free

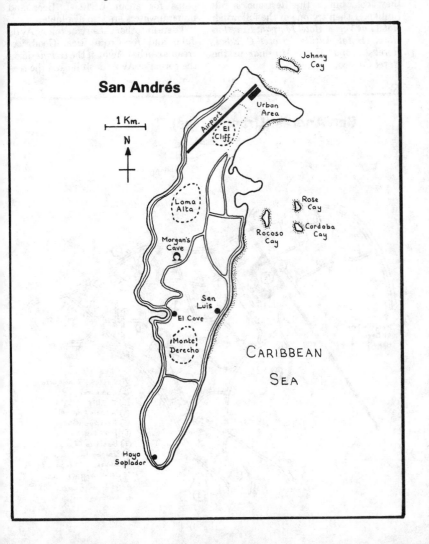

fishing trips in their boats. In the evenings, fishermen and travellers sit around in hammocks and on benches talking and sometimes playing music. Highly recommended.

Most of the cheaper-looking hotels in the main part of town are not as cheap as they look, but if the Restrepo is full (unlikely) then try one of the following: *Hotel Las Vegas, Hotel Morgan, Kingston Hotel, Hotel Antilles, Hotel C Eden, Hotel Europa, Hotel Miramar* or the *Hotel Coliseo*.

Places to Eat

The meals at the *Restrepo* are recommended – good food and large helpings. Otherwise, try the fried fish shack on the beach at the end of Carrera 8 – same road as the Restrepo. Here they sell fresh fish straight out of the sea and breadfruit chips for about US$0.60. Beer and mineral waters are also available.

There are other cheap cafés along Av de Julio and Av Costa Rica. Good ice-creams can be bought at the *Heladeria* on the corner of Av 20 de Julio and the sea-

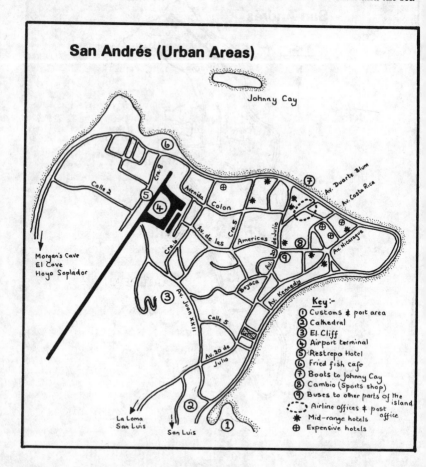

San Andrés (Urban Areas)

Johnny Cay

Morgan's Cave
El Cove
Hoyo Soplador

La Loma
San Luis

San Luis

Calle 2
Cra. 8
Avenida Colon
Av. de las Cras
Americas
Av. Duarte Blum
Av. Costa Rica
Av. Nicaragua
Av. de Julio
Calle 6
Boyaca
Av. Kennedy
Av. Juan XXII
Calle 5
Av. 20 de Julio

Key :-
1. Customs & port area
2. Cathedral
3. El Cliff
4. Airport terminal
5. Restrepo Hotel
6. Fried fish café
7. Boats to Johnny Cay
8. Cambio (Sports shop)
9. Buses to other parts of the island
- - - Airline offices & post office
★ Mid-range hotels
⊕ Expensive hotels

front drive (Av Colombia or Calle 1) but they're not cheap!

PROVIDENCIA

This smaller and completely unspoilt island about 85 km to the north is where you want to head if you're looking for somewhere right off the tourist circuit. It's more hilly than San Andrés – highest spot is 610 metres – and there are waterfalls. There's plenty of seafood and fresh milk available and horses can be hired. It's safe to sleep on the beach; otherwise stay at one of the seven guest houses. The *Hotel Aury* has been recommended but none of them are cheap.

Colombian Amazonia

LETICIA

Leticia, on the Amazon at the tri-border of Colombia, Brazil and Peru, is becoming quite a popular entry/exit point for Amazonian travellers. There are good flight connections from there (or nearby Tabatinga, Benjamin Constant or Ramón Castilla) to other cities in Colombia and also to Manaus (Brazil) and Iquitos (Peru). There are also riverboats to Manaus and to Puerto Leguizamo and Puerto Asís. The latter two are Colombian ports on the Putamayo.

Leticia is, however, a very expensive town. A breakfast of rice, yucca and fried plantain at the market will cost you US$3! And accommodation is heavily booked throughout July and August.

Most people come to Leticia because they're interested in one or more of the aspects of jungle river life – Indian communities, traditional crafts, the fauna and flora of the area, – or simply because they like long riverboat trips. Leticia itself is of little interest and is no longer a 'pioneer' or 'frontier' town – it now has a population of over 15,000.

Most of the trips to the Indian communities and the jungle walks are run by Europeans (often Germans) who came here many years ago specifically for this purpose and they are far from cheap. A one-day trip will cost you about US$50. The ones organised by Hans Heydler who has an office next to the Hotel Anaconda are recommended and should cost you about US$45. Slightly cheaper ones are organised by Guillermo Bueno (tel 72-91). Another person who's worth making the effort to find is an American, Ray Johnston. He exports tropical fish, and if you're willing to involve yourself in organising a trip, he may be prepared to take you along.

If you're a riverboat buff, or would like to make such a trip, remember to set aside sufficient time and don't be too concerned about comfort or amenities. These trips can take weeks, especially to ports on the upper reaches of the rivers, and none of the boats run on any regular schedule. Most are cargo boats and leave when sufficient freight has been accumulated. The conditions on board are often primitive – you sleep in a hammock or on the deck – and food is poor and monotonous. Water is taken straight from the river. There are also plenty of mosquitos on the smaller rivers though rarely any out on the middle of the larger rivers. Depending on the season, finding a boat can take some time. When you have found one, make sure you know whether it includes food. You can often speed things up a little by making enquiries at the Port Captain's office as he will have a list of arrivals and departures and may be able to point out a boat which is going in your direction.

Boats from Leticia to Puerto Leguizamo and Puerto Asís are all cargo boats and only go when the river is high enough – during the 'dry' season you may have to wait for weeks. The journey will take between 10 and 18 days. Boats to Manaus generally leave from Benjamin Constant in Brazil, across the river from Leticia.

If you get stuck, there are flights available from Leticia to Bogotá by a number of airlines in addition to *Avianca*, which flies on Monday, Wednesday, Friday and Saturday and costs US$60. *Satena* flies on Thursday and Sunday and costs US$48. Similarly there are flights available from Tabatinga to Manaus with *Cruzeiro do Sul* and from Ramón Castilla to Iquitos with *TANS*, the Peruvian military airline.

Information

The DAS office is at Carrera 10, Calle 11. This is the only place where you can get a Colombian exit stamp so make sure you do.

If you're changing money here, the money changers give a better rate than the banks. Banks charge 15% commission for changing travellers' cheques.

Places to Stay & Eat

Hotel accommodation is often hard to find in Leticia because it's in such high demand. It's also generally expensive. One of the cheaper places is the *Residencia Monserrate* which is passable but rarely has water and costs US$4.80 a double. There's also a very clean and quiet *residencial* next to the post office for US$12 a double with own bathroom and fan and use of refrigerator.

Others which you can try are the *Residencial Pullman*, the *Hotel Alamania*, which is German-run and very clean; and the *Residencia Copacabana*. The latter has water 24 hours a day. Further up-market is the *Hotel Americano* but it only has water on tap from midnight to 10 am.

For somewhere to eat, try the *La Barra* for typical Colombian food, beer and wine at reasonable prices. Another good place is *La Cabana*.

Getting There & Around

There are taxis and colectivos (US$0.30-$0.40) from Leticia to Tabatinga (Brazil).

There is a twice daily ferry in either direction between Leticia and Benjamin

Constant (Brazil) which takes 1½ hours. There are also occasional ferries to Ramón Castilla (Peru).

PUERTO ASÍS

One of the last ports on the upper reaches of the Putamayo River, Puerto Asís is worth visiting if you want to see something of jungle river-life but don't have the time for a longer trip down to Leticia.

Places to Stay

The *Residencia Gigante* has been recommended as clean and pleasant and costs US$3.20 a double. Water is drawn from a well. If it's full, try the *Residencia San Martín*, Carrera 20 No 11-45 (basic but OK), the *Residencias Patiño* or the *Hotel Meri*.

There is a DAS office in Puerto Asís and an Ecuadorian consulate.

Getting There

Air There are regular flights from Puerto Asís to Bogotá via Puerto Leguizamo, Florencia and Neiva three times a week by *Satena*. They leave Bogotá on Mondays, Wednesdays and Fridays at 7 am. To Florencia it costs US$43 and to Pto Leguizamo it's US$45.50.

Bus The easiest way to get to Puerto Asís is by bus from Pasto which costs US$6, and takes about 10 hours over mountainous, but fairly good, gravel roads.

Riverboat There are riverboats to Puerto Leguizamo from Puerto Asís which take two to three days and cost US$13.50 to US$18. The Colombian military also runs large boats about once a week which cost much less (around US$4.50 plus about US$2.50 per day for food) so they're worth enquiring about. In Pto Leguizamo enquire at their office (Oficina Naval de Ministerio de Defensa) on the waterfront one block from the post office.

PUERTO LEGUIZAMO

Located down-river from Puerto Asís, this river port is a good place to see the Huitoto Indians who are one of the more important Indian tribes in this area.

Places to Stay

For somewhere to stay check out the *Residencia Volver* which is friendly and cheap though basic at US$3.50 a double or US$2.50 if you have your own hammock.

Ecuador

The smallest of the Andean republics, with the highest population density in Latin America, Ecuador covers three distinct geographical regions ranging from lush, tropical coastal lowlands, through the high Andean plateau, down to the jungle-covered Oriente in the Amazon basin. Politically, it's one of the most stable countries in South America and has an atmosphere which is quite different from that of its two neighbours, Colombia and Peru. If you compare it to Colombia, one of the main reasons for this difference is the makeup of its population. Ecuador is one of three Andean republics – the other two being Peru and Bolivia – in which almost half the population is pure Indian.

Until fairly recently, the Indians had a distinctly separate cultural, political, physical and economic identity from the mestizos and those of unmixed European extraction. They had their own villages – mostly in the high, barren valleys of the Andean plateau – their own life-styles, crafts and language. Most of them owned little or no land, were condemned to scratching a bare living from the soil under difficult conditions, and were seen by the mestizos and blancos merely as a source of cheap or free labour for the plantations of the coast and the lowlands in the south of the country. They were denied a voice in national politics, were largely outside the money economy and had little sense of belonging to anything other than their own immediate village or tribe.

However, things are beginning to change under a limited land reform programme so that today quite a few groups have banded together to form cooperatives which own their own land and market their own produce. Tourist interest in the colourful and distinctive crafts which some of the highland groups

produce, particularly the Otavalo Indians, has also accelerated the process of bringing them into the money economy and is enabling them to enjoy a somewhat higher standard of living. On the other hand, they have a traditional lack of interest in growing rich and while this limits the amount of commercial activity they're prepared to get involved in, it tends to make them friendlier and more easy-going than their mestizo counterparts. Their fatalistic attitude towards life probably originated long before the Spanish arrived, and is perhaps a reflection of the often harsh conditions which Andean living dictates. It's surely also a reflection of the fortunes of a history which has until very recently left them dispossessed, disenfranchised and exploited for everything they've got.

Though Ecuador is no longer ruled by a military junta and has an elected civilian government of sorts (only *literate* adult citizens over the age of 18 are qualified to vote), it still has one of the lowest literacy rates of the continent with less than half the children between the ages of six and 15 attending school. Because of centuries of neglect, most of the Indians are illiterate, so their ability to influence national politics is severely limited.

The Incas first arrived in Ecuador around 1450 and founded a settlement where Quito stands today. Unlike Cuzco though, none of that settlement remains, as the stone was used to construct the Spanish city which was built there after the conquest. There are, however, substantial Inca ruins at Ingapirca near Cuenca which display the same mortarless, polished stone techniques of construction found on the monuments at Cuzco, Pisáq and Machu Picchu. They are the only ones remaining in Ecuador.

When the Inca emperor, Huayna Capac, divided the empire between his two sons, Atahualpa and Huascar just before the arrival of the Spanish, the former chose Quito as his capital while the latter retained Cuzco. Civil war was the inevitable outcome of this division and while Atahualpa emerged as the victor, he was enticed into a trap by Pizarro at Cajamarca, and then strangled after he had fulfilled the ransom set by the conquistadores. Atahualpa's death led not only to the collapse of much of the Inca empire but also to Pizarro laying claim to all the lands which the Incas had conquered. Given the avarice of various groups of conquistadores however, Pizarro's claims didn't go undisputed and he was forced at short notice to dispatch an army north to secure Quito and forestall an attempt by Pedro de Alvarado, who was marching south from Colombia to take it from him.

This was the first taste of the squabbling and assassinations which were to go on between rival groups of conquistadores for the next 30 years until the Spanish throne was finally able to establish its authority at Lima. In that time, not only did Pizarro replace Benalcázar with his brother Gonzalo at Quito and have Diego de Almagro executed – both of these two comrades-in-arms were responsible for heading off Alvarado's attempt to take Quito – but was himself assassinated. In the meantime Gonzalo fitted out an expedition into the Amazon lowlands under the command of Francisco de Orellano to search for gold.

Orellano neither returned nor found any gold, but his expedition floated down the Amazon and eventually reached the Atlantic Ocean, thus becoming the first Europeans to cross the continent in this way. The Herzog film, *Aguirre, Wrath of God*, is based on this expedition, as well as the later expedition of 1560 by Ursua, Guzman and Aguirre down the Huallaga River. If you get the chance it's well worth seeing. It paints the conquistadores in their true colours as fractious, back-stabbing, gold-obsessed thugs, and the

church as totally hypocritical. Gonzalo eventually met his match in Pedro de la Gasca, a priest sent out by the Spanish throne, who captured Gonzalo and had him executed after his supporters had deserted him.

Having established the authority of the Spanish throne, Ecuador was to experience some 300 years of relative peace – at least for the ruling class – until, as with the other colonies, the demand for independence gathered force in the late 18th century. During that time Quito became the Audiencia for the area, under the Viceroyalty of Peru, and a major cultural centre. A marriage between the arts of mediaeval Spain and those of the Inca empire took place, and the legacy of this fertile union has left Quito as one of the most attractive and interesting of the South American capitals. It's not only the world's second highest capital city at 2850 metres (only La Paz is higher), but one of steep, narrow, cobbled streets with well-preserved colonial architecture, shady plazas and parks, impromptu Indian street markets and old churches and monasteries with facades and interiors decorated in a unique style by Indian craftsmen. As you might expect, it's a very popular watering hole for travellers.

An attempt was made at setting up an independent government in 1809 but it came to nothing as Quito was too strongly garrisoned by Royalist troops. It wasn't until Sucre, with an army of Venezuelans and Colombians, defeated the Spanish forces at the battle of Pichincha in 1822 that independence was secured. The country was induced by Bolívar to join with Venezuela and Colombia to form the Republic of Gran Colombia, but the union was short-lived and in 1830 Ecuador followed Venezuela's lead and split off. At the time this happened, the Indian provinces around Pasto, in what is today southern Colombia, attempted to join with Ecuador but were prevented from doing so by the Colombian army.

The politics of the country throughout

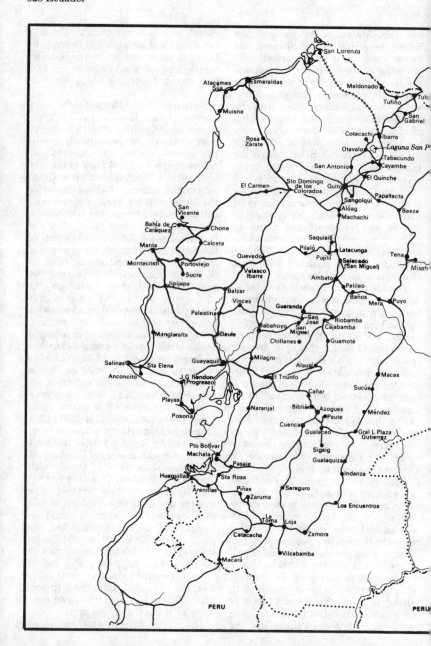

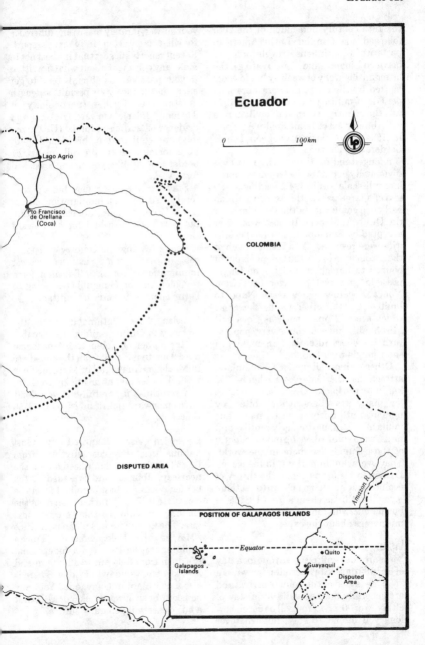

Ecuador

0   100 km

Lago Agrio

Pto Francisco
de Orellana
(Coca)

COLOMBIA

Amazon R.

DISPUTED AREA

POSITION OF GALAPAGOS ISLANDS

— Equator —

Quito

Galapagos
Islands

Guayaquil

Disputed
Area

the 19th century and much of the 20th followed the familiar Latin American pattern of a continuous struggle for power between Liberals and Conservatives, the latter an oligarchy of wealthy landowners backed by the church. There were long periods of military rule and only in 1979 was the country returned to civilian rule with the election of Jaime Roldos Aguilera. In 1984 the conservative León Febres Cordero was elected.

A long-standing dispute with Peru over sovereignty of part of the Oriente erupted into full-scale war in 1941, leading to the loss of a large part of this territory which had once come within the boundaries of the Quito Audiencia. Its loss was never accepted by Ecuador and in 1980 hostilities were resumed. As a result, much of the border area in the the Oriente is out of bounds to foreigners and it's no longer possible to travel by river boat from Nueva Rocafuerte down the Napo to Iquitos. On the other hand, the areas which are still open, such as Coca and Misahuallí, have become very popular with travellers interested in making a short jungle river trip.

Other than Ecuador's mainland attractions, the Galapagos Islands, 600 km out in the Pacific Ocean, are a magnet for many travellers. Uninhabited by humans until fairly recently, its unique fauna and flora, particularly reptiles and birds, were able to develop independently of those found elsewhere in the world. They were an important influence on Darwin in his formation of the theory of evolution. It's no longer cheap to get there – you'll get little change from US$350 – but no-one who makes the trip has any misgivings about the expense.

VISAS

Visas are not required by anyone for a stay of up to 90 days. Stay permits (known as a 'T3') are issued at the point of arrival and are generally marked valid for a stay of either 15 or 30 days. You will be asked how long you intend to stay, but whatever your answer, it rarely makes any difference to what is written in your passport. Recent reports suggest that it's best not to make any comment about what is written in your passport, as officials tend to get angry and reduce your permitted length of stay even further (particularly at Tulcán border). Onward tickets and evidence of 'sufficient funds' (US$20 per day) are required, but this is unlikely to be enforced unless you roll up at the border looking like you haven't washed for a week.

Stay permits are renewable up to a total of 90 days at immigration offices inside Ecuador. These are easy to obtain but you may be asked for an onward ticket.

Before leaving the country you must get an exit stamp at the nearest immigration office, eg at Tulcán if going to Colombia, or Huaquillas if going to Peru. There is no entry or exit tax.

Peruvian Visas Obtainable from the embassy in Quito (Edificio del España, on the corner of Colón and Amazonas: open 9 am to noon) or from the consulate in Machala, Guayaquil or Macará. They will ask to see an onward ticket in Quito and scrutinise it carefully. If you don't have an onward ticket, an MCO for $150 is acceptable.

Colombian Visas Required by most nationalities, they cost anything from US$5 to $20. If you don't need a visa, the necessary Tourist Card is issued at the border. Visas are best obtained from the consulate in Tulcán rather than from the embassy in Quito as there's much less fuss. The Consulate in Tulcán is in office 204/5 in the Delegación de Tulcán Building by the Parque La Indepencia. It's open from 8.30 am to 12.30 pm and 2.30 to 4 pm Monday to Friday. There is also a consulate in Guayaquil. You may be asked for an onward ticket or MCO but a bus ticket will generally suffice.

MONEY
US$1 = Suc 127 (and rising slowly)

The currency was devalued in May 1982 and is currently floating against the US dollar.

The unit of currency is the Sucre = 100 centavos. There is no black market but the best exchange rates are reportedly in Guayaquil. It's quicker to change money at casas de cambio rather than banks, but the former offer slightly lower rates than the banks. Rodrigo Paz cambios have been recommended by many travellers but there are plenty of others. It's easy to change US dollar travellers' cheques into US dollars cash at cambios but shop around as the commission varies between cambios. It's also unlikely they'll be willing to change more than US$100 at any one time.

It's worth asking travellers coming from Peru what the current rate of exchange is for *soles* since you may be offered a better rate at Huaquillas (Ecuador/Peru border) than you are in Tumbes (the first Peruvian town). You're going to need *some* soles anyway to get you from the border to Tumbes.

If you're planning to visit the Galapagos Islands then take sufficient sucres with you from the mainland to cover the whole visit. Exchange rates are poor on the islands, as they are in the Oriente where it can be difficult to exchange money at all. If you are stuck in a small town in the Oriente, the local bank manager may be able to help you out.

If you are thinking of having money sent to Ecuador then make sure that the bank you nominate will be able to pay you when the money arrives. Some banks in Ecuador will only pay account holders so if you don't have an account they'll send it back and there's nothing you can do about it. Quite a few travellers have been caught out this way. It's also wise to be sure that you can have the money paid out in dollars (or at least US dollar travellers' cheques).

Airport departure tax for international flights is US$5. Airline ticket tax is 10%.

GETTING THERE
To/From Colombia
Almost everyone takes the Quito-Ibarra-Tulcán-Pasto road. Buses are very frequent and if you want to, the entire journey can be done in a day. All formalities are taken care of at Rumicacha on the border.

It's also possible these days to get from Puerto Asís (Colombia) to Lago Agrio (Ecuador) in the Amazon lowlands without too much difficulty. Details in the Colombian chapter.

To/From Peru

You have a choice of crossing the border at Machala or Macará. Possible routes are via Guayaquil-Machala-Huaquillas-Tumbes; Cuenca-Machala-Huaquillas-Tumbes; or Cuenca-Loja-Macará-Sullana. Buses along the first two routes are frequent and the journey can be completed in a day. (See 'Huaquillas' section for details). Along the last route, buses are less frequent. On the Peruvian side, you often have to rely on trucks and there's rarely more than one a day between La Tina (border) and Sullana (six hours along a very poor road) with many checkpoints where foreigners must register. The journey between Macará and Piura takes at least two days and often three.

The Oriente border with Peru is closed at present as a result of the 1980 war so you cannot go from any of Ecuador's river ports downriver to Iquitos.

GETTING AROUND

Air Ecuador's most important domestic airline is *TAME* and apart from flights to the Galapagos, internal flights are quite cheap. The most expensive flight is currently US$16. Almost all *TAME* flights originate or terminate in Quito or Guayaquil.

Two other airlines are *SAN-Saeta*, which has a good schedule of flights between Quito, Guayaquil and Cuenca; and *TAO*, which flies small aircraft between Puyo and Macas in the Oriente.

Bus The main route through the highlands from Tulcán via Quito to Guayaquil and Machala has an excellent system of paved roads. There are frequent buses between most cities and towns and journey times are relatively short, so this will probably be your preferred method of transport.

The roads down to the Pacific coast from the highlands tend not to be as good as those in the highlands themselves, and those which descend to the Oriente are often in poor condition.

Bus companies in most Ecuadorian cities and towns are now concentrated in one, often purpose-built, terminal so it's simplicity itself finding a bus.

From north to south, the main bus routes with fares and journey times are as follows:

Ecuador/Colombian border-Tulcán There are no buses between the border and Tulcán but there are plenty of *busetas* throughout the day which cost US$0.20 per person.

From Tulcán there are frequent buses throughout the day to Quito, Otavalo and Ibarra with several companies. The fare and the journey time depend on whether you take a bus, mini-bus or colectivo. There are also a few daily departures for Domingo and Guayaquil. All these buses leave from the central bus terminal in Tulcán.

Tulcán-Ibarra The fare is US$0.90 and the journey takes two to three hours.

Tulcán-Quito There are frequent buses, minibuses and colectivos throughout the day from before dawn until after midnight along this route. What you pay and how long it takes depends on what sort of transport you take. The bus takes about five hours and costs US$1.50. Be prepared for several police/army checkpoints along the route.

Ibarra-San Lorenzo Before you take a bus

or truck along this stretch think about going by rail. It's one of the few possibilities left in Ecuador these days and is very interesting.

If you do decide to go by road there are frequent buses by several companies, like *Flota Imbabura* and *Transportes Andina* which take about 1½ hours.

Quito-Otavalo There are frequent departures in either direction which cost US$0.75 and take about two hours.

Quito-Guayaquil There are frequent departures daily by *Panaméricana*, *Transportes Ecuador* and *Flota Imbabura* which charge US$2.60 and take about eight hours.

Quito-Ambato There are frequent departures daily by *Panamericana*, *Transportes Ecuador*, *Transportes Patria*, *Transportes Chimborazo*, *Santa*, *Expreso Sucre* and *Cooperativo Baños*. The fare is US$1 and the journey takes about 2½ hours.

Quito-Machala There are eight direct buses per day by *Panamericana*, the first at 6 am and the last at 10 pm, which cost US$3.40 and take about 11 hours.

Quito-Huaquillas There are three direct buses per day by *Panamericana* at 6 pm and 7.50 pm (at 1.30 pm, 3.45 pm and 7 pm from Huaquillas) which cost US$4.25 and take about 14 hours.

Machala-Huaquillas This costs US$0.65 and takes about 1½ hours. In Huaquillas these buses leave from the CIFA terminal down the first street on the right hand side as you head north after crossing the bridge from Peru. They leave for Machala every 15 to 30 minutes.

Guayaquil-Machala There are frequent daily buses by *Transportes Colón*, *Ecuatoriano Pullman* and *Panaméricana* which cost US$1.45 and take about three hours. *Rutas Orenses* also runs mini-buses daily which take 2½ hours.

Guayaquil-Huaquillas *Equatoriano Pullman* does the run at two hour intervals daily. The fare is US$2.65 and the journey takes about 5½ hours. There are also more expensive buses (US$3.20) which do the journey in about four hours. There are frequent daily buses between Machala and Huaquillas if you don't get a direct bus from Guayaquil (eg if you need to stop at Machala for a Peruvian visa).

Quito-Baños Several departures daily by *Cooperativo Baños* which cost US$1.40 and take 3½ hours. If there isn't a bus going to Baños for several hours when you get to the terminal, take a bus to Ambato and change there for one to Baños.

Baños-Riobamba Frequent buses throughout the day which cost US$0.40 and take about one hour. In Riobamba these buses leave from the terminal at the northern end of Calle Espejo.

Quito-Cuenca Several departures daily by *Panaméricana*, *Santa* and *Expreso Sucre*. The fare is US$5 and the journey takes 9½ to 12 hours depending on the type of bus.

Riobamba-Cuenca Direct buses are infrequent and operated only by *Patria* at 5.30 am, 7.30 am and 7.30 pm. The fare is US$2.50 and the journey takes from nine to 12 hours along a gravel road. If you miss these three buses you can still get to Cuenca by taking a Guayaquil bus as far as the junction of El Trionfo (three hours), and then another from there to Cuenca (4½ hours).

Cuenca-Guayaquil Several buses daily which cost US$3.30 and take five to seven hours. There are also mini-buses by *Supertaxis Cuenca* which are more expensive.

Cuenca-Huaquillas Two buses per day at 1 pm and 10 pm by *Azuay* from the main bus station which take about eight hours and cost US$3.

If you'd prefer to enter Peru via the less frequently used Macará-Sullana route, the bus connections are less frequent but the route is much more scenic than the Guayaquil-Machala route.

Cuenca-Loja *Pullman Viajeros* operate minibuses every two to three hours between 10 am and 5 pm which cost

US$2.40 and take about 7½ hours. The road is appalling but 'it's an interesting journey if you can stand the dust'.

Loja-Macará Four buses daily which cost US$2 and takes six to eight hours. From Macará there is a 2½ km walk to the border (or you can catch a pickup for 15c), after which you can take a bus or truck from La Tina (the first Peruvian village) to Sullana.

If you're heading for the Pacific coast of Santa Domingo de los Colorados the main connections are:

Quito-Esmeraldas Several daily departures by *Transportes Esmeraldas* and *Transportes Occidentales* but make sure you get an express bus, as they take two hours less to do the journey. Express buses of the former company leave Quito at 8 am, 12.30 pm and 6.30 pm, cost US$2.40 and take about 5½ hours. The ordinary buses cost US$1.70 and take about seven hours. You can also get a bus from Guayaquil to Esmeraldas with *Transportes Esmeraldas* for US$3, which takes eight hours. Remember that it's difficult to find either transport or accommodation at the start of August because of festivals. There are also buses if you're heading for Santo Domingo de los Colorados (US$1.80, three hours).

From Esmeraldas there are daily buses to Atacames (US$0.20) and Suá (US$0.25). The journey takes about one hour and the last bus from Esmeraldas leaves at 8 pm.

Train At one time Ecuador would qualify for a chapter in any guidebook on Great Railway Journeys of the World. Sadly those days are over as a result of the 1982-83 El Niño floods which swept away not only the line from Quito to Guayaquil but also the one from Quito to Ibarra. The only lines which are left are the Quito-Riobamba section of the former Quito-Guayaquil railway and the Ibarra-San Lorenzo line.

The Ibarra-San Lorenzo line is the most interesting of the two and has been raved about by many travellers who have been on it. Like the former Quito-Guayaquil train, the line starts off high in the barren Andes, plunges down into thick jungle and finally chugs through banana plantations until it reaches San Lorenzo. There are two trains in either direction daily (at 7 am and 1 pm from Ibarra). Unfortunately it's no longer possible to buy tickets the day before so there's a mad scramble for these and for seats on the day of departure. Get there early. Tickets cost US$2. Sit on the right hand side for the best views going down.

The only other line open is the Quito-Riobamba section but few travellers seem to use it these days.

NB Transport details for the Oriente and for the Galápagos Islands are given in the sections on those places.

MARKETS
The principal market days in Ecuador are:

Monday
    Ambato
Tuesday
    Otavalo, Riobamba, Latacunga, Guano
Wednesday
    Riobamba, Pujili
Thursday
    Saquisili
Saturday
    Otavalo, Riobamba, Latacunga
Sunday
    Cuenca, Salcedo, Machachi, Sangolgui

AMBATO
Ambato isn't a particularly interesting town though you may find yourself passing through. It was completely destroyed by an earthquake in 1949 and is now a modern city – Ecuador's fourth largest. The city is famous for its 'Fiesta de Frutas y Flores' which takes place in February. Accommodation is impossible to find around this time unless you book in advance.

Information

The tourist office is in the process of moving and is temporarily housed in the Government Office at the corner of Sucre and Castillo.

Banks won't change money but *Cambiato* on Bolívar changes cash and cheques at reasonable rates.

The post office is on Castillo near the Parque Juan Montalvo.

Things to See

If you're staying overnight, it's worth taking a bit of time to visit the **museum** in the Colegio Bolívar. It has hundreds of stuffed birds, animals and mammals. There's also a good display of photographs taken around 1910 by the Ecuadorian mountaineer Nicolás Martínez. It's open Monday to Friday from 7.30 am to 12.30 pm and 2 to 5 pm; entry is 25c.

Places to Stay

Since most travellers merely pass through Ambato en route to Baños, it's unlikely you'll want to spend the night there. Should you have to, probably the best place is the *Residencial Europa* which costs US$1.40 per person.

Both the *Residencial Nacional* and the *Residencial Americano*, Plaza 12 de Noviembre, are cheaper at US$1.10 per person but they're scruffy and unfriendly.

Other travellers have recommended the *Hotel Vivero*, Mera 504 y Caballos, which charges US$4 per person in rooms without bath.

Places to Eat

The best value is the *Chifa Jao Fua* on Cevallos near Castillo where a good cheap meal costs about US$2. For breakfast try one of the cake shops like *Panadería Zurimar* for coffee, juice, rolls or sandwiches. Super-cheap meals can be had around the market.

For a splurge, try one of the three Swiss restaurants called *El Alamo* - one on Castillo and another round the corner on Bolívar. The *Chifa Hong Kong*, Av 12 de Noviembre 24-30, is also recommended - reasonable prices.

For a bit of nightlife, the *Peña Tunguruhua Bar* on M Eguez south of the market has folklore music evenings on Friday and Saturday nights, but doesn't get going until about 11 pm.

Getting There

The main bus terminal is about two km north of the city centre near the railway station and it has an information office. There are daily departures for Quito, (US$1, three hours); Baños, (US$0.35, 45 minutes); Riobamba, (US$0.50, one hour); Guayaquil, (US$2.25, six hours); Guaranda, (US$0.80, 2½ hours); and Tena, (US$2, six hours).

Baños

Baños is one of the most popular destinations in South America. Travellers gather there from all over the continent. The reason for this is not hard to understand as Baños has one of the most beautiful settings you're ever likely to come across. It's surrounded by lush, forested mountains, river gorges, waterfalls and, as its name suggests, hot springs. If you're looking for somewhere to hang up your bag for a few weeks - or a few months as many travellers do - Baños is one place you could do it.

The area also has a very pleasant subtropical climate and produces citrus fruits, peaches, grapes and sugar cane. About 10 km from town are the Agoyán Falls, though one traveller wrote recently to complain that we'd recommended a visit to them in the last edition, and said that they were 'ugly, dirty and unimpressive'. Check them out for yourself. There are also good trekking possibilities in the area - including one to the crater of the volcano, Altar.

Information

There is no tourist office in Baños but there's also little need for one. It's a small town and all you have to do is ask around in one or other of the restaurants where travellers congregate or at your hotel. If you need trekking or climbing information or maps of the local area, ask at the café at the bus station. The owner there is a guide. The maps he has cost about 15 cents and although they're not great, there's nothing else available.

There is a bank in town, Banco del Pacífico, opposite the Hotel Americano on the corner of Carrera 3 and Calle 2. You can only change up to a maximum of US$50 at any one time. If you need more then go to the large hotel opposite the hot baths.

Things to See

Apart from relaxing, walking is the most popular activity in Baños. There are no 'set' routes as such so just ask around at the hotels and cafés to get an idea of where you'd like to go. The Agoyán Falls are, perhaps, the nearest major attraction. There are buses to and from the centre of town.

There are two lots of thermal springs: one in Baños itself and the other at Salado, about 1½ km out of town on the Ambato road. The latter has several baths each at a different temperature and costs about 10 cents per person. There is also a small zoo about one km out of town on the Riobamba road which is said to be worth visiting. Entry costs a few cents. Horses can be hired in Baños for about US$0.50 per hour – ask for Julio Albán near the Plaza Central.

A walk to the Puente San Martia is worthwhile. It crosses a very deep canyon and 200 metres further on, a footpath descends to a place where the river thunders out of the canyon into a huge whirlpool. To get there, walk one km west of town on the Ambato road and turn right just before the police control.

Places to Stay

One of the most popular places is the *Residencial Patty*, Eloy Alfaro 554 (Calle 4), one block from the market, which costs just over US$1 per person and has hot showers. It's owned by a hospitable woman who offers the use of kitchen, washing facilities and equipment for hire to climb the nearby volcano. It's also possible to arrange horses from there.

Two other very popular places are the *Residencia Teresita*, which is very clean and friendly and costs US$0.70 per person; and the *Residencia Olguita* which has excellent views and is very good value at US$3 per person. In fact the latter was described by one bunch of travellers as 'amongst the world's best value hotels'. There's no hot water there, however.

Another place which has been highly recommended by many travellers is the *Residencial Santa Clara*, Calle 2 three blocks south of the cathedral square on the edge of town and near the thermal springs. It offers very pleasant, large, bright rooms for US$0.80 to $1.70 per person with views of the mountains from the balcony. There are cooking facilities and the owners are very friendly and have equipment for hire if you want to go climbing.

The *Residencial La Delicia 1* on P V Maldonado isn't quite as pleasant as the above but it does have hot water (one shower for 22 rooms!) and costs US$1.35 per person and the front rooms have great views over the plaza.

Going up-market, there is the *Hotel Sangay* near the waterfall which costs US$8.50/$11 a single/double.

There's a municipal camp site with showers and toilets next to the hot baths at the end of Carrera 2 but it's overpriced and will cost you as much as a hotel.

If you're thinking of staying around for a while, houses can be rented for around US$2 per night. One of the best places to ask around for these is at the *El Paisano Restaurant*.

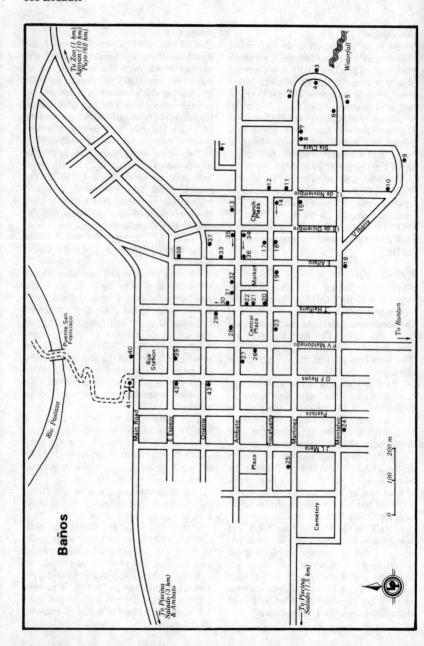

Baños

Places to Eat

Baños is one of those places where recommending any particular restaurant is tantamount to putting your head in the lion's mouth. Everyone has their own favourite and others which they wouldn't be seen dead in. Even local residents fuel the rivalry by writing to Lonely Planet and making outrageously libelous and ridiculous suggestions about the restaurants which they compete with! One thing that is common to most of them, however, is that service is slow so you need patience.

One which has been popular for years is the *Mercedes Restaurant*, across from the cemetery up Carrera 3 between Calles 9 and 10 (Carrera 3 is also known as Luis A Martínez). It's an orange building visible from many parts of town. Its specialties are vegetarian meals but it isn't solely vegetarian. Try the *pastel de mora* (blackberry pie) which everyone agrees is excellent regardless of what else they might think about the place in general. The restaurant has a second-hand book swop-shop with a very good selection.

Equally popular over the years is the *Restoran Monica*, Calle 5 between Carreras 7 and 8 (same street as the Residencial Patty). The service there is slow, casual but friendly and the portions are huge. Similar is the *El Paisano*, and this is one of the few which we haven't had complaints about regarding the cleanliness of the place. However service is just as slow as in the others.

Vegetarians should try the restaurant at the *Hotel Acapulco*. The food is good and the staff are friendly.

For good fish try the *Marisco* in front of the market. The *Pan de Casa* next to the market has received many recommendations for its breakfasts which include whole-wheat bread.

1	La Burbuja Disco
2	New Swimming Pool & Baths
3	Piscina de la Virgen (Hot Baths)
4	Hotel Sangay
5	Hotel Palace
6	Restaurant El Marqués
7	Restaurant El Paisano
8	Hostal El Castillo
9	Sta. Clara Swimming Pool
10	Residencial Villa Sta. Clara
11	Hotel Americano & Restaurant
12	Residencial Sta. Teresita
13	Museum
14	Hotel Guayaquil, Hostal Agoyan, Residencial Acapulco & Restaurant
15	Banco Pacifico
16	Residenciales Anita & Panama
17	Residenciales Mercedes & Lucy
18	Villa Gertrudis
19	Hotel Danubio
20	Town Hall & Clock Tower
21	IETEL
22	Post Office
23	Residenciales Olguita & Los Pinos
24	Hospital
25	Mercedes Restaurant
26	Residencial La Delicia 2
27	Residencial Viena
28	Residencial La Delicia 1 & Bus stop for El Salado
29	Pensión Turismo
30	Pensións Jota, Oriente & Residencial Dumay
31	Hotel Humboldt & Paraiso
32	Chifa Oriental
33	Pensión Patty
34	Residencial Ecuador, Hostal Cordillera, Residencial Puerto del Dorado
35	Residenciales Irmita & Guayas Pensión Quito, Residenciales Bolívar, Santa Fé & Baños
36	Bus stop to Zoo & Agoyan
37	Residencial Cecilita
38	Restaurant Monica
39	Pensión Villa Sta. Clara
40	Sugar cane stalls
41	Residencial El Refugio
42	Residencial Julia
43	Residencial El Rey

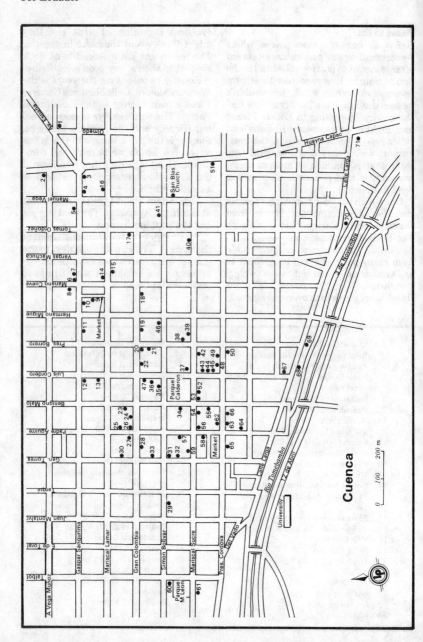

Cuenca

Getting There

The bus terminal is within walking distance of most of the hotels. Buses for Quito (US$1.30, 3½ hours) leave almost every hour or you can take more frequent buses to Ambato and change there. Buses to Riobamba take about one hour and cost 40c.

Buses for the Oriente (Puyo or Tena) usually start in Ambato or Quito and pass through Baños on the way and they are occasionally full.

CUENCA

Founded by the Spanish in 1557, Cuenca is Ecuador's third largest city and one of its most attractive, having retained its colonial atmosphere. The old centre has churches dating from the 16th and 17th centuries, as well as many other old buildings and cobblestone streets. Nearby are the ruins of Ingapirca, Ecuador's only remaining substantial Inca site.

Information

The tourist office is on the 4th floor,

1	Residencial La Alborada	37	Old Cathedral
2	Hostal Londres	38	Cambio Sur Money Changer
3	Hotel España	39	Internacional Hotel Paris
4	Residencial Tito	40	Hotel Atahualpa
5	Hostel El Galeon	41	Ristorante Pizzeria Italiane
6	Pensión Taiwan	42	Teatro Sucre
7	Residencial Florida	43	Cafeteria Roma
8	Pensióna Andaluz	44	Teatro Casa de Cultura
9	Residencial Norte & Colombia	45	Intituto de Folklore
10	Residencial La Ramada	46	MAG Office
11	Restaurant Balcón Quiteño	47	Monsalve English magazines
12	Residencial Atenas	48	Chifa Pack How
13	Hotel Majestic	49	Restaurant La Carreta
14	Cine 9 de Octubre	50	Restaurant El Jardin
15	Residencial Niza	51	Restaurant Casa China
16	Cine España	52	Cambistral Money Changer
17	El Paraiso Vegetarian Restaurant	53	Municipal Hall
18	Residencial Siberia	54	Casa de Cultura
19	Hotel El Conquistador	55	DITURIS office
20	Post Office	56	Flower market
21	IETEL	57	Hotel Catedral
22	Hotel El Dorado	58	Pensión Azuay
23	Hotel Internacional	59	Residencial Granada
24	Residencial Amazonas	60	San Sebastian Church
25	Teatro Cuenca	61	Museum of Modern Art
26	Residencial Sto. Domingo	62	Hotel Alli Tiana
27	Sto. Domingo Church	63	Hotel Milan
28	Hotel Residencial Emperador	64	Restaurant El Inca
29	St. Cenaculo Church	65	San Francisco Church
30	Residencial Paris	66	Hotel Cantabri
31	Hotel Pichincha	67	Hotel Crespo
32	Residencial El Inca	68	Hotel Crespo Annex
33	Gran Hotel	69	Municipal Museum
34	New Cathedral	70	Inca ruins
35	Pio Pio Chicken Restaurant	71	Banco Central Museum
36	TAME		

Edificio Carmerlo, on the corner of Calles Mariscal Sucre and Benigno Malo 725. The information they have is limited but the staff are very helpful. They don't have much information about Ingapirca so if you're planning on going there and can read Spanish, get hold of a copy of the booklet, *Ingapirca, Guía para Visitantes*, from a bookshop. It costs a few cents.

There is a casa de cambio on the main plaza which will change travellers' cheques. Forget the banks.

Some travellers have suggested that *AeroPeru* tickets can be bought relatively cheaply in Cuenca. If you're heading to Peru it might be worth checking this out.

The *TAME* office is by the central plaza and is open weekdays from 9.30 am to 12.30 pm and 2 to 5 pm.

The post office is on the corner of Gran Colombia and Presidente Borrero.

Things to See
The principal Indian market is on Thursdays in the 9 de Octubre and San Francisco areas. It's mainly basketware, clothes and textiles.

The **Municipal Museum**, Calle Larga between Calles P Cordero and P Borrero, is worth visiting. It's divided into four sections. One features archaeology and contains ceramics, metal weapons and jewellery from the Canari, Chordeleg and Inca periods. Another has a display of oil paintings from the colonial period and there's also an historical section. It's open Mondays to Fridays from 8 am to 1 pm and from 3 to 5 pm.

The **Padre Crespi Museum**, Colegio Salesiano, documents Padre Crespi's contention that the Phoenicians reached Cuenca by way of the Amazon, but it's been closed indefinitely since the Padre's death in 1982.

On Avenida Todos los Santos there are some rather lacklustre **Inca ruins**. There are some fine niches and walls but most of the stonework was destroyed to construct colonial buildings.

If you're looking for handicrafts, pay a visit to the *Productos Andinos*, Gran Colombia No 6-24 between Benigno Malo and P Cordero. It's run by an Indian cooperative.

Places to Stay
Many travellers stay at the *Residencial El Inca*, Calle Gral Torres 842 between Bolívar and Sucre, which is reasonably good value at just over US$1 per person. It's clean, has attractive decor and the staff are very friendly. Beware of the wiring system if you're taking a hot shower – a friend nearly burnt the place down a couple of years ago but the staff were most apologetic and spent half the night making sure she got her shower in the end.

Somewhat better is the *Hotel Emperador*, on the corner of Gran Colombia and Oadre Aguirre, which costs US$1.50 a single and is clean and comfortable.

Two others which are worth trying are the *Residencial Colombia*, Mariano Cueva 1163, which has hot water all day and a baggage safe which you can use if you want to go hiking in El Cajas National Park; and the *Pensión Norte*, Mariano Cueva 1161. The Colombia costs US$1.25 a single and the Norte US$0.70 a single (with hot shower).

A bit more expensive is the *Residencia Niza*, Calle Lamar 4-51. It is clean, has hot water and costs US$2.10 a single.

Places to Eat
There are many cheap restaurants along Calle Sangurima such as the *Balcón Quiteño* and the *Chifa Familiar*. Also try the *Cafeteria Roma* which has good lasagna on Sundays. Vegetarians could try the very simple *El Paraiso Restaurant* on Tomas Ordoñez. There's a 24 hour snack bar at the bus terminal and a decent restaurant that's open during the day.

For a minor splurge go to the *El Tunel* near the Residencial El Inca.

Getting There

Air The airport is conveniently located on Avenida España only two km from the centre of town. Buses pass the terminal frequently and a taxi would cost about US$0.50.

There are daily flights to Guayaquil for US$10 and to Quito for US$16.

Bus The new, well organised bus terminal is also on Avenida España on the way to the airport, about 1½ km from the centre. Buses for the terminal leave from the bus stop on Padre Aguirre by the flower market.

Buses leave for Guayaquil (US$2.50, five hours) every few minutes. Buses for Azogues (US$0.25, 45 minutes) leave at least every hour and many continue to Cañar (US$0.45, 1½ hours). There are buses for Quito (US$3, nine to 14 hours) about every hour. There are also daily buses to Machala, Saraguro, Loja, Macas and Gualaquiza.

AROUND CUENCA

Ingapirca

The main place of interest outside Cuenca is the Inca site of Ingapirca, about 50 km north of the city. It's well worth visiting if you have the time to spare. The structures were built with the same mortarless, polished-stone technique as those at Cuzco, Pisaq and Machu Picchu. Excavation and reconstruction work is still going on.

At Ingapirca there is a small village with a craft shop/museum by the church on the plaza that's occasionally open. There are no restaurants or accommodation and the few shops sell only the most basic food items. At Cañar, a village close by, there is a couple of basic pensións.

There are hot sulphur baths about 10 km from Tambo (take the bus marked 'Baños').

There is an Indian market at Ingapirca on Fridays next to the church.

Places to Stay In the past if you wanted to stay at Ingapirca you had to go back to Tambo where there is a simple hospedaje, or to San Pedro where there is a similar place. These days, however, there is a *refugio* at the ruins which is clean and free of charge but you need to take a sleeping bag with you. There's even a bathroom, table and fireplace. If you want to stay there you'll have to chase up the key for the place.

Getting There Visiting Ingapirca is not a straightforward affair as there are no direct buses and the railway was closed after the 1983 floods. A few tourist agencies in Cuenca organise day trips but charge US$15 per person. For a small group it would be better to hire a taxi for the day – about US$20.

To get there by public transport, first take a bus from Cuenca to Cañar (US$0.45, 1½ hours). About two km before Cañar there is a signposted turnoff to Ingapirca. Get off the bus there and wait for a pickup to take you the 15 km to the ruins. The fare is about 35c.

El Cajas

Other travellers have suggested a visit to El Cajas, a high altitude park (around 4200 metres), where you can go trekking or trout fishing in the many lakes. There is a *refugio* where you can stay free and a kitchen with a gas stove but the caretaker is reported to be reluctant to make a fire – it gets very cold up there. Bring your own food and plenty of warm clothing. Before you visit the park you must get a permit from the Ministerio de Agricultura on Simon Bolívar in Cuenca. This costs US$0.25 per day. They also have (inaccurate) maps for about 15 cents.

ESMERALDAS, ATACAMES, SUÁ & MUISNE

If you're heading south, the beaches of Ecuador are the last places where you will be able to enjoy a warm sea. South of Tumbes, the first main town in Peru, and all the way down the rest of the Pacific coast there are plenty of good beaches, but the sea is as cold as a witch's tit because of the Humboldt current which sweeps up from the Antarctic. There are beaches south-west of Guayaquil (Playas, for example), but they tend to be over-crowded, and are popular with people from Guayaquil on weekends so are relatively expensive. The beaches around Esmeraldas are more laid-back and accommodation costs are lower.

The town of Esmeraldas itself is dirty and pretty expensive so you need to head south from there in the direction of Atacames, Suá and Muisne. Atacames is popular with French travellers but even this place and Suá are fairly commercial-ised these days so if you want something really laid-back then go to Muisne or even Cojimies. At these latter places you can sling up a hammock, rent a room in one of the small hotels or even sleep on the beach. Don't, however, leave your belongings lying around unattended, or they'll walk.

Information

There is a tourist office in Esmeraldas at Calle Bolívar 541 (2nd floor), half a block from the main plaza.

Money changers don't exist and it may be that the banks will not change money so bring sucres with you.

Places to Stay & Eat

Esmeraldas If you arrive in Esmeraldas too late to get down to either Atacames or Suá, try the *Hotel Dominguez* just off the main plaza between the bus companies' offices. It's good value for what it offers but has only cold water showers. If it's full, try the *Hotel Bolívar*, where you can get a room for around US$0.50 a single. The *Hotel Colón* is very run-down so avoid staying there if possible.

For somewhere to eat, try the *Asia Restaurant* on the main plaza which serves good food and has friendly staff. The *Miramar*, which is a hut on the beach at the end of the No 1 bus route is also worth trying. It serves some of the best crab in South America.

Atacames Atacames may not be quite what you're looking for. Recent reports suggest that the beach is muddy and there's a lot of garbage strewn around. Also, if you're going to sleep out on the beach, do it as a group as there are plenty of thieves around and you need to keep an eye on your belongings.

Accommodation tends to be expensive and not very good value. An exception is the *Residencial Doña Pichu* which is a pleasant, homely place near the plaza which also offers good, cheap food. North of Atacames, about half an hours walk along the beach, is *El Chavalito* where there are chalets for about US$1.25 per person. There's no fresh water but it's a quiet and relaxing spot.

The *Hotel Atacames* at the beginning of the village is good value but it does cost about US$2.50 a double. Avoid the *Residencial Primavera* (very poor value) and especially the *Hotel Balboa*, which is virtually derelict, the staff are sullen, the doors are made of cardboard, the mattresses mildewed and stinking of urine and the bar is gutted. And they'll have the nerve to ask you for US$3.40 a single.

More acceptable is the *Hotel Tahiti* further down the beach where they have rooms for US$1.10 per person or you can rent a *cabaña* for US$4.20 (regardless of numbers). The toilets are always dirty and blocked and there are cold showers only.

Further down the beach still is the *San Baye*. Old rooms cost US$1.25 per person. They also have new rooms facing the beach with private bath. Water is very irregular. There are hammocks, a verandah and a 'permanently drunk security guard'. The place is often full and there's a loud disco not far away which pounds away until 2 am.

Continuing on down the beach you'll come to *Chavelito Hotel*. It's clean and

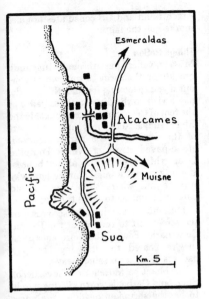

friendly and popular with gringos but there's only well-water available.

Avoid going to Atacames at weekends as it gets overcrowded with people from Quito. Also, there's frequently a water shortage in the village; many times there is only running water on Wednesdays and Sundays.

Most people eat at one or other of the restaurants on the beach. There are quite a few of these and most of them offer seafood, *ceviche* being a speciality. Very popular are the *Maribel* (cheap good food), *Comedor Popular* (also good and cheap) and the *Paco Paco* (very popular but slightly more expensive). There is also the *Dorde Jacobo* and the *Salcon Atacames* which is decked out as a kind of Wild West bar and is worth a visit if you want some local action.

In Atacames itself there is the *Borgoña*, a French restaurant which offers excellent food and generous amounts but it tends to be about twice the price of the beach restaurants. Expect a meal for two to come to about US$8.

Suá There are now quite a lot of hotels at Suá though some are quite primitive. Try the *Residencia Quito* or the *Suá* which both charge US$1.50 per person. More expensive is the *Motel Chaguaramas* on the beach at US$8 a double.

For food, try the *Motel Chaguaramas*. The *Hotel España*, also on the beach, has a discotheque which costs about US$0.30 during the week but is more expensive at the weekends.

Muisne Muisne is only two hours away from Atacames by bus and is much quieter. There are several cheap *residencias* and restaurants in the village. Perhaps the best value is the *Residencial Narcisita* which costs US$1.50 per person. Otherwise try the *Pension Reina* where you can rent a *cabaña* on the beach for US$2.25 without own bath or US$3.25 with own bath. There are cooking facilities. It's a very relaxed place and the beach is superb.

For somewhere to eat, try the *Comedor Moneda* or the *Comedor Martha*, but don't expect anything after 7.30 pm.

From Muisne you can walk south along the beach to **Cojimies** but you'll need to cross several rivers along the way and the fishermen who have boats for this are generally out to make a fast buck. It's perhaps better to catch a boat direct from the muelle which costs about US$3 and takes 3 to 4 hours.

From Cojimies there are buses to **Bahía de Caráquez** which take 4 to 5 hours and cost about US$4. In Bahía de Caráquez stay at *Pension Miriam* which is unremarkable but okay for US$1.

Getting There

Local buses (*Transportes Suá*) run from Esmeraldas to Atacames and Suá approximately every half hour from 6.30 am to 7 pm and take about one hour (US$0.20 to Atacames and $0.25 to Suá). They leave from the main plaza and late buses tend to get packed out so buy a ticket early.

It's possible to walk from Atacames to

Suá along the beach and around the rocky headland when the tide is out – about 20 minutes.

To get to Muisne you need to take an early bus from either Esmeraldas or Atacames (7 am and 7.45 am, three hours and US$0.65). At the last stop, take a motorised canoe to Muisne (about half an hour, US$0.40).

GUAYAQUIL

Guayaquil is Ecuador's largest city and principal port, with a population of over a million. It's a lively, modern place with a number of small parks and gardens and a wide waterfront boulevard known as the Malecón. It's also an expensive place and except for the oldest part of town where there are some delightful colonial streets, it isn't very interesting. Like any major port city, however, it does throb with nightclubs and discotheques if you're looking for some action after spending time in the highlands.

Information

The tourist office is at Malecón 23-21 at the junction with Av Olmedo (tel 510445/512926). Free maps of the city are available and English is spoken. The office is closed between noon and 3 pm.

Guayaquil has the best foreign exchange rate in Ecuador. There are at least a dozen casa de cambios on Avenida 9 de Octubre, and there's one at the airport which is open at weekends to meet incoming international flights.

One of the best bookshops for English-language books is the *Librería Cientifica*, Luque 222. There's also a book exchange at *Nuevos Horizontes*, 6 de Marzo 924.

For tourist card extensions there's an immigration office in the government building (Palacio de Gobierno) on the waterfront.

The Peruvian consulate is on the sixth floor of the building at the corner of Avenida 9 de Octubre and Chile. It's open from 8.30 am to 1 pm and 2 to 5 pm Monday to Friday. The Colombian, Argentinian and US consulates are also marked on the map.

Things to See

Most travellers pass through Guayaquil quickly on their way to somewhere else, but if you're looking for something to do, pay a visit to the district of **Las Peñas** at the foot of Cerro Santa Ana alongside the River Guayas. The most interesting part of the district is the narrow, curved, stone-paved street of Numa Pompilio Llona which is full of old colonial houses. It starts from the small plateau half-way up the hill where there are two old cannons pointing towards the river.

The main nightclub and disco area is in the streets off to the left of the Parque Centenario. Few of them are cheap, as they're geared to emptying the pay packets of sailors on shore leave.

The **Municipal Museum**, on the corner of Sucre and Carbo, is worth visiting if only to see the shrunken heads – *tzantzas* – made by certain tribes of the Oriente. Most of them have been reduced to fist-size without their original features being lost! There's also an archaeological section featuring exhibits from the various coastal cultures of Ecuador and a very good craft collection. It is open Monday to Friday between 9 am and 12 noon and 3 to 7 pm, on Saturday from 10 am to 3 pm and on Sunday from 10 am to 1 pm; entry costs 30c.

The nearest beaches to Guayaquil are at **Salinas** due west of Guayaquil. There are buses there from Guayaquil with *CICA*, Calle Juan Pio Motufar near the intersection with Calle Colón, throughout the day from 4 am to 9 pm. The journey takes three hours and costs US$1.10. At Salinas stay at *Residencial Rachel* two blocks back from the main road which goes along the beach. It costs US$3 a double. The *Hotel Tivoli* is cheaper but 'grotty'.

Places to Stay

Some of the cheapest places are clustered

around the junction of Chiriboga and Chimborazo. They include the *Residencias Ayacucho, Hotel El Cisme, Residencias Mar del Plata, Hotel Florida, Hotel Boston* (Chimborazo 711), and the *Residencias Roma* (Ayacucho 415). The Boston doubles as a brothel (as do many of them) but you can get a room there for US$1.15 a single with fan and handbasin. It can be noisy because of the thin partition walls. Another cheapie which has been recommended is the *Pacific Hotel*, Sucre 533. It's friendly, quiet, clean, secure and costs US$2.15 per person in a room without own bath or US$2.75 per person with own bath.

Closer to the centre is the *Hotel Turistica*, Baquerizo Moreno 903 near the junction with Junín, which costs US$6 a double with own bath but it's dirty and has no hot water. Avoid this place if you are a single woman or two women travelling together. We've had reports that the manager may try to force his way into your room at night.

Much better is the *Residencial Pauker*, Moreno 902, which is run by a Chinese family and has excellent showers with hot water, but there's no longer a restaurant there. It costs US$2.40/$4.20 a single/ double. You can leave excess gear there while you go to the Galapagos.

The *Hotel Londres* has also been recommended. The rooms are somewhat dark but it's in a good location and is quiet. Another recommendation is the *Residencias Comercio*, on the left after the Hotel Casino coming from the riverfront.

Places to Eat

The main restaurant street is 9 de Octubre where numerous places spill out onto the pavements. They aren't particularly cheap but the food is generally good and there's a wide choice available. They're excellent places in which to hang out during the evenings and watch the world go by.

One place which has been recommended is the *El Capitano Restaurant* in the Hotel Oro Verde. It offers a typical Ecuadorian-style buffet meal for US$3 plus 16% but the drinks are expensive.

If you're looking for fish or vegetarian food try the *El Camino Restaurant*. The prices are reasonable. Cheaper food and fruit is available in the market and at the *Restaurant Sucre*, Calle Sucre, where you can get good almuerzos. There are also a number of cheap cafés around the bus terminals.

A great place to go for a drink in Guayaquil is the boat *El Pirato*, which is moored on the waterfront opposite Av 9 de Octubre. It's only slightly more expensive than other places and it's a good place for watching the river.

Getting There

Air Simon Bolívar international airport is close to the centre. Bus No 2 goes there from the Malecón.

There are many flights to all parts of the country with *TAME* and *SAN-Saeta*. Some destinations include: Loja, US$9.50; Machala, US$7.50; Macará, US$9.50; Cuenca, US$9.50; and Manta, US$8.50.

Bus A new bus terminal just beyond the airport has almost been finished but at the moment the bus companies are scattered all over the city.

For the Santa Elena peninsula take *Transportes Villamil* or *Co-op Posorja* which have frequent buses to Playas (US$0.65, 1¾ hours) and Posorja (US$0.80, two hours). *Co-op Libertad* and *CIFA* have buses to Salinas (US$1, 2½ hours).

For the south and Peru, take *CIFA, Transportes Rutas Orenses, Ecuatoriana Pullman* or *Co-op El Oro* to Machala (US$1.50, 3½ hours) and Huaquillas (US$2, five hours). *Transportes Loja* has one bus at 6.30 pm to the border at Macará (US$4, 12 hours) and five buses to Loja (US$3.20, 10 hours).

Several companies have buses leaving hourly for Cuenca (US$2.20 to $2.60, five

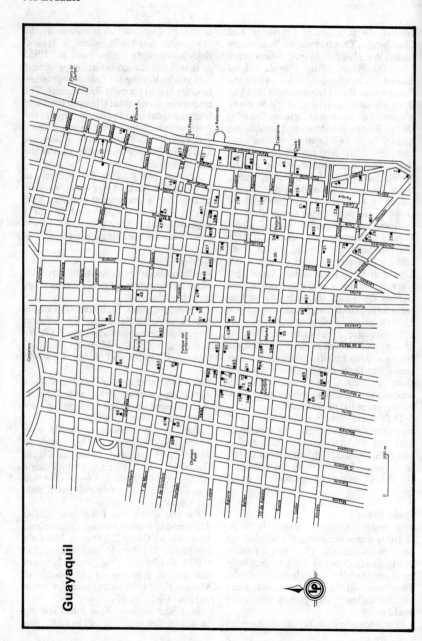

Guayaquil

1. Dituris Tourist Office
2. Hotel Humboldt
3. Hotel Orquidea Internacional
4. Hotels Santa Maria, Nacional
   & Luz de America
5. Hotel Italia
6. Palacio Municipal
7. Palacio de Gobierno
8. Metropolitan Touring
9. Colombian & Argentine Conuls
10. Bank of America
11. Ecuatoriana
12. Banco Pacifico Museo
    de Archaeologia & Hotel Moneda
13. Hotel Metropolitan
14. Hotel Ramada
15. Restaurant Napoli
16. Post Office & IETEL
17. Libreria Cientifica
18. Church & Plaza of San Francisco
19. Church & Plaza of La Merced
20. Milagro Bus Companies
21. Museo Municipal & Library
22. Gran Chifa
23. Cifa Buses
24. Hotel Los Angeles
25. Hotel Residencial Espejo
26. Transportes Sucre
27. Residencial El Cisne
28. Transportes Rutas Orenses
29. Residencial Maria
30. Ecuatoriana Pullman Buses
31. Co-op El Oro Buses
32. Flota Bolívar
33. Hotel Boston
34. Cathedral
35. Gran Hotel Guayaquil
36. La Palma & Cyrano Pavement Cafés
37. Cine Metro
38. Residencial Comercio
39. San & Saeta Airlines
40. Peruvian Consul
41. Hotel Casino Boulevard,
    Teatro Guayaquil, TAME Airline
    & Galasam Tours (Edificio Pasaje)
42. Hotel Pauker
43. Hotel Tourist
44. Lansa Air
45. Hotel San Juan
46. Residencial Imperio
47. Cine 9 de Octubre
48. Hotel Imperial
49. Hotel Regina
50. Hotel Londres
51. Hotel Centenario
52. Buses San Luis & Transportes Oriental
53. Transportes Esmeraldas Buses
54. Residencial Centro
55. Hotel El Inca
56. Hotel Ecuatoriano
57. Residencial Medellin
58. Hotel Marco Polo
59. Hotel La Buena Esperanza
60. Cine Imperio
61. Flota Imbabura Buses
62. Transportes Occidental & Cine Presidente
63. Supertaxis Cuenca, Transportes
    Ecuador & Hotel Ecuador
64. Hotel Delicia
65. Hotel Colón
66. Co-op Libertad Buses
67. Co-op Posorja Buses
68. Transportes Villamil Buses
69. Cica Buses
70. Transportes Patria & CITA Buses
71. Transportes Zaracay
72. Hotel Astoria & Transportes
    Gran Colombia Buses
73. Transportes Andino Buses
74. FBI Buses
75. Cine Quito
76. Hotel Sanders
77. Hotel Alexander
78. Cine Tauro
79. Transportes Urdaneta Buses
80. Transportes Panamerica &
    Transportes Cotopaxi
81. Casa de Cultura (Cine &
    Archaeology Museum)
82. Cine Centenario
83. Transportes Santa Buses
84. Transportes Loja Buses
85. Reina del Camino Buses
86. Rutas Ecuatorianas Buses
87. Machiavello Tours
88. US Embassy & Banco Central
    Archaeology Museum
89. Hotel Oro Verde

to seven hours). *Supertaxis Cuenca* and *Buses San Luis* have the faster smaller buses.

For Riobamba and Ambato, take *CIFA* or *Transportes Andino*.

Buses to Quito (US$2.50, seven to nine hours) leave frequently with *Flota Imbabura* and *Panamericana*.

There are also buses to Esmeraldas, Portoviejo, Bahía de Caráquez and Babahoyo.

Boat The ferry service across the river to Durán is frequent, costs a few cents and makes a great sightseeing trip. The ferry dock is on Malecón at the foot of Avenida J Montalvo. Avoid the temptation to take a taxi there via the bridge as it will cost you at least US$6.

The *Pinzón* and *Piquero* for the Galápagos leave from Dock 4. For shipping information, ask the Capitanía on the Malecón at the foot of Avenida Ballen.

Getting Around

Airport The airport is on Avenida de las Américas about five km north of the centre. Buses leave from across the road outside the terminal. A taxi to the centre will cost about US$3.

Bus '2 Especial' takes about half an hour to get to the airport and runs along the Malecón.

Bus The local bus system is complicated and crowded and it's easier to walk.

HUAQUILLAS

This dusty town on the border with Peru is the one through which most travellers pass on their way south. It is not of interest itself but you may have to stay overnight.

There's a busy street market by the border and the place is full of Peruvians on shopping trips.

If you're leaving Ecuador, it's best to get rid of your sucres and arrive in Peru with dollars.

Places to Stay

There are a number of small pensiónes. None of them are remarkable in any respect and the one you stay at will depend to a large extent on which has a room vacant. The *Residencia Huaquillas* is one of the cheapest but most travellers stay at either the *Hotel Continental*, which is basic, clean but very noisy and costs US$0.85 each; or the *Hotel Guayaquil*, next to the Pensión Loja directly behind the Immigration office.

Adequate meals can be found at the *Pensión Loja* in a small square off the main drag. Also reasonable are the *Restaurant Mini* and the *Restaurant Chic*, both behind the Hotel Guayaquil. If you want to kill time in the evening, there are a number of small bars with jukeboxes down the last street on the left before the bridge (border).

Crossing the Border

Remember you must have an exit stamp before you can cross the border into Peru. Get this at the Immigration office on the main drag (open 8 am to 12 noon and 2 to 5 pm). If your entry stamp was marked 'T3' then there is no exit tax. Some travellers with their own vehicles have been asked for Suc 100 'fee' for having their carnet stamped. This is completely unofficial and you're not obliged to pay but if you choose not to, expect to have to hang around for a couple of hours until they get tired of the game.

Onward tickets and 'sufficient funds' are officially required for entry to Peru but unless you look totally derelict, it will rarely be enforced. The only thing customs are likely to do is cursorily search your baggage.

At one time currency dealers in Huaquillas used to offer excellent rates for those wanting Peruvian soles. This is no longer the case but things do change from time to time, especially with inflation being what it is in Peru, so ask travellers coming from Peru what the rate is and then decide for yourself. In any case, you're going to need *some* soles to get you as far as Tumbes.

On the Peruvian side (now called Aguas Verdes) you have to show your passport to the bridge guard but official formalities take place at the immigration building about three km from the border. About 300 metres from the bridge there are taxis and colectivos to take you there.

From the border there are both colectivos and buses to Tumbes.

IBARRA

The first major town after Tulcán at a height of 2225 metres, Ibarra is an old colonial place with some interesting buildings and a few pleasant plazas.

The Quito-San Lorenzo railway line runs through here if you're heading that way although there are no longer any trains between Quito and Ibarra.

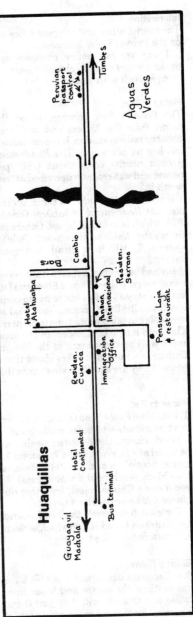

Information

The tourist office and the post office are on the Parque Pedro Moncayo.

There are no money changers and banks are unwilling to change money, so bring enough with you.

Places to Stay

The *Pensión San Lorenzo*, round the corner from the Astoria and one block from the railway station, is recommended but has no hot water. The *Residencias Astoria* nearby costs about US$1 per person and was recently described as 'not worth it.'

If you don't like either of these, try the pleasant *Residencial Imbabura*, Oviedo 3-33, which is in an old house. Otherwise there's the *Residencial Familial*, Calle 9, Carrera 7, which is clean and good value.

Instead of staying in Ibarra itself many travellers go to the village of **Esperanza** (10 km) and stay at *Aida's* house which costs less than US$1 per person. Good food is available but takes a long time to prepare. There are magic mushrooms in the area and a walk to the summit of the Volcan Cuilche is a must and takes about three hours. There are excellent views from the top.

Places to Eat

Try the *Café Pushkin* on Olmedo Cr 10 for good breakfasts and home-made bread.

Good, cheap, three-course meals can be found at *El Caribe*, Calle 7, Carrera 7; and at *Sergio's* near the Hotel Imbabura (one block south of the main plaza). If you'd like a Chinese meal, try either the *Nuevo China* or the *Rono Oriente*.

For good fish there's the *Marisquería Las Redes* on Oviedo Cl 26 which is clean and reasonably priced.

Getting There

Bus The main bus terminal is about 1½ km south of the centre and buses from Quito and Otavalo will drop you there. There are local buses to the centre for 5c.

From this terminal there are frequent departures for Quito, Tulcán (US$0.80, 2½ hours) and Otavalo.

Buses for the 15 minute ride to San Antonio De Ibarra leave frequently, or you could walk – it's only five km.

Train There is one departure daily to San Lorenzo and it's best to try and persuade the station officials that you want to buy a ticket the day before, otherwise you'll be battling with the hordes for a seat on the day of departure as the train is a converted school bus mounted on a railway chassis, so seats are limited.

AROUND IBARRA

San Antonio de Ibarra

While you are staying in Ibarra, pay a visit to the village of San Antonio de Ibarra which is almost a suburb of Ibarra itself. It's a woodcarving centre with a pleasant main square.

The most famous of the woodcarving shops is *Galería Luís Potosí*. Sr Potosí is famous throughout Ecuador and sells his work all over the world.

Places to Stay The only place is the *Hostería Los Nogales* where rooms are US$2.50 per person and meals are available in the bar.

La Esperanza

The village of La Esperanza, 10 km south of Ibarra, has become a popular place among travellers looking for a bit of peace and quiet. There's nothing to do except talk to the locals and take walks in the surrounding countryside.

To get there, take a bus from Sanchez y Cifuentes Cr 11 in Ibarra.

Places to Stay There's one very basic and friendly hotel – the *Casa Anita* – which also has simple, cheap meals.

LOJA

The most southerly major city in Ecuador, Loja is populated mainly by people of

European descent and mestizos. It's not of outstanding interest in itself, though the surrounding countryside is beautiful. Nearby is the town of Vilcabamba, made famous some years ago through an article, which appeared in a Sunday colour supplement, on the numerous centenarians who live in the area. The article put forward various theories on the reason for their longevity. Loja is a possible overnight stop if you're en route to Peru via the border crossing at Macará.

Information

The only place to change money is the Banco Central on the corner of Antonio Eguiguren and Sucre, but the rate is so low that it's better to change money in Macará.

The post office is in the municipal building on the north side of the main plaza.

The main market day is Sunday but Saturday and Monday are also busy days.

Places to Stay

The *Hotel Mexico*, José A Eguiguren 15-71, is perhaps the best value. It costs about US$1 per person for a large pleasant room with hot water in the showers.

The others are more expensive, though two places which are clean, friendly and secure are the *Residencia Santa Marianita*; and the *Hotel Miraflores*, which is somewhat over-priced at US$2.20 a single. If they're full, try the *Paris*. It too is clean and has hot showers.

There are plenty of other hotels near the market on 10 de Agosto but they tend to be noisy. The best of the bunch is the *Saraguro Internacional*. The *Hotel Americano* has also been recommended but has inadequate washing facilities.

Places to Eat

On the west side of the main plaza you have the choice of Chinese or Italian at the *Chifa Asia* and the *Pizzeria Geminis*. Around the corner, the *Cafeteria Glacier* is good for breakfast and snacks.

There's excellent food at the Chinese restaurant, *East China*, Jirón R Eguiguren 14-82, one block from the main plaza.

Getting There

There are many bus terminals, but the main one is the Transportes Loja Terminal on the corner of Avenida 10 de Agosto and Guerrero. Buses are often booked up so you should book early. There are four buses daily to Quito (US$4.50, 18 hours), four to Macará (US$1.80, seven hours), five to Guayaquil (US$3.20, 11 hours), four to Machala (US$2.10, eight hours) and one night bus to Huaquillas (US$2.90, 10 hours).

MACARÁ

Macará is a small and unimportant town on the Peruvian border. The faster and more convenient coastal route carries almost all the international traffic and the main advantage of the route through Macará is the scenic descent from Loja.

There are very few people who will change money – just ask around until you find someone.

Places to Stay & Eat

There are three cheap and basic hotels in the town centre. There's no hot water but with the climate there it's no real problem.

The *Hotel Internacional* is conveniently located over the Transportes Loja bus terminal so it is often both full and noisy. The *Hotel Amazonas* is on the same street but is a good deal quieter. The *Hotel Guayaquil* is above a shop and you should ask at the shop about rooms. All these places cost about US$1 per person.

There are a couple of basic restaurants opposite the bus terminal but they are only open at meal times. For snacks at other times try the *Fuente de Soda*, which isn't great but there's little else.

Getting There

There are daily buses to Loja, (US$1.80, seven hours, three per day); Machala, (US$2.60, 12 hours); Guayaquil, (US$4, 15 hours); Quito, (US$5.20, 22 hours); and Santo Domingo, (US$4.50, 18 hours).

These journeys are tiring and uncomfortable and it's best to break the journey at Loja.

Crossing the Peruvian Border

Macará is about an hours walk from the border at Río Macará. Pickups leave the market once or twice an hour for 15c.

The border is open from 8 am to 6 pm daily with irregular lunch hours. Formalities are fairly relaxed as long as your papers are in order. For those who need a visa for Peru, there is a consulate in Macará on Bolívar which is open from 9 am to 1 pm Monday to Friday.

At the border there is one fly-blown restaurant where you can get a cold drink.

MACHALA

Machala isn't a town you'd visit on purpose but it is on the main road between Guayaquil and the Peruvian border at Huaquillas. Also, for those who need a Peruvian visa, there is a consulate there.

Information

There's a tourist office on the second floor of the office on the corner of Avenida Bolívar and Guayas. The casa de cambio at Paez 17-23 takes cash and cheques.

The Peruvian Consulate is now at Av 3a Sur past Av Guayas (four streets east of the main plaza, then four streets south). It's open Monday to Friday from 8 am to 1 pm. Visas take a couple of hours to issue and are valid for multiple re-entry.

In the unlikely event that you are acquainted with Murwillumbah's (New South Wales, Australia) annual Banana Festival, you'll be pleased to know that Machala has a similar one in September.

Places to Stay & Eat

As Machala has a better selection of hotels than Huaquillas, you're probably better off staying there and heading for the border early the next day. As the border doesn't open until 8 am, a 6 am start will get you there in time.

The best cheap hotel is the *Residencial Pichincha* which charges US$1.20 per person. *Residencias La Internacional* is good value at US$2 per person.

The *Restaurant Chifa Central* has a wide variety of good food. There are several places on or within a block of the main square. For breakfast, the *Rizzo Hotel* has been recommended.

1	Hotel & Bus Ecuatoriana	14	Hotel Oro
2	Ciudad de Piñas Buses	15	Resdidencial Pichincha
3	Cifa Buses to Guayaquil	16	Cinema
4	Encalada Hotel	17	Residencial Machala
5	Rutas Orenses	18	Residencial La Internacional
6	Chifa Central Restaurant	19	IETEL
7	Residencial Mercy	20	Panamericana Buses
8	Hotel Perla Del Pacifico	21	Transportes Occidentales
9	Money Exchange	22	Residencial de Oro
10	Gran Hotel Machala	23	Dituris Office (2nd floor)
11	Residencial Paula	24	Cifa Buses to Huaquillas
12	Teatro Tauro	25	Rizzo Hotel
13	Residencial Almache	26	Peruvian Consul

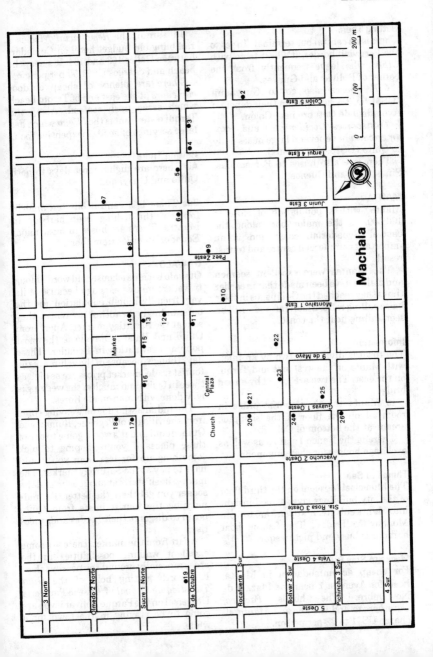

Machala

3 Norte
Olmedo 2 Norte
Sucre 1 Norte
9 de Octubre
Rocafuerte 1 Sur
Bolivar 2 Sur
Pichincha 3 Sur
4 Sur

Colón 5 Este
Tarqui 4 Este
Junín 3 Este
Páez 2 Este
Montalvo 1 Este
9 de Mayo
Guayas 1 Oeste
Ayacucho 2 Oeste
Sta. Rosa 3 Oeste
Vela 4 Oeste
5 Oeste

Market
Central Plaza
Church

200 m
100
0

Getting There

There is no central bus terminal. To get to the Peruvian border, it's best to go with *CIFA*, who leave frequently from the corner of Bolívar and Guayas.

CIFA buses also go to Guayaquil (US$1.50, 3½ hours) from their depot on Avenida 9 de Octubre near Colón.

Transportes Occidentales and *Panamericana* have several large buses daily to Quito (US$3.40, 12 hours).

There are also buses to Esmeraldas, Piñas, Loja and Cuenca.

MANTA

Manta, with a population of close to 100,000, is the major port along the central Ecuadorian coast and is an important commercial centre and tourist resort.

The Mantas were excellent seamen and claims have been made that in earlier times they reached the Galápagos in their balsa sailing rafts. Small rafts can still be seen sailing near the coast.

Information

The town is divided in two by an inlet, with Manta on the west side and Tarqui on the east. The two are joined by a road bridge.

In Manta there's a tourist office in room 1J on the floor of the shopping arcade at the bottom of Calle 8.

There is the Banco Pacifico as well as exchange houses for changing money.

Things to See

The **Municipal Museum** on the third floor of the city buildings gives a good insight into Manta culture. It's open 9 am to 3 pm Monday to Friday. The fishing boat harbour is busy and picturesque.

Places to Stay & Eat

For cheap accommodation in Manta, head for Avenida 1 near the Plaza 4 de Noviembre. The hotels *Pacifico, Chimborazo* and the *Pensión Manta* all charge US$1 to $2 per person.

In Tarqui, the *Residencial Niza* is a rambling old budget hotel on Comedors between Calles 103 and 104. It's near the beach and charges US$1.50 per person.

There are plenty of cheap outdoor *comedors* at the east end of Tarqui beach which serve fresh seafood. Along the Tarqui waterfront is the *Lligua* which has large servings of good, inexpensive food.

Getting There

Air There are flights most days to both Quito and Guayaquil.

Bus There is a central bus terminal in front of the fishing boat harbour in **Mantra**. There are buses to most major Ecuadorian cities from there.

OTAVALO

Otavalo became a household word among travellers many years ago because of its very friendly Indian population and the outstandingly beautiful weavings they sold at the Saturday market. Apart from Quito and Baños, Otavalo is the most popular destination in Ecuador. These days though, because of the volume of the tourist trade, market prices are as high as those in Quito and much of the weaving is now done with man-made fibres.

The Indians who do the weaving come from the villages of Peguche, Iluman and Quinchuqui and it's worth going to one of these places if you're hoping to pick something up for less than you would have to pay at the Saturday market. The market itself starts at about 5 am and the sooner you get there the better. By mid-morning the tourist buses from Quito begin to disgorge their hordes and prices rise.

Apart from the market, there are some excellent walking possibilities in the area, especially around the nearby lakes. It's worth getting hold of the *Guía Turistica de Otavalo* from the Papelería Universal on the Parque Bolívar if you are going to be staying in the town for a while.

Places to Stay

Accommodation is tight on Fridays because of the Sunday market, so try to arrive mid-week. The *Hotel Riviera*, off the main street, has been popular for a number of years. It's run by a Belgian woman (Ali Micui), costs US$1.70 per person and has a folklore evening on Fridays.

The *Pensión Vaca No 2*, on the corner of Bolívar and Morales, is a quiet, friendly place with good views of the volcanos from the balcony. It's good value at about US$1 a single. Similar in price and quality is the *San Lorenzo*, Calle Sucre 10-7. Both the Vaca and the San Lorenzo have dormitory style accommodation if you prefer it and want to save a little money.

Also good value is *Pension Otalvo*. It's friendly, clean and has hot water in the mornings. There are good views from the roof. It costs US$1.20 per person. You can change money there – cash or cheques – at rates slightly better than the bank.

Another place which is worth trying is the *Residencia Santa Ana*, Calle Colón. It has large, clean rooms, hot water, a pleasant courtyard and serves good, cheap breakfasts. A single costs US$1.25. Another traveller wrote in to say that the *Residencial La Herradura* had the nicest single rooms at US$1.25 per person.

Places to Eat

Good vegetarian food and cheeseburgers can be found at *Ali Micui*, Plaza de los Ponchos. It's also a popular meeting place for travellers. *Mama Rosita's* is also popular and offers good, cheap food, especially pancakes (though one traveller suggested you might need a strong constitution to handle these) and omelettes stuffed with avocado. The latter cost about US$0.40 and are good value.

The *Comedor Cristal*, 50 metres from the plaza, offers good set meals. There are two Chinese restaurants if you're looking for a change – *Chifa Tien An Men* (near Moreno and Bolívar) and the *Sopa China*.

Also highly recommended is the Korean restaurant, *Casa de Corea*, opposite the Hotel Riviera. Try their Filippino chicken. Others have recommended the *El Sandwich Viajero*, Sucre 10-02. The people there are very friendly and speak English. They have a house just out of town which can be rented on very favourable weekly or monthly terms.

For a splurge try the *Restaurant Parenthasis*, a French restaurant which has been highly rated – 'camembert, cordon blue, Chilean wines and good service'.

Getting There

Bus The main bus terminal is at the Plaza Copacabana. A 50c taxi ride will take you to most hotels. Buses to Quito arrive and depart from there.

A couple of blocks away on Avenida Calderón, is *Transportes Otavalo* which has frequent buses to Ibarra.

Train The trains only run to Ibarra and there are daily departures at 8 am, 1 and 5 pm and the fare is about 10c. It's a slow and uncomfortable trip and is used by the poorest people. For this reason, it could be very interesting.

AROUND OTAVALO

Most of the Indians live and work in the nearby villages of **Peguche, Quinchuquí** and **Ilumán**, which are loosely strung together on the north-east side of the Pan American Highway a few km from Otavalo.

In **Agato**, on the east side of Lago San Pablo, you can visit the *Cooperativa Tahuantisuyo* where they make traditional but expensive weavings on back-strap looms.

Cotacachi, a small village 15 km from Otavalo, is famous for it's leatherwork. You can find almost anything in the way of leather goods in the shops strung out along the main street. Market day is

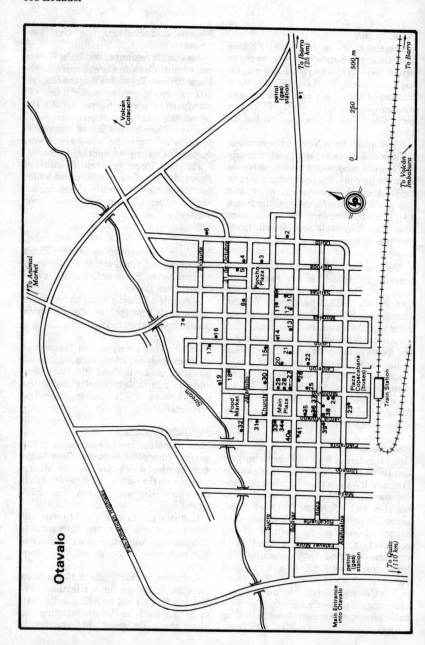

Otavalo

Saturday. There is one hotel which charges US$15 a double, and the building is over two centuries old. There are buses every hour from Otavalo.

Quito

At 2850 metres above sea level, Quito is the world's second highest capital city and a gem of colonial architecture. Its location at the foot of the volcano, Pichincha (4776 metres), is equally superb. The old part of the city, which dates from the early 16th century, consists of steep, narrow and often cobbled streets lined with low adobe houses with whitewashed walls and red-tiled roofs. There are numerous old and often huge monasteries and churches with amazing stone-carved facades and glittering interiors. The streets are lively and colourful and it's a delight to explore this part of the city on foot. Many Indians dressed in traditional costume flock into the city from neighbouring towns and villages to sell their weaving, clothes and agricultural products, and impromptu street markets and stalls are a common sight.

The new part of town with its wide boulevards, modern buildings, tourist hotels, offices and shops sprawls out along the plain to the west of the old city, and is where most of the embassies, banks and travel agencies are located.

Information

The tourist office is at Reina Victoria 514 at the junction with Roca (tel 239044). It has plenty of information and maps and can supply details of how to get to the Galápagos Islands. There are branch offices at the Palacio Municipal, Plaza Independencia, in the old town and at the

1   Hotel Yamor Continental
2   Fire Station
3   Peña de los Chaskis
4   Ali Micui Restaurant
5   Residencial Centenario
6   Bahai Institute
7   Parenthese Restaurant
8   Residencia Samar-Huasy
9   Public toilet
10 Hat shop
11 Residencial El Indio
12 Pensión Vaca 2
13 Residencial La Herradura
14 Pollo Koko Rico Chicken Restaurant
15 El Mesón de Arragon Re
16 Residencias Santa Ana
17 Residencial Colón
18 Local villages bus departures
19 Cockfight Stadium
20 Restaurant Centro Latino (chicken)
21 Cine Bolívar
22 Transportes Otavalo

23 Bar Huasipungo
24 Pensión Residencial Los Andes
25 Residencia Otavalo
26 Camba Huasy Chicken Restaurant
27 Stationary & Restaurant Copacabana
28 Banco Del Pichincha
29 Royal Restaurant Cafeteria & Camba Huasy Fuente de Soda (ice-cream)
30 Mama Rosita Restaurant
31 Café El Triunfo
32 Police Station
33 Drug Store
34 IETEL & Post Office
35 Chifa Tien An Men
36 Casa de Korea Restaurant
37 Hotel Otavalo & Golden Eagle Restaurant
38 Riviera-Sucre Hotel
39 Apollo Theatre
40 Chifa Restaurant Pekin
41 Industria Papelera Stationer

international airport, but many travellers have described the latter as useless.

It is best to change money at a casa de cambio rather than a bank. *Rodrigo Paz* is a popular change house at Venezuela 659 and on Av Amazonas, but it doesn't always give the best rates so shop around. If you're thinking of buying any Peruvian soles in Quito be sure to check with travellers who have recently come from there before you do it as rates in Ecuador are often poor.

Almost all the travel agents and airline offices are in the streets between Parque El Ejido and Av Colón, especially along Av Amazonas.

The Immigration office, where you get tourist card extensions, is at Avenida Amazonas 3149 (or 2639 – the two different numbers appear within a few metres of each other but it's the same place!) between Av Marina de Jesús and Av de la República, off Parque El Hippodrome. It's open from 8.30 am to 12 noon and 2.30 to 6 pm. Take bus No 15 from Av Pichincha. Getting an extension can soak up time so take something to read while you wait.

Good maps, suitable for hiking, can be bought at the Instituto Geográfico Militar at the top of the hill behind the Casa de la Cultura.

There are several post offices but the best one for receiving and sending mail is the central office on Calle Benalcázar behind the Plaza Independencia.

The *TAME* ticket office nearest the old town is at Avenida 10 de Agosto 239.

The American Express Agents in Quito are Ecuadorian Tours, Av Amazonas 339. Their mailing address is c/o Amex, Aptdo 2605, Quito.

The Peruvian Embassy, Edificio del España (on the corner of Av Colón and Av Amazonas), is open from 9 am to noon for visas. You will be asked for an onward ticket or an MCO for at least US$150 despite the fact that this is no longer necessary for entry to Peru. If this is going to present difficulties then try to get your visa elsewhere. Visas take one day to issue.

The bookshop, Libri Mundi, J L Mera 851 at the junction with Veintimilla (Mera is between Amazonas and Reina Victoria), is probably the best in Quito. It stocks books in English, French, German, Italian and Spanish. Open seven days a week.

Language Schools

There are three places in Quito to learn Spanish and there are classes at various levels. The Quito Spanish School (tel 515845) is at Avenida Colombia 1140 and Yaguachi. The postal address is PO Box 39-C, Quito. They offer four and six-week courses and provide accommodation with local families. All inclusive costs for a four week course is US$340, or for six weeks is US$480.

If you prefer group classes and will provide your own accommodation, try the Catholic University at Avenida 12 de Octubre and Robles. They have six-week courses for about US$50 and they will provide you with a student card.

We've had two enthusiastic recommendations for the *Quito Escuela de Idioma*, Marchena 130 with 10 de Agosto (Casilla 39-C), run by Sr Edgar J Alvarez. It offers one-to-one, seven-hour daily sessions with trained instructors. Ideally you need four to six weeks to get to reasonable fluency. The courses cover speaking, reading and writing as well as cultural and other topics. It's self-paced and involves visits to museums, hikes and other innovations. You have the choice of living-in with a local family or just attending classes. The cost with live-in is US$338 (four weeks) or US$478 (six weeks) which includes meals. If you just want to attend classes without living-in, it costs US$52 per week. Very good value especially if you live with a family.

Things to See

Of the many churches in Quito, don't miss **La Compañía**, Calle G Moreno, a

Jesuit church built in the 17th century which has the most ornately sculptured facade and interior of any church in the city. It also has a stunning main altar of gold as well as many gilded side altars. Most of the work done on this church was executed by Indian craftsmen. It's open daily from 10 to 11 am and 1 to 6 pm.

The church and monastery of **San Francisco**, in a large cobbled square off Calle Cuenca, is also worth visiting for its beautiful carved ceiling, enormous gold altar and very fine woodcarvings in the choir. It's one of the oldest churches in South America and is Quito's largest.

Santo Domingo Church, on Plaza Santo Domingo, also merits a visit for its fine interior craftsmanship, especially the wood carvings.

Two of the best museums in the city are housed in the Banco Central de Ecuador, Av 10 de Agosto. They are the **Archaeological Museum** on the 5th floor which has pre-Colombian artefacts and a gold display; and the **Museo Colonial y de Arte Religioso** on the 6th floor. Both are open Tuesday to Friday from 9.30 am to 8 pm and on Saturday and Sunday from 10 am to 5 pm. Entry is free on Sundays and on weekdays between 6 and 8 pm. At other times it costs US$0.20 (or $0.10 with a student card).

Two other museums worth visiting are the **Museum of Colonial Art** (possibly closed for restoration) at the junction of Calle Cuenca and Calle Mejía; and the **Museo de San Francisco** attached to the church and monastery of San Francisco, which is open Monday to Saturday from 9 to 11.30 am and 3 to 5.30 pm. It has displays of paintings, sculpture and woodwork – there are some beautiful old bureaux made from different types of wood and inlaid with mother-of-pearl. Entry costs US$0.20. The **Casa de la Cultura Ecuatoriana** on the west side of the Parque de Mayo is worth a visit for its unique collection of musical instruments and other exhibits.

One of Sucre's former residences – now a museum known as the **Museo Histórico Casa de Sucre** – is at the junction of Venezuela and Sucre and is worth visiting just for the house itself – a beautiful old colonial villa. It's open from 9 am to 12 noon and 3 to 6 pm.

Some of the most well-preserved colonial houses are to be found along Calle Ronda (also called Morales), which is a continuation of 24 de Mayo, going downhill. It's one of the most photographed streets in Ecuador.

Superb views over Quito can be had from the top of Cerro Panecillo, the hill to the west of the old town, which is topped by the huge statue of the Virgin of Quito. To get to the top you can either walk up the steep flights of steps which start just past the Hotel Gran Casino on Calle G Moreno or take a bus from Av 24 de Mayo.

For somewhere shady to relax during the day, try either the **Parque El Ejido** or the **Alameda**. On weekends they're both thronged with Ecuadorian families who go there to picnic and play games.

Places to Stay

For years the most popular place has been the *Hotel Gran Casino*, Calle G Moreno 330. It's so popular that it's been nicknamed the 'Gran Gringo.' Recent reports suggest that it's getting somewhat run down but that doesn't seem to affect its popularity. You either love it or hate it. It's a huge place with fairly clean showers and toilets, hot water, a sauna (about US$0.90), sometimes a TV, a moderately useful noticeboard and its own restaurant (which is still very good and cheap). Rooms cost US$1/$1.55 a single/double without own bath and US$3 a double with own bath. There are also triple rooms. The restaurant won't serve non-residents if they're busy or if they don't feel like it. If you're planning on going to the Galapagos Islands then it's worth staying there – at least for a few days – because there are always a lot of people there who have the same idea and they'll probably have done a lot of leg-work to find out the cheapest way to do it. Talking to them can save you a lot of time and money.

Another place where many travellers stay is the *Hotel Astoria*, Calle Loja 630. It's cheaper than the Gran Casino at US$0.90 per person, but tends to be a bit dark depending on which room you're given, and it only has cold showers.

Three other places which are recommended and not overflowing with gringos are: *Hotel Monasterio*, Calle 24 de Mayo, which costs US$1 per person and has hot water but is 'dingy and dirty'; *Hotel Viena*, Calle Flores 421 near the corner with Chile, which has spacious and clean rooms with hot showers and costs US$1.25 per person or US$1.70 a double, though the beds have seen better days; and the *Hotel Sucre*, Plaza San Francisco, where you can get a huge double room with balcony for less than US$2, though the rooms on the roof are not so good.

Three others you could try are the *Hotel Venecia*, Moreno and Rocafuerte, at US$2 a single; the *Hotel Ecuador*, Flores near the Viena, which costs US$1.70 but is a bit grubby; and the *Hotel Quitumbe* which costs US$3.40 a double and has hot water. The *Hostal Minerva*, Calle Loja, has also been recommended at US$1.25 a (large) single, but make sure you use your own lock on the door.

Somewhat up-market is the *Hotel San Agustín*, Flores near the Hotel Ecuador, which costs US$5 a double.

One correspondent suggested the *Casa Familiar* run by Monica Bendorf, a Danish nurse, which he said was very good but he didn't let us know the address. She has 12 beds only and a common room and cooking facilities. It costs about twice the price of the usual budget hotels.

If you don't like any of these or they happen to be full, there are plenty of other hotels scattered around the old town ranging from cheap to expensive, and some of the cheaper ones are indicated on the street map.

The other main hotel area – mostly fairly expensive – is in the streets east of Parque El Ejido where the majority of the airline offices, travel agents and many restaurants are situated. It's a popular tourist area but you shouldn't expect to find anything cheap. If you want to stay there, first ask other travellers you meet if they have any suggestions. One of the cheaper places is the *Residencia Bethania*, on the corner of Presidente Wilson and Juan León Mera which costs US$4 per night. It's clean and has hot water and its own restaurant.

Places to Eat

If you're staying at the *Hotel Gran Casino* it's certainly worth eating there at least some of the time as far as quality and prices go. If you want up-to-the-minute information on almost anywhere on the continent, then this is the place to visit.

A good vegetarian restaurant in this area is the *Govinda*, Esmeraldas 853 near the junction with Venezuela, run by the Centro Cultural Hindu de Ecuador. You can eat very well for just US$1 though the choice is limited. It's open from 9 am to 8 pm daily. They also have a health food shop and run meditation and yoga courses.

The *Mariana de Jesús y Hungría* close to Av Amazonas, run by a friendly Colombian, has been recommended. It's very clean and the service is excellent.

Over in the new part of town, a very popular meeting place for travellers and other tourists is the *Fuente* on Av Amazonas at the junction with Jorge Washington and close to Rodrigo Paz casa de cambio. It sells fairly cheap snacks like hamburgers and full meals for about twice what you would pay in the old town.

Two other good places in this area are *La Delicia*, Av 6 de Deciembre 1325, which has a good, three-course lunch for about US$0.40; and *La Llama* on the Alameda near the junction with 7 de Septiembre, a grilled-chicken house and one of the best in Quito. A quarter of a chicken with salad and potatoes will cost you around US$0.50. It also offers steaks and sausages.

Two other places in the new part of town which have been recommended are the *Restaurant Amis*, Roca 549; and the *Chifa Fenix*, Jeronimo Carrion 761, both of which are cheap and good (eat for about US$1). For a splurge, try the *Hotel Colón* where they have an all-you-can-eat buffet-banquet for US$3 per head between 11 am and 3 pm on Sundays.

For some local music in the evenings, try the *Taberna Quiteña*, in the old town at the corner of Calle Manabí and Luis Vargas, and in the new town at Avenida Amazonas 1259 and Colón, which has free music on weekends. They serve typical Ecuadorian food which is expensive but you don't need to order much.

Getting There

Air There are flights to the Galápagos daily except Sundays. You usually have to change planes in Guayaquil but your luggage is transferred. The return flight is US$350 for non-residents.

Bus There are literally hundreds of buses per day going to places throughout the country. Some of the major destinations are:

	cost	hours
Ambato	US$1	3
Bahía de Caráquez	US$3.50	8
Baños	US$1.30	3½
Coca	US$3	13
Cuenca	US$4	9 to 14
Guaranda	US$1.50	5
Guayaquil	US$1.50	5
Lago Agrio	US$2.60	8
Latacunga	US$0.80	2
Loja	US$4.50	18
Machala	US$3.40	11
Manta	US$3.50	8
Portoviejo	US$3.50	8
Puyo	US$1.80	8
Riobamba	US$1.40	4
Santo Domingo	US$1	2½
Tena	US$2.60	9

Train There is a daily *autoferro* to Riobamba (US$0.70, five hours) at 2 pm which goes via Latacunga (US$0.30, two hours) and Ambato (US$0.50, 3½ hours). The train is crowded and you should buy tickets in advance on the day of departure, but the ticket office often doesn't open until an hour before departure so there is a mad scramble.

Getting Around

All long-distance buses going south, west and east of Quito depart from the bus terminal, Terrestre del Sur, about 5½ km from the centre of the city. To get there, take bus No 10 from the Plaza Santo Domingo. Bus departure times are printed on page two of the daily newspaper, *El Comercio*.

Northbound buses leave from several terminals grouped in three or four blocks on the streets to the north-west of the Parque El Ejido. Buses to Otavalo (US$0.75, 2½ hours), Ibarra (US$0.90, three hours) and Tulcán (US$1.50, 5½ hours) leave from Calles 18 de Septiembre and Manuel Larrea.

To the airport take a blue double-decker London bus which begins from the Casa de Cultura and runs along Avenida Amazonas. Other buses to the airport are Nos 1 or 16, or the Iñaquito, Aeropuerto or Panecillo buses – the latter all have 'aeropuerto' on the windscreen. There are also minibuses for US$2 and taxis for US$6. If you're coming from the airport, taxi drivers will tell you that you won't be allowed on the buses with a pack – this isn't true.

Other useful buses include No 3 (El Panecillo-Plaza 24 de Mayo-Calle G Moreno-Av Pichincha-Av Amazonas); and Nos 1 and 2 (Plaza Sto Domingo-Av 10 de Agosto).

The railway station is at Avenida P Vicente Maldonado near Llangunates, about two km south of the old town. Most buses going to the bus terminal go there as well.

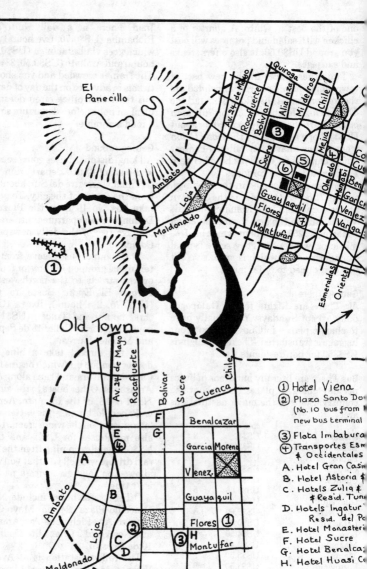

① Hotel Viena
② Plaza Santo Do
   (No. 10 bus from
   new bus terminal
③ Flota Imbabura
✝ Transportes Esm
   & Occidentales
A. Hotel Gran Casi
B. Hotel Astoria &
C. Hotels Zulia &
   & Resid. Tun
D. Hotels Ingatur
   Resid. del Po
E. Hotel Monasteri
F. Hotel Sucre
G. Hotel Benalca;
H. Hotel Huasi Ce

Quito

Key:-
1. Railway Station
2. Supertaxis del Sur (minibuses)
3. San Francisco church & monastery
4. Museo de Arte Colonial
5. Post Office
6. Cathedral, Govt. Palace, La Compañía church & main plaza
7. San Agustín church
8. The Alameda
9. El Ejido park
10. American Express & airline offices
11. Tourist Office
12. Peruvian Embassy
13. Flota Imbabura Transportes Andina Buses to Otavalo, Ibarra and Tulcán

New Town

0   600 m

AROUND QUITO
Mitad del Mundo

The most famous excursion is to the equator at Mitad del Mundo about 22 km north of Quito. There is a large stone monument and a museum (which may be closed for restoration). En route to the equator, the road passes an intriguing highway art gallery where famous Latin American artists have painted roadside billboards with weatherproof paints. The works, some two dozen of them, are stretched out along the highway.

Getting There To get there take a Mitad del Mundo bus, which leaves about every half hour from the corner of Calle Cuenca and Chile, and goes north out of town along Avenida América. The journey takes about an hour and costs 15c.

Sangolquí

The Indian market closest to the capital is the Sangolquí Sunday market. Frequent local buses go there from the Plaza Marin on the corner of Calle Chile and M de Solanda.

RIOBAMBA

A few years ago Riobamba was famous for its enormous Saturday market which rivalled those at Oaxaca in Mexico and Huancayo in Peru. It filled nine separate plazas and connecting streets and attracted up to 10,000 Indians from the surrounding countryside. It was an unforgettable experience, and was one of *the* places in Ecuador to go if you were looking for native handicrafts and weaving. Unfortunately, it's been moved into a new building and has lost much of the colourful atmosphere which made it famous. The move has also considerably reduced its size and there are far fewer crafts for sale and many more plastic consumer articles. Recent reports suggest that it's hardly worth going to anymore.

Riobamba is in the centre of an extensive and scenic road network so you should try and plan your arrival and departure for daylight hours.

Information

The tourist office is at 5 de Junio 2306 at the junction with Primera Constituente. The staff are friendly but not particularly efficient.

The Banco Internacional is the only place to change money. It's on the corner of L Borges and G Moreno.

The post office is on the third floor of an office building on Primera Constituente, almost opposite the Teatro T Leon.

Things to See & Do

The **Museo de Arte Religioso** in the old church of La Concepción is famous and worth visiting. The building has been beautifully restored and there's a variety of paintings, sculptures and religious artefacts. The huge, gem-encrusted gold monstrance is said to be priceless. It's on Argentinos at the corner of Larrea and is open Tuesday to Saturday from 9 am to 12.30 pm and 3 to 6.30 pm, Sundays and holidays during the morning only, and Monday it's closed.

If you're interested in mountaineering, Sr Enrique Veloz (tel 960196) is the president of the Asociación de Andinismo de Chimborazo and is an experienced mountaineer. He can guide you himself or arrange a guide. For a close look at Chimborazo, you can hire a pick-up from near the railway station. This will take you as far as the parking lot below the climbers' hut and should cost about US$10 to $15 depending on the vehicle and your bargaining skill.

Places to Stay

Many of the cheapies are around the railway station and so tend to be noisy. One which is relatively quiet is the *Hotel Atahualpa*. It costs US$1 a single and has hot water. Three doors away is the *Hotel Colonial* which is similarly priced – ask for a room at the back as the front ones are very noisy.

The *Residencial Camba Huasi*, 10 de Agosto opposite the railway station, is also good value at US$2 a double. Whatever you do, *don't* stay at the *Residencial Chimborazo*, Guayaquil 30-17 opposite the station. One traveller who, judging from his letter never expected more than basic amenities in budget hotels, had this to say about the place: 'It was dirty, dingy, the toilets were blocked and I'm amazed my stuff didn't get nicked. Wouldn't recommend it to my worst enemy. And the bed was crawling!'

For something a bit up-market, the old-fashioned *Hotel Metro* on L Borges near the railway station has friendly staff and good clean rooms for US$3.50 per person.

Places to Eat

The four-course lunch for US$0.70 at the *Restaurant Kikirimian* on G Moreno near Primera Constituente is recommended.

The *Hotel Metro* near the station offers good, cheap food and is worth a try – you can eat there for US$1 to $2. *La Biblia*, on the corner of Primera Constituente and Miguel León, and the Chinese restaurant, *Chifa Internacional*, 10 de Agosto near the main plaza, are also recommended. The latter also has very cheap good breakfasts.

Another place to try for breakfast is the *Restaurant Cafeteria El Pailón* on Pichincha near L Borges.

Getting There

Bus The main bus terminal is about two km north-west of the town centre, but not all buses leave from it. There are frequent buses to Quito (US$1.40, four hours) and Guayaquil (US$1.75, five hours). At 7 and 9 pm there are buses for Machala (US$2.75, 10 hours) and Huaquillas (US$3.25, 12 hours) if you're heading for Peru. *Patria* have three buses daily at 5.30 am, 7.30 am and 7.30 pm for Cuenca (US$2.50, nine to 12 hours).

Three blocks south of the main terminal is a smaller terminal with frequent local buses to Cajabamba and Balbanera.

Buses to the Oriente leave from the bus terminal at the corner of Avenidas Espejo and Luz Elisa Borja, four km away. A taxi between the two terminals costs about US$0.50.

Train With the closure of the line to Guayaquil and Cuenca following the El Niño floods of 1982, there is only one daily *autoferro* to Quito which leaves at 5 am, costs US$0.70 and takes five hours.

SAN LORENZO

Quite a few travellers come to this Pacific port close to the border with Colombia in order to travel down the coast to Limones and Esmeraldas. It's an interesting place to spend a bit of time.

The population is almost entirely of African descent and there's a relaxed

Caribbean atmosphere especially down the main street in the evening. The town is built around a series of tidal creeks with most of the houses on stilts. Also the journey there on the *autoferro* from Ibarra is the last of the spectacular railway journeys still operating in Ecuador.

Information

There is no proper money changing facilities, but if you ask around, you'll find people who'll change small amounts of Colombian currency or US dollars.

If you arrive in San Lorenzo by boat from Colombia, there is no immigration office, so ask at the police station or tourist office about getting your passport stamped – you may have to go to Quito.

Bring insect repellent with you to San Lorenzo – the mosquitos are voracious!

Places to Stay & Eat

There are several cheap places to stay – none of them remarkable. Try the *Residencial Ibarra*, two or three blocks from the boat pier above the restaurant of the same name, which is clean and friendly and costs US$1.25 a single. Mosquito nets are provided. The cinema next door can be noisy.

Apart from the *Ibarra*, you can eat seafood at *La Red* or in the market.

Getting There

Boat The boat/bus trip to Esmeraldas runs on a fixed schedule: 6.30 am, 8.30 am, 10.30 am and 12.30 pm but only the 6.30 and 8 am boats connect with the buses at La Tola which go to Esmeraldas. All the boats go via Limones and the through fare to Esmeraldas is US$3. San Lorenzo to La Tola takes about 2½ hours and the bus trip from La Tola to Esmeraldas takes about 4½ hours. A new road is being built between Montalvo and Esmeraldas so the trip should be quicker in future. The first part of the journey by boat to Limones or La Tola is highly recommended and goes through

mangrove swamps teeming with wild life – especially pelicans. Accommodation in Limones and La Tola is worse than in San Lorenzo, so many travellers make the straight through trip to Esmeraldas.

There are boats most days to Tumaco (Colombia) but make sure you have all the necessary visas. The journey is done in motorised dugouts, takes most of the day and costs about US$7. It can be both very wet and very sunny, so be prepared.

TULCÁN

Almost everyone passes through this border town on their way to or from Colombia. There's only one thing to see there if you have some time to spare, and that's the cemetery – the place is famous for its topiary.

Information

Change only enough money to get to Quito, as the rates are very poor compared with those in the capital. Money changers in the bus terminal offer better rates than those at the border. The only place which will change travellers' cheques is Rodrigo Paz casa de cambio in the town centre (Bolívar 1548).

The Colombian Consulate is on the 2nd floor of the IESS Building, Plaza de la Independencia. It's not obvious, so you may need to ask. It's open until 4 pm (but closed from 12.30 to 2.30 pm) and is much less hassle than the embassy in Quito. It seems however, to be demanding US$20 from some people for what should be the free Tourist Card, as well as an onward ticket (they will accept tickets ex-Quito, ex-Caracas and even ex-Lima) though one New Zealander went through recently without having to grease the consul's palm with so much as a penny.

Places to Stay

Since it's unlikely you'll be doing anything except staying overnight, the most convenient place to stay is one of the cheap pensiónes opposite the bus terminal. They're about two km from the centre of town on the main road going south. One of the best in this area is the *Residencias Avenida*. It's clean and friendly and has hot water. A single costs US$1. Also opposite the bus terminal is the *Residencial Ecuador* which costs US$1.25 but has small rooms and is dark. Close by is the *Residencial Española* (no sign, ask at the Kathy Restaurant below) which has nice rooms but poor washing facilities and cold water only.

As is usual in highland towns, there are public hot showers (Baños Calientes Santa Terisita) if you can't face a cold one.

At the border there's only one place to stay and it's expensive – singles/doubles for US$10/$14.

Places to Eat

Many travellers recommend the restaurant in the bus station, but there's also the *Pollo a la Brasa* about four doors away from the Avenida, which serves excellent barbecued chicken and cold beers. For more authentic Ecuadorian food, the *Restaurant Danubio* is clean, quiet and pleasant but has a limited menu.

Out by the border there are plenty of stalls selling snacks.

Getting There

Bus The main bus terminal is inconveniently located 3½ km uphill from the town centre. Local buses run along Avenida Bolívar and go to the terminal.

There are frequent departures to Quito (US$1.50, five hours) and Ibarra (US$0.90, three hours). There are also departures for Santo Domingo and Guayaquil.

Buses for Tufino and Maldonado by *Co-operativa Transportes Norte* leave from the corner of Junín and Arellano.

Crossing the border

Fourteen-seater minibuses for the border leave Tulcán throughout the day from Parque Isidro Ayora and cost about US0.20. Return buses from the border will cost the same, but for a little extra you should be able to persuade the driver to take you the extra 3½ km to the Tulcán bus terminal if you are in a hurry to head south.

The border is open daily from 8 am to 12 noon and 1 to 5.45 pm. If you're leaving Ecuador from here, you have to get an exit stamp and return your tourist card. If you've overstayed you're visa by a few days, a (genuine) fine of about $10 is payable; if it's several months, expect a hefty fine or a trip back to Quito.

THE ORIENTE

Ecuador's riverine eastern lowlands have become very popular in the past few years. The area is one of lush jungle, scattered Indian communities, oil-drilling rigs and rough pioneer towns. Most of the towns are dirty and unattractive and certainly aren't for those of a sensitive disposition, but the area is outstandingly beautiful and the Indian villages are well worth making the effort to go and see.

Many travellers follow the Quito-Baños-Puyo-Tena-Misahuallí-Coca-Lago Agrio-Baeza-Quito circuit, or at least part of it. Using a combination of bus, colectivo and boat, the route can be covered in one week but going at this pace wouldn't allow you to get far off the beaten track. It's best to plan on about two weeks. All the places mentioned are connected to the highlands by road and have regular bus services, but they aren't all connected to each other, so where there is no road, riverboats have to be taken.

Getting There

There are two main bus services which will get you down into the lowlands:
(1) **Quito-Baeza** Buses at 8.30 am, 12.30, 3.30 and 6.30 pm by *Cooperativa Centinela del Norte* (Calle José Lopez No 2, Quito). The trip takes three hours and offers spectacular views. The fare is US$1.20.

There is only one hotel at Baeza, the *Hotel Samay*, which costs US$1.30, is clean and basic with a pleasant balcony but has no hot water. In the unlikely event that it's full, you can go four km to the village of Borja, where there is a simple pension.

If you want something to do while you're there, visit the 145-metre-high **San Rafael Falls**. To get there either hitch or take a bus along the road to Lago Agrio and get off when you see the INECEL sign (about 2½ hours). From there, follow the steep path down to the bridge (about 45 minutes) and don't worry about the prohibited entry sign – the people working down there are very friendly. The falls are another 15 minutes walk from the bridge. There is a basic lodge in the nearby village of El Reventadora (15 km) where you can stay the night if you wish.

From Baeza there are buses to Lago Agrio and to Tena. To Lago Agrio it takes about five hours and costs US$1.70. To Tena it takes about two hours and costs US$1.

In Tena stay at the *Residencia Enmita* opposite the bus terminal. It's pricey at US$2.10 but for that you get a good clean room with toilet and shower. There is a clean restaurant downstairs. Avoid the *Residencia Roma* if possible as it's dirty, noisy and smelly though it only costs about US$1.

From Lago Agrio the road runs south to Coca (Puerto Francisco de Orellana). There are several daily buses along this stretch, the first at 6 am. Get there half an hour before they're due to leave as they often depart early. They cost about US$1 and take 2½ to three hours. Between Coca and Quito there are three buses daily with two companies; one of them is the *Cooperativa Baños* which terminates at the Terrestre de Sur in Quito. The first bus from Coca leaves at 7 am, the last at 3 pm, and the fare is US$1.40. The journey involves crossing several rivers by ferry – these ferries don't operate in the rainy season and at these times you have to take a canoe, which some travellers have described as 'a wet, soggy, unpleasant experience.' The buses take about 12

hours. *Transportes Occidental* are also now running three buses daily in either direction between Quito and Lago Agrio.

If for any reason you can't get a bus out of Coca, there are five flights per week to Quito by *TAME* but they are often booked out days ahead. From Coca to Misahuallí you must take a boat (described later). At the moment, you can forget about going to Nuevo Rocafuerte on the Ecuador/Peru border because of political tensions. To do the trip you need written permission from the military authorities in Coca (Batallón de la Selva 57, Montecristi, which is over the bridge on the left), but this is almost always refused.

There are several hotels in Lago Agrio – it's an oil workers' dormitory town. They're all pretty shoddy, and the best of the bunch is perhaps the *Hotel Oro Negro*, which charges US1.50; and the *Residencia Hilton*. The *Residencial Putumayo* has fans and mosquito nets and charges US$2 per night. The best value meals are at the restaurant in the *Hotel Utopia* where a hearty set-meal costs US$1. The *Hostal El Cofan* restaurant is the best in town and not too expensive.

From Lago Agrio, a trip to the village of San Pablo de Kantesiya on the Río Aguarico is recommended. The village has about 30 houses, all built on stilts. The Secoya Indians who live there will rent you one of these houses for about US$0.40. Wood for fires is provided but you need to bring food, something to sleep on, cooking utensils and matches. The villagers are very friendly and there are plenty of jungle paths to explore. To get to San Pablo take a bus or hitch to Chiritza where the road ends (US$0.35, about two hours). From there take a boat to San Pablo, which costs US$4.25 per person on the way out, but as much as US$8.50 on the return trip because the boatmen know you can't get back otherwise. The boat trip takes about two hours. Boats going to San Pablo are easy to find – there is at least one a day – but boats in the opposite direction are more difficult to get, especially in heavy rain, so be prepared for two or three days wait.

In Coca, stay at the *Pensión Rosita* near the bridge which costs US$1.20 per person and is one of the few hotels in town with running water; or at the *Hotel Auca* which costs US$4 for a room with a fan – and you need one! Another place which has been recommended is the *Hotel Oasis* which is cheaper. The *Hotel Auca* has a decent restaurant, and the next best is the *Restaurant El Rey*, which is in a rather sleazy but quite safe area.

One traveller suggested that it's possible to make much cheaper trips into the jungle from Coca than it is from Misahuallí. Two good guides he suggested to contact there are San Miguel and Edward – ask for them at the navy office at the harbour (this is where you have to check in if you arrive from Misahuallí by boat). The only drawback about going on a jungle trip from Coca is that there are not many travellers there so it's hard to get a group together.

From Coca you can take a boat one hour down the River Napo to *Hacienda Primavera* where you can camp or rent a room for US$2 per person. There's also a restaurant at the hacienda which serves good, fairly cheap food. The area around the ranch is very pleasant and interesting jungle hikes are possible from there.

(2) **Baños-Puyo-Napo** There are frequent buses along this route which cost US$1 and take about three hours. From Napo to Misahuallí you must take a colectivo. The alternative route to Misahuallí is by bus from Baños to Tena, and from there by colectivo, about six hours in total.

If you stay in Puyo, there's a good choice of hotels. Two which have been recommended are the *Hotel Granada* and *Pensión Victoria*, both near the bus terminal, which cost US$1.20 a single. The Granada is run by friendly people and has a restaurant which serves good

food. More expensive, but recommended are the hotels *California* and *Europa*, next door to one another on 9 de Octubre between Marin and Atahualpa. They both charge US$2.50 per person with shared facilities, or US$3 in rooms with own bath. For somewhere to eat in Puyo, try the *Rincón Ambateño* on Atahualpa, or for breakfast there's the *Mistral*, also on Atahualpa.

One of the best hotels in Misahuallí is the *Hotel Balcón Napo*, on the main plaza, which costs US$1.30 per person. Also on the main plaza but slightly cheaper is the *Pension Posada*. Another place you could try is the *Hotel El Paisano* which has a few spacious rooms at US$1 each and good vegetarian food. A little distance from the town on the beach between the two rivers is the *Pension Sasha*. It has bamboo-lined rooms and clean sheets and costs US$1. Finally, there's the *Hotel Jaguar* which costs just over US$1 per person and is good value.

For somewhere to eat try the *Paisano Restaurant* on the edge of town which serves excellent vegetarian food for US$1 per meal and has been recommended. Many travellers go there to get a group together to go on jungle tours. It's also a good place to meet guides (of which there are some 24 in Misahuallí). The *Restaurant Dayuna* is also popular and serves excellent fish and chips.

From Misahuallí you can take trips into the jungle with a guide – the average cost is US$16 to $21 per person per day. Generally a minimum of six people is needed. One guide we've had consistently good reports about for years is Douglas Clarke, a lepidopterist, who has now been joined by a partner, Adonis Muñoz, an ornithologist. Both are dedicated people. They offer tours of up to 10 days – the longer your trip the better – on short trips you'll see only insects and birds as a rule. Contact these people at the Dayuna Restaurant. There are other guides to be found and most are very good. You should, however, avoid Hector Fluvial.

Some years ago a traveller described his outfit as 'a gang of fat slobs'. Only very recently we've had confirmation that nothing has improved from another traveller who decided to ignore our warning and wished he hadn't. Another thing to avoid are guided day trips – it's hardly worth the money. If that's all you have time for then borrow a pair of rubber boots and take off on your own.

From Misahuallí to Coca there is a daily boat at 11.30 am, which is US$5.50 and takes up to 9½ hours. It's a motorised canoe with no shelter, so dress accordingly. After buying your ticket you must report to the harbour police with your passport – it's the last building on the road to the beach. In the opposite direction, the canoe departs at 8 am. Note that if you're going to Coca from Misahuallí you won't arrive in time to catch the last bus to Quito and will have to spend the night there.

The Galápagos Islands

Very few people have not heard of the Galápagos Islands and their unique wildlife. A scattered archipelago of volcanic islands rising to 3000 metres, about 600 km west off the Ecuadorian coast, they were first brought to the attention of the scientific world by Charles Darwin. In formulating his theory of the origin of species, Darwin was strongly influenced by what he saw on the Galápagos. The islands have been popularised in more recent years by TV documentaries and naturalists. Because the sea which surrounds them is cooled by the Humboldt current from the Antarctic they have a range of different climates from desert to sub-tropical forest.

When discovered by the Spanish in the early 1500s, the islands were uninhabited. It's been established that they were never connected with the mainland and so the life forms which existed there were able to develop completely independently of those found anywhere else in the world. Their most famous residents are, of course, the giant tortoises. Unfortunately, once the islands were discovered, their numbers were sadly reduced over the centuries by the crews of ships looking for food. They are now being bred and protected at the Charles Darwin biological research station on Santa Cruz Island.

It's not cheap getting to the Galápagos Islands. Part of the reason for this is that the government doesn't want to see them inundated with tourists to the detriment of the wildlife. The other part of the equation is to milk tourists for as much money as they're willing to pay.

SANTA CRUZ

Although five islands are inhabited, only one, Santa Cruz, is visited frequently by travellers. It has the greatest population and most travellers stay in the small town of Puerto Ayora. There is a variety of hotels there, as well as restaurants and shops and it's the place to organise a tour from.

Information

There are plans to open a permanent tourist office, but in the meantime the Charles Darwin Research Station has an exhibition hall, information kiosk and tortoise-raising pens, but they do not organise tours. During the busy season, self-styled tour agents set up shop near the Las Ninfas Restaurant.

Money changing facilities are not very good and you should change travellers' cheques on the mainland. The bank does not usually change money. There is a shop (marked on the map) which will change cheques at a poor rate. Other shops will sometimes change money, as will some hotels if you're staying there.

The Capitanía can give you information about boats to the mainland. TAME has an office open from 8 am to 12 noon Monday to Thursday and on Saturday; and from 2 to 5 pm Monday to Friday.

Things to See & Do

If you have to wait around in Puerto Ayora for a day or so until there are enough people to go on a tour, there are quite a few things you can do do spend the time. A visit to the Charles Darwin Research Station, where there's the tortoise hatchery, corral and a good museum and exhibition, is recommended. There's also a tortoise reserve near Santa Rosa on the road to the airport where you can see tortoises in their natural habitat. There are buses to Santa Rosa from where you can walk to the reserve. You can also rent horses there for a nominal price.

If you want to go swimming there is a good beach on the other side of Puerto Ayora at Tortuga Bay (see map). If you have whole days to spare you can take day trips to some of the closer islands such as Plazas and Santa Fe. One of the boats which goes there is the *Santa Cruz*. Enquire about it at the office next to the waterfront bakery. These trips are easy to make since you often don't need a group as there are usually sufficient Ecuadorian people signed up already to make that unnecessary. The cost of the trips are about US$12 including lunch.

Snorkelling Donning a mask and snorkel opens up a whole new world. Baby sea lions may come up and stare through your mask, various species of rays come slowly undulating by and penguins dart past you in a stream of bubbles. There are hundreds of species of fish and you can watch the flapping shapes of sea turtles as they circle you. Snorkelling also lets you observe the more sedentary forms of marine life. Sea urchins, starfish, sea anemones, algae and crustaceans combine in an exotic display of underwater life.

You may be able to buy a snorkel and mask in sports shops in Quito or Guayaquil, but if you definitely plan on visiting the

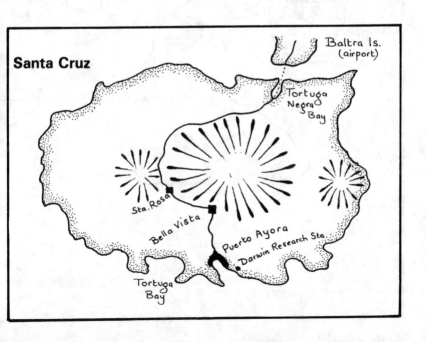

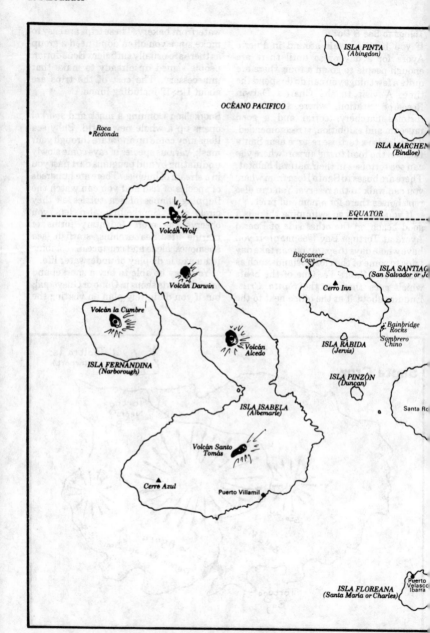

TOWER ISLAND
(Isla Genovesa)

Galápagos Islands

0   20   40 km

A SEYMOUR

ISLA BALTRA
ort   Bellavista

Plaza Islands
ISLA SANTA CRUZ
(Indefatigable)

ros
llavista

Point Nuñez

adamy
Bay

ISLA SANTA FÉ
(Barrington)

ISLA SAN CRISTÓBAL
(Catham)

Puerto Baquerizo
Moreno
El Progresso

ISLA ESPAÑOLA   Gardner
(Hood)

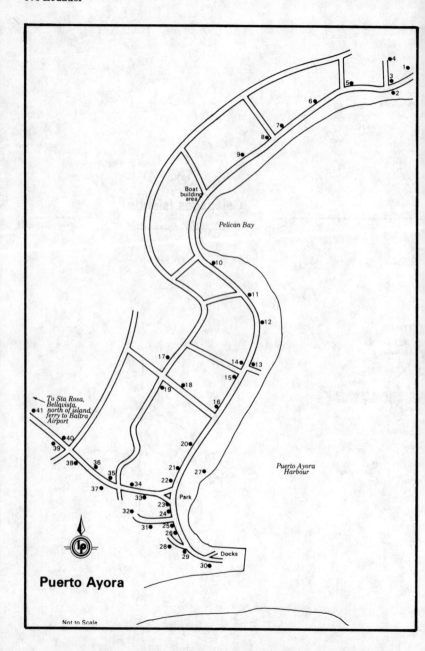

Puerto Ayora

Not to Scale

islands, consider bringing them from home to ensure a good fit and to enable you to dive when you feel like it. It may also be possible to borrow them on Santa Cruz.

Places to Stay

The cheapest way to stay on the islands is to put your own food together and camp. However, you are only allowed to camp in certain designated areas and you must first get permission from the National Park Office. The sites are: *Charles Darwin Research Station* and *Tortuga Bay* (both on Santa Cruz); *Post Office Bay* (Floreana); *James Bay* and *Volcan Celdo* (both on Santiago).

For budget travellers the best place to stay in Puerto Ayora is *Angermeyer's*. This place has private cabins set in a beautiful tropical garden with outdoor cooking and washing facilities and good bathrooms. It's excellent value at US$1.20 per person. Both Mrs Angermeyer and her husband, Gus, are mines of information about the islands and which boats are available for tours. If it's full then go to the *Hotel Gloria* next door. This is also very good value at US$1 per person. If both are full then ask around for Lucretia, an islander who rents out beds very cheaply in his own house – it's ultra-basic!

There are plenty of other hotels but they are more expensive. Hotels such as the *Palmeras*, *Salinas* and *Santa Cruz* all charge about US$4 per person.

The *Hotel Galapágos* charges US$29/ $52/$75 for singles/doubles/triples and, as you might expect, has all the facilities.

Places to Eat

There are not many restaurants where you can eat cheaply. *Los Gemellos* has good seafood but very slow service. The *Pizzeria* just before Angermeyer's serves

1	Entrance to Darwin Research Centre 1/2 km to first buildings	22	Micro Mercado
2	Hotel Galapagos	23	Radio Station
3	Cemetery	24	Church
4	Camping permitted	25	INGALA Office
5	Fragata Bar & Boutique	26	Post Office
6	Bar La Peña	27	Capitania de Puerto
7	Hotel Angermeyer	28	Bakery
8	Comercial Pelican Bay Store	29	Souvenirs
9	Pensión Gloria	30	Las Ninfas Restaurant
10	Hotel Sol y Mar	31	Hotel Castro
11	Banco Nacional de Fomento	32	Hotel Nynfas
12	Church	33	Hospital
13	Hotel Lobo de Mar	34	Store buys $ Travellers Cheques
14	Booby Trap Disco	35	Café
15	Town Hall (Municipalidad)	36	Hotel Darwin
16	Hotel Elizabeth & Store	37	Pharmacy
17	Cinema	38	TAME
18	Hotel Salinas	39	School
19	Hotel Palmeras	40	Tunnel Restaurant
20	La Terraza Bar	41	Hotel Santa Cruz
21	Hotel Colón (& Raul Jeria)		

reasonable food and the owner speaks English. For good health-food try the *Café Bambu. Las Ninfas Restaurant* is the main meeting place during the day. They serve decent meals. The *Fragata Bar* is good for snacks and meeting people.

In the evening, the rowdiest action is at the *La Terraza Bar*. The *Booby Trap Bar* is quieter and serves food.

Getting There

Until recently, you needed about US$400 to pay a visit to the Galápagos (including a boat trip around the islands). It's probably still wise to put aside that amount but if you find you can do it cheaper then think yourself lucky.

The good news however, is that there are always a lot of impecunious travellers at the Hotel Gran Casino in Quito who put a lot of energy and time into working out the cheapest way to get there. That's why it's worth staying there when you get to Quito. Even without a student card, or proof that Charles Darwin was your great-grandfather, you'll more than likely be able to pick up a return air ticket to the Galápagos from the Gran Casino for US$120 with *TAME*, the military airline. This means that with the cost of a tour and food you could go there and back for around US$300. Just how long this will last we can't tell but it's worth asking to see if it still applies. If it doesn't, but you have a student card, then get in touch with *CEPTEJ* at the Catholic University, Av 12 de Octubre, because they also have student tickets available to the Galápagos.

If you don't have a student card there's still hope. First of all, make sure you write 'Estudiante' on the form which you fill in when you enter Ecuador. With a photostat of this form (plus two photos and US$5) or an out of date student card you can buy a new student card at the Catholic University.

Not only that, but there are ways of getting there even cheaper if you're prepared to do some leg-work and string-

pulling. If you're a biology student and have confirmation of this on headed notepaper from your university or college then you're entitled to a return flight to the Galápagos with *TAME* for just US$45. United States and West German nationals can get such a letter from their respective embassies. With such a letter you first go to the Señor General Commandante de la FAE in the Ministerio de Defensa. Here you get a radiogramme which you take to the Colegio Militar two to three blocks beyond the airport and there buy your ticket. Ecuadorians get first preference so you may not be able to fly on the day you choose.

We've also had a letter from an Israeli traveller who reported that Israeli nationals get a deal with the same airline whereby they can buy a return air ticket for US$75.

If you don't have a student card or a letter confirming that you are a biology student or if the Gran Casino or the Catholic University are no longer able to offer their US$120 return flights, then you're up for the full amount.

As far as sailing to the Galápagos goes, the cheapest passages are offered by *TRAMFSA*, Villamil 315, 1st floor (close to the tourist office). They operate the freighter *Piquero* which has accommodation for eight passengers (sometimes extended up to 30 though most of these would have to sleep on deck). The boat does the run to the islands twice a month taking three days to get there. It then spends around seven days unloading at various ports before returning to Guayaquil. The one-way fare is about US$90. The *Piquero* usually docks at Muelle 4 on the Malecón near the junction of Junín and Malecón.

The *Piquero* is fine if you happen to be in Guayaquil at the right time but if you're not or your time is limited anyway then it's best to fly. *TAME* offer the cheapest tickets (apart from the various deals already mentioned). They have daily flights at 11 am from Guayaquil except on Sundays which cost US$312 return. There are also daily flights from Quito which cost US$353 return. If you book at short notice they may tell you that the plane is full – this is rarely the case so it's worth turning up and going standby. There isn't much point in asking at the office in town what the chances are of getting on. *TAME* agents are notoriously uninformed. Ask four different people and you'll get four different answers. *TAME* has offices at Av 10 de Agosto 239, Quito, and at the Edificio Gran Pasaje, Av 9 de Octubre 424, Guayaquil. If you have difficulty getting a ticket at the latter, go to *Galasam* (Economic Galápagos Tours) on the 11th floor of the same building.

All planes land at Baltra airport, an old US air base, on a small island just off the coast of Santa Cruz Island. When you land you'll first have to pay the entrance fee for the National Park which is now US$30 (payable in US dollars). Buses meet incoming planes and take passengers to the ferry for US$0.40. The ferry to Santa Cruz Island costs a further US$0.15, and from the far side you take either a truck or jeep (about 1½ hours) to Puerto Ayora, the main town, on the south side of the island. The fare is US$1.20.

Make sure you take enough sucres with you to the islands from either Quito or Guayaquil as exchange rates on the islands are poor.

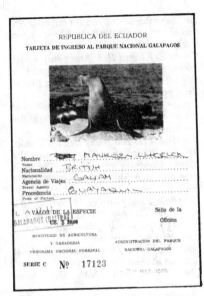

REPUBLICA DEL ECUADOR
TARJETA DE INGRESO AL PARQUE NACIONAL GALAPAGOS

Nombre .... ROBT MAUREEN WHEELER
Name
Nacionalidad .... BRITISH
Nacionality
Agencia de Viajes .... GALYAM
Travel Agency
Procedencia .... GUAYAQUIL
Point of Parture

VALOR DE LA ESPECIE   Sello de la
US $ 30,00   Oficina

MINISTERIO DE AGRICULTURA
Y GANADERIA   ADMINISTRACIÓN DEL PARQUE
PROGRAMA NACIONAL FORESTAL   NACIONAL GALAPAGOS

SERIE C   Nº 17123

Visiting the Other Islands

There are very few regular boats between the islands so if you want to see anything of the wildlife you must charter a boat. The cost of these is presently running at US$20 to $25 per person per day but you must bargain for this price. It should include food but beware of forcing the price too low if you like a decent meal every evening. You might think you're getting a bargain but all that will happen is that you'll get a tiny or indifferent meal each night and if you complain they'll threaten to cut the tour short. Naturally you need to get a small group together, which is not difficult. Many of the boats are converted trawlers though there are one or two yachts. The average trip lasts 7 to 10 days. Among the better boats are:

Daphne, Goldrina, Poseidon and *Angelito* (the latter has good food).
Normita skippered by Joselito, a friendly guy who will do his best to see that you have a good trip.
Mistral This is Frenchman Max's yacht.

He has scuba-diving equipment on board and his wife generally does the cooking on a trip – excellent food.

Cristo Rey I and II A larger ship which takes seven or more people and is skippered by Raul Jeria – ask for him at the Capitania del Puerto.

Xavier Another larger ship with lots of room on board. Ask for Allesandro Padrana.

Narcissa This is a really beautiful ship. Ask for Victor Lopez who lives near the Mesón Conchita restaurant. The best time to catch him is between 2 and 4 pm.

Española A boat with eight berths and a good crew. The owner is called Ramon. A recent letter, however, complained about the quantity of food served.

Lobo de Mar The owner lives in the Hotel Lobo de Mar on the waterfront.

The *San Juan* has also been recommended.

Avoid the *Diomede* because although it's cheap (US$16 per day) the food is deficient and the crew is said to be lazy.

You can, of course, book a tour (with or without flight tickets) before you go to the Galápagos but this is going to cost you considerably more than it would to make your own arrangements when you get to Puerto Ayora. There's also very little you can do on a pre-booked tour if it turns out that the tour wasn't quite what you were given to believe. We get quite a few complaints about the quality of pre-booked tours, one of the worst being about *Galasam* (Economic Galápagos Tours), Pinto 523 y Amazonas, Quito and 9 de Octubre, Gran Pasaje Building (11th floor), Guayaquil. They also now have an office in Toronto (Galápagos Tours, 161 Dupont St, Toronto M5R 1V5).

Whether you pre-book a tour or organise it when you get there, it's sensible to head off possible disputes by agreeing in advance with the boat's captain exactly what is included. Important here is a complete itinerary – vagueness or unwillingness to provide one probably indicates problems later on. Crews are prone to go off socialising at various points on a trip and this can lead to a lot of wasted time and the cancellation of visits to outlying islands.

Make sure you visit Española (Hood) – for the birds and marine iguanas; and Isabella – the only place, apart from the Darwin Research Station, where you can see giant land tortoises in the wild. If you're thinking of snorkelling (eg on Floreana) then take a wet suit; the water can be really cold.

You'll probably enjoy your trip around the islands more if you have some background information. You can get this by picking up a copy of the book *The Galápagos Guide*, at the Charles Darwin Research Station in Academy Bay. It costs about US$2.50. You can generally also find it in Quito and Guayaquil bookshops. Another book worth having (but which you're unlikely to find on the islands) is *Galápagos: The Flow of Wilderness*, published by the Sierra Club and Ballantine Books. It's probably too large to cart around in a rucksack so read it before you set off.

The few regular ferries which connect the islands include:

Puerto Ayora-San Cristóbal The post-boat, *San Pedro II*, does the trip once a week departing Puerto Ayora on Tuesday afternoon (arriving Wednesday morning) and San Cristóbal on Wednesday afternoon (arriving Thursday morning). There's also an irregular navy supply boat, the *Pinta* – ask at the Capitania del Puerto.

Puerto Ayora-Floreana The post-boat *San Pedro II* departs once every fortnight and takes about 10 hours. There are also occasional freight boats. Contact the Capitania for details.

Puerto Ayora-Isabela The post-boat also occasionally visits this island. Enquire at the Capitania.

Guyana, Surinam & French Guiana

The Guianas are a legacy of the British, Dutch and French attempts to get a slice of the colonial action in South America. Neither the Spanish nor the Portuguese ever really accepted these 'incursions' on what they regarded was their divine right – to divide the whole continent between them. They were in no position to effectively do anything about it, however, because of the nature of the land – lowland swamps and jungle highlands – and the ease with which military expeditions could be mounted from the heavily fortified British, Dutch and French West Indies. As a result, disputes simmer even today over land boundaries. Venezuela claims almost the whole of Guyana and Brazil occasionally makes noises about the borders of Surinam (formerly Dutch Guiana) and French Guiana though belligerence rarely reaches a pitch comparable to Guatemalan claims over Belize.

Guyana has a unique population mix for this part of the world, consisting of approximately equal numbers of people of Asian Indian and African origin, both of whom manage to retain their own largely separate cultures. In addition there is a small proportion (about 5%) of pure-blooded Amerindians who, until very recently, lived an undisturbed tribal life in the forests of the interior; and a small northern European community (about 1%).

The Asian Indian element is the result of a system of indentured labour introduced by the British following the abolition of slavery in 1834. Until that time the plantations of cotton, coffee, sugar and tobacco had been worked by slaves brought from Africa. When they were 'freed' most of them deserted the plantations and set up their own small holdings forcing the plantation owners to look elsewhere for a source of labour. By the first decade of the 20th century, a quarter of a million Asian Indian labourers had served their time in the colony. Most of them returned home at the end of their indenture but others settled, giving rise to the present population mix. Most people live on the coastal belt, a good quarter of them in Georgetown itself.

The first northern European settlements in what is now Guyana were made by the Dutch in the early 1600s. The British set up colonies in what is now Surinam and French Guiana. Their early history was turbulent and subject to the varying military fortunes of the Dutch, British and French navies in the Caribbean and to the outcome of various wars fought in Europe. At one point, the British colony in Surinam was traded for the Dutch colony in New York. In this way Dutch influence remained paramount in the Guianas until the French Revolution and the advent of the Napoleonic Wars in Europe, at the end of which Britain gained Guyana, the French got Guyane, and the Dutch retained Surinam. Independence for Guyana came in 1966 and since that time there's been a lot of heavy political activity centred around the tension between black and Asian-Indian interests.

Guyana hit the news in 1979 following the mass 'suicide' of thousands of members of a secretive and rigidly-controlled North American evangelical religious sect which had set up a huge farming commune in the interior of the country under the leadership of a Rev Jones. Though undoubtedly much of the story remains to be told, he apparently decided that the holocaust was on its way and commanded his followers to commit suicide by drinking cyanide. 'Suicide' was just a euphemism, since from all accounts many did so only at gunpoint. The scandal rocked the Guyanese government and destroyed much of the credibility of the Prime Minister who, it was alleged, accepted bribes from the sect in return for land concessions at their 'Jonestown' settlement.

Apart from a few tribes of Amerindians, the interior of the country is largely unpopulated and consists of virgin jungle and barren highlands. Roads are few and far between and travel is rough and time-consuming. The only road connections are along the coast to Surinam. Bauxite is mined in the interior.

Since the Jonestown scandal, tourism has not been encouraged so you may find obstacles in your path if you're trying to get a visa.

VISAS

Required by all except nationals of Western Europe (Portugal and West Germany excepted), Commonwealth countries and the USA. The length of stay given on arrival is arbitrary and there's

little rhyme or reason about what you get. Onward tickets are generally asked for and sometimes they also want to see how much money you have. A ticket from Georgetown to Lethem or to Surinam is generally acceptable as an onward ticket. If you wish to visit the interior you must first get a permit from the Home Department, 6 Brickdam, Georgetown. If you're a journalist or photographer by trade don't advertise the fact or you may be refused entry. Baggage searches are thorough. The Bom Fim border on the Lethem-Boa Vista road is reported to be fairly easy going.

MONEY
US$1 = G$2.50

The unit of currency is the Guyanese dollar = 100 cents. Import or export of Guyanese currency is allowed up to G$40 – there are strict currency controls so don't try leaving with more than this amount.

Guyana isn't a cheap country. Expect to pay around US$16 for a hotel (less at Government Rest Houses) and around US$2 for a simple meal.

Airport departure tax for international flights is US$10.

GETTING THERE & AROUND
The only way you can get into Guyana without flying is by road from either Brazil or Surinam. Even if you enter by road from Brazil you will still have to fly from Lethem to Georgetown. There are no road connections with Venezuela.

From Brazil, there are daily buses at 8 am from Boa Vista to Bom Fim which take about three hours and cost US$4. From Bom Fim you must walk five km to the River Tacutu (border) and cross it by dug-out (US$0.80). Bom Fim is about 2½ km from Lethem.

If you're going in the opposite direction, the buses leave Bom Fim for Boa Vista at 2 pm. If you're heading south from

Georgetown by plane to Lethem, don't expect to get to Boa Vista the same day as the planes are usually late and you'll miss the bus at Bom Fim. Stay overnight at Lethem. Passport formalities on the Guyanese side are completed at Lethem. On the Brazilian side they are completed at Bom Fim.

If you're heading for Surinam, there are buses as far as Springlands on the Berbice River (border) and a ferry into Surinam from there. First get a bus to Rosignol (US$2.60) then a ferry to New Amsterdam (35c) followed by another bus to Springlands (US$0.20, about 2½ hours). A taxi from Georgetown to Springlands will cost about US$8 per person.

As far as internal transport goes, other than the road link with Surinam, you have to fly. Guyana Airways have a flight to Lethem at 11.45 am daily except Sundays. The fare is US$36 one-way. Flights to Kaieteur Falls have been discontinued though there is a possibility of getting on a military flight – try the Guyana Defence Force in Georgetown. The only reliable way of getting to these falls is through *Guyana Overland Tours* in Georgetown. They offer an excellent tour which doesn't cost much more than the flight. The trip takes four to five days. The only drawback is that you must get a group together.

GEORGETOWN

If you like Belize then you'll like this place too. It's quite unlike any other capital city in South America. It has that character and atmosphere which only wooden buildings can give a place. Some of the largest are the City Hall, the cathedral (one of the tallest wooden buildings in the world other than those in Karelia, north-west Russia/Finland), the Law Courts and the President's House. There would have been many more but for a fire in 1945 which destroyed much of the town. Georgetown is actually built below the high water mark and has to be protected from the sea by an embankment and a system of dykes which are opened at low tide. It's quite an attractive town, built along the lines of the old Dutch canals, on the banks of the Demerara River.

Information

The main post office is on North Rd. It's

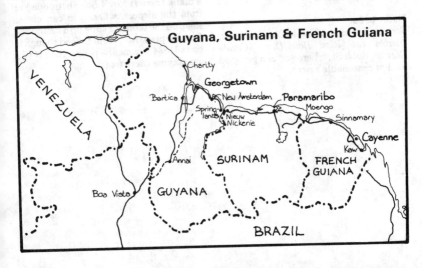

open from 7.30 am to 4 pm. The main bus terminal is at Stabroek Market Square. A taxi (colectivo) from the airport to town costs G$14 per person (35 km).

Things to See

Georgetown is a pleasant place to walk around though once you've seen it there isn't much to do. Do make sure you visit the Stabroek Market in Water St, where you can buy just about anything including Benares brassware.

Botanists should go to the Botanical Gardens (entry free) which are very extensive and have good collections of palms, orchids and the Victoria Regia lilies.

Places to Stay

Some of the best deals in accommodation are found in boarding houses, like those in Belize. Try *Bill's Guest House*, 46 High St (very good); *Ark Guesthouse*, Croal St; the *Elizabeth Guest House*, Wellington St; or the *Rima Guest House*, Middle St. You should be able to get a room there for about US$10. Another colourful place you might like to try is *Aunt Aggies*, 69 Main St. This is a cheap place used partially by whores.

Places to Eat

For a mixed Indian/Creole/Chinese menu, there's the *Rice Bowl/Doc's Creole Corner*, Robb St, where you can get good food at reasonable prices.

Two good Chinese restaurants are the *Kwang Chow*, Camp St and Regent St; and the *Chinese Dragon*, Robb St and Avenue of the Republic. If you'd like some action in the evenings, give the *Grub Inn* a spin – dancing and cheap Creole food.

LETHEM

Lethem is just a small border town on the Brazilian/Guyanese border, which you must pass through if you're going to or coming from Brazil, but it is a very, very friendly town. It's more than likely one or more people will invite you to go with them to nearby Amerindian villages and markets or even to a waterfall of which there are several in the area.

Places to Stay

There's really only one hotel in the town (although there's another some considerable distance from the town), and it costs US$16 per night. The best thing to do is try to get into the *Government Rest House* where you can stay free – they only charge for meals (US$1.20 for breakfast and US$2 for lunch or supper). Ask for either Mrs Matthews or Mr Ching.

Another place you could try if you score a blank there is *Roy's Bar* about one km from the airport, where you can either sleep on the tables or sling up a hammock free. He prepares excellent food though it costs US$4 per meal – pretty good if you are staying there free.

Paraguay

There are probably very few people in the west who, if asked, could rub together two facts about Paraguay. This isn't very surprising. It is remote, landlocked, rarely gets even a one-liner in the media and has been ruled for the past 28 years by one of the world's longest-reigning iron-fisted dictators. Only Kim Il-Sung of North Korea outdoes President Alfredo Stroessner in the longevity stakes.

Until recently, Paraguay shared with Bolivia the dubious distinction of being Latin America's poorest and most backward nation. However, its fortunes are beginning to change quite dramatically with the construction of the Itaipú dam on the Paraná River which, it is estimated, will produce six times as much electricity as the Aswan Dam when it comes fully on line in 1988. This dam is being constructed in partnership with Brazil. Further down the Paraná, another dam – the Yacyretá Dam – is being constructed, this time in partnership with Argentina. Yet another is being considered between the two.

Paraguay, Brazil and Argentina make somewhat strange bed partners. Only a little over 100 years ago Brazil and Argentina were responsible for battering Paraguay back into the Stone Age. It's a pattern that has been repeated several times in Paraguay's history.

Unlike the rest of Spanish America, Paraguay declared its independence from Spain without having to fight a war of liberation – and as early as 1811. Two of its earliest dictators were unusual in that they weren't cut from the same mould as most others in Latin America at the time. Both Francia and his successor, Lopez, went all-out to destroy the power of the landowners and the merchants and to put the country onto the path of autonomous, self-sustained development without recourse to foreign capital. Politically, they would have given Amnesty Inter-national apoplexy but by 1865 Paraguay had telegraphs, railroads, numerous factories making construction materials, textiles, paper, crockery and gunpowder, and the highest literacy rate in Latin America. It made its own steel and even had a merchant navy fleet on the Paraná with a shipyard at Asunción. Almost all the land was publicly owned and holdings were granted to peasants in return for permanent occupation and cultivation but without the right to sell. Even the pre-conquest practice of raising two crops per year instead of one had been revived. All this had been achieved without Paraguay owing a cent to foreign creditors.

This all took place at a time when British merchant bankers were providing the bulk of the funds for the development and exploitation of the natural resources of Brazil and Argentina and British merchants were flooding Uruguay with finished products from their factories. Being denied access to Paraguay wasn't to their liking. They were not the only source of mounting pressure however, because as Paraguay had no direct access to the sea, its exports were at the mercy of its two powerful neighbours who frequently imposed arbitrary taxes and hold-ups. There was also constant political rivalry between Brazil and Argentina for control of Uruguay. As a result of British mediation, the two countries had formally recognized Uruguay as an independent buffer state between them in 1828. Unfortunately, this wasn't to be the beginning of internal peace in Uruguay or the end of foreign intervention.

An independent Uruguay was obviously of paramount importance for Paraguay and its access to the ocean. When, in 1852, Brazilian forces overthrew the Argentinian dictator Rosas on Argentinian soil and subsequently encouraged lawless bands of cowboys to raid Paraguay from the Rió Grande do Sul, it was the last straw for Paraguay. Though heavily outnumbered, Lopez sent the Paraguayan army into Uruguay in an attempt to force the Brazilians out of that country. His act precipitated the War of the Triple Alliance (1865-70) in which Paraguay fought Argentina, Uruguay and Brazil. The Bank of London, Baring Bros and Rothschilds financed the allied war effort. When it was over, half the population of Paraguay had been wiped out and only 10% of those who were left were male. Paraguayan prisoners were marched off to work as slaves on the coffee plantations of São Paulo, Paraguay's industrial installations were looted and the land parcelled out into huge estates under private ownership.

Paraguay never quite recovered from that disaster and its politics fell into the familiar pattern of coup and counter-coup throughout the rest of the 19th and much of the early 20th century, with heavy interference from both Argentina and Brazil. Impoverished as Paraguay was, it nevertheless went to war again between 1929 and 1935, this time with Bolivia over a dispute about sovereignty of the Chaco. This time the conflict was engineered by rival western oil companies which had their eye on concessions should their prospecting activities turn up huge reserves of oil. No oil was found and though Paraguay was the victor in the war, it was once again at the expense of development and a massive number of lives.

Paraguay's post-independence experiment with socialism (of a sort) and self-sufficiency wasn't the first time this had been tried. At the beginning of the 17th century, Jesuit missionaries, over whom the civil authorities had little or no control, persuaded the Guaraní Indians who had fled to the forests, rather than become virtual slaves on the estates of the Spanish conquerors, to come and settle on their reducciónes – sort of communal villages. Under the protection of the missionaries, around 150,000 Indians were able to build permanent communities, work the land communally and to revive and breathe fresh life into their traditional crafts, arts and music. Money was banned as a medium of exchange and any business with outsiders had to be conducted at an appropriate distance from the reducciónes.

Although the communities established in the north eventually had to be abandoned because of the rapacious slave-raiding parties that frequently crossed the border from Brazil, the ones in the south were an outstanding success and viewed with alarm and envy by the large landowners. There was nothing, however, they could do while the Jesuits retained their influence at the Vatican. But the Jesuit's days were numbered. They eventually became such a threat to Papal authority itself that something was bound to give. So when their grip on the Vatican was finally broken, about 160 years after the establishment of the reducciónes, the Spanish king took the opportunity to expel them from the colonies. Stripped of protection, the reducciónes were looted, whole communities herded to the slave markets of Brazil and others forcibly put to work on the estates of plantation owners in Paraguay. Many Indians, however, escaped once again to the relative safety of the forest. The ruins of the reducciónes can be seen today near Trinidad, a small town close to Encarnación.

Remarkably, the idea of self-sufficient communities didn't die there. In 1926 the first wave of Mennonites arrived. The government allowed them to set up self-governing communities, conduct their affairs in German and agreed to honour their religious pledge which prohibits military service. Today the Mennonites are a very prosperous section of the nation with their centre at Filadelfia in the heart of the Chaco. There they raise corn, soybeans, peanuts, cotton and produce dairy products. Mennonites are also found in Mexico, Belize, Colombia, Bolivia, Brazil, Argentina and Uruguay. Other successful agricultural projects have been set up more recently by the Japanese, who number over 1000. Taiwan is also involved in various agricultural experiments. There was even an Australian rival to the Mennonite settlements at the turn of the century – known as Nueva Australia. It's now more or less defunct and there are very few surviving members.

The most recent wave of immigration has come from South Korea. There are no less than 10,000 Koreans in Paraguay, most of them in Asunción itself! They have virtually taken over many of the service industries and the rag trade. Walk down any of the main streets in Asunción and you could almost imagine you were in Seoul – there are Korean signs everywhere, on pharmacies, hotels, restaurants, watch repair shops and clothing stores. You'll probably find yourself staying in one of

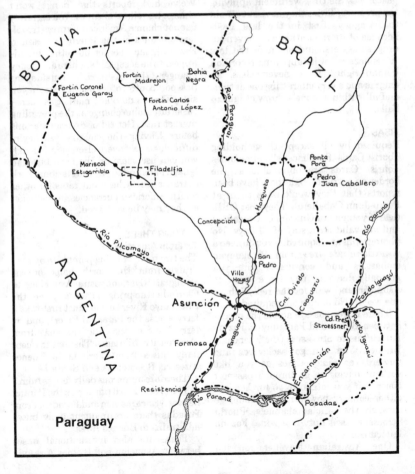

Paraguay

their hotels – they are very well run with typically high Korean standards of cleanliness and maintenance.

Paraguay is changing fast and won't be the South American backwater that it has been for much longer. It's still controlled, of course, by Alfredo Stroessner whose political slogan beams out in neon from the top of a building on the Plaza de los Heroes in Asunción ('Paz, trabajo, bienestar'), yet even he is having to come to terms with popular pressure. In the past it was the US government applying the pressure. Twice they have cut off aid to Paraguay, first in the late 1960s because of its reputation as a haven for drug smugglers, and again in the late 1970s because of its appalling record on human rights. It is, nevertheless, an enigma and a very interesting one at that, and all within a stone's throw of Iguazú Falls.

VISAS

Required by all except those holding Tourist Cards. For almost all nationalities Tourist Cards are obtainable at the border on entry (though there have been reports that they won't issue them at Pedro Juan Caballero). They cost US$3 (less if you pay in Guaraní or Cruzeiros) and are valid for a stay of 90 days. No photographs are required. If you do need a visa these are free from Paraguayan embassies and consulates but you normally have to pay for a telex to Asunción and wait for the reply (about one week). No photos are required.

There is free passage across the border between Brazil and Paraguay at Foz do Iguaçu/Puerto Stroessner (the Friendship Bridge). You can go backwards and forwards as many times as you like without having to go through passport control. If you intend to go further into either country however, you should go through the official channels. Puerto Stroessner is a duty-free zone. Foz do Iguaçu is not.

One Australian traveller reported recently that despite being given a visa, he was turned back at the border because he had old Nicaraguan visas in his passport.

MONEY
US$1 = G660 (floating)

The unit of currency is the Guaraní = 100 centimos. There are no restrictions on the import or export of local currency. It's best to change money at a casa de cambio. We've had reports that banks won't change travellers' cheques. You certainly cannot change American Express travellers' cheques at the Puerto Stroessner/ Foz do Iguaçu border but other brands appear to be acceptable. There are money changers (for cash) right outside the passport control office on the Paraguayan side. There's no black market as such – casas de cambio change at the prevailing market rate. Get rid of excess Guaranís before leaving the country as they're difficult to reconvert elsewhere (though you can use them on the local buses to Iguaçu Falls and to pay the National Park entrance fee). Check out rates for other South American currencies in Asunción as they may be very good.

GETTING THERE
To/From Argentina
The two main crossing points are by road bridge from the north bank of the Paraguai River, opposite Asunción, to Clorinda (the bridge is actually over the Pilcomayo River so you must first take a ferry across the Paraguai River), and by ferry across the Río Paraná from Encarnación to Posadas. There are frequent daily buses from Clorinda to Buenos Aires via Resistencia and Santa Fé.

There are numerous daily ferries from 7 to 11 am and 2 to 6 pm across the Paraná between Encarnación and Posadas. From Posadas there are frequent daily buses and trains to Buenos Aires.

There are also international buses between Asunción and Buenos Aires via

Formosa, Resistencia, Santa Fé and Rosario. Three companies cover this route: *Brujula*, *Godoy* and *La Internacional*. Their schedules are:

Servicio Diferencial
    Brujula on Monday, Wednesday and Friday at 2 pm; *Godoy* on Tuesday, Thursday and Saturday at 2 pm; and *La Internacional*, daily, except Saturday, at 7 pm.
Servicio Convencional
    Brujula on Tuesday, Thursday and Saturday at 4 pm; *Godoy* on Monday, Wednesday and Friday at 4 pm; and *La Internacional*, daily, except Thursday, at 8 am.

If you only want to go as far as Resistencia there are daily buses at 6 am and 5 pm. The fares on the above buses are: Formosa, US$3.70; Resistencia, US$6.30; Santa Fé, US$24.20 'conven', US$32 'diferen'; Rosario, US$25 'conven', US$32.80 'diferen'. There are connections to Cordóba at Rosario.

To/From Brazil

To get to Brazil you can either cross the Friendship Bridge from Puerto Stroessner to Foz do Iguaçu and go on from there to the Iguazú Falls, or cross at the twin towns of Pedro Juan Caballero/Ponta Porã further north. From Ponta Porã there are daily buses to Campo Grande and a train twice daily in either direction (at 6.40 and 8.45 am from Ponta Porã). There is also the possibility of going by cargo boat from Asunción to Corumbá along the Río Paraguay.

There are also international buses to Blumenau and Florianopolis by *Catarinense* on Tuesday, Thursday and Saturday at 1 pm; to Curitiba (US$8.60), São Paulo (US$12.20, 9 am daily) and Rio de Janeiro (US$15.30, Wednesday and Sunday at 9 am) by *Pluma*; and to Curitiba and São Paulo daily (except Friday and Saturday), at 9 am and on Saturday at 6 pm by *Rapido Yguassu SA*.

Pluma, *Rapido Yguassu* and *Nuestra Señora de la Asuncion* all operate daily buses to Foz do Iguaçu (*Pluma* runs several daily; the other two once daily only). The journey takes about 5½ hours and costs US$3.50. If you're heading for Foz it's best to take one of these international buses since they take you through both passport controls. You may save up to US$0.50 by taking an internal bus as far as Puerto Stroessner, walking over the bridge and then taking another local bus into the centre of Foz but it will take you much longer.

To/From Bolivia

Getting into Bolivia across the Chaco can take several days but don't attempt it in the rainy season (October to April). It's no problem at all getting as far as Mariscal Estigarribia. There are buses three times a week from Asunción on Tuesday and Thursday at 10 pm and on Saturday at 6.30 pm by *Nasa*. The road is surfaced almost as far as Filadelfia. At Mariscal Estigarribia you need to have your passport checked by the commanding officer at the army base (between 1 and 4 pm) before going any further. There's a small *pension* run by a German man close to the base where you can get a room and food for the night. From there to Fortín Garay, the last Paraguayan village, the track isn't too bad but you must hitch hike (the usual form of transport is petrol trucks). Paraguayan exit stamps are obtained from the commanding officer of the army base at Fortín Garay.

It's another 13 km or so from there to the actual border post (passport check) and then another 3 km from there to the Bolivian border post of Villazón (not to be confused with the town of the same name close to the Argentina border). It's possible to stay at either of these border posts if you arrive late in the day. Bolivian passport formalities are completed at Villazón. From there to Boyuibe (where petrol and water are available) it's a rough road but you should be able to cover it in a day. You might even be able to get as far as Camiri (another 65 km) the same day.

If you're doing this trip from Paraguay you need a permit from the Bolivian consulate in Asunción before you set off. In the opposite direction you need to get a permit from the police in Camiri. Take insect repellent with you – the flies and mosquitos can be outrageous.

To/From Uruguay

Two companies operate international buses between Asunción and Montevideo via Argentina and Brazil. The route is from Asunción to Encarnación, across the river to Posadas and then down through Argentina to Paso de los Libres, across into Brazil at Uruguaiana and then down to the Uruguay border at Bella Union and from there to Montevideo. Depending on what passport you hold, you will need transit visas for both Argentina and Brazil (though the Argentinians aren't too fussy if you haven't got one). If you hold a British passport it can take two weeks or longer to get an Argentine transit visa.

Tacuary have a bus once a week on Mondays at 9 am and *COIT* have a bus on Wednesdays and Saturdays at 8 am. The journey takes 25 hours and costs US$25. They're good buses with *semi-leito* seats, a toilet on board and drinks available.

GETTING AROUND
Bus

There's an extensive network of buses through Paraguay and most of the main roads are surfaced.

Asunción-Encarnación Four companies cover this route: *Rapido Yguassu* (at 7.45 am, 11.30 am, 5.30 and 11.30 pm daily); *La Encarnacena* (at 12.30 am, 8.30 am, 12 noon, 5 and 11 pm daily); *Alborada* (at 1.30, 4.15, 7 and 9.30 am and 1, 10.30 and 11.30 pm daily); and *Flecha de Oro* (at 12.30, 3, 5.30 and 8.30 am and 3, 6 and 9 pm daily). The journey takes about six hours.

Asunción-Puerto Stroessner There are at least 10 buses daily in either direction shared more or less equally between *Rapido Yguassu* and *Nuestra Señora de la Asunción*. The journey takes about 4½ hours and costs US$2.70.

Asunción-Concepción/Pedro Juan Caballero *Transportes Amambay* covers this route. They have buses daily at 10 am, 5.30 pm (both via Concepción) and 7.30 pm – direct. The journey to Concepción takes about five hours and to Pedro Juan Caballero 11 to 12 hours but there are major road works in progress so expect long delays. *Transportes y Turismo Paraguay (TTP)* also runs a daily bus to Concepción at 2.30 am (returns from Concepción at 12.30 pm daily) via Pozo Colorado. *NASA* also have less frequent buses.

Asunción-Filadelfia *NASA* operates buses to Filadelfia on Tuesday, Thursday, Saturday and Sunday at 7.30 am and on Wednesday and Sunday at 10 pm. The trip takes about seven hours along a good surfaced road. They also run buses to Mariscal Estigarribia on Tuesdays and Thursdays at 10 pm and on Saturdays at 6.30 pm, and to Campo Aceval on Monday, Wednesday and Thursday at 7.30 am.

Train

Trains in Paraguay are of the wood-burning steam engine variety and are really only for railway buffs – because they're so slow. The line from Asunción to Encarnación is, however, a pleasant journey and worth considering if you're not in a hurry. There are two trains per week in either direction (on Tuesdays and Thursdays at 6 pm from Asunción) which take about 26 hours and cost US$1.54 in 1st class and US$1.32 in 2nd class.

Boat

Flota Mercantil del Estado, Calle Estrella 672/682, Asunción, operate boats on the Paraguai River between Asunción and Concepción on a regular schedule. They leave Asunción every week on Tuesdays at 8 am, take 24 hours and cost US$8.30 (1st class) and US$5.45 (2nd class). Return times from Concepción depend on whether the boats continue on from Concepción to Bahia Negra – make enquiries since not all boats do this. First class consists of two and four-berth cabins. Men and women are separated in the four-berth first class cabins and in second class. The boats are excellent and it's a fine trip for both photography and relaxing. There is a restaurant on board. Book tickets at the office in Asunción.

There are a number of other smaller boats which go upriver but not on any regular schedule – enquire at the small dock next to the large one. You can also find cargo boats from there going to Corumbá (Brazil) – fares by negotiation.

Asunción

Asunción is the capital of Paraguay and the only city of any size in the country (population about 600,000). Back in the days of the Conquest it had the brief distinction of being the most important Spanish city in the southern half of the continent but its influence gradually waned with the growth of Buenos Aires. Large parts of the city are still in the traditional low-rise Spanish colonial style but skyscrapers are gradually rising in the centre. It's still very relaxing and there are even old trams which service parts of the city. It's quite a contrast to the larger cities of Argentina and especially of Brazil.

Information

The tourist office is on the junction of Alberdi and Oliva. They have maps of Asunción but precious little else. It's open 7 am to 12 noon and 3 to 6 pm. If you want information on the Chaco, contact the International Federation of Auto Clubs, on the corner of Brasíl and 25 de Mayo.

There are a number of casas de cambio in the streets adjacent to the Plaza de los Heroes particularly along Chile, Alberdi and 14 de Mayo. The rates can vary quite a bit so check them out before changing. Street dealers often offer less than the cambios. On Sundays you can change cash and cheques in the Plaza de Heros.

The Instituto Britanico is on Peru 615 on the corner with Azara; and the US Peace Corps office is on Brasil 365.

The English-language newspapers, *Buenos Aires Herrald* and the *Latin America Daily Post* are available at news stands on the Plaza de los Heroes. They're often better than *Time* or *Newsweek* and certainly cheaper.

Embassies

Argentina
Banco Nacional de Argentina, on the corner of Chile and Palma. Open Monday to Friday from 7 to 11 am.

Bolivia
Gral Bruguez 2002 near the junction with E Ayala (tel 226622).

Brazil
Banco do Brasil, Plaza de los Heroes. Open Monday to Friday from 8 am to 12 noon.

Uruguay
Av Brasil at the junction with Siria.

Things to See

The **Botanical Gardens**, 6½ km from Asunción, are worth visiting if you'd like to go for a walk in pleasant surroundings though botanically they're not exceptionally interesting. What is very interesting is the museum within the grounds which has some very good displays especially of insects, snakes and Siamese twins (of all things!). Entry to the museum is free. To get to the Gardens take local bus No 35 from along Cerro Corá. They're frequent and cost a few cents. The driver will tell you where to get off though you can't really miss the main gate anyway. Entry costs about seven cents plus US$0.15 per person if you want to camp there.

In the centre itself, it's worth strolling along the Avenida Republica where,

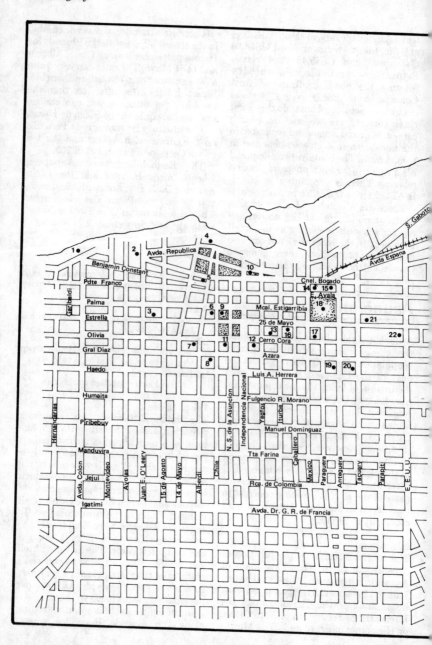

Asunción

1 Boat Dock & Customs
2 Government Palace
3 Flda Mercantil del Estado Boat Office
4 Legislative Palace
5 Post Office
6 Argintinian Office
7 Tourist Office
8 LAB
9 Plaza de les Herces
10 Cathedral
11 Brazillian Consulate
12 restaurant Germania
13 Hotel Hispania
14 Railway Station
15 Hotel Italia
16 Hotel Rosa
17 Residencial Antequra
18 Plaza Uruguay
19 Residencial Antequera
20 Hotel Lord
21 Restaurant Horizonte
22 Buon Appetito
24 Buffalo Saloon
25 Japanese Restaurant
26 Kang Nan Korean Restaurant

To Botanical Gardens

Avda. Gral. Artiges

Sarmiento

Avda. Saltos de Gualra

Avda. Mcal. Lopez

To Airport

Constitucion

Curubay IV

Pai Perez

23

Avda. Peru

Cnel. Luis Irrazabel

Rca. Francesa

Mayor Fleitas

Brazil

To Bus Terminal &
Pto. Pte Stroessner
Encarnacion

24
25
26

among other things, you can see the Cathedral and the Government Palace. There are good views across the river from many places.

One traveller suggested visiting the former Australian colony of **Nueva Australia** (now re-named *Hugo Stroessner*) about two hours by bus from Asunción. To get there take a bus to Colonel Oviedo on the road to Puerto Stroessner and ask the driver to let you off at the Hugo Stroessner turn-off (it's about halfway between San José and Colonel Oviedo). There's a café at the turn-off which does good cheap meals. From there it's another eight km to the colony – you can usually hitch a ride in a bullock cart with the local *campesinos*, many of whom are grandsons of the Australians who went there at the turn of the century. When you get to the colony, ask for Ricardo Smith. He's one of the few surviving members of the colony and will show you around and may offer you a meal.

It's also worth visiting **San Bernadino**, an hours drive by bus from Asunción. It's a relaxing, hilly area and you may well meet other travellers there. The cheapest place to stay is the *Santa Rita Hotel* in the village. Otherwise there is the *Casino Hotel* just outside the village. It's expensive if you want to stay there but it's a good place to dance and drink.

Places to Stay

There's a wide choice of budget hotels in Asunción so you'll have no trouble finding a room.

The cheapest place in town and one which has been popular with travellers for years is the Korean-run *Hotel Hispania*, Cerro Corá 265. It's a bizarre looking place which appears to have been designed by someone who took a fancy to re-creating French lingerie in concrete. It's a bit run-down and very basic but the sheets are crisp and clean, the walls freshly whitewashed, the rooms all have fans and there are no bugs. The communal showers are usually cold but the

management assured me there was hot water available (if there isn't – ask). It's very good value at US$1.25 each regardless of whether you occupy a single or a double room and it includes coffee and bread in the morning.

Another very cheap place is the *Hotel Italia*, Col Bogado 638 very close to the railway station. It's a large old place, Paraguayan-run and friendly. It's clean and the bathrooms have hot water. It costs US$1.55 a single or US$0.95 per person in rooms with more than one bed.

Of a much better standard are the *Hospedaje Oasis*, Azara 736; and the *Residencial Antiquera*, Antiquera 630. Both are Korean-run and I highly recommend the Antiquera. The Oasis is very clean and friendly, has new pleasant decor and a courtyard. It costs US$1.55 per person with own bath or share bath with one other room. There are hot showers. The Antiquera is run by a very friendly family, it's spotlessly clean both in the rooms and the communal showers and it's quiet, comfortable and pleasantly decorated. It costs US$2.35/$2.80 a single/double without bathroom (hot water in the communal showers) and without breakfast. You can wash clothes and dry them on the roof and there's use of a refrigerator.

Somewhat more expensive is the *Hotel Rosa*, 25 de Mayo 352. This is Taiwanese-run, is very clean and pleasant and has a relaxing, leafy courtyard upstairs. It costs US$3.15/$4.70 a single/double with own bathroom, hot water and air-conditioning.

Similar is the *Residencial Familiar*, Eligio Ayala 843, which is also very clean and run by a friendly family. It costs US$3.50 a double without own bath and US$5.50 a double with own bath including breakfast. Another in this range is the *Hotel Lord*, Tacuary 576. Again, it's Korean-run but the management are somewhat indifferent. It costs US$3.90/$6.25 a single/double with own bathroom.

Two others which you might like to try are the *Hotel Damasco*, Caballero 294, an old place with high ceilings, Korean-run and Paraguayan-staffed (giggly girls), which costs US$2.35/$4.70 a single/double without own bath and US$3.15 per person in rooms with their own bath; and the *Hotel Atlantico*, Mexico, which is Paraguayan-run but the management are indifferent. It costs US$3.90/$6.90 a single/double with own bathroom, hot water and breakfast.

The *Hotel Ipiranga*, Cerro Corá on the corner of Mexico, is also reasonable value at US$4.70 a double with own bathroom, hot water and including breakfast but Cerro Corá is a noisy street so you won't sleep much after 6.30 am in the front rooms.

Places to Eat

One of the best restaurants in Asunción is the *Restaurant Germania*, Cerro Corá 180. It's very popular with local people and has a quiet, fragrant, leafy courtyard as well as two internal rooms. They serve excellent food and the portions are generous. Most dishes cost around US$1 except for the special cuts of steak. The staff are friendly.

Similar is the *Restaurant Horizonte*, 25 de Mayo 809. This is a good, clean place which has been pleasantly refurbished and has a verandah. It's Korean-run, offers good food and generous portions and the prices are reasonable. Grilled fish, mixed salad, palm hearts, chips, a beer and one soft drink cost US$2.50. They also do good breakfasts. For snacks (*empanadas*) or for breakfast, the *Koki Bar*, Gral Diaz 235 near the junction with Chile, is a good bet. The staff are friendly and the food is good.

For a splurge, try the *Buon Appetito*, 25 de Mayo 1199. This restaurant is in an old town-house with a corner courtyard and is great for lunch or for sitting around with a bottle of wine during the siesta. It's a little on the expensive side but not by much.

With so many Koreans in town you might expect plenty of Korean restaurants,

and indeed there are. You can get the real thing at the *Kang Nan*, Av Peru 1129. This is the one rated as best by the Korean community. It's a little bit expensive (though we did, after all, order *pulgogi* – the most expensive dish in any Korean restaurant) but it's very cheap in comparison to Korean restaurants in neighbouring countries. The food is excellent and the service is great. If you're into Japanese food there is a restaurant quite close to this on Fariña close to the junction with Av Peru.

As far as bars go, there's quite a choice. Check out the *Choppería Chico*, Estados Unidos 422 between 25 de Mayo and Cerro Corá. It's run by a German and has large, chunky bar furniture, a pleasant atmosphere and a good sound system. Meals are available too. For a beer and/or a game of pool, the *Super Star Bar*, Azara 798, is a good bet. Don't be put off by the name – it isn't like that at all. It's pleasant, friendly, has two pool tables and the drinks are at normal prices. It's popular with local youths in the afternoons. The *Bar de la Estación* at Eligio Ayala 587 has also been recommended.

Many of the places where you can hear Paraguayan folk music have a cover charge and food can be expensive so make sure you know what you are getting into. Try the *Hermitage* at 15 de Agosto; the *Paraguay-Choferes del Chaco* (some distance from the centre); *Restaurant El Rosedal*, Estados Unidos and Figueroa; and the beer garden opposite the Hospital Bautista, Av Argentina, Villa Mora.

Getting Around

The long-distance bus terminal is a long way from the centre of the city at Av Republica Argentina and Av Fernando da la Mora. To get from there to the city centre take local bus Nos 8 (the best), 31 or 38. They take about 15 minutes and cost US$0.10. The stop is on the main road opposite the front of the bus terminal. From the centre of the city to the terminal these buses are best caught on Calle Cerro Corá. If you're taking a bus from the terminal or going there to buy a ticket there's an entry charge of about eight cents to get inside! Buy your token at one of the bus offices on either side of the barrier.

Between the airport and the city centre take local bus Nos 30 or 206. There are also more expensive minibuses available. The airport is 15 km from the centre and a taxi costs about US$7.

CONCEPCIÓN

A small town north of Asunción on the banks of the Paraguaí with a population of about 35,000, Concepción has an interesting market but otherwise is just a way station en route to the Brazilian border at Pedro Juan Caballero. It's also the terminus of the boat trip up the river from Asunción.

Places to Stay & Eat

There's a very limited choice of hotels in Concepción. One of the cheapest places to stay is the hotel above the *Bar Victoria*. Otherwise, try for one of the cheaper rooms without bathroom at the *Hotel Frances*. Good, reasonably priced food can be found at the *Hotel Paraguay*.

ENCARNACIÓN

Facing the Argentinian town of Posadas across the Paraná River, Encarnación has that weathered, rural look about it – dusty streets, bullock carts and gauchos – but it's a busy port as well. It's also likely to change dramatically over the next few years as it has become a supply centre for the Yacyreta Dam further down river which is being jointly built by Paraguay and Argentina.

Things to See

The main point of interest (other than that the town is a crossing point into Argentina) are the ruins of the Jesuit *reducción* at Trinidad about 20 km north-west of the town. The ruins are not only extensive but also quite substantial despite the ravages of time. Reconstruction work is going on at present. You can get there either by bus from Encarnación (about half an hour) or get a group together and hire a colectivo. There's a very friendly café right next to the ruins where you can buy a good meal but there's no accommodation in Trinidad itself.

There's another equally impressive Jesuit ruin at San Ignacio Mirí on the Posadas-Iguazú road across the river which is worth visiting if you're heading in that direction.

Places to Stay

Most of the cheapies are around the railway station. They include the *Hospedaje Comercio* and the *Hospedaje El Torbellino*. Another very friendly place with excellent food but very basic facilities is the *Pensión Villa Alegre*, Antequerra 951. The *Hotel Suizo* has also been recommended as a cheap place to stay and has very friendly staff.

FILADELFIA

This is the main Mennonite town in the centre of the Chaco. If you're interested in seeing what they do out there, it's worth a visit. For accommodation it's best to ask around for a room in a house as the few hotels are pretty expensive. If you can't find a place on the first day you arrive, stay at the *Hotel Loma Plata* in the meantime. It is in a small village outside Filadelfia itself.

PEDRO JUAN CABALLERO

This Paraguayan border town is in fact a twin town, since it's part of the Brazilian border town of Ponta Porã. There is no border as such – you just walk from one to the other whenever you like. If you're travelling further into Brazil however, you need to go about it officially. First visit the Delegación de Gobierno in the Paraguayan half for an exit stamp, then the Federal police in the Brazilian half for an entry stamp. If you need a visa for

Brazil, there is a Brazilian consulate in P J Caballero.

There wouldn't be any real reason to stay there, but if you arrive late in the evening you could stay at the *Hotel Peral Fa*. This is about as cheap as you will find. The bus terminal is about opposite the Brazilian consulate.

Peru

Peru, more than any other South American country, was the crucible which nourished one of the world's greatest and most fascinating civilisations, and as far as we know, it did this without any contact with simultaneous developments in Europe, Asia and Africa. The Inca are the most well-known of the branches of this civilisation but there are many others whose origins go back into the mists of time and whose ruins dot the Peruvian countryside. No other South American country can compare with Peru as a ruin-hunter's paradise, and thousands of travellers make the journey there every year in search of the legend which these people left. Indeed the legend is alive and well and no-one who sets eyes on Machu Picchu, the Nazca lines, Chachapoyas, the Moche pyramids or the vast adobe ruins of Chan Chan is going to go away disappointed.

The Spanish conquest shattered the very foundations of this indigenous culture and its destruction has had a profound effect on the Peruvian psyche ever since. On the one hand, the descendants of the people who created that amazing civilisation without any knowledge of the wheel, iron, heavy draught animals or the written word look inwards to the fragments which survive after centuries of oppression and, on the other, the blancos and mestizos look to Spain for their cultural roots.

Like Ecuador and Bolivia, Peru is an example of a dual society. The Indians (better known as campesinos these days), who still make up about half of the country's population, are a disenfranchised and dispossessed people looked on with veiled contempt by the blancos and mestizos who, until recently, have regarded them as little more than lazy, coca-chewing savages who can be ignored in the affairs of the nation.

However times are changing, albeit slowly. The Sendero Luminoso Maoist guerrillas in the highlands around Ayacucho may well be an isolated movement committed to using violence in the face of oppression and they are certainly inspired by a mestizo intellectual but, out of all proportion to their actual numbers, they are forcing the government to a realisation that the arrogant prejudices of the past must be broken and that drastic and genuine reform is an urgent necessity.

So too, the increasing numbers of tourists who flock to Peru to see the colourful festivals and markets of the campesinos and the ruined achievements of their predecessors, have prompted the government to heavily promote their culture. This may well have restored to them some degree of respect and has brought modest wealth to some communities, yet the vast majority are still condemned to a bleak existence scratching a bare living from the soil in the harsh environment of the 3000-metre-high Andean plateau. They have one of the lowest literacy rates on the continent and most live on a diet which is deficient in everything but starch. Many are outside the money economy entirely and some two million of them speak only Quechua, the main Indian language. It was not until very recently that this language was made the second official language of Peru and was introduced into the schools. Not that most campesino children get much chance to attend school.

The contemptuous attitude toward the indigenous population goes right back to the Spanish conquest. Pizarro and his band of ruthless and desperate adventurers arrived in Peru when the Inca empire was at its height and spread over what is today most of Peru, Bolivia, Ecuador and the northern parts of Chile and Argentina. Most of the Spanish

invaders came from the poverty-stricken provinces of Extramadura and Andalusia and were in search of gold and an easy life.

They were fortunate in having arrived at a time when the Inca empire lay in a weakened state following a civil war between Huayna Capac's two sons, Huascar and Atahualpa, for sole control of the empire. Had Pizarro arrived at any other time it is possible that the Incas could have held the Spanish at bay and the history of South America might have been quite different. As it is, Pizarro lured Atahualpa, the victor in the civil war, into a trap at Cajamarca. An enormous ransom in gold and silver was set for Atahualpa's release yet, as soon as it was fulfilled, Pizarro had the Inca emperor strangled. The empire fell apart – though not as abruptly as some historians suggest – and the stage was set for the wholesale destruction of a unique culture.

With an avarice little short of staggering, the Spanish conquistadores combed the empire for every precious-metal object they could lay their hands on and in their haste to exploit gold and silver deposits, herded millions of Indians to their deaths as forced labourers in the mines and on the plantations established by Pizarro's successors.

After the Spanish throne asserted its authority over the new colonies, most of this gold and silver found its way back to Spain where it was squandered in high living and in financing the numerous wars which Spain waged in attempts to gain political and military supremacy in Europe. Meanwhile, in South America, the collective-farming system – the basis of Inca society – was destroyed. The huge plantations of corn, yucca, kidney bean, peanut and sweet potato which had once fed a large part of the population fell into ruin, as did the magnificent system of aqueducts and water channels which once provided irrigation for them. The Indian cities were torn down to provide building stone for the new Spanish cities which rose in their place, and the Catholic religion was imposed rigorously, using any possible means to effect conversion however superficial. Every aspect of colonial life was controlled by the policy-makers in Spain and designed to ensure the maximum return of benefits to the mother country.

Nevertheless, although Peru became the glittering centrepiece of its overseas empire, Spain couldn't have everything its own way. Many ancient customs, particularly religious beliefs and practices, merely went underground to re-surface later in a different guise. The cult of the Virgin Mary and Catholicism's numerous saints and martyrs provided a convenient medium through which the Indian gods could be reborn and kept alive. The Church was well aware of this development and of how superficial conversion was in most cases, but in those early days of empire it dared not challenge it for fear of widespread revolt. As a result, Catholicism in the highlands of Ecuador, Peru and Bolivia is very different from that found elsewhere in the southern part of the continent. Attend any Indian fiesta and see for yourself how strongly pagan they are.

The fact that the Spanish weren't able to suppress such a vital culture entirely comes as no surprise when you take a look at the history of pre-Columbian Peru. The Incas were merely the inheritors of an amalgam of cultural threads which can be traced back to 2000 BC, when a coastal civilisation sprang up near present-day Supe. It was followed by the Chavín culture, which also started on the coast but quickly spread up into the mountains. Its influence eventually stretched from Piura to Pisco. The most important ruins of this culture stand at Chavín de Huantar near Huáraz.

The next major development came with the rise of the Nazca in the south and the Mochica in the north, both of which flourished between 400 and 800 AD. The Nazca, of course, as any UFO convert must know, were responsible for creating the gigantic animal and geometric figures cut into the stony desert near the town of the same name. They are the subject of endless speculation as to their inspiration and purpose, though it can probably be said that von Daniken's claims are a little far-fetched. Maria Reiche's contention that they represent an ancient calendar is far more plausible.

The Mochica are noted for their exceptionally beautiful and realistic designs on pottery, examples of which you can see in almost any museum in Peru. They were also responsible for building the largest pre-Columbian structures in South America – the pyramids of the sun and moon a few km south of Trujillo. Unlike the stone pyramids of Teotihuacán in Mexico, the Moche pyramids were constructed out of millions of adobe bricks.

The southern coastal cultures gradually spread into the altiplano and contributed to the rise of the Tihuanaco civilisation around the southern end of Lake Titicaca between the 10th and 13th centuries. Although they were the originators of the cult of the weeping Sun God – adopted as the state religion by the Incas who were to follow – very little else is known about them other than what can be gleaned from the ruins which they left at Tihuanaco, in what is today northern Bolivia.

The Incas themselves entered the chronicles of history in the 11th century in the valley of the Urubamba near Cuzco. They were contemporaries of the Chimú whose capital at Chan Chan near Trujillo covered an enormous area (some 25 square km) and included step pyramids, walled compounds, irrigated gardens and gigantic stone-lined reservoirs. At its height, Chan Chan ruled over 1000 km of coast up into Ecuador and had a well-developed mass-production system of pottery and fabric manufacture as well as gold artefacts. The wealthy city eventually fell to the Incas in the last phase of Inca expansion in the mid-1400s.

What the Incas themselves contributed to the cultural evolution of South America was not so much a further refinement of the arts – with the exception of their superb mortarless stone building technique – but an efficient and centralised social and military organisation, excellent communications and a vast programme of public works designed to irrigate the desert, prevent soil erosion in the mountains and increase crop yields. Many of the terraces which were built at this time are still in use today and can be seen at their best in the Urubamba valley. Research suggests that the system worked well, as far as ensuring that there were adequate supplies of food, though of course there was a price to pay.

Social cohesion was maintained by the imposition of a state religion and language (Quechua) and by re-settling groups of Quechua speakers whose loyalty could be relied on in newly conquered areas. The Incas also adopted an ingenious system of manipulating the remembered histories of the various tribes and cultures which they conquered. Since no script had been invented by any of the South American cultures, everything had to be orally transmitted from one generation to another. So in order to integrate newly conquered peoples into their empire, the Incas introduced a class of officials whose function was to selectively forget or alter essential parts of their history and traditions and weave what remained into the 'official' Inca history, with the Incas, naturally, cast in the role of civiliser. Stalin would have been green with envy at how successful they were in this venture as can be gleaned from how little we know about other cultures which flourished in Peru before the arrival of the Spanish.

The Inca empire, like that of the Aztecs, was pyramidal in structure but with the important difference that the head of state, the Sapa Inca, was a hereditary ruler and regarded as the incarnation of the Sun God. His authority

and that of his regional governors was absolute, as was submission to the *ayllu*, or basic earth-cell commune, for the farmer. Personal freedom as we understand it today did not exist – not that it did anywhere anywhere else in the world at that time. This extreme centralisation of authority goes some way to explain how a small and ridiculously outnumbered band of Spaniards were able to take over an empire by capturing and murdering one person.

The truth of the matter was that it didn't collapse quite so precipitously. Aware of the precarious nature of his conquest, Pizzaro was forced to maintain appearances by installing a puppet emperor, Manco II, at Cuzco in 1534. For two years there was an uneasy co-existence between the Incas and the Spaniards until the greed and cruelty of the conquerors grew to such a pitch that an explosion was inevitable. Manco II gathered together an army of 50,000 warriors and besieged Cuzco. He came within a hair's breadth of victory but at the last minute was forced to retreat to Ollantaytambo and from there, being no match for the Spanish cavalry, to Vitcos. Shortly after this he was surprised there by a Spanish force led by Almagro and Pizarro's brother, Gonzalo. His forces were decimated, his son captured and the remnants of his army were forced to retreat to Vilcabamba on the edge of the sierra. A new capital was founded at Vilcabamba and all bridges into the kingdom were cut and passes heavily garrisoned. From this citadel, Manco II was able to continually harass the Spanish forces as far away as Ayacucho and Lima, while constructing a modern army using captured Spaniards, horses and war materials.

Meanwhile, jealousies and rivalries split the conquistadores into several camps. Pizarro had Almagro executed for conspiracies real or imagined and then was himself assassinated by Almagro's supporters. They in turn were hunted by Pizarro's brother and forced to take refuge at Vilcabamba. This marriage of convenience between sworn enemies lasted only a short time and, in 1545 after an attempt to negotiate peace with a viceroy sent out by the Spanish throne to establish royal authority over the conquistadores, Manco was assassinated by the Spaniards who had taken refuge with him.

Manco's son, Titu Cusi, succeeded his father but refused to leave Vilcabamba despite assurances of a safe passage, being rightfully suspicious of the Spanish. Missionaries were sent to Vilcabamba in an attempt to Christianise the Indians but they met with little success and in the end made such a nuisance of themselves that they were expelled. In the meantime, Titu Cusi died of pneumonia and was replaced by his son, Tupac Amaru. The Spanish Viceroy, angered by the expulsion of the missionaries, decided to wipe out the last vestiges of the Inca empire and attacked Vilcabamba in 1572 with an overwhelmingly superior army. After a number of set-backs, the armies of Tupac Amaru were routed but Tupac himself escaped, leaving Vilcabamba in flames and everything of value was taken away and hidden in the jungle. The bulk of this treasure has never been found and the legend of it has continued to attract adventurers right up to the present day. Vilcabamba itself wasn't rediscovered until the 1960s but what was truly a 'lost city of the Incas' – Machu Picchu – was rediscovered by Hiram Bingham in the early 1900s. This legendary place with its incomparable setting is today *the* attraction of Peru.

Following the destruction of Vilcabamba, Tupac Amaru foolishly allowed himself to be lured back to Cuzco by the promise of an amnesty. Typically, the Spanish had him tortured to death along with his chieftains and followed this up by hunting down and murdering anyone connected with the royal line. The Inca empire finally died. There were further Indian revolts in 1780 under the leadership of the self-styled Tupac Amaru II and again in 1814, but the same fate befell Tupac Amaru II as did his Vilcabamba predecessor – he, his wife, his children and his supporters were tortured to death in the Plaza de Armas at Cuzco.

After the consolidation of Spanish power, Lima became the centre of the enormous viceroyalty of Peru, covering the whole of Spanish South America until, as a result of increasing immigration, development and corruption, it became too unwieldy an administrative unit. It was then split up into three, with new Viceroyalties being established at Bogotá and Buenos Aires. By the time the Napoleonic Wars engulfed Europe and most of Central and South America were clamouring for independence, there was probably no area of Latin America less ready for revolt than Peru. Centuries of easy money, privilege and the abundance of slave labour had resulted in a colony dominated by wealthy *peninsulares* (Spanish citizens born in Spain) and *criollos* (people of Spanish origin born in the colonies). They saw little reason to revolt against the Spanish crown and this was well understood by San Martín, who had shipped his Army of the Andes up to Peru after completing the liberation of Argentina and Chile. Much to the annoyance of his lieutenants, San Martín waited a long time before advancing on Lima as he saw no point in 'liberating' a city which was subsequently going to be politically hostile. Nevertheless, Lima was entered in 1821 and the independence of Peru declared with much of the country still under the control of Royalist troops commanded by the Viceroy, La Serna.

Being too weak to face them in pitched battle, San Martín sailed for Guayaquil to solicit help from Bolívar. Just what happened at that historic meeting between the two leading lights of the independence movement isn't known except that Bolívar had no sympathy for San Martín's monarchical ideas and the

military assistance which he offered was insufficient. San Martín retired to Europe disillusioned and it was left to Bolívar and Sucre to complete the liberation of Ecuador, Peru and Bolivia with their victory over the Royalists at Ayacucho.

Other than an abortive attempt at federation with Bolivia in the 1830s and a brief war with Spain in 1866, the first 50 or so years of independence passed uneventfully. It was during this period that nitrate began to be used extensively as a fertiliser by the industrialised nations. There were large deposits of it in the Atacama desert which until then was enclosed within the borders of Bolivia and Peru. The existence of this nitrate had been common knowledge for centuries but it had previously only been of value in the manufacture of gunpowder. Suddenly the desert became a very interesting tract of real estate. Both Bolivia and Peru had traditionally neglected this area and it was the Chileans who were to begin the exploitation of the deposits. Encouraged by British business interests and others, it wasn't too long before a convenient pretext was found for a dispute over sovereignty. In the war that followed, known as the War of the Pacific (1879-1883), Chile defeated both Bolivia and Peru, depriving the former of its Pacific littoral and the port of Antofagasta, and the latter of its southernmost territory up as far as Tacna. The losers have never accepted the loss of their territory and every so often, either in concert or individually, they threaten to go to war with Chile in order to regain the lands which they lost. The last time this happened was in 1978 when there was a good deal of sabre-rattling in Bolivia with some degree of support from Peru.

Like other Latin American nations, Peru has had a long history of coups and military dictatorships sprinkled here and there with periods of civilian rule. Reform has been desperately slow. One of the most radical attempts was made by Haya de la Torre who formed the Alianza

Popular Revolucionaria Americana in 1924. The 'Apristas,' as they were known, advocated the return of the land to the Indian communities, an economic programme which would enable those farmers to get beyond mere subsistence farming, a campaign to eliminate illiteracy, and progressive labour laws. Faced with this, the ruling oligarchy panicked and hounded la Torre for three decades, five years of which he spent in political asylum at the Colombian embassy in Lima. He was eventually allowed to return to the political arena and campaign for election in 1962, having made suitable pro-capitalist and pro-landowner noises. Although he won, the military immediately annulled the election result.

The next attempt at land and labour reform was made in 1968 when armed forces led by General Velasco Alvarado deposed the civilian president Belaúnde Terry whose economic programme, though well-intentioned, had become alarmingly extravagant and was leading to the resurgence of the Apristas. Alvarado wasn't a typical Latin American military dictator at all and saw the army not as champions of the status quo but as an agent for change. He nationalised North American oil companies but in such a way that he avoided US retaliatory sanctions and embarked on a programme of radical land reform. For a while the *campesinos* enthusiastically took up his lead and began organising farming collectives on land granted to them by the new government but it all came to an abrupt end in 1975 with another military coup. Politics took a sharp turn to the right. The farming collectives were starved of funds and much of the land was given back to its former owners. Nevertheless, inflation began to get out of control and the economy rapidly deteriorated. The IMF was reluctant to provide a loan until the USSR offered what the Peruvians needed. Then the IMF miraculously came up with US\$600 million.

Civilian elections were again held in 1980 and Belaúnde Terry was returned to the Presidency. This time he proceeded more cautiously with reform but the economic climate was against him. With the industrialised nations in recession, the price of oil consuming vast amounts of most Third World countries' budgets and the US dollar riding high, Peru was faced with drastically reducing the budget for social and economic reform in order to finance its external debt repayments. Opposition to the government grew apace and in the elections of 1985 APRA at last found itself in power with Alan García its President. One of García's first announcements was that repayments on Peru's external debt would be limited to 10% of the country's earnings from exports. It remains to be seen whether his government can maintain and even accelerate the pace of economic and land reform in Peru and so carry the people with him but, at present, he continues to ride a wave of huge popular support. Other Latin American countries enthusiastically welcomed his stand on external debt repayments and were themselves in the process of rescheduling their own debt repayments.

Peru is, without doubt, most travellers' favourite Latin American country and deservedly so. Having been the cradle of civilisation and then the centre of the Spanish American empire, it has endless fascinating and incomparable archaeological sites, romantic and unspoilt colonial towns and colourful, rustic, Indian villages. Before you visit Peru read some books on the Indian civilisations that developed and get an idea of which of the sites you'd like to explore. One of the most readable accounts is *The Ancient Sun Kingdoms of the Americas* by Victor Wolfgang von Hagen, Paladin 1973 (in English).

Though it is important as such, Peru isn't just an archaeologist's dream. It's a country of countless variations from the bizarre, narrow, sandy desert which runs the length of the coast, to the snow-covered peaks which rise to over 6000 metres from the Andean altiplano (itself around 3000 metres) and down to the lush rainforests of the Amazon basin. There are superb Indian markets with weavings and carpets you won't see anywhere else in the world; riotous fiestas of fantasy and legend which often rage non-stop for as long as a week; one of the highest and largest inland lakes – Titicaca – where whole villages live (and play football!) on reed rafts; some of the most spectacular railway journeys in the world – not to mention bus journeys – and, of course, the Inca Trail to Machu Picchu through the magnificent Urubamba River valley.

Not a great deal has changed in Peru since colonial times. Travel in many places is still an adventure into dust, rocks and punctures. Somehow it just adds to the memory and however rough you might have felt after 18 hours on a bus through the highlands, you'll want to be back there within weeks of leaving! Whatever you do, don't attempt to rush Peru. Nothing gets rushed here, and you can afford not to be – the cost of living is one of the lowest on the continent.

VISAS

These are not required by nationals of Austria, Belgium, Canada, Denmark, Finland, France, Germany (West), Greece, Irish Republic, Italy, Japan, Luxembourg, Netherlands, Norway, Portugal, Spain, Sweden, Switzerland, UK and USA. The usual permitted length of stay is 90 days but this is sometimes reduced to 30 days depending on your nationality. Extensions up to the full 90 days are easy to get, cost US$20 (payable in soles) and take 48 hours. No onward ticket or 'sufficient funds' are asked for up to an additional 60 days but if you want 90 days then you must have an onward ticket. The Immigration office in Lima is at Av 28 de Julio No 1145.

Avoid overstaying your visa as fines for this are high – US$20 per day for the first day rising to US$50 per day.

MONEY

US$1 = 17,800 soles (cash) & 17,000 soles (cheques) (late 1985)

At present Peru is in the process of changing over from one unit of currency (the old *sol*, plural *soles*), to another (the new *inti*). The relationship between the two units is 1000 sol = 1 inti. So far only inti coins have been minted and there are no inti bank notes but this will change so keep an eye on the situation. The new inti coins look very similar to the old sol coins so it's easy to be confused. Unscrupulous shopkeepers and the like are obviously going to take advantage of this for some time to come so watch out. There should be no such confusion with bank notes (the smallest bank note is 500 soles).

Peru's economy, like those of Bolivia, Brazil and Mexico to name just three, is in bad shape and inflation hovers at well over 100%. As a result, the rate of exchange is rising constantly against the US dollar (and other hard currencies) so you're advised not to change a lot of money at once. Indeed, changing money in Peru is one of those chores which you'll get used to very quickly – even though you'll have to do it two or three times a week. It doesn't pay to change money at banks, not only because their rates are generally poor but because it's time-consuming (there are a lot of forms to fill in) and, if you're changing cheques, they're likely to be minutely scrutinised and treated like forgeries. Banks also charge commission and there's often a limit on how much you can change at one time (usually US$100). Always change cheques either at a casa de cambio (very quick, no fuss and no commission) or privately at a shop which stocks imported goods (and so needs hard currency to buy them with).

With cash you have the choice of the shops, casas de cambio or street changers. There are plenty of the latter in the main cities, usually congregated along certain streets. It's technically illegal to do this but you wouldn't know it, given the openness with which they conduct their business in full view of the police and the army. Be sure to count your money carefully if you change on the street, though few people seem to have problems.

There's no check on how many soles you bring into or take out of the country.

In the same way that you can buy soles for US dollars on the street or at a casa de cambio, you can also buy US dollars for soles. Naturally, the transaction is pegged in favour of the dealer but if you want to re-convert excess soles before you leave Peru then it's well worth it. Expect to pay 2-4% depending on who you change with and where. Don't expect to be able to do this at Jorge Chavín airport in Lima.

Airport departure tax for international flights is US$10. Government tax on international airline tickets is a numbing 21% and even 9% on domestic flights. Buy the former elsewhere!

You can buy film in almost any town or city in Peru but it's naturally more expensive at major tourist sites so avoid buying it in those areas. In Lima and Arequipa you can expect to pick up Fuji colour negative film (36 frames) for about US$2.50. The same in Kodak or Agfa is about US$3.50. It's possible to buy the same, but several months out of date, for less than US$2 (it's rarely been refrigerated). Slide film is more difficult to find and there's rarely any choice other than ASA 100. Expect to pay US$7.50 to $8 for 36 frames excluding developing.

COSTS

It's very difficult to quote costs accurately in Peru because the exchange rate changes so rapidly. As an example, in early '85 a museum might have charged 10,000 soles admission, say about US$2. By mid-year it would have become US$1, by the end of the year US$0.50. Perhaps they then multiply the admission charge by five and make it 50,000 soles which brings the charge back up to US$2.50. So prices quoted depend very much on when they were last adjusted for inflation. Restaurant and hotel prices tend to be adjusted much more often than museum prices or local transport costs.

THEFT

Keep your wits about you in this country and especially when walking down crowded streets with bags on your shoulders. Keep cameras and other valuables out of sight. Keep nothing in the back pockets of trousers and have bags in front of your body. Thieves often work in groups of three or more so beware of being distracted while the rest go to work. Take special care in crowded situations – bus and train stations (especially while boarding buses or trains) and markets are the most notorious places.

The favourite trick at present (this happens to almost everyone) is that one of them squirts washing-up liquid or shampoo onto the back of your shoulder and then points this out to you. The mess distracts your attention, the thieves move in professing concern, their hands roving over your clothing. Then suddenly they melt back into the crowds or simply take to their heels. You've lost your wallet and/or the contents of your bag. All this happens in broad daylight in full view of hundreds of people. Cuzco and Lima are the major blackspots. Unfortunately you have to be suspicious of anybody who tries to talk to you.

If you have something stolen it's not worth the time and trouble reporting it unless the value is over US$20. If it is over US$20 go to the PIP office or, if there is no PIP office, to the Guardia Civil (the latter may not be able to speak any English so you'll need a good command of Spanish or an interpreter). Before you go there you need to buy *papel sellado* (stamped paper) which you get for a few cents at any *papellería* (stationer's). At the PIP you make a statement about the circumstances and itemise what was stolen along with the estimated value. The PIP officer will type this out on the *papel sellado* and then take it to his chief to be signed and rubber-stamped. They'll give you a copy which you must keep if you intend making an insurance claim when you return home.

If you have to go to a Guardia office, they will only deal with you if you say the loss happened in the immediate area. If you say it happened elsewhere they'll send you back there to report it. If you're not sure when it happened or simply can't afford the time or expense of backtracking, then use your imagination. After all, if you've had something stolen, what difference does it make when or where? – you still lost it.

If you have your passport stolen then, in most cases, it's back to Lima for a time-consuming and expensive experience in getting it replaced. Most embassies will insist on telexing the passport office in the country of your origin – for which you must pay. When you've been issued with a new one you'll have to go to the Immigration Office to get a new stamp in it. For this you'll need a photocopy of the first few pages of your new passport and another sheet of *papel sellado*. Both of these are available in the foyer. The new stamp is generally issued the same day.

GETTING THERE
To/From Ecuador

In the north the main point of entry is by road from Machala (Ecuador) to Tumbes (Peru) via Huaquillas/Aguas Verdes (border). Between the border and Tumbes you have the choice of colectivo or bus. If you're coming from Ecuador, try to get to Tumbes early in the day as competition for tickets on the long-distance buses heading south can be heavy.

There is another, less-used route between Ecuador and Peru along the Piura-Sullana-Macará-Loja road via La Tina (border). There are several changes of bus involved along this route as well as five checkpoints on the Peruvian side and three more on the Ecuadorian side. *Transportes Chiclayo* cover the section between Piura and Sullana (several buses daily) but after that there are no buses through to La Tina so you must hitch with trucks. There's usually two a day, which generally cost about US$1 and take six hours – it's a very poor road. From La Tina to the first Ecuadorian town you must take a colectivo or walk, after which there are buses to Loja and Cuenca. You'll be lucky to do Piura to Cuenca in less than three days.

Both these border crossings are open from 8 am to 6 pm. All passport formalities take place at the border.

To/From Chile

Entry to Chile is by road or rail from Tacna to Arica. There are buses and colectivos between the two, but the colectivos are much faster and more convenient. They cost US$1.75 and take one hour. The driver handles all the passport formalities though there may be a cursory baggage check at the Chilean customs. Otherwise there are no problems at either border. In Tacna the colectivos can be found along Mendoza (see the street map). In Arica they are at the junction of Chacabuco and Colón.

If you don't want to stay in Tacna on your way south then there are buses direct from Arequipa to Arica (and vice versa) by *TEPSA*. These are sleeper buses which take only 19 passengers and the fare is US$7. Meals are served on the coach.

There are also two trains in either direction between Tacna and Arica at 11 am and 2 pm from both places. The fare is about US$1 and the journey takes about 1½ hours.

To/From Bolivia

There are a number of choices if you're heading to or from Bolivia:

Puno-La Paz via Copacabana This is possibly the most interesting route and the one favoured by most travellers. The first leg of the journey is by bus or colectivo from Puno to Yungayo and then to Copacabana or direct to Copacabana. Most travellers take one of the daily minibuses or colectivos which go direct to Copacabana. They leave at 8 am, cost about US$3.50 and take four hours. Book a seat in advance at either the *Turis Coop* colectivo office or at one of the travel agents, all of which are along Calle Tacna. The same companies also sell through-tickets to La Paz (US$6, six to seven hours) involving a change to a normal bus (no further charge) at Copacabana. Between Copacabana and La Paz you have to take a ferry across the Straits of Tiquina but this doesn't involve changing buses. It's a good surfaced road all the way from Puno to La Paz via Copacabana. All passport formalities take place at the border. You can change money at Yungayo and the rate is often better than in Bolivia.

Puno-La Paz direct The second choice is from Puno to La Paz direct via Desaguadero and Guaqui. There are daily departures, usually at 8 am, by minibus from Puno to the border at Guaqui where you change to a normal bus for the ride into La Paz. The journey takes eight hours and costs US$6. Most of the buses stop at Tiahuanaco (the pre-Inca archaeological site) for half an hour to give you time to see the ruins. Passport formalities are all taken care of at the border. The road between Puno and Guaqui is surfaced and in excellent condition but from Guaqui to La Paz it's very rough. There is a passport check at Desaguadero.

Puno-La Paz hovercraft route The third choice is a bus-hovercraft-bus combination which involves taking a bus from Puno to Juli, followed by a hovercraft from there to Copacabana, and then another bus to La Paz. It's considerably more expensive than the first two routes at US$128, though the hovercraft does stop off at the *Island of the Sun* giving you time to see the Inca ruins there. The first bus leaves Puno at 7 am and you arrive in La Paz about 6.30 pm.

Puno-La Paz steamer route The fourth choice is a Lake Titicaca steamer and train combination which costs US$23.50. The steamer, the *Inca*, departs Puno on Wednesdays at 8 pm (and on the return trip from Guaqui on Fridays at the same time), and arrives in Guaqui 13 hours later where passengers transfer to a train which takes them to La Paz (a three-hour journey). The price of the ticket covers the steamer and the train as well as a bunk and meals on board the steamer. The main disadvantage of this route is that the steamer sails at night so you don't see Lake Titicaca. If you do decide to take it, tickets must be bought at the wharf on Wednesday evening at 6 pm.

Puno-La Paz via Lake Ticaca boat A fifth possibility is the trip offered by *Transturin* for US$55. The boat stops at the Island of the Sun. The bus departs Puno at 6.30 am and you arrive in La Paz at 6 pm. Bookings at Av Giron Taina 201 in Puno, and Av Comacho 1321 La Paz.

To/From Brazil

The only direct route (other than flying) between Peru and Brazil is by riverboat. The first leg of the journey is from Iquitos to Islandia which is very close to Tabatinga (Brazil) and Leticia (Colombia) (there are local ferries between all these places). There are no regular departures as such but riverboats generally leave several times per week. The trip should cost about US$10 without food though sometimes this fare can include food. Often there are no cabins so you need a hammock and mosquito net. There are further details in the chapter on Brazil.

If you decide to go this way you first have to get to Iquitos. There are no roads from the rest of Peru to Iquitos so you must either fly or first go to Pucallpa (where the road ends) and take a riverboat from there to Iquitos. One riverboat which has been recommended along this stretch is the *Otita* captained by Sr Samuel. It departs Thursday at 5 pm and arrives Sunday. The fare is US$18 including food. The crew are friendly and trustworthy and the boat stops at several towns and villages en route to pick up or put down cargo and passengers. Another bunch of travellers recently paid US$13 per person without food on a cargo boat between Pucallpa and Iquitos.

GETTING AROUND

Air

Peru's internal air routes are shared by two companies, *AeroPeru* and *Faucett*. As with other Andean countries, domestic air fares are relatively cheap – often not much more than three times the price of the equivalent bus fare – so it's worth considering making a few hops here and there if your time is limited, if the road is rough, or if you've simply had enough of interminable bus journeys over boulder-strewn river beds. Where the two airlines fly the same routes their prices are the same and except on the major routes, they generally share the days of the week between them. If you're thinking of taking a few flights then get hold of a copy of each airline's flight schedule and price list as soon as you can. There's little point in giving a comprehensive table of flights and fares here as these change too frequently.

There is a third internal airline run by the Peruvian military called *Grupo 8*. It has an extensive schedule of flights, especially to towns in the lowlands east of the Andes and its fares are about half those of *AeroPeru* or *Faucett* so, wherever possible, fly with *Grupo 8* if you want to save money. Their Lima-Cuzco flight for instance costs US$35 as opposed to US$84 with the others. *Grupo 8* may not have offices in some town centres (like Cuzco) so you have to go out to the airport and get your name on the list they keep there. Peruvians are given priority over foreigners so it helps to get your name on the waiting list as soon as possible. They're especially useful for flights between Iquitos and Pucallpa or Yurimaguas.

There is a 9% government tax on internal flights.

Both *AeroPeru* and *Faucett* are often criticised for delays, cancellations and over-booking, especially on flights in the mountains. No compensation is offered for any inconvenience this may cause, so if it's vital that you make an international flight connection in Lima, don't leave flying back there from some other city in Peru until the day before – you might not make it. Always re-confirm a booking 24 hours before departure regardless of what a ticket clerk may have told you to the contrary.

Bus

Buses (and colectivos) are the major means of transportation in Peru. There are a number of large companies which cover most of the long-distance routes – *TEPSA, Roggero, Sudamericana, Hidalgo, Ormeño* and *Morales Moralitos* – and you'll find them in most major towns and cities. If possible, avoid *Morales Moralitos* buses – they've earned the well-deserved nickname, *Morales Mortalitos.*

Elsewhere, particularly in the mountains and along minor roads, smaller companies cover more localised routes. Where roads are surfaced (the coast road and a number of major routes into the highlands), the buses tend to be fairly new, relatively comfortable and reasonably punctual though this isn't universally the case (we've had bad reports about TEPSA, for instance).

Many roads in the mountains and those leading down from the mountains into the Amazon basin can be as rough as hell and journeys can take a long, long time. Buses along these routes are often badly maintained bone-shakers, filled to over-flowing with anyone and anything that can be crammed into them. Tyres are frequently bald, resulting in punctures which can increase the length of your journey by many hours. The seating – for what it's worth – is fine for young children but can become excruciating for adults because of the extremely limited leg-room. Fortunately, there aren't many accidents but it's a good idea to do a preliminary check on the sort of buses which various competing companies are running along any particular route and take what appears to be the best. It

doesn't always work because some companies run both fairly new and geriatric buses along the same route and there's no way of telling what you're going to get until it turns up.

Bus terminals in Peru are becoming almost as notorious as railway stations for baggage rip-offs. It's getting so blatant in some places that you can hand up a piece of baggage on one side of the bus to whoever is stacking them on the roof and it will instantly disappear down the other side. Meanwhile, the other piece you put down on the ground while handing up the first one has also disappeared! Get a friend or another traveller to keep an eye on things and carry bags up onto the roof yourself. Once they're up on the roof, hang around and keep an eye on them until the bus is ready to go. Don't make any assumptions.

Many long-distance buses travel at night, which is a nuisance as far as taking in the sights is concerned. The only way you can avoid this is by travelling in short hops and not trying to go too far in one day.

Keep an eye out for special offers on fares. Quite a few companies seem to be doing this these days and it can considerably reduce the cost of a journey.

In a book of this size it's impossible to provide a complete schedule of buses for a country the size of Peru, nor would it be particularly viable since they change constantly. Instead we concentrate on providing details of the major routes: The Coastal Highway – Tumbes-Trujillo-Lima -Pisco -Nazca -Arequipa -Tacna; Routes into the Highlands – Trujillo-Cajamarca, Trujillo/Chimbote/Lima-Huaráz; Lima-Cuzco – via Huancayo, Ayacucho & Abancay, or via Pisco, Nazca & Abancay; Arequipa-Puno; Routes into the Amazon Basin.

The Coastal Highway

Tumbes-Trujillo-Lima-Pisco-Nazca-Arequipa-Tacna The main companies which cover this highway are *TEPSA, Roggero,*

Ormeño, Expreso Cruz del Sur and *Sudamericana.* Between Tumbes and Lima most of the departures are at night though there are one or two daytime services. All the buses stop at Trujillo and usually also at Sullana, Piura and Chiclayo. Between Trujillo and Lima they generally stop at Chimbote, Casma and Paramonga. You book only as far as you want to go but on some buses priority is given to passengers who want to do the complete Tumbes-Trujillo or Trujillo-Lima sections. Some buses are exclusively for those doing the long hauls and you cannot get on these at intermediate stations.

Between Lima and Arequipa there is a much greater choice of day and night-time departures. All the buses stop at Pisco, Ica and Nazca. Again, you only book as far as you want to go but on some buses priority is given to those doing the Lima-Arequipa long-haul. Similarly, there are buses reserved exclusively for those doing the Lima-Arequipa run and although they stop at intermediate points you cannot get on there.

If you are catching a bus at an intermediate stop between Tumbes and Trujillo, Trujillo and Lima or Lima and Arequipa then expect it to be late. Very rarely do they arrive on time.

It's a good idea to book tickets in advance (one day before or earlier on the same day is sufficient as a rule). You should certainly do this in Tumbes if you're going south as there's a lot of competition and not many buses.

A comprehensive schedule of buses along this major highway is pointless, not only because you can generally find a bus on the same day you want to leave, but also because it would probably be out of date within six months. What is more useful is knowing where the various bus companies have their offices/terminals, which is marked on the relevant street maps; and the following information on journey times and approximate costs.

Tumbes-Trujillo-Lima Most of the departures are around 7 pm. The only company which has daytime departures is *TEPSA* at 1 and 2 pm. The journey to Trujillo takes about 16 to 17 hours and to Lima from 24 to 28 hours. The fare to Trujillo varies from US$7.50 to $8.40, and to Lima US$12 to $14, depending on the company. From Tumbes to Trujillo book early in the day if you want to be sure of a seat. A colectivo to Lima will cost you around US$20.

Trujillo-Lima In addition to the long-distance buses already mentioned there are also buses by *Peru Express* and *Empresa Chinchay-Suyo.* Most departures out of Trujillo are at night, though there's a chance of catching a daytime bus which originated in Tumbes if there are passengers getting off at Trujillo. The journey to Lima takes eight to nine hours and costs US$7. A colectivo will cost about US$10 and take seven to eight hours.

Trujillo-Chimbote Chimbote is the best place to get buses to Huaráz as you have a choice of day buses, some of which go via Huallanca and Caráz (Cañon del Pato) and others which go via Casma. From Trujillo there are only night-time buses. Whichever way you go, the landscape is spectacular so it doesn't make sense to go at night and miss it all. Buses to Chimbote from Trujillo are operated by *TEPSA, Empresa Cajamarca* (Av Colón 589), *Empresa El Aguila* (Calle Nicaragua) and *Empresa Chinchay-Suyo.* The service is frequent especially with *El Aguila* (16 buses daily between 5 am and 8 pm). The journey takes about 2½ hours and costs US$1.30 to $1.75 depending on the company. A colectivo will cost US$2.25 and take about two hours.

Lima-Pisco *Ormeño, Roggero* and *Expreso Cruz del Sur* have daily departures to Pisco and Nazca. The journey takes about 3-1/2 hours and costs US$2.30.

Lima-Nazca This run is covered by the same companies which do the Lima-Pisco leg and the frequency of the service is the same. The journey takes about 7½ hours and costs US$4.

Lima-Arequipa Daily departures in either direction by *TEPSA, Roggero, Sudamericana* and *Cruz del Sur*. The journey takes about 17 to 18 hours and the fare is US$10. Book in advance if possible. A colectivo will cost about US$12 to $14 and can take as little as 12 hours.

Pisco-Nazca Daily departures in either direction by *Roggero* and *Ormeño*. Tickets cost US$2.30 and US$2.55 respectively. The journey takes about 6½ hours.

Nazca-Arequipa *Roggero, Cruz del Sur* and *Ormeño* all have daily departures in either direction. The journey takes about 10-1/2 hours and costs US$4.40 to $6.60 depending on the company. *Cruz del Sur* are the cheapest.

Arequipa-Tacna Many departures daily in either direction by *Ormeño, Cruz del Sur, TEPSA* and *Sudamericana*. The journey takes about eight hours and costs US$3 to $3.50 depending on the company. *TEPSA* also operates international buses direct to Arica (Chile) which cost US$7.

Routes into the Highlands

Trujillo-Cajamarca *TEPSA, Empresa Díaz, Empresa Cajamarca* and *Empresa Cóndor* all have at least one departure daily. The journey takes eight to nine hours and costs US$2.50. A colectivo will cost about US$5.

Chiclayo-Cajamarca There are three buses daily in either direction with *El Cumbre* and *Di-az*. You must book in advance.

Trujillo-Huaráz The only trouble with going direct from Trujillo to Huaráz is that there are no direct daytime buses. *Empresa Chinchay-Suyo* (near Calle España) leave daily at 7.30 pm and take about eight hours. If you want to do it during the day and see the spectacular landscape of the Cañon del Pato then take a bus from Chimbote or Casma instead, as they have buses in the daylight hours.

Chimbote-Huaráz *Transportes Moreno Hnos* has one daily bus at 8 am which takes eight to nine and hours and costs US$5. The buses go via the Cañon del Pato and Caraz. It's a bad road and not for the faint-hearted but there are some very beautiful views. The same company has another bus at 7 am which goes via Casma instead of the Cañon del Pato and it's slightly cheaper.

Casma-Huaráz This is the same bus as described earlier and is the one you should take if you don't fancy the journey through the Cañon del Pato. There's also a 9 pm bus from Casma to Huaráz.

Lima-Huaráz The following companies all have daily services in either direction at about 9.30 am and 9.30 pm – *Rodriguez, Ormeño, Expreso Ancash* (Av Carlos Zavala 145, Lima), and *Empresa Huaráz* (Leticia 550, Lima). The journey takes about 8-1/2 hours along good paved roads and costs US$5.50. Rodriguez buses have been recommended but avoid *El Trome*. A colectivo costs around US$10.50 and will take about six hours.

Bus connections between the various towns of the Cordillera Blanca are included under the Huaráz & The Cordillera Blanca section.

Lima-Cuzco Routes via Lima-Cuzco via Huancayo, Ayacucho and Abancay

Lima-Huancayo Several bus companies cover this route including *Hidalgo* (probably the best line), *Etusca* (also good), *Sudamericana, Centroandino* and *Empresa Ayacucho*. The journey takes eight hours and costs US$3. Several colectivo companies also cover this route including Comité 12 (Montevideo 736, Lima), Comité 22 (Ayacucho 997, Lima) and Comité 30. The colectivos cost US$6.50 and take five to seven hours. You also have the alternative of the train along this route.

Huancayo-Ayacucho This is a route which most bus companies cover at night. *Hidalgo, Etusca, Transportes Andinos, Flota Cóndor* and *Empresa Ayacucho* all have one, sometimes two departures daily in the late afternoon. The only company which runs a daytime service is *Transportes Gutarra* which departs at 5 am daily. The journey takes about 14 hours but can take considerably longer during the rainy season as parts of the road are as rough as hell. The fare varies from US$5 to US$7.50. It's a beautiful trip so try to do it by day. All buses are heavily booked in January because of fiestas which take place in many towns in the area. Be warned, however, that your safety cannot be guaranteed around Ayacucho because of the activities of the Sendero Luminoso, the Maoist guerrillas. Buses have been ambushed though this is a rare occurrence.

Ayacucho-Abancay There's no guarantee that you will be able to find a bus between these two towns at present because of Sendero Luminoso activities. Most of the companies have withdrawn their services. If the situation is quiet then *Hidalgo* is the company to make enquiries with. They operate the Lima-Cuzco run via Abancay, Andahuaylas, Ayacucho and Pisco usually four days a week but if you find yourself stuck then you'll have to fly.

Ayacucho-Cuzco The same applies to this route because the road goes first to Abancay.

Lima-Cuzco There are two ways to do this at present but bear in mind the warning about guerrilla activities in the area. The first route goes via Abancay, Andahuaylas, Ayacucho and Pisco and is covered by *Hidalgo*. There are four departures per week in either direction, from Cuzco on Monday, Wednesday, Thursday and Friday at 7.30 am. The journey takes about 42 hours and costs US$13.35. Journey times and fares to intermediate stops from Cuzco are as follows: Abancay, six hours, US$2.65; Ayacucho, 21 hours, US$8.65; and Pisco, 38 hours, US$11.35.

The second route is via Abancay, Nazca and Ica and is covered by *Señor de Animas*, *Ormeño* and *Morales Moralitos*

(which should be avoided). *Señor de Animas* has four departures per week from Cuzco on Tuesday, Wednesday, Friday and Sunday at 7 am. The journey takes 36 hours and costs US$15.20. Journey times and fares to intermediate stops from Cuzco are: Nazca, 30 hours, US$7.65; and Ica, 32 hours, US$12.65. *Ormeño* has three departures per week from Cuzco on Wednesday, Friday and Sunday at 7 am. The journey takes the same time as *Señor de Animas* and costs US$17.30. Fares to intermediate stops from Cuzco are: Abancay, US$4; Nazca, US$15.30; and Pisco US$16.

It's a very rough road between Cuzco and Nazca and you'll be extremely lucky to get there in the scheduled time. Punctures are common. Most buses don't make Cuzco-Nazca in less than 45 hours.

The Southern Highlands

Cuzco-Puno Only two bus companies now cover this route – it seems that most people go by rail. The reason for this is that the road is quite rough in parts and the bus takes longer. There's also little difference in price between first class on the train and the bus, and in second class the train is actually cheaper. Both *Cruz del Sur* and *San Cristobal* have two departures daily, one in the morning and the other in the afternoon. The journey takes about 12 hours and costs US$6.

Arequipa-Puno Four bus companies cover this route including *San Cristóbal* and they all have departures between 4 and 6 pm. The journey takes about 13 hours and costs US$5. There are also colectivos, such as *Comité 3* and *Comité 2 Sur Peruano* which do the journey in about eight hours and cost US$10 to $12. From Puno, *Comité 3* depart daily at 10 am and *Comité 2* depart daily at 3 pm. If you want to go direct from Arequipa to Cuzco the only company which operates a through bus is *San Cristóbal*. It has two departures weekly (from Cuzco on Wednesday and Sunday at 9 am). The journey takes about 20 hours and costs US$10.

Routes into the Amazon Basin

There are basically two routes into the interior from the mountains. The first starts from Cajamarca and follows the (rough) roads via Celendín and Chachapoyas through the Sierras to Rioja. From there to Moyobamba or Yurimaguas you'll probably have to fly as the 'roads' are atrocious. It is possible to walk, but it's an ambitious trek which takes about a week and you need guides. The area is, however, honeycombed with extensive and often jungle-engulfed Inca and other ruins. Again, guides are essential if you want to explore them. The landscape is amazing and the roads hair-raising.

The second route follows what is known as the Central Highway which begins at Lima and ends at Pucallpa passing through La Oroya, Cerro de Pasco, Huánuco and Tingo María en route. The road along this route is much better than the one between Cajamarca and Rioja, but even so, in the rainy season it can take a week to get from Lima to Pucallpa.

From Cajamarca The first part of the journey is by bus (*Empresa Atahualpa* is the best) to Celendín – they go twice daily, take about six hours and cost US$1.75. If you need to stay overnight try the *Hotel Maxmar*, the *José Galves*, the *Amazonas* or the *Hotel Jorge Girón*. They're all fairly cheap. From Celendín to Chachapoyas you have to take a truck (usually one per week), or one of the infrequent minibuses which usually go on Mondays and occasionally on Thursdays as well. The hair-raising journey takes 15 to 17 hours and should cost around US$3.50. Ask at the Hotel Maxmar when transport is going.

For somewhere to stay in Chachapoyas, try the *Marañón* which is the best of the cheapies. If it's full, your next best bet is either the *Chachapoyas* or the *Amazonas*. For somewhere to eat, the *Bar Chacha*, Plaza de Armas, serves good meals for US$1 to $2. You must register with the PIP on arrival in town.

At Kuelap near Chachapoyas is a huge, ruined pre-Inca mountain-top fortress which is perhaps every bit as impressive as Machu Picchu and certainly fits the image of a genuine 'Lost City' better because it hasn't been cleared. The first explorations of the area were done by Gene Savoy in 1960. Little has happened since then due to lack of money and interest by the government (and official fears about antiquities being looted). The origins of the ruins go back to around 1350-1400 AD. The builders were a non-Inca people who came into contact with the Incas when the latter were expanding their empire. Inca chronicles described them as 'fair-skinned fierce fighters' and mummies found in the area have distinctly Caucasian features (taller than most Indians, low cheek bones and occasional blonde hair). It's not known where these people originated but their ruined fortresses and cities are incredible. Very few outsiders have seen them so far.

If you'd like to see them, go first to Tingo (not to be confused with Tingo María) near Chachapoyas (by *camionette*) where there is one hotel. From there you can walk to the ruins at Kuelap in about four hours (it only takes 2½ hours to get back as it's downhill). There is a hostal at the ruins which has beds, blankets, food and drink and it's a great place to spend a few peaceful days exploring the ruins. Local people are friendly and there are fantastic views.

If you want to find out more about the ruins in this area contact a priest in Chachapoyas called Parróco Pablo Rodriguez Arista – everyone knows him; just ask. He's very knowledgeable about the area and willing to assist anyone considering making the trip. He may provide you with maps and letters of introduction to the headmen of the villages you will pass through – he knows them personally. The people in these villages are reported to be among the friendliest in Peru. On the other hand, it isn't necessary to contact him unless you specifically want to as you don't need a guide to find the main ruins. The police in Tingo will point you in the right direction (but don't leave gear with them – things have been known to disappear from bags left there).

From Chachapoyas the road goes to Rioja via Pedro Ruiz and Nueva Cajamarca. If you find direct transport it should cost US$6 and take about 15 hours. You can always find transport during the dry season even if you have to do it in stages. There are always plenty of pick-ups available between Pedro Ruiz and Chachapoyas and the scenery between the two is beautiful. From Nueva Cajamarca to Rioja the road is surfaced. In Rioja stay at either the *Restaurante Los Olivos* or the *Hostal Rioja*. There's also a pleasant, cheap hostal at Pedro Ruiz. During the dry season you can easily get from Rioja to Moyobamba (US$1) or Tarapoto (US$5, about 3½ hours) by colectivo. In the rainy season the road can become impassable. From Moyobamba there are riverboats downriver to Yurimaguas and Iquitos.

While in Moyobamba, stay at the *Hotel Monterrey*. In Tarapoto there is the *Hostal El Soreno* which is clean and costs less than US$1 and the *Hostal America* which has rooms with attached bath for US$3. In the nearby village of Lamas there is a good museum depicting Indian life and there's an Indian settlement which you can visit.

From Lima It is possible to take a bus all the way from Lima to Pucallpa and vice versa if you want to do the journey in one hop. *Arellano, TEPSA* and *León de Huánuco* all do runs there via Tingo María and Huánuco. The journey takes 24 to 32 hours and costs US$14. In the wet season (November to March) the journey can take a week. Have plenty of warm clothes with you – it gets bitterly cold at night. It's probably better to break the journey into stages and stay overnight in Huánuco and Tingo María.

On the first stage of the journey you

have the choice of taking a bus direct to Huánuco from Lima (takes about 15 hours and costs US$8) or a train. The train is the same as the one which goes daily – except on Sundays – at 7.40 am to Huancayo, but you have to change at La Oroya and take the 2.30 pm train from there to Cerro de Pasco. The only problem with the trains is that the one from Lima is often late and you miss the connection at La Oroya which means you have to overnight there. Also if you take the train to Cerro de Pasco you may well have to spend the night there. It's a good idea to consider taking pick-ups from La Oroya to Tingo María but have warm clothes as the journey can be very cold. Both La Oroya and Cerro de Pasco are pretty grim and desolate places but if you need to stay at La Oroya try the *Hotel Lima* which is clean and friendly and provides plenty of blankets.

For somewhere to stay in Huánuco there are the *Internacional, Astoria* or *Imperial*, all of which are cheap, clean and good value. The Internacional has hot water in the mornings in the common bathrooms. If you arrive late in Huánuco you may find places full, so don't discount the possibility of paying considerably more for accommodation than you bargained for. For food, try *Las Palmeras*, the *Tokio* or *El Imán* (the last two are off the main square). All have good, cheap food.

There are frequent buses (US$1.75) and colectivos (US$2) to Tingo María which take about four hours. There's also a daily bus to Pucallpa which costs US$4.50. If you're heading back to Lima from Huánuco there are daily buses which cost US$8 and take about 15 hours as well as colectivos for US$10. The latter leave at 4 am and should be booked the night before at General Prado 607.

In Tingo María try the *Cuzco* or *Raimundo* first, as they are both cheap and clean. If they're full – and hotels here often are – then try the *Imperial, Royal* and the *Marco Antonio* which are somewhat up-market and rooms have their own bathrooms. Another place which has been recommended is the *Hotel Viena* which is cheap and clean and has showers. Two good places to eat are the *Restaurant Tingo*, on the main street; and the *La Cabaña Hotel*. Another place worth trying if you want to splurge is the *Café Rex*, Av Raimondi 500, run by a friendly Swiss woman who offers excellent European food.

Buses from Tingo María to Pucallpa cost US$4.50 and take eight to 11 hours. *La Perla* and *Nor-Oriente* are two companies which do this run. In the rainy season the journey can take three days. On this last leg, the road passes through the magnificent Boquerón Padre Abad, a canyon four km long and two km wide. It's an awesome experience of sheer rock faces, lush tropical rainforest, waterfalls, and a raging torrent at the bottom of the canyon.

Riverboats from Pucallpa to Iquitos don't run on any fixed schedule and at certain times of the year can be very difficult to find. A good place to ask around at is the Amazonas hotel in Pucallpa as they proprietor tends to know what's going on. Some boats are better than others but the average fare to Iquitos is around US$18 to $25 including food or US$13 without food on a cargo boat. There are generally no cabins so you'll need a hammock and mosquito net. Food isn't usually up to much – beans and rice with the odd piece of fish thrown in and many people get diarrhoea so take something to stop you up. The trip should take four to six days assuming there isn't much off-loading and on-loading en route. One boat which has been recommended is the *Otita* skippered by Sr Samuel. If you can't find a boat all the way to Iquitos then first take one to Requena, about two-thirds of the way. From there, there are launches to Iquitos every second day which take about 12 hours and cost US$5.

Train

Apart from the short stretch down the Urubamba Valley from Cuzco to Machu Picchu, there are really only three major lines of interest to travellers plus a short section between Tacna and Arica (Chile).

Lima-Huancayo This is one of the highest railways in the world and goes over a pass which rises to 5000 metres. The line branches at La Oroya (one of the most desolate areas you will ever clap eyes on!) – one section heading north-west to Cerro de Pasco where there are road connections to Tingo María and Pucallpa, and the other section heading south-east to Huancayo and Huancavelica. If you're heading for Cerro de Pasco you must change at La Oroya. The train to Huancayo is cheaper than the bus though only marginally if you go 1st class.

The Lima-Huancayo train leaves on Tuesday, Thursday and Saturday from Lima; and on Monday, Wednesday and Friday from Huancayo. The journey takes about nine hours. The fare is US$3 (1st class) and US$2 (2nd class). Lima to La Oroya costs US$2.40 (1st class) and US$2 (2nd class). Tickets go on sale the day before departure from 9 am in Lima and from 10 am in Huancayo. Get there early. Meals (breakfast and lunch) are served on the train if you're not taking your own food and cost US$1.50 per meal.

If you want to go on to Huancavelica from Huancayo there is a stopping train at 7 am daily except Sundays in either direction which departs at 7.30 am and arrives at 1.50 pm. The fares are US$2.60 (autovagon), US$1.60 (1st class) and US$1.20 (2nd class). If you're heading for Cerro de Pasco, there is a daily train from La Oroya which costs US$1.35 and leaves at 2.30 pm regardless of whether the train from Lima has arrived or not.

Cuzco-Puno Although there are buses between Cuzco and Puno, most travellers prefer to take the train. Indeed, it's so popular that the colectivo services between the two cities only operate on Sunday when there is no train.

Trains depart Cuzco (Av El Sol railway station) at 7.30 am and Puno at 7.25 am daily except Sundays and arrive at the opposite end at about 5.30 to 6 pm. The fares are US$7.15 (1st class) and US$5.20 (2nd class). Lunch is served on the train and costs US$1.50. Soft drinks and beer are also available. In the tourist season (June to September) there is heavy competition for tickets. In Cuzco they go on sale from 10 to 11 am and 2 and 5 pm the day before departure. In Puno they are on sale between 6.30 and 8 am and between 8 and 9.30 pm the day before departure. You cannot book further ahead than this. It is possible to buy a ticket on the day of departure as well but there is no guarantee you will be able to get a 1st class ticket – they're usually sold out by then and only 2nd class will be available as these can only be bought on the day of departure. There is no change involved at Juliaca.

The railway authorities do their best to separate foreigners and Peruvians in order to minimise the incidence of theft. If going from Puno to Cuzco on this line, hotel proprietors or their employees board the train several stops before Cuzco and try to sell you their accommodation. That gives you plenty of time to bargain for a room at often much less than they would normally charge and they'll usually throw in a free ride to the hotel from the station.

Cuzco-Arequipa This is basically the same train as the one to Puno (7.30 am daily) except that at Juliaca the Pullman car 'Cuzco-Arequipa' is detached from the train and later tacked on to the Puno-Arequipa night train, arriving in Arequipa at 6 am. Second class passengers must change carriages. While it stands in the station at Juliaca, the Pullman car is locked so you don't have to worry about thieves. If you're in 2nd class, however, be

very careful – never leave your bags unattended. The fares are US$12.60 (1st class) and US$9.15 (2nd class). Booking times in Cuzco are the same as for the Cuzco-Puno train.

Puno-Arequipa You have a choice on this line of day or night trains but it's strongly recommended that you take a day train not only because you'll see nothing of the landscape at night but because this line is by far the worst in Peru for rip-offs. This warning cannot be over-emphasized – a ridiculous number of travellers have something stolen on this train. Never go to sleep leaving bags unattended and if you're in a group then take it in turns to watch the bags. As on the Cuzco-Puno trains, the railway authorities do their best to separate foreigners and Peruvians to minimise theft but it hasn't eliminated it.

The day trains depart Puno at 7.25 am on Tuesday, Thursday and Saturday and Arequipa at 7.30 am on Monday, Wednesday and Friday. The night trains depart Puno at 7.45 pm daily and Arequipa at 10 pm daily. The journey takes about 11 hours and costs US$6.65 (1st class) and US$4.85 (2nd class). As with the Cuzco-Arequipa train, there is also an Arequipa-Cuzco Pullman car on the night trains which is detached at Juliaca and then added to the daytime Puno-Cuzco train. In Puno buy tickets the day before between 6.30 and 8 am and 7 and 9.30 pm. Second class tickets can only be bought on the day of departure.

If you take a night train then take plenty of warm clothes as it gets very cold.

Tacna-Arica There are daily trains in either direction at 8 am and 2 pm daily. From Arica they depart daily at 10.30 am and 4.30 pm. The fare is about US$1 and the journey takes about 1½ hours. If you're leaving Peru, get your passport stamped at Immigration in Tacna before taking the train.

Cuzco-Machu Picchu The trains on this line are covered in the Cuzco and Urubamba Valley section later.

Warning

Peruvian trains and railway stations are notorious for rip-offs. Never for a second take your eyes off your baggage or anything else you want to see again. Never allow yourself the luxury of falling asleep unless you've made arrangements with a friend to watch the baggage constantly. All the lines are worked by professional thieves. All they need is five seconds and they'll wait all day or night for the opportunity. They also work in groups using the familiar ploy of creating a distraction to take your attention off your baggage.

It may be worth paying the extra dollar or so for the buffet car service. You get a reserved seat, you don't have to buy any food or drink and the carriage doors are locked at all times and manned by an attendant.

ABANCAY

Abancay is really just a way station en route either from Ayacucho to Cuzco or from Lima to Cuzco via Nazca. There isn't any good reason to stop there unless you're going by bus from Ayacucho to Cuzco, in which case it's well to remember that although this journey should take 24 hours it can take three days!

Places to Stay & Eat

Most travellers stay at the *Hotel Gran* on the same street as the bus terminals. It

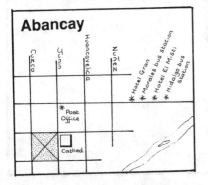

costs US$2 a single and is clean. If it's full, try the *Hotel El Misti*, also on the same street, or the *Abancay* or the *Alojamiento Centenario*.

For a place to eat, the *Quinta del Peñon* is recommended.

Arequipa

Although Arequipa is Peru's second largest city (population 400,000) and the commercial centre of the south, it has retained its colonial atmosphere. Sitting at the foot of the impressive, snow-capped volcano, El Misti (5843 metres), it consists almost entirely of low buildings constructed out of white volcanic stone. Founded in 1540, it's full of magnificent old churches, colonial mansions and a labyrinthine nunnery which is a city within a city. To complement its buildings it has a quiet, ethereal kind of charm quite different from the run-down, smog- and noise-filled streets of Lima. Civic pride runs high here and you'll hear many local people half-seriously boast about the 'Republica de Arequipa'.

On another level, it's a lively centre of folk music and you'll never be short of a *peña* to go to in the evening.

Information

The tourist office is at La Merced 117. It's open from 8 am to 1 pm Monday to Friday but it's of dubious value. Free but very sketchy maps of the city are available.

For changing money there is a casa de cambio at Santo Domingo 119 which stays open till 6 pm. Street money changers congregate on the first block of Santo Domingo (there called Moral) walking away from the Plaza de Armas.

The Argentine Consulate is at Mercaderes 212, Room 704. Open 8 am to 1 pm Monday to Friday. At the same address but in Room 400, you'll find the Chilean Consulate. The Bolivian Consulate is at Pierola 209, Room 321.

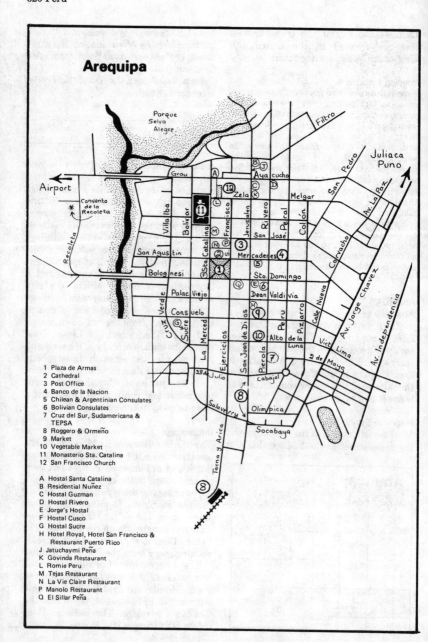

Arequipa

1 Plaza de Armas
2 Cathedral
3 Post Office
4 Banco de la Nacion
5 Chilean & Argentinian Consulates
6 Bolivian Consulates
7 Cruz del Sur, Sudamericana & TEPSA
8 Roggero & Ormeño
9 Market
10 Vegetable Market
11 Monasterio Sta. Catalina
12 San Francisco Church

A Hostal Santa Catalina
B Residential Nuñez
C Hostal Guzman
D Hostal Rivero
E Jorge's Hostal
F Hostal Cusco
G Hostal Sucre
H Hotel Royal, Hotel San Francisco & Restaurant Puerto Rico
J Jatuchaymi Peña
K Govinda Restaurant
L Romie Peru
M Tejas Restaurant
N La Vie Claire Restaurant
P Manolo Restaurant
Q El Sillar Peña

There's a local branch of the Peruvian Andenisto Club run by Señor Zarate at his photographic studio and camera repair shop at Santo Domingo 416. He's a local guide and mountain rescue organiser who is very friendly and enthusiastic and charges fair prices if you want his services as a guide. Even if you don't, he's more than happy to give advice and sell detailed maps of the area.

Most long-distance buses have their terminals on San Juan de Dios between Alta de Luna and Salaverry. Colectivos are also on San Juan de Dios and Salaverry.

Things to See

The city's biggest attraction is the **Monasterio de Santa Catalina** between Santa Catalina and Bolívar. It's a city within a city – narrow, cobbled streets, houses, gardens, fountains, churches, bakeries and even a cemetery. Until fairly recently it was functioning as a convent and outsiders were barred. The few nuns who still remain occupy only a very small part of the walled complex, the remainder is open to the public. You can spend hours wandering around this place and there's a café where you can buy snacks and drinks. Its only disappointing feature is that there are very few artefacts left from the days when the nuns used to live there (perhaps they lived very frugally?), but the gardeners have made up for that with pots of flowering plants and small gardens on every street corner. Entry costs about US$1.50 and it's open from 9 am to 4 pm. There are no student reductions.

Another place not to miss is the **Iglesia y Claustros de la Compañia**, an ornate Jesuit church on Santo Domingo on the corner of the Plaza de Armas. Its beautiful, sculptured stone facade is the first thing you'll see, but inside is the **Chapel of San Ignacio** which was completely painted in luxuriant jungle scenes by Indian painters of the Cuzco school hundreds of years ago. There is a small entry charge to the chapel.

Other ecclesiastical buildings worth visiting are the **Basilica Catedral** on the Plaza de Armas and the **Church and Monastery of San Francisco** on Zela, which is open from 6 to 8 pm only. The **Museum Archaeological** is only of minor interest but the **Municipal Museum** (entry by donation) has quite an interesting collection – lots of old photographs, interesting models on Arequipa and a three-dimensional map of the country from the coast up to the mountains. Over the bridge on Calle Ayacucho is the well-kept **La Recoleta Franciscan Monastery** which has an Amazon museum.

There are some Nazca-like scratchings in the desert near Arequipa at a place called **Toro Muerto**. They're not as famous or on such a grand scale as those at Nazca but nevertheless very interesting. The problem is getting there as there are no buses and a colectivo would be expensive. If you'd like to take a look, contact the curator of the local museum as he often goes there on weekends.

Places to Stay

Arequipa is good news for budget travellers. You'll have no problem finding a good place to stay which offers excellent value for money. The most popular hotel among travellers is the *Hostal Residencial Guzman* (tel 22 7142), Jirón Jerusalén 408, a traditional one-storey house with rooms around a sunny, central courtyard. It costs US$2.50/$3/$4 a single/double/triple all without own bathroom. The singles are actually a bed in a small dormitory. There's usually enough hot water in the bathrooms but it can run out if demand is heavy. Clean sheets are provided and the manager is very hospitable.

Another place which deserves to be popular but which isn't too well known at present is the *Hostal Sucre* (tel 21 9196) Calle Sucre 407. It's very pleasant, has a courtyard, cafeteria and bar and hot water in the bathrooms. It costs US$1.65/$3.10 a single/double without own bathroom. There are doubles with own bathroom for US$3.30.

Somewhat more expensive than these, but pleasant and friendly, is the *Hostal Nuñez*, Jerusalén 528. All the rooms have their own bathroom with hot water and cost US$3.30/$4.45 a single/double. Similar is the *Hostal Rivero*, Rivero 420 on the corner with Ayacucho. It's spotlessly clean, friendly and has hot water all day.

Also in this area above the Plaza de Armas is the *Hostal Santa Catalina*, Santa Catalina 500, which costs US$2.50 to $4 for rooms without own bathroom. Clean sheets are provided and there's hot water in the communal bathrooms.

If cost is your major consideration then there's a good choice of cheaper places. The *Hostal Cuzco*, Plaza de Armas near the corner with Bolognesi, offers small double rooms without own bathroom for US$2.20. There are no single rooms but there's hot water and a cheap restaurant on the balcony overlooking the plaza. Also good value is the *Hostal Royal*, San Juan de Dios between Valdivia and San Camilo, where the manager is very friendly and welcoming. The rooms are small but clean, there's plenty of hot water all day and you'll probably meet other travellers there.

Similar is the *Hostal Mercaderes*, Mercaderes 142 next to the post office. It's a little tatty at the edges but it does have hot water and costs US$1.30/$2 a single/double. Even cheaper but without any atmosphere or hot water is the *City Hotel*, Consuelo 211, which costs US$1.10/$2 a single/double.

Jorge's Hostal (tel 21 3988) Santo Domingo 110, is worth trying if you want to stay near the plaza. It's a modern place, is very clean and has it's own restaurant. Rooms cost US$1.55/$2.45/$3.10 a single/double/triple without own bath and US$3.30/$3.90 a single/double with own bath. There's plenty of hot water. Good value for money.

On the plaza itself is the *Hostal El Mirador* near the corner with Mercaderes. This is another pleasant place and costs US$2.20 a single without own bathroom and US$3.90 a double with own bathroom. The *Hostal Tradicion* on Sucre 113 at US$1.50 per person has been described as above average and excellent value.

Places to Eat

La Vie Claire in the alley at the back of the cathedral is excellent and you'll find some of the tastiest vegetarian food you're ever likely to come across. Service is fast, the prices are a breeze (less than US$0.50 for a good meal) and they have salads, soups, quiche and other pies, yogurt, fruit juices, milk shakes and sandwiches. Also very good indeed is *Govinda*, Jerusalén 402, run by the Hari Krishna people (no proselytising here). They have all the usual Indian vegetarian food as well as a set meal-of-the-day which is excellent value at less than US$0.50 (dhal, subji, chapatti, dessert and tea). For breakfast it offers muesli with wild honey.

Somewhat more expensive but with an extensive range of dishes and huge submarine sandwiches is *Manolo*, San Francisco near the junction with Moral. A delicious chicken milanesa or *lomo saltada* with chips costs about US$1. Don't drink the beer there – it's twice the price of other places. The *Lluvia de Oro*, Jerusalén 308, is also very popular with travellers. If you're looking for fish, try *El Batuta* on the bottom side of the Plaza de Armas. It's reasonable but nothing special. A meal costs about US$1.

For a splurge the best place to go is *La Tejas Restaurant*, Santa Catalina 206 opposite the monastery. This restaurant has one of the best atmospheres in the city. The food is excellent, well-presented and prices are reasonable. Even beers are the normal price. It's run by Alejandro Ybarra and his wife who are from Argentina. There's often live folklore music on Friday and Saturday evenings (no extra charge). Also opposite Santa

Catalina *El Quinque* is another atmospheric place with a beautiful vaulted room and very good food. Some say it's even better than La Tejas.

If you want to fix your own food or organise a picnic there's a supermarket on the Plaza das Armas or you can get superb bread and lots of wine, cheese and so on at *Las Americas* on Jerusale'n. Arequipa has its own beer – *Arequipena*.

Peñas

You can hear folkmusic any night of the week from 7 pm onwards at *El Sillar*, Santo Domingo 118. You can't see this place from the street, so go under the archway and across the courtyard to the far side. It's something of a tourist spot but there's usually a lively crowd and the music is excellent. Drinks are expensive and there's a cover charge of about US$0.50. Just round the back of this place is a disco which is popular with local young people.

Two very popular peñas, especially with local people (you will rarely meet any tourists there), are *Jatuchaymi*, Jerusalén 522; and *Romie*, Zela 202 opposite the San Francisco monastery. The *Jatuchaymi* is open several nights per week including Saturday (but closed Sunday) from 9 pm and is very friendly and informal, always boisterous and good fun. It's a large place, there's plenty of room to dance (the locals will plead, beg and insist that you do!) and the drinks are cheap. There's a cover charge of about US$0.50. It stays open till *late*! The *Romie* has a very good reputation among locals because of the quality of the music but it's a much smaller place than the Jatuchaymi. It's open Wednesday to Saturday nights only.

Another peña you may see advertised is the *Peña de José*, Av Mariscal Castilla 929. Ask at your hotel for directions.

Getting Around

Airport Transport Catch the No 3 blue bus marked 'Zamacola' or 'Aeropuerto' for the airport. The trip takes approximately 20 minutes and the bus leaves from the corner of La Merced and Palacio Viejo. You can also catch it at Puente Grau – the bridge at the bottom of Selva Alegre. The bus doesn't go right to the airport terminal, and you will have to walk the last 200 metres, but the driver will tell you when and where to get off! A taxi there will cost about US$1.50. There's a US$2 airport tax.

Warning

Arequipa railway station is notorious for pickpockets and thieves, as is the Arequipa-Puno train. Don't leave anything to chance – there's always somebody keeping an eye on what you take your eyes off. Arequipa's market has razor artists so keep a tight grip on your bag.

AYACUCHO

Ayacucho occupies an important place in the history of Peru. It was there on 9 December 1824 that the final battle for independence from Spain was fought. Though the Spanish city was founded in 1539, the area was important long before that as a major cross-roads of the Inca empire. Today, it's a peaceful, easy-going mountain city full of beautiful old colonial buildings with shady patios and a colourful market. The surrounding area, unfortunately, is far from peaceful and is the stronghold of the Sendero Luminoso (Shining Path) guerrillas. The game of cat and mouse between these guerrillas and the Peruvian army is brutal and ruthless. Atrocities have been committed by both sides. Though Ayacucho itself is quite safe, you're advised not to explore the surrounding area. A number of foreigners who have done this in the recent past have disappeared and later been found hacked to death. All sides involved in this conflict – the guerrillas, the army and the campesinos – are very suspicious of outsiders.

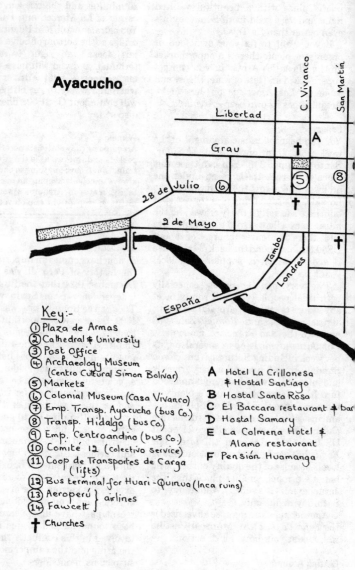

Ayacucho

Key:-
1. Plaza de Armas
2. Cathedral & University
3. Post Office
4. Archaeology Museum (Centro Cultural Simon Bolívar)
5. Markets
6. Colonial Museum (Casa Vivanco)
7. Emp. Transp. Ayacucho (bus Co.)
8. Transp. Hidalgo (bus Co.)
9. Emp. Centroandino (bus Co.)
10. Comité 12 (colectivo service)
11. Coop de Transportes de Carga (lifts)
12. Bus terminal for Huari-Quinua (Inca ruins)
13. Aeroperú ⎱ airlines
14. Fawcett ⎰ airlines

✝ Churches

A Hotel La Crillonesa & Hostal Santiago
B Hostal Santa Rosa
C El Baccara restaurant & bar
D Hostal Samary
E La Colmena Hotel & Alamo restaurant
F Pensión Huamanga

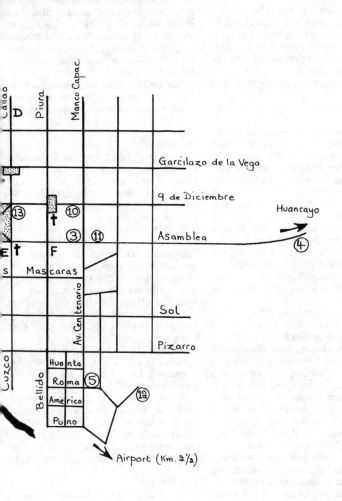

Information

The tourist office is at Asamblea 138. It's closed on weekends. They have useful leaflets about the area and sketch maps of the city. Similar information is available from the AeroPeru office on the Plaza de Armas (Parque Sucre).

There is presently a curfew from 8.30 pm to 6 am.

Things to See

My own favourite in Ayacucho is the **Museo Casa Vivanco**, on 28 de Julio, which shares premises with the PIP. The building itself is perhaps of more interest than the collection of pots they have there – it's a superb colonial villa with a quiet courtyard. Admission to the museum is free.

Also, don't miss the **Archaeological Museum** in the *Centro Cultural Simon Bolívar* on the outskirts of town past the hospital and the nightclub. The collection of pots and stone figures is relatively small but very well displayed. There is a small entrance fee.

It's worth visiting the 17th-century cathedral, on the Plaza de Armas, and its **Museum of Religious Art**, for which there is a small entry charge. Next door to the cathedral is the university, founded in 1677, closed in 1886, and re-opened in 1958. It's principally of interest for the building which houses it, though you might meet young people there who'll show you where the action is.

Other churches of interest include **San Francisco de Asís, La Compañía de Jesús, Santa Clara, Santo Domingo** and **Santa Teresa**. Ayacucho has some 33 churches, many of them no longer used as such but most of them gems of colonial architecture.

Outside Ayacucho at **Vilcashuamán** are some fine examples of Inca stone masonry and agricultural terracing. The church there stands on top of what was once an Inca sun temple. The village was an important cross-roads of the Inca empire and a provincial capital. If it's safe to do so, get a group together and take a colectivo. There's a market there on Wednesdays. If you're on your own, enquire at Ayacucho Tours, San Martín 406, as they do trips there, including a visit to the famous battlefield for around US$5.

The main market in Ayacucho is on Vivanco. It happens every day and it has some of the most beautiful *mantas* you'll find anywhere in Peru or Bolivia.

Places to Stay

La Colmena, Jirón Cuzco, is still the most popular place to stay though it's not the cheapest. It's exceptionally clean, quiet and has hot water but the staff tend to be indifferent. It costs US$3 a single with your own bathroom.

If you'd like something cheaper, try the *Hotel La Crillonesa*, Jirón Vivanco 165 (also called Calle Nazereno), close to the market. It's good value and clean, and although none of the rooms have their own bathrooms/toilets, hot water is available all day. If it's full, you could try the *Hostal Santiago* which is next door. It isn't as clean as the Crillonesa but it also has hot water all day.

Another place which has been recommended is the *Hotel Magdalena*, Av Centenario 277. All the rooms have their own bathrooms.

For something up-market, try the *Hostal Santa Rosa*, Jirón Lima, a modern building but built traditionally with a shady courtyard. The hotel has its own restaurant which regularly puts on folk music evenings – open to non-residents.

Places to Eat

El Alamo, next door to the Colmena, serves excellent food at reasonable prices (including fried fish 'n' chips for those yearning for a taste of home). Their mixed salads are particularly good. They sometimes put on folk music evenings.

Another very good place to try is *El Baccara* on the corner of the Plaza de Armas and Jirón Lima. Like the Alamo, they offer an excellent range of good food at reasonable prices. This restaurant also has a bar which is usually pretty lively and is a good place to meet local people. The doors close around 10 pm, but if you're in there having a good time either with a bunch of travellers or local people the owner generally keeps the beer and laughter flowing until he falls asleep on the counter.

If you're in search of more ethnic dishes, try one of the cheap cafés on Vivanco or San Martín between Grau and 2 de Mayo. You can eat in any of them for much less than a dollar. For snacks, there's a good café on the top side of the Plaza de Armas (on the opposite side from the cathedral) which does good sandwiches and coffee.

Another good place to eat – meals at meal times, snacks at other times – is the café in the university. To get there go through the main entrance on the Plaza de Armas, across the patio and down the corridor on the right-hand side, then turn left at the end of the corridor. *Los Portales* on the Plaza de Armas is also good and cheap and has live folk music in the evenings.

If you're looking for something to do in the evening keep an eye out for leaflets advertising folk music evenings. There are quite a few places which put these on, such as the *Hostal Santa Rosa* and the *Hotel Turistico*, and they'll all let non-residents in for a small entry fee.

Getting There
Air If you're flying to Lima you have a choice of both *AeroPeru* and *Faucett* (latter at Jirón Lima 196), but if you're flying to Cuzco then you have to take *AeroPeru*. The Ayacucho-Cuzco flight is notorious for cancellations and over booking and if it's cancelled they not only won't compensate you for extra nights you have to spend in Ayacucho, but if you complain they call the police! There is a flight every day but don't make any assumptions until you have a boarding pass – a confirmed ticket is about as useful as the money to pay for one. If a backlog has accumulated because of cancellations, the scene at the airport can approach mayhem. If that's the case, obey the law of the jungle and you might make it. Local bus No 2 goes from the Plaza de Armas to the airport (first bus at 6 am). A colectivo will cost about 200 soles per person.

CAJAMARCA
Cajamarca is the place where Pizarro ambushed the Inca emperor, Atahualpa, and held him ransom until he fulfilled a pledge to fill a room with gold and silver – the *Cuarto de Rescata* which still stands today. Pizarro typically didn't fulfill his part of the bargain and had Atahualpa strangled. The Spanish town hasn't changed a great deal since colonial times and is set in a beautiful valley which is ideal for walking. The remains of several pre-Columbian civilisations dot the valley.

Information
The tourist office is next to the Belén monuments (*Conjunto de Belén*) one block from the Plaza de Armas. The main post office is at Jirón Lima 406. *AeroPeru* is at Jirón Amalia Puga 525.

The main bus terminals are near the junction of Ayacucho and Urteaga.

Things to See
Cajamarca's most famous landmark is the **Cuarto de Rescata** (Ransom Room) but how much interest can you wring from an empty room? Of far more interest is the small museum in the education department of the university near Calle Revilla, open from 8 am to 12 noon and 2 to 5 pm. It contains objects belonging to a pre-Inca society which flourished in the Cajamarca valley.

Also worth seeing is the **Museo de Arte Colonial** in the Convento de San Francisco. A good place to get a bird's eye view of the town and the surrounding countryside is

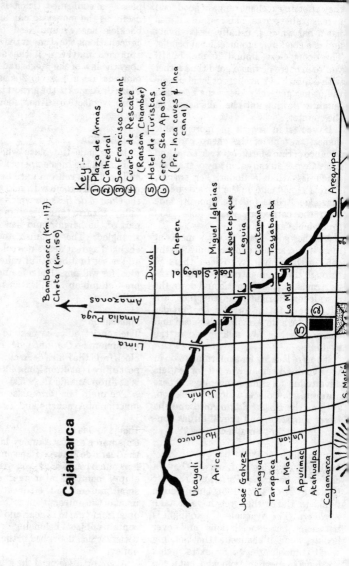

Cajamarca

Key:-
1. Plaza de Armas
2. Cathedral
3. San Francisco Convent
4. Cuarto de Rescate (Ransom Chamber)
5. Hotel de Turistas
6. Cerro Sta. Apolonia (Pre-Inca caves & Inca canal)

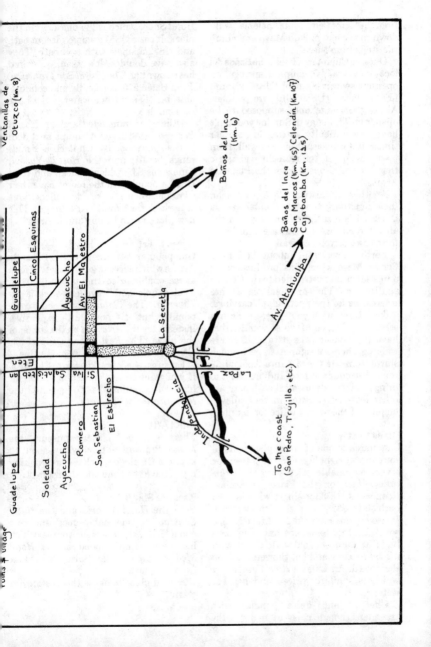

Ruins + Village

Guadelupe
Soledad
Ayacucho
Guadelupe
Cinco Esquinas
Ayacucho
Av. El Maestro

Ventanillas de Otuzco (km. 8)

Baños del Inca (km. 6)

Eten
Santisteban
Silva
Romero
San Sebastian
El Estrecho

La Secreta

La Paz

Independencia

To the coast
(San Pedro, Trujillo, etc.)

Av. Atahualpa

Baños del Inca (km. 6)
San Marcos (km. 65) Celendín (km 107)
Cajabamba (km. 125)

from the top of **Cerro Santa Apolonia** – walk down to the end of 2 de Mayo and climb the steps from there.

Outside Cajamarca itself, the **Baños del Inca** – natural hot sulphur springs, an open-air swimming pool (US$0.50) and private baths (US$0.70) – are popular. Although they're only supposed to be open from Thursday to Sunday you won't have any difficulty getting in at other times. It's a pleasant six km walk from town though if you're feeling geriatric there are mini-buses from the Plaza de Armas.

Another interesting place – once an Inca sanctuary – is the **Ventanillas de Otuzco**. It's eight km from town on the airport road. Again, there are mini-buses from town or you can walk.

Further away still (about 14 km) is **Cumbe Mayo** which has pre-Inca caves and a sanctuary attributed to the Chavín civilisation. The artificial caves are interesting for their petroglyph carvings. Take a torch with you. There is no bus service to Cumbe Mayo so you'll either have to walk or take a taxi. If you're walking, there's a signposted path which starts from the Cerro Santa Apolonia – it's well-trodden as local Indians use it to bring their goods to market. There are other less-known ruins in the valley – enquire at the tourist office for details.

Places to Stay

Cajamarca is one of those places where you can stay right in the centre of town for a very reasonable price – try the *Gran Hotel Plaza* on the Plaza de Armas. Rooms cost US$2 a single without own bath and US$2.30 a single with own bath. It also has an annexe at 2 de Mayo No 585 which isn't quite as pleasant. The main building has a lot of old world charm with a good balcony and hot showers. Also on the Plaza de Armas is the *Hotel Casablanca* which is similarly priced and has hot water.

Cheaper and quite popular with travellers though noisy at night is the *Hotel Sucre* which is 1½ blocks from the plaza. It costs US$1 a single without bath and US$2 a single with own bath. They also have doubles. It's clean, quiet and has its own bar. The *Hostal San Francisco*, Jirón Belén 570, is friendly and comfortable but has no hot water. Prices are reasonable.

Others recommended are the *Hostal Beccera* (no sign) on Arequipa next door to the *Amazonas* (which itself is a mid-range hotel); and the *Hostal Yusovi*, Amazonas 637, which is clean and costs US$3 a double. All the rooms have their own bathroom. Other travellers have suggested the *Hostal Atahualpa*. This new place is good value and is clean.

Places to Eat

One popular restaurant on the Plaza de Armas which serves a good variety of food at reasonable prices and is popular with local people and travellers alike is *La Taverna*. The *Salas* also used to be popular but it's now quite expensive. Instead, try the *Arlequin* on the corner of the plaza. The *Restaurant Central* has also been recommended as good value.

For an excellent breakfast go to *Charlie's*. If you want to try something different, like *cuy* (guinea pig), go to the *Restaurante del Rescata*.

CHICLAYO

There is a good pottery museum, the *Museo Braning*, at **Lambayeque** about 10 km from Chiclayo which is worth visiting if you have the time and the interest.

Places to Stay & Eat

Both the *Hotel Madrid* and the *Hotel Central* are reasonably good and cost about US$1.20 per person. Another which has been recommended is the *Hotel Mediterraneo*, Calle Balta, one block from the plaza.

A good place to eat is the *Restaurant Roma*.

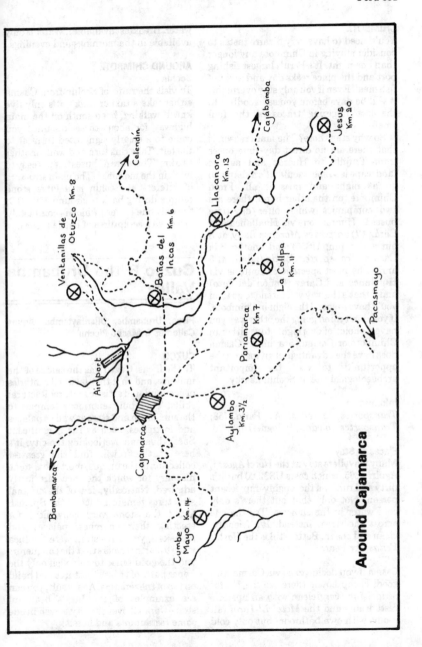

Around Cajamarca

Jesus Km. 20

Cajábamba

Llacanora Km. 13

Celendín

Baños del Incas Km. 6

Ventanillas de Otuzco Km. 8

La Collpa Km. 11

Pacasmayo

Pariamarca Km. 7

Airport

Aylambo Km. 3½

Cajamarca

Bambamarca

Cumbe Mayo Km. 14

CHIMBOTE

You'd need to have very bizarre tastes to consider staying in Chimbote any longer than one night. It's Peru's largest fishing port and the place reeks day and night of fish meal. Even if you only stay overnight, it will be days before you say goodbye to the last lingering traces of the foul smell.

So why stay there? The main reason is that there are no direct day-time buses from Trujillo to Huaráz and as the landscape is so spectacular it's a shame to go at night and miss it all. From Chimbote, on the other hand, there are two companies which offer day-time buses to Huaráz, one via Huallanca and Caráz (*Transportes Morenos* daily at 8 am and 8 pm; US$5) and another via Casma (*Transportes Soledad*; daily at 8 am). The most spectacular route is via Huallanca and Caráz (Cañón del Pato) and if that's the way you intend to go then you'll have to spend the night in Chimbote. If you don't mind going the other way you have a choice of overnight stops either in Chimbote or Casma. Staying at Casma does have the advantage of giving you the opportunity to visit the important archaeological site at Sechín nearby.

Information
Transportes Morenos, Av Parlo 758; *Transportes Soledad*, Bolognesi 752.

Places to Stay
Many travellers stay at the *Hotel Agosto*, Aguirre 265, which costs US$2.20 but it's dirty and run by a thoroughly unpleasant person. Not only that but there's only cold water in the showers. Try the one across the street instead. It's friendly, clean and cheap. Better still is the *Hostal Venus*, Av Pedro.

Casma If you decide to go via Casma, two good, cheap hotels there are the *Hostal Madeleine* (very clean with an upstairs restaurant) and the *Motel El Farol* (all rooms with own bathroom but only cold water. Breakfast available). Water is only available in the mornings and evenings.

AROUND CHIMBOTE
Sechín
To visit the ruins of Sechín from Casma either take a taxi or walk – it's only five km. If walking, head south on the main highway for about three km until you come to a clearly signposted turn-off to the left. Take this turn and walk another two km. There are no buses but it's easy to hitch in the mornings. The main structure of interest at Sechín is a large stone temple dating back to around 1500 BC; the only one in Peru which is completely faced with sculptures of battle scenes.

Cuzco & the Urubamba Valley

Pisac, Urubamba, Ollantaytambo, Aguas Calientes & Machu Picchu

CUZCO

To the Incas, Cuzco was the centre of the universe, and on it they lavished centuries of accumulated artistic and architectural skills. They built enormous temples to the sun, moon and stars as well as palaces and fortresses, such as the magnificent Sacsayhuaman overlooking the city. It's here that you will find the greatest collection of the unique, mortarless stone masonry for which the Incas are justly admired. Naturally, few of the original structures remain intact as the Spanish found the stone very convenient for erecting their churches, palaces and mansions, yet so resistant were the Inca walls to earth tremors that the conquerors had the good sense to demolish only the upper parts of these structures and build on top of the remains. As a result, you can see examples of the Inca's beautiful stone-work all over the city – even inside some restaurants and hotels!

Unlike the Tenochtitlán of the Aztecs, Cuzco was too remote to function as a capital for the new Spanish colonies which depended very heavily on sea-going communications. So although it remained an important regional centre, Lima became the centre of the new empire. Nevertheless, Cuzco remains the cultural centre of the Quechua people and tens of thousands of travellers flock here every year in search of legends, ruins, music, markets and, according to a *Time* magazine article, cocaine. But then *Time* is always hungry for an eye-grabbing headline.

No-one goes away disappointed. It's the Oaxaca/Guanajuato/Chichén Itzá of Peru, all rolled into one and it isn't just Inca ruins and Quechua culture that it offers. Cuzco features some of the world's most remarkable monuments to the fusion of two very different and vibrant cultures. If that were not enough, the incomparable setting of the nearby Urubamba Valley, with its numerous archaeological sites, must offer one of the world's most fascinating and intriguing journeys back in time. This is, of course, where you will find Machu Picchu, the legendary 'Lost City of the Incas'.

Information

The tourist office is at Capilla Lourdes on the corner of Loreto and the Plaza de Armas next to La Compañia church. There's also an information kiosk at the airport. The office on the plaza is very well organised and very helpful. They have free maps of the city, of the Urubamba Valley and of the Inca Trail to Machu Picchu (the latter is really just a rough sketch map and of limited use) as well as all the information you're ever likely to need about bus and rail time-tables and fares, hotels, restaurants, night spots, folklore evenings, museum opening times and lots more. Their hotel prices, however, are likely to be wildly out of date – but then that's something with which all guidebooks have to contend!

There are large-scale maps pinned to walls detailing areas of interest and it's also the place you should buy the combination entrance ticket for the museums, churches and archaeological sites. These are sold from 8 am to 12 noon and 3 to 5 pm, cost US$10 (US$5 for student card holders) and are valid for 10 days. It's payable in soles so the exact amount varies depending on the exchange rate.

The best place to change money is at a casa de cambio or in a hotel. You need to shop around to find out who is offering the best rate of exchange – this varies considerably. There are a number of casas de cambio on and just off the Plaza de Armas. Stash your money carefully before leaving a change house. Thieves keep a sharp eye on such places. People do offer to change money on the streets especially around the plaza but, unlike Arequipa and Lima, for instance, it's not a very good idea. Cuzco seethes with thieves. It may be all right out of the tourist season.

American Express is represented by Lima Tours, Avenida Sol 567 (PO Box 531, Cuzco). They will hold clients' mail but only offer a limited range of Amex services. They don't, for instance, issue travellers' cheques, so if you need to buy more or want stolen ones replaced you have to go to Lima.

The Immigration office is at Calle Santa Teresa 364 (tel 222741).

The main post office on Avenida Sol has a strange method of sorting the *lista de correos* letters. They're put into separate male and female sections! Most of the time they get it right though just how they divine the sex of an initial when no other indication is given remains a mystery. All the same, if you're expecting mail and there's nothing for you, ask them to sort through the other section – they're used to these requests!

For used paperbacks (in English, French, German and Spanish), the bookshop at Mantas 191 near the Plaza

San Francisco is one of the best. It isn't particularly cheap. They will also buy books from you.

Consulates

Bolivia
    Pasaje España, Av Pardo (tel 231412)
France
    Portal Espinar 142 (tel 233091)
Spain
    Calle Saphy 440 (tel 223243)
West Germany
    Av Tullumayo 874 (tel 224262)

Airlines

AeroPeru
    Av Sol 600 (tel 233051)
Faucett
    Av Sol 567 (tel 221871)
Grupo 8
    Airport terminal
Lloyd Aero Boliviano
    Av Sol 348 (tel 229900)
Viasa
    Calle Heladeros 167
Eastern Airlines
    Av Sol 954 (tel 221386)

With both AeroPeru and Faucett you must reconfirm bookings at least 24 hours before departure regardless of what you may be told to the contrary when you buy the ticket.

Place Names The spelling of street names in Cuzco can be confusing. *C* and *Q* – and to a lesser extent *K* – are not only interchanged with gay abandon but are often doubled up. For example, Quera may also be spelt Qquera or Ccuera; Tecsecocha may also be spelt Tecseccocha and Tecseqocha; and Manco Capac can also be spelt Manko Qapaq.

Things to See & Do

Before you set off to see the sights of Cuzco and the Urubamba Valley (Sacred Valley of the Incas) go to the tourist office on the Plaza de Armas and buy a combination entrance ticket. You can also buy them at the entrance to Sacsayhuaman, and if your student card

is out of date you'd be advised to get the tickets there. These entitle you to see the Cathedral, the Church of San Blas, Museo de Santa Catalina, Museo Religioso, Museo Regional and Qoricancha (all in Cuzco) and Pikillacta, Sacsayhuaman, Qenqo, Puca Pucara, Tambomachay, Pisac, Chinchero and Ollantaytambo (all outside of Cuzco).

Many travellers think US$10 is expensive (though surely no-one can complain at US$5 for students?) but a lot of this money is used to fund further excavations and reconstruction. Peru is really strapped for finance (especially for social welfare and agriculture) and the temptation to withdraw funding for all non-essential projects must be enormous. Don't knock it too much! It is still possible to pay to get into each individual place but you'd be throwing money down the drain if you did this.

If you're going to be spending a long time in Cuzco or you have a consuming interest in colonial architecture or archaeology then it's worth buying a copy of the local guide, *Exploring Cuzco* by Peter Frost which is on sale at most bookshops in Cuzco for around US$2.

A word of caution: Cuzco can easily develop into a breathless, sight-seeing marathon, gawping at one solid gold, glittering, bejewelled monstrance after another; traipsing through vast galleries full of mediocre and dolorous religious 'art'; and anxiously dashing from one Inca ruin to the next intent on seeing the lot. You can't consume Cuzco in this way without saturation. Not only that, but if you try to gobble it up like that you'll miss out on a lot of other things which the place has to offer such as a colourful (non-craft) market; a bunch of folk musicians you unexpectedly run into in an obscure café; or an Indian wedding where someone thrusts a pot of *chicha* into your hands and you get endless amusement all afternoon trying to learn the fancy footwork of the local dances. There are many possibilities. Real people live in

Cuzco too and they don't live in the past. Give yourself some time and don't shun distractions and opportunities to experience something else.

Inca Ruins

The most impressive of these is the fortress of **Sacsayhuaman**, overlooking Cuzco. There you can see three parallel levels of fortifications constructed out of enormous rocks – some of them weighing an estimated 30 tonnes – which all fit together perfectly without the use of any mortar. Across the parade ground, which they face, is the solid rock throne where the Sapa Inca is reputed to have sat while reviewing his troops. It was at Sacsayhuaman that the Incas made their last stand against Pizarro's forces before retreating down the Urubamba Valley. These days it's the setting for the annual festival *Inti Raymi*, on 24 June, which is one of the largest and most colourful of all Peruvian festivals and not to be missed if you're in the area about that time. Get there two weeks before, otherwise you'll find hotel accommodation almost impossible to get. Fresh excavation work is going on behind the parade ground so there may be even more to see in future.

To get to Sacsayhuaman simply walk up Calle Suecia from the Plaza de Armas, bearing slightly right onto Resbalosa and then turn sharp right when you reach the tarmac road that goes up to the ruins. It shouldn't take you more than half an hour to walk there.

From Sacsayhuaman you can carry on along the same tarmac road to **Qenqo**, **Puca Pucara** and **Tambomachay**. You can't miss them: they're all by the side of the road though Tambomachay is quite a walk (about 4 km). Qenqo and Puca Pucara, on the other hand, are only about a 15 to 20 minute walk from Sacsayhuaman.

In Cuzco itself, you can see the best examples of Inca stonework along Loreto which starts on the Plaza de Armas alongside the tourist office. One side of this street once formed the walls of the Palace of the Women of the Sun, and the other side the Palace of the Serpents. Other superb examples can be found along San Agustín and along Triunfo. About half-way along the second block of Triunfo, from the Plaza de Armas on the right-hand side, is the famous 12-angled stone.

What remains of the **Temple of the Sun (Qoricancha)** – a huge five-chambered structure – can be seen inside and outside the church of Santo Domingo. Excavations, which have been going on since the disastrous earthquake of 1950, have revealed four of the original chambers. Included in these excavations is the curved wall below which, in Inca times, was a 'garden' of gold and silver replicas of maize and other important food plants. You can see this curved wall best from outside the church. It's open 8.30 am to 12 noon and 2 to 5 pm Monday to Saturday.

Churches & Colonial Mansions

In the centre of the city is the early 17th century baroque **Cathedral** built on the site of the Palace of Viracocha. It's worth visiting for its ornate interior, choir stalls and its main altar of solid silver. Entry is via the attached chapel of El Triunfo on the corner of Triunfo and the Plaza de Armas. It's open 10 am to 12 noon and 3 to 6 pm Monday to Saturday and 3 to 6 pm on Sunday.

The most beautiful church in the centre however, is **La Compañia de Jesus**, the Jesuits' church built on the side of the Palace of the Serpents. It's open 11 am to 12 noon and 5 to 6.30 pm daily. Two other churches you should visit are **La Merced** and **Santa Catalina**. The former, first built in 1534 and rebuilt in the late 17th century, is noteworthy for its beautiful cloisters in the attached monastery and for its museum which contains many objects of historical interest. Like Santa Catalina, part of La Merced is still a functioning nunnery despite the fact that the public can now see the church; and part of the building is a museum. La Merced is open 8.30 am to 12 noon and 2.30 to 5.30 pm Monday to Saturday. Santa Catalina is open 9 am to 12 noon and 3 to 6 pm every day except Friday.

Also worth a quick visit is the church of **San Blas**. The pulpit there is a masterpiece of mestizo wood carving. It's open 10 am to 12 noon and 3 to 6 pm Monday to Saturday and from 3 to 6 pm on Sunday.

Most of the outstanding colonial mansions now also double as museums. One of the most important is the **Regional History Museum** housed in the Palacio del Almirante which formerly belonged to Admiral Francisco Maldonado. It has displays of Inca agricultural implements and wooden locks, colonial furniture and paintings of the Cuzco school. It's open 9 am to 12 noon and 2 to 5 pm Monday to Saturday. Another is the **Museum of Religious Art**, housed in the Palacio Arzobispal, on the corner of Herrajes and Hatunrumiyoc, which displays paintings of the Cuzco school and colonial furniture. It's open Monday to Saturday from 8 am to noon and 3 to 6 pm.

The **Archaeological Museum**, Calle Tigre 115 near the junction with Plateros, has an excellent collection of pre-Columbian artefacts including examples of Inca gold work (you may have to ask to see the latter as they tend to be kept under lock and key). It also contains a very good display of woven fabrics. The museum is open daily from 7.15 am to 1 pm during the first three months of the year and 7.45 am to 12.30 pm and 3 to 6 pm Monday to Friday for the rest of the year. Entry costs about US$1 (no student reductions).

Around Cuzco

The **Urubamba Valley** naturally offers the most spectacular Inca ruins, but it's also worth making a trip to **Raqchi** on the Cuzco-Puno road where there is a unique Inca construction standing 13½ metres high. It's the only Inca structure, yet discovered, which used pillars to support the roof and the only one with adobe walls

standing on top of a stone base. The complex includes stone baths. It was once thought to be the fabled Temple of Viracocha but archaeologists now think it was more likely a textile factory.

If you're thinking of staying in the area overnight, the nearest places to stay are in Tinta. There are no hotels in Raqchi – it's just a tiny village. In Tinta, try the *Casa Communal* which has dormitory-style accommodation and serves good food for US$0.65. Food is also available at a few other shops and cafés and Tinta is a good place to see primitive farming techniques practised.

Raqchi is also famous throughout Peru for its annual festival of dance and music which takes place one week before *Inti Raymi*. Performers flock there from all over Peru to take part in the festival and there are special trains from Cuzco at the time. To get to Raqchi during the rest of the year take a *San Cristobal* bus from Av Huascar 120, Cuzco. They leave about every hour throughout the day, cost US$1 and take about four hours.

Places to Stay

As you might expect of a city which attracts thousands of visitors every year, Cuzco has an almost endless variety of hotels to choose from. Unfortunately, many of the cheaper places are dingy, cold and scruffy with hot water only rarely available. This is especially true of the budget hotels along San Agustín, many of which used to be popular. They include the *Hostal Palermo, Hostal Royal* and the *Hotel Central*. The only one which looks vaguely pleasant is the *Hotel Panamericana*, San Agustín 339, which has a courtyard, heavily carved wooden staircases and balconies and is kept clean and tidy. It costs US$1 to $1.50 per person, depending on whether you have a bathroom or not.

Another cheapie which used to be popular much nearer the centre but which again, you'd probably only consider if money is really tight, is the *Hostal*

Bolívar, Tecsecocha 2 near the junction with Procuradores. It's very basic but costs only US$0.50 per bed.

Much better value if you want to pay as little as possible but stay right in the centre is either the *Hostal del Procuradores*, Procuradores 366; or the *Hostal Residencial La Casona*, Procuradores 50. Both are pleasant, rustic old places set around small courtyards and cost about US$2 per person.

Another popular place which is good value are the rooms at the school run by the Santo Domingo Convent, Ahuacpinta 600 (look for the sign, 'Colegio Estatal Gratuito San Martín de Porras'). Go through the gate there and round to the far side of the new cream-coloured building on the left hand side. They rent out double rooms for US$1.75 per person, there's hot water all day and you can leave excess gear there safely while you do the Inca Trail or whatever. The rooms are very clean and many travellers recommend this place.

The most popular hotels among travellers, however, are along Plateros/Saphi and Suecia off the top side of the Plaza de Armas. The best value for money is undoubtedly the *Hospedaje Suecia*, Suecia 332. This is a really cosy, thoughtfully-decorated, clean and comfortable hospedaje with rooms around a small, glass-roofed courtyard. The staff are very friendly, rooms cost just US$1 per person and there are hot showers. Unfortunately, because it's small it's often full.

Next are two very similar places close to each other: the *Hotel Caceres*, Plateros 368; and the *Plateros*, Plateros 340, with the former possibly the better of the two. They're both large, traditional wood and adobe hotels where you can almost always find a room. The staff are friendly, the rooms secure, clean sheets are provided (as well as blankets) and there's plenty of hot water for three hours in the mornings and evenings. Rooms, all without bathroom, start from less than US$2 and go up to nearly US$6 for a room with four beds.

More expensive but very popular indeed is the *Hostal Familiar*, Saphi 661. This courtyard place has been very tastefully renovated and has a captivating atmosphere. Doubles are US$3.50 without a bathroom and US$4 with a bathroom. In the tourist season it's likely you will be quoted US$5.50. There's plenty of hot water all day. Make sure you get there early in the day if you want a room.

Other places which are good value and very reasonably priced are:

Hostal Residencial Milan, Trinitarias 237. This place is quite a way from the plaza but very convenient for the Machu Picchu railway station and the Indian market (a photographer's paradise). The staff are very friendly and there's a baggage safe, cafeteria and hot water all day. Rooms cost US$2 to $3.50 depending on size and whether or not they have a bathroom. Some rooms are better than others. They also have rooms for four people for US$5 without own bathroom.

Hostal Chavin, Matara 215. A colonial house with patio converted to a hotel. All the rooms have their own bath and there's hot water all day. There's also a baggage safe. The prices are similar to the Milan.

Gran Hotel Imperio, Chaparro 121. This is a very large hotel very close to the Machu Picchu railway station which often caters for the volunteers of archaeological digs in the Urubamba Valley. It's a clean place with hot water all day and costs US$1 per person without own bath and US$1.50 per person with own bath.

Hostal Bellavista, Av Santiago 100, almost on the bridge over the railway (the Urubamba railway line) and about 10 minutes walk from the Plaza de Armas. It costs US$3 a double with own bath and constant hot water. It's brand new and very clean, there is a laundry service and the staff are friendly.

Hostal San Blas, Cuesta San Blas 526. Close to San Blas church, this hotel is good value at US$2 per person with own bath and hot water.

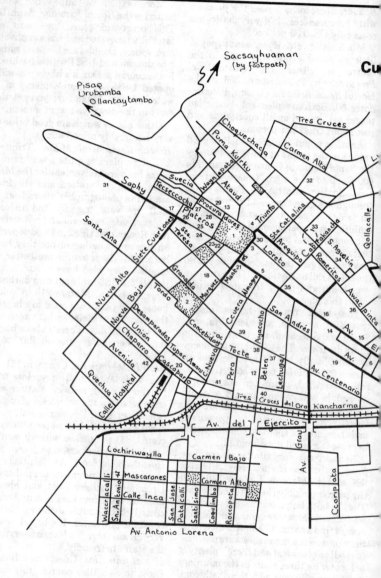

Cu

Sacsayhuaman
(by footpath)

Pisaq
Urubamba
Ollantaytambo

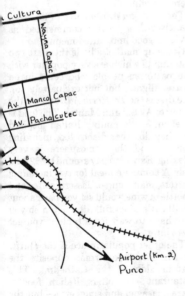

1 Plaza de Armas
2 Plaza San Francisco
3 Tourist Office
4 Cathedral & Iglesia del Triunfo
5 Money Exchange Houses &
  Museum of Popular Art
6 Post Office
7 Railway Station for Macchu Picchu
8 Railway Station for Puno,
  Juliaca & Arequipa
9 Hidalgo Bus Terminal
10 San Cristobal Bus Terminal
11 Minibuses to Pisaq & Urubamba
12 Morales Moralitas Bus Terminal
13 Ormeña Booking Office
14 Aeroperu & Avianca
15 Fawcett Airline Office
16 Lima Tours &
  American Express Agents
17 Archeology Museum
18 Regional History Museum
  (Casa Garcilaso)
19 Carmen Alto Bus Terminal
20 Main Market
21 Trattoria Adriano
22 Qhatuchay & Los Violinos
  Restaurant & Peña
23 Hotel Samari, Hotel Espaderos &
  Govinda
24 Choperia Cusco
25 Hostal Plateros
26 Hotel Cacebes
27 Hostal Bolivar
28 Hostal del Procuradores &
  Residencial la Casona
29 Hospedaje Suecia
30 Paititi Restaurant
31 Hostal Familiar
32 Hostal San Blas
33 Hostal Palermo,
  Hostal Royal &
  Hotel Central
34 Hotel Panamericana
35 Del Angel Hotel
36 Dormitorio Santo Domingo
37 Hostal Portales
38 Hostal Colonial
39 Hostal Chavin
40 Hostal Belen
41 Hostal Residencial Milan
42 Gran Hotel Imperio

Places to Eat

The restaurant scene in Cuzco has improved by leaps and bounds over the last few years and you'll be spoilt for choice. Most of the popular restaurants, bars and nightclubs are on the Plaza de Armas, Procuradores, Plateros and Mantas, though probably the cheapest places are along Santa Clara (the continuation of Mantas towards Machu Picchu railway station), Procuradores and Espaderos (the street between the Plaza de Armas and the Plaza Cabildo on the top side of the two). This isn't always the case because you can still buy chicken, chips and salad on the Plaza de Armas (at *Mario's*) for less than US$1.

El Corsario (popularly known as *Chez Maggy*) has been popular for years but has moved premises and is now on Espaderos. It's still excellent value, does good spaghetti and pizza and is very popular with travellers. The *Chifa Hawaii* (formerly the Chifa Dragon), Plateros, has also been popular for years. It still offers what is probably the best Chinese food in Cuzco. Also on Plateros near the junction with the Plaza de Armas is the *Choperia Cusco*. This is a new tastefully decorated place which looks expensive but isn't. It's very popular at lunch times. You can have chicken and chips (about US$1), salads (US$0.50) and omelettes (US$0.50) and breakfast for US$0.80 to $1 depending on whether you want American or Continental.

The almost unpronounceable *Haylliys*, again on Plateros, has been recommended by many travellers for its good food. It is open early in the morning for breakfast. If you like yoghurt then try the *Café Paris* near the Café Ayllu on the Plaza de Armas. *Café Ayllu* is a very pleasant coffee bar with good tea, toast, cakes and classical music. The Paris has contemporary music. You can get a good breakfast with quick service at *Piccolo* on the top side of the Plaza de Armas. Ham and eggs or a large sandwich with coffee should cost US$0.75 to $1.

Vegetarians have a good choice here too. *God's Food*, Procuradores 398, has a good varied menu at reasonable prices. So too does *Govinda*, Espaderos next to the Hostal Espaderos, which offers the usual high quality, Indian-style vegetarian food associated with Hari Krishna restaurants. Likewise, the *Restaurant Vegetariano*, Procuradores 36, has a very good varied menu (such as Greek salads and soups) and the prices are very reasonable. The *Inti Café* on Procuradores has also been recommended for vegetarian food.

Another place which could be very good is the *Restaurant La Casa Antigua* on Procuradores. The food is good and the atmosphere would be excellent if there were more people and they lit the fire in there at night.

The *Café San Antonio* in La Plaza San Francisco has been recommended as having a good and varied menu.

Going up-market a little there are two restaurants which are very popular with gringos (often people who come in on charter flights, but not exclusively so). The first is the *Trattoria Adriano*, on the corner of Av Sol and Mantas. The food is excellent – it's mainly Italian-inspired but they do other dishes too, including trout – and the atmosphere is very relaxing. Expect to pay around US$2 for a dish. A complete meal for two including starters, main course, dessert, coffee and a bottle of wine would set you back about US$10. It's often full after 7 pm so you may have to wait for a table if you get there later.

The other popular place is the *Paititi* on the Plaza de Armas opposite the bottom side of the Cathedral. This restaurant also offers Italian food – pizzas, lasagna and spaghettis – but the pizza portions are niggardly. The lasagna, on the other hand, is good value at about US$2 per dish. This place is very popular because it puts on live folklore music every night during the tourist season from 8 pm onwards. Don't go to eat there until about 7.45 pm because if you finish your meal before 8 pm (when the tourists flock in) the waiters turn into mafia heavies and almost strong-arm you out so they can seat someone else. At these times they also fawn over groups of obvious tourists and ignore anyone else. Someone ought to give them coins coated with super-glue. The place sucks.

If possible, avoid the *Do-Re-Mi* on the top side of the plaza near Suecia. The food is relatively expensive but nothing special and the soups are just warmed-up 'Maggi' with liberal amounts of cornflour. There are bored folklore musicians and enthusiastic dancers but service is excruciatingly slow and the bill – when you finally get it – is just a figment of the imagination heavily biased in the cashier's favour. It takes all night to sort it out.

Peñas

There are many restaurants and bars around the Plaza de Armas and along Procuradores and Av Sol which put on live folklore music. Some of them however, only do it in the tourist season and a few of the restaurants are more interested in customer turn-over than anything else.

There are two *peñas*, though, which are excellent and very friendly indeed. The first is the *Qhatuchay* on the first floor half way along the Plaza de Armas on the Plateros side. This is probably the best *peña* in South America. It's usually open every night from 8 pm until early morning and has non-stop bands from 9 pm onwards. There's no cover charge (though the bands may pass the hat around), it's informal in the extreme, always riotous and very friendly. There's no food available and they only have beers, pisco and soft drinks (at almost normal prices). Go there once and you'll return every night!

Right next door to the Qhatuchay and also on the first floor is *Los Violinos*. This is a restaurant/*peña* which looks something like a converted barn. It's informal, there's no cover charge and meal prices are very reasonable. There's usually music every night from 8 pm. A blackboard down at street level has information about what's on in the evening. Highly recommended. Try it for a meal instead of going to the Paititi.

El Tronquito on Plateros has been recommended. It has good food, good music and is not touristy.

You'll come across posters advertising other *peñas* from time to time, usually during the tourist season, so keep an eye out.

Getting Around

There are local buses to the airport from the city centre but it's hardly worth it with a rucksack on your back and the possibility of theft. A taxi costs just US$1. Around town taxis generally cost about US$0.50.

There are local buses from Cuzco to Raqchi (Inca ruins) on the Puno road from Huascar 120. A bus to Pisac is about US$0.50.

THE URUBAMBA VALLEY

The Urubamba Valley, or Sacred Valley of the Incas as it's sometimes known, offers a unique experience that cannot be matched anywhere else in South America. There you will find the greatest collection of Inca ruins on the continent, stretching all the way from Pisac to Machu Picchu and, if you're into bush walking, beyond there to Vilcabamba. Also in this valley, from Km 88 on the Cuzco-Machu Picchu railway line, is the famed Inca Trail, which is studded with superb ruins like those of Sayajmarca, Phuyupatamarca and Wiñay Wayna.

But it isn't just the ruins which draw travellers from the four corners of the globe. The setting itself is something else again, with snow-covered peaks rising to over 6000 metres, lush jungle and dramatic gorges. All the way from Pisac to Ollantaytambo you'll see the agricultural terraces – many of them still used – carved out of the steep mountain slopes by the Incas. Mix all this with a colourful

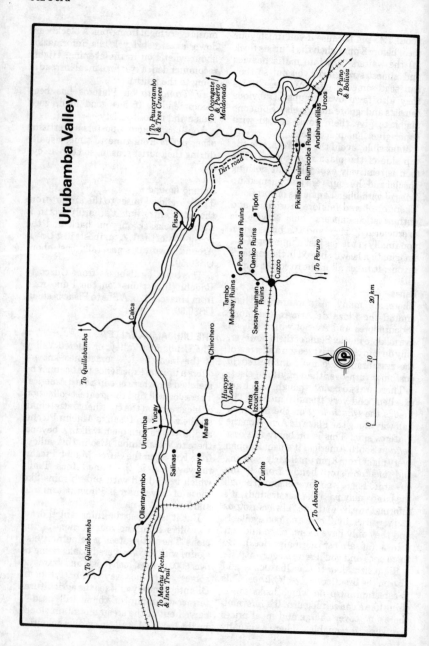

Urubamba Valley

craft market and hot springs and you have Peru in a nutshell.

Getting Around

Bus Cuzco is connected to Pisac, Calca and Urubamba by a fleet of new minibuses which run from the early morning until late in the afternoon (last bus back from Urubamba to Cuzco about 3.30 pm). There is a sort of vague half-hourly schedule but it's safer to say they go when full. The terminus in Cuzco is along Recoleta. In Pisac you pick them up at the bridge over the Urubamba river and in Urubamba town you pick them up at the petrol station on the main road through the valley. Cuzco to Urubamba costs about US$1.20 and takes about 1½ hours.

There are no buses between Urubamba and Ollantaytambo so here you must take a pick-up or hitch. The pick-ups go when they're full, get even fuller along the way and take about half an hour. The charge should be about US$0.20.

Transport between Ollantaytambo and Quillabamba is much less frequent though there are usually two or three trucks daily in either direction. Ask around in the plaza at Ollantaytambo.

Train

Cuzco-Ollantaytambo-Machu Picchu-Quillabamba These are the trains to take if you are visiting Ollantaytambo, the Inca Trail, Machu Picchu or Quillabamba and unlike the trains to Puno and Arequipa, they depart from San Pedro station. Between Cuzco and Machu Picchu you can take any train but most people take either the *autovagon* or the tourist train since they are much quicker than the ordinary train and depart at more convenient times (though they are more expensive).

If you want to get on or off at Ollantaytambo, Km 88 (for the Inca Trail) or Aguas Calientes (just before Machu Picchu station – which is actually called 'Ruinas') then you have to take the ordinary stopping trains. The same applies if you want to go to Quillabamba. These ordinary trains are always late but usually predictably so – half an hour at Aguas Calientes is normal. If you only bought a one-way ticket out of Cuzco and are catching a train back from Ruinas, Aguas Calientes or Ollantaytambo then buy your return ticket before you get on the train – they're more expensive if you buy them on the train itself.

The train schedules are:

Cuzco-Quillabamba ordinary trains at 5.30 am and 2 and 10.30 pm.
Cuzco-Ruinas *autovagons* at 7 and 8 am, and a tourist train at 8.20 am, journey time about three hours. **Ruinas-Cuzco** *autovagons* at 3.05 and 4.10 pm, tourist train 5.30 pm (this one takes four hours).
Ruinas/Aguas Calientes-Cuzco ordinary trains at 7.50 am and 4.40 pm, four hours.

All these trains are daily services, except that on Sundays there is only one ordinary train in either direction (at 4.40 pm from Aguas Calientes to Cuzco), and they're often cancelled completely.

In Cuzco, tickets for the *autovagons* and the tourist train are sold the day before departure from 10 am to 12 noon and 2.30 to 4 pm. You can also buy them on the day of departure between 6.30 and 8.20 am. Tickets for the ordinary trains are sold the day before departure from 9.30 am to 12 noon and 4 to 5 pm and on the day, are sold between 4 am and 5.30 pm.

Student reductions are not available on the railway fares themselves but they are on the entry fee into Machu Picchu so if you're buying a return ticket from Cuzco, be sure to show the railway clerk your student card.

Return tickets on the *autovagons* cost US$12 but they don't include the entry fee to Machu Picchu or the bus fare from the railway station to the site (a further US$6.35). Return tickets on the tourist train cost US$15.65 (or US$13.30 if you have a student card) and they do include the entry fee and the bus fare from the station to the site. You can buy one-way tickets on the tourist train for US$4.65 but they exclude the entry fee and bus fare (the latter two cost US$4.75, or US$2.40 with student card, and US$1.60 respectively). One-way tickets on the *autovagons* cost US$5.60.

Fares (excluding entry fee and bus fare) on the ordinary train from Cuzco are:

Station	1st Class	2nd Class
Ollantaytambo	US$1.15	US$0.90
Aguas Calientes	US$1.90	US$1.50
Ruinas	US$1.95	US$1.50
Quillabamba	US$2.95	US$2.30

If you decide to take local trains for whatever reason then be very careful about thieves. These trains are notorious for rip-offs. The same is true of the railway station in Cuzco, only even more so. The tourist train and the *autovagons* are generally fairly safe these days since they are heavily policed (and expensive) so thieves rarely get on.

A fleet of minibuses transports passengers from Machu Picchu railway station up to the site entrance. The return fare is US$1.60 if you don't have a railway ticket which includes this. Buy your ticket at Ruinas station. If you've just completed the Inca Trail, you have the choice of walking down to the Ruinas station (very well signposted and shouldn't take more than 20 to 30 minutes – local children run down in 10 minutes) or taking the bus from the hotel at the site entrance (half fare one-way).

PISAC

Pisac is famous for its magnificent Inca ruins and colourful Sunday market. You really need to spend a whole day (at least!) exploring the ruins as they're spread out over a large area on very steep mountain slopes. There's some beautiful stone-work to be seen as well as the remains of temples, fortresses, living quarters and terraces – the latter are still

in use. Some sensitive reconstruction has been done on some of the houses. There are stupendous views down the valley in either direction. To get to the ruins from the town, take the path which goes up-hill from the left-hand side of the church on the plaza.

The Sunday market is still worth visiting but over the last few years it's become very touristy. It used to start at about dawn and the best prices you could get were before the tourist buses arrived at about 10 am. These days many of the traders don't even arrive until about an hour before the tourists are due. Other travellers report that a better market can be found at Chinchero.

Places to Stay

There's are only three places unless you can find a room to rent in a private house. Electricity supplies can be sporadic so have candles handy.

The best place if you're on a budget is the *Hostal Pisaq* on the main plaza. Beds cost about US$2 per person per night. After that there is the *Pension Roma* close to the bridge over the Urubamba river. It's definitely nothing to write home about unless you have a fertile imagination. It's dirty, dingy and run by a reincarnation of Mother Hubbard. Don't expect running water when you need it and although meals are available in the evening, they're inedible, so eat elsewhere. The cost of a bed in the (mixed) dormitory won't even damage the thread in your pocket.

The only other place is the *Albergue Turistico Chongo Chico*. With a name like that you'd expect something special and indeed it is. It's a very up-market hotel which caters for well-heeled tourists. It costs US$12 for bed, dinner and breakfast. It's clean, well-run, has excellent food and information on the area. English is spoken. You can also camp in the grounds for a small fee.

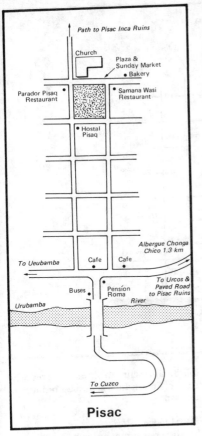

Path to Pisac Inca Ruins

Church

Plaza & Sunday Market
• Bakery

Parador Pisaq • Restaurant

• Samana Wasi Restaurant

• Hostal Pisaq

Albergue Chonga Chico 1.3 km

To Ueubamba

Cafe   Cafe

To Urcos & Paved Road to Pisac Ruins

Buses •

Pension Roma

Urubamba   River

To Cuzco

Pisac

Places to Eat

If you're not staying at the Chongo Chico, the best place to eat is the tourist café on the bottom side of the plaza. The food is pretty good and prices are reasonable. There's also another reasonable restaurant diagonally opposite this near the top side of the plaza. The cafés on the main road close to the Roma and facing the Urubamba river bridge are also worth checking out. The standard is about the same as street-stall food. Near the main square there's a bakery where you can get excellent bread straight from the oven.

URUBAMBA

Though somewhat larger than Pisac, Urubamba is a sleepy town with nothing much going on. It's unlikely you would want to stay there overnight – it's best to carry on to Ollantaytambo.

Places to Stay

There are a number of hotels in Urubamba. The *Hotel Urubamba*, Jiron Bolognesi, is an attractive colonial house and reasonably good value at US$1 per person per night.

OLLANTAYTAMBO

This beautiful and tranquil village is the ideal place to use as a base from which to explore the rest of the valley, or just as somewhere to relax. Like Cuzco and Pisac it has some spectacular and extensive Inca ruins, most of them enclosed within a temple fortress. The unfinished temple, begun by Pachacuti, contains some of the largest stones ever used by the Inca builders. The village itself is constructed on top of Inca foundations so you can see typical Inca stonework down almost any street. Don't miss this village on your way to or from Machu Picchu; it's the sort of place that's very difficult to leave once you have soaked up its atmosphere for a few days.

Ollantaytambo is the last place that you can buy food and drink for the Inca Trail – there's nothing on the trail itself. The two tiendas on the top side of the plaza stock most basic things including tinned fish and meat, a strange-tasting variety of plain chocolate and the local firewater (similar to Pisco). Fresh bread can be bought from the bakery every evening. There is no camping equipment for hire in the village.

Places to Stay

The most popular place used to be the *Albergue* but they no longer take individual travellers, though local expatriates suggest you might get in there outside the tourist season. These days

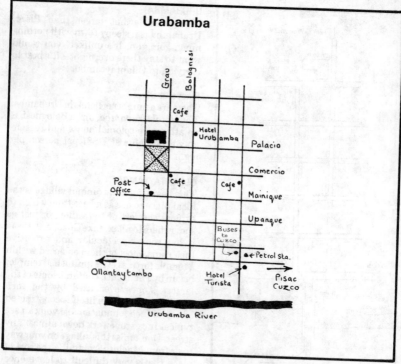

they cater for trekking companies and pre-booked groups and charge US$5 per person per night.

The cheapest places are the *Restaurant Alcazar*, which is friendly and adequate and costs US$0.65 per person in two-bed rooms (they only have two of these rooms); and the *Hostal El Tambo*, which is considerably larger, equally friendly, and offers basic rooms around a quiet courtyard for US$0.65 per person although it only has cold showers.

The *Parador Turistico* has rooms from US$4. This large, traditional house has rooms on two storeys around a peaceful courtyard. The bedrooms are on the first floor, some of them overlooking the ruins. Like many buildings in Ollantaytambo the foundations are of Inca stonework. The rooms are spartan and bare and the

toilet and washing facilities are extremely basic but downstairs is the best restaurant in town.

Places to Eat

The best restaurant by far in this village is the *Parador* and although it isn't cheap (by Peruvian standards) the food and the setting are excellent. Trout, fresh from the river, is superb – for two people about US$2.50. For average Peruvian fare, try the *Restaurant Alcazar*, the *La Nusta Restaurant* or the *Restaurant Ollantay*. The latter two are on the plaza.

THE INCA TRAIL

For those without the time, the experience or the money to pay for the guide and equipment necessary for the more remote

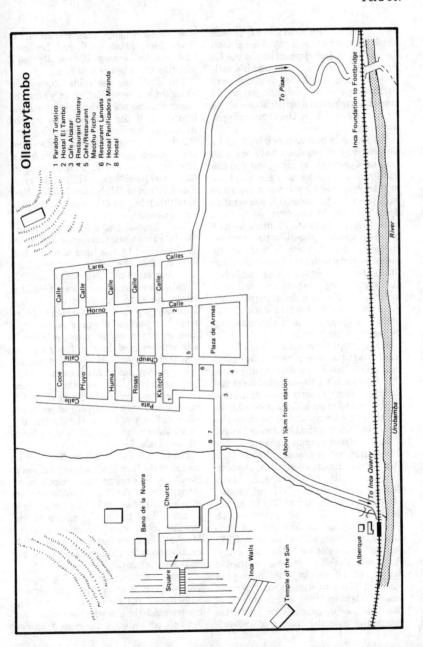

Ollantaytambo

1 Parador Turistico
2 Hostal El Tambo
3 Cafe Alcazar
4 Restaurant Ollantay
5 Cafe/Restaurant Macchu Picchu
6 Restaurant Lanusta
7 Hostal Panificadora Miranda
8 Hostal

To Pisac

Inca Foundation to Footbridge

River

Urubamba

Calles

Lares

Calle   Calle   Calle   Calle   Calle

Horno

Calle

Plaza de Armas

Ccoe   Ptuyo   Huma   Rosas   Kkitchu   Chaupi

Pata

Calle   Calle

2

5

6

4

1

3

About ½km from station

8 7

Bano de la Nustra

Church

Square

Inca Walls

Temple of the Sun

To Inca Quarry

Alberque

treks, the Inca Trail offers an experience which cannot be found anywhere else on the continent (except perhaps in the La Paz area). There's no doubt that it's well-trodden these days, but it's still very worthwhile and any feelings you might have of being part of a herd will quickly be blown away by the magnificent landscape.

It's probably best to hire a tent (and a sleeping bag, if you don't have one with you) as it gets cold at night, but you can cut down on the amount of gear you have to take with you by sharing a gas stove with several other people. If you want to keep the weight of your pack to a minimum, concentrate on dried foods – packet soups, muesli-type cereals, chocolate, etc. A torch is more-or-less essential and a water bottle very useful to fill in the gaps between watering holes. Give some thought to taking a small hand axe too, if you want a fire at night. Loose wood is difficult to find around the regular camping sites as it's been used up by previous trekkers.

Many people also take a bag of coca leaves and a ball of ash (banana leaf ash is the best). Chewing coca leaves alleviates the effects of high altitude and gives you the extra energy to carry you over the first 4000-plus metre pass. Coca leaves can be bought very cheaply and legally from any tienda in Cuzco or the Urubamba Valley.

You can rent camping gear in Cuzco from a number of places. They include *Inca Treks*, Procuradores 354; *Andean Adventures*, Procuradores 332; *Luren Tours*, Plaza de Armas 177; and another place at Plaza de Armas 265 (near Los Violinos *peña*). Hire charges are much the same. A tent should cost US$1.50 to $2 per day; a foam rubber 'mattress' US$1 per day; and a gas stove US$0.50 a day. For a tent you must leave a returnable deposit of US$80 to $100 plus your passport. Gas canisters to run the stove can be bought for US$4 each from most of the hire companies. None of these companies (nor the tourist office) will store excess baggage while you are on the Trail. Most hotels in Cuzco, however, now offer this service. It's usually free if you stay there before and after.

The Trail and the ruined Inca cities along the way were 'lost' shortly after the Conquest and not rediscovered until the beginning of the 20th century by the American explorer Hiram Bingham. Bingham's accounts of his explorations are good reading – *Lost City of the Incas: The Story of Machu Picchu and its Builders* (New York, 1948), and *Across South America* (Houghton Mifflin, New York 1911). Many of them are available in bookshops in Cuzco.

The Spanish never actually found Machu Picchu so it truly was a lost city of the Incas but by the time the dust had settled after the collapse of the Inca successor state at Vilcabamba in 1595, Vilcabamba also became lost. Bingham came close to rediscovering it but dismissed the outer works which he came across as part of a minor settlement. Another 50 years were to elapse before it was rediscovered in the 1960s by the explorer Gene Savoy. His excellent account of his journey and of his discovery of the high jungle cities of the pre-Inca Chachapoyas civilisation is well worth reading and may whet your appetite for more difficult trails in the Andes. It's called *Vilcabamba: Last City of the Incas* (Robert Hale, London 1971).

You should plan on taking five days to complete the Inca Trail, or longer if you'd like time to explore the various ruins along the way. You can – if you're in good physical shape or pushed for time – do it in three days but you'd miss a lot by treating it as merely a race to get to Machu Picchu as fast as possible. Full details about the trail itself can be found on the accompanying maps.

There have been quite a few reports over the last year or two about armed robberies on the Inca Trail. It's usually the lone individuals who are picked out but this isn't always the case. We have

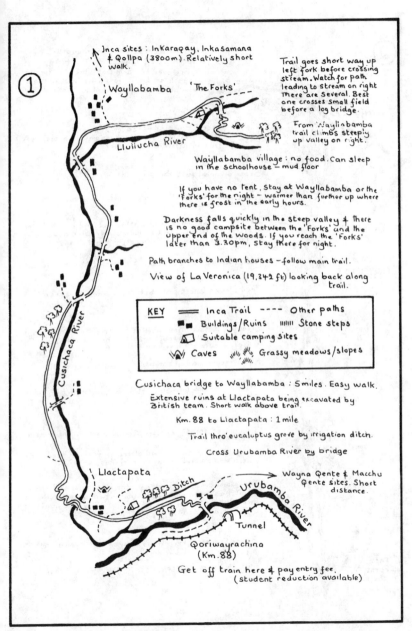

① Inca sites : Inkaraqay, Inkasamana & Qollpa (3800m). Relatively short walk.

Wayllabamba   'The Forks'

Lluliucha River

Trail goes short way up left fork before crossing stream. Watch for path leading to stream on right. There are several. Best one crosses small field before a log bridge.

From Wayllabamba trail climbs steeply up valley on right.

Wayllabamba village : no food. Can sleep in the schoolhouse – mud floor.

If you have no tent, stay at Wayllabamba or the 'Forks' for the night – warmer than further up where there is frost in the early hours.

Darkness falls quickly in the steep valley & there is no good campsite between the 'Forks' and the upper end of the woods. If you reach the 'Forks' later than 3.30pm, stay there for night.

Path branches to Indian houses – follow main trail.

View of La Veronica (19,342 ft) looking back along trail.

KEY   ═══ Inca Trail   ---- Other paths
▪ Buildings/Ruins   ⅢⅢ Stone steps
⌂ Suitable camping sites
⋀ Caves   ᚚᚚ Grassy meadows/slopes

Cusichaca River

Cusichaca bridge to Wayllabamba : 5 miles. Easy walk.

Extensive ruins at Llactapata being excavated by British team. Short walk above trail.

Km. 88 to Llactapata : 1 mile

Trail thro' eucalyptus grove by irrigation ditch.

Cross Urubamba River by bridge

Llactapata   Ditch   Urubamba River

Wayna Qente & Macchu Qente sites. Short distance.

Tunnel

Qoriwayrachina (Km. 88)

Get off train here & pay entry fee. (student reduction available)

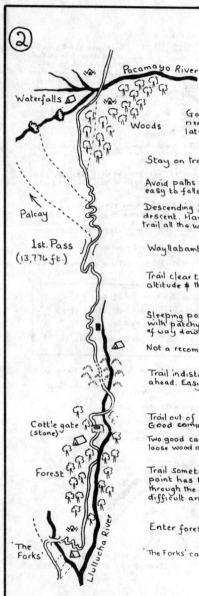

② Pacamayo River

Waterfalls

Woods

Palcay

1st. Pass
(13,776 ft.)

Cattle gate
(stone)

Forest

'The Forks'

Llullucha River

When you reach the Pacamayo you are approx. half way to Macchu Picchu. Once over the 2nd pass the Trail is mostly downhill or on the level though elevation stays around 10,000 ft.

Good camp sites, caves & sweet water — next possibility at Runkuraqay (2 hours). If late in afternoon, stay here.

Stay on trail just above woods.

Avoid paths to left. Carry on straight down valley. Trail easy to follow.

Descending 1st Pass, trail washed out / indistinct. Steep descent. Hard on knees & ankles. Can pick out line of trail all the way to Runkuraqay from 1st Pass.

Wayllabamba to 1st Pass: 6¼ miles (About 5 hours' walk).

Trail clear to first path but slow climbing due to altitude & thin air.

Sleeping possibilities either at herder's hut (stone walls with patchy straw roof) or stone sheep corral about ⅓ of way down to the stream from trail.

Not a recommended campsite — very cold at night.

Trail indistinct through pasture but reappears on ridge ahead. Easy to spot.

Trail out of forest, crosses stream & into alpine pasture. Good camping site.

Two good campsites in small clearings in forest. Very little loose wood around. Frost in mornings.

Trail sometimes runs along edge of stream and at one point has been washed away — here you must walk through the stream itself for about 50–100 yards. Not difficult and trail easy to follow.

Enter forest. Steep trail. Stay on left bank of stream.

'The Forks' campsite has a shelter — no sides, just a roof.

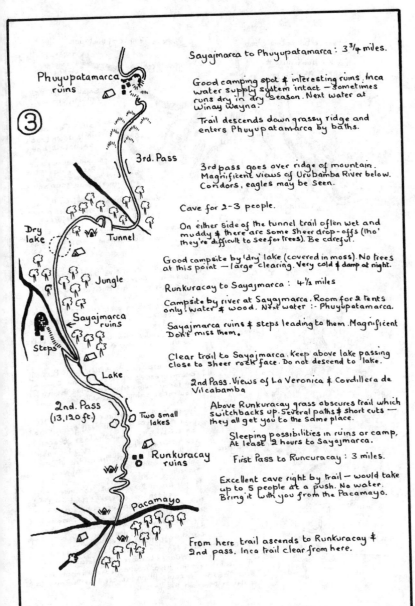

Phuyupatamarca ruins

③

3rd. Pass

Dry lake

Tunnel

Jungle

Sayajmarca ruins

Steps

Lake

2nd. Pass
(13,120 ft.)

Two small lakes

Runkuracay ruins

Pacamayo

Sayajmarca to Phuyupatamarca : 3¾ miles.

Good camping spot & interesting ruins. Inca water supply system intact — sometimes runs dry in dry season. Next water at Winay Wayna.

Trail descends down grassy ridge and enters Phuyupatamarca by baths.

3rd pass goes over ridge of mountain. Magnificent views of Urubamba River below. Condors, eagles may be seen.

Cave for 2-3 people.

On either side of the tunnel trail often wet and muddy & there are some sheer drop-offs (tho' they're difficult to see for trees). Be careful.

Good campsite by 'dry' lake (covered in moss). No trees at this point — large clearing. Very cold & damp at night.

Runkuracay to Sayajmarca : 4½ miles

Campsite by river at Sayajmarca. Room for 2 tents only. Water & wood. Next water :- Phuyupatamarca.

Sayajmarca ruins & steps leading to them. Magnificent Don't miss them.

Clear trail to Sayajmarca. Keep above lake passing close to sheer rock face. Do not descend to 'lake.

2nd Pass. Views of La Veronica & Cordillera de Vilcabamba

Above Runkuracay grass obscures trail which switchbacks up. Several paths & short cuts — they all get you to the same place.

Sleeping possibilities in ruins or camp, At least 2 hours to Sayajmarca.

First Pass to Runcuracay : 3 miles.

Excellent cave right by trail — would take up to 5 people at a push. No water. Bring it with you from the Pacamayo.

From here trail ascends to Runkuracay & 2nd pass. Inca trail clear from here.

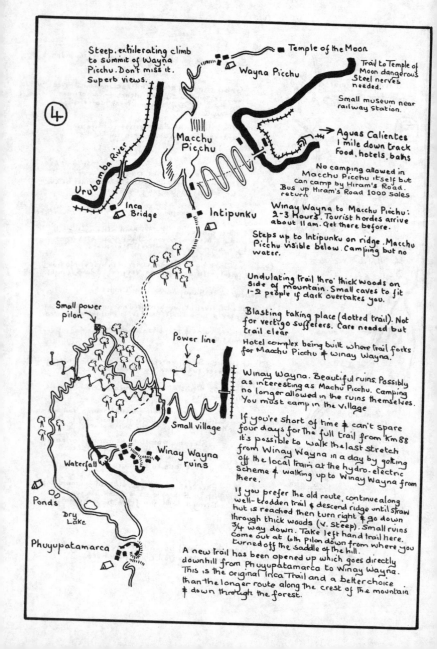

heard of a whole group of people who were relieved of their valuables. Nevertheless, it does seem safer to travel as a group. If you're really worried, armed police can be hired for US$5 per day.

MACHU PICCHU

The 'Lost City of the Incas' is Peru's crowning glory. It's probably the most famous and spectacular archaeological site in the entire Americas and you'll never see anything quite like this place anywhere else. It straddles a narrow saddle of mountain, high above a U-bend in the Urubamba River, against a backdrop of snow-capped peaks, which rise to over 6000 metres high. The sight which greets you as you pass through the portals of Intipunku early in the morning on the last day of the Inca Trail is pure magic. What an incredible place this must once have been! And for those with a little nerve there's the *piéce de résistance* – climbing up the hair-raising stone steps to the top of Wayna Picchu (Huayna Picchu) which overlooks Machu Picchu and has the Temple of the Moon as well as other ruins on its summit.

When Hiram Bingham found this place it was engulfed in jungle. Since then a tremendous amount of clearing and restoration work has been done, which includes thatching some of the buildings and getting the original water courses working again. It's a romantic place – a place for dreaming – and it needs time.

As it is such a wonder, the site is naturally overrun with hordes of well-heeled tourists, at certain times of the year, all anxious to consume its sights in a few short hours. You can avoid this onslaught by exploring the site between dawn and about 10.30 am and between 3 and 6 pm. In the meantime, climb Wayna Picchu – very few day-trippers get up there as it takes too long. You are not allowed to start the climb up to Wayna Picchu after 1 pm.

Entry to Machu Picchu costs about US$5, or US$2.50 with a student card.

This ticket entitles you to entry on two consecutive days without further charge. If you want the student reduction the officials will demand to see your passport as well as the student card to make sure that you have 'Student' in the occupation section of your passport. You may have problems if it doesn't say that. Tell them you left your passport at the hotel in Cuzco because you'd been warned about thefts on the train. The site opens at 6.30 am.

Expensive soft drinks and outrageously expensive meals and accommodation are available at the *Tourist Hotel* just outside the ticket gate – a double is US$65 to $75 a night! Some of the waiters and staff can be extremely off-hand with backpackers, they obviously make more in tips from the day tourists, so if you're on a budget this is not the place to stay. The outside cafeteria does terrible food at very expensive prices. There are cheaper soft drinks, beer and ice cream at the snack shop/shack on the other side of the road from the hotel.

Accommodation is available for those who want it at Aguas Calientes, a short distance down the railway line from Machu Picchu. There is now a hostal at Wiñay Wayna, two to three hours down the Inca trail, which costs less than US$1 and meals cost about US$1.

AGUAS CALIENTES

For budget travellers who want to spend a few days at Machu Picchu, this is the place to stay. It's also well known for its thermal springs which are just perfect to relax in if you've come off the Inca Trail. To get there from Machu Picchu simply walk down the railway line from Ruinas station towards Cuzco. It's a couple of km at the most.

Entry to the hot springs costs US$0.10 and the old woman who collects it will chase you if you try to avoid paying. Unfortunately, in the tourist season, a lot of people use those springs and there are only two baths (one tepid and the other relatively hot). It can get scummy by late afternoon and, if you're concerned about catching giardia (women in particular), then it might not be a good idea to use them at those times. Better to go there after midnight by which time the inflowing water should have cleaned them out. You also don't have to pay at this time.

Places to Stay

The best place is the Q'oñi Unu (Quechua for 'Aguas Calientes'). It's run by Bill Kaiser (a North American) and his wife, Margarita (a Cusqueña). They offer one of the most relaxing places to stay in the whole of South America and it's excellent value – just US$1.30 per person in a two-bed room and US$2 (for two people) in what they call the 'honeymoon room' with a double bed. The rooms, beds and showers are spotless and there's hot water at all hours (electric), but what gives this place it's atmosphere is the warm and informal welcome which these two people offer. Ask any volunteer worker where they stay when they go to Machu Picchu and you'll get the same answer. By the time you read this they will also have some newly completed (modern) rooms available with or without own bathroom. They'll also do you breakfast (eggs, bread, butter and coffee) for around US$1. I can't recommend this place enough. Bill also acts as a guide if you want to explore the Inca trails and ruins of the Vilcabamba area.

If that place is full then try the Hostal Los Caminantes overlooking the railway tracks which costs US$1.10/$2 for singles/doubles without own bath; has doubles with own bathroom for US$2; and rooms with three, four and five beds for US$0.65 per person. The Hostal Machu Picchu, on the opposite side of the tracks, costs US$1.10 per person in the dormitory rooms or more in private rooms. There's hot water in both places and the Caminantes also has a restaurant and bar. Up the street towards the hot springs there is a fairly new and large Albergue Juventil (Youth Hostel). This is very popular with groups, is modern, very clean and OK if you like these sort of places but it's relatively expensive at US$3 per person including breakfast or US$2.50 without breakfast. Quite a few travellers have recommended it.

Places to Eat

There are a lot of small cafés by the railway tracks and one opposite the Youth Hostel. They all try in their own way but with varying success. Please yourself where you eat but the best of the bunch are, without doubt, the Samana and El Refugio. The former is run by a young Peruvian who has a very good idea what type and standard of food travellers are looking for. Prices are very reasonable, service is quick, and there's a relaxing atmosphere with a good selection of music. The El Refugio is equally good.

The food at El Mirador on the main street has been highly recommended.

If you'd like a game of snooker or pool then go to the restaurant just opposite the Youth Hostel (open all day).

HUANCAYO

Situated in a major wheat-growing area at 3261 metres, Huancayo is famous for its enormous Sunday market and is generally the first town where travellers stop in the mountains above Lima. It's a predominantly Indian area and the Sunday market attracts them in their thousands from far and wide.

Information

The tourist office is on Calle Real 695 and is part of the Ministry of Industry office.

The Banco de la Nación is on Calle Real 144. If you have difficulty changing travellers' cheques, try the State Tourist Hotel.

Huancayo Tours, Calle Real 543, organises tours to nearby villages and towns with English-speaking guides.

Things to See

The big attraction is the Sunday market which brings together probably the largest collection of handicrafts you're ever likely to see in Peru – woven ponchos, blankets, wall hangings and carpets, bags, belts, carved gourds, silverware, antiques real and imagined, fruit and vegetables. The variety and quantity of goods for sale is staggering but get there as early as possible if you want to find any bargains. Many well-heeled tourists come from Lima for the day and all the traders know it so they're often unwilling to bargain at all. But, whatever else you do at this market, *be constantly on the watch for thieves*. It crawls with bag snatchers, bag slashers, pick-pockets and every other kind of rip-off merchant. Very few people come through unscathed.

If you find the prices in the Sunday market rather higher than you expected, it's worth visiting some of the nearby towns and villages where the crafts are made – many of these places also have their own, more localised, markets. The nearest place is **Hualhuas**, a beautiful Indian village in its own right, where alpaca goods are woven. It's almost within walking distance of Huancayo though it's probably better to take a bus. Catch them in the Plaza Inmaculada (marked Local bus terminal on the street map). The journey takes about 15 minutes.

San Jerónimo near Concepción, 22 km north-west of Huancayo, is worth visiting if you're interested in fine filigree silverwork. The local market there is on Wednesdays. Buses leave from the Plaza Amazonas in Huancayo.

Further away still, 18 km beyond Concepción, is **Jauja**, which Pizarro had built as the provisional capital of Peru before Lima was founded. There are colourful markets there on Wednesdays and Sundays, and a number of substantial Inca and Huanca ruins, within walking distance, on the hills overlooking the town. There are plenty of daily buses and colectivos to Jauja from Huancayo.

If you're looking for crafts on any day other than Sunday, try visiting the **Centro Regional de Artesanías**, Jirón Brasilia 200, which sells woven fabrics, carved gourds, ceramics and many other things. It's open Monday to Friday from 8 am to 12 noon and 2 to 6 pm. Also on Saturdays and Sundays from 10 am to 12 noon and 3 to 5 pm.

Places to Stay

A very popular place is the *Hotel Dani*, Giraldez 485. It has hot water, cooking facilities and in many ways is like a small youth hostel. The staff are very friendly and it's good value at US$1.50 per person. Also good value, clean and friendly is the *Hotel Balderon*. It has has hot water and good food such as trout, apple pie and yogurt.

If those places are full then try the *Hotel Santo Domingo*, Calle Ica 675, a quiet, friendly place with a pleasant courtyard but it tends to be very cold. The beds aren't the best I've ever slept in, but there is hot water some of the time. It costs US$2 a double. Better is the *Hotel Prince*, Av Calixto, which also costs US$2 a double with own bathroom and vaguely hot water in the mornings and evenings. The rooms tend to be warmer than those at the Santo Domingo.

Two others of similar standard are the *Hotel Real*, Calle Real, which is quiet, friendly, has hot water and large rooms; and the *Hotel Centro*, Calle Loreto, at about the same price. Opposite the Centro is the *Hotel Roma* at Loreto 447, which is another small, friendly place with good beds and clean sheets but no showers. It's suggested you avoid the *Hotel Ferrocarril*, Calle Giraldez, which is now very run-down and dirty. Similarly, the *Hotel Mandarin*, Calle Amazonas, is no longer very good value.

Places to Eat

There are plenty of restaurants offering

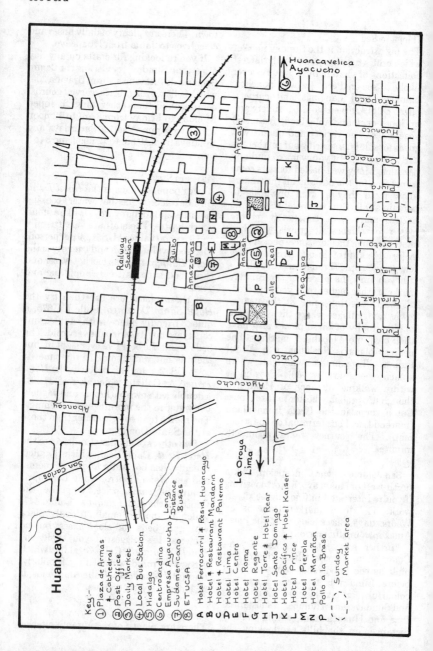

Huancayo

Key:-
1. Plaza de Armas
   † Cathedral
2. Post Office
3. Daily Market
4. Local Bus Station
5. Hidalgo
6. Centroandina
   Empresa Ayacucho
7. Sudamericano
8. ETUCSA

A. Hotel Ferrocarril † Resid. Huancayo
B. Hotel † Restaurant Mandarin
C. Hotel † Restaurant Palermo
D. Hotel Lima
E. Hotel Centro
F. Hotel Roma
G. Hotel Regente
H. Hotel Torre † Hotel Rear
I. Hotel Santa Domingo
J. Hotel Pacifico † Hotel Kaiser
K. Hotel Prince
L. Hotel Prerola
M. Hotel Marañon
P. Pollo a la Brasa

Sunday Market area

Huancavelica
Ayacucho

La Oroya
Lima

Railway Station

Long Distance
Buses

chicken and chips (*pollo a la brasa con papas*), on the Giraldez side of the Plaza de Armas, which are popular with travellers. They're all about the same price and most of them also sell tostadas, which are cheaper. There's an excellent little café next to the Hotel Prince which serves 'businessmen's lunches' at very reasonable prices – three courses plus maize beer and a fruit punch.

The *Restaurant Internacional*, just off the Plaza de Armas, has also been recommended as having very good food at reasonable prices. There's also a vegetarian restaurant on Calle Loreto near the Hotel Roma.

In the Sunday market, head for the *Restaurant El Padrino*. It offers some of the best food in Huancayo – chicken plus mashed potatoes and plantain with salad, for instance. They often have a local harp player there all afternoon. He's a superb musician and also plays at the Hotel Turista in the evenings – at the Turista you'll have to pay to get in.

Getting There & Around

You need to plan ahead if you want a bus or colectivo to Ayacucho. Few of the colectivo services have regular cars going there, so if you prefer a colectivo you'll have to put in some leg-work to get a small group together. *Hidalgo* and *ETUSCA* have the better buses to Ayacucho but they're often booked up days in advance. *Centroandino* use their roughest buses along this route and they overcrowd them excessively – 'full' on the booking form means nothing. They literally fill the corridor with anybody and anything which happens to turn up around departure time. And that's not all – they continue to pick people up en route. Avoid this company if possible. One look at the tyres on their buses and you won't feel like getting on in a hurry.

Bicycles can be hired from Turismo Huancayo Ltd, Calle Real 356, and Huancayo Tours, Calle Real 543. A deposit is necessary.

Huaráz & the Cordillera Blanca

Huaráz is the main population centre of the Cordillera Blanca – the most spectacular mountain area in the entire Andes chain. It contains some of the highest peaks in South America, including Huascarán which at 6768 metres, is the seventh highest mountain in South America. It's a very popular trekking area with a variety of trails ranging from easy to difficult. If you've ever trekked in the Himalaya – and even if you haven't – you'll love this area. It also contains some of the most important archaeological ruins in Peru. Chavín de Huantar, Yaino and Wilcahuaín are among them.

The Cordillera Blanca and the Callejón de Huaylas were the centres of the worst disaster, in terms of the number of lives lost, in the history of the Americas. On 31 May 1970 an earthquake ripped through the area, followed by tremors lasting all night. Almost every town was levelled, 80,000 people were killed and over a million left homeless. About 90% of Huaraz was destroyed and about 15,000 of its inhabitants killed, but the town which took the brunt of the disaster was Yungay. Some 15 million cubic metres of granite fell from the west face of Huascarán, bringing with it another three million cubic metres of ice. In just three minutes this incredible avalanche picked up more earth, rode a cushion of air all the way down to the Santa River (14 km), and hurtled on a further 50 km past Caráz to the hydro-electric plant in the Cañon de Pato. Part of this terrifying mass of rock, mud and ice jumped a 200-metre-high ridge and buried Yungay, along with 18,000 of its inhabitants.

Reconstruction has been going on ever since, aided by disaster funds donated by many countries, particularly Cuba, Switzerland, Russia and West Germany. Although many lives and buildings have

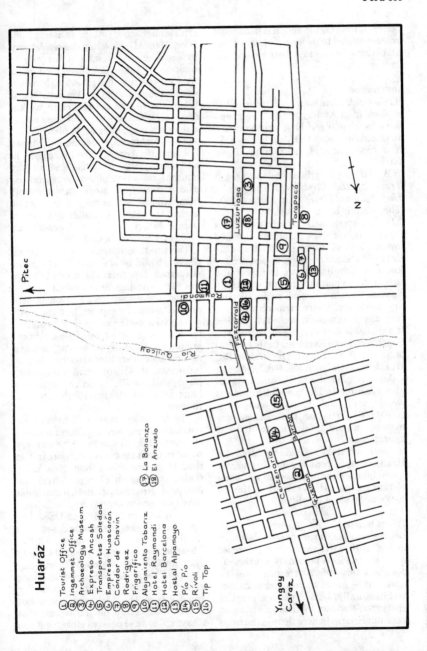

Huaráz

1. Tourist Office
2. Ingemmet Office
3. Archaeology Museum
4. Expreso Ancash
5. Transportes Soledad
6. Empresa Huascarón
7. Cóndor de Chavín
8. Rodríguez
9. Frigorífico
10. Alojamiento Tabariz
11. Hotel Raymondi
12. Hotel Barcelona
13. Hostal Alpamayo
14. Pío Pío
15. Rívoli
16. Tip Top
17. La Bonanza
18. El Anzuelo

been lost forever, the area has been more or less restored to its former state, except that it now has a much better communications network.

Information

The tourist office is on Av Fitzcarral half a block from Av Raymondi. The people are very friendly and have a good range of information about trekking in the area. You can photostat their maps if you like.

By far the best book on the area is *Trails of the Cordilleras Blancas & Huayhuash of Peru* by Jim Bartle (1980). This superb book, written by someone who has spent half his life wandering around this region, contains detailed descriptions of every centimetre of 18 different treks in the area; all you need to know on accommodation, transport and eating in the main towns and villages; a Spanish/Quechua/English pocket dictionary; maps and instructions on where to find any information you may require. It's available in Huaráz itself, or from the South American Explorers Club in Lima, or direct from 771 W Dry Creek Rd, Healdsburg, California 95448, USA.

Another guide book, *Yuraq Janka*, is also available in Huaráz and has maps which are good for the geography (1:100,000), but the trails which are marked should only be treated as approximate.

Tents for trekking can be hired for US$3 per day at various places in Huaráz. Avoid taking rice or beans with you when you go trekking as they take a long time to cook and so use a lot of fuel.

Things to See

Because most of the towns were flattened in the 1970 earthquake, the priorities were to provides homes as quickly as possible afterwards. As a result, few of the towns have much to recommend them architecturally, but do make a point of visiting **Wilcahuaín** (Willcawain), seven km from Huaraz, where there is the ruins

of a Tiahuanaco-style temple dating from about 1000 AD. Probably the easiest way to get there is to walk – the site is signposted. Take the Yungay road down Av Centenario and turn off right when you see the sign about one km out of town. When you've seen the main site, walk a further 500 metres and you'll come across some even more impressive ruins.

The **Archaeology Museum** (Museo Regional de Ancash), Av Luzuriaga, is well worth visiting. It has a small but unusual collection of artefacts and includes dozens of stone carvings and monoliths from Chavín, set in a small park at the rear of the building. It's open from 8.30 am to 4.30 pm Tuesdays to Fridays. Entry costs US$0.95.

The pre-Inca fortress temple ruins of **Chavín** should not be missed. The main structures date from about 600 BC and the stone carvings are in excellent condition. There used to be seven underground levels to explore but the 1970 earthquake destroyed all but two. You need a torch to explore these underground levels. Many of the best carvings and monoliths are now in archaeological museums at Huaráz and Lima, but plenty still remain, including the famous Lanzón monolith inside the temple tunnel.

The best way to get to Chavín from Huaráz is to trek over the mountains from Olleros (37 km). It's an easy hike and very popular, but if for any reason you can't do this, there are buses from Huaráz by *Condor de Chavín* (Tarapacá 312) and *Empresa Huascarán*. Both companies have one service per day and both leave between 10 and 11 am, cost US$2 and take four to five hours. These buses go on to Huari (about seven hours, US$3). There is also a company called *Chavín Tours* in Huaraz which offer one-day tours to Chavín with a Spanish speaking guide. The trips take 10 to 11 hours with two hours at the ruins and cost about US$4. There are a few basic hotels at Chavín plus an expensive albergue if you want to stay the night – more choice at Hauri if you can find transport there.

Places to Stay

There's a good selection of places in Huaráz but in the high season (July to September) many hotels put their prices up so you may have to shop around a little. In the past the cheapest and most popular place to stay was with Pepe who offered very cheap accommodation on the fifth floor of the Hotel Barcelona. Pepe is still in Huaráz but he now owns the *Hotel Cataluna* on Calle Raymondi. Cheap dormitory accommodation is available as well as private single and double rooms. There's plenty of information available on trekking and what to see. You can also hire trekking equipment here. English, French, German and Hebrew (!) spoken.

A room in the *Hotel Barcelona*, Raymondi 612, will cost US$2.50 a double without bath, and US$4.50 a double with bath. There's no hot water but they will store your excess gear while you're away trekking.

Very popular these days with travellers is the *Hostal Los Andes*, Tarapacá 316 next to a Bata shoe shop. It has a choice of dormitory beds for US$0.60 and a few rooms. There is occasional hot water in the bathrooms. The very friendly woman who runs the hostal often meets incoming buses. Another which has been recommended is the *Holiday Inn*, Cruz Romero 593 (no sign but it's run by the Quintana family). It's a new place which has bright clean rooms and hot water in the bathrooms. There's a free laundry service.

Good accommodation can be found for US$1 per person in Sra Gonzales' house at Nueva Granada 519. She's very hospitable and there's plenty of hot water available. The house of Sr Lopez on the outskirts of town has also been recommended. The family is friendly, there's hot water and the rooms upstairs are excellent. Similar is the *Hostal Quito*, Tarapacá 316, which is quiet, very clean and friendly. It's an unnamed house next door to Transportes Condor de Chavín – just ring the bell. Another in the same bracket is the *Casa Edwards*, one block towards town from Roggero bus station next to a florist. It costs US$1.50 per person.

The *Pensión Maguina* at Calle Tarapaca 643 has also been recommended and the señora will prepare a traditional meal of Guinea pig for about US$1 per person. There is a courtyard and good views over the town from the balcony.

Two other hotels which have been suggested are the *Hostal Alpamayo*, Leoncio Prado 126, near the stadium, which has three-bed rooms for about US$1.50 per person and hot showers; and the *Hotel Raymondi*, Raymondi 820, with hot water in the mornings only. You can leave excess gear at the Alpamayo free of charge while you go trekking. Another cheapie is the *Alojamiento Tabariz*, but it only has cold water.

Another recommendation is the *Edwards Inn* where the English-speaking owner is helpful with trekking information and transport arrangements.

Places to Eat

The *Pío Pío Restaurant*, Centenario 329, is very popular and serves excellent cheap meals. Others in the same price range worth trying are the *Rivoli*, Guzman Barrón 244; *La Bonanza*, Luzuriaga 643; and the *Tip Top*, Raymondi 615.

If you like seafood, try the *El Anzuelo*. It's in an alley behind La Fontana on Luzuriaga, but get there early as they often run out by 1 pm.

One of the best Chinese restaurants is the *Chifa Canton*, Raymondi 809. It's very popular and prices are reasonable. The *Chifa Familia* also has good food but it's a little more expensive.

For breakfasts, the *Los Portales*, Luzuriaga 463; and *Fuente de Soda Gipsy*, Luzuriaga 492, have been recommended.

Trekking in the Cordillera Blanca

Before you set off on any treks, buy a copy of *Trails of the Cordilleras Blanca & Huayhuash of Peru* by Jim Bartle (available in Huaráz). In this book are descriptions of 18 treks in the Cordillera Blanca and others in the Cordillera Huayhuash ranging from easy (no experience, equipment, guides or pack animals required) to difficult.

The best maps of the area are available from *Ingemmet*, Guzman Barrón 582, Huaráz. They have two series available (1:100,000 with 200 metre contours) – Cordillera Blanca (two sheets), US$3.50; and Cordilleras Huayhuash & Raura (one sheet), US$2. Other maps are available from the *Instituto Geográfico Militar*, Av Aramburú 1119, Lima. They have six sheets which cover the whole area (US$3 per sheet) on a scale of 1:100,000 with 50-metre contours but the names of the mountains, canyons and villages are often wrong and trails inaccurately marked.

If you're going on one of the more ambitious trails and need a guide, they are easy to find in Huaráz, Chiquián and Musho. The National Parks Office (Parque Nacional Huascarán), behind the Ministerio de Agricultura in Huaráz, is a good place to enquire about guides, porters and cooks. Standard rates are presently US$8 a day for a first class porter or guide and US$4 to $5 a day for an unqualified guide or porter. Burros (mules) cost about US$1 per day. These rates exclude food, which you also have to provide, but guides and porters generally bring their own camping equipment.

Supplies for trekking are adequate in Huaráz, Caráz and, to a lesser extent, Pomabamba, but elsewhere they're in short supply. The best store in Huaráz is *Bodega Santillana*, Centenario 417. Other good ones are *Papicho*, Los Libertadores 132; and *Tienda Ortiz*, on the corner of Luzuriaga and Raymondi. Kerosene can be bought at all gas stations but over 4000 metres you can't use it to run a *Primus* or *Optimus* stove. At this altitude and above you will have to use *benzina*. Trekking equipment can be hired from Pepe at the Hotel Cataluna on Raymondi. Tents cost about US$2 per day and stoves US$1.50 per day.

THE CHAVÍN TRAIL

This is one of the easiest and most popular trails in the Cordillera Blanca, though in terms of mountain views it's one of the least interesting. From Huaráz, to get to Olleros where the trail starts, take one of the many pick-up trucks from the Frigorífico (the fish and meat market) on Tarapacá. The fare is about US$0.25. If you can't find one, take a Recuay/Catac bus from the same market and get off at Puente Bedoya, from where it's a two-km walk up the track to Olleros.

The walk to Chavín should take three days. Remember that nights get cold so bring camping equipment and plenty of warm clothes. A guide isn't necessary along this trail as the route is clear most of the way. Where it gets indistinct all you have to remember is that, apart from a very short section (marked on the map), the trail stays on the south side of the streams the whole way.

There are a number of basic hotels in Chavín, the best two being the *Hotel Monte Carlo* and the *Hotel Monterrey*. Both are cheap and clean. The *Hotel Inca* is also cheap and friendly but the bathrooms are filthy. There's also the expensive *Albergue de Turistas* about seven km from Chavín on the road to Huari.

A good place to eat in Chavín is the *Comedor de Cooperativa de Chavín* behind the main church (closed Wednesdays and Thursdays). There are no banks in Chavín.

The Chavín ruins are open daily from 8 am to 12 noon and from 2 to 4 pm. Entry costs US$0.65, or US$0.50 with a student card.

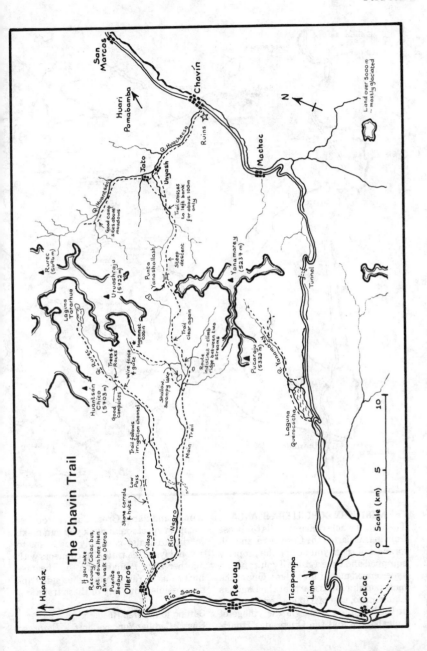

The Chavin Trail

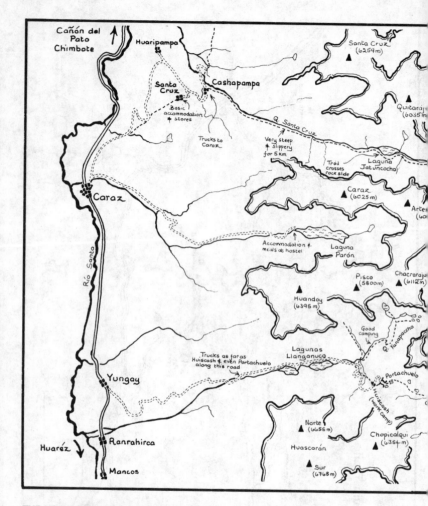

THE NORTHERN CORDILLERA BLANCA

There are a whole range of trails to choose from in this part of the Cordillera, though for most of them you need to be properly equipped and have a guide if you're not an experienced mountain walker. One of the most popular hikes starts at the Lagunas Llanganuco, east of Yungay, and ends up at Cashapampa going via the village of Colcabamba and the Quebradas Huari-pampa and Santa Cruz. This is probably the most spectacular walk you can make in the area and generally takes six to seven days. This trail also connects with another from Pomabamba via the pre-Inca ruins of Yaino. Numerous side trips are possible along any of these trails.

Getting to the Trail Heads
Huaráz-Carhuaz-Yungay-Caráz *Empresa*

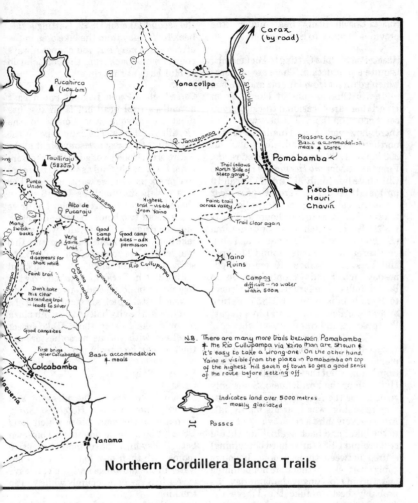

Map labels:

Carax (by road)

Pucahirca (6046m)

Yanacollpa

Q. Jancapampa

Río Shiulla

Pleasant town
Basic accommodation,
meals & stores
Pomabamba

Piscobamba
Hauri
Chavín

Trail follows
North side of
steep gorge

Taulliraju (5830m)

Punta Unión

Río Tingopampa

Highest
trail – visible
from Yaino

Faint trail
across valley

Trail clear again

Alto de Pucaraju

Many switch-backs

Good camp sites

Good camp sites – ask permission

Very faint trail

Trail disappears for
short while

Faint trail

Laguna O'griococha

Laguna Huecrococha

Río Cullupampa

Yaino Ruins

Camping
difficult – no water
within 500m

Don't take
this clear
ascending trail
– leads to silver
mine

Good campsites

First bridge
after Colcabamba

Basic accommodation
& meals

Colcabamba

Yaqueria

Yanama

N.B. There are many more trails between Pomabamba
& the Río Cullupampa via Yaino than are shown &
it's easy to take a wrong one. On the other hand,
Yaino is visible from the plaza in Pomabamba on top
of the highest hill south of town so get a good sense
of the route before setting off.

Indicates land over 5000 metres
– mostly glaciated

Passes

Northern Cordillera Blanca Trails

Moreno Hermanos and *Suiza Peruana* have daily buses every half hour or so in **either direction from 6 am to 6 pm. The fare from Huaráz to Caráz is US$1.** Colectivos are also available along the same route. They cost about US$1.40 per person and take about one hour. They leave from near the junction of Fitzcarral and Raymondi in Huaráz and from the Plaza de Armas in Caráz.

There are usually several trucks per day between Caráz and Cashapampa. The best time to find them is around noon in Caráz and between 5 and 6 am in Cashapampa. They may or may not call at Santa Cruz. The journey from Caráz to Cashapampa takes about two or three hours (less in the opposite direction) and costs US$0.50 to $0.60.

Huaráz-Chavín-Huari See under the previous 'Things to See' section.

Huaráz-Pomabamba Getting to Pomabamba is quite a production. There are no buses which go direct from Huaráz and the bus route via Chavín ends at Huari. From Huari there are occasional trucks but you can't count on them. The best way to get there, however, is via Huallanca on the northern route, a total distance of about 300 km, only 72 km of it on paved roads. First take a *Moreno Hermanos* Huaráz to Chimbote bus (daily at 7 am, 11 am and 9 pm) and get off at Tres Cruces near Yurucmarca. This part of the journey takes about three to four hours and costs US$2. Buses which start out in Lima (*Empresa Marino*, Jr Ayacucho 1140), pass through Chimbote around 3 to 5 pm and Tres Cruces about 10 pm on Wednesday and Sundays only and go to Pomabamba. The fare from Tres Cruces to Pomabamba is about US$5. Return buses from Pomabamba to Lima depart Wednesdays and Sundays at 6 am.

Yungay-Lagunas Llanganuco There are plenty of trucks which go up this valley from Yungay but they don't all go as far as Huiscash or the Portachuelo. Some only go as far as the first lake, so ask how far they're going when arranging a lift. Alternatively, hire a colectivo to take you to the lakes and back again. This should cost around US$8 (after hard bargaining) shared between three people. If you're going on a trek and therefore not planning on returning to Yungay the same day, it's probably best to take the *Virgen del Rosario* truck which goes as far as the Portachuelo. It officially only goes on Wednesdays and Sundays, but something goes every day between June and August because of demand. It should leave at 6 am but often doesn't go until 10 am. The fare should be US$1.

For those not going on a trek, there are many smaller and faster trucks which take tourists up as far as the upper end of

the second lake for US$2. Getting a ride back to Yungay from the lake area in the afternoon is easy but you cannot always count on one back from the Portachuelo or Huiscash at that time.

Caráz-Laguna Parón Laguna Parón isn't actually a trail head but is an absolute must for anyone who comes to the Cordillera Blanca. The canyon below the lake offers the most awesome sight in the entire area. Colectivos go to the lake from outside Caráz city hall as soon as there are five or six passengers wanting to go. The fare can be as much as US$16 return shared between the six people. The drive takes about two hours in either direction and the driver will generally wait at the lake for up to two hours but make sure this is agreed before you set off. If you'd like to stay up at the lake, the municipal authorities in Caráz have taken over the Ingemmet building and converted it into a basic hostel which also provides meals. Enquire at the city hall on the main plaza if you'd like to stay there. Take insect repellent with you as horseflies around the lake can be a real pain.

Places to Stay
Caráz

Most people stay at the pleasant and friendly though basic *Hotel La Suiza Peruana* on the main plaza which costs US$1/$1.50 a single/double without own bath. They also have more expensive rooms with their own bath. There is hot water in the mornings and you can leave excess luggage here securely while you go trekking.

Another good place to stay is at Professor Bernardino Aguilar Prieto's house at San Martín 1143 a few doors down from the Suiza. He has six double or triple rooms available at US$1 per person including breakfast (milk, bread and honey). He knows a lot about trekking in the area and will help to arrange vehicles to visit the lakes.

Two other hotels you can try if these are

full are the *Hostal Carás* and the *Hotel El Cafetal*. Both have hot water and are clean and friendly. If you want to stay at the hostel at Laguna Parón (US$1.60 per person), ask at city hall on the main plaza.

Another possibility is the *Hostal Chavin* on the main square. It's a new place, is cheap and has hot water.

A good restaurant in Caráz is the *Restaurante Carás* on the main plaza which has good, cheap meals.

Colcabamba

Several families offer basic accommodation to trekkers. One of the most popular is the Calonge family, who live just below the village plaza, and who've virtually made their home into a pleasant hostel. They charge about US$0.75 per person per night. A simple meal will cost about US$0.60. Some travellers say it's overpriced but OK for a night.

Pomabamba

Most people stay at the basic hotel near the main plaza. There is a bank in Pomabamba.

Yungay

Señor Blanco's hostel in the eucalyptus grove behind the hospital is popular. It has a very peaceful atmosphere and costs US$1 per person in dormitory-style rooms. Breakfast and dinner are available at a cost of US$1.40 per meal. You can store luggage safely if you go trekking. If it's full, try *Hostal Gledel*, Av Arias Graziana, which is cheap and clean and the owner, Señora Gamboa, is very hospitable. There's no hot water. Beds cost about US$1.20 per night and meals are available too.

If you're not eating at either of these places, try the *Alojamiento Acuña*, which serves good meals.

The tourist office in Yungay is on the main plaza.

IQUITOS

The main centre of population in Peruvian Amazonia, Iquitos is completely cut off from the rest of the country by road. Access is only possible by plane or riverboat – the latter from Yurimaguas or Moyobamba on the Río Marañon and Pucallpa on the Río Ucayali. Like Manaus in Brazil, Iquitos took part in the rubber boom at the beginning of the 20th century and then went into a long decline when the bottom fell out of the market. Prosperity returned with the discovery of oil and the town is now an expensive, fast-developing regional centre.

Information

The tourist office is at Prospero 218. Maps of the town are available.

The casa de cambio at Prospero 375 offers good rates for cash. Only banks will change travellers' cheques, and at a poor rate.

If you leave Iquitos by air make sure you get an exit stamp from immigration before going to the airport.

The airline *Grupo Aereo 8*, Hualaga 309, is part of *TANS*, the military airline, and offers flights which are half the price of those on either *AeroPeru* or *Faucett*.

Things to See

Iquitos didn't participate in the rubber boom (1890-1920) to anywhere near the same extent as Manaus, so there's nothing to see here on the grand scale of the Opera House. There are, on the other hand, a number of old mansions constructed by the rubber barons which are faced in outstanding glazed tiles. Most travellers find themselves in Iquitos because they want to travel by riverboat down to Leticia (Colombia) or Manaus (Brazil), or because they have come by riverboat from Pucallpa or Yurimaguas.

A number of guided jungle trips are available from Iquitos but they're not particularly cheap. One of the least expensive is by *Artesanías La Chamita*, Jirón Putumayo 157, which offers week-long trips to jungle villages for US$18 per person per day. Two other outfits which offer one, two or three-day excursions up various rivers and have their own lodges where you stay overnight are *Amazon Lodge Safari Tours*, Av Putumayo 165; and *Explorama*, Putumayo 150, both of them close to the Plaza de Armas. Expect to pay around US$40 for a one-day tour, US$85 to $95 for a two-day tour and US$115 for a three-day tour, though in the low season it's possible to bargain the rates down. At these times you may get three days and two nights all inclusive for just US$40 per person.

Another company which is recommended is *Tamshiyacu Lodge*, Putumayo 184 (tel 233976). Lucho, who runs this outfit, has three small camps strung out along the river well away from the usual tourist routes. They offer fishing, swimming, jungle trekking, canoeing by day or night and their prices are very reasonable at US$30 per person per day which includes transport, food, guides and overnight accommodation. The highlight of their tours is the wilderness expedition down the Yarapa River (about 120 km from Iquitos). They keep their groups small – six to eight people at the most. Lucho is very helpful and will check out the boats you intend to take further down-river at no extra charge.

Although most of the available excursions are tourist set-ups some travellers who've been on them say that they were worth the money.

Of the jungle resorts near Iquitos, **Quistococha** is reputedly the best of them and has specimens of all the animals found in the jungle (though in cages). To get there take a truck (about US$0.30) from the junction of Abtao and Elias Aguirre.

Places to Stay

A relatively cheap place is the *Hostal Lima* which costs US$5 a double. The hostal has its own restaurant. The *Hostal La Pascana*, Pevas 133, three blocks from the Plaza de Armas, has been highly recommended. It costs US$5.50 a double with own bathroom and there's a pleasant courtyard where you can get breakfast for US$1. The staff are friendly and you can store excess baggage safely.

Others which are worth trying if these are full are the *Residencia Internacional*, Calle Lima (rooms with both communal bathrooms and private bathroom available, electric fans in the rooms); and the *Tarapacá*, Calle Tarapacá.

For something slightly up-market, try the *Isabel* (very good and clean) or the *Hostal Alfert*, Garcia Sanz 001, a new place which is great value and has friendly management. Another good place is the *Maynas*, Próspero 388, which is very clean and hospitable.

Places to Eat

An excellent fish restaurant is the *El Mesón*, Jirón Napo where you can eat for about US$2. The *Chifa Wang Wu*, Arica on the right hand side walking towards Belén, offers tasty Chinese food for around US$2; and the *Pollo Broaster*, Prospero 466, offers fried chicken, which would rival that which the Colonel turns out, for around US$0.60. The *Chifa Central* has also been recommended for Chinese food.

Good cakes and snacks are available at Prospero 366. Another similar place is at Prospero 415 where there are good snacks, coffee, ice-cream and milk shakes.

Getting There

Air If you can't find a riverboat or don't have the time, check out where *Grupo 8* is flying to. Failing that, *AeroPeru* flies to Yurimaguas twice weekly for US$45 and five times weekly to Pucallpa for US$51. Both *AeroPeru* and *Faucett* fly to Tarapoto, further on than Yurimaguas, virtually everyday for US$45. There's also a small airline company (office at Ramón Castilla 353, Iquitos) which flies to Yurimaguas on Fridays and is much cheaper than the other airlines.

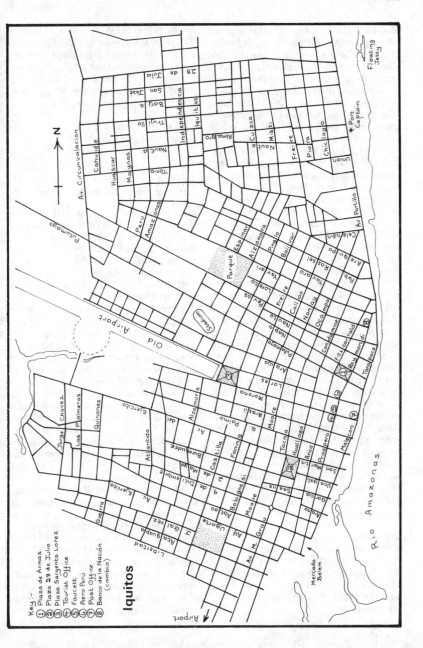

Key:-
① Plaza de Armas
②ⓐⓝ Plaza 28 de Julio
③ⓜ Plaza Sargento Lorez
④ Faucett
⑤ Tourist Office
⑥ Aero Perú
⑦ Post Office
⑧ Banco de la Nación (cambio)

Iquitos

Riverboat Boats going all the way to Manaus are very infrequent so it's best to go first to Ramón Castilla or Islandia (the floating town close to Tabatinga). Take a ferry from there to either Leticia (Colombia) or Benjamin Constant (Brazil) and then find a boat going to Manaus. One of the best places to look for boats going to Ramón Castilla is the *Agencia General de Representaciones*, Bermudez 445, which faces the Plaza 28 de Julio. The office should know which boats are going, but you should also ask around at the end of Tawara West.

If you hear that it's going, the *Oro Negro* is a boat that many travellers have recommended. The fare should be around US$10 excluding food. There are generally no cabins on these boats – just sling up a hammock. The food will be rice and beans cooked in river water plus whatever can be picked up en route. If you want to vary your diet, take canned food with you.

For boats going to Pucallpa or Yurimaguas – a six to 10-day trip – ask around the following agencies: *Bellavista*, Tarapacá 596; *Hurtado*, Av Grau 1223; *Casa Pinto*, Sargento Flores 164; and *Meneses*, Jirón Lima. Also ask down at the wharfs. The cheapest boats should cost about US$13, though of course if there are cabins and you want the luxury of a berth, you'll pay considerably more. As with the boats to Ramón Castilla, the meals are mainly rice and beans, so take some canned food with you.

Many people pick up enteritis (and sometimes worse things) on these boat trips so have some prophylactic tablets at the ready. Dysentery is also fairly common.

JULIACA

Few travellers seem to go to Juliaca these days but it is worth a trip if you're looking for alpaca clothing as these things are generally slightly cheaper than in Puno and the quality tends to be better.

Places to Stay & Eat

The *Hotel Victoria* has double rooms without own bathroom for about US$1.50. It's clean and basic but only cold water is available in the bathrooms. Cheaper is the *Hotel Juliaca* at US$0.75 per room but the sanitation leaves much to be desired.

The *El Dorado Restaurant*, Calle Union, has good food.

Lima

Once the capital of the vast viceroyalty of Peru which included Ecuador, Colombia, Bolivia, Chile and Argentina as well as Peru itself, Lima was a city of wealth and luxury which few others could rival during the 17th and early 18th centuries. Founded in 1535, it was almost completely destroyed by earthquake in 1746. It's now South America's fourth largest city with a population exceeding five million, and though it is surrounded by seemingly endless shanty towns occupied by people from the mountains who come looking for work, the centre itself is quite compact.

While parts of the centre still retain a certain colonial flavour and the Plaza de Armas is quite impressive, much of this area is dirty, dusty, decayed and litter-strewn. Only in the richer suburbs of Miraflores and San Isidro and along the Paseo de la Republica in the centre is any effort made to plant trees and tend gardens.

Nevertheless, it's well worth spending some time here as there are plenty of interesting places to see, museums to visit, street markets, and cafés which put on folk music. From June to October it doesn't exactly have the world's most agreeable climate. Between these months a thick sea mist hangs almost continually over the city, making it damp, grey and depressing. You may need warm clothes in the evenings during this period.

Information

The tourist office is at Jirón Unión (Belen) 1066, and is open Monday to Friday from 8 am to 7 pm. They're very helpful and have brochures and maps. There is a branch office at the junction of Av Diagonal and Figari, Miraflores.

Look out for the monthly magazine, *Peru. Where, When, How . . .* , which is worth getting hold of. It's free and distributed round most of the higher class hotels and restaurants.

Most of the casas de cambio are spread out along Colmena, Ocoña and Unión. The rates vary from one to the other so it's worth shopping around. They take both cheques and cash. There are also a large number of money changers on the street at the junction of Ocoña and the Plaza San Martín and outside the Hotel Gran Bolivar. It's all very informal but watch out for thieves after you have changed. No-one with any sense changes money in a bank these days – it takes too much time, the rates are poor and travellers' cheques are often treated like forgeries.

If you're going trekking in the mountains or heading anywhere off the beaten track, it's worth getting in touch with the *South American Explorers Club*, Av Portugal 146, between Av Bolivia and Av España, three blocks from the Av Alfonso Ugarte, (postal address: Casilla 3714, Lima 100). They're very helpful, have plenty of information and good maps of almost all the established treks. They also produce a magazine, *South American Explorer*, which is worth subscribing to. Club membership costs US$25 per year and includes four issues of the magazine. The club is open to non-members from 10 to 11 am on weekdays.

The Immigration office is at Av 28 de Julio 1145. Visa renewals cost US$20 and are issued in 48 hours. As long as you don't ask for an extension of more than 60 days, you probably won't be asked for an onward ticket or 'sufficient funds'.

The main post office is at Jirón Junín, west of the Plaza de Armas. Open Monday to Saturday from 8 am to 6 pm and on Sunday from 8 am to 12 noon. The lista de correos here is good – they hand you the pile and you do the sorting.

American Express is represented at Lima Tours, Jirón Union (Belen) 1040, near the junction with Plaza de San Martín. Open for collection of clients' mail between 9 am and 5.30 pm.

The Spanish language school, *Centro de Idiomas de Lima*, Av Manuel Olguin 215, Monterrico, Lima (tel 350601), offer a number of six-hour-per-day courses. The courses include 'Getting Ready in Spanish 1' (a one-week course, total 30 hours, US$300); 'Getting Ready in Spanish 2' (a two-week course, total 60 hours, US$400) and the 'Immersion Course' (a four-week course, total 120 hours, US$650). They can also arrange for you to stay with families locally. Write to PO Box 772, Lima 100.

One traveller suggested that it may be possible to get a job teaching English if you enquire at the *Asociación Cultural Peruano Britanica*, Av Arequipa 3495.

Embassies

Argentina
  Pablo Bermudez 143 (2nd floor), (tel 245984). Open Monday to Friday 8 am to 1 pm.

Australia
  Natalio Sánchez 220 (6th floor), (tel 288315). Open Monday, Wednesday and Friday from 8 am to 2 pm and Tuesday and Thursday from 8 am to 5 pm.

Bolivia
  Los Castaños 235, San Isidro, (tel 228231). Open Monday to Friday from 8.30 am to 1.30 pm.

Brazil
  Cmdte Espinar 181, Miraflores, (tel 462635). Open Monday to Friday from 8 am to 1 pm.

Canada
  La Libertad 132, (tel 463890). Open Monday to Friday from 8.30 to 11 am.

Chile
  Av Javier Prado Oeste 790, San Isidro, (tel 407965). Open Monday to Friday from 8.45 am to 12.30 pm

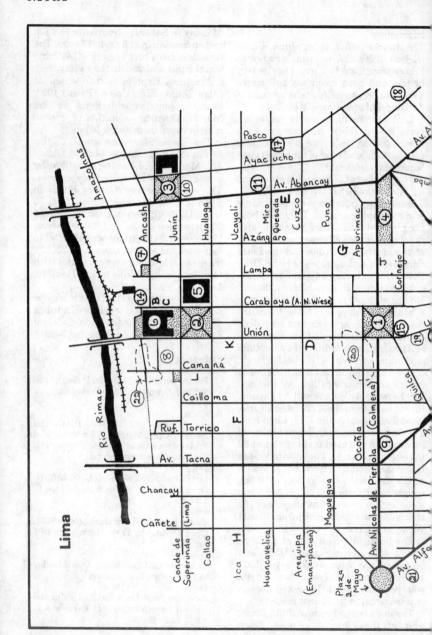

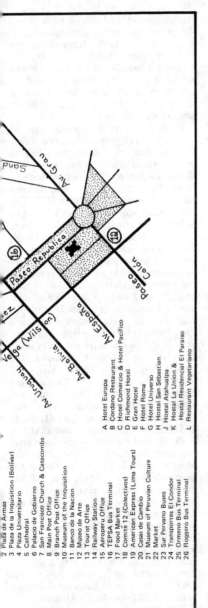

2 Plaza de Armas
3 Plaza de la Inquisition (Bolívar)
4 Plaza Universitario
5 Cathedral
6 Palacio de Gobierno
7 San Francisco Church & Catacombs
8 Main Post Office
9 Branch Post Office
10 Museum of the Inquisition
11 Banco de la Nacion
12 Museo de Arte
13 Tourist Office
14 Railway Station
15 Aeroperu Office
16 TEPSA Bus Terminal
17 Food Market
18 Comité 12 (Colectivos)
19 American Express (Lima Tours)
20 Casas de Cambio
21 Museum of Peruvian Culture
22 Market
23 Sur Pervano Buses
24 Transportes El Condor
25 Ormeno Bus Terminal
26 Roggero Bus Terminal

A Hotel Europa
B Cordano Restaurant
C Hotel Comercio & Hotel Pacifico
D Richmond Hotel
E Gran Hotel
F Hotel Roma
G Hotel Universo
H Hostal San Sebastian
J Hostal Atahualpa
K Hostal La Union &
  Hostal Residencial El Paraiso
L Restaurant Vegetariano

Colombia
Arequipa 2685, Lince, (tel 407835). Open Monday to Friday from 9 am to 12.30 pm.

Ecuador
Las Palmeras 356, San Isidro, (tel 228138). Open Monday to Friday from 9 am to 1 pm.

France
Plaza Francia 234, (tel 238618). Open Monday to Friday from 9 am to 12 noon.

Japan
Av San Felipe 356, Jesús Maria, (tel 614041). Open Monday to Friday from 9 am to 12.30 pm and 3.30 to 5.30 pm.

New Zealand
Av Salaverry 3006, San Isidro, (tel 621890).

Netherlands
Av Principal 190, San Borja, (tel 401599). Open Monday to Friday from 8.30 am to 3.30 pm.

UK
Washington Building, 12th floor, Plaza Washington, (tel 283830). Open Monday to Thursday from 10 am to 3 pm and Friday from 10 am to 1 pm.

USA
Garcilaso de la Vega 1400, (tel 286000). Open Monday to Friday from 10 am to 1 pm.

West Germany
Av Arequipa 4202, Miraflores, (tel 459997). Open Monday to Friday from 9 am to 12 noon.

Bus Terminals

TEPSA and *Morales Moralitos*, Paseo de la Republica, opposite the Sheraton Hotel.
Empresa Rodríguez, Av Roosevelt 354.
Hidalgo Av Bausate y Meza 1535.
Roggero Av Grau 711.
Ormeño Zavala Loayza 177.
Expreso Cajamarca, Nicholas de Pierola 1163.
Expreso Sudamericana, Nicholas de Pierola 1153.
Carmen Alto, Garcia Naranjo 354-366.

Almost all the colectivo services have their offices either on or immediately around the Parque Universitario.

Airlines

Most of the airlines serving Peru have

their offices along Nicholas de Pierola (Colmena). Those which don't include *AeroPeru* (Plaza San Martín); *Faucett* (Jr Unión); *British Airways* (Plaza San Martín); *British Caledonian* (Torrico 822); *Ecuatoriano* (Cailloma 802); and *Canadian Pacific Airways* (Paseo de la Republica 138).

Things to See

Two colonial buildings in the centre of the city worth visiting are the **Cathedral** and the **Torre Tagle Palace**. On the Plaza de Armas, the cathedral has been partly reconstructed several times as a result of earthquake damage. It has some superb woodcarvings, a coffin supposedly containing the remains of Pizarro, and the Museum of Religious Art. Entry costs US$1, or US$0.50 with a student card.

The Torre Tagle Palace on Jirón Ucayali was built in 1735 and is the city's best surviving example of colonial architecture. Though occupied by the Foreign Ministry, visitors are allowed to enter a number of the courtyards and balconies from 2 to 4 pm on Saturdays.

Another church which is a must is the **Convento de San Francisco de Jesús**, Jirón Ancash opposite the Hotel Europa. It has an interesting museum containing historical and religious exhibits dating back to the Conquest. There are also extensive underground catacombs containing thousands of skeletons, many of them lying where they were placed hundreds of years ago, and others thoughtfully arranged into pretty patterns by some enterprising soul. Guided tours through the museum and catacombs take place approximately every half hour. Entry costs US$0.50 and it's open from 10 am to 1 pm and 3 to 6 pm daily.

A little further away from the centre on Plaza Bolívar at Junín 548 (no sign but it's the building with the classical frontage) is the **Palace of the Inquisition**, now a museum. The Inquisition was established in 1570 and not abolished until 1813. You can get a good idea of how

compassionate the Catholic Church was then when you see the gory collection of wax dummies being tortured in the dungeons there! Entry is free and the museum is open Monday to Friday from 9 am to 2 pm and 3 to 8 pm, and on Saturdays from 9 am to 1 pm. The ceiling in the main chamber is a magnificent piece of wood carving.

There is naturally a whole range of museums in a city the size and importance of Lima, but two which shouldn't be missed in the Pueblo Libre district are the **Museum of Anthropology and Archaeology**, Plaza Bolívar; and the **Rafael Larco Herrera Museum**, Av Bolívar 1515. The former has an excellent and well-displayed collection of artefacts from the Chimú, Paracas, Nazca, Mochica, Chavín, Pachacamac and Inca civilisations. It's very good on stonework and not too heavy on pottery, and has a number of carefully constructed scale models of such Inca citadels as Pisaq, Wiñay Winay and Machu Picchu. Entry costs US$0.50, or US$0.25 if you have a student card. It's open Tuesday to Sunday from 10 am to 6 pm. To get there from the centre, take the microbus No 2 from Colmena at the junction with Rufino Torrico, bus No 12 from the corner of Tacna and Emancipación or bus No 41 from the corner of Emancipación and Cusco. Other possible buses are Nos 21, 24, 42 and 48 from the Parque Universitario.

The **Rafael Herrera Museum** is very good on pottery especially from the Chimú and Mochica periods as well as having the best collection of erotic pottery of any museum in Peru. It also has some rare pre-Colombian examples of weaving, several mummified weavers who were buried with their looms, and a small gold collection. It's open Monday to Saturday from 9 am to 1 pm and 3 to 6 pm. Entry costs US$3, or US$1.50 with a student card. To get there from the centre, take microbus No 37 from Nicholas de Pierola or bus No 23 from the Av Abancay.

Two other museums worth visiting are

the **National Museum of Art**, Paseo Colón near the junction with Paseo de la Republica; and the **Museum of Peruvian Culture**, Av Alfonso Ugarte 650. The former has an excellent range of exhibits which chronicle the development of Peruvian culture and art from 2000 years ago to the present. It has pottery sections, weavings, mummies, carved wooden colonial furniture, paintings of the Cuzco school and precious-metal objects. It also puts on films and lectures every Friday evening from April onwards and several daily screenings of a slide show covering numerous aspects of Peruvian life. Entry costs US$0.65 (half price with a student card) and the museum is open Tuesday to Sunday from 9 am to 7 pm except on public holidays.

The Museum of Peruvian Culture is mainly a folk museum and is very good on craftwork and Indian costumes. If you're thinking of buying a carved gourd, check out this museum's collection before you do. Entry costs US$0.25. It's open Monday to Friday from 10 am to 5 pm.

The **Gold Museum** is part of the **Museo Miguel Gallo** and is at Av de Molina 1110 in the Monterrico suburb. The gold exhibits are in vaulted chambers in the basement. On the ground floor is one of the best small-arms collections in the world. Entry costs US$3, or US$1.50 with a student card and the museum is open daily from 12 noon to 7 pm. To get there take bus No 67 from Av Alfonso Ugarte or bus No 2 from the Plaza San Martín. If you take the latter, change in Miraflores on the corner of Av **Arequipa** and **Angamos** to microbus No 72.

Many travellers have recommended the **Amano Museum**, Retiro 160 (off the 11th block of Angamos in the Miraflores suburb). This museum has exhibits rarely seen anywhere else because they are very fragile – textiles, jewels and pottery. Ring 412909 and make a reservation for one of the guided tours which take place at 2, 3, 4 or 5 pm – you can't just turn up there.

Other travellers have recommended a visit to the **Parque de las Leyendas** between Lima and Callao. It was built and designed to re-create the three regions of Peru – the coast, the altiplano and the Amazon jungle beyond the mountains – and is stocked with the appropriate plants and animals. It's open every day, except Monday, from 9 am to 5 pm and costs US$0.35 entry. To get there from the centre of Lima take microbus No 75 from Jirón Azángaro.

One of the largest street markets for clothes, footwear and household goods is at the back of the main post office facing the Rimac river and the railway line. For curios, jewellery, clothes and all manner of other interesting items take a stroll down Unión between the Plaza de Armas and the Plaza San Martín. There are two shifts, one from around lunch time to 5 pm and another in the evening.

Another good street market happens on Sundays all along Av Abancay and spilling into Av Cusco. Most of what is for sale is domestic household items but there are a lot of other things such as strange herbs, books you're not likely to find anywhere else and clothes. Most of the curio shops for such things as carved gourds, *mantas*, old coins, mounted tarantula and butterfly collections and pottery are found along Colmena and along Unión between the Plaza San Martín and Paseo de la Republica. Prices are surprisingly reasonable.

Miraflores is the Lima beach resort – neither the beach or the sea are particularly attractive and the steep cliffs are eroded and dusty. Miraflores itself, however, is quite pleasant to wander around. There are many interesting stalls in the main square in the evening – look for the stalls selling giant tarantulas in glass display boxes.

Places to Stay

There are a number of very cheap hotels in the centre which have been popular with travellers for years but you shouldn't expect anything very special. Many are definitely on the decaying side.

An old favourite is the *Hotel Europa*, Jirón Ancash 376, which costs from US$1.50 to $3 for rooms without own bathroom. Slightly better perhaps is the *Hotel Richmond*, Jirón Unión 706. The huge marbled entry hall with its stained glass windows is quite impressive but the rooms are somewhat run-down. Nevertheless, it's very popular with budget travellers. Rooms cost about US$1 to $2 without bathroom, or US$1.50 to $2.50 with bathroom. There are hot showers and a baggage store which costs US$0.20 per day for a maximum of 30 days.

Also quite popular is the *Hostal La Unión*, Unión 442 which is actually in a courtyard off Unión and one floor above the *Pension Unión* which is similarly priced. It's not easy to find this place as you have to go through an alley which is lined with bookshops. It's a friendly place, clean and secure but it only has one bathroom and there's not always enough hot water to satisfy demand.

Also worth trying if these are full and cost is your major consideration is the *Hotel Comercio*, Jirón Agostino Wiese opposite the side of the Government Palace. This is definitely a museum piece being a bizarre cross between a Dickensian orphanage, a warehouse and a New Orleans bawdy house. It's a huge, decrepit, moth-eaten place and somewhat grim but with a strange kind of lingering charm. These days it even sports a one-star rating (surely this is a joke?). It costs US$1.50 to $3 without own bathroom and hot showers are extra.

In this category, avoid the *Hotel Pacifico* very close to the Comercio. It's even cheaper than the Comercio but very grim and ultra-basic.

Going up-market a little, try the *Hostal Residencial El Paraiso*, Unión 428. This is a very clean and tidy place where rooms cost US$3/$3.50, or with bathroom they're US$5 to $6 for a double. There are hot showers and the rooms are secure.

Slightly more expensive but very good value and popular with Peruvian families is the *Hotel Universo*, Azangaro 754A. It's a very clean place and costs US$2.35/$3.35 a single/double without own bathroom and US$3/$4/$5 a single/double/triple with own bathroom. There is hot water in the showers.

Also in this category is the *Gran Hotel*, Av Abancay 54, which must at one time have been quite a smart hotel. It's still fairly well maintained and popular with travelling salesmen. Rooms cost US$3/$5 for singles/doubles without own bathroom, US$4/$7 with own bathroom. The *Hostal Atahualpa*, Colmena 1170 close to the Parque Universitario, has similar prices but being on such a noisy street, isn't really worth it.

Going further up-market there are two very popular hotels. Perhaps the better, but not the cheaper, of the two is the *Hostal San Sebastian*, Jirón Ica 712 at the junction with Cañete. It's run by a very friendly family who are well clued on what travellers want. The rooms are very pleasant, totally secure, there's hot water 24 hours a day (electric heaters) and a cafeteria, but what sets the place apart from other hotels is the roof-top courtyard where you can always be sure of meeting other travellers. Rooms cost US$4/$7/$9 a single/double/triple without own bath. Not cheap but highly recommended.

Similar is the *Hostal Roma*, Jirón Ica 326. The rooms are very clean and well-maintained and there's hot water 24 hours a day. It costs US$4 to $7 for a double with own bathroom.

Other travellers have enthusiastically recommended the *Hostal Rinasumiento*, Parque Hernan Velarde 52. It's run by Enrique and Marta who are very friendly people and they offer 12 rooms, some with shared bathroom and others with private bath. The charge is US$5 to $16 depending on what you want. The house has a beautiful and relaxing garden patio.

If you're thinking of staying in Miraflores rather than the centre of Lima, there is a *Youth Hostel* (tel 475374) at Av Larco 1247, which is very close to the beach and costs US$1.60 per night in the dormitory. There are no cooking facilities but there is a fairly cheap basic restaurant inside. There are also restaurants on the other side of the road. Close to the Youth Hostel is a very good, second-hand bookstore, *Libreria Alemania*, Av Larco 1150, which has books in English, French and German at a tenth of the price you would pay for them in central Lima.

For a private room with a Peruvian family in the same suburb, General Borgoño 280 (tel 471704) has been recommended. It costs US$10 per person including breakfast. It's quiet and clean and has hot water all day. You can store luggage here safely while you go elsewhere. It's about 15 minutes from the centre of the city.

Places to Eat

The *Cordano Hnos Café* on the corner of Agostino N Wiese and Ancash opposite the railway station, has been popular for many years. It consists of a dining room where you can get a cheap fixed-menu meal at lunch times and a bar with good a-la-carte menu at both lunch and dinner times. You'll find travellers here throughout the day, but especially at night. It's relatively good value and also offers house wines at very competitive prices, but watch out for 'scarface', one of the waiters – it seems he's taken a dislike to travellers.

At Jirón Carabaya 149 beside the palace and just off the Plaza de Armas, *El Meson de Palacio* is a glossy little snack bar which does excellent sandwiches.

There are quite a number of cafés on the west side of the Jirón Unión which offer Peru's national dish – *ceviche*. This consists of raw fish, raw shellfish, sliced onions, peppers and sometimes other fresh vegetables marinated in a lemon and oil dressing. It's very tasty and you should try it at least once, even if you've never eaten raw fish. It's not always cheap so check out the prices in several places.

On Jirón Unión itself between the Plaza de Armas and Plaza San Martín there are any number of restaurants offering fried chicken, chips and salad and several others offering more traditional Peruvian fare. At the latter places the dishes available are often displayed in a refrigerator at the front of the restaurant so if you're not familiar with the names this doesn't present any problem. Prices are very reasonable and all the restaurants are very clean. *Las Vegas* at 810 is a good example. It's a popular little snack bar and ice-cream place and gets crowded at lunch time.

Vegetarians should try the *Restaurant Vegetariano El Curasol*, Camaná 327. You can get a very good set-meal at lunch times for around US$0.60. The *Hindu Govinda*, Azangaro 149, run by the Hare Krishna people, has reasonable food although their interpretations of Indian food are sometimes a bit strange. The more expensive *Bircher Berner* in Miraflores has been highly recommended.

Miraflores has all sorts of restaurants including some good pizzerias and many places with tables and chairs outside and an almost Mediterranean feel. Pizzas are US$2 to $4 and wine is US$2 a bottle.

For breakfast try the *Versailles*, Plaza San Martín 974. It offers two eggs, bread and tea/coffee for US$0.65, or the same but with juice and chips for US$0.85. It's closed on Saturday mornings.

There are plenty of restaurants along Av Nicolas de Pierola from Plaza San Martín, including some more expensive places like the *Chalet Suisse* at 560, which is good if you want to temporarily escape from South America with main courses at US$2.50 to $3. There are some good bakeries along here like the *Munich Cakehouse* or the *Kudan Pastileria & Tea Bar*.

Wine There are only two widely available brands of Peruvian wine – Tacame and

Ocucaje. They're not cheap in shops – US$3 to $4 – but the mark-up in restaurants is only a dollar or so. Tacame red is pretty good – a solid full-bodied red. And the Ocucaje Reisling ain't bad either!

Peñas

The best of these is the *Hatuchay*, Trujillo 228 on the other side of the river from the Government Palace. It's open Wednesday, Friday and Saturday nights from about 9 pm onwards. Similar is the *Korikancha*, Recuay 854 in the Breña suburb. It's open on Friday and Saturday nights. There's a small cover charge at each place. Other travellers have written to us to recommend two unnamed places at Cailloma 889 and Cailloma 633. The latter has local musicians on Wednesdays and at weekends.

There's a good piano bar in the basement of Jirón Unión 1041 (no sign but it's between Lima Tours and the Restaurant Wony). The place has been done out to resemble a Bavarian beer cellar and is actually owned by a German. It can get very lively when there are a few people down there. Prices are only slightly above normal.

Getting Around

Airport Transport Jorge Chávez International Airport is 16 km from the centre of the city. There are several ways of getting to and from the airport. A taxi will cost US$2.50 to $3, though if you can't speak Spanish well, expect to pay considerably more – the airport tourist office will tell you the fare is US$10 but you should be able to get them down to about half that! Fares increase at night. Service bus No 106M goes there from the Plaza 2 de Mayo (cheapest way).

The *Trans Hotel* bus, Camana 828 in central Lima or Ricardo Palma 280 in Miraflores, runs a 24-hour service every half hour or so. The fare is about US$0.75. To find this bus on arrival at the airport, turn right out of the terminal building and walk to the end of the footpath.

Colectivos, which take five people, leave all day from 6 am to 6 pm from Colmena 733 in front of the Galeria International. They cost about US$0.50 per person plus US$0.30 for each piece of luggage.

Around Town Buses have a standard fare of about US$0.10. Taxis are very cheap – they start at less than US$1 and you can get a long way in Lima for US$1.50.

AROUND LIMA
Pachacamac

The nearest Inca site to Lima is at Pachacamac, about 31 km down the coast in the Lurín valley. The site was a pilgrimage and ceremonial centre, the origins of which go back as far as 200 BC. The Temple to the Creator God, built on terraces with rooms for sacrificial ceremony, is the main ruin. There is also the ruin of a temple to the Sun God built by Pachacutec after the Incas conquered the area in 1470, as well as the remains of reservoirs and irrigation works. The easiest way to get there is to get a small group together and hire a colectivo.

NAZCA

Nazca sits in the middle of an oasis surrounded by desert on the coastal plain south of Lima and is, of course, world famous for its enormous and mysterious lines and figures scratched into the stony desert some 22 km north of the town. Maria Reiche, who has studied the lines for over 30 years and who still lives in the town, has dated them at around 1000 BC, which would mean that they predated the actual Nazca civilisation by over 1000 years. Nazca itself reached its peak around 800 AD. She's of the opinion that the lines represent a pre-Inca calendar and that, because they can only be appreciated from the air, the people who created them had discovered how to fly in hot-air balloons. There is evidence for

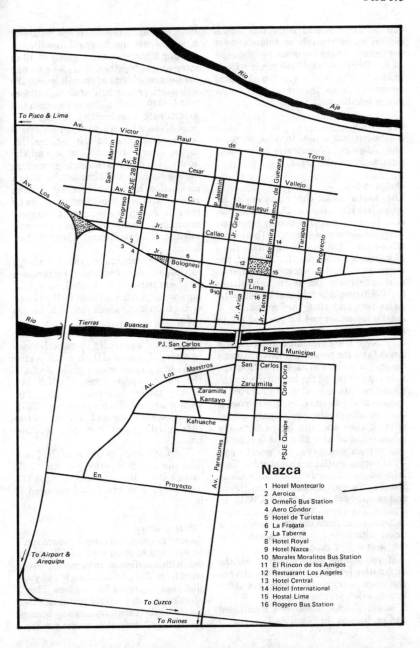

Nazca

1 Hotel Montecarlo
2 Aeroica
3 Ormeño Bus Station
4 Aero Cóndor
5 Hotel de Turistas
6 La Fragata
7 La Taberna
8 Hotel Royal
9 Hotel Nazca
10 Morales Moralitos Bus Station
11 El Rincon de los Amigos
12 Restuarant Los Angeles
13 Hotel Central
14 Hotel International
15 Hostal Lima
16 Roggero Bus Station

this on pottery and from pits which display scorching in the middle of some of the figures. There are other people, such as von Daniken, who have made a lot of money writing books which make more eccentric claims than hers. No doubt you're familiar with them.

Information

All the bus companies (*Ormeño, Roggero* and *Morales Moralitos*) have their terminals on Calle Lima.

Things to See

The **Nazca Lines** can only really be appreciated from the air. Three companies offer light aircraft flights over the lines. They are *Aeroica, Aerocondor* (both with offices on Calle Lima) and *Aero Montecarlo* (office in the hotel of the same name). All these companies offer 45 minute flights in four-seater light planes for US$20 (you'll be told that US$40 is the usual fare and that they're making a special reduction just for you but not to tell anyone else – nonsense!).

Before you are pressured into buying a ticket (and the pressure consists of some twenty guys who will hassle you from the moment you get off the bus all the way to a hotel reception desk) it's a good idea to enquire at the Monte Carlo Hotel to see if they are offering their customary special offer. If they are, you buy a normally priced ticket on *Aero Montecarlo* (US$20) and you can then stay at the hotel for just US$1 per person (for one night only). This is a bargain because the Monte Carlo Hotel is the second best hotel in Nazca and normally charges US$7 to US$15 for a room. The Hotel Nazca may also offer half-price accommodation if you buy a ticket with *Aero Condor* or *Aeroica* but this isn't such a good deal.

If you simply can't afford this, the alternative is to take a bus or colectivo to the tower next to the lines, but don't expect to see very much.

Maria Reiche, whom we mentioned earlier, lives at the Hotel de Turistas, Jr Bolognesi, and she is still prepared to give a lecture on the Nazca Lines in the evening if you can get a group of 10 or more people together. You can also buy her illustrated book at these lectures. It's well worth getting hold of though it does cost US$10. She's a fine old woman but unfortunately her health is failing.

The Nazca Lines are not the only sight worth seeing while you're in the area. Out in the desert, some 30 km beyond the airstrip, is a vast and fascinating cemetery dating back to the time of the Nazca civilisation. Exposed are scores of human skulls and other bones bleached white by the sun, as well as a number of complete mummies, some with the wrapping missing off the skull but still with the hair intact.

Closer to town are the ruins of a large fortress and tithe collection centre which has been partially excavated, as well as aqueducts which were built by the Nazca civilisation and which are still in use today.

Visits to both the cemetery and the fortress and aqueducts by colectivo can be arranged at most of the hotels in Nazca and usually come with a guide. Some of the guides speak some English but usually they're Spanish-speaking. The usual charge is US$3 per person or US$6 if you're on your own and each of the two sites usually takes from two to three hours.

There is a small museum on the Plaza de Armas which is perhaps worth a visit though it's a bit expensive at US$0.25 considering how small and cramped it is.

Places to Stay

As soon as you get off a bus in Nazca you'll be besieged by local guys all filling your ear with conflicting information about what is on offer and all trying to sell you a flight ticket over the Nazca Lines. They'll all offer you a free taxi ride to the hotel but this is hardly necessary anyway because no hotel in Nazca is further than three minutes walk from any other. However, if you are thinking of taking a flight over the lines remember that the *Hotel Monte Carlo* may still be offering its flight/accommodation deal mentioned earlier. If it is, it doesn't make any sense to stay anywhere else.

The most popular budget hotel in Nazca is the *Hotel Nazca* on Calle Lima. It's run by a very friendly family who are keen on maintaining high standards. The rooms are small but clean and the showers and toilets are scrubbed out daily. There's hot water available and you can leave your bags safely in reception if you are leaving late in the day. Rooms cost US$1.30/$2.20 a single/double without own bathroom.

Also very good value is the *Hostal Lima*, Calle Tacna near the junction with the main plaza. The hotel offers very clean rooms with hot showers for US$1.30/$2 a single/double without own bath and US$2.20/$2.90 a single/double with bathroom. There is an attached restaurant with reasonable prices. If you want something cheaper than this then try the *Hotel Royal*, Calle Lima. It's very basic and often full but costs just US$0.55/$1.10 a single/double without own bath.

If you want something better than these then try the *Hotel Internacional*, Av Maria Reiche. This costs US$3.80/$5 a single/double with own bathroom and hot water. The hotel has its own bar but no restaurant.

At the top end of the market are the *Hotel de Turistas*, Jr Bolognesi (US$20/$28 a single/double); and the *Hotel Monte Carlo*, Jr Callao 115 (US$7 to $10 a single and US$9 to $15 a double). Both have their own bar, restaurant and swimming pool.

Places to Eat

La Taberna, Calle Lima, is very popular with travellers but somewhat cliched. Nevertheless, it offers very good food and attentive service though it is more expensive than most other restaurants. Alcoholic drinks are about twice the price that they are elsewhere. Very good value is the *El Rincon de los Amigos*, Calle Lima 582, which offers barbecued chicken. It's popular with travellers and locals alike. For an excellent, cheap, set-menu meal at lunch times try the *Hostal Lima* on the Plaza de Armas.

Two places where you can find *ceviche* at reasonable prices are the *Los Angeles*, Jr Bolognesi just off the Plaza de Armas; and *La Fragata*, Jr Bolognesi in the block next to the Hotel de Turistas, which is popular with local people and is sometimes closed in the evenings. The *Los Angeles* is also a good place for breakfast.

PISCO

Pisco is an old colonial town notable in the history of Peru as the spot where General San Martín landed during the liberation struggle. It's of interest to travellers on account of the nearby necropolis of the Paracas civilisation which flourished in the area between 700 and 300 BC, and for the figure (known as the 'candelabra') which is carved into the side of a hill overlooking the town. A little further south, a beach resort and nature reserve are being developed.

Things to See

Most of what there is to see lies outside the town of Pisco itself. One of the most interesting trips you can make is a boat ride out to the **Ballestas Islands**, which are a source of guano and also have seal and sea lion colonies on them. On the way out you can get the best views of the candelabra carved into the hillside. The boats cost around US$4 per person and take about five hours in total. Book the boats at the Hostal Pisco on the Plaza de Armas. A bus leaves there at 7 am (no extra charge) to take you to the boats.

Apart from this there is the necropolis at **Paracas** and a small archaeological museum which houses many of the finds that have been made there. A colectivo from Pisco to Paracas should cost about US$0.50.

Some 50 km from Pisco on the road to Huaytará and Ayacucho is **Tambo Colorado**, a very well preserved pre-Inca ruin with a number of wall paintings which have survived the ravages of time. You can get there and back from Pisco in a day by taking either the *Oropesa* bus (which goes to Huancavelica) at 10 am or the *Huaytarino* bus (which goes to Huaytará) at noon. The journey takes about 1½ hours and costs US$1 – get off about 20 minutes after Humay when the road goes right through the middle of the site. When you want to return, simply wait at the caretaker's house for a bus or truck.

Places to Stay

The three cheapest hotels have all had consistently bad press and been described by many travellers as very run-down, filthy and insecure. They are the *Hotel Comercio*, *Hotel Progreso* and the *Hotel Peru*. It's suggested you avoid them if possible. The Hotel Peru costs US$1.50 per person and the staff are not particularly friendly.

Instead, stay at the *Hostal Pisco* on the Plaza de Armas which isn't too bad and costs US$2 per person. Food and drink at the attached *El Candelabra* restaurant is above average in price but relatively good value.

Places to Eat

La Cabina Restaurant, opposite the Hotel Peru, offers some of the best food in Pisco. Their *lomo* sandwiches (steak with onions, tomato and chips) are a real bargain. If you're hanging out for seafood, try the *El Flamingo* in the same building as the Comercio on the main plaza. The food is excellent. Another seafood place is the *Oros Restaurant* which is a bit cheaper than the Flamingo. The set lunches at the *Restaurant Las Vegas* on the plaza have also been recommended.

PUCALLPA

Like many other places in the Amazon basin, Pucallpa is a relatively expensive boom town. Logging, oil and cocaine are the biggest money spinners around there, the latter being the most important. Stay clear of it. There are millions of dollars involved and curiosity is neither appreciated nor tolerated. The army is involved in a running battle with the cultivators, the processors and the carriers but bribes and rivalry between the army and the police severely limit the effectiveness of the campaign. The road ends at Pucallpa but most travellers go there to get a riverboat down to Iquito.

Information

The tourist office is at 2 de Mayo 111.

Places to Stay

The best of the cheapies is the *Europa* which is very clean. If it's full then try either the *Amazonas* or the *Hostal Los Angeles* which are also fairly cheap and reasonably clean. The Amazonas is also the best place to enquire about boats going downriver to Iquitos.

Another place which has been suggested is the *Hotel España* which costs US$3.50 per person. Two others which have been used by travellers in the past are the *Mercedes* and the *Alex*, though they're a little on the expensive side.

Places to Eat

The *Chifa Hong Kong* and the *Restaurant d'Onofrio* both serve good food but they're not particularly cheap.

AROUND PUCALLPA
Lago Yarinacocha

If you have the money and the time then it's worth spending a few days at Lago Yarinacocha, 30 minutes by bus from Pucallpa. There are a number of places to stay, some of them expensive, others fairly cheap. You can swim, rent motorboats (about US$12 per day) or dug-outs (about US$2.50 to $3 per day) and visit local Indian villages. For more information enquire at the tourist office.

PUERTO MALDONADO

To find yourself in Puerto Maldonado – presently a gold rush town – you'd have to be hell-bent on going the hard way through the Amazon jungles to Cobija (Bolivia) or Rio Branco (Brazil). It's not a particularly interesting town and it has some peculiar quirks of climate too. Normally, the temperature hovers around 37 to 40°C but freezing winds sweeping down from the Andes can send it rapidly down towards zero. As a result, the fauna in this part of the jungle is very different from fauna elsewhere.

Places to Stay

Puerto Maldonado is an expensive town and because there is a gold rush on, it can be very hard to find cheap accommodation. Some of the cheapest are the *Toni, Moderno, Chávez* and the *Central*.

If they are full, then try the *Oriental* (on the Plaza) or the *Wilson*. If you have no luck or you'd like a touch of luxury, try the *State Tourist Hotel* on the banks of the Tambopata River.

Places to Eat

Meals in this town will cost you at least double what you would pay anywhere else in Peru, except perhaps in Iquitos. With that in mind, try the *Juanito* on the Plaza de Armas.

Puno

Because it's the largest Peruvian town on the shores of Lake Titicaca and on the main road from Cuzco to La Paz (Bolivia), Puno has become a major tourist centre over the last few years. Services are now very good and there's plenty to do in the evenings.

Lake Titicaca is, of course, the site of the legendary origin of the Incas. A pageant is held in the town every year on 5 November to celebrate the arrival of Manco Capac and his wife from the waters of the lake. There's also a much larger festival, the Virgen de la Candelaria, from 1 to 15 February.

For the rest of the year the main points of interest are the Indian-inhabited islands in the lake, particularly the floating reed islands of Uros. The islands can be visited from Puno and though they tend to be very touristy these days they're still worth visiting. The Indians not only live on reed islands but sail reed boats too, and it was these that inspired Thor Heyerdahl. Craftsmen from Suriqui, a Bolivian town on the lake, were responsible for constructing his reed boats, *Ra II* and *Tigris*.

Information

The tourist office is on Cajamarca between Ancash and Ayacucho on the 2nd floor. It's open Monday to Friday from 7 am to 2 pm. They have maps of the town and details of how to get to the islands in the lake, but not a great deal else.

There are several casas de cambio but the best one is on Lima close to the junction with Grau and opposite the Monterrey. The rates are generally better than in Cuzco and they take both cash and travellers' cheques.

The Bolivian Consulate is on Jr Junín, between Jr Giraldo and Jr Deza diagonally opposite the Hostal Arequipa. It's open Monday to Friday from 8.30 am to 12.30 pm and 2.30 to 4.30 pm. On the door is a notice saying that *all* tourists need a visa for Bolivia if they are crossing the border at Yunguyo from 14th to 23rd of each month. This maybe only a temporary measure so check it out. Visas cost US$5, no photos required, and are issued on the spot.

Warning The Puno-Arequipa train is a thieves' paradise. A horrifying proportion of travellers who take it get ripped off.

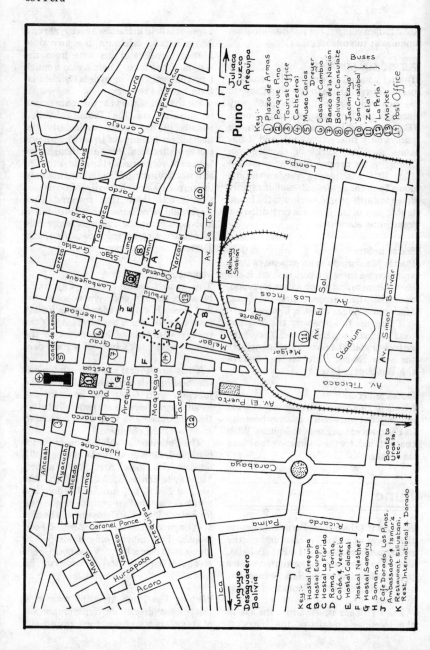

Puno

Key:—
1. Plaza de Armas
2. Parque Pino
3. Tourist Office
4. Cathedral
5. Museo Carlos
   Dreyer
6. Casa de Cambio
7. Banco de la Nación
8. Bolivian Consulate
   Buses
9. 'Jacantaya'
10. 'San Cristóbal'
11. 'La Perla'
12. 'Zela'
13. Market
14. Post Office

Key:—
A. Hostal Arequipa
B. Hostal Europa
C. Hostal La Florida
D. Roma, Torino,
   Colón & Venecia
E. Hostal Colonial
F. Hostal Nesther
G. Hostal Sanary
H. Samana
J. Café Dorado, Los Pinos,
   Ambassador & Ismar's
K. Restaurant Sillustani,
   Rest. Internacional & Dorado

You must be extremely careful if you don't want to join their ranks. Don't for a second take your eyes off anything you want to see again. The Puno-Cuzco train isn't as bad but you're advised to keep your wits about you.

Things to See

Uros Islands These floating reed islands are well worth visiting even though they're tourist traps. They're constructed out of the reeds which grow in the shallower parts of the lake. As the old reeds rot away under water, new layers are added on the surface. There are houses, schools and even a football pitch on one of them – the first pitch I've ever encountered which bounced as I ran across it! I'd love to see a whole team play on it! You'll be charged for any photographs you take on these islands and you'll probably be pressured into buying one of the model reed boats which are made there.

To get to the Uros Islands you can either arrange a trip with one of the travel agencies along Tacna or with one of the touts who go round the hotels. There are usually two trips a day, one at 9 am (returning by 12 noon) and another at 2.30 pm (returning by 5.30 pm). They all charge the same – US$5 per person. You can also hire your own boat by going down to the *muelle* (quay). Boat owners usually ask for US$20 for the whole boat, so get a group together first.

Taquile Island This island is much further out in the lake than the Uros Islands (about 24 km from Puno) and in order to see it properly you should plan to stay overnight. There are quite a few pre-Inca and Inca ruins there as well as Inca terracing. The Indians who live there, save for a few, speak only Quechua and derive most of their income from selling well-made woollen goods to tourists and by providing them with places to stay.

Accommodation on the island is organised by the community craftwork cooperative and is in private homes (there are no hotels). Prices are fixed at US$0.50 per person per night excluding food. It's best to try to get a place to stay close to the village as there are one or two cafés there where you can find basic meals. You may also arrange to have a family cook for you. The food is usually all right but lacks variety. It's advisable to take along a sleeping bag as well, as accommodation is fairly primitive. Sweets or fruit for the kids also helps. There are several restaurants around the main square.

Three to four boats leave the *muelle* in Puno daily for Taquile (usually between 8 and 9 am, cost about US$3 return and take about four hours. Recent reports suggest this island is getting as touristy as the Uros Islands yet many travellers continue to write favourably about it.

Amantani Island Amantani is similar to Taquile but even more tranquil. The boats there from Puno cost US$1.90 one-way and take five to six hours, calling briefly at one or other of the Uros islands on the way. Accommodation is in private homes in groups and the minimum charge is US$7.50 for four people including three meals a day. People are hospitable but the staple diet is potatoes and more potatoes. One family which has been recommended is that of Sn Florentino Yanarica Cari. Their farm is about two km from where the boat lands. It's very basic but the family is very friendly and they cook good food.

Sillustani The partially restored ruins of burial towers built by the Colla tribe, who pre-dated the Incas, can be seen at Sillustani, 32 km north-west of Puno. The site is quite extensive and if you liked the Inca stonework in and around Cuzco then you shouldn't miss a trip to these as they're quite bizarre. It is possible to get there by bus but it's hardly worth it as there are plenty of colectivos from the travel agencies along Tacna which will

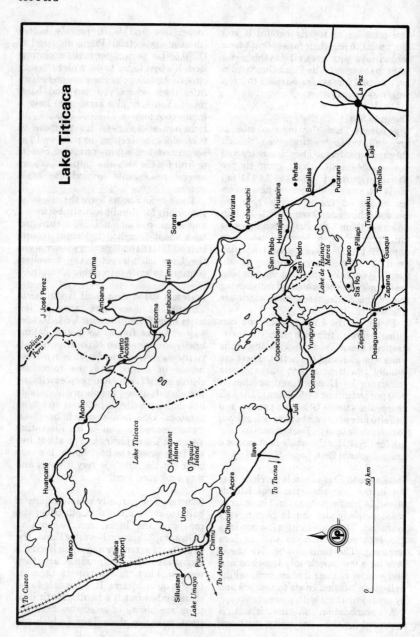

Lake Titicaca

50 km

0

To Cuzco

To Arequipa

To Tacna

La Paz

Peñas
Batallas
Pucarani
Laja
Tambillo
Tiwanaku
Pillapi
Guaqui
Taraco
Sta Ro
Zapana
Desaguadero
Zepita
Yunguyo
Copacabana
Pomata
Juli
Ilave
Acora
Chucuito
Chimu
Puno
Juliaca (Airport)
Taraco
Huancané
Moho
Puerto Acosta
Escoma
Carabuco
Ambana
Timusi
Chuma
J José Perez
Sorata
Warizata
Achachachi
San Pablo
Huatajata
San Pedro
Huapina
Huarina

Lake de Huiñay Marca

Lake Titicaca

Amantani Island
Taquile Island

Uros

Sillustani
Lake Umayo

Bolivia
Peru

take you there for US$2 each. The road is surfaced the whole way and the drive takes about one hour. There's an entry fee of US$0.15. The museum at the site is hardly worth the bother. Most of the colectivos leave at 2.30 pm.

Chucuíto South-east of Puno, there's an Inca sundial close to the village of Chucuíto. The village also has houses with carved stone doorways and a small museum in the church of Santo Domingo. The church of La Asunción is worth a visit.

In Puno itself, drop into the market which offers good llama and alpaca wool articles. There are also carved stone amulets and models of the Uros reed boats.

The **museum** on Conde de Lemos near the junction with Destua is well worth a visit. It's mainly devoted to archaeology. There is an entry fee of US$0.25.

Places to Stay

During winter the nights can get bitterly cold in Puno and budget hotels never provide heating and rarely enough blankets. A sleeping bag is very useful.

Most of the real cheapies have rooms from under US$1 to about US$1.50 – *Hostal Rosario*, Moquegua 325; *Hotel Torino*, Libertad 126; *Hostal Roma*, Libertad 115; and the *Venecia*, Tacna – have no hot showers and are very basic.

Slightly better is the *Hostal Colonial*, Arequipa between Libertad and the Parque Pino. It offers small, basic rooms and you'll be told there is hot water. There are indeed the Brazilian-type electric heaters in the showers but the electricity supply is either not connected or they're very unwilling to turn it on. It's always the same story – 'In another hour'; but it never comes.

Another cheapie which has been popular for years is the *Hostal Colón*, Tacna 290, which is basic, friendly and has its own restaurant. Rooms are also

around US$1 with *cama matrimonial* or for a double without own bathroom.

The most popular hotel in Puno – and with good reason – is the *Hotel Europa*, Alfonso Ugarte 112 near the corner with Tacna. It's run by very friendly people and although a little tatty at the edges these days it's kept very clean and the hot showers are like Iguazu Falls (you can get a shower anytime from 6 to 9 pm. The rooms cost from about US$1 to $3 depending on whether they have an attached bathroom or not. There are clothes washing and drying facilities on the roof. You can also lock up baggage safely while you go elsewhere.

Similar, and one which many travellers have recommended, is the *Hostal Arequipa*, Arequipa 153. This is a fairly modern place, friendly and has hot water all day (very unusual in Puno). The beds are comfortable, there's a laundry service and early breakfasts are available if you want them. Rooms cost US$2 a double without own bath and US$3 a double with bath. They also have singles.

Three other places which many people have recommended are the *Hotel Monterrey*, corner Lima and Grau with rooms from US$1.50 to $4; the *Hostal Nesther*, Destua between Arequipa and Moquegua; and the *Hostal Samary*, Destua between Arequipa and Lima. These three are somewhat more expensive than the previous hotels. The Monterrey has its own cafeteria.

In this same bracket is the *Hostal Lima*, Tacna 248, which costs US$1.50/$2 a single/double without own bath and US$2.50/$4 a single/double with bath. There is hot water (only between 6 and 9 pm) in this reasonably modern and clean but rather dull hotel.

For something a bit up-market, the new *Hostal Real* at Av El Sol 841 has been recommended.

If your hotel doesn't have hot water there are public hot showers on Av El Sol next to the dry cleaners near the Juliaca bus terminal. Bring your own soap.

Places to Eat

Two of the most popular restaurants are the *Sillustani* and the *Restaurant Internacional* both on the corner of Moquegua and Libertad. The Sillustani has the better atmosphere and the service is quicker but it's somewhat more expensive and, unless there's a crowd in there, it can be cold. The Internacional is a modern place and usually warm but the service is very slow although the food is good when it arrives. It also lays on folk music during the high season (no cover charge).

Also very popular are the *Samana*, Puno 334 between Arequipa and Lima; and the restaurant at the *Hotel Samary*, Destua between Arequipa and Lima. The Samana has folklore shows from 9.30 pm onwards (taped music at other times), very good mulled wine and what must be one of Puno's only fireplaces. There's no cover charge. You can also change money there at a very good rate. The Samary offers meals for less than US$1. Their 'trout of the casa' includes rice, chips, salad, vegetables, a fried egg and avocado! It's not very good.

On Lima between Libertad and Lambayeque there are four restaurants which are worth trying out. They are *Ismar's* (No 371), *Restaurant Los Pinos* (No 341), *Restaurant Ambassador* (No 347), and the *Café Dorado* (No 361). Ismar's and the Ambassador are probably the best of the bunch but the Café Dorado is also capable of turning out good food although the kitchen doesn't look at all hygienic. The Dorado often puts on folklore shows in the high season. The Ambassador reputedly offers the best trout in Puno though it's not particularly cheap.

The *Café Sumac Wasi*, Melgar 109 near the junction with Tacna, offers traditional fare and advertises itself as open 24 hours a day.

As far as bars go, try the *Bar Café Delta*, on the corner of Libertad and Moquegua opposite the Restaurant Internacional, which has cheap drinks and is popular with local people. There's also a bar opposite the Hotel Monterrey on Lima which has been highly recommended. There are two other bars on Moquegua between Libertad and Arbulu.

For coffee and snacks try either *Hielo Rico* in the Parque Pino or *Ito's Bar & Restaurant* on the Plaza de Armas.

TACNA

Forty-two km from the Chilean border, Tacna is the last major town in Peru going south. Following the War of the Pacific between Chile, on one side, and Peru and Bolivia on the other, Tacna remained in Chilean hands from 1880 to 1929 after which it was handed back to Peru. During that time the Chileans attempted to put their stamp on the place and built a large number of schools. As a result, Tacna has the highest literacy rate in Peru. It's also one of Peru's cleanest and most modern cities.

Information

The tourist office at Av Bolognesi 2088 is a very long way from the centre so it's hardly worth going out there. The *Touring y Automovil Club de Peru* is at Av 2 de Mayo 55.

There are plenty of people offering to change money along Av Bolognesi. Casas de cambio are along San Martín and Av Bolognesi. It's better to change soles into Chilean pesos in Tacna rather than in Arica. You should also buy Chilean pesos there if you are going to Arica on a weekend as it can be difficult to change money at this time in Arica.

Things to See

If you have time on your hands in Tacna have a look at the **cathedral** designed by Eiffel of the Eiffel Tower fame; and the **Railway Museum** at the railway station, which is excellent and has maps, blueprints and Pacific war memorabilia as well as old steam engines and rolling

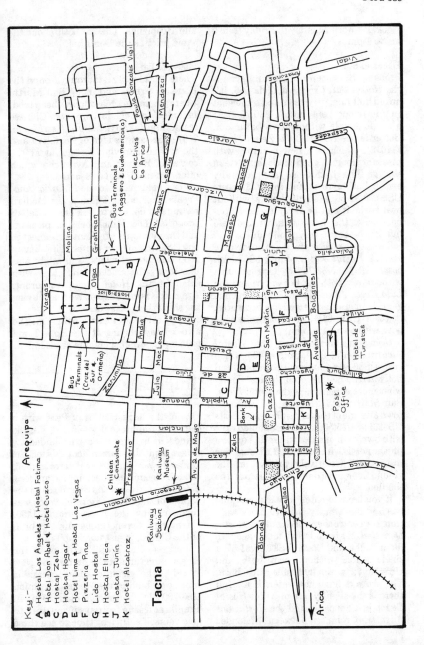

Key:-
A Hostal Los Angeles & Hostal Fatima
B Hotel Don Abel & Hotel Cuzco
C Hostal Zela
D Hostal Hogar
E Hotel Lima & Hostal Las Vegas
F Pizzeria Pino
G Lido Hostal
H Hostal El Inca
J Hostal Junin
K Hotel Alcatraz

Tacna

stock. It's open Monday to Friday from 9 am to 1 pm.

Places to Stay

Probably the cheapest place in Tacna is the *Hostal San Cristóbal*, Zela 666. It's an old building, very basic and somewhat run-down but it only costs US$0.70/$1.35 a single/double without own bathroom. Better is the *Hostal Zela*, Zela 374 (tel 711012), which is a new building with pleasant rooms, good beds and clean sheets. The bathrooms are generally awash but there is hot water. It costs US$0.90/$1.65 a single/double without own bath. It can be noisy up to 10 pm because of the downstairs bar and café but otherwise it's very good value.

Two other places which are good value are the *Hostal Junín*, Junín 88, which costs US$1.65/$2.75 a single/double without own bath but hot water; and the *Lido Hostal*, San Martín 876A, which is very clean and secure and has hot water. It costs US$1.65/$2.55 a single/double both with own bathroom.

Going up-market, try the *Hostal Alcatraz* (tel 724991), Bolívar 295, which costs US$3.30 a double with own bath and hot water. They have no singles. Somewhat more expensive is the *Hotel Lima*, San Martín 442, right in the centre of town and one of the largest hotels. It costs US$2.30/$4/$5.50 a single/double/triple with own bath and hot water. It's quite a plush hotel with carpeted floors, two restaurants (relatively pricey) on the ground floor and a dance hall/disco on the top floor.

If you have to catch an early morning bus and don't fancy the five-block walk from the centre then check out the *Hostal Don Abel* on Melendez which is adequate for a night and costs US$1.35/$1.55 a single/double without own bath and US$1.45/$2 a single/double with bath. The showers have hot water. If it's full there is the slightly less pleasant *Hostal Cuzco* just opposite; and the *Hostal Los Angeles*, Grohman between Melendez and Hospiglios. They're both about the same price as the Don Abel.

Places to Eat

There are a lot of restaurants around the Plaza de Armas and along San Martín where you can get reasonably cheap food. Included in this lot are two Chinese restaurants (eg *Saywa Chifa*, San Martín 753). The same is true of Zela. Try also the typical Peruvian restaurant at the corner of Bolívar and Ayacucho which offers set-meals and a-la-carte.

For a splurge, go to the *Pizzaria Pino*, Pasaje Libertad 79. This is a very modern restaurant, done up to look like an Italian trattoria. The atmosphere is pleasant and the pizzas are excellent but expect to pay US$2 to $2.50 per person. They have a good selection of wines. You might also like to try the chicken and chips with salad at the *Hotel Lima* restaurant. Again, this is more expensive than buying the same thing elsewhere.

If you're looking for action there may be a rock band playing at the Hotel Lima from 9 pm onwards; enquire at reception.

Trujillo

One of the largest cities of Peru with a population approaching 500,000, Trujillo stands in a large oasis surrounded by desert and the barren foothills of the Andes. It was founded by Pizarro in 1536, though the area had been important long before the arrival of the Spaniards as the capital of the Chimú empire, which was conquered by the Incas around 1450. Chan Chan, the enormous ruined capital of the Chimú, is just north of Trujillo.

Just south of Trujillo are two of the largest structures of the prehistoric New World – the gigantic adobe pyramids which were built by the Moche civilisation (150-700 AD). You should plan to stay in Trujillo at least a few days if you want to give yourself sufficient time to see these places as well as Trujillo itself, which retains a good deal of its colonial atmosphere.

Information

The tourist office is at Av España 2335 on the 2nd floor. There's only a small sign so it's not obvious. On the 1st floor is a college. It only has limited information and is open erratic hours. Good maps and information are also available from the Touring y Automóvil Club del Perú on Almagro 707 but you're more likely to get a map (US$0.20) from the Libreria Ayacucho at 570 Ayacucho.

The casa de cambio on the Plaza de Armas at the junction with Pizarro offers good rates for cash but they won't take travellers' cheques. To change these you must go to the casa de cambio round the corner from the *Faucett* office but expect to be charged a lot of commission. Banks (and Trujillo has a surprising number of surprisingly grand banks) do change travellers' cheques and they don't take all that long over it.

Immigration (for visa extensions) is on 3rd floor, Edificio Demarco, Diego de Almagro 225. Go there in the morning, pick up the necessary forms and take them to the Banco de la Nacion on the corner of Independencia and Gamarra. Pay your US$20 fee and get the forms stamped. Next buy a sheet of *sexto* paper from the people outside the bank and take this and the stamped form back to immigration. Some two hours later you'll get your visa extension. No onward ticket or 'sufficient funds' are asked for as long as you only want another 60 days. If you ask for 90 days you must have an onward ticket and they have to telephone Lima.

Most long-distance bus terminals are grouped around the junction of Costa Rica and Av La Marina. *TEPSA* is on Almagro between Grau and Av España.

Things to See

In Trujillo itself, make sure you visit the **Archaeological Museum**, Calle Bolívar

446, which has a good collection of Moche and Chimú pottery as well as many other exhibits. It's open from 8 am to 1 pm from January to March, and from 8 am to 12 noon and 3 to 6 pm during the rest of the year. Unfortunately it was closed down in '85 and there was some discussion as to whether it would re-open.

Chan Chan The crumbling adobe ruins of the Chimú capital, Chan Chan, are about five km north of Trujillo and form the largest archaeological site in Peru. The ruins cover some 28 square km in all and are dominated by nine palaces of the Chimú kings, though there are also the remains – some of them well-preserved – of temples, workshops, warehouses, canals and the homes of ordinary people.

The Chimú were once rivals of the Incas and controlled an empire which stretched from Guayaquil to Paramonga, north of Lima. When finally conquered by the Incas, the city was allowed to fall into ruin, but the tombs of the kings were not looted for their treasures. That, typically, was left to the Spaniards. Today, part of Chan Chan – Tschudi – has been reconstructed and this is what most people visit. If you wander off to visit other parts of the site it's suggested that you don't do it alone as there's a danger of being mugged. The main area which tourists visit is now policed at the weekends because of this.

To get to Chan Chan, take one of the frequent minibuses which you can pick up on Junín. They take about 20 minutes and cost a few cents. You can also get there on the buses to Huanchaco from the market place on San Agustín off Bolívar; ask the driver to let you off at Tschudi. Entry to Tschudi costs US$0.50 (half price for students) and is also valid for entry to Arco Iris (Huaca del Dragón).

Arco Iris, a restored temple from the Mochica civilisation, is close to Chan Chan and is well worth a visit. Either get a colectivo from Tschudi if you are there, or if coming direct from Trujillo, take a bus

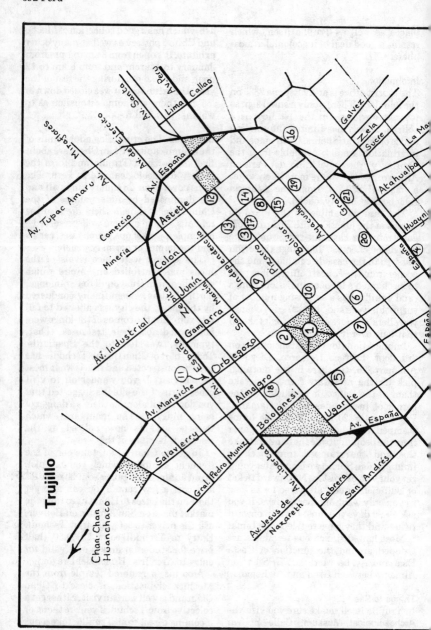

2 Hotel Touristas
3 Hotel San Martin
4 Tourist Office
5 Post Office
6 Archeological Museum
7 Aeroperu
8 Vegetarian Restaurant
9 Banco de la Nacion
10 Fawcett Airline Office
11 Bus Stop for Chan Chan & Huanchaco Beach
12 TEPSA Ticket Office
13 Peru Express (to Lima & Chiclayo)
14 Empresa Diaz Terminal (to Cajamarca)
15 Empresa Chinchaysuyo (to Lima, Piura, Chiclayo & Chimbote)
16 Roggera Bus Terminal
17 Hotel Americano
18 Immigration Office
19 Hostel Lima
20 Hotel Opt-Gar
21 Restaurant Criollo Grau

to La Esperanza from the same place as the buses to Chan Chan. There is a small museum at this latter site which is worth seeing. Entry is free.

The Moche Pyramids – Huaca del Sol & Huaca de la Luna These are the largest pre-Columbian structures in South America and date from the Moche civilisation which flourished from 150 to 700 AD. They are of a similar size to the pyramids at Teotihuacán in Mexico. The site is littered with pot shards from the Moche era. It's a good idea to take a torch along with you in case it's still possible to enter the pyramids. There are direct VW minibus colectivos to the site from the corner of Av Los Incas and Av Zela (Av Los Incas is the continuation of Costa Rica) or you can hire a colectivo. It's also possible to get close to the site by taking any bus marked 'Salaverry' but you must let the driver know where you want to get off and it's difficult to see the pyramids from the inside of a crowded bus. A taxi there and back with an hour or two to look around will cost about US$6.

It's best to visit the pyramids in the early morning as by noon the wind whips up the sand and conditions can be unpleasant. Huaca del Sol is the larger of the pyramids and Luna is the one at the base of the hill – it's further away but more impressive. There's nobody around at this splendidly barren site apart from the odd visitor or local villager.

Places to Stay
The *Hotel Americano*, Pizarro 758-768, has been popular for a number of years and is still very good but there is no hot water in the showers. Rooms range from US$1.50 to $3. Water is scarce in Trujillo and most hotels are only supplied with it for two hours per day. If you want hot water then go to the *Hotel Premier* which costs US$2.75 per person.

The *Hotel Chan Chan*, several blocks from the Plaza da Armas has been recommended. It costs US$4 for a double

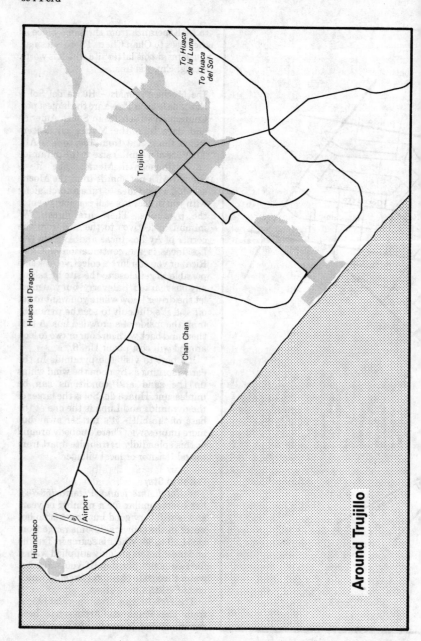

To Huaca
de la Luna

To Huaca
del Sol

Trujillo

Huaca el Dragon

Chan Chan

Huanchaco

Airport

Around Trujillo

and has a common room with a TV and daily newspapers.

Hostal Lima at Av Ayacucho 718 (between Colon and Juni'n) is a real cheapie with rooms from US\$1 to \$2. The *Pension Carmen de Vanini*, Av Larco 237, has also been recommended. Other cheaper hotels include the *Premier* at Gamarra 631 with rooms at US\$2 to \$4; or the *San José* at 515 Grau with rooms at US\$2.50 to \$4. The *San Martin* at San Martin 749 is a flashier place at about US\$4 to \$5.

If you wanted a much more up-market place have a look at the very pleasant old *Hotel de Turistas de Trujillo*, right on the Plaza de Armas. Rooms are about US\$8/\$10 for singles/doubles. Even if you don't stay here have a look inside because it's a fine old building. They often have a good exhibition in the front room and there are some interesting old aerial photographs of Trujillo.

Places to Eat

The cheapest places are the restaurants in the modern covered market and the street stalls on the corner of Grau and Gamarra (between 7 pm and 1 am). There are also several cheap restaurants opposite the Hotel Americano. One is the *De Marco Restaurant*, Pizarro 725, which is moderately expensive but it's a nice little place with white tablecloths, wine and the food is very good. At lunchtime you can have a complete meal from their 'menu economica' for about US\$0.70! Their desserts and ice-cream are great too.

Just up from the Dam Marco at Pizarro 749, the *Bar Romano* is also a fine looking place. The expensive *Hotel Opt Gar* at Jiron Gamarra 796 at the corner of Grau has an excellent little snack bar right on the corner. At Grau 630 the *Restaurant Criollo Grau* is a big, straightforward place with tablecloths and good honest criollo food.

For seafood, try the *Cebicheria Esquina*, on the corner of Orbegozo and Grau, where you can eat for about US\$1. The staff are very friendly. Try their *corvina con salsa de mariscos*. *El Meson de Cervantes* at Pizarro 654 is another more expensive place with a pleasant open courtyard.

Getting Around

Taxis around town cost a standard US\$0.50. A taxi to the airport costs about US\$2.50.

HUANCHACO

Many travellers prefer to stay not in Trujillo itself but just up the coast at the village of Huanchaco past the ruins of Chan Chan. It's a somewhat dusty and grubby little fishing village/beach resort just beyond the airport. The ruins of a large but deserted old church overlook the town and you can see reed canoes like the ones at Lake Titicaca along the beach. When the fish are running hundreds of people drop lines in from the pier and haul small fish out at an amazing rate. The beach is OK but, like anywhere in Peru, the sea isn't particularly warm.

Places to Stay

At Huanchaco, the *Hostería Sol y Mar* is *the* place to stay and has been popular for many years. It's a fairly luxurious budget hotel and costs US\$2.50 to \$5. The double rooms have their own bathroom and many have a balcony but there's no hot water. The staff are very friendly and there are laundry facilities.

If you're on a tight budget the cheapest place is at *Lola's* house which costs about US\$0.50 per person per night. If it's full, go to the *Hotel Bracamonte* which has a number of excellent chalets, each with its own bathroom, for US\$2 per person. The owner (same name as the hotel) is very friendly. There is a swimming pool at this hotel as well as a pleasant garden. There's no hot water.

If you're staying in Huanchaco for a while then ask around for rooms to let in private houses (around US\$0.50).

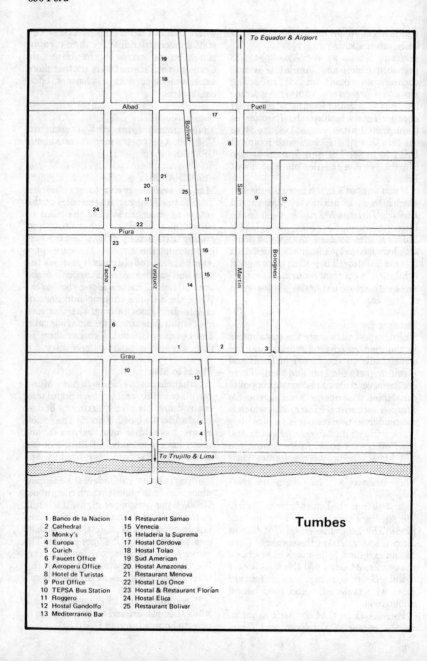

To Equador & Airport

Abad

Puell

Bolivar

San

Piura

Tacna

Vasquez

Martin

Bolognesi

Grau

To Trujillo & Lima

Tumbes

1 Banco de la Nacion
2 Cathedral
3 Monky's
4 Europa
5 Curich
6 Faucett Office
7 Aeroperu Office
8 Hotel de Turistas
9 Post Office
10 TEPSA Bus Station
11 Roggero
12 Hostal Gandolfo
13 Mediterraneo Bar

14 Restaurant Samao
15 Venecia
16 Heladeria la Suprema
17 Hostal Cordova
18 Hostal Tolao
19 Sud American
20 Hostal Amazonas
21 Restaurant Menova
22 Hostal Los Once
23 Hostal & Restaurant Florían
24 Hostal Elica
25 Restaurant Bolivar

Places to Eat

There are a number of excellent seafood restaurants along the promenade, but prices differ from one place to the next so you need to check them out before sitting down. The *Lucho del Mar* is popular for its ceviche but the service is slow and erratic. Similar is *Le Picolo* run by a German and French couple which offers excellent cheap food. *El Penon* has good straightforward food, *El Poseidon* is also a basic, cheap place; or there's the *El Ereza*.

Getting There

There are frequent buses and minibuses from Trujillo via Chan Chan which take half an hour and cost about US$15. Otherwise, take a colectivo for US$0.30. A taxi to the airport will cost about US1.50.

TUMBES

Tumbes became a part of Peru only recently, having been captured from the Ecuadorians in 1941 during a war over ownership of what is today part of Peru's Amazon basin. There isn't anything to see there and most travellers simply pass through on their way to somewhere else. Tumbes has terrible, voracious mosquitoes.

Information

There is a bank in Tumbes, which is open until 11.30 am only, but it will change travellers' cheques at a decent rate of exchange.

Places to Stay

Two of the most popular hotels with travellers are the *Hotel Florían* opposite the El Dorado bus office and the *Hostal Amazonas* next to the Roggero bus office. They both cost about US$2 to $3 with own bath but cold showers only.

Other hotels which you could try if these are full are the *Hotel Elica*, Av Tacna behind the Roggero and TEPSA bus terminals; and the *Hotel Italia*, Grau 733.

Avoid the *Hotel Gandolfo* which is revoltingly filthy and frequently gets hassled by the immigration police. At the other extreme Tumbes has an amazingly modern (and expensive) *Hotel de Turistas* – why does a grubby little town like this deserve such a place?

Places to Eat

The *Restaurant Florían* (part of the Hotel Florían) serves good fish. Three other places which serve good seafood are the *Pez Espada*, *Restaurant Curich* (Plaza de Armas) and *Tito's*, Alfonso Ugarte 212, two blocks from the Plaza de Armas. Curich has a straightforward menu and pleasantly cold beer.

The *Mediterraneo Bar* on the Plaza de Armas is a popular bar and is a good place to watch the activity in the square. Good ice cream at the *Heladeria La Suprema*.

Getting There

A colectivo to the Ecuador border is about US$1 per person including the stop at the immigration office a couple of km down the road from the actual border. A bus all the way through to Lima from Tumbes costs about US$17, to Trujillo about US$10.

Uruguay

You might be forgiven for thinking that Fray Bentos was another name for corned beef – and you wouldn't be too far off the mark. It's in Fray Bentos that Uruguay's largest meat-processing plant is situated. The country's huge herds of sheep and cattle are the backbone of its economy and have been since the beginning of the century. Uruguay once exported more meat than Argentina.

These days, apart from its continuing importance as a meat producer, the country is unremarkable yet it was once one of the world's most advanced nations as far as social welfare goes and was well ahead of Europe or the USA at the time.

As early as 1915 legislation was already in force providing for an eight-hour working day, holidays with pay, old-age pensions, free medical treatment, legalised divorce (for a largely Catholic country!) and the nationalisation of essential industries and services such as electricity, telephones, transport, banks, insurance, port facilities and chemical products. Capital punishment and bull-fighting had been abolished and the Church disestablished. These remarkable reforms were largely the work of one man – José Batlle y Ordonez.

A former political journalist who edited his own newspaper, Batlle believed that Uruguayan political and social life throughout the 19th century were the result of corruption and excessive presidential power, so when he became the leader of the liberal party (the Colorados), he persuaded them that they ought to make themselves worthy of popular support by ensuring honest elections. Not only did he do this but when his first term as president came to an end, he announced that he would observe the habitually ignored clause in the Constitution which prohibited a president from serving two consecutive terms in office. This was an action unprecedented in South American politics at the time, yet it seemed to work, for he was re-elected to the presidency four years later.

Naturally the opposition conservative party (the Blancos), were outraged by his reforms and branded him insane, but they never managed to convince anyone that he was acting out of any motive other than sincere conviction. Batlle's influence was felt a long time after his death, but the idealism on which his reforms were based, as well as much of their substance, was gradually whittled away. There was never any meaningful attempt at land reform or to re-invest profits in livestock production and more efficient management. Some 500 families continued to monopolise the land and to control the bulk of the capital invested in industry and the banks. They were more interested in investing their money abroad and frittering away their time at ritzy beach resorts than in doing anything about increasing productivity on their ranches. Their profits remained high, despite low yield, because of the low costs – most ranches provided work for barely two people per 1000 hectares and even then for only part of the year.

With so few jobs available in the countryside, workers began to flock to the cities, adding to unemployment there. Social tension began to rise and in the 1960s Latin America's first urban guerrilla organisation was formed, the Tupamaros. Organised on a cellular basis to make infiltration extremely difficult, they were for a time very successful in their armed resistance to the weak and corrupt government of Jorge Areco, and later to that of General Bordaberry, who overthrew the civilian government in a military coup in 1973. The Tupamaros gained a lot of sympathy from large sections of the community by distributing money robbed from banks and casinos, seizing food trucks and driving them into poor neighbourhoods, and pilfering government documents which exposed the truth about official corruption, tax evasion and fraud.

Faced with their inability to significantly infiltrate the movement, the government panicked and brought in CIA and FBI advisers, but when one of them was kidnapped and then shot after the government refused to release imprisoned Tupamaros in exchange, a state of siege was declared. Almost all civil liberties were suspended, Congress closed, labour and student organisations outlawed and over 5000 opponents of the regime thrown into prison. Torture became commonplace during interrogations. By casting the dragnet over anyone and everyone who

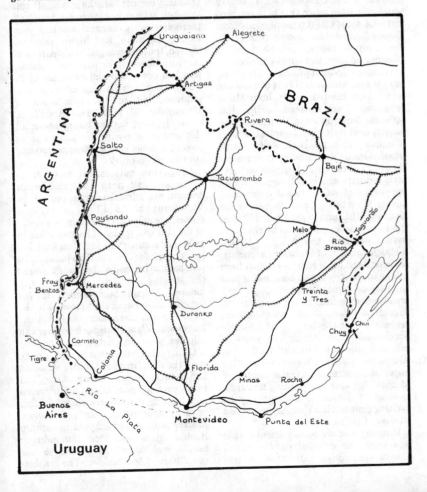

Uruguay

could be even vaguely suspected of being either involved with or in sympathy with the Tupamaros, the movement was finally crushed, yet precisely nothing had been done to ameliorate the intolerable conditions which had given rise to the movement in the first place.

Very little has changed since those days of the early 1970s except that over 100,000 people have since emigrated and the trend shows no sign of diminishing. It's certainly a tragic reversal for a country which offered so much that between 1836 and 1926 some 650,000 immigrants from Europe flocked there, mostly from Spain and Italy (Uruguay is the smallest Hispanic country in South America).

Things are beginning to change, however, since the election in late 1984 of a civilian government headed by Dr Julio Maria Sanguinetti, yet it treads a thin line between bankruptcy and getting the country back on its feet. Despite the years of military rule, the basic welfare state remains intact and funding it consumes about 70% of the GNP. Uruguay has very little industry and is still dependent on the whims of international commodity buyers. With talk of protectionism in the air at the EEC and in the United States, the future doesn't look too bright. This hasn't deterred the Frente Amplio coalition (made up of Christian Democrats, socialists and more radical groups) from taking to the streets and demanding that the pace of change be speeded up. They are also demanding, as are the people in Argentina, that those army officers responsible for the murder and torture which took place during the years of military rule are brought to justice. Almost every week witnesses yet another huge demonstration in the centre of Montevideo, each one pushing forward a new set of demands. It's certainly an exciting time to visit Uruguay if you're a student of politics.

Uruguay – or the *banda oriental* as it was known in colonial days – hasn't always seemed so attractive. It was largely ignored by the Spanish for nearly 200 years after their arrival in this part of the world. Indeed, it was the Portuguese from Brazil who founded Colonia in 1680 as a rival to Buenos Aires. Meanwhile cattle which had been released from some of the early Spanish expeditions had multiplied rapidly. The herds which they produced were followed by roving bands of gauchos, who killed them for food and to sell their hides. Argentine ranchers gradually began to see the potential in all this and set up headquarters here and there, employing the gauchos to look after herds. As more and more ranchers arrived, the land was gradually parcelled out into huge *estancias*. The gauchos, who had never laid claims to any of it, were left out entirely. Increasing Spanish influence led to the foundation of Montevideo in 1726. The Brazilians, naturally, were not too happy about all this and as a result, Uruguay was to become a battlefield for influence throughout the 19th century.

Uruguayan nationalism was late in developing and until 1800 the *banda oriental* was administered as part of the Viceroyalty of La Plata. A national conscience came about partly as a result of the British capture of Buenos Aires in 1806. The occupation didn't last long, but long enough for US$1 million in loot to be sent back to London and paraded around the streets. The sight of such wealth induced British businessmen to get together a merchant fleet stocked to the gunwales with manufactures (until the Napoleonic Wars, the Spanish-American colonies were prohibited from trading with any other nation but Spain). By the time the fleet arrived, the Argentinians had re-taken Buenos Aires and they had to be content with taking Montevideo and landing their wares there. British naval reinforcements arrived several months later and attempted to capture Buenos Aires but were resoundingly beaten and forced to accede to the evacuation of Montevideo. The inhabitants of that city, however, had enjoyed seven months of unprecedented activity and prosperity and were very reluctant from then on to revert to their former status as poor cousins of the *porteños*. In 1808 they declared themselves independent of Buenos Aires.

Three years later, the Brazilians pressed their claims to the *banda oriental* and invaded the country. A long and bloody war of attrition began under the leadership of the Uruguayan patriot, Atigas, but he was forced to flee to Paraguay in 1820, after which the struggle was taken up by Lavalleja. The Brazilians were finally beaten at Ituzaingo in 1827. British merchants were none too happy about seeing their lucrative trade disrupted during this struggle and so, following the defeat of the Brazilians, intervened in 1828 and were instrumental in getting both Argentina and Brazil to relinquish their claims on the country. In August 1828, Uruguay was declared independent.

It was a fragile arrangement and marked neither the beginning of internal peace nor the end of foreign intervention. The country was divided into two rival factions, one supported by Argentina and the other by Brazil. Civil war, intrigue, assassination and dictatorship tore the guts out of the country throughout the 19th century. All this led to involvement in the War of the Triple Alliance in 1865 as a result of Brazilian interference in Argentinian and Uruguayan affairs, and the dispatch of a Paraguayan army into Uruguay in an attempt to force the Brazilians to leave. Uruguay would probably never have been dragged into that war had not the dictator Flores been supported by Brazil.

Few travellers visit Uruguay, mainly because it's somewhat off the beaten track and the Iguazú Falls act as a huge magnet drawing people directly from Argentina into Brazil. But Montevideo, where over half the population live, is worth visiting and it's just as easy to get to Iguazú from there as it is from Buenos

Aires. If you've just visited Iguazú and are heading south, it's a pleasant alternative to an otherwise long and monotonous journey from Posadas to Buenos Aires.

VISAS

These are required by all except nationals of Western Europe, Canada, Israel, Japan, Seychelles and the USA. The normal permitted length of stay is 90 days. If you need a visa these cost US$6.50 and take 24 hours to issue.

Argentine visas The Consulate-General is at Rio Branco 1281. It's open from 2 to 7 pm but you must apply for visas between 2 and 5 pm and collect between 6 and 7 pm. It's very busy in there. Transit visas (three days maximum) for British passport holders take 15 days to come through and you must pay for a telex to Buenos Aires (about US$8 to $9). They also tend to give you the run-around between different officials.

Bolivian visas The Consulate-General is at Rio Branco 1320 (4th floor) – you have to go into the *galeria* to find the lift. It's open Monday to Friday from 2 to 6 pm and the staff speak English. They're very pleasant people and will give you a visa while you wait as long as you're not South Korean in which case you have to pay for a telegram to La Paz (US$25) and wait for an answer!

Brazilian visas The Consulate-General is at Bulevar Artigas 1257 (take bus No 14 from 18 de Julio, US$0.15; or a taxi, about US$1). For most people there's no problem. All you need is one photo and it's issued while you wait. If you're Korean, however, or you have stayed in Brazil for six months and then nipped over the border to get a fresh visa (as one Australian that I met there had) then you've got big problems. They'll tell you they have to telex Brasília (which *you* pay for) and that the reply may be a *month* in coming!! Onward tickets (a return

Montevideo-Pôrto Alegre bus ticket with *ONDA* or *TTL* is sufficient), credit cards, lots of green-backs all speed things up somewhat and the young woman who deals with enquiries there is very helpful. In other words, get your visa renewed in Brazil – not outside – if you've already been there six months.

Peruvian Visas The Consulate-General is at Soriano 1124. It's open Monday to Friday from 9 am to 2 pm. Visas cost US$4 (in dollars) and take 24 hours. No problems.

MONEY
US$1 = 120 pesos (and rising slowly)

The unit of currency is the New Uruguayan Peso = 100 centimos. There are no restrictions on the import or export of local currency.

The centre of Montevideo is peppered with casas de cambio and you can freely exchange any currency you like. You can also buy US cash dollars there and change US dollar travellers' cheques into US cash dollars. The commission is very low. In Brazil you can *not* buy US cash dollars at a casa de cambio or at a bank. You can only buy them on the parallel market (*mercado paralelo*) and although this is quite legal, you pay heavily over the odds for them (around 25-30% is average). If you're heading for Brazil, therefore, it makes a lot of sense to pick up as many cash dollars in Uruguay as you dare carry otherwise you're going to find Brazil relatively expensive.

There is an airline ticket tax of 3% for all tickets bought in Uruguay. The departure tax for international flights is US$2.50.

ACCOMMODATION
If you have come from the Andean countries or from Brazil you are going to find accommodation in Uruguay quite expensive. US$5 to $7 a double would be average for a reasonable hotel though, of course, there are cheaper, more basic places.

If you're thinking of spending any time in Uruguay and especially if you intend to explore the countryside it's worth considering using the Youth Hostels. Full details can be obtained from the national headquarters, *Asociación de Alberguistas del Uruguay*, Calle Pablo de Maria 1583, Montevideo (tel 98-1324). The office is open from 2 to 7 pm. Hostels cost on average US$1.50 per night (though some are cheaper – the one at Paysandú costs only US$0.75). Some are conveniently located in main towns, but a few are in out-of-the-way places. The most useful are:

Colonia Suiza
  Hotel del Prado, Nueva Helvecia, Colonia (tel 169)
Montevideo
  Canelones 935, corner of Río Branco.
Paysandú
  Gran Bretaña 872 (tel 4247).
Piriápolis
  Simon del Pino 21136, behind Hotel Argentino.
Rocha
  Albergue Valisas, above the castle on the beach.

GETTING THERE
To/From Argentina
There is almost a bewildering number of ways to get to Argentina. The price you pay depends on the time it takes and the number of changes of transport you are prepared to accept so take your pick. These are possibilities in order of cost:

Bus and Ferry via Carmelo & Tigre
(US$9.85 one-way; US$18.20 return)
There are two bus departures to Carmelo from Montevideo daily from Monday to Saturday at 6.15 am, which take four hours. The ferries depart Carmelo at 10.30 and 11 am, and the trip to Tigre takes four hours. On Sundays, there are two bus departures at 7.15 and 9 am and

the ferries from Carmelo leave at 12 noon and 2 pm.

From Tigre to Montevideo, there are daily ferries at 8 and 8.30 am with the buses to Montevideo leaving Carmelo at 12 noon and 12.30 pm).

It may still be possible to get a 10% reduction on the cost of the launch between Carmelo and Tigre if you have a Youth Hostel membership card. Make sure you enquire about this when you buy your combined bus/launch ticket. From Tigre to Buenos Aires take a train to Retiro Station (in the centre of Buenos Aires) on the Mitre Suburban Line. They leave approximately every 10 minutes and take about 50 minutes.

Entirely by Bus
(US$13 one-way; US$26 return.)
There are three bus companies which offer this service. They are COT, Sarandi 699; CITA, Av del Libertador 1446 (tel 910419); and ONDA, Ibicuy 1309 (tel 900187).

The buses depart Montevideo daily at 8 am, 9 and 10 pm arriving Buenos Aires at 5 pm, 6 and 7 am respectively. In the opposite direction they depart Buenos Aires daily at 10 am, 9 and 10 pm arriving Montevideo at 7 pm, 6 and 7 am.

The Buquebus by Ferry via Colonia
(US$13 one-way; US$26 return.)
This route is operated by COT, Sarandi 699 (tel 912266); and Ferry Rios Uruguayas, Colonia 963 (tel 915066). The ferries are the Silva Acia and the Ciudad de Colonia.
Departures from Montevideo Monday to Saturday at 12.30 am and 8.30 am, and on Sundays at 4 pm. The trip to Buenos Aires takes about six hours.

From Buenos Aires, departures are daily at 8 am, and Sunday to Friday at 6.30 pm.

Ferry via Colonia
(US$18.70 one-way; US$35.35 return.)
This route is operated by ONDA, San José 1145 (tel 912333); and Ferryturismo, Rio Branco 1368 (tel 900045).

Departures from Montevideo daily at 9.15 am, and daily except Sunday at 4.15 pm. This trip to Buenos Aires takes six to seven hours.

From Buenos Aires, departures are daily at 7 am.

Aliscafos BELT via Colonia
(US$19.45 one-way; US$36.85 return.)
This route is operated by Aliscafos BELT, Rio Negros 1356 (tel 905063), and Plaza Cagancha 1327 (tel 904032).
Departures from Montevideo to Buenos Aires at 6.15 and 9.15 am, 1.15 and 4.15 pm daily; journey time about four hours.

From Buenos Aires, departures are daily at 7.50 and 10.50 am, and 2.50 and 5.50 pm.

ARCO Bus/Flight via Colonia
(US$19.80 one-way; US$37.70 return.)
This route is operated by ARCO, Plaza Libertad 1340.
Departures from Montevideo daily at 3 pm, on Monday to Saturday at 6 am, and on Sunday at 10 am. Total journey time to Buenos Aires is about three hours.

From Buenos Aires, departures are daily at 7 pm, Monday to Saturday at 10 am, and Sunday at 2 pm.

Aliscafos/Alimar via Colonia
(US$20 one-way; US$38 return.)
This route is operated by ONDA, San José 1133 (tel 982287).
Departures from Montevideo to Buenos Aires daily at 6.20 and 9.30 am, and 1.20 and 4.25 pm, journey time four hours.

From Buenos Aires, departures are daily at 8 and 11 am, and 3 and 6 pm.

All these are ways of getting to or from Montevideo/Colonia and Buenos Aires. On the other hand, there are other ways of getting into Argentina which don't necessarily end up in Buenos Aires. These routes simply involve crossing the River Uruguay which forms one border between the two countries.

There are international bridges across the river between Fray Bentos and Gualeguaychu and between Paysandú and Concepcíon. Further north is the

Salto Grande dam across the river some 20 km north of Salto with a road across the top, so the third possibility is from Salto to Concordia. There is also still a ferry operating directly between Salto and Concordia. There are five per day in either direction on weekdays, three on Saturdays and two on Sundays. The ferry costs US$1 and takes 15 minutes.

To/From Brazil

The routes into Brazil are all by road. The main route these days is via the coastal highway (very good surfaced road) via Chuy to Pelotas and on to Pôrto Alegre. The border actually runs down the centre of Chuy. If you take a Uruguayan bus to Chuy you'll be dropped outside the Hotel Chuy. Uruguayan immigration is one km back down the road to Montevideo and Brazilian immigration is two km down the road to Pelotas. There are frequent daily buses from the Brazilian side to Pelotas and Pôrto Alegre.

The other main highway from Treinta y Tres or Melo to Pelotas goes via the Mauá bridge and the border towns of Río Branco and Yaguarão (Brazil). It isn't used as much as the coastal route these days. Brazilian customs are on the international bridge and immigration in the town of Jaguarão. There are also frequent daily buses from Yaguarão to Pelotas.

Another route crosses the border via Rivera and Livramento, which are actually one town (free movement between the two but go through official channels if going further into either country). From Livramento there is a daily bus to Pôrto Alegre. The bus terminals in either place are only a few blocks from the border. The cheapest places to stay in Rivera are the *Hotel Montevideo*, Av Brasil 879 near the railway station; and the *Hotel Agraciada*, Calle Agraciada 646, but both are dormitory style hotels. If you want your own room try the *Hotel Sarandi*, Calle Sarandi 777, which costs US$1.75 a single. It's very clean and has good facilities.

You cannot get direct from Rivera to Foz do Iguaçu as there are no public transport connections – you must first go to Pôrto Alegre.

The last possibilities are across the bridges between Artigas and Quarai and between Bella Unión and Barra do Quarai (en route to Uruguaiana). You would take the latter if you were heading for Paraguay. This road crosses the Uruguay River into Argentina at Uruguaiana and heads for Posadas on the Paraná River opposite Encarnación in Paraguay. Without changing local buses many, many times you cannot get to Iguaçu Falls entirely through Brazil from either of these last two crossing points.

Direct Buses: Montevideo-Pôrto Alegre via Chuy and Pelotas

Both *ONDA* and *TTL* offer direct buses between the two cities. The buses are quite luxurious and coffee is available on board. You have to get off at the Brazilian border and go through a baggage search – it's not very thorough. It's cheaper to do the journey in stages but the savings are not that great – about US$10 minus the cost of accommodation en route. The schedules and fares of the direct buses are:

ONDA, Ibicuy 1309, Montevideo (tel 983570/983444).

Daily from Montevideo at 8 pm and from Pôrto Alegre at 10 pm. The journey takes 12 hours and the fare is US$24.50. If you just want to go as far as Pelotas the fare is US$20.

TTL, Plaza Libertad 1385, Montevideo (tel 915482/908419).

Daily from Montevideo at 10 pm and from Pôrto Alegre at 8 pm. The journey takes 12½ hours and costs US$24.50; or just US$20 as far as Pelotas. There are also sleeper coaches available from Montevideo on Fridays only and from Pôrto Alegre on Thursdays only but the fare on these is US$48.80.

Both *ONDA* and *TTL* also have direct buses (or connections at Pôrto Alegre) to Florianopolis, Curitiba and São Paulo but you pay through the nose for this and it's much cheaper to do the journey in stages using Brazilian buses.

To/From Paraguay

Uruguay has no common border with Paraguay but there are direct buses between Montevideo and Asunción. This is a good way of getting to the Iguaçu Falls rather than going via Pôrto Alegre and Curitiba though it is cheaper to do the journey in stages. Doing it in stages, however, takes considerably longer. The route is from Montevideo to Bella Unión then across the international bridge to Barra do Quarai in Brazil, up to Uruguaiana then across the river to Paso de los Libres in Argentina, up to Posadas then across the river to Encarnación in Paraguay and finally on to Asunción. Two companies operate buses along this route:

COIT, Paraguay 1473, Montevideo (tel 916619/908906) and at both the Terminal de Buses and Eligio Ayala 693, Asunción (tel 96197).

The buses depart Montevideo on Wednesday and Saturday at 1 pm and from Asunción on Wednesday and Saturday at 8 am. The fare is US$25 and the journey takes about 25 hours. The buses are air-conditioned, the seats semi-sleepers and drinks are available on board.

Tacuary, Paraguay 1311, Montevideo (tel 984121-3) and at the Terminal de Buses, Asunción.

The buses depart Montevideo on Fridays at 2 pm; and Asunción on Mondays at 9 am. The fares and journey times are the same as for *COIT*.

Since these buses go through both Brazil and Argentina you must have transit visas for both countries (where required). This is also what the bus office will tell you. However, the Argentine Consulate in Montevideo will tell you you don't need a transit visa. This isn't true because when you turn up at the border the officials will demand to see one though they'll almost always let you through after a little persuasion (since it's obvious you're en route to Paraguay).

If you have a British passport then you can't use these buses unless you have an Argentine transit visa. You can get these from the Consulate in Montevideo but they take 15 days to come through and you have to pay for the cost of a telex to Buenos Aires (US$8 to $9).

GETTING AROUND

Bus Buses in Uruguay are fast, comfortable and have an extensive network. One of the largest lines is *ONDA* which has its terminal on Plaza Cagancha in Montevideo. Another similar company is *COT* which has its terminal just below *ONDA* on Plaza Libertad. There are, however, several other smaller lines which operate along the same routes, and though their buses may not be as luxurious as *ONDA*, they're often just as fast and may be slightly cheaper.

There are too many departures daily to most large centres of population to be worth listing. When you want to go, just turn up and buy a ticket; except during summer when you should try to book in advance as buses fill up rapidly then.

Some examples of fares from Montevideo are:
Colona US$3.75, journey time three hours; Chuy US$7.05; Durazno US$3.75; Fray Bentos US$6.50; Florida US$2.50; Mercedes US$5.84; Paysandú US$9.75, six to seven hours depending on the route; Rio Branco US$8.75; and Salto US$10.45.

Train Railways aren't really worth considering in Uruguay as they're so slow (over 7½ hours to Fray Bentos from Montevideo and over 26 hours to Artigas from Montevideo) but they are about half the price of the buses so if you're trying to save money you might want to use them here and there. Railway buffs might also like to take one or more short journeys.

There are plenty of departures daily

from Montevideo to various cities and these are all clearly displayed at the station. As an example, Montevideo-Salto by train costs US$5.50 (or US$8.40 with a sleeping berth) and takes 16 hours. By bus it costs US$10.50 and takes about nine hours.

Montevideo

Founded by the Spanish in 1726, Montevideo is the capital of Uruguay and by far the country's largest city. Over half the population of the country lives there (about 1½ million) and the city dominates the commercial and cultural life of the nation. It's a very lively and modern city with some astonishing and architecturally interesting buildings, especially down the city's main drag, the Av 18 de Julio.

The atmosphere is quite unlike that in other Spanish-American capitals. This can be put down partly to the very mixed, almost entirely European population and also partly to the architecture which displays distinctly Parisian and, to a lesser extent, Islamic influences. Very few colonial-style buildings remain, though where they do the city authorities have embarked on a programme of preservation and landscaping. There's a lot of civic pride in Montevideo and you won't find the sort of decaying and decrepit areas close to the centre like you would in Lima or Santiago.

There is an endless number of bars, restaurants and discotheques where you can find some action in the evenings. Most of them are along the wide Rambla, which snakes all along the southern shoreline right up to the resort town of Punta del Este, where the rich have their villas. The city is also peppered with cinemas which show a wide variety of American, European and Spanish-American films and tickets are very cheap indeed.

That's one aspect of the city. The other is its political energy which bursts out frequently in huge street demonstrations and rallies. Hardly a week goes by without one group or another taking to the streets (they're usually peaceful). You'll end up with a fist full of leaflets after each one. They're interesting reading.

Information
The tourist office is at Lavalleja 1409 (4th floor) on the corner of Plaza Cagancha (Libertad). The people are very friendly and helpful, speak English, have superb maps of Montevideo and the suburbs (free) and a lot of other leaflets about other areas of Uruguay. They're well worth a visit. There's also an information kiosk on Plaza Cagancha opposite the *ONDA* bus station but it's closed in winter. The information kiosk at the international airport is hardly worth visiting. They have no information on hotels under US$15 per night and a map which might be useful for a fledgling taxi driver but nothing else. Boredom prevails.

Most of the casas de cambio are on 18 de Julio between the Plaza Cagancha and the Plaza Independencia. All of them take travellers' cheques and cash but rates vary so it's worth walking around. Some stay open until late at night.

There's a good coin-op laundrette called *Laverap*, Colonia 1327 between Yaguaron and Ejido next door to a cinema. Charges are US$1 (washing), US$1.50 (drying) and US$0.35 (service).

For baggage repairs, good reasonably priced leather work is done by Raul Cohen, *Casa Meco*, Rio Branco 1209 (tel 910919).

Useful Addresses
Main Post Office
    Calle Buenos Aires, on the corner of Misiones.
American Express
    Mercedes 942.
Bus Terminals
    Most of these are either on Plaza Cagancha or on one of the streets running into it.

Embassies

See under 'VISAS' in the introductory section of this chapter.

Things to See

There are a number of good museums in Montevideo but one you shouldn't miss is the **Museo del Gaucho** in the Banco de la República Oriental del Uruguay building on the corner of Av 18 de Julio and the Plaza del Entrevero. This museum chronicles the history of the famous gauchos of Uruguay and has superb displays of their leather and silverwork, the tools of their trade and their weapons. Below it, on a lower floor, is another museum detailing the history of bank notes and coins in Uruguay. The building in which it is housed is also worth seeing. Entry is free. It's usually open Tuesday to Friday but is sometimes closed in the mornings.

Two others which are worth seeing are the historic houses of **Casa Lavalleja** (Museo Histórico Nacional), Zabala 1464; and the **Casa Rivera**, Rincón 437. You must, however, wear a jacket and tie to see these.

A visit to the **Mercado del Puerto**, on the corner of Piedras and Castellanos in the old part of town, is a must. It still functions as a meat and vegetable market but a lot of restoration work has been done on and around the place recently so there are now a number of very attractive bars and restaurants there too. It's a popular place to go and eat or sit around and have a beer or wine.

Railway buffs should go down to the railway station and see the old steam engines which are displayed to the side of the main building in a small park. It's a pity they're in a somewhat sorry state of preservation.

For a superb view of the whole of Montevideo go to the **Palacio Municipal** on the corner of Av 18 de Julio and Ejido and take the lift up to the 11th floor where there's an open-air terrace all the way around the building. On the mezzanine above the terrace is a bar and restaurant but it's only open in the summer months.

Stretching along the whole of the metropolitan waterfront are nine bathing beaches which are very popular with the people of the city during summer. One of those closest to the centre, Playa Pocitos, is regarded as the Copacabana of Montevideo. On the other hand, the further east from the centre you go, the cleaner the beaches become. They're peppered with bars, restaurants, yachting clubs, discotheques and night clubs. If you want to check them out, hop on a No 104 bus from Calle San José. This will take you right past them all as far as Playa Miramar, which is beyond Playa Carrasco.

Places to Stay

The *Youth Hostel*, Canelones 935 (tel 98-1324), is probably the cheapest place to stay in Montevideo. It costs about US$1.50 per person per night. There are no cooking facilities and it's closed between 10 am and 5 pm.

There are not many budget hotels in Montevideo (at least not for the price you would pay in Brazil or the Andean countries). One which is good value is the *Hotel City*, Buenos Aires 462 (tel 957580) opposite the main post office. It has hot water and costs US$3.80 a double with own bathroom and US$4.40 a double with a larger outside bathroom.

Also good value is the *Nueva Pension Ideal*, Soriano 1073 (tel 982913), which costs US$2.20/$3.80 a single/double with own bath and hot water. The rooms are small and some of them are partitioned 'cells' in what must, at one time, have been a courtyard. In this price range you could also try the *'Habitaciones'* (no other name), Rincón 706, which costs US$2.70 per person without own bath and US$3.80 per person with own bath. There is hot water but no heating.

Going up-market a little, try the *Hotel Aramaya*, Av 18 de Julio 1103 next to the Plaza Cagancha. It costs US$3.50/$4.50 a

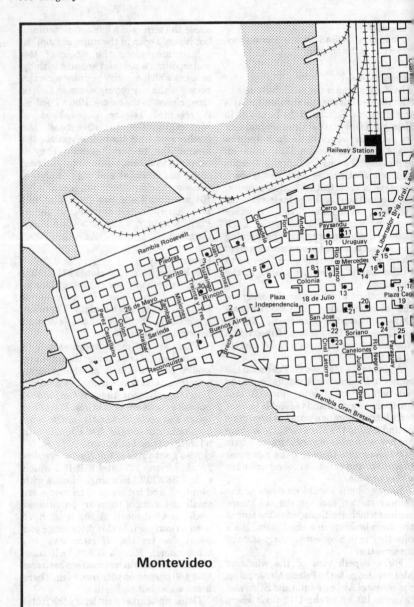

Montevideo

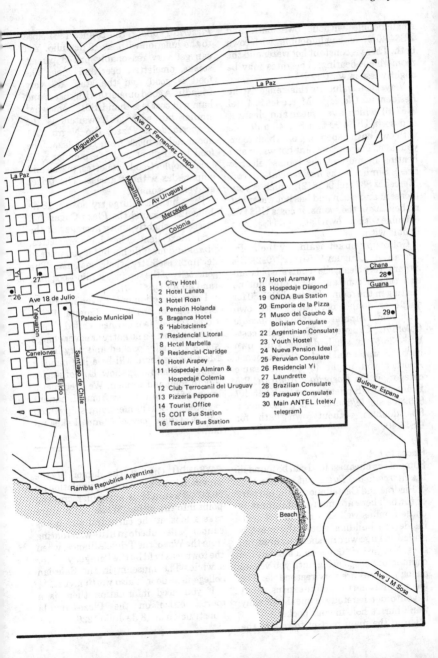

1 City Hotel
2 Hotel Lanata
3 Hotel Roan
4 Pension Holanda
5 Braganca Hotel
6 'Habitaciones'
7 Residencial Litoral
8 Hotel Marbella
9 Residencial Claridge
10 Hotel Arapey
11 Hospedaje Almiran &
   Hospedaje Colemia
12 Club Terrocanil del Uruguay
13 Pizzeria Peppone
14 Tourist Office
15 COIT Bus Station
16 Tacuary Bus Station
17 Hotel Aramaya
18 Hospedaje Diagond
19 ONDA Bus Station
20 Emporia de la Pizza
21 Musco del Gaucho &
   Bolivian Consulate
22 Argentinian Consulate
23 Youth Hostel
24 Nueva Pension Ideal
25 Peruvian Consulate
26 Residencial Yi
27 Laundrette
28 Brazilian Consulate
29 Paraguay Consulate
30 Main ANTEL (telex/
   telegram)

single/double without own bath and US$4.40/$7 a single/double with own bath. There is constant hot water and the rooms have heating. The rates may be slightly less in winter.

Very good value in this range is the *Residencial Claridge*, Mercedes 924 (tel 915746), which is very clean and pleasant and costs US$4.90 to US$5.45 a double with own bath depending on which room you take. There's constant hot water and heating in most of the rooms (electric fires). Similar is the *Residencial Litoral*, Mercedes 887 (tel 905812), which is very pleasant and clean and has hot water but no heating in the rooms. It costs US$4.35 a double without own bath and US$5.45 a double with.

Going up-market again, try the *Hotel Arapey*, Av Uruguay 925 (tel 907032). It's elegant, very clean, the rooms are pleasant and there's constant hot water but no heating in the rooms. It costs US$7.50 for single or double occupancy with own bathroom. Similar is the *Hospedaje Colonial*, Uruguay 967, which costs US$4.35/$7 a single/double with own bath, hot water and heating in the rooms. Another you might try in the same category is the *Hospedaje Almiran*, Rio Branco 1518. It offers rooms for US$5.40/$10.85 a single/double. They also have a few doubles without own bath for US$5.40.

Places to Eat

Some of the cheapest food can be found in the *Mercado del Puerto*, at the junction of Piedras and Castellanos in the old part of town. There are many restaurants to chose from as well as a number of grills inside the building where the meat is grilled on large wire meshes over charcoal fires. You just sit down on a stool at the counter and keep eating until you've had enough. Prices are very reasonable. The restaurants tend to be more expensive but if you order carefully a meal certainly won't burn a hole in your pocket,

Up in the main part of town, try the *Pizzeria Peppore*, Rio Branco 1364 close to the junction with Av 18 de Julio. You can get very reasonably priced pizzas, steaks, omelettes, beer and wine. The food is good and the staff are very friendly. A good omelette with cheese and ham will cost less than US$1. Somewhat similar but with gruff waiters is the *Emporia de la Pizza*, Rio Negro 1311 about half a block from the plaza. The food is excellent and it's popular with local people. Good omelettes, pizzas and empanadas without grease. The prices are very reasonable.

For a bit of a splurge try *Soko's*, 18 de Julio 1250 beyond the Plaza Cagancha. Prices are slightly above average but the food is excellent. They have omelettes, pizzas and meat dishes but if you want to be impressed try their lasagna. The generosity of the servings is mind-boggling (and all for US$1.30).

For some action in the evening try the *Disco-Bar* at the Hotel Lanata, Plaza Constitución (sometimes called Plaza Matriz). There's no entry or cover charge and it's usually packed and very lively. Most nights there will be a live band, a conjurer(!) and strip show. Lots of singles – both men and women. We even met a bunch of Korean officers from a Liberian-registered, British merchant ship which had a Greek captain and Pakistani crew!

PAYSANDÚ One of the larger of the provincial towns, with a population of 80,000, Paysandú is a popular crossing point into Argentina. While you're there take a look at the cathedral which has cannon balls embedded in its walls dating from the War of the Triple Alliance, when the town was held by the Paraguayans for a while. The museum in the Salesian college next door is also worth a visit.

If you need information there is a tourist office on the Plaza de la Constitución at 18 de Julio 1226.

Places to Stay

The *Youth Hostel*, Gran Bretaña 872, is the best deal in town and costs just US$0.75. It's basic but very friendly. If you don't want to stay there, try either the *Bary Pensión Popular* or the *Lobato*, Leandro Gómex 1415, both of which are budget hotels.

PUNTA DEL ESTE

This is one of the most ritzy beach resorts in South America and as you might expect, a very expensive place to stay. There is cheap accommodation in the nearby town of **Maldonado** at the *Hospedaje Ituzaingo*, Calle Ituzaingo. It's run by an Irishman who is very helpful. From Maldonado you can visit the seal colony on Isla de Lobos.

SALTO

This is the largest major centre of population in Uruguay as you go north up the Río Uruguay. There are daily ferries across the river to Concordia in Argentina.

Places to Stay

Again, the best place in town is the *Youth Hostel*, Colegio Oriental, Invernizzi 80.

Venezuela

Only Brazil can match Venezuela for the incredible contrasts which exist between the urban centres and the countryside. Much of the highland massif south of the Orinoco River is natural grassland with fantastic views, to the horizon on all sides, of strange mountain formations dropping down to endless, impenetrable rain-forests honeycombed with huge, silt-laden rivers. It's wild, vast, beautiful and largely uninhabited. Nothing much has changed there for thousands of years. It was only in 1937 that the world's highest falls – Angel Falls (979 metres) – were discovered in this area by an American aviator. Facts like that are a good indication of how little this region has been explored.

That's one face of Venezuela, and entering the country this way ill-prepares you for the onslaught of elevated motor-ways, enormous skyscraper complexes and the endless torrents of traffic which oil money has made out of Caracas, Maracaibo and some of the coastal towns. A few years ago someone scrawled in huge letters outside the Nuevo Circo bus terminal in Caracas, 'El capitalismo convirta a Caracas en un inferno' – a pretty apt description of what life is like for many people down in the concrete jungle amid all the speed, noise and fumes.

It isn't really any worse than a lot of other big cities around the world though, and in some ways it's a lot better. Caracas' setting, in the bottom of a fertile valley up against the massive green wall of the Parque Avila, is one of the most beautiful in the world. The affluent suburbs on the slopes of the mountains, with their hectares of landscaped gardens and flowering trees, are delightfully pleasant and peaceful, while down in the working districts it's pure bedlam. Perhaps though, it's just the difference between money and the lack of it which makes the contrast seem so great.

As with many other big cities in South America, hundreds of thousands of people flock to Caracas in search of the illusive dream of wealth, or even just a job. They come mainly from the rural areas of Venezuela but also from other South American republics. For many it's the start of years of drudgery and a hand-to-mouth existence in a tin shack without amenities, trying to hold down one menial job after another. Housing is very expensive, flats are very difficult to find and there is always more demand than supply. This is one reason why many of the budget hotels around the centre are more or less permanently full. Most of them double as brothels. Yet despite the breathless pace of life, most people you meet are very friendly and helpful especially after they've had their morning slug of what must be the world's most caffeinated coffee!

From the time the Spanish arrived, right up to 1917, Venezuela was a relatively unimportant agricultural backwater with a small population. The early settlers went panning for gold but yields were so small that they quickly abandoned the search in favour of agriculture along the coast and in the central highlands. It was another 150 years, however, before they began to spread out and settle the *llanos* – and then only patchily, and this pattern of settlement is reflected today in the vast empty spaces of the south.

Apart from three brief rebellions against colonial rule in the 1700s, the country had a relatively uneventful history. All this changed at the beginning of the 19th century when Venezuela gave to Latin America its greatest-ever cult figure, Simon Bolívar. 'El Libertador', as he is known, together with his most able lieutenant, Sucre, were to be responsible

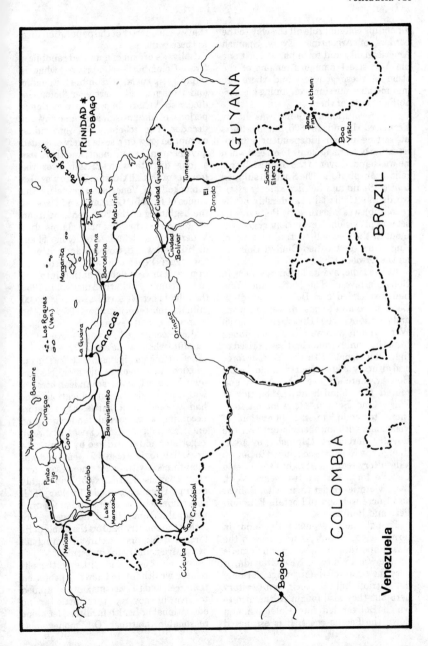

for ending colonial rule all the way to the borders of Argentina. Every Spanish American city and town has at least one plaza or street named after one or the other of these generals and there are innumerable museums containing memorabilia of both of them.

The revolutionary flame was lit by Francisco Miranda in 1806, but his efforts at setting up an independent administration at Caracas came to an end when he was handed over to the Spanish by his fellow conspirators. The Spanish shipped him to Spain and he died shortly afterwards in a Cadiz jail. Leadership of the revolution was taken over by Bolívar, who set up a provisional revolutionary government at the sleepy little trading town of Angostura (now called Ciudad Bolívar) on the Orinoco River.

At the time, events in Europe were in Bolívar's favour. The Napoleonic Wars had just ended and Bolívar's agent in London was able to raise money and arms and recruit over 5000 British ex-Peninsula War veterans who were being demobbed from the armies which had been raised to fight Napoleon. With this British force and an army of horsemen from the *llanos*, Bolívar marched over the Andes and routed the Spanish at the battles of Vargas and Boyacá. He went on from there to complete the liberation of Venezuela with another victory over the Royalist forces at Caraboba in 1821, though the Royalists continued to put up a desultory rear-guard fight from Puerto Cabello for a further two years. With these victories under their belts, Bolívar and Sucre went on to liberate Ecuador, Peru and Bolivia.

Though both economically and in terms of population Venezuela was the least important of the areas which made up the Viceroyalty of New Granada, it bore the brunt of the fighting. Not only did patriots fight on their own territory here but they also fought in the armies which Bolívar led into Colombia and down the Pacific coast. It is estimated that over a quarter of the population died in these wars.

Bolívar's dream of a unified republic – Gran Colombia – comprising what is today Venezuela, Colombia, Ecuador and Panama, fell apart even before he died and Venezuela was to experience periods of despotism and anarchy for decades. The economy fell into ruins; corruption grew on a scale rarely exceeded anywhere on the continent; and there was a long dispute with Britain over the frontier of British Guiana. There was also a blockade of Venezuelan ports by the navies of Britain, Germany and Italy, at the beginning of the 20th century, in an effort to press their financial claims after Venezuela had defaulted on loans. Then, in 1917, oil was discovered and within a few years Venezuela was transformed from a penniless debtor nation into the richest country in Latin America. In 1980 the value of petroleum sales was US$18,000 million, representing about 95% of the country's export revenue.

Just before oil was discovered, a *caudillo* who saw the advantages of being allied to foreign big business (like Díaz in Mexico) took over as dictator. He was Juan Vicente Gómez, an Andean *mestizo* with almost no formal education, who had worked as a cattle hand before becoming a successful landowner and entering politics. Gómez was a shrewd negotiator and considered by many to be *brujo*. His regime lasted 27 years and was maintained with even more savagery than Díaz used in Mexico. Thoroughly corrupt, Gómez creamed off a share of all government transactions and amassed a personal fortune. He did, however, see to it that the country paid off the whole of its foreign debt, once again becoming an attractive country for investment.

On the other hand, little of the oil-related wealth filtered down to people on the street, and the vast majority continued to live in poverty with little or no educational or health facilities, let alone reasonable housing. Oil money also resulted in a neglect of agriculture. Food had to be imported in increasing amounts and prices rose rapidly. When Gómez died the people of Caracas went on the rampage burning down the houses of his relatives and supporters and even threatened to set fire to the oil installations on Lake Maracaibo.

After Gómez's death, an oligarchy of military officers and landowners took over but were overthrown in 1945 in a coup d'état staged by junior army officers aware of the popular discontent with military rule. They were determined to end the ascendancy of the elderly generals who had survived from the Gómez era. A civilian government was put into office headed by Betancourt, the founder of the left-wing Acción Democratica.

Given the forces competing for influence at that time however, Betancourt acted too hastily in trying to convert Venezuela into a welfare state and even went so far as to attempt to exclude from government the very same army officers who had put him there. The inevitable coup took place with Colonel Perez Jímenez emerging as the leader. Once in control, Jímenez began to ruthlessly crush all opposition to his rule, but at the same time he ploughed the oil money back into public works, workers' flats in Caracas and into industries which would help diversify the economy.

Spectacular buildings in Caracas and increasing foreign ownership of Venezuela's natural resources and commercial life however, were a poor substitute for a better standard of living and access to political power. Opposition to Jímenez' rule grew and in 1958 he was overthrown by a coalition of civilians and junior military officers. An election was held shortly afterwards and Betancourt was again elected president. He put an end to the former dictator's solicitous policy towards foreign big business but he was careful this time not to act too impetuously. Since then there has been an orderly transfer of power and the country is one of the most stable on the continent. Nevertheless, a lot of food still has to be imported, and this fact, together with the affluence which oil creates, makes Venezuela a somewhat expensive country. If you're on a budget, a long stay here will mean a shorter stay somewhere else.

VISAS

Tourist Cards (Tarjetas de Ingreso) are required by all. If they're issued by a consulate they are valid for 90 days (only 30 days at Boa Vista, Brazil), extendable to 180. If they're issued by an airline they're only valid for 60 days and not extendable – airlines can issue them to nationals of all Western European countries except Portugal and Spain, and to nationals of Australia, Canada, Israel, Japan, New Zealand and the USA. Tourist Cards are free and no photographs are required. The amount of hassle you have to go through at consulates to get hold of one depends on where you apply. Most places don't ask to see an onward ticket but in Colombia and Brazil they do, and they also often want to see how much money you have. You may also be asked for a Yellow Fever vaccination certificate.

There was another bizarre twist to this a few years ago when the consulate in Cúcuta, Colombia, not only demanded to see an onward ticket and an International Health Card but also demanded that you had a test for syphilis at a clinic nearby. Naturally you had to pay for this. It's quite possible that that particular consul has now been replaced.

Borders are usually fairly easy-going (except at Santa Elena). There's often a cursory baggage search but they're principally interested in girlie books and the consumer goods which Venezuelans bring with them – there are always plenty of arguments about these, so if you're on a bus, expect to be held up for at least an hour.

Visa extensions are expensive at US$70!

MONEY
US$1 = B$15 (and rising slowly)

The unit of currency is the Bolívar (B$) = 100 centimos. There is no limit on the import or export of local currency and there's no black market. The Banco Royal Venezolana doesn't charge commission for changing travellers' cheques. Outside Caracas, and especially in the eastern part of the country, however, you'll be very lucky to find a bank which will change travellers' cheques. Some banks won't even change US cash dollars. Not only that, but even in Caracas, some banks will change American Express cheques but won't change Thomas Cook's, some will change Cook's but not Amex. You never know what the situation is going to be. We even had one report about a bank which would sell American Express cheques but wouldn't cash them! Take cash with you and change at shops (poor rate as a rule) or casas de cambio.

The airport tax for international flights varies from one airport to the next. The maximum is B$20.

GETTING THERE
Many travellers from Europe and North America use Venezuela as a gateway to South America since cheap tickets are available from many European cities and from Miami. Details of those flights and where to find them are given in the 'Getting There' chapter at the beginning of this book. Other than those flights, Venezuela has road and air connections with Colombia and Brazil and air connections with Trinidad and the Netherlands Antilles. There are no air or road connections with Guyana. The only way to get there is via Brazil by ferry and (very rough) road.

To/From Colombia
Coastal Route: Maracaibo-Maicao-Santa Marta There are four or five buses daily in either direction between Maracaibo and Maicao. They depart Maracaibo at 5.45, 7, 8 and 9.30 am and 3.30 pm and Maicao at 8.30 and 11 am, and 1 and 3 pm. Colombian border officials demand to see an onward ticket.

From Maicao there are frequent daily buses to Barranquilla by *Línea Dorada*. The smuggling which occurs on this run from Maicao to Santa Marta and Barranquilla has become legendary. One traveller wrote recently to say that his bus was stopped no less that 25 times!

The Highland Route: Mérida-San Cristóbal-Cúcuta
There are no longer buses between Mérida and San Cristóbal so you must take a *por puesto*. There are plenty of these everyday. They cost about US$5 and take five to six hours. From San Cristóbal there are *por puestos* daily to San Antonio (the Venezuelan border town) which cost about US$1.50 and take about four hours. A taxi across the border will cost about US$2. From the Colombian side of the border there are a number of buses daily to Cúcuta. Before you leave San Antonio make sure you get your Venezuelan exit stamp at Calle 4A just before the international bridge or the Colombians will send you back. Once in Colombia, you must report to the DAS office in Cúcuta either at the airport or at Calle 17 No 2-60.

To/From Brazil
There's only one road which runs between Venezuela and Brazil and it's gravel so be prepared for numerous delays during the wet season. For the rest of the year it's pretty good. The road runs from Ciudad Bolívar via Tumeremo and El Dorado to Santa Elena (on the Venezuela/Brazil border) and then on to Boa Vista. Buses on the Venezuelan section run only as far as Km 88 (south of El Dorado). Between there and Santa Elena you must either hitch or hire a Land-Rover or jeep. There's transport everyday. A vehicle which takes five passengers will cost about US$12 per person; and one which

takes six will cost about US$9.60. You can pick up these jeeps at Tumeremo, El Dorado or Km 88 and there's little difference in price between them. The journey from El Dorado to Santa Elena takes about eight hours. A flight from Ciudad Bolívar to Santa Elena will cost about US$25. *Aeropostal* have daily flights but they're often booked up in advance.

From Santa Elena there is a bus to Boa Vista daily at 8 am by *União Cascavel* from outside the Hotel Auyantepuy. It costs US$2.50 and takes about seven hours. Get there early if you want a good seat and pay in cruzeiros if possible (it's cheaper that way). Expect thorough searches of baggage at both borders.

To/From Netherlands Antilles

There are ferries to Aruba and Curaçao three times per week but check at the ferry office for the exact times as they change frequently. The ferries go from La Vela de Coro (ferry office on Av Independencia, Coro) and Punto Fijo on the Paraguaná Peninsula, north-west of Maracaibo. The ferries should take about four hours but bureaucracy can triple the journey time. The fare from Coro to Curaçao is US$17 but in the opposite direction it is US$43! You must have a return or onward ticket at either end and you won't be allowed in until you buy one. This applies to Dutch people as well. Be at the ferry for passport and customs formalities several hours before it's due to go. Buy tickets on the morning of departure. There's a bar and restaurant on the ferry.

To/From Trinidad

There are no longer any ferries from the Venezuelan mainland to Trinidad, or flights between Maturin and Port of Spain which means you have to fly either from Caracas or Isla Margarita. The fares are US$98 (Caracas-Port of Spain) and US$71 (Isla Margarita-Port of Spain). However, there are complications. The

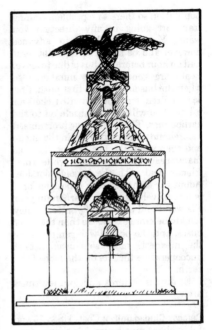

authorities in Port-of-Spain may not accept a return ticket to Isla Margarita or Caracas as an onward ticket and may demand that you buy a ticket back to your own country before letting you in. To get around this crazy situation (at least partially) it's best to visit the Caribbean islands on the way to South America rather than on the way back home. That way you'll probably have an acceptable onward ticket.

GETTING AROUND

Bus

There are no railways of any importance in Venezuela. All travelling is done by bus or *por puesto* (shared taxi). Buses are generally fast, comfortable and efficient and all main roads are surfaced, except the one which heads down to Brazil from Ciudad Bolívar. There are frequent daily buses between all major centres of population so there's no problem finding transport going in any direction you want. You should book in advance however and be at the terminal at least half an hour before the bus is due to leave. Seats are generally not numbered so when the bus arrives, it's first push, first seated. Frequently people with tickets for a later bus will try to muscle on to the earlier ones. The locals have it organised beforehand – one or two get in the queue and then when the bus arrives claim as many seats as they need while their friends deal with the luggage outside. Adopt the same strategy if possible or if you're travelling alone, sharpen up your elbows. Avoid *Aerobus* if you can – they tend to be more expensive than the other buses, and the people who run them are the meanest, most sour-faced set of uncooperative fuckers on the face of the earth.

Examples of fares and journey times are:

Caracas-Ciudad Bolívar Costs US$5.75 and takes about nine hours. It's a poor road.
Ciudad Bolívar-El Dorado Costs US$4.50 and takes about 7½ hours.
Caracas-Mérida Costs US$6 and takes 11 to 13 hours. *Expreso Mérida* is recommended.
Caracas-Valencia Costs US$1.50 and takes two to 2½ hours.
Valencia-Coro Costs US$3.20 and takes about five hours.
Caracas-Maturin Costs US$4.40 and takes seven hours.

Ferry
Venezuela has a number of off-shore possessions, the main ones being Los Roques north of La Guaira, and Margarita Island north of Cumaná. Ferries to Los Roques go from La Guaira, and to Margarita from Puerto La Cruz, Cumaná and Carúpano.

Puerto La Cruz-Punta de Piedras Daily ferries at 7 am, 12 noon, 4 and 8 pm in either direction. In addition to these ferries there is a fast boat, the *Gran Cacique I*, which does the journey in 2½ hours and costs US$11.65.

Cumaná-Punta de Piedras There are ferries twice a day at 8 am and 5 pm which return at 7 am and 5 pm. The journey takes 3½ hours. There is also a fast boat, the *Gran Cacique II*, which takes 1½ hours and costs US$7.

Caracas

Until oil was discovered in 1917, Caracas was a relatively small and unhurried place with its colonial buildings more or less intact. Since WWII, however, it has grown faster than any other South American capital city except São Paulo. Today it's at least 15 km long with a population exceeding four million. The centre, El Silencio (which is anything but silent at any hour of the day or night!), is fast becoming a concrete jungle and the pace of life is super-fast. Oil money has been used to create vast and impressive high-rise complexes, freeways and more recently, a subway.

Because it's so spread out, very few places are within easy reach of each other and the intricacy of the local bus system isn't something you're likely to work out in a hurry. On the other hand, the city is very impressively situated against the steep green wall of the Parque Ávila which contrasts with all the speed, noise and fumes down in the valley bottom.

Information
The tourist office is on the 37th floor, Torre Oeste – 'the service is lousy but the views over the city are great'. There is a branch office at the international airport at Maiquetía.

The best cambios to change money at are the *Italcambios*. There are two of these, one on the Av Urdaneta (Centro) and the other on Av Casanova. Some branches of the Bank of Venezuela will change travellers' cheques, some won't.

Useful addresses

American Express
  In the Centro Commercial de Tamanaco.
Aeropostal
  Bloque 1, El Silencio (tel 483 4144).
Avensa
  Corner of El Chorro, Av Universidad, Edificio 29 (tel 45 5244).
Viasa
  Centro Commercial de Tamanaco.

Embassies

Brazil
  Av San Juan Bosco, corner of 8 Transversal, Quinta San Antonia Urb Altamira.
Britain
  Edificio Mercedes (3rd floor), near the Centro Commercial de Tamanaco.
Colombia
  Av Luis Roche between 6 and 7 Transversal, Quinta 53, Urb Altamira (tel 324 318). Open from 8 am to noon only for visas. To get there catch bus marked 'Chacaito.'
Ecuador
  Av Andrés Bello, Centro Empresarial Andrés Bello, Torre Ceste, Oficina Nos 131 and 132.
Guyana
  Calle Real de Sabana Grande, corner of Av Los Jabillo, Edificio Continental, 17th floor.
Trinidad & Tobago
  4a Avenida between 7 and 8 Transversal, Urb La Floresta.

Things to See

In the centre of the city, the **Casa Natal del Libertador** – Bolívar's birthplace – is worth visiting, though it's not the original house. This one is a reconstruction ordered by the dictator Gómez in the 1920s. It is open weekdays, except Monday, from 9 am to noon and 3 to 6 pm, and on Saturday and Sunday from 10 am to 1 pm. Next door is the **Museo Bolivariano** which has exhibits of historical interest from the wars of liberation.

Another museum well worth visiting is the **Museo de Bellas Artes**, Plaza Morelos, Parque Los Caobos, which has an excellent display of contemporary art. It's open daily, except Monday, from 9 am to noon and 3 to 5.30 p.m. Entry is free.

It's also well worth the effort to see the **Museo de Arte Contemporáneo**, Edificio Anauco near the Hilton Hotel in the Parque Central. It has a truly amazing display of 'cyber-kinetic' art, the likes of which you have probably never seen before. It's open Tuesday to Friday from 12 noon to 7 pm, on Saturday from 11 am to 9 pm and on Sunday from 11 am to 7 pm.

If you want to get away from the noise and fumes of the traffic for a while, try either the **Jardín Botánico** or the **Parque Los Caobos**.

It's also interesting to wander around some of the smarter suburbs to check out how the other half live – try some of the streets around the Tamanaco Hotel or the American Embassy.

Take a bus marked 'Macuto Sheriton' from the bus station opposite the Nuevo Circo to the beaches past La Guaira. It takes about an hour and costs US$0.30. There are showers and other facilities and the water is safe.

Places to Stay

The budget hotel area is right outside the Nuevo Circo bus terminal. What hotel you stay in will more than likely depend simply on which one has a vacant room. Many outsiders who come to work in Caracas stay more or less permanently in budget hotels and a lot of rooms are rented by whores, so be prepared for a little bit of leg work in searching for a place to stay.

One of the best places is the *Pensión San Biagio*, Av Lecuna, which has clean sheets and a friendly manager. There are no fans but it's cool enough at night to do without them. The showers and toilets are clean.

Two others which are popular are the *Hotel Ber-Mar* and the *Hotel San Roque*,

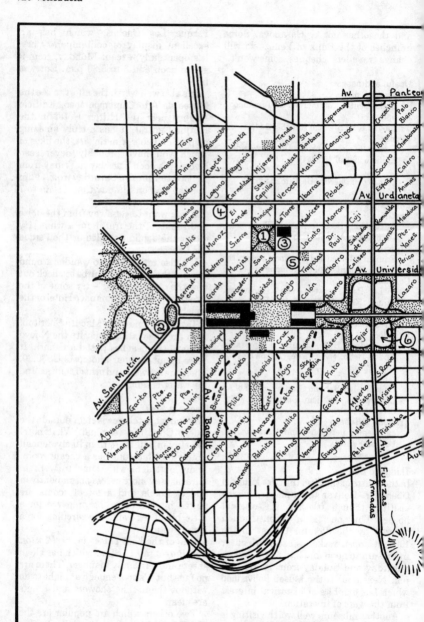

Caracas (El Silencio & El Conde)

Key:-
1. Plaza Bolívar
2. Plaza O'Leary
3. Cathedral
4. Post Office
5. Casa Natal del Libertador & Museo Bolivariano
6. Nuevo Circo bus terminal
7. Museo de Arte Colonial
8. Museos de Bellas Artes & Natural Sciences
9. Caracas University

Area of budget hotels & cheap cafes. (Blow-up of this area on separate map).

both opposite the Nuevo Circo bus station. They both cost US$3.20/$6.40 a single/double and although they're frequently used by whores and their clients, they're clean and secure. Also in the same area is the *Hotel Bella Italia* which is reasonable value at US$6.40 a double. Similar is the *Hotel ABC*, Av Lecuna, which costs US$7.20 a double.

Moving further afield, the *Posadas Turistical Andrés Bello*, Av La Salle, Quinta Bucaral, Los Caobos, is worth a try. It's very clean, has its own restaurant and baggage lockers are available. To get there take the metro to Plaza Venezuela and then walk about 15 minutes uphill.

The *Posada Cecilia*, Av Costa, has also been recommended as a hostel for students on Calle Los Abogados. To get to it, you need to take a bus or *por puesto* to 'Santa Monica'. The latter costs US$2.80 per person.

Places to Eat

There are quite a few *pollo a la brasa* cafés scattered around the Nuevo Circo bus station but the chicken tends to be very greasy so you'll probably only use them as a stop-gap. Much better is the *Restaurant Ritz* on Pichincha opposite the Nuevo Circo. This has been popular for years and is still good value. The nearby *El Meson del Viajero* isn't such good value and is relatively expensive.

The *Restaurant Vegetariano*, Norte 9 and Av Este, has been recommended by many travellers. It's a little way from the budget hotel area but well worth the walk. It isn't entirely vegetarian (it serves fish too). The main vegetarian meal on offer is served *smorgasbord* style with a choice of six items. You can eat as much as you like and drink as much juice as you can put down all for about US$2.40. Very good value.

Commonwealth citizens can join the British Commonwealth Association for less than US$1. It's in Altamira on Quinta Alborada at Av 7 with Transversal 9.

For some entertainment in the evening there are many discos, including *La Jungla*, Plaza de la Castellana; and *Number Two*, Av Principal de la Castellana.

Getting Around

The Nuevo Circo bus terminal at El Silencio (in the centre) is the long-distance bus terminal. Adjacent to it is the municipal bus station.

Like many other huge South American cities, Caracas now has a metro (underground railway) which is the most convenient and quickest form of transport but, unfortunately, you can't use it if you have a rucksack or other large bag. It's open Monday to Saturday from 6 am to 9 pm and on Sundays from 9 am to 9 pm. The fares are US$0.20 (up to five stations), US$0.25 (up to 10 stations) and US$0.30 (more than 10 stations). Use it whenever you can.

Maiquetía airport (for domestic flights) and Simon Bolívar International airport are next to each other 28 km from Caracas near the port of La Guaira on the Caribbean coast. The bus between them and the centre of Caracas leaves the centre from Av 17 Sur between Av Mexico and Av Lecuna east of the Nuevo Circo bus terminal. It takes 45 minutes and costs US$1.50 plus a small charge for each piece of luggage. Coming from the airports, ignore the taxi drivers who will swear blind that there are no buses. If you can't find the airport bus then take a local bus to Catia which has a stop on the main road, on the far side of the car park as you come out of the airport terminal. This bus costs just a few cents. From Catia there are public buses to Caracas which again cost just a few cents.

CIUDAD BOLÍVAR

This Spanish colonial city on the south bank of the Orinoco at one of the river's narrowest points, occupies an important place in Latin American history. It was

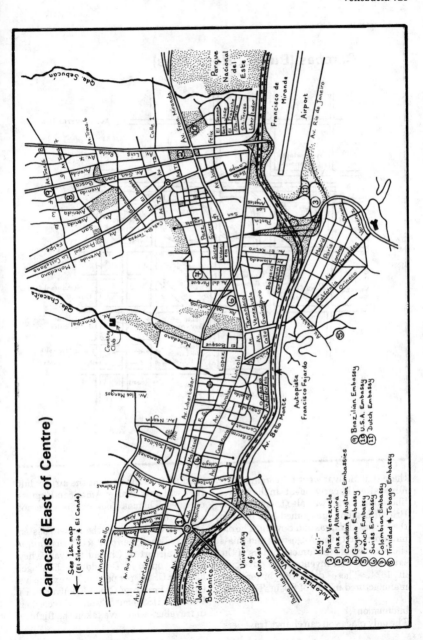

Caracas (East of Centre)

See 1st. map (El Silencio & El Conde)

Key:-
1. Plaza Venezuela
2. Plaza Altamira
3. Canadian & Austrian Embassies
4. Guyana Embassy
5. French Embassy
6. Swiss Embassy
7. Colombian Embassy
8. Trinidad & Tobago Embassy
9. Brazilian Embassy
10. U.S.A. Embassy
11. Dutch Embassy

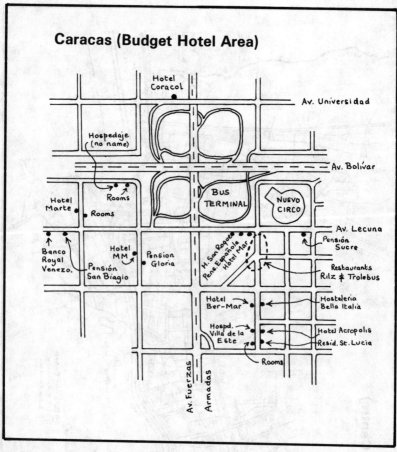

Caracas (Budget Hotel Area)

Hotel Coracol

Av. Universidad

Hospedaje (no name)

Av. Bolívar

Rooms

Hotel Marte

Rooms

BUS TERMINAL

NUEVO CIRCO

Av. Lecuna

Banco Royal Venezo.

Hotel MM

Pensión Gloria

Pensión San Biagio

H. San Roque
Pens Española
Hotel Mar

Pensión Sucre

Restaurants Rilz & Trolebus

Hotel Ber-Mar

Hostelería Bella Italia

Hospd. Villa de la Este

Hotel Acropolis

Resid. St. Lucia

Rooms

Av. Fuerzas Armadas

there that Bolívar went to reorganise his forces after the early defeats in the wars of liberation, and it was also there that the British Legionnaires joined him prior to the battles of Vargas and Boyacá. The old name of the city was Angostura and this is the place where the famous bitters of the same name were invented by a physician in 1824. These days the bitters are manufactured in Port of Spain, Trinidad.

Information

The only place you can change travellers'
cheques is in the bank at the airport but they will only change American Express cheques. Thomas Cook cheques are not acceptable.

If you'd like to see the **Angel Falls** en route to Brazil then contact *Transmandu* at the airport in Ciudad Bolívar. They will fly you to El Dorado via the Angel Falls for US$45 per person. It's expensive (the bus fare from Ciudad Bolívar to El Dorado is US$5) but is 'worth it' according to travellers who have taken the flight.

Things to See

Much of the town retains its colonial atmosphere and is worth exploring on foot. The docks are also worth visiting to see the amazing variety of river craft. It's possible to find boats going up to Puerto Ayacucho but they're few and far between.

There is an interesting art and pottery museum on Paseo Orinoco.

Places to Stay & Eat

Two of the cheaper places to stay are the *Pensión Boyacá*, Calle Babilonia; and the *Pensión Panamericana*, Calle Rocia 6, both of which are basic but clean and comfortable and cost around US$2.40 per person.

For something slightly better, try the *Hotel Muno*, on the corner of Paseo Orinoco and Calle Amazonas, which is good value, clean and has excellent views of the river and the bridge. It costs US$6.40 a double. There are others along Paseo Orinoco, but avoid the *Pension Yocoima* – it's a pigsty.

Two places to try on Paseo Orinoco for a meal are the *La Playa* and *Las Cibeles*.

Getting There & Around

The bus terminal is at the junction of Av República and Av Sucre and there are many mini-buses from there to Paseo Orinoco where there are many hotels.

Buses to Caracas leave about every two hours from 9 am to 9 pm.

EL DORADO

This is more or less the last village of any size before Santa Elena on the Venezuela/ Brazil border though public buses now go beyond there to Km 88. Apart from its famous jail where 'Papillon' stayed for a while, it's a fairly unremarkable place but you may find yourself staying overnight if you're heading towards Brazil.

Places to Stay

If you want a free place to sling a hammock ask at the prison. The police there are friendly and may let you do this. Alternatively, there's the *Hotel El Dorado* and the *Hotel San Antonio*, both of which charge about US$4.

Other than those places there is the *Campamento Turistico* owned by Sidney Coles. It's a good deal more expensive than the others mentioned. Sidney Coles organises eight to 10-day tours to Angel Falls, but there must be a minimum of eight people wanting to go.

If you don't want to stay at El Dorado then carry on further south to Km 85 (known as Las Claritas) where you should ask for Luis and Jorge Gonzales, two very friendly people who offer camping in their grounds just outside the village. They also have thatched-roof Indian-style bungalows for less than US$1.

Getting There

There are many daily buses to Cuidad Bolívar for US$3.50, and one to Caracas at 2 pm.

MARACAIBO

Maracaibo is Venezuela's second largest city and the centre of its oil industry – oil derricks pepper Lake Maracaibo. The city, however, is of little interest to travellers and it's unlikely you'd want to stay longer than overnight. The bus terminal is on the edge of the city one km south of the old part of town.

Places to Stay & Eat

Finding a cheap hotel in Maracaibo can be problematical because many of the oil workers live in the cheap accommodation. Two of the cheapest are the *Hotel San Remo*, pretty rough; and the *Santa Ana*, opposite the Occidente garage on Av 3 between Ciencias and Venezuela.

Opposite the bus station, two or three houses from the main road, you can rent rooms with fan for US$3.

Two good places to eat are the *La Friulana*, Calle 95, Av 3 (meals for US$2); and the *Central Lunch*, Calle 98 (Chinese food).

MATURÍN

Maturín isn't of any interest in itself unless you're travelling to or from Trinidad – the cheapest flights to Trinidad are from Maturín. Halfway between Maturín and Cumana, however, is the **Cueva del Guáchero**, 10 km from the small town of Caripe. It's well worth a visit if you have the time. The cave was discovered by Humboldt and is at least eight km long, though visitors normally only go two km to the **Pozo del Viento** where there are strange stalactite formations and eerie sounds. Inside the cave live countless sightless birds known as *Guácheros*. They pour out of the mouth of the cave around 9 pm and return around 4 am with their pouches full of fruit.

The caves are open daily from 7 am to 4.30 pm and a guide is compulsory. It's best to get there early as visits are only done in groups of a minimum of 10 people. The charge is usually US$5 per hour. Torches, cameras and backpacks are prohibited. Wear old clothes to visit the caves, as you have to wade through streams and scramble over rocks here and there.

To get to Caripe take a bus or *por puesto* from Caracas to Cumana and then another bus or *por puesto* to Caripe (about US$2). From Caripe to the caves there are only taxis available so bargain hard. If coming from Maturín, there are only *por puestos* available so it's a seller's market – bargain hard.

There are hotels in Caripe if you need to stay the night. The cheapest are the *Venecia* and the *San Francisco*, which has its own restaurant which serves delicious meals. At the caves there is a café which sells delicious coconut *batidos* for just a few cents.

Places to Stay

Most of the cheapies in Maturín are priced around US$3 a double. There are plenty of them and you won't find anything cheaper than this. Try the *Trinidad*, good value, clean, English spoken; the *Europa* (same standard as the Trinidad); or the *Tamanaco*.

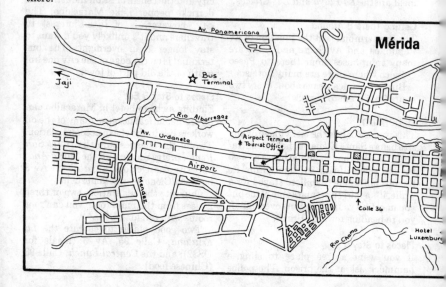

Mérida

Founded in 1558 and within sight of Pico Bolívar, the country's highest mountain (at 5007 metres), Mérida is probably Venezuela's most pleasant city and because it's a university town, there are a lot of young people there. It retains a good deal of its colonial atmosphere, though this is changing as the city expands.

Information

There are two tourist offices, both on the main highway through the town at the northern and southern entrances to the city.

Things to See

The high point of a visit to Mérida is to take the world's highest cable car to Pico Espejo (4765 metres) in four stages. The cable car normally operates from Tuesdays to Sundays and on holidays and costs US$4.80 return (half price to student card holders). The first trip up goes at 8 am and the last at noon. The last trip down is

at 2 pm. It's best to go up as early as possible as clouds obscure the view later on. You'll get the best between November and June. You can visit the highest village in Venezuela, Los Nevados, if you get off at Redonda station (the last but one from the top). There is a path from the station which leads to the village but it's a four-hour walk so you'll probably have to stay the night there (ask around for a room in a private house). Warm clothes, gloves, etc can be hired at the station in Mérida. Try to book in advance in the high season as there is a quota of 200 people per hour. If you don't want to walk back to the cable car station at La Redonda you can carry on to El Morro, Las Tienditas and from there take a bus back to Mérida.

To go walking in the mountains (eg from La Redonda to Los Nevados) you need two permits and you need to get them in the right order. Get the first from the Oficina de Inparque, Avenida 4, four blocks up from the Plaza Bolívar in Mérida. Next you must go to the Defensa Civil near the Estadio Santa Rosa. Even if you only walk down from the cable car

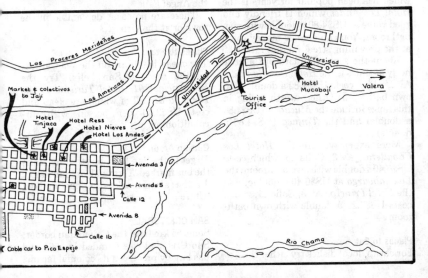

station at La Redonda to the station below (about 1½ hours and very pleasant) you will still need the first permit. Other than the cable railway, there are two museums which are worth visiting in Mérida. The first is the **Museo de Arte Colonial** in the Parque La Isla (open Tuesday to Friday from 9 am to 12 noon and 3 to 6 pm, on Saturdays from 3 to 6 pm, and on Sundays from 10 am to noon and 3 to 6 pm); and the **Jardín Acuario** which is an exhibition centre devoted to the crafts and lifestyle of the Andean peasants. It's open daily, except between 12 noon and 2 pm, and costs US$0.50.

While you're in Mérida, it's worth making a day trip to **Jají**, famous for its colonial architecture. A *por puesto* should cost about US$1 per person each way. If you'd like to stay the night there, try the *Posada de Jají*, which has its own restaurant (good food).

Places to Stay

Probably the cheapest place is the *Italia* which is basic but clean and costs US$1.60 a single. Similar is *Hotel Los Nives* which costs US$2.40 a single. One which has been popular for years is the *Hotel Los Andes* which is friendly and good value at US$4.80 a double with own bathroom. You can change money there at the prevailing street market rate.

About the same standard but a little noisy at times is the *Hotel Don Candido*, Av 2, which costs US$4.80 a double with own bathroom. Others worth trying in this range include the *Mucabaji* (US$4.80 a double) and the *Tinjaca* (US$4.80 a double).

More expensive are the *Hotel Los Caballeros*, Av 3, Calle 25, which costs US$6.40 a double with own bathroom; the *Luxembourgo* at US$6.40 a double; and the *Hotel Principe* Av 3, Calle 31, which costs US$7.20 a double with own bathroom.

Places to Eat

For cheap, local dishes try either the *Los Nevados*, Av 2 No 18-57; or the *Comedor Popular*, Calle 23 No 6. For Chinese food, the *Pekin*, Avenida 3, offers set lunches for US$3.

For vegetarian meals go to the *Anforade Aquarius*, Av 2 No 18-23, which is very friendly and has excellent cheap food. Two other places with reasonably priced food are the *Chipen Restaurant* and *La Paellera*.

Getting Around

The new bus station is a long way from the centre of town. Take a *por puesto*, from across the road from the Plaza Bolívar, which costs a few cents. On the way back the *por puesto* will be tagged 'Terminal Sur.'

PUERTO ORDAZ

Puerto Ordaz is part of the Ciudad Guyana complex and is what you should ask for if you're heading for the latter as few Venezuelans know it as Ciudad Guyana. It's not a particularly interesting place in itself and it's very spread out but it's one of the places for taking a plane to the Angel Falls.

There are no casas de cambio in the town or at the airport.

Places to Stay

The cheap hotels are off the Via Caracas on the road to San Felix. Try the *Residencias 101, Hotel Turismo* or the *Hotel Jardin* all of which are clean and cost US$2.40 per person with air-conditioning.

Getting Around

To get to the San Felix bus terminal take the bus marked 'Terminal' or 'San Felix'. To the airport take the bus marked 'Utare'.

SAN CRISTÓBAL

Some 55 km from the Colombian border, San Cristóbal was founded in 1561 and has largely preserved its colonial facade.

There isn't a great deal to see there but you may find yourself stopping overnight either on your way to or from Colombia.

Places to Stay & Eat

The *Hotel del Sur*, Avenida 8 on the right hand side as you walk towards town from the bus station, has been a popular place to stay for years. It's basic but clean and very friendly and costs US$2.40 a single plus less than US$1 for breakfast.

Similar is the *Hotel Americano*, Calle 8, which is good value at US$2.40 a single. There are other cheapies on Avenida 6A just off the main plaza which are similarly priced.

For a good, cheap meal there's the *Bella Napoli* near the Plaza Bolívar.

SANTA ELENA

Santa Elena is a growing frontier town on the Brazilian/Venezuelan border which you will have to pass through if you're travelling overland between Brazil and Venezuela. It's a pleasant enough town with fairly expensive accommodation and restaurant facilities, but there's no bank and absolutely nothing to see. If you're heading for Brazil you need to get an exit stamp from the Immigration office, which is on the northern edge of town on the hillside above the Corpovén petrol station. The office is open Monday to Friday from 8.30 am to 12 noon and 2 to 5.30 pm, and on Saturday and Sunday from 9.30 am to 12 noon.

Money can be changed either at the supermarket/tienda opposite the Mac-King or at the Hotel Auyantepuy, but the rates are relatively poor. Travellers' cheques cannot be changed there.

Places to Stay

Three of the cheapest places are the *Hotel Auyantepuy*, opposite the Mac-King, which is very clean and costs US$2.40 per person or US$5.60 a double; the *Hotel Mac-King*; and the *Hospedaje Roraima* both about the same price as the Auyantepuy. The *Hotel Brasilia* is also reasonably priced. The only trouble with the rooms in many of these cheap places is that they're just semi-partitioned hardboard boxes, so if someone in the next room is kicking up the dust you don't get any sleep.

If none of these suit you, then shell out the extra and stay at the *Hotel Fronteras*. It's a modern place and has rooms with attached bathrooms.

Places to Eat

Meals are expensive in Santa Elena but you can get an excellent, filling soup made of meat, beans, potatoes and barley at the café next door to the Hotel Mac-King. Apart from this, try the *Las 4 Esquinas* or the *Gran Sabana*.

Getting There

There is a daily jeep to El Dorado and Tumeremo from the Hotel Roraima at 7 am for US$11.

ANGEL FALLS

The Angel Falls are the highest in the world at 979 metres and, until recently were outside the scope of budget travellers. They're still fairly expensive to get to but just about affordable these days. The cost of a return flight from Puerto Ordaz to Canaima, one night in the hotel there and a short canoe trip comes to US$35.

You can do it even cheaper if you're prepared to camp, though this means walking a few km to get away from the hotel. If you do this, you need to bring all your own food and anything else you might need because there are no shops or facilities at Canaima for people who are not staying at the hotel. If you do eat independently at the hotel it's going to work out very expensive (they charge US$2.50 for breakfast and US$10 for lunch or dinner). For walkers, there are no trails all the way to the Falls so it's down to the hotel launch. This only operates in the wet season (June to December) as the rivers are too shallow at other times, so if you go there during the dry season, you'll have to be content with just seeing the Falls from the air on arrival at Canaima. Contact *Avensa* about the flights in Puerto Ordaz or any travel agent.

It's also possible to see the Falls (from the air) if you take a flight from Ciudad Bolívar to El Dorado with *Transmandu* who operate out of Ciudad Bolívar airport. They charge US$45 per person for this flight.

Index

731

Thanks to:

Wayne Asher (UK); Nick Anderson (USA); Bruce Anderson (Australia); Michael Aaronson (USA); Gill Albury (Australia); Betty Alden (Belize); Robert Aronoff (USA); Harry Boehme (USA); Eric van Bemmel (Japan); Stephen Bailey & Julia Kirby (Australia); Christopher Brown (UK); Neal Buckow (USA); Ian Butterss (Australia); Robert Barnes (Australia); Wendy Blue (NZ); Hans-Petter Buvollen (Netherlands); Keith Brockway (NZ); Kevin Bell (Australia); Peter Berke & Marianne Ravn (Denmark); Graham Boyle (Australia); Mark Babington (UK); John Baker (UK); Prue Biddle & Moise Sokal (c/o UK); Tony Brand (UK); Bernire Brown (NZ); Frances Brown (UK); Paul Bennet (Wales); Martin Buckridge (UK); Hans Petter Buvollen (Netherlands); Geoff Crofts; Ian Chadwick (Paraguay); Rod Clarke (Australia); Marg Connolly (Australia); Tom Connell (USA); Sid Cullen (Australia); Greg Comer (NZ); Donald Daus (USA); Bob Detwiler (USA); George Duffy (Canada); George Dunsham (USA); Bo Danielsen (Sweden); Richard Davies (Mexico); Denise Elson (Australia); Pamela Engle (USA); Cliff Elliott (USA); Dave Erskine (USA); Linda Farthing (USA); Thomas Frellesen & Johan Skjoldborgs (Denmark); Aner Gurvitz (Israel); Andrew Griffith (Canada); Jon Gibson (Australia); Tony Goodman (UK); Willy Gunther (W Germany); Simon Garth (UK); Johannes de Geus (Netherlands); Ann Marie & Goldie (USA); Ruth Haigh (UK); David Heinicke (Australia); Alison Hartley & Isobel Ogilvie (UK); Martin Howell (UK); Arthur Hallett; Janet & John Hoolachan (USA); James Hickman (UK); Dermot Hall (NZ); Jo Hanson (UK); Ian Harrison (Australia); Jane Horton & Mick Hammond (Mexico); Richard & Robyn Hawkes (NZ); Kevin Healey (Australia); Rene & Eva de Heer (Netherlands); Steven Heller (Canada); Dr Norbert Holtschmidt (W Germany); Dr David & Sally Hillebrant (UK); Danilo Ilic (Sweden); Yves Jacobs & Sophie Teyssier (France); V Jacobsen (Denmark) (thanks for your many letters!); Ray Kamil (Australia); Ian F Kerr (Canada); Malcolm Keir (UK); John King (Australia); David Kuhn (USA); Ken Lancaster (Hong Kong); Keith A Liker (USA); Christy Lanzl (USA); Sally Lush & Jim Ackroyd (NZ); Gait Leferink (Netherlands); Gabriel Estenssoro L (Bolivia); Charles Lloyd (UK); Carlton Lee (USA); Peter Lonsdale (NZ); Gordon Ludt (Canada); Bob Liepa (Canada); Teresa Lewis (USA); Peggy Lynin (USA); Mike Lewis and Sally Moore (UK); Denis Marks (Venezuela); Marielle de Natris & Toine Knipping (didn't say where from but thanks for your incredibly informative letter!); Jean Luc Matte (Canada); Patsy Morgan (Australia); Luke G McNamara (Australia); Lisa & Pat McCarthy (UK); Bart & Suzi Mickler (Belize); Mitch Martin (USA); Paul Mollatt (UK); Jenny Mortimer (Australia); Paul Mollatt (UK); Nigel Marsden (NZ); Malcolm McFrederick & Alistair Brown (UK); Sandra Moore (UK); John Nettleship (USA); Judith Nisbet (Australia); Bhakta Nomal (Ecuador); John Oldale (UK); John O'Conner (NZ); Jan Orleanski (Poland) (thanks for your many letters Jan!); Joe Parascandau (Canada); Kees & Pieter van Vleit & Jan van der Plas (Netherlands); Michael Pessehais (Australia); Joe Quilligan (Australia); Christina Quigley & Daniel Ortiz (Ecuador); Knud Rosenstand (Denmark); Lucy Robertson (UK); Tom & Jytte Rahbek (Denmark); Rob Rachowiecki (UK); Larry Reid (Canada); Tapas Saha (India); Gary Saunderson (Australia); Ted Stroll (USA); Justine Schneider (Peru); Gerard Steil (Luxembourg); Terry Stein (USA); Garth Swinburn (NZ); J Straue (Australia); Bo Svensson (Sweden); Kirra Shepard (USA); Kirk A Sackett (USA); William Seffusatti (Brazil); Ben Snelden (Netherlands); Christopher Stetson (USA); Mike Shawcross (UK); Werner Simon (W Germany); Ross Smillie (Canada); Ulla Siljeholm (Sweden); Mike Saunders (USA); Bill Shaw (Falkland Is); Tetsuo Tokuda (Japan); Russel Thomas (USA); Simon Watson Taylor (UK); Karen Trabjerg & friend (Denmark); Mark Voskamp (Holland); Per Skeimo & Anders Volle (Norway); Steve Vincent (UK); Ingrid Versteeg (Canada); Richard Walford (UK); Perre Willems (Belgium); Janelle Wallace (Australia); Frederick Watson (UK); Lilian Wardell (Ireland); Anthony E C Wolseley-Wilmsen (UK); D Wilson (UK); Dieter Weber (Switzerland); Russel Willis (Australia); Anselm Wright (Belize); Akira Yoshida (Japan); Sarah Colley (USA/UK); Ems Zuidgeest (Holland).

Temperature

To convert °C to °F multipy by 1.8 and add 32

To convert °F to °C subtract 32 and multipy by ·55

Length, Distance & Area

	multipy by
inches to centimetres	2.54
centimetres to inches	0.39
feet to metres	0.30
metres to feet	3.28
yards to metres	0.91
metres to yards	1.09
miles to kilometres	1.61
kilometres to miles	0.62
acres to hectares	0.40
hectares to acres	2.47

°C		°F
50		122
45		113
40		104
35		95
30		86
25		75
20		68
15		59
10		50
5		41
0		32

Weight

	multipy by
ounces to grams	28.35
grams to ounces	0.035
pounds to kilograms	0.45
kilograms to pounds	2.21
British tons to kilograms	1016
US tons to kilograms	907

A British ton is 2240 lbs, a US ton is 2000 lbs

Volume

	multipy by
Imperial gallons to litres	4.55
litres to imperial gallons	0.22
US gallons to litres	3.79
litres to US gallons	0.26

5 imperial gallons equals 6 US gallons
a litre is slightly more than a US quart, slightly less
than a British one

Lonely Planet

Lonely Planet published its first book in 1973. Tony and Maureen Wheeler had made a lengthy overland trip from England to Australia and, in response to numerous 'how do you do it?' questions, Tony wrote and they published *Across Asia on the Cheap*. It became an instant local best-seller and inspired thoughts of a second travel guide. A year and a half in South-East Asia resulted in their second book, *South-East Asia on a Shoestring*, which they put together in a backstreet Chinese hotel in Singapore in 1975. The 'yellow book', as it quickly became known, soon became *the* guide to the region and has gone through five editions, always with its familiar yellow cover.

Soon other writers started to come to them with ideas for similar books – books that went off the beaten track and took an adventurous approach to travel, books that 'assumed you knew how to get your luggage off the carousel,' as one reviewer described them. Lonely Planet grew from a kitchen table operation to a spare room and then to its own office. It also started to develop an international reputation as the Lonely Planet logo began to appear in more and more countries. In 1982 *India – a travel survival kit* won the Thomas Cook award for the best guidebook of the year.

These days there are over 60 Lonely Planet titles. Nearly 30 people work at our office in Melbourne, Australia and another half dozen at our US office in Oakland, California.

At first Lonely Planet specialised exclusively in the Asia region but these days we are also developing major ranges of guidebooks to the Pacific region, to South America and to Africa. The list of walking guides is growing and Lonely Planet is producing a unique series of phrasebooks to 'unusual' languages. The emphasis continues to be on travel for travellers and Tony and Maureen still manage to fit in a number of trips each year and play a very active part in the writing and updating of Lonely Planet's guides.

Keeping guidebooks up to date is a constant battle which requires an ear to the ground and lots of walking, but technology also plays its part. All Lonely Planet guidebooks are now stored and updated on computer, and some authors even take lap-top computers into the field. Lonely Planet is also using computers to draw maps and eventually many of the maps will be stored on disk.

The people at Lonely Planet strongly feel that travellers can make a positive contribution to the countries they visit both by better appreciation of cultures and by the money they spend. In addition the company tries to make a direct contribution to the countries and regions it covers. Since 1986 a percentage of the income from each book has gone to aid groups and associations. This has included donations to famine relief in Africa, to aid projects in India, to agricultural projects in Nicaragua and other Central American countries and to Greenpeace's efforts to halt French nuclear testing in the Pacific. In 1988 over $40,000 was donated by Lonely Planet to these projects.

Lonely Planet Distributors

Australia & Papua New Guinea Lonely Planet Publications, PO Box 88, South Yarra, Victoria 3141.
Canada Raincoast Books, 112 East 3rd Avenue, Vancouver, British Columbia V5T 1C8.
Denmark, Finland & Norway Scanvik Books aps, Store Kongensgade 59 A, DK-1264 Copenhagen K.
Hong Kong The Book Society, GPO Box 7804.
India & Nepal UBS Distributors, 5 Ansari Rd, New Delhi – 110002
Israel Geographical Tours Ltd, 8 Tverya St, Tel Aviv 63144.
Japan Intercontinental Marketing Corp, IPO Box 5056, Tokyo 100-31.
Netherlands Nilsson & Lamm bv, Postbus 195, Pampuslaan 212, 1380 AD Weesp.
New Zealand Transworld Publishers, PO Box 83-094, Edmonton PO, Auckland.
Singapore & Malaysia MPH Distributors, 601 Sims Drive, #03-21, Singapore 1438.
Spain Altair, Balmes 69, 08007 Barcelona.
Sweden Esselte Kartcentrum AB, Vasagatan 16, S-111 20 Stockholm.
Thailand Chalermnit, 108 Sukhumvit 53, Bangkok 10110.
UK Roger Lascelles, 47 York Rd, Brentford, Middlesex, TW8 0QP
USA Lonely Planet Publications, PO Box 2001A, Berkeley, CA 94702.
West Germany Buchvertrieb Gerda Schettler, Postfach 64, D3415 Hattorf a H.
All Other Countries refer to Australia address.

Guides to the Americas

Alaska - a travel survival kit
A definitive guide to one of the world's most spectacular regions - including detailed information on hiking and canoeing.

Canada - a travel survival kit
Canada offers a unique combination of English, French and American culture, with forests mountains and lakes that cover a vast area.

Chile & Easter Island - a travel survival kit
Chile has one of the most varied geographies in the world, including deserts, tranquil lakes, snow-covered volcanoes and windswept fjords. Easter Island is covered, in detail.

Ecuador & the Galapagos Islands - a travel survival kit
Ecuador is the smallest of the Andean countries, and in many ways it is the easiest and most pleasant to travel in. The Galapagos Islands and their amazing inhabitants continue to cast a spell over every visitor.

Mexico - a travel survival kit
Mexico has a unique blend of Indian and Spanish culture and a fascinating historical legacy. The hospitality of the people makes Mexico a paradise for travellers.

Guides to the Americas

Peru – a travel survival kit
The famed city of Machu Picchu, the Andean altiplano and the Amazon rainforests are just some of Peru's attractions. All the facts you need can be found in this comprehensive guide.

South America on a shoestring
An up-dated edition of a budget travellers bible that covers Central and South America from the USA-Mexico border to Tierra del Fuego. Written by the author The New York Times called "the patron saint of travellers in the third world".

Baja California – a travel survival kit
Mexico's Baja peninsula offers a great escape, right at California's back door. This comprehensive guide follows the long road south from raucous border towns like Tijuana, to resorts, untouched villages and deserted villages.

Colombia – a travel survival kit
Colombia is the land of emeralds, orchids and El Dorado. You may not find the mythical city of gold, but you will find an exotic, wild and beautiful country.

Bolivia – a travel survival kit
Bolivia offers safe and intriguing travel options – from isolated villages in the Andes and ancient ruins to the incredible city of La Paz.

Lonely Planet Guidebooks

Lonely Planet guidebooks cover virtually every accessible part of Asia as well as Australia, the Pacific, Central and South America, Africa, the Middle East and parts of North America. There are four main series: 'travel survival kits', covering a single country for a range of budgets; 'shoestring' guides with compact information for low-budget travel in a major region; trekking guides; and 'phrasebooks'.

Mail Order

Lonely Planet guidebooks are distributed worldwide and are sold by good bookshops everywhere. They are also available by mail order from Lonely Planet, so if you have difficulty finding a title please write to us. US and Canadian residents should write to Embarcadero West, 112 Linden St, Oakland CA 94607, USA and residents of other countries to PO Box 88, South Yarra, Victoria 3141, Australia.

Indian Subcontinent
India
Hindi/Urdu phrasebook
Kashmir, Ladakh & Zanskar
Trekking in the Indian Himalaya
Pakistan
Kathmandu & the Kingdom of Nepal
Trekking in the Nepal Himalaya
Nepal phrasebook
Sri Lanka
Sri Lanka phrasebook
Bangladesh

Africa
Africa on a shoestring
East Africa
Swahili phrasebook
West Africa

Middle East
Egypt & the Sudan
Jordan & Syria
Yemen

North America
Canada
Alaska

Mexico
Mexico
Baja California

South America
South America on a shoestring
Ecuador & the Galapagos Islands
Colombia
Chile & Easter Island
Bolivia
Peru

Lonely Planet Update

We collect an enormous amount of information here at Lonely Planet. Apart from our research there's a steady stream of travellers' letters full of the latest news. For over 5 years much of this information went into a quarterly newsletter (and helped to update the guidebooks). The new paperback *Update* includes this up-to-date news and aims to supplement the information available in our guidebooks. There will be four editions a year (Feb, May, Aug and Nov) available either by subscription or through bookshops. Subscribe now and you'll save nearly 25% off the retail price.

Each edition has extracts from the most interesting letters we have received, covering such diverse topics as:
• how to take a boat trip on the Yalu River
• living in a typical Thai village
• getting a Nepalese trekking permit

Subscription Details

All subscriptions cover four editions and include postage. Prices quoted are subject to change.

USA & Canada – One year's subscription is US$12; a single copy is US$3.95. Please send your order to Lonely Planet's California office.

Other Countries – One year's subscription is Australian $15; a single copy is A$4.95. Please pay in Australian $, or the US$ or £ Sterling equivalent. Please send your order form to Lonely Planet's Australian office.

Order Form

Please send me

☐ One year's subscription – starting next edition.   ☐ One copy of the next edition.

Name (please print) ....

Address (please print) ....

....

....

Tick One

☐ Payment enclosed (payable to Lonely Planet Publications)

Charge my   ☐ Visa   ☐ Bankcard   ☐ MasterCard   for the amount of $ ....

Card No .... Expiry Date ....

Cardholder's Name (print) ....

Signature .... Date..

US & Canadian residents
   Lonely Planet, Embarcadero West, 112 Linden St,
   Oakland, CA 94607, USA
Other countries
   Lonely Planet, PO Box 88, South Yarra, Victoria 3141, Australia